review of Medical Microbiology

15th edition

review of
Medical Microbiology

ERNEST JAWETZ, MD, PhD
Professor of Microbiology and Medicine,
Lecturer in Pediatrics
University of California School of Medicine
San Francisco

JOSEPH L. MELNICK, PhD
Distinguished Service Professor of Virology and Epidemiology
Baylor College of Medicine
Houston

EDWARD A. ADELBERG, PhD
Professor of Human Genetics
Yale University School of Medicine
New Haven

LANGE Medical Publications   Los Altos, California 94022

A Concise Medical Library for Practitioner and Student

Current Medical Diagnosis & Treatment 1982 (annual revision). Edited by M.A. Krupp and M.J. Chatton. 1113 pp.   1982

Current Pediatric Diagnosis & Treatment, 7th ed. Edited by C.H. Kempe, H.K. Silver, and D. O'Brien. 1106 pp, *illus.*   1982

Current Surgical Diagnosis & Treatment, 5th ed. Edited by J.E. Dunphy and L.W. Way. 1138 pp, *illus.*   1981

Current Obstetric & Gynecologic Diagnosis & Treatment, 3rd ed. Edited by R.C. Benson. 1001 pp, *illus.*   1980

Harper's Review of Biochemistry (formerly **Review of Physiological Chemistry**), 18th ed. D.W. Martin, Jr., P.A. Mayes, and V.W. Rodwell. 614 pp, *illus.*   1981

Review of Medical Physiology, 10th ed. W.F. Ganong. 628 pp, *illus.*   1981

Review of Medical Pharmacology, 7th ed. F.H. Meyers, E. Jawetz, and A. Goldfien. 747 pp, *illus.*   1980

Basic & Clinical Immunology, 3rd ed. Edited by H.H. Fudenberg, D.P. Stites, J.L. Caldwell, and J.V. Wells. 782 pp, *illus.*   1980

Basic Histology, 3rd ed. L.C. Junqueira and J. Carneiro. 504 pp, *illus.*   1980

Clinical Cardiology, 3rd ed. M. Sokolow and M.B. McIlroy. 763 pp, *illus.*   1981

General Urology, 10th ed. D.R. Smith. 598 pp, *illus.*   1981

General Ophthalmology, 9th ed. D. Vaughan and T. Asbury. 410 pp, *illus.*   1980

Correlative Neuroanatomy & Functional Neurology, 17th ed. J.G. Chusid. 464 pp, *illus.*   1979

Principles of Clinical Electrocardiography, 10th ed. M.J. Goldman. 415 pp, *illus.*   1979

Handbook of Obstetrics & Gynecology, 7th ed. R.C. Benson. 808 pp, *illus.*   1980

Physician's Handbook, 20th ed. M.A. Krupp, L.M. Tierney, Jr., E. Jawetz, R.L. Roe, and C.A. Camargo. 774 pp, *illus.*   1982

Handbook of Pediatrics, 13th ed. H.K. Silver, C.H. Kempe, and H.B. Bruyn. 735 pp, *illus.*   1980

Handbook of Poisoning: Prevention, Diagnosis, & Treatment, 10th ed. R.H. Dreisbach. 578 pp.   1980

Lithographed in USA

Table of Contents

Preface

The authors' intention in preparing this *Review* has been to make available a comprehensive, accurate, up-to-date presentation of those aspects of medical microbiology that are of particular significance in the fields of clinical infections and chemotherapy. The book is directed primarily at the medical student, house officer, and practicing physician. However, because the necessity for a clear understanding of microbiologic principles has increased in recent years as a result of important developments in biochemistry, genetics, immunology, virology, chemotherapy, and other fields of direct medical significance, a considerable portion of this *Review* has been devoted to a discussion of the relevant basic science aspects. It is to be expected that the inclusion of these sections will extend the book's usefulness to students in introductory microbiology courses as well. In general, details of technique and procedure have been excluded.

With the appearance of the Fifteenth Edition, the authors are pleased to report that Spanish, German, French, Italian, Portuguese, Serbo-Croatian, Japanese, Polish, Albanian, and Indonesian translations have proved successful. Greek, Chinese, Russian, and Arabic translations are in progress.

The authors wish to reaffirm their gratitude to everyone who assisted them with the preparation of this edition and to all those whose comments and criticisms have helped to keep the biennial revisions of this *Review* accurate and up to date. We are especially grateful to the following for their help: Janet S. Butel, John Conte, Mary Estes, Margaret Ann Fraher, Moses Grossman, Carlyn Halde, Lavelle Hanna, and F. Blaine Hollinger.

Ernest Jawetz
Joseph L. Melnick
Edward A. Adelberg

San Francisco
May, 1982

SI Units of Measurement in the Biologic Range

Prefix	Abbreviation	Magnitude
kilo-	k	10^3
deci-	d	10^{-1}
centi-	c	10^{-2}
milli-	m	10^{-3}
micro-	μ	10^{-6}
nano-	n	10^{-9}
pico-	p	10^{-12}

These prefixes are applied to metric and other units. For example, a micrometer (μm) is 10^{-6} meter (formerly micron, μ); a nanogram (ng) is 10^{-9} gram (formerly millimicrogram, mμg); and a picogram (pg) is 10^{-12} gram (formerly micromicrogram, $\mu\mu$g). Any of these prefixes may also be applied to seconds, units, mols, equivalents, osmols, etc. The Angstrom (A, 10^{-7}) is now expressed in nanometers (eg, 40 A = 4 nm).

Before the discovery of microorganisms, all known living things were believed to be either plant or animal; no transitional types were thought to exist. During the 19th century, however, it became clear that the microorganisms combine plant and animal properties in all possible combinations. It is now generally accepted that they have evolved, with relatively little change, from the common ancestors of plants and animals.

The compulsion of biologists to categorize all organisms in one of the 2 "kingdoms," plant or animal, resulted in a number of absurdities. The fungi, for example, were classified as plants because they are largely nonmotile, although they have few other plantlike properties and show strong phylogenic affinities with the protozoa.

In order to avoid the arbitrary assignment of transitional groups to one or the other kingdom, Haeckel proposed in 1866 that microorganisms be placed in a separate kingdom, the **Protista.** As defined by Haeckel, the Protista included algae, protozoa, fungi, and bacteria. In the middle of the current century, however, the new techniques of electron microscopy revealed that the bacteria differ fundamentally from the other 3 groups in their cell architecture. The latter share with the cells of plants and animals the advanced type of structure called **eukaryotic;** the bacteria possess a more primitive type of structure called **prokaryotic.** (The 2 types of cell structure are described in Chapter 2.) The term protist is currently used to refer only to the eukaryotic microorganisms, the assemblage of bacterial groups being referred to collectively as prokaryotes.

The term algae has long been used to refer to all chlorophyll-containing microorganisms that produce gaseous oxygen as a by-product of photosynthesis. Electron microscopy, however, has revealed that one major group—formerly called blue-green algae—are in fact true prokaryotes, and they have thus been renamed **cyanobacteria.***

Three groups of prokaryotes—methanogens, extreme halophiles, and thermoacidophiles—have been found to share a set of properties that distinguish them clearly from all other prokaryotes. It has been pro-

posed that these organisms represent the most primitive cell types and that they should therefore be classified separately as the **archaebacteria.** An analysis of the base sequences of the ribosomal RNA of these and other organisms shows that the archaebacteria are only distantly related to other bacteria; there are also major differences in the composition of their cell walls and membranes and in their metabolism.

Thus, a current classification of microorganisms might read as follows:

I. Protists (eukaryotic)
  A. Algae
  B. Protozoa
  C. Fungi
  D. Slime molds (sometimes included in the fungi)
II. Prokaryotes
  A. Bacteria
  B. Cyanobacteria
  C. Archaebacteria

The bacteria include 2 groups, the **chlamydiae (bedsoniae)** and the **rickettsiae,** which differ from other bacteria in being somewhat smaller ($0.2-0.5 \mu m$ in diameter) and in being obligate intracellular parasites. The reasons for the obligate nature of their parasitism are not clear; there is some evidence that they depend on their hosts for coenzymes and complex energy-rich metabolites such as ATP, to which their membranes may be permeable.

Viruses are also classed as microorganisms, but they are sharply differentiated from all cellular forms of life. A viral particle consists of a nucleic acid molecule, either DNA or RNA, enclosed in a protein coat, or **capsid.** The capsid serves only to protect the nucleic acid and to facilitate attachment and penetration of the virus into the host cell. Viral nucleic acid is the infectious principle; inside the host cell it behaves like host genetic material in that it is replicated by the host's enzymatic machinery and also governs the formation of specific (viral) proteins. Maturation consists of assemblage of newly synthesized nucleic acid and protein subunits into mature viral particles; these are liberated into the extracellular environment.

A number of transmissible plant diseases are caused by **viroids,** small, single-stranded, covalently

Bergey's Manual of Determinative Bacteriology, 8th ed. Williams & Wilkins, 1974.

closed circular RNA molecules existing as highly base-paired rodlike structures; they do not possess capsids. Their molecular weights are estimated to fall in the range of 75,000–100,000. It is not known whether they are translated in the host into polypeptides or whether they interfere with host functions directly (as RNA); if the former is true, the largest viroid could only be translated into the equivalent of a single polypeptide containing about 55 amino acids.

Viroid RNA is replicated by the DNA-dependent RNA polymerase of the plant host; preemption of this enzyme may contribute to viroid pathogenicity.

The general properties of animal viruses pathogenic for humans are described in Chapter 27. Bacterial viruses are described in Chapter 9.

PROTISTS

The protists share with true plants and animals the type of cell construction called eukaryotic ("possessing a true nucleus"). In such cells the nucleus contains a set of chromosomes that are separated, following replication, by an elaborate mitotic apparatus. The nuclear membrane is continuous with a ramifying endoplasmic reticulum. The cytoplasm of the cell contains self-replicating organelles (mitochondria and, in photosynthetic cells, chloroplasts), as well as microtubules and microfilaments. Motility organelles (cilia or flagella) are complex multistranded elements.

Algae

The term "algae" refers in general to chlorophyll-containing protists. The algae are divided into 6 phylogenetic groups, for descriptions of which the reader is referred to Smith GM: *Cryptogamic Botany*, 2nd ed. Vol 1: *Algae and Fungi*. McGraw-Hill, 1955.

Protozoa

In Smith's classification of algae, several types of photosynthetic, flagellated, unicellular forms are included that many textbooks class with the protozoa. These include members of Volvocales in Chlorophyta, members of Euglenophyta, the dinoflagellates in Pyrrophyta, and some of the golden browns in Chrysophyta. These have not been classified as algae arbitrarily but because definite phylogenetic series are recognized that link them to typical algal forms.

On the other hand, these photosynthetic flagellates probably represent transitional forms between algae and protozoa; according to this view, the protozoa have evolved from various algae by loss of chloroplasts. They thus have a polyphyletic origin (ancestors in many different groups). Indeed, mutations of flagellates from green to colorless have been observed in the laboratory. The resulting forms are indistinguishable from certain protozoa.

The most primitive protozoa are thus the flagellated forms. "Protozoa" are unicellular, nonphotosynthetic protists. From the flagellated forms appear to have evolved the ameboid and the ciliated types; intermediate types are known that have flagella at one stage in the life cycle and pseudopodia (characteristic of the ameba) at another stage. The simplest classification of protozoa would be the following (see also p 497).

Phylum: Protozoa
  Class I: Mastigophora. The flagellate protozoa.
  Class II: Sarcodina. The ameboid protozoa. (Some also form flagella.)
  Class III: Sporozoa. Parasites with complex life cycles that include a resting or spore stage.
  Class IV: Ciliata. The ciliate protozoa. High degree of internal organization.

Fungi

The fungi are nonphotosynthetic protists growing as a mass of branching, interlacing filaments ("hyphae") known as a mycelium. Although the hyphae exhibit cross-walls, the cross-walls are perforated and allow the free passage of nuclei and cytoplasm. The entire organism is thus a coenocyte (a multinucleate mass of continuous cytoplasm) confined within a series of branching tubes. These tubes, made of polysaccharides such as chitin, are homologous with cell walls. The mycelial forms are called **molds;** a few types, **yeasts,** do not form a mycelium but are easily recognized as fungi by the nature of their sexual reproductive processes and by the presence of transitional forms.

The fungi probably represent an evolutionary offshoot of the protozoa; they are unrelated to the actinomycetes, mycelial bacteria which they superficially resemble. Fungi are subdivided as follows:

Class I: Zygomycotina (the phycomycetes). Mycelium usually nonseptate; asexual spores produced in indefinite numbers within a structure called a sporangium. Sexual fusion results in formation of a resting, thick-walled cell termed a zygospore. *Example: Rhizopus nigricans* (no known pathogens).
Class II: Ascomycotina (the ascomycetes). Sexual fusion results in formation of a sac, or ascus, containing the meiotic products as 4 or 8 spores (ascospores). Asexual spores (conidia) are borne externally at the tips of hyphae. *Examples: Trichophyton (Arthroderma), Microsporum (Nannizzia), Blastomyces (Ajellomyces).*
Class III: Basidiomycotina (the basidiomycetes). Sexual fusion results in formation of a club-shaped organ called a basidium, on the surface of which are borne the 4 meiotic products (basidiospores). Asexual spores (conidia) are borne externally at the tips of hyphae. *Example: Cryptococcus neoformans (Filobasidiella neoformans).*

Class IV: Deuteromycotina (the imperfect fungi). This is not a true phylogenetic group but rather an artificial class into which are temporarily placed all forms in which the sexual process has not yet been observed. Most of them resemble ascomycetes morphologically. *Examples: Epidermophyton, Sporothrix, Candida.*

The evolution of the ascomycetes from the phycomycetes is seen in a transitional group, members of which form a zygote but then transform this directly into an ascus. The basidiomycetes are believed to have evolved in turn from the ascomycetes.

Although the fungi are classified on the basis of their sexual processes, the sexual stages are difficult to induce and are rarely observed. Descriptions of species thus deal principally with various asexual structures, including the following: (See Figs 25–1 to 25–9 for drawings of some of these structures.)

A. Sporangiospores: Asexual spores borne internally inside a sac known as a sporangium. In terrestrial forms, the sporangium is borne at the tip of a filament called a sporangiophore. These structures are characteristic of the phycomycetes.

B. Conidia: Asexual reproductive units that develop along one of 2 basic pathways. "Blastic" conidia develop from an enlargement of some part of the conidiophore (conidiogenous hypha) prior to delimitation by a septum. "Thallic" conidia differentiate from a whole cell after a septum has formed. The blastic type of conidia show many modifications that may be given specific names. When a sexual stage has not been recognized for a given fungus, the form of conidia it produces is used as a basis for classification within the imperfect fungi.

C. Arthrospores: Thallic conidia formed by segmentation and disarticulation of a filament of a septate mycelium into separate cells. They are properly called **arthroconidia.**

D. Chlamydospores: Thallic conidia formed as enlarged, thick-walled cells within a hypha. They remain a part of the mycelium, surviving after the remainder of the mycelium has died and disintegrated.

E. Blastospores: Simple blastic conidia produced as buds that then separate from the parent cell. They are properly called **blastoconidia.**

Slime Molds

These organisms are characterized by the presence, as a stage in the life cycle, of an ameboid multinucleate mass of cytoplasm called a **plasmodium.** The creeping plasmodium, which reaches macroscopic size, gives rise to walled spores that germinate to produce naked uniflagellate swarm spores or, in some cases, naked nonflagellated amebas ("myxamebae"). These usually undergo sexual fusion before growing into typical plasmodia again.

The plasmodium of a slime mold is analogous to the mycelium of a true fungus. Both are coenocytes; but in the latter, cytoplasmic flow is confined to the branching network of chitinous tubes, whereas in the former the cytoplasm can flow (creep) in all directions.

PROKARYOTES

The prokaryotes form a heterogeneous group of microorganisms distinguished from protists by the following criteria: size range (0.2–2 μm for the smallest diameter); cell construction; and unique systems of genetic transfer (see Chapter 4).

Photosynthesis occurs within several subgroups of bacteria, as well as in all cyanobacteria. The cyanobacteria include a variety of prokaryotic forms that overlap bacteria and eukaryotic algae in their range of cellular sizes. They possess the same chlorophylls as the eukaryotic algae and oxidize H_2O to gaseous oxygen in their photosynthesis. By these properties they differ from the photosynthetic bacteria, which have specialized chlorophylls and do not produce gaseous oxygen.

Both the cyanobacteria and the photosynthetic bacteria contain their photosynthetic pigments in a series of lamellae just under the cell membrane. In some photosynthetic bacteria, these lamellae differentiate under certain environmental conditions into ovoid or spherical bodies called chromatophores. In contrast, the eukaryotic algae always contain their photosynthetic pigments in autonomous cytoplasmic organelles (chloroplasts). There is strong evidence to support the hypothesis that the chloroplasts of eukaryotic algae and plants evolved from endosymbiotic cyanobacteria.

The cyanobacteria exhibit a type of motility called "gliding" or "creeping," the mechanism of which is unknown. Many nonphotosynthetic bacteria also possess gliding motility; some of these resemble certain cyanobacteria so closely that they are believed to be "colorless blue-greens" that have lost their photosynthetic pigments in the course of evolution.

No further generalizations can be made about the prokaryotes. The reader is referred instead to the descriptions of the various bacterial groups in Chapter 3.

SUMMARY

A theory of evolutionary relationships between the above groups is diagrammatically presented in Fig 1–1. Listed at the right are the major groups of present-day microorganisms; the horizontal scale indicates time, and the vertical scale indicates relative evolutionary advance. Thus, the earliest cell type to emerge on earth was presumably anaerobic and prokaryotic. From this ancestral type, 3 parallel lines of evolution diverged, leading to (1) photosynthesis; (2) aerobic respiration; and (3) such eukaryotic structural features as microtubular systems and nuclear complexity ("proto-eukaryotes").

The contemporary eukaryotes are pictured as arising by a sequence of further events: (1) establishment

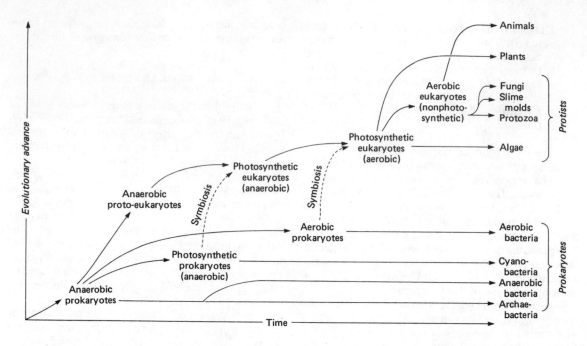

Figure 1–1. Evolutionary relationships of the major groups of microorganisms.

of endosymbiosis between a cyanobacterium and an anaerobic proto-eukaryotic cell, the chloroplast evolving from the endosymbiont; and (2) evolution of the mitochondrion, either from an endosymbiotic aerobic prokaryote or by segregation of part of the eukaryotic nucleus. Although mitochondria share many properties with bacteria, their DNA more closely resembles that of the eukaryotic nucleus in possessing highly reiterated sequences as well as introns; thus, both theories are at this time equally tenable.

These 2 events would have produced an aerobic photosynthetic eukaryote comparable to present-day higher algae. Loss of the chloroplast would account for the appearance of protozoa and ultimately of fungi and slime molds.

Anaerobic bacteria and archaebacteria, according to this line of reasoning, represent forms that have evolved with relatively little change from the earliest prokaryotic groups. The evolutionary origin of present-day viruses, on the other hand, is obscure. A reasonable hypothesis is that they have evolved from their respective host cell genomes, escaping the normal control mechanisms of the cell and acquiring capsids.

•   •   •

References

Books

Ainsworth GC, Sparrow FK, Sussman AS (editors): *The Fungi, An Advanced Treatise*. Academic Press, 1973.

Bold HC, Wynne MJ: *Introduction to the Algae: Structure and Reproduction*. Prentice-Hall, 1978.

Carlile MJ, Skehel JJ (editors): *Evolution in the Microbial World: 24th Symposium of the Society for General Microbiology*. Cambridge Univ Press, 1974.

Diener TO: *Viroids and Viroid Diseases*. Wiley-Interscience, 1979.

Laskin AT, Lechevalier HA (editors): *CRC Handbook of Microbiology*, 2nd ed. Vol I. *Bacteria*. Vol II. *Fungi, Algae, Protozoa and Viruses*. CRC Press, 1977.

Levandowsky M, Hutner SH (editors): *Biochemistry and Physiology of Protozoa*, 2nd ed. Academic Press, 1980.

Luria SE et al: *General Virology*. Wiley, 1978.

Margulis L: *Symbiosis in Cell Evolution: Life and Its Environment on the Early Earth*. Freeman, 1981.

Moulder JW: *The Psittacosis Group as Bacteria*. Wiley, 1964.

Ragan MA, Chapman DJ: *Biochemical Phylogeny of the Protists*. Academic Press, 1978.

Sleigh M: *The Biology of Protozoa*. University Park Press, 1975.

Smith GM: *Cryptogamic Botany*, 2nd ed. Vol 1. McGraw-Hill, 1955.

Stanier RY, Adelberg EA, Ingraham J: *The Microbial World*, 4th ed. Prentice-Hall, 1976.

Articles & Reviews

Barghoorn ES: The oldest fossils. *Sci Am* (May) 1971;**224**:30.

Bruenn JA: Virus-like particles of yeast. *Annu Rev Microbiol* 1980;**34**:49.

Cloud P: Evolution of ecosystems. *Am Sci* 1974;**62**:54.

Diener TO: Viroids: Structure and function. *Science* 1979; **205**:859.

Fox GE et al: The phylogeny of prokaryotes. *Science* 1980; **209**:457.

Horowitz NH, Hubbard JS: The origin of life. *Annu Rev Genet* 1974;**8**:393.

Knoll AH, Barghoorn ES: Precambrian eukaryotic organisms: A reassessment of the evidence. *Science* 1975;**190**:52.

Lemke PA: Viruses of eukaryotic microorganisms. *Annu Rev Microbiol* 1976;**30**:105.

Rackwitz HR et al: DNA-dependent RNA polymerase II of plant origin transcribes viroid RNA into full length copies. *Nature* 1981;**291**:297.

Raff RA, Mahler HR: The nonsymbiotic origin of mitochondria. *Science* 1972;**177**:575.

Sänger HL et al: Viroids are single-stranded covalently closed circular RNA molecules existing as highly base-paired rod-like structures. *Proc Natl Acad Sci USA* 1976;**73**:3852.

Schopf JW: Precambrian microorganisms and evolutionary events prior to the origin of vascular plants. *Biol Rev* 1970; **45**:319.

Schwartz RM, Dayhoff MO: Origins of prokaryotes, eukaryotes, mitochondria and chloroplasts. *Science* 1978; **199**:395.

Van Valen LM, Maiorana VC: The archaebacteria and eukaryotic origins. *Nature* 1980;**287**:248.

Woese CR, Magrum LJ, Fox GE: Archaebacteria. *J Mol Evol* 1978;**11**:245.

2 | Cell Structure

OPTICAL METHODS

The Light Microscope

The resolving power of the light microscope under ideal conditions is about half the wavelength of the light being used. (Resolving power is the distance that must separate 2 point sources of light if they are to be seen as 2 distinct images.) With yellow light of a wavelength of 0.4 μm, the smallest separable diameters are thus about 0.2 μm. The **useful magnification** of a microscope is that magnification that makes visible the smallest resolvable particles. Microscopes used in bacteriology generally employ a 90-power objective lens with a 10-power ocular lens, thus magnifying the specimen 900 times. Particles 0.2 μm in diameter are therefore magnified to about 0.2 mm and so become clearly visible. Further magnification would give no greater resolution of detail and would reduce the visible area (field).

Further improvement in resolving power can be accomplished only by the use of light of shorter wavelengths. The **ultraviolet microscope** uses wavelengths of about 0.2 μm, thus allowing resolution of particles with diameters of 0.1 μm. Such microscopes, employing quartz lenses and photographic systems, are too expensive and complicated for general use.

The Electron Microscope

Using a beam of electrons focused by magnets, the electron microscope can resolve particles 0.001 μm apart. Viruses, with diameters of 0.01–0.2 μm, can be easily resolved.

An important technique in electron microscopy is the use of "shadowing." This involves depositing a thin layer of metal (such as platinum) on the object by placing it in the path of a beam of metal ions in a vacuum. The beam is directed obliquely, so that the object acquires a "shadow" in the form of an uncoated area on the other side. When an electron beam is then passed through the coated preparation in the electron microscope and a positive print made from the "negative" image, a 3-dimensional effect is achieved (eg, Figs 2–21, 2–22, and 2–23).

Other important techniques in electron microscopy include the use of ultrathin sections of embedded material; a method of freeze-drying specimens, which prevents the distortion caused by conventional drying procedures; and the use of negative staining with an electron-dense material such as phosphotungstic acid (eg, Fig 27–35).

The **scanning electron microscope** provides 3-dimensional images of the surfaces of microscopic objects (eg, Fig 3–1). The object is first coated with a thin film of a heavy metal and then scanned by a downward-directed electron beam. Electrons scattered by the heavy metal are collected and focused to form the final image.

Darkfield Illumination

If the condenser lens system is arranged so that no light reaches the eye unless reflected from an object on the microscope stage, structures that provide insufficient contrast with the surrounding medium can be made visible. This technique is particularly valuable for observing organisms such as the spirochetes, which are difficult to observe by transmitted light.

Phase Microscopy

The phase microscope takes advantage of the fact that light waves passing through transparent objects, such as cells, emerge in different phases depending on the properties of the materials through which they pass. A special optical system converts difference in phase into difference in intensity, so that some structures appear darker than others. An important feature is that internal structures are thus differentiated in living cells; with ordinary microscopes, killed and stained preparations must be used.

Autoradiography

If cells that have incorporated radioactive atoms are fixed on a slide, covered with a photographic emulsion, and stored in the dark for a suitable period of time, tracks appear in the developed film emanating from the sites of radioactive disintegration. If the cells are labeled with a weak emitter such as tritium, the tracks are sufficiently short to reveal the position in the cell of the radioactive label. This procedure, called autoradiography, has been particularly useful in following the replication of DNA, using tritium-labeled thymidine as a specific tracer (Fig 4–1).

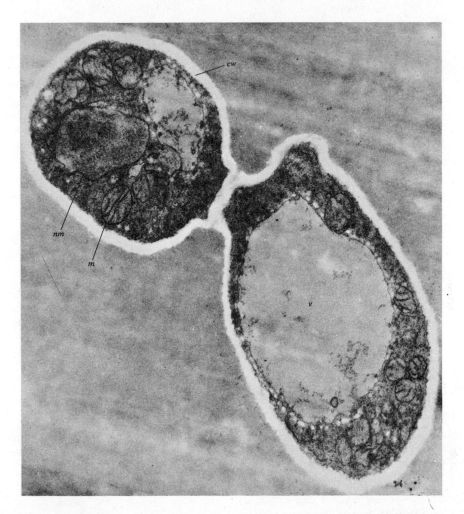

Figure 2–1. Thin section of a eukaryotic cell. A dividing cell of the unicellular yeast *Lipomyces* (17,500 ×). *n* = nucleus; *nm* = nuclear membrane; *v* = vacuole; *m* = mitochondrion; *cw* = cell wall. Electron micrograph taken by Dr CF Robinow. (From Stanier RY, Doudoroff M, Adelberg EA. *The Microbial World*, 2nd ed. Copyright © 1963. By permission of Prentice-Hall, Inc, Englewood Cliffs, NJ.)

EUKARYOTIC CELL STRUCTURE

The principal features of the eukaryotic cell are shown in the electron micrograph in Fig 2–1. Note the following structures.

Nucleus

The nucleus is bounded by a membrane (**nm**) that is continuous with the endoplasmic reticulum. The chromosomes, embedded in the nuclear matrix, are not distinguishable. The mitotic apparatus is not present at this stage in the division cycle.

Cytoplasmic Structures

The cytoplasm of eukaryotic cells is characterized by the presence of an endoplasmic reticulum, vacuoles, self-reproducing plastids, and an elaborate cytoskeleton composed of microtubules, mi-

crofilaments, and intermediate filaments about 10 nm in diameter.

The **endoplasmic reticulum** is a network of membrane-bounded channels. In some regions of the endoplasmic reticulum, the membranes are coated with ribosomes; proteins synthesized on these ribosomes pass through the membrane into the channels of the endoplasmic reticulum, through which they can be transported to other parts of the cell. A related structure, the **Golgi apparatus,** pinches off vesicles that can fuse with the cell membrane, releasing the enclosed proteins into the surrounding medium.

The plastids include **mitochondria,** which contain in their membranes the respiratory electron transport system, and chloroplasts (in photosynthetic organisms). The plastids contain their own DNA, which codes for some (but not all) of their constituent proteins and transfer RNAs.

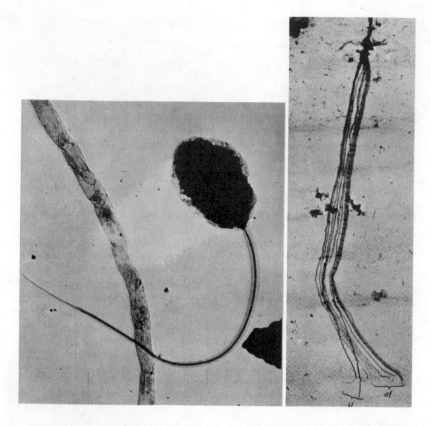

Figure 2–2. Eukaryotic flagella (3000 ×). *Left:* A zoospore of the fungus *Allomyces,* with a single flagellum. *Right:* A partially disintegrated flagellum of *Allomyces,* showing the 2 inner fibrils *(if)* and 9 outer fibrils *(of).* (Courtesy of Manton I et al: *J Exp Bot* 1952:3:204.)

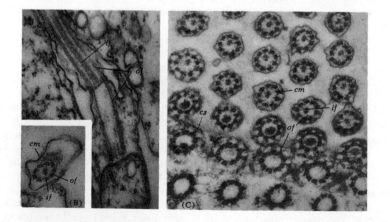

Figure 2–3. Fine structure of eukaryotic flagella and cilia (31,500 ×). *(A)* Longitudinal section of a flagellum of *Bodo,* a protozoon, showing kinetoplast *(k)* from which extend the outer fibrils *(of).* Note the origin of the inner fibrils *(if)* at the cell surface. *(B)* Cross section of same flagellum near the surface of the cell, showing outer fibrils *(of),* inner fibrils *(if),* and extension of cell membrane *(cm). (C)* Cross section through surface layer of the ciliate protozoon *Glaucoma,* which cuts across a field of cilia just within the cell membrane (lower half) as well as outside the cell membrane (upper half). *cs* = cell surface. Electron micrographs taken by Dr D Pitelka. (From Stanier RY, Doudoroff M, Adelberg EA: *The Microbial World,* 2nd ed. Copyright © 1963. By permission of Prentice-Hall, Inc, Englewood Cliffs, NJ.)

The cytoskeleton includes arrays of **microtubules,** which play a role in cytoplasmic membrane function and cell shape as well as forming the mitotic spindle and flagellar components; arrays of actin- and myosin-containing **microfilaments,** which provide the mechanism of ameboid motility; and the **intermediate filaments,** whose function is not yet known.

Surface Layers

The cytoplasm is enclosed within a lipoprotein cell membrane, similar to the prokaryotic cell membrane illustrated in Fig 2–10. Most animal cells have no other surface layers; many eukaryotic microorganisms, however, have an outer **cell wall,** which may be composed of a polysaccharide such as cellulose or chitin or may be inorganic, as in the silica wall of diatoms.

Motility Organelles

Many eukaryotic cells propel themselves through water by means of protein appendages called **cilia** or **flagella** (cilia are short; flagella are long). In almost every case the organelle consists of a bundle of 9 fibrils surrounding 2 central fibrils (Figs 2–2 and 2–3). The fibrils are assembled from microtubules.

PROKARYOTIC CELL STRUCTURE

The prokaryotic cell is simpler than the eukaryotic cell at every level, with one exception: the cell wall may be more complex.

Nucleus

The prokaryotic nucleus can be seen with the light microscope in stained material (Fig 2–4). It is Feulgen-positive, indicating the presence of DNA. The negatively charged DNA is at least partially neutralized by small polyamines and magnesium ion, but histonelike proteins have recently been discovered in

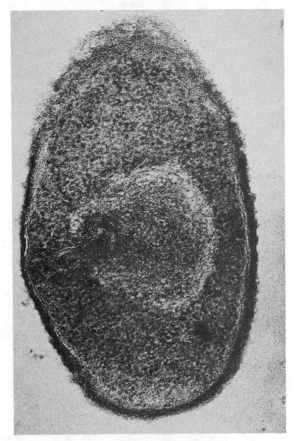

Figure 2–5. Electron micrograph of a thin section of *Bacillus subtilis,* showing the DNA in contact with a mesosome. (From Ryter A, Jacob F: Membrane et ségrégation nucléaire chez les bactéries. Page 267 of: *Proceedings of the 15th Colloquium on Protides of the Biological Fluids.* Vol 15. Peeters H [editor]. 1967.)

bacteria and presumably play a role similar to that of histones in eukaryotic chromatin.

Electron micrographs such as Fig 2–5 reveal the absence of a nuclear membrane and of a mitotic apparatus. The nuclear region is filled with DNA fibrils; the DNA of the bacterial nucleus can be extracted as a single continuous molecule with a molecular weight of $2–3 \times 10^9$ (see Chromosome Structure, Chapter 4). It may thus be considered to be a **single chromosome,** approximately 1 mm long in the unfolded state.

The nucleus can be isolated by gentle lysis of bacteria, followed by centrifugation. The structures thus isolated consist of DNA associated with smaller amounts of RNA, RNA polymerase, and possibly other proteins. The DNA appears to be looped around an RNA core, which serves to hold the DNA in its compact form.

Bacterial DNA, isolated directly on the electron microscope supporting film by gentle lysis of the cells in physiologic salt solution, is seen to have a beaded structure similar to that of eukaryotic chromatin (Fig 2–6).

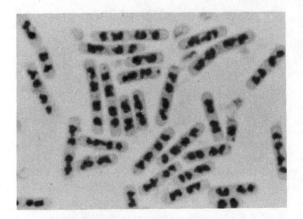

Figure 2–4. Nuclei of *Bacillus cereus* (2500 ×). (Courtesy of Robinow C: *Bacteriol Rev* 1956; **20**:207.)

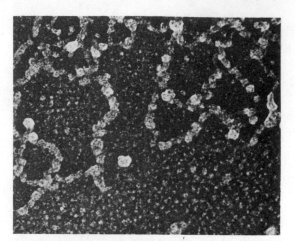

Figure 2–6. Bacteriophage λ DNA prepared by lysing infected cells with lysozyme in 0.15 M NaCl directly on an electron microscope supporting film. The beaded substructure shows a 13-nm repeating pattern. (From Griffith JD: Visualization of prokaryotic DNA in a regularly condensed chromatin-like fiber. *Proc Natl Acad Sci USA* 1976;**73**:563.)

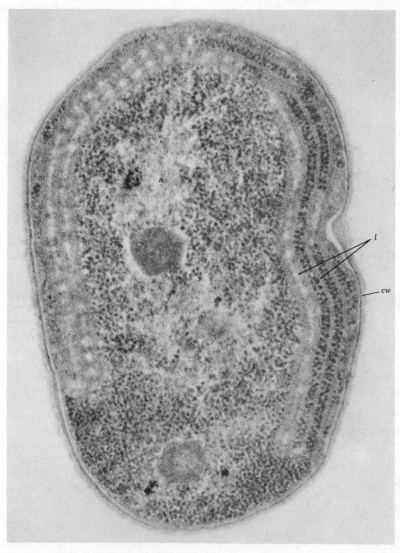

Figure 2–7. Thin section of a cyanobacterium, *Anacystis* (80,500 ×). *l* = lamellae bearing photosynthetic pigments; *cw* = cell wall; *n* = nuclear region. (Reprinted by permission of the Rockefeller Institute Press, from Ris H, Singh RN: *J Biophys Biochem Cytol* 1961;**9**:63.)

The electron microscopy of serial thin sections through bacterial cells shows that the DNA is associated at one point with an invagination of the cell membrane (Fig 2–5). This attachment is thought to play a key role in the segregation of the 2 sister chromosomes following chromosomal replication (see Cell Division). The genetics and chemistry of the bacterial chromosome are presented in Chapter 4.

Cytoplasmic Structures

Prokaryotic cells lack autonomous plastids, such as mitochondria and chloroplasts. The electron transport enzymes are localized instead in the cell membrane; in photosynthetic organisms, the photosynthetic pigments are localized in **lamellae** underlying the cell membrane (Fig 2–7). In some photosynthetic bacteria, the lamellae may become convoluted and pinch off into discrete particles called **chromatophores.**

Bacteria often store reserve materials in the form of insoluble cytoplasmic **granules,** which are deposited as osmotically inert, neutral polymers. In the absence of a nitrogen source, carbon source material is converted by some bacteria to the polymer **poly-β-hydroxybutyric acid** (Fig 2–8) and by other bacteria to various polymers of glucose such as starch and glycogen. The granules are used as carbon sources when protein and nucleic acid synthesis is resumed.

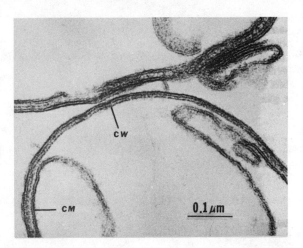

Figure 2–9. The cell membrane. Fragments of the cell membrane (CM) are seen attached to the cell wall (CW) in preparations made from *Escherichia coli.* (From Schnaitman CA: Solubilization of the cytoplasmic membrane of *Escherichia coli* by Triton X-100. *J Bacteriol* 1971; **108**:545.)

Similarly, certain sulfur-oxidizing bacteria convert excess H_2S from the environment into intracellular granules of elemental **sulfur.** Finally, many bacteria accumulate reserves of inorganic phosphate as granules of polymerized metaphosphate, called **volutin.** Volutin granules are also called **metachromatic granules** because they stain red with a blue dye. They are characteristic features of corynebacteria (see p 214).

Microtubular structures, characteristic of eukaryotic cells, are generally absent in prokaryotes. In a few instances, however, the electron microscope has revealed bacterial structures that resemble microtubules.

Cytoplasmic Membrane

A. Structure: The bacterial cytoplasmic membrane, also called the cell membrane, is visible in electron micrographs of thin sections (Fig 2–9). It is a typical "unit membrane," composed of phospholipids and proteins; Fig 2–10 illustrates a model of membrane organization. The membranes of prokaryotes are distinguished from those of eukaryotic cells by the absence of sterols, the only exception being mycoplasmas that incorporate sterols into their membranes when growing in sterol-containing media.

Convoluted invaginations of the cytoplasmic membrane form specialized structures called **mesosomes** (Fig 2–11). There are 2 types: septal mesosomes, which function in the formation of cross-walls during cell division; and lateral mesosomes. The bacterial chromosome (DNA) is attached to a septal mesosome (see Cell Division, below). More extensive ramifications of the cytoplasmic membrane into the cytoplasm are found in bacteria with exceptionally active electron transport systems (eg, photosynthetic and nitrogen-fixing bacteria).

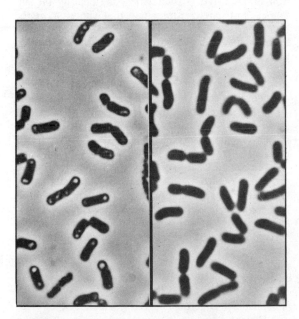

Figure 2–8. Poly-β-hydroxybutyric acid granules (1900 ×) Formation and utilization of the polymer by *Bacillus megaterium.* **Left:** Cells grown on glucose plus acetate, showing granules (light areas). **Right:** Cells from the same culture after 24 hours' further incubation in the presence of a nitrogen source but without an exogenous carbon source. The polymer has been completely metabolized. Phase contrast photomicrograph taken by Dr JF Wilkinson. (From Stanier RY, Doudoroff M, Adelberg EA: *The Microbial World,* 2nd ed. Copyright © 1963. By permission of Prentice-Hall, Inc, Englewood Cliffs, NJ.)

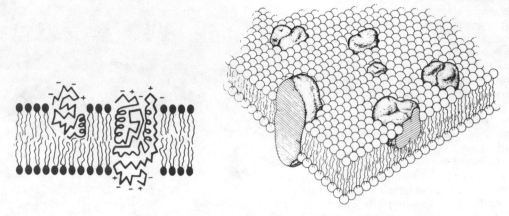

Figure 2–10. A model of membrane structure. Folded polypeptide molecules are visualized as embedded in a phospholipid bilayer, with their hydrophilic regions protruding into the intracellular space, extracellular space, or both. (From Singer SJ, Nicolson AL: The fluid mosaic model of the structure of cell membranes. *Science* 1972;**175**:720. Copyright © 1972 by the American Association for the Advancement of Science.)

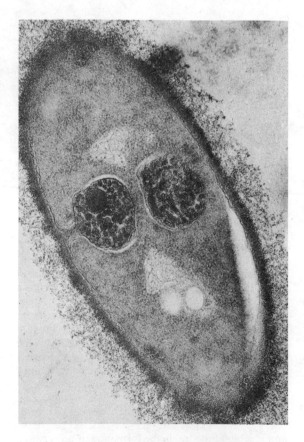

Figure 2–11. Septal mesosomes. A septal mesosome, formed as a concentric fold of the plasma membrane, grows inward. The new transverse septum is seen forming at the base of the concentric mesosome. Cell division will occur by fusion of the membrane layers surrounding the mesosome. (From Ellar DJ, Lundgren D, Slepecky RA: Fine structure of *Bacillus megaterium* during synchronous growth. *J Bacteriol* 1967;**94**:1189.)

B. Function: The major functions of the cytoplasmic membrane are (1) selective permeability and transport of solutes; (2) electron transport and oxidative phosphorylation, in aerobic species; (3) the excretion of hydrolytic exoenzymes; (4) bearing the enzymes and carrier molecules that function in the biosynthesis of DNA, cell wall polymers, and membrane lipids; and (5) bearing the receptors and other proteins of the chemotactic systems.

1. Permeability and transport–The membrane is both a permeability barrier (lipophobic solutes do not penetrate passively) and a permeability link: specific protein systems (permeases) are present that either facilitate the passive diffusion of specific solutes or catalyze energy-dependent active transport against a gradient.

There are 2 types of active transport. In primary systems (''pumps''), metabolic energy is used to drive solutes through the membrane against their concentration gradients. In aerobic bacteria, the primary pump is the electron transport system, which uses the energy derived from substrate oxidation to export protons (see Chapter 5). As illustrated in Fig 5–2, the exported protons reenter the cell via the membrane ATPase; the energy derived from this ion flow is used by the ATPase to synthesize ATP from ADP plus inorganic phosphate. In anaerobic bacteria, which lack the electron transport system, the system is reversed: proton export takes place through the ATPase, at the expense of energy derived from the breakdown of ATP.

In mammalian cells, the primary pump of the cytoplasmic membrane is Na^+-K^+ ATPase, which pumps 3 sodium ions out of and 2 potassium ions into the cell for each ATP molecule converted to ADP and inorganic phosphate.

In secondary systems, the energy stored in the cation gradients and membrane potential produced by the pumps is used to actively transport solutes, such as amino acids and sugars, into the cell. This is accomplished by cotransport systems: the carrier binds cation and solute, transporting both simultaneously. Since the cation gradient is directed strongly inward, the combined electrochemical gradient drives the solute into the cell against its own concentration gradient.

The cell also has specific protein carriers in the membrane to facilitate the diffusion of solutes either into or out of the cell. Thus, if the cell is placed in a medium containing a high concentration of an amino acid, it can equilibrate that amino acid by facilitated diffusion in the absence of a coupled energy source.

Bacteria use the transport of potassium ion to regulate their turgor pressure. An increase in external osmolarity at constant K^+ concentration activates the expression of genes coding for a set of K^+ transport proteins and also increases the activity of those proteins.

In addition to true transport, in which a solute is moved across the membrane without change in structure, bacteria use a process called **group translocation** to effect the net uptake of certain sugars (eg, glucose and mannose), the substrate becoming phosphorylated during the transport process. A membrane carrier protein is first phosphorylated in the cytoplasm at the expense of phosphoenolpyruvate; the phosphorylated carrier then binds the free sugar at the exterior membrane face and transports it into the cytoplasm, releasing it as sugar-phosphate.

2. Electron transport and oxidative phosphorylation—The cytochromes and other enzymes of the respiratory chain, including certain dehydrogenases, are located in the cytoplasmic membrane, most or all being concentrated in the mesosomes. The bacterial cytoplasmic membrane is thus a functional analog of the mitochondrial inner membrane—a relationship which has been taken by many biologists to support the theory that mitochondria have evolved from symbiotic bacteria. The mechanism by which ATP generation is coupled to electron transport is discussed in Chapter 5.

3. Excretion of hydrolytic exoenzymes—All organisms that rely on macromolecular organic polymers as a source of nutrients (eg, proteins, polysaccharides, lipids) excrete hydrolytic enzymes that degrade the polymers to subunits small enough to penetrate the cytoplasmic membrane. Higher animals excrete such enzymes into the lumen of the digestive tract; bacteria excrete them directly into the external medium (in the case of gram-positive cells) or into the space (the "periplasmic space") between the peptidoglycan layer and the outer membrane of the cell wall in the case of gram-negative bacteria (see Cell Wall, below). Excreted proteins are synthesized as preproteins carrying a hydrophobic sequence of about 20 amino acids at the N-terminal end. This leader or "signal" sequence binds the ribosome to the inner face of the cell membrane; the signal sequence initiates the passage of the polypeptide through the membrane and is ultimately cleaved off to release the mature excreted protein.

4. Biosynthetic functions—The cytoplasmic membrane is the site of the carrier lipids on which the subunits of the cell wall are assembled (see Synthesis of Cell Wall, Chapter 5), as well as of the enzymes of cell wall biosynthesis. The enzymes of phospholipid synthesis are also localized in the cytoplasmic membrane. Finally, some proteins of the DNA replicating complex are present at discrete sites in the membrane, presumably in the septal mesosomes to which the DNA is attached.

5. Chemotactic systems—Attractants and repellents bind to specific receptors in the bacterial membrane (see Flagella, below). There are at least 20 different chemoreceptors in the membrane of *Escherichia coli,* some of which also function as a first step in the transport process.

C. Antibacterial Agents Affecting the Cell Membrane: Detergents, which contain lipophilic and hydrophilic groups, disrupt cytoplasmic membranes and kill the cell (see Chapter 7). One class of antibiotics, the polymyxins, consists of detergentlike cyclic peptides that selectively damage membranes containing phosphatidylethanolamine, a major component of bacterial membranes. A number of antibiotics specifically interfere with biosynthetic functions of the cytoplasmic membranes—eg, nalidixic acid, phenethyl alcohol, and novobiocin inhibit DNA synthesis; and novobiocin also inhibits teichoic acid synthesis.

A third class of membrane-active agents is the ionophores: compounds that permit rapid diffusion of specific cations through the membrane. Valinomycin, for example, specifically mediates the passage of potassium ions. Some ionophores act by forming hydrophilic pores in the membrane; others act as lipid-soluble ion carriers that behave as though they shuttle back and forth within the membrane. Ionophores can kill cells by discharging the membrane potential, which is essential for oxidative phosphorylation as well as for other membrane-mediated processes; they are not selective for bacteria but act on the membranes of all cells.

Cell Wall

The internal osmotic pressure of most bacteria ranges from 5 to 20 atmospheres as a result of solute concentration via active transport. In most environments, this pressure would be sufficient to burst the cell were it not for the presence of a high-tensile-strength cell wall (Fig 2–12). The bacterial cell wall owes its strength to a layer composed of a substance variously referred to as murein, mucopeptide, or **peptidoglycan** (all are synonyms). The structure of peptidoglycan will be discussed below.

Bacteria are classified as gram-positive or gram-negative according to their response to the Gram staining procedure. This procedure, named for its inventor, was developed in an attempt to selectively stain bacteria in infected tissues. The cells are first stained with crystal violet and iodine and then washed with acetone or alcohol. The latter step decolorizes gram-negative bacteria but not gram-positive bacteria.

The difference between gram-positive and gram-negative bacteria has been shown to reside in the

Figure 2–12. Cell walls of *Streptococcus faecalis,* removed from protoplasts by mechanical disintegration and differential centrifugation (11,000 ×). (Courtesy of Salton M, Horne R: *Biochim Biophys Acta* 1951;7:177.)

cell wall: gram-positive cells can be decolorized with acetone or alcohol if the cell wall is removed after the staining step but before the washing step. Although the chemical composition of gram-positive and gram-negative walls is now fairly well known (see below), the reason gram-positive walls block the dye-extraction step is still unclear.

In addition to giving osmotic protection, the cell wall plays an essential role in cell division as well as serving as a primer for its own biosynthesis. Various layers of the wall are the sites of major antigenic determinants of the cell surface, and one layer—the lipopolysaccharide of gram-negative cell walls—is responsible for the nonspecific endotoxin activity of gram-negative bacteria. The cell wall is, in general, nonselectively permeable; one layer of the gram-negative wall, however—the outer membrane—hinders the passage of relatively large molecules (see below).

The biosynthesis of the cell wall and the antibiotics that interfere with this process are discussed in Chapter 5.

A. The Peptidoglycan Layer: Peptidoglycan is a complex polymer consisting, for the purposes of description, of 3 parts: a backbone, composed of alternating N-acetylglucosamine and N-acetylmuramic acid; a set of identical tetrapeptide side chains attached to N-acetylmuramic acid; and a set of identical peptide cross-bridges (Fig 2–13). The backbone is the same in all bacterial species; the tetrapeptide side chains and the peptide cross-bridges vary from species to species, those of *Staphylococcus aureus* being illustrated in Fig 2–13. In many gram-negative cell walls, the cross-bridge consists of a direct peptide linkage between the diaminopimelic acid (DAP) amino group of one side chain and the carboxyl group of the terminal D-alanine of a second side chain.

The tetrapeptide side chains of all species, however, have certain important features in common. Most

have L-alanine at position 1 (attached to N-acetylmuramic acid); D-glutamate or substituted D-glutamate at position 2; and D-alanine at position 4. Position 3 is the most variable one: most gram-negative bacteria carry diaminopimelic acid at this position, to which is linked the lipoprotein cell wall component discussed below. Gram-positive bacteria may carry diaminopimelic acid, L-lysine, or any of several other L-amino acids at position 3.

Diaminopimelic acid is a unique element of prokaryotic cell walls and is the immediate precursor of lysine in the bacterial biosynthesis of that amino acid (Fig 5-1). Bacterial mutants that are blocked prior to diaminopimelic acid in the biosynthetic pathway grow normally when provided with diaminopimelic acid in the medium; when given L-lysine alone, however, they lyse, since they continue to grow but are specifically unable to make new cell wall peptidoglycan.

The fact that all peptidoglycan chains are cross-linked means that each peptidoglycan layer is a single giant molecule. In gram-positive bacteria there are many peptidoglycan layers, comprising up to 90% of the cell wall material; in gram-negative bacteria there is only one layer—or at most 2 layers—comprising only 5–20% of the wall material.

Several prokaryotic groups, collectively called the archaebacteria, lack a peptidoglycan layer. In some species within this group, a similar polymer exists containing N-acetyl sugars and 3 L-amino acids; muramic acid and D-amino acids are absent. In other archaebacteria, a protein layer is present instead. These organisms, which also show major differences in their lipids and RNAs, occupy extreme environments in nature and have been proposed to represent the most primitive forms of cellular life on earth (see Chapter 1).

B. Special Components of Gram-Positive Cell Walls: Most gram-positive cell walls contain considerable amounts of **teichoic acids,** which may form up to 50% of the dry weight of the wall and 10% of the dry weight of the total cell. In addition, some gram-positive walls may contain polysaccharide molecules.

1. Teichoic acids–These are water-soluble polymers, containing ribitol or glycerol residues joined through phosphodiester linkages (Fig 2–14A). There are 2 types: wall teichoic acid, covalently linked to peptidoglycan; and membrane teichoic acid (lipoteichoic acid), covalently linked to membrane glycolipid and concentrated in mesosomes. Some gram-positive species lack wall teichoic acids, but all appear to contain membrane teichoic acids.

The teichoic acids constitute major surface antigens of those gram-positive species that possess them, and their accessibility to antibodies has been taken as evidence that they lie on the outside surface of the peptidoglycan layer. Their activity is often increased, however, by partial digestion of the peptidoglycan; thus, much of the teichoic acid may lie between the cytoplasmic membrane and the peptidoglycan layer, possibly extending upward through pores in the latter (Fig 2–14B).

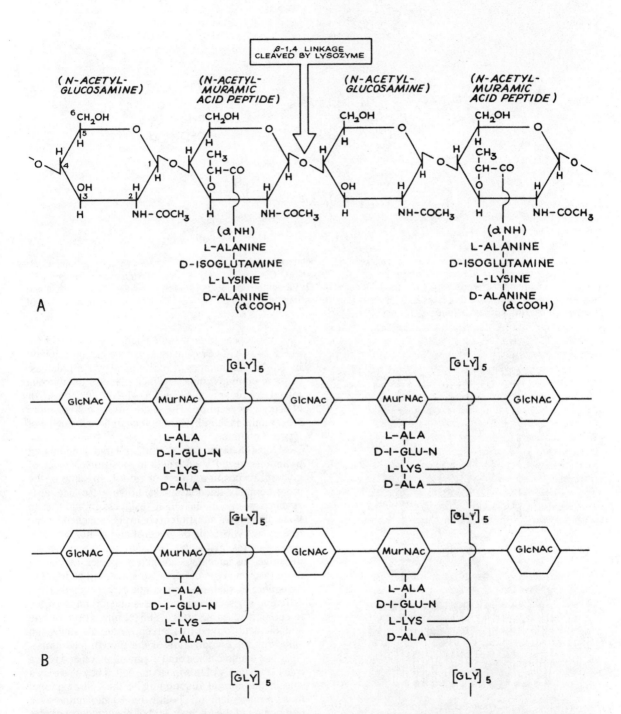

Figure 2–13. *A:* A segment of the peptidoglycan of *Staphylococcus aureus*. The backbone of the polymer consists of alternating subunits of N-acetylglucosamine and N-acetylmuramic acid connected by β-1,4 linkages. The muramic acid residues are linked to short peptides, the composition of which varies from one bacterial species to another. In some species, the L-lysine residues are replaced by diaminopimelic acid, an amino acid that is found in nature only in prokaryotic cell walls. Note the D-amino acids, which are also characteristic constituents of prokaryotic cell walls. The peptide chains of the peptidoglycan are cross-linked between parallel polysaccharide backbones, as shown in Fig 2–13B. *B:* Schematic representation of the peptidoglycan lattice that is formed by cross-linking. Bridges composed of pentaglycine peptide chains connect the α-carboxyl of the terminal D-alanine residue of one chain with the ε-amino group of the L-lysine residue of the next chain. The nature of the cross-linking bridge varies among different species.

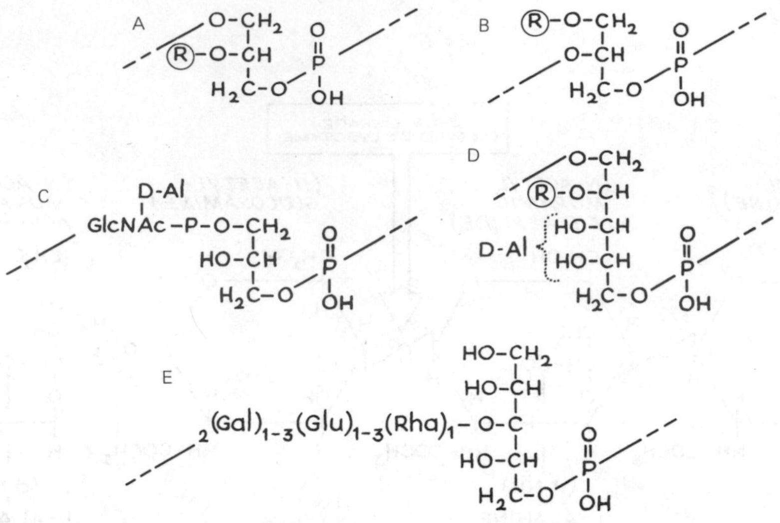

Figure 2–14A. Repeat units of some teichoic acids. *A:* Glycerol teichoic acid of *Lactobacillus casei* 7469 (R = D-alanine). *B:* Glycerol teichoic acid of *Actinomyces antibioticus* (R = D-alanine). *C:* Glycerol teichoic acid of *Staphylococcus lactis* I3. D-Alanine occurs on the 6 position of N-acetylglucosamine. *D:* Ribitol teichoic acids of *Bacillus subtilis* (R = glucose) and *Actinomyces streptomycini* (R = succinate). (The D-alanine is attached to position 3 or 4 of ribitol.) *E:* Ribitol teichoic acid of the type 6 pneumococcal capsule.

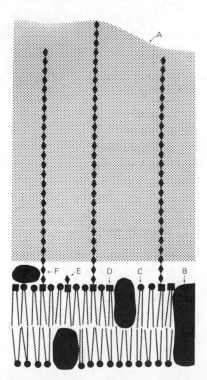

Figure 2–14B. Lipoteichoic acids. A model of the cell wall and membrane of a gram-positive bacterium, showing lipoteichoic acid molecules extending through the cell wall. The wall teichoic acids, covalently linked to muramic acid residues of the peptidoglycan layer, are not shown. A = cell wall; B = protein; C = phospholipid; D = glycolipid; E = phosphatidyl glycolipid; F = lipoteichoic acid. (From Van Driel D et al: Cellular location of the lipoteichoic acids of *Lactobacillus fermenti* NCTC 6991 and *Lactobacillus casei* NCTC 6375. *J Ultrastruct Res* 1971;**43**:483.)

The repeat units of some teichoic acids are shown in Fig 2–14A. The repeat units may be glycerol, joined by 1,3- or 1,2-linkages; ribitol, joined by 1,5-linkages; or more complex units in which glycerol or ribitol is joined to a sugar residue such as glucose, galactose, or N-acetylglucosamine. The chains may be 30 or more repeat units in length, although chain lengths of 10 or less are common.

Most teichoic acids contain large amounts of D-alanine, usually attached to position 2 or 3 of glycerol or position 3 or 4 of ribitol. In some of the more complex teichoic acids, however, D-alanine is attached to one of the sugar residues. In addition to D-alanine, other substituents may be attached to the free hydroxyl groups of glycerol and ribitol: eg, glucose, galactose, N-acetylglucosamine, N-acetylgalactosamine, or succinate. A given species may have more than one type of sugar substituent in addition to D-alanine; in such cases it is not certain whether the different sugars occur on the same or on separate teichoic acid molecules. The composition of the teichoic acid formed by a given bacterial species can vary with the composition of the growth medium.

The teichoic acids bind magnesium ion and play a role in the supply of this ion to the cell. They also play a role in the normal functioning of the cell envelope; thus, replacement of choline by ethanolamine as a component of the teichoic acid of pneumococci causes the cells to resist autolysis and to lose the ability to take up transforming DNA (see Chapter 4).

2. Polysaccharides–The hydrolysis of gram-positive walls has yielded, from certain species, neutral sugars such as mannose, arabinose, galactose, rhamnose, and glucosamine and acidic sugars such as glucuronic acid and mannuronic acid. It has been proposed that these sugars exist as subunits of polysac-

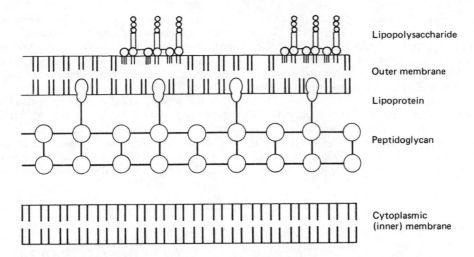

Figure 2–15. A model of the gram-negative cell envelope.

charides in the cell wall; the discovery, however, that teichoic acids may contain a variety of sugars (see Fig 2–14A) leaves the true origin of these sugars uncertain.

C. Special Components of Gram-Negative Cell Walls: Gram-negative cell walls contain 3 components that lie outside of the peptidoglycan layer: lipoprotein, outer membrane, and lipopolysaccharide (Fig 2–15).

1. Lipoprotein–Molecules of an unusual lipoprotein cross-link the outer membrane and peptidoglycan layers. The protein component contains 57 amino acids, representing repeats of a 15-amino-acid sequence; it is peptide-linked to diaminopimelic acid residues of the peptidoglycan tetrapeptide side chains. The lipid component, consisting of a diglyceride thioether linked to a terminal cysteine, is noncovalently inserted in the outer membrane (Fig 2–15).

2. Outer membrane–The outer membrane is a phospholipid bilayer in which a large fraction of the phospholipids of the outer leaflet are replaced by lipopolysaccharide (LPS) molecules (see below). Like the cytoplasmic membrane, the outer membrane is a fluid mosaic containing a set of specific proteins embedded in a phospholipid matrix.

The major proteins of the outer membrane, named according to the genes that code for them, have been placed into several functional categories on the basis of mutants in which they are lacking. The **matrix porins,** exemplified by OmpC, D, and F of *E coli* and *Salmonella typhimurium,* are trimeric proteins that penetrate both faces of the outer membrane. They form relatively nonspecific pores that permit the free diffusion of small (up to about 600 molecular weight) hydrophilic solutes across the membrane. A second group of pore-forming proteins, exemplified by LamB and Tsx, show greater specificity: LamB, which is the receptor for lambda bacteriophage, is responsible for most of the transmembrane diffusion of maltodextrins; Tsx, the receptor for T6 bacteriophage, is responsible for most of the transmembrane diffusion of nucleosides. LamB allows some passage of other solutes, however; its relative specificity may reflect weak interactions of solutes with configuration-specific sites within the channel.

A third group of major proteins are nonporins: they include OmpA, which participates noncovalently in the anchoring of the outer membrane to the peptidoglycan layer and is also the sex pilus receptor in F-mediated bacterial conjugation (see Chapter 4); lipoproteins, described above; and a protein designated ''a'' by one group and ''3b'' by another, which may be a protease and also functions as a regulator of capsular polysaccharide biosynthesis.

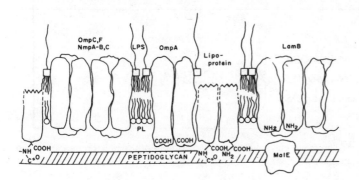

Figure 2–16. Schematic representation of the molecular organization of the major proteins in the outer membrane of gram-negative bacteria. LPS = lipopolysaccharide; PL = phospholipid; Omp, Lam, Nmp = major proteins of the outer membrane; MalE = periplasmic binding protein for maltodextrins. (From Osborn MJ, Wu HCP: Proteins of the outer membrane of gram-negative bacteria. *Annu Rev Microbiol* 1980; **34:**369. Reproduced, with permission, from the *Annual Review of Microbiology,* Vol 34. © 1980 by Annual Reviews, Inc.)

The outer membrane also contains a set of less abundant, so-called minor proteins, many of which are involved in the transport of specific small molecules such as vitamin B_{12} and the iron siderophores. They show high affinity for their substrates and probably function like the classic carrier transport systems of the inner (cytoplasmic) membrane.

In addition to their functions in transport and their functions as phage receptors and conjugation receptors, outer membrane proteins have been implicated in the control of DNA replication and cell division. The outer membrane also serves as a barrier to the diffusion of large molecules (hence the greater resistance of gram-negative bacteria to many antibiotics) and as a protective envelope for hydrolytic enzymes and binding proteins that accumulate in the periplasmic space (the space between the outer membrane and the peptidoglycan layer).

The topology of the major proteins of the outer membrane, based on cross-linking studies and analyses of functional relationships, is shown in Fig 2–16. These proteins are synthesized on ribosomes bound to the cytoplasmic surface of the inner membrane; how they are transferred to the outer membrane

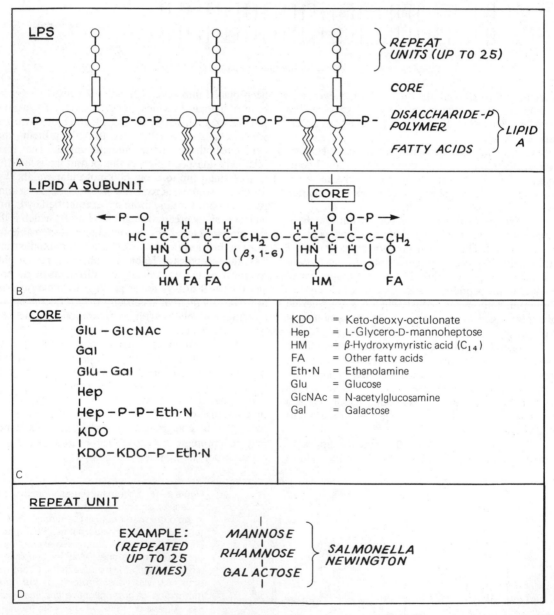

Figure 2–17. The lipopolysaccharide LPS of the gram-negative cell envelope. *A:* A segment of the polymer, showing the arrangements of the major constituents. *B:* The structure of lipid A. *C:* The polysaccharide core. *D:* A typical repeat unit (*Salmonella newington*).

is still uncertain, but one hypothesis suggests that transfer occurs at regions of adhesion between the inner and outer membranes, which regions are visible in the electron microscope.

3. Lipopolysaccharide (LPS)–The lipopolysaccharide of gram-negative cell walls consists of a complex lipid, called lipid A, to which is attached a polysaccharide made up of a core and a terminal series of repeat units (Fig 2–17A).

Lipid A consists of a chain of glucosamine disaccharide units connected by pyrophosphate bridges, to which are attached a number of long chain fatty acids (Fig 2–17B). β-Hydroxymyristic acid, a C_{14} fatty acid, is always present and is unique to this lipid; the other fatty acids vary according to the bacterial species.

The polysaccharide core, shown in Fig 2–17C, is constant in all gram-negative species. Each species, however, contains a unique repeat unit, that of *Salmonella newington* being shown in Fig 2–17D. The repeat units are usually linear trisaccharides or branched tetra- or pentasaccharides.

LPS, which is extremely toxic to animals, has been called the **endotoxin** of gram-negative bacteria because it is firmly bound to the cell surface and is released only when the cells are lysed. When LPS is split into lipid A and polysaccharide, all of the toxicity is associated with the former. The polysaccharide, on the other hand, represents a major surface antigen of the bacterial cell—the so-called **O antigen.** Antigenic specificity is conferred by the terminal repeat units, which form a sort of molecular fur on the cell surface. The number of possible antigenic types is very great: over 1000 have been recognized in *Salmonella* alone.

LPS is attached to the outer membrane by hydrophobic bonds. It is synthesized on the cytoplasmic membrane and transported to its final exterior position. Its function is unknown; although mutants lacking various parts of the polysaccharide grow normally in culture, mutants lacking lipid A have never been observed. An essential role for lipid A is thus postulated.

D. Enzymes That Attack Cell Walls: The β-1,4 linkage of the peptidoglycan backbone is hydrolyzed by the enzyme **lysozyme,** which is found in animal secretions (tears, saliva, nasal secretions) as well as in egg white. Gram-positive bacteria treated with lysozyme in low-osmotic-strength media lyse; if the osmotic strength of the medium is raised to balance the internal osmotic pressure of the cell, free protoplasts are liberated (Fig 2–18). The outer membrane of the gram-negative cell wall prevents access of lysozyme unless disrupted by an agent such as EDTA*; in osmotically protected media, cells treated with EDTA-lysozyme form **spheroplasts** that still possess remnants of the complex gram-negative wall, including the outer membrane.

Bacteria themselves possess a number of **autolysins,** hydrolytic enzymes that attack peptidoglycan, including glycosidases, amidases, and peptidases. These enzymes presumably play essential functions in cell growth and division, but their activity is most apparent during the dissolution of dead cells (autolysis).

Enzymes that degrade bacterial cell walls are also found in cells that digest whole bacteria, eg, protozoa and the phagocytic cells of higher animals.

E. Cell Wall Growth: As the protoplast increases in mass, the cell wall is elongated by the intercalation of newly synthesized subunits into the various wall layers. In streptococci, intercalation into the principal antigen-bearing layer is localized to the equatorial region of the cell wall (Fig 2–19); in some gram-negative bacteria, a process of random intercalation has been inferred, although localized intercalation followed by rapid displacement or turnover could produce the same appearance. In *E coli,* growth of the outer membrane framework takes place exclusively at the cell poles, specialized components such as phage receptors and permeases being inserted randomly into

*Ethylenediaminetetraacetic acid, a chelating agent.

 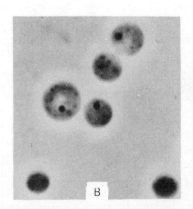 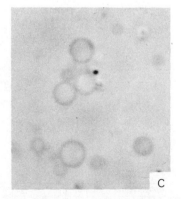

Figure 2–18. *Bacillus megaterium* phase contrast photomicrographs (3000 ×). *A:* Before treatment. *B:* Protoplasts liberated following treatment with lysozyme and sucrose. *C:* After treatment with lysozyme alone; the empty structures are cytoplasmic membranes. (Courtesy of Weibull C: *J Bacteriol* 1963; **66:**688.)

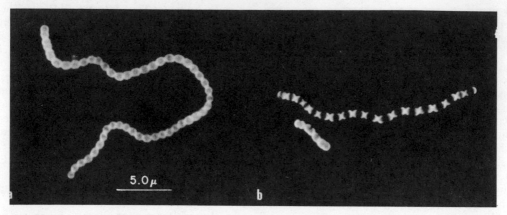

Figure 2–19. Growth of the bacterial cell wall. *(a)* Chain of streptococci, stained with fluorescent antibody directed against cell wall antigens. *(b)* After 15 minutes' growth in the absence of antibody. New cell wall material, unstained by antibody, has been deposited in the equatorial region of each cell. (From Cole RM, Hahn JJ: Cell wall replication in *Streptococcus pyogenes. Science* 1962; **135**:722. Copyright © 1962 by the American Association for the Advancement of Science.)

this framework. The peptidoglycan layer of *E coli* appears to grow by randomly located intercalations.

F. Protoplasts, Spheroplasts, and L Forms: Removal of the bacterial cell wall may be accomplished by hydrolysis with lysozyme or by blocking peptidoglycan biosynthesis with an antibiotic such as penicillin. In osmotically protective media, such treatments liberate protoplasts from gram-positive cells and spheroplasts (which retain the outer membrane) from gram-negative cells.

If such cells are able to grow and divide, they are called **L forms.** L forms are difficult to cultivate and usually require a medium that is solidified with agar as well as having the right osmotic strength. L forms are produced more readily with penicillin than with lysozyme, suggesting the need for residual peptidoglycan.

Some L forms are capable of reverting to the normal bacillary form upon removal of the inducing stimulus. Thus, they are able to resume normal cell wall synthesis. Other L forms, however, are stable and never revert. The factor that determines their capacity

to revert may again be the presence of residual peptidoglycan, which normally acts as a primer in its own biosynthesis.

Some bacterial species produce L forms spontaneously. The spontaneous or antibiotic-induced formation of L forms in the host may produce chronic infections, the organisms persisting by becoming sequestered in protective regions of the body. Since L-form infections are relatively resistant to antibiotic treatment, they present special problems in chemotherapy. Their reversion to the bacillary form can produce relapses of the overt infection.

Capsule & Glycocalyx

Many bacteria synthesize large amounts of extracellular polymer when growing in their natural environments. With one known exception (the poly-D-glutamic acid capsule of *Bacillus anthracis*), the extracellular material is polysaccharide (Table 2–1). When the polymer forms a condensed, well-defined layer closely surrounding the cell, it is called the **capsule** (Fig 2–20A); when it forms a loose meshwork of

Table 2–1. Chemical composition of the extracellular polymer in certain bacteria.*

Organism	Polymer	Chemical Subunits
Bacillus anthracis	Polypeptide	D-Glutamic acid
Leuconostoc mesenteroides	Dextran	Glucose
Streptococcus pneumoniae (pneumococcus)	Complex polysaccharides (many types), eg,	
	Type II	Rhamnose, glucose, glucuronic acid
	Type III	Glucose, glucuronic acid
	Type VI	Galactose, glucose, rhamnose
	Type XIV	Galactose, glucose, N-acetylglucosamine
	Type XVIII	Rhamnose, glucose
Streptococcus spp	Hyaluronic acid	N-Acetylglucosamine, glucuronic acid
Streptococcus salivarius	Levan	Fructose
Acetobacter xylinum	Cellulose	Glucose
Enterobacter aerogenes	Complex polysaccharide	Glucose, fucose, glucuronic acid

*From Stanier RY, Doudoroff M, Adelberg EA: *The Microbial World,* 3rd ed. Copyright 1970. By permission of Prentice-Hall, Inc, Englewood Cliffs, NJ.

Figure 2–20A. *Bacillus megaterium,* stained by a combination of positive and negative staining (1400 ×). (See section on staining, below.) (Courtesy of Welshimer H: *J Bacteriol* 1953; **66**:112.)

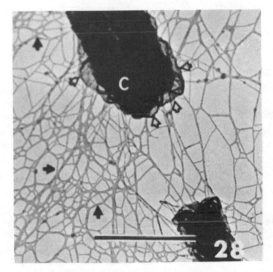

Figure 2–20B. *Klebsiella pneumoniae* cells (C), surrounded by glycocalyx (solid arrows). (From Cagle AD: Fine structure and distribution of extracellular polymer surrounding selected aerobic bacteria. *Can J Microbiol* 1975; **21**:395.)

fibrils extending outward from the cell, it is called the **glycocalyx** (Fig 2–20B). In some cases, masses of polymer are formed which appear to be totally detached from the cells but in which cells may be entrapped; in these instances, the extracellular polymer may be referred to simply as a "slime layer." Extracellular polymer is synthesized by enzymes located at the surface of the bacterial cell. *Streptococcus mutans,* for example, uses 2 enzymes—glucosyl transferase and fructosyl transferase—to synthesize long chain dextrans (poly-D-glucose) and levans (poly-D-fructose) from sucrose.

The capsule contributes to the invasiveness of pathogenic bacteria: encapsulated cells are protected from phagocytosis unless they are coated with anticap-

sular antibody. The glycocalyx plays a major role in the adherence of bacteria to surfaces in their environment, including the cells of their plant and animal hosts. *S mutans,* for example, owes its capacity to adhere tightly to tooth enamel to its glycocalyx. Bacterial cells of the same or different species become entrapped in the glycocalyx, which forms the layer known as plaque on the tooth surface; acidic products excreted by these bacteria cause dental caries (see p 282). The essential role of the glycocalyx in this process—and its formation from sucrose—explains the correlation of dental caries with sucrose consumption by the human population.

Flagella

A. Structure: Bacterial flagella are threadlike appendages composed entirely of protein, 12–30 nm in diameter. They are the organs of locomotion for the forms that possess them. Three types of arrangement are known: **monotrichous** (single polar flagellum), **lophotrichous** (tuft of polar flagella), or **peritrichous** (flagella distributed over the entire cell). The 3 types are illustrated in Figs 2–21, 2–22, and 2–23.

A bacterial flagellum is made up of a single kind of protein subunit called flagellin; the flagellum is formed by the aggregation of subunits to form a hollow cylindric structure. If flagella are removed by mechanically agitating a suspension of bacteria, new flagella are rapidly formed by the synthesis, aggregation, and extrusion of flagellin subunits; motility is restored within 3–6 minutes. The flagellins of different bacte-

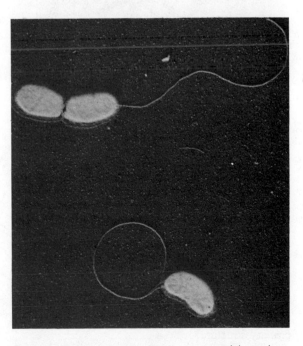

Figure 2–21. *Vibrio metchnikovii,* a monotrichous bacterium (7500 ×). (Courtesy of van Iterson W: *Biochim Biophys Acta* 1947; **1**:527.)

Figure 2–22. Electron micrograph of *Spirillum serpens,* showing lophotrichous flagellation (9000 ×). (Courtesy of van Iterson W: *Biochim Biophys Acta* 1947; **1**:527.)

Figure 2–24. Electron micrograph of a negatively stained lysate of *Rhodospirillum molischianum,* showing the basal structure of an isolated flagellum. (From Cohen-Bazire G, London L: Basal organelles of bacterial flagella. *J Bacteriol* 1967; **94**:458.)

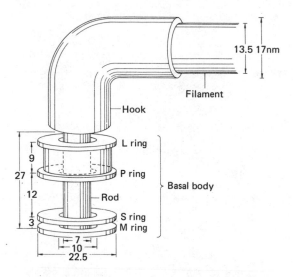

Figure 2–25. Basal structure of the bacterial flagellum. Diagram interpreting the structure seen in Fig 2–24. (From De Pamphilis ML, Adler J: Fine structure and isolation of the hook-basal body complex of flagella from *Escherichia coli* and *Bacillus subtilis. J Bacteriol* 1971; **105**:384.)

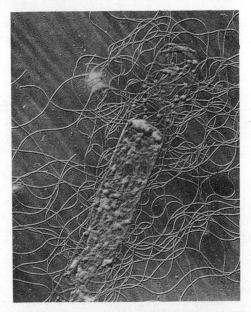

Figure 2–23. Electron micrograph of *Proteus vulgaris,* showing peritrichous flagellation (9000 ×). Note basal granules. (Courtesy of Houwink A, van Iterson W: *Biochim Biophys Acta* 1950; **5**:10.)

rial species presumably differ from one another in primary structure.

The flagellum is attached to the bacterial cell body by a complex structure consisting of a hook and a basal body. The basal body bears a set of rings, one

pair in gram-positive bacteria and 2 pairs in gram-negative bacteria. An electron micrograph and interpretative diagrams of the gram-negative structure are shown in Figs 2–24 and 2–25; the rings labeled L and P are absent in gram-positive cells.

B. Motility: Bacterial flagella are semirigid helical rotors to which the cell imparts a spinning movement. Rotation appears to be driven by the flow of protons into the cell down the gradient produced by the primary proton pump (see above); in the absence of a metabolic energy source, it can be driven by a proton-motive force generated by ionophores.

When a peritrichous bacterium swims, its flagella associate to form a posterior bundle that drives the cell forward in a straight line. At intervals the flagella reverse their direction of rotation and momentarily dissociate, causing the cell to tumble until swimming resumes in a new, randomly determined direction.

This behavior confers on the bacterium the property of **chemotaxis:** a cell that is moving away from the source of a chemical attractant tumbles and reorients itself more frequently than one that is moving toward the attractant, the result being the net movement of the cell toward the source. The presence of a chemical attractant (such as a sugar or an amino acid) is sensed by specific receptors located in the cell membrane (in many cases the same receptor also participates in membrane transport of that molecule). The bacterial cell is too small to be able to detect the existence of a spatial chemical gradient (ie, a gradient between its 2 poles); rather, experiments show that it detects temporal gradients, ie, concentrations that decrease with time when the cell is moving away from the attractant source and increase with time when the cell is moving toward it.

Some compounds act as repellents rather than attractants. The mechanism by which cells respond to attractants and repellents involves a cGMP-mediated methylation and demethylation of specific proteins in the membrane. Attractants cause a transient inhibition of demethylation of these proteins, while repellents stimulate their demethylation.

Pili (Fimbriae)

Many gram-negative bacteria possess rigid surface appendages called pili (Latin ''hairs'') or fimbriae (Latin ''fringes''). They are shorter and finer than flagella; like flagella, they are composed of protein subunits. Two classes can be distinguished: ordinary pili, which play a role in the adherence of symbiotic bacteria to host cells; and sex pili, which are responsible for the attachment of donor and recipient cells in bacterial conjugation (see Chapter 4). Pili are illustrated in Fig 2–26, in which the sex pili have been coated with phage particles for which they serve as specific receptors.

The virulence of certain pathogenic bacteria depends on the production not only of toxins but also of ''colonization antigens,'' which are now recognized to be ordinary pili. In enteropathogenic *E coli* strains, both the enterotoxins and the colonization antigens (pili) are genetically determined by transmissible plasmids, as discussed in Chapter 4.

One group of gram-positive cocci, the streptococci, bears a layer of fimbriae that are the site of the major surface antigen, the M protein. Lipoteichoic acid, associated with these fimbriae, is responsible for the adherence of group A streptococci to epithelial cells of their hosts.

Endospores

Members of several bacterial genera are capable of forming endospores (Fig 2–27). The 2 most common are gram-positive rods: the obligately aerobic genus *Bacillus* and the obligately anaerobic genus *Clostridium*. The other bacteria known to form endospores are the gram-positive coccus *Sporosarcina* and the rickettsial agent of Q fever, *Coxiella burnetii*. These organisms undergo a cycle of differentiation in

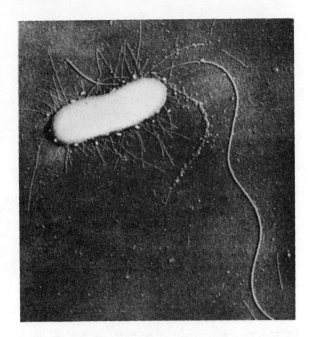

Figure 2–26. Surface appendages of bacteria. Electron micrograph of a cell of *Escherichia coli* possessing 3 types of appendages: ordinary pili (short, straight bristles); a sex pilus (longer, flexible, with phage particles attached); and several flagella (longest, thickest). Diameters: Ordinary pili: 7 nm; sex pili: 8.5 nm; flagella: 25 nm. (Courtesy of Dr J Carnahan and Dr C Brinton.)

response to environmental conditions: under conditions of nutritional depletion, each cell forms a single internal spore that is liberated when the mother cell undergoes autolysis. The spore is a resting cell, highly resistant to desiccation, heat, and chemical agents; when returned to favorable nutritional conditions and activated (see below), the spore germinates to produce a single vegetative cell.

A. Sporulation: The sporulation process begins when nutritional conditions become unfavorable, depletion of the nitrogen or carbon source (or both) being the most significant factor. Sporulation occurs massively in cultures that have terminated exponential growth as a result of such depletion.

Sporulation involves the production of many new structures, enzymes, and metabolites along with the disappearance of many vegetative cell components. These changes represent a true process of **differentiation:** A series of genes whose products determine the formation and final composition of the spore is activated, while another series of genes involved in vegetative cell function is inactivated. These changes involve an alteration in the specificity of RNA polymerase.

The sequence of events in sporulation is highly complex: asporogenous mutants reveal at least 12 morphologically or biochemically distinguishable stages, and at least 30 operons (including an estimated 200 structural genes) are involved. During the process,

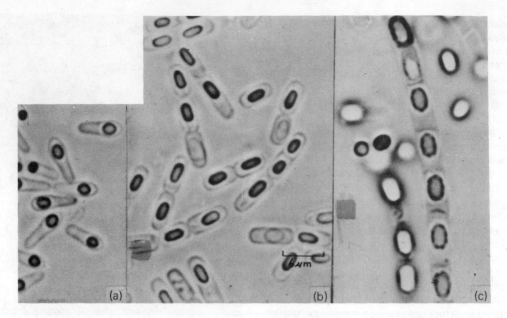

Figure 2–27. Sporulating cells of *Bacillus* species. *A:* Unidentified bacillus from soil. *B: B cereus. C: B megaterium.* (From Robinow CF, in: *The Bacteria.* Vol 1. Gunsalus IC, Stanier RY [editors]. Academic Press, 1960.)

some bacteria release peptide antibiotics, which may play a role in regulating sporogenesis.

Morphologically, sporulation begins with the isolation of a terminal nucleus by the inward growth of the cell membrane (Fig 2–28). The growth process involves an infolding of the membrane so as to produce a double membrane structure whose facing surfaces correspond to the cell wall–synthesizing surface of the cell envelope. The growing points move progressively toward the pole of the cell so as to engulf the developing spore.

The 2 spore membranes now engage in the active synthesis of special layers that will form the cell envelope: the **spore wall** and **cortex,** lying between the facing membranes; and the **coat** and **exosporium,** lying outside of the facing membranes. In the newly isolated cytoplasm, or **core,** many vegetative cell enzymes are degraded and are replaced by a set of unique spore constituents. A thin section of a sporulating cell is shown in Fig 2–29.

B. Properties of Endospores:

1. Core–The core is the spore protoplast. It contains a complete nucleus (chromosome), all of the components of the protein-synthesizing apparatus, and an energy-generating system based on glycolysis. Cytochromes are lacking even in aerobic species, the spores of which rely on a shortened electron transport pathway involving flavoproteins. A number of vegetative cell enzymes are increased in amount (eg, alanine racemase), and a number of unique enzymes are formed (eg, dipicolinic acid synthetase). The energy for germination is stored as 3-phosphoglycerate rather than as ATP.

The heat resistance of spores is due in part to their dehydrated state and in part to the presence of large

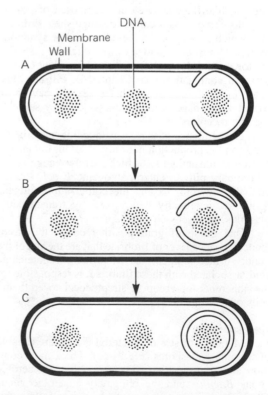

Figure 2–28. The sporulation process. *A:* Inward growth of an invagination of the cell membrane. *B:* Membrane growing points move toward the pole of the cell. *C:* Fusion of membranes completes the isolation of the spore protoplast.

amounts (5–15% of the spore dry weight) of calcium dipicolinate, which is formed from an intermediate of the lysine biosynthetic pathway (Fig 5–11). In some way not yet understood, these properties result in the stabilization of the spore enzymes, most of which exhibit normal heat lability when isolated in soluble form.

2. Spore wall–The innermost layer surrounding the inner spore membrane is called the spore wall. It contains normal peptidoglycan and becomes the cell wall of the germinating vegetative cell.

3. Cortex–The cortex is the thickest layer of the spore envelope. It contains an unusual type of peptidoglycan, with many fewer cross-links than are found in cell wall peptidoglycan. Cortex peptidoglycan is extremely sensitive to lysozyme, and its autolysis plays a key role in spore germination.

4. Coat–The coat is composed of a keratinlike protein containing many intramolecular disulfide bonds. The impermeability of this layer confers on spores their relative resistance to antibacterial chemical agents.

5. Exosporium–The exosporium is a lipoprotein membrane containing some carbohydrate.

C. Germination: The germination process occurs in 3 stages: activation, initiation, and outgrowth.

1. Activation–Even when placed in an environment that favors germination (eg, a nutritionally rich

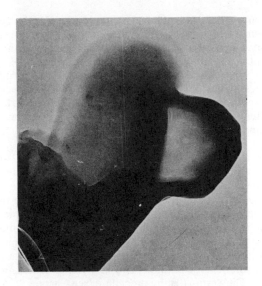

Figure 2–30. Electron micrograph of germinating spore of *Bacillus mycoides.* (Courtesy of Knaysi G, Baker R, Hillier J: *J Bacteriol* 1947; **53**:525.)

medium), bacterial spores will not germinate unless first activated by one or another agent that damages the spore coat. Among the agents that can overcome spore dormancy are heat, abrasion, acidity, and compounds containing free sulfhydryl groups.

2. Initiation–Once activated, a spore will initiate germination if the environmental conditions are favorable. Different species have evolved receptors that recognize different effectors as signalling a rich medium: thus, initiation is triggered by L-alanine in one species and by adenosine in another. Binding of the effector activates an autolysin that rapidly degrades the cortex peptidoglycan. Water is taken up, calcium dipicolinate is released, and a variety of spore constituents are degraded by hydrolytic enzymes.

3. Outgrowth–Degradation of the cortex and outer layers results in the emergence of a new vegetative cell consisting of the spore protoplast with its surrounding wall (Fig 2–30). A period of active biosynthesis follows; this period, which terminates in cell division, is called outgrowth. Outgrowth requires a supply of all nutrients essential for cell growth.

STAINING

Stains combine chemically with the bacterial protoplasm; if the cell is not already dead, the staining process itself will kill it. The process is thus a drastic one and may produce artifacts.

The commonly used stains are salts. **Basic** stains consist of a colored cation with a colorless anion (eg, methylene blue$^+$ chloride$^-$); **acidic** stains are the reverse (eg, sodium $^+$ eosinate$^-$). Bacterial cells are rich in nucleic acid, bearing negative charges as phosphate

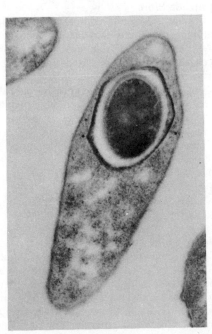

Figure 2–29. Thin section through a sporulating cell of a bacillus (33,000 ×). Electron micrograph taken by Dr CL Hannay. (From Stanier RY, Doudoroff M, Adelberg EA: *The Microbial World,* 2nd ed. Copyright © 1963. By permission of Prentice-Hall, Inc, Englewood Cliffs, NJ.)

groups. These combine with the positively charged basic dyes. Acidic dyes do not stain bacterial cells and hence can be used to stain background material a contrasting color (see Negative Staining, below).

The basic dyes stain bacterial cells uniformly unless the cytoplasmic RNA is destroyed first. Special staining techniques can be used, however, to differentiate flagella, capsules, cell walls, cell membranes, granules, nuclei, and spores.

Gram Stain

An important taxonomic characteristic of bacteria is their response to Gram's stain. The gram-staining property appears to be a fundamental one, since the Gram reaction is correlated with many other morphologic properties in phylogenetically related forms (see Chapter 3). An organism that is potentially gram-positive may appear so only under a particular set of environmental conditions and in a young culture.

The gram-staining procedure (see Chapter 26 for details) begins with the application of a basic dye, crystal violet. A solution of iodine is then applied; all bacteria will be stained blue at this point in the procedure. The cells are then treated with alcohol. Gram-positive cells retain the crystal violet–iodine complex, remaining blue; gram-negative cells are completely decolorized by alcohol. As a last step, a counterstain (such as the red dye safranin) is applied so that the decolorized gram-negative cells will take on a contrasting color; the gram-positive cells now appear purple.

The basis of the differential Gram reaction is the structure of the cell wall, as discussed earlier in this chapter.

The Acid-Fast Stain

Acid-fast bacteria are those that retain carbolfuchsin (basic fuchsin dissolved in a phenol-alcohol-water mixture) even when decolorized with hydrochloric acid in alcohol. A smear of cells on a slide is flooded with carbolfuchsin and heated on a steam bath. Following this, the decolorization with acid-alcohol is carried out, and finally a contrasting (blue or green) counterstain is applied. Acid-fast bacteria (*Mycobacterium* species and some of the related actinomycetes) appear red; others take on the color of the counterstain.

Negative Staining

This procedure involves staining the background with an acidic dye, leaving the cells contrastingly colorless. The black dye nigrosin is commonly used. This method is used for those cells or structures difficult to stain directly (Fig 2–20A).

The Flagella Stain

Flagella are too fine (12–30 nm in diameter) to be visible in the light microscope. However, their presence and arrangement can be demonstrated by treating the cells with an unstable colloidal suspension of tannic acid salts, causing a heavy precipitate to form on the cell walls and flagella. In this manner, the apparent diameter of the flagella is increased to such an extent

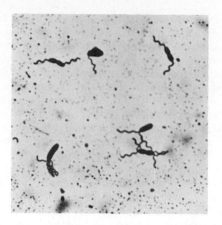

Figure 2–31. Flagella stain of *Pseudomonas* species. (Courtesy of Leifson E: *J Bacteriol* 1951; **62:**377.)

that subsequent staining with basic fuchsin makes the flagella visible in the light microscope. Fig 2–31 shows cells stained by this method.

In multitrichous bacteria, the flagella form into bundles during movement, and such bundles may be thick enough to be observed on living cells by darkfield or phase contrast microscopy.

The Capsule Stain

Capsules are usually demonstrated by the negative staining procedure or a modification of it (Fig 2–20A). One such "capsule stain" (Welch method) involves treatment with hot crystal violet solution followed by a rinsing with copper sulfate solution. The latter is used to remove excess stain because the conventional washing with water would dissolve the capsule. The copper salt also gives color to the background, with the result that the cell and background appear dark blue and the capsule a much paler blue.

Staining of Nuclei

Nuclei are stainable with the Feulgen stain, which is specific for DNA.

The Spore Stain

Spores are most simply observed as intracellular refractile bodies in unstained cell suspensions or as colorless areas in cells stained by conventional methods. The spore wall is relatively impermeable, but dyes can be made to penetrate it by heating the preparation. The same impermeability then serves to prevent decolorization of the spore by a period of alcohol treatment sufficient to decolorize vegetative cells. The latter can finally be counterstained. Spores are commonly stained with malachite green or carbolfuchsin.

MORPHOLOGIC CHANGES
DURING GROWTH

Cell Division

In general, bacteria reproduce by binary fission. Following elongation of the cell, a transverse cell membrane is formed, and subsequently a new cell wall. In bacteria, the new transverse membrane and wall grow inward from the outer layers, a process in which the septal mesosomes are intimately involved (Fig 2–11). The nuclei, which have doubled in number preceding the division, are distributed equally to the 2 daughter cells.

Although bacteria lack a mitotic spindle, the transverse membrane is formed in such a way as to separate the 2 sister chromosomes formed by chromosomal replication. This is accomplished by the attachment of the chromosome to the cell membrane. According to one model, the completion of a cycle of DNA replication triggers active membrane synthesis between the sites of attachment of the 2 sister chromosomes, which are pushed apart by the inward growth of the transverse membrane (Fig 4–4). The deposition of new cell wall material follows, resulting in the elongation and eventual doubling of the cell envelope.

Cell Groupings

If the cells remain temporarily attached following division, certain characteristic groupings result. Depending on the plane of division and the number of divisions through which the cells remain attached, the following arrangement may occur in the coccal forms: chains (streptococci), pairs (pneumococci), cubical bundles (sarcinae), or flat plates. Rods may form pairs or chains.

Following fission of some bacteria, characteristic postfission movements occur. For example, a "whipping" motion can bring the cells into parallel positions; repeated division and whipping results in the "palisade" arrangement characteristic of diphtheria bacilli.

Life Cycle Changes

As bacteria progress from the dormant to the actively growing state, certain visible changes take place. The cells tend to become larger, granules disappear, and the protoplasm stains more deeply with basic dyes. When growth slows down again, a gradual change in the reverse direction takes place. Finally, in very old cultures there appear morphologically unusual cells called involution forms. These include filaments, buds, and branched cells, many of which are nonviable.

●　　●　　●

References

Books

Beachey EH (editor): *Bacterial Adherence: Receptors and Recognition.* Series B, Vol 6. Chapman & Hall, 1980.

Fuller R, Lovelock DW (editors): *Microbial Ultrastructure.* Academic Press, 1976.

Goldberger RF: *Molecular Organization and Cell Function.* Plenum, 1980.

Gould GW, Hurst A (editors): *The Bacterial Spore.* Academic Press, 1969.

Inouye M (editor): *Bacterial Outer Membranes: Biogenesis and Functions.* Wiley-Interscience, 1980.

Leive L (editor): *Membranes and Walls of Bacteria.* Dekker, 1973.

Parish JH: *Developmental Biology of Prokaryotes.* Univ of California Press, 1980.

Rosen B (editor): *Bacterial Transport.* Dekker, 1978.

Stanier R et al (editors): *Relations Between Structure and Function in the Prokaryotic Cell.* No. 28 of: *Symposia of the Society for General Microbiology.* Cambridge Univ Press, 1978.

Tipper DJ, Gauthier TT: Structure of the bacterial endospore. Page 3 in: *Spores.* Vol 5. Halvorson HO, Hanson R, Campbell LL (editors). American Society for Microbiology, 1972.

Articles & Reviews

Archibald AR: The structure, biosynthesis and function of teichoic acid. *Adv Microb Physiol* 1974;**11:**53.

Aronson AI, Fitz-James P: Structure and morphogenesis of the bacterial spore coat. *Bacteriol Rev* 1976;**40:**360.

Beachey EH, Ofek I: Epithelial cell binding of group A streptococci by lipoteichoic acid on fimbriae denuded of M protein. *J Exp Med* 1976;**143:**759.

Begg KJ, Donachie WD: Growth of the *Escherichia coli* cell surface. *J Bacteriol* 1977;**129:**1524.

Berg H: Chemotaxis in bacteria. *Annu Rev Biophys Bioeng* 1975;**4:**119.

Berg H: How bacteria swim. *Sci Am* (Aug) 1975;**233:**36.

Cagle GD: Fine structure and distribution of extracellular polymer surrounding selected aerobic bacteria. *Can J Microbiol* 1975;**21:**395.

Cairns J: The chromosome of *Escherichia coli*. *Cold Spring Harbor Symp Quant Biol* 1963;**28:**43.

Clasener H: Pathogenicity of the L-phase of bacteria. *Annu Rev Microbiol* 1972;**26:**55.

Costerton JW, Geesey GG, Cheng KJ: How bacteria stick. *Sci Am* (Jan) 1978;**238:**86.

Costerton JW, Ingram JM, Cheng KJ: Structure and function of the cell envelope of gram-negative bacteria. *Bacteriol Rev* 1974;**38:**87.

Doetsch RN, Sjoblad RD: Flagellar structure and function in eubacteria. *Annu Rev Microbiol* 1980;**34:**69.

Doi RH: Genetic control of sporulation. *Annu Rev Genet* 1977;**11:**29.

Elwell LP, Shipley PL: Plasmid-mediated factors associated with virulence of bacteria to animals. *Annu Rev Microbiol* 1980;**34:**465.

Fox EN: M proteins of group A streptococci. *Bacteriol Rev* 1974;**38**:57.

Giesbrecht P, Wecke J, Reinicke B: On the morphogenesis of the cell wall of staphylococci. *Int Rev Cytol* 1976;**44**:225.

Gould GW, Dring GJ: Mechanisms of spore heat resistance. *Adv Microb Physiol* 1974;**11**:137.

Greenwalt JW, Whiteside TL: Mesosomes: Membranous bacterial organelles. *Bacteriol Rev* 1975;**39**:405.

Gunn RB: Co- and counter-transport mechanisms in cell membranes. *Annu Rev Physiol* 1980;**42**:249.

Henning U: Determination of cell shape in bacteria. *Annu Rev Microbiol* 1975;**29**:45.

Hübscher V et al: Novel histone H2A-like protein of *Escherichia coli*. *Proc Natl Acad Sci USA* 1980;**77**:5097.

Inouye M: Lipoprotein of the outer membrane of *Escherichia coli*. *Biomembranes* 1979;**10**:141.

Inouye M, Halegoua S: Secretion and membrane localization of proteins in *Escherichia coli*. *CRC Crit Rev Biochem* 1980;**7**:339.

Kaback HR: Transport across isolated bacterial cytoplasmic membranes. *Biochim Biophys Acta* 1972;**265**:367.

Kandler O, König H: Chemical composition of the peptidoglycan-free cell walls of methanogenic bacteria. *Arch Microbiol* 1978;**118**:141.

Keynan A: The transformation of bacterial endospores into vegetative cells. *Symp Soc Gen Microbiol* 1973;**23**:85.

Kleppe K, Ovrebö S, Lossius I: The bacterial nucleoid. *J Gen Microbiol* 1979;**112**:1.

Knox KW, Wicken AJ: Immunological properties of teichoic acids. *Bacteriol Rev* 1973;**37**:215.

Konings WN: Active transport of solutes in bacterial membrane vesicles. *Adv Microb Physiol* 1977;**15**:175.

Koshland DE Jr: A response regulator model in a simple sensory system. *Science* 1977;**196**:1055.

Laimins LA, Rhoads DB, Epstein W: Osmotic control of *kdp* operon expression in *Escherichia coli*. *Proc Natl Acad Sci USA* 1981;**78**:464.

Lambert PA, Hancock IC, Baddiley J: Occurrence and function of membrane teichoic acids. *Biochim Biophys Acta* 1977;**472**:1.

Lanyi JK: The role of Na$^+$ in transport processes of bacterial membranes. *Biochim Biophys Acta* 1979;**559**:377.

Lo TC: The molecular mechanisms of substrate transport in gram-negative bacteria. *Can J Biochem* 1979;**57**:289.

Machtigen NA, Fox CF: Biochemistry of bacterial membranes. *Annu Rev Bacteriol* 1973;**42**:575.

Manson MD et al: A protonmotive force drives bacterial flagella. *Proc Natl Acad Sci USA* 1977;**74**:3060.

Neilands JB: Transport functions of the outer membrane of enteric bacteria. *Horiz Biochem Biophys* 1978;**5**:65.

Nikaido H, Nakae T: The outer membrane of gram-negative bacteria. *Adv Microb Physiol* 1979;**20**:163.

Osborn MJ: Structure and biosynthesis of the bacterial cell wall. *Annu Rev Microbiol* 1969;**38**:501.

Osborn MJ, Wu HCP: Proteins of the outer membrane of gram-negative bacteria. *Annu Rev Microbiol* 1980;**34**:369.

Pettijohn DE: Prokaryotic DNA in nucleoid structure. *CRC Crit Rev Biochem* 1976;**4**:175.

Ryter A: Association of the nucleus and the membrane of bacteria: A morphological study. *Bacteriol Rev* 1968;**32**:39.

Salton MRJ: Membrane associated enzymes in bacteria. *Adv Microb Physiol* 1974;**11**:213.

Salton MRJ, Owen P: Bacterial membrane structure. *Annu Rev Microbiol* 1976;**30**:451.

Schleifer KH, Hammes WP, Kandler O: Effect of endogenous and exogenous factors on the primary structure of bacterial peptidoglycan. *Adv Microb Physiol* 1976;**13**:246.

Schleifer KH, Kandler O: Peptidoglycan types of bacterial cell walls and their taxonomic implications. *Bacteriol Rev* 1972;**36**:407.

Shively JM: Inclusion bodies of prokaryotes. *Annu Rev Microbiol* 1974;**28**:167.

Silverman M, Simon MI: Bacterial flagella. *Annu Rev Microbiol* 1977;**31**:397.

Slater M, Schaechter M: Control of cell division in bacteria. *Bacteriol Rev* 1974;**38**:199.

Smith H: Microbial surfaces in relation to pathogenicity. *Bacteriol Rev* 1977;**41**:475.

Springer MS, Goy MF, Adler J: Protein methylation in behavioural control mechanisms and in signal transduction. *Nature* 1979;**280**:279.

Ward JB: Teichoic and teichuronic acids: Biosynthesis, assembly and location. *Microbiol Rev* 1981;**45**:211.

Warth AD: Molecular structure of the bacterial spore. *Adv Microb Physiol* 1978;**17**:1.

Wilson DB: Cellular transport mechanisms. *Annu Rev Biochem* 1978;**47**:933.

Worcel A, Burgi E: Properties of a membrane-attached form of the folded chromosome of *Escherichia coli*. *J Mol Biol* 1974;**82**:91.

PRINCIPLES OF CLASSIFICATION

Although it may be said of the higher organisms that no 2 individuals are exactly alike, it is nevertheless true that such individuals tend to form clusters of highly similar types. Furthermore, between any 2 clusters there is generally a sharp discontinuity. It is common practice to speak of each cluster as a **species.**

For hundreds of years, biologists have been naming and describing species of plants, animals, and microorganisms. Having at hand a large number of such names and accompanying descriptions, the next step was to compile this information in some orderly and systematic manner, ie, to classify it. In order to understand the problems and limitations of bacterial classification, it is necessary first to discuss 2 fundamental issues: the meaning of the term "species," and the types and purposes of classification.

"Species" Defined

A "species" is a stage in the evolution of a population of organisms. To understand this, it is necessary to consider how species originate in higher plants and animals with obligatory sexual life cycles.

A. Evolution in Higher Organisms: Organisms having obligatory sexual life cycles are characterized by populations that maintain relatively homogeneous gene pools by interbreeding. Divergent evolution occurs when 2 segments of a homogeneous population become geographically isolated from each other: The barrier to interbreeding between the 2 groups allows each to evolve along its own path, eventually becoming sufficiently different in physiology or behavior (or both) to prevent further interbreeding, even if the geographic barrier is overcome. Such populations are said to be "physiologically isolated"; the point in evolution at which physiologic isolation occurs is thus a highly significant one and is therefore chosen as the point at which new species are said to have arisen. A "species" may thus be defined as follows: "A given stage of evolution at which actually or potentially interbreeding arrays of forms become segregated into two or more separate arrays which are physiologically incapable of interbreeding."*

*Dobzhansky T: *Genetics and the Origin of Species.* Columbia Univ Press, 1957.

B. Evolution in Bacteria: Unlike higher plants and animals, bacteria (and many other microorganisms) multiply almost entirely vegetatively. There is thus no mechanism by which discontinuous "species" can arise; instead, mutations accumulate so as to produce gradients of related types. As bacteria evolve to occupy their niches more and more efficiently, divergent lines of evolution will occur to the extent that the niches differ; groups of related ecologic types can thus often be recognized, but within each group there may be few real discontinuities. The term "species" thus has little meaning when applied to bacteria; it cannot even be defined, as it can for sexually reproducing organisms. Bacterial taxonomists must be purely arbitrary in deciding to what extent 2 types must differ before being classed as different "species."

In recent years, the techniques of molecular genetics have introduced new criteria for determining the degree of evolutionary relatedness between different bacteria. In one such technique, the DNA is extracted from pure cultures of the types in question and their relative base compositions determined. The parameter most often used is the mole percent of guanine (G) plus cytosine (C) in the total DNA; the G + C content may be directly measured or indirectly calculated from buoyant density or melting point determinations. For 2 organisms to be considered closely related, their G + C contents must be closely similar (although such similarity is not proof of relatedness).

Within a well-defined, closely-knit group such as the aerobic spore-forming bacilli, much higher degrees of relatedness can be recognized by the relative abilities of heat-denatured DNAs from different strains to reanneal with each other during slow cooling. Such reannealing reflects the existence in the 2 types of DNA of homologous nucleotide sequences.

A third technique is based on base sequence homologies in ribosomal RNA. The 16S RNA is digested to short oligonucleotides, which are readily sequenced; phylogenetic relatedness is considered to be proportionate to the number of oligonucleotide sequences held in common by 2 species. Since ribosomal RNA sequences have been highly conserved during evolution, such analyses can detect relations between even distantly related species.

Types & Purposes of Classification

While many sorts of systematic compilations are conceivable, only 2 are generally used in taxonomy: keys, or "artificial classifications"; and phylogenetic, or "natural," classifications.

A. Keys: In a "key," descriptive properties are arranged in such a way that an organism on hand may be readily identified. Organisms that are grouped together in a "key" are not necessarily related in the phylogenetic sense; they are listed together because they share some easily recognizable property. It would be perfectly reasonable, for example, for a key to bacteria to include a group such as "bacteria forming red pigments," even though this would include such unrelated forms as *Serratia marcescens* and purple sulfur bacteria. The point is that such a grouping would be useful; the investigator having a red-pigmented culture to identify would immediately narrow the search to a relatively few types.

B. Phylogenetic Classification: A phylogenetic classification groups together types that are **related,** ie, those that share a common ancestor. Species that have arisen through divergent evolution from a common ancestor are grouped together in a single genus; genera with a common origin are grouped in a single family, etc. Recognition of phylogenetic relationships in higher organisms is greatly aided by the existence of fossil remnants of common ancestors and by the multitude of morphologic features that can be studied. Bacteria, on the other hand, have not been preserved as recognizable fossils and exhibit relatively few morphologic properties for study. Evolutionary trends are thus difficult to determine or even to guess at, and a valid phylogenetic classification of bacteria is a long way from being realized.

Computer Taxonomy of Bacteria

Taxonomy by computer has been developed for groups of bacteria in which a large number of strains exist that can be described in terms of 100 or more clear-cut taxonomic properties (eg, presence or absence of certain enzymes, presence or absence of certain pigments, presence or absence of certain morphologic structures). The computer compares the data and prints out a list of the strains in such an order that each strain is followed in the list by the strain with which it shares the most characteristics. When this is done, the list often reveals several broad subgroups of strains, each subgroup characterized by a large number of shared common characteristics. The median strain within each subgroup can then be arbitrarily considered as a type species.

Bergey's Manual of Determinative Bacteriology

There is no universally accepted natural classification of bacteria, since there is no mechanism for the evolution of discrete bacterial species and we can discern only broad outlines of bacterial evolution. A few groups, such as the photosynthetic bacteria, have been thoroughly classified by studies with enrichment cultures, but we do not know how such major groups

are related to each other. The few evolutionary lines that are discernible will be presented later in this chapter.

In spite of these objections, however, an attempt at a phylogenetic classification of bacteria has been published in the USA as *Bergey's Manual of Determinative Bacteriology.** First published in 1923, it has now reached its 8th edition. The 6th edition, in 1948, grouped the bacteria in 6 orders containing 36 families. The 7th edition, in 1957, rearranged the genera into 10 orders and 47 families. The 8th edition, in 1974, groups the bacteria into 19 "parts" (eg, spirochetes, spiral and curved bacteria, gram-negative aerobic rods and cocci), each of which contains numerous genera. In some parts, the genera are grouped into families and orders; in others, they are not.

In view of the divergent views that exist regarding bacterial classification, it is probable that the *Manual* will undergo further major changes with each edition. We will therefore not follow Bergey's classification in this chapter but instead will describe the major groups of bacteria, using common names. We will also refer to the medically important genera, about which there is good agreement among bacteriologists.

Bergey's Manual does serve several useful purposes, however, if we ignore its attempt to represent a phylogeny. First, it represents an exhaustive compilation of names and descriptions; second, the latest edition includes a completely practical although artificial key to the genera, as an aid to identification of newly isolated types. The *Manual* has a companion volume, called *Index Bergeyana,* containing the literature index, the host and habitat index, and descriptions of organisms that the editors consider inadequately described or whose taxonomic positions are uncertain.

In 1980, the International Committee on Systematic Bacteriology published an approved list of bacterial names.† This list of about 2500 species replaces a former list that had grown to over 30,000; since January 1, 1980, only the new list of names has been considered valid, and the reinstatement of discarded names, the addition of new ones, or any other changes require publication in *International Journal of Systematic Bacteriology*.

An informal classification of the bacteria is presented in the following pages and in Table 3–1. The cyanobacteria and archaebacteria are discussed in Chapter 1.

DESCRIPTIONS OF THE PRINCIPAL GROUPS OF BACTERIA

A key to the principal groups of bacteria is presented in Table 3–1. Four major groups can be recognized on the basis of mechanism of movement and

*Buchanan RE, Gibbons NE (editors): *Bergey's Manual of Determinative Bacteriology,* 8th ed. Williams & Wilkins, 1974.
†Skerman VBD, McGowan V, Sneath PHA (editors): Approved lists of bacterial names. *Int J Systematic Bacteriol* 1980;**30**:225.

Table 3–1. Key to the principal groups of bacteria (listing the genera that include species pathogenic for humans).

	Genera
I. Flexible, thin-walled cells, motility conferred by gliding mechanism: **Gliding Bacteria**	
II. Flexible, thin-walled cells, motility conferred by axial filament: **Spirochetes**	*Treponema* *Borrelia* *Leptospira*
III. Rigid, thick-walled cells, immotile or motility conferred by flagella: **Eubacteria**	
A. Mycelial (actinomycetes)	*Mycobacterium* *Actinomyces* *Nocardia* *Streptomyces*
B. Simple unicellular	
1. Obligate intracellular parasites	*Rickettsia* *Coxiella* *Chlamydia*
2. Free-living	
a. Gram-positive	
(1) Cocci	*Streptococcus* *Staphylococcus*
(2) Nonsporulating rods	*Corynebacterium* *Listeria* *Erysipelothrix*
(3) Sporulating rods	
Obligate aerobes	*Bacillus*
Obligate anaerobes	*Clostridium*
b. Gram-negative	
(1) Cocci	*Neisseria*
(2) Nonenteric rods	
Spiral forms	*Spirillum*
Straight, very small rods	*Pasteurella* *Brucella* *Yersinia* *Francisella* *Haemophilus* *Bordetella*
(3) Enteric rods	
Facultative anaerobes	*Escherichia* (and related coliform bacteria) *Salmonella* *Shigella* *Klebsiella* *Proteus* *Vibrio*
Obligate aerobes	*Pseudomonas*
Obligate anaerobes	*Bacteroides* *Fusobacterium*
IV. Lacking cell walls	*Mycoplasma*

Figure 3–1. Scanning electron micrograph of fruiting bodies of the myxobacterium *Chondromyces crocatus,* prepared by J. Pangborn and P. Grilione. (From Stanier RY, Adelberg EA, Ingraham JL: *The Microbial World,* 4th ed. Copyright © 1976. By permission of Prentice-Hall, Inc, Englewood Cliffs, NJ.)

forms it is accompanied by rapid flexing of the cells. No locomotor organelles have yet been identified. The thin cell walls of gliding bacteria are typical of gram-negative bacteria.

There are 3 main assemblages within the gliding bacteria: unicellular forms called **myxobacteria,** characterized by their ability to aggregate into elaborate fruiting structures (Fig 3–1); **cytophagas,** non-fruiting unicellular forms differing markedly from the myxobacteria in the guanine-plus-cytosine content of their DNA; and **filamentous gliding bacteria,** including 2 sulfur-oxidizing genera *(Beggiatoa* and *Thiothrix)* as well as several heterotrophs (eg, *Saprospira, Vitreoscilla,* and *Leucothrix).* None of these groups includes forms that are pathogenic for humans.

Spirochetes

The spirochetes are thin-walled, flexible, helical rods. They propel themselves by undulation of an axial filament that is wound about the cell body. The axial filament is formed from 2 tufts of polar flagella lying between the cell membrane and cell wall (Fig 3–2); it can be freed by enzymatic digestion of the outer envelope (Fig 3–3). Three genera contain important pathogens for humans: *Treponema, Borrelia,* and *Leptospira* (see Chapter 20).

Eubacteria

The eubacteria include stalked, budding, and mycelial organisms as well as simple unicellular forms. Since there are no pathogens among the stalked and budding forms, they will not be considered further here.

A. Mycelial Forms (Actinomycetes): The mycelial (branching filamentous) growth of these gram-positive organisms confers on them a superficial

character of cell wall: gliding bacteria, spirochetes, eubacteria, and mycoplasmas.

Gliding Bacteria

This heterogeneous group of bacteria have in common a motility mechanism called gliding. Gliding requires contact with a solid substrate; in unicellular

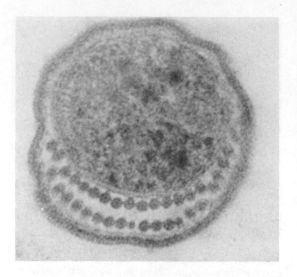

Figure 3–2. Cross section of a large spirochete, showing the location of the fibrils of the axial filament between the cell membrane and the cell wall (258,000 ×). (Reproduced, with permission, from Listgarten MA, Socransky SS: Electron microscopy of axial fibrils, outer envelope and cell division of certain oval spirochetes. *J Bacteriol* 1964; 88:1087.)

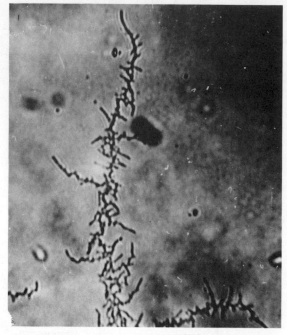

Figure 3–4. The surface growth on agar of *Mycobacterium fortuitum* (600 ×). Photomicrograph by Gordon R and Lechevalier H. (From Stanier RY, Doudoroff M, Adelberg EA: *The Microbial World,* 3rd ed. Copyright © 1970. By permission of Prentice-Hall, Inc, Englewood Cliffs, NJ.)

resemblance to the fungi, strengthened by the presence—in higher forms—of external asexual spores, or conidia. The resemblance ends there, however. The actinomycetes are prokaryotic organisms, whereas the fungi are eukaryotic; in the lower actinomycetes (eg, mycobacteria; Fig 3–4) the mycelium breaks up into typical unicellular bacteria. In one group, the Actinoplanes, sporangia are formed that rupture to release flagellated bacilli. The bacilli ultimately lose their flagella and initiate new mycelial growth.

1. Mycobacteria–Members of the genus *Mycobacterium*, which includes the agents of tuber-

culosis, are acid-fast organisms: they are relatively impermeable to dyes, but once stained they resist decolorization with acidified organic solvents. Their acid-fastness, along with their tendency to form a pellicle at the surface of aqueous media, is due to their high content of lipids: lipids may account for up to 40% of the dry weight of the cell and up to 60% of the dry weight of the cell wall. They include true waxes along with glycolipids. The only other bacteria containing lipids of these types are corynebacteria and certain

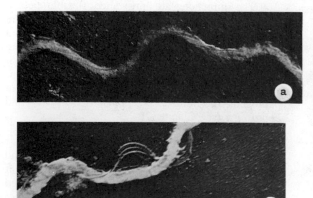

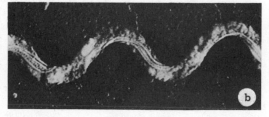

Figure 3–3. *Treponema pallidum.* Electron micrographs showing axial filament. *(a)* Without digestion. *(b)* After 20 minutes of tryptic digestion. *(c)* After 10 minutes of peptic digestion. (Courtesy of Swain RHA: *J Pathol Bacteriol* 1955;69:117.)

Figure 3–5. Early growth, a species of *Nocardia* (490 ×). (Courtesy of Ordal EJ: *The Biology of Bacteria,* 3rd ed. Heath, 1948.)

nocardiae, which also tend to be acid-fast. The mycobacteria are characterized further in Chapter 17.

2. *Nocardia* and *Actinomyces* –These 2 genera form much more advanced mycelia than do the mycobacteria, but they too tend to break up in older cultures to form irregularly shaped cells. A typical young mycelium of *Nocardia* is shown in Fig 3–5.

Actinomyces species are typically anaerobes, but some are facultative anaerobes, tolerating oxygen and capable of growth in air; *Nocardia* species are aerobes, and many are acid-fast. Both groups include pathogens for humans.

3. Higher actinomycetes–Several genera (eg, *Streptomyces, Micromonospora*) remain fully mycelial, reproducing by externally borne asexual spores, or conidia (Fig 3–6). Although their normal habitat is

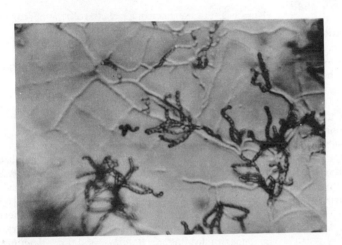

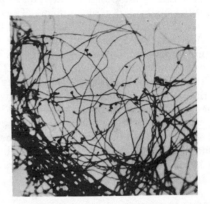

Figure 3–6. Streptomycetaceae. *Left:Streptomyces,* showing chains of aerial conidia (780 ×). ***Right:*** *Micromonospora,* showing single conidia on short lateral branches. (From Stanier RY, Doudoroff M, Adelberg EA; *The Microbial World,* 2nd ed. Copyright © 1963. By permission of Prentice-Hall, Inc, Englewood Cliffs, NJ.)

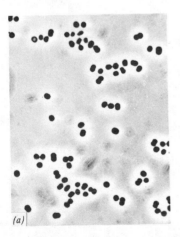

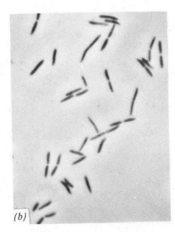

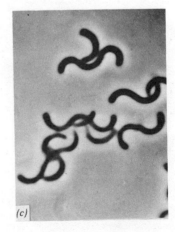

Figure 3–7. The cell shapes that occur among unicellular true bacteria. *(a)* Coccus. *(b)* Rod. *(c)* Spiral. (Phase contrast, 1500 ×.) (From Stanier RY, Doudoroff M, Adelberg EA: *The Microbial World,* 3rd ed. Copyright © 1970. By permission of Prentice-Hall, Inc, Englewood Cliffs, NJ.)

the soil, some *Streptomyces* species may contaminate wounds or scratches and initiate abscesses similar to those caused by nocardiae.

The higher actinomycetes, notably *Streptomyces,* are medically significant principally for their production of a wide array of antibiotics that act against bacteria (see Chapter 10). Since the actinomycetes are themselves bacteria, they must have special mechanisms to protect themselves against the antibiotics they liberate. In *Streptomyces azureus,* for example, which produces the ribosome-binding antibiotic thiostrepton, binding to its own ribosomes is prevented by the methylation of a single adenosine residue in the 23S ribosomal RNA.

B. Unicellular Forms: These bacteria include spheres (cocci), straight rods (bacilli), and helical forms (spirilla), as illustrated in Fig 3–7.

1. Obligate intracellular parasites–Two groups—the rickettsiae (genera *Rickettsia* and *Coxiella*)—and the smaller chlamydiae (genus *Chlamydia*)—are obligate intracellular parasites and include pathogens for humans. They are gram-negative. The basis of their obligate parasitism is unknown, although they may depend on the host for energy-rich compounds and coenzymes. They are described more fully in Chapters 21 and 22.

2. Free-living forms–The majority of the bacteria pathogenic for humans fall into this group. The medically important genera are grouped in Table 3–1 according to their gram-staining properties, their morphology, and (in the case of the gram-negative rods) whether or not they normally inhabit the intestinal tract of humans and other mammals. They are discussed in detail in Chapters 14–19.

Mycoplasmas

The mycoplasmas (Fig 3–8) are highly pleomorphic, wall-less bacteria. They resemble the L forms that are produced by the removal of the cell wall of eubacteria; unlike L forms, however, mycoplasmas never revert to the walled state, and there are no an-

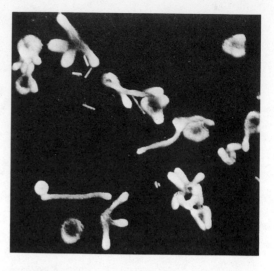

Figure 3–8. Electron micrograph of cells of a member of the *Mycoplasma* group, the agent of bronchopneumonia in the rat (1960 ×). (Reproduced, with permission, from Klieneberger-Nobel E, Cuckow FW: A study of organisms of the pleuropneumonia group by electron microscopy. *J Gen Microbiol* 1955; **12**:99.)

tigenic relationships between mycoplasmas and eubacterial L forms.

Four genera have been classified as mycoplasmas, based on morphologic criteria: *Mycoplasma, Spiroplasma, Acholeplasma,* and *Thermoplasma.* Analysis of base sequence homologies in 16S ribosomal RNA has shown that the first 3 of these genera are related to the gram-positive line of clostridial ancestry leading to *Bacillus* and *Lactobacillus; Thermoplasma,* on the other hand, belongs to the archaebacteria, a group only distantly related to the bacteria (see Chapter 1).

Human pathogens of the genus *Mycoplasma* are described in Chapter 23.

•   •   •

References

Books

Alexander M: *Microbial Ecology*. Wiley, 1971.

Barile MF, Razin S (editors): *Cell Biology*. Vol 1 of: *The Mycoplasmas*. Academic Press, 1979.

Buchanan RE, Gibbons NE (editors): *Bergey's Manual of Determinative Bacteriology*, 8th ed. Williams & Wilkins, 1974.

Sneath PHA, Sokal RR: *The Principles and Practice of Numerical Classification*. Freeman, 1973.

Stanier RY, Adelberg EA, Ingraham JL: *The Microbial World*, 4th ed. Prentice-Hall, 1976.

Starr MP et al (editors): *The Prokaryotes: A Handbook on Habitats, Isolation, and Identification of Bacteria*. Springer-Verlag, 1981.

Tully JG, Whitcomb RF (editors): *Human and Animal Mycoplasmas*. Vol 2 of: *The Mycoplasmas*. Academic Press, 1979.

Whitcomb RF, Tully JG (editors): *Plant and Insect Mycoplasmas*. Vol 3 of: *The Mycoplasmas*. Academic Press, 1979.

Articles & Reviews

Becker Y: The chlamydia: Molecular biology of procaryotic obligate parasites of eucaryotes. *Microbiol Rev* 1978;**42**:274.

Holt SC: Anatomy and chemistry of spirochetes. *Microbiol Rev* 1978;**42**:114.

Jones D, Sneath PHA: Genetic transfer and bacterial taxonomy. *Bacteriol Rev* 1970;**34**:40.

Kaiser D et al: Myxobacteria: Cell interactions, genetics, and development. *Annu Rev Microbiol* 1979;**33**:595.

Mandel M: New approaches to bacterial taxonomy: Perspectives and prospects. *Annu Rev Microbiol* 1969;**23**:239.

Ormsbee RA: Rickettsiae (as organisms). *Annu Rev Microbiol* 1969;**23**:275.

Razin S: The mycoplasmas. *Microbiol Rev* 1978;**42**:414.

Sanderson KE: Genetic relatedness in the family Enterobacteriaceae. *Annu Rev Microbiol* 1976;**30**:327.

Schachter J, Caldwell HD: Chlamydiae. *Annu Rev Microbiol* 1980;**34**:285.

Skerman VBD, McGowan V, Sneath PHA (editors): Approved lists of bacterial names. *Int J Systematic Bacteriol* 1980;**30**:225.

Woese CR, Magrum LJ, Fox GE: Archaebacteria. *J Mol Evol* 1978;**11**:245.

Woese CR et al: Phylogenetic analysis of the mycoplasmas. *Proc Natl Acad Sci USA* 1980;**77**:494.

4 | Microbial Genetics

THE PHYSICAL BASIS OF HEREDITY

In formulating a general concept of mechanisms of inheritance, 2 basic biologic phenomena must be accounted for: **heredity,** or stability of type (eg, the progeny formed by the division of a unicellular organism are generally identical with the parent cell); and the rare occurrence of **heritable variations.** Genetic and cytologic analyses of plant, animal, and microbial cells have established that the physical basis for both of these phenomena is the **gene** (the genetic determinant controlling the properties of organisms). The genes are located along the threadlike **chromosomes** in the cell nucleus. The chromosomes undergo duplication (replication) prior to cell division; when the cell divides, each daughter cell receives an identical set of chromosomes and therefore an identical set of genes.

Replication is usually an exact process, which accounts for heredity; any given gene, however, has a low probability of **mutation,** and mutation accounts for variation. Mutated genes are usually stable and are replicated in the new form in subsequent generations. A gene mutation thus causes a heritable change in one or more properties of the organism.

In eukaryotic and prokaryotic cells (see Chapter 1), the chemical substance of the chromosome which is responsible for both gene replication and gene function is deoxyribonucleic acid (DNA). In viruses, it can be either DNA or RNA (ribonucleic acid). One of the basic problems of genetics is thus to explain gene replication, mutation, and function in terms of nucleic acid structure. In the following sections this problem will be discussed with particular reference to the prokaryotic chromosome of the bacterium *Escherichia coli*. In general, however, the material to be presented applies equally to the chromosomes of eukaryotes: protozoa, fungi, slime molds, and algae.

THE PROKARYOTIC CHROMOSOME

Chromosome Structure

The electron micrograph in Fig 2–5 shows the bacterial nucleus to be a packed mass of DNA fibers. When bacterial DNA is extracted and purified by ordinary chemical methods, a preparation is obtained having an average molecular weight of about 5×10^6. In the intact cell, however, the bacterial nucleus consists of a single continuous DNA molecule, or chromosome, with a molecular weight of 2 to 3×10^9, which is sheared into several hundred fragments by the extraction procedure. Using gentler methods, Cairns was able to extract the unbroken chromosome of *E coli* (Fig 4–1). Cairns's pictures showed the bacterial chromosome to be a continuous DNA structure approximately 1 mm long. The structure of the DNA molecule is now well known: it consists of a double helix made up of 2 complementary polynucleotide strands in each of which purine and pyrimidine bases are arranged along a backbone made of alternating deoxyribose and phosphate groups (Fig 4–2). The 2 strands are held together by hydrogen bonds between neighboring bases; the stereochemistry is such that hydrogen bonds can be formed only between adenine and thymine (A-T pair) and between guanine and cytosine (G-C pair) (Fig 4–3). Thus, a sequence of bases along one strand such as G-C-C-A-C-T-C-A must be matched on the opposite strand by the complementary sequence of C-G-G-T-G-A-G-T.

The chromosome of *E coli,* with a molecular weight of 3×10^9, contains about 5×10^6 base-pairs. It has been shown both by genetic analysis and by autoradiography to be a circular structure.

Chromosome Replication

In viruses, prokaryotic cells, and eukaryotic cells, DNA has been shown to replicate according to a semiconservative mechanism. The complementary strands separate, each then acting as a **template** on which is assembled a complementary strand by the enzymatic polymerization of nucleotide subunits. The sequence of bases in the new strand is rigidly dictated by the hydrogen bonding possibilities described above; ie, wherever the template carries adenine the new strand will acquire a thymine, etc. Replication thus leads to the formation of 2 new double helices, each identical with the original double helix.

The bacterial chromosome replicates sequentially along the entire structure, starting at a specific sequence of about 240 base-pairs called the **replication origin.** According to a model proposed by Jacob and Brenner, the replication origin is attached to a mesosomal site on the cell membrane; when replica-

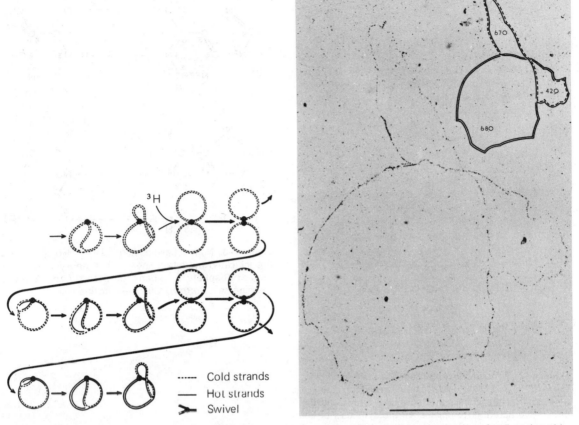

Figure 4–1. Replication of the circular chromosome of *E coli*. *Left:* Diagram showing that introduction of radioactive tritium (^{3}H) toward the end of a replication cycle would lead, 2 cycles later, to a chromosome labeled as found experimentally. Replication begins at the "swivel" and proceeds counterclockwise along the 2 complementary strands of the DNA double helix. *Right:* Autoradiograph of a chromosome extracted from an Hfr cell of *E coli* 2 generations after addition of ^{3}H. Grain counts per unit length in the regions indicated by solid lines are double those in the regions indicated by dashed lines. The numbers in the insert are the lengths (in micrometers) between the 2 forks. (Courtesy of Cairns J: *Cold Spring Harbor Symp Quant Biol* 1963;**28**:43.)

tion is initiated, the chromosome moves past the membrane attachment site, unwinding and replicating as it goes (Fig 4–4). Separation of the 2 daughter chromosomes is accomplished by localized membrane synthesis; later, a transverse cell wall will form between the DNA attachment sites.

The Jacob-Brenner model is yet to be confirmed experimentally. Although there is much evidence for the attachment of the replication origin to the membrane, evidence for continuing attachment of the replicating fork (as represented in Fig 4–4) is still inconclusive.

In Figs 4–1 and 4–4, replication is shown to proceed in one direction along the duplex molecule of DNA. Such unidirectional replication has indeed been verified for some circular DNA viruses and is consistent with observations of DNA transfer between conjugating bacteria (Figs 4–12 and 4–13). Vegetative chromosomal replication, however, is normally bidirectional: 2 replicating forks may move away simultaneously from the replicator site, meeting approx-

imately halfway around the chromosome. This observation may be reconciled with Cairns's autoradiographs by the finding that the cell is capable of both types of replication (unidirectional and bidirectional), depending on the growth conditions.

In a bacterial cell, several different genetic (DNA) structures may be present and replicating independently at the same time, eg, chromosome, sex factor, and bacteriophage genomes. The term **replicon** has been coined to describe an independent unit of replication.

Chromosome Function

The chromosome, consisting of about 5×10^6 nucleotide pairs, is functionally subdivided into segments, each of which determines the amino acid sequence and hence the structure of a discrete protein. These proteins, as enzymes and as components of membranes and other cell structures, determine all the properties of the organism. A segment of chromosomal DNA that determines the structure of a

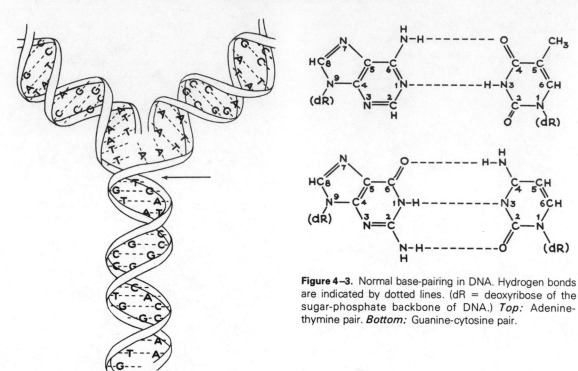

Figure 4–3. Normal base-pairing in DNA. Hydrogen bonds are indicated by dotted lines. (dR = deoxyribose of the sugar-phosphate backbone of DNA.) *Top:* Adenine-thymine pair. *Bottom:* Guanine-cytosine pair.

Figure 4–2. Structure and replication of DNA according to the Watson and Crick model. The vertical double strand is unwinding at the point indicated by the arrow, and the 2 arms have acted as templates for the synthesis of complementary strands. Synthesis is proceeding downward along the vertical double strand.

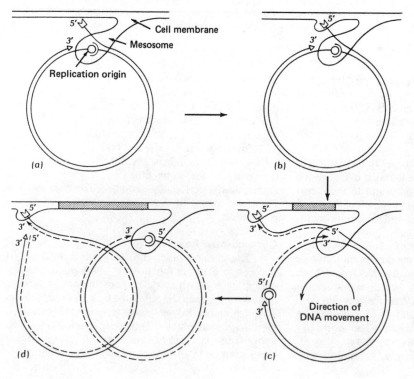

Figure 4–4. Replication of the bacterial chromosome, according to the model of Jacob and Brenner. *(a)* The chromosome is attached to a mesosome at the replication origin site, which serves as a swivel. One of the strands is broken. *(b)* The 5' end of the broken strand attaches to a new site in the membrane. *(c)* The chromosome rotates counterclockwise past the mesosomal attachment site, at which is fixed the replicating enzyme system. Newly synthesized strands are shown as dashed lines. The attachment sites are separated by localized membrane synthesis (shown by shaded area). *(d)* The cycle of replication has been completed. The final step will be the joining of the free ends of one strand of the new chromosome (solid line). (From Stanier RY, Doudoroff M, Adelberg EA: *The Microbial World,* 3rd ed. Copyright © 1970. By permission of Prentice-Hall, Inc, Englewood Cliffs, NJ.)

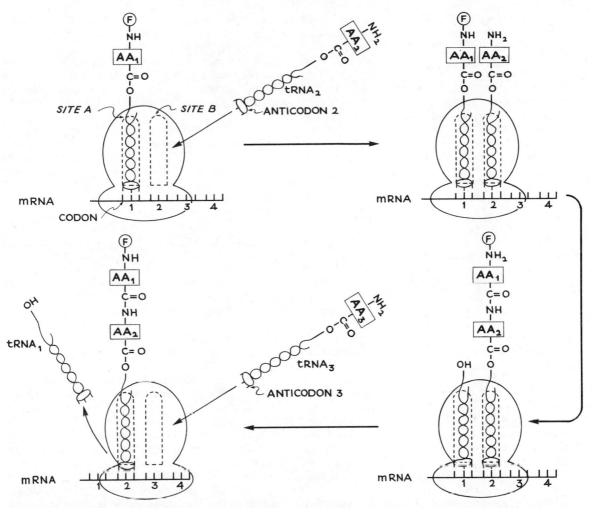

Figure 4–5. Four stages in the lengthening of a polypeptide chain on the surface of a 70S ribosome. *Top left:* A tRNA molecule bearing the anticodon complementary to codon 1 at one end and AA_1 at the other, binds to site A. AA_1 is attached to the tRNA through its carboxyl group; its amino nitrogen bears a formyl group (F). *Top right:* A tRNA molecule bearing AA_2 binds to site B; its anticodon is complementary to codon 2. *Bottom right:* An enzyme complex catalyzes the transfer of AA_1 to the amino group of AA_2, forming a peptide bond. (Note that transfer in the opposite direction is blocked by the prior formylation of the amino group of AA_1.) *Bottom left:* The ribosome moves to the right, so that sites A and B are now opposite codons 2 and 3; in the process, $tRNA_1$ is displaced and $tRNA_2$ moves to site A. Site B is again vacant and is ready to accept $tRNA_3$ bearing AA_3. (When the polypeptide is completed and released, the formyl group is enzymatically removed.) (Redrawn and reproduced by permission of Stanier RY, Doudoroff M, Adelberg EA: *The Microbial World,* 3rd ed. Copyright © 1970. Prentice-Hall, Inc, Englewood Cliffs, NJ.)

discrete protein is called a **gene.** The mechanism by which the sequence of nucleotides in a gene determines the sequence of amino acids in a protein is as follows:

(1) An RNA polymerase forms a single polyribonucleotide strand, called "messenger RNA" (mRNA), using DNA as a template; this process is called **transcription.** The mRNA has a nucleotide sequence complementary to one of the strands in the DNA double helix.

(2) Amino acids are enzymatically activated and transferred to specific adapter molecules of RNA, called "transfer RNA" (tRNA). Each adapter molecule has at one end a triplet of bases complementary to a triplet of bases on mRNA, and at the other end its specific amino acid. The triplet of bases on mRNA is called the **codon** for that amino acid.

(3) mRNA and tRNA come together on the surface of the ribosome. As each tRNA finds its complementary nucleotide triplet on mRNA, the amino acid that it carries is put into peptide linkage with the amino acid of the preceding (neighboring) tRNA molecule. The ribosome moves along the mRNA, the polypeptide growing sequentially until the entire mRNA molecule has been translated into a corresponding sequence of amino acids. This process, called **translation,** is diagrammed in Fig 4–5.

Thus, the nucleotide sequence of the DNA gene represents a code that determines, through the mediation of mRNA, the structure of a specific protein. In many cases such proteins act as subunits that polymerize to form active enzymes; many high-molecular-weight enzymes are now known to be made up of subunits having molecular weights in the range of 10^4 to 10^5. The triplet code requires that a gene governing the formation of a protein of molecular weight 40,000 should contain on the order of 1000 nucleotide pairs; the chromosome of *E coli* thus has sufficient DNA for 5000 such genes.

THE EUKARYOTIC CHROMOSOME

Chromosome Structure

In contrast to that of the bacterial genome, the DNA of the eukaryotic nucleus is divided among a set of distinct chromosomes. Each chromosome consists of a single continuous, linear DNA molecule, associated tightly with a set of basic proteins called histones and with varying degrees of tightness to a large number of nonhistone proteins. As isolated from the cell, this complex of DNA and proteins is called **chromatin.**

Studies with isolated chromatin show that the DNA molecule is wrapped around histone complexes to form beaded structures called **nucleosomes.** This primary structure is then subject to several further orders of coiling to produce the chromosome as it exists in interphase; at mitosis, a further coiling occurs to bring about the condensation of the chromosomes into their visible, rodlike shapes.

The organization of the DNA in eukaryotic chromosomes differs from that in the prokaryotic chromosome in at least 3 significant ways. First, the genes governing sets of closely related functions appear not to be clustered to form operons, as they are in bacteria; coordinate control of their expression must therefore be based on a different mechanism. Second, the genes of eukaryotic organisms are in many cases not continuous base sequences, as they are in prokaryotes; instead, a given gene may be present as a set of DNA segments that are interrupted by intervening sequences, or "introns." The entire sequence is transcribed, but the RNA molecule that is originally formed is processed by enzymes that excise the introns and splice together the coding segments to form the final mRNA molecule. Third, eukaryotic chromosomes contain a high proportion of repetitious DNA: sequences that are repeated in the genome anywhere from 100 times to 100,000 times or more.

Mitosis

Eukaryotic cells undergo a regular cycle of events associated with the division process. Periods of active DNA replication—the S (for "synthesis") phase—alternate with periods of mitosis (M phase), during which the 2 products of chromosomal replication, called chromatids, are segregated into the 2 daughter cells produced by cell division.

At the completion of the S phase, each chromosome is present as a pair of sister chromatids, joined at a specific site called the centromere. At mitosis, a mitotic spindle is formed, and the chromosomes become arranged on the spindle in a flat plane called the metaphase plate. Spindle fibers attach to the chromatids at the centromeres, the chromatids separate, and the 2 chromatids of each chromosome are moved to opposite poles of the cell by the spindle fibers. Cell division segregates the 2 groups of chromatids into the 2 daughter cells; the cycle is completed when they traverse the next S phase. This process ensures that each daughter cell receives a complete set of chromosomes, identical to that of every other mitotic cell.

Organelles

The early recognized phenomenon of maternal inheritance revealed the existence of genetic determinants in the cytoplasm of eukaryotic cells, and these cytoplasmic determinants were ultimately found to reside in DNA molecules within cytoplasmic organelles: the mitochondria and the chloroplasts of photosynthetic cells.

The mitochondria, for example, contain small circular DNA molecules that code for certain mitochondrial components, including a set of transfer RNAs, ribosomal RNAs, and a number of membrane proteins. Although most mitochondrial proteins are coded by nuclear genes, many mutations that affect mitochondrial function (and thus the phenotype of the cell) can occur in the mitochondrial DNA. In particular, mutations causing resistance of the cell to some of the drugs that inhibit mitochondrial protein synthesis (such as chloramphenicol) have been shown to occur in the mitochondrial DNA.

The mitochondria of eukaryotes share many properties with those of prokaryotes, including membrane-associated electron transport systems, small circular DNA genomes, and ribosomal systems with characteristic structures and patterns of antibiotic sensitivity. These similarities have led to the popular theory of organellar evolution from prokaryotic symbionts of proto-eukaryotic cells. Whether this theory is correct or not, the eukaryotic cell must be viewed as a complex system with at least 2 independent genomes: (1) the set of chromosomes in the nucleus and (2) the DNA molecules of the cytoplasmic organelles; mutations occurring in either genome can change the phenotype of the cell.

MUTATION

Mutation at the Molecular Level

Any change in the nucleotide sequence of a gene constitutes a mutation. The different forms of a gene produced by mutations are called **alleles.**

A. Types of Sequence Changes: The sequence

of nucleotides in DNA can change in either of 2 ways: by the substitution of one base-pair for another as the result of a replication error; or by breakage of the sugar-phosphate backbone, with subsequent deletion or insertion of a DNA segment.

1. Base-pair substitution–The most frequent types are those in which the pyrimidine is replaced by a different pyrimidine and the purine by a different purine, eg, A-T replaced by G-C, or T-A by C-G. These are called **transitions.** In the less frequent type, a pyrimidine is replaced by a purine and vice versa; these are called **transversions.**

2. Insertions and deletions–Occasionally, during replication, a single base-pair or 2 adjacent base-pairs are inserted into or deleted from the DNA structure. This shifts the translation "reading frame" of the coded message from that point on, forming an entirely new set of triplets, or codons. For example, if a portion of the correct message reads –/AGG/CTC/CAA/GCC/GAT/TGG–, deletion of the fourth base changes the message to –/AGG/TCC/AAG/CCG/ATT/GG–. Such mutations are called **frame shift mutations;** their effects on translation are discussed below.

Much larger insertions and deletions may also occur, involving segments that span one or more entire genes.

B. Spontaneous Mutation:

1. Mechanisms–The most common spontaneous mutations represent replication errors: the template mechanism of replication described earlier may function imperfectly, so that—for example—a G is inserted opposite a T. Such mismatches occur frequently but are usually corrected by a $3' \rightarrow 5'$ exonuclease "proofreading" function of DNA polymerase that recognizes and excises mismatched base-pairs. Base-pair substitutions thus can arise as a consequence of failure in template action of the DNA together with failure in the proofreading function of the polymerase.

Base-pair substitutions can also arise as a consequence of a tautomeric shift of electrons in a purine or pyrimidine ring. For example, thymine normally exists in the keto state, in which state it forms 2 hydrogen bonds with adenine. If, however, thymine exists in the rare enol state at the moment that it is acting as a template during replication, it will form 3 hydrogen bonds with guanine instead (Fig 4–6). The new strand will then carry a guanine in place of adenine and will form a G-C pair at the next round of replication, replacing the original A-T pair.

Frame shift mutations (small insertions or deletions) can also arise spontaneously; they are thought to arise as a result of a single-strand nicking of the DNA adjacent to a run of identical base-pairs. The nicked strand may be displaced, looping out a segment carrying one or 2 of the identical bases and leaving a gap which is then filled in by a DNA polymerase; the result is an insertion of one or 2 bases in that strand which is faithfully replicated at future generations. Alternatively, the nick may be widened to a gap by an exonuclease; the gap may then be closed by a displacement and looping out of the opposite strand, leading to a small deletion.

Large deletions and insertions occur by yet other mechanisms, some of which are mediated by transposons (see below).

2. Mutator genes–A mutator gene is an allele of a normal gene which, by virtue of its altered function, causes a general increase in the spontaneous mutation rate over the entire genome. Three types of mutator genes have been identified: (1) Mutations in DNA polymerase genes, causing either a loss of fidelity of the polymerase or a decrease in $3' \rightarrow 5'$ exonuclease proofreading function. (2) Mutations causing large distortions in the relative pool sizes of the 4 nucleotide triphosphates as a result of alterations in their relative rates of biosynthesis. A large excess of one nucleotide triphosphate leads to an increased rate of substitution of that base for a correct base during replication. (3) Mutations causing a failure in **mismatch repair.** Endonucleases are present in the cell that recognize distortions in the double helix caused by mismatched base-pairs; they can distinguish between the template strand and the new strand, excising the mismatched base from the latter. The gap thus formed is filled in by a polymerase. Recognition of the new strand is based

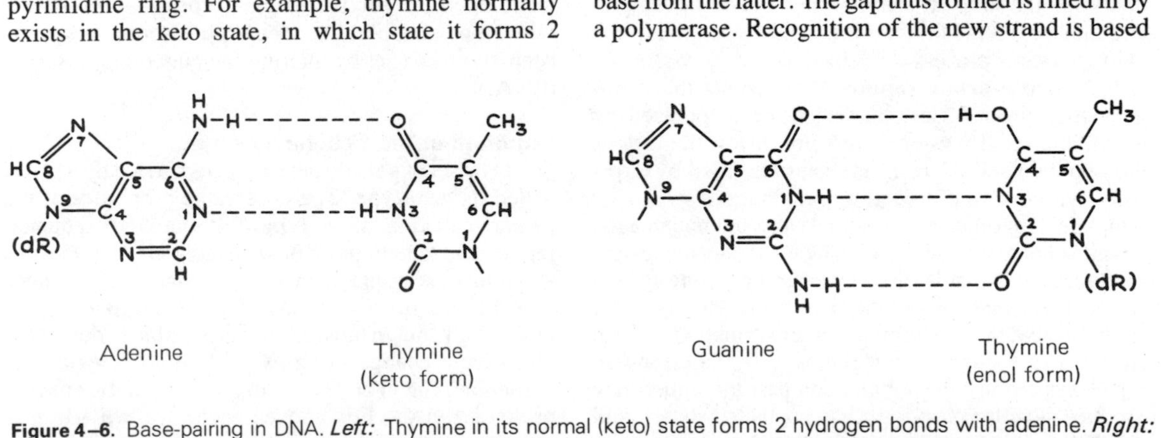

Adenine   Thymine   Guanine   Thymine
                 (keto form)   (enol form)

Figure 4–6. Base-pairing in DNA. *Left:* Thymine in its normal (keto) state forms 2 hydrogen bonds with adenine. *Right:* Thymine may exist in the enol state as the result of rare tautomeric shift of electrons. In this state, thymine forms 3 hydrogen bonds with guanine. If the tautomeric shift occurred during replication, guanine would be incorporated into DNA in place of adenine, and a G-C pair would ultimately replace an A-T pair in the nucleotide sequence. (dR = deoxyribose of the sugar-phosphate backbone of DNA.)

on the fact that DNA is **methylated:** a methylase adds a methyl group to an occasional purine ring shortly after the new strand has been synthesized. The brief lag in methylation, however, means that the new strand is relatively undermethylated, and it is this state that is recognized by the mismatch repair enzyme system. Mutator alleles include mutants defective in the endonuclease itself as well as mutants defective in methylase: the latter mutants' DNA lacks the methyl groups on which strand recognition depends, so that excision of the correct base (on the template strand) takes place as often as excision of the "wrong" base on the new strand.

C. Mutagenic Agents: Mutations are induced by a variety of physical and chemical agents, which directly or indirectly cause a general increase in the mutation rate.

1. Physical agents–Radiations with wavelengths absorbed by the cell are mutagenic, including visible light, ultraviolet light, and all ionizing radiations. Heat is also mutagenic.

2. Chemical agents–Chemical mutagens can be divided into 2 classes: those that act directly and those that require conversion by cellular enzymes to the active form.

The direct-acting mutagens include nitroso compounds, alkylating agents, base analogs, nitropyrenes, and a number of anticancer drugs such as methotrexate, dactinomycin, and hydroxyurea. The compounds that require activation include polycyclic aromatic hydrocarbons such as benzpyrene and the aflatoxins.

D. Mechanisms of Induced Mutation:

1. Increased frequency of replication errors–A number of mutagens, including base analogs, alkylating agents, and deaminating agents such as nitrous acid, act by increasing the frequency of mismatches during replication.

2. Stabilization of loopouts–A number of mutagenic compounds, such as acridines, are called stacking agents: They interact with the bases of the double helix so as to stabilize the looped-out single-stranded segments that are intermediates in the frame shift mutation process described above.

3. Error-prone repair–Most agents that damage DNA produce lesions which are recognized by enzymatic repair systems. In some cases, the lesions are removed and the resulting gaps are filled by error-free systems that use the undamaged strand as template. In other cases, however, an undamaged strand is not available. In such cases, the repair system produces a gap that is filled by an **error-prone** system which adds bases at random. Ultraviolet light, for example, causes pyrimidine dimer formation on one strand; if the dimer is not removed by an error-free repair system in time, replication past the dimer may produce a duplex carrying a gap opposite a dimer, and gap-filling is accomplished by an error-prone system. Alternatively, the replication polymerase may itself insert a wrong base opposite a lesion rather than skipping to produce a gap.

The enzymes of the error-prone repair systems are inducible. They are greatly increased in cells that have been treated with DNA-damaging agents.

E. Effects of Mutation on Translation:

1. Nonsense mutations–With 3 exceptions, transfer RNAs are present in the cell for each of the 64 possible nucleotide triplets, or "codons," in messenger RNA. The exceptions are UAG, UAA, and UGA; they are called "nonsense codons." When a ribosome reaches a nonsense codon in the translation process described above, polypeptide chain formation is terminated. One or more of the 3 nonsense codons function as natural chain terminators in the synthesis of proteins; if a nonsense codon is formed within a gene by mutation of a "sense" codon, only a partial polypeptide is produced. Such mutations are called **nonsense mutations.**

2. Suppressor mutations–A mutation that restores the function of a gene inactivated by a previous mutation is called a **suppressor mutation.** For example, the frame shift mutation described on p 41, in which a single base was deleted, can be suppressed by a single base insertion at a nearby site. In the above case, imagine that a second frame shift mutation causes insertion of a G between the seventh and eighth bases. The sequence now reads –AGG/TCC/AGA/GCC/GAT/TGG–. Note that the final sequence differs from the normal sequence only in the second and third codons; if these code for amino acids that are not critical to the functioning of the protein produced by this gene, normal activity will have been at least partially restored. In contrast, either frame shift mutation by itself produces an unending string of missense codons within the gene; by random chance, at least one new triplet will be a nonsense codon leading to chain termination.

Suppressor mutations can also occur at other places on the chromosome (**extragenic** suppressors). The extragenic suppressor loci are genes that code for components of the translation system, such as tRNA; by mutation, they alter one or another component so as to compensate for the original coding error in the DNA. For example, one such suppressor mutation has been shown to act by altering the anticodon in serine tRNA.

Mutation at the Cellular Level

The set of genetic determinants carried by a cell is called its **genotype.** The observable properties of the cell are called its **phenotype.** Without DNA sequencing, a gene mutation can only be recognized if it brings about an observable phenotypic change; such changes may be described in terms of gross morphology or physiology, but in most cases it is possible to define the phenotypic change in terms of the loss or gain of a particular protein or its function (eg, a specific enzyme or its activity). For convenience, we will discuss phenotypic change in terms of enzyme activity only.

A. Phenotypic Expression in Uninucleate Cells:

1. Gain mutations–When a mutation confers on

the cell the ability to synthesize an active enzyme, there is no detectable lag between the time of mutation and the beginning of enzyme synthesis.

2. Loss mutations–Most cell proteins are stable. In *E coli,* for example, there is no protein turnover in actively growing cells, and a turnover of only about 5% per hour in resting cells. Thus, when a mutation causes the synthesis of a functional enzyme to stop, the cell remains enzymatically active. If the cell continues to grow, however, the amount of preexisting enzyme per cell is halved at each generation. After 7 generations, the progeny of the original mutant will each have less than 1% of the wildtype enzyme level.

This **phenotypic lag** has certain practical consequences. For example, the sensitivity of bacteria to attack by viruses (bacteriophages, or "phages") depends upon the presence in the cell wall of specific receptor sites. The mutation to phage resistance reflects the loss of synthesis of phage receptor. If such mutations are induced, the phage resistance phenotype will not be detected until a sufficient number of generations has taken place to dilute out the original receptors. In other words, there is a **delay in phenotypic expression.**

B. Phenotypic Expression in Multinucleate Cells:

1. Gain mutations–Many microbial cells are multinucleate. *E coli,* for example, has an average of about 4 nuclei per cell during exponential growth. When a gain mutation occurs in a multinucleate cell, the mutant nucleus synthesizes the new active enzyme and phenotypic expression is immediate. A gain mutation is thus **dominant;** the active form ("allele") of the gene is expressed, and the inactive allele is not.

2. Loss mutations–When, in a multinucleate cell, a loss mutation occurs, only the mutant nucleus ceases to make active enzyme, whereas the other nuclei continue. The loss mutation is thus **recessive** and is not expressed in the original cell. After several generations, however, the mutant nucleus will have segregated into a separate cell (Fig 4–7). Phenotypic expression of a loss mutation must thus await both phenotypic lag and nuclear segregation.

Mutation at the Population Level

A. Mutant Frequency and Mutation Rate:

1. Relation between frequency and rate–The proportion of mutants in a cell population is the **mutant frequency.** Frequencies ranging from 1×10^{-5} to 1×10^{-10} are commonly observed when individual phenotypes are considered. The frequency of mutants in a given culture reflects 3 independent parameters: (1) The probability that a cell will mutate during a given interval, such as a generation. This is the **mutation rate.** (2) The distribution in time of mutational events over the growth period of the culture. For example, exceptionally early mutations will produce extremely large **clones** of mutant progeny. (A clone constitutes the total progeny of a single cell.) (3) The growth rates of the mutant cells relative to the parental type.

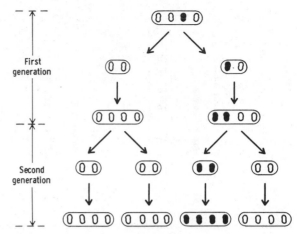

Figure 4–7. Segregation of a mutant nucleus. The nucleus containing the mutation is shown in black. If the mutation occurs in a cell with 4 nuclei, 2 generations are required before a pure mutant cell is produced.

2. Measurement of mutation rate–The mutation rate can be related to average mutant frequencies by a complex equation that takes into account all of the above parameters. However, there are methods that permit a direct determination of the number of mutations which have occurred in a culture (as opposed to the number of mutant cells in the culture) and thus permit a simple estimation of the mutation rate.

The mutation rate is commonly expressed in units of "mutations per cell per generation"; in other words, the probability that a mutation will occur during the event of a single cell doubling in size and dividing to become 2 cells. When one cell goes through 2 successive generations to become 4 cells, for example, 3 such "cell-doubling events" occur (Fig 4–7). In general terms, when N_0 cells increase to form N_1 cells, the number of doubling events is equal to $N_1 - N_0$. The mutation rate (**a**) is thus expressed by the simple formula

$$a = \frac{M}{N_1 - N_0}$$

where **M** = the number of mutations occurring during the growth of N_0 cells to form N_1 cells.

The number of mutations (M) that have occurred in a culture during a measured interval of growth can be determined by depositing an inoculum on a membrane filter and placing the filter on top of an agar medium that permits every cell to initiate colony formation. After a limited period of incubation during which the colonies develop to only microscopic size, the membrane is moved to a different agar medium that permits only the desired mutant type to continue growth. Each large colony that ultimately develops represents a **single mutational event** that occurred when N_0 cells (the inoculum) increased to N_1 cells (the number of cells present at the time that the medium was changed).

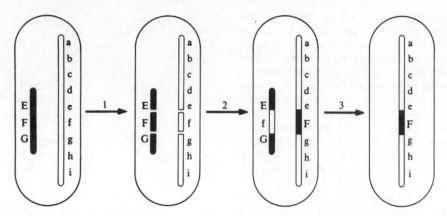

Figure 4–8. Genetic recombination in partial zygotes. The open bar represents the recipient cell chromosome, with genes lettered a–i. The solid bar represents an exogenote that has been transferred from a donor cell. An exchange of segments bearing the alleles of gene f, followed by cell division and segregation, leads to a recombinant cell. See Fig 4–9 for the detailed mechanism by which broken ends are reciprocally rejoined. (From Stanier RY, Doudoroff M, Adelberg EA: *The Microbial World,* 2nd ed. Copyright © 1963. By permission of Prentice-Hall, Inc, Englewood Cliffs, NJ.)

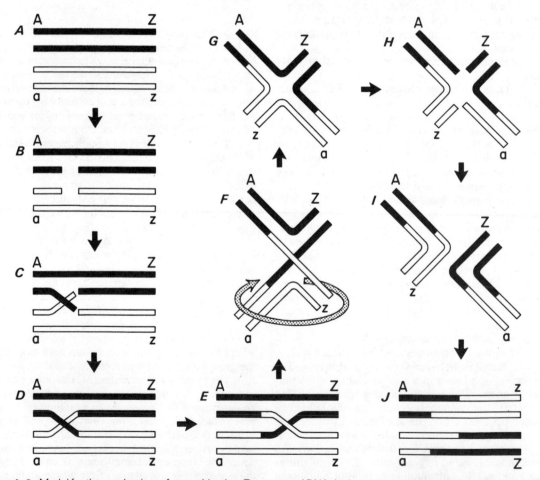

Figure 4–9. Model for the mechanism of recombination. Two parental DNA duplexes are represented by the pairs of shaded and unshaded bars, with one duplex carrying the markers A and Z; the other, a and z. *(A)* Duplexes pair. *(B)* Breakage of two strands occurs. *(C), (D)* The broken segments are reciprocally rejoined. *(E)* The crossover point is laterally displaced. *(F), (G)* Rearrangement of the diagram. *(H)* The other strands are broken and partially digested. *(I)* Localized repair and reciprocal rejoining. *(J)* Rearrangement of the diagram to show the heterozygosity within each duplex at the site of crossing over, a phenomenon that can be demonstrated readily in certain phage crosses. (After Potter H, Dressler D: In vitro system from *Escherichia coli* that catalyzes generalized genetic recombination. *Proc Natl Acad Sci USA* 1978; **75**:3698.)

B. Selection:

1. Relative selection—Although any given type of mutant may be present in a culture at very low frequency (eg, 10^{-6}), small differences between the mutant and parent in either growth rate or death rate can lead to tremendous population shifts. For example, consider a culture containing 10^7 penicillin-sensitive (pen-s) cells and 10^1 penicillin-resistant (pen-r) cells. If the pen-s cells have a generation (doubling) time of 60 minutes and the pen-r cells a generation time of 50 minutes, then after 3 transfers of the culture, permitting 30 generations of the pen-s cells, the frequency of pen-r cells will have changed from 1×10^{-6} to 1×10^{-4}—a 100-fold increase. After 3 more transfers, 1% of the culture will be penicillin-resistant.

2. Absolute selection—In medical or microbiologic practice, microbial populations are commonly subjected to absolute selection, either consciously or unconsciously. For example, growth of the above-described culture in the presence of penicillin will lead to the death of all pen-s cells, so that the final culture will be 100% pen-r after one transfer. Since most mutants occur in cultures at very low frequencies, absolute selection is generally employed for their detection. The usual practice is to plate the culture on an agar medium that will permit only the sought-for mutant type to form colonies.

INTERCELLULAR TRANSFER & GENETIC RECOMBINATION IN BACTERIA

The Formation of Bacterial Zygotes

In eukaryotic organisms, the diploid cell formed by the fusion of 2 haploid sexual cells (gametes) is called the **zygote.** Zygotes may also be formed in bacteria, but true cell fusion does not normally take place; instead, part of the genetic material of a donor cell is transferred to a recipient cell, and the recipient thus becomes diploid for only a part of its genetic complement. In the partial zygote, the genetic fragment from the donor is called the **exogenote** and the genetic complement of the recipient is called the **endogenote.** Exogenote and endogenote usually pair and recombine immediately after transfer. This recombinational step occurs by breakage and reunion of the paired genotes (Figs 4–8 and 4–9).

During succeeding nuclear and cell divisions, the **recombinant chromosome** is segregated into a single haploid cell. This cell can be experimentally detected by plating the partial zygotes on a selective medium on which only recombinants can grow.

The 3 processes by which recombination normally occurs in bacteria differ from each other primarily in the mechanism of the transfer process. These processes—transformation, transduction, and plasmid-mediated conjugation—are briefly summarized in the following sections.

Although DNA transfer and partial zygosis are the normal processes by which bacteria recombine, complete zygosis can be artificially induced by removing the bacterial cell wall and fusing the resulting protoplasts with agents such as polyethylene glycol. In *Bacillus subtilis,* for example, up to 10% of the treated protoplasts yield cells that, after reversion to walled bacilli, contain both parental genomes. These biparental types segregate true recombinants as well as parental segregants during further cell divisions.

Mechanism of Recombination

A model for the mechanism of recombination between 2 DNA molecules is shown in Fig 4–9. Evidence for this model comes from electron micrographs of DNA molecules extracted from cells (or from in vitro preparations) in which plasmid recombination was taking place: structures are seen that correspond to the intermediates labeled F and G in the figure.

Restriction & Modification

Bacterial cells of many species contain 2 enzymes with complementary functions. One enzyme **modifies** all the DNA in the cell by methylating bases at a few specific sites on the DNA. The other enzyme degrades all DNA that is not so modified; this process is called **restriction.** Restriction and modification may have evolved to protect the cell from the lytic attack of DNA viruses (bacteriophages; see Chapter 9).

The degrading enzymes are called **restriction endonucleases;** the DNA site recognized by a particular restriction endonuclease is a specific sequence of 6–8 base-pairs that constitute a palindrome, ie, the sequence reads the same in both directions, starting from the 3' end of each strand. For example, the restriction endonuclease of *E coli* called EcoR1 recognizes the sequence

$$\downarrow$$
$$- - \; G \; A \; \overset{*}{A} \; T \; T \; C \; - -$$
$$- - \; C \; T \; T \; \underset{*}{A} \; A \; G \; - -$$
$$\uparrow$$

cutting it at the symmetric sites indicated by the arrows. The asterisks represent the sites that are methylated by the modifying enzyme of *E coli*, thus protecting the sequence from endonuclease attack.

When a zygote is formed by the transfer of DNA between bacterial strains with different specificities of restriction and modification, the DNA that penetrates the recipient is rapidly degraded in most of the cells. In a few cells, however, the exogenote may escape restriction and recombination can take place.

For example, conjugation between *E coli* strain B and *E coli* strain K12 yields recombinants at an extremely low frequency. From such crosses, however, a few recombinants can be isolated that are K12 strains carrying strain B's genes for modification and restriction. Such recombinants show high frequencies of recombination with *E coli* strain B. Restriction and modification similarly affect the transfer of phages from one strain of bacterium to another (see p 114).

Almost every bacterial species produces a unique restriction endonuclease in terms of its DNA recognition site. The availability of this large series of specific enzymes has made possible the technologies of genetic engineering based on recombinant DNA, as discussed on pp 59–61.

TRANSFORMATION

In transformation, the recipient cell takes up soluble DNA released from the donor cell. In some cases, transforming DNA is released spontaneously; eg, it is found in the extracellular slime of certain *Neisseria* species. Usually, however, it is necessary to extract the DNA from donor cells by chemical procedures and to protect it from degradation by DNases.

Transformation occurs only in bacteria that are capable of taking up high-molecular-weight DNA from the medium. Originally discovered in the pneumococcus, it was subsequently discovered to occur in a number of other bacterial species, both gram-positive and gram-negative. Gram-positive species include the pneumococcus *(Streptococcus pneumoniae)* and *Bacillus subtilis;* gram-negative species include the gonococcus *(Neisseria gonorrhoeae)* and *Haemophilus influenzae.* Transformation also occurs in *E coli* in the presence of high concentrations of calcium ion. In some species, transformable cells are capable of taking up DNA from any source, although they form genetic recombinants only if the donor is a closely related organism. This specificity reflects the requirement of endogenote and exogenote to pair before exchanges can take place: pairing of DNA molecules demands close homology of nucleotide sequences.

Transformation may be considered to occur in 3 steps: binding of high-molecular-weight DNA to the cell surface; uptake of the bound DNA through the cell membrane; and integration of the donor DNA fragment into the recipient cell's chromosome. Only the first 2 stages occur in transformation with plasmid DNA, which becomes reestablished in the recipient cell as an autonomous replicon.

In *Neisseria,* cells are competent to bind DNA at all times; in the other transformable species, competence develops only at certain stages in the cell cycle or under a particular growth regimen and requires formation of competence factors by the cell. These factors include specific DNA-binding proteins of the cell membrane.

The mechanisms by which specifically bound DNA enters the cell appear to differ in gram-positive and gram-negative cells. In the gram-positive pneumococcus, externally bound double-stranded DNA is nicked by a membrane-bound endonuclease. Entry is then initiated, at which time the nicks become double-stranded breaks. Entry of the fragments proceeds with the digestion of one of the 2 strands. In the gram-positive species *H influenzae,* a specific 11-base-pair sequence is bound to a membrane protein complex; there are approximately 600 randomly distributed copies of this sequence in the *Haemophilus* chromosome: roughly one per 4 kilobases. Each cell takes up 5 or 6 bound DNA molecules, the DNA remaining double-stranded during entry. These differences in uptake mechanism presumably reflect the different structures of the cell envelope in gram-positive and gram-negative cells.

The uptake of DNA by *E coli* cells, which requires a high concentration of calcium ion, presumably takes place by an entirely different mechanism. The uptake mechanism for plasmid DNA also differs from that for chromosomal DNA, as indicated by different ion requirements and by the requirement for circular DNA in plasmid transformation of *B subtilis.*

The final stage of transformation—integration—appears to be similar in both gram-positive and gram-negative organisms: one of the 2 strands of a segment of the recipient's DNA is replaced by a single strand of donor DNA, forming a heteroduplex. The heteroduplex molecule segregates a recombinant daughter duplex at the next round of DNA replication.

It is not clear whether transformation requires the expenditure of metabolic energy by the recipient cell. Transformation in *B subtilis*—but not in *E coli*—requires the maintenance of a membrane potential; ATP appears not to be required in either species.

TRANSDUCTION BY BACTERIOPHAGE

In transduction, a fragment of donor chromosome is carried to the recipient by a bacteriophage that has been produced in the donor cell. Transduction is generally observed with temperate bacteriophages, ie, those capable of forming prophages (see Chapter 9); certain mutants of virulent phages, however, may also effect transduction.

Transduction occurs in many bacterial genera, both gram-negative and gram-positive. Transduction may be generalized or restricted: in **generalized transduction,** the phage has a roughly equal chance of carrying any segment of the donor's chromosome; in **restricted transduction,** the transducing particles carry only those segments that are immediately adjacent to the site of prophage attachment.

(or specialized)

Restricted Transduction

The mechanism of prophage attachment is shown in Fig 9–4, for phage λ(lambda). When λ is induced, λ DNA is detached from the chromosome by the reversal of the steps shown in Fig 9–4; detachment is followed by phage replication, maturation, and host cell lysis. As a rare event (about 10^{-6} to 10^{-5} of the cells), the crossover event occurs at a different position, generating a circle of DNA in which part of the λ genome has been replaced by a segment of host chromosome (Fig 4–10). The recombinant circles, lacking certain essential phage genes, are usually defective; they cannot replicate or mature unless the cell is simultaneously infected with a normal phage that supplies the missing phage gene products. When this occurs,

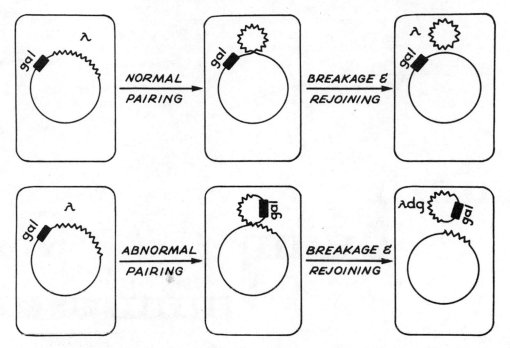

Figure 4–10. *Upper Row:* Detachment of λ prophage to form a normal λ vegetative DNA. *Lower Row:* Detachment of λ prophage to form λdg DNA, which will mature as a transducing particle. ("λdg" is an abbreviation for "lambda defective carrying gal genes.")

the cell lyses and liberates both normal phage particles and "transducing particles."

When a transducing particle is adsorbed by a recipient cell, it injects its DNA in the normal fashion; the recipient thus receives a segment of the donor's chromosome as part of a phage genome that integrates with the recipient's chromosome to become a prophage. The transduced donor genes are expressed in the recipient cell, even though they are inserted within a prophage.

Generalized Transduction

Although generalized transducing phages may occasionally incorporate host DNA by the mechanism described above, the great majority of their transducing particles contain only host DNA; it thus appears that phage heads can be assembled around condensed segments of host DNA as well as around condensed phage genomes. The products of certain phage genes are essential for normal head assembly; presumably these "morphopoietic factors" complex with phage DNA and provide a matrix for assembly of the head subunits. Transducing phage particles may thus arise when morphopoietic factors complex with fragments of host DNA of the right size. As in restricted transduction, only about one particle in 10^5 or 10^6 is a transducing particle.

It has been found that phage P1, a typical generalized transducing phage, does not form a prophage that is integrated into the host chromosome. Instead, the prophage occupies an independent site in the cell. This difference is compatible with the differ-

ent mechanisms of formation of transducing particles.

In generalized transduction, part of the donor cell DNA is degraded; the rest is integrated into the recipient cell's chromosome as a double-stranded fragment.

In the pneumococcus, a phage-associated gene transfer process has been discovered that exhibits transformationlike as well as transductionlike properties. In this system, host genes are packaged in DNase-resistant particles that adsorb to recipient cells in a phagelike manner. Unlike transduction, however, entry of the DNA requires recipient competence and endonuclease action and becomes DNase-sensitive. It is not known whether this mixed mode of transfer occurs in other host-phage systems.

High-Frequency Transduction

In restricted transduction, the transducing particle contains part of a phage genome linked to a segment of host DNA. When this is injected into the recipient, the entire DNA structure becomes integrated into the bacterial chromosome. The transduced recipient then produces a clone of cells, every one of which carries the defective prophage plus the extra segment of donor DNA. If these cells also carry a normal prophage (as a result of simultaneous infection of the original recipient by a normal particle and a transducing particle), then, on induction, a lysate is produced in which half of the particles are transducing particles. This is the phenomenon of "high-frequency transduction."

Abortive Transduction

In many generalized transductions, failure of the

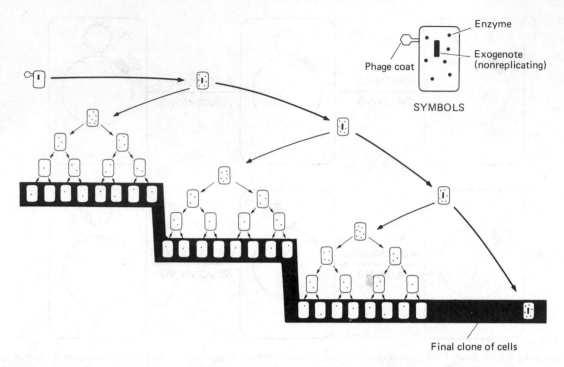

Figure 4–11. Abortive transduction. At each division only one of the daughter cells receives the active gene. The other cell goes through a few cell divisions, until the active gene product (eg, enzyme) is diluted out. Plating an abortive transductant produces a minute colony, in which only one cell is capable of further growth and division. (From Stanier RY, Doudoroff M, Adelberg EA: *Microbial World,* 3rd ed. Copyright © 1970. By permission of Prentice-Hall, Englewood Cliffs, NJ.)

exogenote to be integrated may lead to persistence without replication. Thus, when the zygote divides, only one of the daughter cells receives the exogenote. In further cell generations, the exogenote is again transmitted without replicating, so that only one cell in the clone at any given time is a partial diploid. This situation is called ''abortive transduction''; the exogenote appears to be maintained in circular form by a host cell protein, accounting for its resistance to nuclease attack.

In abortive transduction, the genes of the exogenote function normally. Thus, if a gal⁺/gal⁻ cell is produced by an abortive transduction, the cell in which the nonreplicating gal⁺ gene resides will produce the galactose-fermenting enzyme. During further generations, the clone of cells arising from each gal⁻ segregant will produce no more enzyme, and the enzyme will be diluted out by the cell division process. If a gal⁺/gal⁻ abortive transductant is plated on a medium in which galactose is the sole source of carbon and energy, it will produce a minute colony (containing about 10^6 cells) after 4 days of growth as a result of the limited production of the galactose-fermenting enzyme. (A normal gal⁺ cell would produce a very large colony, containing over 10^9 cells, in 2 days of growth.) The production of a minute colony as the result of abortive transduction is shown in Fig 4–11.

PLASMID–MEDIATED CONJUGATION

Plasmids

Bacteria are hosts to small, extrachromosomal genetic elements called plasmids. Plasmids are dispensable to the cell under ordinary conditions of growth. Their presence is detectable when the genes they carry confer new properties on the host, and they are generally named for these properties. Some examples are as follows:

(1) Sex factors–These mediate chromosome transfer by the mechanism described below. The most widely studied is F, the sex factor found in *E coli* K12.

(2) Col factors–These carry genes that cause their hosts to produce **colicins,** proteins that are lethal toxins for coliform bacteria. Most members of this group are small (less than 10 megadaltons of DNA), are present in the cell in many copies (20–100), and are nonconjugative—lacking the gene system mediating self-transfer.

(3) Resistance (R) factors–These carry genes conferring on the host cell resistance to various antimicrobial agents, such as antibiotics. A single plasmid, for example, may carry separate genes for resistance to streptomycin, chloramphenicol, tetracyclines, and sulfonamides. In some cases it has been possible to dissociate the plasmid into several smaller ones: an element called resistance transfer factor (RTF), carrying the genes governing the intracellular transfer process; and separate elements called R determinants, carrying the resistance genes. In other cases, the various elements remain tightly linked, and the entire plasmid is then referred to as an R factor.

(4) Penicillinase plasmids of staphylococci– These plasmids carry a gene that causes the cell to produce a potent penicillinase, thus rendering it resistant to penicillin. They differ from R factors in that they are not capable of transfer by conjugation. They can be carried from cell to cell, however, by phage-mediated transduction.

(5) Degradative plasmids of *Pseudomonas*– These plasmids carry sets of genes determining the enzymes of catabolic pathways, such as the enzymes for the degradation of camphor, toluene, octane, or salicylic acid.

(6) Virulence plasmids– A number of plasmids carry genes whose products contribute to the relative pathogenicity of the host cell. These plasmids include the enterotoxin and colonization antigen plasmids of enteropathogenic *E coli* strains and a staphylococcal plasmid carrying a gene for exfoliative toxin.

As will be discussed below, plasmids share many properties with bacterial viruses (phages). They are of major clinical significance, not only because they may carry genes for resistance to therapeutic drugs and for virulence factors but also because some of them mediate gene transfer—a process that leads to the emergence of strains with new combinations of antigenic and virulence properties.

A. Physical Properties: All plasmids discovered to date are circular, double-stranded DNA molecules. Their molecular weights range from 3×10^6 to 1×10^8, which is sufficient to code for 5–160 average polypeptides.

B. Replication: Plasmid DNA replicates while maintaining a supercoiled, circular state. Replicating plasmid DNA can be isolated in the form of "relaxation complexes," in which the DNA is bound to proteins that appear to provide the following functions: (1) binding of the DNA to the membrane replicator site; (2) nicking and unwinding of the strands to permit replication; and (3) resealing of the nicks. Replication is bidirectional in some plasmids and unidirectional in others.

Plasmids regulate their own replication, such that each plasmid exhibits a typical copy-number ratio (ratio of plasmid copies to chromosome copies in the cell). In general, the small nonconjugative plasmids have high copy-number ratios whereas the large conjugative plasmids have copy-number ratios closer to 1. Plasmid replication is unusually sensitive to inhibition by such agents as acridine dyes and ultraviolet light; by using these agents at threshold doses, cells can be "cured" of their plasmids.

Even in plasmids having a copy-number ratio of 1, partition between daughter cells following replication is highly efficient. This is effected by a plasmid DNA site called *par*, which is the functional equivalent of the eukaryotic chromosomal centromere. It may act by binding to a cell membrane site or, alternatively, by associating with the host chromosome.

C. Incompatibility: Plasmids can be classified into a number of incompatibility groups; 2 members of the same group cannot coexist in the same cell. This phenomenon may involve competition for a specific attachment site in the cell membrane or may reflect the action of group-specific repressors. Members of the same incompatibility group are closely related, as indicated by the extensive hybridization of their DNAs.

D. Self-Transfer:

1. Gram-negative bacteria– Many—but not all—plasmids of gram-negative bacteria are conjugative: they carry the genes (called the *tra* genes) mediating their own transfer by the process of cell conjugation. There are 12 or more *tra* genes arranged in an operon (see below); some of these code for the production of the **sex pilus.**

Plasmid transfer in gram-negative bacteria begins with the extrusion of a sex pilus, a protein thread several times the length of the cell. The tip of the sex pilus adheres to gram-negative cell walls. Any gram-negative cell that it touches becomes tethered to the plasmid-containing cell; shortly thereafter, the 2 cells become bound together at a point of direct wall-to-wall contact, possibly by retraction of the pilus into the donor cell (Fig 4–12).

Binding of the recipient cell to the donor pilus requires the presence of specific receptor sites on the recipient cell's surface. In certain conjugation-deficient mutants, one of the major proteins of the outer membrane is missing and the lipopolysaccharide is altered, indicating a role for both of these components in pair formation.

Following specific pair formation, the plasmid undergoes a special type of replication called "transfer replication," one parental strand passing into the recipient and the other remaining in the donor cell (Fig 4–13). Complementary strands are synthesized in the donor and recipient simultaneously with transfer. The daughter molecules are circularized by ligase action immediately after transfer replication is complete.

With the use of a micromanipulator, tethered cells have been separated and isolated before becoming permanently coupled by direct contact. Some of the isolated cells produced recombinant clones, suggesting that DNA can be transferred through the sex pilus. However, most—if not all—transfers occur after the cells are in direct, wall-to-wall contact.

No cytoplasm, nor any cell material other than DNA, passes from donor to recipient. The mating couples eventually break apart, resulting in 2 plasmid-containing cells where there had been one before.

2. Gram-positive bacteria– Several antibiotics produced by members of the genus *Streptomyces* have been found to be determined by plasmid genes, and some of these plasmids are transferable from one streptomycete to another. The process resembles conjugation in that direct hyphal contact is necessary, but the molecular details of the process are not understood. The best known such plasmid is SCP1, which carries the genes for the biosynthetic pathway producing the

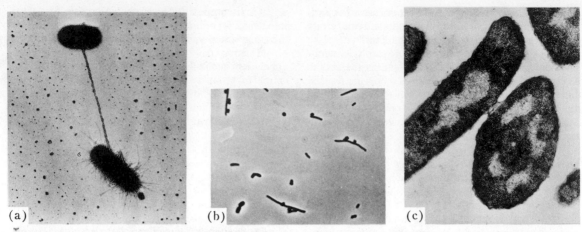

Figure 4–12. *(a)* A male and a female cell joined by an F pilus. The F pilus has been "stained" with male-specific RNA phage particles. The male cell also possesses ordinary pili, which do not adsorb male-specific phages and which are not involved in mating. *(b)* Mating pairs of *E coli* cells. Hfr cells are elongated. *(c)* Electron micrograph of a thin section of a mating pair. The cell walls of the mating partners are in intimate contact in the "bridge" area. (Electron micrograph [*a*] by Carnahan J and Brinton C. From Stanier RY, Doudoroff M, Adelberg EA: *The Microbial World,* 3rd ed. Copyright © 1970. By permission of Prentice-Hall, Inc, Englewood Cliffs, NJ. Photographs [*b*] and [*c*] from Gross JD and Caro LG: DNA transfer in bacterial conjugation. *J Mol Biol* 1966; **16**:269.)

antibiotic methylenomycin. SCP1 also carries the genes responsible for transfer by a mechanism which has some similarities to that of plasmid-mediated chromosome transfer in gram-negative bacteria.

Plasmid-mediated conjugation also occurs in members of the gram-positive genus *Streptococcus*. In *Streptococcus lactis*, the ability to ferment lactose is conjugally transmitted as a plasmid-borne β-galactosidase *(lac)* gene. A series of conjugative plasmids have been analyzed in *Streptococcus faecalis*, carrying genes for hemolysin, bacteriocin, and single or multiple drug resistance. These plasmids can mobilize other (nonconjugative) plasmids as well as chromosomal markers.

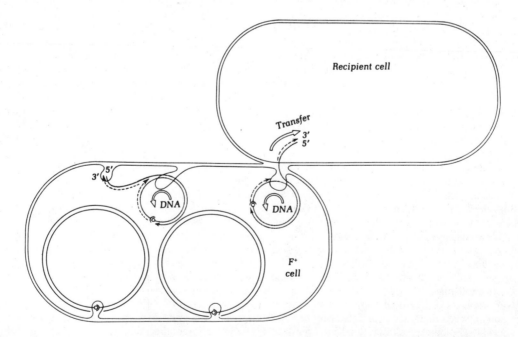

Figure 4–13. An F+ cell, containing 2 autonomous F replicons and 2 chromosomes, is shown conjugating with a recipient cell. Replication of F is proceeding according to the mechanism outlined in Fig 4–4. The F at the left is replicating within the host cell; the F at the right is being driven into the recipient by replication. (From Stanier RY, Doudoroff M, Adelberg EA: *The Microbial World,* 3rd ed. Copyright © 1970. By permission of Prentice-Hall, Inc, Englewood Cliffs, NJ.)

An unusual feature of the *S faecalis* mating system is the production by recipient cells of specific **sex pheromones**—diffusible proteins that stimulate donor cell aggregation (with each other and with recipient cells) and, if the donor cells are preinduced by the pheromone, increase the frequency of donor plasmid transfer as much as a million-fold. When a recipient cell acquires a given plasmid, it ceases to produce the pheromone specific for that plasmid but continues to excrete pheromones that act on donor cells harboring other conjugative plasmids.

E. Recombination: Plasmids undergo crossing over with each other and with the host chromosome, depending on the extent of their base sequence homologies or on the presence of transposable elements (see below). Since both plasmids and chromosome are circular, an odd number of crossovers serves to integrate the 2 DNA structures, which then replicate as a single unit. An even number of crossovers, on the other hand, brings about an exchange of segments.

A plasmid capable of integrating with the bacterial chromosome is called an **episome.** When integration occurs, a double replicon is formed bearing both a chromosomal and a plasmid replicator site. In some cases, replication continues to start at the chromosomal replicator; in others (eg, at nonpermissive temperatures in mutants temperature-sensitive for DNA synthesis), replication of the entire structure is taken over by the plasmid replicator, a phenomenon known as "integrative suppression."

F. Mobilization: If a gram-negative cell harbors 2 plasmids, one self-transferable and the other not, the former may bring about the simultaneous transfer of the latter—ie, the latter is "mobilized." Mobilization is brought about when the 2 plasmids are either permanently or transiently integrated by a crossover; mobilization can also occur without integration if the nontransferable plasmid simply lacks one or more gene functions (eg, pilus formation) that the self-transferable plasmid can provide.

The bacterial chromosome may also be mobilized by integration with a self-transferable plasmid. If the integration is relatively stable, the cell in which it has occurred may give rise to a clone, every cell in which is capable of chromosome transfer. The strain obtained by isolation of such a clone is called **Hfr,** for "high-frequency recombination"; chromosome transfer by Hfr strains is described below.

Some chromosome-mobilizing plasmids are found among the R and Col factors; others have no other detectable effect on the host and are known simply as "sex factors."

G. Population Dynamics: Plasmids are occasionally irreversibly lost by their host cells and hence would ultimately disappear from bacterial populations in nature if their loss were not compensated by cell-to-cell transfer and replication. As discussed above, such transfer may occur either by conjugation or by phage transduction. The rates of loss and transfer are such as to maintain each type of plasmid in a small percentage of the natural host population at any given time. When selection is applied, however, as in the case of R factor selection by antibiotics, a majority of host cells may harbor a given type of plasmid (see below).

The transmission frequency of plasmids is limited mainly by the efficiency of pilus formation, which in most host strains is repressed to a level of 10^{-5} per cell, and by species specificity. For example, F (the sex factor of *E coli* K12), which is totally nonrepressed, is transferred from one *E coli* strain to another with a frequency of 1.0, but from *E coli* to *Proteus mirabilis* at a frequency of 1×10^{-5} or less.

H. Cell Properties Determined by Plasmid Genes:

1. Drug resistance–In gram-negative bacteria, genes governing resistance to such drugs as neomycin, kanamycin, streptomycin, chloramphenicol, tetracyclines, penicillins, and sulfonamides are found on one or another plasmid in various combinations. In the gram-positive staphylococci, genes governing resistance to such agents as penicillin, erythromycin, and heavy metals (eg, Hg^{2+} and Co^{2+}) are found on plasmids. Genes conferring resistance to the same agents may also be found on the chromosome, but in such cases they do so by different mechanisms. Most plasmid-governed resistance is mediated by enzymatic inactivation of the drug (eg, by acetylation or phosphorylation), whereas chromosome-mediated resistance usually reflects a lowered affinity of its target molecule for the drug. These findings are compatible with the fact that plasmids are (by definition) dispensable to the cell: Only chromosomal genes can confer resistance by structurally altering the binding site for the drug, since the genes determining the structures of indispensable cell components must themselves be indispensable.

2. Virulence–Enteropathogenic strains of *E coli* of porcine or human origin cause diarrheal illnesses by the liberation of enterotoxins. Two types have been recognized: a heat-labile toxin (LT) and a heat-stable toxin (ST) (see p 229). Both are determined by plasmid genes. Other plasmids of *E coli* carry genes determining surface hairs (pili) that serve as "colonization antigens": only strains possessing these pili can adhere to host epithelial cells and establish themselves in sufficient numbers to cause disease.

Plasmid-borne genes can contribute to host cell virulence in other ways. The colicinogenic plasmid Col V, for example, determines enzymes that synthesize cell-associated, hydroxamate-containing iron-sequestering compounds which are induced in media containing low concentrations of iron. It is believed that invasiveness of symbiotic bacteria depends heavily on the ability of the bacteria to compete with their mammalian host cells for iron; most *E coli* strains isolated from bacteremias carry Col V, suggesting a role for the Col V–determined iron-sequestering system in host cell virulence. The invasiveness of the human pathogen *Yersinia enterocolitica* has also been shown to be plasmid-determined, although in this case the mechanism is not known.

3. Production of antimicrobial agents–Antimicrobial agents include antibiotics, which are the products of metabolic pathways, and polypeptide toxins. A number of these agents are encoded by plasmid genes, including some antibiotics of *Streptomyces*, bacteriocins (such as colicins), and microcins—oligopeptides produced by certain strains of *E coli*.

4. Other properties—As discussed above, plasmids are known that encode enzymes of special catabolic pathways (in *Pseudomonas*), enzymes of nitrogen fixation (in *Klebsiella*), and tumorigenicity for host plants (in *Agrobacterium tumefaciens*).

I. Relation to Viruses: Bacterial viruses possess all of the properties described above for plasmids; a *Pseudomonas* phage has even been found to promote conjugation. The major difference thus appears to be the ability of phages to form mature, protein-coated virions that can be liberated and passed to other cells through the medium. Their many similarities suggest a close evolutionary relationship between phages and plasmids.

J. Clinical Significance: The ease with which plasmids can transfer from cell to cell and the strong selection that chemotherapy has exerted for drug resistance have combined to produce striking results. In Japan, for example, the frequency of R-governed multiple-resistance *Shigella* strains rose from 10–20% in 1955 to 80% in 1968. In England, multi-resistant *Salmonella typhimurium* first appeared in 1961 and rose to 21% of all *S typhimurium* isolates by 1964.

In general, 60–90% of resistance markers in the gram-negative pathogens are carried on transferable plasmids. Although the experimentally determined rate of transfer of resistance in vivo is very low, epidemiologic evidence indicates that such transfer accounts for the rapid rise in incidence of drug-resistant strains of gram-negative pathogens.

The use of antibiotics as feed supplements for domestic animals has led to a large increase (by selection) in R factors among the normal gram-negative flora of such animals, and such R factors are transmissible to humans. For example, one study carried out in England showed a much higher incidence of bacteria carrying multiple-resistance R factors in the fecal contents of farm workers who were in contact with antibiotic-fed pigs than in a control group who were in contact only with normal pigs.

RTFs (plasmids carrying the genes for self-transfer but not for drug resistance) have also been discovered to be extremely common in the bacterial flora of humans and animals. For example, 20 out of 60 *E coli* strains isolated from healthy humans and animals were found in one study to carry RTFs, as did 15 out of 21 enteropathogenic strains isolated from patients. (RTFs are detected in the following way: strain A, which is being screened for the presence of an RTF, is mated with strain B, which carries only a nontransferable R determinant. Strain B is then mated with a third strain—strain C—which is plasmid-free. The transfer of the R determinant from strain B to strain C reveals the presence of an RTF acquired from strain A.)

Chromosome Transfer

A. The F⁻, F⁺, and Hfr States: Cells of *E coli* K12 which carry F are called F⁺; those which have lost it are called F⁻. F⁺ cells will transfer replicas of their sex factors to F⁻ cells by the process described above.

In a population of F⁺ cells, the integration of F and chromosome occurs about once per 10^5 cells at each generation; the cells in which this occurs, and the clones that arise from them, are called Hfr (see above). Integration does not always occur at the same site on the bacterial chromosome. There are 8 or 10 preferred sites, containing insertion sequences (see below) or base-pair regions homologous with regions on F. Fig 4–14 illustrates the integration at one of these sites.

The integration process is reversible; in a population of Hfr cells, detachment by a second crossover occurs about once per 10^5 cells at each generation. Thus, every F⁺ population contains a few Hfr cells, and every Hfr population contains a few F⁺ cells.

B. DNA Transfer by Hfr Donors: When a suspension of Hfr cells is mixed with an excess of F⁻ cells, every Hfr cell will attach to an F⁻ cell and initiate replicative transfer. Since F and the chromosome have merged to form a single replicon, chromosomal DNA as well as F DNA passes into the recipient (Fig 4–15).

The order in which chromosome markers move into the recipient depends on the chromosomal site at which F has become integrated, as illustrated in Fig 4–16.

DNA transfer proceeds at a constant rate in each mating pair: approximately 5×10^4 base-pairs per

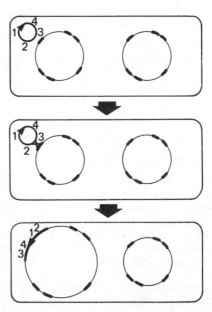

Figure 4–14. The attachment of F to chromosome. The sex factor (F) is shown as a smaller circle, not drawn to scale. The dark segments along the chromosome (larger circle) represent sites having base-pair homology with F DNA. The numbers represent regions of F DNA; the arrowhead represents the site at which the circle breaks at the time of conjugal transfer.

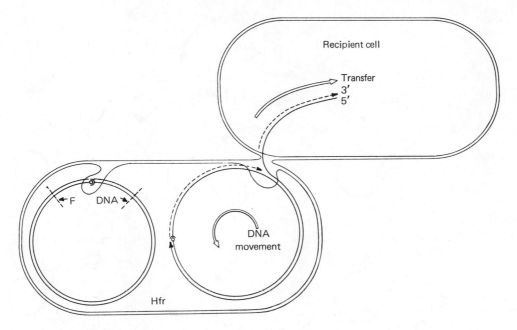

Figure 4–15. DNA transfer by an Hfr cell. Since F and chromosome are integrated, F replicative transfer causes the sequential transfer of chromosomal DNA. (From Stanier RY, Doudoroff M, Adelberg EA: *The Microbial World,* 3rd ed. Copyright © 1970. By permission of Prentice-Hall, Inc, Englewood Cliffs, NJ.)

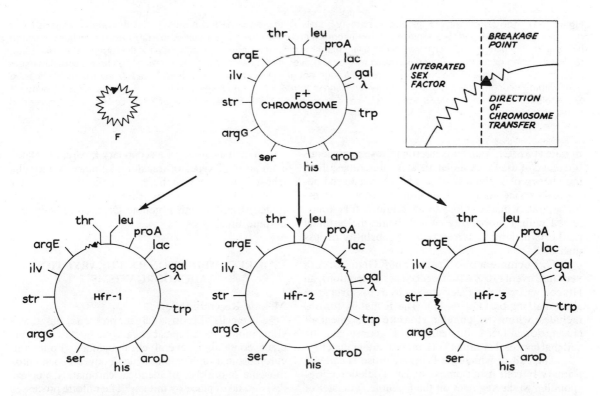

Figure 4–16. Integration of the sex factor and F⁺ chromosome to produce 3 different Hfr males. The upper circle represents the F⁺ chromosome; only a few of the known genetic loci, or "markers," are shown. The lower circles represent cases in which the sex factor (F) has integrated with the chromosome between argE and thr, between lac and gal, and between str and argG, respectively. (The 3- and 4-letter symbols represent genes governing biochemical activities of the cell, eg, "lac," the set of loci governing the utilization of β-galactosides; "his," the set of loci governing the biosynthesis of histidine, etc.) See Fig 4–13 for mechanism of integration.

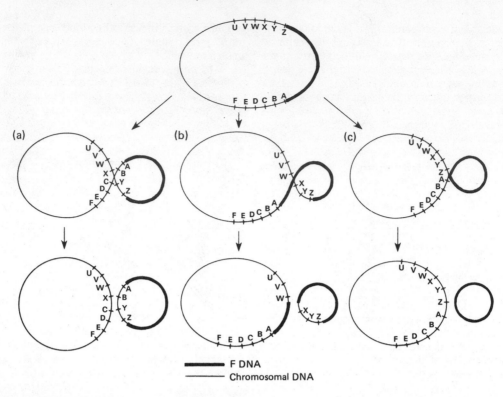

Figure 4–17. The generation of F genotes, in primary F' cells. At the top is an Hfr chromosome, with the integrated F DNA at the right. Letters A –F and U –Z represent chromosomal markers. *(a)* Exceptional pairing in a different region has generated an F genote containing a full complement of F DNA, plus chromosomal genes from both sides of the former attachment site. *(b)* Pairing in an exceptional region, followed by crossing over, generates an F genote carrying the chromosomal markers XYZ. The chromosome of the primary F' contains a segment of F DNA and has a deletion of the XYZ segment. *(c)* Crossing over within the original region of pairing between F and chromosome regenerates a normal F. (From Stanier RY, Doudoroff M, Adelberg EA: *The Microbial World,* 3rd ed. Copyright © 1970. By permission of Prentice-Hall, Inc, Englewood Cliffs, NJ.)

minute at 37 °C. Transfer is interrupted by spontaneous breakage of the DNA molecule at random times; thus, the chance of a given marker's being transferred decreases exponentially with its distance from the transfer origin. A marker close to the origin will be transferred with a probability of 1.0, while the terminal marker will be transferred with a probability of less than 0.01.

C. Formation and Transfer of F Genotes: As a very rare event (10^{-8}–10^{-6} per cell per generation), an Hfr cell will undergo F detachment by a crossover in an abnormal region (Fig 4–17). The F that is formed includes within its circular structure a segment of chromosomal DNA; it is called an **F genote,** and the cell that carries it is called F' (F prime), rather than F⁺.

The cell in which the F genote arose is called a primary F' cell; its chromosome has a deletion corresponding to the segment on the F genote. Transfer of the F genote to a normal F⁻ cell gives rise to a secondary F' strain, in which part of the chromosome is present in the diploid state. Crossing over occurs at a high rate in such cells, so that the F genote undergoes alternate integration and detachment from the chromosome.

When a culture of a secondary F' strain is mated with an F⁻, 2 types of transfer take place: some cells (those in which F is at that moment detached) transfer only the F genote; others (those in which F is integrated) transfer both F genote DNA and contiguous chromosomal DNA.

RECOMBINATION IN EUKARYOTIC MICROORGANISMS

Meiotic Recombination

The cells of protists (algae, protozoa, fungi, and slime molds) have typical eukaryotic nuclei, each nucleus containing several chromosomes. Following chromosomal replication, which converts each chromosome into a pair of identical chromatids, nuclear division takes place by mitosis. The mitotic processes segregate one chromatid of each pair into each daughter cell.

Some eukaryotic protists multiply in the diploid state, a clone of diploid cells arising from a zygote formed by the fusion of 2 haploid gametes. Each diploid nucleus thus contains 2 haploid sets of chromosomes, one from each parent. The 2 homologs of a particular chromosome will often differ by mutation at several genetic loci, ie, the cell will be heterozygous for those genes. The mutationally different forms of the same gene are called **alleles.**

Just after replication, then, each chromosome is represented by 4 chromatids, one pair from each parent. At meiosis, 2 sequential divisions segregate the 4 chromatids into 4 separate nuclei. The cells containing these nuclei may act immediately as gametes, fusing to restore the diploid condition, or—in some species—may give rise to clones of haploid cells, delaying the fusion event to a later stage in the life cycle.

New combinations of genes are produced during meiosis in 2 ways: (1) the random segregation of the chromatids during the division events scrambles the original parental sets of chromosomes, so that a given meiotic product receives some chromatids from one set and some from the other; and (2) during the first meiotic division, the 2 homologs of each chromosome pair, and a chromatid from one homolog may exchange segments with a chromatid from the other homolog by a recombinational (crossing over) event.

Gene Conversion

Consider a heterozygous marker on one of the chromosomes in the diploid cell. Call the dominant allele A and the recessive allele a; the 4 chromatids must carry the set A, A, a, a both at the start and at the end of meiosis. In exceptional cases, however, the 4 products of meiosis are found to carry the alleles A, A, A, a, ie, one of the a alleles has been converted to the A form during the meiotic process. This phenomenon, called gene conversion, may be explained by the following sequence of events: (1) Single-strand breaks occur in the chromatid DNA; (2) the breaks are widened into gaps by exonuclease attack; (3) the gaps are repaired by a DNA polymerase, *using one of the opposite parental strands as template;* and (4) the gaps are closed by polynucleotide ligase. Such events occur frequently in the region of a crossover but may also occur elsewhere on the chromosome.

Mitotic Recombination

During the multiplication of heterozygous diploid cells by mitosis, homologous chromosomes do not normally pair. As a rare event, they may do so, however, and in the process chromatids may exchange segments just as in meiosis. As shown in Fig 4–18, the ensuing random segregation of chromatids will result—in 50% of cases—in daughter cells that are homozygous for all loci distal to the crossover. The cell receiving the homozygous recessive alleles will then show a change from the dominant phenotype of the heterozygous parent to the recessive phenotype.

Heterokaryosis & Parasexuality in Fungi

Many fungi multiply in the haploid condition. When 2 mutationally different strains of the same species come into contact, hyphal fusion may occur to produce a mycelium in which the 2 parental types of nuclei commingle. Such a mycelium is called a **heterokaryon.**

On rare occasions, nuclear fusion may occur, producing a truly diploid heterozygous nucleus. When this nucleus is segregated into a uninucleate spore, germination will give rise to a diploid heterozygous mycelium. During mitotic growth, successive losses of one homolog of each chromosome pair may restore the haploid condition. The resulting haploids are genetic recombinants, since homolog loss is random with respect to parental origin; furthermore, genetic exchanges may have occurred by mitotic crossing over.

This cycle of events—the fusion of haploid nuclei to form a diploid nucleus and the return to haploidy by homolog loss—is called **parasexuality.** It provides a mechanism for genetic recombination in imperfect fungi but may be of little importance in fungi with a sexual stage in their life cycle.

Recombination in Cytoplasmic Organelles

The mitochondrial ribosomes of yeast are sensitive to certain inhibitors of protein synthesis such as chloramphenicol, erythromycin, and spiramycin that have no effect on cytoplasmic ribosomes. Mutants resistant to these inhibitors have been isolated and the mutations shown to reside in mitochondrial DNA. When different mitochondrial mutants of the yeast *Saccharomyces cerevisiae* are crossed and the resulting diploid cells allowed to undergo meiosis, the haploid progeny are found to contain recombinant mitochondria, with new combinations of mitochondrial genes.

The chloroplasts of algae and higher plants also contain their own DNA. In the unicellular green alga *Chlamydomonas,* mutants resistant to inhibitors of chloroplast ribosomal synthesis of protein have been isolated; the mutations reside in the chloroplast DNA. In experiments analogous to those done with yeast, sexual crosses between haploid algal cells carrying different chloroplast mutations yielded progeny containing genetically recombinant chloroplasts.

GENES OF STRUCTURE & GENES OF REGULATION

A gene that determines the structure of a particular protein (eg, an enzyme) is called a **structural gene.** The activity of a structural gene, in terms of production of messenger RNA for enzyme synthesis, is strictly regulated in the cell. It has been shown that many structural genes lie adjacent to specific sites concerned with the regulation of structural gene activity. Such a site is called an **operator.** Under certain conditions, the cell produces cytoplasmic proteins called **repressors;** when an operator gene binds its specific repressor, the structural gene adjacent to it is prevented from producing mRNA and is thus inactivated. In many cases, a series of structural genes determining a series of coordinated enzymes (eg, the enzymes of a particu-

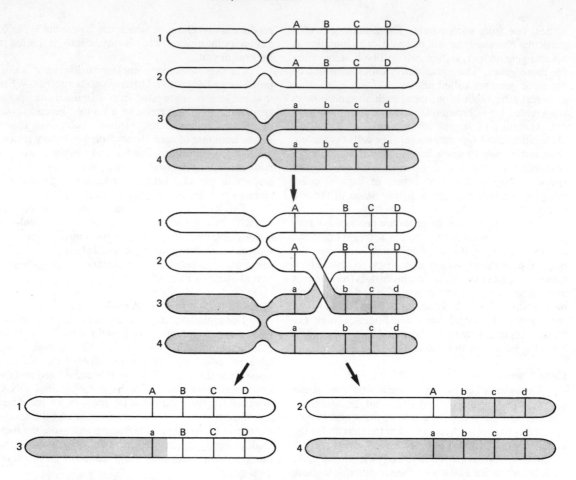

Figure 4–18. Mitotic recombination. *(Top)* Two homologs of a heterozygous cell, carrying dominant (A, B, C, D) and recessive (a, b, c, d) alleles at 4 loci, pair at mitosis. *(Middle)* Crossing over between heterologous chromatids occurs. *(Bottom)* Chromatids separate at mitosis. If chromatids 2 and 4 segregate together (a random event occurring in 50% of such mitoses), a daughter is produced that is **homozygous recessive** at all loci distal to the crossover site.

lar metabolic pathway) form a continuous segment of DNA under the control of a single adjacent operator gene. A gene sequence under the coordinated control of a single operator is called an **operon.**

Each specific type of repressor molecule of the cell must, of course, be formed by its own structural gene. A gene concerned with the production of a repressor is called a **regulator gene.** Both operator genes and regulator genes can be detected when they occur in mutant form. For example, the operator can mutate to a state in which it is unable to bind repressor. The operon now functions under all conditions and is said to be "derepressed."

Mutations of the regulator gene produce phenotypes similar to those produced by mutations of the corresponding operator gene. For example, a mutated regulator gene may fail to make repressor, giving rise to the derepressed phenotype (Fig 4–19). Regulator genes can be distinguished from operator genes, however, by the behavior of diploid cells carrying one normal gene and one mutated gene. In such diploids the derepressed state is dominant if the mutation has

altered the operator gene but recessive if the mutation has inactivated the regulator gene.

Note that the set of structural genes which make up an operon is transcribed as a unit, forming a polygenic mRNA molecule. Transcription begins at the operator end of the operon; a nonsense mutation in one of the genes proximal to the operator may stop translation not only of that gene but also of all genes in the operon distal to it. Such mutations are called **polar mutations;** the polarity of nonsense mutations reflects the inability of a ribosome, once discharged from the mRNA, to reinitiate translation further downstream.

Operons are characteristic of prokaryotic cells; they are rare or absent in eukaryotic organisms.

TRANSPOSABLE ELEMENTS

Transposable elements are specific DNA sequences, copies of which move to new positions in the genome; their replication and movement are catalyzed by enzymes they themselves encode. These events

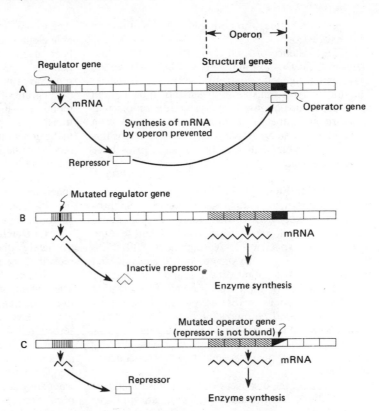

Figure 4–19. Genetic regulation of enzyme synthesis. The product of the regulator gene, the repressor, prevents the functioning of the operon, which it controls by binding to the operator site. Mutations at either the regulator gene or the operator gene can interfere with repression, thus permitting enzyme synthesis. (*Note:* Enzyme inducers generally act by inactivating repressors. In feedback repression of biosynthetic enzymes, however, the repressor is normally inactive and must be activated by the biosynthetic end product. See p 78.)

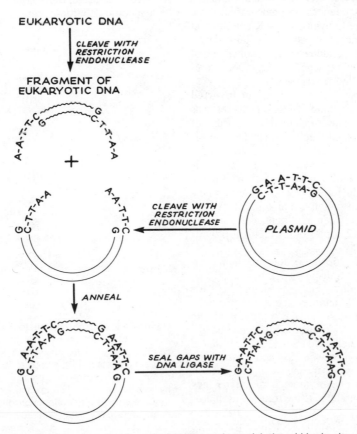

Figure 4–20. The insertion of a fragment of eukaryotic DNA into a bacterial plasmid by in vitro procedures. See text.

have profound effects on both genome evolution and gene expression.

The existence of such elements was first recognized in the 1930s by McClintock, who observed the movement of genetic controlling elements in maize. The discovery of transposable elements in bacteria in the 1960s made possible an analysis of their molecular structure and function; similar elements have been found in yeast and *Drosophila,* and close relationships between such elements and the tumor viruses have been recognized.

Transposable Elements in Prokaryotes

A. Structure: Transposable elements in prokaryotes were discovered when a series of polar mutations in an *E coli* operon were found to represent the insertions of specific DNA sequences 800–1400 base-pairs in length. By heteroduplex analysis and DNA-DNA hybridizations, it was found that copies of a small number of these specific sequences (called **insertion sequences** or **ISs**) are present at numerous sites on the *E coli* chromosome as well as on many plasmids and phage genomes. ISs are transposed as discrete elements and are integrated at new sites by mechanisms that are independent of DNA sequence homology.

Soon after the discovery of ISs, it was found that many of the R determinants of R factors are similarly transposable; in every such case, the R determinant is flanked by repeated sequences. In some cases, these repeated sequences are known ISs; the R determinant for kanamycin resistance, for example, is flanked by 2 copies of IS1 (Fig 4–21). Such elements, consisting of repeated sequences flanking a gene coding for an unrelated function, are called **transposons.**

All ISs and transposons terminate in **inverted repeats** 20–40 base-pairs long. These repeats serve as recognition sites for enzymes that mediate a variety of reactions, including not only replication and transposition but also the deletion of DNA segments adjacent to the transposable element. When such an element is transposed from one replicon to another within the same cell, replicon fusion may occur as an intermediate step. Replicon fusion can also occur by normal recombination between replicons carrying the identical element, the 2 copies of the element providing sequence homology.

Transposons code for one or more proteins, including an enzyme ("transposase") that catalyzes their own transposition. The transposon Tn3, for example, encodes for β-lactamase (conferring penicillin resistance), transposase, and a repressor of the transposase. Probably all transposable elements, including ISs, code for their own transposases. If that is the case, the distinction between ISs and transposons becomes a minor one, a transposon being an insertion sequence that carries one or more additional genes coding for functions unrelated to the transposition process itself.

B. Transposition: Transposition takes place by a process that combines recombination and replication:

At the completion of the process, the original transposable element remains in position, and a new copy has been inserted within a "target site" elsewhere in the genome. The new copy may appear within the same replicon or in a different replicon; in the latter case, a cointegrate structure—representing the fusion of the 2 replicons—may occur as an intermediate stage in the transposition process. In all cases, the process results in the generation of short (5–11 base-pairs long) direct repeats of target DNA on each side of the transposed sequence.

Transposable elements show a wide range of specificity for target sites, ranging from elements having no detectable specificity to those having only a single integration site.

C. Deletion: Deletions of DNA segments immediately adjacent to a transposable element occur at rates that are 100- to 1000-fold higher than the spontaneous background for the remainder of the genome. The deletion mechanism appears to be closely related to that of transposition.

D. Excision: When a transposable element inserts within a functional gene, that gene is inactivated for normal expression. Such events appear as loss mutations such as auxotrophy. The mutant genes are frequently found to revert back to normal expression; when they do, the transposed element is found to have been precisely eliminated. This elimination is not associated with further transposition but rather appears to be a specific deletion event.

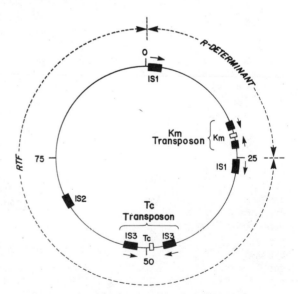

Figure 4–21. Map of the R factor R6-5. The coordinates (0, 25, 50, 75) are distances in kilobases. The R determinant carrying the kanamycin resistance (Km) gene is bounded by 2 direct repeats of IS1; a copy of IS2 is present in the RTF region. A tetracycline resistance (Tc) transposon, bounded by reverse repeats of IS3, is also inserted in the RTF region. Km is itself part of a transposon; the inverted repeats that bound it have not been identified with any of the known IS elements. (After Cohen SN, Kopecko DJ: *Fed Proc* 1976; 35:2031.)

Transposable Elements in Eukaryotes

A. Yeast: A transposable element called Ty1 has been discovered in *Saccharomyces cerevisiae*. Ty1 is a 5.6-kilobase sequence that is present in the yeast genome in about 35 copies. It carries a repeated sequence 338 base-pairs long at each end; this sequence, in turn, is present in the genome in about 100 copies. Ty1 generates 5-base-pair repeats of target DNA and can inactivate functional genes by insertion.

S cerevisiae has a locus controlling mating type, depending on which allele—a or α—is present. A given strain may switch between the a and α phenotypes, but this change does not reflect mutation. Rather, the a and α genes are separately and silently stored at other specific loci; a copy of the a or α gene is occasionally transposed into the mating-type locus, displacing the preexisting allele and becoming expressed. The a and α genes thus belong to a special class of transposable elements.

B. Mammalian Tumor Viruses: A number of integrated tumor viruses have been found to be flanked by 0.6-kilobase direct repeats. Furthermore, sarcoma, leukemia, and mammary tumor viruses of mice generate 5- to 6-base-pair repeats in their target DNA. These viruses thus share fundamental molecular properties with the transposable elements.

Genetic Roles of Transposable Elements

A. Gene Expression: Transposable elements contain transcriptional promoters, transcriptional termination signals, and nonsense condons. Their insertion adjacent to (or within) a functional gene can thus lead to the switching on or switching off of that gene's expression.

The long-known phenomenon of flagellar phase variation in *Salmonella* is explained by the presence of an 800-base-pair sequence that seems closely related to the transposable elements. This sequence, called PD, lies immediately adjacent to an operon containing the gene for the H2 type of flagellin and a repressor of the unlinked gene for the H1 type of flagellin. PD contains a transcriptional promoter; when present in the correct orientation, PD's promoter switches on the H2 gene and the H1 repressor, so that the flagella are made exclusively of the H2 flagellin. Occasionally, however, the PD sequence inverts; now, neither the H2 gene nor the H1 repressor is expressed, and the flagella are made exclusively of H1 flagellin. The inversion event is controlled by a *trans*-acting, closely-linked gene called *rh2*; *rh2* presumably codes for the enzyme catalyzing the inversion.

It has been proposed that sequences closely related to—and perhaps evolved from—transposable elements govern the orderly sequence of gene expression changes that take place during differentiation and that aberrant transposition events may be responsible for the abnormal gene expression associated with some malignant transformations. These are areas of intensive current investigation.

B. Genome Evolution: Evolution depends on the forces of selection acting upon new genes arising by mutation and upon new combinations of genes arising by recombination. In mitotic and meiotic crossing over, recombination takes place by breakage and reunion events within regions of DNA homology. Transposable elements are now seen to provide another mechanism of evolution: blocks of genes become rearranged through transpositions, replicon fusions, deletions, and inversions, independent of sequence homologies. Such rearrangements have apparently played a major role in the evolution of viruses, plasmids, and prokaryotic genomes. The emergence of new, multiple drug resistance R factors is a modern manifestation of this phenomenon.

MOLECULAR CLONING OF DNA

Only part of the DNA of any genome is directly involved in coding for amino acid sequences in proteins. Other, noncoding regions function in such processes as DNA replication, recombination, the control of gene expression, and the structural organization of the chromosome. In many cases, this is accomplished by short base-pair sequences in the DNA that serve as binding sites for specific proteins or RNA molecules; in other cases, it seems likely that recognition sites are provided by secondary structures in the DNA, formed by internal base-pairing in regions of repeated base sequences.

To obtain definitive information concerning such processes, it is necessary to perform a **functional analysis of DNA structure:** Specific segments of DNA of known base-pair sequence must be altered and rearranged in known ways, then reintroduced into host cells or put into in vitro systems to determine the effects of the changes on specific functions. Such functional analysis has been made possible by 3 major technical advances: (1) the ability to determine the complete base-pair sequence of DNA molecules ("DNA sequencing"); (2) the ability to synthesize DNA sequences 20 or more base sequences in length (performed by automatic machines); and (3) the ability to carry out the **molecular cloning of DNA.** These techniques not only permit the functional analysis of DNA structure but also make possible the production in large quantities of almost any desired gene product, eg, otherwise scarce hormones, enzymes, and antigens.

Principles of Molecular Cloning

Molecular cloning involves the following steps, the details of which are discussed below: (1) DNA from any desired source is cleaved into fragments of appropriate size. (2) The fragments are spliced into a **vector,** ie, a circular replicon such as a plasmid or a viral genome. (3) By the process of transformation, the vector is introduced into a host cell in which it can replicate. (4) After replication of the vector, which provides an enormous amplification of the original DNA fragment, the vector is isolated and the inserted fragment cleaved back out and purified. Alternatively, the host-vector system may be designed so as to permit the efficient expression of genes carried by the foreign DNA segment, with the aim of isolating the gene product rather than the gene itself.

The techniques of molecular cloning are commonly referred to as "recombinant DNA technology."

DNA Splicing

The fragments of DNA to be spliced are provided with **cohesive ends**—short, single-stranded extensions complementary to each other. This can be done by adding complementary homopolymers such as poly-dA to the 3' ends of one molecule and poly-dT to the 3' ends of another; usually, however, it is done by cleaving the DNA with a **restriction endonuclease.**

The production of cohesive ends by restriction endonucleases is based on their property of making staggered cuts in short palindromic sequences, as illustrated on p 57. Bacteria produce a wide variety of species-specific endonucleases, each recognizing a different palindromic sequence; by screening through a battery of such enzymes, one can usually find an enzyme that cleaves the vector at a single site and cuts the donor DNA into fragments without cleaving within the base sequence of interest. The fragments and the linearized vector, cleaved with the same restriction endonuclease, are mixed under conditions that promote the annealing (hydrogen bonding) of their complementary ends, following which the gaps are sealed by polynucleotide ligase (Fig 4–20).

Vectors

Molecular cloning of DNA can be done in any propagatable host cells, provided that a suitable vector is available. Animal virus genomes, for example, can be used to clone DNA in animal tissue culture cells, and plasmids are available for cloning in yeast. In bacteria, the vector may be either a plasmid or a bacteriophage genome (bacteriophages are described in Chapter 9).

A. Plasmid Vectors: When a plasmid vector is reintroduced into a host bacterium, it establishes itself as an independent replicon. The "infected" cell then gives rise to a clone every cell of which contains one or more copies of the vector with its foreign DNA insert. The clone can be expanded by large-scale mass culture, the plasmid DNA reextracted, and the foreign DNA reisolated.

Plasmid vectors have been specially engineered for this purpose. Those in general use now have some or all of the following properties: (1) The plasmid may be amplified to reach 40–50% of the total cellular DNA (up to 2000 copies per cell) by providing a final period of incubation in the presence of chloramphenicol. (2) The plasmid contains one each of several different restriction sites, so that a restriction enzyme suitable for the donor DNA may be chosen. (3) Markers are present that permit the selection of vectors with inserted DNA sequences as well as the selection of host cells that have been infected with the vector. (4)

If expression of an inserted gene is desired, the insertion site is adjacent to a high-efficiency promotor of transcription. (5) The vector contains a minimum of essential plasmid DNA, making room for larger inserts. (An upper size limit is imposed by increasing instability as the size of the overall vector is increased.)

B. Bacteriophage Vectors: The sequence of a bacteriophage such as lambda (see Chapter 9) can be isolated, cleaved with a restriction endonuclease, and spliced to a foreign DNA insert. The phage DNA can then be reintroduced into bacterial host cells, where it undergoes a lytic cycle of infection; the host cells eventually burst, each liberating several hundred infectious virions (protein-coated phage genomes). After repeated cycles of infection have destroyed all host cells, the virions are harvested and their DNA extracted. Alternatively, a phage vector may be used which has been engineered so that it may be propagated either lytically, as described above, or as a nonlytic plasmid.

For virion production, the process by which phage DNA is packaged with the capsid (phage coat) limits to about 10% the amount of DNA that can be added. However, lambda contains a dispensable region amounting to about 25% of its total DNA; replacing this region with foreign DNA allows a total of about 35%, or about 17,000 base-pairs, to be cloned. This method has the added advantage that infectious particles are formed only from phage genomes carrying DNA inserts, since the correct amount of DNA must be present for packaging to proceed.

Selection of Cloned DNA Segments

In some cases, the segment of DNA to be cloned may be available as a relatively pure material—eg, as cDNA (reverse transcripts of highly purified messenger RNAs), as synthetic DNA molecules, or as DNA fragments that can be purified on the basis of their high copy-number in vivo. In many cases, however, a "shotgun" approach is used: Total DNA is cleaved, all possible fragments are spliced into a population of vector molecules, and this mixture is used to transform host cells. The problem, then, is to detect those clones of bacteria (or phage plaques) that carry the particular sequence of interest.

If a cloned gene is expressed in the host cell, it is often possible to devise a technique that will permit only those cells carrying the desired gene to form colonies. In most cases, however, the gene is not expressed and can only be detected by the use of a "probe," consisting of radioactive RNA or DNA complementary to the sequence of interest. Colonies of cells or phage plaques are produced on nitrocellulose filters, denatured in situ, and their DNA allowed to anneal with the probe. The filters are washed to remove excess, nonannealed probe; autoradiography then reveals those clones containing DNA complementary to the probe, and live cells or viruses are recovered from replica plates made beforehand.

Radioactive probes depend on the availability of a small amount of a radioactive RNA or DNA complementary to part or all of the sequence of interest. In many cases, such probes are obtained as mRNA (or DNA made by reverse transcription of mRNA), isolated from specialized cells in which that mRNA is a major species. The availability of techniques for synthesizing DNA molecules of any desired sequence up to 20 or more bases in length, however, adds another approach: If one knows the amino acid sequence of the polypeptide coded for by the gene in question, the DNA sequence of that gene can be deduced and a portion of it synthesized for use as a probe.

Expression of Cloned DNA

Transcription of the cloned DNA will occur if the inserted fragment carries its own promoter (RNA polymerase binding site) or if the vector carries a properly spaced promoter adjacent to the insertion site. The correct translation of eukaryotic sequences, however, requires that the host system possess the enzyme for processing RNA transcripts; thus, prokaryotic host cells cannot be used to express cloned eukaryotic genes that contain introns. For such genes, translation in bacterial host cells is made possible by the cloning of cDNA made from mRNA that has already been processed in the eukaryotic donor cell.

Genes & DNA Segments Cloned

The rapid development of improvements in cloning techniques has made the list of cloned segments much too long to tabulate here, and the list is increasing rapidly. The techniques lend themselves to commercial applications, since microorganisms expressing genes that code for useful products can be grown on a scale of tens of thousands of gallons. The commercial production of a variety of medically useful hormones and antigens, as well as many industrially useful enzymes, will soon be carried out with microorganisms carrying cloned segments of DNA.

Recombinant DNA technology is also being used to produce improved strains of microorganisms for use in industrial processes such as fermentations and biochemical conversions. It will almost certainly be used to produce improved strains of plants, thanks to a plasmid that can be transferred from the bacterium *Agrobacterium tumefaciens* to plant cells, and holds promise for animal husbandry as well. Finally, recombinant DNA technology opens the way to future applications in the treatment of human genetic disease as a source of normal genes for gene replacement therapy.

• • •

References

Books

Adelberg E (editor): *Papers on Bacterial Genetics,* 2nd ed. Little, Brown, 1966.

Beckwith JR, Zipser D (editors): *The Lactose Operon.* Cold Spring Harbor Laboratory, 1970.

Bukhari AI et al (editors): *DNA Insertion Elements, Plasmids and Episomes.* Cold Spring Harbor Laboratory, 1977.

Chirikjian JG: *Gene Amplification and Analysis.* Elsevier, 1981.

Cold Spring Harbor Symposia on Quantitative Biology: Vol 45. *Moveable Genetic Elements.* Cold Spring Harbor Laboratory, 1981.

Falkow S: *Infectious Multiple Drug Resistance.* Pion, 1975.

Goldberger RF (editor): *Gene Expression.* Plenum Press, 1979.

King RC: *A Dictionary of Genetics,* 2nd ed. Oxford Univ Press, 1972.

Kornberg A: *DNA Replication.* Freeman, 1980.

Lewin B: *Gene Expression.* Vol 1: *Bacterial Genomes,* 1974; Vol 2: *Eukaryotic Chromosomes,* 2nd ed. 1980; Vol 3: *Plasmids and Phages,* 1977. Wiley-Interscience.

Miller JH, Reznikoff WS: *The Operon.* Cold Spring Harbor Laboratory, 1978.

Mitsuhashi S, Hashimoto H (editors): *Microbial Drug Resistance.* Vol 1, 1976; Vol 2, 1979. University Park Press.

Old RW, Primrose SB: *Principles of Gene Manipulation: An Introduction to Genetic Engineering.* Univ of California Press, 1980.

Setlow JK, Hollander A (editors): *Genetic Engineering, Principles and Methods.* Plenum Press, 1980.

Stent GS, Calendar R: *Molecular Genetics, An Introductory Narrative,* 2nd ed. Freeman, 1978.

Strathern JN et al (editors): *The Molecular Biology of the Yeast Saccharomyces.* Cold Spring Harbor Laboratory, 1981.

Watson JD: *The Molecular Biology of the Gene,* 3rd ed. Benjamin, 1976.

Woese CR: *The Genetic Code: The Molecular Basis for Genetic Expression.* Harper & Row, 1967.

Wu R (editor): *Recombinant DNA.* Vol 68 of: *Methods in Enzymology.* Academic Press, 1979.

Articles & Reviews

Auerbach C, Kilben BJ: Mutation in eukaryotes. *Annu Rev Genet* 1971;**5**:163.

Bachmann BJ, Low KB: Linkage map of *Escherichia coli* K-12, edition 6. *Microbiol Rev* 1980;**44**:1.

Beckwith J, Rossow P: Analysis of genetic regulatory mechanisms. *Annu Rev Genet* 1974;**8**:1.

Birky CW: Transmission genetics of mitochondria and chloroplasts. *Annu Rev Genet* 1978;**12**:471.

Bridges BA: Recent advances in basic mutation research. *Mutat Res* 1977;**44**:149.

Brill WJ: Biochemical genetics of nitrogen fixation. *Microbiol Rev* 1980;**44**:499.

Calos MP, Miller JH: Transposable elements. *Cell* 1980; **20**:579.

Chakrabarty AM: Plasmids in *Pseudomonas. Annu Rev Genet* 1976;**10**:7.

Chilton MD: *Agrobacterium* Ti plasmids as a tool for genetic engineering in plants. *Basic Life Sci* 1979;**14**:23.

Clark AJ, Warren GJ: Conjugal transmission of plasmids. *Annu Rev Genet* 1979;**13**:99.

Clewell DB: Plasmids, drug resistance, and gene transfer in the genus *Streptococcus*. *Microbiol Rev* 1981;**45**:409.

Clewell DB, Brown BL: Sex pheromone cAD₁ in *Streptococcus faecalis:* Induction of a function related to plasmid transfer. *J Bacteriol* 1980;**143**:1063.

Cohen SN, Shapiro JA: Transposable genetic elements. *Sci Am* (Feb) 1980;**242**:40.

Cox EC: Bacterial mutator genes and the control of spontaneous mutation. *Annu Rev Genet* 1976;**10**:135.

Dawid IB et al: Application of recombinant DNA technology to questions of developmental biology: A review. *Dev Biol* 1979;**69**:305.

Drake JW, Baltz RH: The biochemistry of mutagenesis. *Annu Rev Biochem* 1976;**45**:11.

Elwell LP, Shipley PL: Plasmid-mediated factors associated with virulence of bacteria to animals. *Annu Rev Microbiol* 1980;**34**:465.

Gots JS, Benson CE: Biochemical genetics of bacteria. *Annu Rev Genet* 1974;**8**:77.

Hanawalt PC et al: DNA repair in bacteria and mammalian cells. *Annu Rev Biochem* 1979;**48**:783.

Hardy KG: Colicinogeny and related phenomena. *Bacteriol Rev* 1975;**39**:464.

Hartman PE, Roth JR: Mechanisms of suppression. *Adv Genet* 1973;**17**:1.

Helinski DR: Bacterial plasmids: Autonomous replication and vehicles for gene cloning. *CRC Crit Rev Biochem* 1979;**7**:83.

Henner BJ et al: The *Bacillus subtilis* chromosome. *Microbiol Rev* 1980;**44**:57.

Hopwood DA: Extrachromosomally determined antibiotic production. *Annu Rev Microbiol* 1978;**32**:373.

Hopwood DA, Merrick MJ: Genetics of antibiotic production. *Bacteriol Rev* 1977;**41**:595.

Hotchkiss RD, Gabor MH: Biparental products of bacterial protoplast fusion showing unequal parental chromosome expression. *Proc Natl Acad Sci USA* 1980;**77**:3553.

Kimball RF: The relation of repair phenomena to mutation induction in bacteria. *Mutat Res* 1978;**55**:85.

Lacey RW: Antibiotic resistance plasmids of *Staphylococcus aureus* and their clinical significance. *Bacteriol Rev* 1975;**39**:1.

Levinthal M: Bacterial genetics excluding *E coli*. *Annu Rev Microbiol* 1974;**28**:219.

Low KB: *Escherichia coli* K-12 F-prime factors, old and new. *Bacteriol Rev* 1972;**36**:587.

Low KB, Porter RD: Modes of gene transfer and recombination in bacteria. *Annu Rev Genet* 1978;**12**:249.

Miller WL: Use of recombinant DNA technology for the production of polypeptides. *Adv Exp Biol Med* 1979;**118**:153.

Petes TD: Molecular genetics of yeast. *Annu Rev Biochem* 1980;**49**:845.

Potter H, Dressler D: In vitro system from *Escherichia coli* that catalyzes generalized genetic recombination. *Proc Natl Acad Sci USA* 1978;**75**:3698.

Radman M et al: Replication fidelity: Mechanisms of mutation avoidance and mutation fixation. *Cold Spring Harbor Symp Quant Biol* 1979;**43**:937.

Riggs AD et al: Synthesis, cloning and expression of hormone genes in *Escherichia coli*. *Recent Progr Horm Res* 1980;**36**:261.

Roberts RJ: Restriction and modification enzymes and their recognition sequences. *Gene* 1980;**8**:329.

Roth JR: Frameshift mutations. *Annu Rev Genet* 1974;**8**:319.

Rowbury RJ: The replication of bacterial plasmids. *Sci Progr* 1978;**65**:231.

Sanderson KE, Hartman PE: Linkage map of *Salmonella typhimurium*, edition 5. *Microbiol Rev* 1978;**42**:471.

Schwesinger MD: Additive recombination in bacteria. *Bacteriol Rev* 1977;**41**:872.

Simon M et al: Genes whose mission is to jump. *Science* 1980;**209**:1370.

Sisco KL, Smith HO: Sequence-specific DNA uptake in *Haemophilus* transformation. *Proc Natl Acad Sci USA* 1979;**76**:972.

Smith HO: New insights into how bacteria take up DNA during transformation. *Am J Trop Med Hyg* 1980;**29**:1085.

Tomizawa J et al: Initiation of DNA synthesis in *Escherichia coli*. *Annu Rev Biochem* 1979;**48**:999.

Topal MD, Fresco JR: Complementary base pairing and the origin of substitution mutations. *Nature* 1976;**263**:285.

Venema G: Bacterial transformation. *Adv Microb Physiol* 1979;**19**:245.

Vosberg HP: Molecular cloning of DNA: An introduction into techniques and problems. *Hum Genet* 1977;**40**:1.

Wigler M et al: Transformation of mammalian cells with genes from procaryotes and eucaryotes. *Cell* 1979;**16**:777.

Willetts N, Skurray R: The conjugation system of F-like plasmids. *Annu Rev Genet* 1980;**14**:41.

Witkin EM: Ultraviolet mutagenesis and inducible DNA repair in *Escherichia coli*. *Bacteriol Rev* 1976;**40**:869.

Microbial Metabolism | 5

THE ROLE OF METABOLISM IN BIOSYNTHESIS & GROWTH

Major Functions Served by Metabolism

The major function of any microbial cell is growth. Other functions, such as motility, luminescence, and synthesis of capsular substances, also exist but are often dispensable. Growth is defined as the orderly increase in mass or number of all components of the cell; cell multiplication is a common but not essential consequence of growth. In some microorganisms, such as certain slime molds, growth is accompanied by repeated nuclear division but not by cell division. The result is the formation of a greatly enlarged, multinucleate cell, or "coenocyte."

Since the major cell components (chromosomes, protein-synthesizing systems, enzymes, membranes, walls, flagella) are made up of macromolecules, the major function served by the metabolism of a microbial cell can be more precisely stated in terms of the **synthesis of macromolecules.** These macromolecules are assembled from their respective subunits: proteins from amino acids; nucleic acids from nucleotides; polysaccharides from simple sugars; and lipids from glycerol or other alcohols, fatty acids, and (in phospholipids) special subunits such as choline.

In every case, the condensation of subunits to form a macromolecule requires that the subunit be **activated**—ie, coupled by means of a suitable energy-rich bond to a substituent group such as phosphate (P), pyrophosphate (PP), adenosine monophosphate (AMP), or coenzyme A (CoA). The energy of the activating group's linkage then provides the energy needed for the condensation, and the activating group is split off in the process. In general, the ultimate source of the energy in such activating groups is adenosine triphosphate (ATP).

The arrangement (sequence) of subunits in the ultimate macromolecule is determined in one of 2 ways. In nucleic acids and in proteins, it is **template-directed:** DNA serves as template for its own synthesis and for the synthesis of the various types of RNA; messenger RNA serves as template for the synthesis of proteins. In carbohydrate and lipids, on the other hand, the arrangement of subunits is determined entirely by enzyme specificities.

Given these systems for the orderly and directed condensation of subunits, the principal functions of metabolism are seen to be 3-fold: (1) to generate the subunits themselves from intermediates of metabolism, (2) to generate ATP from adenosine diphosphate (ADP) and inorganic phosphate, and (3) to generate reducing power (as $NADP \cdot H_2$) for those instances in which the substrates taken from the medium are more oxidized than the overall products of biosynthesis.

The Generation of the Subunits of Macromolecules

The subunits of macromolecules include fatty acids, monosaccharides, amino acids, purines, and pyrimidines. All of these may be furnished by the medium; however, many microorganisms can synthesize the entire complement from suitable sources of carbon (eg, glucose), nitrogen (eg, ammonia), and sulfur (eg, sulfate). All biosynthetic pathways are under negative end product regulation, including both repression of enzyme synthesis and inhibition of enzyme action, so that subunits are not synthesized if they are available in the medium (see below). The availability of such compounds is greatly increased by the action of specific transport systems in the microbial cell membrane that produce internal concentrations of subunits 100-fold or more over the external concentrations.

When a subunit is unavailable, the microbial cell synthesizes it by a biosynthetic pathway. All biosynthetic pathways originate from a relatively small number of metabolic intermediates. All of the aliphatic amino acids, for example, derive from just 4 intermediates: pyruvate, 3-phosphoglycerate, oxalacetate, and α-ketoglutarate. The aromatic ring of phenylalanine, tyrosine, and tryptophan derives from a condensation of D-erythrose 4-phosphate and phosphoenolpyruvate, and most of the carbon skeleton of histidine comes from pentose phosphate. These relationships are shown schematically in Fig 5–1.

The pyrimidine ring is formed by the addition of a carbamyl group to aspartic acid, followed by ring closure; the purine ring is built up by condensations involving glycine, formate, CO_2, and amido or amino groups from glutamine and aspartic acid. The fatty acids are all synthesized primarily from acetate as a building block, while the simple sugars are formed by a series of transformations starting with hexose phosphate.

All of these biosynthetic pathways are outlined in

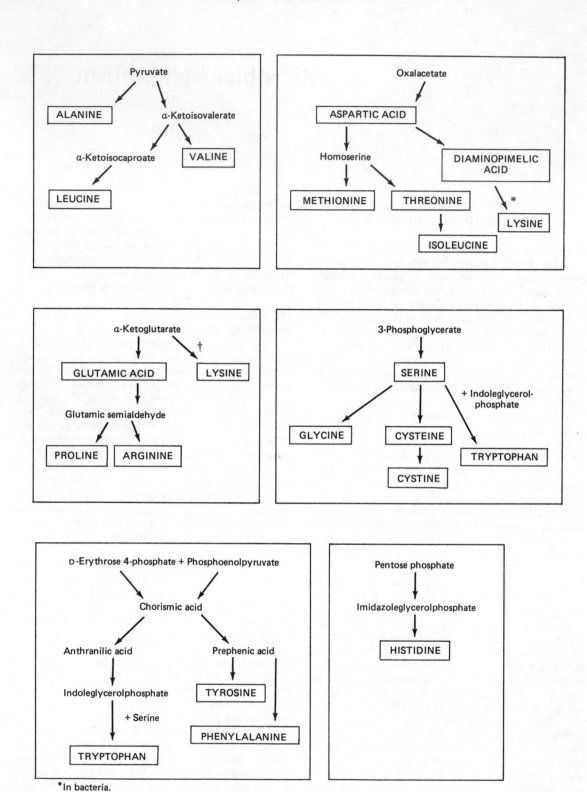

Figure 5–1. Biosynthetic families of amino acids. (In many cases, the arrow represents 2 or more sequential reactions.)

Table 5–1. Pathways of carbohydrate metabolism.

Pathway	Key Intermediates Generated
Embden-Meyerhof pathway	Glucose 1-phosphate 3-Phosphoglyceraldehyde Phosphoenolpyruvate (PEP) Pyruvate
Direct oxidative pathway	Pentose phosphates D-Erythrose 4-phosphate
Pyruvate decarboxylation	Acetyl-CoA CO_2
Tricarboxylic acid (TCA) cycle (and its replenishment by PEP carboxylation)	Oxalacetate α-Ketoglutarate CO_2

other sources. (See, for example, Martin DW, Mayes PA, Rodwell VW: *Harper's Review of Biochemistry,* 18th ed. Lange, 1981.) They are essentially the same in all organisms that possess them. Different organisms lack one or another biosynthetic enzyme system, however, and in such cases the macromolecular subunits must be furnished by the environment. Humans, for example, require 8 amino acids in their diet.

The subunits, then, either are supplied by the environment or are derived through biosynthetic pathways from a number of **key intermediates** of metabolism. As shown in Table 5–1, these intermediates are in turn generated by relatively few metabolic pathways that are common to most organisms. Note that the tricarboxylic acid cycle, the enzymes of which form oxalacetate and α-ketoglutarate, cannot by itself produce *net* amounts of these intermediates. Rather, as these intermediates are drained from the cycle into biosynthetic pathways, they are replenished by the carboxylation of phosphoenolpyruvate (PEP) to form oxalacetate.

The Generation of ATP

There are 2 general mechanisms for the generation of ATP by nonphotosynthetic organisms: substrate phosphorylation and oxidative phosphorylation. In both cases, bond energy from a metabolic intermediate is used to create a molecule of ATP from ADP and inorganic phosphate (P_i).

A. Substrate Phosphorylation: This term is used to describe the 2 steps in the Embden-Meyerhof pathway at which an energy-rich phosphate bond is created: (1) The oxidation of 3-phosphoglyceraldehyde by NAD in the presence of P_i produces 1,3-diphosphoglyceric acid, and the new phosphate group is then transferred to ADP. (2) The dehydration of 2-phosphoglyceric acid redistributes the bond energy of the molecule so that the phosphate bond of the product, phosphoenolpyruvate, is energy-rich and transferable to ADP also.

An analogous process occurs when α-ketoglutarate is oxidized to succinic acid in the tricarboxylic acid cycle. One of the intermediates in this process is succinyl-CoA; the energy of the CoA bond can then be used to form ATP from ADP plus P_i.

B. Electron Transport Phosphorylation: In respiration, pairs of electrons are transported from an ultimate electron donor (such as NADH) to an ultimate electron acceptor (such as O_2). This process involves an **electron transport chain,** in which electrons are passed sequentially from one electron carrier to another of increasing oxidation-reduction potential. A typical chain might be as follows (the arrows denote the passages of electrons, and the numbers in parentheses are the approximate oxidation-reduction potentials in volts under standard conditions—25 °C, all reactants at 1.0 M, pH 7.0):

Organic → NAD → Flavoprotein → Quinone →
substrate (−0.32) (−0.20) (−0.07)

Cytochrome b → Cytochrome c → Cytochrome a → O_2
(+0.01) (+0.22) (+0.34) (+0.81)

The free energy change accompanying the passage of a pair of electrons from NADH to O_2 is sufficient to generate 3 molecules of ATP from ADP plus P_i. The mechanism by which the flow of electrons is coupled to ATP generation is diagrammed in Fig 5–2.

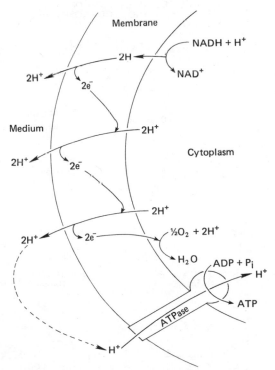

Figure 5–2. The coupling of electron transport in respiration to the generation of ATP. The indicated movements of protons and electrons are mediated by carriers (flavoprotein, quinone, cytochromes) that are associated with the membrane. The flow of protons down their electrochemical gradient, via the membrane ATPase, furnishes the energy for the generation of ATP from ADP and P_i. See text for explanation. (After Harold FM: Chemiosmotic interpretation of active transport in bacteria. *Ann NY Acad Sci* 1974;**227**:297.)

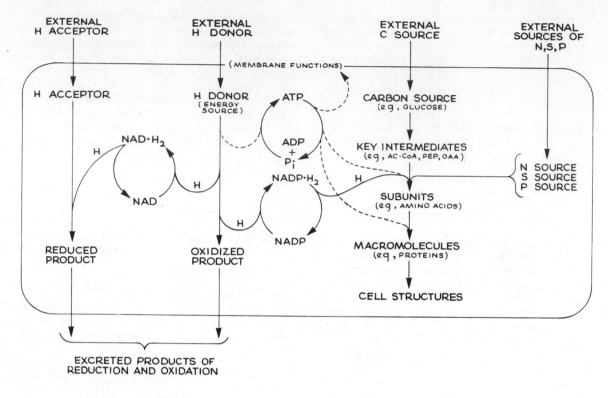

Figure 5–3. Relationships between nutrition, metabolism, and growth.

Glucose 6-phosphate → 6-Phospho-gluconate → 2-Keto-3-deoxy-6-phosphogluconate → Pyruvate + Glyceraldehyde 3-phosphate

Figure 5–4. The Entner-Doudoroff pathway.

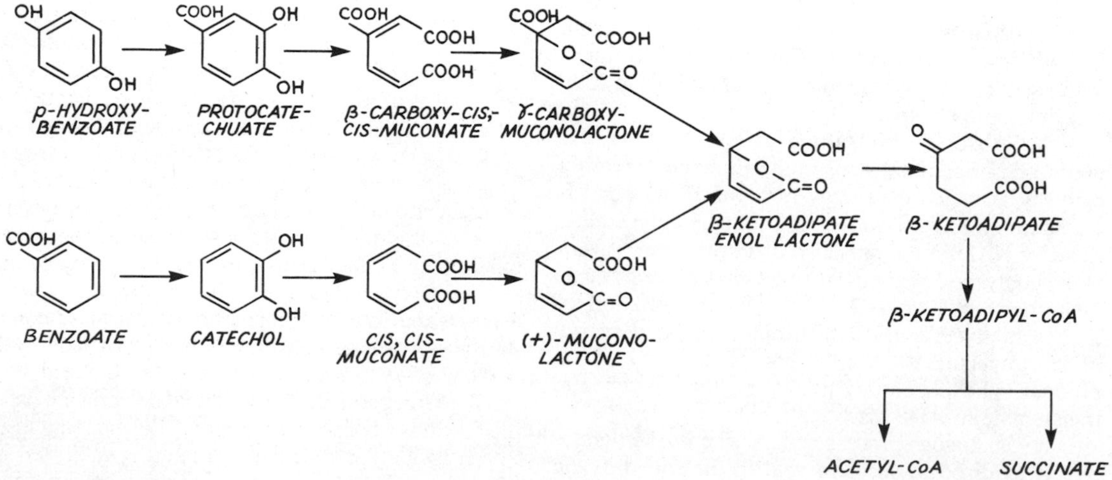

p-HYDROXY-BENZOATE → *PROTOCATE-CHUATE* → *β-CARBOXY-CIS,-CIS-MUCONATE* → *γ-CARBOXY-MUCONOLACTONE*

BENZOATE → *CATECHOL* → *CIS, CIS-MUCONATE* → *(+)-MUCONO-LACTONE*

β-KETOADIPATE ENOL LACTONE → *β-KETOADIPATE*

β-KETOADIPYL-CoA

ACETYL-CoA   *SUCCINATE*

Figure 5–5. The β-ketoadipate pathway. (After Stanier RY, Adelberg EA, Ingraham JL: *The Microbial World,* 4th ed. Prentice-Hall, 1976.)

The electron transport carriers are embedded in the cell membrane in an oriented manner such that the passage of electrons is accompanied by the transfer of protons (H^+) from the interior to the exterior of the membrane. Since the membrane is otherwise impermeable to protons, the result is a **proton gradient,** and the membrane is said to be "energized." The energy of the proton gradient can be used by the cell to drive a number of processes, including active transport of other ions and small organic molecules, flagellar rotation, and ATP generation.

ATP is generated when protons reenter the cell at the sites of membrane-bound ATPase complexes. Each of these complexes includes a proton-conducting channel that spans the membrane; the flow of electrons through this channel is coupled to the enzymatic conversion of ADP plus P_i to ATP. Uncoupling agents such as dinitrophenol are lipid-soluble molecules that promote the direct passage of protons through the membrane, thus dissipating the proton gradient.

The membrane-bound ATPase can be used by the cell in the reverse manner: ATP stored in the cell can be hydrolyzed, driving protons out of the cell and generating a proton gradient that can be used for other energy-requiring processes such as the transport of amino acids into the cell.

The Generation of Reducing Power

Many of the oxidative steps of catabolism, in which ATP is generated, are coupled with the reduction of NAD or NADP. If the compound being used as carbon source is as reduced as or more reduced than the overall products of biosynthesis, its oxidation will generate the required reducing power. If the carbon source is more oxidized than the overall products of biosynthesis, however, net reducing power is achieved by the oxidation of additional carbon source molecules to CO_2.

Summary: Nutrition in Relation to Metabolism

The relationships outlined above are summarized in Fig 5–3. Microbial cells must take in from the medium, as a minimal set of requirements, a carbon source, an energy source, and sources of elements (N, S, P, etc). Metabolism of the carbon source provides key intermediates from which the cell can synthesize the subunits of the macromolecules. Oxidation of the energy source provides both ATP and reducing power to drive these biosyntheses, as well as ATP for the activation of the subunits. The activated subunits are polymerized to form the macromolecules, which self-assemble to form cell structures. The net result is cell growth; it is usually, but not always, accompanied by cell division.

The carbon source and energy source may be the same molecule (eg, glucose) or different molecules (eg, CO_2 as carbon source, NH_3 as energy source). Cells which lack any biosynthetic pathway must obtain the end product of that pathway from the medium, as a "growth factor." If biosynthetically competent cells are presented with an end product they will preferentially use it, shutting off endogenous synthesis.

The medium must also furnish the cell with a terminal H acceptor in order for oxidations to occur. For aerobes, this is O_2; for anaerobes, it may be an organic compound or an organic by-product of the catabolism of the carbon source. Thus, many bacteria can grow fermentatively using glucose as the source of carbon, as the source of energy, and (through its catabolism) as the H acceptor.

METABOLIC PATHWAYS UNIQUE TO MICROORGANISMS

Pathways of Catabolism

Table 5–1 lists the principal pathways, common to all groups of organisms, by which the key intermediates for biosynthesis are formed. In certain microorganisms these have been supplemented by several unique pathways, including the following:

A. The Entner-Doudoroff Pathway: In addition to the Embden-Meyerhof and the direct oxidative pathways, many microorganisms break down hexose via the Entner-Doudoroff pathway (Fig 5–4), first discovered in the bacterium *Pseudomonas saccharophila.*

B. The β-Ketoadipate Pathway: Many microorganisms, notably bacteria of the genus *Pseudomonas,* can oxidize aromatic compounds via the β-ketoadipate pathway to acetyl-CoA and succinate, which then enter the tricarboxylic acid cycle (Fig 5–5). Other oxidizable aromatic acids funnel into this pathway via the intermediates shown, eg, benzene is oxidized to catechol, toluene is oxidized to benzoic acid, and so on.

Pathways of Biosynthesis

A. The Glyoxylate Cycle: A special problem of biosynthesis arises in the case of microorganisms that are furnished acetate as the sole source of carbon for growth under aerobic conditions. Since, under aerobic conditions, acetate is completely oxidized to CO_2 in the tricarboxylic acid cycle, this pathway cannot provide a net synthesis of C_4 compounds necessary for many biosynthetic pathways. Instead, acetate is metabolized by the set of reactions shown in Fig 5–6.

Note that with each turn of the cycle, 2 molecules of acetate (activated as acetyl-CoA) are converted to one molecule of succinate. Note also that several enzymes of this pathway are also those of the tricarboxylic acid cycle; indeed, the glyoxylate cycle and the tricarboxylic acid cycle go simultaneously when acetate is the sole carbon source. Under these conditions, the 2 unique enzymes of the glyoxylate cycle (isocitritase and malate synthetase) are induced.

B. Nitrogen Fixation: Certain bacteria are capable of fixing atmospheric nitrogen (N_2) and reducing it to NH_3 inside the cell; the reduction is catalyzed by nitrogenase. The electrons for the reduction are transferred from a suitable donor to enzyme-bound N_2 through an electron transport chain consisting of

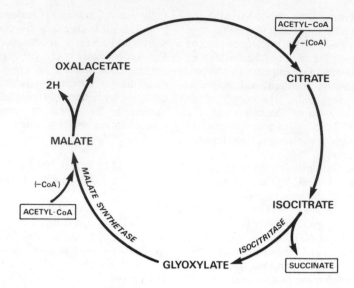

Figure 5–6. The glyoxylate cycle.

ferredoxin, azoferredoxin, and molybdoferredoxin; the reduction also requires ATP. The isolated enzyme system is quite sensitive to inhibition by molecular oxygen.

Some nitrogen-fixing bacteria exhibit this activity only when living symbiotically with a host organism. These include *Rhizobium* (in legumes), *Frankia* (in nonlegumes), and certain cyanobacteria (in lichens). Free-living nitrogen-fixing bacteria occur in many genera; they include obligate aerobes (eg, *Azotobacter, Beijerinckia*), facultative anaerobes (eg, *Klebsiella, Enterobacter, Bacillus*), and obligate anaerobes (eg, *Clostridium, Desulfovibrio*).

The symbiotic rhizobia inhabit the root tissues of leguminous plants (peas, beans, alfalfa, etc), causing formation of root nodules. In the nodule, true hemoglobin is formed; its role may be to lower the redox potential within the nodule and thus protect the bacterial nitrogenase system from inhibition by oxygen.

The role of nitrogen fixation in the nitrogen cycle of the biosphere is discussed on p 105.

C. The Synthesis of Carbohydrates From CO_2: A special mechanism is found in organisms that use CO_2 as the sole source of carbon for the production of intermediates. This occurs in photosynthetic organisms and in bacteria that obtain their energy by the oxidation of inorganic substances. In such organisms, CO_2 is converted to carbohydrate according to the general scheme shown in Fig 5–7. Note the requirement for 12 molecules of $NADPH_2$ for each molecule

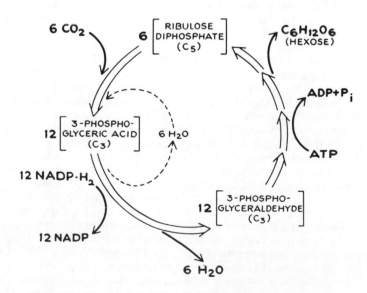

Figure 5–7. Path of carbon in photosynthesis and autotrophy.

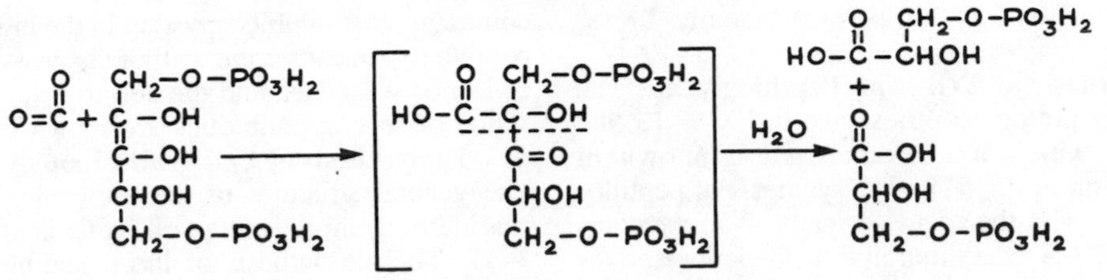

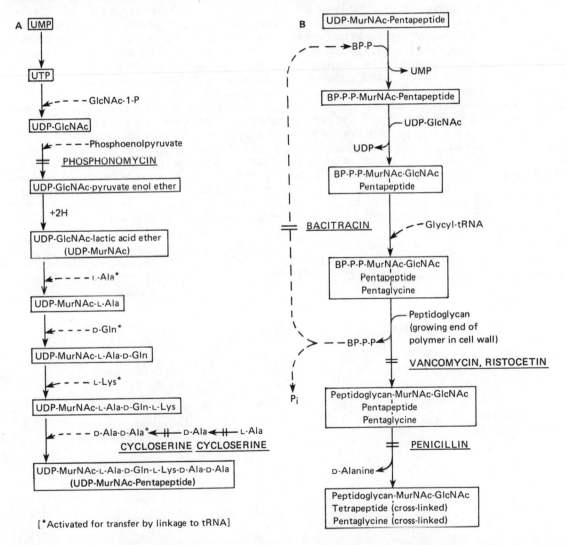

Figure 5–8. Synthesis of 3-phosphoglyceric acid.

of hexose produced. These are furnished by noncyclic photophosphorylation or (in the case of autotrophic bacteria) by the oxidation of reduced inorganic substances from the environment. The key step in this cycle is the fixation of CO_2 by ribulose diphosphate to form 3-phosphoglyceric acid (Fig 5–8).

The conversion of 3-phosphoglyceric acid to hexose and ribulose diphosphate via 3-phosphoglyceraldehyde is a complex process involving 12 separate enzymatic reactions. (For further details, see Elsden SR: Photosynthetic and lithotrophic carbon dioxide fixation. In: *The Bacteria.* Vol 3: *Biosynthesis.* Gun-

Figure 5–9. The biosynthesis of cell wall peptidoglycan, showing the sites of action of 6 antibiotics. BP = bactoprenol; MurNAc = N-acetylmuramic acid; GLcNAc = N-acetylglucosamine. *(A)* Synthesis of UDP-N–acetylmuramic acid–pentapeptide. *(B)* Synthesis of peptidoglycan from UDP-N-acetylmuramic acid–pentapeptide, UDP-N-acetylglucosamine, and glycyl residues. (See Fig 2–13 for structure of peptidoglycan.)

salus IC, Stanier RY [editors]. Academic Press, 1962.)

D. Synthesis of Cell Wall Peptidoglycan: The structure of peptidoglycan is shown in Fig 2–13; the pathway by which it is synthesized is shown in simplified form in Fig 5–9. The synthesis of peptidoglycan begins with the stepwise synthesis in the cytoplasm of UDP-N-acetylmuramic acid-pentapeptide. N-Acetylglucosamine is first attached to UDP and then converted to UDP-N-acetylmuramic acid by condensation with phosphoenolpyruvate and reduction. The amino acids of the pentapeptide are sequentially added, each addition catalyzed by a different enzyme and each involving the split to ATP to ADP + P_i.

The UDP-N-acetylmuramic acid-pentapeptide is attached to bactoprenol (a lipid of the cell membrane) and receives a molecule of N-acetylglucosamine from UDP. The pentaglycine derivative is next formed in a series of reactions using glycyl-tRNA as the donor; the completed disaccharide is polymerized to an oligomeric intermediate before being transferred to the growing end of a glycopeptide polymer in the cell wall. Finally, cross-linking is accomplished by a transpeptidation reaction in which the free amino group of a pentaglycine residue displaces the terminal D-alanine residue of a neighboring pentapeptide.

The biosynthetic pathway is of particular importance in medicine, as it provides a basis for the selective antibacterial action of several chemotherapeutic agents. Unlike their host cells, bacteria are not isotonic with the body fluids. Their contents are under high osmotic pressure, and their viability depends on the integrity of the peptidoglycan lattice in the cell wall being maintained throughout the growth cycle. Any

compound that inhibits any step in the biosynthesis of peptidoglycan causes the wall of the growing bacterial cell to be weakened and the cell to lyse. The sites of action of several antibiotics are shown in Fig 5–9.

E. Synthesis of Cell Wall Lipopolysaccharide: The general structure of the antigenic lipopolysaccharide of gram-negative cell walls is shown in Fig 2–17. The biosynthesis of the repeating end-group, which gives the cell wall its antigenic specificity, is shown in Fig 5–10. Note the resemblance to peptidoglycan synthesis: in both cases, a series of subunits is assembled on a lipid carrier in the membrane and then transferred to open ends of the growing polymer fabric of the cell wall.

F. Synthesis of Extracellular Capsular Polymers: The capsular polymers, a few examples of which are listed in Table 2–1, are enzymatically synthesized from activated subunits. No membrane-bound lipid carriers have been implicated in this process. The presence of a capsule is often environmentally determined: dextrans and levans, for example, can only be synthesized using the disaccharide sucrose (fructose-glucose) as the source of the appropriate subunit, and their synthesis thus depends on the presence of sucrose in the medium.

G. Synthesis of Reserve Food Granules: When nutrients are present in excess of the requirements for growth, bacteria convert certain of them to intracellular reserve food granules. The principal ones are starch, glycogen, poly-β-hydroxybutyrate (PBHB), and volutin, which consists mainly of inorganic polyphosphate. The type of granule formed is species-specific. The granules are degraded when exogenous nutrients are depleted.

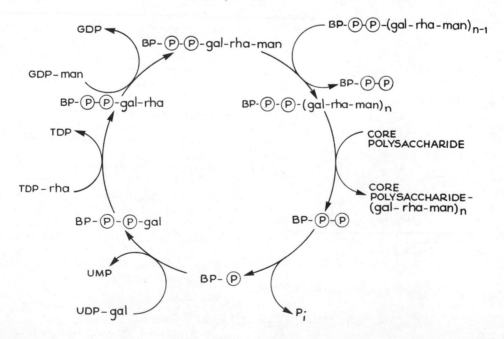

Figure 5–10. Synthesis of the repeating unit of the polysaccharide side chain of *Salmonella newington* and its transfer to the lipopolysaccharide core. BP = bactoprenol.

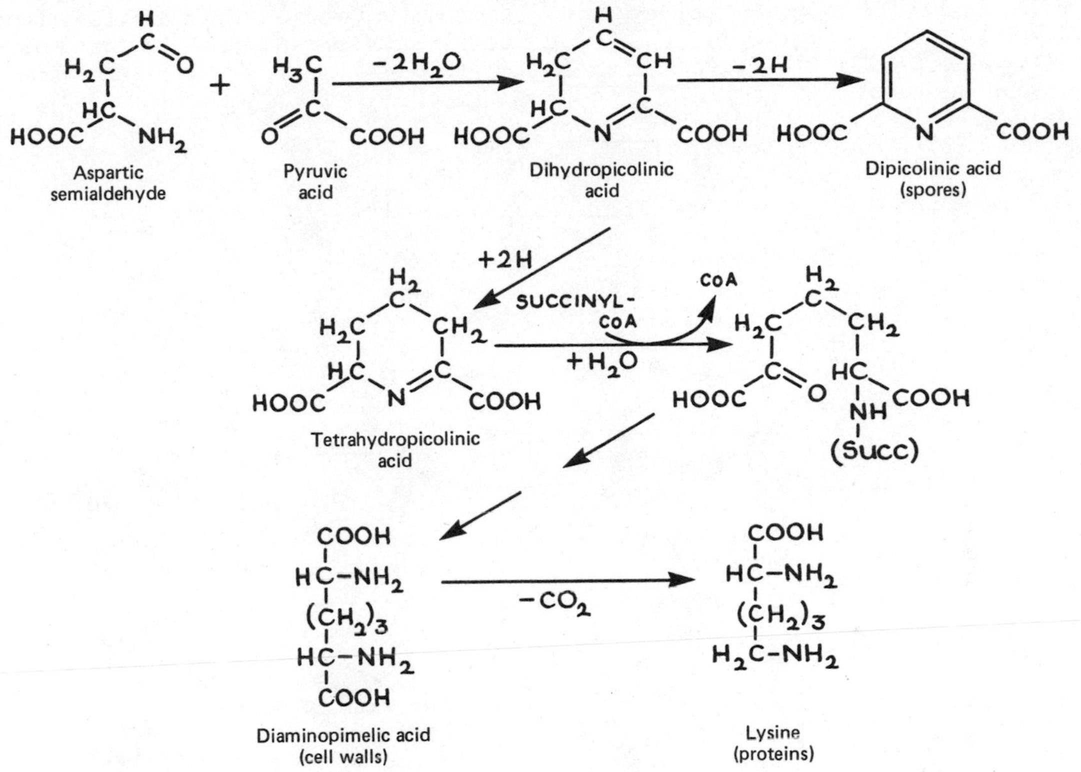

Figure 5–11. The biosynthesis of dipicolinic acid, diaminopimelic acid, and lysine.

H. Synthesis of Dipicolinic Acid, Diamino-pimelic Acid, and Lysine: Bacteria require 2 unique metabolites for their structure: diaminopimelic acid, for the peptidoglycan layer of the cell wall (see Chapter 2); and dipicolinic acid, for endospores. These compounds arise as intermediates in the bacterial biosynthetic pathway for L-lysine, shown in Fig 5–11.

PATTERNS OF MICROBIAL ENERGY–YIELDING METABOLISM

In the nonphotosynthetic bacteria, ATP is generated by oxidation-reduction reactions that may be treated as coupled half-reactions of the following general types:

Oxidation half-reaction: H donor $\xrightarrow{-2H}$ Oxidized product

Reduction half-reaction: H acceptor $\xrightarrow{+2H}$ Reduced product

(where H stands for one electron plus one proton)

When the redox potentials of the 2 half-reactions are sufficiently different, the energy of the reaction may be coupled with the formation of a molecule of ATP from ADP plus P_i.

Different groups of microbes are capable of using different types of H donors and H acceptors. H donors may be either organic or inorganic compounds; H acceptors may be molecular oxygen, inorganic compounds, or organic compounds. The overall process of oxidation-reduction is called "respiration" if the passage of electrons occurs in a membrane-bound respiratory electron transport chain, generating ATP by the mechanism discussed earlier. In aerobic respiration, the terminal acceptor is molecular oxygen; in anaerobic respiration, the terminal acceptor is another substrate of relatively high oxidation-reduction potential, such as nitrate ion, sulfate ion, or fumarate, depending on the organism.

Altogether, 5 patterns exist, as shown in Table 5–2. Note that mammalian tissues obtain ATP exclusively by pattern III (aerobic respiration of organic H donors) with the exception of the lactic acid fermentation in muscle. All parasitic microorganisms use either pattern III or pattern V (fermentation); many are facultative, being able to grow fermentatively under anaerobic conditions but switching preferentially to respiration under aerobic conditions.

Pattern III: The Aerobic Respiration of Organic H Donors

For every naturally occurring organic compound, a microorganism exists that is capable of catabolizing it. Some bacteria can oxidize only one or a few H

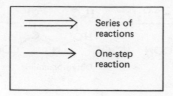

Series of reactions

One-step reaction

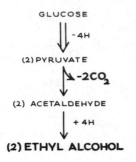

Figure 5–12. Ethyl alcohol fermentation.

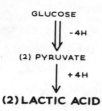

Figure 5–13. Lactic acid homofermentation.

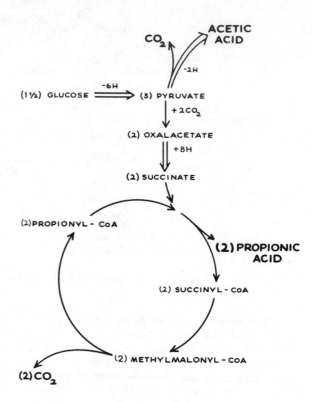

Figure 5–15. Propionic acid fermentation.

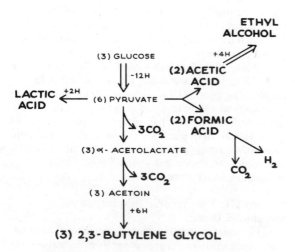

Figure 5–14. Butylene glycol fermentation.

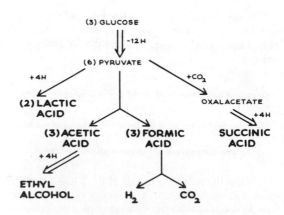

Figure 5–16. Mixed acid fermentation.

Table 5–2. Patterns of energy-yielding oxidation-reduction reactions used by microorganisms.

H DONOR	H ACCEPTOR		
	O_2 (Aerobic Respiration)	NO_3^-, SO_4^{2-}, Fumarate (Anaerobic Respiration)	Organic Compounds (Fermentation)
Inorganic substances	I. Aerobic respiration of inorganic substances Example: *(Nitrosomonas)* $NH_3 \rightarrow NO_2^-$ $O_2 \rightarrow H_2O$	II. Anaerobic respiration of inorganic substances Example: *(Thiobacillus denitrificans)* $S \rightarrow SO_4^{2-}$ $NO_3^- \rightarrow N_2$	(None)
Organic substances	III. Aerobic respiration of organic substances Example: (Many organisms) Glucose $\rightarrow CO_2$ $O_2 \rightarrow H_2O$	IV. Anaerobic respiration of organic substances Example: *(Desulfovibrio)* Lactic acid $\rightarrow CO_2$ $SO_4^{2-} \rightarrow H_2S$	V. Fermentation of organic substances Example: *(Streptococcus)* −4H Glucose $\rightarrow$ 2 pyruvate ↓ +4H 2 lactic acid

donors (eg, a limited number of carbohydrates); others, such as certain pseudomonads, can oxidize at least 100.

Pattern V: Fermentation

Fermentations are metabolic processes in which both H donor and H acceptor are organic compounds. We will consider them in 3 groups.

A. Fermentations Based on the Embden-Meyerhof Pathway: Almost all of the fermentations carried out by clinically significant bacteria fall into this group. They are characterized by the oxidation of carbohydrate to pyruvate via the Embden-Meyerhof

pathway, generating (per molecule of glucose, for example) 2 net molecules of ATP and 2 molecules of $NADH_2$. NAD is regenerated from $NADH_2$ by the reduction of pyruvate—either directly, as in lactic acid homofermentation, or indirectly, as in the others.

The different fermentations of this group are thus characterized by the reduction products formed from pyruvate, reflecting the enzymatic constitutions of different species. The major products of fermentation, listed in Table 5–3, form the basis for many diagnostic laboratory tests.

The details of the enzymatic pathways are presented in Figs 5–12 to 5–17.

Table 5–3. Microbial fermentations based on the Embden-Meyerhof pathway.

Fermentation	Organisms	Products
Ethyl alcohol (Fig 5–12)	Some fungi (notably some yeasts)	Ethyl alcohol, CO_2.
Lactic acid (homofermentation) (Fig 5–13)	*Streptococcus* Some species of *Lactobacillus*	Lactic acid (accounting for at least 90% of the energy source carbon).
Butylene glycol (Fig 5–14)	*Enterobacter* *Aeromonas* *Bacillus polymyxa*	Ethyl alcohol, acetoin, 2,3-butylene glycol, CO_2, lactic acid, acetic acid, formic acid. (Total acids = 21 mol.[*])
Propionic acid (Fig 5–15)	*Clostridium propionicum* *Propionibacterium* *Corynebacterium diphtheriae* Some species of: *Neisseria* *Veillonella* *Micromonospora*	Propionic acid, acetic acid, succinic acid, CO_2.
Mixed acid (Fig 5–16)	*Escherichia* *Salmonella* *Shigella* *Proteus*	Lactic acid, acetic acid, formic acid, succinic acid, H_2, CO_2, ethyl alcohol. (Total acids = 159 mol.[*])
Butyl alcohol-butyric acid (Fig 5–17)	*Butyribacterium* *Zymosarcina maxima* Some species of: *Clostridium* *Neisseria*	Butyl alcohol, butyric acid, acetone, isopropanol, acetic acid, ethyl alcohol, H_2, CO_2.

*Per 100 mol of glucose fermented.

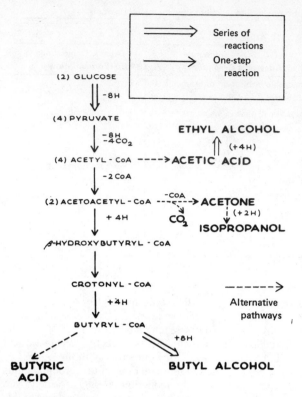

Figure 5–17. Butyl alcohol–butyric acid fermentation.

B. Fermentations Based on the Hexose Monophosphate Shunt: Two fermentations begin with the formation of 6-phosphogluconate from glucose: heterolactic fermentation, carried out by certain harmless lactic acid bacteria; and bacterial alcoholic fermentation, carried out by the nonparasitic species *Zymomonas mobilis.* Their mechanisms are outlined in Fig 5–19.

C. Miscellaneous Special Pathways: Several unique pathways exist, including the following:

1. *Bifidobacterium*–This unusual bacterium is the predominant organism in the intestinal tract of breast-fed infants; it disappears upon weaning. Its fermentation is outlined in Fig 5–18.

2. Clostridia–A number of clostridia, including the agents of tetanus and botulism, carry out fermentations in which the H donor and H acceptor are amino acids taken from the medium. For example, *Clostridium tetani* is capable of the following pair of oxidation-reductions:

$$\text{Alanine} \xrightarrow{-4H} \text{Acetic acid} + NH_3 + CO_2$$

$$2 \text{ Glycine} \xrightarrow{+4H} 2 \text{ Acetic acid} + 2 NH_3$$

3. Methane fermentation–Certain strict anaerobes, called methanogens, carry out the follow-

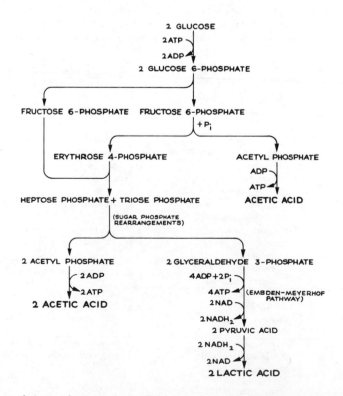

Figure 5–18. The pathway of glucose fermentation by *Bifidobacterium.* (From Stanier RY, Doudoroff M, Adelberg EA: *The Microbial World,* 3rd ed. Copyright © 1970. By permission of Prentice-Hall, Inc, Englewood Cliffs, NJ.)

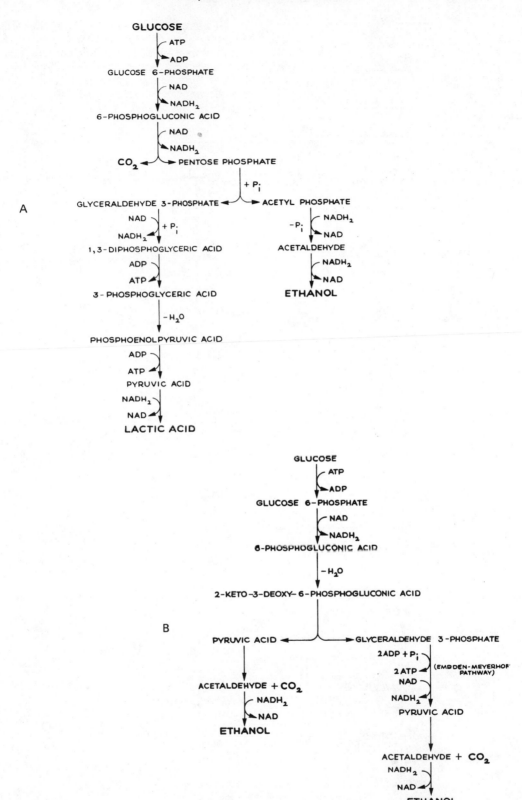

Figure 5–19. *A:* The bacterial heterolactic fermentation of glucose. *B:* Mechanism of the alcoholic fermentation of glucose by the bacterium *Zymomonas mobilis.* (From Stanier RY, Doudoroff M, Adelberg EA: *The Microbial World,* 3rd ed. Copyright © 1970. By permission of Prentice-Hall, Inc, Englewood Cliffs, NJ.)

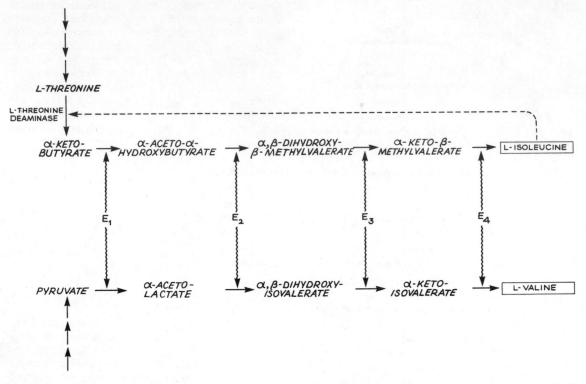

Figure 5–20. Feedback inhibition of L-threonine deaminase by L-isoleucine (dashed line). The pathways for the biosynthesis of isoleucine and valine are mediated by a common set of 4 enzymes, as shown.

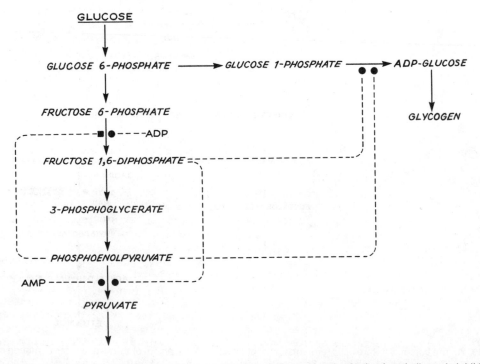

Figure 5–21. Regulation of glucose utilization by a combination of allosteric activation(...●) and allosteric inhibition (...■). (After Stanier RY, Adelberg EA, Ingraham JL: *The Microbial World,* 4th ed. Prentice-Hall, 1976.)

ing reaction; how it is coupled with ATP generation is not clear:

$$\overset{*}{C}H_3COOH \longrightarrow \overset{*}{C}H_4 + CO_2$$

THE REGULATION OF METABOLIC PATHWAYS

In their normal environment, microbial cells regulate their metabolic pathways so efficiently that no intermediate or subunit is made in excess. Each metabolic reaction is regulated not only with respect to all others in the cell but also with respect to the concentrations of nutrients in the environment. Thus, when a sporadically available carbon source suddenly becomes abundant, the enzymes required for its catabolism increase in both amount and activity; conversely, when a subunit (such as an amino acid) suddenly becomes abundant, the enzymes required for its biosynthesis decrease in both amount and activity.

The regulation of enzyme activity as well as enzyme synthesis provides both fine control and coarse control of metabolic pathways. For example, the inhibition of enzyme activity by the end product of a pathway constitutes a mechanism of fine control, since the flow of carbon through that pathway is instantly and precisely regulated. The inhibition of enzyme synthesis by the same end product, on the other hand, constitutes a mechanism of coarse control. The preexisting enzyme molecules continue to function until they are diluted out by further cell growth, although unnecessary protein synthesis ceases immediately.

The mechanisms by which the cell regulates enzyme activity and enzyme synthesis are discussed in the following sections.

The Regulation of Enzyme Activity
A. Enzymes as Allosteric Proteins: In many cases, the activity of an enzyme catalyzing an early step in a metabolic pathway is inhibited by the end product of that pathway. Such inhibition cannot depend on competition for the enzyme's substrate binding site, however, because the structures of the end product and the early intermediate (substrate) are usually quite different. Instead, such inhibition depends on the fact that regulated enzymes are **allosteric:** each enzyme possesses not only a catalytic site, which binds substrate, but also one or more other sites that bind small regulatory molecules, or **effectors.** The binding of an effector to its site causes a conformational change in the enzyme such that the affinity of the catalytic site for the substrate is reduced (allosteric inhibition) or increased (allosteric activation).

Allosteric proteins are usually polymeric. In some cases the subunits are identical, each subunit possessing both a catalytic site and an effector site; in other cases, the subunits are different, one type possessing only a catalytic site and the other only an effector site.

B. Feedback Inhibition: The general mechanism which has evolved in microorganisms for regulating the flow of carbon through biosynthetic pathways is the most efficient that one can imagine. The end product in each case allosterically inhibits the activity of the first—and only the first—enzyme in the pathway. For example, the first step in the biosynthesis of isoleucine not involving any other pathway is the conversion of L-threonine to α-ketobutyric acid, catalyzed by threonine deaminase. Threonine deaminase is allosterically and specifically inhibited by L-isoleucine and by no other compound (Fig 5–20); the other 4 enzymes of the pathway are not affected (although their synthesis is repressed, as discussed below).

C. Allosteric Activation: In some cases it is advantageous to the cell for an end product or an intermediate to activate rather than inhibit a particular enzyme. In the breakdown of glucose by *Escherichia coli,* for example, overproduction of the intermediates glucose 6-phosphate and phosphoenolpyruvate signals the diversion of some glucose to the pathway of glycogen synthesis; this is accomplished by the allosteric activation of the enzyme converting glucose 1-phosphate to ADP-glucose (Fig 5–21).

D. Cooperativity: Many polymeric enzymes, possessing more than one substrate binding site, show cooperative interactions of substrate molecules. The binding of substrate by one catalytic site increases the affinity of the other sites for additional substrate molecules. The net effect of this interaction is to produce an exponential increase in catalytic activity in response to an arithmetic increase in substrate concentration.

The Regulation of Enzyme Synthesis
A. Regulatory Proteins: As discussed in Chapter 4, enzyme synthesis is controlled by regulatory proteins, each produced by a specific regulator gene (Fig 4–19). The regulatory proteins are allosteric: one site binds to an operator region of DNA, either potentiating transcription of an adjacent region or blocking it; the other site binds an effector molecule, which alters the affinity of the DNA binding site. Regulatory proteins that potentiate gene transcription—and thus enzyme synthesis—are called **activators;** those that block enzyme synthesis by interfering with transcription are called **repressors.**

B. Enzyme Induction: In microorganisms, many of which have evolved the ability to use a variety of sporadically occurring carbon sources, the enzymes for the catabolism of these carbon sources are **inducible:** they are synthesized only when the carbon source is present in the medium. Most such enzymes are under "negative control," ie, their synthesis is normally blocked by specific repressors. Induction of enzyme synthesis occurs when an inducer molecule (usually the substrate of the catabolic pathway) enters the cell and binds to the effector site of the repressor; such binding alters the repressor so that it can no longer bind to its cognate site on DNA, and enzyme synthesis begins.

In a few cases, inducible enzymes have been found to be under "positive control," ie, transcription requires the binding to DNA of an activator protein, which is in turn activated by the binding (at an effector site) of the inducer molecule.

C. End Product Repression: The regulation of biosynthetic pathways demands a response opposite to that found in catabolic pathways: instead of enzyme synthesis being induced when the substrate of the pathway becomes available, enzyme synthesis is repressed when the end product of the pathway is made in excess or becomes available as a nutrient. Thus, the repressor of a biosynthetic enzyme is normally unable to bind to the operator site on DNA and gains this ability only when it has bound its specific effector, ie, the end product of the pathway.

Feedback repression, as we may call this phenomenon, differs from feedback inhibition of enzyme activity in that the synthesis of every enzyme in the pathway is repressed. In some cases (notably in bacteria), this is accomplished by the action of a repressor on an **operon** (see Chapter 4), blocking transcription of a polygenic messenger RNA (mRNA).

Base sequence analysis of several polygenic mRNAs for amino acid biosynthesis operons has revealed the presence of a leader sequence rich in codons for the amino acid in question—eg, the mRNA for the tryptophan operon has a leader sequence containing several adjacent tryptophan codons (UGG). The mRNA also contains sequences that give it 2 mutually exclusive, alternate base-pairing configurations. This situation has led to a proposed model of feedback repression called "translational control of transcription termination," or "attenuation." According to the model, when the tryptophan concentration is high, for example, all tryptophan tRNA molecules are charged, and translation of the leader sequence proceeds normally until the ribosome reaches a terminator codon. The presence of a ribosome at this site blocks one of the alternative base-pairing configurations; the other configuration is thus permitted and acts as a transcription termination signal. Alternatively, when the tryptophan concentration is low, uncharged tryptophan tRNA molecules cause stalling of the ribosomes in the leader region. Base-pairing then occurs in the other configuration, and transcription proceeds to completion.

D. Catabolite Repression: Many of the enzymes of catabolic pathways are subject to a regulation process called **catabolite repression.** If the cell is provided with a rapidly metabolizable energy source, such as glucose, the enzymes that degrade alternative sources of energy cease to be synthesized. For example, β-galactosidase, which hydrolyzes lactose, is not synthesized by cells when glucose is present.

The synthesis of all enzymes subject to catabolite repression is under the positive control of a protein called CAP (catabolite activator protein). CAP binds to DNA at sites adjacent to each gene governing a catabolite repressible enzyme and activates the gene's transcription; CAP, in turn, is activated by 3',5'-cAMP. When a rapidly metabolizable substrate such as glucose binds to the cell membrane, the internal concentration of cAMP falls and synthesis of the catabolite repressible enzymes ceases.

Patterns of Regulation in Branched Biosynthetic Pathways

Many biosynthetic pathways are branched, each branch leading to a different, indispensable end product. Aspartic acid, for example, is the starting point for a pathway that branches out to form lysine, methionine, threonine, and isoleucine (Fig 5–22). It would clearly be fatal if the presence in excess of any one of these end products were to shut off the entire pathway starting at aspartate, yet to be efficient the cell must regulate the early steps in the pathway as well as the late ones.

A number of different solutions to this problem have evolved:

A. Isofunctional Enzymes: The first step in the

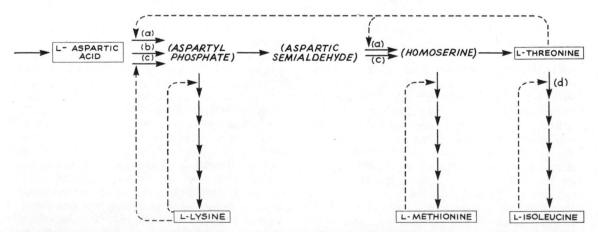

Figure 5–22. Regulation of a branched pathway by feedback inhibition (dashed lines). (a), (b), and (c) are isofunctional aspartokinases; (a) and (c) also catalyze the third step in the pathway. (d) is L-threonine deaminase. Feedback repression of enzyme synthesis is not shown. (After Stanier RY, Adelberg EA, Ingraham JL: *The Microbial World,* 4th ed. Prentice-Hall, 1976.)

pathway is catalyzed by 2 or more different enzymes with the same catalytic activity. For example, there are 3 aspartokinases in *E coli,* labeled (a), (b), and (c) in Fig 5–22. Enzymes (a) and (c) also catalyze the third step in the pathway, reducing aspartic semialdehyde to homoserine. Enzyme (a) is both inhibited and repressed by threonine; enzyme (b) is repressed by methionine; and enzyme (c) is both inhibited and repressed by lysine. Thus, if one of the 3 end products of the branched pathway is present in excess, the flow of carbon through the common pathway is proportionately reduced. (Note in Fig 5–22 that the final branches of the pathway are separately controlled by their respective end products.)

B. Sequential Feedback Inhibition: Fig 5–23 illustrates a second solution to the problem of regulating the early steps of a branched pathway. The 2 end products inhibit the first steps in their own branches, causing the accumulation of a common intermediate. The latter compound then serves as the feedback inhibitor of the first step in the common pathway.

C. Concerted and Cumulative Feedback Inhibition: In still other cases, the enzyme catalyzing the first step of a branched pathway possesses 2 or more effector sites, each binding a different end product. In **concerted feedback inhibition,** all effector sites must be occupied for the enzyme to be inhibited. In **cumulative feedback inhibition,** each end product causes partial inhibition; the effects of binding more than one end product are additive. The latter is the more efficient of the 2 mechanisms.

D. The Diversity of Microbial Regulatory Systems: Different groups of microorganisms have evolved different mechanisms for regulating the same pathway. In the aspartate pathway shown in Fig 5–22, for example, aspartokinase is regulated by the use of separately inhibited isofunctional enzymes in the enteric bacteria but by concerted feedback inhibition in *Pseudomonas.* Thus, regulatory systems appear to have developed late in the evolution of the different microbial groups.

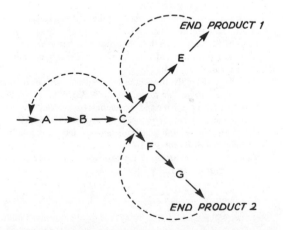

Figure 5–23. Regulation of a branched biosynthetic pathway by sequential feedback inhibition (dashed lines).

THE REGULATION OF RNA SYNTHESIS

The mechanisms described above for the regulation of enzyme (protein) synthesis all act at the level of transcription and hence regulate messenger RNA (mRNA) synthesis. The 2 classes of stable RNA— ribosomal (rRNA) and transfer (tRNA)—are regulated together by a different set of mechanisms that are as yet poorly understood. However, the following generalizations can be made: (1) The synthesis of stable RNA is closely geared to the growth rate of the cell as determined by nutrient supply. In rich media, allowing high rates of protein synthesis and short doubling times, the rate of synthesis of stable RNA increases; in poor media, allowing only low rates of protein synthesis and long doubling times, the rate of synthesis of stable RNA decreases. At all growth rates, the amount of stable RNA made by the cell is precisely that which is sufficient to support the permitted level of protein synthesis. (2) Regulation of stable RNA synthesis is not effected by varying the concentration of RNA precursors (nucleotide triphosphates) but by varying the number of RNA polymerase molecules actively engaged in transcribing the *rRNA* and *tRNA* genes.

One mechanism by which stable RNA synthesis is coupled to protein synthesis has been partially elucidated. When protein synthesis is arrested—eg, by depriving the cell of an essential amino acid—2 regulatory molecules are rapidly synthesized on the ribosomes, ppGpp and ppGppp.* These molecules, in turn, effect the repression of stable RNA synthesis. In *E coli,* a mutation in the gene called *rel* (for "relaxed synthesis of RNA") abolishes the production of the 2 guanosine polyphosphates, and stable RNA synthesis continues in the absence of protein synthesis.

Additional mechanisms must exist for the regulation of stable RNA synthesis, however, since the modulation of such synthesis as a function of growth rate is normal in the *rel* mutants.

THE REGULATION OF DNA SYNTHESIS & CELL DIVISION

In bacteria, the rate of DNA polymerization is a constant at a given temperature. In *E coli* cells growing at 37 °C, for example, chromosome replication takes 40 minutes. In rich media, however, cells may double in as few as 20 minutes; this increase, which requires a corresponding increase in the rate of DNA synthesis, does not reflect a change in the rate of polymerization but rather an increase in the number of replication forks. In other words, a new round of replication begins before the previous round has been completed.

There is a precise relationship between the timing of DNA replication and cell division. For example, in *E coli* at 37 °C, cell division occurs 20 minutes after completion of chromosomal replication. Since both

*ppGpp: guanosine-3′,5′-di(diphosphate); ppGppp: guanosine-3′-diphosphate-5′-triphosphate.

(R), the replication period, and (D), the period between replication and division, are constant, totaling 60 minutes, the following situations may occur: (1) At doubling times of less than 60 minutes, a second round of replication begins during D and each daughter cell receives a chromosome containing a replication fork. (2) At a doubling time of 60 minutes or longer, each daughter cell receives a chromosome without a replication fork.

Thus, the *E coli* cell is so regulated that (1) rounds of DNA replication are initiated at intervals equal to the doubling time of the culture, and (2) a cell division event occurs at a precise interval (eg, 60 minutes at 37 °C) after each initiation event. If DNA synthesis is selectively inhibited, cell elongation continues but cell division is prevented.

The regulation of DNA replication and cell division appears to be achieved through the synthesis of specific proteins; if protein synthesis is blocked, ongoing rounds of DNA replication are completed, but the initiation of new rounds of replication is blocked, as is cell division.

•   •   •

References

Books

Barker HA: *Bacterial Fermentations.* Wiley, 1957.

Cohen GN: *Biosynthesis of Small Molecules.* Harper, 1967.

Cold Spring Harbor Symposia on Quantitative Biology: Vol 26: *Cellular Regulatory Mechanisms.* Vol 28: *Synthesis and Structure of Macromolecules.* Cold Spring Harbor Laboratory, 1961, 1963.

Dagley S, Nicholson E: *An Introduction to Metabolic Pathways.* Wiley, 1970.

Doelle HW: *Bacterial Metabolism,* 2nd ed. Academic Press, 1975.

Gunsalus IC, Stanier RY (editors): *The Bacteria.* Vol 2: *Metabolism.* Vol 3: *Biosynthesis.* Academic Press, 1961, 1962.

Haddock BA, Hamilton WA (editors): *Microbial Energetics: Society for General Microbiology Symposium 27.* Cambridge Univ Press, 1977.

Kornberg A: *DNA Replication.* Freeman, 1980.

Lehninger AL: *Biochemistry,* 2nd ed. Worth, 1975.

Lehninger AL: *Bioenergetics,* 2nd ed. Benjamin, 1971.

Mandelstam J, McQuillen K (editors): *The Biochemistry of Bacterial Growth,* 2nd ed. Wiley, 1973.

Ornston LN, Sokatch JR (editors): *The Bacteria.* Vol 6: *Bacterial Diversity.* Academic Press, 1978.

Rosen BP (editor): *Bacterial Transport.* Dekker, 1978.

Watson JD: *Molecular Biology of the Gene,* 3rd ed. Benjamin, 1976.

Articles & Reviews

Blumberg PM, Strominger JL: Interaction of penicillin with the bacterial cell: Penicillin-binding proteins and penicillin-sensitive enzymes. *Bacteriol Rev* 1974;**38:**291.

Bourgeois S et al: Repressors. *Adv Protein Chem* 1976;**30:**1.

Dawes EA, Senior PJ: The role and regulation of energy reserve polymers in microorganisms. *Adv Microb Physiol* 1973;**10:**136.

Downie JA et al: Membrane adenosine triphosphatases of prokaryotic cells. *Annu Rev Biochem* 1979;**48:**103.

Evans WC: Biochemistry of the bacterial catabolism of aromatic compounds in anaerobic environments. *Nature* 1977;**270:**17.

Finnerty WR: Physiology and biochemistry of bacterial phospholipid metabolism. *Adv Microb Physiol* 1978;**18:**177.

Fraenkel DA, Vinopal RT: Carbohydrate metabolism in bacteria. *Annu Rev Microbiol* 1973;**27:**69.

Giesbrecht P et al: On the morphogenesis of the cell wall of staphylococci. *Int Rev Cytol* 1976;**44:**225.

Haddock BA, Jones CW: Bacterial respiration. *Bacteriol Rev* 1977;**41:**47.

Harold FM: Membranes and energy transduction in bacteria. *Curr Top Bioenerg* 1977;**6:**83.

Hirsch J, Schleif R: Electron microscopy of gene regulation: The L-arabinose operon. *Proc Natl Acad Sci USA* 1976;**73:**1518.

Iaccarino M et al: Regulation of isoleucine and valine biosynthesis. *Curr Top Cell Regul* 1978;**14:**29.

Mitchell P: Vectorial chemiosmotic processes. *Annu Rev Biochem* 1977;**46:**996.

Monod J, Changeux J, Jacob F: Allosteric proteins and cellular control systems. *J Mol Biol* 1963;**6:**306.

Morris JG: The physiology of obligate anaerobiosis. *Adv Microb Physiol* 1975;**12:**169.

Mortenson LE, Thorneley RNF: Structure and function of nitrogenase. *Annu Rev Biochem* 1979;**48:**387.

Nierlich DP: Regulation of bacterial growth, RNA and protein synthesis. *Annu Rev Microbiol* 1978;**32:**393.

Priest FG: Extracellular enzyme synthesis in the genus *Bacillus. Bacteriol Rev* 1977;**41:**711.

Tang M-S, Helmstetter CE: Coordination between chromosome replication and cell division in *Escherichia coli. J Bacteriol* 1980;**144:**1148.

Tonn SJ, Gander JE: Biosynthesis of polysaccharides by prokaryotes. *Annu Rev Microbiol* 1979;**33:**169.

Troy FA: The chemistry and biosynthesis of selected bacterial capsular polymers. *Annu Rev Microbiol* 1979;**33:**519.

Umbarger HE: Amino acid biosynthesis and its regulation. *Annu Rev Biochem* 1978;**47:**532.

Yanofsky C: Attenuation in the expression of bacterial operons. *Nature* 1981;**289:**751.

Cultivation of Microorganisms | 6

Cultivation is the process of propagating organisms by providing the proper environmental conditions: nutrients, pH, temperature, and aeration. Other factors that must be controlled include the salt concentration and osmotic pressure of the medium and such special factors as light for photosynthetic organisms.

NUTRITION

The provision of nutrients for the growth of an organism is called nutrition. In the following discussion, the nutrients are classified according to their role in metabolism.

Hydrogen Donors

All chemosynthetic organisms require an energy source in the form of H donors (ie, oxidizable substrates). In addition, photosynthetic organisms require H donors in order to carry on photosynthesis. Types of compounds that can serve as H donors are discussed in Chapter 5.

Hydrogen Acceptors

H acceptors are required in energy-yielding oxidation-reduction reactions. For aerobes, gaseous oxygen (O_2) is required. Anaerobes require either inorganic compounds (sulfate, nitrate, fumarate) or organic compounds. In the latter case, either the carbon source or a fragment derived from it by catabolism usually serves; in a few instances, however, there is a requirement for a unique H acceptor that must be present in the medium.

Carbon Source

All organisms require a source of carbon for synthesis of the numerous organic compounds that comprise protoplasm. For photosynthetic and lithotrophic organisms, CO_2 is the sole source. Other organisms use the organic energy source as carbon source also; in addition, they require small amounts of CO_2 for such purposes as the carboxylation of phosphoenolpyruvate to form 4-carbon biosynthetic intermediates, the formation of carbamoyl phosphate as a precursor of arginine and pyrimidines, and the biosynthesis of the purine ring. In most cases, sufficient CO_2 is produced

Table 6–1. Sources of nitrogen in microbial nutrition.

Compound	Valence of N
NO_3^-	+5
NO_2^-	+3
N_2	0
NH_3	−3
$R–NH_2$	−3

in catabolism to satisfy this requirement; however, growth frequently cannot be initiated unless CO_2 is present in the environment.

Nitrogen Source

Many cell constituents, principally the proteins, contain nitrogen; in bacteria, nitrogen accounts for approximately 10% of the dry weight of the cell.

The form in which nitrogen is required depends on the organism's enzymatic reducing abilities; a given microbial species may obtain it from the environment in one or more of the forms shown in Table 6–1.

When the nitrogen source is $R–NH_2$ (R = organic radical), the organism uses it by deamination to NH_3, which is then incorporated into nitrogenous compounds; or by direct transfer of the amino group to suitable acceptors (transamination); or by both methods:

$$R–CH–COOH + R_1–C–COOH \xrightarrow{\text{Transamination}}$$
$$\quad | \qquad\qquad\qquad ||$$
$$\quad NH_2 \qquad\qquad\quad O$$

| Amino donor | Amino acceptor |

$$R–C–COOH + R_1–CH–COOH$$
$$\quad || \qquad\qquad\qquad |$$
$$\quad O \qquad\qquad\qquad NH_2$$

| Deaminated donor | Aminated acceptor |

Most microorganisms can use NH_3 as the sole nitrogen source. The principal reaction by which NH_3

is introduced into organic molecules is the reaction catalyzed by glutamic dehydrogenase:

$$HOOC-\underset{\underset{O}{\|}}{C}-CH_2-CH_2-\underset{\underset{O}{\|}}{C}-COOH \xrightarrow[\substack{+2H \\ from \\ NADPH}]{+NH_3}$$

α-Ketoglutaric acid

$$HOOC-\underset{\underset{O}{\|}}{C}-CH_2-CH_2-\underset{\underset{NH_2}{|}}{CH}-COOH + H_2O$$

Glutamic acid

Distribution of the nitrogen into other compounds can then be effected by transamination between glutamic acid and various keto acids and by modification of the new amino acids thus formed.

A limited number of microorganisms can fix atmospheric nitrogen (N_2) by converting it to NH_3 in the cell. Some bacteria can use nitrate as a nitrogen source, reducing it to the level of NH_3 in the cell.

Minerals

In addition to carbon and nitrogen, living cells require a number of other minerals for growth:

A. Sulfur: Like nitrogen, sulfur is a component of many organic cell substances; the bulk of it occurs as sulfhydryl (–SH) groups in proteins. Some organisms require organic sulfur (R–SH) or H_2S, but most species can reduce sulfate (SO_4^{2-}) to the organic form.

B. Phosphorus: Phosphate (PO_4^{3-}) is required as a component of ATP, of nucleic acids, and of such coenzymes as NAD, NADP, and flavins. Phosphate is always assimilated as free inorganic phosphate.

C. Enzyme Activators: Numerous minerals are needed as enzyme activators. Magnesium ion (Mg^{2+}) and ferrous ion are also found in porphyrins: magnesium in the chlorophyll molecule and iron as a part of the coenzymes of the cytochromes and peroxidases. Mg^{2+} and K^+ are both essential for the function and integrity of ribosomes. Ca^{2+} is required as a constituent of gram-positive cell walls, although it is dispensable for gram-negative bacteria. In formulating a medium for the cultivation of most microorganisms, it is necessary to provide sources of potassium, magnesium, calcium, and iron, usually as their ions (K^+, Mg^{2+}, Ca^{2+}, and Fe^{2+}). Many other minerals are required but are adequately provided as contaminants of tap water and of other medium ingredients.

The uptake of iron, which forms insoluble hydroxides at neutral pH, is facilitated in many bacteria and fungi by their production of **siderochromes** — compounds that chelate iron and promote its transport as a soluble complex. They include hydroxamic acids ($-CONH_2OH$), called sideramines, and derivatives of catechol (eg, 2,3-dihydroxybenzoylserine). Plasmid-determined siderochromes play a major role in the invasiveness of some bacterial pathogens (see Chapter 4).

Growth Factors

A growth factor is an organic compound which a cell must contain in order to grow but which it is unable to synthesize. Many microorganisms, when provided with the nutrients listed above, are able to synthesize all of the organic constituents of the cell, including amino acids (the subunits of proteins), vitamins (for coenzymes), purines and pyrimidines (components of nucleic acids), fatty acids (components of fats and lipids), and other compounds.

Each of these essential compounds is synthesized by a discrete sequence of enzymatic reactions; each enzyme is produced under the control of a specific gene. When an organism undergoes a gene mutation resulting in failure of one of these enzymes to function, the chain is broken and the end product is no longer produced. The organism must then obtain that compound from the environment: the compound has become a **growth factor** for the organism.

Different microbial species vary widely in their growth factor requirements. The compounds involved are found in and are essential to all organisms; the differences in requirements reflect differences in synthetic abilities. Some species require no growth factors, while others (like some of the lactobacilli) have lost, during evolution, the ability to synthesize as many as 30–40 essential compounds and hence require them in the medium. This type of mutation can be readily induced in the laboratory.

ENVIRONMENTAL FACTORS AFFECTING GROWTH

A suitable growth medium must contain all the nutrients required by the organism to be cultivated, and such factors as pH, temperature, and aeration must be carefully controlled. A liquid medium is used; the medium can be gelled for special purposes by adding agar or silica gel. Agar, a polysaccharide extract of a marine alga, is uniquely suitable for microbial cultivation because it is resistant to microbial action and because it dissolves at 100 °C but does not gel until cooled below 45 °C; cells can be suspended in the medium at 45 °C and the medium quickly cooled to a gel without harming them.

Nutrients

On the previous pages the function of each type of nutrient is described and a list of suitable substances presented. In general, the following must be provided: (1) Hydrogen donors and acceptors: about 2 g/L. (2) Carbon source: about 1 g/L. (3) Nitrogen source: about 1 g/L. (4) Minerals: sulfur and phosphorus, about 50 mg/L of each; trace elements, 0.1–1 mg/L of each. (5) Growth factors: amino acids, purines, pyrimidines, about 50 mg/L of each; vitamins, 0.1–1 mg/L of each.

For studies of microbial metabolism it is usually necessary to prepare a completely synthetic medium in which the characteristics and concentration of every ingredient are exactly known. Otherwise it is much cheaper and simpler to use natural materials such as yeast extract, protein digest, or similar substances. Most free-living microbes will grow well on yeast extract; parasitic forms may require special substances found only in blood or in extracts of animal tissues.

For many organisms, a single compound (such as an amino acid) may serve as energy source, carbon source, and nitrogen source; others require a separate compound for each. If natural materials for nonsynthetic media are deficient in any particular nutrient, they must be supplemented.

Hydrogen Ion Concentration (pH)

Most organisms have a fairly narrow optimal pH range. The optimal pH must be empirically determined for each species. Most organisms grow best at a pH of 6.0–8.0, although some forms have optima as low as pH 2.0 *(Thiobacillus thiooxidans)* and others have optima as high as pH 8.5 *(Alcaligenes faecalis)*.

Temperature

Different microbial species vary widely in their optimal temperature ranges for growth: psychrophilic forms grow best at low temperatures (15–20 °C); mesophilic forms grow best at 30–37 °C; and thermophilic forms grow best at 50–60 °C. Most organisms are mesophilic; 30 °C is optimal for many free-living forms, and the body temperature of the host is optimal for symbionts of warm-blooded animals. The upper end of the temperature range tolerated by any given species correlates well with the general thermal stability of that species' proteins as measured in cell extracts.

Aeration

The role of oxygen as hydrogen acceptor is discussed in Chapter 5. Many organisms are obligate aerobes, specifically requiring oxygen as hydrogen acceptor; some are facultative, able to live aerobically or anaerobically; and others are obligate anaerobes, requiring a substance other than oxygen as hydrogen acceptor and being sensitive to oxygen inhibition.

The toxicity of O_2 results from its reduction by enzymes in the cell (such as flavoproteins) to hydrogen peroxide (H_2O_2) and the even more toxic free radical, superoxide (O_2^-). Aerobes and aerotolerant anaerobes are protected from these products by the presence of superoxide dismutase, an enzyme that catalyzes the reaction

$$2O_2^- + 2H^+ \rightarrow O_2 + H_2O_2$$

and by the presence of catalase, an enzyme that catalyzes the reaction

$$2H_2O_2 \rightarrow 2H_2O + O_2$$

One exception to this rule is the lactic acid bacteria, aerotolerant anaerobes that do not contain catalase. This group relies instead on peroxidases, which reduce H_2O_2 to $2H_2O$ at the expense of oxidizable organic substrates. All strict anaerobes lack both superoxide dismutase and catalase; the former enzyme is indispensable for survival in the presence of O_2.

Hydrogen peroxide owes much of its toxicity to the damage it causes to DNA. DNA repair–deficient mutants are exceptionally sensitive to hydrogen peroxide; the *recA* gene product, which functions in both genetic recombination and repair, has been shown to be more important than either catalase or superoxide dismutase in protecting *Escherichia coli* cells against hydrogen peroxide toxicity.

The supply of air to cultures of aerobes is a major technical problem. Vessels are usually shaken mechanically to introduce oxygen into the medium, or air is forced through the medium by pressure. The diffusion of oxygen often becomes the limiting factor in growing aerobic bacteria; when a cell concentration of $4–5 \times 10^9$/mL is reached, the rate of diffusion of oxygen to the cells sharply limits the rate of further growth.

Obligate anaerobes, on the other hand, present the problem of oxygen exclusion. Many methods are available for this: reducing agents such as sodium thioglycolate can be added to liquid cultures; tubes of agar can be sealed with a layer of petrolatum and paraffin; the culture vessel can be placed in a container from which the oxygen is removed by evacuation or by chemical means; or the organism can be handled within an anaerobic glove-box.

Ionic Strength & Osmotic Pressure

To a lesser extent, such factors as osmotic pressure and salt concentration may have to be controlled. For most organisms the properties of ordinary media are satisfactory, but for marine forms and organisms adapted to growth in strong sugar solutions, for example, these factors must be considered. Organisms requiring high salt concentrations are called **halophilic;** those requiring high osmotic pressures are called **osmophilic.**

Most bacteria are able to tolerate a wide range of external osmotic pressures and ionic strengths because of their ability to regulate internal osmolality and ion concentration. Osmolality is regulated by the active transport of K^+ ions into the cell; internal ionic strength is kept constant by a compensating excretion of the positively charged organic polyamine putrescine. Since putrescine carries several positive charges per molecule, a large drop in ionic strength is effected at only a small cost in osmotic strength.

CULTIVATION METHODS

Two problems will be considered: the choice of a suitable medium and the isolation of a bacterial organism in pure culture.

The Medium

The technique used and the type of medium selected depend upon the nature of the investigation. In general, 3 situations may be encountered: (1) one may need to raise a crop of cells of a particular species that is on hand; (2) one may need to determine the numbers and types of organisms present in a given material; or (3) one may wish to isolate a particular type of microorganism from a natural source.

A. Growing Cells of a Given Species: Microorganisms observed microscopically to be growing in a natural environment may prove exceedingly difficult to grow in pure culture in an artificial medium. Certain parasitic forms, for example, have never been cultivated outside the host. In general, however, a suitable medium can be devised by carefully reproducing the conditions found in the organism's natural environment. The pH, temperature, and aeration are simple to duplicate; the nutrients present the major problem. The contribution made by the living environment is important and difficult to analyze; a parasite may require an extract of the host tissue, and a free-living form may require a substance excreted by a microorganism with which it is associated in nature. Considerable experimentation may be necessary in order to determine the requirements of the organism, and success depends upon providing a suitable source of each category of nutrient listed at the beginning of this chapter. The cultivation of obligate parasites such as rickettsiae is discussed in Chapter 28.

B. Microbiologic Examination of Natural Materials: A given natural material may contain many different microenvironments, each providing a niche for a different species. Plating a sample of the materials under one set of conditions will allow a selected group of forms to produce colonies but will cause many other types to be overlooked. For this reason it is customary to plate out samples of the material using as many different media and conditions of incubation as is practicable. Six to 8 different culture conditions are not an unreasonable number if most of the forms present are to be discovered.

Since every type of organism present must have a chance to grow, solid media are used and crowding of colonies is avoided. Otherwise, competition will prevent some types from forming colonies.

C. Isolation of a Particular Type of Microorganism: A small sample of soil, if handled properly, will yield a different type of organism for every microenvironment present. For fertile soil (moist, aerated, rich in minerals and organic matter) this means that hundreds or even thousands of types can be isolated. This is done by selecting for the desired type. One gram of soil, for example, is inoculated into a flask of liquid medium that has been made up for the purpose of favoring one type of organism, eg, aerobic nitrogen fixers *(Azotobacter)*. In this case the medium contains no combined nitrogen and is incubated aerobically. If cells of *Azotobacter* are present in the soil, they will grow well in this medium; forms unable to fix nitrogen will grow only to the extent that the soil has introduced contaminating fixed nitrogen into the medium. When the culture is fully grown, therefore, the percentage of *Azotobacter* in the total population will have increased greatly; the method is thus called "enrichment culture." Transfer of a sample of this culture to fresh medium will result in further enrichment of *Azotobacter*; after several serial transfers, the culture can be plated out on a solidified enrichment medium and colonies of *Azotobacter* isolated.

Liquid medium is used to permit competition and hence optimal selection, even when the desired type is represented in the soil as only a few cells in a population of millions. Advantage can be taken of "natural enrichment." For example, in looking for kerosene oxidizers, oil-laden soil is chosen, since such soil is already an enrichment environment for such forms.

Enrichment culture, then, is a procedure whereby the medium is prepared so as to duplicate the natural environment ("niche") of the desired microorganism, thereby selecting for it. An important principle involved in such selection is the following: The organism selected for will be the type whose nutritional requirements are barely satisfied. *Azotobacter*, for example, grows best in a medium containing organic nitrogen, but its minimum requirement is the presence of N_2; hence it is selected for in a medium containing N_2 as the sole nitrogen source. If organic nitrogen is added to the medium, the conditions no longer select for *Azotobacter* but rather for a form for which organic nitrogen is the minimum requirement.

When searching for a particular type of organism in a natural material, it is advantageous to plate the organisms obtained on a differential medium if available. A differential medium is one that will cause the colonies of a particular type of organism to have a distinctive appearance. For example, colonies of *Escherichia coli* have a characteristic iridescent sheen on agar containing the dyes eosin and methylene blue (EMB agar). EMB agar containing a high concentration of one sugar will also cause organisms which ferment that sugar to form reddish colonies. Differential media are used for such purposes as recognizing the presence of enteric bacteria in water or milk and the presence of certain pathogens in clinical specimens from patients.

Table 6–2 presents examples of enrichment culture conditions and the types of bacteria they will select.

Isolation of Microorganisms in Pure Culture

In order to study the properties of a given organism, it is necessary to handle it in pure culture free of all other types of organisms. To do this, a single cell must be isolated from all other cells and cultivated in such a manner that its collective progeny also remain isolated. Several methods are available.

A. Plating: Unlike cells in a liquid medium, cells in or on a gelled medium are immobilized. Therefore, if few enough cells are placed in or on a gelled medium, each cell will grow into an isolated colony.

Table 6-2. Some enrichment cultures.

Constituents of all media: $MgSO_4$, K_2HPO_4, $FeCl_3$, $CaCl_2$, $CaCO_3$, trace elements.

Nitrogen Source	Carbon Source	Atmosphere	Illumination	Predominant Organism Initially Enriched
N₂	CO₂	Aerobic or anaerobic	Dark	None
			Light	Cyanobacteria
	Alcohol, fatty acids, etc	Anaerobic	Dark	None
		Air	Dark	*Azotobacter*
	Glucose	Anaerobic	Dark	*Clostridium pasteurianum*
		Air	Dark	*Azotobacter*
NaNO₃	CO₂	Aerobic or anaerobic	Dark	None
			Light	Green algae and cyanobacteria
	Alcohol, fatty, acids, etc	Anaerobic	Dark	Denitrifiers
		Air	Dark	Aerobes
	Glucose	Anaerobic	Dark	Fermenters
		Air	Dark	Aerobes
NH₄Cl	CO₂	Anaerobic	Dark	None
		Aerobic	Dark	*Nitrosomonas*
		Aerobic or anaerobic	Light	Green algae and cyanobacteria
	Alcohol, fatty acids, etc	Anaerobic	Dark	Sulfate or carbonate reducers
		Aerobic	Dark	Aerobes
	Glucose	Anaerobic	Dark	Fermenters
		Aerobic	Dark	Aerobes

The ideal gelling agent for most microbiologic media is **agar,** an acidic polysaccharide extracted from certain red algae. A 1.5–2% suspension in water dissolves at 100 °C, forming a clear solution that gels at 45 °C. Thus, a sterile agar solution can be cooled to 50 °C, bacteria or other microbial cells added, and then the solution quickly cooled below 45 °C to form a gel. (Although most microbial cells are killed at 50 °C, the time-course of the killing process is sufficiently slow at this temperature to permit this procedure. See Fig 7–3.) Once gelled, agar will not again liquefy until it is heated above 80 °C, so that any temperature suitable for the incubation of a microbial culture can subsequently be used. In the pour-plate method, a suspension of cells is mixed with melted agar at 50 °C and poured into a Petri dish. When the agar solidifies, the cells are immobilized in the agar and grow into colonies. If the cell suspension was sufficiently dilute, the colonies will be well separated, so that each has a high probability of being derived from a single cell. To make certain of this, however, it is necessary to pick a colony of the desired type, suspend it in water, and replate. Repeating this procedure several times ensures that a pure culture will be obtained.

Alternatively, the original suspension can be streaked on an agar plate with a wire loop. As the streaking continues, fewer and fewer cells are left on the loop, and finally the loop may deposit single cells on the agar. The plate is incubated and any well-isolated colony is then removed, resuspended in water, and again streaked on agar. If a suspension (and not just a bit of growth from a colony or slant) is streaked, this method is just as reliable and much faster than the pour-plate method.

B. Dilution: A much less reliable method is that of extinction dilution. The suspension is serially diluted and samples of each dilution are plated. If only a few samples of a particular dilution exhibit growth, it is presumed that some of these cultures started from single cells. This method is not used unless plating is for some reason impossible. An undesirable feature of this method is that it can only be used to isolate the predominant type of organism in a mixed population.

● ● ●

References

Books

Alexander M: *Microbial Ecology*. Wiley, 1971.

Guirard BM, Snell EE: Nutritional requirements of microorganisms. Pages 33–93 in: *The Bacteria*. Vol 4: *Physiology of Growth*. Gunsalus IC, Stanier RY (editors). Academic Press, 1962.

Meynell GG, Meynell E: *Theory and Practice in Experimental Bacteriology*. Cambridge Univ Press, 1965.

Precht H (editor): *Temperature and Life*. Springer, 1973.

Schlegel HG (editor): *Enrichment Culture and Mutant Selection*. Fischer (Stuttgart), 1965.

Stanier RY, Adelberg EA, Ingraham JL: *The Microbial World*, 4th ed. Prentice-Hall, 1976.

Articles & Reviews

Brown AD: Aspects of bacterial response to the ionic environment. *Bacteriol Rev* 1964;**28**:296.

Carlsson J, Carpenter VS: The *recA*[+] gene product is more important than catalase and superoxide dismutase in protecting *Escherichia coli* against hydrogen peroxide toxicity. *J Bacteriol* 1980;**142**:319.

Fridovich I: Oxygen, boon and bane. *Am Sci* 1975;**63**:54.

Fridovich I: Superoxide dismutases. *Annu Rev Biochem* 1975;**44**:147.

Hassan HM, Fridovich I: Physiological function of superoxide dismutase in glucose-limited chemostat cultures of *Escherichia coli*. *J Bacteriol* 1977;**130**:805.

Hutner SH: Inorganic nutrition. *Annu Rev Microbiol* 1972;**26**:313.

Morris JG: The physiology of obligate anaerobiosis. *Adv Microb Physiol* 1975;**12**:169.

Nielands JB: Hydroxamic acids in nature. *Science* 1967;**156**:1443.

Wang CC, Newton A: Iron transport in *Escherichia coli:* Roles of energy-dependent uptake and 2,3-dihydroxybenzoylserine. *J Bacteriol* 1969;**98**:1142.

The Growth & Death of Microorganisms | 7

DEFINITION & MEASUREMENT OF GROWTH

The Meaning of Growth

Growth is the orderly increase in all of the components of an organism. Thus, the increase in size that results when a cell takes up water or deposits lipid is not true growth. Cell multiplication is a consequence of growth; in unicellular organisms, multiplication leads to an increase in the number of individuals making up a population or a culture.

The Measurement of Growth

Microbial growth can be measured in terms of cell concentration (the number of cells per unit volume of culture) or of cell density (dry weight of cells per unit volume of culture). These 2 parameters are not always equivalent because the average dry weight of the cell varies at different stages in the history of the culture. Nor are they of equal significance: In studies on microbial biochemistry or nutrition, cell density is the significant quantity; in studies on microbial inactivation, cell concentration is the significant quantity.

A. Cell Concentration: The viable cell count (Table 8–1) is usually considered the measure of cell concentration. However, the general practice is to measure the light absorption or light scattering of a culture by photoelectric means and to relate viable counts to optical measurements in the form of a standard curve. By means of the standard curve, all further optical readings can be converted to cell concentration. However, it is essential that a separate standard curve be determined for each stage in the growth of the culture so that differences in average cell size can be taken into account.

B. Cell Density: Since it is technically difficult to perform a large number of dry weight measurements, and since such measurements are accurate only with relatively large amounts of cells, various indirect methods are used. These include photoelectric measurements, nitrogen determination, and centrifugation in special vessels. In each case it is necessary to construct a standard curve equating the measurement values with known dry weights.

EXPONENTIAL GROWTH

The Growth Constant

Since the 2 new cells produced by the growth and division of a single cell are each capable of growing at the same rate as the parent cell, the number of cells in a culture increases with time as a geometric progression—ie, exponentially.

The rate of growth of a culture at a given moment is directly proportionate to the number of cells present at that moment. This relationship is given by the following equation:

$$\frac{dN}{dt} = kN \qquad \ldots (1)$$

Integration of the above expression gives

$$N = N_0 e^{kt} \qquad \ldots (2)$$

where N_0 is the number of cells at time zero and N is the number of cells at any later time t.

In equation (2) above, k is the growth constant. Solving the equation for k gives

$$k = \frac{\ln(N/N_0)}{t} \qquad \ldots (3)$$

Thus, k represents the rate at which the natural logarithm of cell number increases with time and can be determined graphically as shown in Fig 7–1.

The Generation

In practice it is customary to express the growth rate of a microbial culture in terms of generations per hour. For organisms that reproduce by binary fission, a generation is defined as a doubling of cell number. Thus, the number of cells (N) increases with generations (g) as follows:

g	N
0	1
1	2
2	4
3	8
4	16
5	32

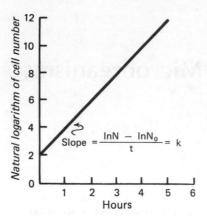

Figure 7–1. The rate at which the natural logarithm of cell number increases with time.

This relationship can be expressed as follows:

$$N = N_0 2^g \qquad \ldots (4)$$

Combining equations (2) and (4), we find

$$N_0 e^{kt} = N_0 2^g \qquad \ldots (5)$$

Equation (5) can be rearranged to give

$$\frac{g}{t} = \frac{k}{\ln 2} \qquad \ldots (6)$$

Equation (6) thus relates g/t (generations per hour) with k, the growth constant.

The number of generations per hour is usually determined by plotting cell number against time on a semilogarithmic scale and reading off directly the time required for the number to double. For example, if such a plot shows the doubling time ("generation time") to be 40 minutes, the growth rate of the culture is said to be 1.5 generations per hour.

Alternatively, the generation time can be calculated directly from equation (4), which can be solved for g (the number of generations) as follows:

$$g = \frac{\log N - \log N_0}{\log 2} \qquad \ldots (7)$$

For example, if an inoculum of 10^3 cells grows exponentially to 1×10^9 cells, then

$$g = \frac{\log(10^9) - \log(10^3)}{\log 2} = \frac{9 - 3}{0.3} = \textbf{20 generations}$$

If, for example, this growth required 13.3 hours, the growth rate was 20/13.3, or 1.5 generations per hour.

THE GROWTH CURVE

If a liquid medium is inoculated with microbial cells taken from a culture that has previously been grown to saturation and the number of viable cells per milliliter determined periodically and plotted, a curve of the type shown in Fig 7–2 is usually obtained. The curve may be discussed in terms of 6 phases, represented by the letters A–F (Table 7–1).

Table 7–1. Phases of microbial death curve.

Section of Curve	Phase	Growth Rate
A	Lag	Zero
B	Acceleration	Increasing
C	Exponential	Constant
D	Retardation	Decreasing
E	Maximum stationary	Zero
F	Decline	Negative (death)

The Lag Phase (A)

The lag phase represents a period during which the cells, depleted of metabolites and enzymes as the result of the unfavorable conditions that obtained at the end of their previous culture history, adapt to their new environment. Enzymes and intermediates are formed and accumulate until they are present in concentrations that permit growth to resume.

If the cells are taken from an entirely different medium, it often happens that they are genetically incapable of growth in the new medium. In such cases a long lag may occur, representing the period necessary for a few mutants in the inoculum to multiply sufficiently for a net increase in cell number to be apparent.

The Exponential Phase (C)

During the exponential phase, the mathematics of which has already been discussed, the cells are in a steady state. New cell material is being synthesized at a constant rate, but the new material is itself catalytic

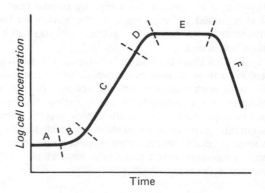

Figure 7–2. Cell concentration curve.

and the mass increases in an exponential manner. This continues until one of 2 things happens: Either one or more nutrients in the medium become exhausted, or toxic metabolic products accumulate and inhibit growth. For aerobic organisms, the nutrient that becomes limiting is usually oxygen: When the cell concentration exceeds about 1×10^7/mL (in the case of bacteria), the growth rate will decrease unless oxygen is forced into the medium by agitation or by bubbling in air. When the cell concentration reaches $4-5 \times 10^9$/mL, the rate of oxygen diffusion cannot meet the demand even in an aerated medium, and growth is progressively slowed.

The Maximum Stationary Phase (E)

Eventually, the exhaustion of nutrients or the accumulation of toxic products causes growth to cease completely. In most cases, however, cell turnover takes place in the stationary phase: there is a slow loss of cells through death, which is just balanced by the formation of new cells through growth and division. When this occurs, the total cell count slowly increases although the viable count stays constant.

The Phase of Decline (the Death Phase, F)

After a period of time in stationary phase, which varies with the organism and with the culture conditions, the death rate increases until it reaches a steady level. The mathematics of steady-state death are discussed below. Frequently, after the majority of cells have died, the death rate decreases drastically, so that a small number of survivors may persist for months or even years. This persistence may in some cases reflect cell turnover, a few cells growing at the expense of nutrients released from cells that die and lyse.

THE MAINTENANCE OF CELLS IN EXPONENTIAL PHASE

Cells can be maintained in exponential phase by transferring them repeatedly into fresh medium of identical composition while they are still growing exponentially. Two devices have been invented for carrying out this process automatically: the chemostat and the turbidostat.

The Chemostat

This device consists of a culture vessel equipped with an overflow siphon and a mechanism for dripping in fresh medium from a reservoir at a regulated rate. The medium in the culture vessel is stirred by a stream of sterile air; each drop of fresh medium that enters causes a drop of culture to siphon out.

The medium is prepared so that one nutrient limits growth yield. The vessel is inoculated, and the cells grow until the limiting nutrient is exhausted; fresh medium from the reservoir is then allowed to flow in at such a rate that the cells use up the limiting nutrient as fast as it is supplied. Under these conditions, the cell concentration remains constant and the growth rate is directly proportionate to the flow rate of the medium.

The chemostat thus provides a steady-state culture of exponentially growing cells and permits regulation of the growth rate. However, its disadvantage is that growing cells are always in a state of semistarvation for one nutrient and must be grown at less than maximum rate to achieve good regulation. These disadvantages are not present in the turbidostat.

The Turbidostat

This device resembles the chemostat except that the flow of medium is controlled by a photoelectric mechanism that measures the turbidity of the culture. When the turbidity exceeds the chosen level, fresh medium is allowed to flow in. Thus, the cells can grow at maximum rate at a constant cell concentration. The growth rate can be controlled in the turbidostat only by varying the nature of the medium or the culture conditions (eg, temperature).

SYNCHRONOUS GROWTH

In ordinary cultures, the cells are growing nonsynchronously: at any moment, cells are present in every possible stage of the division cycle. The culture must be synchronized if one is to study the sequence of events occurring in a single cell during the division cycle.

Synchrony has been achieved for a variety of microorganisms by several techniques. Some microorganisms, for example, go through one or 2 synchronous divisions when diluted from a stationary phase culture into fresh medium. In many cases, however, it is necessary to bring the cells into synchrony by a more involved process. Pneumococci, for example, will divide synchronously after several alternating periods of incubation at high and low temperature. *Escherichia coli* has been synchronized by 2 different methods: in one, a thymine-requiring mutant is starved for thymine until viability begins to drop. Replacing thymine in the culture then causes the surviving cells to undergo several synchronous divisions. In the other method, a heavy cell suspension is deposited in a filter paper pile. As the adsorbed cells divide, the newly formed daugther cells are released from the filter paper; they can be recovered as a synchronously dividing population by washing the paper briefly with warm medium.

Synchrony only persists for 1–4 cycles. After that time the cells become more and more out of phase until their division times become completely random.

GROWTH PARAMETERS

Physiologic studies may be carried out by introducing controlled variations in individual environmental factors and then quantitatively determining the effect of such variations on bacterial growth. To be most useful, experiments of this type should involve determination of meaningful growth parameters. Growth parameters that may be determined include total growth and exponential growth rate.

Total Growth

A culture eventually stops growing when one of 3 things occurs: (1) when one or more nutrients are exhausted; (2) when toxic products accumulate; or (3) when an unfavorable ion equilibrium develops (eg, unfavorable pH).

If total growth (G) is limited by exhaustion of a nutrient, then

$$G = KC \qquad \ldots (8)$$

where K is a constant and C is the initial concentration of the limiting nutrient. Such an equation implies a straight-line relationship between C and G.

Exponential Growth Rates

If some nutrient is initially present at a sufficiently low concentration, metabolic intermediates will be formed at a limited rate and the overall growth rate will be a function of the concentration of the limiting nutrient. Experiments show that a hyperbolic curve results, in accordance with the following general equation:

$$R = R_K \frac{C}{C_1 + C} \qquad \ldots (9)$$

where R = Growth rate
R_K = Maximum rate reached with increasing concentration of nutrient
C = Concentration of the limiting nutrient
C_1 = Value of C at which $R = \frac{1}{2} R_K$

Total growth is a useful parameter in many microbial assays; for example, in the assay of a vitamin or a carbon source in some natural material. For most physiologic studies, however, growth rate is the most meaningful parameter. One method, for example, is to compare concentrations of nutrients or inhibitors that give half-maximal growth rates.

DEFINITION & MEASUREMENT OF DEATH

The Meaning of Death

For a microbial cell, death means the irreversible loss of the ability to reproduce (grow and divide). The empiric test of death is the culture of cells on solid media: a cell is considered dead if it fails to give rise to a colony on any medium. Obviously, then, the reliability of the test depends upon choice of medium and conditions: A culture in which 99% of the cells appear "dead" in terms of ability to form colonies on one medium may prove to be 100% viable if tested on another medium. Furthermore, the detection of a few viable cells in a large clinical specimen may not be

possible by directly plating a sample, as the sample fluid itself may be inhibitory to microbial growth. In such cases, the sample may have to be diluted first into liquid medium, permitting the outgrowth of viable cells before plating.

The conditions of incubation in the first hour following treatment are also critical in the determination of "killing." For example, if bacterial cells are irradiated with ultraviolet light and plated immediately on any medium, it may appear that 99.99% of the cells have been killed. If such irradiated cells are first incubated in a suitable buffer for 20 minutes, however, plating will indicate only 10% killing. In other words, irradiation determines that a cell will "die" if plated immediately but will live if allowed to repair irradiation damage before plating.

A microbial cell that is not physically disrupted is thus "dead" only in terms of the conditions used to test viability.

The Measurement of Death

When dealing with microorganisms, one does not customarily measure the death of an individual cell but the death of a population. This is a statistical problem: Under any condition that may lead to cell death, the probability of a given cell's dying is constant per unit time. For example, if a condition is employed that causes 90% of the cells to die in the first 10 minutes, the probability of any one cell dying in a 10-minute interval is 0.9. Thus, it may be expected that 90% of the surviving cells will die in each succeeding 10-minute interval, and a death curve similar to those shown in Fig 7–3 will be obtained.

The number of cells dying in each time interval is thus a function of the number of survivors present, so that death of a population proceeds as an exponential process according to the general formula

$$S = S_0 e^{-kt} \qquad \ldots (10)$$

where S_0 is the number of survivors at time zero, and S is the number of survivors at any later time t. As in the case of exponential growth, $-k$ represents the rate of exponential death when the fraction $ln \, (S/S_0)$ is plotted against time.

The one-hit curve shown in Fig 7–3A is typical of the kinetics of inactivation observed with many antimicrobial agents. The fact that it is a straight line from time zero (dose zero)—rather than exhibiting an initial shoulder—means that a single "hit" by the inactivating agent is sufficient to kill the cell, ie, only a single target must be damaged in order for the entire cell to be inactivated. Such a target might be the chromosome of a uninucleate bacterium or the cell membrane; conversely, it could not be an enzyme or other cell constituent that is present in multiple copies.

A cell that contains several copies of the target to be inactivated exhibits a multi-hit curve of the type shown in Fig 7–3B. Extrapolation of the straight-line portion of the curve to the ordinate permits an estimate of the number of targets (eg, 4 in Fig 7–3B).

Sterilization

In practice, we speak of ''sterilization'' as the process of killing all of the organisms in a preparation. From the above considerations, however, we see that no set of conditions is guaranteed to sterilize a preparation. Consider Fig 7–3, for example. At 60 minutes, there is one organism (10^0) left per milliliter. At 70 minutes there would be 10^{-1}, at 80 minutes 10^{-2}, etc. By 10^{-2} organisms per milliliter we mean that in a total volume of 100 mL, one organism would survive. How long, then, does it take to ''sterilize'' the culture? All we can say is that after any given time of treatment, the probability of having any surviving organisms in 1 mL is that given by the curve. After 2 hours, in the above example, the probability is 1×10^{-6}. This would usually be considered a safe sterilization time, but a thousand-liter lot might still contain one viable organism.

Note that such calculations depend upon the curve's remaining unchanged in slope over the entire time range. Unfortunately, it is very common for the curve to bend upward after a certain period, as a result of the population being heterogeneous with respect to sensitivity to the inactivation agent. Extrapolations are dangerous and can lead to errors such as those encountered in early preparations of sterile poliovaccine.

The Effect of Drug Concentration

When antimicrobial substances (drugs) are used to inactivate microbial cells, it is commonly observed that the concentration of drug employed is related to the time required to kill a given fraction of the population by the following expression:

$$C^n t = K \qquad \ldots(11)$$

In this equation, C is the drug concentration, t is the time required to kill a given fraction of the cells, and n and K are constants.

This expression says that, for example, if $n = 5$ (as it is for phenol), then doubling the concentration of the drug will reduce the time required to achieve the same extent of inactivation 32-fold. That the effectiveness of a drug varies with the fifth power of the concentration suggests that 5 molecules of the drug are required to inactivate a cell, although there is no direct chemical evidence for this conclusion.

In order to determine the value of n for any drug, inactivation curves are obtained for each of several concentrations, and the time required at each concentration to inactivate a fixed fraction of the population is determined. For example, let the first concentration used be C_1 and the time required to inactivate 99% of the cells be t_1. Similarly, let C_2 and t_2 be the second concentration and time required to inactivate 99% of the cells. From equation (11), we see that

$$C_1{}^n t_1 = C_2{}^n t_2 \qquad \ldots(12)$$

Solving for n gives

$$n = \frac{\log t_2 - \log t_1}{\log C_1 - \log C_2}$$

Thus, n can be determined by measuring the slope of the line that results when $\log t$ is plotted against $\log C$ (Fig 7–4). If n is experimentally determined in this manner, K can be determined by substituting observed values for C, t, and n in equation (11).

ANTIMICROBIAL AGENTS

Definitions

The following terms are commonly employed in connection with antimicrobial agents and their uses.

A. Bacteriostatic: Having the property of inhibiting bacterial multiplication; multiplication resumes upon removal of the agent.

B. Bactericidal: Having the property of killing bacteria. Bactericidal action differs from bacteriostasis only in being irreversible; ie, the ''killed'' organism

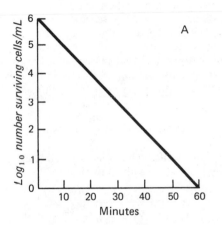

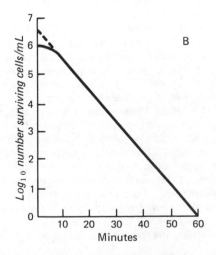

Figure 7–3. Death curve of microorganisms. *A:* Single-hit curve. *B:* Multi-hit curve. The straight-line portion extrapolates to 6.5, corresponding to 4×10^6 cells. The number of targets is thus 4×10^6, or 4 per cell.

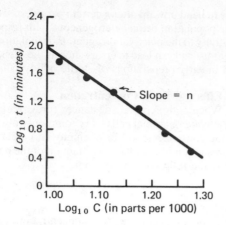

Figure 7–4. Relationship between drug concentration and time required to kill a given fraction of a cell population.

can no longer reproduce, even after being removed from contact with the agent. In some cases the agent causes lysis (dissolving) of the cells; in other cases the cells remain intact and may even continue to be metabolically active.

C. Sterile: Free of life of every kind. Sterilization may be accomplished by filtration (in the case of liquids or air) or by treatment with microbicidal agents. Since the criterion of death for microorganisms is the inability to reproduce, sterile material may contain intact, metabolizing microbial cells.

D. Disinfectant: A chemical substance used to kill microorganisms on surfaces, but too toxic to be applied directly to tissues.

E. Septic: Characterized by the presence of pathogenic microbes in living tissue.

F. Aseptic: Characterized by absence of pathogenic microbes.

Possible Modes of Action

Antibacterial agents may affect cells in a variety of ways, many of which are poorly understood. Some broad generalizations can be made, however. At high concentrations many agents are so destructive that, among other things, the cell proteins precipitate from the colloidal state ("coagulate"). Under certain conditions, some agents may specifically disrupt the cell membrane. Many of the cell's essential enzymes possess sulfhydryl (–SH) groups and can only function if these remain free and reduced; hence agents that oxidize or combine with sulfhydryl groups are strongly inhibitory. Finally, many agents may act by interfering with one or a few specific enzymatic reactions (chemical antagonism).

A. Protein Denaturation: Proteins exist in a folded, 3-dimensional state determined by intramolecular covalent disulfide linkages and a number of noncovalent linkages such as ionic, hydrophobic, and hydrogen bonds. This state is called the **tertiary structure** of the protein; it is readily disrupted by a

number of physical or chemical agents, causing the protein to become nonfunctional. The disruption of the tertiary structure of a protein is called protein denaturation.

B. Disruption of Cell Membrane or Wall: The cell membrane acts as a selective barrier, allowing some solutes to pass through and excluding others. Indeed, some compounds are actively transported through the membrane, becoming concentrated within the cell. The membrane is also the site of many enzymes involved in the biosynthesis of components of the cell envelope. Substances that concentrate at the cell surface may alter the physical and chemical properties of the membrane, preventing its normal function and therefore killing or inhibiting the cell.

The cell wall acts as a corseting structure, protecting the cell against osmotic lysis. Thus, agents that destroy the wall (eg, lysozyme) or prevent its normal synthesis (eg, penicillin) may bring about lysis of the cell.

C. Removal of Free Sulfhydryl Groups: Enzyme proteins containing cysteine have side chains terminating in sulfhydryl groups. In addition to these, at least one key coenzyme (coenzyme A, required for acyl group transfer) contains a free sulfhydryl group. Such enzymes and coenzymes cannot function unless the sulfhydryl groups remain free and reduced. Oxidizing agents thus interfere with metabolism by tying neighboring sulfhydryls in disulfide linkages:

$$R-SH + HS-R \xrightarrow{-2H} R-S-S-R$$

Many metals such as mercuric ion likewise interfere by combining with sulfhydryls:

$$\begin{matrix} R-SH \\ R-SH \end{matrix} + \begin{matrix} Cl \\ | \\ Hg \\ | \\ Cl \end{matrix} \longrightarrow \begin{matrix} R-S \\ R-S \end{matrix}\!\!\!>\!Hg + 2HCl$$

There are many sulfhydryl enzymes in the cell; therefore, oxidizing agents and heavy metals do widespread damage. The exact reason for the requirement of free sulfhydryl groups is not certain, although in many cases (eg, coenzyme A) they probably represent the normal site of substrate attachment.

D. Chemical Antagonism: The interference by a chemical agent with the normal reaction between a specific enzyme and its substrate is known as "chemical antagonism." The antagonist acts by combining with some part of the holoenzyme (either the protein apoenzyme, the mineral activator, or the coenzyme), thereby preventing attachment of the normal substrate. ("Substrate" is here used in the broad sense to include cases in which the inhibitor combines with the apoenzyme, thereby preventing attachment to it of coenzyme.)

An antagonist combines with an enzyme because of its chemical affinity for an essential site on that enzyme. Enzymes perform their catalytic function by virtue of their affinity for their natural substrates;

hence any compound structurally resembling a substrate in essential aspects may also have an affinity for the enzyme. If this affinity is great enough, the "analog" will displace the normal substrate and prevent the proper reaction from taking place.

Many holoenzymes include a mineral ion as a bridge either between enzyme and coenzyme or between enzyme and substrate. Chemicals that combine readily with these minerals will again prevent attachment of coenzyme or substrate; for example, carbon monoxide and cyanide ($-C\equiv N$) combine with the iron atom in the porphyrin enzymes and prevent their function in respiration.

Chemical antagonists can be conveniently discussed under 2 headings: antagonists of energy-yielding processes, and antagonists of biosynthetic processes. The former include poisons of respiratory enzymes (carbon monoxide, cyanide) and of oxidative phosphorylation (dinitrophenol); the latter include analogs of the building blocks of proteins (amino acids) and of nucleic acids (nucleotides). In some cases the analog simply prevents incorporation of the normal metabolite (eg, 5-methyltryptophan prevents incorporation of tryptophan into protein), and in other cases the analog replaces the normal metabolite in the macromolecule, causing it to be nonfunctional. The incorporation of *p*-fluorophenylalanine in place of phenylalanine in proteins is an example of the latter type of antagonism.

Reversal of Antibacterial Action

In the section on definitions, the point was made that bacteriostatic action is, by definition, reversible. Reversal can be brought about in several ways:

A. Removal of Agent: When cells that are inhibited by the presence of a bacteriostatic agent are removed by centrifugation, washed thoroughly in the centrifuge, and resuspended in fresh growth medium, they will resume normal multiplication.

B. Reversal by Substrate: When a chemical antagonist of the analog type forms a dissociating complex with the enzyme, it is possible to displace it by adding a high concentration of the normal substrate. Such cases are termed "competitive inhibition." The ratio of inhibitor concentration to concentration of substrate reversing the inhibition is called the **antimicrobial index;** it is usually very high (100–10,000), indicating a much greater affinity of enzyme for its normal substrate.

C. Inactivation of Agent: An agent can often be inactivated by adding to the medium a substance that combines with it, preventing its combination with cellular constituents. For example, mercuric ion can be inactivated by addition to the medium of sulfhydryl compounds such as thioglycolic acid.

D. Protection Against Lysis: Osmotic lysis can be prevented by making the medium isotonic for naked bacterial protoplasts. Concentrations of 10–20% sucrose are required. Under such conditions penicillin-induced protoplasts remain viable and continue to grow as L forms.

Resistance to Antibacterial Agents

The ability of bacteria to become resistant to antibacterial agents is an important factor in their control. The mechanisms by which resistance is acquired are discussed on p 121.

Physical Agents

A. Heat: Application of heat is the simplest means of sterilizing materials, provided the material is itself resistant to heat damage. A temperature of 100 °C will kill all but spore forms of bacteria within 2–3 minutes in laboratory-scale cultures; a temperature of 121 °C for 15 minutes is utilized to kill spores. Steam is generally used, both because bacteria are more quickly killed when moist and because steam provides a means for distributing heat to all parts of the sterilizing vessel. Steam must be kept at a pressure of 15 lb/sq in above atmospheric pressure to obtain a temperature of 121 °C; autoclaves or pressure cookers are used for this purpose. For sterilizing materials that must remain dry, circulating hot air electric ovens are available; since heat is less effective on dry material, it is customary to apply a temperature of 160–170 °C for 1 hour or more.

Under the conditions described above (ie, excessive temperatures applied for long periods of time), heat undoubtedly acts by denaturing cell proteins and by disrupting cell membranes.

B. Radiation: Ultraviolet light is sometimes used as a sterilizing agent. Its action is due in part to the production of peroxides (R–O–O–R) in the medium, which in turn act as oxidizing agents. Some of the more penetrating radiations, such as x-rays, ionize (and hence inactivate) the cell constituents through which they pass. However, some of the effect of x-ray irradiation can be traced again to peroxide formation, since cells can be partially protected by the exclusion of oxygen during irradiation.

Much of the killing action of radiation, however, is due to a direct effect on the nucleic acids of the cell. The major effect of ultraviolet absorption by DNA is the production of cross-links between neighboring pyrimidine residues (production of pyrimidine dimers).

Bacteria contain several enzymatic systems for the repair of DNA that contains pyrimidine dimers. One system, called **photoreactivation,** consists of an enzyme that cleaves the pyrimidine dimers. This enzyme is activated by visible light; hence, cells that have been "killed" by ultraviolet light can be reactivated by exposure to intense light of wavelength 400 nm. A second system is called the **excision repair** system. It requires the action of 4 enzymes operating in succession: (1) a specific endonuclease that makes single-strand cuts on either side of the dimer, excising it from the DNA; (2) a 3' exonuclease, which widens the gap in the DNA strand by sequential digestion; (3) DNA polymerase, which fills in the gap by lengthening the 3' end, using the opposite strand as template; and (4) polynucleotide ligase, which rejoins the free ends.

Both photoreactivation and excision repair function in nonreplicated DNA duplexes. Replication of DNA past an unrepaired lesion (pyrimidine dimer) will usually be lethal, since it will produce a new duplex with a gap opposite a dimer; nevertheless, one or more repair systems exist for **postreplicative repair.** One of these systems has been proposed to be recombinational: the exchange of undamaged segments between daughter duplexes. Another system, which may or may not involve recombination, is called the **error-prone repair** system because it is responsible for the mutations that are induced by ultraviolet light (see below).

The relative resistance of different bacterial strains to radiation and other agents that directly damage DNA is due to the relative effectiveness of their repair enzyme systems.

Chemical Agents

Because antibacterial agents must be safe for the host organism under the conditions employed (selective toxicity), the number of commonly used antibacterial agents is much lower than the number of cell poisons and inhibitors available. Thus cyanide, arsenic, and other poisons are not included below because of the limitations on their practical usefulness.

A. Alcohols: Compounds with the structure $R-CH_2OH$ (where R means "alkyl group") are toxic to cells at relatively high concentrations. Ethyl alcohol (CH_3CH_2OH) and isopropyl alcohol ($[CH_3]_2CHOH$) are commonly used. At the concentrations generally employed (70% aqueous solutions), they act as protein denaturants.

B. Phenol: Phenol and many phenolic compounds are strong antibacterial agents. At the high concentrations generally employed (1–2% aqueous solutions), they denature proteins.

C. Heavy Metal Ions: Mercury, copper, and silver salts are all protein denaturants at high concentrations but are too injurious to human tissues to be used in this manner. They are commonly used at very low concentrations, under which conditions they act by combining with sulfhydryl groups. Mercury can be made safer for external use by combining it with organic compounds (eg, Mercurochrome, Merthiolate). Except when used on clean skin surfaces, these organic mercurials are of doubtful practical value, since they are readily inactivated by extraneous organic matter.

D. Oxidizing Agents: Strong oxidizing agents inactivate cells by oxidizing free sulfhydryl groups. Useful agents include hydrogen peroxide, iodine, hypochlorite, chlorine, and compounds slowly liberating chlorine (chloride of lime).

E. Alkylating Agents: A number of agents react with compounds in the cell to substitute alkyl groups for labile hydrogen atoms. The 2 agents of this type that are commonly used for disinfection purposes are formaldehyde (sold as the 37% aqueous solution **formalin**) and **ethylene oxide.** Ethylene oxide gas, rendered inexplosive by mixture with 90% CO_2 or a fluorocarbon, is the most reliable disinfectant available for dry surfaces. It is extensively used for the disinfection of surgical instruments and materials, which must be placed in special vacuum chambers for the purpose.

F. Detergents: Compounds that have the property of concentrating at interfaces are called "surface-active agents," or "detergents." The interface between the lipid-containing membrane of a bacterial cell and the surrounding aqueous medium attracts a particular class of surface-active compounds, namely, those possessing both a fat-soluble group and a water-soluble group. Long chain hydrocarbons are very fat-soluble, while charged ions are very water-soluble; a compound possessing both structures will thus concentrate at the surface of the bacterial cell.

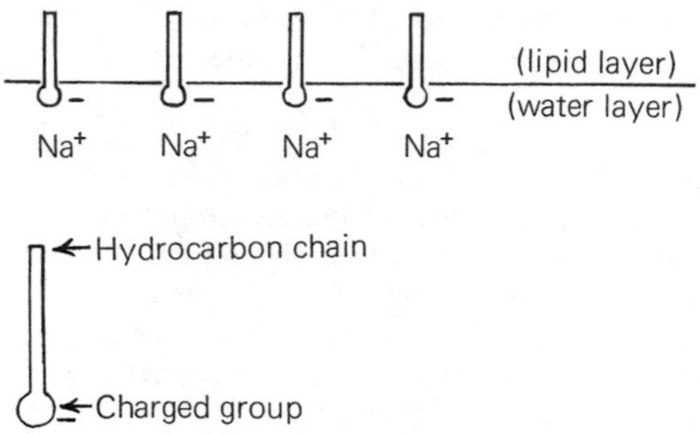

Two general types of such surface-active agents, or detergents, are known: anionic and cationic.

1. Anionic detergents–Detergents in which the long chain hydrocarbon has a negative charge are called "anionic." These include soaps (sodium salts of long chain carboxylic acids); synthetic products resembling soaps except that the carboxyl group is replaced by a sulfonic acid group; and bile salts, in which the fat-soluble portion has a steroid structure. Some examples are shown in Figs 7–6, 7–7, and 7–8.

The synthetic detergents have advantages in solubility and cost over the natural soaps (obtained by saponification of animal fat). Bile salts are notable in that they completely dissolve pneumococcal cells, thus providing an aid in identification.

2. Cationic detergents–The fat-soluble moiety can be made to have a positive charge by combining it with a quaternary (valence = +5) nitrogen atom (Fig 7–5).

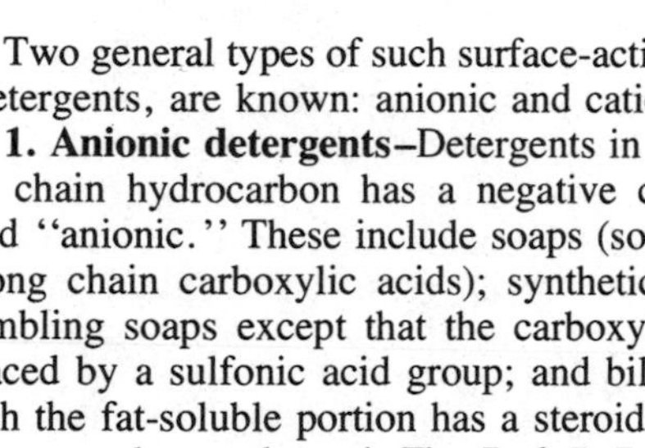

Figure 7–5. Alkyldimethylbenzylammonium chloride.

$$CH_3CH_2CH_2CH_2CH_2CH_2CH_2CH_2CH_2CH_2CH_2CH_2CH_2CH_2CH_2 \overset{\overset{\displaystyle O}{\|}}{C}-O^-Na^+$$

Figure 7–6. Sodium salt of palmitic acid (a soap).

$$CH_3CH_2CH_2CH_2CH_2CH_2CH_2CH_2CH_2CH_2CH_2CH_2 -O-\overset{\overset{\displaystyle O}{\|}}{\underset{\underset{\displaystyle O}{\|}}{S}}-O^-Na^+$$

Figure 7–7. Sodium lauryl sulfate (a synthetic anionic detergent, Duponol WA).

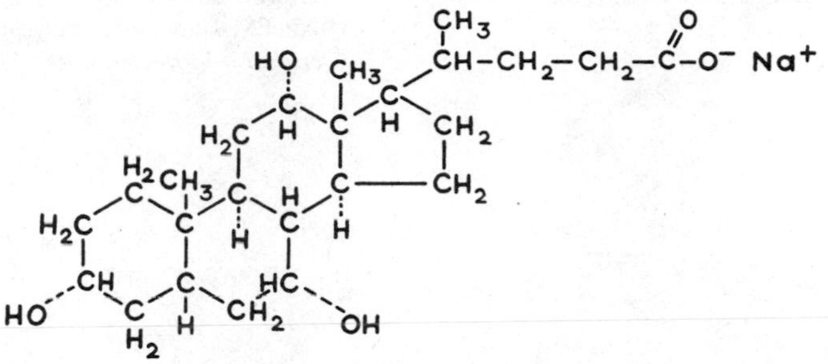

Figure 7–8. Sodium salt of cholic acid (a bile salt).

Since the detergents concentrate at the cell membrane, and since the latter is a delicate, essential cell component, the inference is drawn that detergents act by disrupting the normal function of the cell membrane. Support for this view comes from experiments showing that cells exposed to detergents leak soluble nitrogen and phosphorus compounds into the medium.

Chemotherapeutic Agents

To be a useful chemotherapeutic agent, a compound must be either bacteriostatic or bactericidal in vivo (action not reversed by substances in host tissues or fluids) and at the same time remain noninjurious to the host. These requirements for in vivo effectiveness and selective toxicity narrow the list of important chemotherapeutic agents to a very few compounds, including the sulfonamides, the antibiotics, and the antituberculosis agents.

The natures and modes of action of these drugs are discussed in Chapter 10.

Response to DNA Damage: The SOS Response

A variety of agents, both physical and chemical, produce lesions in DNA that trigger a set of reactions collectively termed "the SOS response." The process begins with the enzymatic cleavage and partial digestion of one DNA strand, leaving a single-stranded region on the other. The recA protein (product of the *recA* gene) binds to the single-stranded DNA and is converted to an active form with 2 unrelated functions: It initiates recombinational events, and it acts as a protease, cleaving certain repressors. Some of these are repressors of prophages, such as lambda; others are repressors of genes whose products are involved in DNA repair. The end result of the SOS response is thus 3-fold: (1) the rate of recombination is greatly increased; (2) prophages are induced to enter the vegetative phase (see Chapter 9); and (3) DNA repair systems are induced. One or more of these inducible repair systems is error-prone, resulting in the appearance of induced mutations (see Chapter 4).

• • •

References

Books

Gunsalus IC, Stanier RY (editors): *The Bacteria*. Vol 4: *Physiology of Growth*. Academic Press, 1962.

Hanawalt PC & others (editors): *DNA Repair Mechanisms*. Academic Press, 1978.

Hugo WB (editor): *Inhibition and Destruction of the Microbial Cell*. Academic Press, 1971.

Lawrence CA, Block SS (editors): *Disinfection, Sterilization, and Preservation*. Lea & Febiger, 1968.

Mandelstam J, McQuillen K (editors): *The Biochemistry of Bacterial Growth*, 2nd ed. Wiley, 1973.

Meynell GG, Meynell E: *Theory and Practice in Experimental Bacteriology*. Cambridge Univ Press, 1965.

Articles & Reviews

Allen JG et al: Phosphonopeptides, a new class of synthetic antibacterial agents. *Nature* 1978;**272**:56.

Lehmann AR, Bridges BA: DNA repair. *Essays Biochem* 1977;**13**:71.

Moseley BE, Williams E: Repair of damaged DNA in bacteria. *Adv Microb Physiol* 1977;**16**:99.

Novick A: Growth of bacteria. *Annu Rev Microbiol* 1955; **9**:97.

Scherbaum OH: Synchronous division of microorganisms. *Annu Rev Microbiol* 1960;**14**:283.

Senez JC: Some considerations on the energetics of bacterial growth. *Bacteriol Rev* 1962;**26**:95.

Witkin EM: Ultraviolet mutagenesis and DNA repair in *Escherichia coli*. *Bacteriol Rev* 1976;**40**:869.

WATER

Methods of Study

A. Quantitative Analysis: Bacteria cannot be accurately counted by microscopic examination unless there are at least 100 million (10^8) cells per milliliter. Natural bodies of water, however, rarely contain more than 10^5 cells per milliliter. The method employed is therefore the plate count: A measured volume of water is serially diluted (see below), following which 1 mL from each dilution tube is plated in nutrient agar and the resulting colonies counted. Since only cells able to form colonies are counted, the method is also known as the "viable count."

A typical example of serial dilution would be the following: One milliliter of the water sample is aseptically transferred by pipette to 9 mL of sterile water. The mixture is thoroughly shaken, yielding a 1:10 dilution. (For obvious reasons, this is also known as the "10^{-1}" dilution.) The process is repeated serially until a dilution is reached that contains between 30 and 300 colony-forming cells per milliliter, at which point several 1-mL samples are plated in a nutrient medium. Since the original sample may have contained up to 1 million (10^6) viable bacteria, it is necessary to dilute all the way to 10^{-5}, plate 1-mL samples from each dilution tube, and then count the colonies only on those plates containing 30–300 colonies. The reasons for these numerical limits are that with over 300 colonies the plate becomes too crowded to permit each cell to form a visible colony, whereas with below 30 colonies the percent counting error becomes too great. (The statistical error of sampling can be calculated as follows: The standard deviation of the count equals the square root of N, where N equals the average of many samples. Ninety-five percent of all samples will give counts within 2 standard deviations of the average. For example, if the average count is 36, then 95% of all samples will lie between 24 and 48 [36 ± 12]. In other words, within 95% confidence limits a sample count of 36 has an error of plus or minus 33%.) Assume that the above procedure has been carried out with the results shown in Table 8–1. The 10^{-3} dilution has a suitable number of colonies, the others being either too high or too low for accuracy. The original water sample is calculated to have contained 72,000 (72×10^3) viable cells per milliliter.

B. Qualitative Analysis: The methods of plating and enrichment culture (see Chapter 6) are used to obtain a picture of the aquatic bacterial population. Although such methods are satisfactory for general biologic studies, they are inadequate for the purpose of sanitary water analysis; this involves the detection of intestinal bacteria in water, since their presence indicates sewage pollution and the consequent danger of the spread of enteric diseases (see Chapter 18). Since any enteric bacteria would be greatly outnumbered by other types present in the water samples, a selective technique is necessary in order to detect them. Two widely used procedures for sanitary water analysis are as follows:

1. Tube method–Dilutions of a water sample are inoculated into tubes of a medium which is selective for coliform bacteria and in which all coliform bacteria but few noncoliform bacteria will form acid and gas. Such media include MacConkey's medium, which contains bile salts as inhibitors of noncoliform bacteria; lactose-containing media; and glutamate-containing media. Cultures showing both acid and gas may then be subjected to further tests to confirm the presence of *Escherichia coli* or closely related enteric gram-negative rods. Such tests include streaking cultures on a lactose-peptone agar containing eosin and methylene blue (EMB agar), on which *E coli* forms characteristic blue-black colonies with a metallic sheen; subculturing at 44 °C; and a series of diagnostic biochemical tests (see Chapter 18, p 231).

2. Membrane filtration method–A large measured volume of water is filtered through a sterilized

Table 8–1. Example of a viable count.

Dilution	Plate Count*
Undiluted	Too crowded
10^{-1}	to count
10^{-2}	510
10^{-3}	72
10^{-4}	6
10^{-5}	1

*Each count is the average of 3 replicate plates.

membrane of a type that retains bacteria on its surface while permitting the rapid passage of smaller particles and water. The membrane is then transferred to the surface of an agar plate containing a selective differential medium for coliform bacteria. Upon incubation, coliform bacteria give rise to typical colonies on the surface of the membrane. The advantages of this method are speed (the complete test takes less than 24 hours) and quantitation, the number of coliform cells being determined for a given volume of water.

Nature of the Environment & of the Bacterial Population

A. The Environment: Natural bodies of water contain nutrients in sufficient quantities to support populations of specialized groups of microorganisms. Few if any of these cause diseases in humans; the presence of human pathogens in water indicates contamination either from the soil or from the deliberate discharge of sewage.

B. The Bacterial Population: Pathogens that reach the water from soil represent organisms liberated from animal or human excrement or from the bodies of animals or humans who have died of infectious disease. Of the latter group, only the spores of the anthrax bacillus (*Bacillus anthracis*) are able to survive in the soil for a significant length of time. The major pathogens in water, then, are those originating in excreta: *Salmonella typhi* and other salmonellae, *Vibrio cholerae, Shigella dysenteriae, Escherichia*, and *Leptospira* among the bacteria; a number of enteric viruses, including infectious hepatitis and poliovirus; and the protozoon *Entamoeba histolytica*. *Francisella tularensis*, the agent of tularemia, may also be transmitted in drinking water contaminated by infected animals. Waterborne diseases may be acquired by drinking or washing food utensils in contaminated water or by eating shellfish that concentrate pathogenic microorganisms when filter-feeding in contaminated water.

When sufficiently diluted in a large body of water, coliform bacteria survive for only short periods of time; a positive test for such bacteria may usually be taken as evidence of recent contamination. Some rivers and harbors are now so polluted with sewage-derived organic nutrients, however, that coliform bacteria may not only survive but may maintain significant populations by slow multiplication.

Bacteria that enter the soil from septic tanks or other sources of human excrement are rapidly filtered out in fine soils or sandstone, but in coarse soils or in limestone formations, enteric bacteria may pollute water supplies several miles from the source of contamination. In general, contamination is limited to the upper layers of the soil; deep waters contain very low numbers of bacteria, usually of the harmless types that survive well in soil.

Control of Bacteria in Water

Bacteria are controlled in water only in connection with sanitation measures. Three problems are encountered: the sanitation of drinking water, the sanitation of swimming pools, and the purification of sewage.

A. Sanitation of Drinking Water: Since drinking water supplies may at any time become contaminated with sewage and cause an epidemic of enteric disease, water supplies for large cities are usually filtered and chlorinated. The presence of only 0.5 parts per million of free chlorine will rid the water of enteric pathogens. Before chlorination, however, the majority of the bacteria are usually removed by filtration through beds of sand. In "slow sand filters," removal of bacteria is actually accomplished by their adsorption on the gelatinous film of slime-forming microbes that builds up in the sand layers. In "rapid sand filters," chemicals are first added to coagulate organic matter and bacteria; after the precipitate is settled out or is removed mechanically, rapid filtration through clean sand completes the purification.

B. Sanitation of Swimming Pools: The rapidity with which bathers may exchange pathogenic organisms makes the sanitation of swimming pools a major problem. The problem is effectively handled by maintaining free chlorine concentrations of 0.5 parts per million. Coliform bacteria are used as indicators of pollution, as in the case of drinking water, but staphylococci of human origin persist longer than coliforms in chlorine-treated water, and their presence is thus a more sensitive indicator of pollution.

C. Sewage Purification: In modern cities, domestic sewage is pumped through a disposal plant that accomplishes the following general objectives:

1. Screening–Bulky, nondecomposable material is screened and removed (bottles, paper, boxes, gravel, etc).

2. Sludge formation–The screened sewage is allowed to settle in large tanks. The sediment, containing much of the organic matter and microorganisms, is called **sludge.** It is drained off at the bottom of the tank and separated from the supernatant, which still contains large amounts of putrescible organic matter. The sludge and supernatant are then treated separately as described below.

The amount of organic matter in the supernatant can be greatly reduced if, instead of simply allowing sludge to form by settling, an activated sludge is caused to form by aeration of the sewage. As air is forced through the sewage, a floc, or precipitate, is formed, the particles of which teem with actively oxidizing microbes. After a period of time, during which the organic matter is oxidized to a very great extent, the sludge is allowed to settle. The supernatant and part of the sludge are removed for treatment as described below, and part of the sludge is returned to the tank to activate fresh sewage.

3. Sludge digestion–The sludge obtained by either process described above consists of organic matter rich in bacteria and other microbes. It is then pumped to anaerobic tanks where fermentation is allowed to go on for weeks or months. Much of the organic matter is converted to gases (CO_2, CH_4, NH_3,

H_2, and H_2S). The methane content of the gas may be as high as 75%, and the collected gas may consequently be burned, with the production of useful heat. When fermentation is complete, the sludge is removed and disposed of in one of several ways: it may be dried and discarded or dried and sold as fertilizer (nitrogen may have to be added), or it may be pumped into a large body of water.

4. Disposal of supernatant–The supernatant, after chlorination, may be pumped into a large body of water. When none is nearby, however, the supernatant must be treated to remove remaining putrescible material as well as enteric bacteria. This is accomplished by aerating and filtering the fluid: it is sprayed over a bed of sand or broken stone, which then filters it as in the process described earlier for drinking water purification. The aeration is necessary to ensure formation of an oxidizing microbial film on the filter-bed particles.

MILK

Methods of Study

A. Quantitative Analysis: Bacteria in milk are counted either directly under the microscope or by plate count. The direct procedure has been rigidly standardized and is known as the "Breed count." The plate count method employs a medium containing skimmed milk in addition to other ingredients, ensuring maximal development of colonies of milk-inhabiting organisms.

Most procedures connected with the bacteriologic analysis of milk have been devised as tests of the safety of the product for human consumption. In addition to the counting procedures, a rough index of bacterial activity in milk is provided by the reductase test. Bacteria contain many enzymes that reduce various substrates. Various dyes are available that are susceptible to bacterial reduction ("reductase activity") and change color when reduced. These dyes thus serve as indicators; in a typical test, a standard amount of a dye such as methylene blue is added to a measured volume of milk, and the time necessary for it to change from blue to colorless is determined. Grade A raw milk that is to be pasteurized, for example, should show a reduction time under standard conditions of 6 hours or more.

B. Qualitative Analysis: The types of organisms present in milk are determined by the procedures described above for water bacteriology. Although coliform bacteria are frequently present in milk, they are derived from the cow and are not usually pathogenic for humans. They are thus not useful indicators of contamination with human pathogens.

Nature of the Environment & of the Bacterial Population

A. The Environment: Milk constitutes an ideal bacterial habitat, consisting of emulsified fat droplets and physiologic concentrations of salts, sugars, and proteins dissolved in water. Milk also contains enzymes originating in the animal. Sugar is present in the form of lactose, a disaccharide in which glucose is linked to one of its stereoisomers, galactose. The pH of fresh milk is about 6.8, which is within the optimal range for most bacteria. As normally handled (in filled containers), milk tends to be anaerobic.

B. The Bacterial Population: Because bacteria invade milk as dust-borne contaminants, almost any type may be present. Milk constitutes a typical enrichment culture medium, however, and so only the most suited types will predominate. The first organism to flourish in milk is usually *Streptococcus lactis,* which ferments the lactose principally to lactic acid. As the pH drops, other species, such as *Lactobacillus casei* and *Lactobacillus acidophilus,* may replace *S lactis* as the predominant type. If the milk is kept at body temperature, *Enterobacter (Aerobacter) aerogenes* and *Escherichia coli* may be favored.

Other organisms that may develop in milk under special conditions include anaerobic sporeformers (clostridia), *Streptococcus faecalis* and related enterococci, *Pseudomonas aeruginosa* (producing blue pigment), and lactose-fermenting yeasts. The presence of pathogens in milk is discussed below.

Ecology

A. Effect of the Environment on Bacteria: The environmental factors that most affect the bacterial population are the degree of anaerobiosis, the temperature, the presence of lactose as the principal sugar, and the pH (which drops as fermentation ensues). The selective effect of these factors has been described above.

B. Effect of Bacteria on Milk:

1. Souring–Milk, whether raw or pasteurized (see below), will sour on standing, mainly as a result of the production of lactic acid by *S lactis* or by the lactobacilli. Many dairy products are purposely allowed to sour in this way, as in the manufacture of buttermilk, butter, sour cream, yogurt, and cheese. When *E coli* or *E aerogenes* propagates, mixed acid or butylene glycol fermentations take place; these organisms produce less acidity than lactic acid bacteria but cause the production of gas and unpleasant flavors.

2. "Abnormal fermentations"–All changes due to microbial activity other than souring are referred to as "abnormal fermentations," although many of the processes involved are not fermentative. Included are gas formation by yeasts or bacteria; "ropiness," due to gum secretion by bacteria; "sweet curdling," due to secretion by bacteria of the protein-coagulating enzyme rennin; various color productions due to pigment-forming bacteria; and digestion of milk proteins and fats by bacterial enzymes (proteolytic and lipolytic).

Control of Bacteria in Milk

It has not yet proved economically feasible to sterilize milk completely except by drastic heating, and this destroys the flavor of fresh milk. (Heat sterilization is used in the production of canned evaporated milk.) However, because contaminated milk is a method of transmission of many diseases, rigid control is necessary.

A. Diseases Transmitted by Milk: Two general classes of disease may be transmitted by milk: those transmitted from the animal, the causative microbe being able to infect both animals and humans; and those transmitted from other contaminating sources, which are ultimately derived from infected persons.

1. Transmission from the animal–Tuberculosis and undulant fever are the most important of these diseases. Both are transmissible from animal to animal or from animal to human. The route from the animal's tissues to the milk is not definitely known, but it is possible that *Brucella* organisms, which cause undulant fever, may be secreted directly from the blood-stream into the udder.

Cows are also subject to infections with group A streptococci, salmonellae, *Staphylococcus aureus,* and *Coxiella burnetii,* the agent of Q fever; any of these may be shed from the udder directly into the milk, reaching densities of 10^3/mL or higher, and may cause outbreaks of disease in human populations. *S aureus* is liberated in milk by cows suffering from mastitis and produces an enterotoxin that causes a well-known type of food poisoning (see p 147).

2. Transmission from infected persons–Milk that is not handled under scrupulously clean conditions may at any time become contaminated by dust or droplets bearing pathogenic microorganisms. Still more likely is direct infection from diseased milk-handlers and dairy workers. The diseases most commonly transmitted by contaminated milk are typhoid fever and other salmonelloses; dysentery, tuberculosis, and streptococcal infections.

B. Control of Pathogenic Bacteria in Milk: Since many diseases transmitted by milk are the result of milk contamination, an obvious control measure is to insist on sanitary procedures in milk production and bottling. Communities that enforce the provisions of their own Medical Milk Commission with regard to "Certified Raw Milk" or of the USPHS with regard to "Grade A Raw Milk" supervise the production of milk under sanitary conditions. However, even the most sanitary handling procedures cannot prevent the transmission of tuberculosis or undulant fever from infected animals, and the only safe milk is therefore that which has been pasteurized. In the USA, it is the general practice to check all dairy cattle by the tuberculin test; an agglutinin test is used to detect infection with *Brucella.*

Pasteurization may be carried out by maintaining the milk at 62 °C for 30 minutes and then rapidly cooling it; this will kill all pathogenic bacteria that may be present, although many harmless forms (eg, *S lactis*) survive. Alternatively, pasteurization can be accomplished by heating an extremely thin layer of milk for 3–5 seconds at 74 °C. Pasteurization is the only procedure that renders milk absolutely safe without destroying its flavor and palatability. Even the heating processes used in producing dried milk products are insufficient to guarantee freedom from pathogens;

salmonellae have been detected in such products, and staphylococcal food poisoning outbreaks have been traced to batches of dried milk.

C. Safety Standards: A very sensitive, practical method used to determine whether milk has been properly pasteurized is known as the **phosphatase test,** which consists of quantitatively determining the activity of the enzyme phosphatase in a sample of the milk. Because this enzyme is more resistant than any pathogenic bacterium to pasteurization, its destruction indicates that the milk is safe. Phosphatase activity indicates improper pasteurization or adulteration with raw milk.

A satisfactory phosphatase test, however, does not guarantee that the milk has not become contaminated by handlers after pasteurization. To determine this, milk is analyzed for the presence of coliform organisms by the procedures described in the section on water bacteriology, above. Even a negative coliform test does not eliminate the possibility that diphtheria or streptococcal organisms may have been introduced. The best protection against this danger is the insistence on sanitary procedures of dairies and medical examination of milk handlers.

FOODS

Methods of Study

The plate count and enrichment culture methods are also used for the examination of foods. Solid food samples must be ground and suspended in liquid for dilution and plating; care must be taken to avoid introducing bacteria from other sources during preparation of the sample. Coliform analysis is carried out on food samples as well as on water and milk to determine whether fecal contamination has occurred.

Nature of the Environment & of the Bacterial Population

A. Meat: The interior of intact meat is usually sterile or nearly so unless taken from an infected animal. The surface, however, becomes contaminated from dust or from handling immediately upon dismemberment of the animal. Any organotrophic bacterium may be found, including those from soil, dung, or human handlers.

B. Ground Meat: The grinding process introduces the surface contaminants into the interior of the meat and may also warm the meat enough to encourage considerable bacterial multiplication. The interior of the meat is somewhat anaerobic, and fermentative organisms are enriched for. The number of bacteria in ground meat is so high that a count of 10 million per gram is considered a safe maximum. (Since such counts are made on aerobic plates, the many obligate anaerobes present are not included in this figure.)

C. Fish: The general picture is similar to that for unground meat, but the bacterial population will include many marine halophilic and psychrophilic forms. The "phosphorescence" of spoiling fish is due to the growth of luminescent marine bacteria (such as *Achromobacter*) on the surface.

D. Shellfish: These become contaminated during handling, but they also bear organisms acquired from their marine environment. Shellfish gathered near a sewage outlet will contain numbers of sewage bacteria, including both pathogenic enterobacteria and viruses. Outbreaks of typhoid fever have frequently arisen from the consumption of contaminated shellfish, and outbreaks of infectious hepatitis have been traced to oysters contaminated with the viral agent of this disease. Oysters are often "planted" near sewage outlets because they fatten rapidly on sewage. In recent years it has become mandatory that such oysters be transported to clean water and left there long enough to have cleansed themselves of sewage organisms before they are marketed.

E. Fruits and Vegetables: Most vegetables have a considerable surface contamination of soil organisms. Fruits acquire a surface flora through dust contamination and handling. Fruits and vegetables with tough skins are fairly proof to penetration by bacteria unless bruised; soft fruits and vegetables will spoil much more readily. Acid fruits offer a selective environment for yeasts and molds; otherwise, a typical array of soil microorganisms is found.

The number of microbial cells contaminating the surfaces of fruits and vegetables varies over a wide range. For example, on the unwashed surfaces of leafy vegetables, the count may be as high as $2 \times 10^6/g$. On the unwashed surfaces of tomatoes, counts as high as $5 \times 10^3/cm^2$ have been recorded; on washed tomatoes, the counts vary between 4 and $7 \times 10^2/cm^2$.

F. Eggs: Bacteria may be incorporated into eggs from infected ovaries or oviducts; otherwise, the interiors of eggs are usually sterile. The surface becomes contaminated immediately after laying, but penetration of the egg by bacteria is normally prevented by a dry, mucilaginous coating on the surface. This coating is easily removed, however, by washing or overhandling, in which case the interior of the egg becomes contaminated. Bacteria on eggs come from soil and from the feces of the birds. A mixed flora is common, but fermenters predominate inside the egg. Egg products, like ground meat, show the result of mixing surface contaminants throughout the material; counts are similar to those of ground meat.

G. Bread: The flour from which bread is made contains polysaccharide carbohydrates and protein; fats are added in the form of "shortening." Hydrolysis of the polysaccharides by the yeast added to make the bread rise, and partial hydrolysis of the protein by enzymes in the flour, yield a mixture that is ideal for bacterial growth. Baking kills most microorganisms, but spores of bacilli, clostridia, and fungi persist and will germinate to produce a new flora unless preservatives are added.

Ecology

A. Effect of Environment on Bacterial Population: When organisms begin to grow in food products,

selection will determine the predominant type (eg, fermentative organisms are selected for in the anaerobic interior of ground meat). Variables that most affect bacterial growth are moisture, factors permitting penetration (bruising of fruits, washing of eggs, etc), and autolysis ("self-dissolving"); as cells die, enzymes are released that dissolve cell walls and protoplasts to a variable extent depending upon the tissue and the environmental conditions. The "ripening" or "tenderizing" of meat, for example, is a result of autolysis. Autolysis results in digestion of polysaccharides, proteins, and fats, rendering the product much more susceptible to bacterial growth.

B. Effect of Bacteria on Food: The interest in food bacteriology is focused on spoilage and disease transmission. Since pathogens affect the consumer rather than the food, only spoilage need be considered here. Disease transmission is discussed below.

Spoilage is the result of microbial growth in or on food. The metabolic activity associated with growth causes both a breakdown of the food substance and the release of the products of fermentation, digestion, and other processes. Spoilage may be defined as the process by which food is rendered aesthetically unfit for human consumption. Only rarely is spoilage accompanied by actual poisoning of the food. (The term food poisoning is restricted to infection by enteric pathogens contaminating food, or ingestion of food containing exotoxins produced by staphylococci or *Clostridium botulinum*.)

Unpleasant odors and tastes are produced by "putrefactive" organisms, ie, those that digest proteins and produce H_2S, sulfhydryl compounds, or amines. These compounds, while not poisonous in the concentrations involved, have vile smells. Molds produce a musty odor and taste, and some bacteria produce great quantities of slime (as in "ropy bread"). Eggs have a high sulfur content, and their spoilage results in H_2S production, rendering them completely unpalatable.

Many fungi produce poisonous substances called **mycotoxins,** which cause serious — sometimes fatal — diseases if ingested. They also produce a variety of **hallucinogens,** such as lysergic acid. The mycotoxins of importance to humans include the toxins of the poisonous mushrooms, the toxins of *Claviceps purpurea* (ergot, a parasite of rye), and the **aflatoxins.**

The aflatoxins are produced by the fungus *Aspergillus flavus*; they are highly toxic (as well as carcinogenic) for animals. Aflatoxins have caused serious damage to livestock when their feed has become contaminated with *A flavus*. The risk to humans is unknown; there is strong circumstantial evidence, however, based on epidemiologic data, that aflatoxins may cause cirrhosis and cancer of the liver in parts of the world where human foodstuffs are subject to aflatoxin contamination (eg, India and Africa). Aflatoxins have been found in the food and in the urine of children in India who exhibited cirrhosis of the liver.

Control of Bacteria in Food

A. Prevention of Spoilage: For some foods, such as meats, much can be accomplished to prevent contamination through the use of sanitary procedures. Fruits and vegetables, however, already have a rich surface flora from their natural environment, and contamination during handling plays a relatively minor role. In the case of meat, fruit, eggs, and vegetables, it is important to prevent penetration of the food by bacteria (see above). Most effort, however, is directed toward preservative measures; the following measures are used either singly or in combination.

1. Irradiation–Ultraviolet light is used to reduce surface contamination of food materials and equipment in many types of food processing but is relatively ineffective. Irradiation with high-penetration gamma rays has proved to be much more effective and is used to extend the ''shelf life'' of packaged nonsterilized food products, including those preserved by chilling, freezing, drying, heating, or the addition of chemical preservatives.

2. Low temperature–Bacterial activity is markedly slowed at refrigeration temperatures and virtually negligible at temperatures below freezing. Refrigeration and freezing are well-known methods of food preservation and need no further discussion here.

3. Drying–Foods kept completely dry will stay preserved indefinitely, since moisture is essential to microbial activity. Examples of dried foods are hay, raisins, ''cured'' meat, powdered eggs, and powdered milk. All of these contain dormant microorganisms and will spoil if exposed to humidity.

4. Heat–A temperature of 121 °C for 15 minutes is utilized to kill heat-resistant bacterial spores. Such conditions are obtainable with steam at a pressure of 7 kg/2.5 cm² (15 lb/sq in) above atmospheric pressure. Industrial autoclaves and home pressure cookers are used for heat sterilization of canned foods.

5. Salt–Most bacteria are unable to grow at high salt concentrations. Meat and fish are often ''salt-cured'' by immersion in brine or by rubbing salt into the surface.

6. Sugar–High sugar concentrations produce osmotic pressures that are too high for most bacteria, although permitting the growth of molds. Many fruits are packed in syrup, and meat is sometimes rubbed with or mixed with sugar instead of salt (''sugar-cured'' ham).

7. Smoking–Smoke contains volatile bactericidal substances that are gradually absorbed by the meat or fish being smoked. The smoking process is slow, however, and the food is often salt-treated first to prevent spoilage early in the process.

8. Chemical preservatives–Only a few chemicals are useful preservatives at concentrations harmless to humans. Calcium propionate, for example, is used to prevent growth of molds in bread; sodium benzoate is used in cider and some vegetable products; and sulfur dioxide is used to preserve sausages, pickles, and soft fruits used in the manufacture of jams, jellies, and alcoholic beverages. Nitrites, used in the curing of meats, are bacteriostatic. Sorbic acid, a 6-carbon unsaturated fatty acid, and sorbates are used as fungistatic agents in various foods, particularly cheeses.

9. Acids–Many foods that are soured for the purpose of flavor are thereby preserved, since few bacteria can tolerate the pH values produced by the lactic acid or acetic acid bacteria. Examples are buttermilk, pickles, sauerkraut, and vinegar.

B. Prevention of Disease Transmission: Since few of the preservative measures listed above are bactericidal, it is essential that pathogenic organisms be prevented from contaminating food. The infectious diseases transmissible by food are *Shigella* and *Salmonella* infections, dysentery, and streptococcal infection. Salmonellae other than *S typhi* are widespread contaminants of poultry and eggs in the USA.

The principal bacterial toxins that may be produced in food and cause poisoning are those of staphylococci, *Clostridium perfringens*, *Clostridium botulinum*, *Escherichia coli*, *Vibrio parahaemolyticus*, and *Bacillus cereus*. *C botulinum* is an obligate anaerobe; it is usually found in improperly sterilized canned foods. Since the canning industry now observes rigid standards of sterilization, most cases of botulism arise from home-canned foods, although outbreaks of botulism from ingestion of commercially canned foods have occurred recently. Proper methods of autoclaving (pressure-cooking) foods can prevent botulism. Although foods suspected of containing botulinus toxin can probably be made safe by boiling for more than 20 minutes at 100 °C, the extreme potency of the toxin suggests that no reliance should be placed on this procedure and that suspect foods should be discarded.

Staphylococci grow well in meats and dairy products, where they produce a potent exotoxin. This can usually be prevented by careful refrigeration and sanitary measures to prevent their introduction into foods.

Typhoid fever, *Salmonella* infections, and dysentery are enteric diseases transmitted by fecal contamination of food. They are preventable only by rigid sanitation control and medical examination of food handlers. *Salmonella* infection may also be acquired by the ingestion of meat or eggs from infected animals.

AIR

The air does not constitute a microbial habitat; microbial cells exist in the air as accidental contaminants or as air-dispersed fungal spores. Many pathogens are transmitted through the air on dust particles or on the dry residues of saliva droplets, and control measures are attempted for this reason.

Types of Infectious Particles

In addition to naturally dispersed fungal spores, pathogenic microorganisms occur in the air associated with 2 types of particles: the residues of evaporated exhalation droplets (**droplet nuclei**), and the much

Table 8–2. Characteristics of and control measures for airborne infections.

	Droplet Nuclei	Dust Particles
Source of particles in air	Evaporation of droplets expelled from the respiratory tract by sneezing, coughing, and talking (in decreasing order of effectiveness).	Movements that cause the shedding of particles from skin and clothing; air turbulence sufficient to redistribute previously settled dust.
Settling behavior	Remain suspended indefinitely as a result of minor air turbulence (average settling velocity in still air, 1.2 cm/min).	Settle rapidly to the ground (average settling velocity, 46 cm/min). Redistributed by major air turbulence.
Organisms per particle	Rarely more than one.	Usually many.
Access to susceptible tissues and significance in disease	Deposited in lungs; probably responsible for most pulmonary infections.	Deposited on external surfaces and in upper respiratory tract.
Epidemiologic characteristics	Propagated epidemics (disease transmitted serially from person to person).	Epidemics associated with specific places as reservoirs of infection.
Control measures	Ventilation; ultraviolet irradiation of the air; evaporation of glycols.	Prevention of accumulation of infectious material (eg, by sterilization of clothing and bedding); prevention of dispersal (eg, by oiling of floors and bedding, and by proper design of ventilation system).

larger **dust particles.** These 2 types of particles are very different with respect to their source, their settling behavior, their significance in disease, and the methods that must be used to assess them and to control them. Some of these differences are summarized in Table 8–2.

Viability of Airborne Organisms

Both dust-borne and droplet nuclei–borne organisms lose viability in air, and the kinetics of survival are similar to those shown in Fig 7–3. Usually the curve changes slope sharply, revealing the presence of a more resistant fraction, even in experiments dealing with a single type of organism. The presence of 2 populations with different death rates probably reflects differences in the microenvironments of the particles rather than genetic differences in the organisms. The death rates are markedly affected by the humidity and temperature of the air, and there are great differences in death rates among different species of organisms. In general, organisms that are normally airborne (eg, *Mycobacterium tuberculosis*) are more resistant to inactivation than organisms that are normally waterborne (eg, *E coli*).

Epidemiology of Droplet Nuclei-Borne Infections

In propagated epidemics, succeeding crops of cases, or "generations," occur as a result of the incubation period that intervenes between successive cases. At each generation, the relationship between the number of new cases (C), the number of infectors (I), and the number of susceptibles (S) is given by the equation*

$$C = KIS \qquad \ldots(1)$$

where K is a constant representing the effective contact rate.

*The equations in this section are from Riley R, O'Grady F: *Airborne Infection.* Macmillan, 1961.

For droplet nuclei–borne infections, K is related to the volume of air (s) breathed by a susceptible, the number of infectious doses (i) liberated by an infector, and the volume of air (V) that passes through the space in which contact occurs, all measured over the same interval of time, by the equation

$$K = si/V \qquad \ldots(2)$$

For an epidemic to occur, C/I must exceed 1; the greater the ratio C/I, the more severe the epidemic. Since equation (1) can be rearranged as

$$C/I = KS \qquad \ldots(3)$$

it is seen that the severity of an epidemic is directly proportionate to K, the effective contact rate, and to S, the number of susceptibles.

These simple equations have been used to make some illuminating calculations. For example, in a measles epidemic occurring in a school where contact took place only in a well-defined classroom area, K was estimated by equation (1) to be 0.1. Since both s and V were known, i could be calculated from equation (2); it was found to be 270. Thus, each infector liberated enough measles virus to infect 270 persons. This represented about one infectious dose per 3000 cubic feet of air, which was the volume breathed by 10 children during the time interval used for the calculation. Thus, under such conditions, one child in 10 could be expected to be infected. (Since, however, the distribution of particles in air is random, there is about one chance in 3 under such conditions that no child would be infected. Chance thus may play a significant part in deciding whether an epidemic will occur.)

Epidemiology of Infections Associated With Air-Dispersed Fungal Spores

A number of serious respiratory diseases (mycoses) result from the inhalation of fungal cells that have been dispersed as airborne spores or as contaminants of airborne dust particles. These diseases include infections with *Coccidioides immitis, Histoplasma capsulatum,* and *Blastomyces dermatitidis* (see Chapter 25). Fungal cells are also the agents of a number of occupational allergic diseases: Farmer's lung, for example, is a form of allergic alveolitis caused by thermophilic actinomycetes growing in moldy hay, and a significant percentage of farmers working with harvested grain develop allergies to a variety of fungal spores.

Control of Indoor Airborne Infections

Some control measures for dust-borne infections are indicated in Table 8–2. The accumulation of infectious organisms on fabrics can be minimized by a bactericidal rinse at the end of the laundering process or by heat sterilization when feasible. The dispersal of dust can be minimized by the oiling or other wetting of blankets and floors; however, the design of the ventilation system often limits what can be accomplished by such measures.

The control measures for droplet nuclei-borne infections include the following:

A. Sanitary Ventilation: If equations (2) and (3) above are combined, it is found that

$$C/I = si/V_s \qquad \ldots (4)$$

where V_s is the volume of air per susceptible. Thus, the severity of an epidemic as well as its probability of being initiated (which is proportionate to C/I) is inversely proportionate to V_s. In order to achieve a value of C/I less than 1, the corresponding V_s may require one **air change per minute** under ordinary circumstances of room size and occupancy. This is more than 5 times that supplied by ordinary ventilation systems. A very large improvement can be achieved by the use of laminar flow ventilation systems.

B. Ultraviolet Irradiation: The use of ultraviolet light can accomplish the equivalent of one air change per minute by the killing of airborne organisms. This can be done either by installing high-intensity ultraviolet lamps in the air supply ducts or by irradiating the air in the upper levels of the room by indirect lamps. The latter method requires good mixing of upper and lower air, but this condition does obtain in many situations. Ultraviolet barriers, or "curtains," can also be set up at room entrances so that personnel can pass through quickly and avoid radiation injury.

C. Chemical Disinfection: Propylene glycol and some related compounds are effective germicides in the vapor phase. They presumably act by condensing on droplet nuclei and dehydrating the nuclei-borne organisms. This method is only successful within a narrow range of relative humidities and is therefore not always reliable.

D. Evaluation: Control measures against dust-borne and droplet nuclei-borne infections must be separately evaluated by methods that assay only the appropriate particles. The best criterion of success is the lowering of the incidence of disease; in practice,

however, it is almost impossible to design valid controls for comparison. For this reason, there are very few data that permit a valid evaluation of the efficacies of the methods listed above, and in some trials neither ultraviolet irradiation systems nor chemical vapor disinfection was found to reduce the incidence of airborne infections.

When the data indicate that a control measure has failed, it can mean either that the transmission route being controlled is not significant in the spread of the disease being studied or that the exposure to the disease is taking place outside of the controlled area.

SOIL

The earth is covered with green plants that rapidly convert nitrate, sulfate, and CO_2 into organic matter. The plants die—or are eaten by animals that in turn die—and so return the elements to the soil in organic form. The nitrogen and sulfur are then present principally as the amino ($-NH_2$) and sulfhydryl ($-SH$) groups of proteins; the carbon is present principally in the form of the reduced "carbon skeletons" of carbohydrates, proteins, fats, and nucleic acids.

Without a mechanism for the "mineralization" of these elements, the surface of the earth would long ago have been depleted of the nitrate, sulfate, and CO_2 needed for plant growth, and life on the earth would have ceased. But, as we have seen in the previous sections on metabolism, such a mechanism does exist in the form of microbial metabolic activities. Thus, nitrogen, sulfur, and carbon are constantly undergoing cycles of transformation from the oxidized, inorganic state to the reduced, organic state and back again.

One other major element, phosphorus (as phosphate), is converted to organic form during plant growth, being incorporated chiefly into nucleic acids. On return to the soil, nucleic acids are hydrolyzed by microbial enzymes, again liberating free phosphate. No oxidation or reduction is involved.

These cycles, and hence all life on earth, are completely dependent on the metabolic activities of soil microorganisms. A gram of typical fertile soil contains on the order of several million bacteria, a million fungal spores, 50,000 algae, and 25,000 protozoa. The top 6 inches of such soil may contain more than 2 tons of microorganisms per acre.

The Nitrogen Cycle (See Fig 8–1.)

A. Decomposition: The proteins of organic matter are digested by many microorganisms to free amino acids, from which ammonia (NH_3) is then liberated by deamination. Urea, the principal form in which higher animals excrete nitrogen, is hydrolyzed to NH_3 and CO_2 by various urea-decomposing bacteria.

B. Oxidation of Ammonia: Soil rich in ammonia from decomposing organic matter is abundantly occupied by cells of *Nitrosomonas*, which obtain their energy for growth by oxidizing NH_3 to nitrite (NO_2^-). As nitrite is formed, the *Nitrobacter* cells that are

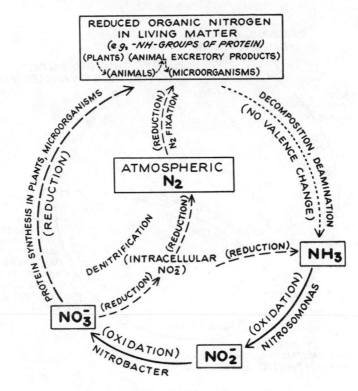

Figure 8–1. The nitrogen cycle.

present multiply and convert the nitrite to nitrate (NO_3^-).

C. Nitrate Reduction and Denitrification: Nitrate serves as the final hydrogen acceptor for various anaerobic bacteria, being reduced by some to NH_3 and by others to gaseous N_2. In the former case no nitrogen is lost from the soil, since the ammonia usually stays in solution as ammonium ion (NH_4^+); N_2 escapes, however, and the latter process is hence termed "denitrification."

D. Conversion of Nitrate to Organic Nitrogen: Green plants, as well as many microorganisms, convert nitrate to organic nitrogen and reduce it once again to amino groups, thus completing the cycle.

E. Nitrogen Fixation: One other important source of nitrogen is the atmosphere. Atmospheric nitrogen is reduced to organic nitrogen by nitrogen-fixing bacteria, balancing the losses due to denitrification. This process, although a reduction, is not a mechanism for anaerobic respiration but rather a means of obtaining nitrogen. Many nitrogen fixers, in fact, are aerobes. Two types of fixation are distinguished; symbiotic and nonsymbiotic (see p 67).

The Sulfur Cycle (See Fig 8–2.)

A. Decomposition: Following digestion, the sulfur-containing amino acids are broken down by many microorganisms, and in the process H_2S is released.

B. Oxidation of H_2S to Free Sulfur: H_2S spon-taneously oxidizes to S in the presence of oxygen; in addition, it is oxidized as an energy source by certain chemolithotrophs and as a hydrogen donor by some photosynthetic bacteria.

C. Oxidation of S to SO_4^{2-}: Certain chemolithotrophs and photosynthetic bacteria oxidize sulfur to sulfate.

D. Conversion of Sulfate to Organic Sulfur: This process is analogous to the conversion of nitrate to organic nitrogen in the nitrogen cycle.

E. Sulfate Reduction: *Desulfovibrio* uses SO_4^{2-} as the final hydrogen acceptor in anaerobic respiration.

The Carbon Cycle (See Fig 8–3.)

The valence changes of carbon are frequently associated with valence changes of oxygen, hence the inclusion of an "oxygen cycle." Since anaerobic respiration of organic matter may involve electron transfer from carbon to sulfate or nitrate, the sulfur and nitrogen cycles are also "geared" to the carbon cycle. By "gearing" we mean that the organic carbon oxidation is coupled with a reduction of nitrate or sulfate by electron transfer.

A. Green Plant Photosynthesis and Aerobic Oxidation: For each molecule of CO_2 reduced in photosynthesis, one molecule of O_2 is produced from H_2O. This process just balances the reduction of O_2 to H_2O in aerobic oxidations, so that the oxygen content of the atmosphere remains remarkably constant at about 20%.

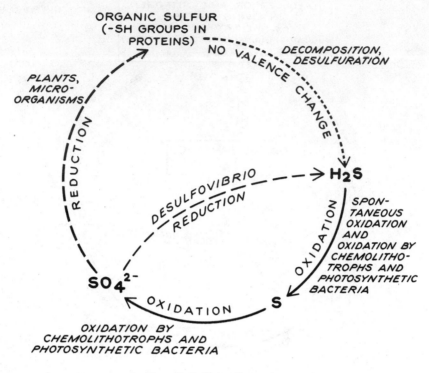

Figure 8–2. The sulfur cycle.

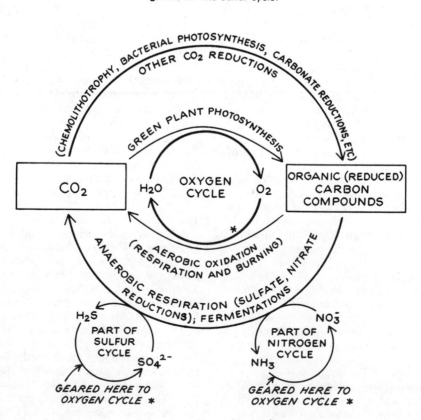

Figure 8–3. The carbon cycle.

MICRO – EXAM II

- Strep
- Staph
- Neisseriae
- Hemophilus ; Bordetella
- Zoonotic Dis's.
- Gr(+) Rods.
- Mycobact.
- (Phagocytosis)

B. Other CO_2 Reductions: A relatively small amount of CO_2 is reduced to organic carbon by processes that do not result in the formation of oxygen. These processes include chemolithotrophic reduction, bacterial photosynthesis, carbonate reduction in anaerobic respiration, and CO_2 fixations in chemoorganotrophic nutrition.

C. Anaerobic Respiration: Anaerobic organotrophs oxidize carbon compounds to CO_2 with nitrate, sulfate, or organic molecules as electron acceptors. When nitrate or sulfate is reduced, their respective cycles are affected; reoxidation of the nitrogen and sulfur is usually accomplished aerobically, causing a half-turn of the oxygen cycle.

● ● ●

References

Books

Alexander M: *Microbial Ecology.* Wiley, 1971.

Graham HD (editor): *The Safety of Foods,* 2nd ed. Avi, 1980.

Gregory PH: *The Microbiology of the Atmosphere,* 2nd ed. Wiley, 1973.

Gregory PH, Monteith JL (editors): *Airborne Microbes.* Cambridge Univ Press, 1967.

Hawker LE, Linton AH: *Micro-organisms: Function, Form and Environment,* 2nd ed. University Park Press, 1979.

Hers JFP, Winkler KC (editors): *Airborne Transmission and Airborne Infection: 6th International Symposium on Aerobiology.* Wiley, 1973.

Hugo WB (editor): *Inhibition and Destruction of the Microbial Cell.* Academic Press, 1971.

Jay JM: *Modern Food Microbiology,* 2nd ed. Van Nostrand, 1978.

Lawrence CA, Block SS (editors): *Disinfection, Sterilization, and Preservation.* Lea & Febiger, 1968.

Lynch JM, Poole NJ: *Microbial Ecology: A Conceptual Approach.* Wiley, 1979.

Riley R, O'Grady F: *Airborne Infection.* Macmillan, 1961.

Stanier RY, Adelberg EA, Ingraham JL: *The Microbial World,* 4th ed. Prentice-Hall, 1976.

Tyrell DAJ: *Airborne Microbes.* Cambridge Univ Press, 1967.

Articles & Reviews

Cosgrove DJ: Microbial transformations in the phosphorus cycle. *Adv Microb Physiol* 1977;**1**:95.

Diet and aflatoxin toxicity. *Nutr Rev* 1971;**29**:181.

Focht DD, Verstraete W: Biochemical ecology of nitrification and denitrification. *Adv Microb Ecology* 1977;**1**:135.

La Rivière JWM: Microbial ecology of liquid waste treatment. *Microb Ecology* 1977;**1**:215.

Nakamura M, Schulze JA: *Clostridium perfringens* food poisoning. *Annu Rev Microbiol* 1970;**24**:359.

Stark AA: Mutagenicity and carcinogenicity of mycotoxins: DNA binding as a possible mode of action. *Annu Rev Microbiol* 1980;**34**:235.

Taber WA: Wastewater microbiology. *Annu Rev Microbiol* 1976;**30**:263.

Wogan GN: Aflatoxin risks and control measures. *Fed Proc* 1968;**27**:932.

9 | Bacteriophage

Bacteria are host to a special group of viruses called bacteriophage, or "phage." Although any given phage is highly host-specific, it is probable that every known type of bacterium serves as host to one or more phages. Phages have not been successfully used in therapy. They are important, however, because they furnish ideal materials for studying host-parasite relationships, virus multiplication, and molecular genetics.

LIFE CYCLES OF PHAGE & HOST

Fig 9–1 summarizes the potential life cycles of bacterial cells infected with double-stranded DNA phages. Single-stranded DNA phages and RNA phages are discussed in later sections.

Fig 9–1 shows the following:

(1) Life cycle of uninfected bacterium: An uninfected bacterium may reproduce by binary fission, showing no involvement with phage.

(2) Adsorption of free phage: When an uninfected bacterium is exposed to free phage, infection will take place if the cell is sensitive. Bacteria may also be genetically resistant to phage infection; such cells lack the necessary receptors on their surfaces. (Contrast this with "immunity" due to the presence of prophage. See p 113.)

When infection takes place, the phage is adsorbed onto the cell surface and the nucleic acid of the phage

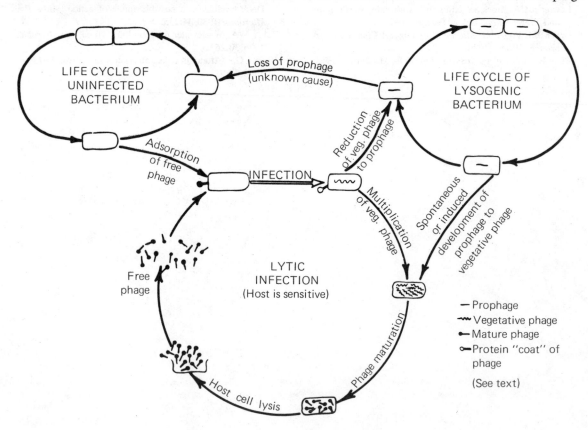

Figure 9–1. Phage-host life cycles.

penetrates the cell. In this state, the phage nucleic acid is called "vegetative phage."

(3) Lytic infection: The injected vegetative phage material may be reproduced, forming many replicas. These mature by acquisition of protein coats, following which the host cell lyses and free phage is liberated.

(4) Reduction of vegetative phage to prophage: Many phages, termed "temperate," are capable of reduction to prophage as an alternative to producing a lytic infection. The bacterium is now lysogenic (see pp 112–114); after an indeterminate number of cell divisions, one of its progeny may lyse and liberate infective phage.

(5) Loss of prophage: Occasionally a lysogenic bacterium may lose its prophage, remaining viable as an uninfected cell.

METHODS OF STUDY

Assay

Since phages (like all viruses) multiply only within living cells, and since their size precludes direct observation except with the electron microscope, it is necessary to follow their activities by indirect means. For this purpose, advantage is taken of the fact that one phage particle introduced into a crowded layer of dividing bacteria on a nutrient agar plate will produce a more or less clear zone of lysis in the opaque film of bacterial growth. This zone of lysis is called a "plaque"; it results from the fact that the initially infected host cell bursts (lyses) and liberates dozens of new phage particles, which then infect neighboring cells. This process is repeated cyclically until bacterial growth on the plate ceases as a result of exhaustion of nutrients and accumulation of toxic products. When handled properly, each phage particle produces one plaque, any material containing phage can thus be titrated by making suitable dilutions and plating measured samples with an excess of sensitive bacteria. The plaque count is analogous to the colony count for bacterial titration.

Isolation & Purification

In order to study the physical and chemical properties of phage, it is necessary to prepare a large batch of purified virus as free as possible of host cell material. For this purpose, a liquid culture of the host bacterium is inoculated with phage and incubated until the culture is completely lysed. The now clear culture fluid, or lysate, contains in suspension only viral particles and bacterial debris. These materials are easily separated from each other by differential centrifugation. The centrifuged pellet of phage material can be resuspended and washed in the centrifuge as often as needed and may then be used for chemical and physical analysis in the laboratory or for electron microscopy.

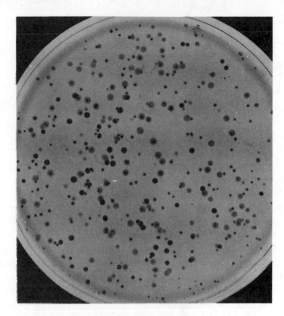

Figure 9–2. Different phage plaque types. (Courtesy of Stent GS.)

PROPERTIES OF PHAGE

One group of phages has been studied more extensively than any other: certain phages that attack *Escherichia coli* strain B (coliphages). Of the numerous coliphages, 7 have been selected for intensive study. Unless otherwise noted, the information given below applies to this group, which has been numbered T1 through T7.

Morphology

A typical phage particle consists of a "head" and a "tail." The head represents a tightly packed core of nucleic acid surrounded by a protein coat, or capsid. The protein capsid of the head is made up of identical subunits, packed to form a prismatic structure, usually hexagonal in cross section. The smallest known phage has a head diameter of 25 nm; others range from 55 × 40 nm up to 100 × 70 nm.

The phage tail varies tremendously in its complexity from one phage to another. The most complex tail is found in phage T2 and in a number of other coli and typhoid phages. In these phages, the tail consists of at least 3 parts: a hollow core, ranging from 6 to 10 nm in width; a contractile sheath, ranging from 15 to 25 nm in width; and a terminal base-plate, hexagonal in shape, to which may be attached prongs, tail fibers, or both. Electron micrographs of phage preparations embedded in electron-dense material such as phosphotungstate show the phages to exist in 2 states: in one, the head contrasts highly with the medium, the sheath is expanded, and the base-plate appears to have a series of prongs. In the second state, the head is of low contrast, the sheath is contracted, and the base-plate is now revealed to have 6 fibers attached to it. The

PHAGE T2

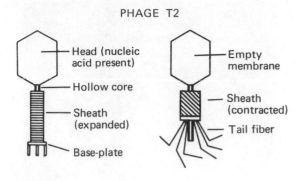

Figure 9–3. Diagrams of phage T2 based on electron micrographic observation.

former state presumably represents active phage, containing nucleic acid; the latter state presumably represents phage that has ejected its nucleic acid (eg, into a host cell). These 2 states are diagrammed in Fig 9–3.

A number of other tail morphologies have been reported. In some of these, sheaths are visible but the contracted state has not been observed; and in one case no sheath can be seen. The phages also vary with respect to the terminal structure of the tail: some have base-plates, some have "knobs," and some appear to lack specific terminal structures.

The phage tail is the adsorption organ for those phages that possess them. Some phages lack tails altogether; in the RNA phages, for example, the capsid is a simple icosahedron.

Although most phages have the head-and-tail structure described above, some **filamentous phages** have been discovered that possess a very different morphology. One of these, called "fd," has been characterized in some detail. It is a rod-shaped structure measuring 6 nm in diameter and 800 nm in length. It contains DNA and protein, which are complexed in a manner that is not completely understood. The DNA may be intertwined with the protein, rather than forming a core.

Chemistry

Phage particles contain only protein and one kind of nucleic acid. Most phages contain only DNA; however, phages that contain only RNA are also known. In the T-even phages, the nucleic acid makes up about 50% of the dry weight and consists of a single molecule (called the phage chromosome) with a molecular weight of 1.3×10^8, sufficient to code for about 200 different proteins of molecular weight 30,000. In phages T2, T4, and T6, a unique base (hydroxymethylcytosine) is present to which are attached short chains of glucose units. This pyrimidine has never been found in the nucleic acid of the uninfected bacterial host.

The proteins that make up the head, the core, the sheath, and the tail fibers are distinct from each other; in each case, the structure appears to be made of repeating subunits.

An unusual phage called PM2 has been isolated from a culture of a marine pseudomonad. PM2 is a double-stranded DNA phage in which the virion is surrounded by a lipoprotein membrane and contains 2 enzymes: an endonuclease that converts the phage DNA to the linear form within the host, and a DNA-dependent RNA polymerase.

PHAGE REPRODUCTION

Adsorption

The kinetics of phage adsorption have been thoroughly analyzed, and the process has been shown to be a first-order reaction; the rate of adsorption is proportional to the concentration of both the phage and the bacterium. Under optimal conditions, the observed rates are compatible with the assumption that almost every collision between phage and host cell results in adsorption. If the bacteria are mixed with an excess of phage, adsorption will continue until as many as 300 particles are adsorbed per cell.

Before the phage can be adsorbed onto the host cell, the phage surface must be modified by attachment of positively charged cations (the nature and number of cations varying from one phage to another) and, in some cases, the amino acid tryptophan. Each phage is quite specific with regard to the cofactors required for adsorption.

The bacterial surface, ie, the cell wall, is complex and heterogeneous. In gram-negative bacteria, there appear to be 3 distinct layers: an inner layer composed of peptidoglycan, the outer membrane, and lipopolysaccharide (see Chapter 2). Different bacterial strains are highly specific with regard to the phages that they will adsorb. For example, a strain able to adsorb phages T2, T4, and T6 can give rise to mutants unable to adsorb one or another of these viruses. This specificity has been found to reside in the cell wall; when cell walls are isolated and purified, they exhibit the same adsorption patterns as the cells from which they are prepared. The factors in the cell wall responsible for adsorption appear to be discrete, localized "receptors"; the receptors for phages T3, T4, and T7 reside in the lipopolysaccharide layer, whereas the receptors for phages T2 and T6 reside in the outer membrane. Ability to adsorb phage is obviously a factor in the determination of bacterial sensitivity to infection.

In certain phages (eg, phages T2, T4, T6), the attachment of phage particles (or of empty phage capsids) causes a profound change in the cell membrane: at low phage multiplicities, the membrane becomes permeable to small molecules; and at high multiplicities the cell lyses ("lysis from without"). Even a single phage or ghost particle will affect the membrane, causing not only a permeability change but also the inhibition of host DNA and protein synthesis.

Penetration

Phages with contractile tails, such as the T-even

phages (Fig 9–3), behave as hypodermic syringes, injecting the phage DNA into the cell. In phage T4, it has been found that the triggering of DNA injection requires the maintenance of a membrane potential by the host cell.

The filamentous DNA phages penetrate the host cell by a different mechanism. The entire phage structure penetrates the cell wall; the major protein of the phage coat is then deposited on the cell membrane, which is penetrated by the phage DNA. A minor coat protein enters the cytoplasm along with the DNA.

Intracellular Development of DNA Phages

Some phages always lyse their host cells shortly after infection, generally in a matter of minutes and usually before the host cell can divide again. (See "lytic infection" cycle in Fig 9–1.) The process of intracellular development is as follows:

(1) For several minutes following infection (eclipse period), active phage is not detectable by artificially induced premature lysis (eg, by sonic oscillation). During this period, a number of new proteins ("early proteins") are synthesized. These include certain enzymes necessary for the synthesis of phage DNA: a new DNA polymerase, new kinases for the formation of nucleoside triphosphates, and a new thymidylate synthetase. The T-even phages (T2, T4, T6), which incorporate hydroxymethylcytosine instead of cytosine into their DNA, also cause the appearance of a series of enzymes needed for the synthesis of hydroxymethylcytosine, as well as an enzyme that destroys the deoxycytidine triphosphate of the host. Later on in the eclipse period, "late proteins" appear, which include the subunits of the phage head and tail as well as lysozyme that degrades the peptidoglycan layer of the host cell wall. All of these enzymes and phage proteins are synthesized by the host cell using the genetic information provided by the phage DNA.

(2) During the eclipse period, up to several hundred new phage chromosomes are produced; as fast as they are formed, they undergo random exchanges of genetic material (see below).

In many phages, the linear DNA molecule that enters the cell has cohesive ends consisting of short complementary base sequences. Base pairing of these cohesive ends converts the DNA from the linear to the circular form; circularization is completed by a ligase-catalyzed sealing of the single-stranded gaps. Replication then occurs in the circular state, by either a simple-circle or a rolling-circle mechanism.

(3) The protein subunits of the phage head and tail aggregate spontaneously (self-assemble) to form the complete capsid. In the case of a complex capsid such as that of phage T4, capsid formation results from the coming together of 3 independent subassembly lines: one each for the head, the tail, and the tail fibers. Each subassembly proceeds in a defined sequence of protein additions.

(4) Maturation consists of irreversible combination of phage nucleic acid with a protein coat. The mature particle is a morphologically typical infectious virus and no longer reproduces in the cell in which it was formed. If the cells are artificially lysed late in the eclipse period, immature phage particles are found in which the DNA and protein are not yet irreversibly attached, so that the DNA is easily removed.

Lysis & Liberation of New Phage

Phage synthesis continues until the cell disintegrates, liberating infectious phage. The cell bursts as a result of osmotic pressure after the cell wall has been weakened by the phage lysozyme. (The exceptions are the filamentous DNA phages, in which the mature virus particles are extruded through the cell wall without killing the host.)

REPLICATION OF RNA PHAGES

When a molecule of viral RNA enters the cytoplasm of the host cell, it is immediately recognized as messenger RNA by the ribosomes, which bind to it and initiate its translation into viral proteins. One such viral protein is a complex enzyme, RNA polymerase. This enzyme brings about the replication of the viral RNA: it polymerizes the ribonucleoside triphosphates of adenine, guanine, cytosine, and uracil, using viral RNA as template.

The first step in the process of RNA replication is the formation of double-stranded intermediates, in which the entering viral RNA strand (called the "plus" strand) is hydrogen-bonded to the complementary "minus" strand synthesized by the polymerase. The polymerase now uses the double-stranded molecule as a template for the repeated synthesis of new plus strands, each new plus strand displacing the previous one from the double-stranded intermediate.

As the newly synthesized plus strands are released from the replicative intermediate, they are either used by the polymerase to form a new double-stranded intermediate or are assembled into mature virions by the attachment of coat protein subunits.

The complete nucleotide sequence of one RNA phage, MS2, has been determined. It is a single molecule, 3566 nucleotides in length, and contains 3 functional genes coding respectively for the RNA polymerase, the coat protein, and a second protein called the "A protein." The single-stranded RNA molecule is capable of folding back on itself and forming double-stranded regions by base-pairing; the secondary structure that results appears to play a major role in the regulation of viral RNA replication and translation.

PHAGE GENETICS

Phage particles exhibit the same 2 fundamental genetic properties that are characteristic of organized cells: general stability of type and a low rate of heritable variation (see Chapter 4).

Phage Mutation

All phage properties are controlled by phage genes and are subject to change through gene mutation. The mechanisms of gene mutation described in Chapter 4 apply equally well to phages; indeed, most of our knowledge concerning the chemical basis of mutation comes from studies on phage genetics.

Phage Recombination

If a bacterium simultaneously adsorbs 2 related but slightly different DNA phage particles, both can infect and reproduce; on lysis, the cell releases both types. When this occurs, many of the progeny are observed to be recombinants. Recombination takes place between pairs of phage DNA molecules and is repeated many times between different, random pairs of replicating phage DNA before maturation. Three-way recombinants are therefore possible in a cell simultaneously infected with 3 parental phage types.

Genetic Maps

The relative positions on the phage chromosome of mutant loci involved in phage structure or phage reproduction can be determined by a combination of genetic and physical mapping procedures. In genetic mapping, 2 different mutants are propagated simultaneously in the same host cell, and the frequency of their recombination is measured: the lower the frequency, the shorter the distance between the 2 loci. In physical mapping, heteroduplexes are made between single strands of DNA from normal phage and deletion mutants; examination in the electron microscope reveals the location of the deletion in the form of a non–base–paired region.

Some procedures have been used to produce detailed maps of phage chromosomes. An example of such a map is given in Fig 9–5 for the phage λ. The genes lettered A–W on the map were originally identified as conditional lethal mutations that were suppressed in a host strain carrying a particular suppressor gene; their functions were later identified by electron microscopy and biochemical analyses.

Phage genomes vary widely in size. The smallest known phage genome, that of the RNA phage MS2, has only 3 genes, as described above. In contrast, the largest phages contain sufficient DNA to code for about 200 proteins of average size; genes are present for coat proteins, morphogenesis, enzymes and regulators of phage replication, glycosylation of phage DNA, inhibitors of host restriction enzymes, enzymes that degrade host DNA, DNA repair enzymes, recombination enzymes, and proteins involved in integration and excision of prophage DNA.

LYSOGENY

Prophage

Earlier in this chapter it was mentioned that some phages ("temperate phages") fail to lyse the cells they infect and then appear to reproduce synchronously with the host for many generations. Their presence can be demonstrated, however, because every so often one of the progeny of the infected bacterium will lyse and liberate infectious phage. To detect this event it is necessary to use a sensitive indicator strain of bacterium, ie, one that is lysed by the phage. The bacteria that liberate the phage are called "lysogenic"; when a few lysogenic bacteria are plated with an excess of sensitive bacteria, each lysogenic bacterium grows into a colony in which are liberated a few phage particles. These particles immediately infect neighboring sensitive cells, with the result that plaques appear in the film of bacterial growth; in the center of each plaque is a colony of the lysogenic bacterium.

A culture of lysogenic bacteria can also be centrifuged, removing the cells and leaving the temperate phage particles in the supernatant. Their number can be measured by plating suitable dilutions of the supernatant on a sensitive bacterial indicator strain and counting typical plaques.

The release of infectious phage in a culture of lysogenic bacteria is restricted to a very few cells of any given generation. For example, in one bacterial type about 1 in 200 lyse and liberate phage during each generation; in another type it may be 1 in 50,000. The remainder of the cells, however, retain the potentiality to produce active phage and transmit this potentiality to their offspring for an indefinite number of generations.

With the rare exceptions mentioned, lysogenic bacteria contain no detectable phage, either as morphologic, serologic, or infectious entities. However, the fact that they carry the potentiality to produce, generations later, phage with a predetermined set of characteristics means that each cell must contain one or more specific noninfectious structures endowed with genetic continuity. This structure is termed "prophage."

The Nature of Prophage

Two entirely different prophage states are found in different phages. In one state, discovered in phage λ, the prophage consists of a molecule of DNA integrated with the host chromosome. The chromosomes of E coli and of phage λ are circular; the length of the phage chromosome is about one-fiftieth that of the bacterial chromosome. Both the phage and bacterial chromosomes carry a specific **attachment site.** The bacterial attachment site is immediately adjacent to the *gal* locus (see Fig 4–16); the phage attachment site is similarly located at a specific point on the phage genetic map. When λ infects a cell of E coli, recombination between the 2 attachment sites occurs, with the result that the 2 circles are integrated (Fig 9–4). This integration process requires the action of a phage gene product: phage mutants defective in this gene (the *int* locus) are unable to lysogenize the cell.

A number of coliphages are of the λ type: their prophages integrate with the host chromosome at specific attachment sites. One phage, called Mu, is unusual in that it is capable of integrating at totally

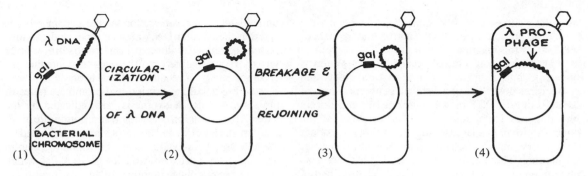

Figure 9–4. The integration of prophage and host chromosome. *(1)* The phage DNA is injected into the host. *(2)* The ends of the phage DNA are covalently joined to form a circular element. *(3)* Pairing occurs between a sequence of bases adjacent to the *gal* locus and a homologous sequence on the phage DNA. *(4)* Breakage and reciprocal rejoining ("crossing over") within the region of pairing integrates the 2 circular DNA structures. The integrated phage DNA is called prophage. The length of λ DNA has been exaggerated for diagrammatic purposes. It is actually 1–2% of the chromosomal length.

random sites on the chromosome, including sites within bacterial genes. Such integrations result in the inactivation of the gene in question and produce the appearance of mutations.

In the other state, discovered in phage P1, the phage chromosome circularizes and enters a state of "quiescent" replication that is synchronous with that of the host; no phage proteins are formed. The prophage in the "P1 type" of system is not integrated with the chromosome; its replication is analogous to that of plasmids.

Further Properties of the Lysogenic System

A. Immunity: Lysogenic bacteria are immune to infection by phage of the type already carried in the cell as prophage. When nonlysogenic cells are exposed to temperate phage, many permit phage multiplication and are lysed, while other cells are lysogenized. Once a cell carries prophage, however, neither it nor its progeny can be lysed by homologous phage. Adsorption takes place, but the adsorbed phage simply persists without reproducing and is quickly "diluted out" by continued cell division.

It has been shown that temperate phages cause the appearance in the cytoplasm of a repressor substance that inhibits multiplication of vegetative phage. Repressor also blocks the detachment of prophage (which otherwise would occur by the reversal of the integration process described above) as well as the expression of other phage genes (eg, formation of phage proteins). The establishment of the lysogenic state is thus dependent on the production and action of repressor. The λ repressor has been isolated and characterized as a protein that specifically binds to λ DNA.

The immunity of a lysogenic cell to homologous phage, mediated by a repressor, is clearly different from the phenomenon of "resistance" to virulent phage exhibited by certain bacteria. In the latter case, resistance is caused by failure to adsorb the phage.

B. Induction: "Vegetative phage" is defined as rapidly reproducing phage on its way to mature infective phage, whereas "prophage" reproduces synchro-

nously with the host cell. On rare occasions prophage "spontaneously" develops into vegetative (and later into mature) phage. This accounts for the sporadic cell lysis and liberation of infectious particles in a lysogenic culture. However, the prophage of practically every cell of certain lysogenic cultures can be induced by various treatments to form and liberate infectious phage. For example, ultraviolet light will induce phage formation and liberation by most of the cells in a lysogenic culture at a dose that would kill very few nonlysogenic bacteria.

Induction requires the inactivation or destruction of repressor molecules present in the cell. Phage mutants have been obtained that produce thermolabile repressors: these phages can be induced simply by raising the temperature to 44 °C. Agents such as ultraviolet light that damage host DNA induce prophage development by the following series of reactions the end result of which is the inactivation of phage repressor: (1) The DNA lesions are recognized by specific endonucleases that digest a short segment of one strand. (2) The single-stranded regions thus formed bind a protein called the recA protein (product of the *recA* gene), which acts as a protease. (3) The recA protein cleaves the phage repressor molecules, which have also bound to the single-stranded regions of DNA. Oligonucleotides, produced in the first step, are required to activate repressor cleavage.

C. Mutation to Virulence: When virulent phage is mixed with bacterial cells, all of the infected cells lyse. When temperate phage is mixed with nonlysogenic bacteria, some of the cells reproduce the phage and are lysed, while others are lysogenized.

Temperate phage can mutate to the virulent state. Two types of virulent mutants have been found. In one type, the mutation has made the phage resistant to the repressor, so that it can multiply even in lysogenic cells that are otherwise immune; in the other type, the phage has lost the ability to produce repressor. Virulent mutants of temperate phages are quite different from the naturally virulent phages such as T2. The latter cause the appearance of enzymes that degrade host DNA and stop the synthesis of ribosomal RNA, whereas the former do not interfere with the normal metabolism of the host in this manner.

D. Effect on Genotype of Host: When a lysogenic phage, grown on host "A," infects and lysogenizes host "B" of a different genotype, some of the cells of host "B" may acquire one or more closely linked genes from host "A." For example, if the phage is grown in a lactose-nonfermenting host, about 1 in every million cells infected becomes lactose-fermenting. The transferred property is heritable. This phenomenon, called "transduction," is described in more detail in Chapter 4.

In other instances, phage genes may themselves determine new host properties. For example, the toxin of *Corynebacterium diphtheriae* and the toxins of many clostridia are determined by genes carried in prophage DNA. In *Salmonella*, phage infection confers a new antigenic surface structure on the host cell. The acquisition of new cell properties as the result of phage infection is called "phage conversion." Phage conversion differs from transduction in that the genes controlling the new properties are found only in the phage genome and never in the chromosome of the host bacterium.

Genetic Regulation of Phage Reproduction

The vegetative and prophage modes of temperate phage reproduction are regulated by a complex series of genes that govern the transcription of different segments of the phage DNA. One such system of regulation, for the phage λ, is shown in Fig 9–5A.

It should be recalled that λ DNA is circularized immediately after penetration of the cell membrane and that the circular DNA may be replicated and ultimately combined with coat proteins to form mature virions, or alternatively may be integrated into the host chromosome by a recombinational event.

In Fig 9–5B, transcriptional promoters (sites of initiation of mRNA synthesis) are indicated by the letter *P*; termination sites for transcription are indicated by the letter *T*; and operator sites are indicated by the letter *O*. These symbols are shown on the map in italics to distinguish them from the genes A–W, which code for various phage proteins not directly involved in transcription regulation.

A. Regulation of Vegetative Replication and Maturation: Gene activity involved in productive phage growth occurs in 3 phases: (1) In the "immediate-early" phase, transcription initiates at promoters P_L and P_R, proceeds left and right respectively, and terminates at the ends of the N and cro genes. These termination sites are designated T_L and T_{R1}; some rightward transcripts extend further, to termination site T_{R2}. (2) In the "delayed-early" phase, the N gene product (protein) acts as an antitermination factor, allowing the above transcriptions to extend further through the genes for replication, recombination, and regulation. (3) In the "late" phase, the cro protein acts at operators O_L and O_R to reduce the initiation of early mRNA transcription from promoters P_L and P_R respectively. Also, Q protein activates rightward transcription from the promoter P'_R, which continues through the lysis, head, and tail genes. (Remember that the genome is circular, the m and m′ ends being joined during this phase.)

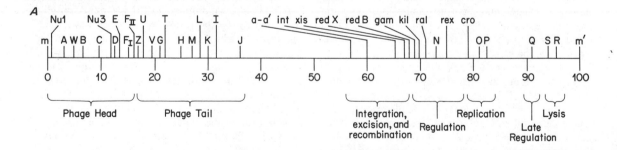

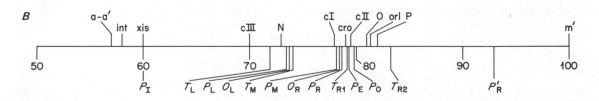

Figure 9–5. *A.* Genetic map of λ phage. During the replication phase, the 2 ends of the DNA (m−m′) are joined to form a circular molecule. The regulatory genes controlling transcription are omitted, being shown in *B,* below. For the functions of the different loci, see the reference given at the end of this caption. Note the clustering of genes for related structures and activities. *B.* Map of λ genes regulating gene activity. See text for explanation. (After Echols H, Murialdo H: Genetic map of bacteriophage lambda. *Microbiol Rev* 1978;**42**:577.)

B. Regulation of Lysogenic Development: Different genes are involved in the establishment and maintenance of lysogeny: (1) In the "establishment" phase, the cII and cIII proteins activate leftward transcription from the promoters P_E and P_I, thus transcribing the cI and int genes; the cII and cIII proteins also inhibit rightward transcription of the lysis genes. (2) In the "maintenance" phase, the cI protein acts at operators O_L and O_R to repress nearly all transcription from promoters P_L and P_R. The cI protein also regulates its own synthesis by controlling leftward transcription from the promoter P_M. Transcription from this site is stimulated by low cI protein concentrations and inhibited by high cI protein concentrations.

The choice between the lytic and lysogenic modes of phage development depends on the relative concentrations of the cI protein (the "λ repressor") and the cro protein; the former is required for lysogeny and the latter for lytic growth. Both proteins bind to 3 repressor binding sites within the O_R operator; whether transcription from the adjacent P_R promotor is inhibited or stimulated depends on their patterns of binding.

C. DNA Replication: Replication starts at the site marked ori and requires the activities of the proteins coded by phage genes O and P.

D. Integration and Excision of Prophage: The a–a' attachment site is recognized by the int protein, catalyzing integration by crossing over at a specific attachment site on the host chromosome. Excision, brought about by a second crossover event, requires the activities of both the int and xis proteins.

E. Cleavage of the Circular DNA: Prior to its packaging in virions the circular DNA must be cleaved at a specific site (m–m') to form linear molecules. This requires the activity of the A protein as well as the presence of phage head precursors.

Restriction & Modification

The phenomena of restriction and modification, as described in Chapter 4, were discovered as a result of their effects on phage multiplication. It was observed that if phage λ is grown in *E coli* strain K12, only about 1 in 10^4 particles can multiply in strain B. The few that succeed, however, liberate progeny that infect B with an efficiency of 1.0 but infect strain K12 with an efficiency of 10^{-4}.

It was shown that DNA of particles formed in K12 is modified by a K12 enzyme so as to be immune to degradation in K12. In strain B, however, the DNA of such particles is rapidly degraded by the restricting enzyme of the host. The few particles that escape restriction are modified by the specific modification enzyme of strain B; the progeny formed are now susceptible to degradation in K12 but not in B. The modifying enzymes have been shown to act by methylating bases at specific sites in the DNA.

Certain temperate phages carry genes that govern the formation of new modification and restriction enzymes in the host. Thus, *E coli* cells carrying P1 prophage will degrade all DNA not modified in a P1-containing cell.

As discussed in Chapter 4, a given restricting enzyme recognizes a particular site on DNA and causes cleavage at that site unless the site has already been protected by the homologous modifying enzyme. Restriction appears to be a mechanism by which a cell protects itself against invasion by foreign DNA. Some phages have been found to have mechanisms for resisting restriction: Phages T3 and T7, for example, produce an early protein that inhibits the host restriction endonuclease; in other cases, the phage codes for enzymes that modify its DNA (eg, by glycosylation) so as to block the action of the restriction enzymes.

•　　•　　•

References

Books

Hayes W: *The Genetics of Bacteria and Their Viruses,* 2nd ed. Blackwell, 1968.

Hershey AD (editor): *The Bacteriophage Lambda.* Cold Spring Harbor Laboratory, 1971.

Stent G: *The Molecular Biology of Bacterial Viruses.* Freeman, 1963.

Stent G (editor): *Papers on Bacterial Viruses,* 2nd ed. Little, Brown, 1965.

Stent G, Calendar R: *Molecular Genetics,* 2nd ed. Freeman, 1978.

Articles & Reviews

Barksdale L, Arden SB: Persisting bacteriophage infection, lysogeny, and phage conversion. *Annu Rev Microbiol* 1976;**28**:265.

Bernstein C: DNA repair in bacteriophage. *Microbiol Rev* 1981;**45**:72.

Boyer HW: DNA restriction and modification mechanisms in bacteria. *Annu Rev Microbiol* 1971;**25**:153.

Broker TR, Doermann AH: Molecular and genetic recombination of bacteriophage T4. *Annu Rev Genet* 1975;**9**:213.

Craig NL, Roberts JW: *E coli* recA protein-directed cleavage of phage λ repressor requires polynucleotide. *Nature* 1980;**283**:26.

Echols H, Murialdo H: Genetic map of bacteriophage lambda. *Microbiol Rev* 1978;**42**:577.

Fiers W et al: Complete nucleotide sequence of bacteriophage MS2 RNA: Primary and secondary structure of the replicase gene. *Nature* 1976;**260**:500.

Hemphill HE, Whiteley HR: Bacteriophages of *Bacillus subtilis. Bacteriol Rev* 1975;**39**:257.

Herskowitz I, Hagen D: The lysis-lysogeny decision of phage λ: Explicit programming and responsiveness. *Annu Rev Genet* 1980;**14**:399.

Horne RW, Wildy P: Symmetry in virus structure. *Virology* 1961;**15**:348.

Koerner JF et al: Shutoff of host macromolecular synthesis after T-even bacteriophage infection. *Microbiol Rev* 1979;**43**:199.

Kotewicz M et al: Characterization of the integration protein of bacteriophage λ as a site-specific DNA-binding protein. *Proc Natl Acad Sci USA* 1977;**74**:1511.

Laval F: Endonuclease activity associated with purified PM2 bacteriophage. *Proc Natl Acad Sci USA* 1974;**71**:4965.

Lemke PA: Viruses of eukaryotic microorganisms. *Annu Rev Microbiol* 1976;**30**:105.

Lindberg AA: Bacteriophage receptors. *Annu Rev Microbiol* 1973;**27**:205.

Lwoff A: The concept of virus. *J Gen Microbiol* 1957;**17**:239.

Lwoff A, Horne R, Tournier P: A system of viruses. *Cold Spring Harbor Symp Quant Biol* 1962;**27**:51.

Marvin DA, Wachtel E: Structure and assembly of filamentous bacterial viruses. *Nature* 1975;**253**:19.

Meyn MS, Rossman T, Troll W: A protease inhibitor blocks SOS functions in *Escherichia coli:* Antipain prevents λ repressor inactivation, ultraviolet mutagenesis, and filamentous growth. *Proc Natl Acad Sci USA* 1977;**74**:1152.

Miller RC: Replication and molecular recombination of T-phage. *Annu Rev Microbiol* 1975;**29**:355.

Ptashne M et al: How the lambda repressor and cro work. (Review.) *Cell* 1980;**19**:1.

Spoerel N, Herrlich P, Bickle TA: A novel bacteriophage defence mechanism: The anti-restriction protein. *Nature* 1979;**278**:30.

Sussman R et al: Interaction of bacteriophage λ repressor with non-operator DNA containing single-strand gaps. *Proc Natl Acad Sci USA* 1978;**75**:5817.

Szybalski EH et al: A comprehensive molecular map of bacteriophage lambda. *Gene* 1979;**7**:217.

Valentine R, Ward R, Strand M: The replication cycle of RNA bacteriophages. *Adv Virus Res* 1969;**15**:1.

Witmer HJ: Regulation of bacteriophage T4 gene expression. *Prog Mol Subcell Biol* 1976;**4**:53.

Antimicrobial Chemotherapy | 10

Although various chemicals have been used for the treatment of infectious diseases since the 17th century (eg, quinine for malaria and emetine for amebiasis), chemotherapy as a science began with Paul Ehrlich. He was the first to formulate the principles of selective toxicity and to recognize the specific chemical relationships between parasites and drugs, the development of drug-fastness in parasites, and the role of combined therapy in combating this development. Ehrlich's experiments in the first decade of the 20th century led to the arsphenamines, the first major triumph of planned chemotherapy.

The current era of rapid development in antimicrobial chemotherapy began in 1935, with the discovery of the sulfonamides by Domagk. In 1940, Chain and Florey demonstrated that penicillin, which had been observed in 1929 by Fleming, could be made into an effective chemotherapeutic substance. During the next 25 years, chemotherapeutic research largely centered around antimicrobial substances of microbial origin called antibiotics. The isolation, concentration, purification, and mass production of penicillin was followed by the development of streptomycin, tetracyclines, chloramphenicol, and many other agents. Although these substances were all originally isolated from filtrates of media in which their respective molds, or *Streptomyces,* had grown, several have subsequently been synthesized. In recent years chemical modification of molecules by biosynthesis has been a prominent method of new drug development. Brief summaries of antimicrobial agents commonly employed in medical treatment are presented at the end of this section.

MECHANISMS OF ACTION OF CLINICALLY USED ANTIMICROBIAL DRUGS

Selective Toxicity

An ideal antimicrobial agent exhibits *selective toxicity,* ie, it interferes—at concentrations tolerated by the host—with some metabolic or synthetic process that exists only in the infectious organism and not in the cells of the host. At present, the concept of true selective toxicity applies to the penicillins and cephalosporins, which act only against bacteria. How-

ever, many other antimicrobials exhibit sufficient selective toxicity to be effective chemotherapeutic agents in the treatment of infectious disease.

At the cellular and subcellular level, most antimicrobial agents function in one of 4 major ways:

(1) Inhibition of cell wall synthesis.

(2) Alteration of cell membrane permeability or inhibition of active transport across cell membrane.

(3) Inhibition of protein synthesis (ie, inhibition of translation and transcription of genetic material).

(4) Inhibition of nucleic acid synthesis.

Antimicrobial Action Through Inhibition of Cell Wall Synthesis
(*Examples:* **Bacitracin, Cephalosporins, Cycloserine, Penicillins, Ristocetin, Vancomycin.**)

In contrast to animal cells, bacteria possess a rigid outer layer, the cell wall. It maintains the shape of the microorganism and "corsets" the bacterial cell, which has a high internal osmotic pressure. The internal pressure is 3–5 times greater in gram-positive than in gram-negative bacteria. Injury to the cell wall (eg, by lysozyme) or inhibition of its formation may lead to lysis of the cell. In a hypertonic environment (eg, 20% sucrose), damaged cell wall formation leads to formation of spherical bacterial "protoplasts" limited by the fragile cytoplasmic membrane. If such "protoplasts" are placed in an environment of ordinary tonicity, they may explode. This is an irreversible action and leads to cell death.

The cell wall contains a chemically distinct complex polymer "mucopeptide" ("murein," "peptidoglycan") consisting of polysaccharides and a highly cross-linked polypeptide. The polysaccharides regularly contain the amino sugars N-acetylglucosamine and acetylmuramic acid. The latter is found only in bacteria. To the amino sugars are attached pentapeptide chains. The final rigidity of the cell wall is imparted by cross-linking of the peptide chains (eg, through pentaglycine bonds) as a result of transpeptidation reactions carried out by several enzymes. The peptidoglycan layer is much thicker in the cell wall of gram-positive bacteria than in the cell wall of gram-negative bacteria.

All penicillins and all cephalosporins are selective inhibitors of bacterial cell wall synthesis through inhibition of the terminal cross-linking of the linear glycopeptides—the "transpeptidation" reaction. The initial step consists of the binding of the drug to cell receptors at least some of which are transpeptidation enzymes. After attachment of the drug, the transpeptidation reaction is inhibited and peptidoglycan synthesis is blocked by penicillins and cephalosporins. The next step in drug action probably involves the removal or inactivation of an inhibitor of autolytic enzymes in the cell wall. This activates the lytic enzyme and results in lysis if the environment is isotonic. In a markedly hypertonic environment (eg, 20% sucrose), the cells change to protoplasts, covered only by the fragile cell membrane. In such protoplasts, synthesis of proteins and nucleic acids may continue for some time.

The inhibition of the transpeptidation enzymes by penicillins and cephalosporins may be due to a structural similarity of these drugs to acyl-D-alanyl-D-alanine. The transpeptidation reaction involves loss of a D-alanine from the pentapeptide.

The remarkable lack of toxicity of penicillins to mammalian cells must be attributed to the absence of a bacterial type cell wall, with its peptidoglycan, in animal cells. The difference in susceptibility of gram-positive and gram-negative bacteria to various penicillins or cephalosporins probably depends on structural differences in their cell walls (eg, amount of peptidoglycan, presence of receptors and lipids, nature of cross-linking, activity of autolytic enzymes) that determine penetration, binding, and activity of the drugs.

Some 6-beta-amidinopenicillanic acid derivatives, eg, mecillinam, are active against gram-negative but not against gram-positive bacteria. They do not affect final transpeptidation in cell wall synthesis but act by other mechanisms; they may exhibit synergism with several penicillins.

Insusceptibility to penicillins is in part determined by the organism's production of penicillin-destroying enzymes (beta-lactamases). Beta-lactamases open the beta-lactam ring of penicillins and cephalosporins and abolish their antimicrobial activity. Certain penicillins (eg, cloxacillin) and other compounds (eg, clavulanic acid) have a high affinity for the beta-lactamase produced by some gram-negative bacteria, eg, *Haemophilus*. They bind the enzyme but are not hydrolyzed by it and thus protect simultaneously present hydrolyzable penicillins (eg, ampicillin) from destruction. This is a form of "synergism" of known mechanism. A fixed combination of clavulanic acid, 250 mg, with amoxicillin, 500 mg, given orally 3 times daily, is being tested for efficacy in beta-lactamase–producing *Haemophilus influenzae* infections.

Two other types of resistance mechanisms may exist. One is due to the absence of some penicillin receptors and occurs as a result of chromosomal mutation; the other results from failure of the beta-lactam drug to activate the autolytic enzymes in the cell wall. As a result, the organism is inhibited but not killed. Such "tolerance" has been observed especially with staphylococci.

Several other drugs, including bacitracin, van-comycin, ristocetin, and novobiocin, inhibit early steps in the biosynthesis of the peptidoglycan. Since the early stages of synthesis take place inside the cytoplasmic membrane, these drugs must penetrate the membrane to be effective. For these drugs, inhibition of peptidoglycan synthesis is not the sole mode of antibacterial action.

Cycloserine, an analog of D-alanine, interferes also with peptidoglycan synthesis. This drug blocks the action of alanine racemase, an essential enzyme in the incorporation of D-alanine in the pentapeptide of peptidoglycan. Phosphonopeptides also inhibit enzymes needed for early synthesis of peptidoglycans.

Antimicrobial Action Through Inhibition of Cell Membrane Function
(*Examples:* **Amphotericin B, Colistin, Nystatin, Polymyxins.**)

The cytoplasm of all living cells is bounded by the cytoplasmic membrane, which serves as a selective permeability barrier, carries out active transport functions, and thus controls the internal composition of the cell. If the functional integrity of the cytoplasmic membrane is disrupted, purine and pyrimidine nucleotides and proteins escape from the cell, and cell damage or death ensues. The cytoplasmic membrane of bacteria and fungi has a different structure and can be more readily disrupted by certain agents than can the membranes of animal cells. Consequently, selective chemotherapeutic activity is possible.

The outstanding examples of this mechanism are the polymyxins acting on gram-negative bacteria (polymyxins selectively act on membranes rich in phosphatidylethanolamine and act like cationic detergent) and the polyene antibiotics acting on fungi. However, polymyxins are inactive against fungi, and polyenes are inactive against bacteria. This is because sterols are present in the fungal cell membrane and absent in the bacterial cell membrane. Polyenes must interact with a sterol in the fungal cell membrane prior to exerting their effect. Bacterial cell membranes do not contain that sterol and (presumably for this reason) are resistant to polyene action—a good example of cell individuality and of selective toxicity. Conversely, polymyxins will not act on the sterol-containing cell membranes of fungi.

Antimicrobial Action Through Inhibition of Protein Synthesis
(*Examples:* **Chloramphenicol, Erythromycins, Lincomycins, Tetracyclines; Aminoglycosides: Amikacin, Gentamicin, Kanamycin, Neomycin, Streptomycin, Tobramycin, Etc.**)

It is established that chloramphenicol, tetracyclines, aminoglycosides, erythromycins, and lincomycins can inhibit protein synthesis in bacteria. Puromycin is an effective inhibitor of protein synthesis in animal and other cells. The concepts of protein synthesis are undergoing rapid change, and the precise mechanism of action is not fully established for these drugs.

Bacteria have 70S ribosomes, whereas mammalian cells have 80S ribosomes. The subunits of each type of ribosome, their chemical composition, and their functional specificities are sufficiently different to explain why antimicrobial drugs can inhibit protein synthesis in bacterial ribosomes without having a major effect on mammalian ribosomes.

In normal microbial protein synthesis, the mRNA message is simultaneously "read" by several ribosomes, which are strung out along the mRNA strand. These are called polysomes.

A. Aminoglycosides: The mode of action of streptomycin has been studied far more than that of other aminoglycosides (kanamycin, neomycin, gentamicin, tobramycin, amikacin, etc), but probably all act similarly. The first step is the attachment of the aminoglycoside to a specific receptor protein (P 12 in the case of streptomycin) on the 30S subunit of the microbial ribosome. Second, the aminoglycoside blocks the normal activity of the "initiation complex" of peptide formation (mRNA + formyl methionine + tRNA). Third, the mRNA message is misread on the "recognition region" of the ribosome, and as a result, the wrong amino acid is inserted into the peptide, resulting in a nonfunctional protein. Fourth, aminoglycoside attachment results in the breakup of polysomes and their separation into "monosomes" incapable of protein synthesis. These activities occur more or less simultaneously, and the overall effect is usually an irreversible event—killing of the cell.

Chromosomal resistance of microbes to aminoglycosides principally depends on the lack of a specific protein receptor on the 30S subunit of the ribosome. Plasmid-dependent resistance to aminoglycosides depends on the production by the microorganism of adenylylating, phosphorylating, or acetylating enzymes that destroy the drugs. A third type of resistance consists of a "permeability defect," perhaps due to absence of active transport of the aminoglycoside into the cell so that the drug cannot reach the ribosome. Sometimes at least, this is plasmid-mediated.

B. Tetracyclines: Tetracyclines bind to the 30S subunit of microbial ribosomes. They inhibit protein synthesis by blocking the attachment of charged aminoacyl-tRNA. Thus, they prevent introduction of new amino acids to the nascent peptide chain. The action is usually inhibitory and reversible upon withdrawal of the drug. Resistance to tetracyclines results from changes in permeability of the microbial cell envelope. In susceptible cells, the drug is concentrated from the environment and does not readily leave the cell. In resistant cells, the drug is not actively transported into the cell or leaves it so rapidly that inhibitory concentrations are not maintained. This is often plasmid-controlled.

C. Chloramphenicol: Chloramphenicol attaches to the 50S subunit of the ribosome. It interferes with the binding of new amino acids to the nascent peptide chain, largely because chloramphenicol inhibits peptidyl transferase. Chloramphenicol is mainly bacteriostatic, and growth of microorganisms resumes

(ie, drug action is reversible) when the drug is withdrawn. Microorganisms resistant to chloramphenicol produce the enzyme chloramphenicol acetyltransferase, which destroys drug activity. The production of this enzyme is usually under control of a plasmid.

D. Macrolides (Erythromycins, Oleandomycins): These drugs bind to the 50S subunit of the ribosome, and the binding site is a 23S rRNA. They may interfere with formation of initiation complexes for peptide chain synthesis or may interfere with aminoacyl translocation reactions. Some macrolide-resistant bacteria lack the proper receptor on the ribosome (through methylation of the rRNA). This may be under plasmid or chromosomal control.

E. Lincomycins (Lincomycin, Clindamycin): Lincomycins bind to the 50S subunit of the microbial ribosome and resemble macrolides in antibacterial activity and mode of action. There may be mutual interference between these drugs. Chromosomal mutants are resistant because they lack the proper binding site on the 50S subunit.

Antimicrobial Action Through Inhibition of Nucleic Acid Synthesis
(*Examples:* **Nalidixic Acid, Novobiocin, Pyrimethamine, Sulfonamides, Trimethoprim, Rifampin.**)

Drugs such as the actinomycins are effective inhibitors of DNA synthesis. Actually, they form complexes with DNA by binding to the deoxyguanosine residues. The DNA-actinomycin complex inhibits the DNA-dependent RNA polymerase and blocks mRNA formation. Actinomycin also inhibits DNA virus replication. Mitomycins result in the firm cross-linking of complementary strands of DNA and subsequently block DNA replication. Both actinomycins and mitomycins inhibit bacterial as well as animal cells and are not sufficiently selective to be employed in antibacterial chemotherapy.

Rifampin inhibits bacterial growth by binding strongly to the DNA-dependent RNA polymerase of bacteria. Thus, it inhibits bacterial RNA synthesis. The mechanism of rifampin action on viruses is different. It blocks a late stage in the assembly of poxviruses.

The halogenated pyrimidines, eg, IUDR (5-iodo-2'-deoxyuridine, idoxuridine, IDU), can block the synthesis of functionally intact DNA and thus interfere with the replication of infective DNA viruses. IUDR can interfere with the incorporation of thymidine into viral DNA, and IUDR itself may be incorporated to form nonfunctional DNA. The systemic administration of IUDR is not feasible because of severe toxicity. Local application of IUDR to DNA virus-producing cells (in herpes simplex keratitis) can result in significant suppression of viral replication in vivo. Other inhibitors of DNA replication, eg, adenine arabinoside, are used in systemic antiviral chemotherapy.

Nalidixic and oxolinic acid, used principally as

urinary antiseptics, are potent inhibitors of DNA synthesis. They block DNA gyrase. It is not known whether the effect in vivo depends solely on this action.

For many microorganisms, p-aminobenzoic acid (PABA) is an essential metabolite. It is used by them as a precursor in the synthesis of folic acid, which serves as an important step in the synthesis of nucleic acids. The specific mode of action of PABA involves an adenosine triphosphate (ATP)-dependent condensation of a pteridine with PABA to yield dihydropteroic acid, which is subsequently converted to folic acid. Sulfonamides are structural analogs of PABA.

p-Aminobenzoic
acid (PABA)

Basic ring
structure
of sulfonamides

Sulfonamides can enter into the reaction in place of PABA and compete for the active center of the enzyme. As a result, nonfunctional analogs of folic acid are formed, preventing further growth of the bacterial cell. The inhibiting action of sulfonamides on bacterial growth can be counteracted by an excess of PABA in the environment (competitive inhibition). Animal cells cannot synthesize folic acid and must depend upon exogenous sources. Some bacteria, like animal cells, are not inhibited by sulfonamides. Many other bacteria, however, synthesize folic acid as mentioned above and consequently are susceptible to action by sulfonamides.

Tubercle bacilli are not markedly inhibited by sulfonamides, but their growth is inhibited by PAS (p-aminosalicylic acid). Conversely, most sulfonamide-susceptible bacteria are resistant to PAS. This suggests that the receptor site for PABA differs in different types of organisms.

Trimethoprim (3,4,5-trimethoxybenzyl pyrimidine) inhibits dihydrofolic acid reductase 50,000 times more efficiently in bacteria than in mammalian cells. This enzyme reduces dihydrofolic to tetrahydrofolic acid, a stage in the sequence leading to the synthesis of purines and ultimately of DNA. Sulfonamides and trimethoprim each can be used alone to inhibit bacterial growth. If used together, they produce sequential blocking in the sequence, resulting in a marked enhancement (synergism) of activity. Such sulfonamide (5 parts) + trimethoprim (1 part) mixtures have been used in the treatment of urinary tract infections, enteric fevers, and many other bacterial and parasitic infections (malaria, pneumocystis pneumonia).

Pyrimethamine (Daraprim) also inhibits dihydrofolate reductase, but it is more active against the enzyme in mammalian cells and therefore is more toxic than trimethoprim. Pyrimethamine plus sulfonamide is the current treatment of choice in toxoplasmosis and some other protozoal infections.

RESISTANCE TO ANTIMICROBIAL DRUGS

There are many different mechanisms by which microorganisms might exhibit resistance to drugs. The following are fairly well supported.

(1) Microorganisms produce enzymes that destroy the active drug. *Examples:* Staphylococci resistant to penicillin G produce a beta-lactamase that destroys the drug. Other beta-lactamases are produced by gram-negative rods. Gram-negative bacteria resistant to aminoglycosides (by virtue of a plasmid) produce adenylylating, phosphorylating, or acetylating enzymes that destroy the drug. Gram-negative bacteria may be resistant to chloramphenicol if they produce a chloramphenicol acetyltransferase.

(2) Microorganisms change their permeability to the drug. *Examples:* Tetracyclines accumulate in susceptible bacteria but not in resistant bacteria. Resistance to polymyxins is also associated with a change in permeability to the drugs. Streptococci have a natural permeability barrier to aminoglycosides. This can be partly overcome by the simultaneous presence of a cell-wall–active drug, eg, a penicillin. Resistance to amikacin and to some other aminoglycosides may depend on a lack of permeability to the drugs, apparently due to impaired active transport across cell membranes.

(3) Microorganisms develop an altered structural target for the drug (see also ¶ 5, below). *Examples:* Chromosomal resistance to aminoglycosides is associated with the loss or alteration of a specific protein in the 30S subunit of the bacterial ribosome that serves as a binding site in susceptible organisms. Erythromycin-resistant organisms have an altered receptor on the 50S subunit of the ribosome, resulting from methylation of a 23S ribosomal RNA.

(4) Microorganisms develop an altered metabolic pathway that bypasses the reaction inhibited by the drug. *Example:* Some sulfonamide-resistant bacteria do not require extracellular PABA but, like mammalian cells, can utilize preformed folic acid.

(5) Microorganisms develop an altered enzyme that can still perform its metabolic function but is much less affected by the drug than the enzyme in the susceptible organism. *Example:* In some sulfonamide-susceptible bacteria, the tetrahydropteroic acid synthetase has a much higher affinity for sulfonamide than for PABA. In sulfonamide-resistant mutants, the opposite is the case.

ORIGIN OF DRUG RESISTANCE

The origin of drug resistance may be genetic or nongenetic.

Nongenetic Origin

Active replication of bacteria is usually required for most antibacterial drug actions. Consequently, microorganisms that are metabolically inactive (nonmultiplying) may be phenotypically resistant to drugs. However, their offspring are fully susceptible. *Example:* Mycobacteria often survive in tissues for many years after infection yet are restrained by the host's defenses and do not multiply. Such "persisting" organisms are resistant to treatment and cannot be eradicated by drugs. Yet if they start to multiply (eg, following corticosteroid treatment of the patient), they are fully susceptible to the same drugs.

Microorganisms may lose the specific target structure for a drug for several generations and thus be resistant. *Example:* Penicillin-susceptible organisms may change to L forms during penicillin administration. Lacking most cell wall, they are then resistant to cell wall inhibitor drugs (penicillins, cephalosporins) and may remain so for several generations as "persisters." When these organisms revert to their bacterial parent forms by resuming cell wall production, they are again fully penicillin-susceptible.

Genetic Origin

Most drug-resistant microbes have emerged as a result of genetic changes and subsequent selection processes. Genetic changes may be chromosomal or extrachromosomal and can be transferred from one bacterial species to another by a variety of mechanisms.

Bacteria contain chromosomes made of a double-stranded circular molecule of DNA. These chromosomes are supercoiled and folded within the cell to allow for orderly segregation into the daughter cells. Bacterial chromosomes replicate semiconservatively and sequentially. In some bacteria, replication is known to proceed bidirectionally.

A. Chromosomal Resistance: This develops as a result of spontaneous mutation in a locus that controls susceptibility to a given antimicrobial. The presence of the antimicrobial drug serves as a selecting mechanism to suppress susceptibles and favor the growth of drug-resistant mutants. Spontaneous mutation occurs with a frequency of 10^{-7} to 10^{-12} and thus is an infrequent cause of the emergence of clinical drug resistance in a given patient. Chromosomal mutants are most commonly resistant by virtue of a change in a structural receptor for a drug. Thus, the P 12 protein on the 30S subunit of the bacterial ribosome serves as a receptor for streptomycin attachment. Mutation in the gene controlling that structural protein results in streptomycin resistance. A narrow region of the bacterial chromosome contains structural genes that code for a number of drug receptors, including those for erythromycin, lincomycin, aminoglycosides, and others.

B. Extrachromosomal Resistance: Bacteria also contain extrachromosomal genetic elements called plasmids. Plasmids are circular DNA molecules, have 1–3% of the weight of the bacterial chromosome, and may exist free in the bacterial cytoplasm or may be integrated into the bacterial chromosome at times. Some plasmids carry their own genes for replication and transfer. Others rely on genes in other plasmids.

R factors are a class of plasmids that carry genes for resistance to one—and often several—antimicrobial drugs and heavy metals. Plasmid genes for antimicrobial resistance often control the formation of enzymes capable of destroying the antimicrobial drugs. Thus, plasmids determine resistance to penicillins and cephalosporins by carrying genes for the formation of beta-lactamases. Plasmids code for enzymes that destroy chloramphenicol (acetyltransferase); for enzymes that acetylate, adenylylate, or phosphorylate various aminoglycosides; for enzymes that determine the active transport of tetracyclines across the cell membrane; and for others.

Genetic material and plasmids can be transferred by the following mechanisms:

(1) Transduction: Plasmid DNA is enclosed in a bacterial virus and transferred by the virus to another bacterium of the same species. *Example:* The plasmid carrying the gene for beta-lactamase production can be transferred from a penicillin-resistant to a susceptible *Staphylococcus* if carried by a suitable bacteriophage. Similar transduction occurs in salmonellae.

(2) Transformation: Naked DNA passes from one cell of a species to another cell, thus altering its genotype. This can occur through laboratory manipulation (eg, in recombinant DNA technology) or perhaps spontaneously.

(3) Bacterial conjugation: A unilateral transfer of genetic material between bacteria of the same or different genera occurs during a mating (conjugation) process. This is mediated by a fertility (F) factor that results in the extension of sex pili from the donor (F^+) cell to the recipient. Plasmid or other DNA is transferred through these protein tubules from the donor to the recipient cell. A series of closely linked genes, each determining resistance to one drug, may thus be transferred from a resistant to a susceptible bacterium. Such a resistance transfer factor (RTF) is the commonest method of spread of multidrug resistance among various genera of gram-negative bacteria.

(4) Transposition: A transfer of short DNA sequences (transposons, transposable elements) occurs between one plasmid and another or between a plasmid and a portion of the bacterial chromosome within a bacterial cell.

Cross-Resistance

Microorganisms resistant to a certain drug may also be resistant to other drugs that share a mechanism of action. Such relationships exist mainly between agents that are closely related chemically (eg, polymyxin B–colistin: erythromycin-oleandomycin;

neomycin-kanamycin), but they may also exist between unrelated chemicals (erythromycin-lincomycin). In certain classes of drugs, the active nucleus of the chemical is so similar among many congeners (eg, tetracyclines) that full cross-resistance is to be expected.

Limitation of Drug Resistance

Emergence of drug resistance in infections may be minimized in the following ways: (1) maintain sufficiently high levels of the drug in the tissues to inhibit both the original population and first step mutants; (2) simultaneously administer 2 drugs that do not give cross-resistance, each of which delays the emergence of mutants resistant to the other drug (eg, ethambutol and isoniazid in the treatment of tuberculosis); and (3) avoid exposure of microorganisms to a particularly valuable drug by restricting its use, especially in hospitals.

Clinical Implications of Drug Resistance

In 1936, when sulfonamides were first employed for the treatment of gonorrhea, practically all strains of gonococci were susceptible, and most cases were cured by these drugs. Six years later, the majority of strains were resistant, and most cases failed to respond to sulfonamide therapy but were still highly susceptible to penicillin. The resistance of most gonococci to penicillin has increased markedly, and beta-lactamase–producing gonococci have appeared, first in the Philippines and West Africa and more recently in some endemic foci in the USA (eg, Los Angeles). Until 1962, meningococci were regularly susceptible to sulfonamides. Subsequently, sulfonamide-resistant meningococci spread widely. Sulfonamides have now lost their usefulness in the prevention and treatment of meningococcal infections. In 1944, the vast majority of strains of staphylococci isolated from hospitalized patients or members of hospital staffs were found to be sensitive to penicillin. By 1948, 65–85% of staphylococci in hospitals were resistant to penicillin as a result of drug selection pressures through heavy use of penicillin in hospitals. Tetracycline resistance emerged similarly. Thus, a majority of "hospital staphylococci" are resistant to both penicillin G and tetracycline, and treatment requires beta-lactamase-resistant penicillins. Tetracycline-resistant pneumococci and group A streptococci have also appeared. In 1982, staphylococci in the community are 60–80% resistant to lactamase-susceptible penicillins and often also to tetracyclines.

Pneumococci were once uniformly susceptible to penicillin G. In 1963, relatively resistant pneumococci appeared in New Guinea. In 1977, outbreaks of disease due to pneumococci that were resistant to penicillin (as well as tetracycline and other drugs) occurred in South Africa, with wide dissemination of such organisms among hospital personnel.

A similar situation has developed with respect to gram-negative enteric organisms, especially in hospitals. The excessive use of drugs leads to suppression of drug-susceptible microorganisms and favors the survival of drug-resistant ones. This "selection pressure" of drugs in the hospital environment gradually brings about prevalence of drug-resistant bacteria — especially *Enterobacter, Proteus, Pseudomonas, Serratia* —and fungi.

To a limited extent, drug-resistant mutants have arisen in tuberculosis. They may complicate the treatment of individual patients in whom they arise and may be transmitted to contacts, giving rise to primary drug-resistant infections. This problem has been marked among migrants from Southeast Asia, where indiscriminate distribution of antituberculosis drugs is rampant.

In closed environments—eg, hospitals or military establishments—the intensive exchange of drug-resistant organisms between persons and their spread by fomites greatly contribute to the problem. The possibility also exists that certain drug-resistant organisms may exhibit enhanced virulence or ability to disseminate.

DRUG DEPENDENCE

Certain organisms are not only resistant to a drug but require it for growth. This has been best demonstrated for streptomycin. When streptomycin-dependent meningococci are injected into mice, progressive fatal disease results only if the animals are treated simultaneously with streptomycin. In the absence of streptomycin, the microorganisms cannot proliferate, and the animals remain well. This phenomenon probably plays no role in human infection. Drug-dependent bacteria have been used in live vaccines for animals.

ANTIMICROBIAL ACTIVITY IN VITRO

Antimicrobial activity is measured in vitro in order to determine (1) the potency of an antibacterial agent in solution, (2) its concentration in body fluids or tissues, and (3) the sensitivity of a given microorganism to known concentrations of the drug.

Measurement of Antimicrobial Activity

Determination of these quantities may be undertaken by one of 2 principal methods: dilution or diffusion.

Using an appropriate standard test organism and a known sample of drug for comparison, these methods can be employed to estimate either the potency of antibiotic in the sample or the "sensitivity" of the microorganism.

A. Dilution Tests: Graded amounts of antimicrobial substances are incorporated into liquid or solid bacteriologic media. The media are subsequently inoculated with test bacteria and incubated. The end point is taken as that amount of antimicrobial substance required to inhibit the growth of, or to kill, the test bacteria.

B. Diffusion Method: A filter paper disk, a porous cup, or a bottomless cylinder containing measured quantities of drug is placed on a solid medium that has been heavily seeded with the test organisms. After incubation, the diameter of the clear zone of inhibition surrounding the deposit of drug is taken as a measure of the inhibitory power of the drug against the particular test organism. Obviously, this method is subject to many physical and chemical factors in addition to the simple interaction of drug and organisms (eg, nature of medium and diffusibility, molecular size, and stability of drug). Nevertheless, standardization of conditions permits quantitative assay of drug potency or sensitivity of the organism.

When determining bacterial sensitivity by the diffusion method, most laboratories use disks of antibiotic-impregnated filter paper. A concentration gradient of antibiotic is produced in the medium by diffusion from the disk. As the diffusion is a continuous process, the concentration gradient is never stable for long; but some stabilization can be achieved by allowing diffusion to start before bacterial growth begins. The greatest difficulties arise from the varying growth rates of different microorganisms and must be corrected by varying the density of the inoculum.

Since it is not feasible to state directly the antibiotic concentration in the medium at any given distance from the diffusion center, interpretation of the results of diffusion tests must be based on comparisons between dilution and diffusion methods. Such comparisons have been made, and international reference standards have been established. Linear regression lines can express the relationship between log of minimum inhibitory concentration in dilution tests and diameter of inhibition zones in diffusion tests.

Use of a single disk for each antibiotic with careful standardization of the test conditions permits the evaluation of "susceptibility" for a microorganism by comparing the size of the inhibition zone against a standard of the same drug (Kirby-Bauer method).

It is fundamentally wrong to regard inhibition around a disk containing a certain amount of antibiotic as implying sensitivity to the same concentration of the antibiotic per milliliter of medium, blood, or urine.

Factors Affecting Antimicrobial Activity

Among the many factors that affect antimicrobial activity in vitro, the following must be considered because they significantly influence the results of tests.

A. pH of Environment: Some drugs are more active at acid pH (eg, nitrofurantoin); others at alkaline pH (eg, aminoglycosides, sulfonamides).

B. Components of Medium: Sodium polyanethol sulfonate and other anionic detergents inhibit aminoglycosides. PABA in tissue extracts antagonizes sulfonamides. Serum proteins bind penicillins in varying degrees, ranging from 40% for methicillin to 98% for dicloxacillin.

C. Stability of Drug: At incubator temperature, several antimicrobial agents lose their activity. Chlortetracycline is inactivated rapidly and penicillins more slowly, whereas aminoglycosides, chloramphenicol, and polymyxin B are quite stable for long periods.

D. Size of Inoculum: In general, the larger the bacterial inoculum, the lower the apparent "sensitivity" of the organism. Large bacterial populations are less promptly and completely inhibited than small ones. In addition, the likelihood of the emergence of a resistant mutant is much greater in large populations.

E. Length of Incubation: In many instances, microorganisms are not killed but only inhibited upon short exposure to antimicrobial agents. The longer incubation continues, the greater the chance for resistant mutants to emerge or for the least susceptible members of the microbial population to begin multiplying as the drug deteriorates.

F. Metabolic Activity of Microorganisms: In general, actively and rapidly growing organisms are more susceptible to drug action than those in the resting phase. "Persisters" are metabolically inactive organisms that survive long exposure to a drug but whose offspring are fully susceptible to the same drug. A specialized form of "persisters" might be L forms of bacteria. Under treatment with drugs that inhibit cell wall formation, cell wall–deficient forms may develop in certain tissues possessing suitable osmotic properties (eg, medulla of kidney). These protoplasts could persist in tissues while the drug (eg, penicillin) was administered and might later revert to intact bacterial forms, causing relapse of disease.

ANTIMICROBIAL ACTIVITY IN VIVO

The problem of the activity of antimicrobial agents in vivo is much more complex than in vitro. It involves not only drug and parasite but also a third factor, the host. The interrelationships of host, drug, and parasite are diagrammed in Fig 10–1. Drug-parasite and host-parasite relationships are discussed in the following paragraphs. Host-drug relationships (absorption, excretion, distribution, metabolism, and toxicity) are dealt with mainly in pharmacology texts.

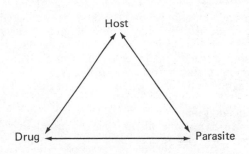

Figure 10–1. Interrelationships of host, drug, and parasite.

DRUG–PARASITE RELATIONSHIPS

Several important interactions between drug and parasite have been discussed in the preceding pages. The following are additional important in vivo factors.

Environment

The environment in the test tube is constant for all members of a microbial population. In the host, however, varying environmental influences are brought to bear on microorganisms located in different tissues and in different parts of the body. Therefore, the response of the microbial population is much less uniform within the host than in the test tube.

A. State of Metabolic Activity: In the test tube, the state of metabolic activity is relatively uniform for the majority of microorganisms. In the body it is diverse; undoubtedly, many organisms are at a low level of biosynthetic activity and are thus relatively insusceptible to drug action. These "dormant" microorganisms often survive exposure to high concentrations of drugs and subsequently may produce a clinical relapse of the infection. Alternatively, cell wall–deficient forms may be insusceptible to drugs that inhibit cell wall formation.

B. Distribution of Agent: In the test tube, all microorganisms are equally exposed to the drug. In the body, the antimicrobial agent is unequally distributed in tissues and fluids. Many drugs do not reach the central nervous system effectively. The concentration in urine is often much greater than the concentration in blood or tissue. The lesion induced by the microorganism may protect it from the drug. Necrotic tissue or pus may adsorb the drug and thus prevent its contact with bacteria.

C. Location of Organisms: In the test tube, the microorganisms come into direct contact with the drug. In the body they may often be located within tissue cells. Drugs enter tissue cells at different rates. Some (eg, tetracyclines) reach about the same concentration inside monocytes as in the extracellular fluid. With others (eg, streptomycin) the intracellular concentration is only a small fraction (perhaps 5–10%) of the extracellular concentration.

D. Interfering Substances: In the test tube, drug activity may be impaired by binding of the drug to protein or to lipids or by interaction with salts. The biochemical environment of microorganisms in the body is very complex and results in significant interference with drug action. The drug may be bound by blood and tissue proteins or phospholipids; it may also react with nucleic acids in pus and may be physically adsorbed onto exudates, cells, and necrotic debris. In necrotic tissue the pH may be highly acid and thus unfavorable for drug action (eg, aminoglycosides).

Concentration

In the test tube, microorganisms are exposed to an essentially constant concentration of drug. In the body this is not so.

A. Absorption: The absorption of drugs from the intestinal tract (if taken by mouth) or from tissues (if injected) is irregular. There is also a continuous excretion as well as inactivation of the drug. Consequently, the available levels of drug in body compartments fluctuate continuously, and the microorganisms are exposed to varying concentrations of the antimicrobial agent.

B. Distribution: The distribution of drugs varies greatly with different tissues. Some drugs penetrate poorly into certain tissues (eg, central nervous system) or body cavities (eg, pleural space). Drug concentrations following systemic administration may therefore be inadequate for effective treatment. In such situations the drug may be administered locally (eg, injection of drugs into the central nervous system). On surface wounds or mucous membranes, local (topical) application of poorly absorbed drugs permits highly effective local concentrations without toxic side-effects. Drug concentrations in urine are often much higher than in blood.

C. Variability of Concentration: The critical consideration in antimicrobial therapy is the necessity of maintaining an effective concentration of the drug in contact with microorganisms at their site of proliferation or establishment in the tissues for a sufficient length of time to cause eradication of infecting organisms. Because the drug is administered intermittently and is absorbed and excreted irregularly, the levels constantly fluctuate at the site of infection. In order to maintain sufficient drug concentrations for a sufficient time, the time-dose relationship has to be considered. The larger each individual drug dose, the longer the permissible interval between doses. The smaller the individual dose, the shorter the interval that will ensure adequate drug levels. A good general rule in antimicrobial therapy is as follows: Give a sufficiently large amount of an effective drug as early as possible and continue treatment long enough to ensure eradication of infection; but give an antimicrobial drug only when it is indicated by rational choice.

HOST–PARASITE RELATIONSHIPS

Host-parasite relationships may be altered by antimicrobial drugs in several ways.

Alteration of Tissue Response

The inflammatory response of the tissue to infections may be altered if the drug suppresses the multiplication of microorganisms but does not eliminate them from the body, and an acute process may in this way be transformed into a chronic one. Conversely, the suppression of inflammatory reactions in tissues by corticosteroids may reduce the effectiveness of bacteriostatic drugs. The administration of antineoplastic drugs depresses inflammatory reactions and immune responses and consequently leads to enhanced susceptibility to infection and diminished response to antimicrobial drugs.

Alteration of Immune Response

If an infection is modified by an antimicrobial drug, the immune response of the host may also be altered. An example will suffice to illustrate this phenomenon:

Infection with beta-hemolytic group A streptococci is followed frequently by the development of antistreptococcal antibodies and occasionally by rheumatic fever. If the infective process can be interrupted early and completely with antimicrobial drugs, the development of an immune response and of rheumatic fever can be prevented (presumably by rapid elimination of the antigen). Drugs and doses that rapidly eradicate the infecting streptococci (eg, penicillin) are more effective in preventing rheumatic fever than those that merely suppress the microorganisms temporarily (eg, tetracycline.)

Alteration of Microbial Flora

Antimicrobial drugs affect not only the infecting microorganisms but also susceptible members of the normal microbial flora of the body. An imbalance is thus created that in itself may lead to disease. A few examples will serve:

(1) In hospitalized patients who receive antimicrobials, the normal microbial flora is suppressed. This creates a partial void that is filled by the organisms most prevalent in the environment, particularly drug-resistant "hospital" staphylococci, *Pseudomonas*, fungi, etc. Such superinfecting organisms subsequently may produce serious drug-resistant infections.

(2) In women taking tetracycline antibiotics by mouth, the normal vaginal flora may be suppressed, permitting marked overgrowth of *Candida*. This leads to unpleasant local inflammation (vaginitis) and itching that is difficult to control.

(3) In the presence of urinary tract obstruction, the tendency to bladder infection is great. When such urinary tract infection due to a sensitive microorganism (eg, *Escherichia coli*) is treated with an appropriate chemotherapeutic drug, the organism may be eradicated. However, very often a reinfection due to drug-resistant *Proteus, Pseudomonas,* or *Enterobacter* occurs after the drug-sensitive microorganisms are eliminated. A similar process accounts for respiratory tract superinfections in patients being given antimicrobials for chronic bronchitis or bronchiectasis.

(4) In persons receiving antimicrobial drugs by mouth for several days, parts of the normal intestinal flora may be suppressed. Drug-resistant organisms may establish themselves in the bowel in great numbers and may precipitate serious enterocolitis (see p 136).

CLINICAL USE OF ANTIBIOTICS

Selection of Antibiotics

The rational selection of antimicrobial drugs depends upon the following:

A. Diagnosis: A specific etiologic diagnosis must be formulated. This can often be done on the basis of a clinical impression. Thus in typical lobar pneumonia or acute urinary tract infection, the relationship between clinical picture and causative agent is sufficiently constant to permit selection of the antibiotic of choice on the basis of clinical impression alone. Even in these cases, however, as a safeguard against diagnostic error, it is preferable to obtain a representative specimen for bacteriologic study before giving antimicrobial drugs.

In most infections, the relationship between causative agent and clinical picture is not constant. It is therefore important to obtain proper specimens for bacteriologic identification of the causative agent. As soon as such specimens have been secured, chemotherapy can be started on the basis of the "best guess." Once the causative agent has been identified by laboratory procedures, chemotherapy can be modified as necessary.

The "best guess" of a causative organism is based on the following considerations, among others: (1) the site of infection (eg, pneumonia, urinary tract infection); (2) the age of the patient (eg, meningitis; neonatal, young child, adult); (3) the place where the infection was acquired (hospital, community); (4) mechanical predisposing factors (intravenous drip, urinary catheter, respirator, exposure to vector); and (5) predisposing host factors (immunodeficiency, corticosteroids, transplant, cancer chemotherapy, etc).

When the causative agent of a clinical infection is known, the drug of choice can often be selected on the basis of current experience (see Table 10–2). At other times, laboratory tests for antibiotic sensitivity (see below) are necessary to determine the drug of choice.

B. Sensitivity Tests: Laboratory tests for antibiotic sensitivity are indicated in the following circumstances: (1) when the microorganism recovered is of a type that is often resistant to antimicrobial drugs (eg, gram-negative enteric bacteria); (2) when an infectious process is likely to be fatal unless treated specifically (eg, meningitis, septicemia); (3) in certain infections where eradication of the infectious organisms requires the use of drugs that are rapidly bactericidal, not merely bacteriostatic (eg, infective endocarditis). The laboratory aspects of antibiotic sensitivity testing are discussed in Chapter 26.

C. Serum Assay of Bactericidal Activity: This test determines directly whether adequate amounts of the correct drugs are being administered to the patient from whom a causative organism has been isolated. Serum is obtained during therapy, diluted, inoculated with the previously isolated organism, and incubated. Subcultures at intervals must indicate bactericidal activity in significant serum dilutions (depending upon inoculum size and time after drug administration, usually at least 1:5) to suggest adequate therapy (see Chapter 26).

Dangers of Indiscriminate Use

(1) Widespread sensitization of the population,

with resulting hypersensitivity, anaphylaxis, rashes, fever, blood disorders, cholestatic hepatitis, and perhaps connective tissue diseases.

(2) Changes in the normal flora of the body, with disease resulting from "superinfection" due to overgrowth of drug-resistant organisms.

(3) Masking serious infection without eradicating it. For example, the clinical manifestations of an abscess may be suppressed while the infectious process continues.

(4) Direct drug toxicity, particularly with prolonged use of certain agents. Important examples are aplastic anemia due to inappropriate use of chloramphenicol; renal damage or auditory nerve damage due to aminoglycoside antibiotics.

(5) Development of drug resistance in microbial populations, chiefly through the elimination of drug-sensitive microorganisms from antibiotic-saturated environments (eg, hospitals) and their replacement by drug-resistant microorganisms.

ANTIMICROBIAL DRUGS USED IN COMBINATION

Indications

Possible reasons for employing 2 or more antimicrobials simultaneously instead of a single drug are as follows:

(1) Prompt treatment in desperately ill patients suspected of having a serious microbial infection. A good guess about the most probable 2 or 3 pathogens is made, and drugs are aimed at those organisms. Before such treatment is started, it is essential that adequate specimens be obtained for identifying the etiologic agent in the laboratory. Suspected gram-negative or staphylococcal sepsis and bacterial meningitis in children are the foremost indications in this category at present.

(2) To delay the emergence of microbial mutants resistant to one drug in chronic infections by the use of a second or third non–cross-reacting drug. The most prominent example is active tuberculosis of an organ, with large microbial populations.

(3) Mixed infections, particularly those following massive trauma or those involving vascular structures. Each drug is aimed at an important pathogenic microorganism.

(4) To achieve bactericidal synergism (see below). In a few infections, eg, enterococcal sepsis, a combination of drugs is more likely to eradicate the infection than either drug used alone. Unfortunately, such synergism is unpredictable, and a given drug pair may be synergistic for only a single microbial strain. Occasionally, simultaneous use of 2 drugs permits significant reduction in dose and thus avoids toxicity but still provides satisfactory antimicrobial action.

Disadvantages

The following disadvantages of using antimicrobial drugs in combinations must always be considered:

(1) The doctor may feel that since several drugs are already being given, everything possible has been done for the patient. This attitude leads to relaxation of the effort to establish a specific diagnosis. It may also give a false sense of security.

(2) The more drugs that are administered, the greater the chance for drug reactions to occur or for the patient to become sensitized to drugs.

(3) The cost is unnecessarily high.

(4) Antimicrobial combinations usually accomplish no more than an effective single drug.

(5) On very rare occasions, one drug may antagonize a second drug given simultaneously (see below).

Mechanisms

When 2 antimicrobial agents act simultaneously on a homogeneous microbial population, the effect may be one of the following: (1) indifference, ie, the combined action is no greater than that of the more effective agent when used alone; (2) addition, ie, the combined action is equivalent to the sum of the actions of each drug when used alone; (3) synergism, ie, the combined action is significantly greater than the sum of both effects; (4) antagonism, ie, the combined action is less than that of the more effective agent when used alone.

All these effects may be observed in vitro (particularly in terms of bactericidal rate) and in vivo. Antagonism is sharply limited by time-dose relationships and is therefore a rare event in clinical antimicrobial therapy. Antagonism resulting in higher morbidity and mortality rates has been most clearly demonstrated in bacterial meningitis. It occurred when a bacteriostatic drug (which inhibited protein synthesis in bacteria) such as chloramphenicol or tetracycline was given with a bactericidal drug such as a penicillin or an aminoglycoside. Antagonism occurred mainly if the bacteriostatic drug reached the site of infection before the bactericidal drug, if the killing of bacteria was essential for cure, and if only minimal effective doses of either drug in the pair were present. Antagonism can be overcome by large excess amounts of drug in the pair—a common event clinically—and it very rarely affects the outcome of clinical therapy.

Synergism

Antimicrobial synergism can occur in several types of situations. Synergistic drug combinations must be selected by complex laboratory procedures.

(1) Sequential block of a microbial metabolic pathway by 2 drugs. Sulfonamides inhibit the use of extracellular p-aminobenzoic acid by some microbes for the synthesis of folic acid. Trimethoprim or pyrimethamine inhibits the next metabolic step, the reduction of dihydro- to tetrahydrofolic acid. The simultaneous use of a sulfonamide plus trimethoprim is effective in some bacterial infections (eg, urinary tract, enteric) and in some parasitic infections (*Pneumocystis carinii*, malaria). Pyrimethamine plus a sulfonamide is used in toxoplasmosis.

(2) One drug may greatly enhance the uptake of a second drug and thereby greatly increase the overall bactericidal effect. Penicillins enhance the uptake of aminoglycosides by enterococci. Thus, a penicillin plus an aminoglycoside may be essential for the eradication of *Streptococcus faecalis* or *Streptococcus* group B infections, particularly sepsis or endocarditis. Similarly, carbenicillin plus gentamicin may be synergistic against some strains of *Pseudomonas*. Cell wall inhibitors (penicillins and cephalosporins) may enhance the entry of aminoglycosides into other gram-negative bacteria and thus produce synergistic effects.

(3) One drug may affect the cell membrane and facilitate the entry of the second drug. The combined effect may then be greater than the sum of its parts. Polymyxins have been synergistic with trimethoprim-sulfamethoxazole or rifampin against *Serratia,* and amphotericin has been synergistic with flucytosine against certain fungi, eg, *Cryptococcus*.

Another known and possibly beneficial effect of a drug combination depends on inhibition of the bacterial enzyme that destroys a drug. Thus, beta-lactamase-producing *Haemophilus* infections may be treated more effectively with a mixture of amoxicillin with clavulanic acid (which inhibits beta-lactamase) than by amoxicillin alone.

The effects that can be achieved with combinations of antimicrobial drugs vary with different combinations and are specific for each strain of microorganism. Thus no combination is uniformly synergistic. Combined effects cannot be predicted from the behavior of the microorganism toward single drugs.

Combined therapy should not be used indiscriminately; every effort should be made to employ the single antibiotic of choice. In resistant infections, detailed laboratory study can at times define synergistic drug combinations that may be essential to eradicate the microorganisms.

ANTIMICROBIAL CHEMOPROPHYLAXIS

Anti-infective chemoprophylaxis implies the administration of antimicrobial drugs to prevent infection. In a broader sense, it also includes the use of antimicrobial drugs soon after the acquisition of pathogenic microorganisms (eg, after compound fracture) but before the development of signs of infection.

Useful chemoprophylaxis is limited to the action of a specific drug on a specific organism. An effort to prevent all types of microorganisms in the environment from establishing themselves only selects the most drug-resistant organisms as the cause of a resulting infection. In all proposed uses of prophylactic antimicrobials, the risk of the patient's acquiring an infection must be weighed against the toxicity, cost, inconvenience, and enhanced risk of superinfection resulting from the "prophylactic" drug.

Prophylaxis in Persons of Normal Susceptibility Exposed to a Specific Pathogen

In this category, a specific drug is administered to prevent one specific infection. Outstanding examples are the injection of benzathine penicillin G, 1.2 million units intramuscularly once every 3–4 weeks, to prevent reinfection with group A hemolytic streptococci in rheumatic patients; prevention of meningitis by eradicating the meningococcal carrier state with rifampin, 600 mg orally twice daily for 2 days, or minocycline, 100 mg every 12 hours for 5 days; prevention of syphilis by the injection of benzathine penicillin G, 2.4 million units intramuscularly, within 24 hours of exposure; prevention of plague pneumonia with tetracycline, 0.5 g twice daily for 5 days, when exposed to infectious droplets; and prevention of clinical rickettsial disease (but not of infection) by the daily ingestion of 1 g tetracycline during exposure.

Early treatment of an asymptomatic infection is sometimes called "prophylaxis." Thus, administration of isoniazid, 6–10 mg/kg/d (maximum, 300 mg daily) orally for 6–12 months, to an asymptomatic person who converts from a negative to a positive tuberculin skin test may prevent later clinically active tuberculosis.

Prophylaxis in Persons of Increased Susceptibility

Certain anatomic or functional abnormalities predispose to serious infections. It may be feasible to prevent or abort such infections by giving a specific drug for short periods. Some important examples are listed below:

A. Heart Disease: Persons with congenital or acquired abnormalities of the heart valves are unusually susceptible to implantation of microorganisms circulating in the bloodstream. This bacterial endocarditis can sometimes be prevented if the proper drug can be used during periods of bacteremia. Viridans streptococci enter the bloodstream from the upper respiratory tract. Large numbers of these organisms are pushed into the circulation during dental procedures and operations on the mouth or throat. At such times, the increased risk warrants the use of a prophylactic antimicrobial drug aimed at viridans streptococci, eg, the injection of procaine penicillin G, 600,000 units intramuscularly 1–2 hours before the procedure and once daily for 2 days thereafter. In addition, 600,000 units of aqueous penicillin G is injected intramuscularly just prior to the procedure. It may be that an aminoglycoside should be given together with penicillin for optimal bactericidal effect. Alternatively, penicillin V, 2 g orally, can be given before the procedure, followed by 500 mg every 6 hours for 8 doses afterward. In persons hypersensitive to penicillin or those receiving daily doses of penicillin for prolonged periods (for rheumatic fever prophylaxis), erythromycin, 2 g daily orally, can be substituted to cover penicillin-resistant viridans streptococci in the throat.

Enterococci cause 5–15% of cases of bacterial endocarditis. They reach the bloodstream from the urinary or gastrointestinal tract or from the female genital tract. During surgical procedures in these areas, persons with heart valve abnormalities can be given prophylaxis directed against enterococci, eg, penicillin G, 5 million units, plus gentamicin, 3 mg/kg intramuscularly daily, beginning on the day of surgery and continuing for 2 days.

During and after cardiac catheterization, blood cultures may be positive in 10–20% of patients. Many of these persons also have fever, but very few acquire endocarditis. Prophylactic antimicrobials do not appear to influence these events.

B. Respiratory Tract Disease: Persons with functional and anatomic abnormalities of the respiratory tract—eg, emphysema or bronchiectasis—are subject to attacks of "recurrent chronic bronchitis." This is a recurrent bacterial infection, often precipitated by acute viral infections and resulting in respiratory decompensation. The most common organisms are pneumococci and *H influenzae*. Chemoprophylaxis consists of giving tetracycline or ampicillin, 1 g daily orally, during the "respiratory disease season." This is successful only in patients who are not hospitalized; otherwise, superinfection with *Pseudomonas, Proteus,* or yeasts is common. Similar prophylaxis of bacterial infection has been applied to children with mucoviscidosis who are not hospitalized. In spite of this, such children contract complicating infections caused by *Pseudomonas* and staphylococci. Trimethoprim-sulfamethoxazole is effective as a prophylactic against *Pneumocystis* pneumonitis in children.

C. Recurrent Urinary Tract Infection: In certain women who are subject to frequently recurring urinary tract infections, the daily oral intake of nitrofurantoin, 200 mg daily, trimethoprim (40 mg)-sulfamethoxazole (200 mg) daily, or methenamine mandelate or hippurate, 2–3 g daily, can markedly reduce the frequency of symptomatic recurrences over periods of many months—perhaps years—until resistant microorganisms appear.

Certain women frequently develop symptoms of cystitis after sexual intercourse. The ingestion of a single dose of antimicrobial drug (200 mg nitrofurantoin, 250 mg cephalexin, etc) can prevent this postcoital cystitis by early inhibition of growth of bacteria moved into the proximal urethra or bladder from the introitus during intercourse.

D. Opportunistic Infections in Severe Granulocytopenia: Patients with leukemia or neoplasm develop profound leukopenia while being given antineoplastic chemotherapy. When the neutrophil count falls below 1000/μL, they become unusually susceptible to opportunistic infections, most often gram-negative sepsis. In some cancer centers, such individuals are given a drug combination (eg, vancomycin, gentamicin, cephalosporin) directed at the most prevalent opportunists at the earliest sign—or even without clinical evidence—of infection. This is continued for several days until the granulocyte count rises again. Retrospective studies suggest that there is some benefit to this procedure.

In other centers, such patients are given oral insoluble antimicrobials (neomycin + polymyxin + nystatin) during the period of granulopenia to reduce the incidence of gram-negative sepsis. Some benefit has been reported from this approach.

Prophylaxis in Surgery

A major portion of all antimicrobial drugs used in hospitals is employed on surgical services with the stated intent of "prophylaxis." The administration of antimicrobials before and after surgical procedures is sometimes viewed as "banning the microbial world" both from the site of the operation and from other organ systems that suffer postoperative complications. Regrettably, the provable benefit of antimicrobial prophylaxis in surgery is much more limited.

Several general features of "surgical prophylaxis" merit consideration.

(1) In clean elective surgical procedures (ie, procedures during which no tissue bearing normal flora is traversed, other than the prepared skin), the disadvantages of "routine" antibiotic prophylaxis (allergy, toxicity, superinfection) generally outweigh the possible benefits.

(2) Prophylactic administration of antibiotics should generally be considered only if the expected rate of infectious complications approaches or exceeds 5%. An exception to this rule is the elective insertion of prostheses (cardiovascular, orthopedic), where a possible infection would have a catastrophic effect.

(3) If prophylactic antimicrobials are to be effective, a sufficient concentration of drug must be present at the operative site to inhibit or kill bacteria that might settle there. Thus, it is essential that drug administration begin 1–3 hours before operation.

(4) Prolonged administration of antimicrobial drugs tends to alter the normal flora of organ systems, suppressing the susceptible microorganisms and favoring the implantation of drug-resistant ones. Thus, antimicrobial prophylaxis should last only 1–3 days after the procedure to prevent superinfection.

(5) Systemic antimicrobial levels usually do not prevent wound infection, pneumonia, or urinary tract infection if physiologic abnormalities or foreign bodies are present.

In major surgical procedures, the administration of a "broad-spectrum" bactericidal drug from just before until 1 day after the procedure has been found effective. Thus, cefazolin, 1 g intramuscularly given 2 hours before gastrointestinal, gallbladder, or orthopedic operations and again at 2, 10, and 18 hours after the end of the operation, results in a demonstrable lowering of the risk of deep infections at the operative site. Similarly, in cardiovascular surgery, antimicrobials directed at the commonest organisms producing infection are begun just prior to the procedure and continued for 2 or 3 days thereafter. While this prevents drug-susceptible organisms from producing endocarditis, pericarditis, or similar complications, it may favor the implantation of drug-resistant bacteria or fungi.

Other forms of surgical prophylaxis attempt to reduce normal flora or existing bacterial contamination at the site. Thus, the colon is routinely prepared not only by mechanical cleansing through cathartics and enemas but also by the oral administration of insoluble drugs (eg, neomycin, 1 g, plus erythromycin, 0.5 g, every 4–6 hours) for 1–2 days before operation. In the case of a perforated viscus resulting in peritoneal contamination, there is little doubt that immediate treatment with an aminoglycoside, a penicillin, or clindamycin reduces the impact of seeded infection. Similarly, grossly infected compound fractures or war wounds benefit from a penicillin or cephalosporin plus an aminoglycoside. In all these instances, the antimicrobials tend to reduce the likelihood of rapid and early invasion of the bloodstream and tend to help localize the infectious process—although they generally are incapable of preventing it altogether. The surgeon must be watchful for the selection of the most resistant members of the flora, which tend to manifest themselves 2 or 3 days after the beginning of such "prophylaxis"—which is really an attempt at very early treatment.

In all situations where antimicrobials are administered with the hope that they may have a "prophylactic" effect, the risk from these same drugs (allergy, toxicity, selection of superinfecting microorganisms) must be evaluated daily, and the course of prophylaxis must be kept as brief as possible.

Topical antimicrobials (intravenous tube site, catheter, closed urinary drainage, within a surgical wound, acrylic bone cement, etc) may have limited usefulness but must always be scrutinized with suspicion.

DISINFECTANTS

Disinfectants and antiseptics differ from systemically active antimicrobials in that they possess little selective toxicity: they are toxic not only for microbial parasites but for host cells as well. Therefore, they can be used only to inactivate microorganisms in the inanimate environment or, to a limited extent, on skin surfaces, but they cannot be administered systemically and are not active in tissues.

The antimicrobial action of disinfectants is determined by concentration, time, and temperature, and the evaluation of their effect may be complex. The known modes of action of several classes of chemical disinfectants are described in Chapter 7. A few examples of disinfectants that are used in medicine or public health are listed in Table 10–1.

Table 10–1. Practical chemical disinfectants.

Disinfection of inanimate environment	
Table tops, instruments	5% Lysol or other phenolic compound
	1–10% formaldehyde
	2% aqueous glutaraldehyde
	0.1% mercury bichloride
	Quaternary ammonium compounds (0.1%)
Excreta, bandages, bedpans	1% sodium hypochlorite
	5% Lysol or other phenolic compound
Air	Propylene glycol mist or aerosol
	Formaldehyde vapor
Heat-sensitive instruments	Ethylene oxide gas
Disinfection of skin or wounds	
	Washing with soap and water
	Soaps or detergents containing 2% hexachlorophene or 1.5% trichlorocarbanilide or chlorhexidine
	2% tincture of iodine
	70% ethyl alcohol; 70–90% isopropyl alcohol
	Povidone-iodine (water-soluble)
	Nitrofurazone, 0.2% jelly or solution
Topical application of drugs to skin or mucous membranes	
In candidiasis	Gentian violet, 1:2000
	Nystatin cream, 100,000 units/g
	Candicidin ointment, 0.6 mg/g
	Miconazole, 2% cream
In burns	Silver nitrate, 0.5%
	Mafenide acetate cream
	Silver sulfadiazine
In dermatophytosis	Undecylenic acid powder or 5–10% cream
	Tolnaftate cream, 1%
In pyoderma	Ammoniated mercury, 2–5% ointment
	Bacitracin-neomycin-polymyxin ointment
	Potassium permanganate, 0.01%
Topical application of drugs to eyes	
For gonorrhea prophylaxis	1% silver nitrate
For bacterial conjunctivitis	Sulfacetamide ointment
	Chloramphenicol ointment

ANTIMICROBIAL DRUGS FOR SYSTEMIC ADMINISTRATION

PENICILLINS

The penicillins are derived from molds of the genus *Penicillium* (eg, *Penicillium notatum*) and obtained by extraction of submerged cultures grown in special media. The most widely used natural penicillin at present is penicillin G. From fermentation brews of *Penicillium*, 6-aminopenicillanic acid has been isolated on a large scale. This makes it possible to synthesize an almost unlimited variety of penicillinlike compounds by coupling the free amino group of the penicillanic acid to free carboxyl groups of different radicals.

All penicillins share the same basic structure (see 6-aminopenicillanic acid in Fig 10–2). A thiazolidine ring (a) is attached to a beta-lactam ring (b) that carries a free amino group (c). The acidic radicals attached to the amino group can be split off by bacterial and other amidases. The structural integrity of the 6-aminopenicillanic acid nucleus is essential to the biologic activity of the compounds. If the beta-lactam ring is enzymatically cleaved by beta-lactamases (penicillinases), the resulting product, penicilloic

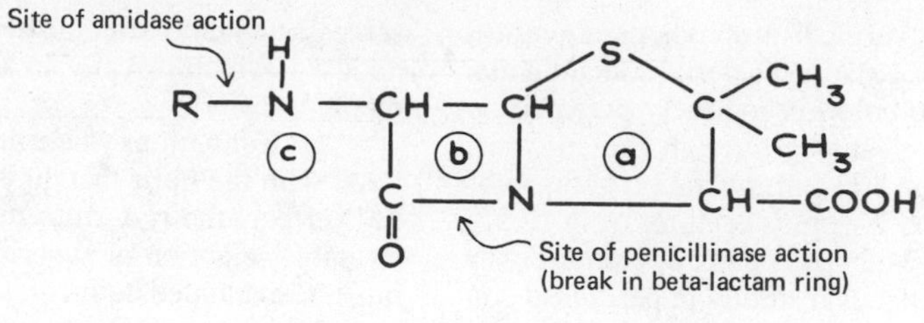

6-Aminopenicillanic acid

The following structures can each be substituted at the R to produce a new penicillin.

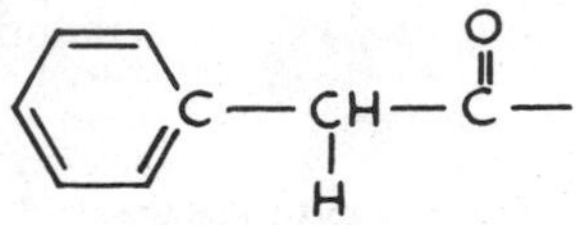

Penicillin G (benzylpenicillin):

High activity against gram-positive bacteria. Low activity against gram-negative bacteria. Acid-labile. Destroyed by beta-lactamase; 60% protein-bound.

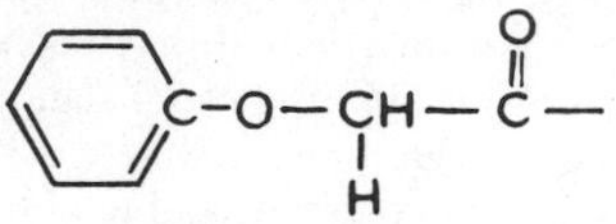

Penicillin V (phenoxymethyl penicillin):

Similar to penicillin G, but relatively acid-resistant.

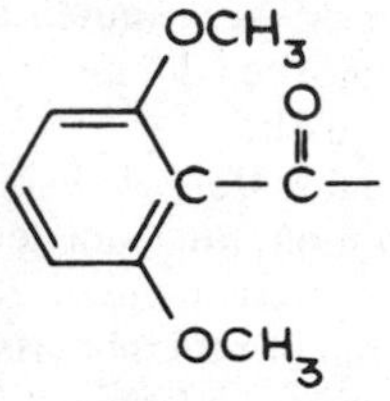

Methicillin (dimethoxyphenylpenicillin):

Lower activity than penicillin G but resistant to penicillinase. Acid-labile. 40% protein-bound.

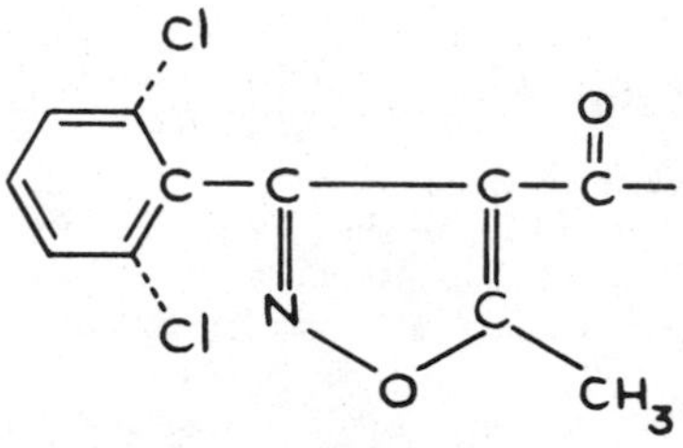

Oxacillin; cloxacillin (one Cl in structure); dicloxacillin (2 Cls in structure); flucloxacillin (one Cl and one F in structure) (isoxazolyl penicillins): Similar to methicillin in penicillinase resistance, but acid-stable. Highly protein-bound (95–98%).

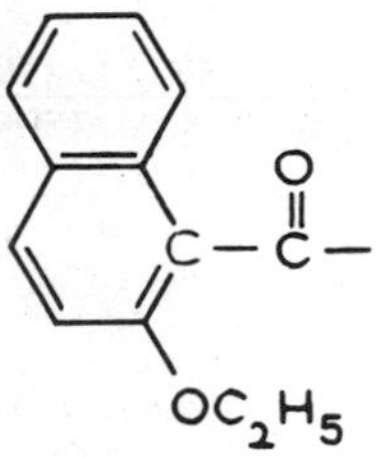

Nafcillin (ethoxynaphthamidopenicillin):

Similar to isoxazolyl penicillins; less strongly protein-bound (90%); less nephrotoxic than methicillin.

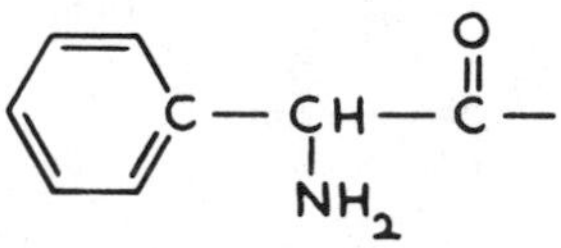

Ampicillin (alpha-aminobenzylpenicillin):

Similar to penicillin G (destroyed by beta-lactamase), but acid-stable and more active against gram-negative bacteria. Carbenicillin has $-COONa$ instead of the $-NH_2$ group.

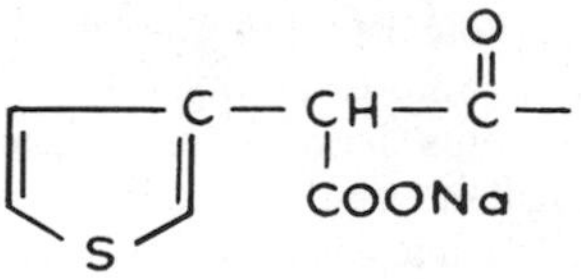

Ticarcillin:

Similar to carbenicillin but gives higher blood levels.

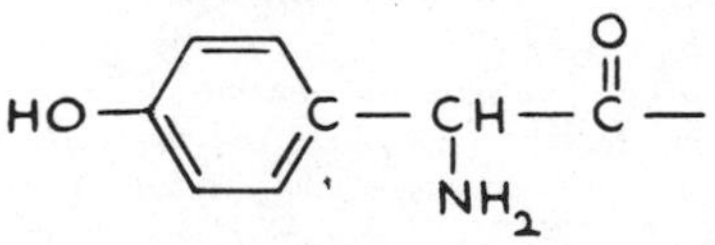

Amoxicillin:

Similar to ampicillin but better absorbed; gives higher blood levels.

Figure 10–2. Structures of some penicillins.

Table 10—2. Drug selections, 1981—1982.

Suspected or Proved Etiologic Agent	Drug(s) of First Choice	Alternative Drug(s)
Gram-negative cocci		
Gonococcus	Penicillin[1], ampicillin, tetracycline[2]	Spectinomycin, cefoxitin
Meningococcus	Penicillin[1]	Chloramphenicol, sulfonamide
Gram-positive cocci		
Pneumococcus *(Streptococcus pneumoniae)*	Penicillin[1]	Erythromycin[3], cephalosporin[4]
Streptococcus, hemolytic groups A, B, C, G	Penicillin[1]	Erythromycin[3], cephalosporin[4]
Streptococcus viridans	Penicillin[1] plus aminoglycoside(?)	Cephalosporin, vancomycin
Staphylococcus, nonpenicillinase-producing	Penicillin[1]	Cephalosporin, vancomycin
Staphylococcus, penicillinase-producing	Penicillinase-resistant penicillin[5]	Vancomycin, cephalosporin
Streptococcus faecalis (enterococcus)	Ampicillin plus aminoglycoside	Vancomycin
Gram-negative rods		
Acinetobacter (Mima-Herellea)	Gentamicin	Minocycline, amikacin
Bacteroides (except *B fragilis)*	Penicillin[1] or chloramphenicol	Clindamycin
Bacteroides fragilis	Clindamycin, cefoxitin	Metronidazole, chloramphenicol
Brucella	Tetracycline plus streptomycin	Streptomycin plus sulfonamide[6]
Enterobacter	Gentamicin or amikacin	Chloramphenicol
Escherichia		
Escherichia coli sepsis	Gentamicin or kanamycin	Cephalosporin, ampicillin
Escherichia coli urinary tract infection (first attack)	Sulfonamide[7] or TMP-SMX[8]	Ampicillin, cephalosporin[4]
Haemophilus (meningitis, respiratory infections)	Chloramphenicol	Ampicillin, TMP-SMX[8]
Klebsiella	Cephalosporin or gentamicin	Chloramphenicol
Legionella pneumophila (pneumonia)	Erythromycin	Tetracycline
Pasteurella (Yersinia) (plague, tularemia)	Streptomycin or tetracycline	Sulfonamide[6], chloramphenicol
Proteus		
Proteus mirabilis	Penicillin or ampicillin	Kanamycin, gentamicin
Proteus vulgaris and other species	Gentamicin or amikacin	Chloramphenicol, tobramycin
Pseudomonas		
Pseudomonas aeruginosa	Gentamicin plus carbenicillin	Polymyxin, amikacin
Pseudomonas pseudomallei (melioidosis)	Tetracycline	Chloramphenicol
Pseudomonas mallei (glanders)	Streptomycin plus tetracycline	Chloramphenicol
Salmonella	Chloramphenicol or ampicillin	TMP-SMX[8]
Serratia, Providencia	Gentamicin, amikacin	TMP-SMX[8] plus polymyxin
Shigella	Ampicillin or chloramphenicol	Tetracycline, TMP-SMX[8]
Vibrio (cholera)	Tetracycline	TMP-SMX[8]
Gram-positive rods		
Actinomyces	Penicillin[1]	Tetracycline
Bacillus (eg, anthrax)	Penicillin[1]	Erythromycin
Clostridium (eg, gas gangrene, tetanus)	Penicillin[1]	Tetracycline, cephalosporin[4]
Corynebacterium	Erythromycin	Penicillin, cephalosporin
Listeria	Ampicillin plus aminoglycoside	Tetracycline
Acid-fast rods		
Mycobacterium tuberculosis	INH plus rifampin or ethambutol[9]	Other antituberculosis drugs
Mycobacterium leprae	Dapsone, clofazimine	Amithiozone, rifampin
Mycobacteria, atypical	Ethambutol plus rifampin	Rifampin plus INH
Nocardia	Sulfonamide[6]	Minocycline
Spirochetes		
Borrelia (relapsing fever)	Tetracycline	Penicillin
Leptospira	Penicillin[1]	Tetracycline
Treponema (syphilis, yaws)	Penicillin[1]	Erythromycin, tetracycline
Mycoplasma	Tetracycline	Erythromycin
Chlamydia trachomatis, Chlamydia psittaci	Tetracycline, sulfonamide[6]	Erythromycin, chloramphenicol
Rickettsiae	Tetracycline	Chloramphenicol

[1] Penicillin G is preferred for parenteral injection; penicillin V for oral administration. Only highly sensitive microorganisms should be treated with oral penicillin.

[2] All tetracyclines have similar activity against microorganisms and comparable therapeutic activity and toxicity. Dosage is determined by the rates of absorption and excretion of different preparations.

[3] Erythromycin estolate is the best-absorbed oral form but carries greatest risk of hepatitis.

[4] Cefazolin, cephapirin, cephalothin, cefamandole, and cefoxitin are parenteral cephalosporins; cephalexin and cephradine the best oral forms.

[5] Parenteral nafcillin or oxacillin. Oral dicloxacillin, cloxacillin, or oxacillin.

[6] Trisulfapyrimidines and sulfisoxazole have the advantage of greater solubility in urine over sulfadiazine for oral administration; sodium sulfadiazine is suitable for intravenous injection in severely ill persons.

[7] For previously untreated urinary tract infection, a highly soluble sulfonamide such as sulfisoxazole or trisulfapyrimidines is the first choice. TMP-SMX[8] is acceptable.

[8] TMP-SMX is a mixture of 1 part trimethoprim plus 5 parts sulfamethoxazole.

[9] Either or both.

acid, is devoid of antibacterial activity. However, it carries an antigenic determinant of the penicillins and acts as a sensitizing hapten when attached to carrier proteins.

The different radicals (R) attached to the aminopenicillanic acid determine the essential pharmacologic properties of the resulting drugs. The clinically important penicillins in 1982 fall into 4 principal groups: (1) Highest activity against gram-positive organisms, spirochetes, and some others but susceptible to hydrolysis by beta-lactamases and acid-labile (eg, penicillin G). (2) Relatively resistant to beta-lactamases but lower activity against gram-positive organisms and inactive against gram-negatives (eg, nafcillin). (3) Relatively high activity against both gram-positive and gram-negative organisms but destroyed by beta-lactamases (eg, ampicillin, carbenicillin, ticarcillin). (4) Relatively stable to gastric acid and suitable for oral administration (eg, penicillin V, cloxacillin, amoxicillin). Some representatives are shown in Fig 10–2. Most penicillins are dispensed as sodium or potassium salts of the free acid. Potassium penicillin G contains about 1.7 mEq of K^+ per million units (2.8 mEq/g). Procaine salts and benzathine salts of penicillin provide repository forms for intramuscular injection. In dry form, penicillins are stable, but solutions rapidly lose their activity and must be prepared fresh for administration.

Antimicrobial Activity

The initial step in penicillin action is binding of the drug to cell receptors. These are proteins, and at least some of them are enzymes involved in transpeptidation reactions. From 3 to 7 receptors (or more) per cell can be present. After penicillin molecules have attached to the receptors, peptidoglycan synthesis is inhibited as final transpeptidation is blocked. A final bactericidal event is the removal of an inhibitor of autolytic enzymes in the cell wall. This activates the autolytic enzymes and results in cell lysis. Organisms with defective autolysin function are inhibited but not killed by beta-lactam drugs, and they are said to be "tolerant."

Since active cell wall synthesis is required for penicillin action, metabolically inactive microorganisms, L forms, or mycoplasmas are insusceptible to such drugs.

Penicillin G and penicillin V are often measured in units (1 million units = 0.6 g), but the semisynthetic penicillins are measured in grams. Whereas 0.002–1 μg/mL of penicillin G is lethal for a majority of susceptible gram-positive organisms, 10–100 times more is required to kill gram-negative bacteria (except neisseriae). The activity of penicillins also varies with their protein binding, which ranges from 40% to more than 95% for different drugs.

Resistance

Resistance to penicillins falls into several categories: (1) Production of beta-lactamases by staphylococci, gram-negative bacteria, *Haemophilus,*

gonococci, and others. More than 50 different beta-lactamases are known, most of them produced under the control of bacterial plasmids. (2) Lack of penicillin receptors (transpeptidases, etc) or inaccessibility of receptors because of permeability barriers of bacterial outer membranes. These are often under chromosomal control. (3) Failure of activation of autolytic enzymes in cell wall can result in inhibition without killing bacteria, eg, "tolerance" of some staphylococci. (4) Failure to synthesize peptidoglycans, eg, in mycoplasmas, L forms, or metabolically inactive bacteria.

Absorption, Distribution, & Excretion

After intramuscular or intravenous administration, absorption of most penicillins is rapid and complete. After oral administration, only 5–30% of the dose is absorbed, depending on acid stability, binding to foods, presence of buffers, etc. After absorption, penicillins are widely distributed in tissues and body fluids. Protein binding is 40–60% for penicillin G, ampicillin, and methicillin; 90% for nafcillin; and 95–98% for oxacillin and dicloxacillin. For most rapidly absorbed penicillins, a parenteral dose of 3–6 g/24 h yields serum levels of approximately 1–6 μg/mL.

Special dosage forms have been designed for delayed absorption to yield drug levels for long periods. After a single intramuscular dose of benzathine penicillin, 1.5 g (2.4 million units), serum levels of 0.03 unit/mL are maintained for 10 days and levels of 0.005 unit/mL for 3 weeks. Procaine penicillin given intramuscularly yields therapeutic levels for 24 hours.

In many tissues, penicillin concentrations are similar to those in serum. Lower levels occur in eyes and the central nervous system. However, in meningitis, penetration is enhanced, and levels of 0.2 μg/mL occur in the cerebrospinal fluid with a daily parenteral dose of 12 g. Thus, meningococcal and pneumococcal meningitis are treated with systemic penicillin, and intrathecal injection has been abandoned.

Most of the absorbed penicillin is rapidly excreted by the kidneys. About 10% of renal excretion is by glomerular filtration and 90% by tubular secretion. The latter can be partially blocked by probenecid to achieve higher systemic and cerebrospinal fluid levels. In the newborn and in persons with renal failure, penicillin excretion is reduced and systemic levels remain elevated longer.

Clinical Uses

Penicillins are the most widely used antibiotics, particularly in the following areas.

Penicillin G is the drug of choice in infections caused by streptococci, pneumococci, meningococci, spirochetes, clostridia, aerobic gram-positive rods, nonpenicillinase-producing staphylococci and gonococci, and some others (eg, *Bacteroides melaninogenicus*). Most of these infections respond to daily doses of penicillin G, 0.4–4 g, often given by intermittent intramuscular injection. Much larger amounts (6–50 g/d) are given by intermittent addition (every 2–6 hours) to an intravenous infusion in serious or complicated infections due to susceptible organisms. Sites for such intravenous infusions are subject to thrombophlebitis and superinfection; they must be kept scrupulously clean and changed every other day. Oral administration of penicillin V in daily doses of 1–4 g is indicated in minor infections. Oral administration is subject to so many variables that it should not be relied upon in seriously ill patients unless serum levels are monitored.

Penicillin G is inhibitory for enterococci *(S faecalis)* but for bactericidal effects (eg, in enterococcal endocarditis) an aminoglycoside must be added. Penicillin G in ordinary doses is excreted in sufficiently high concentrations into the urine to inhibit some gram-negative organisms in urinary tract infections, particularly *Proteus mirabilis*. However, this treatment fails in the presence of large numbers of beta-lactamase–producing bacteria in urine.

Benzathine penicillin G is a salt of very low solubility given intramuscularly for low but prolonged drug levels. A single injection of 1.2 million units (0.7 g) is satisfactory treatment for group A streptococcal pharyngitis. The same injection once every 3–4 weeks is satisfactory prophylaxis against group A streptococcal reinfection in rheumatic carditis. A dose of 2.4 million units 1–3 times at weekly intervals is effective in early syphilis.

Infection with beta-lactamase–producing staphylococci is the only indication for the use of lactamase-resistant penicillins, eg, nafcillin or oxacillin (6–12 g intravenously for adults, 50–100 mg/kg/d intravenously for children); cloxacillin or nafcillin, 2–6 g/d by mouth, can be given for milder staphylococcal infections.

Ampicillin, 2–3 g/d, can be given orally for treatment of some urinary tract infections with coliforms. In larger doses, ampicillin suppresses *Salmonella* enteric fevers. For bacterial meningitis in small children, ampicillin, 300 mg/kg/d intravenously, is the present choice, but lactamase-producing *H influenzae* is on the increase. Such infections can perhaps be treated by the simultaneous administration of ampicillin or amoxicillin with clavulanic acid. The latter binds the beta-lactamase and thus protects the penicillin (see p 118). That may apply to staphylococcal infection in the future. Amoxicillin is better absorbed and gives higher levels than ampicillin. Carbenicillin resembles ampicillin but is more active against *Pseudomonas* and *Proteus*. Up to 30 g intravenously is given daily, usually in conjunction with gentamicin, 5 mg/kg/d. Ticarcillin is more active than carbenicillin, and the daily dose is therefore 12–16 g/d.

Side-Effects

Penicillins possess less direct toxicity than any of the other antimicrobial drugs. Most serious side-effects are due to hypersensitivity.

A. Toxicity: Very high doses (more than 30 g/d intravenously) may produce central nervous system concentrations that are irritating. In patients with renal failure, smaller doses may produce encephalopathy, delirium, and convulsions. With such doses, direct cation toxicity (K^+) may also occur. Lactamase-resistant penicillins occasionally cause granulocytopenia. Oral penicillins can cause diarrhea. Carbenicillin may cause a bleeding tendency.

B. Allergy: All penicillins are cross-sensitizing and cross-reacting. Any material (including milk, cosmetics) containing penicillin may induce sensitization. The responsible antigens are degradation products, eg, penicilloic acid, bound to host protein. Skin tests with penicilloyl-polylysine, with alkaline hydrolysis products, and with undegraded penicillin identify many hypersensitive persons. Among positive reactors to skin tests, the incidence of major immediate allergic reactions is high. Antibodies to penicillin (IgG) are not correlated with allergic reactions except rare hemolytic anemia. A history of a penicillin reaction in the past is not reliable, but the drug must be administered with caution to such persons, or a substitute drug should be chosen.

Allergic reactions may occur as typical anaphylactic shock, typical serum sickness type reactions (urticaria, joint swelling, angioneurotic edema, pruritus, respiratory embarrassment within 7–12 days of penicillin dosage), and a variety of skin rashes, fever, nephritis, eosinophilia, vasculitis, etc. The incidence of hypersensitivity to penicillin is negligible in children but may be 1–5% among adults in the USA. Acute anaphylactic life-threatening reactions are very rare (0.05%). Corticosteroids can sometimes suppress allergic manifestations to penicillins.

CEPHALOSPORINS

Fungi of *Cephalosporium* species yield several antibiotics called cephalosporins. They resemble penicillins, are resistant to beta-lactamases, and are active against both gram-positive and gram-negative bacteria. The nucleus of the cephalosporins, 7-aminocephalosporanic acid, closely resembles the nucleus of penicillin, 6-aminopenicillanic acid. The cephamycin drugs are similar but are made by actinomycetes.

The intrinsic activity of the natural cephalosporins is low, but attachment of various R groups has yielded several compounds of high therapeutic activity and low toxicity. The cephalosporins have molecular weights of about 420; they are freely soluble in water and relatively stable. Cephalothin, cefazolin, cephapirin, cefamandole, cefotaxime, and cefoxitin must be injected parenterally, since they are not well absorbed from the gastrointestinal tract. Serum levels of 10–20 μg/mL are reached with cephalothin, 8–12 g/d intravenously, and 20–50 μg/mL with cefazolin, 4 g/d intramuscularly or intravenously. The drugs are distributed widely in tissues but penetrate poorly into the central nervous system. Cephalosporins should not be used in meningitis. Cephalexin and cephradine are sufficiently well absorbed from the gut to give serum

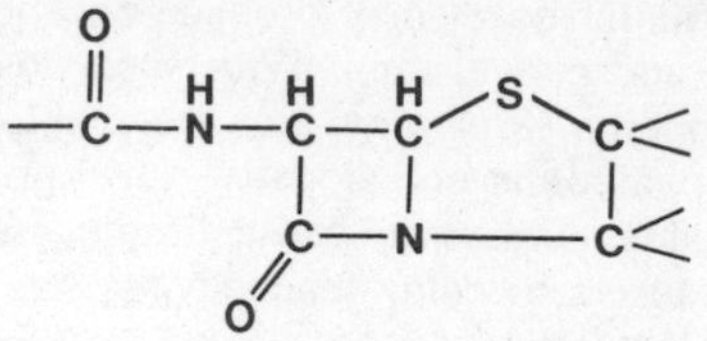

Aminopenicillanic acid

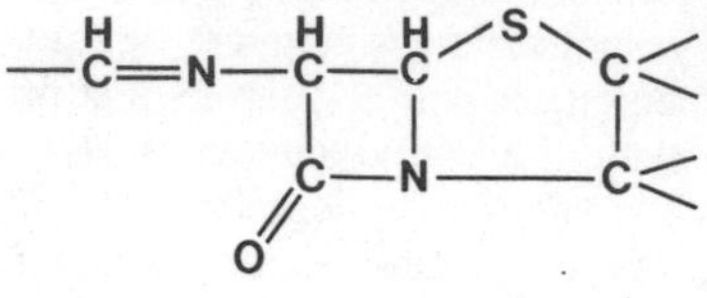

Amidinopenicillanic acid

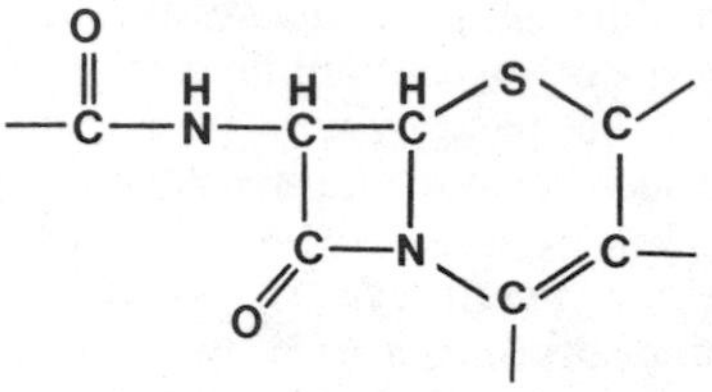

Cephalosporanic acid

levels of 10 μg/mL. Urinary and respiratory tract infections can be treated, but these oral drugs are rarely suitable for treatment of major systemic infections.

Activity

The cephalosporins are active in concentrations of 10 μg/mL or less against gram-positive organisms, including penicillinase-producing staphylococci, and against many gram-negative bacteria. Typically, many strains of *Klebsiella*, coliforms, and *Proteus* remain susceptible to cephalosporins, whereas *Enterobacter*, *Serratia*, and *Pseudomonas* are resistant. The antistaphylococcal activity of the cephalosporins is comparable to that of penicillinase-resistant penicillins. Most enterococci, *Serratia, Acinetobacter, Proteus*, and some strains of coliforms are resistant to 10 μg/mL but may be inhibited by the levels reached in urine (300–500 μg/mL). Cefoxitin and cefotaxime are active against several anaerobes, including *Bacteroides*. The cephalosporins, like penicillins, interfere with transpeptidation of peptidoglycans in cell wall synthesis. They are moderately or highly resistant to many beta-lactamases. In spite of the lack of primary indications, cephalosporins were in 1981 in the USA a leading item in drug budgets, particularly in hospitals. Many new drugs in this class are in testing stages and clinical trials. Cephalosporins are the principal drugs in surgical chemoprophylaxis.

Side-Effects

A. Allergy: Cephalosporins can be sensitizing, and specific hypersensitivity reactions, including anaphylaxis, can occur. Because of the chemical difference in drug nucleus structure, the antigenicity of cephalosporins differs from that of penicillins. Con-

sequently, many individuals who are hypersensitive to penicillins can tolerate cephalosporins. The degree of cross-allergenicity between penicillins and cephalosporins remains controversial (6–16%). Some cross-antigenicity can be demonstrated in vitro.

B. Toxicity: Pain on injection, thrombophlebitis, rashes, and granulocytopenia. Diarrhea, nausea, and vomiting occur with oral cephalosporins.

THE TETRACYCLINE DRUGS

The tetracyclines have the basic structure shown below. The following radicals occur in the different chemical forms:

	R	R_1	R_2	Renal Clearance (mL/min)
Tetracycline	—H	—CH$_3$	—H	65
Chlortetracycline	—Cl	—CH$_3$	—H	35
Oxytetracycline	—H	—CH$_3$	—OH	90
Demeclocycline	—Cl	—H	—H	35
Methacycline	—H	=CH$_2$*	—OH	31
Doxycycline	—H	—CH$_3$	—OH	16
Minocycline	—N(CH$_3$)$_2$	—H	—H	< 10

*No hydroxyl at C6.

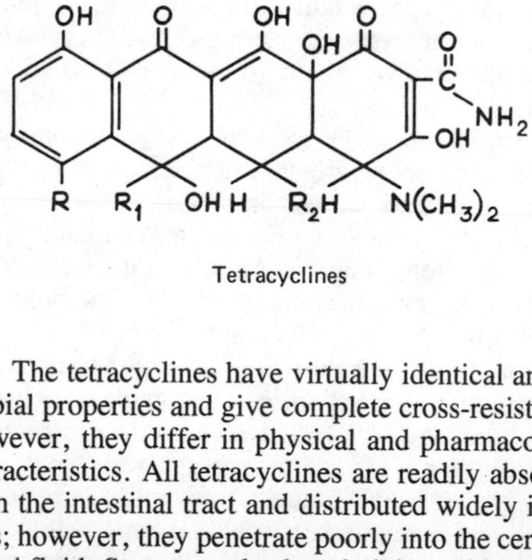

Tetracyclines

The tetracyclines have virtually identical antimicrobial properties and give complete cross-resistance. However, they differ in physical and pharmacologic characteristics. All tetracyclines are readily absorbed from the intestinal tract and distributed widely in tissues; however, they penetrate poorly into the cerebrospinal fluid. Some can also be administered intramuscularly or intravenously. They are excreted in stool and into bile and urine at varying rates. With doses of tetracycline hydrochloride of 2 g daily orally, blood levels reach 8 μg/mL. Demeclocycline, methacycline, minocycline, and doxycycline are excreted more slowly; similar blood levels are achieved by daily doses of 0.6, 0.3, 0.2, and 0.1 g, respectively.

Activity

Tetracyclines are concentrated by susceptible bacteria and inhibit protein synthesis by inhibiting the binding of aminoacyl-tRNA to the 30S unit of bacterial ribosomes. Resistant bacteria fail to concentrate the drug. This resistance is under the control of transmissible plasmids.

The tetracyclines are principally bacteriostatic agents. They inhibit the growth of susceptible gram-positive and gram-negative bacteria (inhibited by 0.1–10 μg/mL) and are drugs of choice in infections caused by rickettsiae, chlamydiae, and *Mycoplasma pneumoniae*. Tetracyclines are used in cholera to shorten excretion of vibrios, and in shigellosis. They provide an alternative to penicillin for gonococcal infections and are sometimes employed to treat *Brucella* or *Pasteurella* infections, in combination with streptomycin. Minocycline is active against many strains of *Nocardia* and can eradicate the meningococcal carrier state. Low doses of tetracycline for many months are given for acne to suppress both skin bacteria and their lipases, which promote inflammatory changes.

Tetracyclines do not inhibit fungi and may even stimulate the growth of yeasts. They temporarily suppress parts of the normal bowel flora. Their therapeutic usefulness is limited by the occurrence of "superinfections": while one microorganism is suppressed, another is permitted to multiply freely and produce pathogenic effects. This has occurred particularly with tetracycline-resistant *Pseudomonas, Proteus,* staphylococci, and yeasts.

Side-Effects

The tetracyclines produce varying degrees of gastrointestinal upset (nausea, vomiting, diarrhea), skin rashes, mucous membrane lesions, and fever in many patients, particularly when administration is prolonged and dosage high. It is not definitely known what part is played by allergy and what part by direct toxicity. Replacement of bacterial flora (see above) occurs commonly. Overgrowth of yeasts on anal and vaginal mucous membranes during tetracycline administration leads to inflammation and pruritus. Overgrowth of organisms in the intestine may lead to enterocolitis.

Tetracyclines are deposited in bony structures and teeth, particularly in the fetus and during the first 6 years of life. Discoloration and fluorescence of the teeth occur in newborns if tetracyclines are taken for prolonged periods by pregnant women. In pregnancy, hepatic damage may occur. Outdated tetracycline can produce renal damage. Demeclocycline causes photosensitization. Minocycline can cause marked vestibular disturbances.

Bacteriologic Examination

Because of its instability in vitro, chlortetracycline often appears less active than the other members of the group. Antimicrobial efficacy of the tetracyclines is virtually identical, so that only one stable tetracycline need be included in antibiotic sensitivity tests. Cross-resistance of microorganisms to tetracyclines is virtually complete; an organism resistant to one of the drugs may be assumed to be resistant to the others also.

CHLORAMPHENICOL

Chloramphenicol is a substance produced originally from cultures of *Streptomyces venezuelae* but now manufactured synthetically.

Crystalline chloramphenicol is a stable compound that is rapidly absorbed from the gastrointestinal tract and widely distributed into tissues and body fluids, including the central nervous system and cerebrospinal fluid; it penetrates well into cells. Most of the drug is inactivated in the liver by conjugation with glucuronic acid or by reduction to inactive arylamines. Excretion is mainly in the urine, 90% in inactive form. Although chloramphenicol is usually administered orally (2 g daily gives blood levels up to 10 μg/mL), the succinate can be injected intravenously in similar dosage.

Chloramphenicol

Activity

Chloramphenicol is a potent inhibitor of protein synthesis in microorganisms. It blocks the attachment of amino acids to the nascent peptide chain on the 50S unit of ribosomes by interfering with the action of peptidyl transferase. Chloramphenicol is principally

Table 10–3. Blood levels of some commonly used antibiotics at therapeutic dosages in adults.

	Route	Daily Dose	Expected Mean Concentration per mL Blood or per gram Tissue
Penicillin	IM	0.6–1 million units	1 unit
	Oral	0.6 million units	0.2 unit
Nafcillin	IV	6–12 g	5–30 μg
Cloxacillin, dicloxacillin	Oral	2–4 g	3–12 μg
Ampicillin	Oral	2–3 g	3–4 μg
	IV	4–6 g	10–40 μg
Carbenicillin	IV	30 g	100–200 μg
Ticarcillin	IV	18 g	100–200 μg
Cephalothin	IV	8–12 g	10–20 μg
Cefazolin	IM	2–4 g	20–50 μg
Cefoxitin, cefamandole	IV	4–12 g	40–80 μg
Tetracyclines	Oral	2 g	6–8 μg
Chloramphenicol	Oral	2 g	8–10 μg
Erythromycin	Oral	2 g	0.5–2 μg
Amikacin	IM	1 g	20–30 μg
Gentamicin, tobramycin	IM	0.3 g	3–6 μg
Vancomycin	IV	2 g	10–20 μg
Clindamycin	IV	2.4 g	3–6 μg
Polymyxin B	IV	0.15 g	1–3 μg

bacteriostatic, and its spectrum is similar to that of the tetracyclines. Dosage and blood levels are similar to those of the tetracyclines. Chloramphenicol is a drug of possible first choice in (1) meningitis due to *N meningitidis* or *S pneumoniae;* (2) *H influenzae* infections not susceptible to ampicillin; (3) *Salmonella* enteric fevers; and (4) brain abscess.

Chloramphenicol resistance is due to destruction of the drug by an enzyme (chloramphenicol acetyltransferase) that is under plasmid control.

Side-Effects

Chloramphenicol infrequently causes gastrointestinal upsets. However, prolonged administration of more than 3 g daily to adults regularly results in abnormalities of early forms of red blood cells, elevation of serum iron, and anemia. These changes are reversible upon discontinuance of the drug. Very rare individuals exhibit an apparent idiosyncrasy to chloramphenicol and develop severe or fatal depression of bone marrow function. The mechanism of this aplastic anemia is not understood, but it is distinct from the dose-related reversible effect described above. For these reasons the use of chloramphenicol is generally restricted to those infections where it is clearly the most effective drug by laboratory test or experience.

In premature and newborn infants, chloramphenicol can induce collapse ("gray syndrome") because the normal mechanism of detoxification (glucuronide conjugation in the liver) is not yet developed.

Bacteriologic Examination

Chloramphenicol is very stable and diffuses well in agar media. For these reasons, it tends to give larger zones of growth inhibition by the "disk test" than the tetracyclines, even when tube dilution tests show identical effectiveness. An enzymatic assay (using acetyltransferase) permits estimation of chloramphenicol concentration in body fluids.

ERYTHROMYCINS
(Macrolides)

Erythromycin is obtained from *Streptomyces erythreus* and has the chemical formula $C_{37}H_{67}NO_{13}$. Drugs related to erythromycin are spiramycin, oleandomycin, and others. These drugs give complete cross-resistance but are less effective than erythromycin.

Erythromycins attach to a receptor (a 23S rRNA) on the 50S subunit of the bacterial ribosome. They inhibit protein synthesis by interfering with translocation reactions and the elongation of the peptide chain. Resistance to erythromycins results from an alteration (methylation) of the rRNA receptor. This is under control of a transmissible plasmid. The activity of erythromycins is greatly enhanced at alkaline pH.

Erythromycins in concentrations of $0.1-2\ \mu g/mL$ are active against gram-positive organisms, including pneumococci, streptococci, and corynebacteria. *Mycoplasma, Chlamydia trachomatis, Legionella pneumophila,* and *Campylobacter fetus* are also susceptible. Resistant variants occur in susceptible microbial populations and tend to emerge during treatment. This is especially true in staphylococcal infections.

Erythromycins are substitutes for penicillins in persons hypersensitive to the latter. Erythromycin stearate, succinate, or estolate, 0.5 g every 6 hours orally, yields serum levels of $0.5-2\ \mu g/mL$. Special forms (erythromycin gluceptate or lactobionate) are given intravenously in a dose of 0.5 g every 8–12 hours (40 mg/kg/d).

Undesirable side-effects are drug fever, mild gastrointestinal upsets, and cholestatic hepatitis as a hypersensitivity reaction, especially to the estolate. Hepatotoxicity may be increased during pregnancy.

CLINDAMYCIN & LINCOMYCIN

Lincomycin (derived from *Streptomyces lincolnensis*) and clindamycin (a chlorine-substituted derivative) resemble erythromycins in mode of action, antibacterial spectrum, and ribosomal receptors but are chemically distinct. Clindamycin is very active against *Bacteroides.*

The drugs are acid-stable and can be given by mouth or by injection of 600 mg intravenously 3–4 times daily (10–20 mg/kg/d). Serum levels reach 3–6 $\mu g/mL$, and the drugs are widely distributed in tissues, except the central nervous system. Excretion is mainly through liver, bile, and urine.

Probably the most important indication for intravenous clindamycin is the treatment of severe anaerobic infections, including those caused by *Bacteroides fragilis.* Lincomycins have also been suggested for treatment of gram-positive coccal infections in persons hypersensitive to penicillins, but erythromycins may be preferable. Successful treatment of staphylococcal infections of bone with lincomycins has been recorded. Lincomycins should not be used in meningitis. Clindamycin has been prominent in antibiotic-associated colitis caused by *Clostridium difficile.* This organism is generally clindamycin-resistant and gains prominence in bowel flora during treatment with this—or occasionally other—drugs. It produces a necrotizing toxin and results in pseudomembranous colitis, which may be fatal. Early diagnosis and treatment with oral vancomycin are necessary.

VANCOMYCIN

Vancomycin is an amphoteric material produced by *Streptomyces orientalis,* dispensed as the hydrochloride. It has a high molecular weight (3300) and is poorly absorbed from the intestine.

Vancomycin is markedly bactericidal for staphylococci, enterococci, and some clostridia. The drug inhibits early stages in cell wall mucopeptide synthesis. Drug-resistant strains do not emerge rapidly. The dosage is 0.5 g every 6–12 hours intravenously (injected in a 30-minute period) for serious systemic staphylococcal or enterococcal infections, including endocarditis, especially if resistant to nafcillin. Oral vancomycin, 0.25–0.5 g, is indicated in pseudomembranous antibiotic-associated colitis (see Clindamycin and p 213).

Undesirable side-effects are thrombophlebitis, skin rashes, nerve deafness, and occasionally kidney damage.

BACITRACIN

Bacitracin is a polypeptide obtained from a strain of *Bacillus subtilis*. It is stable and poorly absorbed from the intestinal tract or from wounds. Its best use is for topical application to skin, wounds, or mucous membranes.

Bacitracin is mainly bactericidal for grampositive bacteria, including penicillin-resistant organisms. For topical use, concentrations of 500–2000 units per milliliter of solution or gram of ointment are used. In combination with polymyxin B or neomycin, bacitracin is useful for the suppression of mixed bacterial flora in surface lesions.

Bacitracin is toxic for the kidney, causing proteinuria, hematuria, and nitrogen retention. For this reason, it has no place in systemic therapy. Bacitracin is said not to induce hypersensitivity readily.

POLYMYXINS

Polymyxin B and polymyxin E (colistin) are basic polypeptides, poorly absorbed from the intestinal tract but readily absorbed after injection. They are not widely distributed in tissues and body fluids. Unless locally introduced, they do not reach the spinal fluid or pleural or joint space. Colistin is dispensed as a methanesulfonate complex and produces fewer side-effects than polymyxin B sulfate.

Activity

The polymyxins are strongly bactericidal against gram-negative bacilli, including *Pseudomonas,* that are resistant to other antibiotics. Polymyxins coat the bacterial cell membrane and destroy its active transport and function as a selective permeability barrier. They act like cationic detergents.

In tissues, polymyxins are strongly bound to membranes rich in phosphatidylethanolamine and are inhibited by pus. This limits their availability for antibacterial action.

Polymyxin B sulfate can be injected intramuscularly or intravenously (2.5 mg/kg/d) in serious gram-negative infections, including *Pseudomonas* sepsis. It can be given intrathecally (up to 5 mg/d) for *Pseudomonas* meningitis. Colistin methanesulfonate (3–5 mg/kg/d) intramuscularly for urinary tract infections contains a local anesthetic and causes less pain than polymyxin B given intramuscularly.

Side-Effects

The polymyxins produce reversible central nervous system side-effects, including drowsiness, abnormal sensations, and ataxia. Pain at the site of intramuscular injection necessitates simultaneous administration of a local anesthetic. In doses exceeding 2.5 mg/kg/d, damage to the kidney may occur, particularly if renal function is impaired.

Bacteriologic Examination

The polymyxins are large molecules and diffuse poorly through agar. Consequently, inhibition zones in "disk tests" are always very small, even when the organism is shown to be highly sensitive by the tube dilution test. Organisms highly sensitive in vitro (inhibited by 0.1–1 μg/mL) may not respond in vivo if parenchymatous organs are involved in the infection. In susceptible strains of bacteria, resistance to polymyxins rarely develops.

AMINOGLYCOSIDES

Aminoglycosides are a group of drugs sharing chemical, antimicrobial, pharmacologic, and toxic characteristics. At present, the group includes streptomycin, neomycin, kanamycin, amikacin, gentamicin, tobramycin, sisomicin, netilmycin, and others. All inhibit protein synthesis of bacteria by attaching to and inhibiting the function of the 30S subunit of the bacterial ribosome. Resistance is based on (1) a deficiency of the ribosomal receptor (chromosomal mutant), (2) enzymatic destruction of the drug (plasmid-mediated transmissible resistance of clinical importance), or (3) lack of permeability to the drug molecule and lack of active transport into the cell. The last factor can be chromosomal in nature (eg, streptococci are relatively impermeable to aminoglycosides), or it can be plasmid-mediated (clinically significant resistance among gram-negative enteric bacteria). Anaerobic bacteria are often resistant to aminoglycosides because transport through the cell membrane is an energy-requiring process that is oxygen-dependent.

All aminoglycosides are more active at alkaline pH than at acid pH. All are potentially ototoxic and nephrotoxic, though to different degrees. All can accumulate in the presence of renal failure; therefore, marked dosage adjustments must be made when nitrogen retention occurs. Aminoglycosides are used most widely against gram-negative enteric bacteria or when there is suspicion of sepsis. In the treatment of bacteremia or endocarditis caused by fecal streptococci or some gram-negative bacteria, the aminoglycoside is given together with a penicillin that enhances permeability and facilitates the entry of the aminoglycoside. Aminoglycosides are selected according to recent susceptibility patterns in a given area or hospital until susceptibility tests become available on a specific isolate. All positively charged aminoglycosides and polymyxins are inhibited in blood cultures by sodium polyanethol sulfonate and other polyanionic detergents. Some aminoglycosides (especially streptomycin) are useful as antimycobacterial drugs.

1. NEOMYCIN & KANAMYCIN

Kanamycin is a close relative of neomycin, with similar activity and complete cross-resistance. Paromomycin is also closely related and is used in amebiasis. These drugs are stable, poorly absorbed from the intestinal tract, readily absorbed and distributed after intramuscular injection, and slowly excreted in the urine. Kanamycin is less toxic than neomycin, and only kanamycin is used systemically in children.

Kanamycin is bactericidal for many gram-negative bacilli, including some strains of *Proteus,* but ineffective against *Pseudomonas* and *Serratia.* Kanamycin, 15 mg/kg/d, is administered in serious infections due to gram-negative organisms that are resistant to other drugs. Oral doses of 4–6 g daily are used for reduction of intestinal flora preoperatively but are ineffective in most bacterial diarrheas except those caused by enteropathogenic *E coli.* Neomycin is limited to topical application to skin wounds or gut.

Neomycin and kanamycin may cause renal damage and nerve deafness without warning signs. Intraperitoneal administration of 3–5 g has induced respiratory paralysis, which can be overcome by neostigmine.

2. AMIKACIN

Amikacin is a semisynthetic derivative of kanamycin. It is relatively resistant to several of the enzymes that inactivate gentamicin and tobramycin and therefore can be employed against some microorganisms resistant to the latter drugs. However, bacterial resistance due to impermeability to amikacin is increasing. Many gram-negative enteric bacteria, including many strains of *Proteus, Pseudomonas,* enterobacteria, and *Serratia,* are inhibited by 1–20 μg/mL amikacin in vitro. After the injection of 500 mg amikacin intramuscularly every 12 hours (15 mg/kg/d), peak levels in serum are 10–30 μg/mL. Some infections caused by gram-negative bacteria resistant to gentamicin respond to amikacin. Central nervous system infections require intrathecal or intraventricular injection of 1–10 mg daily.

Like all aminoglycosides, amikacin is nephrotoxic and ototoxic (particularly for the auditory portion of the eighth nerve). Its levels should be monitored in ts with renal failure.

3. GENTAMICIN

In concentrations of 0.5–5 μg/mL, gentamicin is bactericidal for many gram-positive and gram-negative bacteria, including many strains of *Proteus, Serratia,* and *Pseudomonas.* Gentamicin is ineffective against streptococci and *Bacteroides.*

After intramuscular injection of 3–5 mg/kg/d, serum levels reach 3–6 μg/mL and the drug is widely distributed. Gentamicin is indicated in serious infections caused by gram-negative bacteria insusceptible to other drugs, when up to 7 mg/kg/d has been used. Gentamicin may precipitate with carbenicillin in vitro, but enhancement of bactericidal action against *Pseudomonas* occurs sometimes in vivo.

Gentamicin is nephrotoxic and ototoxic, particularly in impaired renal function, which predisposes to cumulation and toxic effects. Gentamicin sulfate, 0.1%, has been used topically in creams or solutions for infected burns or skin lesions. Such creams tend to select gentamicin-resistant bacteria, and patients receiving them must remain in strict isolation.

4. TOBRAMYCIN

This aminoglycoside, available since 1975, has an antibacterial spectrum similar to that of gentamicin but is more active than the latter against *Pseudomonas* species. Although there is some cross-resistance between gentamicin and tobramycin, it is unpredictable in individual strains. Separate laboratory susceptibility tests are therefore necessary.

The pharmacologic properties of tobramycin are virtually identical to those of gentamicin. The daily dose of tobramycin is 3–5 mg/kg/d intramuscularly, divided in 3 equal amounts and given every 8 hours. Such dosage produces blood levels of 2–5 μg/mL in the presence of normal renal function. About 80% of the drug is excreted by glomerular filtration into the urine within 24 hours of administration. In uremia, the drug dosage must be reduced. A formula for such dosage is 1 mg/kg every (6 × serum creatinine level) hours. However, monitoring of blood levels is desirable in uremia.

Like other aminoglycosides, tobramycin is ototoxic and nephrotoxic. It should not be used concurrently with other drugs having similar adverse effects or with diuretics, which tend to enhance aminoglycoside tissue concentrations.

5. STREPTOMYCIN

Streptomycin was the first aminoglycoside—it was discovered in the 1940s as a product of *Streptomyces griseus.* It was studied in great detail and became the prototype of this class of drugs. For this reason, its properties are listed here, although widespread resistance among microorganisms has greatly reduced its clinical usefulness. Dihydrostreptomycin

Streptidine   Streptobiosamine

Streptomycin

has been abandoned altogether because of excessive ototoxicity.

After intramuscular injection, streptomycin is rapidly absorbed and widely distributed in tissues except the central nervous system. Only 5% of the extracellular concentration of streptomycin reaches the interior of the cell. Absorbed streptomycin is excreted by glomerular filtration into the urine. After oral administration it is poorly absorbed from the gut; most of it is excreted in feces.

Activity

Like other aminoglycosides, streptomycin inhibits protein synthesis in bacteria.

The streptomycins are bactericidal against susceptible microorganisms (inhibited in vitro by 0.1–20 μg/mL). The therapeutic effectiveness of streptomycin is limited by the rapid emergence of resistant mutants.

Streptomycin may be given in a dosage of 1 g/d intramuscularly with a penicillin in enterococcal endocarditis to enhance bactericidal action. In tularemia and plague, it is given with tetracyclines. In tuberculosis, 1 g is injected intramuscularly twice weekly (or daily), together with one or 2 other antituberculosis drugs (isoniazid, rifampin).

Resistance

All microbial strains produce streptomycin-resistant chromosomal mutants with relatively high frequency. Chromosomal mutants have an alteration in the P 12 receptor on the 30S ribosomal subunit. Plasmid-mediated resistance results in enzymatic destruction of the drug. In tuberculosis, combination with isoniazid or other antituberculosis drugs results in a marked delay in the emergence of resistance.

Side-Effects

A. Allergy: Fever, skin rashes, and other allergic manifestations may result from hypersensitivity to streptomycin. This occurs most frequently upon prolonged contact with the drug, in patients receiving a protracted course of treatment (eg, for tuberculosis), or in medical personnel preparing and handling the drug. (Nurses preparing solutions should wear gloves.)

B. Toxicity: Streptomycin is markedly toxic for the vestibular portion of the eighth cranial nerve, caus-

ing tinnitus, vertigo, and ataxia, which are often irreversible. It is moderately nephrotoxic.

Bacteriologic Examination

When sensitivity determinations with streptomycin are carried out in liquid media, a single resistant organism in the inoculum may grow out rapidly, although the bulk of the population is streptomycin-sensitive. Conversely, testing on solid media may fail to reveal the presence of resistant mutants in the population unless a very large inoculum is employed.

SPECTINOMYCIN

This is an aminocyclitol antibiotic (related to aminoglycosides) for intramuscular administration. Its sole application is in the treatment of gonorrhea in individuals believed to be hypersensitive to penicillin or in those failing to respond to penicillin or tetracycline. One injection of 2 g produces blood levels of 100 μg/mL. About 5–10% of gonococci are probably resistant. There is usually pain at the injection site, and there may be nausea and fever.

ISONIAZID
(Isonicotinic Acid Hydrazide, INH)

Isoniazid has little effect on most bacteria but is strikingly active against mycobacteria, especially *Mycobacterium tuberculosis*. Most tubercle bacilli are inhibited by 0.1–1 μg/mL of isoniazid in vitro, but large populations of tubercle bacilli usually contain some isoniazid-resistant organisms. For this reason, the drug is employed in combination with other antimycobacterial agents (especially ethambutol or rifampin) to reduce the emergence of resistant tubercle bacilli. Isoniazid has been shown to exert competitive antagonism against pyridoxine-catalyzed reactions in *E coli*, but the antimycobacterial action appears to involve inhibition of the synthesis of mycolic acids. Isoniazid and pyridoxine are structural analogs. Patients receiving isoniazid excrete pyridoxine in excessive amounts, which results in peripheral neuritis. This can be prevented by the administration of pyridoxine, 0.3–0.5 g daily, which does not interfere with the

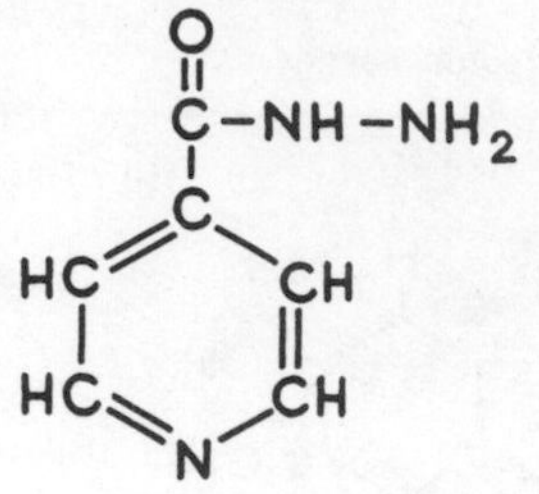

O
‖
C—NH—NH$_2$

Isoniazid

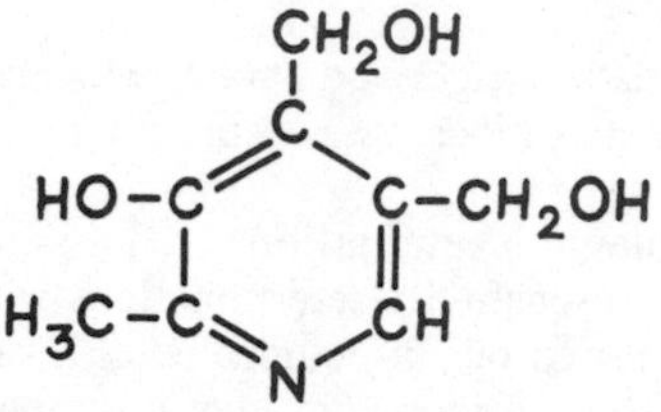

CH$_2$OH

HO—C   C—CH$_2$OH

H$_3$C—C   CH

Pyridoxine

antituberculosis action of isoniazid.

Isoniazid is rapidly and completely absorbed from the gastrointestinal tract and is in part acetylated and in part excreted in the urine. In the ordinary systemic dose of 4–6 mg/kg/d, toxic manifestations (eg, hepatitis) are infrequent, and blood levels reach an average of 0.5 μg/mL. Isoniazid freely diffuses into tissue fluids, including the cerebrospinal fluid. In tuberculous meningitis, 8–10 mg/kg/d is given for many weeks.

In converters from negative to positive tuberculin skin tests who have no evidence of disease, isoniazid, 300 mg daily for 1 year, may be used "prophylactically."

ETHAMBUTOL

Ethambutol is a synthetic, water-soluble, heat-stable D-isomer of the structure shown below.

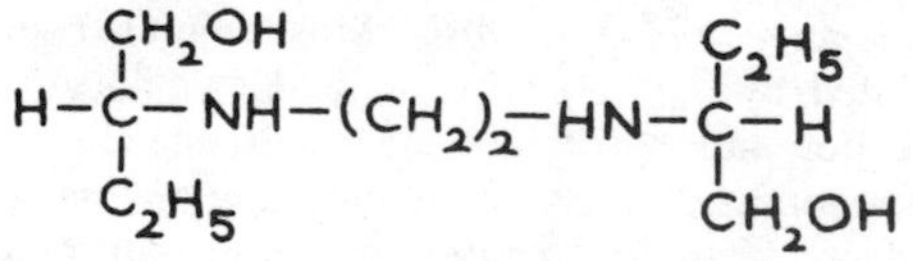

CH$_2$OH   C$_2$H$_5$
| |
H—C—NH—(CH$_2$)$_2$—HN—C—H
| |
C$_2$H$_5$ CH$_2$OH

Ethambutol

Many strains of *M tuberculosis* are inhibited in vitro by ethambutol, 1–5 μg/mL. The mechanism of action is not known.

Ethambutol is well absorbed from the gut. Following ingestion of 15 mg/kg, a blood level peak of 1–4 μg/mL is reached in 2–4 hours. About 20% of the drug is excreted in feces and 50% in urine, in unchanged form. Excretion is delayed in renal failure. About 15% of absorbed drug is metabolized by oxida-

tion and conversion to a dicarboxylic acid. In meningitis, ethambutol appears in the cerebrospinal fluid.

Resistance to ethambutol emerges fairly rapidly among mycobacteria when the drug is used alone. Therefore, ethambutol is given in combination with other antituberculosis drugs, most commonly isoniazid.

Ethambutol, 15 mg/kg, is usually given as a single daily dose. Hypersensitivity to ethambutol occurs infrequently. The commonest side-effects are visual disturbances; reduction in visual acuity, optic neuritis, and perhaps retinal damage occur in some patients given 25 mg/kg/d for several months. Most of these changes apparently regress when ethambutol is discontinued. However, periodic visual acuity testing is mandatory during treatment. With 15 mg/kg/d, visual disturbances are very rare.

RIFAMPIN

Rifampin is a semisynthetic derivative of rifamycin, an antibiotic produced by *Streptomyces mediterranei*. It is active in vitro against some gram-positive and gram-negative cocci, some enteric bacteria, mycobacteria, chlamydiae, and poxviruses. Although many meningococci and mycobacteria are inhibited by less than 1 μg/mL, highly resistant mutants occur in all microbial populations in a frequency of 1 in 10^7 or greater. The prolonged administration of rifampin as a single drug permits the emergence of these highly resistant organisms. There is no cross-resistance to other antimicrobial drugs.

Rifampin binds strongly to DNA-dependent RNA polymerase and thus inhibits RNA synthesis in bacteria and chlamydiae. It blocks a late stage in the assembly of poxviruses, perhaps interfering with envelope formation.

Rifampin is well absorbed after oral administration, widely distributed in tissues, and excreted mainly through the liver and to a lesser extent into the urine. With oral doses of 600 mg, serum levels exceed 5 μg/mL for 4–6 hours and urine levels may be 10–100 times higher.

In tuberculosis, a single oral dose of 600 mg daily (10–20 mg/kg/d) is administered together with ethambutol, isoniazid, or another antituberculosis drug in order to delay the emergence of rifampin-resistant mycobacteria. A similar regimen may apply to atypical mycobacteria. In short-term treatment schedules for tuberculosis, rifampin, 600 mg orally, is given first daily (together with isoniazid) and then 2 or 3 times weekly for 6–9 months. However, no less than 2 doses weekly should be given to avoid a "flu syndrome" and anemia. Rifampin is effective in leprosy.

An oral dose of 600 mg twice daily for 2 days can eliminate a majority of meningococci from carriers. Unfortunately, some highly resistant meningococcal strains are selected out by this procedure. In urinary tract infections and in chronic bronchitis, rifampin is not useful because resistance emerges promptly.

Rifampin imparts an orange color to urine and sweat, which is harmless. Occasional adverse effects include rashes, thrombocytopenia, and impairment of liver function.

AMINOSALICYLIC ACID (PAS)

p-Aminosalicylic acid closely resembles *p*-aminobenzoic acid and sulfonamides. Most bacteria are not inhibited by PAS, but tubercle bacilli are usually inhibited by PAS, 1–5 μg/mL, whereas atypical mycobacteria are resistant. In susceptible mycobacterial populations, PAS-resistant mutants tend to emerge. The simultaneous use of a second antituberculosis drug inhibits this development.

Aminosalicylic acid

PAS, 8–12 g daily orally, was commonly given in combination with streptomycin or isoniazid as antituberculosis therapy. However, full oral doses of PAS were commonly associated with severe gastrointestinal side-effects. Therefore, the use of PAS has been largely abandoned.

AMPHOTERICIN B

Amphotericin B is a complex antibiotic polyene produced by a *Streptomyces* species and has negligible antibacterial properties although it strongly inhibits the growth of several pathogenic fungi in vitro and in vivo. Amphotericin binds to sterols on the fungal cell membranes and disturbs their function. The microcrystals of the drug are dispensed with sodium deoxycholate and a buffer to be dissolved in dextrose solution. It is injected intravenously in daily doses of 0.4–0.8 mg/kg/d (with an initial dose of 5 mg/d) and can be given intrathecally up to 0.8 mg every other day in meningitis. Amphotericin B appears to be the most effective agent available for the treatment of disseminated coccidioidomycosis, blastomycosis, histoplasmosis, cryptococcosis, and candidiasis. It frequently produces marked toxic effects, including fever, chills, nausea and vomiting, renal failure, hypokalemia, and anemia. When it is used together with flucytosine, synergism may occur.

FLUCYTOSINE

5-Fluorocytosine is an oral antifungal compound of relatively low toxicity. Flucytosine, 5 μg/mL, inhibits many strains of *Candida, Cryptococcus,* and *Torulopsis* and some strains of other fungi. Oral doses of 150 mg/kg/d are well absorbed and widely distributed in tissues, including cerebrospinal fluid. Although the drug is relatively well tolerated, prolonged high serum levels often cause depression of bone marrow, loss of hair, skin rashes, and abnormal liver function. With 3–8 g administered daily in divided doses, there has been prolonged remission of fungemia and meningitis caused by susceptible organisms. Resistant mutants occur frequently, and, for this reason, simultaneous use of amphotericin B has been proposed. This delays resistance and may result in synergistic antifungal action, especially in cryptococcal meningitis.

GRISEOFULVIN

Griseofulvin is an antibiotic obtained from certain *Penicillium* species. It has no effect on bacteria or fungi producing systemic mycoses but suppresses dermatophytes, particularly *Microsporum audouini* and *Trichophyton rubrum*. Daily oral doses of 1 g are given for weeks or months. The absorbed drug is deposited in diseased skin, bound to keratin. Toxic effects include headache, drowsiness, skin rashes, and gastrointestinal disturbances. Ultramicrosized griseofulvin (Gris-Peg) is absorbed twice as effectively as microsized griseofulvin.

ANTIFUNGAL IMIDAZOLES

These are drugs that increase membrane permeability and inhibit synthesis of sterols (ergosterol) in fungal cell membranes, among other actions. Clotrimazole, 10-mg troches orally 5 times daily, can suppress oral candidiasis. Miconazole, 2% cream, is used in dermatophytosis and vaginal candidiasis. Miconazole has been given intravenously in systemic mycosis but is quite toxic. Ketoconazole, 200–400 mg orally once daily for many weeks, dramatically improves chronic mucocutaneous candidiasis, vaginal candidiasis, and paracoccidioidomycosis. It has therapeutic benefits in pulmonary coccidioidomycosis and histoplasmosis but not in meningitis due to these fungi.

Adverse effects include nausea, vomiting, headache, skin rashes, and occasional elevations in transaminase levels.

CYCLOSERINE

Cycloserine is an antibiotic active against many types of microorganisms, including coliforms, *Pro-*

teus, and tubercle bacilli. It acts by inhibiting the incorporation of D-alanine into peptidoglycan of bacterial cell walls by blocking alanine racemase. It is occasionally used in urinary tract infections (15–20 mg/kg/d orally) but often causes neurotoxic side-effects or shock and is therefore rarely used.

THE NITROFURANS

The nitrofurans are synthetic nitrofuraldehyde compounds that are strongly bactericidal in vitro for many gram-positive and gram-negative bacteria. Most nitrofurans are very insoluble in water. Some compounds (eg, nitrofuraldehyde semicarbazone, Furacin) are effective topical antibacterial agents used in surgical dressings and virtually unabsorbed.

Nitrofurantoin (Furadantin) is absorbed after oral administration and excreted in the urine. With daily doses of 400–600 mg, urine concentrations reach 100–200 μg/mL, sufficient to inhibit most organisms commonly encountered in urinary tract infections. Activity is limited to the urine. In the bloodstream, no antibacterial effect occurs because the drug is bound to blood proteins. Thus, nitrofurantoin has no effect on systemic infections but is a good urinary antiseptic (see below). Sodium nitrofurantoin can be given intravenously but likewise acts only in the urine.

Gastrointestinal intolerance is the commonest side-effect of orally administered nitrofurantoin, but occasionally hemolytic anemia, skin rashes, hepatitis, pneumonitis, and other effects have been observed.

SULFONAMIDES

The sulfonamides are a large group of compounds with the basic formula shown on p 120. By substituting various R-radicals, a series of compounds is obtained with somewhat varying physical, pharmacologic, and antibacterial properties. The basic mechanism of action of all of these compounds appears to be competitive inhibition of *p*-aminobenzoic acid (PABA) utilization. The simultaneous use of sulfonamides with trimethoprim results in the inhibition of sequential metabolic steps and possible antibacterial synergism (see p 120).

The sulfonamides are bacteriostatic for some gram-negative and gram-positive bacteria, chlamydiae, nocardiae, and some protozoa. Several special sulfones (eg, dapsone) are employed in the treatment of leprosy.

The "soluble" sulfonamides (eg, trisulfapyrimidines, sulfisoxazole) are readily absorbed from the intestinal tract after oral administration of 4–8 g daily and are distributed in all tissues and body fluids (required blood levels: 8–12 mg/dL). The sodium salts of sulfonamides may be injected intravenously. Most sulfonamides are excreted rapidly in the urine. Some (eg, sulfamethoxypyridazine, sulfadimethoxine) are excreted very slowly and give high tissue and low urine

levels. At present, sulfonamides are particularly useful in the treatment of nocardiosis and first attacks of urinary tract infections due to coliform bacteria. By contrast, many meningococci, shigellae, group A streptococci, and organisms causing recurrent urinary tract infections are now resistant. A mixture of 5 parts sulfamethoxazole plus 1 part trimethoprim is widely used in urinary tract infections, shigellosis, and salmonellosis and may be effective in treating other gram-negative bacterial infections and *Pneumocystis carinii* pneumonia.

Trimethoprim alone, 100 mg orally every 12 hours, can be effective treatment for uncomplicated urinary tract infections. Its widespread use in Finland has led to widespread bacterial resistance there.

The "insoluble" sulfonamides (eg, phthalylsulfathiazole) are poorly absorbed from the intestinal tract and exert their action largely by inhibiting the microbial population within the lumen of the tract. They are given in a dosage of 8–15 g orally daily for 4–7 days to prepare the large bowel for surgery.

Resistance

Microorganisms that do not use extracellular PABA but, like mammalian cells, can use preformed folic acid are resistant to sulfonamides. In some sulfonamide-resistant mutants, the tetrahydropteroic acid synthetase has a much higher affinity for PABA than for sulfonamides. The opposite is true for sulfonamide-susceptible organisms.

Side-Effects

The soluble sulfonamides may produce side-effects that fall into 2 categories:

A. Allergic Reactions: Many individuals develop hypersensitivity to sulfonamides after initial contact with these drugs and, on reexposure, may develop fever, hives, skin rashes, and chronic vascular diseases such as polyarteritis nodosa.

B. Direct Toxic Effects: There may be fever, skin rashes, gastrointestinal disturbances, depression of the bone marrow leading to anemia or agranulocytosis, hemolytic anemia, and toxic effects on the liver and kidney. Some of the toxic action on the kidney can be prevented by keeping the urine alkaline and the water intake adequate; by using mixtures of sulfonamides such as trisulfapyrimidines (which are relatively more soluble than a single drug); or by employing sulfisoxazole, which is highly soluble in urine.

Bacteriologic Examination

When culturing specimens from patients receiving sulfonamides, the incorporation of PABA (5 mg/dL) into the medium overcomes sulfonamide inhibition.

METRONIDAZOLE

Metronidazole is an antiprotozoal drug used in treating *Trichomonas, Giardia,* and amebic infections. The usual dosage is 250–500 mg 3 times daily orally for 10 days. It also has striking effects against anaerobic bacteria, especially *Bacteroides* species and *Gardnerella vaginalis*. It may be effective in preoperative preparation of the colon. Adverse effects include stomatitis, diarrhea, and nausea. There is a question about possible teratogenic activity.

URINARY ANTISEPTICS

These are drugs with antibacterial effects limited to the urine. They fail to produce significant levels in tissues and thus have no effect on systemic infections. However, they effectively lower bacterial counts in the urine and thus greatly diminish the symptoms of lower urinary tract infection. They are used primarily for the suppression of bacteria in the urine of patients with chronic urinary tract infection.

The most prominent urinary antiseptics are methenamine mandelate (Mandelamine) or hippurate, nitrofurantoin, and nalidixic acid. The active compounds are liberated in the urine only and have no systemic effect. Therefore, it is meaningless to perform and report sensitivity tests with these substances in any systemic infection. Nalidixic acid is effective in the urine, but microbial resistance tends to emerge rapidly. Oxolinic acid appears to be similar. Other materials, such as amino acids (methionine) or hippuric acid (cranberry juice), may be ingested in large doses to provide an acid, bacteriostatic urine.

ANTIVIRAL DRUGS

Viruses, because of their structure and method of replication, are not affected by the common antibacterial drugs. However, viral multiplication may be interrupted by a variety of chemicals at various stages. In addition to specific antibody globulins that block penetration of extracellular virus into the cell, several chemicals have found limited application in the treatment of viral infections. The following substances are currently used in the management of clinical viral disease.

Amantadine Hydrochloride

This tricyclic symmetric amine (and its congener rimantadine) inhibits the penetration into susceptible cells, or uncoating, of certain myxoviruses, especially influenza A, but not influenza B. A daily oral dose of 200 mg of amantadine hydrochloride for 3 days before and 7 days after influenza A virus infection reduces the incidence and severity of symptoms. The most marked side-effects noted with this drug are insomnia, dizziness, and ataxia.

Idoxuridine (5-Iodo-2′-deoxyuridine)

This halogenated pyrimidine can inhibit the replication of DNA viruses by becoming incorporated into viral DNA in place of thymidine. Topical application to herpetic keratitis can result in marked improvement. The topically applied drug remains localized in the avascular cornea and inhibits herpesvirus replication. For the treatment of herpetic keratitis, 1 drop of 0.1% solution is instilled into the conjunctival sac every 2 hours around the clock. Ointments containing 0.5% idoxuridine can be applied less frequently. Some toxic effects on corneal epithelium occur after prolonged use.

Idoxuridine is too severely cytotoxic for use in most generalized virus infections.

Cytarabine (cytosine arabinoside, arabinofuranosylcytosine) also inhibits replication of DNA viruses. It has been used topically in herpetic keratitis and systemically in varicella-zoster, but it is more toxic than idoxuridine. In disseminated herpes zoster, it appears to be ineffective.

Vidarabine (Adenine Arabinoside, Ara-A)

Vidarabine appears to be the most effective inhibitor of viral DNA synthesis applicable clinically in 1982, and the least toxic. As a 3% ointment, it is more effective in herpetic keratitis than idoxuridine. Vidarabine, 10–15 mg/kg/d intravenously, can suppress progression of disseminated herpes zoster or herpes simplex. It may be effective in arresting herpetic encephalitis if administered early, before onset of coma. If started later, it may reduce the mortality rate, but neurologic sequelae are devastating. While vidarabine is the least toxic of the antivirals tried systemically, untoward effects are significant, especially if the drug is used for prolonged periods, as in suppressing the viremia of hepatitis.

Methisazone (N-Methylisatin-β-thiosemicarbazone)

This drug can block replication of poxviruses, probably by inhibiting the formation of a structural protein. If administered to contacts of smallpox cases within 1–2 days after exposure, 2–4 g/d orally for 3–4 days (100 mg/kg/d for children) gave striking protection against smallpox.

Generalized or progressive vaccinia in immunodeficient individuals can also be treated with methisazone.

The principal side-effect is vomiting.

Photodynamic Inactivation

Photodynamic inactivation was proposed and widely used as topical therapy for skin or mucous membrane lesions of herpes simplex. It consisted of painting a dye (0.1% proflavine or neutral red) on open herpetic lesions, then irradiating them twice with white light. The dye binds to viral DNA and absorbs the light energy. This inactivates the virus. Experimentally, some success was observed and initial clinical studies were enthusiastic. However, controlled clinical trials failed to prove significant benefit. In cell culture, photodynamic inactivation could transform cells to neoplastic behavior, and such cells then produced transplantable tumors in hamsters. A few cases of Bowen's disease have evolved after treatment of penile herpes. There appears tô be no justification for using photodynamic inactivation in 1982.

Interferons

Interferons are a group of antiviral substances generated by human cells. The human interferons employed in clinical studies until 1982 were prepared from pooled blood leukocytes or from human lymphoid cell lines. In 1982, DNA technology will provide vastly increased yields of interferons for clinical trials. Interferons inhibit virus replication by inducing at least 3 enzymes: (1) a protein kinase that leads to phosphorylation of elongation factor eIF-2, resulting in inhibition of peptide chain growth; (2) oligoisoadenylate, which ultimately results in activation of an RNase that degrades viral mRNA; and (3) a phosphodiesterase that leads to inhibition of peptide elongation. In addition, some interferons act as immunomodulators, and it is this feature that is being tested in cancer therapy trials.

In immunosuppressed patients, human interferons can prevent dissemination of herpes zoster and herpes simplex. They can also suppress the viremia of chronic active hepatitis B. If given before trigeminal ganglion surgery for neuralgia, interferons can suppress the appearance of recurrent lesions of herpes simplex. Other possible antiviral applications of interferons will be explored.

Acyclovir

Earlier known as acycloguanosine, acyclovir is an antiviral drug of good potency against herpesviruses in experimental systems. Acyclovir is phosphorylated by a herpesvirus-specific thymidine kinase and becomes an inhibitor of virus-specific DNA polymerase. The drug appears to be relatively nontoxic and is currently undergoing clinical trial in herpetic infections.

● ● ●

References

Appel GB, Neu HC: The nephrotoxicity of antimicrobial agents. (3 parts.) N Engl J Med 1977;296:663, 722, 784.

Bauer AW et al: Antibiotic susceptibility testing by a standardized single disc method. Am J Clin Pathol 1966;45:493.

Beeuwkes H, Rutgers VH: A combination of amoxicillin and clavulanic acid in the treatment of respiratory tract infections caused by amoxicillin-resistant Haemophilus influenzae. Infection 1981;9:244.

Bennett JE et al: A comparison of amphotericin B alone and combined with flucytosine in the treatment of cryptococcal meningitis. N Engl J Med 1979;301:126.

Bennett WM et al: Drug therapy in renal failure. Ann Intern Med 1980;93:62.

Blumberg PM, Strominger JL: Interaction of penicillin with the bacterial cell: Penicillin-binding proteins and penicillin-sensitive enzymes. Bacteriol Rev 1974;38:291.

Davies J: General mechanisms of antimicrobial resistance. Rev Infect Dis 1979;1:23.

Davis SD: Polymyxins, colistin, vancomycin and bacitracin. In: Antimicrobial Therapy, 3rd ed. Kagan BM (editor). Saunders, 1980.

Falkow S: Infectious Multiple Drug Resistance. Pion Ltd, 1975.

Finland M: Emergence of antibiotic resistance in hospitals, 1935–75. Rev Infect Dis 1979;1:4.

Goldman P: Metronidazole. N Engl J Med 1980;303:1212.

Hirsch MS, Swartz MN: Antiviral drugs. (2 parts.) N Engl J Med 1980;302:903, 949.

Hunt TK et al: Antibiotics in surgery. Arch Surg 1975;110:148.

Jackson GG: Considerations of antibiotic prophylaxis in nonsurgical high risk patients. Am J Med 1981;70:467.

Jacobs MR et al: Emergence of multiply resistant pneumococci. N Engl J Med 1978;299:735.

Jawetz E: The doctor's dilemma. In: Current Clinical Topics in Infectious Diseases. Remington JS, Swartz MN (editors). McGraw-Hill, 1981.

Jawetz E: The use of combinations of antimicrobial drugs. Annu Rev Pharmacol 1968;8:151.

Kaufman RH et al: Treatment of genital herpes simplex infection with photodynamic inactivation. Am J Obstet Gynecol 1979; 132:861.

McCormack WM, Finland M: Spectinomycin. Ann Intern Med 1976;84:712.

McCormack WM et al: Hepatotoxicity of erythromycin estolate during pregnancy. Antimicrob Agents Chemother 1977; 12:630.

Merigan TC et al: Human leukocyte interferon for the treatment of herpes zoster in patients with cancer. N Engl J Med 1978; 298:981.

Meyers FH, Jawetz E, Goldfien A: Review of Medical Pharmacology, 7th ed. Lange, 1980.

Murray BE, Moellering RC Jr: Cephalosporins. Annu Rev Med 1981;32:559.

Neu HC: Comparative studies of cefoxitin and cephalothin: An overview. Rev Infect Dis 1979;1:144.

Novik RP, Morse SI: In vivo transmission of drug resistance factors between strains of Staphylococcus aureus. J Exp Med 1967;125:45.

O'Brien TF et al: International comparison of prevalence of resistance to antibiotics. JAMA 1978;239:1518.

Parker CW: Drug allergy. (3 parts.) N Engl J Med 1975;292: 511, 732, 957.

Petz LD: Immunologic cross-reactivity between penicillins and cephalosporins: A review. J Infect Dis 1978;137 (Suppl): S74.

Rahal JJ: Antibiotic combinations: The clinical relevance of synergy and antagonism. Medicine 1978;57:179.

Restrepo A, Stevens DA, Utz JP (editors): Symposium on ketoconazole. Rev Infect Dis 1980;2:519.

Richards H et al: Trimethoprim-resistance plasmids and transposons in Salmonella. Lancet 1978;2:1194.

Ronald AR, Harding KM: Urinary infection prophylaxis in women. *Ann Intern Med* 1981;**94:**268.

Rubin RH, Swartz MN: Trimethoprim-sulfamethoxazole. *N Engl J Med* 1980;**303:**426.

Sabath LD et al: A new type of penicillin resistance of *Staphylococcus aureus*. *Lancet* 1977;**1:**443.

Salton MRJ, Tomasz A: Mode of action of antibiotics on microbial walls and membranes. *Ann NY Acad Sci* 1974;**235:**5.

Siegel D: Tetracyclines: New look at an old antibiotic. *NY State J Med* 1978;**78:**950.

Sivonen A et al: The effect of chemoprophylactic use of rifampin and minocycline on rates of carriage of *Neisseria meningitidis* in army recruits in Finland. *J Infect Dis* 1978;**137:**238.

Stevens DA et al: Cytosine arabinoside in disseminated zoster. *N Engl J Med* 1973;**289:**873.

Tipper DJ: Mode of action of beta-lactam antibiotics. *Rev Infect Dis* 1979;**1:**39.

Weinstein L, Dalton AC: Host determinants of response to antimicrobial agents. *N Engl J Med* 1968;**279:**467.

Whitley RJ et al: Herpes simplex encephalitis: Vidarabine therapy and diagnostic problems. *N Engl J Med* 1981;**304:**313.

Whitley RJ et al: Vidarabine therapy of neonatal herpes simplex infection. *Pediatrics* 1980;**66:**495.

Winston DJ et al: Infectious complications of human bone marrow transplantation. *Medicine* 1979;**58:**1.

11 | Host-Parasite Relationships

A parasite is an organism that resides on or within another living organism in order to find the environment and nutrients it requires for growth and reproduction. This does not imply that a parasite must harm its host. On the contrary, the most successful parasites achieve a balance with the host that ensures the survival, growth, and propagation of both parasite and host. Thus a majority of host-parasite interactions do not result in disease: the infection remains latent or subclinical.

The relationship between parasite and host is determined both by those characteristics of the parasite that favor establishment of the parasite and damage to the host and by the various host mechanisms that oppose these processes. Among the parasite's attributes are infectivity, invasiveness, pathogenicity, and toxigenicity. These are described below. If the parasite injures the host to a sufficient degree, disturbances will result in the host that manifest themselves as disease.

INFECTION

Infection is the process whereby the parasite enters into a relationship with the host. Its essential component steps in humans and animals are the following:

(1) Entrance of the parasite into the host–The most frequent portals of entry are the respiratory tract (mouth and nose), the gastrointestinal tract, and breaks in the superficial mucous membranes and skin. Surface components of the microbe determine its ability to adhere to epithelial cells. These may be surface proteins (eg, K88 in enteropathic *Escherichia coli*), lipoteichoic acids (in group A streptococci), or others. Some parasites can penetrate intact mucous membrane and skin; still others are passively introduced by arthropods through these layers directly into the lymphatic channels or the bloodstream.

(2) Establishment and multiplication of the parasite within the host–From the portal of entry the parasite may spread directly through the tissues or may proceed via the lymphatic channels to the bloodstream, which distributes it widely and permits it to reach tissues particularly suitable for its multiplication. The biochemical environment of the tissues ultimately de-termines the susceptibility or resistance of a certain host to a given parasite.

Although the process of infection is of paramount interest to medicine, there are 2 other requirements for the perpetuation of a parasitic species: a satisfactory portal of exit of the parasite from the host and an effective mechanism for transmission to new hosts.

ATTRIBUTES OF MICROORGANISMS THAT ENABLE THEM TO CAUSE DISEASE

There is no sharp semantic distinction between the terms "pathogenicity" and "virulence." **Pathogenicity** denotes the ability of microorganisms to cause disease or to result in the production of progressive lesions. **Virulence** introduces the concept of degree, ie, virulent organisms exhibit pathogenicity when introduced into the host in very small numbers. These properties may be subdivided into **toxigenicity** (ability to produce toxic substances) and **invasiveness** (ability to enter host tissues, multiply there, and spread). Different pathogenic microorganisms possess these attributes in varying degrees. Toxigenicity and invasiveness may be under separate genetic control.

Virulence is measured in terms of the number of microorganisms or micrograms of toxin necessary to kill a given host when administered by a certain route. It is usually expressed as LD_{50}, ie, the number of organisms or micrograms that must be administered to kill 50% of the animals.

A few representative substances known to play a role in the production of disease by microorganisms are mentioned below.

Toxins

Microbial toxins are usually grouped as exotoxins or endotoxins. The essential features of each group are listed in Table 11–1.

Pathogenetic Mechanisms in Some Disorders Caused by Microbial Exotoxins

A. Diphtheria: *Corynebacterium diphtheriae* grows in the upper respiratory tract or wounds and produces toxin. The toxin is absorbed, inhibits protein

Table 11—1. Differentiation of exotoxins and endotoxins.

Exotoxins	Endotoxins
Excreted by living cells; found in high concentrations in fluid medium.	Integral part of microbial cell walls of gram-negative organisms liberated upon their disintegration.
Polypeptides, molecular weight 10,000—900,000.	Lipopolysaccharide complexes. Lipid A portion probably responsible for toxicity.
Relatively unstable; toxicity often destroyed rapidly by heat over 60 °C.	Relatively stable; withstand heat over 60 °C for hours without loss of toxicity.
Highly antigenic; stimulate the formation of high-titer antitoxin. Antitoxin neutralizes toxin.	Do not stimulate formation of antitoxin; stimulate formation of antibodies to polysaccharide moiety.
Converted into antigenic, nontoxic toxoids by formalin, acid, heat, etc.	Not converted into toxoids.
Highly toxic; fatal for laboratory animals in micrograms or less.	Weakly toxic; fatal for laboratory animals in hundreds of micrograms.
Do not produce fever in host.	Often produce fever in host.

synthesis, and results in necrosis of epithelium, heart muscle, kidney, and nerve tissue.

Diphtheria toxin is a polypeptide (MW 62,000) that can be lethal in a dose of 40 ng. The essential action is inhibition of peptide chain elongation by inactivating the elongation factor EF-2 (formerly called transferase II). The toxin inactivates EF-2 by catalyzing a reaction that yields free nicotinamide plus an inactive adenosine diphosphate–ribose–EF-2 complex. The arrest of protein synthesis may bring about disruption of normal physiologic functions. Some strains of *Pseudomonas aeruginosa* produce a toxin that has the same mode of action as diphtheria toxin.

B. Tetanus: *Clostridium tetani* contaminates wounds, and the spores germinate in an anaerobic environment (devitalized tissue). Vegetative forms produce toxin (MW 150,000) that reaches the central nervous system by retrograde axon transport and is bound to gangliosides. Toxin increases reflex excitability in neurons of the spinal cord (by blocking release of an inhibitory mediator in motor neuron synapses). The toxin may also affect synaptic transmission at the myoneural junction (perhaps because of accumulation of acetylcholine). Muscle spasms result.

C. Gas Gangrene: Spores of *Clostridium perfringens* and other clostridia (especially *Clostridium ramosum, Clostridium bifermentans, Clostridium histolyticum, Clostridium sporogenes, Clostridium novyi*) are introduced into wounds by soil or feces. In the presence of necrotic tissue (anaerobic environment), spores germinate and vegetative cells produce toxins. Many of these are necrotizing and hemolytic and, together with distention of tissue by gas formed from carbohydrates and interference with blood supply, favor the spread of gangrene. *Clostridium difficile*, and perhaps other clostridia, can produce a necrotizing toxin in the gut that leads to antibiotic-associated colitis.

The alpha toxin of *C perfringens* is a lecithinase and damages cell membranes by splitting lecithin to phosphocholine and diglyceride. Theta toxin also has a necrotizing effect. Collagenases and DNases are produced by various clostridia. Some strains of *C per-*

fringens also produce an enterotoxin (see below).

D. Botulism: *Clostridium botulinum* grows in anaerobic foods (canned, vacuum-packed, etc) and produces a neurotoxin (MW 150,000) of 6 antigenic types. The toxin is absorbed from the gut and carried by the blood to motor nerves. Toxin blocks the release of acetylcholine at synapses and neuromuscular junctions, producing diplopia, dysphagia, respiratory paralysis, and other motor paralyses.

E. Staphylococcal Food Poisoning: Certain strains of *Staphylococcus aureus* produce an enterotoxin while growing in meat, dairy, or bakery products. This enterotoxin (MW 40,000) is resistant to heating at 100 °C for 20 minutes. After ingestion, enterotoxin is absorbed in the gut, where it stimulates neural receptors. From there, impulses are transmitted to medullary centers of gut motility. Vomiting, often projectile, results within hours. Diarrhea is less frequent.

F. Cholera: *Vibrio cholerae* from feces of infected persons contaminates food or drink. Vibrios grow in the small intestine, producing a heat-labile enterotoxin (MW 28,000) that binds to ganglioside receptors on villi of the small intestine. The enterotoxin causes a large increase in adenylate cyclase activity and in the concentration of cAMP in the gut. This results in massive hypersecretion of chloride and water and impaired absorption of sodium in the jejunum and ileum. The effect is massive diarrhea and acidosis.

G. Other Food Poisons: Some strains of *C perfringens, E coli, Vibrio parahaemolyticus, Bacillus cereus*, and others can produce enterotoxins with actions similar to that of *V cholerae*. The enterotoxin is often under control of a plasmid.

H. Streptococcal Erythrogenic Toxin: Some strains of hemolytic lysogenic streptococci produce a toxin that results in a punctate maculopapular erythematous rash, as in scarlet fever. The precise mode of action is uncertain. Production of erythrogenic toxin is under genetic control of a temperate bacteriophage. If phage is lost, the streptococci cannot produce toxin.

Toxin stimulates antitoxin formation, which neutralizes the toxin effect. Thus, a person possessing antitoxin may have pharyngitis when infected with streptococci producing erythrogenic toxin but not get scarlet fever.

I. Other Exotoxins: Other exotoxins are described in Chapters 14 and 18.

Extracellular Enzymes

Certain bacteria produce substances that are not directly toxic but do play an important role in the infectious process.

A. Collagenase: *C perfringens,* in addition to a lecithinase, also produces proteolytic enzymes (collagenases) capable of disintegrating collagen. This promotes the spread of bacilli in tissues.

B. Coagulase: Many pathogenic staphylococci produce a substance (coagulase) that, in conjunction with certain serum factors, coagulates plasma. Coagulase contributes to the formation of fibrin walls around staphylococcal lesions, which help them to persist. Coagulase also causes a deposit of fibrin on the surface of individual staphylococci, which may protect them from phagocytosis or from destruction within phagocytic cells.

C. Hyaluronidases (enzymes hydrolyzing hyaluronic acid, a constituent of the ground substance of connective tissue) are produced by many microorganisms (eg, staphylococci, clostridia, streptococci, pneumococci) and aid in their spread through tissues.

D. Streptokinase (Fibrinolysin): Many hemolytic streptococci produce a substance (streptokinase) that activates a proteolytic enzyme of the plasma (plasminogen → plasmin). This enzyme (also called fibrinolysin) is then able to dissolve coagulated plasma and probably aids in the spread of streptococci through tissues.

E. Hemolysins and Leukocidins: Many microorganisms produce substances that dissolve red blood cells (hemolysins) and probably also tissue cells and leukocytes (leukocidins). Streptolysin O, for example, is produced by group A hemolytic streptococci and is lethal for mice in addition to being hemolytic for a variety of red cells. This substance is readily oxidized and thereby inactivated, but it is reactivated by reducing agents. It is antigenic. The same streptococci also produce oxygen-stable streptolysin S, which is nonantigenic. Clostridia produce a variety of hemolysins, among them the lecithinase previously mentioned. Hemolysins are also produced by staphylococci and many gram-negative rods.

F. Proteases: Many organisms produce proteases that can hydrolyze immunoglobulins. Thus, *Neisseria* species or *Streptococcus* species can cleave local secretory IgA antibodies, preventing adherence, opsonization, and phagocytosis.

Factors in the Invasiveness of Microorganisms

A continuous scale of invasiveness could be drawn up for microorganisms. One end of this scale would be occupied by toxin producers like tetanus or diphtheria; the other, by highly invasive organisms like anthrax or plague, with staphylococci and streptococci in between. The toxin producers are pathogenic principally because of elaboration of poisonous chemical substances without much tissue invasion. Plague or anthrax bacilli produce disease and death because they are able to invade tissues rapidly and multiply extensively, with the production of several toxic materials. Pneumococci or meningococci also spread widely throughout the body. The invasiveness of such organisms may be aided by enzymes favoring spread, such as hyaluronidase or streptokinase, but invasiveness is not clearly related to toxic properties. A part of the invasiveness of microorganisms may be attributed to certain surface components that protect the bacteria from phagocytosis and destruction. Such surface substances may be polysaccharide capsules (eg, pneumococci, meningococci, *Klebsiella pneumoniae, Haemophilus influenzae*), hyaluronic acid capsules and surface "M" proteins (beta-hemolytic streptococci), or a surface polypeptide (anthrax bacilli). Certain microorganisms may be invasive and "virulent" because they survive within phagocytic cells and are resistant to enzymatic attack. Although these various factors contribute to the observed invasiveness of microorganisms, it must be concluded that this behavior is an expression of inherent biochemical properties not yet understood. On the other hand, invasiveness as such is by no means synonymous with disease production. Some infectious agents, eg, viruses, may be widely distributed in the body without causing illness.

How can one prove that a given microorganism really causes a disease? Traditionally, the causative relationship between a microorganism and a disease is established by fulfilling "Koch's postulates": (1) The microorganism must regularly be isolated from cases of the illness. (2) It must be grown in pure culture in vitro. (3) When such a pure culture is inoculated into susceptible animal species, the typical disease must result. (4) From such experimentally induced disease the microorganism must again be isolated.

Although these postulates were adequate to prove the causes of some bacterial diseases, they had to be modified for other infections, particularly for virus diseases, which are highly species-specific for humans.

ATTRIBUTES OF THE HOST THAT DETERMINE RESISTANCE TO MICROORGANISMS

The various factors that operate to prevent infection of a host can be arranged in 2 groups: nonspecific factors, operating against a variety of parasites; and specific factors based on immunologic responses toward specific agents.

SOME MECHANISMS OF NONSPECIFIC HOST RESISTANCE

Physiologic Barriers at the Portal of Entry

A. The Skin: Few microorganisms are capable of penetrating the intact skin, but many can enter sweat or sebaceous glands and hair follicles and establish themselves there. Sweat and sebaceous secretions, by virtue of their acid pH and possibly chemical substances (especially fatty acids), have antimicrobial properties that tend to eliminate pathogenic organisms. Lysozyme, an enzyme that dissolves some bacterial cell walls, and perhaps other enzymes are also present on the skin.

Skin resistance may vary with age. In childhood, susceptibility is high to ringworm infection. After puberty, resistance to such fungi increases markedly with the increased content of saturated fatty acids in sebaceous secretions.

B. Mucous Membranes: In the respiratory tract, a film of mucus covers the surface and is constantly being driven by ciliated cells toward the natural orifices. Bacteria tend to stick to this film. Mucus and tears also contain lysozyme and other substances with antimicrobial properties. For some microorganisms, the first step in infection is their attachment to surface epithelial cells. If such cells have IgA antibody on their surfaces, attachment may be prevented—a host resistance mechanism. In turn, if the organism breaks down the antibody with a protease, this constitutes a "virulence factor." When organisms enter the mucous membrane, they tend to be taken up by phagocytes and transported into regional lymphatic channels that carry them to lymph nodes. These act as barriers toward further spread and can dispose of large numbers of bacteria. The mucociliary apparatus for removal of bacteria in the respiratory tract is aided by pulmonary macrophages. This entire defense system can be suppressed by alcohol, narcotics, cigarette smoke, hypoxia, acidosis, and other harmful influences. Special protective mechanisms in the respiratory tract include the hairs at the nares and the cough reflex, which prevents aspiration.

In the gastrointestinal tract, saliva contains numerous hydrolytic enzymes; the acidity of the stomach inactivates many ingested bacteria (eg, *V cholerae*); and the small intestine contains many proteolytic enzymes and active macrophages.

In the adult vagina, an acid pH is maintained by normal lactobacilli that interfere with the establishment of yeasts, anaerobes, and gram-negative organisms.

It must be remembered that most mucous membranes of the body carry a constant normal microbial flora that itself opposes the establishment of pathogenic microorganisms and has important physiologic functions. (See "bacterial interference," pp 193 and 281.)

Phagocytosis

Microorganisms (and other particles) that enter the lymphatics, lung, bone marrow, or bloodstream are engulfed by any of a variety of phagocytic cells. Among them are polymorphonuclear leukocytes, phagocytic monocytes (macrophages), and fixed macrophages of the reticuloendothelial system (see below). Many microorganisms elaborate chemotactic factors that attract phagocytic cells. Defects in chemotaxis may account for hypersusceptibility to certain infections (eg, Job's syndrome), or they may be familial in nature. Phagocytosis can occur in the absence of serum antibodies, particularly if aided by the architecture of tissue. Thus, phagocytic cells are inefficient in large, smooth, open spaces like pleura, pericardium, or joint but may be more effective in ingesting microorganisms that are trapped in small tissue spaces (eg, alveoli) or on rough surfaces. Such "surface phagocytosis" occurs early in the infectious process before antibodies are available.

Phagocytosis is made more efficient by the presence of antibodies (opsonins) that coat the bacterial surface and facilitate the uptake of bacteria by the phagocyte. Opsonization can occur by 3 mechanisms: (1) Antibody alone can act as opsonin. (2) Antibody plus antigen can activate complement via the classic pathway to yield opsonins. (3) Opsonin may be produced by a heat-labile system where immunoglobulin or other factors activate C3 via the alternative pathway. Macrophages have receptors on their membrane for the Fc portion of antibody and for the C3 component of complement. This aids the phagocytosis of antibody-coated particles.

Hyperosmolality (eg, in the renal medulla) inhibits phagocytosis. Hypophosphatemia depletes ATP in granulocytes and reduces the efficiency of phagocytosis. Neutrophils from patients with diabetes (and perhaps other metabolic disorders) ingest bacteria normally but then are deficient in the ability to kill them. By contrast, during acute infections, the killing power of neutrophils may be increased.

The ingestion of foreign particles, eg, microorganisms, has the following effects on phagocytic granulocytes: (1) Oxygen consumption increases and there is an increased generation of superoxide and an increased release of H_2O_2. (2) Glycolysis increases via the hexose monophosphate shunt. (3) Lysosomes rupture, and their hydrolytic enzymes are discharged into the phagocytic vacuole to form a digestive vacuole, or "phagolysosome." Morphologically, this process appears as "degranulation" of granulocytes. (4) There appear to be no major changes in the synthesis of proteins or nucleic acids.

Granulocytes (polymorphonuclear leukocytes) contain at least 2 types of granules: lysosomes that appear to be "bags" of hydrolytic enzymes and granules consisting of basic proteins that have antibacterial effects but no known enzymatic function, eg, phagocytin or lactoferrin.

The functional mechanisms of intracellular killing of microorganisms in phagocytic granulocytes are not fully known. They include nonoxidative mechanisms (eg, activation of hydrolytic enzymes in contact with microorganisms, action of basic proteins) and oxidative mechanisms. Among the latter, the following have been implicated:

(1) The increased oxidative activity results in accumulation of H_2O_2. In the presence of oxidizable cofactors (halides such as iodine, bromine, chlorine), an acid pH, and the enzyme myeloperoxidase, intensive oxidation results in microbial death.

Children suffering from "granulomatous disease" have granulocytes that ingest microbes normally but lack the subsequent respiratory burst and normal intracellular killing. Such individuals usually die of infection, perhaps because their granulocytes may be specifically deficient in enzymes, eg, an NADH dehydrogenase that produces superoxide. In Chédiak-Higashi syndrome, most microorganisms are phagocytosed normally, but intracellular killing is impaired, perhaps because myeloperoxidase is not released from (abnormal) lysosomes. Ascorbate can correct this defect.

(2) In normal granulocytes, superoxide anion (O_2^-) is generated upon phagocytosis of particles and destroyed by superoxidase dismutase. The superoxide radical may be directly lethal for many microorganisms. "Granulomatous disease" granulocytes have a greatly reduced capacity for generation of superoxide radicals after ingestion of microorganisms. Perhaps this defect is responsible for the impaired killing ability of granulocytes from such patients, which promotes their susceptibility to infections, especially those due to staphylococci. When the bone marrow of patients is suppressed by disease, drugs, or radiation, the number of functional granulocytes falls. If the level drops below 1000 polymorphonuclear neutrophils per microliter, the patient is highly susceptible to "opportunistic" infections by bacteria. Such patients may have their antibacterial defenses boosted temporarily by granulocyte transfusions.

Corticosteroids probably increase the stability of lysosomal membranes. This may contribute to the diminished ability of phagocytes to eradicate bacterial and fungal infection in persons receiving high doses of corticosteroids.

In bacterial infections, the number of circulating neutrophilic leukocytes often increases. In addition, these neutrophils reduce colorless nitroblue tetrazolium (NBT) to intracellular blue-black formazan granules. The presence of more than 10% NBT-positive neutrophils suggests the presence of bacterial infection. Depressed NBT responses occur in patients with defective phagocytic immune mechanisms, eg, chronic granulomatous disease. However, the correlation is not good between defective bactericidal activity and increased NBT-positive neutrophils.

Circulating phagocytic monocytes (macrophages) are derived from monocyte stem cells in bone marrow, have a longer life span than circulating granulocytic phagocytes, and continue their activity at lower pH.

Macrophages in blood have few lysosomal granules until they become "activated." This "activa-tion" results from interaction with immunologically active T lymphoid cells. "Activated" macrophages have many lysosomes and are active in phagocytosis and intracellular killing of a variety of bacteria—not only the ones that induced the initial "activation." Thus, the induction of activated macrophages is immunologically specific, but their subsequent expression is nonspecific.

Intracellular killing in macrophages probably includes mechanisms similar to those described above for granulocytes. However, the role of superoxide anion is less well defined.

All types of phagocytic cells (granulocytes, macrophages in blood, and fixed macrophages of the reticuloendothelial system) may kill ingested microorganisms or may permit their prolonged survival or even their intracellular multiplication. It is evident that the outcome of phagocytosis is determined by a complex set of factors, including the specific nature of the microorganism, the genetic and functional makeup of phagocytic cells, and the preconditioning of these cells.

Reticuloendothelial System

This refers to a functional concept of mononuclear, phagocytic cells in blood, lymphoid tissue, liver, spleen, bone marrow, lung, and other tissues that are efficient in uptake and removal of particulate matter from lymph and bloodstream. It includes cells lining blood and lymph sinuses (Kupffer cells in the liver) and histiocytes of tissues (macrophages). An important function of the spleen, bone marrow, and other reticuloendothelial organs is the filtering of microorganisms from the bloodstream. Patients whose spleens were removed often suffer from bacterial sepsis, particularly with pneumococci. Phagocytosis by reticuloendothelial cells is greatly enhanced by opsonins.

Biochemical Tissue Constituents

Certain animal tissues are resistant to specific bacteria (eg, *Bacillus anthracis*) because of their content of polypeptides, which have antibacterial properties. Such biochemical constituents may determine tissue resistance to infection. Beta lysin of serum can kill some gram-positive bacteria. The nutritional status of the host plays an important role in susceptibility or resistance to a given infection.

The role of interferon in resistance to virus infections is discussed in Chapter 27.

Many normal tissues have a high inherent ability to inhibit proliferation of microorganisms. This resistance is severely impaired by trauma, foreign bodies, disturbances in fluid and electrolyte balance, and depressed inflammatory response (x-ray radiation, corticosteroids, antineoplastic drugs, lymphomas).

Inflammatory Response

Any injury to tissue, such as that following the establishment and multiplication of microorganisms, calls forth an inflammatory response. This begins with

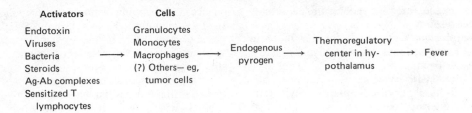

dilatation of local arterioles and capillaries, from which plasma escapes. Edema fluid accumulates in the area of injury, and fibrin forms a network and occludes the lymphatic channels, tending to limit the spread of organisms. Polymorphonuclear leukocytes in the capillaries stick to the walls, then migrate out of the capillaries toward the irritant. This migration is stimulated by substances in the inflammatory exudate (chemotaxis). The phagocytes engulf the microorganisms, and intracellular digestion begins. Soon the pH of the inflamed area becomes more acid, and the cellular proteases tend to induce lysis of the leukocytes. Large mononuclear macrophages arrive on the site and, in turn, engulf leukocytic debris as well as microorganisms and pave the way for resolution of the local inflammatory process.

Several mediators of inflammation have been considered. Prostaglandins (unsaturated fatty acids) increase capillary permeability and vasoconstriction and act in many ways as mediators of inflammatory responses. Their synthesis is inhibited by anti-inflammatory drugs.

Different stages in this inflammatory sequence may predominate with different microorganisms as the inciting cause of the inflammation. The early edema fluid may actually promote bacterial growth. The degree of local fixation depends on the nature of the organism: staphylococci tend to limit their spread through extensive lymphatic thrombi, fibrin walls, etc, precipitated by coagulase, whereas hemolytic streptococci, through the activity of streptokinase (fibrinolysin) and hyaluronidase, tend to spread rapidly through the tissue. Phagocytosis and intracellular residence are destructive to some bacteria (some pyogenic cocci), whereas for others (eg, tubercle bacilli) they serve as a means of transport and protection and even of multiplication.

Fever

Fever does not seem to be helpful in many acute infections, and suppression of fever is not harmful. It is certainly the most common systemic manifestation of the inflammatory response and a cardinal symptom of infectious diseases. Possible mechanisms of fever production must therefore be discussed.

The ultimate regulators of body temperature are the thermoregulatory centers in the hypothalamus. They are subject to physical and chemical stimuli. Direct mechanical injury or the application of chemical substances to these centers results in fever. Neither of these obvious forms of stimulation is present in the many types of fever that are associated with infection, neoplasms, hypersensitivity, and other processes that cause inflammation.

Among the substances capable of inducing fever are the endotoxins of gram-negative bacteria and extracts of normal leukocytes, especially granulocytes, called "endogenous pyrogen." These 2 substances differ as follows:

(1) Endotoxins are heat-stable lipopolysaccharides. After intravenous injection, there is a 60- to 90-minute latent period until the onset of fever. During that time, neutropenia usually develops. Repeated intravenous injection of endotoxin makes the recipient **tolerant:** no response occurs to further injections of endotoxin.

(2) Endogenous pyrogen is heat-labile (destroyed by 90 °C for 30 minutes). After intravenous injection, fever begins in a few minutes, even in endotoxin-tolerant recipients, without the development of neutropenia. Repeated injection of endogenous pyrogen does not induce unresponsiveness.

From many observations it appears that a variety of activators (endotoxins, bacteria, viruses, steroids, antigen-antibody complexes, sensitized T lymphocytes) can act upon several cell types (granulocytes, monocytes, macrophages, perhaps others) and induce them to release endogenous pyrogen. The pyrogen released from different cells may have different characteristics. Endogenous pyrogen is carried by blood to the thermoregulatory center in the hypothalamus, which initiates physiologic responses resulting in fever, eg, increased heat production and heat conservation and reduced heat loss.

Endogenous pyrogen appears to be a protein with a molecular weight of 15,000 and an isoelectric point near 6.9; it is inactivated at pH above 8.0 or by heat and is stabilized by sulfhydryl reducing agents. The endogenous pyrogen derived from cells of one mammalian species acts partially on other species; no tolerance develops upon repeated injections; and activity is increased 100-fold upon injection directly into the hypothalamus.

Some Causes of Persistent Fever of Unknown Origin (FUO) Lasting More Than 3 Weeks

If the usual diagnostic procedures (including thorough bacteriologic and serologic studies) fail to reveal the diagnosis, consider early biopsy or exploratory laparotomy.

(1) Infections (bacterial, fungal, parasitic, viral): Especially mycobacterial infection, liver and biliary tract disease, infective endocarditis, abscesses, urinary tract disease.

(2) Neoplasms: Consider especially those involving the kidneys, lungs, thyroid, liver, pancreas; lymphomas, leukemias, myeloma.

(3) Hypersensitivity diseases: Visceral angiitis, disseminated lupus erythematosus, polyarteritis nodosa, scleroderma, dermatomyositis, rheumatic fever, drug fever, rheumatoid arthritis.

(4) Granulomatous diseases: Regional enteritis, granulomatous hepatitis.

(5) Neurogenic or endocrine disorders: Lesions of brain stem and thalamus; encephalitis, hyperthyroidism; exaggerated circadian temperature variation.

(6) Factitious fever: Malingering.

(7) Miscellaneous: Sarcoidosis, thrombophlebitis, infarction, poisons, drugs, etc.

RESISTANCE & IMMUNITY

In the preceding section were described various properties of the host that give nonspecific resistance to infection. The term "immunity" signifies all those properties of the host that confer resistance to a specific infectious agent. This resistance may be of all degrees, from almost complete susceptibility to complete insusceptibility. Therefore, "resistance" and "immunity" are relative terms implying only that one host is more or less susceptible to a given infection than another host. No inference can be drawn regarding the possible mechanisms of this resistance.

Immunity may be natural or acquired. Acquired immunity may be passive or active.

NATURAL IMMUNITY

Natural immunity is that type of immunity which is not acquired through previous contact with the infectious agent (or with a related species) but is largely genetically determined. Little is known about the mechanism responsible for this form of resistance.

Species Immunity

A given pathogenic microorganism is often capable of producing disease in one animal species but not in another. *Mycobacterium avium* causes tuberculosis in birds but almost never in humans; *B anthracis* infects humans but not chickens (perhaps because of the higher body temperatures of fowl); gonococci infect humans and chimpanzees but no other animal species.

Racial Basis of Immunity

Within one animal species there may be marked racial and genetic differences in susceptibility. Some dark-skinned human races have a 10 times greater chance of developing disseminated coccidioidomycosis following primary infection than light-skinned races. Certain strains of mice are highly susceptible to viral and resistant to bacterial infections. With other strains the opposite is true.

In a few instances the biochemical basis of racial (genetic) immunity is known. For example, a hereditary deficiency of glucose-6-phosphate dehydrogenase occurs in the red blood cells of certain individuals. Such persons are markedly less susceptible to *Plasmodium falciparum* malaria but more susceptible to red cell hemolysis after certain drugs (sulfonamides, primaquine, nitrofurans) than persons with normal red cell enzyme content. Persons with sickle cell anemia are highly resistant to *P falciparum* infection. Blacks may be resistant to *Plasmodium vivax* infection if their red blood cells lack the Duffy surface antigen, which may act as a receptor for the parasite. The genetic basis of several specific defects of immune responses is under study. (See discussion of HLA immune response genes, p 154.)

Individual Resistance

As with any biologic phenomenon, resistance to infection varies with different individuals of the same species and race, following a distribution curve for the host population. Thus, certain individuals may be discovered within a "highly susceptible population" who unaccountably cannot be infected with a certain microorganism even though they have had no previous contact with it. Other individuals have genetic defects (see above) in immunologic responsiveness, antibody production, or phagocyte function that make them unusually susceptible to infections. Nutritional status (eg, protein deficiency may enhance susceptibility; microorganisms may be pathogenic by competing for iron with the host), exposure to ionizing radiation or immunosuppressive drugs, and hormonal balance all greatly influence individual susceptibility.

Differences Due to Age

In general, the very young and the elderly are more susceptible to bacterial disease than persons in other age groups. Many age differences in specific infections can be related to physiologic factors. Thus, bacterial meningitis during the first month of life is often caused by coliform bacteria because bactericidal antibodies to these bacteria are IgM and thus fail to cross the placenta. Gonococcal vaginitis occurs mainly in small girls: near puberty, estrogen production results in epithelial cell cornification and a more acid pH, which induce relative resistance.

Some virus infections (eg, rubella) damage the fetus severely but otherwise produce only mild disease. Rickettsial infections are, by contrast, more severe with advancing age. There are many other examples.

Hormonal & Metabolic Influences

Many known hormones influence susceptibility to infection. Only 2 examples are listed here.

In diabetes mellitus there is increased susceptibility to infections of the vagina and pyogenic infections of tissue. The latter may be due, in part, to altered metabolism, elevated glucose, lowered pH, reduced influx of phagocytic cells, and diminished bactericidal activity of phagocytic cells.

Both in hypoadrenal (Addison's disease) and in hyperadrenal (Cushing's disease) states, susceptibility to infection is increased. Administration of corticosteroids in high doses has similar effects. Bacterial infections are enhanced because of the suppression of the inflammatory response by glucocorticoids. Viral infections (herpes keratitis, varicella) are aggravated by corticosteroids, perhaps because of suppression of interferon production. Huge doses of corticosteroids can directly suppress antibody formation.

Certain clinical associations between an underlying constitutional disorder and a supervening infection are so frequent as to deserve listing:

Sickle cell anemia: *Salmonella* osteomyelitis, pneumococcal bacteremia, meningitis.

Splenectomy: pneumococcal bacteremia.

Diabetes mellitus (especially ketosis): mucormycosis (zygomycosis), probably also increased susceptibility to urinary tract infection; papillary necrosis with pyelonephritis; malignant external otitis caused by *Pseudomonas aeruginosa*.

Cirrhosis, nephrosis: pneumococcal peritonitis.

Hypoparathyroidism: candidiasis.

Pulmonary alveolar proteinosis: nocardiosis.

Lymphocytic leukemia: disseminated herpes zoster, cytomegalovirus.

Immunosuppression by drugs: many "opportunistic" infections—viral, bacterial, fungal, protozoal.

ACQUIRED IMMUNITY

Passive Immunity

By "passive immunity" is meant a state of relative temporary insusceptibility to an infectious agent that has been induced by the administration of antibodies preformed against that agent in another host rather than formed actively by the individual. Because the antibody molecules are decaying steadily while no new ones are being formed, passive protection lasts only a short time—usually a few weeks at most. On the other hand, the protective mechanism is in force immediately upon administration of antibody: there is no lag period such as is required for the formation of active immunity. Antibodies play only a limited role in invasive bacterial infections, and passive immunization (eg, the administration of convalescent serum or globulin) is rarely useful in that type of disease. On the other hand, when an illness is largely attributable to a toxin (eg, diphtheria, tetanus, botulism), the passive administration of antitoxin is of the greatest use because large amounts of antitoxin can be made immediately available for neutralization of the toxin. In certain virus infections (eg, measles, hepatitis A), specific antibodies (such as human pooled gamma globulin) given during the incubation period may result in limitation of virus replication and prevention or modification of the clinical disease.

Passive immunity resulting from the in utero transfer to the fetus of antibodies formed earlier in the mother protects the newborn child during the first months of life against some common infections. Passive immunity (acquired from the mother's blood) may be reinforced by antibodies taken up by the child in mother's milk (mainly colostrum), but that immunity wanes at age 4–6 months.

Active Immunity

Active immunity is a state of resistance built up in an individual following effective contact with foreign antigens, eg, microorganisms or their products. "Effective contact" may consist of clinical or subclinical infection, injection with live or killed microorganisms or their antigens, or absorption of bacterial products (eg, toxins, toxoids). In all these instances the host actively produces antibodies, and the host's cells learn to respond to the foreign material. Active immunity develops slowly over a period of days or weeks but tends to persist, usually for years. A few of the mechanisms that make up the resistance of acquired immunity can be defined.

A. Humoral Immunity: Active production of **antibodies** against antigens of microorganisms or their products. These antibodies may induce resistance because they (1) neutralize toxins or cellular products; (2) have direct bactericidal or lytic effect with complement; (3) block the infective ability of microorganisms or viruses; (4) agglutinate microorganisms, making them more subject to phagocytosis; or (5) opsonize microorganisms, ie, combine with surface antigens that normally interfere with phagocytosis and thus contribute to the ingestion of parasites.

Antibody formation is disturbed in certain individuals with agammaglobulinemia, B cell deficiency, or T cell dysfunction (see Chapter 12).

B. Cellular Immunity: Although antibodies arise in response to foreign antigens, they often play only a minor role in the defense of the organism against invading cells. The central position in such defenses is occupied by cell-mediated immune responses of great complexity, combining immunologically specific and nonspecific features. Circulating thymus-dependent lymphoid cells (see T and B cells, Chapter 12) recognize materials as foreign and initiate a chain of responses that include mononuclear inflammatory reactions; cytotoxic destruction of invading cells (microbial, graft, or neoplastic); "activation" of phagocytic macrophages, which permits them to destroy intracellular organisms; and delayed type hypersensitivity reactions in tissues. In the course of these events, foreign microorganisms or cells are fixed at their point of entry, thus limiting invasiveness (see Tuberculosis, p 220); the phagocytic capacity of cells (polymorphonuclears, macrophages, reticuloendothelial) is enhanced; ingested microbes or cells are more effectively killed, especially in "activated" macrophages (see p 150); and the biochemical environment in tissues is made less favorable for spread and multiplication of the parasite.

GENETIC INFLUENCES

Natural and acquired immunity and predisposition toward specific disease states have a genetic component. Disease susceptibility is in some way related to genes closely associated with the major histocompatibility complex (see Chapter 13), particularly the HLA-D region located on chromosome 6 in humans. Genes in this region are particularly involved in disorders suspected of having an immunologic component; therefore, this region is suspected of carrying

"immune response" genes. An example of a specific correlation is the association of HLA-B27 with ankylosing spondylitis and juvenile arthritis in humans; the association of multiple sclerosis with HLA-Dw2 and of juvenile onset diabetes with HLA-B8 is less regular. The basis for this association of specific genes with specific disease susceptibility is not clear. Possible explanations are that (1) HLA antigens may serve as cell-surface receptors for viruses or toxins; (2) HLA antigen may be incorporated into a viral coat protein; (3) HLA antigens may not themselves be responsible but may be linked to immune response genes that do determine actual susceptibility; and (4) HLA antigens may cross-react with the antigens of bacteria, viruses, or other inciting agents to trigger "autoimmune responses." It is evident that increasing attention will focus on genetic features linking disease susceptibility to major histocompatibility antigens.

• • •

References

Bach FH, van Rood JJ: The major histocompatibility complex: Genetics and biology. (3 parts.) *N Engl J Med* 1976;**295:**806, 872, 927.

Bartlett JG, Onderdonk AB: Virulence factors of anaerobic bacteria. *Rev Infect Dis* 1979;**1:**398.

Beisel WR et al: Single-nutrient effects on immunologic functions. *JAMA* 1981;**245:**53.

Boxer LA et al: Correction of leukocyte function in Chédiak-Higashi syndrome by ascorbate. *N Engl J Med* 1976; **295:**1041.

Chandra RK: Nutritional deficiency and susceptibility to infection. *Bull WHO* 1979;**57:**167.

Densen P, Mandell GL: Phagocyte strategy vs microbial tactics. *Rev Infect Dis* 1980;**2:**817.

Dinarello CA, Wolff SM: Pathogenesis of fever in man. *N Engl J Med* 1978;**298:**607.

Elsbach P: Degradation of microorganisms by phagocytic cells. *Rev Infect Dis* 1980;**2:**106.

Evans AS: Causation and disease: The Henle-Koch postulates revisited. *Yale J Biol Med* 1976;**49:**175.

Herzig RH et al: Successful granulocyte transfusion therapy for gram-negative septicemia. *N Engl J Med* 1977;**296:**701.

Hocking WG, Golde DW: The pulmonary-alveolar macrophage. (2 parts.) *N Engl J Med* 1979;**301:**580, 639.

Klebanoff SJ: Oxygen metabolism and the toxic properties of phagocytes. *Ann Intern Med* 1980;**93:**480.

Mackaness GB: Resistance to intracellular infection. *J Infect Dis* 1971;**123:**439.

Matula G, Paterson PY: Reduction of nitroblue-tetrazolium by

neutrophils in infection. *N Engl J Med* 1971;**285:**311.

Mills EL, Quie PG: Congenital disorders of the functions of polymorphonuclear neutrophils. *Rev Infect Dis* 1980;**2:**505.

Nathan CF et al: The macrophage as an effector cell. *N Engl J Med* 1980;**303:**622.

Newhouse M et al: Lung defense mechanisms. (2 parts.) *N Engl J Med* 1976;**295:**990, 1045.

Olley PM: The prostaglandins. *Am J Dis Child* 1980;**134:**688.

Orskov F: Virulence factors of the bacterial cell surface. *J Infect Dis* 1978;**137:**630.

Peterson PK, Quie PG: Bacterial surface components and the pathogenesis of infectious diseases. *Annu Rev Med* 1981; **32:**29.

Plaut AG: Microbial IgA proteases. *N Engl J Med* 1978; **298:**1459.

Quie PG: Infections due to neutrophil malfunctions. *Medicine* 1973;**52:**411.

Repine JE et al: Bactericidal function of neutrophils from patients with acute bacterial infections and from diabetics. *J Infect Dis* 1980;**142:**869.

Ritzmann SE: HLA patterns and disease associations. *JAMA* 1976;**236:**2305.

Ryan GB: Inflammation and localization of infection. *Surg Clin North Am* 1976;**56:**831.

Smith H: Microbial surfaces in relation to pathogenicity. *Bacteriol Rev* 1977;**41:**475.

Stossel TP: Phagocytosis. (3 parts.) *N Engl J Med* 1974;**290:**717, 774, 833.

Winkelstein JA: Opsonins. *J Pediatr* 1973;**82:**747.

DEFINITIONS & CELLULAR BASIS OF IMMUNE RESPONSES

DEFINITIONS

An **antigen (Ag)** is a substance that stimulates the formation of an **antibody (Ab)** by cells which specifically react with that antigen in a particular animal. Most complete Ags are proteins, but some are polysaccharides or polypeptides. Most Ags are macromolecules with a molecular weight of over 10,000. To act as Ags, substances must be recognized as "foreign" or "nonself" by an animal, since, in general, animals do not produce Abs to their own ("self") proteins.

Antigenic determinants are those portions of Ag molecules that determine the specificity of Ag-Ab reactions. The size of the antigenic determinant group may be quite small in relation to the size of the whole Ag molecule, eg, 5–7 amino acid residues or 3–6 glucose residues.

Haptens are chemicals of low molecular weight that do not by themselves elicit the formation of Abs but can combine with Abs elicited by a large molecule that possesses a structural unit similar to or identical with the hapten. Many simple chemicals and drugs can function as haptens. They can bind to host proteins or other carriers to form complete antigens.

Antibodies (Abs) are proteins that are formed in response to an Ag and react specifically with that Ag or one very closely related to it. Only vertebrates make Abs. Abs are specialized proteins, the immunoglobulins. The behavior of these Abs depends to some extent on the class of immunoglobulins to which they belong.

An **idiotype** is a unique antigenic determinant that is present in the variable domain of a homogeneous antibody. It probably represents the antigenicity of the antigen-binding site. Anti-idiotype antibodies can be prepared by the use of elaborate absorption procedures.

THE CELLULAR BASIS OF IMMUNE RESPONSES

The capacity to respond to immunologic stimuli rests principally in cells of the lymphoid system. In order to make clear normal immune responses as well as clinically occurring immune deficiency syndromes and their possible management, a brief outline of current concepts of the development of the lymphoid system must be presented.

During embryonic life, a stem cell develops in fetal liver and other organs. This stem cell probably resides in bone marrow in postnatal life. Under the differentiating influence of various environments, it can be induced to differentiate along several different lines. Within fetal liver and later in bone marrow, the stem cell may differentiate into cells of the red cell series or of the granulocyte series. Alternatively, the stem cell may turn into a lymphoid stem cell that may differentiate to form at least 2 distinct lymphocyte populations. One population (called T lymphocytes) is dependent on the presence of a functioning thymus; the other (B lymphocytes, analogous to lymphocytes derived in birds from the bursa of Fabricius) is independent of the thymus. Some characteristics of B and T lymphocytes are described below, and some major differences between these 2 types of cells are listed in Table 12–1.

B Lymphocytes

These constitute only about 30% of the recirculating pool of small lymphocytes, being mostly restricted to lymphoid tissue. Their life span is short (days or weeks). The mammalian equivalent of the avian bursa is not known, but it is believed that gut-associated lymphoid tissue (eg, tonsils, Peyer's patches, appen-

Table 12–1. Some differences between T and B cells.

	T Cells	B Cells
Frequency in blood	70%	30%
Frequency in spleen	50%	50%
Immunoglobulins on surface	±	+++
Method of counting	Rosette formation with sheep red cells.	Immunofluorescence with anti-Ig.
Secretion of antibody	−	+
Effector in cell-mediated reactions	+	−
Inactivated by x-ray radiation	−	+
Inactivated by anti-lymphocytic serum	+	−
Recognition of determinants on	Carrier	Hapten

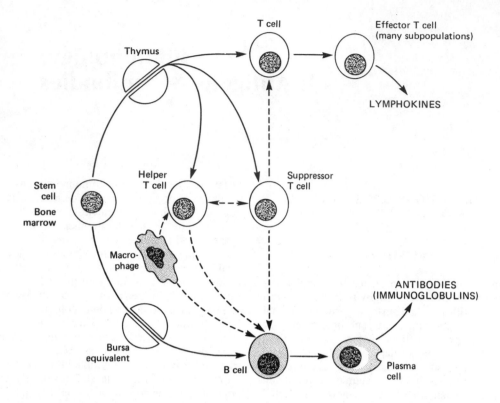

Figure 12–1. Schematic interactions of the immune system.

dix) may be an important source of B lymphocytes. B cells are produced abundantly in the absence of a thymus. B cells have abundant membrane-bound immunoglobulin molecules (about 10^5 per cell). Each cell carries only one type of immunoglobulin, but some carry both IgD and IgM.

B cells can differentiate, proliferate, and mature into plasma cells—large lymphocytes that synthesize specific Abs. Some large lymphocytes can probably revert to small B lymphocytes that have a long life and serve as "memory cells." B cells have various surface receptors, including immunoglobulins and Fc receptors. Attachment of Ag to Ig or of Ag-Ab complex to an Fc receptor provides a stimulus for B cell proliferation. B cell proliferation and "blast cell transformation" can also be stimulated nonspecifically by pokeweed mitogen but not by phytohemagglutinin or concanavalin A.

B cell populations are largely responsible for specific immunoglobulin and Ab production in the host. B cell defects (eg, insufficient numbers, defects in differentiation) lead to inadequate immunoglobulin synthesis but have little to do with cell-mediated immunity. With certain antigens that are large polymers (eg, pneumococcus polysaccharide, anthrax D-glutamic acid polypeptide), B cells alone are stimulated into antibody production, requiring no T cell cooperation. With other antigens that have a smaller number of determinants and require a carrier, T cell cooperation with B cells is needed for antibody production.

T Lymphocytes

These constitute the greater part (65–80%) of the recirculating pool of small lymphocytes. Their life span is long (months or years). Although they are originally derived from bone marrow, they require an intact thymus (at least in early life) before reaching the circulation. Some T cells have receptors for antigens on their surface, but no readily identified immunoglobulins. They tend to give rosette formation with sheep red blood cells. T cells can react with one or a few Ags and then become "immunologically committed" lymphocytes, capable of participating in the cell functions listed below. T cells do not differentiate into immunoglobulin-synthesizing cells and do not produce Ab.

In general, a deficiency of the T cell system manifests itself as a defect in cell-mediated immunity. In view of (E) (see below), however, a T cell defect may also result in impaired antibody synthesis in spite of an intact B cell system.

The precise mechanism by which the thymus controls T cells is not known. In early life, the thymus may be the main intermediate source of T lymphocytes, but their ultimate source is the bone marrow. The thymus exerts some hormonal control over T cells, and hormonal factors have been proposed.

T lymphocytes from an individual sensitized to a given Ag can be stimulated by contact with that Ag to replicate (differentiate) into subpopulations which participate in the following functions:

A. Cell-Mediated Immunity: T cells are responsible for delayed type hypersensitivity reactions to bacterial, viral, fungal, and other antigens. They are a major defense mechanism against many infectious agents and perhaps against neoplastic cells.

B. Graft Rejection, Tumor Immunity: T cells are cytotoxic for grafted cells and for tumor cells. They may also mediate graft-versus-host reactions ("killer T cells").

C. Correlates of Delayed Type Hypersensitivity: T cells release soluble factors that inhibit the migration of macrophages, act as transfer factor, transform other lymphocytes, and are lymphotoxic.

D. Immunologic Memory: T cells divide to form a population of Ag-sensitive cells that have a long life span, thus contributing importantly to immunologic memory.

E. "Helper" T Cells: In response to certain Ags (see above), T cells must cooperate with B cells to permit an antibody response (hence the term "helper" T cells). This is particularly true with haptens and their carriers. The hapten reacts with B cells, but the carrier must react with T cells to yield an Ab response.

F. "Suppressor" T Cells: T cells interact with B cells to inhibit antibody formation. They may also play a role in immune tolerance and in autoimmune phenomena.

G. Nonspecific Stimulation: T cells can be nonspecifically stimulated in culture by mitogens, eg, phytohemagglutinin or concanavalin A.

Some of the above functions are associated with distinct subsets of T cells that can be distinguished on the basis of surface membrane glycoproteins.

Interactions of Lymphoid Cells

The activation of immunocompetent cells is regulated by a complex series of interactions between distinct cell types:

(1) An interaction between macrophages and T cells that is critical for the antigen-stimulated activation of specific T lymphocytes; (2) the "helper" effect exerted by specific T lymphocytes in the activation of B cells and in their differentiation into antibody-secreting plasma cells; (3) the negative regulation ("suppression") exercised by certain T cells on the magnitude and nature of the immune response; (4) the collaboration of separate types of T cells in the differentiation and proliferation of specific cytotoxic effector cells.

The control of lymphoid cell responses and interactions resides in "immune response genes" located in close proximity to the major histocompatibility complex (in humans, HLA—human leukocyte antigen—locus on chromosome 6; see pp 186–187).

Examples of Clinical Immunodeficiency

In a majority of individuals with clinical immunodeficiency, there are complex functional impairments, often involving both B cell and T cell functions. In a few clinical syndromes, the defect is relatively well defined, as illustrated by the examples given in Table 12–2.

Hypersensitivity Reactions

Hypersensitivity or allergic reactions occur in individuals whose reactivity to an Ag has been altered. Reexposure to the same (or a closely related) Ag results in a variety of abnormal reactions. Hypersensitivity reactions are of 2 types: (1) Ab-mediated, or immediate type, reactions and (2) cell-mediated, or delayed type, reactions. Some important differences between the 2 groups are listed in Table 12–3.

From the standpoint of pathogenesis, hypersensitivity reactions have been classified by Gell & Coombs into 4 major types:

Table 12–2. Examples of clinical immunodeficiencies.*

Disorder	Postulated Cell Defect		Observed Immunologic Defect
	B	T	
Congenital X-linked agammaglobulinemia (Bruton's)	+	−	Absent plasma cells, all classes of immunoglobulins extremely deficient. Cellular immunity normal.
Transient hypogammaglobulinemia of infancy	+	−	Usually self-limited.
Selective immunoglobulin deficiency (IgA, IgM, or IgG subclass)	+	(−)	IgA-, IgM-, or IgG-producing plasma cells absent, respective immunoglobulin absent. Cellular immunity normal.
Thymic hypoplasia (DiGeorge's syndrome)	−	+	Immunoglobulins normal but some antibody responses deficient. Cellular immunity defective.
(?) Chronic mucocutaneous candidiasis	−	+	
Immunodeficiency with ataxia-telangiectasia	+	+	Variable deficiency in immunoglobulins and antibodies. Cellular immunity defective for some antigens.
Immunodeficiency with thrombocytopenia and eczema (Wiskott-Aldrich syndrome)	(+)	+	Variable deficiency in immunoglobulins and antibodies. Cellular immunity defective for some antigens.
Immunodeficiency (eg, with thymoma; with short-limbed dwarfism; autosomal recessive, combined, X-linked).	+	+	Extremely deficient antibodies. Cellular immunity defective for all antigens.

*Modified from Cooper MD et al: Classification of primary immunodeficiencies. *N Engl J Med* 1973;**288**:966.
(−) means that there is occasionally a coexisting T cell defect. (+) means that the defect is predominantly T cell but that B cell defects occur also.

Table 12–3. Differences between immediate and delayed hypersensitivity reactions.

	Ab-Mediated or Immediate Type	Cell-Mediated or Delayed Type
Clinical examples	Anaphylactic shock; allergy to pollen, with asthma; serum sickness; some allergies to antibiotics; asthma reaction.	Tuberculin hypersensitivity; allergy to fungi (*Histoplasma*), parasites (trichina), *Rhus* plants (poison ivy or oak), chemicals (nickel); skin graft rejection.
Timing	The reaction begins immediately, ie, within minutes after contact with the allergen, and disappears within 1 hour.	The reaction is delayed. It begins within several hours after contact with the allergen and may last for days.
Histology	The main pathologic reaction consists of dilatation of capillaries and arterioles, with prominent erythema and edema and only limited polymorphonuclear leukocyte infiltration.	The main pathologic reaction consists of inflammatory change with predominant mononuclear cell infiltration and tissue induration.
Passive transfer	The reaction is associated with circulating antibodies and can be transferred passively by means of serum.	The reaction is not associated with circulating Abs and cannot be transferred passively by means of serum. It can often be transferred passively by means of lymphoid cells or their extracts.

I. Anaphylactic Type Hypersensitivity: A special class of Ab (cytotropic Ab, mainly IgE) binds to mast cells and basophils through the Fc fragment. When Ag reacts with these Abs, vasoactive amines and other mediators are liberated and elicit the reaction (see Chapter 13).

II. Cytotoxic Type Hypersensitivity: Ags on the cell surface combine with Ab. This may lead to opsonization and phagocytosis without complement, may facilitate attack by T cells, or may lead to binding of complement, which promotes immune adherence to phagocytes; or the lytic effect may result in membrane damage by complement (see Chapter 13).

III. Complex-Mediated Hypersensitivity: Ags combine with Ab to form complexes that in turn activate complement and Hageman factor (factor XII in blood coagulation) and aggregate platelets, with the consequences shown in Fig 12–2.

IV. Cell-Mediated Hypersensitivity: T lymphocytes carrying specific Ag receptors become activated by contact with that Ag, proliferate, transform, and release a variety of mediators (lymphokines) which in turn act on macrophages, lymphocytes, and other cells to yield the reactions of delayed type hypersensitivity (see Chapter 13).

ANTIBODIES: STRUCTURE & FORMATION

Antibodies (Abs) are immunoglobulins that can react specifically with the Ag that stimulated their production. Immunoglobulins comprise about 20% of total serum proteins, and a variable proportion of immunoglobulins have Ab activity. Abs may be characterized by their chemical, physical, and immunologic properties. Among the prominent physicochemical properties used for classifying Abs are solubility in salts and solvents, electrophoretic mobility, molecular size, and sedimentation in the ultracentrifuge. Electrophoretically, most Abs move with the gamma and beta$_2$ fractions and a few with alpha globulins.

In terms of molecular weight (by ultracentrifugal analysis), Abs fall into 3 main groups: (1) molecular weight 150,000, 7S; (2) 900,000, 19S; and (3) 170,000–400,000, 7S to 11S.

Electrophoresis permits the separation of proteins by migration in an electrical field in paper, starch, gel, etc. From anode toward cathode, albumins migrate slowly the shortest distance, alpha and beta globulins somewhat farther, and gamma globulins faster and farther than the others. **Immunoelectrophoresis** is an important tool in immunoglobulin and antibody identification (see below). The techniques described in this chapter (and others) have indicated that Abs exhibit considerable heterogeneity. Some of this heterogeneity is based on the fact that Abs

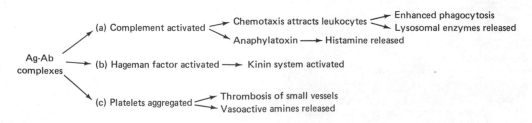

Figure 12–2. Sequence of reactions in complex-mediated hypersensitivity.

Table 12–4. Some characteristics of immunoglobulins.

	IgG	IgM	IgA	IgD	IgE
Sedimentation coefficient	7S	19S	7S or 11S*	7S	8S
Molecular weight	150,000	900,000	170,000 or 400,000*	180,000	190,000
Heavy chain symbol	γ	μ	α	δ	ϵ
Average concentration in normal serum (mg/dL)	1000–1500	60–180	100–400	3–5	0.03
Half-life in serum (days)	23	5	6	3	2.5
Prominent in external secretions	–	–	++	–	+
Percent carbohydrate	4	15	10	18	18
Crosses placenta	+	–	–	?	–
Fixes complement	+	+	–	–	–
Examples of antibodies	Many Abs to toxins, bacteria, viruses; especially late in Ab response	Many Abs to infectious agents, especially early in Ab response; anti-polysaccharide Ab; cold agglutinins	Important as secretory antibody on mucous membranes	No proved Ab activity; present on lymphocyte surface in newborn or in lymphatic leukemia	Binds to mast and basophil cells; raised in allergic and parasitic infections.

*11S, molecular weight 400,000 IgA in external secretions; 7S, molecular weight 170,000 IgA in serum.

to the same Ags belong to different immunoglobulin classes. At present, immunoglobulins are arranged into 5 classes (Table 12–4).

STRUCTURE OF IMMUNOGLOBULINS

In response to a single pure antigen, a large, heterogeneous population of antibody molecules arises from different clones of cells. This made study of the chemical structure of immunoglobulins (Igs) virtually impossible until myeloma proteins were isolated. Myelomas are tumors originating as a clone from a single cell. The Igs produced by myelomas are homogeneous and thus permit chemical analysis of IgG, IgA, IgD, and IgE. In Waldenström's macroglobulinemia (clinically distinct from typical myelomas), a monoclonal IgM is produced. From the study of myeloma proteins, the following generalizations about Ig structure are derived. Quantities of pure monoclonal antibodies can be made artificially by the "hybridoma" technique. This involves the fusion of plasmacytoma (tumor) cells with isolated spleen cells stimulated by a given antigen. The fused "hybridoma" continues to produce the selected monoclonal antibodies in cell culture for long periods.

All immunoglobulins have similar structural patterns but great diversity of antigenic properties and amino acid sequences. Ig molecules are made up of light (small) and heavy (large) polypeptide chains. Each chain consists of a constant carboxyl terminal portion and a variable amino terminal portion, each of which, in turn, is genetically determined by at least one gene. Thus, each Ig chain is coded for by at least 2 genes—one for the constant and one for the variable region. The chains are held together by disulfide bonds (Fig 12–3) and can be isolated by reduction followed by chromatography at acid pH. The chains are folded 3-dimensionally with disulfide bonds to form **domains.** There are variable and constant domains.

Light (L) Chains

These always belong to one of 2 types: κ (kappa) and λ (lambda), with molecular weights of 25,000. Both types occur in all classes of Ig, but any one molecule contains only one type of L chain. Some myeloma tumors secrete homogeneous L chains, either κ or λ type, called Bence Jones proteins, which are excreted in urine. The hereditary human globulin marker Km is located on κ L chains. In primary amyloidosis, the amyloid contains L chains, possibly fragments of autoantibodies.

Heavy (H) Chains

Each of the 5 Ig classes has an antigenically

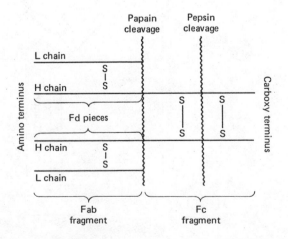

Figure 12–3. Schematic representation of a 7S immunoglobulin (IgG) molecule.

distinct set of H chains (isotypes) with molecular weights of 50,000–70,000. The 5 heavy chain types are called γ in IgG, μ in IgM, α in IgA, δ in IgD, and ϵ in IgE. The portion of H chains that is not involved in the antibody combining site (Fc fragment) carries the sites for various effector reactions (biologic activity), eg, complement fixation, placental transfer, attachment to phagocytic cells, degranulation of mast cells, and skin fixation. It also is the site of the human genetic Gm markers on IgG (with which rheumatoid factors react) and of most of the carbohydrate moiety of Igs. In "heavy chain disease," H chains linked by disulfide bonds are excreted in urine.

Ig fragments resulting from enzymatic treatment of Ig molecules are shown schematically in Fig 12–3.

Treatment of a 7S IgG molecule with papain results in the production of 3 fragments. Two of these are identical Ag-binding Fab fragments (each of which is univalent, containing a single Ag-binding site). The third is the Fc fragment, which carries no Ab activity but a variety of effector reactions (see above).

Treatment of the IgG molecule with pepsin results in similar fragments (see Fig 12–3). Thus, Fab fragments are joined to the Fc fragments by peptide bonds that are readily cleaved by proteases. These act mainly in the "hinge" region.

The piece of heavy chain within the Fab fragment is called the Fd piece.

Combining Site

The biologic activity of an Ab molecule centers on its ability to specifically bind Ags. The combining site is located on the amino terminal end of the Ab molecule (Fig 12–4) and is composed of certain **hypervariable** folded segments within the variable regions of both L and H chains. The active sites of certain Abs are estimated to be just large enough to accommodate 4–6 glucose residues. It has been estimated that of the approximately 650 amino acid residues of an L chain–H chain pair, between 15 and 30 amino acid residues may be involved in each Ab combining site. Antibody specificity is a function of both the amino acid sequence and its 3-dimensional configuration.

Immunoglobulin G (IgG)

IgG comprises about 75% of Igs in normal human sera. Each molecule of IgG consists of 2 L chains and 2 H chains (Fig 12–4) linked by 20 to 25 –S–S– bonds. There are 4 subclasses of IgG (IgG-1 to IgG-4), based on antigenic differences in H chains. Each IgG molecule has only one type of L chain and one type of H chain. IgG is the *only* Ig to cross the placenta and to produce passive cutaneous anaphylaxis. IgG synthesis in humans is about 35 mg/kg/d, and its half-life is about 23 days. Normal adult serum levels (1000–1500 mg/dL) are reached at 2 years of age and decrease from the fourth decade onward.

IgG molecules are probably Y-shaped, with a "hinge region" near the middle of the heavy chain connecting the 2 Fab segments to the Fc segment. The IgG molecule can probably assume various angles at the "hinge." Since each Fab segment has one antigen-binding site, an IgG molecule has a valence of 2. Carbohydrate is less abundant in IgG (4%) than in

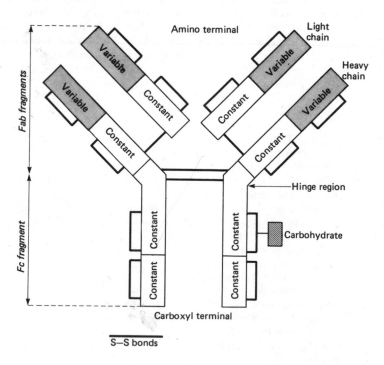

Figure 12–4. Schematic representation of an IgG molecule indicating the location of the constant and the variable regions on the light and the heavy chains.

other Ig classes. Carbohydrate (located on the Fc and occasionally also on Fab segments) may provide binding sites for receptors and may play a role in Ig secretion by plasma cells.

The heterogeneity between IgG subclasses (in antigenicity or amino acid sequence) is less than that between different Ig classes. There are small differences in effector functions among subclasses because of different H chains.

IgG antibodies can probably attach to various tissues through the Fc fragment and participate in anaphylactic (immediate) type reactions.

Immunoglobulin M (IgM)

IgM comprises about 10% of Ig in normal human sera. The greater size of IgM molecules (19S, MW 900,000) is due to 5 units (each similar to one IgG unit) linked through –S–S– bonds near their "hinge regions." Reducing agents (eg, mercaptoethanol) tend to break these linking disulfide bonds and dissociate IgM molecules into 5 subunits of 7–8S, with H chains of molecular weight 70,000. IgM can usually be distinguished from IgG and other Ig classes because treatment with mercaptoethanol results in a loss of agglutinating activity.

Each subunit of IgM consists of 2 L chains and 2 H chains. In addition, there is one J chain (MW 20,000) per 10 L chains of IgM molecules. The J chain is acidic and differs in antigenicity and amino acid composition from the other chains. Its function is uncertain.

Since each IgM molecule has 10 Fab segments, it can combine with up to 10 antigenic sites. It has a valence of from 5 (due to steric hindrance) to 10 (Fig 12–5).

IgM molecules are the earliest antibodies synthesized in response to antigenic stimulation. They fix complement well in the presence of antigen. The rate of IgM synthesis is about 8 mg/kg/d, and the half-life in serum is about 5 days. The fetus synthesizes IgM in utero. Since IgM does not cross the placenta, IgM antibodies in the newborn are thus considered a sign of intrauterine infection. Adult serum levels (60–180 mg/dL) are reached at 6–9 months after birth.

Immunoglobulin A (IgA)

The basic structural unit of IgA corresponds to that of IgG, with 2 H and 2 L chains. While IgG is uniformly a monomer, IgA can occur as a 7S monomer, a 9S dimer, an 11S trimer, and others. With mild reduction, all of these dissociate into 7S monomers. In human serum, IgA comprises about 15% of Ig and occurs either as the 7S monomer or as a polymer in an average concentration of 100–400 mg/dL. The rate of synthesis of serum IgA is about 35 mg/kg/d, and it is rapidly catabolized. In humans and other mammals, IgA is the principal Ig in external secretions (eg, mucus of respiratory, intestinal, urinary, and genital tracts; tears; saliva; milk). This secretory IgA is produced by cells in the various body locations. It exists mainly as a multimer (9S, 11S, etc), contains a J chain (see IgM above) in addition to L and H chains, and also contains another peptide chain called secretory component (MW 60,000). The precise function of the secretory component is not understood. It may be synthesized by specialized cells in the epithelium, whereas IgA molecules are synthesized by plasma cells in the mucous membranes or secretory organs. The production of secretory IgA is stimulated more effectively by local than by systemic infection or antigen administration. IgA (serum or secretory) does *not* fix complement in the presence of antigen but may activate C3 by the alternative pathway. Secretory IgA can neutralize viruses and can inhibit attachment of bacteria to epithelial cells unless cleaved by microbial proteases.

Immunoglobulin D (IgD)

This immunoglobulin was first encountered as a myeloma protein and then found in concentrations of 3–5 mg/dL in normal sera. IgD is rapidly catabolized and has a half-life of only 3 days. IgD has not been proved to have Ab activity. IgD (with IgM) has been demonstrated on the surface of B lymphocytes in cord blood and also on cells in lymphatic leukemia.

Immunoglobulin E (IgE)

In normal sera, IgE is found only in minute concentration (0.03 mg/dL). Intact IgE molecules are 8S, with a molecular weight of 190,000. The H chains of IgE are longer than those of IgG by about 100 amino acid residues, perhaps indicating a special function. IgE mediates allergic reactions in skin and other tissues and, with the Fc fragment, binds to mast cells and basophils. The latter degranulate upon exposure to the specific antigen with the liberation of mediators. (See p 175.) Whereas most Igs are quite heat-stable, IgE loses the ability to sensitize skin after being heated for 4 hours at 56 °C.

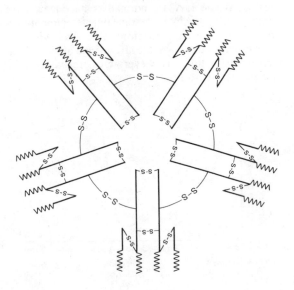

Figure 12–5. Schematic diagram of the pentameric structure of human IgM.

In persons with allergic reactivity of the antibody-mediated (immediate) type, the serum concentrations of IgE are greatly increased. In such individuals, IgE also appears in external secretions and mediates local allergic reactions. The serum level of IgE is increased in parasitic infections (helminthiases).

One or more immunoglobulins may be present in abnormally high concentration in neoplasms of plasma cells (myelomas), in liver disease, in chronic protozoal or microbial infections, and in autoimmune diseases. Deficiencies of specific immunoglobulins often are on a hereditary basis and can be due to absence of specific cells, impaired synthesis, or increased catabolism (see previous section).

Antibody Formation

The mechanism by which Abs are formed has been debated for years. The **instructive theory** proposed that the specificity of an Ab molecule was determined not by its amino acid sequence but by the molding of the peptide chain around the antigenic determinant; the presence of antigen was required to serve as a template. This theory lost favor when it became apparent that Ab-forming cells were devoid of Ag and that Ab specificity was a function of amino acid sequence.

At present, the **clonal selection theory** is widely accepted. It holds that an immunologically responsive cell can respond to only one Ag or a closely related group of Ags and that this property is inherent in the cell before the Ag is encountered. According to the clonal selection theory, each individual is endowed with a very large pool of lymphocytes, each of which is capable of responding to a different Ag; when the Ag enters the body, it selects the lymphocyte that has the best "fit" by virtue of a surface receptor. The Ag binds to this Ab-like receptor, and the cell is stimulated to proliferate and form a clone of cells (clonal amplification). Thus, selected B cells quickly differentiate into plasma cells and secrete Ab that is specific for the Ag which served as the original selecting agent (or a closely related group of antigens).

It appears that each Ab-producing cell makes only one type of immunoglobulin and only one Ab. The receptors on the surfaces of B cells are specific Igs. When this Ig has been selected and bound by a specific Ag, the surface receptor is lost for several hours while the stimulus sets off cell proliferation and differentiation into plasma cells. Each plasma cell makes only one type of heavy chain and one type of light chain. For each chain, one or more genes code for the variable region and one or more genes for the constant region. It is likely that the DNA sequence encoding the variable and constant regions of each chain is transcribed as one cistron. As protein synthesis proceeds, the building of both L and H chains proceeds continuously on separate polyribosomes, starting from the amino terminal, and the completed Ig molecule is assembled in the cell before release.

Although a given cell produces only one Ig type at one time, the so-called **IgM-IgG switch** may occur:

initially, IgM is synthesized; later, the genes controlling the variable regions of the H chain of IgM may recombine with genes controlling the constant regions of IgG so that the IgG later produced is of the same specificity as the earlier IgM.

The initial step in Ab formation is the phagocytosis of Ag by macrophages. These cells present Ag in some form to B cells. (They also present antigen molecules to T cells.) Stimulated B cells differentiate into plasma cells, where immunoglobulin chain synthesis begins on polyribosomes. In some instances (eg, myeloma cells), synthesized chains are excreted; in other instances, L and H chains are assembled with disulfide bonds and the sugar moiety is added before release. Fully assembled IgG may be secreted 30–40 minutes after the onset of synthesis.

With certain Ags, the induction of an Ab response requires the cooperation of B cells with T cells as well as with macrophages. Collaborative effects involve "helper" T cells that recognize the T-dependent antigen by means of IgM-like surface receptor molecules and interact with antigen-specific B cells. Conversely, "suppressor" T cells may inhibit responses by B cells. HLA-linked immune response genes control this B cell–T cell interaction as well as many other aspects of the complex immune response.

The Primary Response

When an animal or human is injected with an Ag—and if this represents the individual's first contact with that Ag—there is a rise in detectable Ab in serum within several days, depending on the route of injection and the dose and nature of the Ag. The Ab concentration then rises to a peak within 1–10 weeks, then drops, and may fall below detectable levels (Fig 12–6). In general, IgM Abs appear earlier than IgG Abs in the primary response. IgM Ab concentrations decline more rapidly than IgG Ab concentrations because IgM and IgA are normally catabolized more rapidly than IgG. Abs made some time after immunization tend to bind Ag more firmly than Ab made soon after immunization—ie, the affinity and avidity of Ab increase with time. However, cross-reactivity may also increase with time.

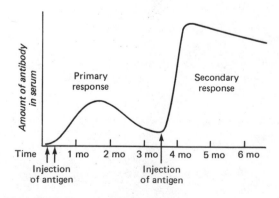

Figure 12–6. Rate of antibody production following initial antigen administration and "booster" injection.

The Secondary Response

When an animal is reinjected with the same Ag weeks, months, or even years after the primary Ab levels have subsided, there is a more rapid Ab response to a higher level—and for a longer period—than in the primary response. This is presumably based on persistence of a substantial number of Ag-sensitive "memory" cells after initial contact with the Ag. The memory for secondary Ab response resides in B cells and, for certain antigens, in both B and T cells. During the secondary response, IgM antibody production may be similar to that in the primary response, whereas IgG antibody production is usually far greater. A secondary response may be elicited with an Ag that is identical with or related to the Ag eliciting the primary response in that individual. This phenomenon ("original antigenic sin") is a useful technique that can be employed in serologic epidemiology of infectious diseases caused by antigenically related but not identical agents (eg, influenza viruses).

Interference With Antibody Formation

When 2 or more Ags are injected simultaneously, the host reacts by producing antibodies to each. Competition of Ags for Ab-producing mechanisms has been observed experimentally, but it plays no practical role. Combined immunization with several Ags is widely used (eg, diphtheria and tetanus toxoids with pertussis vaccine, and live measles-mumps-rubella virus vaccines). The passive administration of a specific antibody interferes with the active production of that same specific antibody by the host. A practical application is the injection of human antibody to Rh antigen into Rh-negative women with Rh-positive partners and children. If the Rh-negative woman is permitted to form antibodies to the fetus's Rh-positive red cells, these antibodies are likely to produce Rh disease in the offspring; but if the Rh-negative woman receives concentrated Rh antibodies before she begins to synthesize Rh antibodies, her antibody production is inhibited and Rh disease of the newborn is prevented (see below).

Human Gamma Globulin

Immune globulin USP is a preparation of gamma globulin derived from large pools of human plasma by low-temperature ethanol fractionation. The preparation contains about 165 mg of gamma globulin per milliliter of solution, representing a 25-fold concentration of Ab-containing globulins of plasma, glycine as stabilizer, and an antibacterial agent. When used, such concentrated gamma globulin is injected intramuscularly or subcutaneously, never intravenously. A 5% solution of gamma globulin in 10% maltose can be given intravenously. It may be employed clinically in the following conditions:

A. Hypo- or Dysgammaglobulinemia With Recurrent Bacterial Infections: Inject 0.6–1 mL/kg body weight (100–165 mg immune globulin per kilogram) once each month, but twice initially. Antimicrobial drugs must also be used.

B. Measles: To prevent clinical disease in nonimmunized children (and interfere with development of active immunity), give 0.25 mL/kg as soon as possible after exposure. To attenuate the disease (and permit development of active immunity), give 0.04 mL/kg within 8 days of exposure. Immune globulin has no effect after the rash has appeared. Attenuation markedly reduces the incidence of complications, but (ideally) all susceptible individuals (except severely immunosuppressed persons) should be vaccinated with live attenuated vaccine (see p 173).

C. Hepatitis A: Use of 0.02 mL/kg once or twice during the incubation period may prevent or modify the disease without interfering with the development of immunity.

Specific Human Gamma Globulins

These are obtained from the blood of individuals who have been immunized with a given antigen and have acquired high concentrations of specific antibody. A few specific indications are listed below.

A. Tetanus: For prevention of tetanus after injury in nonimmunized individuals, 250–500 units of tetanus immune globulin USP will yield serum levels of more than 0.01 unit/mL for several weeks (see p 211). Ten thousand units have been injected intravenously for the treatment of tetanus.

B. Vaccinia: Vaccinia immune globulin (VIG), 0.6–1 mL/kg, can be used in the rare individual who develops progressive vaccinia gangrenosum following smallpox vaccination. Such a person is usually immunodeficient.

C. Rabies: Rabies immune globulin USP (RIG) is prepared from plasma pools with high rabies antibody titer obtained from immunized volunteers. The recommended dose is 20 units/kg. Up to half should be infiltrated around the wound and the rest injected intramuscularly. (Phone the Dallas Distribution Center of Cutter Laboratories: (214) 661-5850. Also available from other Cutter Laboratories distribution centers.) Usually given in conjunction with injections of diploid cell-grown inactivated rabies vaccine, as indicated by the manufacturer, for postexposure immunization against rabies.

D. Mumps: Limited evidence suggests that 20 mL of mumps immune globulin USP may prevent orchitis in adult males.

E. Chickenpox: Varicella-zoster immune globulin (VZIG), 0.15 mL/kg intramuscularly, can prevent the disease when injected into high-risk children within 72 hours of exposure.

F. Rh Disease: $Rh_0(D)$ immune globulin USP can be injected into an Rh-negative mother following delivery of an Rh-positive infant. This prevents Rh isoimmunization of the mother and reduces the risk of hemolytic Rh disease in her next Rh-positive infant.

G. Pertussis: Pertussis immune globulin USP (2–3 mL) may hasten recovery, prevent complications, and reduce the mortality rate in debilitated infants or unimmunized children under 3 years of age.

H. Hepatitis: Hepatitis B immune globulin USP may be given within 7 days of parenteral or mucous membrane exposure to HBsAg-positive material. This is repeated (0.06 mL/kg) 3 weeks later. It is sometimes given to newborns of mothers who became HBsAg-positive late in pregnancy.

ANTIGEN–ANTIBODY REACTIONS

Antigens (Ags) have been defined as substances that can elicit the formation of antibodies (Abs) in a living animal. An animal does not generally produce Abs against its own Ags, ie, it differentiates between "self" and "nonself." Exceptions to this generalization are discussed in Chapter 13.

Antigenic Specificity

Reactions of Ags with Abs are highly specific. This means that an Ag will react only with Abs elicited by its own kind or by a closely related kind of Ag. The majority of antigenic substances are species-specific, and some are even organ-specific within an animal species. Human proteins can easily be distinguished from the proteins of other animals by Ag-Ab reactions and will cross-react only with the proteins of closely related species (eg, anthropoid apes). Within a single species, kidney protein may be distinguished from lung protein, etc. Exceptions to this species-specificity are certain Ags that are widely distributed among animals, particularly protein of the lens of the eye and the so-called **Forssman** or **heterophil antigen,** which is present in the organs of the móuse, dog, cat, horse, fish, and chicken as well as in the red cells of sheep and in some bacteria.

Antigenic specificity is a function of the antigenic determinants, small defined chemical areas on a large antigen molecule. The antigenic determinant may be a small group that is an essential part of the molecule and may repeat itself (eg, egg albumin probably has 5 determinants). Alternatively, the antigenic determinant may be a hapten, a small molecule linked to a larger carrier. Coupling simple chemical groups like $-COOH$, $-SO_3H$, or $-AsO_3H_2$ on a benzene ring with serum protein (by diazo reactions) showed that each of these groups conferred specificity upon the Ag, depending particularly on the position of the radical (ortho-, meta-, or para-) in the aromatic compound.

Ag-Ab reactions are highly specific. Abs usually can distinguish between the homologous Ag (which stimulated their formation) and heterologous, related Ag. The **specificity** of an Ab population depends on its ability to discriminate between Ags of related structure by combining with them to a different extent.

The binding of Ag to Ab does *not* involve covalent bonds but only relatively weak, short-range forces (electrostatic, coulombic, hydrogen bonding, van der Waals forces, etc). The strength of Ag-Ab bonds depends to a large extent on the closeness of fit between the configuration of the antigenic determinant site and the combining site of the Ab. The combining sites on Ab formed against a given antigenic determinant are not all perfect fits. Any antiserum thus contains some Abs with very close fit and relatively strong binding forces and some with poor fit and weaker binding forces. Abs with the best fit and the strongest binding are said to have high **affinity** for the Ag. They have little tendency to dissociate from Ag after binding it (ie, they have high **avidity**). Abs of low avidity tend to dissociate more readily from Ag. Early in the process of immunization, antibody may have relatively low affinity; as immunization proceeds, antibody of increasingly higher affinity is made.

In spite of the very great antigenic specificity, cross-reactions occur between antigenic determinants of closely related structure and their Abs. The sharing of similar antigenic determinants by molecules of different origin leads to unexpected and unpredictable cross-reactions, eg, between human group A red blood cells and type 14 pneumococci. Many microorganisms share antigens (eg, *Haemophilus* and *E coli* O75:K100).

When antigenic proteins are denatured by heating or by chemical treatment, the molecular configuration is somewhat changed. This usually results in the loss of the original antigenic determinants and often leads to the uncovering of new antigenic determinants. Formaldehyde-treated proteins acquire an added antigenicity, and their antisera tend to cross-react with other formaldehyde-treated proteins. However, with gentle formaldehyde treatment of toxins, the original antigenicity may also be preserved, whereas the toxicity of the molecule (eg, exotoxins) may be abolished and the molecule thus converted to a "toxoid" that is immunogenic but nontoxic.

Most microorganisms contain not just one but many Ags to each of which Abs may develop in the course of infection. Among these Ags may be capsular polysaccharides, somatic proteins or lipoprotein-carbohydrate complexes, protein exotoxins, and enzymes produced by the organism. All enzymes appear to be antigenic, and in some but not all cases that portion of the molecule which combines with specific Ab appears to be distinct from the portion of the molecule responsible for enzymatic activity. Many hormones are also antigenic.

Alloantigens (Blood Group Substances)

In general, Abs are elicited only by Ags foreign to the injected animal species (heteroantibodies). However, animals may produce "alloantibodies" against "alloantigens," ie, antigens derived from other individuals of the same species. Outstanding among alloantigens are the blood group substances present in the red cells. There are 4 combinations of the 2 Ags present in erythrocytes. Their presence is under genetic control. The serum contains Ab against the absent Ags. As shown in Table 12–5, Ag and corresponding Ab do not coexist in the same blood. To avoid Ag-Ab reactions that would result in serious

Table 12—5. Determination of blood group by cross-match.

Group	Ags in Red Cell	Abs in Plasma	Determinant Group of Blood Group Ag
O	. . .	a, b	L-Fucose
A	A	b	a-N-Acetyl-galactos-aminoyl-galactose
B	B	a	a-D-Galactosyl-galactose
AB	AB	. . .	. . .

transfusion accidents, all bloods must be carefully matched for transfusion.

In addition to these major alloantigens, certain red blood cells contain other blood group substances capable of stimulating antibodies. Among them is the Rh substance. Abs to Rh are developed when an Rh-negative person is transfused with Rh-positive blood or when an Rh-negative pregnant woman absorbs Rh substance from her Rh-positive fetus who inherited the *D* gene from the father. The development of high-titer anti-Rh$_0$D antibodies in the mother can lead to transplacental passage of IgG to the fetus, with resulting erythroblastosis of the newborn.

Apart from certain "sequestered" Ags—eg, thyroid or lens protein—that can definitely serve as autoantigens, it is not clear what may bring about the autoantigenicity of other organ antigens. Perhaps mobilization from the fixed site or slight alteration of structure, eg, by infection, may predispose to autoimmunization, with consequent disease (see Autoimmune Diseases in Chapter 13).

Rate of Absorption & Elimination of Antigen

One of the features that determines the effectiveness of an Ag as a stimulus for antibody production is its rate of absorption and elimination from the site of administration. Ags differ greatly in their rate of excretion, but the major portion of injected Ag is often eliminated from the host within hours or days. In general, the Ab response will be higher and more sustained if the Ag is absorbed slowly from its "depot" at the site of injection. For this reason, many immunizing preparations employ physical methods to delay absorption. Toxoids are often adsorbed onto aluminum hydroxide. Bacterial or viral suspensions are sometimes prepared with adjuvants that delay absorption and promote tissue reaction to "fix" the Ag at its site of injection. (Adjuvants are discussed in Chapter 13.)

Following intravenous injection of a soluble Ag, the following phases in elimination are observed: (1) equilibration between intra- and extravascular compartments; (2) slow degradation of the Ag; (3) rapid immune elimination, as newly formed Ab combines with persisting Ag to form complexes that are phagocytosed by macrophages and digested.

Kinds of Antibodies

Abs are generally described in terms of their reactions with Ag:

A. Antitoxins: Abs to toxins or toxoids that neutralize or flocculate with the antigen.

B. Agglutinins: Abs that aggregate cells, forming clumps. Agglutinins can only be demonstrated if the Ag is particulate or if it is adsorbed onto the surface of a visible particle of uniform size (red blood cell, latex, bentonite, etc).

C. Precipitins: Abs that form complexes with Ag molecules in solution, forming precipitates. Precipitins can only be demonstrated if the Ag is soluble.

D. Lysins: Abs that, usually together with complement, dissolve the antigenic cells.

E. Opsonins: Abs that combine with surface components of microbial and other particles so that they are more readily taken up by phagocytes.

F. Neutralizing (Protective) Abs: Abs that render the antigenic infective agent (commonly viruses) noninfective.

G. Complement-Fixing Abs: Detected by the consumption of complement by the Ag-Ab complex. These reactions are discussed in detail below.

H. "Blocking," Inhibitory, and Other Nonprecipitating Abs: These combine with Ag but are not grossly detectable unless they are shown to inhibit or "block" a reaction or unless the protein species of Ab can be identified.

•   •   •

Different types of reactions may sometimes be demonstrated with the same Ag and Ab. Often one reaction may be more efficient than another. In general, Ags are multivalent with respect to Ab. Antibody valence is 2 (for IgG, IgA, IgE) or 5–10 (for IgM). In many reactions, Ag and Ab may combine in multiple proportions (see Danysz Phenomenon, p 168).

SEROLOGIC REACTIONS

Serology is the study of reactions between Ags and Abs. It attempts to quantitate these reactions by keeping one reagent constant and diluting the other. Some serologic measurements may be made absolutely quantitative by using the techniques of immunochemistry.

Serologic reactions can be used to identify Ags or Abs, if either of these reagents is known. They are also used to estimate the relative quantity of these reactants. Because of the specificity and sensitivity of Ag-Ab reactions, they find wide application in medicine. Examples are the diagnosis of an infection by detection of Ab titer rise against an etiologic agent (eg, *Salmonella*); the detection of circulating Ag in infection (eg, hepatitis B surface Ag); the "matching" of red blood cells against the serum of a potential recipient; the identification of Ag with sera of known Ab content; and many more.

The type of Ag-Ab reaction applicable to a given situation depends largely on the physical state of the available Ag (see above). Each of the common types of Ag-Ab reactions is taken up in some detail on the following pages. Because the precipitin reaction permits the most accurate chemical quantitative work, it has been studied in the greatest detail. Some of the characteristics observed in precipitin reactions apply generally to all Ag-Ab reactions.

PRECIPITATION REACTIONS

A simple way to demonstrate the presence of Ab against an Ag in solution is to layer a small volume of one over the other in a tube. At the interface, precipitation will occur, forming a ring. This gives qualitative evidence of an Ag-Ab reaction but does not indicate whether one or several Ag-Ab systems are present. If, however, the reaction takes place not in solution but in a semisolid gel, then different Ags and Abs are likely to diffuse at different rates. As a result, optimal proportions for precipitation occur at different sites in the agar, and distinct multiple bands of precipitate form. Double diffusion gel precipitation methods based on this principle are described below. They are used for many different immunologic tests.

Precipitation reactions involving single Ag-Ab systems can be performed quantitatively. A measured quantity of a given antibody is placed in a series of test tubes; varying amounts of the corresponding pure antigen are added, mixed, and allowed to react. A precipitate forms in some tubes, and the quantity of this precipitate, after sedimentation and washing, can be measured accurately in several ways. For example, a total nitrogen determination can be made on the precipitate and the (known) amount of antigen nitrogen subtracted from the total to yield the amount of antibody nitrogen. Or the antigen can be labeled with a radioactive isotope and the amount of radioactivity in the precipitate measured. Other methods can be used as well. When the precipitate is removed and the supernatant examined, 3 zones of antigen-antibody interaction can be discerned. They are shown schematically in Fig 12–7.

(1) A zone of Ab excess, in which uncombined Ab is present.

(2) A zone of equivalence, in which both Ag and Ab are completely precipitated and no uncombined Ag or Ab is present. In this zone there is also maximal complement fixation.

(3) A zone of Ag excess, in which all Ab has combined with Ag and additional uncombined Ag is present. In this zone, precipitation is partly or completely inhibited because soluble Ag-Ab complexes form in the presence of excess Ag.

The field of immunochemistry provides methods for absolute quantitative measurement of Ab that can be applied to a large variety of theoretical and practical problems.*

The initial combination of Ag and Ab takes place almost immediately upon mixing of the reactants. The subsequent formation of larger, visible aggregates requires an hour or more and depends somewhat on the temperature and the total volume of the mixture. The reaction is fastest in the zone of equivalence, where optimal proportions between Ag and Ab exist. The speed of gross precipitation is an index of the zone of equivalence, where complete precipitation of both Ag and Ab takes place and neither is present in excess.

GEL DIFFUSION TESTS

These tests are based on the diffusion of Ag and Ab through a semisolid medium to form stable complexes that can be analyzed visually. The Ouchterlony plate (an agar-coated plate in which wells have been cut to hold Ag and Ab) may be used to identify immunologically active substances and detect their components and relationships. Antigens and antibodies diffusing in all directions will form lines of precipitate when equivalent concentrations of each meet. Typical reaction patterns in angular **double diffusion** are shown in Fig 12–8. These reaction patterns permit the identification of identical antigens, nonidentical antigens, and antigens of partial identity that cross-react.

Single radial diffusion can be used to quantitate an Ag, eg, an immunoglobulin in a mixture. Radial diffusion is based on the quantitative relationship between the amount of Ag placed in a well cut into agar and the diameter of the ring of precipitate that forms with Ab incorporated in the agar. These are then compared to a standard curve obtained with known amounts of Ag and the same Ab-containing plate.

AGGLUTINATION REACTIONS

Whereas the Ag is in solution in precipitation tests, it is particulate in agglutination reactions. It may consist of suspensions of microorganisms, cells (eg,

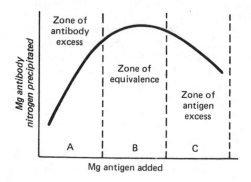

Figure 12–7. The main zones of antigen-antibody interaction.

---

*The techniques, accomplishments, and possibilities of immunochemistry are discussed in Kabat EA: *Kabat & Mayer's Experimental Immunochemistry,* 2nd ed. Thomas, 1971.

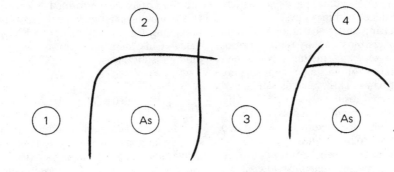

As = Antiserum in wells
1, 2, 3, 4 = Antigens in wells

1 and 2 = Reaction of identity
2 and 3 = Reaction of nonidentity
3 and 4 = Reaction of partial identity (cross-reaction; the "spur" is caused by the fraction of Ab that was not precipitated by Ag 4)

Figure 12–8. Double diffusion precipitin reactions in gel.

red blood cells), or uniform particles like latex or bentonite onto which Ags have been adsorbed. When mixed with specific antiserum, these cells or particles become clumped; the clumps aggregate and finally settle as large, visible clumps, leaving the supernatant clear. If one of the reagents is known, the reaction may be employed for the identification of either Ag or Ab. Thus, the reaction is commonly used to identify, by means of known antisera, microorganisms cultured from clinical specimens. The agglutination reaction is also used to estimate the titer of antibacterial agglutinins in the serum of patients with unknown disease. A rise in Ab titer directed against a specific microorganism occurring during an illness strongly suggests a causal relationship.

Microorganisms possess a variety of antigens, and antibodies to one or more of these may be present in antiserum. A simple example is provided by the antibody response to infection by flagellated bacteria. Antibodies may be directed against the flagellar surface antigen, the somatic antigens, or both. The type of macroscopic agglutination may also be distinctive; the flagellar Ag-Ab complex appears coarse and floccular, whereas the somatic complex is fine and granular.

The agglutination reaction is aided by elevated temperature (37–56 °C) and by movement, which increases the contact between Ag and Ab (eg, shaking, stirring, centrifuging). The aggregation of clumps requires the presence of salts. In the zone of Ab excess (ie, concentrated serum), agglutination may be inhibited owing to the presence of blocking Ab (see Brucellae, p 242). Such a prozone may give the impression that Abs are absent; this error can be avoided only by using serial dilutions of serum.

The agglutination test may be performed microscopically by mixing a loopful of serum with a suspension of microorganisms on a slide and inspecting the result through the low-power objective. This is commonly done for the identification of unknown cultures. For the estimation of the "titer" of agglutinating

Ab in an unknown serum, a macroscopic tube dilution test or a microtiter dilution test may be done: a suitable fixed amount of Ag is added to each tube of a series of serum dilutions, and after thorough shaking, the tubes are incubated at 37 °C for 1–2 hours. The result is determined by looking for sedimented clumps and clear supernatant fluid. The "titer" of the serum is the highest dilution with clearly visible agglutination.

In **co-agglutination,** the Fc fragment of almost any Ab fixes to protein A of staphylococci. Thus, staphylococci with a given attached Ab are agglutinated when mixed with the specific Ag.

THE ANTIGLOBULIN (COOMBS) TEST

This is an indirect agglutination test for the detection of cell-bound or incomplete Abs. Such Abs are by themselves incapable of agglutinating particles but can bind to them firmly. By adding an Ab against the globulin species (eg, antihuman globulin prepared in rabbits), agglutination of the coated particles results. This test has found greatest application in the detection of various anti-red blood cell Abs in hemolytic anemias.

TOXIN–ANTITOXIN REACTIONS

The toxin-antitoxin reactions described below apply only to exotoxins, as exemplified by the toxins of diphtheria, tetanus, or botulism. The following examples of definitions of units apply to diphtheria toxin:

International Unit of antitoxin (IU): The amount of antitoxin in 0.0628 mg of a standard dried antitoxin maintained at the Serum Institute, Copenhagen.

L+ dose: The smallest amount of toxin that, when mixed with 1 unit of antitoxin and injected subcutaneously into a guinea pig weighing 250 g, will cause death within 4 days.

Lf dose (flocculating unit): That amount of toxin which flocculates most rapidly with 1 unit of antitoxin in a series of mixtures containing constant amounts of antitoxin and varying amounts of toxin. (This value is calculated from experimental results.)

Antitoxic potency can be measured by the ability to neutralize the toxin when the mixture is injected into animals or to precipitate toxin in vitro.

Any preparation of toxin contains some molecules of full toxicity and others of low or no toxicity but persistent antigenicity (toxoid). Dried antitoxin, however, is constant in its ability to combine with toxin or toxoid molecules. For this reason, antitoxin is taken as the constant standard for biologic estimation of toxic or antitoxic potency. The L+ dose is usually relied upon. The Lf unit is independent of the toxic activity of a given preparation and is only a function of its antigenic combining power. Thus, it remains constant when a toxin is converted to toxoid by formalin or heat. It is of great importance in the standardization of antigenic quantities of toxoid.

Toxin-antitoxin flocculations are similar to precipitin reactions but show a very sharp zone of equivalence. The reaction is inhibited by both Ag excess and Ab excess; soluble complexes result from either.

Danysz Phenomenon

If toxin is added to antitoxin in several fractions with time intervals between them, then more antitoxin (or less toxin) is necessary to give a neutral end point in injected animals than if all the toxin had been added at once. This is explained by the ability of toxin to combine with antitoxin in multiple proportions. The first fraction of toxin combines with a relatively large amount of the antitoxin present, so that little antitoxin is left to combine with the second fraction. After some time, however, an equilibrium is again reached. The Danysz phenomenon applies similarly to other Ag-Ab reactions, where the dissociation of Ag-Ab complexes is slow.

ABSORPTION REACTIONS

Sera from animals injected with whole microorganisms or from humans who have passed through several infections tend to react with a variety of related Ags. This raises the question whether the serum contains an Ab specific for a given Ag or merely a related Ab that cross-reacts. Such sera may be rendered specific for one antigen by removing related antibodies through absorption with specific Ags. This is done by mixing the serum with concentrated Ag (eg, a dense bacterial suspension), incubating to permit combination, and then centrifuging the precipitate or agglutinated material and removing the supernatant serum. It is now "absorbed" and should no longer contain Abs specific for the absorbing Ag. Such absorptions may be performed with a series of Ags, finally leaving a serum that will react only with a single remaining Ag, for which it is highly specific. This is valuable in "antigenic analysis" of bacteria and other biologic substances.

INHIBITION REACTIONS

In addition to various direct methods of demonstrating and measuring Ag-Ab reactions discussed above, some indirect methods exist that, in essence, use competition for an Ab combining site by 2 antigenic groups or competition for an antigenic group by 2 Abs. They are especially useful when there is no visible evidence of direct reaction between Ag and Ab. Several of these methods are yielding important information regarding the size of the Ab combining site and the structure of antigenic groups. *Examples:* inhibition of precipitation by nonprecipitating Ab or by a fragment of digested Ab; inhibition of viral hemagglutination by Ab; inhibition of the Prausnitz-Küstner reaction by blocking Ab.

IMMUNOFLUORESCENCE
(Fluorescent Antibody Tests, FA)

Certain fluorescent dyes (eg, fluorescein isothiocyanate, rhodamine) can be covalently attached to globulin molecules and thus made visible by using ultraviolet light in the fluorescence microscope. If such fluorescent dyes are conjugated with Ab molecules and all excess is carefully eliminated, such "labeled" Ab may be used to locate and identify specific Ag because of the high specificity of the Ag-Ab bond. By means of such "direct immunofluorescence reactions," bacteria may be identified and viral or other Ags may be located inside cells. In bacteriologic diagnosis, specific direct immunofluorescence is valuable for the rapid identification of group A hemolytic streptococci, *Treponema pallidum,* and other organisms. In special laboratories, immunofluorescence has been applied to the rapid screening of enteric pathogens, *Yersinia,* bacteria causing childhood meningitis, and others.

The "indirect immunofluorescence reactions" involve 3 reagents: Ag + its Ab A + a fluorescent-labeled Ab to Ab A. Any one of the 3 reagents can be unknown. For example, in the serodiagnosis of syphilis, *T pallidum* Ag fixed to a slide is overlaid with the patient's unknown serum and then washed. Fluorescein-labeled antihuman globulin (made in an animal) is then placed on the preparation, which is examined by ultraviolet light. If the patient's serum contains specific Abs to *T pallidum,* brightly fluorescent spirochetes are seen. If the spirochetes do not fluoresce, no specific antitreponemal Abs are present. (See FTA-ABS Test in Chapter 20.)

Immunofluorescence can be used for the detection of viral and bacterial Ags or Abs, tumor Ags, and many others. The indirect test is often more sensitive than the direct immunofluorescence test because more fluorescein-labeled antibodies adhere per antigenic site.

ELECTROPHORESIS METHODS

When an electric current passes through a solution of proteins, the proteins migrate with different velocity from anode to cathode (see p 158). This permits separation of different globulins on some supporting structure, eg, starch, cellulose acetate, paper, gels. This method can be quantitated to permit measurement of different serum proteins in a given sample.

Immunoelectrophoresis combines electrophoretic separation of proteins in a mixture with immune precipitation of the components by Ab. Small wells are cut in a layer of agar on a glass slide, and each is filled with an Ag or mixture of Ags (serum). After electrophoresis with direct current for several hours, a trough is cut in the agar and filled with antiserum. The serum is permitted to diffuse against the electrophoretically separated antigens on the slide. A precipitate arc forms where specific Ag-Ab reactions occur. It can be washed and stained for protein and compared to standards. This method permits (for example) detection of the absence of a specific immunoglobulin in serum, or the presence of an unusually sharp, high peak of an abnormal globulin, as in myeloma.

Counterimmunoelectrophoresis (CIE, double electroimmunodiffusion). This is an extension of immunoelectrophoresis that relies on the movement of Ag toward the anode and of Ab toward the cathode during the passage of electric current through a gel. Ag and Ab are each placed in a well in the gel. As they move toward each other, their meeting and precipitation at an intermediate point is greatly accelerated. Visible precipitin lines develop in 30–60 minutes, and the method is 10 times more sensitive than double diffusion without electric current. The method is limited to acidic antigens. It is most useful for the rapid detection of antigens in body fluids, eg, polysaccharides in cerebrospinal fluid of patients with meningitis caused by *Haemophilus*, pneumococcus, etc.

RADIOIMMUNOASSAY (RIA)

Radioimmunoassays are the most sensitive and versatile methods for the quantitation of substances that are Ags or haptens and can be radioactively labeled. Radioimmunoassay is particularly applicable to the measurement of serum levels of many hormones, drugs, and other biologic materials. The method is based on competition for specific Ab between the labeled (known) and the unlabeled (unknown) concentration of the material. The complexes that form between Ag (or hapten) and Ab can then be separated and the amount of radioactivity determined. The concentration of the unknown (unlabeled) Ag is

determined by comparison with the effect of standards.

Radioallergosorbent test (RAST) is a specialized radioimmunoassay to measure the amount of serum IgE antibodies that react with a specific allergen.

ENZYME–LINKED IMMUNOASSAY

This technique is increasingly popular because it is very sensitive and does not require specialized equipment, as do immunofluorescence and radioimmunoassay. The method depends on conjugation of an enzyme to either an Ag or an Ab and use of the enzyme activity as a quantitative label. Many variations of the method can be constructed, depending on the nature of the enzyme employed and the Ag-Ab system to be measured. A widely employed variant is the **enzyme-linked immunosorbent assay** (ELISA), which can be used to measure either Ag or Ab. To measure Ab, the known Ag is fixed to a solid phase (eg, plastic cup or microplate), incubated with test serum dilutions, washed, and then incubated with anti-immunoglobulin labeled with an enzyme (eg, horseradish peroxidase). Enzyme activity is measured by adding the specific substrate: the color reaction is estimated colorimetrically. The enzyme activity is a direct function of the amount of antibody bound.

To measure Ag, a known specific Ab is fixed to the solid phase, the test material containing Ag is added and washed, and a second enzyme-labeled Ab is added. This test requires that the Ag have at least 2 determinants. After washing, substrate is added and enzyme activity is estimated colorimetrically and related to Ag concentration.

OTHER TYPES OF SEROLOGIC REACTIONS

Protection or Neutralization (Nt) Tests

These are widely employed in the determination of antiviral and a few antibacterial antibodies. They utilize the ability of Ab-containing sera to block the infectivity of these agents upon inoculation of the mixture into susceptible hosts.

Immobilization Tests for *Treponema pallidum*

These tests (TPI) detect antitreponemal antibodies in the serum of infected persons. The test consists of mixing serum with fresh, motile spirochetes from a rabbit chancre and observing their loss of motility in the darkfield microscope. Similar tests can demonstrate the immune adherence of spirochetes to the surface of red blood cells in the presence of specific antibody.

Opsonophagocytic Tests

In these tests, phagocytic cells from the patient (especially polymorphonuclear neutrophils) are mixed with viable bacteria of certain species, or with yeasts, in the presence of serum to observe the rate of ingestion and (by subculture) the rate of intracellular killing. By means of such tests, defects in cellular immunity are studied (see Phagocytosis in Chapter 11). Polymorphonuclear cells from patients with specific deficiencies in phagocytosis and intracellular killing (eg, chronic granulomatous disease) also give abnormally depressed responses in the nitroblue tetrazolium dye test (see Chapter 11).

Ferritin-Labeled Antibody Technique

Electron-dense ferritin can be conjugated with Ab molecules that become visible in the electron microscope. This permits localization of Ag in cells and ultrathin sections examined by electron microscopy.

Hemagglutination Tests, Active & Passive

Red blood cells from various animal species may be clumped by certain viruses. This "active hemagglutination" can be specifically inhibited by Ab to virus, and the hemagglutination inhibition is a convenient serologic test. Red cells also present a convenient surface onto which many types of Ags can be adsorbed. Such coated cells will clump when mixed with Abs to these specific Ags ("passive hemagglutination"). Other convenient particles such as latex or bentonite may substitute for red cells. An IgM in the serum of most patients with rheumatoid disease can be measured by agglutination of latex particles coated with human IgG. Human IgG will be clumped by this IgM "rheumatoid factor." Clinically applicable serologic tests for the diagnosis of infection are listed in Chapter 26.

THE COMPLEMENT SYSTEM

The term complement (C) denotes a complex system of proteins and other factors found in normal serum of vertebrates. Some genes controlling the production of complement components are located on human chromosome 6 in proximity to the *HLA* locus. Some components have enzymatic activity; others are enhancers or inhibitors. Activation of the complement sequence of reactions may occur by the "classic" pathway set off by Ag-Ab reactions or by the "alternative" pathway ("bypass"), which does not require Ag-Ab reactions. The sequence of reactions can lead to the production of biologically active factors (eg, chemotactic factors), to damage of cell membranes (eg, lysis of cells), or to various pathologic processes (eg, nephrotoxic nephritis).

The steps in the complement reaction sequence can most easily be illustrated by the events leading to cell lysis. In the sequence shown in Fig 12–9, E represents a cell membrane carrying an antigenic site (either an intrinsic or artificially attached Ag) and A represents an Ab (IgG, IgM) to that Ag.

Complement of guinea pigs and humans has been studied most extensively. At present, at least 11 distinct components of guinea pig complement are recognized. Complement must either be kept frozen or used in the form of fresh serum to avoid deterioration of some components. On heating at 56 °C, activity is lost completely in 30 minutes. Complement activity depends upon the ionic strength of the medium, pH (optimum, 7.2–7.4), volume (inverse relationship), temperature (optimum, 30–37 °C), and the presence of Ca^{2+} (see step 2) and Mg^{2+} (step 4).

Different animal sera contain different proportions of the various complement components. The component that is lowest in titer or activity in a given serum limits the hemolytic complement activity of that

(1) $E + A \longrightarrow EA$

(2) $EA + C\overline{1} \xrightarrow{Ca^{2+}} EAC\overline{1}$. ($C\overline{1}$ represents the activated form of C1 with enzyme activity; Ca^{2+} is required for the stability of the complex.)

(3) $EAC\overline{1} + C4 \longrightarrow EAC\overline{1,4}$. (The $C\overline{1}$ enzyme, an esterase, has cleaved C4 and C2, part of which attached to the activated complex or the cell membrane.)

(4) $EAC\overline{1,4}, + C2 \xrightarrow{Mg^{2+}} EAC\overline{1,4,2}$. ($Mg^{2+}$ is required for stability of the activated complex; the C4,2, moiety is an enzyme, C3 convertase, active in next step.)

Alternative pathway

(5) $EAC\overline{1,4,2} + C3 \longrightarrow EAC\overline{1,4,2,3} + C3$ fragments with activity of anaphylatoxin and chemotaxis. (Cleavage of C3 occurs either by C3 convertase in the classic pathway or by C3 activator in the alternative pathway.)

(6) $EAC\overline{1,4,2,3} + C5,C6,C7 \longrightarrow EAC\overline{1,4,2,3,5,6,7} + C5$ fragments with anaphylatoxin activity. (The C5,6,7 complex on the cell membrane is chemotactic for polymorphonuclear leukocytes.)

(7) $EAC\overline{1,4,2,3,5,6,7} + C8,C9 \longrightarrow EAC\,\overline{1-9}$. (The final complex results in membrane damage ["holes"], cell damage, or lysis.)

Figure 12–9. Complement reaction sequence.

serum. C1 exists in serum as an aggregate of 3 proteins: C1q, C1r, and C1s. C1q can attach to Ag-Ab complexes or to certain aggregated immunoglobulins (eg, IgM, IgG-1) without any activation. All other components are converted one after another from inactive to activated forms. The final step in cytolysis requires only the production of a single membrane lesion induced by complement action.

Alternative Pathway of Complement Activation

While the "classic" pathway depends on starting the reaction sequence by C1q attaching to Ag-Ab complexes, another pathway exists for activating complement-mediated reactions. A variety of substances can bring about the formation of a C3 activator that cleaves C3 in a fashion analogous to that of C3 convertase in the classic pathway. This "alternative pathway" then proceeds C3–C9, as in the classic pathway shown above. Polysaccharides, lipopolysaccharides, and some immunoglobulin aggregates (eg, IgA, IgE, IgG-4, which do *not* initiate the complement sequence via C1q) activate the **properdin** system as an alternative pathway of complement activation.

The properdin system consists of a unique serum protein (properdin), a glycine-rich beta-glycoprotein (C3 proactivator), and other serum proteins. The activation of this system culminates in cleavage of C3. The reaction sequence then proceeds as in the classic pathway. The properdin system can enhance resistance to gram-negative infections; it is involved in the lysis of erythrocytes from patients with paroxysmal nocturnal hemoglobinuria. The properdin system can also participate in the mediation of immunologic injury (eg, nephritis) and may be defective in sickle cell anemia.

There are other activators of the alternative pathway. Proteolytic enzymes released from lysosomes of phagocytic cells can cleave C3; other proteolytic enzymes involved in the blood coagulation cascade or produced by bacteria can do likewise.

COMPLEMENT–MEDIATED REACTIONS

Immune Hemolysis & Cytolysis

The production of membrane injury of red blood cells by complement acting on Ag-Ab complexes on the membrane is the basis for a sensitive serologic test, the complement fixation (CF) test (see below). Many other types of cells (lymphocytes, tumor cells, etc) are also subject to immune cytolysis.

Some gram-negative bacteria and spirochetes coated with specific Ab go through the sequence of steps (1–7) shown above and exhibit bacteriolysis. It is not clear how often this reaction plays any role in host defenses. Cytolytic reactions may at times cause injury to normal tissues in allergic vasculitis or glomerulitis.

Chemotaxis

Complement bound by Ag-Ab complexes releases chemotactic factors and attracts leukocytes that in turn release lysosomal enzymes and thus cause damage to tissues.

Fragments of C3, C5, and the C5,6,7 complex also attract leukocytes. This may aid in the localization and inactivation of infectious agents or may enhance tissue injury (see step 2, above). This chemotaxis is depressed by alcohol and in cirrhotic patients. Complement components are found attached to Ag-Ab complexes in "complex" diseases, eg, on synovial membranes in rheumatoid arthritis or on glomerular basement membranes in nephritis (see p 177).

Immune Adherence & Opsonization

Fragments of C3 and C5 promote the adherence of Ag-Ab complexes to leukocytes or platelets and the phagocytosis of opsonized (Ab-coated) microorganisms by leukocytes and macrophages.

Anaphylatoxin Effect

Fragments of C3 and C5 can produce degranulation of mast cells with the release of histamine and other mediators. This results in symptoms of vasodilatation, increased capillary permeability, bronchospasm, and other symptoms resembling anaphylaxis.

Hereditary Angioedema

Persons with this disorder are deficient in a normal C1 (esterase) inhibitor (a glycoprotein). Consequently, their serum intermittently has increased C1 activity that liberates a vasoactive kinin from C2. This kinin produces acute, transient local accumulations of edema fluid. C1 activation can be prevented by aminocaproic acid, tranexamic acid, or a special steroid, danazol.

Low Serum Complement Levels

Low serum complement levels—particularly low C3—are encountered in Ag-Ab complex diseases such as lupus erythematosus and acute glomerulonephritis and in cryoglobulinemia.

Hereditary Deficiencies

Hereditary deficiency of certain complement components (eg, C2, C3, C4, C6, C8) may lead to increased susceptibility to infection, eg, *Neisseria* bacteremia.

THE COMPLEMENT FIXATION TEST

Complement fixation (CF) tests depend upon 2 distinct reactions. The first involves Ag and Ab (of which one is known, the other unknown) plus a fixed amount of pretitrated complement. If Ag and Ab are specific for one another, they will combine; the combination will take up ("fix") the added complement. The second reaction involves testing for the presence of free (unattached) complement. This is done by the addition of red cells "sensitized" with specific hemolysin. If complement has been "fixed" by the

Ag-Ab complex, then none will be available for lysis of the sensitized red cells. If the antigen and antibody are *not* specific for each other, or if one of them is lacking, then complement remains free to attach to the sensitized red cells and lyse them. Therefore, a positive CF test gives no hemolysis; a negative test gives hemolysis. This can be written schematically as follows:

I. Specific Ag X + Complement → Complement not bound
II. Specific Ab anti-X + Complement → Complement not bound
III. X + Anti-X + Complement → Complement bound ("fixed")

To detect whether complement is bound or not bound, a hemolytic system (see below) of red blood cells (RBC) + anti-RBC antibody (Ab) is added to each of the mixtures I, II, and III, with these results:

I + RBC + Ab → Lysis of RBC = Negative test
II + RBC + Ab → Lysis of RBC = Negative test
III + RBC + Ab → No lysis of RBC = Positive test

A positive test occurs only if X and anti-X have combined to bind available complement. If Ag (X) does not match specific Ab (Y), no complex will be formed, no complement will be consumed, and lysis of added red cells indicates a negative test. If either Ag X alone or Ab anti-X alone (I or II) inactivates complement, it is unsatisfactory for the test and is called anticomplementary. Anticomplementary Ags or sera are detected by suitable controls in the test. Anticomplementary activity can sometimes be removed by heating or dilution.

For the practical performance of the test, it is necessary to control all reagents and environmental conditions carefully. In order to eliminate any complement that might be present in the serum used as source of Ab, all sera must be inactivated by heating for 30 minutes at 56 °C. To the Ag and the inactivated serum, a carefully titrated amount of complement is added (usually 1.2–2 units). The mixture is then left at 37 °C or in the refrigerator for a specified time to permit interaction of Ag and Ab and "fixation" of complement. Next, the "hemolytic system" is added; this consists generally of a suspension of sheep red cells "sensitized" by the addition of hemolysin (ie, anti-sheep rabbit serum). The mixture is then incubated at 37 °C for 30 minutes and read for hemolysis.

If properly controlled, the CF test is a sensitive method in the diagnostic laboratory. It is used for the identification of antibody and estimation of its titer (with known antigens) or the identification of antigens (with known antibody). The serologic diagnosis of many viral and fungal infections and of some immunologic disorders rests on CF tests (see Chapter 29).

RECOMMENDED ACTIVE IMMUNIZATION

RECOMMENDED SCHEDULE FOR ROUTINE ACTIVE IMMUNIZATION OF CHILDREN
(See Table 12–6.)

RECOMMENDED IMMUNIZATION OF ADULTS FOR TRAVEL

Every adult, whether traveling or not, must be immunized with tetanus toxoid. Purified toxoid "for adult use" must be used to avoid reactions. Every adult should also receive booster vaccination for poliomyelitis (oral live trivalent vaccine) and diphtheria (use purified toxoid "for adult use"). Every traveler must fulfill the immunization requirements of the health authorities of different countries. These are listed in *Health Information for International Travel*, US Public Health Service Publication No. 2045.

Tetanus
Booster injection of 0.5 mL tetanus toxoid, for adult use, every 7–10 years, assuming completion of primary immunization. (All countries.)

Smallpox
In 1980, smallpox was declared eradicated from the world. Smallpox vaccination with vaccinia virus is unnecessary and potentially dangerous. While millions of individuals in the US Armed Forces (and others) continue to receive smallpox vaccine, most countries in the world have abolished the requirement for a valid smallpox vaccination certificate for travelers. Some persons vaccinated prior to 1980 may choose to carry their certificate. For others, a physician's letter indicating that smallpox vaccination is not required and is inadvisable should suffice for the few countries that still maintain such a requirement.

Typhoid
Suspension of killed *Salmonella typhi*. For primary immunization, inject 0.5 mL subcutaneously (0.25 mL for children under 10 years) twice at an interval of 4–6 weeks. For booster, inject 0.5 mL subcutaneously (or 0.1 mL intradermally) every 3 years. (All countries.)

Paratyphoid vaccines are not recommended and are probably ineffective at present.

Yellow Fever
Live attenuated fever virus, 0.5 mL subcutaneously. WHO certificate requires registration of batch number of vaccine. Vaccination available in USA only at approved centers. Vaccination must be repeated at intervals of 10 years or less. (Africa, South America.)

Cholera
Suspension of killed vibrios, including prevalent

Table 12–6. Recommended schedule for active immunization and skin testing of children.

Age	Product Administered	Test Recommended
2 months	DTP[1] TOPV[2]	
4 months	DTP TOPV	
6 months	DTP	
15–19 months	Measles vaccine[3, 4] Mumps vaccine[4] DTP TOPV	Tuberculin test[5]
4–6 years	DTP TOPV	
12–14 years	Td[6] Rubella vaccine[4, 7]	Tuberculin test[5]

[1] **DTP:** Toxoids of diphtheria and tetanus, alum-precipitated or aluminum hydroxide–adsorbed, combined with pertussis bacterial antigen. Suitable for young children. Three doses of 0.5 mL intramuscularly at intervals of 4–8 weeks. Fourth injection of 0.5 mL intramuscularly given about 1 year later.

[2] **TOPV (oral live poliomyelitis virus vaccine):** Trivalent vaccine given 2–3 times at intervals of 6–8 weeks and then as a booster 1 and 4 years later. Monovalent live vaccine rarely used. Inactive (Salk) vaccine is available but recommended only for immunodeficient persons or for initial vaccination of adults.

[3] **Live measles virus vaccine,** 0.5 mL intramuscularly: This is available as a highly attenuated strain in the USA that requires no simultaneous administration of gamma globulin. With less attenuated strains, human gamma globulin, 0.02 mL/kg, was given intramuscularly in a separate site to minimize vaccine reactions. Inactivated measles vaccine should not be used.

[4] **Live mumps virus vaccine (attenuated),** 0.5 mL intramuscularly: This is sometimes given as measles-mumps-rubella vaccine.

[5] The frequency with which **tuberculin tests** are administered depends on the risk of exposure, ie, the prevalence of tuberculosis in the population group.

[6] **Tetanus toxoid and diphtheria toxoid:** Purified, suitable for adults.

[7] **Rubella live virus vaccine (attenuated):** Can be given between age 1 year and puberty. Some physicians recommend rubella vaccine only for prepubertal girls. The entire contents of a single-dose vaccine vial, reconstituted from the lyophilized state, are injected subcutaneously. The vaccine must **not** be given to women who are pregnant or likely to become pregnant within 3 months after vaccination. Women must also be warned that there is a possibility of developing arthralgias and arthritis after vaccination. The cell culture–grown RA 27/3 rubella virus vaccine was licensed in the USA in 1979. No live virus vaccine should be given to immunodeficient persons.

antigenic types. Two injections of 0.5 mL are given intramuscularly 4–6 weeks apart. This must be followed by 0.5-mL booster injections every 6 months during periods of possible exposure. Protection depends largely on booster doses. WHO certificate is valid for 6 months only. (Middle Eastern countries, Asia, occasionally others.)

Plague

Suspension of killed plague bacilli given intramuscularly, 2 injections of 0.5 mL each, 4–6 weeks apart, and a third injection 4–12 weeks later. (Middle Eastern countries, Asia, occasionally South America and others.)

Typhus

Suspension of inactivated typhus rickettsiae given subcutaneously, 2 injections 4–6 weeks apart. Booster doses every 6 months may be necessary.

(Southeastern Europe, Africa, South America.) (Currently not available in the USA and Canada.)

Hepatitis A

No active immunization available. Temporary passive immunity may be induced by the intramuscular injection of human gamma globulin, 0.02 mL/kg every 2–3 months.

Pneumococcal Pneumonia

Elderly travelers or those with chronic respiratory insufficiency may be given pneumococcal polysaccharide vaccine, which was licensed in the USA in 1977.

Rabies

Travelers to rural areas of countries where rabies is prevalent should be considered for preexposure vaccine administration. This involves at least 3 weekly injections of inactivated vaccine plus a booster 3 months later (see p 412).

● ● ●

References

Bloch KJ et al: Gamma heavy chain disease. *Am J Med* 1973;**55**:61.

Cline MJ et al: Monocytes and macrophages: Functions and diseases. *Ann Intern Med* 1978;**88**:78.

Colten HR et al: Genetics and biosynthesis of complement proteins. *N Engl J Med* 1981;**304**:653.

Edelman GM: Antibody structure and molecular immunology. *Science* 1973;**180**:830.

Fearon DT, Austen KF: The alternative pathway of complement: A system for host resistance to microbial infection. *N Engl J Med* 1980;**303**:259.

Flick JA: Human reagins: Antibody of immediate-type hypersensitivity. *Bacteriol Rev* 1972;**36**:311.

Gell PGH, Coombs RRA, Lachmann PJ (editors): *Clinical Aspects of Immunology,* 3rd ed. Blackwell, 1974.

Goodman JW, Wang A-C: Immunoglobulins: Structure, diversity, and genetics. Chapter 4 in: *Basic & Clinical Immunology,* 3rd ed. Fudenberg HH et al (editors). Lange, 1980.

Götz O, Müller-Eberhard HJ: Paroxysmal nocturnal hemoglobinuria: Hemolysis initiated by the C3 activator system. *N Engl J Med* 1972;**286**:180.

Grady GF & others: Hepatitis B immune globulin for accidental exposures among medical personnel. *J Infect Dis* 1978;**138**:625.

Kubo RT et al: IgD, an immunoglobulin on the surface of lymphocytes. *J Immunol* 1974;**112**:1952.

Levin WC (editor): Symposium on myeloma. *Arch Intern Med* 1975;**135**:27.

Liu YS et al: Complete covalent structure of a human IgA immunoglobulin. *Science* 1976;**193**:1017.

McDevitt HO: Regulation of the immune response by the major histocompatibility system. *N Engl J Med* 1980;**303**:1514.

Nusbacher J, Bove JR: Rh immunoprophylaxis. *N Engl J Med* 1980;**303**:935.

Pensky J et al: Properties of highly purified human properdin. *J Immunol* 1968;**100**:142.

Reinherz EL, Schlossman SF: Regulation of the immune response: Inducer and suppressor T-lymphocyte subsets in human beings. *N Engl J Med* 1980;**303**:370.

Robinson JE et al: Diffuse polyclonal B-cell lymphoma during primary infection with Epstein-Barr virus. *N Engl J Med* 1980;**302**:1293.

Rosenthal AS: Regulation of the immune response: Role of the macrophage. *N Engl J Med* 1980;**303**:1153.

Rowlands DT Jr, Daniele RP: Surface receptors in the immune response. *N Engl J Med* 1975;**293**:26.

Ruddy S et al: The complement system of man. *N Engl J Med* 1972;**287**:642.

Siegal FP: Suppressors in the network of immunity. *N Engl J Med* 1978;**298**:102.

Solomon A: Bence-Jones proteins and light chains of immunoglobulins. (2 parts.) *N Engl J Med* 1976;**294**:17, 91.

Tomasi TB: Secretory immunoglobulins. *N Engl J Med* 1972;**287**:500.

Uhr JW et al: Organization of the immune response genes. *Science* 1979;**206**:292.

Unanue ER: Cooperation between mononuclear phagocytes and lymphocytes in immunity. *N Engl J Med* 1980;**303**:977.

Yalow RS: Radio-immunoassay: A probe for the fine structure of biologic systems. *Science* 1978;**200**:1236.

ANTIBODY–MEDIATED HYPERSENSITIVITY

The principal mechanism in a majority of antibody-mediated hypersensitivity reactions is the combination of antibody (Ab) with antigen (Ag) to form complexes that stimulate certain cells to release a variety of mediators. The main reactions in this category are of the anaphylaxis and serum sickness type. Interactions between Ab and red blood cell or platelet Ag usually do not involve the release of mediators.

ANAPHYLAXIS

The experimental demonstration of anaphylaxis involves the following steps:

(1) Sensitization: An adequate sensitizing dose of Ag must be absorbed. In the guinea pig, as little as 0.1 μg of a soluble protein is sufficient.

(2) Waiting period: A waiting period of 2–3 weeks is required. During this period, cytotropic Ab (in guinea pigs, IgE and some IgG) attaches to mast cells and basophilic leukocytes.

(3) "Eliciting injection": The rapid intravenous injection of a massive dose (0.1–10 mg) of the same Ag as used for sensitization permits the Ag to combine with cell-bound Ab rapidly. The complex stimulates the prompt release of mediators that set off the symptoms of anaphylaxis (eg, bronchospasm) within 3–5 minutes.

(4) Passive transfer: If serum is taken after the waiting period (2) from the sensitized animal and injected into the skin of a normal animal, the injected site becomes sensitized in 24 hours (ie, homocytotropic Abs attach to mast cells and basophils). When Ag is given intravenously to such an animal together with a dye (eg, Evans blue), a local anaphylactic reaction at the sensitized site results in a marked increase in capillary permeability that permits the dye to stain the sensitized area of skin. This **passive cutaneous anaphylaxis** is suitable for quantitation of some anaphylactic events.

Anaphylactic reactivity in humans manifests itself as systemic, generalized anaphylaxis or as local anaphylaxis involving skin or respiratory tract or other target tissue.

Generalized anaphylaxis in humans begins within 5–30 minutes after administration of the inciting agent, with flush, urticaria, paroxysmal cough, dyspnea, wheezing, vomiting, cyanosis, circulatory collapse, and shock. Major causes of death are laryngeal edema, massive airway edema, and cardiac arrhythmias. Major causes of generalized anaphylaxis in humans are drugs (eg, penicillins), biologicals (eg, animal sera), insect stings (eg, bee or wasp venom), and foods (eg, shellfish).

Local anaphylaxis in humans begins within a few minutes after contact (inhalation, ingestion) between the responsible Ag and the sensitive shock organ and manifests itself commonly as hay fever, asthma, urticaria, or vomiting. About 10% of the population are prone to become spontaneously sensitized to various environmental Ags (allergens), eg, pollens of ragweed, grasses, or trees; foods, and animal danders. These individuals develop allergic reactions **(atopy)** when exposed to the Ag. There is a marked familial predisposition to this type of disorder, but each individual must become sensitized to the specific allergen before manifesting atopic reactions.

Cutaneous anaphylaxis is seen in the skin test for immediate type hypersensitivity. Two or 3 minutes after 0.1 mL of Ag is injected intracutaneously (often into the flexor surface of the forearm), itching begins at the site, followed by an elevated, blanched irregular wheal surrounded by a zone of erythema ("flare"). This hive (urticarial reaction) reaches a maximum in 10–15 minutes and subsides within less than 1 hour.

Mechanism of Anaphylaxis

As a result of the original sensitization with Ag, specialized, cytotropic Ab is formed that binds to mast cells and basophils, especially in skin, the respiratory tract, and vascular endothelium. In humans, the cytotropic Ab is IgE. When the same Ag is again absorbed, it reaches these cells and results in aggregation of IgE molecules bound to cell surfaces by their Fc fragment. This is the stimulus for the release of pharmacologically active chemical mediators from the cell (degranulation). Aggregated Fc fragments of IgE proteins can also elicit a cell release of mediators even without the presence of Ag. Large amounts of soluble Ag-Ab complexes that are capable of binding complement can also evoke anaphylaxis under special circumstances.

Pharmacologically Active Chemical Mediators

Pharmacologically active chemical mediators released during anaphylaxis include the following:

Histamine (formed by decarboxylation of histidine) occurs in platelets and in granules of tissue mast cells and basophils, cells that—in humans—bind IgE through special sites of the Fc fragment. The histamine released as a result of anaphylaxis results in vasodilatation, increased capillary permeability (edema), and smooth muscle contraction. The relative amount of histamine and of other mediators determines the efficacy of antihistamine drugs in controlling local anaphylaxis. Antihistamines are relatively effective in allergic rhinitis, relatively ineffective in asthma (in which much more SRS-A [see below] is released than histamine).

Serotonin (5-hydroxytryptamine, formed by decarboxylation of tryptophan) occurs mainly in blood platelets and is released from them during anaphylaxis. It dilates capillaries, increases their permeability, and contracts smooth muscle.

Kinins are basic peptides derived from plasma proteins by enzymatic action. Hageman factor in the blood clotting cascade is activated by various substances (eg, Ag-Ab complexes, endotoxins). One of the resulting products, plasmin, activates an enzyme, kallikrein, which splits the basic peptide bradykinin from an alpha globulin in plasma. Bradykinin levels in blood increase in anaphylaxis and cause vasodilatation, increased capillary permeability, and smooth muscle contraction. Other kinins also participate in anaphylactic reactions.

Slow reacting substance (SRS-A) is an acidic lipoprotein released mainly from lung during anaphylaxis. It causes marked smooth muscle contraction and bronchospasm and is not inhibited by antihistamines. The relatively large amount of SRS-A—compared to histamine—in asthma accounts for the virtual lack of effect of antihistamines in that condition.

Eosinophilic chemotactic factor of anaphylaxis (ECF-A) is a mediator released from mast cells that promotes the eosinophilia of immediate allergic reactions.

Other mediators, including prostaglandins, have been implicated in anaphylaxis. Cellular levels of cAMP probably are important regulators of the release of active mediators in anaphylaxis and may explain the influence of emotional states on the intensity of acute allergic reactions. Stimulation of β-adrenergic receptor (eg, by isoproterenol) increases intracellular cAMP levels, causing decreased sensitivity to allergen. Adrenergic effects on the autonomic nervous system may likewise decrease manifestations of anaphylaxis.

The chemical mediators are active for only a few minutes after release. Histamine, serotonin, bradykinin, and SRS-A are enzymatically inactivated. They are resynthesized at a slow rate. The manifestations of anaphylaxis vary among animal species because mediators are released at different rates and in different amounts, and different tissues (''shock organs'') have different sensitivity to mediators. Whereas the respiratory tract (bronchospasm, laryngeal edema) is a principal shock organ in humans, the liver (hepatic veins) plays that role in the dog.

Desensitization

Major manifestations of anaphylaxis depend on the sudden release of large amounts of mediators, usually as a result of a massive dose of Ag suddenly combining with IgE on many mast cells. If, on the other hand, only very small amounts of Ag are administered at 15-minute intervals, complex formation occurs only on a small scale and not enough mediator is released at a given moment to produce a major reaction. This is the basis of **acute desensitization,** which makes it possible to administer a drug or foreign serum to a hypersensitive person. However, days or weeks later, hypersensitivity is restored.

Chronic desensitization (hyposensitization) relies on a different principle. When small amounts of an Ag (especially high-molecular-weight polymerized ragweed Ag) are administered at weekly intervals to a person hypersensitive to that Ag, IgG Abs (blocking Abs) appear in the serum. When a desensitized person is exposed to Ag, the blocking Abs combine with the Ags and prevent their reaching IgE Ab on mast cells and basophils. Consequently, the blocking Ab can prevent allergic reactions.

Blocking antibodies differ from IgE cytotropic Abs (reagins). Reagins bind to human skin, persist there for weeks, are heat-labile, and do not cross the placenta. Blocking Abs are IgG, do not bind to human skin or persist there, are heat-stable, and cross the placenta.

Passive Transfer of Atopy

The serum of a person with atopic hypersensitivity is injected into the skin of a normal person; IgE Ab binds to skin mast cells and sensitizes them during the next 20 hours. Injection of that sensitized skin site with the Ag produces an immediate type wheal-and-flare anaphylactic response of the skin site. In the normal person, that skin site maintains its ability to react to the Ag for several weeks. This **Prausnitz-Küstner (PK) reaction** is commonly used for the identification of important allergens in atopic patients who may have many positive direct skin tests.

Treatment of Anaphylactic Reactions

The purpose of treatment is to counteract the effects of released chemical mediators or to block their action. In systemic anaphylaxis, the main efforts are directed at maintaining ventilation and cardiac function. This implies maintenance of a patent airway, assisted ventilation if necessary, and epinephrine (1:1000 solution), 0.1–0.5 mL given into an intravenous infusion. A soluble corticosteroid may be administered for a later effect, and metaraminol may help to overcome the cardiovascular collapse.

Local anaphylactic reactions tend to respond to epinephrine or aminophylline (7 mg/kg), and their continued activity may be blocked by corticosteroids. Antihistamines are relatively effective in allergic rhinitis but ineffective in asthma.

The release of mediators of allergic reaction from mast cell granules can be inhibited by the administration of cromolyn sodium, a substance that stabilizes lysosomal membranes. This may prevent or terminate an allergic reaction.

Anaphylactoid Reactions

These resemble anaphylaxis but are precipitated by injection of particle suspensions or colloids (barium sulfate, inulin, procaine, etc) that activate Hageman factor, plasmin, kallikrein, and the alternative pathway of the complement sequence. They are unrelated to Ag-Ab reactions or allergy.

Anaphylaxis in Isolated Tissues in Vitro

When an organ (eg, uterus, gut) from a sensitized animal is suspended in a salt solution, addition of the specific Ag results in prompt muscular contraction and liberation of mediators into the solution (Schultz-Dale reaction). This is due to the binding of Ag to cytotropic Ab on tissue mast cells.

Prevention of Anaphylaxis

Since anaphylaxis caused by drugs or biologic products may produce serious or life-threatening illness, a careful history of previous exposure or reaction must be taken before such substances are administered. Skin tests (see p 315) or conjunctival tests* can often predict the presence of hypersensitivity and therefore real risk.

ARTHUS REACTION

This Ab-mediated hypersensitivity reaction requires large amounts of Ag-Ab complexes that fix complement, attract polymorphonuclear leukocytes, and are phagocytosed by them. The cells release lysosomal enzymes that cause tissue damage, typically with vasculitis of blood vessel walls. The lesions subside within several days.

Any class of complement-fixing Ig can mediate the Arthus reaction, but the higher the level of Ab the more intense the lesion; it requires at least 1000 times more Ab than anaphylaxis, and preformed Ag-Ab complexes can elicit it.

Whereas in anaphylaxis the structural changes in tissue are limited to vasodilatation, edema, and a few polymorphonuclear leukocytes, the appearance of the Arthus reaction is much more intensive inflammation. It begins with thrombosis of small vessels surrounded by edema and intense infiltration with polymorphonuclear leukocytes; areas of necrosis then develop in the walls of blood vessels. Neutrophils degenerate, and

*One drop of dilute material is placed into the conjunctival sac. A positive reaction is indicated by itching, redness, and tearing in a few minutes.

the debris is taken up by mononuclear cells and eosinophils. The phagocytosed Ag-Ab complexes are broken down and eliminated, and the inflammation subsides. In humans, lesions corresponding to the Arthus reaction occur sometimes in serum sickness or in hypersensitivity pneumonitis (''farmer's lung'') or allergic alveolitis (see p 182).

SERUM SICKNESS

Persons who receive a large amount of a drug (eg, penicillin) or foreign protein (eg, antiserum) may tolerate these injections well but develop an illness 4–18 days later. Typical serum sickness consists of fever, widespread urticarial eruption, pain and swelling of joints, and enlargement of lymph nodes and spleen. These signs usually subside within a week.

During serum sickness, some tissues exhibit lesions of vasculitis (as in the Arthus reaction) but also vasodilatation, edema, and smooth muscle contraction (as in anaphylaxis). The mechanism is as follows: After a large amount of Ag is injected, its concentration gradually declines and at the same time Ab production starts. The simultaneous presence of Ag and Ab leads to the formation of soluble Ag-Ab complexes that set off the immune response, combining vasculitis with the release of chemical mediators. Serum sickness subsides when the Ag has been eliminated.

IMMUNE COMPLEX DISEASE

Several Ab-mediated hypersensitivity reactions can be elicited by preformed, soluble Ag-Ab complexes (see above). A number of disease entities are attributed to immune complex deposits initiating tissue disorders—although the Ag often is not established. Examples are glomerulonephritis and rheumatoid arthritis. In addition, circulating immune complexes can be detected (by complement binding or by binding to cultured Raji cells) in various disorders ranging from infective endocarditis and viral and parasitic infections to ''autoimmune diseases,'' eg, systemic lupus erythematosus.

Glomerulonephritis in Different Diseases

Acute glomerulonephritis usually follows by several weeks the onset of a group A beta-hemolytic *Streptococcus* infection. During acute glomerulonephritis, the levels of serum complement (especially C3) are usually low, suggesting an Ag-Ab reaction. By immunofluorescence, lumpy deposits of Ig and C3 are seen along basement membranes of renal glomeruli—suggesting the presence of Ag-Ab complexes. Although streptococcal Ags have been infrequently demonstrated in glomeruli, it is assumed that streptococcal Ag-Ab complexes filtered out in glomeruli initiated the reaction and fixed C3.

An analogous lesion with ''lumpy'' immunofluorescent deposits containing Ig and C3 occurs in serum sickness caused by a known foreign protein and in the glomerulonephritis associated with infective endocarditis.

In systemic lupus erythematosus (SLE), patients have circulating Ab to DNA. In the glomerulonephritis of SLE, the lumpy immunofluorescent deposits in glomeruli contain DNA as Ag, Ig (?Ab to DNA), and C3. In other patients with glomerulonephritis (eg, Goodpasture's syndrome), there is linear immunofluorescence along the basement membrane of glomeruli, caused by the combination of basement membrane Ag with Ab and complement.

At least in animals, viral infections can cause glomerulonephritis by an immune complex mechanism. In chronically infected mice, lymphocytic choriomeningitis Ag and its antiviral Ab form complexes that are deposited in glomeruli, bind complement, and initiate inflammatory lesions. The virus of Aleutian mink disease causes a similar immune complex disease with glomerulonephritis.

In penicillin-induced nephritis, the drug binds to tubular basement membrane protein, and Ab to this Ag is formed and deposited. Complement is bound to the complex, and polymorphonuclear leukocytes are attracted to produce the interstitial nephritis.

Rheumatoid Arthritis

Rheumatoid arthritis is a chronic inflammatory joint disease that is particularly common in young women. The synovial fluid contains high concentrations of Ig aggregates, complement, and polymorphonuclear leukocytes. The nature of the Ag is undetermined. The reaction between human immunoglobulins and rheumatoid factors (IgM and IgG molecules that bind to antigenic determinants on the Fc fragments of IgG) is employed diagnostically and might play a causative role.

Autoimmune Diseases

Ag-Ab complexes have been demonstrated in various autoimmune diseases and may participate in their causation (see Chapter 12).

DRUG HYPERSENSITIVITY

Drugs are now among the commonest causes of hypersensitivity reactions, and antibiotics are high on the list. Penicillin hypersensitivity has been studied extensively and is used as an example here.

To induce hypersensitivity, the drug—or a reactive metabolic derivative—must covalently bind to host protein in order to become antigenic. The subsequent allergic reaction is specific for the haptens rather than for the drug itself. Such compounds can induce Ab formation and immediate and delayed type hypersensitivity. The likelihood of any one individual developing hypersensitivity to a given drug is probably influenced by genetic predisposition; the route, duration, and amount of drug exposure; the level of Ab production; and other factors.

In the case of penicillin, some important reactive products are penicilloyl compounds and minor determinant groups. When covalently bound to protein, these can induce Ab-mediated hypersensitivity and local or generalized anaphylaxis.

In order to detect possible hypersensitivity to penicillin, skin tests can be performed with penicilloyl polylysine (which will not itself induce hypersensitivity), with alkaline degradation products (containing minor determinants) of penicillin, or with penicillin itself. An immediate type wheal-and-flare reaction suggests that IgE Abs have become bound to mast cells and that such a reactive person may be subject to generalized anaphylaxis.

In view of the very large number of people who have been given penicillin—many of whom have developed IgE Ab—it is surprising that anaphylactic reactions are so rare. Two possible explanations might be considered: (1) Most persons who develop IgE antipenicilloyl Ab also develop IgG Ab of the same specificity, which may well act as blocking Ab. (2) Penicillin molecules themselves may be univalent for antipenicilloyl Ab and thus may inhibit rather than favor aggregation of IgE Ab. Persons who handle penicillins occupationally may develop contact dermatitis, a form of delayed type hypersensitivity with positive skin test (see below).

Penicilloyl Ab and the corresponding Ag are the basis for the serum sickness that may follow a single penicillin injection as a result of complex formation. Penicilloyl hapten bound to tubular basement membrane was mentioned above as an inciting cause of interstitial nephritis, which is an immune complex disease.

Many different drugs have been incriminated in cytotoxic hypersensitivity reactions that often manifest themselves as hematologic disorders. Thus, hemolytic anemias may result from the attachment of penicillin, phenacetin, quinidine, and other drugs to surface proteins on red blood cells. Autoimmune Abs form, and Ag-Ab complex formation results in hemolysis of the attached cell.

Drugs like apronalide (Sedormid) or quinine attach as haptens to platelets, giving rise to autoantibodies that first clump and then lyse the platelets to produce thrombocytopenia with bleeding tendency. Other drugs, such as hydralazine, may modify host tissue and favor the production of autoantibodies directed against cell DNA. Such patients then have antinuclear factors similar to those found in systemic lupus erythematosus (see p 185).

CELL–MEDIATED HYPER– SENSITIVITY & IMMUNITY

The outstanding differences between Ab-mediated and cell-mediated hypersensitivity reactions are shown in Table 12–3. Cell-mediated hypersensitivity reactions begin several hours after contact with Ag and reach a peak 24–72 hours later. The reactivity can be transferred by lymphoid cells but *not* by serum and consists of inflammatory changes with heavy infiltrates of mononuclear cells. Cell-mediated hypersensitivity is closely related to cell-mediated immunity. For both, the central component is the immunologically committed T lymphocyte and its interactions and products. The prototype of cell-mediated hypersensitivity and of "delayed" type skin reactions is seen in tuberculin hypersensitivity.

TUBERCULIN HYPERSENSITIVITY

Koch's Phenomenon (See Chapter 17.)

When a tuberculous guinea pig is injected subcutaneously with a suspension of tubercle bacilli, there is a massive inflammatory reaction at the injection site that tends to wall off the injected material and often leads to necrosis; this is called Koch's phenomenon. This reaction does not require living tubercle bacilli but occurs similarly with tuberculoprotein (PPD). These soluble preparations produce local inflammatory reactions, particularly edema, infiltration with lymphoid cells and macrophages, hemorrhage, and marked enlargement of the regional lymph nodes; and focal reactions, consisting of hemorrhagic inflammation and dense cellular infiltration within existing tuberculous lesions. Because focal reactions may "stir up" tuberculous activity, administration of excessive doses of tuberculoprotein to hypersensitive individuals during skin tests must be avoided.

Delayed Type Skin Reaction

The typical skin test of the delayed type is exemplified by the tuberculin test. There is no immediate reaction following the intracutaneous injection of tuberculoprotein. After a few hours, redness, edema, and induration develop and tend to increase for 24–48 hours. If the reaction is marked, there may be central blanching, hemorrhage, and necrosis. The redness and edema disappear quickly, but the induration of the skin reaction can be felt for days or weeks. Histologically, the lesion of the skin test is characterized by initial vasodilatation, edema, and polymorphonuclear cell infiltration; this is followed soon afterward by marked and persistent focal accumulation and diffuse infiltration with lymphoid and mononuclear cells. The intensity of the tuberculin skin reaction in the hypersensitive individual bears no relationship to the level of Abs that may be demonstrated. Transfer of lymphoid cells from a skin test–positive person can transfer reactivity to a skin test–negative person.

PASSIVE TRANSFER OF
CELL–MEDIATED HYPERSENSITIVITY

It is not possible to transfer tuberculin or other cell-mediated hypersensitivity with serum. However, viable T lymphocytes taken from a reactive person and transferred to a nonreactive person will temporarily make the recipient reactive (eg, tuberculin-positive). In humans, it is also possible to transfer some reactivity of cell-mediated hypersensitivity by means of nonviable extracts from T lymphocytes. This material has been called "transfer factor."

Properties of "Transfer Factor"

Transfer factor is a stable dialyzable extract of immune lymphocytes with a molecular weight below 2000. Its chemical nature has not been established. After injection of transfer factor, delayed type hypersensitivity begins in 2–7 days and may last for several months. One unit of transfer factor is the dialysate of 5×10^8 leukocytes from a donor who possesses cell-mediated immunity to a specific Ag. The material is dissolved in 1 mL of saline and injected subcutaneously.

The mechanism of transfer factor activity remains uncertain. It can transfer specific delayed type hypersensitivity to tuberculin, streptococcal Ags, coccidioidin, allograft Ags, and others.

In some patients with defects in cell-mediated immunity, transfer factor may temporarily restore competent cell-mediated reactions and delayed type hypersensitivity. In about half of the patients with Wiskott-Aldrich syndrome, transfer factor has resulted in improvement of clinical status, including arrest of chronic infections, eczema, and bleeding tendency. The remissions have lasted about 6 months.

Some patients with severe combined immunodeficiency disease have also shown significant, albeit temporary, improvement. In chronic mycobacterial and fungal infections (eg, disseminated mucocutaneous candidiasis and coccidioidomycosis), transfer factor therapy, combined with antimicrobial drugs, has resulted in encouraging remissions. Improvement has been reported in the immunologic status of patients with various cancers (eg, osteosarcoma and melanoma), but the clinical efficacy of this adjuvant treatment remains to be established.

INDUCTION OF CELL–MEDIATED
HYPERSENSITIVITY

The development of delayed type hypersensitivity is favored by the introduction of small amounts of Ags on cell surfaces or in lipid mixtures called adjuvants. Thus, tuberculin sensitivity can be induced by infection with *Mycobacterium tuberculosis* but also by injection of small amounts of tuberculoprotein together with wax D (a peptidoglycolipid) or tuberculoprotein in Freund's complete adjuvant (see below). If larger amounts of Ag are introduced, there is less cell-mediated hypersensitivity and more Ab response. Whereas very small antigenic determinants (eg, haptens) are effective in inducing Ab responses, cell-mediated responses seem to require larger and more complex structures as determinants of specificity. In other words, cell-mediated responses appear to be carrier-dependent.

The first step in the induction of cell-mediated responses may be the uptake of the Ag by macrophages and its subsequent presentation to the receptors on T lymphocytes. Once suitable lymphocytes have been contacted, these may be stimulated to proliferate and become "sensitized" lymphocytes (see below).

When a person carrying such "sensitized" T lymphocytes is again exposed to the Ag (eg, when a tuberculin skin test is applied), only a few sensitized T lymphocytes are necessary to initiate a cell-mediated hypersensitivity response. The few sensitized T lymphocytes can recruit large numbers of other lymphocytes and macrophages to produce the cellular infiltration characteristic of a cell-mediated reaction. They accomplish this and other effects through release of the following mediators ("lymphokines"), among others.

A. Mediators Affecting Macrophages:

1. Chemotactic factor, which attracts monocytes which then become macrophages.

2. Aggregation factor, which clumps suspended macrophages in vitro.

3. Migration inhibitory factor (MIF), which inhibits the migration of normal macrophages. It is probably an acidic glycoprotein with a molecular weight of 25,000–50,000. This may be the substance that "activates" macrophages (see p 149).

B. Mediators Affecting Polymorphonuclear Leukocytes (PMNs):

1. Leukocyte inhibitory factor, which inhibits migration of PMNs in a manner resembling that of MIF, although it is chemically different. It is a protein with a molecular weight of 68,000 and is inactivated by chymotrypsin.

2. Chemotactic factors for PMNs, basophils, and eosinophils, which selectively attract each type of cell. Factors that promote activity of eosinophil chemotaxis have been extracted from trichina and schistosome larvae.

C. Mediators Affecting Lymphocytes:

1. Blastogenic or mitogenic factor, which causes some lymphocytes to differentiate into large, rapidly dividing blast cells with greatly increased synthesis of DNA. The effect is most readily studied by measuring the incorporation of tritiated thymidine into DNA.

2. Transfer factor (see above).

D. Mediators Affecting Cells in Culture or Affecting Viruses:

1. Lymphotoxin, which can damage or lyse many types of cells.

2. Interferon, which can block virus replication in other cells.

TESTS TO EVALUATE CELL–MEDIATED HYPERSENSITIVITY OR IMMUNITY

The assessment of cell-mediated reactivity is increasingly important as greater numbers of persons suffer from spontaneous or medically induced defects of cell-mediated immunity. Increasing numbers of children with congenital defects survive, and in increasing numbers of patients cell-mediated immunity is suppressed by antitumor drugs, corticosteroids, or immunosuppressive drugs used for organ transplants. In the following tests, it is assumed that defects in cell-mediated reactivity probably indicate defects in cell-mediated immunity to infectious agents.

Skin Tests

Skin tests may be used to determine cell-mediated hypersensitivity to commonly encountered Ags. Most normal persons respond with delayed type reactions to skin test Ags of *Candida, Trichophyton*, mumps, streptokinase-streptodornase, or PPD.

Tests for Competence to Develop Cell-Mediated Hypersensitivity

Simple chemicals applied to human skin in lipid solvents induce cell-mediated hypersensitivity in normal persons. One percent 1-chloro-2,4-dinitrobenzene (dinitrochlorobenzene, DNCB) or dinitrofluorobenzene (DNFB) in acetone is applied to the skin and washed off 24 hours later. When a test dose of 0.03–0.1% of the same chemical is applied to the same area 7–14 days later, a delayed type reaction signifies the competence to develop cell-mediated hypersensitivity.

Skin Graft Rejection

A normal person will reject a skin graft from an unrelated individual in a predictable time sequence of reactions (see below). Inability to reject such a skin graft is strong evidence of impaired cell-mediated responses.

In Vitro Evaluation of Responses of Lymphoid Cells

A. Lymphocyte Blast Transformation: When sensitized lymphocytes are exposed to a specific Ag, they transform into large blast cells (the number and proportion of blasts can be counted) with greatly increased DNA synthesis (the incorporation of tritiated thymidine into DNA can be measured). However, only a small number of cells undergo this *specific* blast transformation. A larger number of T lymphocytes undergo *nonspecific* blast transformation when exposed to mitogens such as phytohemagglutinin (a kidney bean extract), pokeweed mitogen, or concanavalin A (a jack bean extract). The measurements in nonspecific and specific blast transformations are the same.

B. Macrophage Migration Inhibitory Factor: Upon challenge by an Ag to which cultured lymphocytes are sensitive, they elaborate macrophage migration inhibitory factor (MIF). This will inhibit the migration of guinea pig peritoneal macrophages from a capillary tube.

C. Rosette Formation: When incubated with sheep red blood cells, most T lymphocytes form rosettes. Although the mechanism of this effect is not clear, it permits an estimate of the proportion of circulating lymphocytes that behave in this manner. There is good correlation between rosette-forming and MIF-producing T lymphocytes.

CELL–MEDIATED HYPERSENSITIVITY EMPLOYED IN DIAGNOSIS OF INFECTION & ITS LIMITATIONS

Cell-mediated hypersensitivity develops with many types of infection. Delayed type skin reactivity can be a valuable aid in the diagnosis of many infectious processes if it is cautiously interpreted. A positive skin reaction indicates only that the individual has at some time in the past been infected with the specific agent. It provides information about the nature of a specific illness only if conversion from a negative to a positive skin test occurs during the course of the illness. Blood transfusion may passively transfer delayed hypersensitivity by means of sensitized lymphocytes. Furthermore, the general skin reactivity declines markedly in far-advanced stages of many diseases (anergy). Similar anergy may be encountered during the childhood exanthems (measles, chickenpox); thus a tuberculin-positive child may temporarily give a tuberculin-negative reaction during one of these illnesses. Anergy is also a regular feature of sarcoidosis, Hodgkin's disease, and other advanced neoplasms, as well as uremia. Patients receiving large doses of corticosteroids or immunosuppressive drugs (eg, cancer chemotherapy, organ transplants) have marked depression of cell-mediated hypersensitivity and immunity.

Bacterial Infections

Skin tests are useful to support a diagnosis of tuberculosis, tularemia, chancroid, and chlamydial infections (eg, LGV) during the course of the disease. In leprosy, the reaction to lepromin is more an indication of the immunologic state of the disease (ie, tuberculoid) than a help in diagnosis. These and other types of skin tests are described in Chapter 26. Although specific purified protein derivatives are available, mycobacterial infections other than tuberculosis cross-react extensively.

Mycotic Infections

Delayed type skin reactions occur in virtually all deep mycoses. If adequate skin testing material is available and if the concentration used is sufficiently dilute to avoid cross-reactions, the skin tests may be helpful in the diagnosis of past infections such as coccidioidomycosis, histoplasmosis, blastomycosis, and others. Most normal adults give positive skin tests with *Candida* Ags, and a negative test suggests a defect in cell-mediated immunity. In some deep mycoses (eg, histoplasmosis), the skin test itself may result in a significant rise of specific Abs in serum and thus lead to misleading diagnostic serologic tests.

Helminthic Infections

In a majority of parasitic infections—including trichinosis, filariasis, and ascariasis—immediate type skin reactions occur with the application of worm extracts. Some delayed type reactions may also be obtained, especially in *Echinococcus* disease with heated hydatid cyst fluid (Casoni reaction). Skin tests are probably never as specific as refined determinations for Abs in these disorders.

Viral Infections

Cell-mediated hypersensitivity occurs in many viral infections, including herpes simplex, mumps, and vaccinia. In persons repeatedly vaccinated against smallpox, the inoculation of inactive vaccinia virus results in a delayed type reaction. This denotes hypersensitivity to vaccinia Ags and should not be interpreted as immunity to smallpox.

Combined "Immediate" & "Delayed" Reactions

Skin-testing preparations from many infectious agents may produce both Ab-mediated and cell-mediated responses. This is usually due to the presence of multiple Ags in such preparations—some eliciting one response and some another.

RELATIONSHIP OF CELL–MEDIATED REACTIONS & RESISTANCE TO INFECTION

Whereas Abs provide protection against toxin-induced disorders and to a certain extent against virus infections, they play a limited role in host defenses against microbial infections, except in those whose virulence depends on polysaccharide capsules. Cell-mediated reactions are of paramount importance in maintaining resistance to most microbial infections. In some cell-mediated reactions, Abs cooperate in processes of recovery; eg, opsonins facilitate phagocytosis and chemotactic fragments of complement enhance inflammatory reactions and localization of infection. One of the most important contributions of cell-mediated reactions to resistance to infection is the "activation" of macrophages (see p 149). Sensitized T lymphocytes act on normal macrophages and "activate" them to a high level of phagocytic activity and intracellular killing ability. Although the induction of "activated" macrophages is immunologically specific, their subsequent expression is nonspecific.

The role played by Ab-mediated and by cell-mediated reactions, respectively, can be estimated to some extent by noting the types of infection that develop in persons who have a specified immune defect. The absence of complement components (especially C5–C9) favors bloodstream dissemination of neisseriae. Persons with isolated B cell defects and lack of Ab responses may be unusually susceptible to pyogenic coccal (especially pneumococcal) infections but handle intracellular bacterial or fungal and many viral infections normally. Conversely, persons with isolated T cell defects and deficient cell-mediated reactions may be overwhelmed by opportunistic organisms (*Nocardia, Pneumocystis, Candida, Aspergillus*) and incapable of handling mycobacterial or fungal infections. T cell defects and impaired cell-mediated reactions also permit the widespread dissemination of many viral infections (eg, herpes zoster).

Manifestations of hypersensitivity accompany many infectious processes. At times the hypersensitivity is incidental (eg, erythema nodosum in coccidioidomycosis), but at other times the cell-mediated hypersensitivity may significantly enhance the inflammatory reaction in foci of infection (eg, tuberculosis of the lung) and may lead to increased tissue destruction. In still other situations (Koch's phenomenon, p 179), the cell-mediated hypersensitivity reaction may favor localization of the infectious agent and limitation of its spread.

CONTACT ALLERGY TO DRUGS & SIMPLE CHEMICALS

Common allergic skin disorders in humans are attributable to sensitization by contact of skin with many simple chemicals (nickel, formaldehyde), drugs (sulfonamides), cosmetics, plant materials (catechols from poison ivy and poison oak), and others. Chlorogenic acid, a simple phenolic compound of low molecular weight, is a hapten contained in many different plants, eg, coffee beans, castor beans, fruits, and vegetables. It becomes a complete Ag by combining with host protein and can induce respiratory or skin allergy in heavily exposed individuals (eg, coffee workers). Presumably, these materials form covalent bonds with proteins of skin. Induction of cell-mediated hypersensitivity is probably aided by skin lipids or lipid vehicles acting like adjuvants.

Upon skin contact with the offending agent, the sensitized person develops erythema and swelling, itching, vesication, or necrosis in 12–48 hours. Histologically, the reaction is an intense mononuclear cell infiltrate resembling the tuberculin test. Patch testing on a small area of skin reproduces the lesion and can identify the allergen.

ROLE OF LIPIDS, WAXES, & ADJUVANTS IN THE DEVELOPMENT OF CELL–MEDIATED REACTIONS

It has been mentioned above that tuberculoprotein stimulates the development of delayed hypersensitivity reactions only if it is administered together with wax from the tubercle bacillus. The same wax permits sensitization of animals with simple chemicals, such as picryl chloride, which does not elicit hypersensitivity if injected alone. It is conceivable that the strongly allergenic properties of substances applied to the skin (compared with other routes of administration) are aided by the many lipids available in the skin. In general, it appears that the delayed type of hypersensitivity develops best if the allergen is administered in such a fashion as to elicit a focal inflammatory response. Lipids often elicit focal granulomatous tissue lesions.

When weakly antigenic or allergenic materials are mixed with lipids (eg, lanolin or paraffin) and killed tubercle bacilli, they elicit much greater Ab response and cell-mediated reactions than the Ags alone, and occasionally result in the production of "autoimmune" diseases. Such enhancing mixtures (often lanolin + paraffin oil + tubercle bacilli) are referred to as "adjuvants" (eg, Freund's adjuvant).

The main roles of the adjuvant appear to be the favoring of "helper" T cells and the maintenance of long-lasting Ag levels in tissue to be taken up by macrophages and presented to lymphocytes.

EXTRINSIC ALLERGIC ALVEOLITIS (Chronic Recurrent Lung Disease)

A large group of recurrent, debilitating pulmonary disorders is caused by hypersensitivity reactions to inhaled Ags in persons hypersensitive to these Ags. Patients usually have high titers of precipitating Ab against the offending Ag, and immune complex disease has been suspected. However, several features suggest cell-mediated hypersensitivity: delayed onset of reaction, absence of bronchospasm, infiltration of interstitial tissue with mononuclear cells, and, at times, epithelioid cells and granulomas. Although the pathogenesis of the disorders appears to be the same, the inciting agent differs: in farmer's lung, it is micropolyspora from moldy hay; in mushroom worker's lung, *Thermoactinomyces vulgaris* from mushroom compost; in maple-bark disease of paper-mill workers, *Cryptostroma corticale* from moldy bark; in the hypersensitivity pneumonitis of office workers, thermophilic actinomycetes contaminating the air-conditioning system; and in sequoiosis of redwood mill workers, moldy dust from *Sequoia* trees. There are many more.

Opportunistic fungi sometimes establish themselves in the respiratory tract. *Aspergillus* species may grow on bronchial surfaces or in tuberculous cavities, but they may also invade pulmonary tissue and produce granulomas in which hypersensitivity probably plays a role. The lung lesions of schistosomiasis and some other parasitic infestations may be caused by cell-mediated hypersensitivity to the parasite's Ags.

INTERFERENCE WITH CELL–MEDIATED OR ANTIBODY–MEDIATED HYPERSENSITIVITY OR IMMUNITY

Interference by Antibody

A. Antilymphocyte Serum (ALS): Antiserum can be made in one animal species against thymus cells

(T lymphocytes) of a second species. When such antiserum is injected into the second species, it selectively depresses cell-mediated reactions, including allograft rejection. The practical usefulness of ALS is limited by its being a foreign serum. Antilymphoblast globulin is better tolerated in humans.

B. Tumor-Enhancing Antibody: Certain Abs to transplanted tumors interfere with their rejection by the host. This might be attributed to attachment of Ab or Ag-Ab complexes to important tumor cell Ags, thus blocking their recognition or rejection by T lymphocytes.

C. Antibody Formation: Ab present at the time of Ag administration tends to block Ab formation. A practical example is the administration of anti-Rh globulin to Rh-negative mothers immediately after delivery of an Rh-positive infant. The baby's red blood cells entering the mother's circulation (when the placenta separates) tend to induce anti-Rh Ab formation. Such Abs might cause fetal erythroblastosis in a subsequent Rh-positive infant. The Rh globulin rapidly attaches to Rh-positive cells so that they will not act as Ags.

However, in some circumstances, an Ab globulin and the corresponding Ag (eg, tetanus immune globulin and tetanus toxoid) administered simultaneously will not combine if they are given intramuscularly into widely separate areas. This explains the efficacy of emergency prophylaxis of tetanus or analogous problems (eg, rabies).

Interference by Inhibitors of Inflammation or Lymphocyte Proliferation

Corticosteroids and a variety of "immunosuppressive" drugs (eg, azathioprine) given to prolong the survival of organ transplants suppress cell-mediated hypersensitivity and immunity. They are the principal reason for the marked increase in susceptibility of organ transplant recipients to bacterial, mycotic, and protozoal infections, which are often progressive and lethal. Suppression of Ab formation usually is not important clinically.

Many drugs used in the chemotherapy of neoplasms have similar effects. Corticosteroids alone (in high dosage) in immunologic diseases (rheumatoid arthritis, systemic lupus erythematosus, etc) likewise suppress cell-mediated reactions and therefore open the way for the development of infectious ("opportunistic") complications.

Other Types of Interference

Lymphoreticular disorders (Hodgkin's disease, sarcoid, lymphosarcoma) or widely disseminated infections (tuberculosis, coccidioidomycosis, lepromatous leprosy) are typically associated with deficient cell-mediated reactions, including anergy to skin tests. Ab levels are generally normal. If the infection is controlled by treatment, cell-mediated reactivity returns. Transfer factor can accomplish the same result in these disorders for a brief period.

Widespread neoplastic disease also leads to interference with cell-mediated responses. In this situation, cell-mediated skin reactivity has been restored by levamisole (tetrahydro-6-phenyl-imidazothiazole), an anthelmintic drug. The mechanism is not known.

TOLERANCE

Interference by Antigens

Specific immunologic unresponsiveness may be called tolerance. The following features may determine whether an Ag will induce tolerance rather than an immunologic response:

(1) Immunologic maturity of the host: *Examples:*

(a) Neonatal tolerance to allografts (see below).

(b) Vertical transmission of animal viruses: Some tumor viruses and lymphocytic choriomeningitis virus are transmitted from mother to fetus. Viruses multiply in the fetus and persist after birth, but there is little or no Ab response or cell-mediated response. The offspring is tolerant and permits tumor development. On the other hand, if an uninfected mouse offspring matures, it can be infected with viruses, develops an immune response, and resists tumor development.

(2) Structure and dose of antigen: *Example:* If very low or very high doses of an Ag are administered—especially if the Ag lacks aggregated materials—there may be tolerance instead of an immune response. If purified polysaccharides or amino acid copolymers are injected intravenously in huge doses, there may be "immune paralysis"—a lack of response. This tolerance may terminate when much of the antigenic mass has been degraded or excreted or when a cross-reacting Ag is administered. T cells become tolerant more readily and remain tolerant longer than B cells. Intravenous administration of an Ag is more likely to establish tolerance than other routes.

Some Possible Mechanisms for Tolerance

(Combinations of these may occur.)

(1) Failure of macrophages to effectively present the Ag to T cells: Neonatal macrophages lack determinants needed for the Ag-presenting function. Deaggregated materials are not taken up well by macrophages for presentation.

(2) Under some circumstances, it is probable that suppressor T cells engage in inhibiting the reactivity in lymphocytic clones.

(3) Ag administered in very low or very high doses may result in deletion of potentially reactive B cell clones or in deletion of both B cell and helper T cell clones.

Desensitization

Repeated doses of Ag in rapid succession may make the host "tolerant" temporarily in Ab-mediated reactions (through the mechanism shown in [3], above). Desensitization is generally not successful in cell-mediated reactions (see p 176).

Tolerance to Tissue Allografts

(1) If animals of one strain are injected in utero with cells (lymphoid cells, bone marrow) from a second strain, the mature animal of the first strain will accept an allograft from the first strain.

(2) Tolerance is established more readily if the antigenic disparity between donor and recipient is slight rather than major.

(3) Tolerance is established best in the immunologically immature. The timing varies: Mice and rats in utero are immunologically immature; sheep and humans in the third trimester in utero are immunologically mature.

(4) Tolerance in T cells is more effective than in B cells (see above). It may be favored by enhanced activity of "suppressor" T cells.

(5) Graft-versus-host (GVH) reactions: When lymphoid cells are transferred from an immunologically competent donor to an immunodeficient recipient, the donor cells may establish themselves in the recipient but "reject" the host. This can result in growth retardation, runting, or death. GVH reactions are a serious problem in "immunologic reconstitution" by grafts of lymphoid cells, bone marrow, or thymus to immunodeficient children (see p 187).

AUTOIMMUNE DISEASES

Certain disease states are attributed to immune responses of a host to its own tissues. The mechanism of pathogenesis is speculative—often based on circumstantial evidence rather than definitive proof.

In general, the tissue Ags present during fetal and neonatal life are recognized as "self" and so are tolerated by the host. No Abs or cell-mediated reactions are developed to them. On the other hand, Ags not present during fetal or neonatal life are rejected as "not self" and immune responses to them may develop. Very complex interactions are involved.

The differentiation of "self" from "not self" must be an important homeostatic function of the animal body. "Autoimmune disease" may be considered a failure of this homeostatic function, a disorder of immune regulation.

In certain specialized situations, tolerance may be lost and immunologic reaction to host Ags develops. Some possible mechanisms are as follows:

(1) Certain tissues are normally sequestered, so that their Ags have no access to Ab-forming cells. The lens and uveal tract of the eye, sperm, and central nervous system tissue are normally isolated from the circulation and are thus not recognized as "self." Entrance of these Ags into the circulation elicits relatively organ-specific Abs. When these Ags are administered with adjuvant, various disorders such as endophthalmitis, aspermatogenesis, thyroiditis, or encephalitis can be produced experimentally (see below).

(2) Although most Ag-Ab reactions are highly specific, cross-reactions between unrelated Ags do occur. Thus, an Ab formed in response to an extrinsic Ag might by chance cross-react with a tissue Ag of the host. Examples are found among vegetable substances that stimulate Abs reacting with red blood cell Ags, or streptococcal Ags that stimulate Abs reacting with human heart tissue Ags.

(3) It is possible that in certain circumstances native tissue Ags are slightly altered (perhaps by combination with extrinsic haptens) and thus assume a new antigenic specificity. The Ab forming against the hapten-Ag complex may likewise react with the native Ag. In other circumstances, a foreign molecule (eg, a drug) might attach to a cell surface. Abs forming to that foreign molecule can combine with it, and the resulting Ag-Ab complex at the cell surface may injure the cell. (See discussion of apronalide thrombocytopenia, below, for further details.)

(4) In still other situations, it appears that a genetic abnormality determines the ability of certain individuals and their families to manufacture Abs to common host tissue constituents. Thus, in rheumatoid arthritis the IgM or IgG called "rheumatoid factor" may be an Ab to normal human IgG. In systemic lupus erythematosus and related "collagen diseases," Abs are formed to DNA. This may involve an abnormal loss of tolerance. It may be associated with loss of activity of "suppressor" T cells.

The following are oversimplified examples of disorders that may involve "autoimmune" reactions.

Chronic Thyroiditis

If rabbits are repeatedly injected with extracts of homologous thyroid gland, they develop Abs and cell-mediated immunity against thyroid Ags. These can be demonstrated by serologic techniques. At the same time, many of the animals develop chronic thyroiditis that histologically resembles Hashimoto's thyroiditis in humans. Patients suffering from chronic thyroiditis have in their serum specific Abs against thyroid Ags, whereas persons not suffering from thyroid disease lack such Abs. It is probable, therefore, that human thyroiditis develops as an "autoimmune" disease. Thyroid Ags are no longer recognized as "self" by the host; consequently, Abs and cell-mediated reactions are formed against them. It is likely that lymphoid cells are sensitized to thyroid Ags and that these cells provoke the inflammatory process which, in turn, leads to fibrosis and loss of function of the gland. Abs to thyroglobulin may also play a role.

Allergic Encephalitis

When animal brain substance is mixed with adjuvants (see p 182) and injected into other members of the same animal species, many of these animals will develop encephalitis. The experiment can even be performed successfully by removing the frontal lobe from a monkey, mixing the ground brain material with adjuvant, and injecting it intramuscularly into the same monkey. Such an animal may develop demyelinating disease of the central nervous system with disseminated lesions in the brain and cord. Histologically, these lesions greatly resemble "postvaccinal" encephalomyelitis, which occurs in persons who have been repeatedly injected with animal brain material, as in older rabies vaccine.

Experimental allergic encephalitis cannot be transferred passively by serum but can be passively transferred with lymphoid cells. The severity of lesions bears no relationship to antibrain Abs measured by CF, and such Abs may even protect against lesions. The likelihood is great that the illness is based on cell-mediated reactions and that a protein of brain acts as allergen. One such encephalitogenic nonapeptide has been characterized and synthesized.

Diabetes, Myasthenia Gravis, & Hyperthyroidism

In patients with myasthenia gravis, a degenerative central nervous system disease, the serum contains an Ab to the acetylcholine receptors of neuromuscular junctions. Thus, it is possible that the pathogenesis of myasthenia gravis involves an Ab-mediated autoimmune attack on acetylcholine receptors of the neuromuscular junctions.

In at least 2 other disorders—Graves' disease and extreme insulin resistance in diabetes—autoantibodies to hormone receptors have been implicated. Some cases of insulin resistance have circulating Abs to insulin receptors that interfere with insulin binding.

Some cases of Graves' disease (hyperthyroidism) have a circulating Ab to thyrotropin receptors that may block hormone attachment.

It is possible that these are disorders of immune regulation in which the normally functioning suppressor T cells are not functioning. This may result in inappropriate B cell responses and Ab formation. Control of such immune regulation is tentatively placed in immune response genes that are in close proximity to the major histocompatibility complex (HLA region) on chromosomes.

Rheumatic Fever

The development of rheumatic fever is regularly preceded by multiple infections with group A betahemolytic streptococci. There exist cross-reactions between Ags of human heart and streptococci. Certain group A streptococci contain a cell membrane Ag that cross-reacts with human cardiac muscle fibers, especially the sarcolemma. Thus, Abs to the streptococci might react with heart muscle. There is also cross-reactivity between structural glycoproteins of heart valves and streptococcal group-specific carbohydrate. The pathogenetic role of these cross-reacting Abs is not established, but prompt elimination of streptococcal Ags prevents rheumatic fever.

Blood Diseases

Various forms of human hemolytic anemias, granulocytopenias, thrombocytopenias, and other blood disorders have been attributed either to the development of autoantibodies directed against Ags in red blood cells or platelets or to the attachment of Ag-Ab complexes to the cell surface. As a result of such Ag-Ab reactions, cells would be destroyed. The responsible Abs have been demonstrated in a number of instances. For example, in the thrombocytopenic purpura caused by apronalide (Sedormid) or quinine, the sensitive person's serum contains Ab that can lyse platelets onto which the drug has been adsorbed.

Pernicious anemia may represent an "autoimmune" reaction to intrinsic factor, a special protein secreted by parietal cells into the stomach.

Systemic Lupus Erythematosus (SLE) & Other "Collagen Vascular Diseases"

This is a group of human diseases characterized by focal inflammatory lesions, vasculitis, and collagen degeneration. It includes systemic lupus erythematosus (SLE) and other rheumatoid disorders. The causes of these diseases are not known, but typical cases have followed sensitization by drugs, foreign serum, and other immune stimuli. In these diseases, and particularly in systemic lupus erythematosus, a variety of Abs against various normal body constituents have been identified, including autoantibodies to red cell Ag, cellular DNA, clotting factors, etc. The typical LE cell is a granulocyte that has taken up an aggregate of DNA–anti-DNA complex; the intracellular DNA can be identified by immunofluorescence. The complement level in active systemic lupus erythematosus is low, indicating Ag-Ab reactions that bind complement. The nephritis of SLE appears to be an "immune complex disease" (see p 177).

It may be that viruses play a role in the pathogenesis of systemic lupus erythematosus by combining with autoantigens to stimulate immune reactions. There is a 3-fold predominance of black women among patients with systemic lupus erythematosus. A concordance in monozygotic twins emphasizes the role of immunoregulatory genes in the complex origin of these disorders.

In patients with rheumatoid arthritis, a "rheumatoid factor" can be regularly shown by hemagglutination, latex fixation, or precipitation tests. This is an IgM (*rarely* IgG) that reacts with normal human IgG and may be a true autoantibody to IgG. Rheumatoid arthritis may be an "immune complex disease" (see p 177).

TRANSPLANTATION IMMUNITY

Blood groups of the ABO system are transplantation Ags, but they are carbohydrates (see Chapter 12). Most other transplantation Ags are glycoproteins of cell membranes.

It has long been known that an animal will accept a graft of its own tissue (eg, skin) but not that of another of the same species except an identical twin. An autograft is a graft of tissue from one animal onto itself, and it "takes" regularly and permanently. An isograft is a graft of tissue from one individual to another genetically identical individual, and it usually "takes" permanently. A heterograft (xenograft) is a graft from one species to another species. It is always rejected. An allograft (homograft) is a graft from one member of a noninbred species to another member, eg, from one human to another human. It is rejected by the homograft reaction. Initial vascularization and circulation of the graft are good, but after 11–14 days marked reduction in circulation and infiltration of the bed of the graft with mononuclear cells occur, and the graft eventually becomes necrotic and sloughs. In the homograft rejection, a cell-mediated reaction with competent lymphoid cells is of primary importance, but Abs can also participate in the reaction. If a second homograft from the same donor is applied to a recipient who has rejected the first graft, an accelerated ("second-set") rejection is observed in 5–6 days.

The problem of tissue transplantation resides in specific "transplantation (HLA) Ags" that exist in all mammalian cells. These Ags are of a great variety under the control of a number of different "histocompatibility *(HLA)* genes." In inbred strains of mice, at least 14 independently segregating genetic loci for transplantation Ags have been recognized. At each of these loci there exist multiple alleles, so that the number and variety of transplantation Ags are enormous. If inbred mice are cross-mated, the F1 offspring are tolerant of grafts from either parent but either parent rejects the F1 hybrid graft. In humans, the major histocompatibility complex includes at least 4 (or 5) closely linked genes designated *HLA-A, -B, -C, -D (-DR)*. These genetic loci determine strong transplantation Ags. Several other weaker transplantation Ags are determined by other genetic loci. Ags determined by these several genetic loci are defined by their interaction with antisera in the lymphocytotoxicity test or by the mixed lymphocyte reaction. It appears that the newly recognized *DR* genes determine Ags that occur on B lymphocytes and macrophages. The tests by which the Ags are determined are described below. Potent antisera are empirically found in large-scale screening.

The major histocompatibility genetic loci occur on each member of a single chromosome pair (in humans, chromosome 6). For each histocompatibility locus, many alleles exist, controlling expression of specific Ags. Because of this polymorphism, each individual is likely to have at least 4 strong transplantation Ags on cells. The term "haplotype" denotes the products of the major histocompatibility complex in haploid form. Each individual has strong transplantation Ags arranged in pairs of haplotypes, with each haplotype being controlled by the major histocompatibility loci of one chromosome of a pair. Many Ags have now been identified, resulting in thousands of potential haplotypes. Consequently, the likelihood is very small that 2 random individuals would have completely or partly identical haplotypes. Within a family, on the other hand, only 4 haplotypes are involved (2 from each parent), which permits a reasonable opportunity of genetic matching of family members as donors or recipients of transplants. About 25% of

siblings are identical at one haplotype. To characterize the haplotype present in a donor or recipient, both lymphocytotoxicity and mixed lymphocyte culture tests must be done with a broad range of reagents (lymphocytes and sera).

It is also considered essential that donor and recipient be compatible by matching of ABO blood groups. The following procedures are employed in determining the degree of histocompatibility for "matching" donor and recipient of transplants.

A. Mixed Lymphocyte Culture (MLC): This test applies only to living donors and requires 5 days to complete. At present, it is not applicable to cadaver organ transplants. For the test, lymphocytes from donor and recipient are separated from blood. Potential donor cells are treated with mitomycin or radiation to stop DNA replication. The untreated recipient cells are grown in culture with the donor cell Ags. Their response is assayed by the incorporation of tritium-labeled thymidine. The level of cellular radioactivity becomes an indicator of cellular stimulation as a result of exposure to Ags that are recognized as foreign. The greater the disparity of donor and recipient cells, the higher the stimulation of cell growth and of labeled thymidine incorporation into DNA. An ideal match would show similar responses in single or mixed cell cultures. The higher the percentage of relative response is in mixed cell culture (above that in the sum of single cell culture), the greater the antigenic disparity and the less suitable the match.

The mixed lymphocyte culture is particularly useful in selecting the best donor within a family of compatible serologically defined (HLA) types. Mixed lymphocyte culture compatibility takes precedence over the results of HLA typing in donor selection. A recent modification of the mixed lymphocyte culture test is the primed lymphocyte test (PLT), which can give similar results in less than 2 days.

B. Histocompatibility Antigen (HLA) Typing by Lymphocytotoxicity: Viable purified lymphocytes from blood of the tissue donor are added to a panel of standard sera and the recipient's serum. Complement is added, then dye (eosin or trypan blue) and formalin. Cell death occurs if an Ag + Ab + complement reaction takes place. Cell death is established by counting the number of viable cells that exclude the dye (dead cells are stained by dye). An alternative method is to preincubate lymphocytes with ^{51}Cr and determine the release of this isotope as an indication of cell death.

Results of Organ Transplants

If donor and recipient are well matched by mixed lymphocyte culture and histocompatibility Ag typing, the long-term survival of a transplanted organ or tissue is enhanced. In 1981, the 5-year survival rate of 2-haplotype-matched kidney transplants from related donors was near 90%; that of a one-haplotype-matched kidney was near 80%; and that of kidneys from cadaver donors was near 50%. However, the survival rate was higher if the graft recipient had several previous transfusions. The reason for this is much debated.

In one center, well-matched transplants of bone marrow from siblings established themselves in 33 of 37 patients with aplastic anemia, half of whom lived with functioning grafts. However, about 70% of patients with successful marrow grafts exhibited graft-versus-host (GVH) disease (see above). The grafted cells took over from the host in bone marrow transplants following the intensive irradiation and cyclophosphamide treatment for leukemia. The results of graft-versus-host reactions included skin lesions and malfunctions of liver and gut, so that less than one-third of patients with graft-versus-host reactions survived. It is possible that antithymocyte globulin may have some benefit in graft-versus-host disease.

To delay or diminish rejection of transplanted tissue or organs, attempts are made to suppress immunologic rejection mechanisms. At present this involves the administration of corticosteroids, immunosuppressive drugs such as azathioprine or cyclosporin A, antilymphocytic serum, and radiation. Unfortunately, all of these immunosuppressive measures enhance the recipient's susceptibility to endogenous or exogenous infection. Opportunistic "nonpathogenic" microorganisms (bacteria, fungi, viruses, protozoa) may prove fatal to the immunosuppressed transplant recipient. Such disorders as cytomegalovirus pneumonia, *Pneumocystis carinii* pneumonia, or disseminated herpes zoster are prominent examples of endogenous infections that occur mainly in the immunosuppressed. In addition, there is a greatly enhanced susceptibility to the development and spread of neoplasms in such patients (see Chapter 11).

HLA Disease

Histocompatibility Ags also appear to be genetic markers for a variety of diseases. Ankylosing spondylitis and Reiter's disease are associated with the Ag HLA-B27. HLA-B8 and HLA-Dw3 have been associated with a high frequency of "autoimmune" disorders, including insulin-dependent diabetes, systemic lupus erythematosus, Sjögren's syndrome, and others (see p 184). Possible explanations have been suggested in Chapter 11.

The longer a tissue or organ graft survives in the recipient, the greater the chance that tolerance to the graft may be established under the cover of immunosuppressive measures. The establishment of tolerance by means of repeated administration of donor cells into recipients has been attempted only rarely. (See Chapter 12.)

TUMOR IMMUNITY

Animals carrying chemical-induced or virus-induced tumors develop a certain amount of resistance to that tumor which can be demonstrated experimentally although it is usually insufficient to cause complete regression of the tumor.

In the course of neoplastic transformation of cells, new Ags develop at the cell surface that permit the host's immune responses to recognize such cells as "foreign." (Some tumors in adults contain Ag found in *fetal* but not in adult cells. Thus, a carcinoembryonic Ag [CEA] is found in the serum of patients with neoplasms of the gut.) Cell-mediated responses (see p 179) attack these "foreign" tumor cells and tend to limit their proliferation. It is probable that these cell-mediated responses are an effective surveillance system that can eliminate some newly arising clones of neoplastic cells ("forbidden clones").

The tumor Ags also stimulate the development of specific Abs. Some such Abs may be cytotoxic. Others interfere with recognition and disposal of tumor cells by cell-mediated immune responses of the host, and such antitumor Abs (or Ag-Ab complexes) thus produce an enhancement of tumor growth.

Some immunologic features of virus-induced tumors of animals are discussed in Chapter 40.

There is tentative evidence that spontaneously arising human tumors have new cell surface Ags against which the host develops both cytotoxic Abs and cellular hypersensitivity. The possibility is under investigation that enhancement of such immune responses may permit containment of malignant neoplasms. Enhancement by the administration of bacille Calmette Guérin (BCG) into surface tumors (melanomas) has led to tumor regression. Interferon is receiving a trial as an immunomodulator in these same circumstances of tumor therapy.

•   •   •

References

Austen KF: Systemic anaphylaxis in the human being. *N Engl J Med* 1974;**291**:661.

Bach FH, van Rood JJ: The major histocompatibility complex: Genetics and biology. (3 parts.) *N Engl J Med* 1976;**295**:806, 872, 927.

Beaven MA: Histamine. *N Engl J Med* 1976;**294**:319.

Bleich HL, Moore MJ: Release of inflammatory mediators from stimulated neutrophils. *N Engl J Med* 1980;**303**:27.

Blume KG et al: Bone marrow ablation and allogeneic marrow transplantation in acute leukemia. *N Engl J Med* 1980; **302**:1041.

Butterworth AE, David JR: Eosinophil function. *N Engl J Med* 1981;**304**:154.

Byers VS et al: In vitro studies of poison oak immunity. (2 parts.) *J Clin Invest* 1979;**64**:1437, 1449.

Catalona WJ et al: Dinitrochlorobenzene contact sensitization. *N Engl J Med* 1972;**286**:399.

Collins RM: Vaccines and cell-mediated immunity. *Bacteriol Rev* 1974;**38**:371.

Committee on Drugs of the American Academy of Pediatrics: Anaphylaxis. *Pediatrics* 1973;**51**:136.

Dale DC, Petersdorf RG: Corticosteroids and infectious diseases. *Med Clin North Am* 1973;**57**:1277.

David JR: Lymphocyte mediators and cellular hypersensitivity. *N Engl J Med* 1973;**288**:143.

Denman AM: Immunodeficiency and general medicine. *Br Med J* 1980;**281**:1376.

Flax MH: Drug-induced autoimmunity. *N Engl J Med* 1974; **291**:414.

Garraty G, Petz LD: Drug-induced hemolytic anemia. *Am J Med* 1975;**58**:398.

Golden DBK et al: Regimens of hymenoptera venom immunotherapy. *Ann Intern Med* 1980;**92**:620.

Hunt KJ et al: A controlled trial of immunotherapy in insect hypersensitivity. *N Engl J Med* 1978;**299**:157.

Kaliner M et al: Immunologic release of chemical mediators from human nasal polyps. *N Engl J Med* 1973;**289**:277.

Levin AS et al: Transfer factor therapy in immune deficiency states. *Annu Rev Med* 1973;**24**:175.

McCluskey RT, Klasser J: Immunologically mediated renal disease. *N Engl J Med* 1973;**288**:564.

McDonald JC: The biologic implications of HLA. *Arch Intern Med* 1981;**141**:100.

Najarian JS et al: Seven years' experience with antilymphoblast globulin for renal transplantation. *Ann Surg* 1976;**184**:352.

Nathan CF et al: The macrophage as an effector cell. *N Engl J Med* 1980;**303**:622.

Palmer DL, Reed WP: Delayed hypersensitivity skin testing. (2 parts.) *J Infect Dis* 1974;**130**:132, 138.

Parker CW: Drug allergy. (2 parts.) *N Engl J Med* 1975; **292**:511, 732.

Rapaport FT et al: Recent advances in clinical and experimental transplantation. *JAMA* 1977;**237**:2835.

Rimland D et al: Immunization for the internist. *Ann Intern Med* 1976;**85**:622.

Rose NR: HLA and disease. *Arch Intern Med* 1978;**138**:527.

Rosenberg LE, Kidd KK: HLA and disease susceptibility: A primer. *N Engl J Med* 1977;**297**:1061.

Russell PS, Cosimi AB: Transplantation. *N Engl J Med* 1979; **301**:470.

Sbarbaro JA: Skin test antigens: An evaluation whose time has come. *Am Rev Respir Dis* 1978;**118**:1.

Schatz M et al: Immunologic lung disease. *N Engl J Med* 1979; **300**:1310.

Stiller CR et al: Autoimmunity. *Ann Intern Med* 1975;**82**:405.

Stossel TP: Phagocytosis. (3 parts.) *N Engl J Med* 1974;**290**:717, 774, 833.

Theofilopoulos AN et al: Isolation of circulating immune complexes using Raji cells. *J Clin Invest* 1978;**61**:1570.

Toyka KV et al: Myasthenia gravis: Study of humoral immune mechanisms. *N Engl J Med* 1977;**296**:125.

Waldmann TA et al: Disorders of suppressor immunoregulatory cells in the pathogenesis of immunodeficiency and autoimmunity. *Ann Intern Med* 1978;**88**:226.

Weissmann G et al: Release of inflammatory mediators from stimulated neutrophils. *N Engl J Med* 1980;**303**:27.

Williams RC Jr: Immune complexes in human disease. *Annu Rev Med* 1981;**32**:13.

THE STAPHYLOCOCCI

The staphylococci are gram-positive spherical cells, usually arranged in irregular clusters. They grow readily on a variety of media and are active metabolically, fermenting many carbohydrates and producing pigments that vary from white to deep yellow. The pathogenic staphylococci often hemolyze blood and coagulate plasma. Some are members of the normal flora of the skin and mucous membranes of humans; others cause suppuration, abscess formation, a variety of pyogenic infections, and even fatal septicemia. A common type of food poisoning is caused by a heat-stable enterotoxin produced by certain staphylococci. Staphylococci rapidly develop resistance to many antimicrobial agents and present difficult therapeutic problems.

Morphology & Identification

A. Typical Organisms: Spherical cells about 1 μm in diameter arranged in irregular clusters. In liquid cultures, single cocci, pairs, tetrads, and chains are also seen. Young cocci stain strongly gram-positive; on aging, many cells become gram-negative. Staphylococci are nonmotile and do not form spores. Under the influence of certain chemicals (eg, penicillin) they are lysed or changed into L forms, but they are not affected by bile salts or optochin.

Some *Micrococcus* species found free-living in the environment form regular packets of 4 or 8 cocci; their colonies are often yellow, red, or orange.

B. Culture: Staphylococci grow readily on most bacteriologic media under aerobic or microaerophilic conditions. They grow most rapidly at 37 °C but form pigment best at room temperature (20 °C). Colonies on solid media are round, smooth, raised, and glistening, forming varying pigments: *Staphylococcus aureus* is deep golden yellow; *Staphylococcus epidermidis (Staphylococcus albus)* is porcelain white; intermediate shades also occur. Many colonies develop pigment only upon prolonged incubation at 20 °C. No pigment is produced anaerobically or in broth. Various degrees of hemolysis are produced by different strains. Anaerobic cocci *(Peptococcus)* resemble staphylococci in morphology.

C. Growth Characteristics: Staphylococci are able to ferment slowly many carbohydrates, producing lactic acid but not gas. Proteolytic activity varies greatly, but catalase is produced regularly. The extracellular substances produced by pathogenic staphylococci are discussed below.

Staphylococci are relatively resistant to drying, to heat (they withstand 50 °C for 30 minutes), and to 9% sodium chloride but are readily inhibited by certain chemicals, eg, hexachlorophene, 3%. Staphylococci are variably sensitive to many antimicrobial drugs. Resistance falls into several classes: (1) Beta-lactamase production is common, is under plasmid control, and makes the organisms resistant to many penicillins. The plasmids are transmitted by transduction (see p 46). (2) "Methicillin resistance" is independent of beta-lactamase production. The genes probably reside on the chromosome and are sometimes transmissible by transduction. The precise mechanism remains uncertain but is a function of cell wall structure. (3) "Tolerance" implies that staphylococci are inhibited by a drug but not killed by it, ie, there is a very large difference between minimal inhibitory and minimal lethal dose. Tolerance can at times be attributed to a lack of activation of autolytic enzymes of the cell wall. (4) Plasmids can also carry genes for resistance to tetracyclines, erythromycins, and aminoglycosides. Most resistant staphylococci remain susceptible to vancomycin in 1982.

D. Variation: Any culture of staphylococci contains certain organisms that differ from the bulk of the

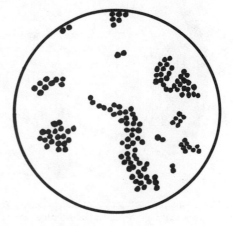

Figure 14–1. Staphylococci from broth culture.

population in cultural characteristics (colony type, pigment, hemolysis), in enzyme equipment, in drug resistance, and in pathogenicity.

Antigenic Structure

Staphylococci contain both antigenic polysaccharides and proteins that permit a grouping of strains to a limited extent. Teichoic acids (polymers of glycerol or ribitol phosphate) linked to cell wall peptidoglycan can be antigenic. Antiteichoic antibodies detected by gel diffusion may be particularly associated with active staphylococcal endocarditis. Surface protein may interfere with phagocytosis. Protein A, a cell wall component (see [b] in Fig 14–2), happens to bind strongly to the Fc portion of any IgG molecule. This makes the Fab portion of an antibody molecule face outward, so that it is free to combine with a specific antigen. This process has found many applications in immunology and diagnostic technology (eg, staphylococcal protein A with an attached specific antibody IgG molecule directed against bacterium X will agglutinate the latter; this is "coagglutination").

Most of the extracellular substances produced by staphylococci are likewise antigenic. Serologic tests have limited usefulness in identifying strains; this can be done by "phage typing." The method is based on the lysis of organisms by one or a series of specific bacteriophages. Such bacteriophage susceptibility (phage type) is a stable genetic characteristic based on surface receptors. It permits the epidemiologic tracing of strains.

Many staphylococcal strains are lysogenic. Production of some toxins is under the control of plasmids or temperate phages.

Toxins & Enzymes

Staphylococci can produce disease both through their ability to multiply and spread widely in tissues and through their production of many extracellular substances. Among the latter are the following:

A. "Exotoxin": A filtrable, thermolabile mixture that is lethal for animals on injection, causes necrosis in skin, and contains several soluble hemolysins which can be separated by electrophoresis. The alpha hemolysin, a protein with a molecular weight of 3×10^4, dissolves rabbit erythrocytes, damages platelets, and is probably identical with the lethal and dermonecrotic factors of exotoxin. Alpha hemolysin also has a powerful action on vascular smooth muscle. Beta hemolysin dissolves sheep erythrocytes (but not rabbit cells) upon incubation for 1 hour at 37 °C and then 18 hours at 10 °C. These hemolysins (and 2 others, the gamma and delta hemolysins) are antigenically distinct and bear no relationship to streptococcal lysins. Exotoxin treated with formalin gives a nonpoisonous but antigenic toxoid that has been used to stimulate antitoxic immunity to staphylococci, albeit without definite clinical benefit.

B. Leukocidin: A soluble material that kills exposed white blood cells of a variety of animal species. It is antigenic but more heat-labile than exotoxin. Its role in pathogenesis is uncertain. Pathogenic staphylococci may not kill white blood cells and may be phagocytosed as effectively as nonpathogenic varieties. However, they are capable of very active intracellular multiplication, whereas the nonpathogenic organisms tend to die inside the cell. Antibodies to leukocidin may play a role in resistance to recurrent staphylococcal infections.

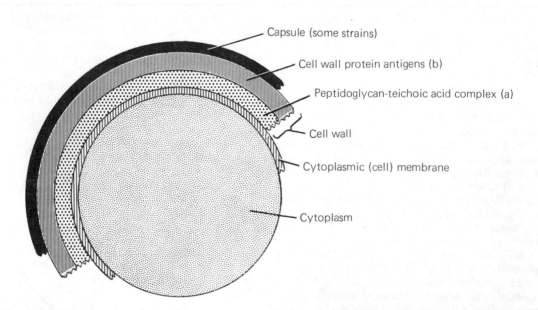

Capsule (some strains)

Cell wall protein antigens (b)

Peptidoglycan-teichoic acid complex (a)

Cell wall

Cytoplasmic (cell) membrane

Cytoplasm

Figure 14–2. Antigenic structure of staphylococci. *(a)* Site of bacteriophage attachment. Species antigens present (antigenic determinant is N-acetylglucosamine linked to polyribitol phosphate). *(b)* Multiple antigens; several widely distributed.

C. Enterotoxin: A soluble material produced by certain strains of staphylococci, particularly strains grown in high concentrations of CO_2 (30%) in semisolid media. Enterotoxin is a protein with a molecular weight of 3.5×10^4. It resists boiling for 30 minutes and the action of gut enzymes and belongs to one of 4 antigenic types (A–D). An important cause of food poisoning, enterotoxin is produced especially when certain staphylococci grow in carbohydrate and protein foods. The gene for enterotoxin production may be on the chromosome, but a plasmid may carry a regulatory protein for active toxin production. Ingestion of 25 μg of enterotoxin B results in vomiting and diarrhea in humans or monkeys. The emetic effect of enterotoxin is probably the result of central nervous system stimulation (vomiting center) after the toxin acts on neural receptors in the gut. Enterotoxin can be assayed by precipitin tests (gel diffusion).

D. Coagulase: By definition, *S aureus* is capable of producing coagulase, an enzymelike protein that clots oxalated or citrated plasma in the presence of a factor contained in many sera. The coagulase-reactive factor of serum reacts with coagulase to generate both esterase and clotting activities in a manner similar to the activation of prothrombin to thrombin. Coagulase may deposit fibrin on the surface of staphylococci, perhaps altering their ingestion by phagocytic cells or their destruction within such cells. Coagulase production is considered synonymous with invasive pathogenic potential.

E. Other Substances: Other extracellular substances produced by staphylococci include a hyaluronidase, or spreading factor; a staphylokinase resulting in fibrinolysis but acting much more slowly than streptokinase; proteinases, lipases, and beta-lactamases; an exfoliative toxin under plasmid control that can cause the "scalded skin syndrome" (see below); and a postulated toxin responsible for the "toxic shock syndrome" seen most notably in menstruating women who use tampons (see below).

Pathogenesis

Staphylococci (particularly *S epidermidis*) are members of the normal flora of the human skin and of the respiratory and gastrointestinal tracts; they are also found regularly in air and human environments. The pathogenic capacity of a given strain of staphylococci is the combined effect of the above-named extracellular factors and toxins together with the invasive properties of the strain, and it covers a wide scale. At one end is staphylococcal food poisoning, attributable solely to the ingestion of preformed enterotoxin; at the other end are staphylococcal bacteremia and disseminated abscesses in all organs. The potential contribution of the various extracellular factors in pathogenesis is evident from the nature of their individual actions.

Pathogenic, invasive staphylococci *(S aureus)* tend to produce coagulase and yellow pigment, be hemolytic, and ferment mannitol. Nonpathogenic, noninvasive staphylococci *(S epidermidis)* tend to be nonhemolytic, white, and coagulase-negative and do not ferment mannitol. Such organisms rarely produce suppuration but may infect orthopedic or cardiovascular prostheses. Some micrococci may produce suppuration like that associated with staphylococcal infections and occasionally cause pneumonia. A micrococcus now called *Staphylococcus saprophyticus* (typically nonpigmented, novobiocin-resistant, and producing acid aerobically from mannitol) has been claimed to be a frequent cause of acute urinary tract infection in young women.

Pathology

The prototype of a staphylococcal lesion is the furuncle or other localized abscess. Groups of staphylococci established in a hair follicle lead to tissue necrosis (dermonecrotic factor). Coagulase is produced and coagulates fibrin around the lesion and within the lymphatics, resulting in formation of a wall that limits the process and is reinforced by the accumulation of inflammatory cells and, later, fibrous tissue. Within the center of the lesion, liquefaction of the necrotic tissue occurs (enhanced by delayed hypersensitivity) and the abscess "points" in the direction of least resistance. Drainage of the liquid central necrotic tissue is followed by the slow filling of the cavity with granulation tissue and eventual healing.

Focal suppuration is typical of staphylococcal infection. From any one focus, organisms may spread via the lymphatics and bloodstream to other parts of the body. Suppuration within veins, associated with thrombosis, is a common feature of such dissemination.

Staphylococci of low invasiveness are involved in many skin infections (eg, acne, impetigo). Staphylococci of phage group II cause bullous exfoliation—the "scalded skin" syndrome—through the production of an exfoliating toxin. "Toxic shock syndrome" usually begins within 5 days of the onset of menses in young women who use tampons. There is an abrupt onset of high fever, vomiting, diarrhea, myalgias, a scarlatiniform rash, and hypotension, with cardiac and renal failure in the most severe cases. The syndrome can recur in successive menstrual periods and is tentatively attributed to a staphylococcal toxin. Staphylococci from toxic shock syndrome patients carry distinct marker proteins. In osteomyelitis, the primary focus of staphylococcal growth is typically in a terminal blood vessel of the metaphysis of long bones, leading to necrosis of bone and chronic suppuration. Staphylococci may be the causative organisms in pneumonia, meningitis, empyema, endocarditis, or sepsis with suppuration in any organ. Anaerobic cocci *(Peptococcus)* participate in mixed anaerobic infections.

Clinical Findings

The picture of a localized staphylococcal infection is that of a "pimple," hair follicle infection, or abscess—usually an intense, localized, painful inflammatory reaction that undergoes central suppuration and that heals quickly when the pus is drained. The wall of fibrin and cells around the core of the abscess tends to prevent spread of the organisms and should not be broken down by manipulation or trauma. If the organisms disseminate and bacteremia ensues, the clinical picture resembles that seen with other bloodstream infections. Secondary localization in an organ or system is accompanied by the symptoms and signs of organ dysfunction and intense focal suppuration.

Food poisoning due to staphylococcal enterotoxin is characterized by a short (1–8 hours) incubation period; violent nausea, vomiting, and diarrhea; and rapid convalescence. There is no fever.

Oral preoperative administration of kanamycin-neomycin has been followed occasionally by enterocolitis associated with staphylococci resistant to that drug. The relationship of this enterocolitis to other forms of antibiotic-associated colitis caused by *Clostridium difficile* toxin is not clear.

Diagnostic Laboratory Tests

A. Specimens: Surface swab, pus, blood, tracheal aspirate, or spinal fluid for culture, depending upon the localization of the process. Antibody determinations in serum are rarely of value.

B. Stained Smears: Typical staphylococci are seen in stained smears of pus or sputum. It is not possible to distinguish saprophytic *(S epidermidis)* from pathogenic *(S aureus)* organisms.

C. Culture: Specimens planted on blood agar plates give rise to typical colonies in 18 hours at 37 °C, but hemolysis and pigment production may not occur until several days later and are optimal at room temperature. From specimens contaminated with a mixed flora, staphylococci can be grown in media containing 7.5% NaCl. Most human staphylococci are not pathogenic for animals. A given *Staphylococcus* is generally considered to be pathogenic if it produces coagulase, ferments mannitol, liquefies gelatin, or hemolyzes blood.

D. Coagulase Test: Citrated rabbit (or human) plasma diluted 1:5 is mixed with an equal volume of broth culture and incubated at 37 °C. A tube of plasma mixed with sterile broth is included as a control. The tubes are inspected for clotting for 1–4 hours.

Growth on tellurite medium may be substituted for coagulase tests. Most coagulase-positive staphylococci reduce tellurite with the production of jet black colonies.

While all coagulase-positive staphylococci are considered pathogenic for humans, certain types of infections, notably infective prosthetic endocarditis, can be caused by coagulase-negative *S epidermidis.*

E. Serologic Tests, Animal Inoculations: These procedures have little practical value. However, phage typing of staphylococci isolated in hospital environments is a useful epidemiologic tool (see below); antibiotic resistance patterns are also helpful.

Treatment

The impression among clinicians that active resis-

tance to staphylococcal infections can be acquired has led to the use of staphylococcal toxoid in persons suffering from recurrent staphylococcal skin infections. There is no good evidence for the efficacy of toxoids in treatment. Staphylococcal vaccines are of even more questionable value.

Many antimicrobial drugs have some effect against staphylococci in vitro. However, the rapid development of resistance to most drugs and the inability of drugs to act in the central necrotic part of the lesions make it difficult to eradicate pathogenic staphylococci from infected persons. Drainage of closed suppurating lesions is essential.

Acute hematogenous osteomyelitis responds well to antimicrobial drugs. In chronic osteomyelitis, surgical drainage and revision is accompanied by long-term administration of appropriate drugs, but eradication of the infecting staphylococci is infrequent. Hyperbaric oxygen has been used to enhance phagocytic and killing capabilities of leukocytes with some benefit in chronic osteomyelitis.

Most persons harbor staphylococci on the skin and in the nose or throat. Even if the skin can be cleared of staphylococci (eg, in eczema), reinfection by droplets will occur almost immediately. Pathogenic organisms are commonly spread from one lesion (eg, furuncle) to other areas of the skin by fingers and clothing. Scrupulous local antisepsis is therefore important to control recurrent furunculosis.

Serious multiple skin infections (acne, furunculosis) occur most often in adolescents and are believed to be favored by hormonal factors. Similar skin infections occur in patients receiving prolonged courses of corticosteroids. In acne, lipases of staphylococci and corynebacteria liberate fatty acids from lipids and thus cause tissue irritation. Lipases can be inhibited by tetracyclines, which are used for long-term treatment.

Because of the frequency of drug-resistant strains, meaningful staphylococcal isolates should usually be tested for antibiotic susceptibility to help in the choice of systemic drugs. Resistance to drugs of the erythromycin group tends to emerge so rapidly that these drugs should not be used singly for treatment of chronic infection. Tetracycline and penicillin resistance, determined by plasmids, can be transmitted among staphylococci by transducing bacteriophages.

Penicillin G-resistant staphylococci from clinical infections always produce penicillinase. They now constitute more than 70% of staphylococcal isolates in US communities and are often susceptible to beta-lactamase-resistant penicillins (see p 132), cephalosporins, or vancomycin. "Methicillin resistance" is independent of beta-lactamase production and occurs in only a small part of the microbial population. Its basis is uncertain, and its clinical frequency varies enormously in different countries and at different times. The selection pressure of lactamase-resistant penicillins is unlikely to be the sole determinant: In Denmark, the isolation rate of "methicillin-resistant" staphylococci was 40% in 1970 and 10% in 1980. In the USA, it was 0.1% in 1970 and— in hospitals—5–10% in 1980. These variations occurred without notable changes in drug use.

In view of the rapid emergence of drug resistance among staphylococci, hospitals have sometimes restricted the use of an antistaphylococcal drug to the treatment of seriously ill patients. Such restriction may greatly prolong the useful period of a new drug. In 1980–1981, vancomycin remains the most widely effective drug against staphylococci.

Epidemiology & Control

Staphylococci are ubiquitous human parasites. The chief sources of infection are accessible human lesions, fomites contaminated from such lesions, and the human respiratory tract and skin. Airborne infection has assumed added importance in hospitals, where a large proportion of the staff and patients carry antibiotic-resistant staphylococci in nose or throat or on the skin. Although cleanliness, hygiene, and aseptic management of lesions ordinarily control the spread of skin infections due to staphylococci, few methods are available to prevent the wide dissemination of staphylococci from carriers. Aerosols (eg, glycols) and ultraviolet irradiation of air have little effect. The most endangered areas in hospitals are the newborn nursery, intensive care units, operating rooms, and cancer chemotherapy wards. Massive introduction of "epidemic" pathogenic staphylococci into these areas may lead to serious clinical disease. Persons with active staphylococcal lesions and carriers may have to be excluded from these areas. In such individuals, the application of topical antiseptics (eg, chlorhexidine or bacitracin cream) to carriage sites (nostrils, perineum, etc) may diminish shedding of dangerous organisms. Antiseptics (eg, hexachlorophene) used on the skin of the newborn diminish colonization by staphylococci, but toxicity presents problems.

In most hospitals, because antibiotics are used extensively, prevalent staphylococci are resistant to commonly employed antimicrobial drugs. Phage typing provides a valuable tool to establish the transmission of "hospital staphylococci" from personnel and patients to newly admitted patients. During outbreaks of staphylococcal disease among newborns or surgical patients, a single phage type usually prevails. Sporadic infections are often caused by several different types. Certain phage types appear to spread much more readily in the environment and acquire drug resistance more rapidly than others. Most drug-resistant staphylococci of hospitals fall into the series of phage types called group III.

Experimentally, it is possible to selectively colonize individuals with nonpathogenic staphylococci (eg, 502A) and thereby prevent colonization with pathogenic staphylococci. This "bacterial interference" can also be applied at times to patients whose lesion-causing staphylococci have been temporarily suppressed by drugs. "Bacterial interference" may have a nutritional basis (eg, competition for a metabolite) or may be due to production of an inhibitor.

THE STREPTOCOCCI

The streptococci are spherical microorganisms, characteristically arranged in chains and widely distributed in nature. Some are members of normal human flora; others are associated with important human diseases attributable in part to infection by streptococci, in part to sensitization to them. They produce a variety of extracellular substances and enzymes. Their ability to hemolyze red blood cells to various degrees is one important basis for classification.

Morphology & Identification

A. Typical Organisms: Individual cocci are spherical or ovoid and are arranged in chains. The cocci divide in a plane perpendicular to the long axis of the chain. The members of the chain often have a striking diplococcal appearance, and rodlike forms are occasionally seen. The lengths of the chains vary widely and are conditioned largely by environmental factors.

Some streptococci elaborate a capsular polysaccharide comparable to that of pneumococci. The majority of group A, B, and C strains (see p 194) produce capsules composed of hyaluronic acid. The capsules are most noticeable in very young cultures. They impede phagocytosis. The streptococcal cell wall contains proteins (M, T, R, antigens), carbohydrates (group-specific), and peptidoglycans (Fig 14–4). From the cell wall, hairlike pili project through the capsule. They consist partly of M protein and are covered with lipoteichoic acid. The latter is important in the attachment of streptococci to epithelial cells.

B. Culture: Most streptococci grow in solid media as discoid colonies, usually 1–2 mm in diameter. Group A strains that produce capsular material often give rise to mucoid colonies. Matt and glossy colonies of group A strains are discussed below. *Peptostreptococcus* grows under anaerobic conditions.

C. Growth Characteristics: Energy is princi-

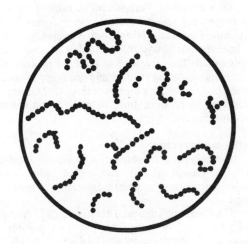

Figure 14–3. Hemolytic streptococci from broth culture.

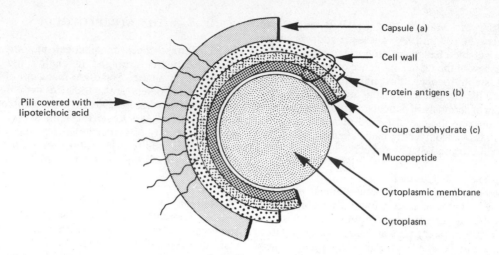

Figure 14–4. Antigen structure of group A streptococcal cell. *(a)* Capsule is hyaluronic acid. *(b)* Cell wall protein antigens M, T, and R. *(c)* Group carbohydrate for group A streptococci is rhamnose-N-acetylglucosamine.

pally obtained from the utilization of sugars. Growth of streptococci tends to be poor on solid media or in broth unless enriched with blood or tissue fluids. Nutritive requirements vary widely among different species. Certain streptococci with stringent growth requirements form colonies only around contaminant organisms ("satellite strep"). They may account for some "negative blood cultures" in endocarditis. The human pathogens are most exacting, requiring a variety of growth factors. Growth and hemolysis are aided by 10% CO_2.

Whereas most pathogenic hemolytic streptococci grow best at 37 °C, group D enterococci grow well between 15 °C and 45 °C. Enterococci also grow in high (6.5%) sodium chloride concentration, in 0.1% methylene blue, and in bile-esculin agar. Most streptococci are facultative anaerobes, but some strains from surgical infections are obligate anaerobes *(Peptostreptococcus)*. Other characteristics are discussed below.

D. Variation: Variants of the same *Streptococcus* strain may show different colony forms. This is particularly marked among group A strains, giving rise to either matt or glossy colonies. Matt colonies consist of organisms that give rise to much M protein. Such organisms tend to be virulent and relatively insusceptible to phagocytosis by human leukocytes. Glossy colonies tend to produce little M protein and are often nonvirulent.

Antigenic Structure

Hemolytic streptococci can be divided into serologic groups (A–U), and certain groups can be subdivided into types. Several antigenic substances are found:

(1) C carbohydrate: This substance is contained in the cell wall of many streptococci and forms the basis of serologic grouping (Lancefield A–U). Extracts of C carbohydrate for "grouping" of strep-

tococci may be prepared by extraction of centrifuged culture with hot hydrochloric acid, nitrous acid, or formamide; by enzymatic lysis of streptococcal cells (eg, with pepsin or trypsin); or by autoclaving of cell suspensions at 15 lb pressure for 15 minutes. The serologic specificity of C carbohydrate is determined by an amino sugar. For group A streptococci, this is rhamnose-N-acetylglucosamine; for group C, rhamnose-N-acetylgalactosamine; for group F, glucopyranosyl-N-acetylgalactosamine.

(2) M protein: This substance is closely associated with virulence of group A streptococci and occurs chiefly in organisms producing matt or mucoid colonies. Repeated passage on artificial media may lead to loss of M protein production, which may be restored by rapidly repeated animal passage. M protein interferes with the ingestion of virulent streptococci by phagocytic cells. Growing L forms of streptococci also produce M protein as well as hyaluronic acid.

M protein determines the type specificity of group A streptococci, as demonstrated by agglutination or precipitation reactions with absorbed type-specific sera. There are more than 60 types in group A. Types are assigned Arabic numbers. In humans, antibodies to an M protein protect against infection with this specific type of group A *Streptococcus*.

(3) T substance: This antigen has no relationship to virulence of streptococci. It is destroyed by acid extraction and by heat and thus is separated from M protein. It is obtained from streptococci by proteolytic digestion (which rapidly destroys M proteins) and permits differentiation of certain types. Other types share the same T substance. Yet another surface antigen has been called R protein.

(4) Nucleoproteins: Extraction of streptococci with weak alkali yields mixtures of proteins and other substances of little serologic specificity, called P substances, which probably make up most of the streptococcal cell body.

Toxins & Enzymes

More than 20 extracellular products that are antigenic are elaborated by group A streptococci, including the following:

(1) Streptokinase (fibrinolysin) is produced by many strains of beta-hemolytic streptococci. It transforms the plasminogen of human serum into plasmin, an active proteolytic enzyme that digests fibrin and other proteins. This process of digestion may be interfered with by nonspecific serum inhibitors and by a specific antibody, antistreptokinase. A skin test with streptokinase-streptodornase is regularly positive in adolescents and adults with normal cell-mediated immunity. It is therefore used as a common test for the latter. Streptokinase has been given intravenously for treatment of pulmonary emboli and venous thromboses.

(2) Streptodornase (streptococcal deoxyribonuclease) is an enzyme that depolymerizes DNA. The enzymatic activity can be measured by the lowering in viscosity of known DNA solutions. Purulent exudates owe their viscosity largely to deoxyribonucleoprotein. Mixtures of streptodornase and streptokinase are used in "enzymatic debridement." They help to liquefy exudates and facilitate removal of pus and necrotic tissue; antimicrobial drugs thus gain better access, and infected surfaces recover more quickly. An antibody to DNase develops after streptococcal infections (normal limit = 100 units), especially after skin infections with pyoderma.

(3) Hyaluronidase is an enzyme that splits hyaluronic acid, an important component of the ground substance of connective tissue. Thus, hyaluronidase aids in spreading infecting microorganisms (spreading factor). Hyaluronidases are antigenic and specific for each bacterial or tissue source. Following infection with hyaluronidase-producing organisms, specific antibodies are found in the serum. Purified hyaluronidase was employed in medical therapy to facilitate the spreading and absorption of fluids injected into tissues.

(4) Erythrogenic toxin is soluble and is destroyed by boiling for 1 hour. It causes the rash that occurs in scarlet fever. Only strains elaborating this toxin can cause scarlet fever. Erythrogenic toxin is elaborated only by lysogenic streptococci. Strains devoid of the temperate phage genome do not produce toxin. A nontoxigenic *Streptococcus,* after lysogenic conversion, will produce erythrogenic toxin. Erythrogenic toxin is antigenic, giving rise to the formation of specific antitoxin that neutralizes the toxin. Persons possessing such antitoxin are immune to the rash though susceptible to streptococcal infection. There exist some minor qualitative differences between the erythrogenic toxins produced by different strains.

Susceptibility to erythrogenic toxin can be demonstrated by the **Dick test:** 0.1 mL of standardized, diluted, erythrogenic toxin (broth culture filtrate) is injected intradermally. Similar material, heat-inactivated, is used as a control. In the absence of significant concentration of antitoxin in the blood, a positive Dick test is seen, consisting of the appearance in 8–24 hours of erythema and edema measuring more than 10 mm in diameter. (This test has been largely abandoned.)

The specific nature of the rash of scarlet fever can be demonstrated by means of the **Schultz-Charlton reaction.** This consists of the injection of specific antitoxin into an area of scarlet fever rash. If the rash is caused by erythrogenic toxin of streptococci, the redness will blanch and fade quickly in the injected area where the antitoxin has neutralized the toxin.

(5) Some streptococci elaborate a **diphosphopyridine nucleotidase** into the environment. This enzyme may be related to the organism's ability to kill leukocytes. Proteinases and amylase are produced by some strains.

(6) Hemolysins: Many streptococci are able to hemolyze red blood cells in vitro in varying degrees. Complete disruption of erythrocytes with release of hemoglobin is called *beta* hemolysis. Incomplete lysis of erythrocytes with the formation of green pigment is called *alpha* hemolysis. "Gamma" sometimes refers to nonhemolytic organisms.

Beta-hemolytic group A streptococci elaborate 2 hemolysins (streptolysins):

Streptolysin O is a protein (molecular weight 60,000) that is hemolytically active in the reduced state (available –SH groups) but rapidly inactivated when oxidized. It combines quantitatively with antistreptolysin O, an antibody that appears in humans following infection with any streptococci that produce streptolysin O. This antibody blocks hemolysis by streptolysin O. This phenomenon forms the basis of a quantitative test for the antibody. An antistreptolysin O (ASO) serum titer in excess of 160–200 units is considered abnormally high and suggests either recent infection with streptococci or persistently high antibody levels following an earlier exposure persisting in a hypersensitive person.

Streptolysin S is the agent responsible for the hemolytic zones around streptococcal colonies on blood agar plates. It is not antigenic. However, sera of humans and animals frequently contain a nonspecific inhibitor that is independent of past experience with streptococci.

Classification of Streptococci

A practical arrangement of streptococci into major categories is based on (1) colony morphology and hemolysis on blood agar; (2) biochemical tests and resistance to physical and chemical factors; (3) immunologic characteristics; and (4) ecologic features. Combinations of the above permit the following arrangement for the sake of convenience:

I. Beta-Hemolytic Streptococci: In general, these produce soluble hemolysins that can be recognized readily on culture, although individual strains may fail to be recognized. They elaborate group-specific carbohydrates. Acid extracts containing these C carbohydrates give precipitin reactions with specific antisera that permit arrangement into groups A–H and K–U. The following are of particular medical relevance and are sometimes referred to by specific names:

Group A—*Streptococcus pyogenes*—contains a majority of human pathogens associated with local or systemic invasion and poststreptococcal disorders caused by immunologic reactions. They are usually bacitracin-sensitive.

Group B—*Streptococcus agalactiae*—are members of the normal flora of the female genital tract and an important cause of neonatal sepsis and meningitis. They hydrolyze sodium hippurate, are rarely bacitracin-sensitive, and give a positive response to the so-called CAMP test (from *C*hristie, *A*tkins, *M*unch, *P*etersen; see *Austr J Exp Biol Med* 1944;**22:**197).

Groups C and G occur sometimes in the pharynx; may cause sinusitis, bacteremia, or endocarditis; and may be mistaken for group A organisms.

Group D includes enterococci (eg, *Streptococcus faecalis, Streptococcus faecium*) and nonenterococci (eg, *Streptococcus bovis, Streptococcus equinus*). **Enterococci** typically grow in the presence of 6.5% NaCl or 40% bile, are inhibited but not killed by penicillins, occur in normal enteric flora, and are found in urinary tract or cardiovascular infections or in meningitis. **Nonenterococci** are also inhibited by 6.5% NaCl or 40% bile but are readily killed by penicillin. They may cause genitourinary tract infections or endocarditis.

Groups E, F, H, and K–U occur infrequently in human disease.

II. Non-Beta-Hemolytic Streptococci: These

commonly exhibit alpha hemolysis or no change on blood plates. The principal members are as follows:

Streptococcus pneumoniae (pneumococci) are bile-soluble, and their growth is inhibited by optochin (ethylhydrocupreine hydrochloride) disks. Their role in disease is discussed in a separate section.

Viridans streptococci, including *Streptococcus salivarius, Streptococcus mitis, Streptococcus mutans, Streptococcus sanguis,* and others, are not bile-soluble, and their growth is not inhibited by optochin disks. They are the most prevalent members of the normal flora in the human respiratory tract and are important for the healthy state of the mucous membranes. As a result of trauma they may reach the bloodstream and are a principal cause of spontaneous infective endocarditis when they settle on abnormal heart valves. Some viridans streptococci (eg, *S mutans*) synthesize large polysaccharides such as dextrans or levans and contribute importantly to the genesis of dental caries.

Group D streptococci includes some strains that produce alpha hemolysis but otherwise behave as enterococci.

Group N streptococci have variable hemolytic ability. They are rarely found in human disease states but produce normal coagulation (''souring'') of milk; they are also called lactic streptococci.

III. Peptostreptococci: These grow only under

anaerobic or microaerophilic conditions and produce variable hemolysis. They participate often in mixed anaerobic infection in the abdomen, pelvis, lung, or brain. They are members of the normal flora of the gut and female genital tract.

Pathogenesis & Clinical Findings

A variety of distinct disease processes are associated with streptococcal infections. The biologic properties of the infecting organisms, the nature of the host response, and the portals of entry of the infection all greatly influence the pathologic picture. Infections can arbitrarily be divided into several categories.

A. Diseases Attributable to Invasion by Beta-Hemolytic Group A Streptococci *(Streptococcus pyogenes):* The portal of entry determines the principal clinical picture. In each case, however, there is a diffuse and rapidly spreading cellulitis that involves the tissues and extends along the lymphatic pathway with only minimal local suppuration. From the lymphatics, the infection rapidly extends to the bloodstream, whereupon bacteremia supervenes.

1. Erysipelas–If the portal of entry is the skin, erysipelas results, with massive brawny edema and a rapidly advancing margin.

2. Puerperal fever–If the streptococci enter the uterus after delivery, puerperal fever develops, which is essentially a septicemia originating in the infected wound (endometritis).

3. Sepsis–Infection of traumatic or surgical wounds with streptococci results in streptococcal sepsis or surgical scarlet fever.

B. Diseases Attributable to Local Infection With Beta-Hemolytic Group A Streptococci and to Their Products:

1. Streptococcal sore throat–The commonest infection due to beta-hemolytic streptococci is streptococcal sore throat. Virulent group A streptococci adhere to the pharyngeal epithelium by means of lipoteichoic acid covering surface pili. In the infant and small child, the sore throat occurs as a subacute nasopharyngitis with a thin serous discharge and little fever but with a tendency of the infection to extend to the middle ear, the mastoid, and the meninges. The cervical lymph nodes are usually enlarged. The illness may persist for weeks. In older children and adults, the disease is more acute and is characterized by intense nasopharyngitis, tonsillitis, and intense redness and edema of the mucous membranes, with purulent exudate; enlarged, tender cervical lymph nodes; and (usually) a high fever. Twenty percent of infections are asymptomatic. A similar clinical picture can occur with infectious mononucleosis, adenovirus infection, diphtheria, and fusospirochetal infection. If the infecting streptococci produce erythrogenic toxin and the patient has no antitoxic immunity, scarlet fever rash occurs. Antitoxin to the erythrogenic toxin prevents the rash but does not interfere with the streptococcal infection. With the most intense inflammation, tissues may break down and form peritonsillar abscesses (quinsy) or Ludwig's angina, where massive swelling of the floor of the mouth blocks air passages.

Streptococcal infection of the upper respiratory tract does not usually involve the lungs. Pneumonia due to beta-hemolytic streptococci is most commonly a sequela to viral infections, eg, influenza or measles, which seem to enhance susceptibility greatly.

2. Streptococcal pyoderma–Local infection of superficial layers, especially in children, is called impetigo. It consists of superficial blisters that break down or of eroded areas whose denuded surface is covered with pus or crusts. It spreads by continuity and is highly communicable in children, especially in hot, humid climates. More widespread infection occurs in eczematous or wounded skin or in burns and may progress to cellulitis. Streptococcal skin infections are often attributable to types 49, 57, and 59–61 and may precede glomerulonephritis but do not often lead to rheumatic fever.

C. Infective Endocarditis:

1. Acute endocarditis–In the course of bacteremia, beta-hemolytic streptococci, pneumococci, staphylococci, or gram-negative bacteria may settle on normal or previously deformed heart valves, producing acute ulcerative endocarditis. Rapid destruction of the valves frequently leads to a fatal outcome in days or weeks. Other organisms are encountered occasionally in this disease, particularly in narcotics users.

2. Subacute endocarditis often involves abnormal valves (congenital deformities and rheumatic or atherosclerotic lesions). Although any organism reaching the bloodstream may establish itself on thrombotic lesions that develop on injured endothelium as a result of circulatory stresses, subacute endocarditis is most frequently due to members of the normal flora of the respiratory or intestinal tract that have accidentally reached the blood. After dental extraction, at least 30% of patients have viridans streptococcal bacteremia. These streptococci, ordinarily the most prevalent members of the upper respiratory flora, are also the most frequent cause of subacute bacterial endocarditis. About 5–10% of cases are due to enterococci. The lesion is slowly progressive, and a certain amount of healing accompanies the active inflammation; vegetations consist of fibrin, platelets, blood cells, and bacteria adherent to the valve leaflets. The clinical course is gradual, but the disease is invariably fatal in untreated cases. The typical clinical picture includes fever, anemia, weakness, a heart murmur, embolic phenomena, an enlarged spleen, and renal lesions.

D. Other Infections: Various streptococci, particularly enterococci, are frequently the cause of urinary tract infections. Anaerobic streptococci *(Peptostreptococcus)* occur in the normal female genital tract, the mouth, and the intestine. They may give rise to suppurative lesions, either alone or in association with other anaerobes, particularly *Bacteroides*. Such infections may occur in wounds, in postpartum endometritis, following rupture of an abdominal viscus, or in chronic suppuration of the lung. Such pus usually has a foul odor. A variety of other streptococci (groups B–L and O) that are usually found in lower animals may also occasionally produce human infections.

Group B streptococci are part of the normal vaginal flora and may affect the newborn. Group B streptococcal infection during the first month of life may present as fulminant sepsis, meningitis, or respiratory distress syndrome. Intrapartum intravenous ampicillin appears to prevent colonization of infants whose mothers carry group B streptococci. Although group B streptococci appear sensitive to penicillin, they are difficult to eradicate from neonatal infection unless an aminoglycoside is also given.

E. Poststreptococcal Diseases (Rheumatic Fever, Glomerulonephritis): Following an acute group A streptococcal infection, there is a latent period of 1–4 weeks, after which nephritis or rheumatic fever occasionally develops. The latent period suggests that these poststreptococcal diseases are not attributable to the direct effect of disseminated bacteria but represent instead a hypersensitivity response that follows streptococcal insult to the affected organs. Nephritis is more commonly preceded by infection of the skin; rheumatic fever, by infection of the respiratory tract.

1. Acute glomerulonephritis develops in some persons 3 weeks following streptococcal infection, particularly with types 12, 4, 2, and 49. Certain strains are particularly nephritogenic. Thus, 23% of children with a skin infection with a type 49 strain developed nephritis or hematuria in one study. However, after random streptococcal infections, the incidence of nephritis is less than 0.5%. Other nephritogenic types are 59–61.

Glomerulonephritis may be initiated by antigen-antibody complexes on the glomerular basement membrane. The most important antigen is probably in the streptococcal protoplast membrane. In acute nephritis, there is blood and protein in the urine, edema, high blood pressure, and nitrogen retention; serum complement levels are low. A few patients die; some develop chronic glomerulonephritis with ultimate kidney failure; the majority recover completely.

2. Rheumatic fever is the most serious sequela to hemolytic streptococcal infection because it results in damage to heart muscle and valves. In some developing countries, rheumatic heart disease still ranks high as a cause of death in young adults. Certain strains of group A streptococci contain cell membrane antigens that cross-react with human heart sarcolemma. Sera from patients with rheumatic fever contain an antibody to these antigens.

The onset of rheumatic fever is often preceded by a group A *Streptococcus* infection 1–4 weeks earlier, although the infection may be mild and may not be detected. Untreated streptococcal infections may be followed by rheumatic fever in up to 3% of military personnel and 0.3% of civilian children. In general, patients with more severe streptococcal sore throats have a greater chance of developing rheumatic fever.

Typical symptoms and signs of rheumatic fever include fever, malaise, a migratory nonsuppurative polyarthritis, and evidence of inflammation of all parts of the heart (endocardium, myocardium, pericardium). The carditis characteristically leads to thickened and deformed valves and to small perivascular granulomas in the myocardium (Aschoff bodies) that are finally replaced by scar tissue. Erythrocyte sedimentation rates, serum transaminase levels, electrocardiograms, and other tests are used to estimate rheumatic activity.

Rheumatic fever has a marked tendency to be reactivated by recurrent streptococcal infections, whereas nephritis does not have this characteristic. The first attack of rheumatic fever usually produces only slight cardiac damage, which, however, increases with each subsequent attack. It is therefore important to protect such patients from recurrent group A hemolytic streptococcal infections by prophylactic penicillin administration.

Diagnostic Laboratory Tests

Specimens to be obtained depend upon the nature of the streptococcal infection. A throat swab, pus, or blood is obtained for culture. Serum is obtained for antibody determinations, particularly antistreptolysin O titer.

A. Stained Smears: Smears from pus often show single cocci or pairs rather than definite chains. Cocci are sometimes gram-negative. If smears of pus show streptococci but cultures fail to grow, anaerobic organisms must be suspected. Smears of throat swabs are rarely contributory because streptococci (viridans) are always present.

Smears from broth cultures of throat swabs 2–3 hours old can be stained with fluorescent group A–specific antibody for the most rapid identification of group A streptococci in clinical disease or carriers.

B. Culture: For rapid identification, all specimens suspected of containing streptococci are cultured on blood agar plates. In addition, if anaerobes are suspected, suitable broth cultures and anaerobic medium must be inoculated. Blood cultures will grow hemolytic group A streptococci (eg, in sepsis) within hours or a few days. However, because certain alpha-hemolytic streptococci or enterococci may grow very slowly, blood cultures in cases of suspected endocarditis should always be incubated for 1–2 weeks before being discarded as negative. Incubation in 10% CO_2 often speeds hemolysis. Slicing into a blood agar plate has a similar effect. The degree and kind of hemolysis (and colonial appearance) may permit placing an organism in a definite group, but serologic grouping and typing by means of precipitin tests should be performed whenever possible for definitive classification and for epidemiologic reasons. Streptococci belonging to group A may be presumptively identified by empirically determined amounts of bacitracin. A bacitracin disk containing 0.04 unit strongly inhibits growth of more than 95% of group A streptococci but rarely those of other groups.

C. Serologic Tests: A rise in antibody titer to many antigens can be estimated, including antistreptolysin O (ASO) (particularly in respiratory disease), anti-DNase and antihyaluronidase (particularly in skin infections), antistreptokinase, "bactericidal" anti-M type-specific antibodies, and others. Antibodies to several streptococcal antigens and enzymes are measured by the sensitive streptozyme test. The antigens are adsorbed onto sheep red blood cells, and agglutination by antibodies occurs within a few minutes on a slide.

Immunity

Resistance against streptococcal diseases is type-specific. Thus, a host who has recovered from infection by one group A streptococcal type is relatively insusceptible to reinfection by the same type but fully susceptible to infection by another type. This resistance is associated with type-specific anti-M antibodies. These are demonstrated in the so-called bactericidal test that exploits the fact that streptococci are rapidly killed after phagocytosis. M protein interferes with phagocytosis, but in the presence of type-specific antibody to M protein, streptococci are killed by leukocytes. The changing patterns of streptococcal disease with increasing age suggest that in the course of infections by beta-hemolytic streptococci the general reactivity to all types is altered, with increasing localization and intensity of inflammatory response.

Immunity against the erythrogenic toxin is based on antitoxin in the blood. This antitoxic immunity protects against the rash of scarlet fever but has no effect on infection with streptococci. Antibody to streptolysin O (antistreptolysin) develops following infection but does not indicate immunity. High titers (> 250 units) indicate recent or repeated infections and are found more frequently in rheumatic individuals than those with uncomplicated streptococcal infections.

Treatment

All beta-hemolytic group A streptococci are sensitive to penicillin G, and most to erythromycin. Some are resistant to tetracyclines. Alpha-hemolytic streptococci and enterococci, on the other hand, vary widely in their susceptibility to antimicrobial agents. Particularly in bacterial endocarditis, antibiotic sensitivity tests are essential to determine which drugs (and in what dosage) may be used for optimal therapy. In these cases, laboratory tests should include determinations of both inhibitory and killing power of drugs or drug combinations. Aminoglycosides often enhance the rate of bactericidal action of penicillin on streptococci, particularly enterococci.

Antimicrobial drugs have no effect on established

glomerulonephritis and rheumatic fever. However, in acute streptococcal infections, every effort must be made to rapidly eradicate streptococci from the patient, eliminate the antigenic stimulus (before day 8), and thus prevent poststreptococcal disease. Doses of penicillin or erythromycin that result in effective tissue levels for 10 days usually accomplish this. Antimicrobial drugs are also very useful in the prevention or early treatment of reinfection with beta-hemolytic group A streptococci in rheumatic subjects.

Epidemiology, Prevention, & Control

A number of streptococci (viridans streptococci, enterococci, etc) are members of the normal flora of the human body. They produce disease only when established in parts of the body where they do not normally occur (eg, heart valves). To prevent such accidents, particularly in the course of surgical procedures on the respiratory, gastrointestinal, and urinary tracts that result in temporary bacteremia, antimicrobial agents are often administered prophylactically to persons with known heart valve deformity.

The ultimate source of group A streptococci is always a person harboring these organisms. The person may have a clinical or subclinical infection or may be a carrier distributing streptococci directly to other persons via droplets from the respiratory tract or skin. The nasal discharges of a person harboring beta-hemolytic streptococci are the most dangerous source of massive contamination with these organisms. The role of contaminated bedding, utensils, or clothing is doubtful. The infected udder of a cow yields milk that may cause epidemic spread of hemolytic streptococci. Immunologic grouping and typing of streptococci are valuable tools for epidemiologic tracing of the transmission chain.

Control procedures are directed mainly at the human source: (1) Detection and early intensive antimicrobial therapy of respiratory and skin infections with group A streptococci. This requires maintenance of adequate penicillin levels in tissues for 10 days (eg, benzathine penicillin G, 1.2 million units given once intramuscularly). Erythromycin is an alternative drug of choice. Prompt eradication of streptococci from early infections can effectively prevent the development of poststreptococcal disease. (2) Antistreptococcal chemoprophylaxis in persons who have suffered an attack of rheumatic fever. This involves giving one injection of benzathine penicillin G, 1.2 million units intramuscularly every 3–4 weeks, or daily oral penicillin or oral sulfonamide. The first attack of rheumatic fever infrequently causes major heart damage. However, such persons are particularly susceptible to reinfections with streptococci that precipitate relapses of rheumatic activity and give rise to cardiac damage. Chemoprophylaxis in such individuals, especially children, must be continued for years. Chemoprophylaxis is not used in glomerulonephritis because of the small number of nephritogenic types of streptococci. An exception may be family groups with a high rate of poststreptococcal nephritis. (3) Eradica-

tion of group A streptococci from carriers. This is especially important when carriers are in "sensitive" areas, eg, obstetric delivery rooms, operating rooms, classrooms, or nurseries. Unfortunately, it is often difficult to eradicate hemolytic streptococci from permanent carriers, and individuals may occasionally have to be shifted away from "sensitive" areas for some time. (4) Dust control, ventilation, air filtration, ultraviolet light, and aerosol mists are all of doubtful efficacy in the control of streptococcal transmission. Milk should always be pasteurized. (5) Group B streptococci account for most cases of neonatal sepsis at present. They are derived from the mother's genital tract, where carriage is asymptomatic. Neonatal illness may be favored by deficiency of maternal antibody. Drug prophylaxis in mother and child has had some success in controlled studies in reducing group B infections.

THE PNEUMOCOCCI

The pneumococci *(Streptococcus pneumoniae)* are gram-positive diplococci, often lancet-shaped or arranged in chains, possessing a capsule of polysaccharide that permits easy "typing" with specific antisera. They are readily lysed by surface-active agents, eg, bile salts. Surface-active agents probably remove or inactivate the inhibitors of cell wall autolysins. The organisms are normal inhabitants of the upper respiratory tract of humans and can cause pneumonia, sinusitis, otitis, bronchitis, meningitis, and other infectious processes.

Morphology & Identification

A. Typical Organisms: The typical gram-positive, lancet-shaped diplococci (Figs 14–5, 14–6, 14–7) are often seen in specimens of young cultures. In sputum or pus, single cocci or chains are also seen. With age, the organisms rapidly become gram-negative and tend to lyse spontaneously.

Autolysis of pneumococci is greatly enhanced by surface-active agents. Lysis of pneumococci occurs in a few minutes when ox bile (10%) or sodium deoxycholate (2%) is added to a broth culture or suspension of organisms at neutral pH. Viridans streptococci do not lyse. The growth of pneumococci is inhibited on solid media around a disk of optochin (ethylhydrocupreine hydrochloride). These tests differentiate between pneumococci and other streptococci that produce alpha hemolysis.

B. Culture: Pneumococci form a small round colony, at first dome-shaped and later developing a central plateau with an elevated rim and alpha hemolysis on blood agar. Growth is enhanced by 5–10% CO_2.

Other identifying points include almost uniform virulence for mice when injected intraperitoneally and the "capsule swelling test," or quellung reaction (Fig 14–7).

C. Growth Characteristics: Most energy is ob-

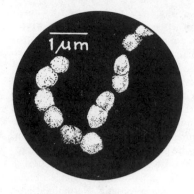

Figure 14 –5. Drawing from electron micrograph of pneumococci.

Figure 14 –6. Pneumococci in stained smear.

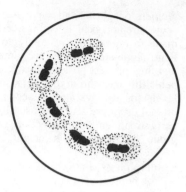

Figure 14 –7. Pneumococci mixed with type-specific antiserum (quellung reaction).

tained from fermentation of glucose, accompanied by the rapid production of lactic acid, which limits growth. Neutralization of broth cultures with alkali at intervals results in massive growth.

D. Variation: Any culture (bacterial population) of pneumococci contains a few organisms unable to produce capsular polysaccharide, which gives rise to rough colonies. The majority are polysaccharide-producing bacteria, which give rise to smooth colonies. Rough forms predominate if the culture is grown in type-specific antipolysaccharide serum.

E. Transformation: When a rough (polysaccharide-less) organism of one type is grown in the presence of DNA extracted from another pneumococcus type, smooth (encapsulated) organisms of the latter type are formed. Similar transformation reactions have been performed that involve changes in drug resistance.

Antigenic Structure

A. Component Structures: The capsular polysaccharide (SSS = specific soluble substance) is immunologically distinct for each of the more than 85 types. The polysaccharide is an antigen that primarily elicits a B cell response (see p 155).

The somatic portion of the pneumococcus contains an M protein that is characteristic for each type and a C carbohydrate that is common to all pneumococci. The C carbohydrate can be precipitated by C-reactive protein, a substance found in the serum of certain patients (see Chapter 26).

B. Quellung Reaction: When pneumococci of a certain type are mixed with an antiserum against that type (specific antipolysaccharide serum) on a microscope slide, the capsule swells markedly. This reaction is useful for quick identification and for "typing" of the organisms (Fig 14–7), either in sputum or in cultures. A polyvalent serum containing antibody to more than 80 types ("omniserum") is a quick method of establishing the presence of pneumococci in fresh sputum by means of microscopy.

Pathogenesis

A. Types of Pneumococci: In adults, types 1–8 are responsible for about 75% of cases of pneumococcal pneumonia and for more than half of all fatalities in pneumococcal bacteremia; in children, types 6, 14, 19, and 23 are frequent causes.

B. Production of Disease: Pneumococci produce disease through their ability to multiply in the tissues. They produce no toxins of significance. The "virulence" of the organism is a function of its capsule, which prevents or delays ingestion of encapsulated cells by phagocytes. A serum that contains antibodies against the type-specific polysaccharide (SSS) protects against infection. If such a serum is absorbed with SSS, it loses its protective power. Animals or humans immunized with a given type SSS are subsequently immune to that type and possess precipitating and opsonizing antibodies for that type SSS.

C. Loss of Natural Resistance: Since 40–70% of humans are at some time or other carriers of virulent pneumococci, the normal respiratory mucosa must possess great natural resistance to the pneumococcus. Among the factors that probably lower this resistance and thus predispose to pneumococcal infection are the following:

1. Abnormalities of the respiratory tract–Other infections (eg, viral) that damage surface cells; abnormal accumulations of mucus (eg, allergy), which protect pneumococci from phagocytosis; bronchial obstruction (eg, atelectasis); and respiratory tract injury due to irritants disturbing the mucociliary blanket.

2. Alcohol or drug intoxication, which depresses phagocytic activity, depresses the cough reflex, and facilitates aspiration of foreign material.

3. Abnormal circulatory dynamics (eg, pulmonary congestion, heart failure).

4. Malnutrition, general debility, sickle cell anemia, hyposplenism, nephrosis.

Pathology

Pneumococcal infection causes an outpouring of

fibrinous edema fluid into the alveoli, followed by red cells and leukocytes, which results in consolidation of portions of the lung. Many pneumococci are found throughout this exudate. The alveolar walls remain normally intact during the infection. Later, mononuclear cells actively phagocytose the debris, and this liquid phase is gradually reabsorbed. The pneumococci are taken up by phagocytes and digested intracellularly.

Clinical Findings

The onset of pneumococcal pneumonia is usually sudden, with fever, chills, and sharp pleural pain. The sputum is similar to the alveolar exudate, being characteristically bloody or rusty. Early in the disease, when the fever is high, bacteremia is present in 15–25% of cases. Before the days of chemotherapy, recovery from the disease began between the fifth and tenth days and was associated with the development of type-specific antibodies. The mortality rate was as high as 30%, depending on age and underlying illness. Bacteremic pneumonia always has the highest mortality rate. With antimicrobial therapy, the illness is terminated promptly; if drugs are given early, the development of consolidation is interrupted.

From the respiratory tract, pneumococci may reach other sites. The sinuses and middle ear are most frequently involved. From the bloodstream (or through extension from the mastoid), the meninges are reached. With the early use of chemotherapy, acute pneumococcal endocarditis has become rare. Pneumococcal pneumonia must be differentiated from pulmonary infarct, atelectasis, neoplasm, congestive heart failure, and pneumonia caused by many other bacteria. Empyema is the commonest complication and requires aspiration and drainage.

Diagnostic Laboratory Tests

Blood is drawn for culture, and sputum is collected for demonstration of pneumococci by smear and culture. Serum antibody tests are impractical. Sputum may be examined in several ways:

(1) Stained smears: Gram-stained film of rusty-red sputum shows typical organisms, many polymorphonuclear neutrophils, and many red cells.

(2) Capsule swelling tests: Fresh emulsified sputum mixed with antiserum gives "capsule swelling" for identification of pneumococci and possible typing.

(3) Culture: Sputum cultured on blood agar in candle jar. Blood culture.

(4) Injection of sputum intraperitoneally into white mice: Animals die in 18–48 hours; heart blood gives pure culture of pneumococci. Peritoneal exudate can be used for quellung reaction.

(5) Pneumococcal meningitis should be diagnosed by prompt examination and culture of cerebrospinal fluid.

Immunity

Immunity to infection with pneumococci is type-specific and depends both on antibodies to SSS and on intact phagocytic function. Vaccines can induce antibody to specific SSS (see below).

Treatment

Type-specific antiserum was formerly administered intravenously to patients who lacked antibodies. Absence of antibodies was determined by the absence of reaction upon intradermal injection of type-specific polysaccharide (Francis test).

Since pneumococci are sensitive to many antimicrobial drugs, early treatment results in rapid recovery, and antibody response seems to play a much diminished role. The penicillins are the drugs of choice. Recently, some drug resistance has appeared: pneumococci resistant to tetracyclines, erythromycin, and lincomycin have been isolated from patients. Pneumococci of greatly increased resistance to penicillin (minimum inhibitory concentration, 4 units/mL) have appeared in New Guinea and elsewhere and have produced hospital-centered outbreaks in South Africa. Some of these pneumococci are resistant to multiple drugs, but no plasmids or beta-lactamase production had been identified as of 1981.

Epidemiology, Prevention, & Control

Pneumococcal pneumonia accounts for about 60–80% of all bacterial pneumonias. It is an endemic disease with a high incidence of carriers. The predisposing factors (see above) are more important in the development of illness than exposure to the infectious agent, and the healthy carrier is more important in disseminating infection than the sick patient.

It is possible to immunize individuals with type-specific polysaccharides. Such vaccines can probably provide 90% protection against bacteremic pneumonia. Among workers in South African gold mines, vaccines containing 12 SSS types have given good antibody response and good protection against disease. A vaccine has also been developed that may particularly benefit children with sickle cell anemia or after splenectomy. It was licensed in the USA in 1977 and includes types 1, 2, 3, 4, 6, 8, 9, 12, 14, 19, 23, 25, 51, and 56. Such vaccines may also be appropriate for elderly, debilitated, or immunosuppressed individuals. In children under 2 years of age and in patients with lymphomas, pneumococcal vaccines have greatly reduced immunogenicity. In such high-risk patients, penicillin prophylaxis must accompany vaccination.

In addition, it is desirable to avoid "predisposing" factors, to establish the diagnosis promptly, and to begin adequate chemotherapy early. At present, fatalities (10%) from pneumococcal pneumonia are limited to young infants, persons older than age 50 years, persons with impaired natural resistance, and those with bacteremia.

THE NEISSERIAE

The neisseriae are a group of gram-negative cocci, usually occurring in pairs. Some members of the group are normal inhabitants of the human respiratory tract and occur extracellularly; others (gonococci, meningococci) are human pathogens and typically occur intracellularly. Members of the group are listed in Table 14–1.

Morphology & Identification

A. Typical Organisms: The typical neisseria organism is a gram-negative diplococcus, approximately 0.8 μm in diameter. Neisseriae are nonmotile and nonsporeforming. Individual cocci are kidney-shaped, with the flat or concave sides adjacent. Older cultures or those exposed to antibiotics may contain swollen, distorted organisms. Meningococci and gonococci autolyze quickly, particularly in an alkaline environment.

B. Culture: In 48 hours on enriched media (eg, Mueller-Hinton, Thayer-Martin), gonococci and meningococci form convex, glistening, elevated, mucoid colonies 1–5 mm in diameter. Colonies are transparent, nonpigmented or yellowish, and nonhemolytic. *Neisseria flavescens, Neisseria subflava,* and *Neisseria lactamica* have a yellow pigment. *Neisseria sicca* produces opaque, brittle, wrinkled colonies.

C. Growth Characteristics: Neisseriae are strict aerobes. They ferment a variety of carbohydrates, forming acid but not gas. Fermentation reactions are summarized in Table 14–1. They produce oxidase.

Meningococci and gonococci grow best on media containing complex organic substances such as blood or animal proteins and in an atmosphere containing 5% CO_2 (eg, candle jar). They are inhibited by some toxic constituents of the medium, such as fatty acids or salts. They are rapidly killed by drying, sunlight, moist heat, and many disinfectants but may survive freezing. They produce autolytic enzymes that result in rapid swelling and lysis in vitro.

NEISSERIA MENINGITIDIS
(Meningococcus)

Antigenic Structure

By agglutination and agglutinin-absorption tests, meningococci can be classified into 4 main groups, designated as A, B, C, and D. Additional serogroups are called X, Y, and Z. Most strains from outbreaks are now A, B, C, or Y. Polysaccharides specific for groups A, B, and C have been isolated. The group A polysaccharide is a polymer of N-acetylmannosamine phosphate. The group C polysaccharide is a polymer of N-acetyl-O-acetylneuraminic acid. Meningococcal antigens are found in blood and cerebrospinal fluid of active severe cases.

The nucleoproteins of meningococci (P substance) have some toxic effect but are not specific for these organisms. Certain DNA extracts are capable of "transformation reactions," inducing streptomycin resistance in meningococci. The composition of cell walls of meningococci resembles that of coliforms; they contain a group-reactive antigen.

Pathogenesis, Pathology, & Clinical Findings

Humans are the only natural hosts for whom meningococci are pathogenic. Mice can be infected intraperitoneally if meningococci of any serologic group are suspended in mucin.

The nasopharynx is the portal of entry of meningococci. There the organisms may form part of the transient flora without producing symptoms or may produce an exudative pharyngitis. From the nasopharynx, organisms may reach the bloodstream, producing a bacteremia (meningococcemia) with high fever and a hemorrhagic rash. There may be fulminant sepsis, disseminated intravascular coagulation, and circulatory collapse (Waterhouse-Friderichsen syndrome). *Neisseria* bacteremia is favored by absence of bactericidal antibody (IgG) or its inhibition by a blocking IgA antibody or a complement deficiency (C6, C7, or C8).

Meningitis is the commonest complication of meningococcemia. It usually begins very suddenly, with intense headache, vomiting, and stiff neck, and progresses to coma within a few hours.

During meningococcemia, there is thrombosis of many small blood vessels in many organs, with perivascular infiltration and petechial hemorrhages.

Table 14–1. Fermentation reactions of neisseriae.

	Dextrose	Acid Formed From			Reduction of	
		Maltose	Sucrose	Lactose	NO₃	NO₂
N meningitidis	+	+	−	−	−	var.
N gonorrhoeae	+	−	−	−	−	−
N sicca	+	+	+	−	−	+
N flavescens	−	−	−	−	−	+
N lactamica	+	+	−	+	−	+
*N catarrhalis**	−	−	−	−	+	+

*Now *Branhamella catarrhalis.* Additional species: *N mucosa, N subflava.*

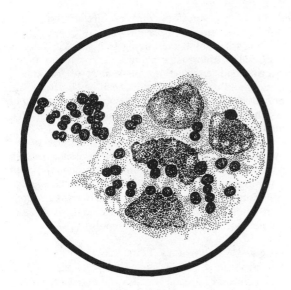

Figure 14–8. Meningococci within a polymorphonuclear leukocyte in spinal fluid.

There may be interstitial myocarditis, arthritis, and skin lesions. In meningitis, the meninges are acutely inflamed, with thrombosis of blood vessels and exudation of polymorphonuclear leukocytes, so that the surface of the brain is covered with a thick purulent exudate.

It is not known what transforms an asymptomatic infection of the nasopharynx into meningococcemia and meningitis, but this can be prevented by specific bactericidal serum antibodies against the infecting strain. Meningococci are readily phagocytosed in the presence of a specific opsonin.

Diagnostic Laboratory Tests

Specimens of blood are taken for culture, and specimens of spinal fluid are taken for smear, culture, and chemical determinations. Nasopharyngeal swab cultures are suitable for carrier surveys. Puncture material from petechiae may be taken for smear and culture.

A. Smears: Gram's stain of the sediment of centrifuged spinal fluid or of petechial aspirate often shows typical *Neisseria* within polymorphonuclear leukocytes or extracellularly. Because meningococci may autolyze rapidly, the fluid must be examined fresh.

B. Culture: Specimens must be promptly plated on heated blood agar (chocolate agar) or Thayer-Martin medium and incubated at 37 °C in an atmosphere of 5% CO_2 (candle jar). A modified Thayer-Martin medium with antibiotics (VCN: vancomycin, colistin, nystatin) favors the growth of neisseriae and inhibits many other bacteria. Spinal fluid or blood generally yields pure cultures that can be further identified by carbohydrate fermentation (see Table 14–1) and agglutination with type-specific (or polyvalent) serum. Direct incubation of freshly drawn spinal fluid at 37 °C may give growth of meningococci.

Colonies of meningococci on solid media, particularly in mixed culture, may be identified by the oxidase test: when the plate is sprayed with tetramethylparaphenylenediamine hydrochloride, meningococcus (and other *Neisseria*) colonies rapidly turn dark purple.

C. Serology: Antibodies to meningococcal polysaccharides can be measured by latex agglutination or hemagglutination tests or by their bactericidal activity.

Immunity

Immunity to meningococcal infection is associated with the presence of specific bactericidal antibodies in the serum. These antibodies develop after subclinical infections with different strains or injection of antigens and are group-specific. The immunizing antigens for groups A and C are the capsular polysaccharides. For group B, the immunizing antigen is not well defined but may constitute membrane proteins. Infants may have passive immunity through IgG antibodies transferred from the mother.

Treatment

Meningococci formerly were uniformly susceptible to sulfonamides, and these were the drugs of choice. Sulfonamide-resistant meningococci are now prevalent, comprising 50–70% of all isolates. Penicillin G has become the drug of choice—or chloramphenicol in persons allergic to penicillins. Antimeningococcus serum is no longer employed therapeutically. High levels of meningococcal antigen in cerebrospinal fluid are associated with neurologic damage.

Epidemiology, Prevention, & Control

Meningococcal meningitis occurs in epidemic waves (eg, military installations; in Brazil, there were more than 15,000 cases in 1974) and a smaller number of sporadic interepidemic cases. Five to 30% of the normal population may harbor meningococci (often nontypable isolates) in the nasopharynx during interepidemic periods. During epidemics, the carrier rate goes up to 70 or 80%. A rise in the number of cases is always preceded by an increased number of respiratory "carriers." In the past, widespread chemoprophylaxis with sulfonamides was successful. Since the appearance of many sulfonamide-resistant meningococci, this is no longer possible. Treatment with penicillin does not eradicate the carrier state. Rifampin, 600 mg twice daily by mouth for 2 days (or minocycline, 100 mg every 12 hours), can often eradicate the carrier state and serve as chemoprophylaxis for household and other close contacts.

Clinical cases of meningitis present only a negligible source of infection, and isolation has therefore only limited usefulness. More important is the reduction of personal contacts in a population with a high "carrier" rate. This is accomplished by good ventilation and avoidance of crowding. Specific polysaccharides of groups A and C can stimulate antibody response and protect susceptible persons against infection. Such vaccines are currently used in selected populations (eg, the military; civilian epidemics). Rifampin prophylaxis is advised for heavily exposed persons.

NEISSERIA GONORRHOEAE
(Gonococcus)

Morphologically and in its behavior in cultures, the gonococcus resembles the meningococcus; however, it does not ferment maltose and differs antigenically. The current epidemic of gonorrhea is associated with a great variety of clinical manifestations.

Antigenic Structure

Gonococci are serologically heterogeneous. The pili in colony types 1 and 2 are immunologically specific but fall into 16 or more antigenic types. Gonococci possess polysaccharides and nucleoproteins similar to those of other neisseriae. Gonococci possess a capsule demonstrated by negative staining. Some immunologic specificity resides in proteins of the "outer membrane complex."

Pathogenesis, Pathology, & Clinical Findings

Gonococci exhibit 4 morphologic types of colonies. Only types 1 and 2 appear to be virulent and possess pili that attach to epithelial cells and help to resist phagocytosis.

Gonococci contain several plasmids; at least one small plasmid (MW 4.5×10^6) carries the gene for beta-lactamase production that makes the gonococcus resistant to penicillin. These plasmids are transmissible by conjugation among gonococci; they may have been acquired from *Haemophilus* or other gram-negative organisms.

Gonococci attach to surface epithelial cells with pili but can be blocked by antipilus antibody. Some gonococci secrete proteases that can break down surface IgA antibodies.

Gonococci attack mucous membranes of the genitourinary tract and the eye, producing acute suppuration that may lead to tissue invasion; this is followed by chronic inflammation and fibrosis. In the male, there is usually urethritis, with yellow, creamy pus and painful urination. The process may extend to the prostate and epididymis. As suppuration subsides, there is fibrosis, sometimes leading to urethral strictures. Urethral infection in men can be asymptomatic. In the female, the infection extends from urethra and vagina to cervix, giving rise to mucopurulent discharge. It may then progress to the oviducts, causing pelvic inflammatory disease, fibrosis, and obliteration of tubes, with consequent sterility. Chronic gonococcal cervicitis or proctitis is often asymptomatic. Gonococci that produce localized infection are often serum-sensitive and relatively resistant to antimicrobials. By contrast, gonococci that enter the bloodstream and produce disseminated infection are usually serum-resistant and quite susceptible to penicillin and other drugs and have specific nutritional

requirements (eg, they may require arginine, hypoxanthine, and uracil for growth).

Gonococcal bacteremia leads to skin lesions (especially hemorrhagic papules and pustules) and to arthritis and tenosynovitis (especially of the knees, ankles, and wrists). Gonococci can be cultured from only 30% of patients with gonococcal arthritis. Other lesions include proctitis, pharyngitis, endocarditis, meningitis, and eye involvement.

Ophthalmia neonatorum, an infection of the eye of the newborn, is acquired during passage through an infected birth canal. The initial conjunctivitis rapidly progresses to involve all structures of the eye and commonly results in blindness. To avoid this disaster, instillation of silver nitrate into the conjunctival sac of the newborn has been made compulsory.

Diagnostic Laboratory Tests

Pus and secretions are taken from the urethra, cervix, prostate, rectal mucosa, or throat for culture and smear. Synovial fluid is sometimes examined in the same way. Blood culture is necessary in systemic illness.

A. Stained Smears: In the acute stage, Gram's stains of smears reveal many intracellular diplococci within pus cells. These give a presumptive diagnosis. In the later, chronic stages, when the secretions are thinner and contain few pus cells, gonococci are often difficult to find and reliance must be placed on culture. Cultured organisms can be quickly identified by immunofluorescence staining.

B. Cultures: Immediately after collection, pus or mucus is streaked on a rich selective medium (eg, Thayer-Martin VCN medium—*Public Health Rep* 1966;**81**:559) and incubated in an atmosphere containing 5% CO_2 (candle jar) at 37 °C. Forty-eight hours later, colonies are subjected to the oxidase test (see above). Subcultures of the organisms may be identified by fermentation reactions (Table 14–1) or by immunofluorescence staining. To avoid overgrowth by contaminants, the culture medium should contain antimicrobial drugs (eg, vancomycin, 3 μg/mL; colistin, 7.5 μg/mL; amphotericin B, 1 μg/mL; and trimethoprim, 3 μg/mL). If immediate incubation is not possible, the specimen should be placed in Transgrow or a similar transport medium.

C. Serology: Antibodies are formed to pili, to various outer membrane proteins, and perhaps to endotoxin fractions. Some IgM of human sera is bactericidal for gonococci in vitro. Gonococci resistant to this serum effect are likely to produce disseminated infection, be susceptible to penicillin and other drugs, and belong to specific auxotypes (ie, be nutritionally deficient) (see above).

In infected individuals, antibodies to gonococcal pili and outer membrane proteins can be detected by several serologic methods, including radioimmunoassay and the ELISA (enzyme-linked immunosorbent assay) test. As yet, however, these tests lack specificity and have little reliability as diagnostic aids.

Immunity

Repeated infections and relapses are the rule rather than the exception in gonococcal infections; resistance to reinfection does not appear to develop as part of the disease process. While a variety of antibodies can be demonstrated, these either are highly strain-specific or have little protective ability—even the IgA on the mucosal surfaces.

Treatment

Local irrigation of the urethra has little effect. Many strains of gonococci are resistant to sulfonamides and to trimethoprim-sulfamethoxazole. During the past 30 years, resistance to penicillin G has gradually risen (presumably by the selection of chromosomal mutants), so that now many strains require 2 units of penicillin G per milliliter for inhibition. This has led to a gradual rise in the recommended dose for treatment: in 1982, a dose of 4.8 million units of procaine penicillin intramuscularly with 1 g probenecid orally is recommended for acute infections.

In 1976, beta-lactamase–producing gonococci made their first appearance. These organisms may have acquired the plasmid that controls enzyme production from *Haemophilus* or some other gram-negative bacteria. By early 1977, these totally penicillin-resistant gonococcal strains had appeared in many parts of the world, but their frequency was still low except in special populations (eg, prostitutes in the Philippines, with a 50% incidence). However, focal outbreaks of beta-lactamase–producing gonococci have occurred in 1980 in California, New York, and elsewhere, and endemic foci are being established. Such infections may require increased use of spectinomycin or—in case of pharyngitis—trimethoprim-sulfamethoxazole in large doses for 5 days. Alternatively, 5-day courses of oral tetracyclines may be effective. Cefoxitin, 1 g intramuscularly twice with an interval of 5 hours between injections, can cure urethritis, cervicitis, and rectal carriage but *not* oropharyngeal gonococcal infection.

Most cases of severe disseminated gonorrhea are still caused by penicillin-susceptible strains, and penicillin G, 10 million units daily for 5–10 days,

seems acceptable therapy. In chronic salpingitis, prostatitis, and other long-established infections, longer courses of treatment are suggested.

In all types of gonorrhea, cure must be established by repeated follow-up, including cultures from involved sites. Since other sexually transmitted diseases may have been acquired at the same time (see discussion of chlamydiae, syphilis, etc), appropriate diagnostic steps must also be taken.

Epidemiology, Prevention, & Control

Gonorrhea is worldwide in distribution, and its incidence has risen steadily since 1955. It is almost exclusively transmitted by sexual contact, principally by women and men harboring asymptomatic chronic infections. The infectivity of the organism is such that a single exposure to an infected sexual partner has a 20–30% chance (or greater) of resulting in infection. The infection rate can be reduced by avoiding sexual promiscuity, rapidly eradicating gonococci from infected individuals by means of early diagnosis and treatment, and finding cases and contacts through education and screening of populations at high risk. The development of a specific serologic test will be crucial for large-scale screening of asymptomatic infections. Mechanical prophylaxis (condoms) provides only partial protection. Chemoprophylaxis cannot be relied upon because of the rise in antibiotic resistance of the gonococcus.

Ophthalmia neonatorum is prevented by the local application to the conjunctiva of the newborn of a substance bactericidal for gonococci on contact, eg, 1% silver nitrate.

OTHER NEISSERIAE

Neisseria (now *Branhamella*) *catarrhalis* and *N sicca* are normal members of the flora of the respiratory tract, particularly the nasopharynx, and do not produce disease. The pigmented neisseriae (*N subflava, N flavescens, N lactamica*) occupy a similar position, but these organisms may on rare occasions cause meningitis or endocarditis.

● ● ●

References

AHA Committee Report: Prevention of rheumatic fever. *Circulation* 1977;**55**:S1.

Ammann AJ et al: Polyvalent pneumococcal polysaccharide immunization in patients with sickle-cell anemia or splenectomy. *N Engl J Med* 1977;**297**:897.

Austrian R: Random gleanings from a life with the pneumococcus. *J Infect Dis* 1975;**131**:474.

Beachey EH, Ofek I: Epithelial cell binding of group A streptococci by lipoteichoic acid on fimbriae. *J Exp Med* 1976;**143**:759.

Berry FA et al: Transient bacteremia during dental manipulation. *Pediatrics* 1973;**51**:476.

Biwas GD et al: High-frequency conjugal transfer of a gonococcal penicillinase plasmid. *J Bacteriol* 1980;**143**:1318.

Brooks GF et al (editors): *Immunobiology of Neisseria gonorrhoeae: Proceedings of a Conference Held in San Francisco, CA, 18—20 Jan 1978.* American Society for Microbiology, 1978.

Broome CV et al: Pneumococcal disease after pneumococcal vaccination. *N Engl J Med* 1980;**303**:549.

Buchanan TM et al: Quantitative determination of antibody to gonococcal pili: Changes in antibody levels with gonococcal infection. *J Clin Invest* 1973;**52**:2896.

Centers for Disease Control: Gonorrhea: CDC-recommended treatment schedules, 1979. *J Infect Dis* 1979;**139**:496.

Facklam RR: Physiological differentiation of viridans streptococci. *J Clin Microbiol* 1977;**5**:184.

Ferrieri P et al: Natural history of impetigo. *J Clin Invest* 1972; **51**:2851.

Fuchs PC et al: CAMP test for presumptive identification of group B streptococci. *J Clin Microbiol* 1978;**7**:232.

Goldschneider I et al: Immunogenicity of group A and group C meningococcal polysaccharides. *J Infect Dis* 1972;**125**:509.

Handsfield HH et al: Asymptomatic gonorrhea in men. *N Engl J Med* 1974;**290**:117.

Handsfield HH et al: Correlation of auxotype and penicillin susceptibility of *Neisseria gonorrhoeae* with sexual preference and clinical manifestations of gonorrhea. *Sex Transm Dis* 1980;**7**:1.

Harder EJ et al: *Streptococcus mutans* endocarditis. *Ann Intern Med* 1974;**80**:364.

Hyams PJ et al: Staphylococcal bacteremia and hexachlorophene bathing: An epidemic in a newborn nursery. *Am J Dis Child* 1975;**129**:595.

Ingram DL et al: Group B streptococcal disease. *Am J Dis Child* 1980;**134**:754.

Jacobs MR et al: Emergence of multiply-resistant pneumococci. *N Engl J Med* 1978;**299**:735.

Jones RB et al: Cefoxitin in the treatment of gonorrhea. *Sex Transm Dis* 1979;**6**:239.

Kaplan EL et al: Immunologic response to group A streptococcal upper respiratory tract infections in very young children. *J Pediatr* 1980;**96**:374.

Kaplan EL et al: Prevention of bacterial endocarditis. (Letter.) *Circulation* 1977;**56**:A139.

Melish ME et al: The staphylococcal scalded-skin syndrome. *J Infect Dis* 1972;**125**:129.

Merrill CW et al: Rapid identification of pneumococci. *N Engl J Med* 1973;**288**:510.

Merrill JP: Glomerulonephritis. (3 parts.) *N Engl J Med* 1974; **290**:275, 313, 374.

Moellering RC et al: Endocarditis due to group D streptococci. *Am J Med* 1974;**57**:239.

Musher DM et al: Infections due to *Staphylococcus aureus*. *Medicine* 1977;**56**:383.

Peacock JE et al: Methicillin-resistant *S aureus:* Introduction and spread within a hospital. *Ann Intern Med* 1980;**93**:526.

Petersen BH et al: *Neisseria meningitidis* and *Neisseria gonorrhoeae* bacteremia associated with C6, C7, or C8 deficiency. *Ann Intern Med* 1979;**90**:917.

Peterson PK et al: Effect of protein A on staphylococcal opsonization. *Infect Immun* 1977;**15**:760.

Punsalang AP, Sawyer WD: Role of pili in virulence of *N gonorrhoeae*. *Infect Immun* 1973;**8**:255.

Recent advances in rheumatic fever control and future prospects: A WHO memorandum. *Bull WHO* 1978;**56**:887.

Shands KN et al: Toxic-shock syndrome in menstruating women. *N Engl J Med* 1980;**303**:1436.

Sparling PF et al: Summary of the conference on penicillin-resistant gonococci. *J Infect Dis* 1977;**135**:865.

Stewart GC, Rosenblum ED: Transduction of methicillin resistance in *Staphylococcus aureus*. *Antimicrob Agents Chemother* 1980;**18**:424.

Stollerman GH: Streptococcal vaccines revisited. *J Lab Clin Med* 1978;**91**:872.

Sumaya CV et al: Pneumococcal vaccine failures. *Am J Dis Child* 1981;**135**:155.

Tuazon CU: Teichoic acid antibodies in the diagnosis of serious infections with *Staphylococcus aureus*. *Ann Intern Med* 1976; **84**:543.

Van de Rijn I et al: Group A streptococcal antigens cross-reactive with myocardium. *J Exp Med* 1977;**146**:579.

Waldvogel FA, Vasey V: Osteomyelitis: The past decade. *N Engl J Med* 1980;**303**:360.

Wallmark G et al: *Staphylococcus saprophyticus:* A frequent cause of acute urinary tract infection among female outpatients. *J Infect Dis* 1978;**138**:791.

Wannamaker LW: Changing concepts in the biology of group A streptococci and in the epidemiology of streptococcal infections. *Rev Infect Dis* 1979;**1**:967.

Washington J: Nutritionally variant streptococci. *Ann Intern Med* 1977;**87**:793.

Weinstein L: "Modern" infective endocarditis. *JAMA* 1975; **233**:260.

Wilson WR et al: Short-term therapy for streptococcal infective endocarditis. *JAMA* 1981;**245**:360.

AEROBIC SPOREFORMING BACILLI

ANTHRAX

The genus *Bacillus* includes large gram-positive rods occurring in chains. They form spores and are aerobes. Most members of this genus are saprophytic organisms prevalent in soil, water, and air and on vegetation, such as *Bacillus cereus* and *Bacillus subtilis*. Some are insect pathogens. *B cereus* can grow in foods and produce an enterotoxin that causes diarrhea by a mechanism similar to that of *Escherichia coli* enterotoxin. Such organisms rarely produce disease in humans (eg, meningitis, endocarditis, endophthalmitis, conjunctivitis, or acute gastroenteritis). *Bacillus anthracis* is the principal pathogen of the genus.

Morphology & Identification

A. Typical Organisms: The typical cells, measuring $1 \times 3-4$ μm, have square ends and are arranged in long chains; spores are located in the center of the nonmotile bacilli.

B. Culture: Colonies are round and have a "cut glass" appearance in transmitted light. Hemolysis is uncommon with anthrax but common with the saprophytic bacilli. Gelatin is liquefied, and growth in gelatin stabs resembles an inverted fir tree.

C. Growth Characteristics: The saprophytic bacilli utilize simple sources of nitrogen and carbon for energy and growth. The spores are resistant to environmental changes, withstand dry heat and certain chemical disinfectants for moderate periods, and persist for years in dry earth. Animal products contaminated with anthrax spores (eg, hides, bristles, hair, wool, bone) can be sterilized by autoclaving.

D. Variation: Variation occurs with respect to virulence, spore formation, and colony form. (In general, virulence is associated with rough colonies.) To minimize variation, living spore suspensions are employed to preserve unstable properties such as virulence.

Antigenic Structure

The capsular substance of *B anthracis*, which consists of a polypeptide of high molecular weight composed of D-glutamic acid, is a hapten. The bacterial bodies contain protein and a somatic polysaccharide, both of which are antigenic.

Pathogenesis

Anthrax is primarily a disease of sheep, cattle, horses, and many other animals; humans are affected only rarely. The infection is usually acquired by the entry of spores through injured skin or mucous membranes, rarely by inhalation of spores into the lung. In animals, the portal of entry is the mouth and the gastrointestinal tract. The spores from contaminated soil find easy access when ingested with spiny or irritating vegetation. In humans, scratches in the skin favor infection.

The spores germinate in the tissue at the site of entry, and growth of the vegetative organisms results in formation of a gelatinous edema and congestion. Bacilli spread via lymphatics to the bloodstream, and they multiply freely in the blood and tissues shortly before and after the death of the animal. In the plasma of animals dying from anthrax, a toxic factor has been demonstrated. This material kills mice or guinea pigs upon inoculation and is specifically neutralized by anthrax antiserum. Its nature is still uncertain.

The exudate in anthrax contains a polypeptide, identical with that in the capsule of the bacillus, which

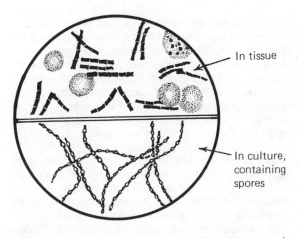

Figure 15–1. Anthrax bacilli in a smear from tissue or culture.

In tissue

In culture, containing spores

is able to evoke histologic reactions similar to those of anthrax infection. Other proteins isolated from exudate stimulate solid immunity to anthrax upon injection into animals. From culture filtrates ("anthrax toxin"), 3 substances have been separated by glass filtration and chromatography: (1) "protective antigen" (a protein), (2) "edema factor," and (3) "toxic factor." Mixtures of (1), (2), and (3) are more toxic in animals, and such mixtures are more immunogenic than single substances.

Another type of anthrax is inhalation anthrax ("woolsorter's disease"). The inhalation of anthrax spores from the dust of wool, hair, or hides results in germination of the spores in the lungs or in tracheobronchial lymph nodes and the production of hemorrhagic mediastinitis, pneumonia, meningitis, and sepsis, which is usually rapidly fatal. In anthrax sepsis, the number of organisms in the blood exceeds 10^7/mL just prior to death.

Pathology

In susceptible animals, the organisms proliferate at the site of entry. The capsules remain intact, and the organisms are surrounded by a large amount of proteinaceous fluid containing few leukocytes from which they rapidly disseminate and reach the bloodstream.

In resistant animals, the organisms proliferate for a few hours, by which time there is massive accumulation of leukocytes. The capsules gradually disintegrate and disappear. The organisms remain localized.

Clinical Findings

In humans, anthrax gives rise to an infection of the skin (malignant pustule). A papule first develops within 12–36 hours after entry of the organisms or spores through a scratch. This papule rapidly changes into a vesicle, then a pustule, and finally a necrotic ulcer from which the infection may disseminate, giving rise to septicemia.

In inhalation anthrax, early manifestations may be mediastinitis, sepsis, meningitis, or hemorrhagic pulmonary edema. Hemorrhagic pneumonia with shock is a terminal event.

While animals often acquire anthrax through ingestion of spores and spread of the organisms from the intestinal tract, this is exceedingly rare in humans. Thus, abdominal pain, vomiting, and bloody diarrhea are rare clinical signs.

Diagnostic Laboratory Tests

A. Specimens: Fluid or pus from local lesion; blood, sputum.

B. Stained Smears: From the local lesion or blood of dead animals; chains of large gram-positive rods are often seen. Identification of anthrax in smears by immunofluorescence techniques is possible at the Centers for Disease Control, Atlanta 30333.

C. Culture: When grown on blood agar plates, the organisms produce nonhemolytic gray colonies with typical microscopic morphology. Carbohydrate fermentation is not useful. In semisolid medium, an-

thrax bacilli are always nonmotile, whereas related nonpathogenic organisms (B cereus) exhibit motility by "swarming." Virulent anthrax cultures kill mice or guinea pigs upon intraperitoneal injection.

D. Ascoli Test: Extracts of infected tissues show a ring of precipitate when layered over immune serum.

E. Serologic Tests: Precipitating or hemagglutinating antibodies can be demonstrated in the serum of vaccinated or infected persons.

Resistance & Immunity

Some animals are highly susceptible (guinea pig), whereas others are very resistant (rat) to anthrax infection. This fact has been attributed to a variety of defense mechanisms: leukocytic activity, body temperature, and the bactericidal action of the blood. Certain basic polypeptides that kill anthrax bacilli have been isolated from animal tissues. A synthetic polylysine has a similar action.

Active immunity to anthrax can be induced in susceptible animals by vaccination with live attenuated bacilli, with spore suspensions, or with protective antigens from culture filtrates (see above). Immune serum is sometimes injected, together with live bacilli, into animals. Anthrax immunization is based on the classic experiments of Louis Pasteur, who in 1881 proved that cultures that had been grown in broth at 42–52 °C for several months lost much of their virulence and could be injected live into sheep and cattle without causing disease; subsequently, such animals proved to be immune. There are great variations in the efficacy of various vaccines, and protection is often far from complete or lasting.

Treatment

Many antibiotics are effective against anthrax in humans, but treatment must be started early. Penicillin is satisfactory treatment except in treatment of inhalation anthrax, in which the mortality rate remains high. Some other gram-positive bacilli may be resistant to penicillin by virtue of beta-lactamase production. Tetracyclines or erythromycin may be effective.

Epidemiology, Prevention, & Control

Soil is contaminated with anthrax spores from the carcasses of dead animals. These spores remain viable for decades. Perhaps spores can germinate in soil at pH 6.5 at proper temperature. Grazing animals infected through injured mucous membranes serve to perpetuate the chain of infection. Contact with infected animals or with their hides, hair, and bristles is the source of infection in humans. Control measures include (1) disposal of animal carcasses by burning or by deep burial in lime pits, (2) decontamination (usually by autoclaving) of animal products, (3) protective clothing and gloves for handling potentially infected materials, and (4) active immunization of domestic animals with live attenuated vaccines. Persons with high occupational risk should be immunized with a cell-free vaccine obtainable from the Centers for Disease Control, Atlanta 30333.

ANAEROBIC SPOREFORMING BACILLI

THE CLOSTRIDIA

The clostridia are anaerobic, gram-positive rods that form spores. Many decompose proteins or form toxins, and some do both. Their natural habitat is the soil or the intestinal tract of animals and humans. Most species are saprophytic organisms in the soil. Among the pathogens are the organisms causing botulism, tetanus, and gas gangrene.

Morphology & Identification

A. Typical Organisms: All species of clostridia are large, gram-positive rods, and all can produce spores. The spores are usually wider than the diameter of the rods in which they are formed. In *Clostridium tetani*, the spore is located at one end of the rod, giving it a drumstick appearance. In the various species, the spore is placed centrally, subterminally, or terminally. Most species of clostridia are motile and possess peritrichous flagella.

B. Culture: Clostridia grow only under anaerobic conditions, established by one of the following means.

1. Agar plates or culture tubes are placed in an airtight jar from which air is removed and replaced by nitrogen with 10% CO_2, or oxygen may be removed by other means (Gaspack).

2. Fluid media are put in deep tubes containing either fresh animal tissue (eg, chopped cooked meat) or 0.1% agar and a reducing agent such as thioglycolate. Such tubes can be handled like aerobic media, and growth will occur from the bottom up to within 15 mm of the surface exposed to air.

C. Colony Forms: Some organisms produce large raised colonies with entire margins (eg, *Clostridium perfringens*); others produce smaller colonies that extend in a meshwork of fine filaments (eg, *C tetani*). Most species produce a zone of hemolysis on blood agar.

D. Growth Characteristics: The outstanding characteristic of anaerobic bacilli is their inability to utilize oxygen as the final hydrogen acceptor. They lack cytochrome and cytochrome oxidase and are unable to break down hydrogen peroxide because they lack catalase and peroxidase. Therefore, H_2O_2 tends to accumulate to toxic concentrations in the presence of oxygen. Clostridia and other obligate anaerobes probably also lack superoxide dismutase and consequently permit the accumulation of the toxic free radical superoxide. Such anaerobes can carry out their metabolic reactions only at a negative oxidation-reduction potential (E_h), ie, in an environment that is strongly reducing.

Clostridia can ferment a variety of sugars; many can digest proteins. Milk is turned acid by some and digested by others and undergoes "stormy fermentation" (ie, clot torn by gas) with a third group (eg, *C*

perfringens). Various enzymes are produced by different species (see below).

E. Antigenic Characteristics: Clostridia share some antigens but also possess specific soluble antigens that permit grouping by precipitin tests.

CLOSTRIDIUM BOTULINUM

This microorganism is worldwide in distribution; it is found in soil and occasionally in animal feces.

Types of *C botulinum* are distinguished by the antigenic type of toxin they produce. Spores of the organism are highly resistant to heat, withstanding 100 °C for at least 3–5 hours. Heat resistance is diminished at acid pH or high salt concentration.

Toxin

During the growth of *C botulinum* and during autolysis of the bacteria, toxin is liberated into the environment. Seven distinct antigenic varieties of toxin—A–G—are known. Types A, B and E are most commonly associated with human illness. Type C produces limberneck in fowl; type D, botulism in cattle. Types A, B, and E toxins have been purified and fractionated to yield a neurotoxic protein (MW 150,000). These are among the most highly toxic substances known: The lethal dose for a human is probably about 1–2 μg. The toxins are destroyed by heating for 20 minutes at 100 °C. Toxin production is under control of a viral gene. Some toxigenic *C botulinum* strains yield bacteriophages that may infect nontoxigenic strains and convert them to toxigenicity.

Pathogenesis

Although *C botulinum* types A and B have been implicated in rare cases of wound infection and botulism, the illness is not an infection. Botulism is an intoxication resulting from the ingestion of food in which *C botulinum* has grown and produced toxin.

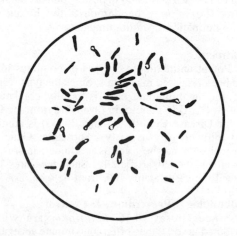

Figure 15–2. *C botulinum* from broth grown under anaerobic conditions.

The most common offenders are spiced, smoked, vacuum-packed, or canned alkaline foods that are eaten without cooking. In such foods, spores of *C botulinum* germinate; under anaerobic conditions, vegetative forms grow and produce toxin.

The toxin acts by blocking release of acetylcholine at synapses and neuromuscular junctions. Flaccid paralysis results. The electromyogram and edrophonium (Tensilon) strength tests are typical.

Clinical Findings

Symptoms begin 18–96 hours after ingestion of the toxic food, with visual disturbances (incoordination of eye muscles, double vision), inability to swallow, and speech difficulty; signs of bulbar paralysis are progressive, and death occurs from respiratory paralysis or cardiac arrest. Gastrointestinal symptoms are not regularly prominent. There is no fever. The patient remains fully conscious until shortly before death. The fatality rate is high. Patients who recover do not develop antitoxin in the blood.

Occasionally, infants in the first months of life develop weakness, signs of paralysis, and electromyographic evidence of botulism. *C botulinum* and botulinus toxin are found in feces but not in serum. It is assumed that *C botulinum* grew in the gut and produced toxin. Most of these infants recover with supportive therapy alone. However, infant botulism may be one of the causes of sudden infant death syndrome. The feeding of honey has been implicated as a possible cause of infant botulism.

Diagnostic Laboratory Tests

Toxin can occasionally be demonstrated in serum from the patient, and toxin may be found in leftover food. Mice injected intraperitoneally die rapidly. The antigenic type of toxin is identified by neutralization with specific antitoxin in mice. *C botulinum* may be grown from food remains and tested for toxin production, but this is rarely done and is of questionable significance. In infant botulism, *C botulinum* and toxin can be demonstrated in bowel contents but not in serum. Toxin may be demonstrated by passive hemagglutination or radioimmunoassay.

Treatment

Potent antitoxins to 3 types of botulinus toxins have been prepared in animals. Since the type responsible for an individual case is usually not known, trivalent (A, B, E) antitoxin (available from the Centers for Disease Control, Atlanta 30333) is administered intravenously as early as possible. Guanidine hydrochloride may be given as an adjunct, and respiration is maintained artificially. Such measures have reduced the case fatality rate from 65% to 25%.

Epidemiology, Prevention, & Control

Since spores of *C botulinum* are widely distributed in soils, they often contaminate vegetables, fruits, and other materials. When such foods are canned or otherwise preserved, they either must be sufficiently heated to ensure destruction of spores or must be boiled before consumption. Strict regulation of commercial canning has largely overcome the danger of large outbreaks, but commercially canned mushrooms and vichyssoise have caused deaths. At present, the chief danger lies in home-canned foods, particularly string beans, corn, peppers, olives, peas, and smoked fish or vacuum-packed fresh fish in plastic bags. Toxic foods may be spoiled and rancid, and cans may "swell"; or the appearance may be innocuous. Home-canned foods should be boiled for more than 20 minutes before consumption. Toxoids are used for active immunization of cattle in South Africa.

CLOSTRIDIUM TETANI

C tetani is worldwide in distribution in the soil and in the feces of horses and other animals. Several types of *C tetani* can be distinguished by specific flagellar antigens. All share a common O (somatic) antigen, which may be masked, and all produce the same antigenic type of toxin. L forms of *C tetani* also produce toxin.

Toxin

Vegetative cells of *C tetani* produce toxin and release it mainly when they lyse. The intracellular toxin is a polypeptide (MW 160,000) that proteolytic enzymes split into 2 fragments of increased toxicity. Purified toxin contains more than 2×10^7 mouse lethal doses per milligram. The toxin, called tetanospasmin, acts in several ways upon the central nervous system. It inhibits release of acetylcholine, thus interfering with neuromuscular transmission, and it can be fixed to cerebral gangliosides. The most important action, however, is the inhibition of postsynaptic spinal neurons by blocking the release of an inhibitory mediator. This results in generalized muscular spasms, hyperreflexia, and seizures.

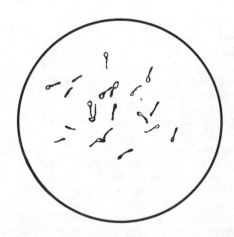

Figure 15–3. *C tetani* from blood agar grown under anaerobic conditions.

Pathogenesis

C tetani is not an invasive organism. The infection remains strictly localized in the area of devitalized tissue (wound, burn, injury, umbilical stump, surgical suture) into which the spores have been introduced. The volume of infected tissue is small, and the disease is almost entirely a toxemia. Germination of the spore and development of vegetative organisms that produce toxin are aided by (1) necrotic tissue, (2) calcium salts, and (3) associated pyogenic infections, all of which aid establishment of low oxidation-reduction potential.

The toxin released from vegetative cells may reach the central nervous system by retrograde axonal transport or via the bloodstream. In the central nervous system, the toxin rapidly becomes fixed to gangliosides in spinal cord and brain stem and exerts the actions described above.

Clinical Findings

The incubation period may range from 4–5 days to as many weeks. The disease is characterized by convulsive tonic contraction of voluntary muscles. Muscular spasms often involve first the area of injury and infection and then the muscles of the jaw (trismus, lockjaw), which contract so that the mouth cannot be opened. Gradually, other voluntary muscles become involved, resulting in tonic spasms. Any external stimulus may precipitate a tetanic seizure. The patient is fully conscious, and pain may be intense. Death usually results from interference with the mechanics of respiration. The mortality rate in generalized tetanus is approximately 50%.

Diagnostic Laboratory Tests

In clinical cases, diagnosis rests on the clinical picture and a history of injury. Anaerobic culture of tissues from contaminated wounds may yield *C tetani*, but neither preventive nor therapeutic use of antitoxin should ever be withheld pending such demonstration. Proof of isolation of *C tetani* must rest on production of toxin and its neutralization by specific antitoxin.

Prevention & Treatment

The results of treatment of tetanus are not satisfactory. Therefore, prevention is all-important. Prevention of tetanus depends upon (1) active immunization with toxoids; (2) proper care of wounds contaminated with soil, etc; (3) prophylactic use of antitoxin; and (4) administration of penicillin.

A. Antitoxin: Tetanus antitoxin, prepared in animals or humans, can neutralize the toxin, but only before it becomes fixed onto nervous tissue. One International Unit of antitoxin is defined as the activity contained in 0.03384 mg of the Second International Standard for Tetanus Antitoxin.

Because of the frequency of hypersensitivity reactions to foreign serum and because of the rapidity with which foreign serum is eliminated, the administration of human antitoxin is preferable. The intramuscular administration of 250–500 units of human antitoxin gives adequate systemic protection (0.01 unit or more per milliliter of serum) for 2–4 weeks. Human tetanus immune globulin is now commercially available. Only if human antitoxin is not available should heterologous (horse, sheep, rabbit) antitoxin be used in a prophylactic dose of 1500–6000 units. Whenever heterologous antitoxin is to be administered, tests for hypersensitivity to the foreign serum protein must be done. Active immunization with tetanus toxoid should always accompany antitoxin prophylaxis.

Patients who develop symptoms of tetanus always receive muscle relaxants, sedation, and assisted ventilation. Sometimes they are given very large doses of antitoxin (3000–10,000 units of human tetanus immune globulin) intravenously in an effort to neutralize toxin that has not yet been bound to nervous tissue. However, the efficacy of antitoxin for treatment is doubtful except in neonatal tetanus, where it may be lifesaving. In neonatal tetanus, treatment with 10,000 units of equine antitoxin seems equivalent to treatment with 500 units of human immune globulin.

B. Surgical Measures: Surgical debridement is vitally important because it removes the necrotic tissue that is essential for proliferation of the organisms. Hyperbaric oxygen has no proved effect.

C. Antibiotics: Penicillin strongly inhibits the growth of *C tetani* and stops further toxin production. Antibiotics may also control associated pyogenic infection.

D. "Booster" Shot: When a previously immunized individual sustains a potentially dangerous wound, an additional dose of toxoid should be injected to restimulate antitoxin production. This "recall" injection of toxoid may be accompanied by antitoxin injected into a different area of the body to provide immediately available antitoxin for the period during which antitoxin levels may be inadequate.

Control

Universal active immunization with tetanus toxoid should be mandatory. Tetanus toxoid is produced by detoxifying the toxin with formalin and then concentrating it. Alum-precipitated or aluminum hydroxide-adsorbed toxoid is employed. Three injections comprise the initial course of immunization, followed by another dose about 1 year later. Initial immunization should be carried out in all children during the first year of life. A "booster" injection of toxoid is given upon entry into school. Thereafter, "boosters" can be spaced 7–10 years apart to maintain serum levels of more than 0.01 unit antitoxin per milliliter. (Some authorities believe that the protective level of antitoxin is 0.1 Lf unit [see p 168] per milliliter of serum.) Tetanus toxoid is often combined with diphtheria toxoid and pertussis vaccine. (For schedule of immunizations, see Table 12–6.)

Control measures are not possible because of the wide dissemination of the organism in the soil and the long survival of its spores. Narcotic addicts are a high-risk group.

CLOSTRIDIA THAT PRODUCE INVASIVE INFECTIONS

Many different toxin-producing clostridia can produce invasive infection (including myonecrosis and gas gangrene) if introduced into damaged tissue. About 30 species of clostridia may produce such an effect, but the commonest in invasive disease are *C perfringens* (90%), *Clostridium ramosum*, *Clostridium bifermentans*, *Clostridium histolyticum*, *Clostridium sporogenes*, *Clostridium novyi*, and some others. *Clostridium difficile* is an important cause of pseudomembranous enterocolitis.

Toxins

The clostridia produce a large variety of toxins and enzymes that result in a spreading infection. Many of these toxins have lethal, necrotizing, and hemolytic properties. In some cases, these are different properties of a single substance; in other instances, they are due to different chemical entities. The alpha toxin of *C perfringens* type A is a lecithinase, and its lethal action is proportionate to the rate at which it splits lecithin (an important constituent of cell membranes) to phosphorylcholine and diglyceride. The theta toxin has similar hemolytic and necrotizing effects but is not a lecithinase. DNase and hyaluronidase, a collagenase that digests collagen of subcutaneous tissue and muscle, are also produced.

Some strains of *C perfringens* produce a powerful enterotoxin. It is heat-labile, has a molecular weight of 35,000, is distinct from other clostridial toxins, and induces profuse diarrhea. The mechanism of action of clostridial enterotoxin resembles that of heat-labile *E coli* enterotoxin. The resulting diarrhea is usually brief and self-limited.

Pathogenesis

Clostridial spores reach tissue either by contamination of traumatized areas (soil, feces) or from the intestinal tract. The spores germinate at low oxidation-reduction potential; vegetative cells multiply, ferment carbohydrates present in tissue, and produce gas. The distention of tissue and interference with blood supply, together with the secretion of necrotizing toxin and hyaluronidase, favor the spread of infection. Tissue necrosis extends, providing an opportunity for increased bacterial growth, hemolytic anemia, and, ultimately, severe toxemia and death.

In gas gangrene, a mixed infection is the rule. In addition to the toxigenic clostridia, proteolytic clostridia and various cocci and gram-negative organisms are also usually present. *C perfringens* occurs in the genital tract of 5% of women. Clostridial uterine infections may follow instrumental abortions. Clostridial bacteremia is a frequent occurrence in patients with neoplasms. In New Guinea, *Clostridium welchii* type C produces a necrotizing enteritis (pigbel) that can be highly fatal in children. Immunization with type C toxoid appears to have preventive value.

The action of *C perfringens* enterotoxin involves marked hypersecretion in the jejunum and ileum, with loss of fluids and electrolytes in diarrhea. The precise mechanism is not established, but it does not appear to involve stimulation of adenylate cyclase or guanylate cyclase.

Clinical Findings

From a contaminated wound (eg, a compound fracture, postpartum uterus), the infection spreads in 1–3 days to produce crepitation in the subcutaneous tissue and muscle, foul-smelling discharge, rapidly progressing necrosis, fever, hemolysis, toxemia, shock, and death. Until the advent of specific therapy, early amputation was the only treatment. At times, the infection results only in anaerobic fasciitis or cellulitis. *C perfringens* food poisoning usually follows the ingestion of 10^6 or more viable organisms (often in unrefrigerated meat dishes) that release enterotoxin upon lysis and cause diarrhea that lasts 1–2 days.

Diagnostic Laboratory Tests

A. Specimens: Material from wounds, pus, tissue.

B. Smears: The presence of large gram-positive, sporeforming rods in gram-stained smears suggests gas gangrene clostridia, but spores are not regularly present.

C. Culture: Material is inoculated into chopped meat–glucose medium and thioglycolate medium and onto blood agar plates incubated anaerobically. The growth from one of the media is transferred into milk. A clot torn by gas in 24 hours is suggestive of *C perfringens*. Once pure cultures have been obtained by selecting colonies from anaerobically incubated blood plates, they are identified by biochemical reactions (various sugars in thioglycolate, action on milk), hemolysis, and colony form. Lecithinase activity is evaluated by the precipitate formed around colonies on egg yolk media. Final identification rests on toxin production and neutralization by specific antitoxin.

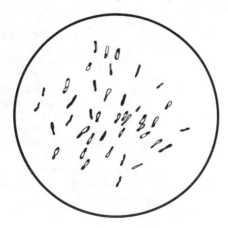

Figure 15–4. Gas gangrene bacilli.

Treatment

The most important aspect of treatment is prompt

and extensive surgical debridement of the involved area and excision of all devitalized tissue, in which the organisms are prone to grow. Administration of antimicrobial drugs, particularly penicillin, is begun at the same time. Hyperbaric oxygen may be of help in the medical management of clostridial tissue infections. It is said to "detoxify" patients rapidly.

Antitoxins are available against the toxins of *C perfringens, C novyi, C histolyticum,* and *Clostridium septicum,* usually in the form of concentrated immune globulins. Since the clinical picture is similar with all species of toxin-forming clostridia, polyvalent antitoxin (containing antibodies to several toxins) has been used. Although such antitoxin is sometimes administered to individuals with contaminated wounds containing much devitalized tissue, there is no evidence for its efficacy. Food poisoning due to *C perfringens* enterotoxin is usually self-limited.

Prevention & Control

Early and adequate cleansing of contaminated wounds and surgical debridement, together with the administration of antimicrobial drugs directed against clostridia (eg, penicillin), are the best available preventive measures. Antitoxins should not be relied on. Although toxoids for active immunization have been prepared, they have not come into practical use.

CLOSTRIDIAL PSEUDOMEMBRANOUS COLITIS

Antibiotic-associated colitis occurs after the prolonged oral administration of clindamycin or other drugs. It has been attributed to the selection of drug-resistant *C difficile* that proliferates in the colon and produces a necrotizing toxin, a glycoprotein (MW 50,000). This toxin can be neutralized by antitoxins to several clostridial toxins, including that of *Clostridium sordellii.* Antibiotic-associated pseudomembranous colitis may have a high mortality rate unless the selecting drug is stopped and oral vancomycin (0.5 g every 6 hours) is given. Until now, all *C difficile* have been sensitive to vancomycin (see also p 136).

•   •   •

References

Arnon SS et al: Intestinal infection and toxin production by *Clostridium botulinum* as one cause of sudden infant death syndrome. *Lancet* 1978;**1**:1273.

Bartlett JG et al: Cephalosporin-associated pseudomembranous colitis due to *Clostridium difficile. JAMA* 1979;**242**:2683.

Bartlett JG et al: Colitis induced by *Clostridium difficile. Rev Infect Dis* 1979;**1**:370.

Caplan ES, Kluge RM: Gas gangrene: Review of 34 cases. *Arch Intern Med* 1976;**136**:788.

Davis JC et al: Hyperbaric medicine in the US Air Force. *JAMA* 1973;**224**:205.

Finegold SM: *Anaerobic Bacteria in Human Disease.* Academic Press, 1977.

George WL et al: Antimicrobial-agent induced colitis: An update. *J Infect Dis* 1979;**140**:266.

Hansen N, Tolo V: Wound botulism complicating an open fracture: A case report and review of the literature. *J Bone Joint Surg [Am]* 1979;**61**:312.

Ihde DC, Armstrong D: Clinical spectrum of infection due to *Bacillus* species. *Am J Med* 1973;**55**:839.

Lamb R: A new look at infectious diseases: Anthrax. *Br Med J* 1973;**1**:157.

Merson MH et al: Botulism in the United States. *JAMA* 1974; **229**:1305.

Midura TF et al: Isolation of *Clostridium botulinum* from honey. *J Clin Microbiol* 1979;**9**:282.

Nathenson G, Zakzewski B: Current status of passive immunity to diphtheria and tetanus in the newborn. *J Infect Dis* 1976; **133**:199.

Pickett J et al: Syndrome of botulism in infancy. *N Engl J Med* 1976;**295**:770.

Stark RL: Biological characteristics of *Cl perfringens. Infect Immun* 1971;**4**:89.

Sugiyama H: *Clostridium botulinum* neurotoxicity. *Microbiol Rev* 1980;**44**:419.

Terranova W et al: Botulism type B: Epidemiologic aspects of an extensive outbreak. *Am J Epidemiol* 1978;**108**:150.

Thomas M et al: Hospital outbreak of *Clostridium perfringens* food poisoning. *Lancet* 1977;**1**:1046.

Tuazon CU et al: Serious infections from *Bacillus* species. *JAMA* 1979;**241**:1137.

Weinstein L: Tetanus. *N Engl J Med* 1973;**289**:1293.

16 | Corynebacteria

Corynebacteria are gram-positive rods, non-motile and nonsporeforming, that often possess club-shaped ends and irregularly staining granules. They are often in characteristic arrangements, resembling "Chinese letters" or palisades. They form acid but not gas in certain carbohydrates. Several species form part of the normal flora of the human respiratory tract, other mucous membranes, and skin. *Corynebacterium diphtheriae* produces a powerful exotoxin that causes diphtheria in humans.

Morphology & Identification

A. Typical Organisms: Corynebacteria are 0.5–1 μm in diameter and several micrometers long. Characteristically, they possess irregular swellings at one end that give them a "club-shaped" appearance. Irregularly distributed within the rod (often near the poles) are granules staining deeply with aniline dyes (metachromatic granules) that give the rod a beaded appearance.

Individual corynebacteria in stained smears tend to lie parallel or at acute angles to one another. True branching is rarely observed in cultures.

B. Culture: On Loeffler's coagulated serum medium, the colonies are small, granular, and gray, with irregular edges. On McLeod's blood agar containing potassium tellurite, the colonies are gray to black because the tellurite is reduced intracellularly. The 3 types of *C diphtheriae* typically have the following appearance on such media: (1) var *gravis* — nonhemolytic, large, gray, irregular, striated colonies; (2) var *mitis* — hemolytic, small, black, glossy, convex colonies; (3) var *intermedius* — nonhemolytic small colonies with characteristics between the 2 extremes. In broth, var *gravis* strains tend to form a pellicle, var *mitis* strains grow diffusely, and var *intermedius* strains settle as a granular sediment.

C. Growth Characteristics: Corynebacteria grow aerobically on most ordinary laboratory media. *Propionibacterium,* a "diphtheroid," is an anaerobe. On Loeffler's serum medium, corynebacteria grow much more readily than other respiratory pathogens, and the morphology of organisms is typical in smears. Acid, but not gas, is formed from some carbohydrates, as illustrated in Table 16–1.

D. Variation and Conversion: Corynebacteria tend to pleomorphism in microscopic and colonial morphology. Variation from smooth to rough forms has been described. Variants from toxigenic strains often are nontoxigenic. When some nontoxigenic diphtheria organisms are infected with bacteriophage from certain toxigenic diphtheria bacilli, the offspring of the exposed bacteria are lysogenic and toxigenic, and this trait is subsequently hereditary. (See Chapter 4, Genetics; and Chapter 9, Bacteriophage.) When toxigenic diphtheria bacilli are serially subcultured in specific antiserum against the temperate phage that they carry, they tend to become nontoxigenic. Thus, acquisition of phage leads to toxigenicity (lysogenic conversion). The actual production of toxin occurs perhaps only when the prophage of the lysogenic *C diphtheriae* becomes induced and lyses the cell. Whereas toxigenicity is under control of the phage gene, invasiveness is under control of bacterial genes.

Figure 16–1. *C diphtheriae* from Loeffler's medium.

Table 16–1. Examples of metabolic reactions.

	Glucose*	Maltose*	Sucrose*	Urease
C diphtheriae	+	+	−	−
C xerosis	+	+	+	−
C pseudodiph-theriticum†	−	−	−	+
C pyogenes (C haemolyticum)	+	+	+	−

*Acid but no gas formed.
†Also called *C hofmannii.*

Antigenic Structure

Serologic differences have been observed between types and within each type of *C diphtheriae*, but no satisfactory classification exists. Serologic tests are not usually employed in identification. Diphtheria toxin contains at least 4 antigenic determinants.

Pathogenesis

Some corynebacteria, notably *Corynebacterium pseudodiphtheriticum, Corynebacterium hofmannii, Corynebacterium xerosis, Corynebacterium pyogenes (Corynebacterium haemolyticum)*, and *Corynebacterium ulcerans*, are commonly called diphtheroids. They are normal inhabitants of the mucous membranes of the respiratory tract, urinary tract, and conjunctiva and rarely cause disease. A number of other diphtheroids cause infections in animals and, rarely, in humans. Anaerobic diphtheroids *(Propionibacterium acnes)* regularly reside in normal skin. They participate in the pathogenesis of acne. They produce lipases, which split off free fatty acids from skin lipids. These fatty acids can produce tissue inflammation and contribute to acne.

In immunosuppressed patients, various corynebacteria behave as opportunists and produce bacteremia accompanied by a high mortality rate, especially during granulocytopenia.

The principal human pathogen of the group is *C diphtheriae*. In nature, *C diphtheriae* occurs in the respiratory tract, in wounds, or on the skin of infected persons or normal carriers. It is spread by droplets or by contact to susceptible individuals; virulent bacilli then grow on mucous membranes and start producing toxin.

All toxigenic *C diphtheriae* are capable of elaborating the same disease-producing exotoxin. In vitro production of this toxin depends largely on the concentration of iron. Toxin production is optimal at 0.14 μg of iron per milliliter of medium but is virtually suppressed at 0.5 μg/mL. Other factors influencing the yield of toxin in vitro are osmotic pressure, amino acid concentration, pH, and availability of suitable carbon and nitrogen sources. The factors that control toxin production in vivo are not well understood.

Diphtheria toxin is a heat-labile polypeptide (MW $\sim$ 60,000) that can be lethal in a dose of 0.1 μg/kg. If disulfide bonds are broken, the molecule can be split into 2 fragments. Fragment B (MW $\sim$ 38,000) has no independent activity but is required for the transport of fragment A into the cell. Fragment A inhibits polypeptide chain elongation—provided nicotinamide adenine dinucleotide (NAD) is present—by inactivating the elongation factor EF-2 (formerly called transferase II). This factor is required for translocation of polypeptidyl-transfer RNA from the acceptor to the donor site on the eukaryotic ribosome. Toxin fragment A inactivates EF-2 by catalyzing a reaction that yields free nicotinamide plus an inactive adenosine diphosphate-ribose-EF-2 complex. An exotoxin with a similar mechanism of operation can be produced by strains of *Pseudomonas aeruginosa*. It is assumed that the abrupt arrest of protein synthesis is responsible for the necrotic and neurotoxic effects of diphtheria toxin.

Corynebacterium minutissimum is the cause of erythrasma, a superficial infection of axillary and pubic skin. The organism produces bright pink fluorescence under ultraviolet light in skin lesions and when cultured on Mueller-Hinton agar.

Gardnerella vaginalis (previously called *Corynebacterium vaginale* or *Haemophilus vaginalis*) is a frequent member of the normal flora of the vagina. It is also associated with vaginitis, discharge, and a "fishy smell" of released amines. It is not agreed whether proliferation of *Gardnerella* alone or in mixture with anaerobes causes this vaginitis, which is promptly suppressed by metronidazole. "Clue cells"—vaginal desquamated epithelial cells covered with many bacteria—aid the diagnosis (see p 251).

Pathology

Diphtheria toxin is absorbed into the mucous membranes and causes destruction of epithelium and a superficial inflammatory response. The necrotic epithelium becomes embedded in exuding fibrin and red and white cells, so that a grayish "pseudomembrane" is formed—commonly over the tonsils, pharynx, or larynx. Any attempt to remove the pseudomembrane exposes and tears the capillaries and thus results in bleeding. The regional lymph nodes in the neck enlarge, and there may be marked edema of the entire neck. The diphtheria bacilli within the membrane continue to produce toxin actively. This is absorbed and results in distant toxic damage, particularly parenchymatous degeneration, fatty infiltration, and necrosis in heart muscle, liver, kidneys, and adrenals, sometimes accompanied by gross hemorrhage. The toxin also produces nerve damage, resulting often in paralysis of the soft palate, eye muscles, or extremities.

Wound or skin diphtheria occurs chiefly in the tropics. A membrane may form on an infected wound that fails to heal. However, absorption of toxin is usually slight and the systemic effects negligible. The "virulence" of diphtheria bacilli is due to their capacity for establishing infection, growing rapidly, and then quickly elaborating toxin that is effectively absorbed. *C diphtheriae* does not actively invade deep tissues and practically never enters the bloodstream.

Clinical Findings

When diphtheritic inflammation begins in the respiratory tract, sore throat and fever usually develop. Prostration and dyspnea soon follow because of the obstruction caused by the membrane. This obstruction may even cause suffocation if not promptly relieved by intubation or tracheostomy. Irregularities of cardiac rhythm indicate damage to the heart. Later, there may be difficulties with vision, swallowing, or movement of the arms or legs. All of these manifestations tend to subside spontaneously.

There is a broad correlation between the type of *C*

diphtheriae and the severity of the disease. In general, var *gravis* infections tend to be more severe than var *mitis,* with a correspondingly higher mortality rate.

In some immunocompromised patients, various diphtheroids can cause pneumonia, endocarditis, and soft tissue and bone infections. When found in blood culture, they pose a problem in interpretation: Are they contaminants from normal skin flora or involved in a pathologic process?

Diagnostic Laboratory Tests

These serve to confirm the clinical impression and are of epidemiologic significance. *Note:* Specific treatment must never be delayed for laboratory reports if the clinical picture is strongly suggestive of diphtheria.

A. Specimens: Swabs from the nose, throat, or other suspected lesions must be obtained before antimicrobial drugs are administered.

B. Smears: Smears stained with alkaline methylene blue or Gram's stain show beaded rods in typical arrangement.

C. Culture: Inoculate a blood agar plate (to rule out hemolytic streptococci), a Loeffler slant, and a tellurite plate, and incubate all 3 at 37 °C. Unless the swab can be inoculated promptly, it should be kept moistened with sterile horse serum so the bacilli will remain viable. In 12–18 hours, the Loeffler slant may yield organisms of typical "diphtherialike" morphology. In 36–48 hours, the colonies on tellurite medium are sufficiently definite for recognition of the type of *C diphtheriae.*

Any diphtherialike organism cultured must be submitted to a "virulence" test before the bacteriologic diagnosis of diphtheria is definite. Such tests are really tests for toxigenicity of an isolated diphtherialike organism. They can be done in one of 3 ways as follows:

1. In vivo test–A culture is emulsified and 4 mL is injected subcutaneously into each of 2 guinea pigs, one of which has received 250 units of diphtheria antitoxin intraperitoneally 2 hours previously. The unprotected animal should die in 2–3 days, whereas the protected animal survives.

2. In vitro test–A strip of filter paper saturated with antitoxin is placed on an agar plate containing 20% horse serum. The cultures to be tested for toxigenicity are streaked across the plate at right angles to the filter paper. After 48 hours' incubation, the antitoxin diffusing from the paper strip has precipitated the toxin diffusing from toxigenic cultures and resulted in lines radiating from the intersection of the strip and the bacterial growth.

3. Tissue culture test–The toxigenicity of *C diphtheriae* can be shown by incorporation of bacteria into an agar overlay of cell culture monolayers. Toxin produced diffuses into cells below and kills them.

Resistance & Immunity

Since diphtheria is principally the result of the action of the toxin formed by the organism rather than invasion by the organism, resistance to the disease depends largely on the availability of specific neutralizing antitoxin in the bloodstream and tissues. It is generally true that diphtheria occurs only in persons who possess no antitoxin or less than 0.01 Lf units/mL (see p 168). Thus, the treatment of diphtheria rests largely on rapid suppression of toxin-producing bacteria by antimicrobials and the early administration of specific antitoxin against the toxin formed by the organisms at their site of entry and multiplication. Antitoxic immunity to diphtheria may be active or passive. The relative amount of antitoxin that a person possesses at a given time can be estimated in one of 2 ways:

A. Titration of Serum for Antitoxin Content: (Too complex for routine use.) Serum is mixed with varying amounts of toxin and the mixture injected into susceptible animals. The greater the amount of toxin neutralized, the higher the concentration of antitoxin in the serum.

B. Schick Test: This test is based on the fact that diphtheria toxin is very irritating and results in a marked local reaction when injected intradermally unless it is neutralized by circulating antitoxin. One Schick test dose (amount of standard toxin that, when mixed with 0.001 unit of the US Standard diphtheria antitoxin and injected intradermally into a guinea pig, will induce a 10-mm erythematous reaction) is injected into the skin of one forearm and an identical amount of heated toxin is injected into the other forearm as a control. (Heating for 15 minutes at 60 °C destroys the effect of the toxin.) The test should be read at 24 and 48 hours and again in 6 days and interpreted as follows:

1. Positive reaction (susceptibility to diphtheria toxin, ie, absence of adequate amounts of neutralizing antitoxin; less than 0.01 Lf units/mL)–Toxin produces redness and swelling that increase for several days and then slowly fade, leaving a brownish pigmented area. The control site shows no reaction.

2. Negative reaction (adequate amount of antitoxin present; usually in excess of 0.02 Lf units/mL of serum)–Neither injection site shows any reaction.

3. Pseudoreaction–Schick test reactions may be complicated by hypersensitivity to materials other than the toxin contained in the injections. A pseudoreaction shows redness and swelling on both arms which disappear simultaneously on the second or third day. It constitutes a negative reaction.

4. Combined reaction–A combined reaction begins like a pseudoreaction, with redness and swelling at both injection sites; the toxin later continues to exert its effects, however, whereas the reaction at the control site subsides rapidly. This denotes hypersensitivity as well as relative susceptibility to toxin.

Treatment

Diphtheria antitoxin is produced in various animals (horses, sheep, goats, and rabbits) by the repeated injection of purified and concentrated toxoid. One International Unit of diphtheria antitoxin = 0.0628 mg of International Standard (Copenhagen). Treatment with antitoxin is mandatory when there is strong clinical suspicion of diphtheria. From 20,000 to 100,000 units are injected intramuscularly or intravenously after suitable precautions have been taken (skin or conjunctival test) to rule out hypersensitivity to the animal serum. The antitoxin should be given on the day the clinical diagnosis of diphtheria is made and need not be repeated. Intramuscular injection may be used in mild cases.

Antimicrobial drugs (penicillin, erythromycin) inhibit the growth of diphtheria bacilli. Although these drugs have virtually no effect on the disease process, they arrest toxin production. They also help to eliminate coexistent streptococci and *C diphtheriae* from the respiratory tracts of patients or carriers.

Antibiotic administration (tetracycline) in acne may inhibit the lipolytic action of anaerobic diphtheroids *(Propionibacterium acnes)*; this reduces tissue inflammation. Variable benefit has been claimed for this treatment of acne.

Epidemiology, Prevention, & Control

Before artificial immunization, diphtheria was mainly a disease of small children. The infection occurred either clinically or subclinically at an early age and resulted in the widespread production of antitoxin in the population. An asymptomatic reinfection during adolescence and adult life served as a stimulus for maintenance of high antitoxin levels. Thus, most members of the population, except children, were immune.

With the introduction of artificial active immunization, the situation has changed. After active immunization during the first few years of life, antitoxin levels are generally adequate until adolescence. However, there are very few cases or carriers of diphtheria in the population, so that the stimulus of subsequent subclinical infections is lacking. Consequently, many adults have no significant amounts of antitoxin and thus are again susceptible to the disease.

Following either natural infection or active immunization, antitoxin levels last only a limited period of time and are subject to great fluctuations. Since the degree of individual resistance varies with the antitoxin titer, all degrees, from complete susceptibility to complete immunity, are likely to be present.

The principal aim of prevention therefore must be to limit the distribution of toxigenic diphtheria bacilli in the population and to maintain as high a level of active immunization as possible.

A. Isolation: To limit contact with diphtheria bacilli to a minimum, patients with diphtheria must be isolated and every effort made to rid them of the organisms. Without treatment, a large percentage of infected persons continue to shed diphtheria bacilli for weeks or months after recovery (convalescent carriers). This danger may be greatly reduced by active early treatment with antibiotics. However, there are some healthy carriers from whom diphtheria bacilli cannot be eradicated with the measures now available. Tonsillectomy is sometimes performed as a last resort.

B. Active Immunization: The following preparations have been employed:

1. Fluid toxoid–A filtrate of broth culture of a toxigenic strain is treated with 0.3% formalin and incubated at 37 °C until toxicity has disappeared. Toxoid is standardized in terms of flocculating units (Lf doses), often as 30 Lf/mL. Three doses of 0.5–1 mL are injected subcutaneously.

2. Alum-precipitated toxoid–Toxoid prepared as above is precipitated with 1–2% potassium alum. This is a somewhat better antigen and remains longer in the subcutaneous tissue. Only 2 injections are required for initial immunization, but the alum-precipitated toxoid may induce hypersensitivity more frequently than fluid toxoid. It is commonly combined with tetanus toxoid and pertussis vaccine in a single injection. Toxoid can also be adsorbed onto aluminum hydroxide or aluminum phosphate for delayed absorption.

Children should receive an initial course of toxoid injections during the first year of life and should have recall ("booster") inoculations at 3–4 and 6–8 years. Adolescents should receive another recall injection. In adults, the incidence of hypersensitivity reactions to toxoids is high, and only purified toxoid (Td) should be used.

3. Toxin-antitoxin mixtures–These have been abandoned because of the danger of dissociation of the "neutral" mixture and the potential serious reactions to the free toxin.

●　●　●

References

Bainton D et al: Immunity of children to diphtheria, tetanus and poliomyelitis. *Br Med J* 1979;**1**:854.

Belsey MA et al: *Corynebacterium diphtheriae* skin infections in Alabama and Louisiana: A factor in the epidemiology of diphtheria. *N Engl J Med* 1969;**280**:135.

Collier RJ: Diphtheria toxin: Mode of action and structure. *Bacteriol Rev* 1975;**39**:54.

Hande KR et al: Sepsis with a new species of *Corynebacterium*. *Ann Intern Med* 1976;**85**:423.

Hodes HL: Diphtheria. *Pediatr Clin North Am* 1979;**26**:445.

Josey WE et al: *Corynebacterium vaginale* in women with leukorrhea. *Am J Obstet Gynecol* 1976;**126**:574.

Kaplan K, Weinstein L: Diphtheroid infections of man. *Ann Intern Med* 1969;**70**:919.

Laird W, Groman N: Tissue culture test for toxigenicity of *C diphtheriae*. *Appl Microbiol* 1973;**25**:709.

McCormack WM et al: Vaginal colonization with *Corynebacterium vaginale*. *J Infect Dis* 1977;**136**:740.

Nathenson G, Zakzewski B: Current status of passive immunity to diphtheria and tetanus in the newborn. *J Infect Dis* 1976;**133**:199.

Pappenheimer AM, Gill DM: Diphtheria. *Science* 1973;**182**:353.

Pearson TA et al: *Corynebacterium* sepsis in oncology patients. *JAMA* 1977:**238**:1737.

Rosenberg EW: Bacteriology of acne. *Annu Rev Med* 1969;**20**:201.

Stamm WE et al: Infection due to *Corynebacterium* species in marrow transplant patients. *Ann Intern Med* 1979;**91**:167.

Thompson HL, Ellner PD: Rapid determination of *Corynebacterium diphtheriae* toxigenicity by counterimmunoelectrophoresis. *J Clin Microbiol* 1978;**7**:493.

Washington JA: Bacteriology, clinical spectrum of diseases, and therapeutic aspects in coryneform bacterial infection. Page 69 in: *Current Clinical Topics in Infectious Diseases*. Vol 2. Remington JS, Swartz MN (editors). McGraw-Hill, 1981.

The mycobacteria are rod-shaped nonsporeforming, aerobic bacteria that do not stain readily but, once stained, resist decolorization by acid or alcohol and are therefore called "acid-fast" bacilli. In addition to many saprophytic forms, the group includes pathogenic organisms (eg, *Mycobacterium tuberculosis, Mycobacterium leprae*) that cause chronic diseases producing lesions of the infectious granuloma type.

MYCOBACTERIUM TUBERCULOSIS

Morphology & Identification

A. Typical Organisms: In animal tissues, tubercle bacilli are thin straight rods measuring about 0.4 × 3 μm. On artificial media, coccoid and filamentous forms are seen. Mycobacteria cannot be classified as either gram-positive or gram-negative. Once stained by basic dyes they cannot be decolorized by alcohol, regardless of treatment with iodine. True tubercle bacilli are characterized by "acid-fastness," eg, 95% ethyl alcohol containing 3% hydrochloric acid (acid-alcohol) quickly decolorizes all bacteria except the mycobacteria. Acid-fastness depends on the integrity of the structure of the waxy envelope (see p 220). The Ziehl-Neelsen technique of staining is employed for identification of acid-fast bacteria. In sputum or sections of tissue, mycobacteria can be demonstrated by yellow-orange fluorescence after staining with fluorochrome stains (eg, auramine, rhodamine).

B. Culture: Three types of media are employed.

1. Simple synthetic media—Large inocula grow on simple synthetic media in several weeks. Small inocula fail to grow in such media because of the presence of minute amounts of toxic fatty acids. The toxic effect of fatty acids can be neutralized by animal serum or albumin, and the fatty acids may then actually promote growth. Activated charcoal aids growth.

2. Oleic acid-albumin media may support the proliferation of small inocula, particularly if Tweens (water-soluble esters of fatty acids) are present (eg, Dubos' medium). Ordinarily, mycobacteria grow in clumps or masses because of the hydrophobic character of the cell surface. Tweens wet the surface and thus permit dispersed growth in liquid media. Growth is often more rapid than on complex media.

3. Complex organic media—Small inocula, eg, specimens from patients, are grown on media containing complex organic substances, eg, egg yolk, animal serum, tissue extracts. These media often contain penicillin or malachite green (eg, Löwenstein-Jensen medium) to inhibit other bacteria.

C. Growth Characteristics: Mycobacteria are obligate aerobes and derive energy from the oxidation of many simple carbon compounds. Increased CO_2 tension enhances growth. Biochemical activities are not characteristic, and the growth rate is much slower than that of most bacteria. The doubling time of tubercle bacilli is 12 hours or more. Saprophytic forms tend to grow more rapidly, proliferate well at 22 °C, produce more pigment, and be less acid-fast than pathogenic forms.

D. Reaction to Physical and Chemical Agents: Mycobacteria tend to be more resistant to chemical agents than other bacteria because of the hydrophobic nature of the cell surface and their clumped growth. Dyes (eg, malachite green) or antibacterial agents (eg, penicillin) that are bacteriostatic to other bacteria can be incorporated into media without inhibiting the growth of tubercle bacilli. Acids and alkalies permit the survival of some exposed tubercle bacilli and are used for "concentration" of clinical specimens and partial elimination of contaminating organisms. Tubercle bacilli are fairly resistant to drying and survive for long periods in dried sputum.

E. Variation: Variation can occur in colony appearance, pigmentation, cord factor production, virulence, optimal growth temperature, and many other cellular or growth characteristics.

F. Pathogenicity of Mycobacteria: There are marked differences in the ability of different mycobacteria to cause lesions in various host species. Examples are shown in Table 17–1.

M tuberculosis and *Mycobacterium bovis* are equally pathogenic for humans. The route of infection (respiratory versus intestinal) determines the pattern of lesions. In developed countries, *M bovis* has become very rare. Some "atypical" mycobacteria (eg, *Mycobacterium kansasii*) produce human disease indistinguishable from tuberculosis; others (eg, *Mycobacterium fortuitum*) cause only surface lesions or act as opportunists.

Table 17–1. Pathogenicity of mycobacteria.

Species	Human	Guinea Pig	Fowl	Cattle
M tuberculosis	+++	+++	–	–
M bovis	+++	+++	–	+++
M kansasii	+++	–	–	–
M avium-intracellulare*	+	–	+++	–
M fortuitum-chelonei*	+	–	–	–
M leprae	++	–	–	–

*Complex

Constituents of Tubercle Bacilli

The constituents listed below are found largely in cell walls. Mycobacterial cell walls can induce delayed hypersensitivity, induce some resistance to infection, and replace whole mycobacterial cells in Freund's adjuvant. Mycobacterial cell contents only elicit delayed hypersensitivity reactions in previously sensitized animals.

A. Lipids: Mycobacteria are rich in lipids. Many complex lipids, fatty acids, and waxes have been isolated from them. In the cell the lipids are largely bound to proteins and polysaccharides. Some such complexes have been isolated. Lipids are probably responsible for most of the cellular tissue reactions to tubercle bacilli. Phosphatide fractions can produce tuberclelike cellular responses and caseation necrosis. Lipids are to some extent responsible for acid-fastness. When mycobacteria are defatted with ether, this staining property is lost. Analysis of the lipids by gas chromatography can reveal species-specific patterns that aid in classification.

Virulent strains of tubercle bacilli form microscopic "serpentine cords" in which acid-fast bacilli are arranged in parallel chains. Cord formation is correlated with virulence. A "cord factor" (trehalose-6,6'-dimycolate) has been extracted from virulent bacilli with petroleum ether. It inhibits migration of leukocytes, causes chronic granulomas, and can serve as an immunologic "adjuvant" (see Chapter 13).

B. Proteins: Each type of mycobacterium contains several proteins that elicit the tuberculin reaction. Proteins bound to a wax fraction can, upon injection, induce tuberculin sensitivity. They can also elicit the formation of a variety of antibodies.

C. Polysaccharides: Mycobacteria contain a variety of polysaccharides. Their role in the pathogenesis of disease is uncertain. They can induce the immediate type of hypersensitivity and can interfere with some antigen-antibody reactions in vitro.

Pathogenesis

Mycobacteria produce no recognized toxins. Organisms in droplets of $1–5~\mu m$ are inhaled and reach alveoli. The disease results from establishment and proliferation of virulent organisms and interactions with the host. Avirulent bacilli (eg, BCG) survive only for months or years in the normal host. Resistance and hypersensitivity of the host greatly influence the development of the disease.

Pathology

The production and development of lesions and their healing or progression are determined chiefly by (1) the number of mycobacteria in the inoculum and their subsequent multiplication, and (2) the resistance and hypersensitivity of the host.

A. Two Principal Lesions:

1. Exudative type–This consists of an acute inflammatory reaction, with edema fluid, polymorphonuclear leukocytes, and, later, monocytes around the tubercle bacilli. This type is seen particularly in lung tissue, where it resembles bacterial pneumonia. It may heal by resolution, so that the entire exudate becomes absorbed; it may lead to massive necrosis of tissue; or it may develop into the second (productive) type of lesion. During the exudative phase, the tuberculin test becomes positive.

2. Productive type–When fully developed, this lesion, a chronic granuloma, consists of 3 zones: (1) a central area of large, multinucleated giant cells containing tubercle bacilli; (2) a mid zone of pale epithelioid cells, often arranged radially; and (3) a peripheral zone of fibroblasts, lymphocytes, and monocytes. Later, peripheral fibrous tissue develops and the central area undergoes caseation necrosis. Such a lesion is called a tubercle. A caseous tubercle may break into a bronchus, empty its contents there, and form a cavity. It may subsequently heal by fibrosis or calcification.

B. Spread of Organisms in the Host: Tubercle bacilli spread in the host by direct extension, through the lymphatic channels and bloodstream, and via the bronchi and gastrointestinal tract.

In the first infection, tubercle bacilli always spread from the initial site via the lymphatics to the regional lymph nodes. The bacilli may spread farther and reach the bloodstream, which in turn disseminates bacilli to all organs (miliary distribution). The bloodstream can be invaded also by erosion of a vein by a caseating tubercle or lymph node. If a caseating lesion discharges its contents into a bronchus, they are aspirated and distributed to other parts of the lungs or are swallowed and passed into the stomach and intestines.

C. Intracellular Site of Growth: Once mycobacteria establish themselves in tissue, they reside principally intracellularly in monocytes, reticuloendothelial cells, and giant cells. The intracellular location is one of the features that makes chemotherapy difficult and favors microbial persistence. Within the cells of immune animals, multiplication of tubercle bacilli is greatly inhibited.

Primary Infection & Reactivation Types of Tuberculosis

When a host has first contact with tubercle bacilli, the following features are usually observed: (1) An acute exudative lesion develops and rapidly spreads to the lymphatics and regional lymph nodes. The "Ghon complex" is the primary tissue lesion (usually in the lung) together with the involved lymph nodes. The exudative lesion in tissue often heals rapidly. (2) The lymph node undergoes massive caseation, which usually calcifies. (3) The tuberculin test becomes positive.

This primary infection type occurred in the past usually in childhood but now is seen frequently in adults who have remained free from infection and therefore tuberculin-negative in early life. In primary infections, the involvement may be in any part of the lung but is most often at the base.

The reactivation type is usually caused by tubercle bacilli that have survived in the primary lesion and rarely by bacilli newly inhaled from the environment. Reactivation tuberculosis is characterized by chronic tissue lesions, the formation of tubercles, caseation, and fibrosis. Regional lymph nodes are only slightly involved, and they do not caseate. The reactivation type almost always begins at the apex of the lung, where the oxygen tension (P_{O_2}) is highest.

The contrast between primary infection and reinfection is shown experimentally in **Koch's phenomenon.** When a guinea pig is injected subcutaneously with virulent tubercle bacilli, the puncture wound heals quickly, but a nodule forms at the site of injection in 2 weeks. This nodule ulcerates, and the ulcer does not heal. The regional lymph nodes develop tubercles and caseate massively. When the same animal is later injected with tubercle bacilli in another part of the body, the sequence of events is quite different: there is rapid necrosis of skin and tissue at the site of injection, but the ulcer heals rapidly. Regional lymph nodes either do not become infected at all or do so only after a delay.

These differences between primary infection and reinfection or reactivation are attributed to (1) resistance and (2) hypersensitivity induced by the first infection of the host with tubercle bacilli. It is not clear to what extent each of these components participates in the modified response in reactivation tuberculosis.

Immunity & Hypersensitivity

Unless a host dies during the first infection with tubercle bacilli, a certain resistance is acquired (see Koch's phenomenon, above), and there is an increased capacity to localize tubercle bacilli, retard their multiplication, limit their spread, and reduce lymphatic dissemination. This can be largely attributed to the ability of mononuclear cells to limit the multiplication of ingested organisms and perhaps to destroy them. Mononuclear cells acquire this "cellular immunity" in the course of initial infection of the host.

Antibodies form against a variety of the cellular constituents of the tubercle bacilli. Antibodies have been determined by precipitation and CF tests and by a hemagglutinating reaction in which sera of tuberculous animals or humans clump red cells that have adsorbed tuberculin. None of these serologic reactions bears any definite relation to the state of resistance of the host.

In the course of primary infection, the host also acquires hypersensitivity to the tubercle bacilli. This is made evident by the development of a positive tuberculin reaction (see below). Tuberculin sensitivity can be induced by whole tubercle bacilli or by tuberculoprotein in combination with the chloroform-soluble wax of the tubercle bacillus, but not by tuberculoprotein alone. Hypersensitivity and resistance appear to be distinct aspects of related cell-mediated reactions.

Tuberculin Test

A. Material: Old tuberculin (OT) is a concentrated filtrate of broth in which tubercle bacilli have grown for 6 weeks. In addition to the reactive tuberculoproteins, this material contains a variety of other constituents of tubercle bacilli and of growth medium. A purified protein derivative (PPD) can be obtained by chemical fractionation of OT and is the preferred material for skin testing. PPD is standardized in terms of its biologic reactivity as "tuberculin units" (TU). By international agreement, the TU is defined as the activity contained in a specified weight of Seibert's PPD Lot # 49608 in a specified buffer. This is PPD-S, the standard for tuberculin against which the potency of all products must be established by biologic assay—ie, by reaction size in humans. First strength tuberculin has 1 TU; intermediate strength has 5 TU; and second strength has 250 TU. Bioequivalency of PPD products is not based on weight of the material but on comparative activity.

B. Dose of Tuberculin: A large amount of tuberculin injected into a hypersensitive host may give rise to severe local reactions and a flare-up of inflammation and necrosis at the main sites of infection (focal reactions). For this reason tuberculin tests in surveys employ 5 TU; in persons suspected of hypersensitivity, skin testing is begun with 1 TU. More concentrated material (250 TU) is administered only if the reaction to the more dilute material is negative. The volume is usually 0.1 mL injected intracutaneously. The PPD preparation must be stabilized with polysorbate-80 to prevent adsorption to glass.

C. Reactions to Tuberculin: In an individual who has not had contact with mycobacteria, there is no reaction to PPD-S. An individual who has had a primary infection with tubercle bacilli develops induration exceeding 10 mm in diameter, edema, erythema in 24–48 hours, and, with very intense reactions, even central necrosis. The skin test should be read in 48 or 72 hours. It is considered positive if the injection of 5 TU is followed by induration 10 mm or more in diameter. Positive tests tend to persist for several days. Weak reactions may disappear more rapidly.

The tuberculin test becomes positive within 4–6 weeks after infection (or injection of avirulent bacilli). It may be negative in the presence of tuberculous infection when "anergy" develops due to overwhelming tuberculosis, measles, Hodgkin's disease, sarcoidosis, or immunosuppressive drugs. A positive tuberculin test may occasionally revert to negative upon isoniazid treatment of a recent converter. After BCG vaccination, a positive test may last for only 3–7 years. Only the elimination of viable tubercle bacilli results in reversion of the tuberculin test to negative. However, persons who had been PPD-positive years ago and are healthy may fail to give a positive skin test.

When such persons are retested 2 weeks later, their PPD skin test—''boosted'' by the recent antigen injection—will give a positive size of induration again. The reactivity to tuberculin can be transferred only by cells—not by serum—from a tuberculin-positive to a tuberculin-negative person.

D. Interpretation of Tuberculin Test: A positive tuberculin test indicates that an individual has been infected with mycobacteria, but it does not indicate active disease. Although tuberculin-positive healthy individuals may have some resistance to widespread disease, in fact most active tuberculosis occurs in persons who have had positive tuberculin tests for months or years. The tuberculin-positive person is at risk of developing disease from reactivation of the primary infection, whereas the tuberculin-negative person is not at risk.

PPDs from other mycobacteria have been prepared. They exhibit some species specificity in low concentrations and marked cross-reactions in higher concentrations (see Other Mycobacteria, p 223).

Clinical Findings

Since the tubercle bacillus can involve every organ system, its clinical manifestations are protean. Fatigue, weakness, weight loss, and fever may be signs of tuberculous disease. Pulmonary involvement giving rise to chronic cough and spitting of blood usually is associated with far-advanced lesions. Meningitis or urinary tract involvement can occur in the absence of other signs of tuberculosis. Bloodstream dissemination leads to miliary tuberculosis with lesions in many organs and a high fatality rate.

Diagnostic Laboratory Tests

Neither the tuberculin test nor any now available serologic test gives evidence of active disease due to the tubercle bacillus. Only isolation of tubercle bacilli gives such proof.

Specimens consist of fresh sputum, gastric washings, urine, pleural fluid, spinal fluid, joint fluid, biopsy material, or other suspected material.

A. Stained Smear: Sputum, or sediment from gastric washings, urine, exudates, or other material, is stained for acid-fast bacilli by the Ziehl-Neelsen technique, by a comparable method, or by fluorescence microscopy with auramine-rhodamine stain. If such organisms are found, this is presumptive evidence of tuberculosis. However, other acid-fast bacilli must be ruled out by culture or animal inoculation.

B. Concentration for Stained Smear: If a direct smear is negative, sputum may be liquefied by addition of 20% Clorox (1% hypochlorite solution) and then centrifuged, and the sediment stained and examined microscopically. This ''digested material'' is unsuitable for culture.

C. Culture: Urine, spinal fluid, and materials not contaminated with other bacteria may be cultured directly. Sputum is first treated with 2% sodium hydroxide or other agents bactericidal for contaminating microorganisms but less so for tubercle bacilli (see Table 17–2). The liquefied sputum is then neutralized and centrifuged and the sediment inoculated into appropriate media. Incubation of the inoculated media is continued for up to 8 weeks.

Isolated mycobacteria should be tested for drug susceptibility.

D. Animal Inoculation: Part of the cultured material may be inoculated subcutaneously into guinea pigs, which are tuberculin tested after 3–4 weeks and autopsied after 6 weeks to search for evidence of tuberculosis. In competent hands, cultures are just as reli-

---

Table 17–2. Identification of acid-fast organisms in sputum specimens.

I. Digest sputum by adding an equal volume of acetylcysteine–trisodium phosphate or 2% sodium hydroxide, shaking with glass beads for 20 minutes at room temperature.

II. Restore neutral pH by adding 25% hydrochloric acid, drop by drop.

III. Inoculate Löwenstein-Jensen medium and incubate at 37 °C. Inspect at 5-day intervals. When colonies appear, make smears and acid-fast stains. If acid-fast organisms are present, proceed as follows:

A. Growth in less than 5 days (rapid growers): Runyon's group IV.*

    1. Aryl sulfate test—

        a. Strongly positive—*M fortuitum.*

        b. Negative or weakly positive—Other group IV mycobacteria, to be identified by sugar fermentations (eg, *M smegmatis, M phlei*).

B. Growth in more than 5–7 days (slow growers):

    1. Niacin test†—

        a. Positive; colonies rough—*M tuberculosis.*

        b. Negative—

            (1) Slow, sparse growth; small, flat colonies—*M bovis,* pathogenic for rabbits and guinea pigs. BCG nonpathogenic.

            (2) Smooth hemispherical colonies—Subculture at 37 °C in 2 tubes of Löwenstein-Jensen medium, one tube kept in light, the other wrapped in foil and kept in darkness.

                (a) Yellow to orange in light, nonpigmented in dark—Photochromogens, *M kansasii* (Runyon's group I).

                (b) Yellow to orange in light and dark—Scotochromogens (Runyon's group II).

                (c) Nonpigmented in light or dark—*M avium-intracellulare* complex (Runyon's group III).

---

*Runyon EH: *Med Clin North Am* 1959;**43**:273.

†Runyon EH et al: *Am Rev Tuberc* 1959;**79**:663.

able. The use of both procedures, however, ensures the highest number of positive results.

E. Serology: CF and HI tests have little value.

Treatment

Physical and mental rest, nutritional buildup, and various forms of collapse therapy were used in the past but have been supplanted by specific chemotherapy. The most widely used antituberculosis drugs at present are isoniazid (isonicotinic acid hydrazide, INH), ethambutol, rifampin, and streptomycin. Unfortunately, resistant variants of tubercle bacilli against each of these drugs emerge rapidly. Treatment is most successful when the drugs are used concomitantly (eg, INH + rifampin; INH + ethambutol; rifampin + ethambutol), thus delaying the emergence of resistant forms. Occasionally, primary infection occurs with tubercle bacilli resistant to one or more drugs. (In the USA, 3–8% of primary infections are caused by INH-resistant *M tuberculosis*. In Asia, the proportion is much greater. This is of concern in the treatment of Asian immigrants to the USA.) Other drugs (eg, ethionamide, pyrazinamide, viomycin, cycloserine) are less frequently employed because of their more pronounced side-effects. The available chemotherapeutic drugs result in suppression of tuberculous activity and eradication of most—but not all—tubercle bacilli. Clinical cure can usually be achieved in 6–12 months. Host factors are important in control of the residual organisms. The sputum-positive patient becomes noninfective within 2–3 weeks after beginning effective chemotherapy.

The following explanations have been advanced for the particular resistance of chronic tuberculosis to chemotherapy: (1) Most bacilli are intracellular, and some drugs (eg, streptomycin) penetrate cells poorly. (2) The caseous material in lesions, although it is itself inimical to bacterial proliferation, interferes with drug action. (3) In chronic lesions tubercle bacilli are nonproliferating, metabolically inactive "persisters" that are not susceptible to drug action.

Epidemiology

The most frequent source of infection is the human who excretes, particularly from the respiratory tract, large numbers of tubercle bacilli. Close contact (eg, in the family) and massive exposure (eg, in medical personnel) make transmission by droplet nuclei most likely. The milk of tuberculous cows is a source of infection where bovine tuberculosis is not well controlled and where milk is not pasteurized.

Susceptibility to tuberculosis is a function of 2 risks: the risk of acquiring the infection and the risk of developing clinical disease after infection has occurred. For the tuberculin-negative person, the risk of acquiring tubercle bacilli depends on exposure to sources of infectious bacilli—principally sputum-positive patients. This risk is proportionate to the rate of active infection in the population, crowding, socioeconomic disadvantage, and inadequacy of medical care. These factors, rather than genetic ones, probably account for the significantly higher rate of tuberculosis in American Indians, Eskimos, and blacks.

The second risk—the development of clinical disease after infection—has a genetic component (proved in animals) and is influenced by age (high risk in infancy and at age 16–21), by undernutrition, and by immunologic status, coexisting diseases (eg, silicosis, diabetes), and individual host resistance factors discussed below.

Infection occurs at an earlier age in urban than in rural populations. Disease occurs only in a small proportion of infected individuals. In the USA at present, active disease represents mainly endogenous reactivation tuberculosis and occurs most commonly among elderly malnourished or alcoholic poor males.

Prevention & Control

(1) Public health measures designed for early detection of cases and sources of infection (tuberculin test, x-ray) and for their prompt treatment until noninfectious.

(2) Eradication of tuberculosis in cattle ("test and slaughter") and pasteurization of milk.

(3) Drug treatment of asymptomatic tuberculin "converters" in the age groups most prone to develop complications (eg, children) and in immunosuppressed persons who were tuberculin-positive in the past.

(4) Immunization: Various living avirulent tubercle bacilli, particularly BCG (bacille Calmette Guérin, an attenuated bovine organism), have been used to induce a certain amount of resistance in those heavily exposed to infection. Vaccination with these organisms is a substitute for primary infection with virulent tubercle bacilli, without the danger inherent in the latter. The available vaccines are inadequate from many technical and biologic standpoints. Nevertheless, in 1980 in London, most tuberculin negative 12-year-olds were given BCG. In Sweden, most 1-year-olds received it. In the USA, the use of BCG is suggested only for tuberculin-negative persons who are heavily exposed (members of tuberculous families, medical personnel). Statistical evidence indicates that an increased resistance for a limited period follows BCG vaccination.

The possible immunizing value of nonliving bacterial fractions is still under investigation.

(5) Individual host resistance: Nonspecific factors may reduce host resistance, thus favoring the conversion of asymptomatic infection into disease. Among such "activators" of tuberculosis are starvation, gastrectomy, and administration of high doses of corticosteroids or immunosuppressive drugs. Such patients may receive INH "prophylaxis."

OTHER MYCOBACTERIA

In addition to tubercle bacilli (*M tuberculosis, M bovis*), other mycobacteria of varying degrees of pathogenicity have been grown from human sources in past decades. These "atypical" mycobacteria were initially grouped according to speed of growth at various temperatures and production of pigments. Photochromogens produced pigment in light but not in darkness; scotochromogens developed pigment when growing in the dark; and nonphotochromogens developed various degrees of pigmentation unrelated to exposure to light (Runyon, *Med Clin North Am* 1959; **43:**273; examples in Table 17–2). More recently, individual species or complexes are defined by additional laboratory characteristics (eg, reduction of nitrate, production of urease or catalase) and certain antigenic features. Most of them occur in the environment, are not readily transmitted from person to person, and are opportunistic.

A few species or complexes that are significant in medicine are outlined below.

A. Mycobacterium kansasii: *M kansasii* is a "photochromogen" that requires complex media for growth at 37 °C. It can produce pulmonary and systemic disease indistinguishable from tuberculosis, especially in patients with impaired immune responses. Sensitive to rifampin, it is often treated with rifampin + ethambutol + INH with good clinical response. The source of infection is uncertain, and communicability is low or absent.

B. Mycobacterium avium-intracellulare Complex: The members of this group grow optimally at 41 °C and produce smooth, soft colonies with little color. Able to infect birds, they cause spontaneous human disease infrequently. Infection with *M intracellulare,* however, is common in the southeastern USA, where the organism occurs in soil and water, and results in skin test reactions to PPD-B. Overt pulmonary disease occurs mainly in immunodeficient persons. Resistance to antituberculosis drugs is common, and disease due to this organism requires treatment with rifampin + ethambutol + streptomycin or cycloserine for many months.

C. Mycobacterium scrofulaceum: This is a scotochromogen occasionally found in water and as a saprophyte in adults with chronic lung disease. It is the commonest cause of chronic cervical lymphadenitis in small children and rarely causes other granulomatous disease. Surgical excision of involved cervical lymph nodes may be curative, whereas resistance to antituberculosis drugs is common. Occasionally, infection responds to combined treatment with INH + rifampin + streptomycin or cycloserine. (*Mycobacterium shulgai* and *Mycobacterium xenopi* are similar.)

D. Mycobacterium marinum and Mycobacterium ulcerans: These organisms occur in water, grow best at low temperature (31 °C), may infect fish, and can produce superficial skin lesions (ulcers, "swimming pool granulomas") in humans. Surgical excision, tetracyclines, and antituberculosis drugs may be tried in therapy.

E. Mycobacterium fortuitum-chelonei Complex: These are saprophytes found in soil and water that grow very rapidly in vitro and form no pigment. They can produce superficial and systemic disease in humans on rare occasions. *M chelonei* has contaminated porcine valves used as prostheses in human cardiac surgery. The organisms are often resistant to commonly used drugs but may be susceptible to amikacin or doxycycline.

Saprophytic Mycobacteria Not Associated With Human Illness

Mycobacterium phlei is frequently found on plants, in soil, or in water. *Mycobacterium gordonae* is similar. *Mycobacterium smegmatis* occurs regularly in human sebaceous secretions, and it might be confused with pathogenic acid-fast organisms. *Mycobacterium paratuberculosis* produces a chronic enteritis in cattle but presumably does not infect humans.

Extracts and PPD prepared from many of these mycobacteria may cross-react with PPD-S from *M tuberculosis,* resulting in positive skin tests in persons who are tuberculin-negative. This is a particular problem if a high proportion of the population becomes hypersensitive to mycobacteria acquired from the environment. Thus, about half of people in the southeastern USA have contact with *M intracellulare-fortuitum* and are PPD-B (derived from that organism)–positive but have never had contact with *M tuberculosis* (although their PPD-S may give weak positive cross-reactions).

M LEPRAE

Although this organism was described by Hansen in 1873 (9 years before Koch's discovery of the tubercle bacillus), it has not been cultivated on nonliving bacteriologic media.

Typical acid-fast bacilli—singly, in parallel bundles, or in globular masses—are regularly found in smears or scrapings from skin or mucous membranes (particularly the nasal septum) in lepromatous leprosy. The bacilli are often found within the endothelial cells of blood vessels or in mononuclear cells. The organisms have not been grown on artificial media. When bacilli from human leprosy (ground tissue, nasal scrapings) are inoculated into foot pads of mice, local granulomatous lesions develop with limited multiplication of bacilli. Inoculated armadillos develop extensive lepromatous leprosy, and armadillos spontaneously infected with leprosy have been found. *M leprae* from armadillo or human tissue contains a unique *o*-diphenoloxidase, perhaps an enzyme characteristic of leprosy bacilli.

Clinical Findings

The onset of leprosy is insidious. The lesions involve the cooler tissues of the body: skin, superficial nerves, nose, pharynx, larynx, eyes, and testicles. The skin lesions may occur as pale, anesthetic macular lesions 1–10 cm in diameter; diffuse or discrete erythematous, infiltrated nodules 1–5 cm in diameter;

or a diffuse skin infiltration. Neurologic disturbances are manifested by nerve infiltration and thickening, with resultant anesthesia, neuritis, paresthesia, trophic ulcers, and bone reabsorption and shortening of digits. The disfiguration due to the skin infiltration and nerve involvement in untreated cases may be extreme.

The disease is divided clinically and by laboratory tests into 2 distinct types: lepromatous and tuberculoid. In the lepromatous type, the course is progressive and malign, with nodular skin lesions; slow, symmetric nerve involvement; abundant acid-fast bacilli in the skin lesions; continuous bacteremia; and a negative lepromin (extract of lepromatous tissue) skin test. In the tuberculoid type, the course is benign and nonprogressive, with macular skin lesions, severe asymmetric nerve involvement of sudden onset with few bacilli present in the lesions, and a positive lepromin skin test. Cell-mediated immunity appears to be markedly defective in lepromatous leprosy.

Systemic manifestations of anemia and lymphadenopathy may also occur. Eye involvement is common. Amyloidosis may develop.

Diagnosis

Scrapings with a scalpel blade from skin or nasal mucosa or from a biopsy of ear lobe skin are smeared on a slide and stained by the Ziehl-Neelsen technique. Biopsy of skin or of a thickened nerve gives a typical histologic picture. No serologic tests are of value. Nontreponemal serologic tests for syphilis frequently yield false-positive results in leprosy.

Treatment

Several specialized sulfones (eg, dapsone [diaminodiphenylsulfone, DDS]) and rifampin suppress the growth of *M leprae* and the clinical manifestations of leprosy if given for many months. Sulfone resistance is beginning to emerge in leprosy. Clofazimine is an oral drug (100–300 mg/d) used in sulfone-resistant leprosy.

Epidemiology

The mode of transmission of leprosy is uncertain. It is believed that susceptibility to infection is greatest in childhood, that the incubation period may extend over many years, and that infected persons usually develop symptoms and signs later in life. Infection is most likely contracted by children from other infected members of the family. Treatment reduces or abolishes the infectivity of patients. Spontaneous leprosy occurs in free-living armadillos.

Prevention & Control

In endemic areas, removal of young children from infected families is employed with some success. Chemotherapy of active cases is good prophylaxis for the community. Chemoprophylaxis with sulfones in close family contacts has been employed. Experimental BCG vaccination has been used in children in endemic areas, with possible benefits. In small children whose parents have infectious lepromatous leprosy, chemoprophylaxis with dapsone (for at least 2 months) is being attempted, together with chemotherapy of the parents.

•   •   •

References

Addington WW: Treatment of pulmonary tuberculosis: Current options. *Arch Intern Med* 1979,**139**:1391.

Barrett-Connor E: The epidemiology of tuberculosis in physicians. *JAMA* 1979;**241**:133.

Bechelli LM et al: BCG vaccination of children against leprosy. *Bull WHO* 1974;**51**:93.

Centers for Disease Control: Guidelines for short-course tuberculosis chemotherapy. *MMWR* 1980;**29**:97.

Comstock GW et al: The prognosis of a positive tuberculin reaction in childhood and adolescence. *Am J Epidemiol* 1974;**99**:131.

Daniel TM, Mahmoud AH, Warren KS: Algorithms in the diagnosis and management of exotic diseases. 16. Tuberculosis. *J Infect Dis* 1976;**134**:417.

Eickhoff TC: The current status of BCG immunization against tuberculosis. *Annu Rev Med* 1977;**28**:411.

Glassroth J et al: Tuberculosis in the 1980s. *N Engl J Med* 1980;**302**:1441.

Grove DI, Warren KS, Mahmoud AA: Algorithms in the diagnosis and management of exotic diseases. 15. Leprosy. *J Infect Dis* 1976;**134**:205.

Gunnels JJ, Bates JH, Swindoll H: Infectivity of sputum-positive tuberculous patients on chemotherapy. *Am Rev Respir Dis* 1974;**109**:323.

Lester TW: Drug-resistant and atypical mycobacterial disease: Bacteriology and treatment. *Arch Intern Med* 1979;**139**:1399.

Mackaness GB: The immunology of antituberculous immunity. *Am Rev Respir Dis* 1968;**97**:337.

Mycobacterial lymphadenitis in adults and children. (Editorial.) *Br Med J* 1976;**1**:658.

Ortbals DW, Marr JJ: A comparative study of tuberculosis and other mycobacterial infections and their association with malignancy. *Am Rev Respir Dis* 1978;**117**:39.

PHS Advisory Committee on Immunization Practices: BCG vaccines. *MMWR* 1979;**28**:241.

Rosenzweig DY: Pulmonary mycobacterial infections due to *Mycobacterium intracellulare-avium* complex. *Chest* 1979;**75**:115.

Runyon EH et al: *Mycobacterium.* In: *Manual of Clinical Microbiology,* 2nd ed. Lennette EH, Spaulding EH, Truant JP (editors). American Society for Microbiology, 1974.

Sbarbaro JA: Tuberculosis. *Med Clin North Am* 1980;**64**:417.

Schaad UB et al: Management of atypical mycobacterial lymphadenitis in childhood: Review based on 380 cases. *J Pediatr* 1979;**95**:356.

Sheagren JM et al: Immunologic reactivity in patients with leprosy. *Ann Intern Med* 1969;**70**:295.

Storrs EE et al: Leprosy in the armadillo. *Science* 1974;**183**:851.

Thompson NJ et al: The booster phenomenon in serial tuberculin testing. *Am Rev Respir Dis* 1979;**119**:587.

Wolinsky E: Nontuberculous mycobacteria and associated diseases. *Am Rev Respir Dis* 1979;**119**:107.

18 | Enteric Gram-Negative Microorganisms

The enteric organisms are a large, heterogeneous group of gram-negative, nonsporeforming rods whose natural habitat is the intestinal tract of humans and animals. They include several families (eg, Enterobacteriaceae and Pseudomonadaceae), and many genera (eg, *Escherichia, Shigella, Salmonella, Enterobacter, Klebsiella, Serratia,* and *Proteus*). The exceedingly complex, confusing, and rapidly changing taxonomy has little bearing on the medical or public health significance of different groups. It is therefore minimized here. Some organisms (eg, *Escherichia coli*) form part of the normal flora of the intestinal tract; others (eg, salmonellae, shigellae) are regularly pathogenic for humans. Enteric bacteria are aerobes, ferment a wide range of carbohydrates, and possess a complex antigenic structure.

Most gram-negative bacteria possess complex lipopolysaccharides in their cell walls. These substances, endotoxins, have a variety of pathophysiologic effects that are summarized below. Many gram-negative enteric bacteria also produce exotoxins of clinical importance. A brief summary is given below. Subsequent sections deal with some prominent groups of enteric bacteria. Many enteric gram-negative rods are of particular concern at present as causes of iatrogenic or hospital-borne infections. Anaerobic gram-negative enteric bacteria, eg, *Bacteroides,* are discussed in Chapter 23.

ENDOTOXINS OF GRAM–NEGATIVE BACTERIA

The endotoxins of gram-negative bacteria are complex lipopolysaccharides derived from bacterial cell walls and often liberated when bacteria lyse. The substances are heat-stable, with molecular weights variously estimated to be between 100,000 and 900,000. The lipopolysaccharide can be extracted (eg, with phenol-water) and has 3 main regions (Table 18–1).

Pathophysiologic Effects

The pathophysiologic effects of all endotoxins are similar regardless of their origin.

The administration of endotoxin to animals or humans results in a series of events in which the endotoxin is taken up by reticuloendothelial or endothelial cells, degraded, or neutralized.

The following are prominently observed clinically or experimentally: fever, leukopenia and hypoglycemia, hypotension and shock, impaired perfusion of essential organs, activation of C3 and complement cascade, intravascular coagulation, and death.

A. Fever: (See p 151.) Normal body temperature is maintained within narrow limits by a balance between heat production and heat loss governed by thermoregulatory centers in the hypothalamus.

Infections (bacteria, viruses, fungi), antigen-antibody complexes, delayed type hypersensitivity reactions, certain steroids, and endotoxins can result in fever production. These insults act on various cells (granulocytes, monocytes, probably others) and result in the release of endogenous pyrogen that acts on the thermoregulatory center to "set" it at a higher level.

Injection of endotoxin gives fever after 60–90 minutes, the time needed to release endogenous pyrogen. Injection of the latter gives fever within 30 minutes. Repeated injection of endogenous pyrogen gives the same fever response each time. Repeated injection

Table 18–1. Composition of lipopolysaccharide "endotoxins" in the cell walls of gram-negative bacteria.

Chemistry	Common Name
(a) Repeating oligosaccharide (eg, man-rha-gal) combinations make up type-specific haptenic determinants (outermost on cell wall).	(a) O-specific polysaccharide; "somatic antigen" of "smooth" colonies. Induce specific immunity.
(b) (N-Acetylglucosamine, glucose, galactose, heptose.) Same in all gram-negative bacteria.	(b) Common core polysaccharide ("rough" colony antigen). Induce some nonspecific resistance to gram-negative sepsis.
(c) Backbone of alternating heptose and phosphate groups linked through KDO (2-keto-3-deoxy-octonic acid) to lipid. Lipid is linked to peptidoglycan (by glycoside bonds). (See p 18.)	(c) Lipid A with KDO responsible for primary toxicity.

of endotoxin gives less and less fever response ("tolerance"—due in part to reticuloendothelial blockade and in part to IgM antibodies to lipopolysaccharide).

B. Leukopenia: Bacteremia with gram-negative organisms is often accompanied by early leukopenia. Injection of endotoxins produces early leukopenia. In both instances, a secondary leukocytosis occurs later. The early leukopenia coincides with the temperature rise resulting from liberation of endogenous pyrogen from leukocytes and other cells. Endotoxin enhances glycolysis in many cell types and leads to hypoglycemia.

C. Hypotension: Early in gram-negative bacteremia, there may be widespread arteriolar and venular constriction (chill) followed by peripheral vascular dilatation, increased vascular permeability, decrease in venous return, lowered cardiac output, stagnation in the microcirculation, peripheral vasoconstriction, shock, and impaired organ perfusion and its consequences (eg, anuria). Injection of endotoxins can duplicate this complex sequence. Endotoxins can activate the release of vasoactive substances—eg, serotonin, kallikrein, and kinins—to initiate the sequence. Disseminated intravascular coagulation (DIC; see below) contributes to these vascular changes. However, vascular changes leading to shock may also occur in infections with gram-positive bacteria and viruses that contain no endotoxins.

D. Impaired Organ Perfusion and Acidosis: As a result of vascular reactions, hypotension, and shock, vital organs (kidneys, heart, liver, lungs, and brain) become anoxic and perform inadequately. This in turn may aggravate the vascular problems. Poor perfusion of tissues also results in accumulation of organic acids and metabolic acidosis (especially lactic acidosis).

E. Activation of C3 and Complement Cascade: Endotoxins are among the many different agents that can activate the "alternative pathway" of the complement cascade. C3 can be activated by endotoxins in the absence of preceding activation of C1,4,2, precipitating a variety of complement-mediated reactions (anaphylatoxins, chemotactic responses, membrane damage, etc) and a drop in serum complement components (C3,5–9).

F. Disseminated Intravascular Coagulation (DIC): DIC is a frequent complication of gram-negative bacteremia, although it can also occur in other infections. Endotoxin activates factor XII (Hageman factor)—the first step of the intrinsic clotting system—and thus the "coagulation cascade" is set into motion, which culminates in the conversion of fibrinogen to fibrin. At the same time, plasminogen can be activated by endotoxin to plasmin (a proteolytic enzyme), which can attack fibrin with the formation of fibrin split products. Reduction in platelets and fibrinogen and detection of fibrin split products are evidence of DIC.

Injection of endotoxin leads to platelets sticking to vascular endothelium and occlusion of small blood vessels. That, in turn, causes ischemic or hemorrhagic necrosis in various organs. Heparin can sometimes prevent lesions of DIC. Clinically, hemorrhagic necrosis of skin occurs frequently in meningococcemia and *Pseudomonas* sepsis, and suggestive DIC occurs frequently in severe gram-negative bacteremias.

Shwartzman phenomenon. This is probably a specialized model for DIC precipitated by endotoxin. If an animal is injected intradermally with endotoxin and injected intravenously with endotoxin the following day, necrosis of the prepared skin site occurs in a few hours. If endotoxin is given intravenously on 2 successive days, DIC occurs. It resembles histologically the DIC seen in gram-negative bacteremias. It has been suggested that the first dose of endotoxin "blocked" the reticuloendothelial system, so that it was unable to efficiently remove the second endotoxin dose. The reticuloendothelial system can be "blocked" by carbon particles or corticosteroid treatment instead of by the first endotoxin dose.

G. Death: Death may occur as a result of massive organ dysfunction, shock, and DIC. It is not directly related to the amount of endotoxin that can be found circulating in the bloodstream. Endotoxin levels can be assayed by the "*Limulus* test": a lysate of amebocytes from the horseshoe crab (*Limulus*) gels in the presence of 0.0001 μg/mL of endotoxin. However, this test is not entirely specific and has no prognostic value at present.

H. Other Biologic Actions of Endotoxins: Experimentally, small amounts of endotoxins can enhance resistance to ionizing radiation and to infection, perhaps by stimulating the removal of bacteria by the reticuloendothelial system. In pregnant animals, endotoxin can produce decidual hemorrhage, premature labor, and abortions. Pregnant women with active urinary tract infections caused by gram-negative bacteria may have premature labor and consequently a high perinatal mortality rate of offspring. This may be caused by endotoxins originating in the urinary tract.

Immunologic Features of Reactions to Endotoxins

From birth, humans constantly encounter lipopolysaccharides on the surfaces of gram-negative bacteria that form the normal flora of the gut. As a result, antibodies are continually being produced to the many antigenic determinants of lipopolysaccharides, and delayed type hypersensitivity is being established. Immunologic responses occur to the O-specific polysaccharides and the core polysaccharides (linked to proteins).

It is known (from studies on cesarean piglets completely free of antibodies) that true "primary toxicity" of endotoxins exists. In humans, this "primary toxicity" is inseparable from immunologic responses.

A. Immediate Type: Endotoxins combine with antibodies. The Ag-Ab complexes with complement can trigger the same type of reactions as attributed to "primary toxicity" of endotoxins: endogenous pyrogen release, coagulopathy, vasoactive substance release, vascular necrosis, etc.

Table 18–2. Acute bacterial diarrheas and "food poisoning."

Organism	Incubation Period (Hours)	Vomiting	Diarrhea	Fever	Epidemiology	Pathogenesis	Clinical Features
Staphylococcus	1–18	+++	+	–	Staphylococci grow in meats, dairy and bakery products and produce enterotoxin.	Enterotoxin acts on receptors in gut that transmit impulse to medullary centers.	Abrupt onset, intense vomiting for up to 24 hours, regular recovery in 24–48 hours. Occurs in persons eating the same food. No treatment usually necessary except to restore fluids and electrolytes.
Bacillus cereus	2–18	+++	++	–	Reheated fried rice causes vomiting or diarrhea.	Enterotoxins formed in food or in gut from growth of B cereus.	After 1–6 hours, mainly vomiting. After 8–16 hours, mainly diarrhea. Both self-limited to less than 1 day.
Clostridium perfringens	8–16	±	+++	–	Clostridia grow in rewarmed meat dishes and produce enterotoxin.	Enterotoxin causes hypersecretion in small intestine.	Abrupt onset of profuse diarrhea; vomiting occasionally. Recovery usual without treatment in 1–4 days. Many clostridia in cultures of food and feces of patients.
Clostridium botulinum	24–96	±	Rare	–	Clostridia grow in anaerobic foods and produce toxin.	Toxin absorbed from gut blocks acetylcholine at neuromuscular junction.	Diplopia, dysphagia, dysphonia, respiratory embarrassment. Treatment requires clear airway, ventilation, and intravenous polyvalent antitoxin (see p 210). Toxin present in food and serum. Mortality rate high.
Escherichia coli (some strains)	24–72	±	++	–	Organisms grow in gut and produce toxin. May also invade superficial epithelium.	Toxin* causes hypersecretion in small intestine ("traveler's diarrhea")†	Usually abrupt onset of diarrhea; vomiting rare. A serious infection in neonates. In adults, "traveler's diarrhea" is usually self-limited in 1–3 days. Use diphenoxylate (Lomotil) but no antimicrobials.
Vibrio parahaemolyticus	6–96	+	++	±	Organisms grow in seafood and in gut and produce toxin, or invade.	Toxin causes hypersecretion in small intestine; stools may be bloody.	Abrupt onset of diarrhea in groups consuming the same food, especially crabs and other seafood. Recovery is usually complete in 1–3 days. Food and stool cultures are positive.
Vibrio cholerae (mild cases)	24–72	+	+++	–	Organisms grow in gut and produce toxin.	Toxin* causes hypersecretion in small intestine.	Abrupt onset of liquid diarrhea in endemic area. Needs prompt replacement of fluids and electrolytes IV or orally. Tetracyclines shorten excretion of vibrios. Stool cultures positive.
Shigella sp (mild cases)	24–72	±	++	+	Organisms grow in superficial gut epithelium and gut lumen and produce toxin.	Organisms invade epithelial cells, blood, mucus, and PMNs in stools. Toxin in Shigella dysenteriae.	Abrupt onset of diarrhea, often with blood and pus in stools, cramps, tenesmus, and lethargy. Stool cultures are positive. Give trimethoprim-sulfamethoxazole or ampicillin or chloramphenicol in severe cases. Do not give opiates. Often mild and self-limited. Restore fluids.
Salmonella sp	8–48	±	++	+	Organisms grow in gut. Do not produce toxin.	Superficial infection of gut, little invasion.	Gradual or abrupt onset of diarrhea and low-grade fever. No antimicrobials unless systemic dissemination is suspected. Stool cultures are positive. Prolonged carriage is frequent.
Clostridium difficile	?	–	+++	+	Drug intake, eg, clindamycin.	Toxin causes epithelial necrosis in colon; pseudomembranous colitis (see p 213).	Especially after abdominal surgery, abrupt bloody diarrhea, and fever. Toxin in stool. Oral vancomycin useful in therapy.
Campylobacter fetus	2–10 days	–	+++	++	Organism grows in jejunum and ileum.	Invasion and toxin production uncertain.	Fever, diarrhea; PMNs and fresh blood in stool, especially in children. Usually self-limited. Special media needed for culture at 43 °C. Erythromycin in severe cases with invasion. Usual recovery in 5–8 days.
Yersinia enterocolitica	?	±	++	+	Fecal-oral transmission. Food-borne. ?In pets.	Gastroenteritis or mesenteric adenitis. Occasional bacteremia.	Severe abdominal pain, diarrhea, fever; PMNs and blood in stool; polyarthritis, erythema nodosum, especially in children. If severe, give tetracycline or gentamicin.

*Toxin stimulates adenylate cyclase activity and increases cAMP concentration in gut; this increases secretion of chloride and water and reduces reabsorption of sodium.
†Heat-stable toxin activates guanylate cyclase and results in hypersecretion.

B. Delayed Type: Cellular hypersensitivity to endotoxin antigens exists. Delayed hypersensitivity can induce reactions attributable to "primary toxicity" of endotoxins: fever, inflammatory lesions, vascular necrosis, etc.

The immune responses can, however, also have a protective role.

C. Tolerance: IgM antibodies to endotoxin can enhance their uptake and degradation by reticuloendothelial cells. This is one form of "tolerance." IgM antibodies may also prevent DIC.

D. Antibodies: High-titer antibodies to the core polysaccharide (glycolipid) can protect humans against shock and death from gram-negative bacteremia.

EXOTOXINS PRODUCED BY AEROBIC GRAM–NEGATIVE ENTERIC BACTERIA

Many enteric bacteria—in addition to their content of endotoxin—produce exotoxins of considerable medical importance. Outstanding features of some of these exotoxins are listed here and are also discussed on pp 146–148. (See also Table 18–2.)

Escherichia coli Enterotoxin

Some strains of *E coli* produce a heat-labile exotoxin that is under the genetic control of a transmissible plasmid. The labile toxin (LT) consists of linked peptides with a total molecular weight of about 80,000. Its subunits A and B have different actions. Subunit B attaches to the G_{M1} ganglioside at the brush border of epithelial cells of the small intestine. Subunit B facilitates the entry of subunit A into the cell, where A (MW 26,000) activates adenylate cyclase. This markedly increases the local concentration of cAMP (cyclic adenosine monophosphate), which results in intense and prolonged hypersecretion of water and chlorides and inhibits the reabsorption of sodium. The gut lumen is distended with fluid, and explosive hypermotility and diarrhea ensue, lasting for several days.

LT is antigenic, and it cross-reacts with the enterotoxin of *Vibrio cholerae*. LT stimulates the production of neutralizing antibodies in the serum (and perhaps on the gut surface) of persons previously infected with enterotoxigenic *E coli*. Persons residing in areas of high prevalence of such organisms (eg, in some developing countries) are likely to possess antibodies and are less prone to develop diarrhea on reexposure to enterotoxigenic *E coli*. A single antitoxin to LT appears to bind LT from different *E coli* and also from *V cholerae*. This provides a potential assay and diagnostic method. Assays for LT include (1) fluid accumulation in the intestine of laboratory animals; (2) typical cytologic changes in cultured cell lines of Chinese hamster ovary or other cells; (3) stimulation of steroid production in cultured adrenal tumor cells; and (4) binding and immunologic assays with standardized antisera to LT.

Some strains of *E coli* produce a heat-stable enterotoxin (ST; MW < 5000) that is under the genetic control of a heterogeneous group of plasmids. Many such strains also produce ST and may produce more severe diarrhea. ST activates guanylate cyclase in enteric epithelial cells and stimulates fluid secretion.

The plasmids carrying the genes for enterotoxins (LT, ST) may also carry genes for colonization factors that facilitate the attachment of *E coli* strains to intestinal epithelium by controlling surface antigens. Recognized colonization factors occur with particular frequency in some serotypes (eg, O78:H11, O6:H16), but others may exist. Certain serotypes of enterotoxigenic *E coli* (eg, O78:H12) are worldwide; others have a limited recognized distribution (eg, O159:H[variable] in Japan, O139:H28 in Brazil). There appears to be a clustering of enterotoxin plasmids in certain serotypes, but it is possible that virtually any *E coli* may acquire an appropriate plasmid. There is no definite association of enterotoxigenic *E coli* with the enteropathogenic strains causing outbreaks of diarrhea in nurseries. Likewise, there is no association between enterotoxigenic strains and those able to invade intestinal epithelial cells.

Enterotoxin of *E coli* appears to be inactivated by bismuth subsalicylate. Suspension of bismuth subsalicylate (Pepto-Bismol), 60 mL 4 times daily by mouth, has been proposed for prophylaxis of traveler's diarrhea caused by enterotoxigenic *E coli*.

Klebsiella pneumoniae Enterotoxin

Some strains of *K pneumoniae* produce a heat-stable enterotoxin that induces hypersecretion of fluids and electrolytes into the lumen of the small intestine and thus gives rise to diarrhea. The enterotoxin appears to have properties very similar to those of the heat-stable enterotoxin of *E coli*. The possibility exists that plasmids carrying appropriate genes have been transferred from *E coli* to make klebsiellae toxigenic; such plasmids may perhaps also have been transferred to a toxigenic *Citrobacter*, and *Enterobacter*, and others.

Pseudomonas aeruginosa Exotoxin

Many strains of *P aeruginosa* can produce an exotoxin in vitro and probably also in vivo that markedly inhibits protein synthesis and causes tissue necrosis. The mechanism of action of that exotoxin appears to be identical in all respects to the mechanism of action of diphtheria exotoxin (see p 146), although the peptide fragments of the *Pseudomonas* toxin may not be identical to those of the diphtheria toxin. Antitoxins to the *Pseudomonas* exotoxin are found in some human sera, including those of patients who have recovered from serious *Pseudomonas* infections. Although the toxin possesses dermonecrotic properties, its precise role in human *Pseudomonas* infections remains unsettled.

Shigella dysenteriae Exotoxin

S dysenteriae type 1 produces a heat-labile exotoxin that affects both the gut and the central nervous system. It is a protein that is antigenic (stimulating production of antitoxin) and lethal for experimental animals. Acting as an enterotoxin, it produces diarrhea as does the heat-labile *E coli* enterotoxin, perhaps by the same mechanism. In humans, it also inhibits sugar and amino acid absorption in the small intestine. Acting as a "neurotoxin," this material may contribute to the extreme severity and fatal nature of *S dysenteriae* infections and to the central nervous system reactions (meningismus, coma) observed in them. Patients with *Shigella flexneri* or *Shigella sonnei* infections develop antitoxin that neutralizes *S dysenteriae* toxin in vitro. This toxic activity is distinct from the invasive property of shigellae in dysentery. The 2 may act in sequence, the toxin producing an early nonbloody, voluminous diarrhea and the invasion of the large intestine resulting in later dysentery with blood and pus in stools.

Enterotoxins are also produced by some strains of *Yersinia enterocolitica, Aeromonas* species, and other enteric bacteria, but their role in pathogenesis is unsettled.

Vibrio cholerae Enterotoxin

V cholerae and related vibrios produce an enterotoxin that closely resembles the LT toxin of *E coli*. The toxin is heat-labile, with a molecular weight of about 80,000, consisting of subunits A (MW 28,000) and B. Ganglioside G_{M1} serves as mucosal receptor for B, which promotes entry of A into the cell. A activates adenylate cyclase and results in prolonged hypersecretion of water and electrolytes, which can lead to severe dehydration, shock, acidosis, and death. The genes for *V cholerae* enterotoxin are on the bacterial chromosome.

The cholera enterotoxin is antigenically related to LT of *E coli* and can stimulate the production of neutralizing antibodies. However, the precise role of antitoxic and antibacterial antibodies in protection against cholera is not clear.

Late-onset *Bacillus cereus* food poisoning (10–18 hours) may be caused by a similar adenylate cyclase–stimulating enterotoxin; the early-onset vomiting (1–6 hours after fried rice) resembles staphylococcal food poisoning.

ENTEROBACTERIACEAE

This is a family of gram-negative nonspore-forming aerobic or facultatively anaerobic rods with diverse ecologic and pathogenetic features. The family is characterized biochemically by the ability to reduce nitrates to nitrites and to ferment glucose, with the production of acid or acid and gas. The oxidase test is negative.

Many other biochemical reactions are of bewildering complexity and variability. Their detection (in United States laboratories) depends to a large extent upon the availability of commercially prepared kits. The latter, in turn, are usually evaluated for statistical significance in the reactions of different strains by

laboratories specializing in this field, including the Centers for Disease Control. A comprehensive approach to the identification of Enterobacteriaceae is presented by Martin and Washington in *Manual of Clinical Microbiology*, 3rd ed., Lennette EH (editor), American Society for Microbiology, 1980.

The nomenclature of these organisms is complex and confusing and changes frequently, especially as genetic relationships are uncovered by DNA homology studies and employed in taxonomy. In subsequent discussions, taxonomy will be minimized and the names employed in the medical literature will be preferred.

Antigenic Structure

Enterobacteriaceae have a complex antigenic structure. The 3 main groups of antigens are O (somatic), H (flagellar), and K (capsular).

O antigens are the most external part of the cell wall lipopolysaccharide and consist of repeating units of polysaccharide. Some O-specific polysaccharides contain unique sugars called dideoxyhexoses. O antigens are resistant to heat and alcohol and usually are detected by bacterial agglutination. Antibodies to O antigens are predominantly IgM and tend to agglutinate O antigens in granular masses.

While each genus of Enterobacteriaceae is associated with specific O groups, a single organism may carry several O antigens, and members of different genera share O antigens. Thus, most shigellae share one or more O antigens with *E coli*. The latter may cross-react with some *Providencia, Klebsiella,* and *Salmonella* species. Many Enterobacteriaceae share the O14 antigen of *E coli*. Occasionally, O antigens may be associated with specific human diseases, eg, O types of *E coli* found in diarrhea or in urinary tract infections (see below).

H antigens are located on flagella and are denatured or removed by heat or alcohol. They are preserved by treating motile bacterial variants with formalin. With anti-H antibodies (mainly IgG), such H antigens agglutinate in fluffy clumps. The determinants in H antigens are a function of the amino acid sequence in flagellar protein (flagellin). Within a single serotype, flagellar antigens may be in either or both of 2 forms, called phase 1 (conventionally designated by lowercase letters) and phase 2 (conventionally designated by arabic numerals) (see Table 18–4). The organism tends to change from one phase to the other; this is called phase variation. H antigens on the bacterial surface may interfere with agglutination by anti-O antibody.

Capsular Antigens

These are external to O antigens on some but not all kinds of Enterobacteriaceae. Some capsular antigens are polysaccharides, including the K antigens of *E coli;* others are proteins. K antigens may interfere with O agglutination by O antisera; they may be associated with virulence (eg, K1 *E coli* is prominent in neonatal meningitis; K antigens of *E coli* cause attachment of the bacteria to epithelial cells prior to diarrhea or urinary tract invasion; Vi antigens of some species of *Salmonella* are associated with invasiveness). Some K antigens of coliform bacteria cross-react with capsular polysaccharides of *Haemophilus influenzae, Streptococcus pneumoniae,* and *Neisseria meningitidis.* Thus, *E coli* O75:K100:H5 can induce antibodies that react with *H influenzae* type b—and may protect against the latter.

The antigenic classification of Enterobacteriaceae often indicates the presence of each specific antigen. Thus, the antigenic formula of an *E coli* may be O55:K5:H21; that of *Salmonella schottmülleri* is 1,4,5,12:b:1,2.

THE COLIFORM BACTERIA

The coliform bacteria are a large and heterogeneous group of gram-negative rods resembling, to some extent, *E coli*. The complexity of the group, the variations in biochemical test results, and the changing ecologic relationships have led to a confusing profusion of names. Besides *E coli*, derived from the intestinal tract, the following groups of organisms are often included among the "coliforms":

(1) The *Klebsiella-Enterobacter-Serratia* group: Typical *K pneumoniae,* originally known as a respiratory pathogen, is now commonly encountered in hospital infections of the respiratory and the urinary tracts. It is characterized by mucoid growth, large polysaccharide capsules, and lack of motility. *Enterobacter aerogenes* is often motile, exhibits less mucoid growth, has small capsules, and may be found free-living as well as in the intestinal tract, in urinary tract infections, and in sepsis. (*Enterobacter* was formerly called *Aerobacter.*) *Serratia marcescens* is a small, usually free-living, gram-negative rod that may produce an intense red pigment in culture. Nonpigmented variants cause iatrogenic sepsis. *Serratia* usually ferments lactose very slowly. *Hafnia (Enterobacter hafniae)* is sometimes associated with gastroenteritis.

(2) The *Arizona-Edwardsiella-Citrobacter* group: These organisms ferment lactose very slowly, if at all. They resemble salmonellae both in biochemical features and, occasionally, in pathogenicity for humans, as when they cause enteritis or sepsis.

(3) The "Providence" group (*Providencia*): These organisms are biochemically related to *Proteus,* deaminate amino acids (eg, lysine), and are encountered free-living or in urinary tract infections, sepsis, etc.

Morphology & Identification

A. Typical Organisms: The coliform bacteria are short gram-negative rods that may form chains. Under unfavorable conditions of culture (eg, exposure to penicillin), long filamentous forms occur. Capsules are rare in *E coli*, more frequent in *Enterobacter,* and large and regular in *Klebsiella.* Motility is present in

most strains of *E coli* and some strains of *Enterobacter;* it is absent in *Klebsiella.*

B. Culture: *E coli* forms circular, convex, smooth colonies with distinct edges. *Enterobacter* colonies are similar but somewhat more mucoid. *Klebsiella* colonies are large and very mucoid and tend to coalesce with prolonged incubation. Hemolysis on blood agar is produced by some strains of *E coli.*

C. Growth Characteristics: *Escherichia* and *Enterobacter* break down many carbohydrates, with the production of acid and gas. *Escherichia* produces approximately equal amounts of CO_2 and H_2 from dextrose; *Enterobacter* produces twice as much CO_2 as H_2. *Serratia* and groups 2 and 3 of coliforms listed above typically ferment lactose slowly or not at all and differ in other biochemical features. *Klebsiella* also ferments many carbohydrates, but variations among strains are great. See Table 18–7.

A few commonly available biochemical tests are as follows:

1. Indole–The ability to produce indole in tryptophan broth, eg, certain *Proteus* species are indole-positive.

2. Methyl red–Growth in 0.5% glucose broth results in pH below 4.5. Klebsiellae are typically methyl red–negative.

3. Voges-Proskauer reaction–Production of acetylmethylcarbinol from dextrose: Klebsiellae are typically Voges-Proskauer–positive, whereas many other Enterobacteriaceae are negative.

Certain enzyme activities, eg, decarboxylases for several amino acids, are commonly used in biochemical differentiation (Table 18–7).

D. Variation: All cultures contain variants and stable mutants with respect to colonial morphology (rough or smooth), antigenic characteristics, biochemical behavior, and virus resistance. *E coli* strain K12 has been extensively studied from the standpoint of plasmid biology, genetics, and sexual recombination of inherited characteristics.

Antigenic Structure

Coliform organisms have a complex antigenic structure, and strains are divergent in their serologic behavior. They are classified by more than 150 different heat-stable somatic O antigens, by more than 100 heat-labile capsular K antigens, and by more than 50 flagellar H antigens. The K antigens occur on surfaces and often interfere with O agglutination unless they are destroyed by heating. The specific K1 antigen on *E coli* is associated with 70% of neonatal coliform meningitis and thus acts as a virulence factor. However, there is no relationship between K1 and enteropathogenicity in neonates.

Klebsiellae form large capsules consisting of polysaccharides (K antigens) covering the somatic (O or R) antigens. Klebsiellae can be identified by capsular swelling tests with specific antisera. Human infections of the respiratory tract are caused particularly by capsular types 1 and 2; those of the urinary tract, by types 8, 9, 10, and 24.

There are many examples of overlapping antigenic structures between coliform and other bacteria. Most Enterobacteriaceae share a common enterobacterial antigen first found in *E coli* O14. The type 2 capsular polysaccharide of klebsiellae is very similar to the polysaccharide of type 2 pneumococci. Many other examples of cross-reactions are known.

Colicins (Bacteriocins)

Many gram-negative organisms produce bacteriocins (colicins, pyocins). These are antibiotic-like bactericidal substances produced by certain strains of bacteria active against some other strains of the same or closely related species. Their production is controlled by plasmids. Colicins are produced by coliform organisms; pyocins by *Pseudomonas*; marcescins by *Serratia*. Bacteriocin production is accompanied by death and lysis of the producing cell. Bacteriocin-producing strains are resistant to their own bacteriocin; thus, bacteriocins can be used for "typing" of organisms.

Pathogenesis & Pathology

The coliform bacteria constitute a large part of the normal aerobic intestinal flora. Within the intestine, they generally do not cause disease and may even contribute to normal function and nutrition. These organisms become pathogenic only when they reach tissues outside the intestinal tract, particularly the urinary tract, the biliary tract, the lungs, the peritoneum, or the meninges, causing inflammation at these sites. When normal host defenses are inadequate, particularly in early infancy, in old age, in the terminal stages of other diseases, after immunosuppression, or with indwelling venous or urethral catheters, coliform bacteria may reach the bloodstream and cause sepsis. In the neonatal period, high susceptibility to coliform sepsis may be caused by the absence of bactericidal IgM antibodies that cannot pass the placenta. *E coli*, especially O serotypes 4, 6, 15, and 75, are the commonest causes of urinary tract infection.

E coli may cause diarrheal disease by means of 2 distinct mechanisms. Some strains produce enterotoxins (see above) by virtue of genes carried in plasmids. Such strains may produce outbreaks in nurseries or in groups of children or adults, where the disease spreads rapidly; these strains may also cause traveler's diarrhea. A second mechanism for the production of diarrhea depends on the ability of certain strains of *E coli* to invade superficial intestinal epithelium as the shigellae do.

Certain O serotypes of *E coli* have been associated with outbreaks of diarrhea among neonates in nurseries (eg, O55, O111, O127). It is possible that some of these "enteropathogenic" strains are more invasive or that they carry plasmids that control enterotoxin production. However, the association between O serotype and "enteropathogenicity" for neonates, leading to diarrhea or sepsis, is far from constant.

Arizona-Citrobacter-Edwardsiella resemble salmonellae and can cause enteritis and sepsis. *Providencia* species are encountered in normal intestinal flora and occasionally in diarrheal disorders. *Citrobacter* and *Serratia* are common in hospitalized patients as opportunistic infections. *Serratia* (usually nonpigmented) can cause pneumonia, bacteremia, and endocarditis—especially in narcotic addicts and hospitalized patients. *Erwinia* species (*Enterobacter agglomerans*) is a plant pathogen resembling coliforms. It has produced bacteremia after administration of contaminated intravenous fluids. All cause urinary tract infections at times and often are resistant to antimicrobial therapy.

K pneumoniae occurs in the respiratory tract and in the feces of about 5% of normal individuals and is the causative agent responsible for a small proportion (about 3%) of bacterial pneumonias. *K pneumoniae* produces extensive hemorrhagic necrotizing consolidation of the lung, which, if untreated, has a high mortality rate (40–90%). Occasionally it produces urinary tract infection or enteritis in children and bacteremia with focal lesions in debilitated patients. Other coliform organisms may also produce pneumonia. Two other klebsiellae are associated with inflammatory conditions of the upper respiratory tract: *Klebsiella ozaenae* has been isolated from the nasal mucosa in ozena, a fetid, progressive atrophy of mucous membranes; and *Klebsiella rhinoscleromatis* from rhinoscleroma, a destructive granuloma of the nose and pharynx.

Calymmatobacterium (Donovania) granulomatis, related to the klebsiellae, causes granuloma inguinale, a venereal disease. It is grown with difficulty on media containing egg yolk. Ampicillin or tetracycline is effective treatment.

Clinical Findings

The clinical manifestations of infections with coliform bacteria depend entirely on the site of the infection and cannot be differentiated by symptoms or signs from processes caused by other bacteria. Coliform bacteremia is often associated with vascular collapse and shock, especially in persons with impaired host defenses subjected to drugs and surgical procedures.

Diagnostic Laboratory Tests

A. Specimens: Urine, blood, pus, spinal fluid, sputum, or other material, as indicated by the localization of the process.

B. Stained Smears: Because gram-negative rods of the coliform group all resemble each other, only the presence of large capsules *(Klebsiella)* is diagnostic. Direct capsule-swelling tests can be performed on klebsiellae visible in fresh specimens.

C. Culture: Specimens are plated both on blood agar and on "differential" media that contain special dyes and carbohydrates; this permits the rapid recognition of lactose-fermenting and non–lactose-fermenting colonies (Table 18–3). On such media, eg, MacConkey's or eosin–methylene blue (EMB) agar, *E coli* colonies have a distinct metallic sheen. Organisms

Table 18–3. Rapid, presumptive identification of gram-negative enteric bacteria.

Lactose Fermented Rapidly	Lactose Fermented Slowly	Lactose Not Fermented
Escherichia coli: Metallic sheen on differential media; motile; flat, nonviscous colonies. *Enterobacter aerogenes:* Raised colonies, no metallic sheen; often motile; more viscous growth. *Klebsiella pneumoniae:* Very viscous, mucoid growth; nonmotile.	*Edwardsiella, Serratia, Citrobacter, Arizona, Providencia, Erwinia*	*Shigella* species: Nonmotile; no gas from dextrose. *Salmonella* species: Motile; acid and usually gas from dextrose. *Proteus* species: "Swarming" on agar; urea rapidly hydrolyzed (smell of ammonia). *Pseudomonas* species: Soluble pigments, blue-green and fluorescing; sweetish smell.

isolated on "differential" media are further identified by biochemical and serologic tests (Table 18–7). Rapid preliminary identification of gram-negative enteric bacteria is often possible (Table 18–3).

Treatment

No single specific therapy is available. The sulfonamides, ampicillin, cephalosporins, chloramphenicol, tetracyclines, polymyxins, and aminoglycosides have marked antibacterial effects against the coliform group, but variation in strain susceptibility is great and laboratory tests for antibiotic sensitivity are essential. Multiple drug resistance is common and is under the control of plasmids that are transmitted by conjugation or transduction. *Serratia* is often resistant to available antimicrobial drugs but may respond to trimethoprim-sulfamethoxazole plus polymyxin. Certain conditions predisposing to infection by these organisms must be corrected surgically, eg, by relief of urinary tract obstruction, closure of perforation in an abdominal organ, or resection of a bronchiectatic portion of lung.

Epidemiology, Prevention, & Control

Coliform bacteria establish themselves in the normal intestinal tract within a few days after birth and from then on constitute a main portion of the normal aerobic microbial flora of the body. *E coli* is the prototype. Finding coliforms in water or milk is accepted as proof of fecal contamination. The presence of either *Escherichia* or *Enterobacter* species or their intermediates in large numbers in drinking water suggests surface contamination.

Control measures are not feasible as far as the normal endogenous flora is concerned. Enteropathogenic *E coli* serotypes and certain "paracolon" bacteria should be controlled like salmonellae. Coliforms constitute a principal problem in hospital infection at present. It is particularly important to recognize that many gram-negative coliform bacteria are "opportunists" that cause illness when they are introduced into debilitated patients. Within hospitals or other institutions, these bacteria are commonly transmitted by personnel, instruments, or parenteral medications. Their control thus depends on hand washing, rigorous asepsis, sterilization of equipment, disinfection,

restraint in ordering intravenous therapy, and strict precautions in keeping the urinary tract sterile.

Immunity

In systemic infections, specific antibodies develop, but it is uncertain whether significant immunity follows infections due to these organisms. Antibodies against the "core" glycolipid of Enterobacteriaceae are associated with protection against the hemodynamic sequelae of gram-negative rod bacteremia. They also reduce the fever response and augment intravascular clearance of certain organisms.

THE *PROTEUS–PROVIDENCIA* GROUP

These are gram-negative, motile aerobic rods that possess the enzyme phenylalanine deaminase. Most species are free-living in water, soil, and sewage, and some may occur in the normal intestinal flora. *Proteus (Morganella) morganii* and *Proteus (Providencia) rettgeri* occur in hospital infections. The *Proteus-Providencia* group ferment lactose not at all or very slowly. *Proteus* species can produce urease, resulting in rapid hydrolysis of urea with liberation of ammonia. In urinary tract infections by *Proteus*, the urine becomes intensely alkaline, promoting stone formation and making acidification virtually impossible. *Providencia* does not produce urease.

Proteus species move very actively by means of peritrichous flagella, resulting in "swarming" on solid media unless inhibited by chemicals (eg, phenylethyl alcohol, CLED [cystine-lactose-electrolyte–deficient agar] medium). Rapid motility may contribute to invasion of the urinary tract.

Motile strains of *Proteus* contain H antigen in addition to the somatic O antigen. Certain strains labeled OX share specific polysaccharides with some rickettsiae. The OX strains are agglutinated by sera from patients with rickettsial diseases (Weil-Felix test). *Proteus*, like the coliform bacilli, produces infections in humans only when it leaves its normal habitat in the intestinal tract. It is frequently found in chronic urinary tract infections and produces bacteremia, pneumonia, and focal lesions in debilitated patients or those receiving intravenous infusions.

There are great variations among strains of *Proteus* in antibiotic sensitivity.

Proteus mirabilis is often inhibited by penicillins. For other members of the group, the most active antibiotics in 1982 are aminoglycosides (amikacin, tobramycin, gentamicin), cephalosporins, (cefamandole, cefoxitin), and chloramphenicol.

THE *PSEUDOMONAS* GROUP

The *Pseudomonas* group is composed of gram-negative motile rods which produce water-soluble pigments that diffuse through the medium. They occur widely in soil, water, sewage, and air.

P aeruginosa is frequently present in small numbers in the normal intestinal flora. It is also found on the human skin. Other *Pseudomonas* species occur in any moist environment but rarely cause disease.

P aeruginosa grows readily on culture media, does not ferment lactose, and forms smooth round colonies with a fluorescent greenish color and a sweetish aromatic odor. From the colonies, bluish-green pigment diffuses into the medium. Some strains hemolyze blood. Among the pigments produced by *P aeruginosa* are pyocyanin, a bluish material soluble in chloroform and water and possessing some antimicrobial activity; and fluorescein, a greenish, fluorescent, water-soluble (but not chloroform-soluble) material (Table 18–3). *P aeruginosa* may also produce a heat-labile exotoxin (see above). *P aeruginosa* is an obligate aerobe.

P aeruginosa is a pathogen only when introduced into areas devoid of normal defenses or when participating in mixed infections. It produces infection of wounds and burns, giving rise to blue-green pus; meningitis, when introduced by lumbar puncture; and urinary tract infection, when introduced by catheters and instruments or in irrigating solutions. Involvement of the respiratory tract, especially from contaminated respirators, results in necrotizing pneumonia. Mucoid *Pseudomonas* strains occur, particularly in patients with pulmonary cystic fibrosis. The organism is often found in otitis externa. Infection of the eye, which may lead to rapid destruction of the eyeball, occurs most commonly after injury or surgical procedures. *P aeruginosa* (and other species, eg, *Pseudomonas cepacia, Pseudomonas putida, Pseudomonas maltophilia*) is resistant to most antimicrobial agents (especially in the presence of Ca^{2+} and Mg^{2+}) and therefore becomes dominant and important when more susceptible bacteria of the normal flora are suppressed. In infants or debilitated persons, it may invade the bloodstream and result in fatal sepsis. This occurs commonly in patients with leukemia or lymphoma who have received antineoplastic drugs or radiation, and in patients with severe burns. In *P aeruginosa* sepsis, verdoglobin (a breakdown product of hemoglobin) or fluorescent pigment can be detected in wounds, burns, or urine by ultraviolet fluorescence. For epidemiologic purposes, strains can be typed by

bacteriophage or by pyocins (see Colicins, above). At least 7 antigenic types of *P aeruginosa* have been defined. Lipopolysaccharides carry antigenic specificity. Vaccine from these types administered to high-risk patients provides some protection against *Pseudomonas* sepsis 10 days later. Such treatment is instituted in cases of leukemia, burns, cystic fibrosis, and immunosuppression.

In 1982, the antimicrobials most useful against *Pseudomonas* include carbenicillin or ticarcillin, singly or in combination with an aminoglycoside; polymyxins are occasionally beneficial in localized infections.

Aeromonas species are free-living gram-negative rods found especially in water. Occasionally they cause opportunistic nosocomial infections. (See also p 279.)

Chromobacterium violaceum (and other species) are gram-negative pigmented rods resembling pseudomonads. They occur in subtropical climates in soil and water and may infect animals and humans through breaks in the skin or via the gut. This may result in abscesses, diarrhea, and sepsis, with many deaths. Chromobacteria are often susceptible to chloramphenicol, tetracyclines, and aminoglycosides.

THE SALMONELLAE

Salmonellae are gram-negative, motile aerobic rods that characteristically ferment glucose and mannose but fail to ferment lactose or sucrose. They are often pathogenic for humans or animals by the oral route. There are more than 1500 serotypes of salmonellae.

Morphology & Identification

Salmonellae are gram-negative nonsporeforming rods that vary in length. Most species are motile with peritrichous flagella, except *Salmonella pullorum-gallinarum*. Salmonellae grow readily on simple media, but they do not ferment lactose or sucrose. From glucose and mannose, they form acid and sometimes gas (Table 18–7). They tend to produce hydrogen sulfide. They survive freezing in water for long periods. Salmonellae are resistant to certain chemicals (eg, brilliant green, sodium tetrathionate, and sodium deoxycholate); such compounds inhibit coliform bacteria and are therefore useful for isolation of salmonellae from feces.

Antigenic Structure

While salmonellae are initially detected by their biochemical characteristics, groups and species must be identified by antigenic analysis. Like other Enterobacteriaceae, salmonellae possess several O antigens (from a total of more than 60) and different H antigens in one or both of 2 phases. Some salmonellae have capsular antigens, referred to as Vi, which may interfere with agglutination by O antisera and may be associated with virulence.

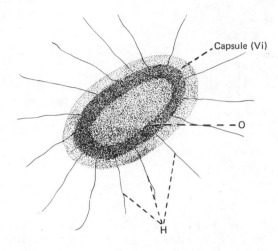

Figure 18–1. Antigenic structure of *Salmonella typhi.*

The Kauffmann-White classification scheme of salmonellae is based on agglutination tests with absorbed antisera, permitting identification of different O and H antigens in an unknown organism. Examples of the group designation of a few named *Salmonella* species are given (Table 18–4) with their antigenic formulas.

For epidemiologic purposes, strains can be identified by lysis by a specific bacteriophage. Such "phage typing" can help in the tracing of isolates and contact cases. It is a function of specific phage receptors.

Variation

Organisms may lose H antigens and become nonmotile. Loss of O antigen is associated with change from smooth to rough colony form. Vi antigen may be lost partially or completely. Antigens may be acquired (or lost) in the process of transduction (see Chapter 4).

Classification

There are 3 primary species: *Salmonella typhi* (one serotype), *Salmonella choleraesuis* (one serotype), and *Salmonella enteritidis* (more than 1500 serotypes). In practice, however, each isolate is classified by antigenic analysis and the assignment of a specific name.

Table 18–4. Representative antigenic formulas of salmonellae.

O Group	Species	Antigenic Formula*
D	*S typhi*	**9, 12,** (Vi):d:—
A	*S paratyphi A*	**1, 2, 12:**a:—
C_1	*S choleraesuis*	**6, 7:**c:**1, 5**
B	*S typhimurium*	**1, 4, 5, 12:**i:**1, 2**
D	*S enteritidis*	**1, 9, 12:**g, m:—

*O antigens: boldface numerals.
(Vi): Vi antigen if present.
Phase 1 H antigen: lower case letter.
Phase 2 H antigen: numeral.

Pathogenesis & Pathology

S typhi and perhaps *Salmonella paratyphi A* and *S schottmülleri* (formerly *Salmonella paratyphi B*) are primarily infective for humans, and infection with these organisms implies acquisition from a human source. The vast majority of salmonellae, however, are chiefly pathogenic in animals that constitute the reservoir for human infection. Involved animals include poultry, pigs, rodents, cattle, pets (from turtles to parrots), and many others.

The organisms virtually always enter via the oral route, usually with contaminated food and drink. The mean infective dose for humans is 10^5–10^8 salmonellae to produce clinical or subclinical infection. Among the host factors that contribute to resistance to *Salmonella* infection are gastric acidity, normal intestinal microbial flora, and local intestinal immunity (see below).

In humans, salmonellae produce 3 main types of disease, but mixed forms are frequent (Table 18–5).

A. The "Enteric Fevers": This syndrome is produced mainly by *S typhi, S paratyphi A,* and *S schottmülleri.* The ingested salmonellae reach the small intestine and enter lymphatics that carry them to the bloodstream. They are then carried by the blood to many organs, including the intestine, where organisms multiply in lymphoid tissue and are excreted in stools.

After an incubation period of 10–14 days, there is fever, malaise, headache, constipation, bradycardia, and myalgia. The fever rises to a high plateau, and the spleen and liver become enlarged. Rose spots are seen briefly in rare cases. The white blood cell count is normal or low. In the preantibiotic era, the chief complications of enteric fever were intestinal hemorrhage and even perforation. The mortality rate was 10–15%. Treatment with chloramphenicol or ampicillin has reduced the mortality rate to less than 1%. Occasional *S typhi* resistant to these drugs has responded to trimethoprim-sulfamethoxazole.

The principal lesions are hyperplasia and necrosis of lymphoid tissue (eg, Peyer's patches), hepatitis, focal necrosis of liver, and inflammation of gallbladder, periosteum, lungs, and other organs and lesions.

B. Bacteremia With Focal Lesions: This is associated commonly with *S choleraesuis* but may be caused by any *Salmonella* serotype. Following oral infection, there is early invasion of the bloodstream (with possible focal lesions in lungs, bones, meninges, etc), but intestinal manifestations are often absent. Blood cultures are regularly positive.

C. Enterocolitis (Formerly "Gastroenteritis"): This is the commonest manifestation of *Salmonella* infection. Eight to 48 hours after ingestion of *Salmonellae* (in the USA, *Salmonella typhimurium* is prominent), there is nausea, headache, vomiting, and profuse diarrhea, with few leukocytes in the stools but rarely blood. Low-grade fever is common, but the episode usually resolves in 2–3 days.

Inflammatory lesions of the small and large intestine are present. Bacteremia is quite rare (2–4%) except in immunodeficient persons. Blood cultures are

Table 18–5. Clinical diseases induced by salmonellae.

	Enteric Fevers	Septicemias	Enterocolitis
Incubation period	7–20 days	Variable	8–48 hours
Onset	Insidious	Abrupt	Abrupt
Fever	Gradual, then high plateau, with "typhoidal" state	Rapid rise, then spiking "septic" temperature	Usually low
Duration of disease	Several weeks	Variable	2–5 days
Gastrointestinal symptoms	Often early constipation; later, bloody diarrhea	Often none	Nausea, vomiting, diarrhea at onset
Blood cultures	Positive in 1st–2nd week of disease	Positive during high fever	Negative
Stool cultures	Positive from 2nd week on; negative earlier in disease	Infrequently positive	Positive soon after onset

usually negative, but stool cultures are positive for salmonellae and may remain positive for several weeks after clinical recovery.

Diagnostic Laboratory Tests

Blood for culture must be taken repeatedly. In enteric fevers and septicemias, blood is often positive in the first week of the disease. Bone marrow cultures may be useful. Urine cultures may be positive after the second week.

Stool specimens also must be taken repeatedly. In enteric fevers, the stools are positive from the second or third week on; in gastroenteritis, during the first week.

Duodenal drainage establishes the location of the organisms in the biliary tract in carriers.

Repeated specimens of blood serum for serology should be taken to demonstrate a rise in titer.

A. Bacteriologic Methods for Isolation of Salmonellae:

1. Enrichment cultures–Put specimen (usually stool) into selenite F or tetrathionate broth, both of which inhibit normal intestinal bacteria and permit multiplication of salmonellae. After incubation for 1–2 days, this is plated on differential and selective media or examined by direct immunofluorescence.

2. Selective medium cultures–The specimen is plated on *Salmonella-Shigella* (SS) agar or on deoxycholate-citrate agar, which favors growth of salmonellae and shigellae over coliform organisms.

3. Differential medium cultures–Eosin-methylene blue, MacConkey's, or deoxycholate medium permits rapid detection of lactose nonfermenters (which include not only salmonellae and shigellae but also *Proteus, Pseudomonas, Serratia*, etc). Gram-positive organisms are somewhat inhibited. Bismuth sulfite medium permits rapid detection of *S typhi*, which forms black colonies because of H_2S production.

4. Final identification–Suspected colonies from solid media are identified by biochemical (Table 18–7) and slide agglutination tests with specific sera.

B. Serologic Methods: Serologic techniques are used for identification of an unknown culture with a known serum (see below) and detection of antibody titer in patients with unknown illness. Serum aggluti-

nins rise sharply during the second and third week of *Salmonella* infection. At least 2 serum specimens should be obtained at intervals of 7–10 days to prove rise in titer.

1. The rapid slide agglutination test is performed by mixing known serum and unknown culture on a slide and observing the mixture under the low-power objective. Clumping, when it occurs, can be observed within a few minutes. This test is particularly useful for preliminary identification of cultures.

2. The tube dilution agglutination test (Widal test)–Serial (2-fold) dilutions of unknown serum are tested against antigens from representative salmonellae. The results are interpreted as follows: (1) High or rising titer of "O" (1:160 or more) suggests that active infection is present. (2) High titer of "H" (1:160 or more) suggests past vaccination or past infection. (3) High titer of "Vi" occurs in some carriers.

Immunity

Infection with *S typhi, S paratyphi,* and *S schottmülleri* usually confers a certain degree of immunity. Reinfection may occur but is often milder. Circulating antibodies to O or Vi are related to resistance to infection and disease. However, relapses may occur in 2–3 weeks after recovery in spite of antibodies. Secretory IgA antibodies may prevent attachment of salmonellae to intestinal epithelium.

Treatment

In severe diarrhea, replacement of fluids and electrolytes is essential. Opiates may be needed to reduce cramps. Two decades ago, chloramphenicol was a drug of choice, then ampicillin. Multiple drug resistance transmitted genetically by plasmids among enteric bacteria plays a role in the problems of treating *Salmonella* infections. Strains of salmonellae resistant to chloramphenicol and ampicillin are becoming more frequent. Trimethoprim-sulfamethoxazole may be a useful drug.

While enteric fevers and bacteremias with focal lesions require antimicrobial treatment, the vast majority of cases of enterocolitis do not, and excretion of organisms may even be prolonged by antimicrobials.

In most carriers, the organisms persist in the gallbladder (particularly if there are stones) and in the biliary tract. Some chronic carriers have been cured by ampicillin alone, but in most cases cholecystectomy must be combined with drug treatment.

Epidemiology

A. Sources of Infection: The sources of infection are food and drink that have been contaminated with salmonellae. The following sources are important:

1. Water–Contamination with feces often results in explosive epidemics.

2. Milk and other dairy products (ice cream, cheese, custard)–Contamination with feces or due to inadequate pasteurization or improper handling. Limited outbreaks traceable to source of supply.

3. Shellfish–Contaminated water.

4. Dried or frozen eggs–From infected fowl or contamination during processing.

5. Dried coconut.

6. Meats and meat products–Either from infected animals (poultry) or contaminated with feces by rodents or humans. Corned beef has often been involved.

7. Animal dyes (eg, carmine) used in drugs, foods, and cosmetics.

8. Household pets, eg, turtles, dogs, and cats.

B. Origin of Contamination: The feces of unsuspected subclinical cases or carriers are a more important source of contamination than frank clinical cases who are promptly isolated, eg, when carriers working as food handlers are "shedding" organisms. Many animals, including cattle, rodents, and fowl, are naturally infected with a variety of salmonellae and have the bacteria in their tissues (meat), excreta, or eggs. The incidence of typhoid fever has decreased, but the incidence of other *Salmonella* infections has increased markedly in the USA. The problem is aggravated by the widespread use of animal feeds containing antimicrobial drugs that favor the proliferation of drug-resistant salmonellae and their potential transmission to humans.

C. Carriers: After manifest or subclinical infection, some individuals continue to harbor organisms in their tissues for variable lengths of time (convalescent carriers or healthy permanent carriers). Three percent of survivors with typhoid become permanent carriers, harboring the organisms in gallbladder, biliary tract, or, rarely, the intestine or urinary tract.

Prevention & Control

Sanitary measures must be taken to prevent contamination of food and water by rodents or other animals that excrete salmonellae. Infected poultry, meats, and eggs must be thoroughly cooked. Carriers must not be allowed to work as food handlers and should observe strict hygienic precautions. Cholecystectomy or ampicillin may eliminate the carrier state.

Two injections of acetone-killed bacterial suspensions of *S typhi*, followed by a booster injection some months later, give partial resistance to small infectious inocula of typhoid bacilli but not to large ones. The vaccines against other salmonellae give less protection and are not recommended.

THE SHIGELLAE

Shigellae are nonmotile, gram-negative, aerobic rods, which—with a few exceptions—do not ferment lactose but do ferment other carbohydrates, producing acid but not gas. Many species share common antigens with one another and with other enteric bacteria. The natural habitat of shigellae is limited to the intestinal tracts of humans and other primates, where a number of species produce bacillary dysentery.

Morphology & Identification

A. Typical Organisms: Slender, unencapsulated, nonmotile, nonsporeforming, gram-negative rods. Coccobacillary forms in young cultures.

B. Culture: Shigellae are facultative anaerobes but grow best aerobically. Convex, circular, transparent colonies with intact edges reach a diameter of about 2 mm in 24 hours. They are commonly recognized on differential media by their inability to ferment lactose, thus remaining colorless while lactose fermenters form colored colonies.

C. Growth Characteristics: All shigellae ferment glucose, none ferment salicin. With the exception of *S sonnei*, they do not ferment lactose. They form acid from carbohydrates but, with the exception of *Shigella newcastle* and *Shigella manchester*, do not produce gas. Shigellae may also be divided into those which ferment mannitol (eg, *S sonnei* and *S flexneri*) and those which do not (eg, *S dysenteriae*) (Table 18–6).

D. Variation: Mutants with different biochemical, antigenic, and pathogenic properties often emerge from parent strains. Variation from smooth (S) to rough (R) colony form is associated with loss of invasiveness.

Table 18–6. Pathogenic species of *Shigella*.

Present Designation	Group and Type	Mannitol	Ornithine Decarboxylase	Earlier Designation
S dysenteriae	A (1–10)	−	−	*S shigae*, Shiga's bacillus
S flexneri	B (1–6)	+	−	*S paradysenteriae*, Flexner subgroup
S boydii	C (1–15)	+	−	*S paradysenteriae*, Boyd subgroup
S sonnei	D 1	+	+	Sonne bacillus

Antigenic Structure

Shigellae have a complex antigenic pattern. There is great overlapping in the serologic behavior of different species, and most of them share O antigens with other enteric bacilli.

The somatic O antigens of shigellae are lipopolysaccharides. Their serologic specificity depends on the polysaccharide. There are more than 40 serotypes. The classification of shigellae relies on biochemical and antigenic characteristics. The principal pathogenic species are shown in Table 18–6.

Pathogenesis & Pathology

The natural habitat of dysentery bacilli is the large intestine of humans, where they can cause bacillary dysentery. *Shigella* infections are practically always limited to the gastrointestinal tract; bloodstream invasion is quite rare. Shigellae are highly communicable: The infective dose is less than 200 organisms (whereas it is $10^5–10^8$ for salmonellae and vibrios). The essential pathologic process is invasion of the mucosal epithelium; microabscesses in the wall of the large intestine and terminal ileum lead to necrosis of the mucous membrane, superficial ulceration, bleeding, and formation of a "pseudomembrane" on the ulcerated area. This consists of fibrin, leukocytes, cell debris, a necrotic mucous membrane, and bacteria. As the process subsides, granulation tissue fills the ulcers and scar tissue forms.

Toxins

Upon autolysis, all shigellae release their toxic somatic antigen. This endotoxin probably contributes to the irritation of the bowel wall.

In addition, *S dysenteriae* produces a heat-labile exotoxin (see above) that may significantly contribute to the neurotoxic and enterotoxic clinical features.

Clinical Findings

After a short incubation period of 1–3 days, there is a sudden onset of abdominal pain, fever, and watery diarrhea. The latter has been attributed to an exotoxin acting in the small intestine. A day or so later, as the infection involves the ileum and colon, the number of stools increase; they are less liquid but often contain mucus and blood. Each bowel movement is accompanied by straining and tenesmus (rectal spasms), with resulting lower abdominal pain. Fever and diarrhea subside spontaneously in more than half of adult cases in 2–5 days. However, in children and the elderly, loss of water and electrolytes may lead to dehydration, acidosis, and even death. The illness resulting from *S dysenteriae* may be particularly severe.

Most persons, on recovery, shed dysentery bacilli for only a short period, but a few remain chronic intestinal carriers and may have recurrent bouts of the disease. Upon recovery from the infection, most persons develop antibodies to shigellae in their blood, but these do not protect against reinfection.

Diagnostic Laboratory Tests

Specimens consist of fresh stool, mucus flecks, and rectal swabs for culture. Large numbers of fecal leukocytes and some blood may often be seen microscopically. Serum specimens, if desired, must be taken 10 days apart to demonstrate rise in titer of agglutinating antibodies.

A. Culture: The materials are streaked on differential selective media (eg, MacConkey's or eosin-methylene blue agar) and on thiosulfate-citrate-bile agar, which suppress coliform and gram-positive organisms. Colorless (lactose-negative) colonies are inoculated into triple sugar iron medium (Table 18–7). Organisms producing acid on the slant and acid and gas in the butt should be discarded; they are either coliforms or paracolon bacilli. *Proteus* is ruled out by the rapid formation of red color in Christensen's urea medium. Organisms that fail to produce H_2S, that produce acid but not gas in the butt and an alkaline slant, and that are nonmotile should be subjected to slide agglutination by specific *Shigella* antisera.

B. Serology: Normal persons often have agglutinins against several *Shigella* species. However, serial determinations of antibody may show a rise of specific antibody. HI tests are promising.

Immunity

Infection is followed by a type-specific antibody response. Injection of killed shigellae stimulates production of antibodies in serum but fails to protect humans against infection. IgA antibodies in the gut may be important in limiting reinfection. They may be stimulated by live attenuated strains given orally as experimental vaccines. Serum antibodies to somatic *Shigella* antigens are IgM.

Treatment

A potent specific antitoxin against *S dysenteriae* exotoxin is available, but convincing proof of its clinical efficacy is lacking. Chloramphenicol, ampicillin, tetracycline, and trimethoprim-sulfamethoxazole are most commonly inhibitory for *Shigella* isolates in 1982 and can suppress acute clinical attacks of dysentery. They often fail to eradicate the organisms from the intestinal tract, however, and permit the carrier state to establish itself. Multiple drug resistance can be transmitted by plasmids, and resistant infection is widespread. It is claimed that a single dose of tetracycline hydrochloride, 2.5 g orally, is effective therapy in adults for acute dysentery caused by either tetracycline-susceptible or tetracycline-resistant shigellae. It is probable that many such cases are self-limited. Opiates should be avoided in *Shigella* dysentery.

Epidemiology, Prevention, & Control

Shigellae are transmitted by "food, fingers, feces, and flies" from person to person. *S dysenteriae* has spread widely in Central and South America. In 1969 in Guatemala, there were 110,000 cases, with 8000 deaths. Mass chemoprophylaxis for limited periods of time (eg, in military personnel) has been tried, but resistant strains of shigellae tend to emerge rapidly. Since humans are the main recognized host of pathogenic shigellae, control efforts must be directed at eliminating the organisms from this reservoir by (1) sanitary control of water, food, and milk; sewage disposal; and fly control; (2) isolation of patients and disinfection of excreta; (3) detection of subclinical cases, particularly in food handlers. Live oral vaccines are being investigated.

THE VIBRIOS

Vibrios are curved, gram-negative, aerobic rods; they are motile, possessing a single polar flagellum. *V cholerae* and related vibrios cause cholera in humans. Other vibrios may cause sepsis or enteritis.

Morphology & Identification

A. Typical Organisms: Upon first isolation, vibrios are comma-shaped, curved rods about 2–4 μm long and are very actively motile by means of a single polar flagellum. They do not form spores. On prolonged cultivation, vibrios may become straight rods, resembling other gram-negative enteric bacteria.

B. Culture: Vibrios produce convex, smooth, round colonies, opaque and granular in transmitted light. They are oxidase-positive.

Most vibrios grow well at 37 °C on defined media containing mineral salts and asparagine as sources of carbon and nitrogen. *V cholerae* grows well on thiosulfate-citrate-bile-sucrose agar. Characteristically, these organisms grow at very high pH (8.5–9.5) but are rapidly killed by acid. Cultures containing fermentable carbohydrates therefore quickly become sterile.

V cholerae regularly ferments sucrose and mannose but not arabinose. When grown in a peptone medium containing adequate amounts of tryptophan and nitrate, it produces indole and reduces nitrate. Upon addition of sulfuric acid, a red color develops (nitroso-indole reaction, "cholera red test"). Glucose inhibits this reaction.

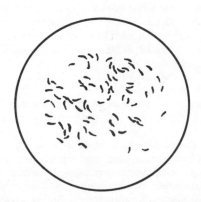

Figure 18–2. Typical organisms of *V cholerae* from broth.

Campylobacter (formerly *Vibrio*) *fetus* has recently emerged as a common cause of acute enteritis. It can be isolated from feces in microaerophilic culture incubated at 43 °C on a medium including vancomycin, polymyxin B, and trimethoprim.

C. Toxins: Cholera vibrios produce an enterotoxin that is heat- and acid-labile. A single antigenic type is known. It causes marked increase in adenylate cyclase activity and cAMP concentration and marked hypersecretion in the small intestine, resulting in massive diarrhea with fluid loss up to 20 L daily (see pp 147 and 230).

Some vibrios (eg, *Vibrio El Tor*) produce soluble hemolysins. Others (*V cholerae*) digest red blood cells without liberating a soluble hemolysin. They remove myxovirus receptors from the red cell surface by means of a receptor-destroying enzyme (RDE), neuraminidase.

Antigenic Structure

Many vibrios share a single heat-labile flagellar H antigen. Antibodies to the H antigen are probably not involved in the protection of susceptible hosts. Cholera vibrios possess somatic O lipopolysaccharides with polysaccharide fractions that confer serologic specificity which places the O antigen in one of 6 groups. Antibodies to the O antigens tend to protect laboratory animals against infections with *V cholerae*. Both group-specific and type-specific O antigens have been found. In vitro—and perhaps in vivo also—vibrios are converted to a protoplastlike, osmotically fragile form in the presence of specific antibody and complement. Lysis occurs unless osmotic protection is provided (eg, 0.5 M lactose).

Pathogenesis & Pathology

Under natural conditions, cholera vibrios are pathogenic only for humans. However, animal models for cholera infection have been devised.

Cholera is not an invasive infection. The organisms never reach the bloodstream but remain localized within the intestinal tract. There they multiply, invade superficial epithelium, and liberate cholera toxin—and perhaps mucinases and endotoxin. Cholera toxin is adsorbed onto epithelial cell gangliosides and stimulates hypersecretion of water and chloride in all parts of the small intestine while inhibiting absorption of sodium. As a result, there is an outpouring of fluid and electrolytes, with resulting diarrhea, dehydration, acidosis, shock, and death.

Vibrio parahaemolyticus causes acute food poisoning with profuse diarrhea after the ingestion of contaminated sea food. No enterotoxin has yet been isolated from this organism.

Another halophilic *Vibrio* (L+, *Vibrio vulnificus*) from sea water can cause intense skin lesions after contact with sea animals (eg, crabs) or can occasionally produce enteritis, bacteremia, and death in elderly or debilitated persons.

Several organisms closely related to vibrios produce disease in horses and cattle, with genital tract

Table 18—7. Biochemical reactions of certain gram-negative enteric bacteria.

Organism	Motility	Glucose	Lactose	Sucrose	Mannitol	H₂S Prod.	Triple Sugar Iron Agar Slant	Triple Sugar Iron Agar Butt	Lysine De-carboxylase	Ornithine De-carboxylase	Arginine De-carboxylase
E coli	+	AG	AG	±	AG	−	A	AG	±	±	±
E aerogenes	±	AG	AG	AG	AG	−	A	AG	+	+	−
Edwardsiella	+	AG	−	−	−	+	±	AG	+	±	±
Citrobacter	+	AG	±	±	+	+	±	AG	−	±	±
Serratia	+	A	±	A	A	−	±	A	+	+	−
K pneumoniae	−	AG	±	±	±	−	±	AG	+	−	−
S typhi	+	A	−	−	A	±	Alk	A	+	−	d+
S paratyphi A	+	AG	−	−	AG	−	Alk	AG	−	+	d+
S typhimurium	+	AG	−	−	AG	+	Alk	AG	+	+	d+
S dysenteriae	−	A	−	−	−	−	Alk	A	−	−	−
S flexneri	−	A	−	±	±	−	Alk	A	−	−	−
S sonnei	−	A	dA	dA	A	−	Alk	A	−	+	−
P vulgaris	+	AG	−	AG	−	+	±A	AG	−	−	−
P mirabilis	+	AG	−	dA	−	+	±A	AG	−	+	−
V cholerae	+	AG	−	A	A	−	A	A	+	+	−
P aeruginosa	+	±	−	±	−	−	Alk	±A	−	−	−
A faecalis	+	−	−	−	−	−	Alk	Alk	−	−	−

(±) Variable   (−) Negative   (AG) Acid and gas   (d) Delayed
(+) Positive   (A) Acid (yellow)   (Alk) Alkaline

infection, abortion, and sepsis. *Campylobacter (Vibrio) fetus* causes invasion of epithelial cells, with blood in stools and occasional bacteremia in humans.

Clinical Findings

After an incubation period of 1–4 days, there is a sudden onset of nausea and vomiting and profuse diarrhea with abdominal cramps. The stools resemble ''rice water'' and contain mucus, epithelial cells, and large numbers of vibrios. There is rapid loss of fluids and electrolytes, which leads to profound dehydration, circulatory collapse, and anuria. The death rate without treatment is between 25 and 50%. *V El Tor* causes a similar diarrheal disease.

The diagnosis of a full-blown case of cholera presents no problem in the presence of an epidemic. However, sporadic or mild cases are not readily differentiated from other diarrheal diseases. *Campylobacter (Vibrio) fetus* can cause acute enteritis with crampy abdominal pain, profuse diarrhea (occasionally bloody), headache, and fever. The illness is usually self-limited within 5–8 days. Sometimes, however, there is bloodstream invasion, with a clinical picture like that of typhoid fever. Deaths are rare. *Campylobacter* may be acquired from dogs with enteritis or from water, or it may be sexually acquired by anal-genital-oral contact. A marine halophilic *Vibrio* may also produce enteritis followed by febrile bacteremia. These organisms are susceptible to erythromycins in vitro, and these drugs may be clinically effective.

V parahaemolyticus causes vomiting, diarrhea, and occasionally fever after an incubation period of 12–24 hours following seafood ingestion. The mechanism of illness is not yet clear; fecal leukocytes are often observed. The enteritis tends to subside spontaneously in 1–4 days with no treatment other than restoration of water and electrolyte balance.

Diagnostic Laboratory Tests

Specimens for culture consist of mucus flecks from stools and, occasionally, vomitus. Growth is rapid on peptone agar, blood agar with pH near 9.0, or thiosulfate-citrate-bile-sucrose agar, and typical colonies can be picked in 18 hours. For enrichment, a few drops of stool can be incubated for 6–8 hours in taurocholate-peptone broth (pH 8.0–9.0) and the organisms stained or subcultured.

Organisms resembling vibrios are further identified by slide agglutination tests, fermentation reactions, and a positive cholera red reaction (see above).

Immunity

Gastric acid provides some protection against cholera vibrios ingested in small numbers.

An attack of cholera is followed by immunity to reinfection, but the duration and actual degree of immunity are not known. In experimental animals, specific antibodies occur in the lumen of the intestine (secretory IgA, ''coproantibodies''). Similar antibodies appear in humans after infection. IgG vibriocidal antibodies in serum develop after infection but last only a few months. The relative role of vibriocidal and antitoxic antibodies in the circulation and in the gut is not established.

Treatment

The most important part of therapy consists of water and electrolyte replacement to correct the severe dehydration and salt depletion. Many antimicrobial agents are effective against *V cholerae*. Oral tetracycline tends to reduce stool output in cholera and shortens the period of excretion of vibrios. In some endemic areas, tetracycline resistance of *V cholerae* has emerged, carried by transmissible plasmids.

Erythromycin, tetracycline, or cephalosporin

may be indicated in *Vibrio* infections with systemic invasion, eg, *Campylobacter* sepsis. However, acute *Campylobacter* diarrhea usually subsides without antimicrobial treatment.

Epidemiology, Prevention, & Control

Cholera is endemic in India and Southeast Asia. From these centers, it is carried along shipping lanes, trade routes, and pilgrim migration routes. The disease is spread by individuals with mild or early illness and by water, food, flies, and person-to-person contact. In many instances, only 1–5% of exposed susceptible persons develop disease. The carrier state seldom exceeds 3 or 4 weeks, and true chronic carriers are rare.

Vibrios survive in water for up to 3 weeks. Since 1960, cholera has spread widely in Africa and the Middle East.

Control rests on education and on improvement of sanitation, particularly of food and water. Patients should be isolated, their excreta disinfected, and contacts followed up. Chemoprophylaxis with antimicrobial drugs may have a place. Repeated injection of a vaccine containing either lipopolysaccharides extracted from vibrios or dense *Vibrio* suspensions can confer limited protection to heavily exposed persons (eg, family contacts) but is not effective as an epidemic control measure. Immunization with cholera toxoid is being studied.

● ● ●

References

Anderson RJ et al: Infectious risk factors in the immunosuppressed host. *Am J Med* 1973;**54**:453.

Blake PA et al: Disease caused by a marine vibrio (L+). *N Engl J Med* 1979;**300**:1.

Blaser MJ et al: Reservoirs for human campylobacteriosis. *J Infect Dis* 1980;**141**:665.

Carpenter CJ: Mechanisms of bacterial diarrheas. *Am J Med* 1980;**68**:313.

Cash RA et al: Response of man to infection with *Vibrio cholerae*. 1. Clinical, serologic, and bacteriologic responses to a known inoculum. *J Infect Dis* 1974;**129**:45.

Cherubin CE et al: Septicemia with non-typhoid *Salmonella*. *Medicine* 1974;**53**:365.

Dinarello CA, Wolff SM: Pathogenesis of fever in man. *N Engl J Med* 1978;**298**:607.

Edwards PR, Ewing WH: *Identification of Enterobacteriaceae*, 3rd ed. Burgess, 1972.

Elin RJ, Wolff SM: Nonspecificity of *Limulus* amebocyte lysate test. *J Infect Dis* 1973;**128**:349.

Field M: Modes of action of enterotoxins from *Vibrio cholerae* and *Escherichia coli*. *Rev Infect Dis* 1979;**1**:918.

Flick MR, Cluff LE: *Pseudomonas* bacteremia: Review of 108 cases. *Am J Med* 1976;**60**:501.

Goldschmidt MC, DuPont HL: Enteropathogenic *Escherichia coli*: Lack of correlation of serotype with pathogenicity. *J Infect Dis* 1976;**133**:153.

Goldstein EJC et al: Isolation of *Eikenella corrodens* from pulmonary infections. *Am Rev Respir Dis* 1979;**119**:55.

Gorbach SL et al: Traveler's diarrhea and toxigenic *Escherichia coli*. *N Engl J Med* 1975;**292**:933.

Guerrant RL et al: Campylobacteriosis in man: Pathogenetic mechanisms and review of 91 blood stream infections. *Am J Med* 1978;**65**:584.

Hornick RB et al: Typhoid fever. (2 parts.) *N Engl J Med* 1970;**283**:686, 739.

Johnson RH et al: *Arizona hinshawii* infections. *Arch Intern Med* 1976;**85**:587.

Jones RJ et al: Controlled trials of a polyvalent *Pseudomonas*

vaccine in burns. *Lancet* 1979;**2**:977.

Ketover BP et al: Septicemia due to *Aeromonas hydrophilia*. *J Infect Dis* 1973;**127**:284.

Klipstein EA, Engert RF: Properties of *Klebsiella pneumoniae* heat-stable enterotoxin. *Infect Immun* 1976;**13**:373.

Levine MM et al: Pathogenesis of *Shigella dysenteriae* 1 dysentery. *J Infect Dis* 1973;**127**:261.

Lüderitz O et al: Lipid A: Structure and biologic activity. *J Infect Dis* 1973;**128** (Suppl):S17.

McCabe WR et al: Humoral immunity to type-specific and cross-reactive antigens of gram-negative bacilli. *J Infect Dis* 1973;**128** (Suppl):S284.

Mandell GL, Douglas RG, Bennett JE (editors): *Principles and Practice of Infectious Diseases*. Wiley, 1979.

Meals RA: Paratyphoid fever: Report of 62 cases. *Arch Intern Med* 1976;**136**:1422.

Rodriguez WJ et al: *Yersinia enterocolitica* enteritis in children. *JAMA* 1979;**242**:1978.

Sommer A et al: Efficacy of cholera vaccination. *Lancet* 1973;**1**:230.

Thomas FE et al: Sequential hospitalwide outbreaks of resistant *Serratia* and *Klebsiella* infections. *Arch Intern Med* 1977;**137**:581.

Tulloch EF et al: Invasive *Escherichia coli* dysentery. *Ann Intern Med* 1973;**79**:13.

Vogel LC et al: *Citrobacter* infections of central nervous system in early infancy. *J Pediatr* 1978;**93**:86.

Warren JW, Hornick RB: Immunization against typhoid fever. *Annu Rev Med* 1979;**30**:457.

Wenzel RP et al: *Providencia stuartii*: Hospital pathogen. *Am J Epidemiol* 1976;**104**:170.

Wilfert CM: *E coli* meningitis: K1 antigen and virulence. *Annu Rev Med* 1978;**29**:129.

Winston DJ et al: Infectious complications of human bone marrow transplantation. *Medicine* 1979;**58**:1.

Young LS et al: Gram-negative rod bacteremia. *Ann Intern Med* 1977;**86**:456.

Yu VL: *Serratia marcescens*. *N Engl J Med* 1979;**300**:887.

19 | Small Gram-Negative Rods

THE BRUCELLAE

The brucellae are small, aerobic, gram-negative coccobacilli that are nonmotile, nonsporeforming, and relatively inactive metabolically. They are obligate parasites of animals and humans and are characteristically located intracellularly. *Brucella melitensis* typically infects goats; *Brucella suis*, swine; *Brucella abortus*, cattle; and *Brucella canis*, dogs (especially beagles). The disease in humans, brucellosis (undulant fever, Malta fever), is characterized by an acute septicemic phase followed by a chronic stage that may extend over many years and may involve many tissues.

Morphology & Identification
A. Typical Organisms: The appearance in young cultures varies from cocci to rods 1.2 μm in length, with short coccobacillary forms predominating. The organisms are gram-negative but often stain irregularly. Capsules can be demonstrated on smooth and mucoid variants. The organisms are nonmotile and nonsporeforming.

B. Culture: On enriched media, small, convex, smooth colonies appear in 2–5 days.

C. Growth Characteristics: Brucellae are adapted to an intracellular habitat, and their nutritional requirements are complex. Some strains have been cultivated on defined media of 18 amino acids, vitamins, salts, and glucose. Fresh specimens from animal or human sources are usually inoculated on trypticase-soy agar or into blood culture media. *B abortus* requires 5–10% CO_2 for growth, whereas the other 3 species grow in air.

Brucellae utilize carbohydrates but produce neither acid nor gas in amounts sufficient for classification. Catalase and oxidase are produced by some strains. Hydrogen sulfide is produced by many strains, and nitrates are reduced to nitrites.

Brucellae are moderately sensitive to heat and acidity. They are killed in milk by pasteurization.

D. Variation: Smooth, mucoid, and rough variants are recognized by colonial appearance and virulence. The typical virulent organism forms a smooth, transparent colony; it tends to mutate to the rough form, which is avirulent.

The serum of susceptible animals contains a globulin and a lipoprotein that suppress growth of nonsmooth, avirulent types and favor the growth of virulent types. Resistant animal species lack these factors, so that rapid mutation to avirulence can occur. D-Alanine has a similar selective effect in vitro.

Antigenic Structure
Different species of brucellae cannot be differentiated by agglutination tests but can be distinguished by agglutinin absorption reactions. It is probable that 2 antigens, A and M, are present in different proportions in 4 species. In addition, a superficial L antigen has been demonstrated that resembles the Vi antigen of salmonellae.

Species differentiation among 4 *Brucella* species is made possible by their characteristic sensitivity to dyes and their production of H_2S. (See Table 19–1.)

Bordetella bronchiseptica is a small gram-negative rod often found in the respiratory tracts of canines. It is related to brucellae and *Haemophilus influenzae*.

Eikenella corrodens is a small gram-negative rod (related to brucellae) that grows on agar and produces pits. It has been isolated from the human respiratory tract, wounds, abscesses, meningitis, and endocarditis. It is of uncertain pathogenicity in the normal host.

Pathogenesis & Pathology
Although each species of *Brucella* has a preferred host, all can infect a wide range of animals, including humans.

The common routes of infection in humans are the intestinal tract (ingestion of infected milk), mucous membranes (droplets), and skin (contact with infected tissues of animals). The organisms progress from the portal of entry, via lymphatic channels and regional

Table 19–1. Differentiation of brucellae.

	Growth in Presence Of		H_2S Production	CO_2 Requirement
	Thionine (1:25,000)	Basic Fuchsin (1:50,000)		
B abortus	–	+	++	+
B melitensis	–	+	–	–
B suis	+	–	+	–
B canis	+	–	–	–

lymph nodes, to the thoracic duct and the bloodstream, which distributes them to the parenchymatous organs. In lymphatic tissue, liver, spleen, bone marrow, and other parts of the reticuloendothelial system, granulomatous nodules form that may develop into abscesses. In such lesions, the brucellae are principally intracellular. Osteomyelitis, meningitis, or cholecystitis also occasionally occurs. The main histologic reaction in brucellosis consists of proliferation of mononuclear cells, exudation of fibrin, coagulation necrosis, and fibrosis. The granulomas consist of epithelioid and giant cells, with central necrosis and peripheral fibrosis.

Persons with active brucellosis react more markedly (fever, myalgia) to injected *Brucella* endotoxin than normal persons. Sensitivity to endotoxin thus may play a role in pathogenesis.

Placentas and fetal membranes of cattle, swine, sheep, and goats contain erythritol, a growth factor for brucellae. The proliferation of organisms in pregnant animals leads to placentitis and abortion in these species. In human placentas, there is no erythritol, and abortion is not part of *Brucella* infection.

Clinical Findings

The incubation period is 1–6 weeks. The onset is insidious, with malaise, fever, weakness, aches, and sweats. The fever usually rises in the afternoon; its fall during the night is accompanied by drenching sweat. There may be gastrointestinal and nervous symptoms. Lymph nodes enlarge, and the spleen becomes palpable. Hepatitis may be accompanied by jaundice. Deep pain and disturbances of motion, particularly in vertebral bodies, suggest osteomyelitis. These symptoms of generalized *Brucella* infection generally subside in weeks or months, although localized lesions and symptoms may continue.

Following the initial infection, a chronic stage may develop, characterized by weakness, aches and pains, low-grade fever, nervousness, and other nonspecific manifestations compatible with psychoneurotic symptoms. Brucellae cannot be isolated from the patient at this stage, but the IgG agglutinin titer may be high. The diagnosis of "chronic brucellosis" is difficult to establish with certainty unless local lesions are present. A high IgG antibody titer is suggestive of *Brucella* activity.

Diagnostic Laboratory Tests

Take blood for culture, biopsy material for culture (lymph nodes, bone, etc), and serum for serologic tests.

A. Culture: Blood or tissues are incubated in trypticase-soy broth and on thionine-tryptose agar. At intervals of several days, subcultures are made on solid media of similar composition. All cultures are incubated in 10% CO_2 and should be observed and subcultured for 6 weeks before being discarded as negative.

If organisms resembling brucellae are isolated, they are typed by H_2S production, dye inhibition, and agglutination by absorbed sera. As a rule, brucellae

can be cultivated from patients only during the acute phase of the illness or during recurrence of activity.

B. Serology: IgM antibodies appear early in the disease. Somewhat later, IgG and blocking antibodies appear. Whereas IgM antibody may persist after recovery (ie, when active infection is terminated spontaneously or by treatment), the finding of a substantial IgG antibody titer indicates active infection and active disease. Usual agglutination tests fail to detect infection with *B canis*.

1. Agglutination test–To be reliable, agglutination tests must be performed with standardized heat-killed, phenolized, smooth *Brucella* antigens available from brucellosis centers and should be incubated at 37 °C for 24 hours. IgG agglutinin titers above 1:80 indicate active infection. Individuals injected with cholera vaccine may develop agglutinin titers to brucellae. If the serum agglutination test is negative in patients with strong clinical evidence of *Brucella* infection, tests must be made for the presence of "blocking" antibodies. These can be detected by adding antihuman globulin to the antigen-serum mixture.

2. Opsonophagocytic test–This test is subject to great variations and is probably not reliable.

3. Blocking antibodies are IgA antibodies that interfere with agglutination by IgG and IgM and cause serologic tests to be negative in low serum dilutions (prozone) although positive in higher dilutions. These antibodies appear during the subacute stage of infection, tend to persist for many years independently of activity of infection, and are detected by the Coombs antiglobulin method.

C. Skin Test: When Brucellergen or a protein *Brucella* extract is injected intradermally, erythema, edema, and induration develop within 24 hours in some infected individuals. The skin test is unreliable. Application of the skin test may stimulate the agglutinin titer.

Immunity

An antibody response occurs with infection, and it is probable that some resistance to subsequent attacks is produced. Immunogenic fractions from *Brucella* cell walls have a high phospholipid content, lysine predominates among 8 amino acids, and there is no heptose (thus distinguishing the fractions from endotoxin).

Treatment

Brucellae may be susceptible to tetracyclines or ampicillin. Symptomatic relief may occur within a few days after treatment with these drugs is begun. However, because of their intracellular location, the organisms are not readily eradicated completely from the host. For best results, treatment must be prolonged. Combined treatment with streptomycin and a tetracycline may be considered.

Epidemiology, Prevention, & Control

Brucellae are essentially animal pathogens transmitted in animal populations by contact with feces, urine, milk, and infected tissues. Infection of humans is accidental, through contact with these same infected materials. The common sources of infection for humans are unpasteurized milk, milk products, and cheese and occupational contact (eg, farmers, veterinarians, slaughterhouse workers) with infected animals. Occasionally the airborne route may be important. Because of occupational contact, *Brucella* infection is much more frequent in men. The majority of infections remain asymptomatic (latent).

Infection rates vary greatly with different animals and in different countries. In the USA, about 4% of cattle are infected, about 15% of cattle herds contain infected animals, and infection in hogs is common. In other countries, infection is much more prevalent. Eradication of brucellosis in cattle can be attempted by test and slaughter, active immunization of heifers with avirulent live strain 19, or combined testing, segregation, and immunization. Cattle are examined by means of agglutination tests.

Active immunization of humans against *Brucella* infection is still experimental. Control rests on limitation of spread and possible eradication of animal infection, pasteurization of milk and milk products, and reduction of occupational hazards wherever possible.

THE PASTEURELLAE
(*Pasteurella, Yersinia, Francisella*)

These are short gram-negative rods showing bipolar staining by special methods. They are nonsporeforming catalase-positive, oxidase-negative aerobic or microaerophilic organisms. All are nonmotile except *Yersinia pseudotuberculosis*. All have animals as their natural hosts. Some species cause hemorrhagic septicemia in various animals (*Pasteurella multocida*); others infect animals and also cause serious disease in humans (*Yersinia pestis*, plague; *Francisella tularensis*, tularemia; *Yersinia enterocolitica*, enteric infection and bacteremia).

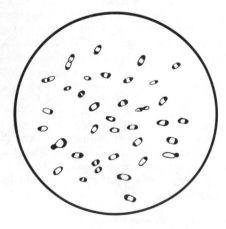

Figure 19–1. Typical organisms of *Y pestis* from smear of lymph node.

Morphology & Identification

A. Typical Organisms: The typical short, ovoid, plump, gram-negative rods are predominant in cultures and in smears from infected tissues. *Y pseudotuberculosis* possesses flagella; other species are nonmotile. Wayson's stain (methylene blue with carbolfuchsin) brings out the bipolar appearance of pasteurellae, causing them to resemble safety pins. Capsules, or "envelopes," around the bacterial body are frequently present. Upon prolonged incubation or in an unfavorable environment, the rods are pleomorphic, varying greatly in size and shape. Long filamentous rods are occasionally seen.

B. Culture: All pasteurellae except *F tularensis* grow on ordinary bacteriologic media, but they grow more rapidly on media containing tissue fluids or blood. Gray, viscous colonies are formed from virulent tissue inocula, but irregular rough colonies occur frequently. *F tularensis* grows from small inocula only on complex media containing blood or tissue extracts and cystine, forming minute droplike colonies in 48–76 hours at 37 °C. All pasteurellae grow readily in the yolk sacs of embryonated eggs.

C. Growth Characteristics: Pasteurellae ferment carbohydrates, forming acid but not gas. There is great variation among strains, and species are not uniform in their biochemical reactions. The temperature for optimal rate of growth is 30 °C for *Y pestis* and 37 °C for *F tularensis,* but the production of certain antigenic components (eg, the protein-carbohydrate complex of fraction I in *Y pestis*) is greater at 37 °C than at 30 °C. *Y pseudotuberculosis* grown at 22 °C is motile; at 37 °C it is nonmotile.

D. Variation: Variants and stable mutants occur commonly with respect to appearance, morphology (eg, motility in *Y pseudotuberculosis*), biochemical characteristics, antigenic makeup, virulence, and drug resistance. Stable, avirulent mutants have been employed for vaccination against plague (eg, strain EV76).

Antigenic Structure

The members of each species of *Pasteurella* fall into certain antigenic patterns; even within each species, however, there are antigenic differences among strains, and different species appear interrelated by serologic tests. All pasteurellae possess somatic O antigens which are toxic for animals and which chemically are lipopolysaccharide-protein complexes. These have been subdivided by chemical fractionation into components of varying immunologic and serologic activity. In *Y pestis,* for example, fraction I, a glycoprotein, confers resistance to phagocytosis and stimulates antibacterial immunity. This fraction is produced at 37 °C but much less at 30 °C; it appears to be located in the outer "envelope" of the plague bacillus. Organisms virulent for guinea pigs produce, in addition to fraction I, a V-W antigen that makes them resist phagocytosis even in the absence of a visible "envelope." V-W alone suffices for full mouse virulence. A pure toxin has been isolated from

Y pestis; it is a homogeneous protein with a molecular weight of 74,000 and an LD_{50} for mice of 1 μg. The "toxin" for mice acts as an adrenergic antagonist and appears to be distinct from the "toxin" for guinea pigs. Some of these antigens appear to be under the genetic control of special plasmids. *Y pestis* is said to produce a distinctive enzyme, isocitrate lyase.

Y pseudotuberculosis carries an H antigen in its flagella when grown at 22 °C. At 37 °C, this antigen does not form and the organisms are universally nonmotile. At least one of the O antigens of *Y pseudotuberculosis* cross-reacts with that of *Y pestis.* Bacteriophages specific for *Y pestis* tend to lyse many strains of *Y pseudotuberculosis,* but they usually do not lyse *P multocida* or *F tularensis.* Bacteriophages that lyse *Y pseudotuberculosis* also lyse certain strains of shigellae or salmonellae. *F tularensis* strains are relatively homogeneous serologically but cross-react with some brucellae. All this indicates close relationship of antigenic constituents among many gram-negative bacteria.

Pathogenesis & Pathology

Some *Pasteurella* species have narrow host ranges, producing disease in only a few types of animals; others affect a large variety of hosts. Pasteurellae generally produce disease by rapid invasion of the host body, multiplying in many tissues until overwhelming sepsis supervenes. When the population of pasteurellae reaches a high level, autolysis probably liberates sufficient "toxin" to be harmful to the host tissues.

Purified plague toxins depress respiration of heart mitochondria in vitro, affecting different animal species to different degrees.

Hemorrhagic Septicemia of Animals

There are varieties of *P multocida* that are pathogenic for one or more of the following animals: rabbits, rats, horses, sheep, fowl, dogs, cats, and swine. The organisms are usually normal inhabitants of the respiratory tracts of animals and may suddenly assume pathogenicity when the host-parasite balance is disturbed. This occurs either (1) when there is unusually rapid passage from one host to another (eg, in the experimental passage of mouse lung with *Pasteurella pneumotropica*), or (2) when host resistance is impaired through drastic environmental changes or intercurrent infections (particularly those due to viruses). Under such circumstances, there may be acute septicemia, with rapid proliferation of bacilli in tissues and bloodstream, high fever, prostration, diarrhea, and death within 12–48 hours. Pathologically, there are serous and hemorrhagic inflammatory changes in all organs and vast numbers of bacilli in the blood. In subacute and chronic disease, necrotic foci form in various organs, and the animals often survive. Human infections with *P multocida* are rare and may follow animal bites. *P multocida* is susceptible to penicillin.

Plague

Y pestis is a parasite of various rodents, eg, rats

and squirrels. It is transmitted from one rodent to another through the bites of fleas who have become infected by sucking the blood of an infected animal. The plague bacilli proliferate vastly in the intestinal tract of the flea and eventually block the lumen of the proventriculus completely, so that no food can pass through. The hungry flea bites ferociously, and the aspirated blood is regurgitated, with an admixture of plague bacilli, into the bite wound. Thus, plague infection is transmitted from rodent to rodent and, occasionally, from rodent to human. It is not usually transmitted from human to human by fleas (although *Pulex irritans* is capable of such transmission). When in the course of human infection pneumonia develops, droplets containing plague bacilli are coughed up. Such droplets are highly infectious by the airborne route and result in primary pneumonic plague in humans, which is usually fatal without chemotherapy and is readily transmitted from person to person. Some plague strains are so highly virulent that infection with a single organism may be lethal.

When plague bacilli enter the host through the bite of a flea, they extend via the lymphatic channels to the regional lymph nodes. Along the lymphatics and in the lymph nodes there is a rapidly spreading hemorrhagic inflammation and the node becomes greatly enlarged, forming a "bubo." Such buboes are usually located in the groin or axilla and may undergo necrosis and become fluctuant. In the lesser forms of plague, the infective process stops there. Often, however, organisms progress via efferent lymphatics and the thoracic duct to the bloodstream, which rapidly disseminates them to all organs, especially to the spleen, liver, lungs, and central nervous system. In parenchymatous organs, hemorrhagic inflammation is followed by development of focal necrosis. There are serosanguineous effusions in the pleura, the peritoneum, and the pericardium, and there may be (plague) meningitis. Terminally, plague bacilli may proliferate freely in the bloodstream.

Pseudotuberculosis

Y pseudotuberculosis produces an infection of birds, rodents, and other animals that is rarely transmitted to humans. The route of transmission has not been established, but it is probable that animals become infected through ingestion of contaminated droppings. Typical lesions consist of whitish nodules, grossly resembling tubercles, in the intestines and the parenchymatous organs. They consist of a necrotic center surrounded by inflammatory cells, but there are no giant or epithelioid cells. The disease tends to be chronic and to progress slowly, but there may be sepsis with rapidly fatal outcome. One clinical form in humans presents as appendicitis, enteritis, and regional lymphadenitis, which tend to subside spontaneously. Serious *Y pseudotuberculosis* sepsis is associated with liver disease.

Yersiniosis

Y enterocolitica is an occasional member of the

human gut flora. It grows best at 25 °C. It can produce febrile diarrhea in dogs and humans, with person-to-person spread on close contact. Severe abdominal pain may suggest appendicitis and lead to operation. There may be ileitis, mesenteric adenitis, hepatic or splenic abscesses, and, rarely, bacteremia or endocarditis. Swine and dogs are sources of infection. Epidemic spread may occur through contaminated food or drink. *Y enterocolitica* can produce an enterotoxin that is similar to the heat-stable one (ST) of *E coli* (see p 229) and that may induce the initial diarrhea.

Tularemia

F tularensis is a parasite of rodents that is adapted to transmission by biting flies (*Chrysops*), ticks (*Dermacentor* and others), and a rabbit louse, all of which transmit the infection among the rodent population and thus maintain the reservoir of infection. Hares, rabbits, and muskrats are the main sources of disease in humans. Handling, skinning, or eating such infected animals or drinking water contaminated by them may result in human infection. *F tularensis* may enter the host via the skin or mucous membranes, through the bites of arthropods, or via the respiratory or gastrointestinal tracts. An ulcerating papule often develops at the site of penetration of the skin or mucous membranes, and the regional lymph nodes enlarge and suppurate. Transitory bacteremia establishes the organisms in various parenchymatous organs, where granulomatous nodules form that often undergo necrosis. As the disease progresses, tularemic pneumonia and septicemia develop that are fatal if untreated. Often the localizing signs are limited to the portal of entry. Thus the clinical picture may be "oculoglandular," following infection via the conjunctiva; "ulceroglandular," following entry through the skin; or "pneumonic," following primary inhalation of infectious droplets. At other times there may be no localizing symptoms whatever and only a febrile systemic illness.

Clinical Findings

Sporadic cases of infections caused by this group of bacteria present difficult diagnostic problems, whereas in epidemics (eg, of plague) the diagnosis is readily apparent. Usually the clinical features of a local lesion, adenopathy, and a bubo in a febrile illness, with a history suggestive of exposure, warrant the performance of laboratory procedures that can establish the diagnosis unequivocally. *Y enterocolitica* produces an enterotoxin similar to the heat-stable one (ST) of *E coli* and can produce febrile diarrhea (see p 229) or abdominal syndromes mimicking appendicitis. The latter can also occur with *Y pseudotuberculosis*.

Diagnostic Laboratory Tests

Blood for culture should be collected repeatedly, as well as blood serum for serologic tests; after an initial specimen in the acute stage, subsequent specimens should be obtained at 12- to 21-day intervals. Sputum for smear and culture must be obtained when pulmonary involvement is probable, and material from local lesions or aspirated material from a suppurating lymph node is required for smear, culture, and animal inoculation. Strict aseptic precautions must be maintained because some pasteurellae are highly infective.

A. Stained Smears: Gram-stained films often show pleomorphic gram-negative organisms ranging from coccal forms to long rods. When plague or tularemia is suspected, immunofluorescence staining can identify the organism rapidly.

B. Cultures: Materials are cultured in rich blood culture media and on blood agar (plates), incubated both aerobically and with 10% CO_2. If tularemia is suspected, specimens should also be cultured on blood-glucose-cysteine agar, as cysteine is a growth requirement for *F tularensis*. To grow *Y enterocolitica* from feces, it is best to enrich stool suspensions in saline at 4 °C for 1–3 weeks before culture. If growth occurs, bacteria may be identified by biochemical and serologic tests (especially immunofluorescence), susceptibility to specific bacteriophages, subculture at 20 °C for motility *(Y pseudotuberculosis),* and animal inoculation. *Note:* Great caution is necessary in handling highly infectious cultures. Sometimes it is difficult to assign a species designation to a *Pasteurella* organism recovered from clinical or pathologic material.

C. Animal Inoculations: One of the important classifying characteristics of the *Pasteurella* group is its ability to cause disease and specific lesions in a variety of laboratory animals (eg, *Y pestis* is pathogenic for white rats and guinea pigs; *Y pseudotuberculosis* for guinea pigs but not for rats). Laboratory animals must be kept in strict isolation and must be rid of ectoparasites before being injected. Animal inoculation is particularly valuable when the specimen is contaminated with other organisms that tend to outgrow pasteurellae in culture. Such organisms frequently are nonpathogenic for laboratory animals and thus permit pasteurellae to produce specific lesions.

D. Serology: In subacute or chronic infections with pasteurellae, recovery of the organism in culture is rarely possible. Diagnosis often depends on the outcome of serologic tests. To be reliable, the antigen must be obtained from a standard source, eg, a state health department.

Agglutination, immunofluorescence, and CF tests can be performed for antibodies to each of the pasteurellae. Very low serum titers are of questionable significance, since some cross-reactions occur with different types of organisms (brucellae, shigellae). A single high titer does not establish the cause of the current disease. Only by a definite rise in serum titer in 2 specimens taken 2 weeks apart can the diagnosis be established. Antiplague sera agglutinate *Y pseudotuberculosis,* but usually not the reverse. Precipitin tests with chemical fractions of *F tularensis* and *Y pestis* can be performed. Precipitins appear in humans after infection but not after injection of killed vaccines. Their development may be suppressed by antimicrobial therapy early in the infection.

E. Skin Test: Intradermal injection of an extract of *F tularensis* gives a delayed positive (tuberculin-like) reaction within 2–4 weeks after infection and for years thereafter. The skin test is specific and rarely causes a rise in agglutination titer.

Immunity

A solid immunity to plague and tularemia follows infection and recovery in each case.

Treatment

Most pasteurellae are sensitive to tetracyclines, chloramphenicol, and aminoglycosides. Streptomycin, often in combination with a tetracycline, is curative in most patients if treatment is begun early in the disease.

Prevention

Vaccines have been prepared from various pasteurellae for the protective inoculation of exposed hosts. Attenuated cultures or killed suspensions of *P multocida* are sometimes employed in the hope of preventing hemorrhagic septicemia in domestic animals. Vaccines against plague and tularemia can be prepared from (1) avirulent live bacteria, (2) heat-killed or formalin-inactivated suspensions of virulent bacteria, or (3) chemical fractions of the bacilli. The first 2 of these have been used on millions of persons in endemic areas and have given some protection that, however, is incomplete and of relatively short duration. Therefore, repeated vaccination of exposed individuals is essential in maintaining effective resistance. Reinfection following recovery from natural plague is quite rare, and immunity is thus presumed to be solid.

No practical or useful vaccines are available for pseudotuberculosis. A living, avirulent vaccine against tularemia has been used in Russia on a large scale.

In endemic areas, plague can be efficiently prevented (even in persons exposed to patients with pneumonic involvement) by the daily administration of 0.5–1 g of tetracycline hydrochloride for 5 days. No spontaneously emerging drug-resistant plague bacilli have as yet been reported.

Epidemiology & Control

Pasteurella infections are animal diseases and are only accidentally transmitted to humans. The risk to humans can be reduced if the animal infection rate can be kept low. This is the principle of control measures. Infections of humans with *P multocida* and *Y pseudotuberculosis* are so rare that active measures against the animal reservoir of infection are not carried out. Tularemia is maintained in wild rodents away from human habitation. Proper precautions when dealing with wild rabbits or muskrats, and thorough cooking, are adequate safeguards in most instances. In areas (eg, Russia, USA), water, grain, or hay contaminated by infected wild rodents or bites of the deer fly (*Chrysops*) may convey *F tularensis* to humans.

Plague, on the other hand, presents an enormous epidemiologic problem. It is essentially an infection of wild rodents (squirrels, field mice, voles, gerbils, etc) and occurs in many parts of the world. The chief enzootic areas are India, East Asia, South Africa, South America, and the western states of the USA and Mexico. In these regions, reservoirs of infection are always present in wild rodents and, intermittently, many animals die from the infection. The infection is transmitted by infective fleas among wild rodents. When the rate of infection rises in wild rodents, rats in urban environments become infected; the rat flea (*Xenopsylla cheopis*) is the chief vector in transmitting the disease to humans. Once plague pneumonia occurs in humans, direct person-to-person transmission through droplets constitutes a serious threat. From cities and harbors, infected rats have been transported across oceans on ships to start new outbreaks in other seaports.

Control measures are directed toward breaking the infection chain at several points: (1) Reduction of wild rodent populations and continuous survey of the rate of plague infection. Practical measures include shooting, trapping, and poisoning. (2) Reduction of rat populations in cities and continuous survey for plague infection in trapped rats. Measures are directed against rats on ships and in harbors. (3) Widespread application of insecticides to kill fleas. (4) Chemoprophylaxis (tetracycline) in all contacts whenever plague is suspected. (5) Prompt and efficient chemotherapy of cases. (Human plague carriers are exceedingly rare.) (6) Active immunization as a supplementary measure in highly endemic areas, in troops, and in persons who may be forced into situations of potential exposure. (7) Strict isolation of plague cases and observation for pneumonic involvement.

THE HEMOPHILIC BACTERIA

This is a heterogeneous group of small, gram-negative, aerobic bacilli that are nonmotile and nonsporeforming and require enriched media, usually containing blood or its derivatives, for isolation. Some are among the normal flora of mucous membranes; others (*H influenzae, Bordetella pertussis*) are important human pathogens.

HAEMOPHILUS INFLUENZAE

Morphology & Identification

A. Typical Organisms: In specimens from acute infections, the organisms are short ($1.5\text{-}\mu$m) coccoid bacilli, sometimes occurring in short chains. Long rods and large spherical bodies are also found. In cultures, the morphology depends both on age and on the medium. At 6–8 hours in rich medium, coccobacillary forms predominate. Later there are longer rods, lysed bacteria, and very pleomorphic forms.

Table 19–2. Characteristics and growth requirements of some hemophilic organisms.

Organism	Hemolysis	Requires X	Requires V	Capsule
H influenzae	–	+	+	+
H parainfluenzae	–	–	+	+
H haemolyticus	+	+	+	–
H suis	–	+	+	+
H haemoglobinophilus	–	+	–	–
B pertussis	+	–	–	+

Organisms in young cultures (6–18 hours) on rich medium have a definite capsule. This capsule is rapidly dissolved by autolytic enzymes and therefore is poorly seen in older cultures. Capsule swelling tests are employed for "typing" *H influenzae* (see below).

B. Culture: On brain-heart infusion agar with blood, small, round, convex colonies with a strong iridescence develop in 24 hours. The colonies on "chocolate" (heated blood) agar take 36–48 hours to develop diameters of 1 mm. Isovitalex in media enhances growth. There is no hemolysis. Around staphylococcal (or other) colonies, the colonies of *H influenzae* grow much larger ("satellite phenomenon").

C. Growth Characteristics: Identification of organisms of the *Haemophilus* group depends in part upon demonstrating the need for certain growth factors called X and V. Factor X acts physiologically as hemin; factor V can be replaced by coenzyme I or II or by nicotinamide nucleoside. The requirements for X and V factors of various *Haemophilus* species are listed in Table 19–2. Carbohydrates are fermented poorly and irregularly.

D. Variation: In addition to morphologic variation, *H influenzae* has a marked tendency to lose its capsule and the associated type specificity. Nonencapsulated variant colonies lack iridescence.

E. Transformation: Under proper experimental circumstances, the DNA extracted from a given type of *H influenzae* is capable of transferring that type specificity to other cells (transformation). Resistance to ampicillin and chloramphenicol is controlled by genes on transmissible plasmids.

Antigenic Structure

Encapsulated *H influenzae* contains capsular polysaccharides of one of 6 types (a–f); these polysaccharides (MW > 150,000) resemble those of pneumococci and sometimes give serologic cross-reactions with pneumococcal types. The capsular antigen of type b is a polyribose-ribitol phosphate (PRP).

The somatic antigen of *H influenzae* consists of at least 2 proteins: the P substance constitutes much of the bacterial body, whereas the M substance is a labile surface antigen. Filtrable endotoxins can be derived from many fluid cultures of *H influenzae*, but their antigenic nature is not clear.

Encapsulated *H influenzae* can be typed by a capsule swelling test with specific antiserum; this test is analogous to the "quellung test" for pneumococci. Analogous typing can be done by immunofluorescence as well.

Pathogenesis

H influenzae produces no exotoxin, and the role of its toxic somatic antigen in natural disease is not clearly understood. The nonencapsulated organism is a regular member of the normal respiratory flora of humans. The encapsulated forms of *H influenzae*, particularly type b, produce suppurative respiratory infections (sinusitis, laryngotracheitis, epiglottis, otitis) and, in young children, meningitis. The blood of many individuals over age 3 years has strong bactericidal power for *H influenzae*, and clinical infections are less frequent. Recently, however, bactericidal antibodies have been absent from 25% of adults, and clinical infections are occurring more often in adults.

The role of *H influenzae* in human influenza of the pandemic type probably was that of a secondary invader producing pneumonitis in the respiratory tract already damaged by influenza virus. On the other hand, it may have been contributory to pandemic influenza in humans, just as *Haemophilus suis* is an essential causative component of swine influenza. Swine influenza is caused by a virus related to influenza type A but requires in addition the presence of *H suis* for the development of clinical symptoms. *H influenzae* is not pathogenic for laboratory animals.

Clinical Findings

H influenzae type b enters by way of the respiratory tract in small children and produces a nasopharyngitis, often with fever. Other types rarely produce disease. There may be local extension with involvement of the sinuses or of the middle ear. *H influenzae* type b and pneumococci are the 2 commonest etiologic agents of bacterial otitis media. The organisms may reach the bloodstream and be carried to the meninges or, less frequently, may establish themselves in the joints. The meningitis thus induced does not differ clinically from other forms of bacterial meningitis in children under age 3 years, and diagnosis rests on bacteriologic demonstration of the organism. *Haemophilus* meningitis is increasing in incidence.

Occasionally, a fulminating obstructive laryngotracheitis with swollen, cherry-red epiglottis develops in babies and requires prompt tracheostomy as a lifesaving procedure. Pneumonitis and epiglottitis due to *H influenzae* may follow upper respiratory tract infections in small children and old or debilitated people.

Diagnostic Laboratory Tests

Specimens consist of nasopharyngeal swabs, pus, blood, and spinal fluid for smears and cultures.

A. Direct Identification: When organisms are present in large numbers in specimens, they may be identified by immunofluorescence or may be mixed directly with specific rabbit antiserum (type b) and a capsule swelling test performed. Counterimmunoelectrophoresis with spinal fluid may be done with specific antiserum to *Haemophilus*. If a precipitate forms, it indicates that the fluid contains high concentrations of specific polysaccharide from *H influenzae* type b.

B. Culture: Specimens are grown on Isovitalex-enriched "chocolate" agar until typical colonies can be identified with the capsule swelling test (in 36–48 hours). *H influenzae* is differentiated from related gram-negative bacilli by the requirements for X and V factors, by hemolysis on blood agar (Table 19–2), and by immunologic means.

Immunity

Infants under age 3 months may have serum antibodies transmitted from the mother. During this time *H influenzae* infection is rare, but subsequently the antibodies are lost. Children often acquire *H influenzae* infections, which are usually asymptomatic but may be in the form of respiratory disease. *H influenzae* is the commonest cause of bacterial meningitis in children from 6 months to 5 years of age. By age 3–5 years, many children have anti-PRP antibodies that promote complement-dependent phagocytosis. Injection of PRP into adults induces the same antibodies, but in children under age 2 years, the present preparations are not immunogenic. The same antibodies can also be induced by cross-reacting *E coli* O75:K100:H5 carried in the gut.

There is a correlation between the presence of bactericidal antibodies and resistance to major *H influenzae* type b infections. It is not known, however, whether these antibodies alone account for immunity. *H influenzae* pneumonia or arthritis can develop in adults with such antibodies.

Treatment

The mortality rate of untreated *H influenzae* meningitis may be up to 90%. Many strains of *H influenzae* type b are susceptible to ampicillin, but some are resistant by virtue of beta-lactamase production controlled by a transmissible plasmid. Most strains are still susceptible to chloramphenicol. In 1982, it is common practice to initially treat suspected *H influenzae* meningitis with both chloramphenicol and ampicillin until definitive microbiologic diagnosis and drug susceptibility are established. Greatest emphasis must be placed on early diagnosis and treatment, for if there is a delay in chemotherapy, the incidence of late neurologic and intellectual impairment is high. Prominent among late complications of influenzal meningitis is the development of a localized subdural accumulation of fluid that requires surgical drainage.

Epidemiology, Prevention, & Control

Encapsulated *H influenzae* type b is transmitted from person to person by the respiratory route. The patient with influenzal meningitis is not an important source of infection. An increasing number of adults lack bactericidal antibody and are susceptible to systemic *Haemophilus* infections. Therefore, immunization with capsular polysaccharides is now being considered for mothers who lack antibody. Available PRP is not adequate vaccine for infants under age 2 years.

Contact with patients suffering from *H influenzae* clinical infection poses little risk for adults but imposes a definite risk for children under age 4 years, for whom possible chemoprophylaxis (?rifampin) must be considered.

BORDETELLA PERTUSSIS

Morphology & Identification

A. Typical Organisms: Short, ovoid, gram-negative bacilli resembling *H influenzae*. With toluidine blue stain, bipolar metachromatic granules can be demonstrated. A capsule is present.

B. Culture: Primary isolation of *Bordetella pertussis* requires enriched media. Bordet-Gengou medium (potato-blood-glycerol agar) that contains penicillin G, 0.5 μg/mL, or blood-charcoal agar that contains cephalexin, 40 μg/mL, is used. When the plates are incubated at 35–37 °C for 3–7 days in a moist environment, "mercury drop" or "pearl" colonies form. The small, faintly staining, gram-negative rods are identified by immunofluorescence staining.

C. Growth Characteristics: The organism is a strict aerobe and forms acid but not gas in glucose and lactose. It does not require X and V factors on subculture.

D. Variation: When isolated from patients and cultured on enriched media, *B pertussis* is in the smooth, encapsulated, virulent phase I. Phase IV is the designation for a rough, nonencapsulated, avirulent form. Phases II and III are intermediates.

Antigenic Structure

B pertussis cells possess many antigens, of which the most external are an agglutinogen and a hemagglutinin. The cell wall contains a heat-stable toxin, the protective antigen, and a histamine-sensitizing factor. Upon disruption of the cell, the protoplasm contains a heat-labile toxin and several other antigens. Phase I variants contain larger amounts of the protective antigens than other variant phases. There are several serotypes of *B pertussis* that may have epidemiologic significance. *B pertussis* contains peptides that promote marked lymphocytosis in the host. This is encountered both in human infection and after administration to experimental animals.

Pathogenesis & Pathology

B pertussis survives for only brief periods outside the human host. There are no vectors. Transmission is largely by the respiratory route from early cases and possibly via carriers. The organism adheres to and multiplies rapidly on the surface of the epithelium in the trachea and bronchi and interferes with ciliary action. The blood is not invaded. Disintegrating organisms liberate a toxin that irritates surface cells, giving rise to catarrhal symptoms and causing marked lymphocytosis. Later there may be necrosis of parts of the epithelium and polymorphonuclear infiltration, with peribronchial inflammation and interstitial pneumonia. Secondary invaders like staphylococci or *H influenzae* may give rise to bacterial pneumonia. Obstruction of the smaller bronchioles by mucous plugs results in atelectasis and diminished oxygenation of the blood. This probably contributes to the frequency of convulsions.

Clinical Findings

After an incubation period of about 2 weeks, the "catarrhal stage" develops, with mild coughing and sneezing. During this stage, large numbers of organisms are sprayed in droplets, and the patient is highly infectious but not very ill. During the "paroxysmal" stage, the cough develops its explosive character and the characteristic "whoop" upon inhalation. This leads to rapid exhaustion and may be associated with vomiting, cyanosis, and convulsions. The white blood count is high (16,000–30,000/μL), with an absolute lymphocytosis. Convalescence is slow. Rarely, whooping cough is followed by encephalitis of unknown origin. Several types of adenovirus can produce a clinical picture resembling that caused by *B pertussis*.

Diagnostic Laboratory Tests

Specimens consist of nasopharyngeal swabs or cough droplets expelled onto a "cough plate" held in front of the patient's mouth during a paroxysm.

A. Culture: Collected mucus or droplets are cultured on modified Bordet-Gengou or blood-charcoal agar (see p 249). The plates are incubated in sealed plastic bags at 35–37 °C for 3–7 days. The antibiotics in the media tend to inhibit other respiratory flora but permit growth of *B pertussis*. The iridescent 1- to 2-mm colonies may be surrounded by a narrow zone of hemolysis. Organisms are identified by immunofluorescence staining or by slide agglutination with specific antiserum.

B. Serology: Serologic tests on patients are of little diagnostic help because a rise in agglutinating or precipitating antibodies does not occur until the third week of illness.

Immunity

Recovery from whooping cough or adequate vaccination is followed by immunity. Second infections may occur but are mild; reinfections occurring years later in adults may be severe. It is probable that the first defense against *B pertussis* infection is the antibody that prevents attachment of the bacteria to the cilia of the respiratory epithelium.

Treatment

B pertussis is susceptible to several antimicrobial drugs in vitro. Administration of erythromycin during the catarrhal stage promotes the elimination of the organisms and may have prophylactic value. Treatment after the onset of the paroxysmal phase rarely alters the clinical course. Oxygen inhalation and sedation may prevent anoxic damage to the brain.

Hyperimmune globulin (prepared from sera of immune persons repeatedly injected with pertussis vaccine), 2.5 mL intramuscularly, may be given to debilitated or unimmunized children very early in the illness with some possible benefit.

Prevention

During the first year of life, every infant should receive 3 injections of killed phase I organisms in proper concentration. This vaccine is usually administered in combination with toxoids of diphtheria and tetanus. Pertussis vaccine appears to be an effective immunogen, though subject to variation in manufacture. Some European preparations are believed to be poorly protective and to give rise to a substantial number of neurologic reactions. Vaccine acceptance is far from universal. An infant exposed to whooping cough without prior immunization can obtain temporary passive protection with hyperimmune globulin. Prophylactic administration of erythromycin for 5 days may also benefit such infants or heavily exposed adults.

Epidemiology & Control

Whooping cough is endemic in most densely populated areas all over the world and also occurs intermittently in epidemic outbreaks. The source of infection is usually a patient in the early catarrhal stage of the disease. The communicability is high, ranging from 30 to 90%. The majority of cases occur in children under age 5 years; most deaths occur during the first year of life.

Control of whooping cough rests mainly on adequate active immunization of all infants.

OTHER ORGANISMS OF THE *HAEMOPHILUS* GROUP

Bordetella (Haemophilus) parapertussis

May produce a disease similar to whooping cough even though it differs from typical *B pertussis* in certain bacteriologic criteria and resembles *B bronchiseptica* bacteriologically. Infection is often subclinical.

Eikenella corrodens (See p 242.)

May be present in upper respiratory tract.

Haemophilus parainfluenzae

Resembles *H influenzae* and is a normal inhabitant of the human respiratory tract; it has been encountered in disease mainly in infective endocarditis.

Haemophilus haemoglobinophilus

Requires X factor but not V factor and has been found in dogs but not in human disease.

Haemophilus suis

Resembles *H influenzae* bacteriologically. Acts synergistically with swine influenza virus to produce the disease in hogs.

Haemophilus haemolyticus

The most markedly hemolytic organism of the group in vitro; it occurs both in the normal nasopharynx and in association with rare upper respiratory tract infections of moderate severity in childhood.

Haemophilus aphrophilus

This organism is sometimes encountered in infective endocarditis and pneumonia. It is present in the normal oral and respiratory tract flora. It is related to *Actinobacillus actinomycetem-comitans* and is occasionally mistaken for *Actinomyces*. Tiny colonies adhere to the sides of broth tubes.

Haemophilus aegyptius (Koch-Weeks Bacillus)

Resembles *H influenzae* closely and has been associated with a highly communicable form of conjunctivitis.

Moraxella lacunata (Morax-Axenfeld Bacillus)

A large gram-negative diplobacillus that is grown with difficulty from purulent exudates in eye infections, especially conjunctivitis. It is found in association with trachoma.

Haemophilus ducreyi

The causative organism of chancroid (soft chancre), a sexually transmitted disease. The chancroid consists of a ragged ulcer on the genitalia, with marked swelling and tenderness. The regional lymph nodes are enlarged and painful.

The small gram-negative rods occur in strands in the lesions, usually in association with other pyogenic microorganisms. *H ducreyi* requires X factor but not V factor. It is grown best from scrapings of the ulcer base on "chocolate" agar containing 1% Isovitalex and vancomycin, 3 μg/mL, and incubated in 10% CO_2 at 35 °C. Suspensions of killed *H ducreyi* serve as a useful skin test antigen for the diagnosis of chancroid (Ducrey's skin test). The test may become positive 1–2 weeks after infection and may remain positive for years. There is no permanent immunity following chancroid infection. Treatment with tetracyclines or sulfonamides often results in healing in 2 weeks.

Gardnerella (Haemophilus) vaginalis

A serologically distinct organism isolated from the normal female genitourinary tract and also associated with vaginitis. In wet smears, this "nonspecific" vaginitis yields "clue cells," which are vaginal epithelial cells covered with many tiny rods, and there is an absence of other common causes of vaginitis such as *Trichomonas* or yeasts. *G vaginalis* (previously called *Corynebacterium* and *Haemophilus*) requires neither X factor nor V factor for growth. Vaginal discharge often has a distinct "fishy" odor and contains many anaerobes in addition to *G vaginalis*. The vaginitis attributed to this organism is suppressed by metronidazole, suggesting an association with anaerobes. Oral metronidazole, 0.75–1 g daily for 1 week, is generally effective.

Bordetella bronchiseptica

A small gram-negative bacillus that inhabits the respiratory tracts of canines and may be associated with pneumonitis. It resembles *B parapertussis* bacteriologically.

●   ●   ●

References

Barkin RM, Pichichero ME: Diphtheria-pertussis-tetanus vaccine: Reactogenicity of commercial products. *Pediatrics* 1979;**63**:256.

Black RE et al: Epidemic *Yersinia enterocolitica* infection due to contaminated chocolate milk. *N Engl J Med* 1978;**298**:76.

Buchanan TM et al: The tularemia skin test. *Ann Intern Med* 1971;**74**:336.

Butler T et al: *Yersinia pestis* infection in Vietnam. *J Infect Dis* 1976;**133**:493.

Dorff GJ et al: Infections with *Eikenella corrodens*: A newly recognized human pathogen. *Ann Intern Med* 1974;**80**:305.

Ferber DM, Brubaker RR: Plasmids in *Yersinia pestis*. *Infect Immun* 1981;**31**:839.

Gaisin A, Heaton CL: Chancroid: Alias the soft chancre. *Int J Dermatol* 1975;**14**:188.

Gardner HL: *Haemophilus vaginalis* vaginitis after 25 years. *Am J Obstet Gynecol* 1980;**137**:385.

Guerrant RL et al: Tickborne oculoglandular tularemia: Review of seasonal and vectorial associations in 106 cases. *Arch Intern Med* 1976;**136**:811.

Hall WH, Manion RE, Zinneman HH: Blocking serum lysis of *Brucella abortus* by hyperimmune rabbit immunoglobulin A. *J Immunol* 1971;**107**:41.

Hammond GW et al: Epidemiologic, clinical, laboratory and therapeutic features of an urban outbreak of chancroid in North America. *Rev Infect Dis* 1980;**2**:867.

Hirschmann JV, Everett ED: *Haemophilus influenzae* infections in adults. *Medicine* 1979;**58**:80.

Honig PJ et al: *H influenzae* pneumonia in children. *J Pediatr* 1973;**83**:215.

Johnson RH, Rumans LW: Unusual infections caused by *Pasteurella multocida*. *JAMA* 1977;**237**:146.

Kendrick PL: Can whooping cough be eradicated? *J Infect Dis* 1975;**132**:707.

Klock LE et al: Tularemia epidemic associated with the deerfly. *JAMA* 1973;**226**:149.

Koplan JP et al: Pertussis vaccine: An analysis of benefits, risks and costs. *N Engl J Med* 1979;**301**:906.

Linnemann CC et al: Use of pertussis vaccine in an epidemic involving hospital staff. *Lancet* 1975;**2**:540.

Linnemann CC, Perry EB: *Bordetella parapertussis*. *Am J Dis Child* 1977;**131**:560.

Martone WJ et al: Tularemia pneumonia in Washington, DC. *JAMA* 1979;**242**:2315.

Medeiros AA, O'Brien TF: Ampicillin-resistant *Haemophilus influenzae*. *Lancet* 1975;**1**:716.

Okamoto K et al: Partial characterization of heat-stable enterotoxin produced by *Yersinia enterocolitica*. *Infect Immun* 1981;**31**:554.

Palmer DL et al: Clinical features of plague in the U.S. *J Infect Dis* 1971;**124**:367.

Peltola H et al: *Haemophilus influenzae* type B capsular polysaccharide in children: A double-blind field study of 100,000 vaccinees 3 months to 5 years of age in Finland. *Pediatrics* 1977;**60**:730.

Pheifer TA et al: Nonspecific vaginitis: Role of *Haemophilus vaginalis* and treatment with metronidazole. *N Engl J Med* 1978;**298**:1429.

Rabson AR et al: Generalized *Yersinia enterocolitica* infection. *J Infect Dis* 1975;**131**:447.

Reddin JL et al: Significance of 7S and 19S brucella agglutinins in human brucellosis. *N Engl J Med* 1965;**272**:1263.

von Reyn CF et al: Epidemiologic and clinical features of an outbreak of bubonic plague in New Mexico. *J Infect Dis* 1977;**136**:489.

Ward JI et al: *Haemophilus influenzae* meningitis: A national study of secondary spread in household contacts. *N Engl J Med* 1979;**301**:122.

Williams JE, Cavanaugh DC: Measuring the efficacy of vaccination in affording protection against plague. *Bull WHO* 1979;**57**:309.

Wise RI: Brucellosis in the United States: Past, present and future. *JAMA* 1980;**244**:2318.

The spirochetes are a large, heterogeneous group of spiral, motile organisms. (See Chapter 3 for general morphologic characteristics.)

One family (Spirochaetaceae) of the order Spirochaetales includes 3 genera of free-living, large spiral organisms. The other (Treponemataceae) includes 3 genera pathogenic for humans: (1) *Treponema*, which causes syphilis, bejel, yaws, and pinta; (2) *Borrelia*, which causes relapsing fever; and (3) *Leptospira*, which causes systemic infections with fever, jaundice, and meningitis.

TREPONEMA PALLIDUM

Morphology & Identification

A. Typical Organisms: Slender spirals measuring about 0.2 μm in width and 5–15 μm in length. The spiral coils are regularly spaced at a distance of 1 μm from each other. The organisms are actively motile, rotating steadily around their central axial filaments. The long axis of the spiral is ordinarily straight but may sometimes bend, so that the organism forms a complete circle for moments at a time, returning then to its normal straight position.

The spirals are so thin that they are not readily seen unless darkfield illumination or immunofluorescent stain is employed. They do not stain well with aniline dyes, but they do reduce silver nitrate to metallic silver that is deposited on the surface, so that treponemes can be seen in tissues (Levaditi silver impregnation).

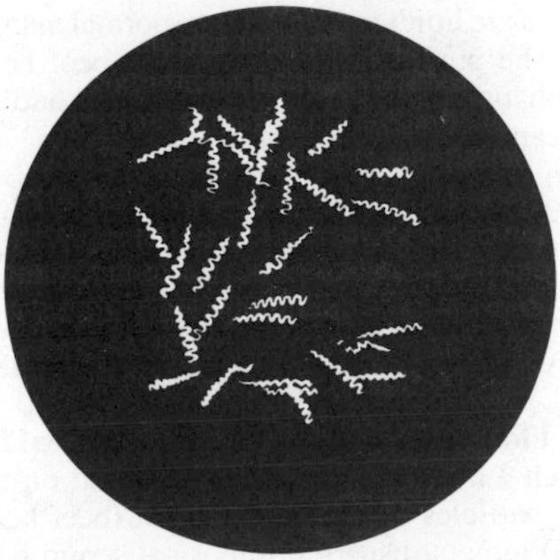

Treponemes ordinarily reproduce by transverse fission, and divided organisms may adhere to one another for some time.

B. Culture: *Treponema pallidum* pathogenic for humans has never been cultured with certainty on artificial media, in fertile eggs, or in tissue culture. Nonpathogenic treponemes (eg, Reiter strain) can be cultured anaerobically in vitro. They are saprophytes antigenically related to *T pallidum*.

C. Growth Characteristics: Because *T pallidum* cannot be grown, no studies of its physiology have been made. The growth requirements for one cultured probably saprophytic strain (Reiter) have, however, been established. A defined medium of 11 amino acids, vitamins, salts, minerals, and serum albumin supports its growth.

In proper suspending fluids and in the presence of reducing substances, *T pallidum* may remain motile for 3–6 days at 25 °C. In whole blood or plasma stored at 4 °C, organisms remain viable for at least 24 hours, which is of potential importance in blood transfusions.

D. Reactions to Physical and Chemical Agents: Drying kills the spirochete rapidly, as does elevation of the temperature to 42 °C also. Treponemes are rapidly immobilized and killed by trivalent arsenicals, mercury, and bismuth. This killing effect is accelerated by high temperatures and can be partially reversed and the organisms reactivated by compounds containing –SH (eg, cysteine, BAL [dimercaprol]). Penicillin is treponemicidal in minute concentrations, but the rate of killing is slow, presumably because of the metabolic inactivity and slow multiplication rate of the organism (estimated division time is 30 hours). Resistance to penicillin has not been demonstrated in syphilis.

E. Variation: A life cycle has been postulated for *T pallidum*, including granular stages and cystlike spherical bodies in addition to the spirochetal form. The occasional ability of *T pallidum* to pass through bacteriologic filters has been attributed to the filtrability of the granular stage.

Figure 20–1. Typical organism of *Treponema pallidum* from tissue fluid in dark field.

Antigenic Structure

The antigens of *T pallidum* are unknown. In the human host, the spirochete stimulates the development of antibodies capable of staining *T pallidum* by indirect immunofluorescence, of immobilizing and killing live motile *T pallidum*, and of fixing complement in the presence of suspensions of *T pallidum* or related spirochetes. The spirochetes also cause the development of a distinct antibodylike substance, reagin, which gives positive complement fixation and flocculation tests with aqueous suspensions of lipids extracted from normal mammalian tissues. Both reagin and antitreponemal antibody can be used for the serologic diagnosis of syphilis.

Pathogenesis, Pathology, & Clinical Findings

A. Acquired Syphilis: Natural infection with *T pallidum* is limited to the human host. Human infection is usually transmitted by sexual contact, and the infectious lesion is on the skin or mucous membranes of genitalia. In about 10% of cases, however, the primary lesion is extragenital (often oral). *T pallidum* can probably penetrate intact mucous membranes, or it may enter through a break in the epidermis.

Spirochetes multiply locally at the site of entry, and some spread to nearby lymph nodes and then reach the bloodstream. In 2–10 weeks after infection a papule develops at the site of infection and breaks down to form an ulcer with a clean, hard base ("hard chancre"). The inflammation is characterized by a predominance of lymphocytes and plasma cells. This "primary lesion" always heals spontaneously, but 2–10 weeks later the "secondary" lesions appear. These consist of a red maculopapular rash anywhere on the body and moist, pale papules (condylomas) in the anogenital region, axillas, and mouth. There may also be syphilitic meningitis, chorioretinitis, hepatitis, nephritis (immune complex type), or periostitis. The secondary lesions also subside spontaneously. Both primary and secondary lesions are rich in spirochetes and highly infectious. Contagious lesions may recur within 3–5 years after infection, but thereafter the individual is not infectious. Syphilitic infection may remain subclinical, and the patient may pass through the primary or secondary stage (or both) without symptoms or signs yet develop tertiary lesions.

In about 30% of cases, early syphilitic infection progresses spontaneously to complete cure without treatment. In another 30% the untreated infection remains latent (principally evident by positive serologic tests). In the remainder the disease progresses to the "tertiary stage," characterized by the development of granulomatous lesions (gummas) in skin, bones, and liver; degenerative changes in the central nervous system (paresis, tabes); or syphilitic cardiovascular lesions, particularly aortitis (sometimes with aneurysm formation) and aortic valve insufficiency. In all tertiary lesions treponemes are very rare, and the exaggerated tissue response must be attributed to some form of hypersensitivity to the organisms. However, treponemes can occasionally be found in the eye or central nervous system in late syphilis.

B. Congenital Syphilis: A pregnant syphilitic woman can transmit *T pallidum* to the fetus through the placenta beginning about the tenth week of gestation. Some of the infected fetuses die and miscarriages result; others are stillborn at term. Others are born live but develop the signs of congenital syphilis in childhood: interstitial keratitis, Hutchinson's teeth, saddle nose, periostitis, and a variety of central nervous system anomalies. Adequate treatment of the mother during pregnancy prevents congenital syphilis. The reagin titer in the blood of the child rises with active infection but falls with time if antibody was passively transmitted from the mother. In congenital infection the child makes IgM antitreponemal antibody.

C. Experimental Disease: Rabbits can be experimentally infected in the skin, testis, and eye with human *T pallidum*. The animal develops a chancre rich in spirochetes, and organisms persist in lymph nodes, spleen, and bone marrow for the entire life of the animal, although there is no progressive disease.

Diagnostic Laboratory Tests

A. Specimens: Tissue fluid expressed from early surface lesions for demonstration of spirochetes; blood serum for serologic tests.

B. Darkfield Examination: A drop of tissue fluid or exudate is placed on a slide and a coverslip pressed over it to make a thin layer. The preparation is then examined under oil immersion with darkfield illumination for typical motile spirochetes.

Treponemes disappear from lesions within a few hours after the beginning of antibiotic treatment.

C. Immunofluorescence: Tissue fluid or exudate is spread on a glass slide, air dried, and mailed to the laboratory. It is fixed, stained with a fluorescein-labeled antitreponeme serum, and examined by means of immunofluorescence microscopy for typical fluorescent spirochetes.

D. Serologic Tests for Syphilis (STS): These use either treponemal or nontreponemal antigens.

1. Nontreponemal antigen tests–The antigens employed are lipids extracted from normal mammalian tissue. The purified cardiolipin from beef heart is a diphosphatidylglycerol. It requires the addition of lecithin and cholesterol or other "sensitizers" to react with syphilitic "reagin." "Reagin" is a mixture of IgM and IgA antibodies directed against some antigens widely distributed in normal tissues. Reagin is found in patients' serum after 2–3 weeks of untreated syphilitic infection and in spinal fluid after 4–8 weeks of infection. Two types of tests determine the presence of reagin.

a. Flocculation tests (VDRL [Venereal Disease Research Laboratories], etc) are based on the fact that the particles of the lipid antigen (beef heart cardiolipin) remain dispersed in normal serum but combine with reagin to form visible aggregates within a few minutes, particularly if the solution is agitated. The rapid plasma reagin (RPR) test is a convenient modification for rapid surveys. Positive VDRL tests revert to negative 6–24 months after effective treatment of early syphilis.

b. Complement fixation (CF) tests (Wassermann, Kolmer) are based on the fact that reagin-containing sera fix complement in the presence of cardiolipin "antigen." It is necessary to ascertain that the serum is not "anticomplementary" (ie, that it does not destroy complement in the absence of antigen).

Both (a) and (b) can give quantitative results. An estimate of the amount of reagin present in serum can be made by performing (a) or (b) with 2-fold dilutions of serum and expressing the titer as the highest dilution that gives a positive result. Quantitative results are valuable in establishing a diagnosis and in evaluating the effect of treatment.

Nontreponemal tests are subject to false-positive results. These either are due to technical difficulties of the test or are "biologic" false positives attributable to the occurrence of "reagins" in a variety of human disorders. Prominent among the latter are other infections (malaria, leprosy, measles, infectious mononucleosis, etc), vaccinations, collagen-vascular diseases (systemic lupus erythematosus, polyarteritis nodosa, rheumatic disorders), and other conditions. Nontreponemal antibody tests may become negative spontaneously in progressive tertiary syphilis; thus, a negative VDRL does not rule out such disease activity.

2. Treponemal antibody tests–

a. Fluorescent treponemal antibody (FTA-ABS) test–A test employing indirect immunofluorescence (killed *T pallidum* + patient's serum + labeled antihuman gamma globulin) shows excellent specificity and sensitivity for syphilis antibodies if the patient's serum, prior to the FTA test, has been absorbed with sonicated Reiter spirochetes. The FTA-ABS test is the first to become positive in early syphilis, and it usually remains positive many years after effective treatment of early syphilis. The test cannot be used to judge the efficacy of treatment. The presence of IgM FTA in the blood of newborns is good evidence of in utero infection (congenital syphilis).

b. TPI test–Demonstration of *T pallidum* immobilization (TPI) by specific antibodies in the patient's serum after the second week of infection. Dilutions of serum are mixed with complement and with live, actively motile *T pallidum* extracted from the testicular chancre of a rabbit, and the mixture is observed microscopically. If specific antibodies are present, spirochetes are immobilized; in normal serum, active motion continues. This test requires live treponemes from infected animals and is hard to perform.

c. *T pallidum* complement fixation test–Spirochetes extracted from syphilomas of rabbits form specific antigens for complement fixation tests that probably measure the same antibody as the TPI test, above. Such spirochetal suspensions are difficult to prepare. Antigens prepared from cultured Reiter spirochetes are occasionally employed in the Reiter complement fixation test.

d. *T pallidum* hemagglutination (TPHA) test–Red blood cells are treated to adsorb treponemes on their surface. When mixed with serum containing antitreponemal antibodies, the cells become clumped. This test is similar to the FTA-ABS test in specificity and sensitivity, but it becomes positive somewhat later in the course of infection.

VDRL and FTA-ABS tests can also be performed on spinal fluid. Antibodies do not reach the cerebrospinal fluid from the bloodstream but are probably formed in the central nervous system in response to syphilitic infection.

Immunity

A person with active syphilis or yaws appears to be resistant to superinfection with *T pallidum*. However, if early syphilis or yaws is treated adequately and the infection is eradicated, the individual again becomes fully susceptible.

Treatment

Penicillin in concentrations of 0.003 unit/mL has definite treponemicidal activity, and penicillin is the treatment of choice. In early syphilis, penicillin levels are maintained for 2 weeks (eg, a single injection of benzathine penicillin G, 2.4 million units intramuscularly); in latent syphilis, benzathine penicillin G, 2.4 million units intramuscularly, is given 3 times at weekly intervals. In neurosyphilis, the same therapy is acceptable, but larger amounts of penicillin (eg, aqueous penicillin G, 20 million units intravenously daily for 2–3 weeks) are sometimes recommended. Other antibiotics can occasionally be substituted. Prolonged follow-up is essential. In neurosyphilis, treponemes occasionally survive such treatment. A typical Jarisch-Herxheimer reaction may occur within hours after treatment is begun. It is probably due to the sudden release of endotoxin from spirochetes.

Epidemiology, Prevention, & Control

At present, the incidence of syphilis (and other sexually transmitted diseases) is rising in most parts of the world. With the exceptions of congenital syphilis and the rare occupational exposure of medical personnel, syphilis is acquired through sexual exposure. An infected person may remain contagious for 3–5 years during "early" syphilis. "Late" syphilis, of more than 5 years' duration, is usually not contagious. Consequently, control measures depend on (1) prompt and adequate treatment of all discovered cases; (2) follow-up on sources of infection and contacts so they can be treated; (3) sex hygiene; and (4) prophylaxis at the time of exposure. Both mechanical prophylaxis (condoms) and chemoprophylaxis (eg, penicillin after exposure) have great limitations. Washing the genitalia after exposure may afford some protection to the male. Several venereal diseases can be transmitted simultaneously. Therefore, it is important to consider the possibility of syphilis when any one sexually transmitted disease has been found.

DISEASES RELATED TO SYPHILIS

These diseases are all caused by treponemes indistinguishable from *T pallidum*. All give biologic true-positive serologic tests for syphilis, and some cross-immunity can be demonstrated in experimental animals and perhaps in humans. All are nonvenereal diseases and are commonly transmitted by direct contact. None of the causative organisms have been cultured on artificial media.

Bejel

Bejel occurs chiefly in Africa but also in the Middle East, in Southeast Asia, and elsewhere, particularly among children, and produces highly infectious skin lesions; late visceral complications are rare. Penicillin is the drug of choice.

Yaws (Frambesia)

Yaws is endemic, particularly among children, in many humid, hot tropical countries. It is caused by *Treponema pertenue*. The primary lesion, an ulcerating papule, occurs usually on the arms or legs. Transmission is by person-to-person contact in children under age 15. Transplacental, congenital infection does not occur. Scar formation of skin lesions and bone destruction are common, but visceral or nervous system complications are very rare. It has been debated whether yaws represents a variant of syphilis adapted to nonvenereal transmission in hot climates. There appears to be cross-immunity between yaws and syphilis. Diagnostic procedures and therapy are similar to those for syphilis. The response to penicillin treatment is dramatic.

Pinta

Pinta is caused by *Treponema carateum* and occurs endemically in all age groups in Mexico, Central and South America, the Philippines, and some areas of the Pacific. The disease appears to be restricted to dark-skinned races. The primary lesion, a nonulcerating papule, occurs on exposed areas. Some months later, flat, hyperpigmented lesions appear on the skin; depigmentation and hyperkeratosis take place years afterward. Late cardiovascular and nervous system involvement probably occurs. Transmission is nonvenereal, either by direct contact or through the agency of a fly *(Hippelates)*. Diagnosis and treatment are the same as for syphilis.

Rabbit Syphilis

Rabbit syphilis *(Treponema cuniculi)* is a natural venereal infection of rabbits producing minor lesions of the genitalia. The causative organism is morphologically indistinguishable from *T pallidum* and may lead to confusion in experimental work.

OTHER SPIROCHETAL ORGANISMS

BORRELIA RECURRENTIS

Morphology & Identification

A. Typical Organisms: *Borrelia recurrentis* is an irregular spiral 10–30 μm long and 0.3 μm wide. The distance between turns varies from 2 to 4 μm. The organisms are highly flexible and move both by rotation and by twisting. *B recurrentis* stains readily with bacteriologic dyes as well as with blood stains such as Giemsa's or Wright's stain.

B. Culture: The organism can be cultured in fluid media containing blood, serum, or tissue; but it rapidly loses its pathogenicity for animals when transferred repeatedly in vitro. Multiplication is rapid in chick embryos when blood from patients is inoculated into the chorioallantoic membrane.

C. Growth Characteristics: Virtually nothing is known of the metabolic requirements or activity of borreliae. At 4 °C, the organisms survive for several months in infected blood or in culture. In some ticks (but not in lice), spirochetes are passed from generation to generation.

D. Variation: The only significant variation of *Borrelia* is with respect to its antigenic structure.

Antigenic Structure

Isolates of *Borrelia* from different parts of the world, from different hosts, and from different vectors (ticks or lice) either have been given different species names or have been designated strains of *B recurrentis*. Biologic differences between these strains or species do not appear to be stable.

Agglutinins, complement-fixing antibodies, and lytic antibodies develop in high titer after infection with borreliae. Apparently the antigenic structure of the organisms changes in the course of a single infection. The antibodies produced initially may act as a selective factor that permits the survival only of anti-

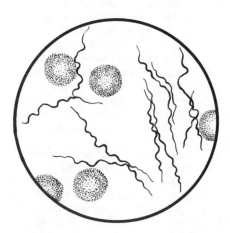

Figure 20–2. *Borrelia recurrentis* in blood smear.

genically distinct variants. The relapsing course of the disease appears to be due to the multiplication of such antigenic variants, against which the host must then develop new antibodies. Ultimate recovery (after 3–10 relapses) is associated with the presence of antibodies against several antigenic variants.

Pathology

Fatal cases show spirochetes in great numbers in the spleen and liver, necrotic foci in other parenchymatous organs, and hemorrhagic lesions in the kidneys and the gastrointestinal tract. Spirochetes have been occasionally demonstrated in the spinal fluid and brains of persons who have had meningitis. In experimental animals (guinea pigs, rats), the brain may serve as a reservoir of borreliae after they have disappeared from the blood.

Pathogenesis & Clinical Findings

The incubation period is 3–10 days. The onset is sudden, with chills and an abrupt rise of temperature. During this time spirochetes abound in the blood. The fever persists for 3–5 days and then declines, leaving the patient weak but not ill. The afebrile period lasts 4–10 days and is followed by a second attack of chills, fever, intense headache, and malaise. There are from 3 to 10 such recurrences, generally of diminishing severity. During the febrile stages (especially when the temperature is rising), organisms are present in the blood; during the afebrile periods they are absent. Organisms appear less frequently in the urine.

Antibodies against the spirochetes appear during the febrile stage, and it is possible that the attack is terminated by their agglutinating and lytic effects. These antibodies may select out antigenically distinct variants that multiply and cause a relapse. Several distinct antigenic varieties of borreliae may be isolated from a single patient's several relapses, even following experimental inoculation with a single organism.

Diagnostic Laboratory Tests

A. Specimens: Blood obtained during the rise in fever, for smears and animal inoculation.

B. Stained Smears: Thin or thick blood smears stained with Wright's or Giemsa's stain reveal large, loosely coiled spirochetes among the red cells.

C. Animal Inoculation: White mice or young rats are inoculated intraperitoneally with blood. Stained films of tail blood are examined for spirochetes 2–4 days later.

D. Serology: Spirochetes grown in culture can serve as antigens for CF tests, but the preparation of satisfactory antigens is difficult. Patients suffering from epidemic (louse-borne) relapsing fever may develop agglutinins for *Proteus* OXK and also a positive VDRL.

Immunity

Immunity following infection is usually of short duration.

Treatment

The great variability of the spontaneous remissions of relapsing fever makes evaluation of chemotherapeutic effectiveness difficult. Tetracyclines, erythromycin, and penicillin are all believed to be effective. Treatment for a single day may be sufficient to terminate an individual attack.

Epidemiology, Prevention, & Control

Relapsing fever is endemic in many parts of the world. Its main reservoir is the rodent population, which serves as a source of infection for ticks of the genus *Ornithodorus*. The distribution of endemic foci and the seasonal incidence of the disease are largely determined by the ecology of the ticks in different areas. In the USA, infected ticks are found throughout the West, especially in mountainous areas, but clinical cases are rare. In the tick, *Borrelia* may be transmitted transovarially from generation to generation.

Spirochetes are present in all tissues of the tick and may be transmitted by the bite or by crushing the tick. The tick-borne disease is not epidemic. However, when an infected individual harbors lice, the lice become infected by sucking blood; 4–5 days later, they may serve as a source of infection for other individuals. The infection of lice is not transmitted to the next generation, and the disease is the result of rubbing crushed lice into bite wounds. Severe epidemics may occur in louse-infested populations, and transmission is favored by crowding, malnutrition, and cold climate.

In endemic areas human infection may occasionally result from contact with the blood and tissues of infected rodents. The mortality rate of the endemic disease is low, but in epidemics it may reach 30%.

Prevention is based on avoidance of exposure to ticks and lice and on delousing (cleanliness, insecticides). No vaccines are available.

LEPTOSPIRAE

Morphology & Identification

A. Typical Organisms: Tightly coiled, thin, flexible spirochetes 5–15 μm long, with very fine spirals 0.1–0.2 μm wide. One end of the organism is often bent, forming a hook. There is active rotational motion, but no flagella have been discovered. Electron micrographs show a thin axial filament and a delicate membrane. The spirochete is so delicate that in the dark field it may appear only as a chain of minute cocci. It does not stain readily but can be impregnated with silver.

B. Culture: Leptospirae grow best aerobically at 30 °C in peptone broth containing 10% inactivated (rabbit) serum. On semisolid meat extract media (Fletcher) containing 10% rabbit serum, round colonies 1–3 mm in diameter develop in 6–10 days. Leptospirae also grow on chorioallantoic membranes of embryonated eggs.

C. Growth Requirements: Leptospirae derive energy from oxidation of long chain fatty acids and cannot use amino acids or carbohydrates as major energy sources. Ammonium salts are a main source of nitrogen. Leptospirae can survive for weeks in water, particularly at alkaline pH.

Antigenic Structure

The main strains of leptospirae isolated from humans or animals in different parts of the world (Table 20–1) are all serologically related and exhibit marked cross-reactivity in serologic tests. This indicates considerable overlapping in antigenic structure, and quantitative tests and antibody absorption studies are necessary for a specific serologic diagnosis. From many strains of leptospirae, a serologically reactive lipopolysaccharide has been extracted that has group reactivity.

Pathogenesis & Clinical Findings

Human infection results usually from ingestion of water or food contaminated with leptospirae. More rarely, the organisms may enter through mucous membranes or breaks in the skin. After an incubation period of 1–2 weeks, there is a variable febrile onset during which spirochetes are present in the blood-stream. They then establish themselves in the parenchymatous organs (particularly liver and kidneys), producing hemorrhage and necrosis of tissue and resulting in dysfunction of those organs (jaundice, hemorrhage, nitrogen retention). The central nervous system is frequently invaded, and this results in a clinical picture of "aseptic meningitis." There may be lesions in skin and muscles also. Often there is episcleral injection of the eye. The degree and distribution of organ involvement vary in the different diseases produced by different leptospirae in various parts of the world (Table 20–1). Many infections are mild or subclinical. Hepatitis is particularly frequent in patients with leptospirosis. It is often associated with elevation of serum creatine phosphokinase, whereas that enzyme is present in normal concentrations in viral hepatitis.

Kidney involvement in many animal species is chronic and results in the elimination of large numbers of leptospirae in the urine; this is probably the main source of contamination and infection of humans. Human urine also may contain spirochetes in the second and third weeks of disease.

Agglutinating, complement-fixing, and lytic antibodies develop during the infection. Serum from convalescent patients protects experimental animals against an otherwise fatal infection. Immunity resulting from infection in humans and animals appears to be specific for leptospirae. Dogs have been artificially immunized with killed cultures of leptospirae.

Diagnostic Laboratory Tests

Specimens consist of blood for microscopic examination, culture, and inoculation of young hamsters or guinea pigs; and serum for agglutination tests.

A. Microscopic Examination: Darkfield examination or thick smears stained by Giemsa's technique occasionally show leptospirae in fresh blood from early infections. Darkfield examination of centrifuged urine may also be positive.

B. Culture: Whole fresh blood can be cultured in diluted serum or on Fletcher's semisolid medium or Stuart *Leptospira* broth (each of which contains 10% rabbit serum).

C. Animal Inoculation: A sensitive technique for the isolation of leptospirae consists of the intraperitoneal inoculation of young hamsters or guinea pigs with fresh plasma or urine. Within a few days, spirochetes become demonstrable in the peritoneal cavity; on the death of the animal (8–14 days), hemorrhagic lesions with spirochetes are found in many organs.

D. Serology: Agglutinating antibodies attaining very high titers (1:10,000 or higher) develop slowly in leptospiral infection, reaching a peak at 5–8 weeks after infection. For agglutination tests, cultured lep-

Table 20–1. Principal leptospiral diseases.

Leptospiral Species*	Source of Infection	Disease in Humans	Clinical Findings	Distribution
L autumnalis	?	Pretibial fever or Ft. Bragg fever	Fever, rash over tibia	USA, Japan
L ballum	Mice	—	Fever, rash, jaundice	USA, Europe, Israel
L bovis	Cattle, voles	—	Fever, prostration	USA, Israel, Australia
L canicola	Dog urine	Infectious jaundice	Influenzalike illness, aseptic meningitis	Worldwide
L grippotyphosa	Rodents, water	Marsh fever	Fever, prostration, aseptic meningitis	Europe, USA, Africa
L hebdomadis	Rats, mice	Seven-day fever	Fever, jaundice	Japan, Europe
L icterohaemorrhagiae	Rat urine, water	Weil's disease	Jaundice, hemorrhages, aseptic meningitis	Worldwide
L mitis	Swine	Swineherd's disease	Aseptic meningitis	Australia
L pomona	Swine, cattle	Swineherd's disease	Fever, prostration, aseptic meningitis	Europe, USA, Australia

*In the view of some, the organisms listed in this table are not different species but serogroups of *Leptospira interrogans*.

tospirae are used live and are observed microscopically for clumping. Cross-absorption of sera may permit identification of a species-specific antibody response. With live suspensions, agglutination may be followed by lysis. Leptospiral cultures can adsorb to red blood cells. These will clump in the presence of antibody. These hemagglutination reactions are group-specific.

Immunity

A solid species-specific immunity (directed against individual serotypes) follows leptospiral infection.

Treatment

In very early infection, antibiotics (penicillin, tetracyclines) have some therapeutic effect but do not eradicate the infection.

Epidemiology, Prevention, & Control

The leptospiroses are essentially animal infections; human infection is only accidental, following contact with water or other materials contaminated with the excreta of animal hosts. Rats, mice, wild rodents, dogs, swine, and cattle are the principal sources of human infection. They excrete leptospirae in urine and feces both during the active illness and during the asymptomatic carrier state. Leptospirae remain viable in stagnant water for several weeks; drinking, swimming, bathing, or food contamination may lead to human infection. Persons most likely to come in contact with water contaminated by rats (eg, miners, sewer workers, farmers, fishermen) run the greatest risk of infection. Children acquire the infection from dogs more frequently than do adults. Control consists of preventing exposure to potentially contaminated water and reducing contamination by rodent control. Dogs can receive distemper-hepatitis-leptospirosis vaccinations.

SPIRILLUM MINOR
(Spirillum morsus muris)

Spirillum minor causes one form of rat-bite fever (sodoku). This very small (3–5 μm) and rigid spiral organism is carried by rats all over the world. The organism is inoculated into humans through the bite of a rat and results in a local lesion, regional gland swelling, skin rashes, and fever of the relapsing type. The frequency of this illness depends upon the degree of contact between humans and rats. The *Spirillum* can be isolated by inoculation of guinea pigs or mice with material from enlarged lymph nodes or blood but has not been grown in bacteriologic media. In the USA and Europe, this disease has been recognized only infrequently. Several other motile gram-negative spiral aerobic organisms can produce spirillum fever. (Kowal J: *N Engl J Med* 1961;**264**:123.)

SPIROCHETES OF THE NORMAL MOUTH & MUCOUS MEMBRANES

A number of spirochetes occur in every normal mouth. Some of them have been named (eg, *Borrelia buccalis*), but neither their morphology nor their physiologic activity permits definitive classification. On normal genitalia, a spirochete called *Borrelia refringens* is occasionally found that may be confused with *T pallidum*. These organisms are harmless saprophytes under ordinary conditions. Most of them are strict anaerobes that can be grown in petrolatum-sealed meat infusion broth tubes to which some tissue has been added.

FUSOSPIROCHETAL DISEASE

Under certain circumstances, particularly injury to mucous membranes, nutritional deficiency, or concomitant infection (eg, with herpes simplex virus) of the epithelium, the normal spirochetes of the mouth, together with cigar-shaped, banded, anaerobic fusiform bacilli (fusobacteria), find suitable conditions for vast increase in numbers. This occurs in ulcerative gingivostomatitis (trench mouth), often called Vincent's stomatitis or Vincent's infection. When this type of process produces ulcerative tonsillitis and massive tissue involvement, it may be called Vincent's angina. It also occurs in lung abscesses where pyogenic microorganisms and *Bacteroides* species have broken down tissue; in bronchiectasis, where anatomic and physiologic disturbances interfere with normal drainage; in leg ("tropical") ulcers with mixed infection and venous stasis; and similar situations.

In all of these instances, necrotic tissue provides the anaerobic environment required by the fusospirochetal flora. The anaerobic conditions in turn prevent rapid healing and may contribute to tissue breakdown. Fusiform bacilli (fusobacteria) coexist with other anaerobes (*Bacteroides, Peptostreptococcus;* see Chapter 23). The fusospirochetal flora is readily inhibited by antibiotics. Antibiotic therapy may thus control gingivostomatitis or angina. However, the fusospirochetal organisms are not primary pathogens. Effective treatment must direct itself against the initial cause of tissue breakdown.

Fusospirochetal disease is generally not transmissible through direct contact, since everybody carries the organisms in the mouth. However, outbreaks occur occasionally in children or young adults. This is attributed to the transmission of a viral agent (eg, herpes simplex virus) in a susceptible population group or to nutritional deficiency and poor oral hygiene ("trench mouth").

• • •

References

Andrew ED, Marrocco GR: Leptospirosis in New England. *JAMA* 1977;**238:**2027.

Babudieri B: The agglutination-absorption test of leptospira. *Bull WHO* 1971;**44:**795.

Butler T et al: *Borrelia recurrentis* infection. *J Infect Dis* 1978;**137:**573.

Center for Disease Control: Syphilis: Recommended treatment schedules, 1976. *Ann Intern Med* 1976;**85:**94.

Clark EG, Danbolt N: The Oslo study of the natural course of untreated syphilis. *Med Clin North Am* 1964;**48:**613.

Fiumara NJ: Treatment of primary and secondary syphilis: Serological response. *JAMA* 1980;**243:**2500.

Harter CA, Benirschke K: Fetal syphilis in the first trimester. *Am J Obstet Gynecol* 1976;**124:**705.

Heimoff LL: The diagnosis of syphilis. *Bull NY Acad Med* 1976;**52:**863.

Hopkins DR: Yaws in the Americas, 1950–1975. *J Infect Dis* 1977;**136:**548.

Johnson RC: The spirochetes. *Annu Rev Microbiol* 1977;**31:**89.

Kampmeier RH: Syphilis therapy: An historical perspective. *J Am Vener Dis Assoc* 1976;**3:**99.

Lee TJ, Sparling F: Syphilis: An algorithm. *JAMA* 1979;**242:**1187.

Malison MD: Relapsing fever. *JAMA* 1979;**241:**2819.

Pavia CS et al: Cell-mediated immunity during syphilis. *Br J Vener Dis* 1978;**54:**144.

Southern PM, Sanford JP: Relapsing fever. *Medicine* 1969;**48:**129.

Tramont EC: Persistence of *T pallidum* following penicillin G therapy. *JAMA* 1976;**236:**2206.

Turner LH: Leptospirosis. *Br Med J* 1973;**1:**537.

Wong M et al: Leptospirosis: Childhood disease. *J Pediatr* 1977;**90:**532.

Rickettsiae are small bacteria that are obligate intracellular parasites and—except for Q fever—are transmitted to humans by arthropods. At least 4 rickettsiae *(Rickettsia rickettsii, Rickettsia conorii, Rickettsia tsutsugamushi, Rickettsia akari)*—and perhaps others—are transmitted transovarially in the arthropod, which serves as both vector and reservoir. Rickettsial diseases (except Q fever) typically exhibit fever, rashes, and vasculitis. They are grouped on the basis of clinical features, epidemiologic aspects, and immunologic characteristics (see Table 21–1).

Properties of Rickettsiae

Rickettsiae are pleomorphic, appearing either as short rods, 600 × 300 nm in size, or as cocci, and they occur singly, in pairs, in short chains, or in filaments. When stained, they are readily visible under the optical microscope. With Giemsa's stain they stain blue; with Macchiavello's stain they stain red and contrast with the blue-staining cytoplasm in which they appear.

A wide range of animals are susceptible to infection with rickettsial organisms. Rickettsiae grow readily in the yolk sac of the embryonated egg (yolk sac suspensions contain up to 10^9 rickettsial particles per milliliter). Pure preparations of rickettsiae can be obtained by differential centrifugation of yolk sac suspensions. Many rickettsial strains also grow in cell culture.

Purified rickettsiae contain both RNA and DNA in a ratio of 3.5:1 (similar to the ratio in bacteria). Rickettsiae have cell walls made up of peptidoglycans containing muramic acid, resembling cell walls of gram-negative bacteria, and they divide like bacteria. In cell culture, the generation time is 8–10 hours at 34 °C.

Purified rickettsiae contain various enzymes concerned with metabolism. Thus they oxidize intermediate metabolites like pyruvic, succinic, and

Table 21–1. Rickettsial diseases.

Disease	*Rickettsia*	Geographic Area of Prevalence	Insect Vector	Mammalian Reservoir	Weil-Felix Agglutination OX19	OX2	OXK
Typhus group							
Epidemic typhus	*Rickettsia prowazekii*	South America, Africa, Asia	Louse	Humans	++	±	−
Murine typhus	*Rickettsia typhi*	Worldwide; small	Flea	Rodents	++	−	−
Scrub typhus	*Rickettsia tsutsugamushi*	Southeast Asia, Japan	Mite*	Rodents	−	−	++
Spotted fever group							
Rocky Mountain spotted fever (RMSF)	*Rickettsia rickettsii*	Western hemisphere	Tick*	Rodents, dogs	+	+	−
Fièvre boutonneuse Kenya tick typhus South African tick fever Indian tick typhus	*Rickettsia conorii*	Africa, India, Mediterranean	Tick*	Rodents, dogs	+	+	−
Queensland tick typhus	*Rickettsia australis*	Australia	Tick*	Rodents, marsupials	+	+	−
North Asian tick typhus	*Rickettsia sibirica*	Siberia, Mongolia	Tick*	Rodents	+	+	−
Rickettsialpox	*Rickettsia akari*	USA, Korea, USSR	Mite*	Mice	−	−	−
RMSF-like	*Rickettsia canada*	North America	Tick*	Rodents	?	?	−
Other							
Q fever	*Coxiella burnetii*	Worldwide	None†	Cattle, sheep, goats	−	−	−
Trench fever	*Rochalimaea quintana*	Rare	Louse	Humans			

*Also serve as arthropod reservoir, by maintaining the rickettsiae through transovarian transmission.
†Human infection results from inhalation of dust.

glutamic acids and can convert glutamic acid into aspartic acid. Rickettsiae lose their biologic activities when they are stored at 0 °C; this is due to the progressive loss of nicotinamide adenine dinucleotide (NAD). All of these properties can be restored by subsequent incubation with NAD. They may also lose their biologic activity if they are starved by incubation for several hours at 36 °C. This loss can be prevented by the addition of glutamate, pyruvate, or adenosine triphosphate (ATP). Subsequent incubation of the starved organism with glutamate at 30 °C leads to recovery of activity.

Rickettsiae may grow in different parts of the cell. Those of the typhus group are usually found in the cytoplasm; those of the spotted fever group, in the nucleus. Thus far, one of the rickettsiae, *Rochalimaea quintana,* has been grown on cell-free media. It has been suggested that rickettsiae grow best when the metabolism of the host cells is low. Thus, their growth is enhanced when the temperature of infected chick embryos is lowered to 32 °C. If the embryos are held at 40 °C, rickettsial multiplication is poor. Conditions that influence the metabolism of the host can alter its susceptibility to rickettsial infection.

Rickettsial growth is enhanced in the presence of sulfonamides, and rickettsial diseases are made more severe by these drugs. Para-aminobenzoic acid (PABA), the structural analog of the sulfonamides, inhibits the growth of rickettsial organisms. Tetracyclines or chloramphenicol inhibits the growth of rickettsiae and can be therapeutically effective.

In general, rickettsiae are quickly destroyed by heat, drying, and bactericidal chemicals. Although rickettsiae are usually killed by storage at room temperature, dried feces of infected lice may remain infective for months at room temperature.

The organism of Q fever is the rickettsial agent most resistant to drying. This organism may survive pasteurization at 60 °C for 30 minutes and can survive for months in dried feces or milk. This may be due to the formation of endospores by *Coxiella burnetii.*

Rickettsial Antigens & Antibodies

A variety of rickettsial antibodies are known; all of them participate in the reactions discussed below. The antibodies that develop in humans after vaccination generally are more type-specific than the antibodies developing after natural infection.

A. Agglutination of *Proteus vulgaris* (Weil-Felix Reaction): The Weil-Felix reaction is commonly used in diagnostic work. Rickettsiae and *Proteus* organisms appear to share certain antigens. Thus, during the course of rickettsial infections, patients develop antibodies that agglutinate certain strains of *P vulgaris*. For example, the *Proteus* strain OX19 is agglutinated strongly by sera from persons infected with epidemic or endemic typhus; weakly by sera from those infected with Rocky Mountain spotted fever; and not at all by those infected with Q fever. Convalescent sera from scrub typhus patients react most strongly with the *Proteus* strain OXK (Table 21–1).

B. Agglutination of Rickettsiae: Rickettsiae are agglutinated by specific antibodies. This reaction is very sensitive and can be diagnostically useful when heavy rickettsial suspensions are available for microagglutination tests.

C. Complement Fixation With Rickettsial Antigens: Complement-fixing antibodies are commonly used in diagnostic laboratories. A 4-fold or greater antibody titer rise is usually required as laboratory support for the diagnosis of acute rickettsial infection. Convalescent titers often exceed 1:64. Group-reactive soluble antigens are available for the typhus group, the spotted fever group, and Q fever. They originate in the cell wall. Some insoluble antigens may give species-specific reactions.

D. Immunofluorescence Test With Rickettsial Antigens: Suspensions of rickettsiae can be partially purified from infected yolk sac material and used as antigens in indirect immunofluorescence tests (see p 168) with patient's serum and a fluorescein-labeled antihuman globulin. The results indicate the presence of partly species-specific antibodies, but some cross-reactions are observed. Antibodies after vaccination are IgG; early after infection, IgM.

E. Passive Hemagglutination Test: Treated red blood cells adsorb soluble antigens and can then be agglutinated by antibody.

F. Neutralization of Rickettsial Toxins: Rickettsiae contain toxins that produce death in animals within a few hours after injection. Toxin-neutralizing antibodies appear during infection, and these are specific for the toxins of the typhus group, the spotted fever group, and scrub typhus rickettsiae. Toxins exist only in viable rickettsiae—inactivated rickettsiae are nontoxic.

Pathology

Rickettsiae multiply in endothelial cells of small blood vessels and produce vasculitis. The cells become swollen and necrotic; there is thrombosis of the vessel, leading to rupture and necrosis. Vascular lesions are prominent in the skin, but vasculitis occurs in many organs and appears to be the basis of hemostatic disturbances. In the brain, aggregations of lymphocytes, polymorphonuclear leukocytes, and macrophages are associated with the blood vessels of the gray matter; these are called typhus nodules. The heart shows similar lesions of the small blood vessels. Other organs may also be involved.

Immunity

In cell cultures of macrophages, rickettsiae are phagocytosed and replicate intracellularly even in the presence of antibody. The addition of lymphocytes from immune animals stops this multiplication in vitro. Infection in humans is followed by partial immunity to reinfection from external sources, but relapses occur (see Brill's disease, p 263).

Clinical Findings

Except for Q fever, in which there is no skin

lesion, rickettsial infections are characterized by fever, headache, malaise, prostration, skin rash, and enlargement of the spleen and liver.

A. Typhus Group:

1. Epidemic typhus–In epidemic typhus, systemic infection and prostration are severe, and fever lasts for about 2 weeks. The disease is more severe and is more often fatal in patients over 40 years of age. During epidemics, the case mortality rate has been 6–30%.

2. Endemic typhus–The clinical picture of endemic typhus has many features in common with that of epidemic typhus, but the disease is milder and is rarely fatal except in elderly patients.

B. Spotted Fever Group: The spotted fever group resembles typhus clinically; however, unlike the rash in other rickettsial diseases, the rash of the spotted fever group usually appears first on the extremities, moves centripetally, and involves the palms and soles. Some, like Brazilian spotted fever, may produce severe infections; others, like Mediterranean fever, are mild. The case mortality rate varies greatly. In untreated Rocky Mountain spotted fever, it is usually much greater in older age groups (up to 60%) than in younger people.

Rickettsialpox is a mild disease with a rash resembling that of varicella. About a week before onset of fever, a firm red papule appears at the site of the mite bite and develops into a deep-seated vesicle that in turn forms a black eschar (see below).

C. Scrub Typhus: This disease resembles epidemic typhus clinically. One feature is the eschar, the punched-out ulcer covered with a blackened scab that indicates the location of the mite bite. Generalized lymphadenopathy and lymphocytosis are common. Localized eschars may also be present in the spotted fever group.

D. Q Fever: This disease resembles influenza, nonbacterial pneumonia, hepatitis, or encephalopathy rather than typhus. There is no rash or local lesion. The Weil-Felix test is negative. Transmission results from inhalation of dust contaminated with rickettsiae from dried feces, urine, or milk.

E. Trench Fever: The disease is characterized by the headache, exhaustion, pain, sweating, coldness of the extremities, and fever associated with a roseolar rash. Relapses occur. Trench fever has been known only among armies during wars in central Europe.

Laboratory Findings

Isolation of rickettsiae is technically quite difficult and so is of only limited usefulness in diagnosis. Whole blood (or emulsified blood clot) is inoculated into guinea pigs, mice, or eggs. Rickettsiae are recovered most frequently from blood drawn soon after onset, but they have been found as late as the 12th day of the disease.

If the guinea pigs fail to show disease (fever, scrotal swellings, hemorrhagic necrosis, death), serum is collected for antibody tests to determine if the animal has had an inapparent infection.

Some rickettsiae can infect mice, and rickettsiae are seen in smears of peritoneal exudate. In Rocky Mountain spotted fever, skin biopsies taken from patients between the fourth and eighth days of illness reveal rickettsiae by immunofluorescence stain.

The most sensitive and specific serologic tests are microimmunofluorescence, microagglutination, and complement fixation. An antibody rise should be demonstrated during the course of the illness.

Treatment

Tetracyclines and chloramphenicol are effective provided treatment is started early. Tetracycline, 2–3 g, or chloramphenicol, 1.5–2 g, is given daily orally and continued for 3–4 days after defervescence. In severely ill patients, the initial doses can be given intravenously.

Sulfonamides enhance the disease and are contraindicated.

The antibiotics do not free the body of rickettsiae, but they do suppress their growth. Recovery depends in part upon the immune mechanisms of the patient.

Epidemiology

A variety of arthropods, especially ticks and mites, harbor *Rickettsia*-like organisms in the cells that line the alimentary tract. Many such organisms are not evidently pathogenic for humans.

The life cycles of different rickettsiae vary:

(1) *Rickettsia prowazekii* has a life cycle limited to humans and to the human louse *(Pediculus corporis* and *Pediculus capitis)*. The louse obtains the organism by biting infected human beings and transmits the agent by fecal excretion on the surface of the skin of another person. Whenever a louse bites, it defecates at the same time. The scratching of the area of the bite allows the rickettsiae excreted in the feces to penetrate the skin. As a result of the infection the louse dies, but the organisms remain viable for some time in the dried feces of the louse. Rickettsiae are not transmitted from one generation of lice to another. Typhus epidemics have been controlled by delousing large proportions of the population with insecticides.

Brill's disease is a recrudescence of an old typhus infection. The rickettsiae can persist for many years in the lymph nodes of an individual without any symptoms being manifest. The rickettsiae isolated from such cases behave like classic *R prowazekii*; this suggests that humans themselves are the reservoir of the rickettsiae of epidemic typhus. Flying squirrels in the USA may provide an extrahuman reservoir, and human cases have occurred after bites by ectoparasites. Epidemic typhus epidemics have been associated with war and the lowering of standards of personal hygiene, which in turn have increased the opportunities for human lice to flourish. If this occurs at the time of recrudescence of an old typhus infection, an epidemic may be set off. Brill's disease occurs in local populations of typhus areas as well as in persons who migrate from such areas to places where the disease does not exist. Serologic characteristics readily distinguish Brill's disease from primary epidemic typhus. Antibodies arise earlier and are IgG rather than the IgM detected after primary infection. They reach a maximum by the tenth day of disease. The Weil-Felix reaction is usually negative. This early IgG antibody response and the mild course of the disease suggest that partial immunity is still present from the primary infection.

(2) *Rickettsia typhi* has its reservoir in the rat, in which the infection is inapparent and long-lasting. Rat fleas carry the rickettsiae from rat to rat and sometimes from rat to humans, who develop endemic typhus. Cat fleas can serve as vectors. In endemic typhus, the flea cannot transmit the rickettsiae transovarially.

(3) *Rickettsia tsutsugamushi* has its true reservoir in the mites that infest rodents. Rickettsiae can persist in rats for over a year after infection. Mites transmit the infection transovarially. Occasionally, infected mites or rat fleas bite humans, and scrub typhus results. The rickettsiae persist in the mite-rat-mite cycle in the scrub or secondary jungle vegetation that has replaced virgin jungle in areas of partial cultivation. Such areas may become infested with rats and trombiculid mites.

(4) *Rickettsia rickettsii* may be found in healthy wood ticks *(Dermacentor andersoni)* and is passed transovarially. Vertebrates such as rodents, deer, and humans are occasionally bitten by infected ticks in the western USA. In order to be infectious, the tick carrying the rickettsiae must be engorged with blood, for this increases the number of rickettsiae in the tick. Thus, there is a delay of 45–90 minutes between the time of the attachment of the tick and its becoming infective. In the eastern USA, Rocky Mountain spotted fever is transmitted by the dog tick *Dermacentor variabilis*. Dogs are hosts to dog ticks but rarely, if ever, serve as a continuing source of tick infection. Most Rocky Mountain spotted fever in the USA now occurs in the eastern and the southeastern regions.

(5) *Rickettsia akari* has its vector in blood-sucking mites of the species *Allodermanyssus sanguineus*. These mites may be found on the mice *(Mus musculus)* trapped in apartment houses in the USA where rickettsialpox has occurred. Transovarial transmission of the rickettsiae occurs in the mite. Thus the mite may act as a true reservoir as well as a vector. *R akari* has also been isolated in Korea.

(6) *Rochalimaea quintana* is the causative agent of trench fever; it is found in lice and in humans, and its life cycle is like that of *R prowazekii*. The disease has been limited to fighting armies. This organism can be grown on blood agar in 10% CO_2.

(7) *Coxiella burnetii* is found in ticks, which transmit the agent to sheep, goats, and cattle. Workers in slaughterhouses and in plants that process wool and cattle hides have contracted the disease as a result of handling infected animal tissues. *C burnetii* is transmitted by the respiratory pathway rather than through the skin. There may be a chronic infection of the udder of the cow. In such cases the rickettsiae are excreted in the milk and occasionally may be transmitted to humans by ingestion or inhalation.

Infected sheep may excrete *C burnetii* in the feces and urine. The placentas of infected cows and sheep contain the rickettsiae, and parturition creates infectious aerosols. The soil may be heavily contaminated from one of the above sources, and the inhalation of infected dust leads to infection of humans and livestock. It has been proposed that endospores formed by *C burnetii* contribute to its persistence and dissemination. *Coxiella* infection is now widespread among sheep and cattle in the USA. *Coxiella* can cause endocarditis in humans in addition to pneumonitis and hepatitis.

Geographic Occurrence

A. Epidemic Typhus: Potentially worldwide, it has disappeared from the USA, Britain, and Scandinavia. It is still present in the Balkans, Asia, Africa, Mexico, and the Andes. In view of its long duration in humans as a latent infection (Brill's disease), it can flourish quickly under proper environmental conditions, as it did in Europe during World War II as a result of the deterioration of community sanitation.

B. Endemic, Murine Typhus: Worldwide, especially in areas of high rat infestation. It may exist in the same areas as—and may be confused with—epidemic typhus or scrub typhus.

C. Scrub Typhus: Far East, especially Burma, India, Ceylon, New Guinea, Japan, and Taiwan. *Trombicula pallida*, the chigger most often found in Korea, maintains the infection among wild rodents of Korea *(Apodemus agrarius),* but only infrequently does it transfer scrub typhus to humans.

D. Spotted Fever Group: These infections occur around the globe, exhibiting as a rule some epidemiologic and immunologic differences in different areas. Transmission by a tick of the Ixodidae family is common to the group. The diseases that are grouped together include Rocky Mountain spotted fever (western and eastern RMSF), Colombian, Brazilian, and Mexican spotted fevers; Mediterranean (boutonneuse), South African tick, and Kenya fevers; North Queensland tick typhus; and North Asian tickborne rickettsiosis.

E. Rickettsialpox: The human disease has been found among inhabitants of apartment houses in the northern USA. However, the infection also occurs in Russia, Africa, and Korea.

F. Q Fever: The disease is recognized around the world and occurs mainly in persons associated with goats, sheep, or dairy cattle. It has attracted attention because of outbreaks in veterinary and medical centers where large numbers of people were exposed to animals shedding *Coxiella*.

Seasonal Occurrence

Epidemic typhus is more common in cool climates, reaching its peak in winter and waning in the spring. This is probably a reflection of crowding, lack of fuel, and low standards of personal hygiene, which favor louse infestation.

Rickettsial infections that must be transmitted to the human host by vector reach their peak incidence at the time the vector is most prevalent—the summer and fall months.

Control

Control is achieved by breaking the infection chain or by immunizing and treating with antibiotics.

A. Prevention of Transmission by Breaking the Chain of Infection:

1. Epidemic typhus–Delousing with insecticide.

2. Murine typhus–Rat-proofing buildings and using rat poisons.

3. Scrub typhus–Clearing from campsites the secondary jungle vegetation in which rats and mites live.

4. Spotted fever–Similar measures for the spotted fevers may be used; clearing of infested land; personal prophylaxis in the form of protective clothing such as high boots, socks worn over trousers; tick repellents; and frequent removal of attached ticks.

5. Rickettsialpox–Elimination of rodents and their parasites from human domiciles.

B. Prevention of Transmission of Q Fever by Adequate Pasteurization of Milk: The presently recommended conditions of "high-temperature, short-time" pasteurization at 71.5 °C (161 °F) for 15 seconds are adequate to destroy viable *Coxiella*.

C. Prevention by Vaccination: Active immunization may be carried out using formalinized antigens prepared from the yolk sacs of infected chick embryos or from cell cultures. Such vaccines have been prepared for epidemic typhus *(R prowazekii)*, Rocky Mountain spotted fever *(R rickettsii)*, and Q fever *(C burnetii)*. However, commercially produced vaccines are not available in the USA in 1982. Cell culture-grown, inactivated suspensions of rickettsiae are under study as vaccines. A live vaccine (strain E) for epidemic typhus is effective and used experimentally but produces a self-limited disease.

D. Chemoprophylaxis: Chloramphenicol has been used as a chemoprophylactic agent against scrub typhus in endemic areas. Oral administration of 3-g doses at weekly intervals controls infection so that no disease occurs even though rickettsiae appear in the blood. The antibiotic must be continued for a month after the initiation of infection to keep the person well. Tetracyclines may be equally effective.

●　●　●

References

Berman SJ, Kundin WD: Scrub typhus in South Vietnam. *Ann Intern Med* 1973;**79**:26.

Bradford WD, Hackett DB: Myocardial involvement in Rocky Mountain spotted fever. *Arch Pathol Lab Med* 1978;**102**:357.

Caughey JE: Pleuropericardial lesion in Q fever. *Br Med J* 1977;**1**:1447.

Donohue JF: Lower respiratory tract involvement in Rocky Mountain spotted fever. *Arch Intern Med* 1980;**140**:223.

Hechemy KE: Laboratory diagnosis of Rocky Mountain spotted fever. *N Engl J Med* 1979;**300**:859.

Hinrichs DJ, Jerrells TR: In vitro evaluation of immunity to *Coxiella burnetii. J Immunol* 1976;**117**:996.

Kimbrough RC et al: Q fever endocarditis in the United States. *Ann Intern Med* 1979;**91**:400.

Ormsbee R et al: Antigenic relationships between typhus and spotted fever groups of rickettsiae. *Am J Epidemiol* 1978;**108**:53.

Philip RN et al: Comparison of serologic methods for diagnosis of Rocky Mountain spotted fever. *Am J Epidemiol* 1977;**105**:56.

Scher MS et al: Initial clinical evaluation of a new Rocky Mountain spotted fever vaccine of tissue culture origin. *J Infect Dis* 1978;**138**:217.

Sheehy TW et al: Scrub typhus: Comparison of chloramphenicol and tetracycline. *Arch Intern Med* 1973;**132**:77.

Tsianabos T et al: Origin and structure of the group-specific complement-fixing antigen of *Rickettsia rickettsii. Appl Microbiol* 1974;**28**:481.

Wells GM et al: Rocky Mountain spotted fever caused by blood transfusion. *JAMA* 1978;**239**:2763.

Wisseman CL, Waddell AD: In vitro studies of rickettsia-host cell interactions. *Infect Immun* 1975;**11**:1391.

Woodward TE: A historical account of the rickettsial diseases. *J Infect Dis* 1973;**127**:583.

22 | Chlamydiae

Chlamydiae are a large group of obligate intracellular parasites closely related to gram-negative bacteria. They are divided into 2 species, *Chlamydia psittaci* and *Chlamydia trachomatis*, on the basis of antigenic composition, intracellular inclusions, sulfonamide susceptibility, and disease production (see below). All chlamydiae exhibit similar morphologic features, share a common group antigen, and multiply in the cytoplasm of their host cells by a distinctive developmental cycle.

Because of their obligate intracellular parasitism, chlamydiae were once considered viruses. Chlamydiae differ from viruses in the following important characteristics:

(1) Like bacteria, they possess both RNA and DNA.

(2) They multiply by binary fission; viruses never do.

(3) They possess bacterial type cell walls with peptidoglycans probably containing muramic acid.

(4) They possess ribosomes; viruses never do.

(5) They have a variety of metabolically active enzymes, eg, they can liberate CO_2 from glucose. Some can synthesize folates.

(6) Their growth can be inhibited by many antimicrobial drugs.

Chlamydiae can be viewed as gram-negative bacteria that lack some important mechanisms for the production of metabolic energy. This defect restricts them to an intracellular existence, where the host cell furnishes energy-rich intermediates.

Developmental Cycle

All chlamydiae share a general sequence of events in their reproduction. The infectious particle is a small cell ("elementary body") about 0.3 μm in diameter with an electron-dense nucleoid. It is taken into the host cell by phagocytosis. A vacuole, derived from the host cell surface membranes, forms around the small particle. This small particle is reorganized into a large one ("initial body") measuring about 0.5–1 μm and devoid of an electron-dense nucleoid. Within the membrane-bound vacuole, the large particle grows in size and divides repeatedly by binary fission. Eventually the entire vacuole becomes filled with small particles derived by binary fission from large bodies to form an "inclusion" in the host cell cytoplasm. The newly formed small particles may be liberated from the host cell to infect new cells. The developmental cycle takes 24–48 hours.

Structure & Chemical Composition

Examination of highly purified suspensions of chlamydiae, washed free of host cell materials, indicates the following: the outer cell wall resembles the cell wall of gram-negative bacteria. It has a relatively high lipid content, and the peptidoglycan perhaps contains muramic acid. Cell wall formation is inhibited by penicillins and cycloserine, substances that inhibit peptidoglycan synthesis in bacteria. Both DNA and RNA are present in both small and large particles. In small particles, most DNA is concentrated in the electron-dense central nucleoid. In large particles, the DNA is distributed irregularly throughout the cytoplasm. Most RNA probably exists in ribosomes, in the cytoplasm. The large particles contain about 4 times as much RNA as DNA, whereas the small, infective particles contain about equal amounts of RNA and DNA.

The circular genome of chlamydiae (MW 7×10^8) is similar to bacterial chromosomes. Chlamydiae contain large amounts of **lipids,** especially phospholipids, which are well characterized.

A toxic principle is intimately associated with infectious chlamydiae. It kills mice after the intravenous administration of more than 10^8 particles. Toxicity is destroyed by heat but not by ultraviolet light.

Staining Properties

Chlamydiae have distinctive staining properties (similar to those of rickettsiae) that differ somewhat at different stages of development. Single mature particles (elementary bodies) stain purple with Giemsa's stain and red with Macchiavello's stain, in contrast to the blue of host cell cytoplasm. The larger, noninfective bodies (initial bodies) stain blue with Giemsa's stain. The Gram reaction of chlamydiae is negative or variable, and Gram's stain is not useful in the identification of the agents.

Fully formed, mature intracellular inclusions are compact masses near the nucleus which are dark purple when stained with Giemsa's stain because of the densely packed mature particles. If stained with dilute Lugol's iodine solution, the inclusions formed by some chlamydiae (mouse pneumonitis, lymphogranuloma venereum [LGV], trachoma, inclusion

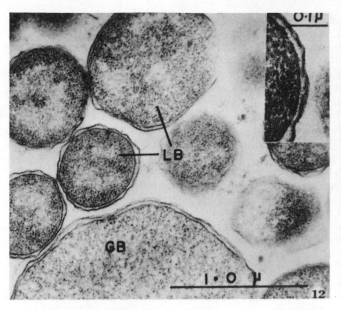 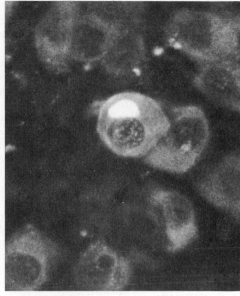

Figure 22–1. Chlamydiae. *Left:* Chlamydiae in various stages of intracellular development. LB = "elementary body" particles with cell walls. GB = "reticulate large body," "initial body." *Right:* Fluorescent inclusion body of *C trachomatis* in epithelial cell (conjunctival scraping) stained with specific fluorescein-labeled antiserum.

conjunctivitis) appear brown because of the glycogen-like matrix that surrounds the particles.

Antigens

Chlamydiae possess 2 types of antigens. Both are probably located in the cell wall. **Group antigens** are shared by all chlamydiae. These are heat-stable lipoprotein-carbohydrate complexes, with 2-keto-3-deoxy-octonic acid as an immunodominant component. Antibody to these group antigens can be detected by complement fixation and immunofluorescence. **Specific antigens** (species-specific or immunotype-specific) remain attached to cell walls after group antigens have been largely removed by treatment with fluorocarbon or deoxycholate. Some specific antigens are membrane proteins that have been purified by immunoadsorption. Specific antigens can best be detected by immunofluorescence. Specific antigens are shared by only a limited number of chlamydiae, but a given organism may contain several specific antigens. Fifteen **immunotypes** of *C trachomatis* have been identified (A, B, Ba, C–K, L1–L3), and the last 3 are LGV immunotypes. The toxic effects of chlamydiae are associated with antigens. Specific neutralization of these toxic effects by antiserum permits similar antigenic grouping of organisms.

A very unstable hemagglutinin capable of clumping some chicken and mouse erythrocytes is present in chlamydiae. This hemagglutination is blocked by group antibody.

Growth & Metabolism

Chlamydiae require an intracellular habitat, presumably because they lack some essential feature of energy metabolism. All types of chlamydiae proliferate in embryonated eggs, particularly in the yolk sac. Some also grow in cell cultures and in various animal tissues. Cells have attachment sites for chlamydiae. Removal of these sites prevents easy uptake of chlamydiae.

Chlamydiae appear to have an endogenous metabolism similar to that of some bacteria but participate only to a limited extent in potentially energy-yielding processes. They can liberate CO_2 from glucose, pyruvate, and glutamate; they also contain dehydrogenases. Nevertheless, they require energy rich intermediates from the host cell to carry out their biosynthetic activities.

Reactions to Physical & Chemical Agents

Chlamydiae are rapidly inactivated by heat. They lose infectivity completely after 10 minutes at 60 °C. They maintain infectivity for years at –50 °C to –70 °C. During the process of freeze-drying, much of the infectivity is lost. Some air-dried chlamydiae may remain infective for long periods.

Chlamydiae are rapidly inactivated by ether (in 30 minutes) or by phenol (0.5% for 24 hours).

The replication of chlamydiae can be inhibited by many antibacterial drugs. Cell wall inhibitors such as penicillins and cycloserine result in the production of morphologically defective forms but are not effective in clinical diseases. Inhibitors of protein synthesis (tetracyclines, erythromycins) are effective in laboratory models and at times in clinical infections. Some chlamydiae synthesize folates and are susceptible to inhibition by sulfonamides. Aminoglycosides have little inhibitory activity for chlamydiae.

Characteristics of Host-Parasite Relationship

The outstanding biologic feature of infection by chlamydiae is the balance that is often reached between host and parasite, resulting in prolonged, often lifetime persistence. Subclinical infection is the rule—and overt disease the exception—in the natural hosts of these agents. Spread from one species (eg, birds) to another (eg, humans) more frequently leads to disease. Antibodies to several antigens of chlamydiae are regularly produced by the infected host. These antibodies have little protective effect. Commonly the infectious agent persists in the presence of high antibody titers. Treatment with effective antimicrobial drugs (eg, tetracyclines) for prolonged periods may eliminate the chlamydiae from the infected host. Very early, intensive treatment may suppress antibody formation. Late treatment with antimicrobial drugs in moderate doses may suppress disease but permit persistence of the infecting agent in tissues.

The immunization of susceptible animals with various inactivated or living vaccines tends to induce protection against death from the toxic effect of living challenge organisms. However, such immunization in animals or humans has been singularly unsuccessful in protecting against infection. At best, immunization or prior infection has induced some resistance and resulted in milder disease after challenge or reinfection.

Classification

Historically, chlamydiae were arranged according to their pathogenic potential and their host range. Antigenic differences were defined by antigen-antibody reactions studied by immunofluorescence, toxin neutralization, and other methods. The 2 presently accepted species and their characteristics are as follows:

(1) *C psittaci:* This species produces diffuse intracytoplasmic inclusions that lack glycogen; it is usually resistant to sulfonamides. It includes agents of psittacosis in humans, ornithosis in birds, meningopneumonitis, feline pneumonitis, and many other animal pathogens.

(2) *C trachomatis:* This species produces compact intracytoplasmic inclusions that contain glycogen; it is usually inhibited by sulfonamides. It includes agents of mouse pneumonitis and several human disorders such as trachoma, inclusion conjunctivitis, nongonococcal urethritis, salpingitis, cervicitis, pneumonitis of infants, and lymphogranuloma venereum.

In nucleic acid hybridization experiments, the 2 species appear not to be closely related.

PSITTACOSIS
(Ornithosis)

Psittacosis is a disease of birds that may be transferred to humans. In humans, the agent, *C psittaci*, produces a spectrum of clinical manifestations ranging from severe pneumonia and sepsis with a high mortality rate to a mild inapparent infection.

Properties of the Agent

A. Size and Staining Properties: Similar to other members of the group (see above).

B. Animal Susceptibility and Growth of Agent: Psittacosis agent can be propagated in embryonated eggs, in mice and other animals, and in some cell cultures. In all these host systems, growth can be inhibited by tetracyclines and, to a limited extent, by penicillins. In intact animals and in humans, tetracyclines can suppress illness but may not be able to eliminate the infectious agent or end the carrier state.

C. Antigenic Properties: The heat-stable group-reactive complement-fixing antigen resists proteolytic enzymes but is destroyed by potassium periodate. It is probably a lipopolysaccharide.

Infected tissue contains a toxic principle, intimately associated with the agent, that rapidly kills mice upon intravenous or intraperitoneal infection. This toxic principle is active only in particles that are infective.

Specific serotypes characteristic for certain mammalian and avian species may be demonstrated by cross-neutralization tests of toxic effect. Neutralization of infectivity of the agent by specific antibody or cross-protection of immunized animals can also be used for serotyping and parallels immunofluorescence.

D. Cell Wall Antigens: Walls of the infecting agent have been prepared by treatment with deoxycholate followed by trypsin. The deoxycholate extracts contained group-reactive complement-fixing antigens, while the cell-walls retained the species-specific antigens. The cell wall antigens were also associated with toxin neutralization and infectivity neutralization.

Pathogenesis & Pathology

The agent enters through the respiratory tract, is found in the blood during the first 2 weeks of the disease, and may be found in the sputum at the time the lung is involved.

Psittacosis causes a patchy inflammation of the lungs in which consolidated areas are sharply demarcated. The exudate is predominantly mononuclear. Only minor changes occur in the large bronchioles and bronchi. The lesions are similar to those found in pneumonitis caused by some viruses and mycoplasmas. Liver, spleen, heart, and kidney are often enlarged and congested.

Clinical Findings

A sudden onset of illness taking the form of influenza or nonbacterial pneumonia in a person exposed to birds is suggestive of psittacosis. The incubation period averages 10 days. The onset is usually sudden, with malaise, fever, anorexia, sore throat, photophobia, and severe headache. The disease may progress no further and the patient may improve in a few days. In severe cases the signs and symptoms of bronchial pneumonia appear at the end of the first week of the disease. The clinical picture often resembles that of influenza, nonbacterial pneumonia, or typhoid fever. The fatality rate may be as high as 20% in untreated cases, especially in the elderly.

Laboratory Diagnosis

A. Recovery of Agent: Laboratory diagnosis is dependent upon the recovery of psittacosis agent from blood and sputum or, in fatal cases, from lung tissues. Specimens are inoculated intra-abdominally into mice, into the yolk sacs of embryonated eggs, and into cell cultures. Infection in the test systems is confirmed by the serial transmission of the infectious agent, its microscopic demonstration, and serologic identification of the recovered agent.

B. Serology: A variety of antibodies may develop in the course of infection. In humans, complement fixation with group antigen is the most widely used diagnostic test. Acute and later phase sera should be run in the same test in order to establish an antibody rise. In birds, the indirect CF test may provide additional diagnostic information. Although antibodies usually develop within 10 days, the use of antibiotics may delay their development for 20–40 days or suppress it altogether.

Sera of patients with other chlamydial infections may fix complement in high titer with psittacosis antigen. In patients with psittacosis, the high titer persists for months and, in carriers, even for years. Infection of live birds is suggested by a positive CF test and by the presence of an enlarged spleen or liver. This can be confirmed by demonstration of particles in smears or sections of organs and by passage of the agent in mice and eggs.

Immunity

Immunity in animals and humans is incomplete. A carrier state in humans can persist for 10 years after recovery. During this period the agent may continue to be excreted in the sputum.

Skin tests with group-reactive antigen are positive soon after infection with any member of the group. Specific dermal reactions may be obtained by the use of some skin-testing antigens prepared by extracting suspensions of agent with dilute hydrochloric acid or with detergent.

Live or inactivated vaccines induce only partial resistance in animals.

Treatment

Tetracyclines are the drugs of choice. Psittacosis agents are not sensitive to aminoglycosides, and most strains are not susceptible to sulfonamides. Although antibiotic treatment may control the clinical evidence of disease, it may not free the patient from the agent, ie, the patient may become a carrier. Intensive antibiotic treatment may also delay the normal course of antibody development. Strains may become drug-resistant.

With the introduction of antibiotic therapy, the fatality rate has dropped from 20% to 2%. Death occurs most frequently in patients 40–60 years of age.

Epidemiology

The term psittacosis is applied to the human disease acquired from contact with birds and also the infection of psittacine birds (parrots, parakeets, cockatoos, etc). The term ornithosis is applied to infection with similar agents in all types of domestic birds (pigeons, chickens, ducks, geese, turkeys, etc) and free-living birds (gulls, egrets, petrels, etc). Outbreaks of human disease can occur whenever there is close and continued contact between humans and infected birds that excrete or shed large amounts of infectious agent. Birds often acquire infection as fledglings in the nest; may develop diarrheal illness or no illness; and often carry the infectious agent for their normal life span. When subjected to stress (eg, malnutrition, shipping), birds may become sick and die. The agent is present in tissues (eg, spleen) and is often excreted in feces by healthy birds. The inhalation of infected dried bird feces is a common method of human infection. Another source of infection is the handling of infected tissues (eg, in poultry rendering plants) and inhalation of an infected aerosol.

Birds kept as pets have been an important source of human infection. Foremost among these were the many psittacine birds imported from South America, Australia, and the Far East and kept in aviaries in the USA. Latent infections often flared up in these birds during transport and crowding, and sick birds excreted exceedingly large quantities of infectious agent. Control of bird shipment, quarantine, testing of imported birds for psittacosis infection, and prophylactic tetracyclines in bird feed help to control this source. Pigeons kept for racing or as pets or raised for squab meat have been important sources of infection. Pigeons populating civic buildings and thoroughfares in many cities are not infrequently infected but shed relatively small quantities of agent.

Among the personnel of poultry farms involved in the dressing, packing, and shipping of ducks, geese, turkeys, and chickens, subclinical or clinical infection is relatively frequent. Outbreaks of disease among birds have at times resulted in heavy economic losses and have been followed by outbreaks in humans.

Persons who develop psittacosis may become infectious for other persons if the evolving pneumonia results in expectoration of large quantities of infectious sputum. This has been an occupational risk to hospital personnel.

Control

Shipments of psittacine birds should be held in quarantine to ensure that there are no obviously sick birds in the lot. A proportion of each shipment should be tested for antibodies and examined for agent. An intradermal test has been recommended for detecting ornithosis in turkey flocks. The incorporation of tetracyclines into bird feed has been used to reduce the number of carriers. The source of human infection should be traced, if possible, and infected birds should be killed.

OCULAR, GENITAL, & RESPIRATORY INFECTIONS DUE TO *CHLAMYDIA TRACHOMATIS*

TRACHOMA

Trachoma is an ancient eye disease, well described in the Ebers Papyrus, which was written in Egypt 3800 years ago. It is a chronic keratoconjunctivitis that begins with acute inflammatory changes in the conjunctiva and cornea and progresses to scarring and blindness.

Properties of *C trachomatis*

A. Size and Staining Properties: See pp 266 and 268.

B. Animal Susceptibility and Growth: Humans are the natural host for *C trachomatis*. Monkeys and chimpanzees can be infected in the eye and genital tract. All chlamydiae multiply in the yolk sacs of embryonated hens' eggs and cause death of the embryo when the number of particles becomes sufficiently high. *C trachomatis* also replicates in various cell lines, particularly when cells are treated with cycloheximide, cytochalasin B, or idoxuridine. *C trachomatis* of different immunotypes replicates differently. Isolates from trachoma do not grow as well as those from LGV or genital infections. Intracytoplasmic replication results in a developmental cycle (see p 266) that leads to formation of compact inclusions with a glycogen matrix in which particles are embedded.

A toxic factor is associated with *C trachomatis* provided the particles are viable. Neutralization of this toxic factor by immunotype-specific antisera permits typing of isolates that gives results analogous to those achieved by typing by immunofluorescence (see p 267). The immunotypes specifically associated with endemic trachoma are A, B, Ba, and C.

Clinical Findings

In experimental infections, the incubation period is 3–10 days. In endemic areas, initial infection occurs in early childhood and the onset is insidious. Chlamydial infection is often mixed with bacterial conjunctivitis in endemic areas, and the 2 together produce the clinical picture. The earliest symptoms of trachoma are lacrimation, mucopurulent discharge, conjunctival hyperemia, and follicular hypertrophy. Biomicroscopic examination of the cornea reveals epithelial keratitis, subepithelial infiltrates, and extension of limbal vessels into the cornea (pannus).

As the pannus extends downward across the cornea, there is scarring of conjunctiva, lid deformities (entropion, trichiasis), and added insult caused by eyelashes sweeping across the cornea. With secondary bacterial infection, loss of vision and blindness occur over a period of years. There are, however, no systemic symptoms or signs of infection.

Laboratory Diagnosis

A. Recovery of *C trachomatis*: Typical cytoplasmic inclusions are found in epithelial cells of conjunctival scrapings stained with fluorescent antibody or by Giemsa's method. These occur most frequently in the early stages of the disease and on the upper tarsal conjunctiva.

Inoculation of conjunctival scrapings into embryonated eggs or cycloheximide-treated cell cultures permits growth of *C trachomatis* if the number of viable infectious particles is sufficiently large. Centrifugation of the inoculum into treated cells increases the sensitivity of the method. The diagnosis can sometimes be made in the first passage by looking for inclusions after 2–3 days of incubation by immunofluorescence, iodine staining, or staining by Giemsa's method.

B. Serology: Infected individuals often develop both group-reactive and immunotype-specific antibodies in serum and in eye secretions. Immunofluorescence is the most sensitive method for their detection. Neither ocular nor serum antibodies confer significant resistance to reinfection.

Treatment

In endemic areas, sulfonamides, erythromycins, and tetracyclines have been used to suppress chlamydiae and bacteria that cause eye infections. Periodic topical application of these drugs to the conjunctivas of all members of the community is sometimes supplemented with oral doses; the dosage and frequency of administration vary with the geographic area and the severity of endemic trachoma. Drug-resistant *C trachomatis* has not been definitely identified except in laboratory experiments. Even a single monthly dose of 300 mg of doxycycline can result in significant clinical improvement, reducing the danger of blindness. Topical application of corticosteroids is not indicated and may reactivate latent trachoma. Chlamydiae can persist during and after drug treatment, and recurrence of activity is common.

Epidemiology & Control

It is believed that over 400 million people throughout the world are infected with trachoma and that 20 million are blinded by it. The disease is most prevalent in Africa, Asia, and the Mediterranean Basin, where hygienic conditions are poor and water is scarce. In such hyperendemic areas, childhood infection may be universal, and severe, blinding disease (resulting from frequent bacterial superinfections) is common. In the USA, trachoma occurs sporadically in some areas, and endemic foci persist on Indian reservations.

Control of trachoma depends mainly upon improvement of hygienic standards and drug treatment.

When socioeconomic levels rise in an area, trachoma becomes milder and eventually may disappear. Experimental trachoma vaccines have not given encouraging results. Surgical correction of lid deformities may be necessary in advanced cases.

GENITAL CHLAMYDIAL INFECTIONS & INCLUSION CONJUNCTIVITIS

C trachomatis, immunotypes D–K, is a common cause of sexually transmitted diseases that may also produce infection of the eye (inclusion conjunctivitis). In sexually active adults, particularly in the USA and western Europe—and especially in higher socioeconomic groups—*C trachomatis* is a prominent cause of nongonococcal urethritis and, rarely, epididymitis in males. In females, *C trachomatis* causes urethritis, cervicitis, salpingitis, and pelvic inflammatory disease. Any of these anatomic sites of infection may give rise to symptoms and signs, or the infection may remain asymptomatic but communicable to sex partners. Up to 50% of nongonococcal or postgonococcal urethritis or the urethral syndrome is attributed to chlamydiae and produces dysuria, nonpurulent discharge, and frequency of urination.

This enormous reservoir of infectious chlamydiae in adults can be manifested by symptomatic genital tract illness in adults or by an ocular infection that closely resembles trachoma. In adults, this inclusion conjunctivitis results from self-inoculation of genital secretions and was formerly thought to be "swimming pool conjunctivitis."

The neonate acquires the infection during passage through an infected birth canal. Inclusion conjunctivitis of the newborn begins as a mucopurulent conjunctivitis 7–12 days after delivery. It tends to subside with erythromycin or tetracycline treatment, or spontaneously after weeks or months. Occasionally, inclusion conjunctivitis persists as a chronic chlamydial infection with a clinical picture indistinguishable from subacute or chronic childhood trachoma in nonendemic areas and usually not associated with bacterial conjunctivitis.

Laboratory Diagnosis

A. Recovery of *C trachomatis:* Scrapings of epithelial cells from urethra, cervix, vagina, or conjunctiva and biopsy specimens from salpinx or epididymis can be inoculated into chemically treated cell cultures for growth of *C trachomatis* (see above). Isolates can be typed by microimmunofluorescence with specific sera. In neonatal—and sometimes adult—inclusion conjunctivitis, the cytoplasmic inclusions in epithelial cells are so dense that they are readily detected in conjunctival exudate and scrapings examined by immunofluorescence or stained by Giemsa's method.

B. Serologic Tests: Because of the relatively great antigenic mass of chlamydiae in genital tract infections, serum antibodies occur much more commonly than in trachoma and are of higher titer. A titer rise occurs during and after acute chlamydial infection.

In genital secretions (eg, cervical), antibody can be detected during active infection and is directed against the infecting immunotype.

Treatment

It is essential that chlamydial infections be treated simultaneously in both sex partners and in offspring to prevent reinfection.

Tetracyclines (eg, doxycycline, 100 mg/d by mouth for 10–20 days) are commonly used in nongonococcal urethritis and in nonpregnant infected females. Erythromycin, 250 mg 4–6 times daily for 2 weeks, is given to pregnant women. Topical tetracycline or erythromycin is used for inclusion conjunctivitis, sometimes in combination with a systemic drug.

Epidemiology & Control

Genital chlamydial infection and inclusion conjunctivitis are sexually transmitted diseases that are spread by indiscriminate contact with multiple sex partners. Neonatal inclusion conjunctivitis originates in the mother's infected genital tract. Prevention of neonatal eye disease depends upon diagnosis and treatment of the pregnant woman and her sex partner. As in all sexually transmitted diseases, the presence of multiple etiologic agents (gonococci, treponemes, *Trichomonas,* herpes, mycoplasmas, etc) must be considered. Instillation of 1% silver nitrate into the newborn's eyes does not prevent development of chlamydial conjunctivitis. The ultimate control of this—and all—sexually transmitted disease depends on reduction in promiscuity, use of condoms, and early diagnosis and treatment of the infected reservoir.

RESPIRATORY TRACT INVOLVEMENT WITH *C TRACHOMATIS*

Adults with inclusion conjunctivitis often manifest upper respiratory tract symptoms (eg, otalgia, otitis, nasal obstruction, pharyngitis), presumably resulting from drainage of infectious chlamydiae through the nasolacrimal duct. Pneumonitis is rare in adults.

Neonates infected by the mother may develop respiratory tract involvement 2–12 weeks after birth, culminating in pneumonia. There is striking tachypnea, paroxysmal cough, absence of fever, and eosinophilia. Consolidation of lungs and hyperinflation can be seen by x-ray. Diagnosis can be established by isolation of *C trachomatis* from respiratory secretions and can be suspected if pneumonitis develops in a neonate who has inclusion conjunctivitis. Systemic erythromycin (40 mg/kg/d) is effective treatment in severe cases.

venereal dis. char by transient genital ulcers + inguinal adenopathy in ♂;

LYMPHOGRANULOMA VENEREUM (LGV)

nodular inflamm. lesion

LGV is a sexually transmitted disease, characterized by suppurative inguinal adenitis, that is common in tropical and temperate zones. The agent is *C trachomatis* of immunotypes L1–L3.

Properties of the Agent

A. Size and Staining Properties: Similar to other chlamydiae.

B. Animal Susceptibility and Growth of Agent: The agent can be transmitted to monkeys and mice and can be propagated in tissue cultures or in chick embryos. Most strains grow in cell cultures; their infectivity for cells is not enhanced by pretreatment with DEAE-dextran.

C. Antigenic Properties: The particles contain complement-fixing heat-stable chlamydial group antigens that are shared with all other chlamydiae. They also contain one of 3 specific antigens (L1–L3), which can be defined by immunofluorescence. Infective particles contain a toxic principle.

Clinical Findings

Several days to several weeks after exposure, a small, evanescent papule or vesicle develops on any part of the external genitalia, anus, rectum, or elsewhere. The lesion may ulcerate, but usually—especially in women—it remains unnoticed and heals in a few days. Soon thereafter, the regional lymph nodes enlarge and tend to become matted and often painful. In males, inguinal nodes are most commonly involved both above and below Poupart's ligament, and the overlying skin often turns purplish as the nodes suppurate and eventually discharge pus through multiple sinus tracts. In females and in homosexual males, the perirectal nodes are prominently involved, with proctitis and a bloody mucopurulent anal discharge. Lymphadenitis may be most marked in the cervical chains.

During the stage of active lymphadenitis, there are often marked systemic symptoms including fever, headaches, meningismus, conjunctivitis, skin rashes, nausea and vomiting, and arthralgias. Meningitis, arthritis, and pericarditis occur rarely. Unless effective antimicrobial drug treatment is given at that stage, the chronic inflammatory process progresses to fibrosis, lymphatic obstruction, and rectal strictures. The lymphatic obstruction may lead to elephantiasis of the penis, scrotum, or vulva. The chronic proctitis of women or homosexual males may lead to progressive rectal strictures, rectosigmoid obstruction, and fistula formation.

Laboratory Diagnosis

A. Smears: Pus, buboes, or biopsy material may be stained, but particles are rarely recognized.

B. Isolation of Agent: Suspected material is inoculated into the yolk sacs of embryonated eggs, into cell cultures, or into the brains of mice. Streptomycin (but not penicillin or ether) may be incorporated into the inoculum to lessen bacterial contamination. The agent is identified by morphology and serologic tests.

C. Serologic Tests: The CF reaction is the simplest serologic test for the presence of antibodies. Antigen is prepared from infected yolk sac. The test becomes positive 2–4 weeks after onset of illness, at which time skin hypersensitivity can sometimes also be demonstrated. In a clinically compatible case, a rising antibody level or a single titer of more than 1:64 is good evidence of active infection. If treatment has eradicated the LGV infection, the complement fixation titer falls. Serologic diagnosis of LGV can employ immunofluorescence, but the antibody is broadly reactive with many chlamydial antigens. A more specific antibody can be demonstrated by counterimmunoelectrophoresis with a chlamydial protein extracted from LGV.

D. Frei Test: Intradermal injection of heat-inactivated egg-grown LGV (0.1 mL) is compared to control material prepared from noninfected yolk sac. The skin test is read in 48–72 hours. An inflammatory nodule more than 6 mm in diameter at the test (but not the control) site constitutes a positive reaction. This can occur with different chlamydiae that share the group-reactive lipopolysaccharide. Thus, the Frei test lacks diagnostic specificity. The preparations of antigen available commercially have given unreliable results and have not been licensed in the USA since 1979.

Immunity

Untreated infections tend to be chronic, with persistence of the agent for many years. Little is known about active immunity. The coexistence of latent infection, antibodies, and cell-mediated reactions is typical of many chlamydial infections.

Treatment

The sulfonamides and tetracyclines have been used with good results, especially in the early stages. In some drug-treated persons there is a marked decline in complement-fixing antibodies, which may indicate that the infective agent has been eliminated from the body. Late stages require surgery.

Epidemiology

The disease is most often spread by sexual contact, but not exclusively so. The portal of entry may sometimes be the eye (conjunctivitis with an oculoglandular syndrome). The genital tracts and rectums of chronically infected (but at times asymptomatic) persons serve as reservoirs of infection.

Although the highest incidence of LGV has been reported from subtropical and tropical areas, the infection occurs all over the world.

Control

The measures used for the control of other sexually transmitted diseases apply also to the control of LGV. Case-finding and early treatment and control of infected persons are essential.

OTHER AGENTS OF THE GROUP

Many mammals are subject to chlamydial infections, mainly with *C psittaci*. Common animal disease entities are pneumonitis, arthritis, enteritis, and abortion, but infection is often latent. Some of these agents may also be transmitted to humans and cause disease in them.

Chlamydiae have been isolated from Reiter's disease in humans, both from the involved joints and from the urethra. The causative role of these agents remains uncertain.

In nonbacterial regional lymphadenitis (cat-scratch fever), a skin test with heat-inactivated pus gives a delayed positive reaction. Chlamydiae have been proposed as a possible cause but without proof. The usefulness of tetracyclines in this syndrome is dubious.

● ● ●

References

Abrams AJ: Lymphogranuloma venereum. *JAMA* 1968;**205:**59.

Beem MO et al: Treatment of chlamydial pneumonia of infancy. *Pediatrics* 1979;**63:**198.

Bowie WR et al: Etiology of nongonococcal urethritis: Evidence for *Chlamydia trachomatis* and *Ureaplasma urealyticum. J Clin Invest* 1977;**59:**735.

Bowie WR et al: Tetracycline in nongonococcal urethritis. *Br J Vener Dis* 1980;**58:**332.

Caldwell HD, Kuo CC: Purification of a *Chlamydia trachomatis* antigen by immunoadsorption with monospecific antibody. *J Immunol* 1977;**118:**437.

Dan M et al: A case of lymphogranuloma venereum of 20 years' duration: Isolation of *C trachomatis* from perianal lesions. *Br J Vener Dis* 1980;**58:**344.

Jawetz E: Chemotherapy of chlamydial infections. *Adv Pharmacol Chemother* 1969;**7:**253.

Mardh PA et al: *Chlamydia trachomatis* infection in patients with acute salpingitis. *N Engl J Med* 1977;**296:**1377.

Mordhorst CH et al: Childhood trachoma in a nonendemic area. *JAMA* 1978;**239:**1765.

Oriel JD, Ridgeway GL: Comparison of erythromycin and tetracycline in the treatment of cervical infection by *Chlamydia trachomatis. J Infection* 1980;**2:**259.

Paavonen J et al: Treatment of nongonococcal urethritis with trimethoprim-sulphadiazine. *Br J Vener Dis* 1980;**56:**101.

Schachter J: Chlamydial infections. (3 parts.) *N Engl J Med* 1978;**298:**428, 490, 540.

Schachter J, Caldwell HD: Chlamydiae. *Annu Rev Microbiol* 1980;**34:**285.

Schachter J et al: Infection with *Chlamydia trachomatis:* Involvement of multiple anatomic sites in neonates. *J Infect Dis* 1979;**139:**232.

Schaffner W et al: The clinical spectrum of endemic psittacosis. *Arch Intern Med* 1967;**119:**433.

Thorsteinsson SB et al: Lymphogranuloma venereum: A cause of cervical lymphadenopathy. *JAMA* 1976;**235:**1882.

23 | Miscellaneous Pathogenic Microorganisms

MYCOPLASMAS (PPLO) & WALL–DEFECTIVE MICROBIAL VARIANTS

Mycoplasmas (previously called pleuropneumonialike organisms or PPLO) are a group of organisms with the following characteristics: (1) The smallest reproductive units have a size of 125–250 nm. (2) They are highly pleomorphic because they lack a rigid cell wall and instead are bounded by a triple-layered "unit membrane." (3) They are completely resistant to penicillin but inhibited by tetracycline or erythromycin. (4) They can reproduce in cell-free media; on agar the center of the whole colony is characteristically embedded beneath the surface ("fried egg" appearance). (5) Growth is inhibited by specific antibody. (6) Mycoplasmas do not revert to, or originate from, bacterial parental forms. (7) Mycoplasmas have an affinity for cell membranes.

L phase variants are wall-defective microbial forms (WDMF) that can replicate serially as nonrigid cells and produce colonies on solid media. Some L phase variants are stable; others are unstable and revert to bacterial parent forms. Wall-defective microbial forms are not genetically related to mycoplasmas. WDMF can result from spontaneous mutation or from the effects of chemicals. Treatment of eubacteria with cell wall–inhibiting drugs or lysozyme can produce WDMF. **Protoplasts** are WDMF derived from gram-positive organisms; they are osmotically fragile, with external surfaces free of cell wall constituents. **Spheroplasts** are WDMF derived from gram-negative bacteria; they retain some outer membrane material (see p 20).

Morphology & Identification

A. Typical Organisms: Mycoplasmas cannot be studied by the usual bacteriologic methods because of the small size of their colonies, the plasticity and delicacy of their individual cells (due to the lack of a rigid cell wall), and their poor staining with aniline dyes. The morphology appears different according to the method of examination (eg, darkfield, immunofluorescence, Giemsa-stained films from solid or liquid media, agar fixation).

Growth in fluid media gives rise to many different forms, including rings, bacillary and spiral bodies, filaments, and granules. Growth on solid media consists principally of plastic protoplasmic masses of indefinite shape that are easily distorted. These structures vary greatly in size, ranging from 50 to 300 nm in diameter.

B. Culture: Many strains of mycoplasmas grow in heart infusion peptone broth with 2% agar (pH 7.8) to which about 30% human ascitic fluid or animal serum (horse, rabbit) has been added. Following incubation at 37 °C for 48–96 hours, there may be no turbidity; but Giemsa stains of the centrifuged sediment show the characteristic pleomorphic structures, and subculture on solid media yields minute colonies.

After 2–6 days on special agar medium incubated in a Petri dish that has been sealed to prevent evaporation, isolated colonies measuring 20–500 μm can be detected with a hand lens. These colonies are round, with a granular surface and a dark center nipple typically buried in the agar. They can be subcultured by cutting out a small square of agar containing one or more colonies and streaking this material on a fresh plate or dropping it into liquid medium. The organisms can be stained for microscopic study by placing a similar square on a slide and covering the colony with a coverglass onto which an alcoholic solution of methylene blue and azure has been poured and then evaporated (agar fixation). Such slides can also be stained with specific fluorescent antibody.

C. Growth Characteristics: Mycoplasmas are unique in microbiology because of (1) their extremely small size and (2) their growth on complex but cell-free media.

Mycoplasmas pass through filters with 450-nm pore size and thus are comparable to chlamydiae or large viruses. However, parasitic mycoplasmas grow on cell-free media that contain lipoprotein and sterol. The sterol requirement for growth and membrane synthesis is unique. Mycoplasmas are resistant to thallium acetate in a concentration of 1:10,000, which can be used to inhibit bacteria.

Many mycoplasmas use glucose as a source of energy; ureaplasmas require urea.

Many human mycoplasmas produce peroxides and hemolyze red blood cells. In cell cultures and in vivo, mycoplasmas develop predominantly at cell surfaces. Many established cell line cultures carry mycoplasmas as contaminants.

D. Variation: The extreme pleomorphism of mycoplasmas is one of their principal characteristics. There is no genetic relationship between mycoplasmas and WDMF or their parent bacteria. The characteristics of WDMF are similar to those of mycoplasmas, but, by definition, mycoplasmas do not revert to parent bacteria or originate from them. WDMF continue to synthesize some antigens that are normally located in the cell wall of the parent bacteria (eg, streptococcal L forms produce M protein and capsular polysaccharide; (see Chapter 14). Reversion of L forms to the parent bacteria is enhanced by growth in the presence of 15–30% gelatin or 2.5% agar, whereas reversion is inhibited by inhibitors of protein synthesis.

Antigenic Structure

Many antigenically distinct species of mycoplasmas have been isolated from animals (eg, mice, chickens, turkeys). In humans, at least 11 species can be identified, including *Mycoplasma hominis, Mycoplasma salivarium, Mycoplasma orale, Mycoplasma fermentans, Mycoplasma pneumoniae, Ureaplasma urealyticum,* and others. The last 2 species are of pathogenic significance.

The species are classified by biochemical and serologic features. The complement-fixing antigens of mycoplasmas are glycolipids. Some species have more than one serotype.

Diseases Due to Mycoplasmas

It is doubtful that WDMF cause tissue reactions resulting in disease. They may be important for the persistence of microorganisms in tissues and recurrence of infection after antimicrobial treatment.

The parasitic mycoplasmas appear to be strictly host-specific, being communicable and potentially pathogenic only within a single host species. In animals, mycoplasmas appear to be intracellular parasites with a predilection for mesothelial cells (pleura, peritoneum, synovia of joints). Several extracellular products can be elaborated, eg, hemolysins.

A. Diseases of Animals: Bovine pleuropneumonia is a contagious disease of cattle producing pulmonary consolidation and pleural effusion, with occasional deaths. The disease probably has an airborne spread. Mycoplasmas are found in inflammatory exudates.

Agalactia of sheep and goats in the Mediterranean area is a generalized infection with local lesions in the skin, eyes, joints, udder, and scrotum; it leads to atrophy of lactating glands in females. Mycoplasmas are present in blood early; in milk and exudates later.

In poultry, several economically important respiratory diseases are caused by mycoplasmas. The organisms can be transmitted from hen to egg and chick. Swine, dogs, rats, mice, and other species harbor mycoplasmas that can produce infection involving particularly the pleura, peritoneum, joints, respiratory tract, and eye. In mice, a *Mycoplasma* of spiral shape (*Spiroplasma*) can induce cataracts.

B. Diseases of Humans: Mycoplasmas have been cultivated from human mucous membranes and tissues, particularly from the genital, urinary, and respiratory tracts and from the mouth. Some mycoplasmas are inhabitants of the normal genitourinary tract, particularly in females. In pregnant women, carriage of mycoplasmas on the cervix has been associated with chorioamnionitis and low birth weight of infants. *U urealyticum* (formerly called T strains of mycoplasmas), requiring 10% urea for growth, is found in some cases of urethritis and prostatitis in men who suffer from "nongonococcal urethritis." This organism and *M hominis* have also been associated infrequently with salpingitis and pelvic inflammatory disease. *U urealyticum* may play a causative role and is suppressed by tetracycline or spectinomycin. However, a majority of cases of "nongonococcal urethritis" are caused by *Chlamydia trachomatis* (see p 271).

Infrequently, mycoplasmas have been isolated from brain abscesses and pleural or joint effusions. Mycoplasmas are part of the normal flora of the mouth and can be grown from normal saliva, oral mucous membranes, sputum, or tonsillar tissue.

M hominis and *M salivarium* can be recovered from the oral cavity of many healthy adults, but an association with clinical disease is uncertain. Over half of normal adults have specific antibodies to *M hominis*.

M pneumoniae is one of the causative agents of nonbacterial pneumonia (see p 276). In humans, the effects of infection with *M pneumoniae* range from inapparent infection to mild or severe upper respiratory disease, ear involvement (myringitis), and bronchial pneumonia (see p 276).

C. Diseases of Plants: Aster yellows, corn stunt, and other plant diseases appear to be caused by mycoplasmas. They are transmitted by insects and can be suppressed by tetracyclines.

Diagnostic Laboratory Tests

Specimens consist of throat swab, sputum, inflammatory exudates, and respiratory, urethral, or genital secretions.

A. Microscopic Examination: Direct examination of a specimen is useless. Cultures are examined as described above.

B. Culture: The material is inoculated onto special solid media (see above) and incubated for 3–10 days at 37 °C (often under anaerobic conditions), or into special broth (see above) incubated aerobically. One or 2 transfers of media may be necessary before growth appears that is suitable for microscopic examination by staining or immunofluorescence. Colonies may have a "fried egg" appearance on agar.

C. Serology: Antibodies develop in humans infected with mycoplasmas and can be demonstrated by several methods. CF tests can be performed with glycolipid antigens extracted with chloroform-methanol from cultured mycoplasmas. HI tests can be applied to tanned red cells with adsorbed *Mycoplasma* antigens. Indirect immunofluorescence may be used. The test that measures growth inhibition by antibody is quite specific. When counterimmunoelectrophoresis is used, antigens and antibody migrate toward each other, and precipitin lines appear in 1 hour. With all these serologic techniques, there is adequate specificity for different human *Mycoplasma* species, but a rising antibody titer is required for diagnostic significance because of the high incidence of positive serologic tests in normal individuals.

Treatment

Many strains of mycoplasmas are inhibited by a variety of antimicrobial drugs, but most strains are resistant to penicillins, cephalosporins, and vancomycin. Tetracyclines and erythromycins are effective both in vitro and in vivo and are, at present, the drugs of choice in mycoplasmal pneumonia.

Epidemiology, Prevention, & Control

Isolation of infected livestock will control the highly contagious pleuropneumonia and agalactia in limited areas. No vaccines are available. Mycoplasmal pneumonia behaves like a communicable viral respiratory disease (see next section).

Mycoplasmal Pneumonia & Nonbacterial Pneumonias

Acute nonbacterial pneumonitis may be due to many different infectious agents, including adenoviruses, influenza viruses, respiratory syncytial virus, parainfluenza type 3 virus, chlamydiae, and *Coxiella burnetii,* the etiologic agent of Q fever. However, the single most prominent causative agent, especially for those between ages 5 and 15, is *M pneumoniae*. Mycoplasmal pneumonia appears to be much more common in military recruit populations than in college populations of comparable age.

The first step in *M pneumoniae* infection is the attachment of the tip of the organism to a receptor on the surface of respiratory epithelial cells. The clinical spectrum of *M pneumoniae* ranges from asymptomatic infection to serious pneumonitis, with occasional neurologic and hematologic (ie, hemolytic anemia) involvement and a variety of possible skin lesions. Bullous myringitis occurs in spontaneous cases and in experimentally inoculated volunteers. Typical cases during epidemic periods might show the following:

The incubation period varies from 1 to 3 weeks. The onset is usually insidious, with lassitude, fever, headache, sore throat, and cough. Initially, the cough is nonproductive, but it is occasionally paroxysmal. Later there may be blood-streaked sputum and chest pain. Early in the course, the patient appears only moderately ill, and physical signs of pulmonary consolidation are often negligible compared to the striking consolidation seen on x-rays. Later, when the infiltration is at a peak, the illness may be severe. Resolution of pulmonary infiltration and clinical improvement occur slowly for 1–4 weeks. Although the course of the illness is exceedingly variable, death is very rare and is usually attributable to cardiac failure. Complications are uncommon, but hemolytic anemia may oc-

cur. The most common pathologic findings are interstitial and peribronchial pneumonitis and necrotizing bronchiolitis.

The following laboratory findings apply to *M pneumoniae* pneumonia: The white and differential counts are within normal limits. The causative *Mycoplasma* can be recovered by culture early in the disease from the pharynx and from sputum. Immunofluorescent stains of mononuclear cells from the throat may reveal the agent. There is a rise in specific antibodies to *M pneumoniae* that is demonstrable by complement fixation, immunofluorescence, passive hemagglutination, and growth inhibition.

A variety of nonspecific reactions can be observed. Cold hemagglutinins for group O human erythrocytes appear in about 50% of untreated patients, in rising titer, with the maximum reached in the third or fourth week after onset. A titer of 1:32 or more supports the diagnosis of *M pneumoniae* infection.

Tetracyclines or erythromycins in full systemic doses (2 g daily for adults) can result in clinical improvement but do not eradicate the mycoplasmas.

M pneumoniae infections are endemic all over the world. In populations of children and young adults where close contact prevails, and in families, the infection rate may be high (50–90%), but the incidence of pneumonitis is variable (3–30%). For every case of frank pneumonitis, there exist several cases of milder respiratory illness. *M pneumoniae* is apparently transmitted mainly by direct contact involving respiratory secretions. Second attacks are infrequent. The presence of antibodies to *M pneumoniae* has been associated with resistance to infection but may not be responsible for it. Cell-mediated immune reactions occur. The pneumonic process may be in part attributed to an immunologic response rather than only to infection by mycoplasmas. Experimental vaccines have been prepared from agar-grown *M pneumoniae*. Several such killed vaccines have aggravated subsequent disease; a degree of protection has been claimed with the use of other vaccines.

On rare occasions, central nervous system involvement has accompanied or followed mycoplasmal pneumonia.

LEGIONELLA PNEUMOPHILA

Legionella is the bacterium responsible for the highly publicized outbreak of respiratory illness that afflicted persons attending an American Legion convention in Philadelphia in 1976. Other outbreaks have been diagnosed retrospectively as far back as 1965 or earlier, and sporadic symptomatic or asymptomatic infection occurred all over the world as long ago as 1947.

Legionella stains poorly—apparently gramnegatively—and is not biochemically similar to any known human pathogen. Its DNA shows no homology to other bacteria, but several distinct *Legionella* species have been identified. They can be grown on complex media, eg, charcoal–yeast extract agar with cycloheximide and antibiotics. In human infections, the organism has been isolated most often from lung biopsies—rarely from pleural fluid, blood, or sputum. The infection is not communicable from patients to contacts but is acquired from environmental sources: inhalation of aerosols or dust associated with air conditioning systems or soil excavation. Some of the organisms have been isolated from the water in evaporative condensers or from streams into which they drained. *Legionella pneumophila* has at least 4 serotypes, and at least 4 other *Legionella* species have been given names. Some produce beta-lactamases.

Asymptomatic infection may be common, revealed only by a rise in specific antibodies. The clinical illness may appear with abrupt onset of high fever, chills, malaise, nonproductive cough, hypoxia, diarrhea, and prostration or delirium. Chest x-rays reveal patchy—often multilobar—consolidation. There may be leukocytosis, hyponatremia, hematuria, and abnormal liver function tests. During epidemics, the mortality rate has been 10–20%.

The diagnosis is usually based on a marked increase in serum antibody titer to *Legionella* antigens detected by immunofluorescence or by immunofluorescence staining of the organism in lung tissue obtained by biopsy or at autopsy. Diagnosis is sometimes made by growing the organisms from specimens obtained during life.

In vitro, *Legionella* is susceptible to several antimicrobial drugs, including erythromycin, rifampin, and cefoxitin. Erythromycin, 500 mg intravenously every 6 hours, has been effective in treatment of human infection, even in immunocompromised patients.

STREPTOBACILLUS MONILIFORMIS

Streptobacillus moniliformis is an aerobic, gram-negative, highly pleomorphic organism that forms irregular chains of bacilli interspersed with fusiform enlargements and large round bodies. It grows best at 37 °C in media containing serum protein, egg yolk, or starch but ceases to grow at 22 °C. In most cultures of the organism, L forms can easily be demonstrated. Subculture of pure colonies of L forms in liquid media often yields the streptobacilli again. All strains of streptobacilli appear to be antigenically identical.

S moniliformis is a normal inhabitant of the throats of rats, and humans can be infected by rat bites. The human disease (rat-bite fever) is characterized by septic fever, blotchy and petechial rashes, and polyarthritis. Diagnosis rests on cultures of blood, joint fluid, or pus; on mouse inoculation; and on serum agglutination tests.

This organism can also produce infection after being ingested in milk—a disease called Haverhill fever, which has occurred in epidemics. Penicillin and perhaps other antibiotics are therapeutically effective.

Rat-bite fever of somewhat different clinical appearance (sodoku) is caused by *Spirillum minor* (see Chapter 20).

LISTERIA MONOCYTOGENES

Listeria monocytogenes is a short, gram-positive, nonsporeforming rod. It has a tumbling end-over-end motility at 22 °C but not at 37 °C. Growth on simple media is enhanced by the presence of blood, ascitic fluid, or glucose. *Listeria* is isolated more readily from pathologic specimens if the tissue is kept at 4 °C for some days before inoculation into bacteriologic media. The organism is a facultative anaerobe and is catalase-positive. Most strains produce a zone of hemolysis on blood agar plates. *Listeria* produces acid but not gas in a variety of carbohydrates. There are several antigenic types.

Spontaneous infection occurs in many animals (domestic and wild) and in humans. In smaller animals (rabbits, chickens) there is a septicemia with focal abscesses in liver and heart muscle and marked monocytosis. A glyceride extracted from *Listeria* can likewise induce monocytosis in rabbits. This cellular reaction, however, is not related to human infectious mononucleosis. *Listeria* infection leads to the production of cold agglutinins for human and sheep red cells as well as specific agglutinating antibodies.

In humans and in ruminants (eg, sheep), *Listeria* may cause meningoencephalitis with or without bacteremia. Listeriosis may be superimposed on lymphoma or immunodeficiency. The diagnosis rests on isolation of the organism in cultures of blood and spinal fluid. A second form of human listeriosis, **granulomatosis infantiseptica,** is an intrauterine infection. The early-onset syndrome results in intrauterine sepsis and death prior to or after delivery. It is caused by serotypes Ia and Ib, rarely IVh. The late-onset syndrome involves no obstetric complications but does cause the development of meningitis in the neonate. It is most often due to type IVb and has a significant mortality rate. The route of infection for adults is sometimes the genital tract. It is probable that asymptomatic infection is rather widespread. Many antimicrobial drugs inhibit *Listeria* in vitro. Ampicillin plus an aminoglycoside, or tetracyclines have resulted in clinical cures.

ERYSIPELOTHRIX INSIDIOSA
(Erysipelothrix rhusiopathiae)

This organism resembles *Listeria* but is nonmotile and produces an entirely different disease. In its smooth form it grows as clear, minute colonies in which short, nonsporeforming rods are arranged in short chains; in its rough form, long filaments predominate.

Growth is aided by blood and glucose in the medium. On blood agar only slight hemolysis is produced. Carbohydrates are fermented irregularly, and catalase is not produced. The antigenic pattern is not established.

Infection with *E insidiosa* occurs in worldwide distribution in a variety of animals, especially hogs. Infection in humans follows skin abrasions from contact with fish, shellfish, meat, or poultry. The infection, called erysipeloid, is limited to the skin. There are pain, edema, and purplish erythema with sharp margins that extends peripherally but clears centrally. Relapses and extension of the lesions to distant areas are common, but there is usually no fever. Rare cases of endocarditis have occurred. There is no permanent immunity following an attack. The diagnosis rests on isolation of the organism in cultures from a skin biopsy. The fragment should be incubated in glucose broth for 24 hours, then subcultured on blood agar plates. Typical clinical appearance in a person with occupational exposure is highly suggestive of infection due to this organism.

Penicillin appears to be the antibiotic of choice.

ACINETOBACTER
(Mima, Herellea)

A group of aerobic gram-negative bacteria (often resembling neisseriae on smears because diplococcal forms predominate in body fluids and on solid media) have been recovered from meningitis and sepsis and have been confused with meningococci. However, they are oxidase-negative. They also have been isolated from blood, sputum, skin, pleural fluid, and urine, but their pathogenic role is not clearly established. In patients with burns or with immunologic deficiency, these organisms become opportunistic pathogens and can produce sepsis. *Acinetobacter* can be grouped into at least 10 antigenic types by means of precipitin tests with enzymatic digests of organisms and specific antisera. They are fairly inactive metabolically and often are antibiotic-resistant, responding most commonly to gentamicin, amikacin, or minocycline. Infections are occasionally induced in hospitals, particularly in late summer, but the source of sepsis is variable. *Acinetobacter calcoaceticus* has been encountered in nosocomial pneumonias and originates in the water of room humidifiers or vaporizers.

BARTONELLA BACILLIFORMIS

This is a gram-negative, very pleomorphic, motile organism that causes **Oroya fever,** a serious infectious anemia, and **verruga peruana,** a skin disorder in humans. The infection is limited to the mountainous areas of the American Andes in tropical Peru, Colombia, and Ecuador and is transmitted by the sandfly *Phlebotomus*.

Bartonella grows in semisolid nutrient agar containing 10% rabbit serum and 0.5% hemoglobin. After about 10 days' incubation at 28 °C, some turbidity develops in the medium and rod-shaped and granular organisms can be seen in Giemsa-stained smears.

Human infection is characterized by the rapid development of severe anemia due to blood destruction, enlargement of spleen and liver, and hemorrhage into the lymph nodes. Masses of bartonellae fill the cytoplasm of cells lining the blood vessels, and endothelial swelling may lead to vascular occlusion and thrombosis. The mortality rate of untreated Oroya fever is about 40%. The diagnosis is made by examining stained blood smears and blood cultures in semisolid medium.

Verruga peruana is a vascular granulomatous skin lesion that occurs in successive crops, lasts for about 1 year, and produces little systemic reaction and no fatalities. *Bartonella* can be seen in the granuloma; blood cultures are often positive, but there is no anemia. Verruga often occurs in persons who have recovered from Oroya fever.

Penicillin, streptomycin, and chloramphenicol are dramatically effective in Oroya fever and greatly reduce the fatality rate, particularly if blood transfusions are also given. Control of the disease depends upon the elimination of the sandfly vectors. Insecticides, insect repellents, and elimination of breeding areas are of value. Prevention with antibiotics may be useful.

BACTEROIDES

This is a large group of nonsporeforming, strictly anaerobic, usually gram-negative bacteria that are very pleomorphic. They may appear as slender rods, branching forms, or round bodies. They grow most readily on complex media, eg, brain-heart infusion agar, in an anaerobic atmosphere containing 10% CO_2.

The capsular polysaccharides of *Bacteroides* appear to be important virulence factors. During infection with *Bacteroides fragilis*, patients develop antibodies to these capsular polysaccharides. *B fragilis* produces a superoxide dismutase and can survive in the presence of oxygen for days. *Bacteroides* species *lack* the typical endotoxin-lipopolysaccharide of gram-negative bacteria.

Bacteroides are normal inhabitants of the upper respiratory, intestinal, and female genital tracts. They constitute more than 99% of the normal fecal flora. The most commonly encountered species are *B fragilis* (particularly in the lower intestine) and *Bacteroides melaninogenicus* (particularly in the oropharynx), and each species can be subdivided into several groups. Classification is based on colonial and biochemical features and characteristic appearance in gas chromatography.

In anaerobic infections (lung, brain, peritoneum, pelvis), *Bacteroides* are often associated with other anaerobic organisms, particularly anaerobic streptococci *(Peptostreptococcus)* and fusiform bacteria

(*Fusobacterium* species), as well as gram-negative aerobic enteric organisms.

Bacteroides may be associated with ulcerative lesions of the skin and mucous membranes; they may produce lung and brain abscesses and empyema; they may cause suppuration in surgical infection such as peritonitis following injury to the bowel, and they may participate in pelvic inflammatory disease. In such anaerobic infections, the pus is often foul-smelling. Bacteremia is common, and endocarditis may develop.

B melaninogenicus and most other *Bacteroides* are susceptible to penicillins. *B fragilis*, on the other hand, is relatively resistant to penicillins due to its production of beta-lactamases but is susceptible to clindamycin, metronidazole, and chloramphenicol. Therefore, anaerobic suppuration above the diaphragm (eg, lung abscess) often responds to penicillin, but suppuration below the diaphragm frequently does not.

VEILLONELLAE

Veillonellae are small, anaerobic, gram-negative cocci that are part of the normal mouth flora. They ferment few sugars and probably are not pathogens.

PSEUDOMONAS (ACTINOBACILLUS) MALLEI & PSEUDOMONAS PSEUDOMALLEI

Pseudomonas mallei is a small, nonmotile, gram-negative, aerobic rod that grows readily on most bacteriologic media and does not ferment lactose. It causes glanders, a disease of horses transmissible to humans. Human infection (often fatal) usually begins as an ulcer of the skin or mucous membranes followed by lymphangitis and sepsis. Inhalation of the organisms may lead to primary pneumonitis.

The disease has been controlled by slaughter of infected horses and mules and at present is very rare. In some countries, laboratory infections are the only source of the disease.

The diagnosis is based on rising agglutinin titers, the mallein skin test, or culture of the organism from local lesions of humans or horses. Human cases can be treated effectively with sulfonamides.

Melioidosis, a disease resembling glanders in humans, occurs in Burma, Vietnam, Guam, the Philippines, and perhaps also in the western hemisphere. It is caused by *Pseudomonas pseudomallei*, which resembles other nonpigmented pseudomonads but is antigenically distinct. The organism occurs in soil, water, and plants and may produce infection in rodents and other animals. Human infection probably originates in any of these sources, but the epidemiology of this disorder is still uncertain.

Melioidosis may manifest itself as an acute or chronic lung disease, may produce abscesses and septicemia, and has a high fatality rate if untreated. *P pseudomallei* is susceptible to many antibiotics in vitro. Chloramphenicol (2 g daily) or gentamicin, alone or in combination, may be the treatment of choice. Trimethoprim-sulfamethoxazole may be effective. Drug resistance emerges frequently. Following an apparent recovery, the results of a passive hemagglutination test constitute positive evidence of past infection. Sometimes latent infection is reactivated as a result of immunosuppression.

AEROMONAS HYDROPHILA

Aeromonas hydrophila is a motile gram-negative rod isolated commonly from water, soil, or foods and rarely from the human intestinal tract. It can be found in the blood in persons with seriously impaired host defenses or endocarditis. It can cause freshwater wound infections. It is occasionally isolated from the feces of patients with diarrhea. Most strains are susceptible to tetracyclines, aminoglycosides, and cephalosporins.

● ● ●

References

Barresi JA: *Listeria monocytogenes:* Cause of premature labor and neonatal sepsis. *Am J Obstet Gynecol* 1980;**136**:410.

Cassell GH, Cole BC: Mycoplasmas as agents of human disease. *N Engl J Med* 1981;**304**:80.

Cordes LG et al: Legionnaires' disease outbreak at an Atlanta, Georgia, country club: Evidence for spread from an evaporative condenser. *Am J Epidemiol* 1980;**111**:425.

Davis WA et al: Human *Aeromonas* infections. *Medicine* 1978;**57**:267.

Edwards EA et al: Longitudinal study of *Mycoplasma pneumoniae* infections in Navy recruits by isolation and seroepidemiology. *Am J Epidemiol* 1976;**104**:556.

Eickhoff TC: Epidemiology of Legionnaires' disease. *Ann Intern Med* 1979;**90**:499.

Finegold SM: *Anaerobic Bacteria in Human Disease.* Academic Press, 1977.

Gantz NM et al: Listeriosis in immunosuppressed patients. *Am J Med* 1975;**58**:637.

Glew RH et al: Infections with *Acinetobacter calcoaceticus (Herellea vaginicola). Medicine* 1977;**56**:79.

Goldschmidt BL et al: Rapid detection of *Mycoplasma* antibody. *J Immunol* 1976;**117**:1054.

Gorbach SL, Bartlett JG: Anaerobic infections. *N Engl J Med* 1974;**290**:1177.

Kasper DL et al: Surface antigens as virulence factors in infections with *Bacteroides fragilis. Rev Infect Dis* 1979;**1**:278.

Kirby BD et al: Legionnaires' disease: Report of 65 nosocomially acquired cases and review of the literature. *Medicine* 1980;**59**:188.

Medoff G et al: Listeriosis in humans. *J Infect Dis* 1971;**123**:247.

Morris GK et al: *Legionella gormanii* sp nov. *J Clin Microbiol* 1980;**12**:718.

Nieman RE, Lorber B: Listeriosis in adults: A changing pattern. Report of eight cases and review of the literature, 1968–1978. *Rev Infect Dis* 1980;**2**:207.

Piggott JA, Hochholzer L: Human melioidosis. *Arch Pathol* 1970;**90**:101.

Platt R et al: Infection with *Mycoplasma hominis* in postpartum fever. *Lancet* 1980;**2**:1217.

Razin S: The mycoplasmas. *Microbiol Rev* 1978;**42**:414.

Retailliau HF et al: *Acinetobacter calcoaceticus*: A nosocomial pathogen with an unusual seasonal pattern. *J Infect Dis* 1979;**139**:371.

Sanford JP: Legionnaires' disease: The first thousand days. *N Engl J Med* 1979;**300**:654.

Stanbridge EJ: A reevaluation of the role of mycoplasmas in human disease. *Annu Rev Microbiol* 1976;**30**:169.

Taylor-Robinson D, McCormack WM: The genital mycoplasmas. (2 parts.) *N Engl J Med* 1980;**302**:1003, 1063.

Thompson SE et al: The microbiology and therapy of acute pelvic inflammatory disease in hospitalized patients. *Am J Obstet Gynecol* 1980;**136**:179.

Visintine AM et al: *Listeria monocytogenes* infection in infants and children. *Am J Dis Child* 1977;**131**:393.

Wenzel RP et al: Field trials of an inactivated *Mycoplasma pneumoniae* vaccine. *J Infect Dis* 1976;**134**:571.

Wolff RL et al: *Aeromonas hydrophila* bacteremia in ambulatory immunocompromised hosts. *Am J Med* 1980;**68**:238.

Normal Microbial Flora of the Human Body | 24

The skin and mucous membranes always harbor a variety of microorganisms that can be arranged into 2 groups: (1) The resident flora consists of relatively fixed types of microorganisms regularly found in a given area at a given age; if disturbed, it promptly reestablishes itself. (2) The transient flora consists of nonpathogenic or potentially pathogenic microorganisms that inhabit the skin or mucous membranes for hours, days, or weeks; it is derived from the environment, does not produce disease, and does not establish itself permanently on the surface. Members of the transient flora are generally of little significance so long as the normal resident flora remains intact. However, if the resident flora is disturbed, transient microorganisms may colonize, proliferate, and produce disease.

ROLE OF THE RESIDENT FLORA

The microorganisms that are constantly present on body surfaces are commensals. Their flourishing in a given area depends upon physiologic factors of temperature, moisture, and the presence of certain nutrients and inhibitory substances. Their presence is not essential to life because "germ-free" animals can be reared in the complete absence of a normal microbial flora. Yet the resident flora of certain areas plays a definite role in maintaining health and normal function. Members of the resident flora in the intestinal tract synthesize vitamin K and aid in the absorption of nutrients. On mucous membranes and skin, the resident flora may prevent colonization by pathogens and possible disease through "bacterial interference" (see Chapter 14).

On the other hand, members of the normal flora may themselves produce disease under certain circumstances. These organisms are adapted to the noninvasive mode of life defined by the limitations of the environment. If forcefully removed from the restrictions of that environment and introduced into the bloodstream or tissues, these organisms may become pathogenic. For example, streptococci of the viridans group are the commonest resident organisms of the upper respiratory tract. If large numbers of them are introduced into the bloodstream (eg, following tooth extraction or tonsillectomy), they may settle on abnormal heart valves and produce subacute infective endocarditis. Small numbers occur transiently in the bloodstream with minor trauma (eg, dental scaling or vigorous toothbrushing). *Bacteroides* are the commonest resident bacteria of the large intestine and are quite harmless in that location. If introduced into the free peritoneal cavity or into pelvic tissues along with other bacteria, as a result of trauma, they cause suppuration and bacteremia. Spirochetes, fusobacteria (fusiform bacilli), and *Bacteroides melaninogenicus* are resident in every normal mouth. In the presence of tissue damage through trauma, nutritional deficiency, or infection, they proliferate vastly in the necrotic tissue, producing "fusospirochetal" disease. There are many other examples, but the important point is that microbes of the normal resident flora are harmless and may be beneficial in their normal location in the host and in the absence of coincident abnormalities. They may produce disease if introduced into foreign locations in large numbers and if predisposing factors are present. For these reasons, members of the resident flora found in disease may be called "opportunists."

NORMAL FLORA OF THE SKIN

Because of its constant exposure to and contact with the environment, the skin is particularly apt to contain transient microorganisms. Nevertheless, there is a constant and well-defined resident flora, modified in different anatomic areas by secretions, habitual wearing of clothing, or proximity to mucous membranes (mouth, nose, and perineal areas).

The predominant resident microorganisms of the skin are aerobic and anaerobic diphtheroid bacilli (eg, *Corynebacterium, Propionibacterium*); nonhemolytic aerobic and anaerobic staphylococci (*Staphylococcus epidermidis, Peptococcus*); gram-positive, aerobic, sporeforming bacilli that are ubiquitous in air, water, and soil; alpha-hemolytic streptococci (*Streptococcus viridans*) and enterococci (*Streptococcus faecalis*); and gram-negative coliform bacilli and *Acinetobacter (Herellea)*. Fungi and yeasts are often present in skin folds; acid-fast, nonpathogenic mycobacteria occur in areas rich in sebaceous secretions (genitalia, external ear).

Among the factors that may be important in eliminating nonresident microorganisms from the skin are the low pH, the fatty acids in sebaceous secretions, and the presence of lysozyme. Neither profuse sweating nor washing and bathing can eliminate or significantly modify the normal resident flora. The number of superficial microorganisms may be diminished by vigorous daily scrubbing with soap containing hexachlorophene, but the flora is rapidly replenished from sebaceous and sweat glands even when contact with other skin areas or with the environment is completely excluded.

NORMAL FLORA OF THE MOUTH & UPPER RESPIRATORY TRACT

The mucous membranes of the mouth and pharynx are often sterile at birth but may be contaminated by passage through the birth canal. Within 4–12 hours after birth, viridans streptococci become established as the most prominent members of the resident flora and remain so for life. They probably originate in the respiratory tracts of the mother and attendants. Early in life, aerobic and anaerobic staphylococci, gram-negative diplococci (neisseriae, *Branhamella*), diphtheroids, and occasional lactobacilli are added. When teeth begin to erupt, the anaerobic spirochetes, *Bacteroides* (especially *B melaninogenicus*), *Fusobacterium* species, and some anaerobic vibrios and lactobacilli establish themselves. *Actinomyces* species are normally present in tonsillar tissue and on the gingivae in adults. Yeasts (*Candida* species) occur in the mouth.

In the pharynx and trachea, a similar flora establishes itself, whereas few bacteria are found in normal bronchi. Small bronchi and alveoli are normally sterile. The predominant organisms in the upper respiratory tract, particularly the pharynx, are nonhemolytic and alpha-hemolytic streptococci and neisseriae. staphylococci, diphtheroids, *Haemophilus*, pneumococci, *Mycoplasma*, and *Bacteroides* are also encountered.

The flora of the nose consists of prominent corynebacteria, staphylococci (*Staphylococcus aureus, S epidermidis*), and streptococci.

The Role of the Normal Mouth Flora in Dental Caries

Caries is a disintegration of the teeth beginning at the surface and progressing inward. First the surface enamel, which is entirely noncellular, is demineralized. This has been attributed to the effect of acid products of bacterial fermentation. Subsequent decomposition of the dentin and cement involves bacterial digestion of the protein matrix.

An essential first step in caries production appears to be the formation of plaque on the hard, smooth enamel surface. The plaque consists mainly of gelatinous deposits of high-molecular-weight glucans in which acid-producing bacteria adhere to the enamel. The carbohydrate polymers (glucans) are produced mainly by streptococci (*Streptococcus mutans*, peptostreptococci), perhaps in association with actinomy-

cetes. There appears to be a strong correlation between the presence of *S mutans* and caries on specific enamel areas. The essential second step in caries production appears to be the formation of large amounts of acid from carbohydrates by streptococci and lactobacilli in the plaque. High concentrations of acid demineralize the adjoining enamel and initiate caries.

In experimental "germ-free" animals, cariogenic streptococci can induce the formation of plaque and of caries. Adherence to smooth surfaces requires both the synthesis of water-insoluble glucan polymers by glucosyltransferases and the participation of binding sites on the surface of microbial cells. (Perhaps carbohydrate polymers also aid the attachment of some streptococci to endocardial surfaces.) Other members of the oral microflora, eg, *Veillonella*, may complex with glucosyltransferase of *Streptococcus salivarius* in saliva and then synthesize water-insoluble carbohydrate polymers to adhere to tooth surfaces. Adherence may be initiated by salivary IgA antibody to *S mutans*. Certain diphtheroids and streptococci that produce levans can induce specific soft tissue damage and bone resorption typical of periodontal disease. Proteolytic organisms, including actinomycetes and bacilli, play a role in the microbial action on dentin that follows damage to the enamel. The development of caries also depends on genetic, hormonal, nutritional, and many other factors. Control of caries involves physical removal of plaque, limitation of sucrose intake, good nutrition with adequate protein intake, and reduction of acid production in the mouth by limitation of available carbohydrates and frequent cleansing. The application of fluoride to teeth or its ingestion in water results in enhancement of acid resistance of the enamel. Control of periodontal disease requires removal of calculus (calcified deposit) and good mouth hygiene.

Periodontal pockets in the gingiva are particularly rich sources of organisms that are rarely encountered elsewhere. While they may participate in periodontal disease and tissue destruction, attention is drawn to them when they are implanted elsewhere, eg, producing infective endocarditis or bacteremia in a granulopenic host. Examples are *Capnocytophaga* species and *Rothia dentocariosa*. *Capnocytophaga* are fusiform, gram-negative, gliding anaerobes; *Rothia* are pleomorphic, aerobic, gram-positive rods. Both probably participate in the complex microbial flora of periodontal disease with prominent bone destruction. In the granulopenic immunodeficient patient, they can lead to serious opportunistic lesions in other organs.

NORMAL FLORA OF THE INTESTINAL TRACT

At birth the intestine is sterile, but organisms are soon introduced with food. In breast-fed children, the intestine contains large numbers of lactic acid streptococci and lactobacilli. These aerobic and anaerobic, gram-positive, nonmotile organisms (eg, *Bifidobac-*

terium) produce acid from carbohydrates and tolerate pH 5.0. In bottle-fed children, a more mixed flora exists in the bowel, and lactobacilli are less prominent. As food habits develop toward the adult pattern, the bowel flora changes. Diet has a marked influence on the relative composition of the intestinal and fecal flora. Bowels of neonates in intensive care nurseries tend to be colonized by abnormal organisms, eg, *Klebsiella, Citrobacter, Enterobacter*.

In the normal adult, the esophagus contains microorganisms arriving with saliva and food. The stomach's acidity keeps the number of microorganisms at a minimum (10^3–10^5/g of contents) unless obstruction at the pylorus favors the proliferation of gram-positive cocci and bacilli. The normal acid pH of the stomach markedly protects against infection with some enteric pathogens, eg, cholera. Administration of cimetidine in peptic ulcer leads to a great increase in microbial flora of the stomach, including many organisms usually prevalent in feces. As the pH of intestinal contents becomes alkaline, the resident flora gradually increases. In the adult duodenum, there are 10^3–10^6 bacteria per gram; in the jejunum and ileum, 10^5–10^8 bacteria per gram; and in the cecum and transverse colon, 10^8–10^{10} bacteria per gram of contents. In the upper intestine, lactobacilli and enterococci predominate, but in the lower ileum and cecum, the flora is fecal. In the sigmoid colon and rectum, there are about 10^{11} bacteria per gram of content, constituting 10–20% of the fecal mass. In diarrhea, the bacterial content may diminish greatly, whereas in intestinal stasis the count rises.

In the normal adult colon, the resident bacterial flora consists of 96–99% anaerobes (*Bacteroides*— especially *Bacteroides fragilis*; anaerobic lactobacilli, eg, *Bifidobacterium*; clostridia [*Clostridium perfringens*, 10^2–10^4/g]; and anaerobic streptococci) and only 1–4% aerobes (gram-negative coliforms, enterococci, and small numbers of *Proteus, Pseudomonas*, lactobacilli, *Candida*, and other organisms). More than 100 distinct types of organisms occur regularly in normal fecal flora. Minor trauma (eg, sigmoidoscopy, barium enema) may induce transient bacteremia in about 10% of procedures.

Intestinal bacteria are important in synthesis of vitamin K, conversion of bile pigments and bile acids, absorption of nutrients and breakdown products, and antagonism to microbial pathogens. The intestinal flora produces ammonia and other breakdown products that are absorbed and can contribute to hepatic coma. Among aerobic coliform bacteria, only a few serotypes persist in the colon for prolonged periods, and most serotypes of *Escherichia coli* are present only over a period of a few days.

Antimicrobial drugs taken orally can, in humans, temporarily suppress the drug-susceptible components of the fecal flora. This is commonly done by the preoperative oral administration of insoluble drugs. For example, neomycin plus erythromycin can in 1–2 days suppress part of the bowel flora, especially aerobes. Metronidazole accomplishes that for anaerobes. When surgery on the lower bowel is performed when the counts are at their lowest, some protection against infection by accidental spill can be achieved. However, soon thereafter the counts of fecal flora rise again to normal or higher than normal levels, principally of organisms selected out because of relative resistance to the drugs employed. The drug-susceptible microorganisms are replaced by drug-resistant ones, particularly staphylococci, *Enterobacter*, enterococci, *Proteus, Pseudomonas, Clostridium difficile*, and yeasts.

The feeding of large quantities of *Lactobacillus acidophilus* may result in the temporary establishment of this organism in the gut and the concomitant partial suppression of other gut microflora.

Growth of young chickens, turkeys, and pigs is greatly accelerated by admixture of antibiotics to the feed. The nature of this phenomenon is not clear; it probably does not occur in humans or ruminants. Antibiotic-fed animals have a predominantly drug-resistant intestinal flora, which may be transmitted to human contacts.

NORMAL FLORA OF THE URETHRA

The anterior urethra of both sexes contains small numbers of the same types of organisms found on the skin and perineum. These organisms regularly appear in normal voided urine in numbers of 10^2–10^4/mL.

NORMAL FLORA OF THE VAGINA

Soon after birth, aerobic lactobacilli (Döderlein's bacilli) appear in the vagina and persist as long as the pH remains acid (several weeks). When the pH becomes neutral (remaining so until puberty), a mixed flora of cocci and bacilli is present. At puberty, lactobacilli reappear in large numbers and contribute to the maintenance of acid pH through the production of acid from carbohydrates, particularly glycogen. This appears to be an important mechanism in preventing the establishment of other, possibly harmful microorganisms in the vagina. If lactobacilli are suppressed by the administration of antimicrobial drugs, yeasts or various bacteria increase in numbers and cause irritation and inflammation. After the menopause, lactobacilli again diminish in numbers and a mixed flora returns. The normal vaginal flora often includes also group B hemolytic streptococci, anaerobic streptococci (peptostreptococci), *Bacteroides* species, clostridia, *Gardnerella (Haemophilus) vaginalis, Ureaplasma urealyticum*, and sometimes *Listeria*. The cervical mucus has antibacterial activity and contains lysozyme. In some women the vaginal introitus contains a heavy flora, resembling that of the perineum and perianal area. This may be a predisposing factor in recurrent urinary tract infections. Vaginal organisms present at delivery may infect the newborn (eg, group B streptococci).

NORMAL FLORA OF THE EYE
(CONJUNCTIVA)

The predominant organisms of the conjunctiva are diphtheroids *(Corynebacterium xerosis)*, neisseriae, and gram-negative bacilli resembling *Haemophilus* (Morax-Axenfeld bacillus, *Moraxella* species). Staphylococci and nonhemolytic streptococci are also frequently present. The conjunctival flora is normally held in check by the flow of tears, which contain antibacterial lysozyme.

•   •   •

References

Aly R et al: Correlation of human in vivo and in vitro cutaneous antimicrobial factors. *J Infect Dis* 1975;**131**:579.

Barksdale L: Identifying *Rothia dentocariosa. Ann Intern Med* 1979;**91**:786.

Bartlett JG et al: Quantitative bacteriology of the vaginal flora. *J Infect Dis* 1977;**136**:271.

Bentley DW et al: The microflora of the human ileum and colon. *J Lab Clin Med* 1972;**79**:421.

Finegold SM: Intestinal bacteria: Their role in physiology. *Calif Med* 1969;**110**:455.

Forlenza S et al: *Capnocytophaga* species: A newly recognized clinical entity in granulocytopenic patients. *Lancet* 1980;**1**:567.

Glickman I: Periodontal disease. *N Engl J Med* 1971;**284**:1071.

Goldmann DA et al: Bacterial colonization of neonates admitted to an intensive care environment. *J Pediatr* 1978;**93**:288.

Gorbach SL, Bartlett JG: Anaerobic infections. *N Engl J Med* 1974;**290**:1177.

Leyden JJ et al: Age-related changes in the resident bacterial flora of the human face. *J Invest Dermatol* 1975;**65**:379.

Levy SB et al: Changes in intestinal flora of farm personnel after introduction of a tetracycline-supplemented feed on a farm. *N Engl J Med* 1976;**295**:583.

McCormack WM et al: Sexually transmitted conditions among women college students. *Am J Obstet Gynecol* 1981;**139**:130.

Scherp HW: Dental caries. *Science* 1971;**173**:1199.

Shooter RA et al: *E coli* serotypes in the faeces of healthy adults over a period of several months. *J Hyg* 1977;**78**:95.

Slade HD: Cell surface antigenic polymers of *Streptococcus mutans* and their role in adherence of the microorganisms in vitro. Page 411 in: *Microbiology 1977*. Schlessinger D (editor). American Society for Microbiology, 1977.

Swenson RM et al: The bacteriology of intra-abdominal infections. *Arch Surg* 1974;**109**:398.

Thadepalli H et al: Anaerobic infections of the female genital tract. *Am J Obstet Gynecol* 1973;**117**:1034.

Many fungi cause plant diseases, but only about 100 of the thousands of known species of yeasts and molds cause disease in humans or animals. Only the dermatophytes and *Candida* are commonly transmitted from one human to another.

For convenience, human mycotic infections may be grouped into superficial, subcutaneous, and deep (or systemic) mycoses. Superficial fungal infections of skin, hair, and nails may be chronic and resistant to treatment but rarely affect the general health of the patient. Deep mycoses, on the other hand, may produce systemic involvement and are sometimes fatal. The actinomycetes are not fungi but filamentous branching bacteria. However, since they produce disease pictures resembling fungal infections, they are discussed in this section.

The deep mycoses are caused by organisms that live free in nature in soil or on decaying organic material and are frequently limited to certain geographic areas. In such areas many people acquire the fungal infection. A majority develop only minor symptoms or none at all, and only a small minority of cases progress to full-blown serious or fatal disease.

Pathogenic fungi generally produce no toxins. In the host they regularly induce hypersensitivity to their chemical constituents. In systemic mycoses, the typical tissue reaction is a chronic granuloma with varying degrees of necrosis and abscess formation.

The general morphology of fungi has been described in Chapter 1. Some typical structures of pathogenic fungi are mentioned below; others are given with the descriptions of specific disease entities.

STRUCTURES OF FUNGI

When grown on suitable media, many fungi produce long, branching filaments. These fungi are commonly called **molds**. Each filament is called a **hypha**. Hyphae may become divided into a chain of cells by the formation of transverse walls, or septa. These are called septate hyphae. As the hyphae continue to grow and branch, a mat of growth called a **mycelium** develops. The part of the growth that projects above the surface of the substrate is called an **aerial** mycelium; the part that penetrates into the substrate and absorbs food is known as the **vegetative** mycelium.

Most fungi reproduce by forming spores through meiosis, during which the chromosome number remains the same. Fungi with only asexual spore formation (or no spore formation) are called **fungi imperfecti**. In the past, most fungi pathogenic for humans were known only in the imperfect (asexual) state. In recent decades, however, the sexual forms of many fungi were discovered and were given new names. Microbiology laboratories and clinicians continue to use the older names (representing asexual replication), but at times the sexual name will also be mentioned here. Fungi are called dimorphic if the tissue form and the free-living form differ markedly.

The following types of sexual spores occur in fungi of medical interest, as a result of mating:

(1) Zygospores: In certain zygomycetes the tips of approximating hyphae fuse, meiosis occurs, and large, thick-walled zygospores develop.

(2) Ascospores: Usually 4–8 spores form within a specialized cell called an ascus, in which meiosis has taken place (Fig 25–1).

(3) Basidiospores: Following meiosis, 4 spores usually form on the surface of a specialized cell called a basidium.

Asexual Reproduction

Conidia are asexual propagules seen in most colonies of fungi of medical interest (Figs 25–1 through 25–3 and 25–5 through 25–9). When no sexual stage is known, classification is based on the morphologic development of conidia. They may form on specialized conidiophores, on the sides or ends of nonspecialized hyphae, or from a hyphal cell (see p 3). Specialized names have been given to each developmental form of conidia. When more than one kind of conidium is produced within a given colony, the small, single-celled conidia are called microconidia, and the large, often multicellular conidia are called macroconidia. The following "spores" represent 3 of the more common types of conidia.

A. Blastospores (Blastoconidia): A simple structure develops by budding, with subsequent separation of the bud from the parent cell (eg, in yeasts) (Fig 25–1).

B. Chlamydospores (Chlamydoconidia): Cells in a hypha enlarge and develop thick walls. These structures are resistant to unfavorable environmental

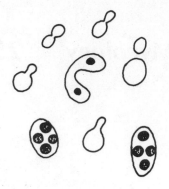

Figure 25–1. *Saccharomyces*. Budding blastospores. Conjugating blastospores. Ascus containing ascospores.

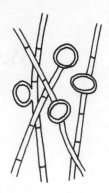

Figure 25–2. Terminal and intercalary chlamydospores.

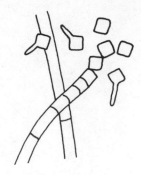

Figure 25–3. *Geotrichum*. Arthrospore formation. Germinating arthrospores.

Figure 25–4. *Rhizopus*. Developing sporangiophores. Sporangiospores released. Rhizoid.

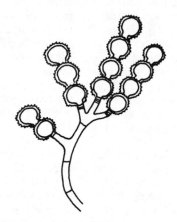

Figure 25–5. *Scopulariopsis*. Conidiophore shows spore scars. Terminal conidium is oldest.

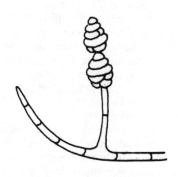

Figure 25–6. *Alternaria*. Black, multicellular conidia in chains. Terminal conidium is youngest.

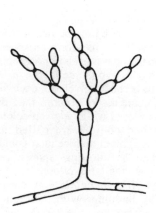

Figure 25–7. *Cladosporium*. Chains of conidia. Terminal conidium is youngest and has budded from subterminal conidium.

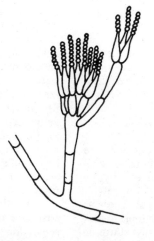

Figure 25–8. *Penicillium*. Conidia form within a phialide. Terminal conidium is oldest.

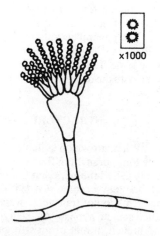

x1000

Figure 25–9. *Aspergillus fumigatus*. Phialides form on top of swollen vesicle. Terminal conidium is oldest. Mature conidia have rough walls.

conditions and germinate when conditions become more favorable for vegetative growth (Fig 25–2).

C. Arthrospores *(Arthroconidia)*: Structures result from a hypha fragmenting into individual cells (eg, in *Coccidioides*) (Fig 25–15).

SUPERFICIAL MYCOSES

The superficial mycoses are caused by fungi that invade only superficial keratinized tissue (skin, hair, and nails) but do not invade deeper tissues. The most important of these are the dermatophytes, a group of closely related fungi classified into 3 genera: *Epidermophyton, Microsporum*, and *Trichophyton*. In keratinized tissue, these form only hyphae and arthrospores. In culture, they develop characteristic colonies and conidia, by means of which they can be divided into species. Sexual spores of some species have been found. Some species are found only in soil and never produce infection. Other soil species may produce disease in humans. Others have evolved to complete parasitism, are communicable, and are not found in soil.

Most dermatophytes are worldwide in distribution, but some species show a higher incidence in certain regions than in others (eg, *Trichophyton schoenleinii* in the Mediterranean, *Trichophyton rubrum* in tropical climates). Many domestic and other animals have infections caused by dermatophytes and may transmit them to humans (eg, *Microsporum canis* from cats and dogs).

Morphology & Identification

Representative colonies form on Sabouraud's agar at room temperature. Conidia formation may be observed by means of slide cultures.

A. *Trichophyton (Arthroderma)*: Microconidia are the predominant spore form. Smooth-walled, pencil shaped macroconidia with blunt ends are rarer. Each species varies in colony morphology and pigmentation. Conidia formation may also vary according to the species under observation (Fig 25–10). The medium on which the fungi grow greatly influences these characteristics. The use of different nutritional media is sometimes needed in order to differentiate among the species.

In culture, colonies of *Trichophyton mentagrophytes* range from granular to powdery, and they usually display abundant grapelike clusters of subspherical microconidia on terminal branches. Some cottony strains develop only rare teardrop-shaped microconidia along the sides of the hyphae. Coiled hyphae are frequent. *T rubrum* usually has some teardrop-shaped microconidia along the sides of the hyphae; in some strains these may be abundant. Colonies often develop a red color on the reverse side. The larger microconidia of *Trichophyton tonsurans* are usually numerous and clavate and may be borne on short branches. Colonies are usually powdery.

B. *Microsporum (Nannizzia)*: Macroconidia are the predominant conidial form (Fig 25–11). They are large, rough-walled, multicellular, and spindle-shaped, and they form on the ends of hyphae. Microconidia are not used as a means of differentiating species. *Microsporum* species usually infect skin and hair but rarely the nails.

M canis forms numerous thick-walled, 8- to 15-celled macroconidia that frequently have curved or hooked spiny tips. A yellow-orange pigment usually develops on the reverse side of the colony. Infected hairs fluoresce a bright green under Wood's light. *Microsporum gypseum* has abundant thinner-walled, 4- to 6-celled macroconidia in buff to brownish colored colonies. *Microsporum audouini* rarely forms conidia in the colony, but many thick-walled chlamydospores may be present. This fungus grows poorly on sterile rice grains, whereas other *Microsporum* species show rapid growth. Infected hairs fluoresce.

C. *Epidermophyton floccosum*: In this monotypic genus, only 1- to 5-celled, club-shaped

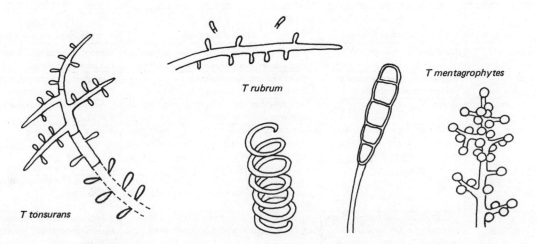

Figure 25–10. *Trichophyton* species. Microconidia and typical macroconidium.

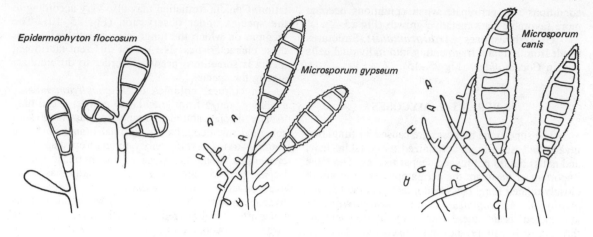

Epidermophyton floccosum

Microsporum gypseum

Microsporum canis

Figure 25–11. Macroconidia and microconidia.

macroconidia (Fig 25–11) are formed in the greenish-yellow colony, which mutates readily to form a sterile white overgrowth. This fungus invades skin and nails but never hair.

Antigenic Structure

Trichophytin, a crude extract from dermatophytes, produces a positive tuberculinlike response in most adults. A galactomannan peptide is the reactive component. The carbohydrate portion is related to an immediate response, whereas the peptide moiety is associated with the delayed response and is believed also to be associated with immunity. Patients without the delayed type reaction or with an immediate type reaction are more susceptible to chronic dermatophytosis. Resistance to infection, both partial and local, may be acquired after the primary infection. This resistance varies in duration and degree depend-

ing on the host, site, and species of fungus causing the infection.

Clinical Findings (See Table 25–1.)

A. Tinea Pedis (Athlete's Foot): This is the most prevalent of all dermatophytoses. The toe webs are infected with a *Trichophyton* species or with *E floccosum*. Initially there is itching between the toes and the development of small vesicles that rupture and discharge a thin fluid. The skin of the toe webs becomes macerated and peels, whereupon cracks appear that are prone to secondary bacterial infection. When secondary infection does occur, lymphangitis and lymphadenitis develop. When the fungal infection becomes chronic, peeling and cracking of the skin are the principal manifestations. Nail infection (tinea unguium) follows prolonged tinea pedis. Nails become yellow, brittle, thickened, or crumbling.

Table 25–1. Some clinical features of dermatophyte infection.

Skin Disease	Location of Lesions	Clinical Appearance	Fungi Most Frequently Responsible
Tinea corporis (ringworm)	Nonhairy, smooth skin.	Circular patches with advancing red, vesiculated border and central scaling. Pruritic.	*Microsporum canis, Trichophyton mentagrophytes*
Tinea pedis* (athlete's foot)	Interdigital spaces on feet of persons wearing shoes.	Acute: itching, red, vesicular. Chronic: itching, scaling, fissures.	*T rubrum, T mentagrophytes, Epidermophyton floccosum*
Tinea cruris (jock itch)	Groin.	Erythematous scaling lesion in intertriginous area. Pruritic.	*T rubrum, T mentagrophytes, E floccosum*
Tinea capitis	Scalp hair. Endothrix: fungus inside hair shaft. Ectothrix: fungus on surface of hair.	Circular bald patches with short hair stubs or broken hair within hair follicles. Kerion rare. *Microsporum*-infected hairs fluoresce.	*M canis, T tonsurans*
Tinea barbae	Beard hair.	Edematous, erythematous lesion.	*T rubrum, T mentagrophytes*
Tinea unguium (onychomycosis)	Nail.	Nails thickened or crumbling distally; discolored; lusterless. Usually associated with tinea pedis.	*T rubrum, T mentagrophytes, E floccosum*
Dermatophytid (id reaction)	Usually sides and flexor aspects of fingers. Palm. Any site on body.	Pruritic vesicular to bullous lesions. Most commonly associated with tinea pedis.	No fungi present in lesion. May become secondarily infected with bacteria.

*May be associated with lesions of hands and nails (onychomycosis).

In the course of dermatophytosis the individual may become hypersensitive to constituents or products of the fungus and may develop allergic manifestations, called dermatophytids (usually vesicles), elsewhere on the body (most often on the hands). The trichophytin skin test is markedly positive in such persons.

B. Tinea Corporis (Tinea Glabrosa, Tinea Cruris) (Ringworm): This is a dermatophytosis of the nonhairy skin of the body that gives rise commonly to the annular lesions of ringworm, with a clearing, scaly center surrounded by a red advancing border that often contains vesicles.

Dermatophytes grow only within dead, keratinized tissue. Fungal metabolic products diffuse through the malpighian layer to cause erythema, vesicle formation, and pruritus. The role of antibody activity is not understood at present. As hyphae age and break up into arthrospores, the cells containing them are shed. This partly accounts for the central clearing of the "ringworm" lesion. Active hyphal growth is into the peripheral "ring" of uninfected stratum corneum. Continuing growth downward into the newly forming stratum corneum of the thicker plantar and palmar surfaces accounts for the persistent infections at those sites.

C. Tinea Capitis (Ringworm of the Scalp): *Microsporum* infection occurs in childhood and usually heals spontaneously by puberty. Untreated *Trichophyton* infections may persist into adulthood. Infection begins on the skin of the scalp, with subsequent growth of the dermatophyte down the keratinized wall of the hair follicle. Just above the hair root, infection of the hair takes place. The fungus continues to grow downward on the upward-growing hair shaft. *Microsporum* species grow primarily as a sheath around the hair (ectothrix), whereas *Trichophyton* species vary in their growth patterns. Some invade the hair shaft (endothrix), making it so fragile that it breaks off within or at the surface of the hair follicle (black-dot ringworm). In infections with other species, the hair breaks a short distance above the scalp, leaving short stubs in a balding, usually circular patch. Redness, edema, scaling, and vesicle formation may be seen. In some patients, a pronounced inflammation called **kerion** may occur around the area of infection and may even resemble pyogenic infection. *T schoenleinii* forms cuplike crusts (scutula) around infected follicles.

Infection with *Trichophyton* species may involve the bearded region of humans (tinea barbae); the highly inflammatory reaction they cause closely resembles pyogenic infections of that area.

Diagnostic Laboratory Tests

Specimens consist of scrapings of both skin and nails and hairs plucked from involved areas. *Microsporum*-infected hairs fluoresce under Wood's light in a darkened room.

A. Microscopic Examination: Specimens are placed on a slide in a drop of 10–20% potassium hydroxide, covered with a coverslip, and examined

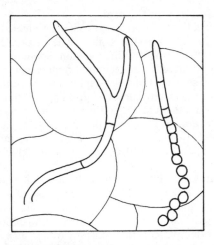

Figure 25–12. Dermatophyte in KOH mount of skin or nail scraping. Branching hyphae. Arthrospore formation.

immediately and then again after 20 minutes. In skin or nails, branching hyphae or chains of arthrospores are seen (Fig 25–12). In hairs, *Microsporum* species form dense sheaths of spores in a mosaic pattern around the hair; *Trichophyton* species form parallel rows of spores outside (ectothrix) or inside (endothrix) the hair shaft.

B. Culture: All final identification of dermatophytes rests on cultures. Specimens are inoculated onto Sabouraud's agar slants, incubated for 1–3 weeks at room temperature, and further examined in slide cultures if necessary.

Treatment

Therapy consists of thorough removal of infected and dead epithelial structures and application of a topical antifungal chemical. Overtreatment often causes dermatophytids. Attempts must be made to prevent reinfection. In widespread involvement, oral administration of griseofulvin for 1–4 weeks has been effective. Nail infections require months of griseofulvin treatment and sometimes surgical removal of the nail.

A. Scalp Infections: In scalp infections, hairs can be plucked manually, clipped, or otherwise epilated. Griseofulvin, 0.125–0.5 g/d orally, may be given for 1–2 weeks. Frequent shampoos and miconazole cream, 2%, or other antifungal agents may be effective if used for weeks.

B. Body Infections: Use miconazole cream, 2%; undecylenic acid cream, 5%; salicylic acid, 3%; or benzoic acid, 5%. In tinea versicolor, selenium sulfide is also effective.

C. Foot Infections:

1. Acute phase–Soak in potassium permanganate 1:5000 until the acute inflammation subsides; then apply antifungal chemicals as described above.

2. Chronic phase–Apply antifungal chemicals as creams at night (as powders during the day) as outlined above. Higher concentrations may be tolerated.

Epidemiology & Control

Infection arises from contact of uninfected skin or hair with infected skin scales or hair stubs. Hyphae then grow into the stratum corneum. Sporadic cases of ringworm infection are acquired from cats or dogs (*M canis*). Epidemics of tinea capitis have been traced to the use of shared barber shop clippers, transfer of infected hairs on seats, and person-to-person contact. Control depends on cleanliness, sterilization of instruments (using hot mineral oil), effective treatment of cases, and reduced contact with infectious materials.

Athlete's foot is found only in people who wear shoes. Infection spreads through the use of common showers and dressing rooms, where infected, desquamated skin serves as a source of infection. No really effective control measures (other than proper hygiene and the use of talc to keep interdigital spaces dry) are available. In many persons, chronic athlete's foot is asymptomatic and becomes activated only in excessive heat or moisture or with unsuitable footwear. Open-toed shoes or sandals are best for general wear.

OTHER SUPERFICIAL MYCOSES

Tinea Versicolor

Growth within the stratum corneum of clusters of spherical, thick-walled budding cells and short bent hyphae of *Malassezia furfur* usually causes no other pathologic signs than fine to brawny scales. Lesions appear principally on the chest, back, abdomen, neck, and upper arms. The lesions range from depigmented to brownish-red and are only of cosmetic importance.

Tinea Nigra

Light brown to blackish macular areas appear most commonly on the palmar or plantar stratum corneum. These are filled with brownish, branched, septate hyphae and budding cells of *Cladosporium werneckii*. No scaling or other reaction develops.

Piedra

Hard black nodules are formed around the scalp hair by *Piedraia hortai*. Softer, white to light brown nodules caused by *Trichosporon cutaneum* form on axillary, pubic, beard, and scalp hair.

SUBCUTANEOUS MYCOSES

The fungi causing the subcutaneous mycoses grow in soil or on decaying vegetation. They must be introduced into the subcutaneous tissue in order to produce disease. In general, lesions spread slowly from the area of implantation. Extension via lymphatics draining the lesion is slow except for sporotrichosis. Each of these fungi has developed a unique morphologic form as a pathogen, except for *Basidiobolus haptosporus* and *Entomophthora coronata*, zygomycetes that grow as branching hyphae within subcutaneous lesions.

1. *SPOROTHRIX SCHENCKII*

Sporothrix schenckii is a fungus that lives on plants or wood and causes sporotrichosis, a chronic granulomatous infection, when traumatically introduced into the skin. There is often a characteristic spread along lymphatics draining the area. The fungus is dimorphic.

Morphology & Identification

The organisms are only rarely seen in pus and tissues from human infections; they may appear as small, round to cigar-shaped, gram-positive budding cells. In cultures at room temperature on Sabouraud's agar, cream-colored to black, folded, leathery colonies develop within 3–5 days. (Pigment formation of different strains of *S schenckii* is variable.) Simple, ovoid conidia are borne in clusters at the tip of long, slender conidiophores (resembling a daisy; see Fig 25–13) as well as along the sides of the thin hyphae. Culture at 37 °C produces spherical to ovoid budding cells.

Antigenic Structure

Heat-killed saline suspensions of cultures (or carbohydrate fractions from them) give positive delayed skin tests in infected humans or animals. A variety of antibodies are also produced by infected patients.

Pathogenesis & Clinical Findings

The fungus is introduced into the skin of the extremities through trauma. A local lesion develops as a pustule, abscess, or ulcer, and the lymphatics leading from it become thickened and cordlike. Multiple subcutaneous nodules and abscesses occur along the lymphatics. Usually there is little systemic illness associated with these lesions, but dissemination of the infection sometimes occurs, especially in debilitated

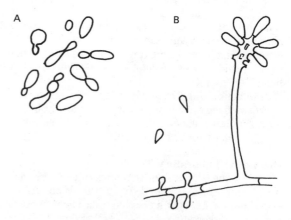

Figure 25–13. *Sporothrix schenckii.* **A:** Blastospores seen in tissue or 37 °C culture. **B:** Conidia formation in 20 °C culture.

patients. Rarely, primary infection in humans occurs through the lung. A variety of animals (rats, dogs, mules, and horses) are found naturally infected.

Histologically, the lesions show both chronic inflammation and granulomas that undergo necrosis.

Organisms in tissue can be identified by specific immunofluorescence. Around rare organisms an eosinophilic antibody complex ("asteroid") may be seen in hematoxylin-eosin stains.

Diagnostic Laboratory Tests

Specimens consist of pus or biopsy from lesions.

A. Microscopic Examination: In human lesions, organisms are seen infrequently, whereas budding cells are abundant in laboratory infections of mice.

B. Culture: On Sabouraud's agar, typical colonies with clusters of conidia are diagnostic. They should convert to yeast morphology during incubation at 37 °C.

C. Serology: Agglutination of yeast cell suspensions or of latex particles coated with antigen occurs in high titer with sera of infected patients.

Treatment

In a majority of cases the infection is self-limited although chronic. Potassium iodide administered orally for weeks has some therapeutic benefit in the cutaneous-lymphatic form. In systemic involvement, amphotericin B is given intravenously.

Epidemiology & Control

S schenckii occurs worldwide in nature on plants (particularly sphagnum moss in the USA), thorns, and decaying wood; in soil; and on infected animals. Occupational exposure of gardeners, nursery workers, miners, and others in contact with plants and wood accounts for most cases. Prevention of trauma in these occupations is effective, since the organism must be passively introduced subcutaneously in order to cause disease.

2. CHROMOMYCOSIS

Chromomycosis is a slowly progressive granulomatous infection of skin caused by several species of black molds. *Phialophora verrucosa*, *Phialophora (Fonsecaea) pedrosoi*, and *Cladosporium carrionii* have been isolated most frequently.

Morphology & Identification

In exudates and tissues these fungi produce dark-brown, thick-walled, rounded cells 5–15 μm in diameter that divide by septation. Septation in different planes with delayed separation may give rise to a cluster of 4–8 cells (Fig 25–14). Cells within superficial crusts of pus may germinate into brown, branching hyphae. Colonies vary in pigmentation from olive-gray to brown to black. The surface is generally velvety, overlying a black, densely interwoven mat of mycelium.

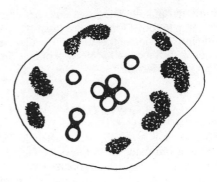

Figure 25–14. Chromomycosis. Pigmented fungal cells seen in giant cell.

A. *P verrucosa*: Conidia are primarily produced by vase-shaped phialides.

B. *P pedrosoi*: Most conidia form in short branching chains with the terminal cell budding to form a new conidium. Conidia may also form without chains directly on the top and sides of a conidiophore. Phialides are rare.

C. *C carrionii*: Only long, branching chains of conidia form on elongated conidiophores.

Pathogenesis & Clinical Findings

The fungi are introduced by trauma into the skin, often of the legs or feet. Slowly, over months or years, wartlike growths extend along the lymphatics of the affected area. Cauliflowerlike nodules with crusting abscesses eventually cover the area, and elephantiasis may result from obstruction and fibrosis of lymph channels. Dissemination to other parts of the body is very rare.

Histologically, the lesions are granulomas; within leukocytes or giant cells the dark-brown, round fungus cells may be seen.

Diagnostic Laboratory Tests

Specimens consist of scrapings or biopsy from lesions.

A. Microscopic Examination: Specimens are placed in 10% potassium hydroxide and examined under a coverglass for the dark, round fungus cells.

B. Culture: Specimens should be cultured on Sabouraud's agar in order that the characteristic conidial structures and arrangement described above may be detected. Pathogenic species are distinguished from similar saprophytic black molds by their inability to digest gelatin.

Treatment

Flucytosine, 150 mg/kg/d orally, and thiabendazole, 25 mg/kg/d orally, can be effective. Surgical removal of lesions and skin grafting may be required.

Epidemiology

Chromomycosis occurs mainly in the tropics. The fungi are saprophytic in nature, probably occurring on vegetation and in soil. The disease occurs chiefly on the legs of barefoot farmers, presumably following traumatic introduction of the fungus. The disease is not communicable. Shoes and protection of legs probably would prevent infection.

3. MYCETOMA

Mycetoma is a localized, swollen lesion with granules that are compact colonies of the causative agent draining from sinuses. It is caused by a variety of fungi and actinomycetes (filamentous bacteria). Mycetoma develops when these soil organisms are implanted by trauma into subcutaneous tissue. The term maduromycosis is often used for those infections caused by fungi, but the clinical disease resembles actinomycotic mycetoma, although therapy is different. Mycetoma occurs worldwide but is primarily a disease occurring in people who do not wear shoes. It is particularly prevalent in tropical Africa.

Morphology & Identification

White, yellow, red, or black granules are extruded in pus. The granules due to fungi consist of intertwined, septate hyphae (3–5 μm), and depending on the species, they may have larger, thick-walled cells at the periphery. The actinomycete granule consists only of filamentous hyphae (1 μm in diameter). *Petriellidium (Allescheria) boydii (Monosporium apiospermum)* is among the more common fungal causes of mycetoma. The gray colony produces abundant ovoid conidia and occasionally ascospores within brown cleistothecia. *P boydii* may also cause opportunistic disease of the lungs and other organs in compromised hosts. Some other fungi causing mycetoma are *Madurella* species, *Phialophora* species, and *Acremonium* species. Each has its own characteristic colonial and microscopic morphology.

The most common causes of "actinomycotic" mycetoma are *Nocardia brasiliensis* and *Actinomadura madurae*. *N brasiliensis* may be acid-fast. These and other pathogenic actinomycetes are differentiated by biochemical tests and chromatographic analysis of cell wall components (see p 302).

Pathogenesis & Clinical Findings

After one of the causative agents has been introduced into the subcutaneous tissue (usually foot, hand, or back) by trauma, abscesses form that may extend through muscle and even into bone, eventually draining through chronic sinuses. The agent can be seen as a compact granule in the pus. Untreated lesions persist for years and extend deeper and peripherally, causing deformity and loss of function.

Histologically, the lesions resemble those of actinomycosis, with prominent abscess formation, granulation tissue, necrotic foci, and fibrosis. Within the abscess the granule is often seen surrounded by an eosinophilic matrix representing host materials and perhaps antigen-antibody complexes.

Diagnostic Laboratory Tests

Some granules have a characteristic morphology as well as color that aids in identification when cultures cannot be made. The diagnosis of mycetoma should never be made unless granules are seen.

Treatment

The actinomycotic mycetomas respond well to sulfonamides and sulfones if therapy is begun early before extensive deformity has occurred. Surgical drainage assists in healing. There is no established therapy for fungal mycetoma. Surgical excision of early lesions may prevent spread.

Epidemiology & Control

The organisms producing mycetoma occur in soil and on vegetation. Barefoot farm laborers are therefore most exposed. Properly cleaning wounds and wearing shoes are reasonable control measures.

SYSTEMIC MYCOSES

The systemic mycoses are caused by soil fungi. Infection is acquired by inhalation, and most infections are asymptomatic. In symptomatic disease, dissemination of infection may occur to any organ, although each fungus tends to attack certain organs. These fungi appear to cause disease in specific persons, in whom disseminated, usually fatal infection takes place. The characteristics of these unique hosts that may predispose to such infections are not clearly understood. All these fungi are dimorphic in that they have a unique morphologic adaptation to existence in tissue or to growth at 37 °C.

1. *COCCIDIOIDES IMMITIS*

Coccidioides immitis is a soil fungus that causes coccidioidomycosis. The infection is endemic in some arid regions of the southwestern USA and Latin America. Infection is usually self-limited; dissemination is rare but may be fatal.

Morphology & Identification

In histologic sections of tissue, in pus, or in sputum, *C immitis* appears as a spherule 15–60 μm in diameter, with a thick, doubly refractile wall (Fig 25–15). Endospores form within the spherule and fill it. Upon rupture of the wall, they are released into surrounding tissue, where they enlarge to form new spherules.

When grown on bacteriologic media or on Sabouraud's agar, a white to tan cottony colony develops. The aerial hyphae form alternating arthrospores and empty cells. Hyphae fragment easily and release the spores. The arthrospores are light, float in air, and are highly infectious. When they are inoculated into animals or inhaled by humans, these infectious spores develop into tissue spherules. Spherules

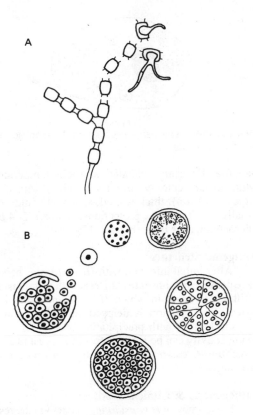

Figure 25–15. *Coccidioides immitis. A:* In soil. Arthrospore formation and germination. *B:* In tissue. Spherule formation with endospores.

can also be produced in the laboratory by cultivation of *C immitis* using specialized methods.

Antigenic Structure

Coccidioidin is a sterile filtrate from broth in which *C immitis* mycelium was grown. Spherulin is a sterile filtrate from broth in which spherules were grown. These materials give positive skin tests (in dilutions up to 1:10,000) in infected persons and serve as antigens in immunodiffusion (precipitin), latex agglutination, and complement fixation tests. In low dilutions (1:10) these antigens cross-react with antigens of other fungi *(Histoplasma, Paracoccidioides).* Polysaccharides have been partially purified from these materials, and they react serologically and in skin tests. Some antisera give highly specific immunofluorescence tests with spherules in tissue.

Pathogenesis & Clinical Findings

Infection is acquired through the inhalation of airborne arthrospores. A respiratory infection follows that may be asymptomatic and may be evident only by the development of precipitating antibodies and a positive skin test in 2–3 weeks; on the other hand, an influenzalike illness, with fever, malaise, cough, and aches, may occur. About 5–10% of individuals in this latter category develop hypersensitivity reactions 1–2

weeks later in the form of erythema nodosum or erythema multiforme. This symptom complex is called "valley fever" or "desert rheumatism" and is self-limited. Some radiologic changes occur in the lungs in more than half of cases, occasionally taking the form of thin-walled cavities. The latter may heal or become chronic.

In fewer than 1% of persons who have been infected with *Coccidioides* does the disease progress to the disseminated, highly fatal form. This occurs much more frequently in some races (eg, Filipinos, blacks, or Mexicans) and is also prominent in pregnant women. Dissemination, if it occurs, usually develops within 1 year of initial infection, either by direct extension of a lesion or by hematogenous spread; meningitis and bone lesions are common. Dissemination denotes some defect in the individual's ability to localize and control infection with *C immitis*. Most persons can be considered immune to reinfection after their skin tests have become positive. However, if such individuals are immunosuppressed by drug or disease, dissemination can occur many years after primary *Coccidioides* infection.

Disseminated coccidioidomycosis is comparable to tuberculosis, with lesions in many organs, bones, and the central nervous system. Histologically, these are typical granulomas with interspersed suppuration. The histologic diagnosis depends on the detection of typical spherules filled with endospores. The clinical course often includes remissions and exacerbations.

Diagnostic Laboratory Tests

Specimens consist of sputum, pus, spinal fluid, biopsy specimens, and blood for serologic diagnosis.

A. Microscopic Examination: Materials should be examined fresh (after centrifuging, if necessary) for typical spherules.

B. Cultures: Cultures can be grown on blood agar at 37 °C and on Sabouraud's agar at 20 °C. *Use extreme caution—arthrospores from cultures are highly infectious.*

C. Animal Inoculation: Mice injected intraperitoneally develop progressive lesions from which *Coccidioides* can be grown.

D. Serology: IgM and IgG antibodies to coccidioidin develop within 2–4 weeks after infection and can be detected readily by immunodiffusion and latex agglutination tests. These titers decline within a few months. Complement-fixing antibodies rise at about the same time and persist in lower titer for 6–8 months but are sometimes undetectable in self-limited infection. By contrast, complement-fixing titers continue to rise if dissemination occurs, and they are a poor prognostic sign. Their fall in titer during treatment suggests improvement. In coccidioidal meningitis, the complement-fixing antibody titer may be high in cerebrospinal fluid and low in serum.

E. Skin Test: (See Antigenic Structure.) The coccidioidin skin test reaches maximum induration (more than 5 mm in diameter) between 24 and 48 hours after injection of 0.1 mL of 1:100 dilution. It is often negative in disseminated disease. Cross-reactions with other fungi occur at a dilution of 1:10. Spherulin is more sensitive than coccidioidin in detecting reactors but may be less specific. Reactions to skin tests tend to diminish in size and intensity some years after primary infection in residents of endemic areas.

Immunity

Following recovery from primary infection with *C immitis* there usually is immunity to reinfection.

Treatment

In most persons, primary infection is self-limited and requires only supportive treatment. In disseminated coccidioidomycosis, intravenous amphotericin B (0.4–0.8 mg/kg/d) continued for months may result in remissions. Systemic miconazole and ketoconazole have occasionally seemed to offer promise. However, therapeutic benefits have been limited in disseminated disease and especially in meningeal involvement. In coccidioidal meningitis, amphotericin B is also given intrathecally, but the long-term results are often poor.

Epidemiology & Control

The endemic area of *C immitis* in the USA includes the arid regions ("lower sonoran life zone") of the southwestern states, particularly the San Joaquin and Sacramento Valleys of California, areas around Tucson and Phoenix in Arizona, and west Texas. *C immitis* also occurs in some arid areas of Central and South America. In these areas the fungus is found in the soil and in rodents, and many humans have been infected, as shown by positive skin tests. The infection rate is highest during the dry months of summer and autumn, when dust is most prevalent. The dust storms in the winter of 1977, following a severe drought in the western USA, were followed by primary infections in previously *Coccidioides*-free areas near San Francisco.

The disease is not communicable from person to person, and there is no evidence that infected rodents contribute to its spread. A certain amount of control can be achieved by reducing dust, paving roads and airfields, planting grass or crops, and using oil sprays.

2. HISTOPLASMA CAPSULATUM

Histoplasma capsulatum is a dimorphic soil fungus occurring in many parts of the world. It causes histoplasmosis, an intracellular mycosis of the reticuloendothelial system. The ascomycetous, sexual stage of the fungus is called *Emmonsiella capsulata*.

Morphology & Identification

H capsulatum forms oval, uninucleate budding cells measuring 2–4 μm in phagocytic cells and on glucose-cysteine blood agar slants or in tissue culture incubated at 37 °C (Fig 25–16). The bud arises at the smaller end of the yeast on a narrow bud base. On

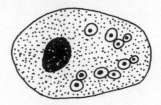

Figure 25–16. *Histoplasma capsulatum*. Macrophage containing blastospores.

Sabouraud's agar incubated at room temperature, white to tan, cottony colonies develop, with either large (8–14 μm), thick-walled, spherical conidia that usually have fingerlike projections, or small (2–4 μm) microconidia, or both (Fig 25–17).

Antigenic Structure

After initial infection with *Histoplasma*, persons have positive responses to skin tests with histoplasmin, a filtrate of broth in which *H capsulatum* has been grown. The reaction is delayed and tuberculinlike. Polysaccharides with precipitating and complement-fixing activity can be isolated from the yeast phase or mycelium. Cross-reactions with blastomycin are significant.

Pathogenesis & Clinical Findings

Infection with *H capsulatum* occurs via the respiratory tract. Inhaled conidia are engulfed by alveolar macrophages and eventually develop into budding cells. Although organisms are soon spread throughout the body, most infections are asymptomatic. The small inflammatory or granulomatous foci in the lungs and spleen heal with calcification. With heavy respiratory exposure, clinical pneumonia may develop. Chronic cavitary histoplasmosis occurs most often in adult males. Severe, disseminated histoplasmosis develops in a small minority of infected individuals, particularly infants and aged or immunosuppressed individuals. The reticuloendothelial system is particularly involved, with lymphadenopathy, enlarged spleen and liver, high fever, anemia, and a high fatality rate.

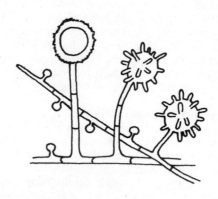

Figure 25–17. *Histoplasma capsulatum*. Macro- and microconidia in culture at 20 °C.

Ulcers of the nose, mouth, tongue, and intestine can occur. In such individuals the histologic lesion shows focal areas of necrosis in small granulomas in many organs. Phagocytic cells (mononuclear or polymorphonuclear leukocytes of the blood, fixed reticuloendothelial cells of liver, spleen, and bone marrow) contain the small, oval yeast cells.

Many animals, including dogs and rodents, are spontaneously infected in endemic areas. Many laboratory animals can be infected with cultures.

Diagnostic Laboratory Tests

Specimens consist of sputum, urine, scrapings from lesions, or buffy coat blood cells for culture; biopsies from bone marrow, skin, or lymph nodes for histology; and blood for serology.

A. Microscopic Examination: The small, ovoid cells may be detected intracellularly in histologic sections or in Giemsa-stained smears of bone marrow or blood. Specific immunofluorescence can identify histoplasma cells in sections or smears.

B. Culture: Specimens are cultured at 37 °C on glucose-cysteine blood agar and on Sabouraud's agar at room temperature. Cultures must be kept for 3 weeks or more. Injection of organisms into mice may yield *Histoplasma* in lesions of spleen and liver upon culture.

C. Serology: Latex agglutination, precipitation, and immunodiffusion tests become positive within 2–5 weeks after infection. Complement fixation titers rise later in the disease; they fall to very low levels if the disease is inactive. With progressive disease, the CF test remains positive in high titer (1:32 or more). Complement-fixing antibody cross-reacts with other fungal antigens. Two precipitin bands can be diagnostic: one (H) connotes active histoplasmosis; the other (M) may arise from repeated skin testing or past contact.

D. Skin Test: The histoplasmin skin test (1:100) becomes positive soon after infection and remains positive for years. It may be negative in disseminated progressive disease. Repeated skin testing stimulates serum antibodies, especially to complement fixation.

Immunity

Following initial infection with *Histoplasma*, most persons appear to develop some degree of immunity.

Treatment

Supportive therapy and rest enable most persons with symptomatic primary pulmonary histoplasmosis to recover. In disseminated disease, systemic treatment with amphotericin B has arrested and, at times, cured the disease, and ketoconazole has shown some promise.

Epidemiology & Control

Histoplasmosis occurs in many parts of the world. In the USA, areas endemic for *H capsulatum* include the central and eastern states. The fungus has been recovered from the soil where human or animal outbreaks of infection have occurred. *Histoplasma* grows abundantly in soil mixed with bird feces (eg, chicken houses) or bat guano (caves). Exposure in such places may result in massive infection with severe disease (eg, cave disease).

In endemic areas it must be assumed that small infective inocula are spread by dust. A large proportion of inhabitants apparently become infected early in life but without symptoms. They develop positive histoplasmin skin tests and occasionally have miliary calcifications in the lungs. The disease is not communicable from person to person. Spraying of formaldchyde on infected soil may destroy *Histoplasma*.

3. *BLASTOMYCES DERMATITIDIS*

Blastomyces dermatitidis is a dimorphic fungus that grows in mammalian tissues as a budding cell and in culture at 20 °C as a mold (Fig 25–18). It causes blastomycosis, a chronic granulomatous disease. Until recently it was recognized only in Canada, the USA, and Mexico and was referred to as "North American blastomycosis." However, it also occurs in Central America and Africa.

A

B

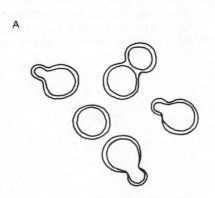
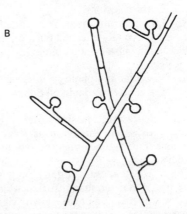

Figure 25–18. *Blastomyces dermatitidis. A:* In tissue or culture at 37 °C. *B:* In culture at 20 °C on Sabouraud's agar.

The ascomycetous sexual stage is called *Ajellomyces dermatitidis*.

Morphology & Identification

In tissue, pus, or exudates, *B dermatitidis* appears as a round, multinucleate, budding cell (8–15 µm) with a doubly refractile wall. Each cell usually has only *one* bud with a broad base. Colonies on blood agar at 37 °C are wrinkled, waxy, and soft, and the cells are morphologically similar to the tissue stage, although short hyphal segments may also be present. When grown on Sabouraud's agar at room temperature, a white or brownish colony develops, with branching hyphae bearing round or ovoid conidia 2–10 µm in diameter on slender terminal or lateral conidiophores.

Antigenic Structure

Extracts of culture filtrates of *Blastomyces* contain blastomycin, probably a mixture of antigens. Blastomycin as a skin test gives positive delayed reactions in some patients but lacks specificity. Cross-reactions with histoplasmin are common. In CF tests, blastomycin is an unreliable antigen, giving cross-reactions with other fungal infections but also reacting to high titer in persons with widespread blastomycosis. Specific animal sera permit the demonstration of budding *Blastomyces* cells in tissues by means of immunofluorescence.

Pathogenesis & Clinical Findings

Human infection probably occurs most commonly via the respiratory tract. Mild and self-limited cases are recognized infrequently. When dissemination occurs, skin lesions on exposed surfaces are most common. They may evolve into ulcerated verrucous granulomas with an advancing border and central scarring. The border is filled with microabscesses and has a sharp, sloping edge. Lesions of bone, prostate, epididymis, and testis occur; other sites are less frequently involved.

Diagnostic Laboratory Tests

Specimens consist of sputum, pus, exudates, urine, and biopsies from lesions.

A. Microscopic Examination: Wet mounts of specimens may show broadly attached buds on thick-walled cells. These may also be apparent in histologic sections.

B. Culture: Cellular morphology is typical on blood agar at 37 °C but often variable on Sabouraud's agar at 20 °C.

C. Animal Inoculation: Massive doses of blastospore cultures injected intravenously or intraperitoneally into mice, guinea pigs, or rabbits are fatal in 5–20 days.

D. Serology: Blastospore antigens may give positive results in CF and immunodiffusion tests. A titer rise in successive sera has more diagnostic significance, but cross-reactions with other fungal antigens are common.

Treatment

Although some benefit has been derived in disseminated cases from treatment with aromatic diamidines (eg, dihydroxystilbamidine), amphotericin B in doses up to 50 mg/d is the current drug of choice. Adjuvant surgical management of lesions is helpful. Relapses are not rare.

Epidemiology

Blastomycosis is a relatively common finding in dogs and some other animals in endemic areas. It is not communicable from animals or humans. It is assumed that both animals and humans are infected by inhaling conidia from *Blastomyces* growing in soil. However, direct isolation from soil has been successful only a few times, and the definitive source of infection remains unknown.

4. *PARACOCCIDIOIDES BRASILIENSIS* (*Blastomyces brasiliensis*)

Paracoccidioides brasiliensis is a dimorphic fungus that causes paracoccidioidomycosis in Latin America.

Morphology & Identification

P brasiliensis resembles *B dermatitidis*. The principal difference is that in tissue and in culture at 37 °C, *P brasiliensis* forms thick-walled yeast cells (10–60 µm in tissue) that characteristically have *multiple* buds (Fig 25–19). At room temperature, cultures are mycelial, with small conidia.

Pathogenesis & Clinical Findings

The infective organism is inhaled, and early lesions occur in the lung. Dissemination occurs later, primarily to the spleen, liver, mucous membranes, and skin. Asymptomatic lung infections may be followed by dissemination, with frequent and severe oral mucous membrane lesions. Lymph node enlargement or gastrointestinal disturbances may be the presenting symptom. Histologically, there is either a granuloma with central caseation or microabscess formation. Organisms are frequently seen in giant cells or in pus and are always characterized by their multiple budding.

Skin tests can be performed using "paracoccidioidin," a sterile filtrate of old broth cultures of the

Figure 25–19. *Paracoccidioides brasiliensis*. In tissue or culture at 37 °C; multiple budding.

organism or extracts of the yeast phase. Some cross-reactions may occur with histoplasmin and blastomycin.

Diagnostic Laboratory Tests

These are essentially the same as for *B dermatitidis*. Animal inoculation is best carried out by the intratesticular route; the developing lesion is cultured for the organism. Paracoccidioidin is used as an antigen in serologic tests. The sera of healthy persons living in endemic areas fail to react in CF or precipitin tests. A significant serum antibody titer denotes tissue involvement with the disease, and complement fixation titers of 1:2048 or more occur in active disease. In immunodiffusion tests, 2 well-defined precipitin lines are said to be diagnostic of paracoccidioidomycosis. In such persons the skin test is also positive.

Treatment

Paracoccidioidomycosis is unique among systemic mycoses in its striking response to systemically administered sulfonamides given for many months. Amphotericin B and ketoconazole have been effective in many sulfonamide-resistant patients.

Epidemiology

Paracoccidioidomycosis occurs mainly in rural areas of Latin America, particularly among farmers. The disease manifestations are much more frequent in males than females, but infection occurs equally in both sexes. The fungus has been isolated from soil. The disease is not communicable.

OPPORTUNISTIC MYCOSES

Fungi that usually do not induce disease may do so in persons who have altered host defense mechanisms. Such opportunists may infect any or all organs of the body. The underlying predisposing condition may allow only certain opportunistic fungi or actinomycetes to infect the host. Often there are several organisms infecting a severely compromised patient. *Candida* and other yeasts may be acquired from an endogenous source. Conidia of other fungi are commonly found in the air. Additional opportunists are *Fusarium, Penicillium, Geotrichum, Paecilomyces, Scopulariopsis*, and a number of black molds. Disease caused by known pathogenic fungi is often accelerated by impaired host defense mechanisms.

1. *CANDIDA* & RELATED YEASTS

Candida albicans is an oval, budding yeast that produces a pseudomycelium both in culture and in tissues and exudates. It is a member of the normal flora of the mucous membranes in the respiratory, gastrointestinal, and female genital tracts. In such locations it may gain dominance and be associated with pathologic conditions. Sometimes it produces systemic progressive disease in debilitated or immunosuppressed patients. It may produce bloodstream invasion, thrombophlebitis, endocarditis, or infection of the eyes and other organs when introduced intravenously (tubing, needles, hyperalimentation, narcotic abuse, etc). Other yeasts (eg, *Torulopsis glabrata*) may be pathogenic under similar circumstances.

Morphology & Identification

In smears of exudates, *Candida* appears as a gram-positive, oval, budding yeast, measuring $2-3 \times 4-6 \mu m$, and gram-positive, elongated budding cells resembling hyphae (pseudohyphae) (Fig 25–20). On Sabouraud's agar incubated at room temperature, soft, cream-colored colonies develop that have a yeasty odor. The surface growth consists of oval budding cells. The submerged growth consists of pseu-

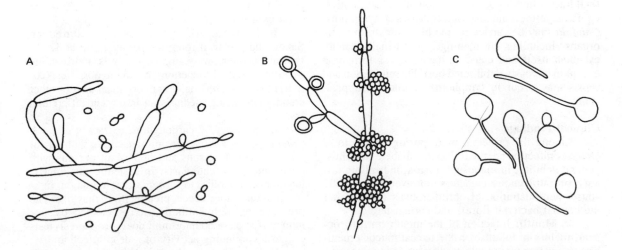

Figure 25–20. *Candida albicans. A:* Blastospores and pseudohyphae in exudate. *B:* Blastospores, pseudohyphae, and conidia in culture at 20 °C. *C:* Young culture forms germ tubes when placed in serum for 3 hours at 37 °C.

domycelium. This is composed of pseudohyphae that form blastospores at the nodes and sometimes chlamydospores terminally. *C albicans* ferments glucose and maltose, producing both acid and gas; produces acid from sucrose; and does not attack lactose. These carbohydrate fermentations, together with colonial and morphologic characteristics, differentiate *C albicans* from the other species of *Candida (Candida krusei, Candida parapsilosis, Candida stellatoidea, Candida tropicalis, Candida pseudotropicalis*, and *Candida guilliermondii)*, which are also occasionally members of normal human flora and occasionally implicated in disease. *Torulopsis glabrata*—an occasional opportunistic pathogen—is a yeast found in the normal vagina, gastrointestinal tract, and soil. Only the budding cells of 24-hour-old cultures of *C albicans* and *C stellatoidea* will form germ tubes in 2–3 hours when placed in serum at 37 °C.

Antigenic Structure

Agglutination tests with absorbed sera show that all *C albicans* strains fall into 2 distinct groups: A and B. Group A appears to be antigenically identical with *C tropicalis*; group B, with *C stellatoidea*. *Candida* extracts for serologic and skin tests appear to consist of mixtures of antigens. They can be detected by precipitation, immunodiffusion, counterimmunoelectrophoresis, and latex agglutination. In disseminated candidiasis, there is a high level of precipitating antibodies against nonmannan antigenic extracts.

Pathogenesis & Pathology

Upon intravenous injection into mice or rabbits, dense suspensions of *C albicans* result in widespread abscesses, particularly in the kidney, and death in less than 1 week.

Histologically, the various skin lesions in humans show inflammatory changes. Some resemble abscess formation; others resemble chronic granuloma. Large numbers of *Candida* are sometimes found in the intestinal tract following administration of oral antibiotics, eg, tetracyclines, but this usually causes no symptoms. *Candida* may be carried by the bloodstream to many organs, including the meninges, but usually cannot establish itself and cause miliary abscess formation except in a grossly debilitated host. Dissemination and sepsis may occur in lymphoma or immunosuppression.

Clinical Findings

Among the principal predisposing factors to *C albicans* infection are the following: diabetes mellitus, general debility, immunosuppression, indwelling urinary or intravenous catheters, intravenous narcotic abuse, administration of antimicrobials (which alter the normal bacterial flora), and corticosteroids.

A. Mouth: Infection of the mouth (thrush) occurs, mainly in infants, on the buccal mucous membranes and appears as white adherent patches consisting largely of pseudomycelium and desquamated epithelium, with only minimal erosion of the membrane. Growth of *Candida* in saliva is enhanced by glucose, antibiotics, and corticosteroids.

B. Female Genitalia: Vulvovaginitis resembles thrush but produces irritation, intense itching, and discharge. Its development is favored by alkaline pH. It is counteracted normally by vaginal bacteria. Diabetes, pregnancy, progesterone, or antibiotic therapy predisposes to disease.

C. Skin: Infection of the skin occurs principally in moist, warm parts of the body, such as the axilla, intergluteal folds, groin, or inframammary folds; it is most common in obese and diabetic individuals. These areas become red and weeping and may develop vesicles.

Candida infection of the interdigital webs of the hands is seen most frequently following repeated prolonged immersion in water; it is most common in homemakers, cooks, vegetable and fish handlers, etc.

D. Nails: Painful, reddened swelling of the nail fold, resembling a pyogenic paronychia, may lead to thickening and transverse grooving of the nails and eventual loss of the nail.

E. Lungs and Other Organs: *Candida* infection may be a secondary invader of lungs, kidneys, and other organs where a preexisting disease is present (eg, tuberculosis or cancer). In uncontrolled leukemia and in immunosuppressed or surgical patients, candidal lesions may occur in many organs. *Candida* endocarditis (often due to *C parapsilosis)* occurs particularly in narcotic addicts or on prosthetic valves.

F. Chronic Mucocutaneous Candidiasis: This disorder is a sign of deficiency of cellular immunity.

Diagnostic Laboratory Tests

Specimens consist of swabs and scrapings from surface lesions, sputum, exudates, and material from removed intravenous catheters.

A. Microscopic Examination: Sputum, exudates, thrombi, etc, may be examined in gram-stained smears for pseudohyphae and budding cells. Skin or nail scrapings are first placed in a drop of 10% potassium hydroxide.

B. Culture: All specimens are cultured on Sabouraud's agar at room temperature and at 37 °C; typical colonies are examined for cells and budding pseudomycelia. Production of chlamydospores (conidia) of *C albicans* on either corn meal agar or other conidia-enhancing media is an important differential test.

C. Serology: A carbohydrate extract of group A *Candida* gives positive precipitin reactions with sera of 50% of normal persons and of 70% of persons with mucocutaneous candidiasis. In systemic candidiasis, the titer of antibodies to *Candida* (agglutination, indirect immunofluorescence, precipitation) may rise. The presence of high antibody titers detected by immunodiffusion or counterimmunoelectrophoresis tests suggests continuing activity of a deep infection.

D. Skin Test: A *Candida* test is almost universally positive in normal adults. It is therefore used as an indicator of competent cellular immunity.

Immunity

Animals can be immunized actively and are then resistant to disseminated candidiasis. Human sera often contain IgG antibody that clumps *Candida* in vitro and may be candidacidal.

Treatment

Orally administered nystatin does not reach tissues and thus is of no avail in disseminated *Candida* infections. Soluble amphotericin B (0.4–0.8 mg/kg/d intravenously), alone or in combination with flucytosine, has been successful in some patients.

Mucocutaneous candidiasis in immunodeficient individuals has occasionally responded to the administration of transfer factor (see p 179).

Oral ketoconazole, 200–400 mg/d, has given good results in some systemic *Candida* infections, including chronic mucocutaneous candidiasis.

Local lesions are best treated by removing the cause, ie, avoiding moisture; keeping areas cool, powdered, and dry; and withdrawing antibiotics. There is no convincing evidence that vaccine therapy is effective. Various chemicals have been employed with more or less success, eg, 1% gentian violet for thrush and parahydroxybenzoic acid esters, sodium propionate, candicidin, or 2% miconazole for vaginitis. Nystatin suppresses intestinal and vaginal candidiasis.

Epidemiology & Control

The most important preventive measure is to avoid interfering with the normal balance of microbial flora and with normal host defenses. *Candida* infection is not communicable, since most individuals harbor the organism under normal circumstances.

2. CRYPTOCOCCUS NEOFORMANS

Cryptococcus neoformans is a yeast characterized by a wide carbohydrate capsule both in culture and in tissue fluids. It occurs widely in nature and is found in very large numbers in dry pigeon feces. Human disease is usually opportunistic.

Morphology & Identification

In spinal fluid or tissue, the organism is round or ovoid, 4–12 μm in diameter, often budding, and surrounded by a wide capsule (Fig 25–21). On Sabouraud's agar at room temperature, the cream-colored colonies are shiny and mucoid. Cultures do not ferment carbohydrates but assimilate glucose, maltose, sucrose, and galactose (but not lactose). Urea is hydrolyzed. In contrast to nonpathogenic cryptococci, *C neoformans* grows well at 37 °C on most laboratory media provided they do not contain cycloheximide. Mating of serotypes A and D or B and C gives rise to mycelia and basidiospores of *Filobasidiella neoformans* or *Filobasidiella bacillispora*.

Antigenic Structure

Four serologic types of capsular polysaccha-rides—A, B, C, and D—have been identified. The capsular antigen may be dissolved in spinal fluid, serum, or urine and can be detected by specific antisera through CF, counterimmunoelectrophoresis, or latex agglutination tests (particles coated with antibody). Several serologic tests also can detect antipolysaccharide antibodies. The presence of these antibodies does not denote increased resistance to recurrence.

Pathogenesis

Infection in humans occurs via the respiratory tract and is either asymptomatic or associated with nonspecific pulmonary signs and symptoms. Very massive inhalation of cells may result in progressive systemic disease in a normal person. Usually, however, cryptococcosis is an opportunistic infection. In immunodeficient or immunosuppressed persons, the pulmonary infection may disseminate systemically and establish itself in the central nervous system and other organs.

Histologically, the reaction varies from mild inflammation to formation of typical granulomas.

Clinical Findings

Infection with *C neoformans* may remain subclinical. The commonest clinical manifestation is a slowly developing chronic meningitis with frequent spontaneous remissions and exacerbations. The meningitis may resemble a brain tumor, brain abscess, degenerative central nervous system disease, or any mycobacterial or fungal meningitis. Cerebrospinal fluid pressure and protein content may be greatly increased and the cell count elevated, whereas the sugar content is normal or low. In addition, there may be lesions of skin, lungs, or other organs.

The course of cryptococcal meningitis may fluctuate over long periods, but ultimately all untreated cases are fatal. The disease is not communicable.

Diagnostic Laboratory Tests

Specimens consist of spinal fluid, exudates, sputum, urine, and serum.

A. Microscopic Examination: Specimens are

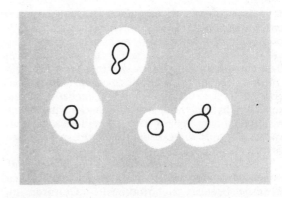

Figure 25–21. *Cryptococcus neoformans.* India ink preparation of spinal fluid.

examined in wet mount, both directly and after mixing with India ink (which makes the large capsule stand out around the budding cell). Immunofluorescent stain is applied to dried smears. Filtration of cerebrospinal fluid through Millipore filters may reveal the organism.

B. Culture: Growth is rapid at 20–37 °C on Sabouraud's agar and other laboratory media provided they do not contain cycloheximide. Urea is hydrolyzed. *C neoformans* colonies produce brown pigment on media that contain substrate for phenol oxidase. Cultured cells should be injected into mice to determine their pathogenicity. (Intraperitoneal or intracerebral injection of *C neoformans* into mice results in a fatal infection from which organisms can be isolated and grown in pure culture.)

C. Serology: Tests for both antigen and antibody can be performed on cerebrospinal fluid and serum. Latex slide agglutination or immunoelectrophoresis reveals antigen. Detection of antigen is diagnostically important. With effective treatment the antigen titer drops. Antibody agglutinates cryptococcal yeast cells or antigen-coated particles.

Treatment

Flucytosine (150 mg/kg/d orally) is effective against many strains of *Cryptococcus*, but resistant mutants may emerge. Amphotericin B (0.4–0.8 mg/kg/d) can also be effective but has many toxic side-effects. The combination of the 2 drugs is given for meningitis for several months, often resulting in prolonged remission. Oral ketoconazole may also be promising.

Epidemiology & Control

Bird droppings containing *C neoformans* are the major source of infection for animals and humans. The organism grows luxuriantly in pigeon excreta, but the birds are not infected. One method of control is reduction of the pigeon population and site decontamination with alkali.

3. ASPERGILLOSIS

Broadly defined, aspergillosis is a group of mycoses with diverse causes and pathogenesis. *Aspergillus fumigatus* is a ubiquitous mold found on decaying vegetation. It may colonize and then invade tissues in the traumatized cornea, burns, wounds, or external ear (otitis externa). It and other *Aspergillus* species become opportunistic invaders in immunodeficient persons or individuals with anatomic abnormalities of the respiratory tract (pulmonary aspergillosis). Various species of *Aspergillus* produce aflatoxins in foods (see p 101).

In tissues, exudates, or sputum, *Aspergillus* species occur as filamentous, septate structures that usually branch dichotomously. Cultures on Sabouraud's agar incubated at 37–40 °C grow as gray–green colonies with a central dome of co-

nidiophores. The latter support characteristic radiating chains of conidia (Fig 25–9). Extracts of cultures are used as antigens in serologic tests, especially in immunodiffusion and immunofluorescence. Divergent results occur in different forms of disease.

Pulmonary aspergillosis may occur in distinct forms. One is a "fungus ball" growing in a preexisting cavity (eg, tuberculous cavity, paranasal sinus, bronchiectasis) in which the *Aspergillus* does not invade tissue. Such patients usually require only treatment for the underlying disorder. They may give significant antibody responses to *Aspergillus* antigens.

A second form is an actively invasive granuloma with *Aspergillus* spreading in the lung, giving rise to necrotizing pneumonia, hemoptysis, and secondary dissemination to other organs. This occurs mainly in immunodeficient or immunosuppressed persons and requires active antifungal drug therapy with flucytosine and amphotericin B. A third form is allergic pulmonary aspergillosis, with asthma, eosinophilia, high serum IgE, and only minimal tissue invasion but abnormal bronchograms. *Aspergillus* antibodies may be demonstrable but have little diagnostic value.

Diagnosis of aspergillosis rests most securely on demonstration of hyphal fragments in tissue biopsies by methenamine-silver stain. Treatment of invasive aspergillosis in immunosuppressed patients is only marginally successful. The same applies to the rare postsurgical *Aspergillus* endophthalmitis that usually leads to rapid loss of the infected eye.

Other fungi that may invade tissues in an immunoincompetent host and produce hyphae that resemble *Aspergillus* species include *Petriellidium, Fusarium,* and *Curvularia,* among others. These may produce disease states resembling the several forms of aspergillosis.

4. ZYGOMYCOSIS
(Mucormycosis, Phycomycosis)

Saprophytic zygomycetes (eg, *Mucor, Rhizopus*) are occasionally found in the tissues of compromised hosts. In persons suffering from diabetes mellitus (particularly with acidosis), extensive burns, leukemia, lymphoma, or other chronic illness or immunosuppression, *Rhizopus* species, *Mucor* species, and other zygomycetes invade and proliferate in the walls of blood vessels, producing thrombosis. This occurs commonly in paranasal sinuses, the lungs, and the gastrointestinal tract and results in ischemic necrosis of surrounding tissue with an intense polymorphonuclear infiltrate.

The organisms are rarely cultured during life but are seen in histologic preparations of tissues as broad, *nonseptate,* irregular hyphae in thrombosed vessels or sinuses with surrounding leukocytic and giant cell response.

In zygomycosis diagnosed during life, intense therapy of the underlying disorder accompanied by systemic amphotericin B therapy and in some cases surgical removal of infected tissue has resulted in remissions and occasional cure.

ACTINOMYCETES

The actinomycetes are a heterogeneous group of filamentous bacteria related to corynebacteria and mycobacteria and superficially resembling fungi. Characteristically, they grow as gram-positive, branching organisms that tend to fragment into bacterialike pieces. Some actinomycetes are acid-fast. Most are free-living, particularly in soil. The anaerobic species are part of the normal flora of the mouth. Some of the aerobic species found in soil (*Nocardia, Streptomyces*) may cause disease in humans and animals.

1. ACTINOMYCOSIS

Actinomycosis is a chronic suppurative disease that spreads by direct extension, forms draining sinus tracts, and is caused by *Actinomyces israelii* and related anaerobic filamentous bacteria, including *Arachnia* species. These form part of the normal flora of the oral cavity, and it is not clear what transforms carriage of the organisms into invasive disease. When they invade tissues, *Actinomyces* species are often associated with other oral bacteria. *Actinomyces bovis* causes "lumpy jaw" in cattle.

Morphology & Identification

In tissue, *Actinomyces* species occur as branching filaments surrounded by suppurating, fibrosing inflammation. The typical finding is a "sulfur granule" in pus (Fig 25–22). It consists of a colony of gram-positive mycelial filaments surrounded by eosinophilic "clubs." The latter may be antigen-antibody complexes.

A. Typical Organism: When a sulfur granule in pus is washed and crushed, it reveals a tangled mass of filaments that readily breaks up into coccoid or bacillary forms which are gram-positive and non–acid-fast and show characteristic V or Y branching.

B. Culture: "Sulfur granules" or other pus containing *Actinomyces* can be washed and inoculated into thioglycolate liquid medium, streaked onto brain-heart infusion agar, and incubated anaerobically at 37 °C. In thioglycolate, *A israelii* grows as fluffy balls near the bottom of the tube, whereas *A bovis* produces general turbidity. On solid media, *A israelii* produces small "spidery" colonies in 2–3 days that become white, heaped-up, irregular, or sometimes smooth, larger colonies in 10 days. Other species may have different colony forms.

C. Growth Characteristics: Of the 3 species most commonly responsible for actinomycosis, *A israelii* does not hydrolyze starch but ferments xylose and mannitol, whereas *A bovis* hydrolyzes starch but does not ferment these sugars. *Arachnia propionica* yields large amounts of propionic acid. Most *Actinomyces* species are nonhemolytic, nonproteolytic, and catalase-negative.

Antigenic Structure

Gel diffusion methods may be used to differentiate *A israelii* from *A bovis* and other filamentous anaerobes that may produce granules in tissues. Species-specific antigens (mainly polysaccharides from the cell wall) occur in acetone extracts of culture supernate. There are at least 2 serotypes of *A israelii*.

Pathogenesis & Pathology

Typical *A israelii* can be found on teeth and in tonsillar crypts of most normal persons. It is likely that trauma (eg, tooth extraction), pyogenic or necrotizing bacterial infection, or aspiration precipitates clinical actinomycosis.

The typical lesion consists of an abscess with central necrosis, surrounded by granulation tissue and fibrous tissue; the pus often contains "sulfur granules" and may drain to the outside through sinuses. Histologically, the lesions are not typical unless sulfur granules can be found or *Actinomyces* cultured. In early lesions a mixed bacterial flora is often seen.

Clinical Findings

The characteristic appearance of actinomycosis is a hard, red, relatively nontender swelling that usually develops slowly. It becomes fluctuant, points to a

A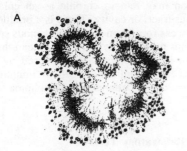
B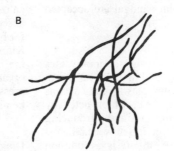
C

Figure 25–22. *Actinomyces israelii.* **A:** Sulfur granule in pus. **B:** In broth culture. **C:** Diphtheroidlike and branching in agar culture.

surface, and eventually drains, forming a chronic sinus tract with little tendency to heal. Lesions extend by contiguity. Dissemination via the bloodstream is very rare.

In about half of cases of actinomycosis, the initial lesion is cervicofacial, involving the face, neck, tongue, or mandible. About one-fifth of cases show predominant involvement of lungs (thoracic actinomycosis), with abscesses or empyema. In a similar number, the primary lesion is in the cecum, appendix, or pelvic organs and may develop multiple draining fistulas (abdominal actinomycosis). *A israelii, A propionica,* and other species may cause similar disease.

Diagnostic Laboratory Tests

Animal inoculation, skin tests, and serologic tests are not useful. Specimens consist of pus from lesions, sinus tracts, or fistulas and sputum or tissue biopsy material.

A. Microscopic Examination: Every effort must be made to find "sulfur granules." These are rinsed, crushed, examined, and cultured. The appearance in wet mount of the central mycelium and peripheral clubs is characteristic (Fig 25–22). If no granules are found, stained smears of gram-positive branching rods and filaments are suggestive.

B. Culture: Material inoculated into thioglycolate medium and streaked onto brain-heart infusion blood agar plates must be incubated anaerobically for at least 2 weeks. The cultures are examined intermittently for characteristic morphology.

Immunity

Actinomyces are part of the normal body flora. It is uncertain whether antibodies or cell-mediated reactions are produced until tissue invasion occurs. Eosinophilic clubs are not present on granules found in tonsillar crypts; these eosinophilic reactions in tissue granules may denote an antigen-antibody complex.

Treatment

Prolonged administration of penicillin, 5–10 million units daily, is effective in many cases. However, drugs may penetrate poorly into the abscesses, and some of the tissue destruction may be irreversible. Surgical drainage and surgical removal are accepted forms of treatment.

Epidemiology

Because of the many free-living actinomycetes and the occurrence of "lumpy jaw" in cattle, it was at one time believed that actinomycosis in humans was acquired from grasses, straws, etc, which acted by traumatizing the mucous membranes and introducing the causative organism. However, it is now established that potentially pathogenic *A israelii* is a common inhabitant of mucous membranes in the mouth, so that no introduction from the outside need be postulated. The disease is never communicable.

Most isolates from human sources are *A israelii*; most isolates from bovine sources are *A bovis*.

2. NOCARDIOSIS

Nocardia species and *Streptomyces* species are aerobic organisms that occur in soil. *Nocardia asteroides* and *Nocardia brasiliensis* are the main causes of nocardiosis, an opportunistic human pulmonary disease that may spread to other parts of the body. These organisms may also produce mycetoma (see p 292).

Morphology & Identification

N asteroides has thin, gram-positive, branching filaments that may fragment into bacillary or coccoid forms. Many isolates are acid-fast when decolorized with 1% sulfuric acid. Bacillary and filamentous forms may be seen in tissue exudates or in pus. Granules similar to those in actinomycosis or mycetoma are never seen, although filamentous clusters and colonies may occur. *Streptomyces* are not acid-fast and do not fragment into bacillary forms.

Nocardia species grow aerobically on many simple media. Growth is variable and slow. Colonies are waxy, with pigmentation varying from yellow to orange or red. White aerial hyphae may form over the surface of the colony. Sporulation occurs by fragmentation into arthrospores. *N asteroides* will not grow in gelatin media and is unable to digest casein, peptonize milk, or ferment carbohydrates. *N brasiliensis* gives positive results in all these tests. All nocardiae are urease-positive. Chromatographic identification of cell wall constituents is used to differentiate species.

Antigenic Structure

Diagnostic and prognostic serologic tests have not yet been developed. Filtrates from *Nocardia* growth in broth can serve as antigen in CF reactions. Antibodies occur in disease, but false-positive reactions occur in mycobacterial infections. Nocardiae and mycobacteria evidently share antigens.

Pathogenesis & Clinical Findings

Nocardiosis begins as a pulmonary infection that may be subclinical or produce pneumonia. The localized lesion may remain chronic as an enlarging abscess, sinus tract, or cavity. There is a predilection for brain abscess formation by hematogenous spread. Kidney lesions may also develop and extend through the cortex to the medulla. Disease caused by these organisms is most commonly seen in immunosuppressed patients or in patients with lymphoma or leukemia.

Diagnostic Laboratory Tests

Specimens consist of sputum, pus, spinal fluid, and biopsy material. Serologic tests are unreliable at present. Sonicated extracts of *Nocardia* species may give precipitin lines with sera of infected persons in immunodiffusion tests.

A. Microscopic Examination: Gram-stained smears show coccal and bacillary forms or tangled masses of branching rods. Some strains are partially acid-fast.

B. Culture: *Nocardia* species grow on most laboratory media but may be inhibited by the presence of antibacterial quantities of antibiotics in the media. Guinea pigs, mice, and rabbits are susceptible to experimental infection.

C. Tissue Sections: Nocardiae are stained by methenamine-silver stain.

Treatment

The sulfonamides are currently the drugs of choice; minocycline is also effective. Surgical drainage or resection may be required. Treatment of the underlying disorder should be attempted.

Epidemiology

Potentially pathogenic nocardiae are ubiquitous in soil and probably enter the body by the respiratory route or through breaks in the skin. Infections in dogs, other pets, and farm animals are fairly common. Mastitis in dairy cattle is at times widespread. Nocardiosis is not communicable.

• • •

HYPERSENSITIVITY TO FUNGI

In the course of many fungal infections, delayed type hypersensitivity develops to one or more antigens of the fungus. This is true whether the organism grows as a saprophyte (see *Aspergillus*) or as an invasive opportunist and whether it grows on surfaces, in cavities, or in tissues. The inhalation of actinomycetes or molds growing in the environment may cause an allergic pneumonitis (see Chapter 13). Hypersensitivity evidenced by positive skin tests with fungal extracts may be helpful in diagnosis, but such skin tests are often negative in persons with disseminated systemic involvement. The return of a positive skin test reaction may be a sign of effective chemotherapy and of improved prognosis.

MYCOTOXINS

Many fungi produce poisonous substances called mycotoxins that can cause acute or chronic intoxication and damage. Ingestion of poisonous mushrooms (eg, *Amanita phalloides*) may cause severe damage to liver, kidney, or bone marrow. Chronic damage or neoplasms may be induced in animals or humans following ingestion of small quantities of toxin or contaminated food (eg, aflatoxin from *Aspergillus flavus*). Derivatives of fungal products (eg, LSD) may cause profound mental derangement.

• • •

References

Aisner J et al: Treatment of invasive aspergillosis: Relation of early diagnosis and treatment to response. *Ann Intern Med* 1977;**86**:539.

Beaman BL et al: Nocardial infections in the United States, 1972–1974. *J Infect Dis* 1976;**134**:286.

Bennett JE: Chemotherapy of systemic mycoses. (2 parts.) *N Engl J Med* 1974;**290**:30, 320.

Bennett JE et al: A comparison of amphotericin B alone and combined with flucytosine in the treatment of cryptococcal meningitis. *N Engl J Med* 1979;**301**:126.

Curry WA: Human nocardiosis: A clinical review with selected case reports. *Arch Intern Med* 1980;**140**:818.

Davies SF et al: Disseminated histoplasmosis in immunologically suppressed patients in a non-endemic area. *Am J Med* 1978;**64**:94.

Davis WA et al: Disseminated *Petriellidium boydii* and pacemaker endocarditis. *Am J Med* 1980;**69**:929.

Dean AG et al: Outbreak of histoplasmosis at an Arkansas courthouse, with 5 cases of probable reinfection. *Am J Epidemiol* 1978;**108**:36.

Drutz DJ, Catanzaro A: Coccidioidomycosis. (2 parts.) *Am Rev Respir Dis* 1978;**117**:559, 727.

Emmons CW et al: *Medical Mycology*, 3rd ed. Lea & Febiger, 1977.

Flynn NM et al: An unusual outbreak of windborne coccidioidomycosis. *N Engl J Med* 1979;**301**:358.

Fraser DW et al: Aspergillosis and other systemic mycoses: The growing problem. *JAMA* 1979;**242**:1631.

Goodwin RA, DesPrez RM: Histoplasmosis. *Am Rev Respir Dis* 1978;**117**:929.

Holmberg K, Berdischewsky M, Young LS: Serologic immunodiagnosis of invasive aspergillosis. *J Infect Dis* 1980;**141**:656.

Kammer RB, Utz JP: *Aspergillus* species endocarditis: The new face of a not so rare disease. *Am J Med* 1974;**56**:506.

Kozinn PJ et al: The precipitin test in systemic candidiasis. *JAMA* 1976;**235**:628.

Levine HB et al: Spherulin and coccidioidin: Cross-reactions in dermal sensitivity to histoplasmin and paracoccidioidin. *Am J Epidemiol* 1975;**101**:512.

Lewis JL, Rabinovich S: The wide spectrum of cryptococcal infections. *Am J Med* 1972;**53**:315.

Lilien LD et al: *Candida albicans* meningitis in a premature neonate successfully treated with 5-fluorocytosine and amphotericin B. *Pediatrics* 1978;**61**:57.

Medoff G, Kobayashi GS: Strategies in the treatment of systemic fungal infections. *N Engl J Med* 1980;**302**:145.

Palmer DL et al: Diagnostic and therapeutic considerations in *Nocardia asteroides* infection. *Medicine* 1974;**53**:391.

Pankey GA, Daloviso JR: Fungemia caused by *Torulopsis glabrata*. *Medicine* 1973;**52**:395.

Peeters F et al: Observations on candidal vaginitis. *Am J Obstet Gynecol* 1972;**112**:80.

Pennington JE: *Aspergillus* lung disease. *Med Clin North Am* 1980;**64**:475.

Restrepo A, Stevens DA, Utz JP (editors): Symposium on ketoconazole. *Rev Infect Dis* 1980;**2**:519.

Restrepo A et al: The gamut of paracoccidioidomycosis. *Am J Med* 1976;**61**:33.

Sarosi GA, Davies SF: Blastomycosis. *Am Rev Respir Dis* 1979; **120**:911.

Satir AA et al: Systemic phycomycosis. *Br Med J* 1971;**1**:440.

Shainhouse JZ et al: Complement fixation antibody test for human nocardiosis. *J Clin Microbiol* 1978;**8**:516.

Varkey B, Rose HD: Pulmonary aspergilloma. *Am J Med* 1976;**61**:626.

Weese WC, Smith IM: Study of 57 cases of actinomycosis over a 36-year period. *Arch Intern Med* 1975;**135**:1562.

Young RC et al: Fungemia with compromised host resistance: A study of 70 cases. *Ann Intern Med* 1974;**80**:605.

Diagnostic medical microbiology is concerned (1) with the etiologic diagnosis of infectious disease by means of the isolation and identification of infectious agents and the demonstration of immunologic responses (antibody, skin reactivity) in the patient; and (2) with the rational selection of antimicrobial therapy and dosage on the basis of laboratory tests.

In the field of infectious diseases, the results of laboratory tests depend largely on the quality of the specimen, the timing of its collection and the care with which it is collected, and the technical proficiency and experience of the laboratory personnel. Although any general physician should be competent to perform a few simple, crucial microbiologic tests—make and stain a smear, examine it microscopically, and streak a culture plate—the technical details of the more involved procedures are usually left to the bacteriologist or virologist and the technicians on the staff. Any physician who deals with infectious processes must know when and how to take a specimen, what laboratory examinations to request, and how to interpret the results.

COMMUNICATION BETWEEN PHYSICIAN & LABORATORY

When a physician sends a blood specimen to the laboratory and requests a chemical determination, the laboratory has no alternative but to employ a single chemical procedure and report the result to the physician. Although that value may be reported higher or lower depending upon variations in the specimen, in the skill and experience of the technician, and in the equipment at hand in the laboratory, the physician generally accepts that value and takes it into account in making the clinical diagnosis. Little would be gained, in this situation, by further communication between the physician and the laboratory.

In microbiologic laboratory diagnosis, the situation is different. No one method is available that will permit the isolation of all possible pathogenic organisms or differentiate them from nonpathogenic ones. Before the laboratory personnel can select the one technique best suited to the isolation of one or another organism, the physician must inform the laboratory of the tentative clinical diagnosis and of the type of infection suspected. This forces the clinician to reason more closely than if "infection" were suspected and all attempts at etiologic diagnosis merely deferred until the laboratory results were returned. Clinical information from the physician can often aid the laboratory in selecting the best methods available for the identification of a causative agent.

In contrast with chemical determinations, microbiologic laboratory procedures are often slow, requiring a series of sequential steps before the answer is reached. Many pathogenic microorganisms grow slowly, and days or even weeks may elapse before their identification. However, it is almost never possible to defer treatment until this laborious process is complete. It is therefore essential that the physician obtain proper specimens, inform the laboratory of the tentative clinical diagnosis, and then begin appropriate treatment with drugs aimed at the organism thought to be responsible for the patient's illness. As the laboratory begins to derive information of clinical significance, it can feed it back to the physician, who can then reevaluate the diagnosis, along with the clinical course of the patient, and perhaps make changes in the therapeutic program. This "feedback" information will consist of preliminary reports of the results of individual steps in the isolation and identification of the causative agent.

SPECIMENS

The results of many diagnostic tests in infectious diseases depend largely upon the selection, timing, and method of collection of specimens. These factors are often more crucial for microbiologic specimens than for those designed to yield chemical data. Microbial agents grow and die, are susceptible to many chemicals, and can be found at different anatomic sites and in different body fluids and tissues during the natural history of most infectious disorders. In general, the successful isolation of an infectious agent carries much more diagnostic weight in the formulation of a diagnosis than failure to do so. Therefore, the specimen must be obtained from the site most likely to yield the infectious agent at that particular stage of illness and must be handled in such a way as to favor survival and growth of the agent. For each type of specimen, suggestions for optimal handling are given in the following paragraphs.

Recovery of an infectious agent is most significant if the agent is isolated from a site normally devoid of microorganisms. Any type of microorganism cultured from blood, cerebrospinal fluid, or joint fluid or from the pleural cavity is a significant diagnostic finding. Conversely, many parts of the body have a normal microbial flora that may be altered by endogenous or exogenous influences. The recovery of potentially pathogenic microorganisms from the respiratory, gastrointestinal, or genitourinary tracts; from wounds; or from the skin must be considered in the context of the normal flora of each particular site. The situation is often further complicated by the presence of mixtures of different microorganisms, each of which may or may not participate in a disease process of that particular tissue. Correlation of bacteriologic information with medical experience is then required to arrive at a meaningful interpretation of the results.

A few general rules apply to all specimens:

(1) A sufficient quantity of specimen must be provided to permit thorough study.

(2) The sample should be representative of the infectious process (eg, sputum, not saliva; pus from the underlying lesion, not from its sinus tract; a swab from the depth of the wound, not from its surface).

(3) Care must be taken to avoid contamination of the specimen by using only sterile equipment and aseptic precautions.

(4) The specimen must be taken to the laboratory and examined promptly. Special transport media may be helpful.

(5) Meaningful specimens must be secured before antimicrobial drugs are administered. If antimicrobial drugs are given before specimens are taken for microbiologic study, drug therapy may have to be stopped and repeat specimens obtained several days later.

The above comments apply particularly to specimens intended for the isolation of bacterial or fungal agents. The isolation of viruses, rickettsiae, or chlamydiae is usually performed only in specialized laboratories. Specimens are often shipped to such laboratories in well-stoppered containers packed in dry ice. All specimens must be accurately labeled and accompanied by adequate instructions, a clearly worded statement of the information desired, and background information.

The type of specimen to be examined is determined by the presenting clinical picture. If symptoms or signs point to involvement of one organ system, specimens are obtained from that source. In the absence of localizing signs or symptoms, repeated blood samples for culturing are taken first. Specimens from other sites are then considered in sequence, depending in part upon the likelihood of involvement of a given organ system in a given patient and in part upon the ease of obtaining the specimen.

SELECTION OF LABORATORY INVESTIGATIONS

Diagnostic tests in infectious diseases fall into 4 classes:

(1) The demonstration of an infectious agent (bacterial, mycotic, viral, protozoal, or helminthic) in specimens obtained from the patient.

(2) The demonstration of a meaningful antibody response in the patient. This frequently involves proof of a rise in specific antibody titer, and therefore requires 2 serum specimens usually obtained at an interval of 10–20 days or longer.

(3) The demonstration of meaningful cell-mediated responses or skin tests to antigens associated with a particular infectious agent.

(4) The demonstration of deviations in a variety of clinical laboratory determinations that nonspecifically suggest or support a suspicion of infectious diseases.

In the following paragraphs, some important applications of these principal classes of tests will be described.

THE DEMONSTRATION OF AN INFECTIOUS AGENT

Laboratory examinations usually include microscopic study of fresh unstained and stained materials and preparation of cultures under environmental conditions that are suitable for growth of a wide variety of microorganisms, including the type of organism most suspect on clinical grounds. If a microorganism is seen or isolated, the physician is notified of its preliminary identification. Complete identification may then be pursued by bacteriologic, mycologic, immunologic, or other techniques. Isolated microorganisms may be tested for susceptibility to antimicrobial drugs or combinations of drugs. In certain types of diseases, assay of antibacterial activity in the patient's serum or urine during treatment may be more informative than drug susceptibility tests (see Chapter 10 and p 318). In all cases in which significant pathogenic microorganisms are isolated before treatment, follow-up examinations during and after treatment are mandatory.

Blood

In the febrile ill patient, with or without localizing signs or symptoms, blood culture is the most useful and most frequently performed test for the detection of systemic infection due to bacteria. Proof of bacteremia is also essential in all persons suspected of having infective endocarditis even when they do not appear acutely or severely ill. In addition to its diagnostic significance, recovery of an infectious agent from the blood provides invaluable aid in guiding antimicrobial therapy. Every effort should therefore be made to isolate the causative organism in bacteremia.

In healthy persons, properly obtained blood cultures remain sterile. Although microorganisms from the normal respiratory and gastrointestinal flora enter the blood occasionally, they are rapidly removed by the reticuloendothelial system. These transients rarely affect the interpretation of blood culture results. If a blood culture yields microorganisms, this fact is of great clinical significance provided that technical error can be excluded. Proper technique in performing the procedure is therefore all-important.

Tissues, tissue fluids, or reducing substances must be used in such a way that the bottom part of the blood culture bottle will provide sufficiently low oxygen tension to permit growth of anaerobes while the top part permits growth of aerobes.

The following rules, rigidly applied, yield reliable results:

(1) Use only sterile equipment and strict aseptic technique.

(2) Apply a tourniquet and locate a fixed vein by touch to minimize probing after insertion of the needle.

(3) Prepare the skin by applying 2% tincture of iodine in widening circles, beginning with the site of proposed skin puncture. Remove iodine with 70% alcohol. Do not touch the skin with the fingers after it has been prepared.

(4) Perform venipuncture and withdraw 10–15 mL of blood.

(5) Add blood to a flask containing 50–100 mL of a rich nutrient medium that will permit the growth of fastidious organisms, eg, trypticase soy broth with 0.05% sodium polyanethol sulfonate, which has anticoagulant and anticomplement properties and inactivates some antimicrobials, such as aminoglycosides.

(6) Take specimens to the laboratory promptly.

In the laboratory, the blood culture bottles are incubated at 37 °C for up to 2 weeks. They are examined for bacterial growth every 2–3 days by inspection, smears, and subcultures. Anaerobic subcultures may be indicated.

In general, there is no significant advantage in arterial over the usual venous blood specimens.

If microorganisms grow from blood cultures, it then becomes necessary to determine their significance by ruling out technical error. Although it is not possible to state conclusively that any given positive blood culture does not reflect bacteremia, the following criteria may be helpful in differentiating "true" positives from contaminated specimens:

(1) Growth of the same type of organism in repeated cultures obtained from separate sites: bacteremia.

(2) Small numbers of several different organisms: suggestive of contamination.

(3) Common skin flora (white staphylococci [*Staphylococcus epidermidis*], diphtheroids [*Propionibacterium*]) occurring in only one of several cultures: suggestive of contamination. (The presence of such organisms in more than one culture, or in the presence of a vascular prosthesis, enhances the likelihood of clinically significant bacteremia.)

(4) "Expected" organisms (eg, viridans streptococci or enterococci in suspected endocarditis) are more apt to be etiologically significant than organisms commonly found as contaminants.

The number of blood specimens that should be drawn for cultures and the period of time over which this should be done depend upon the severity of the clinical illness. In hyperacute sepsis, only 2 or 3 blood cultures can be taken in as many hours before antimicrobial therapy, based on the clinician's "best guess" regarding etiology, is begun. On the other hand, with a chronically ill patient who has suspected endocarditis, 2 cultures may be taken daily for 3 days before drugs are administered. In patients who eventually yield positive blood cultures, growth is usually obtained in the first few cultures taken, although there may be much delay until growth becomes evident. About 90–95% of positive blood cultures in proved cases of infective endocarditis are encountered among the first 5 cultures taken. Consequently, it is reasonable to begin treatment after 5–6 specimens have been obtained.

Virtually every microorganism other than viruses, rickettsiae, and chlamydiae has been grown in blood culture at some time. The following are most commonly found: viridans streptococci; *Streptococcus faecalis;* staphylococci (*Staphylococcus aureus* and others); gram-negative enteric bacteria, including *Escherichia coli, Enterobacter aerogenes,* and *Klebsiella pneumoniae; Proteus* species; *Pseudomonas* species; pneumococci; meningococci; gonococci; *Bacteroides;* salmonellae; brucellae; pasteurellae; *Haemophilus influenzae;* vibrios; leptospirae; *Candida;* and others.

In most types of bacteremia listed above, examination of direct blood smears contributes little. However, in some microbial infections (eg, anthrax, plague, relapsing fever) and parasitic infections (eg, malaria, trypanosomiasis), the etiologic organism can be detected in stained blood films. In some infections (eg, rickettsioses, leptospirosis, spirillosis, psittacosis), inoculation of blood into experimental animals may give positive results more readily than culture.

Urine

At present, bacteriologic examination of the urine is done mainly when signs or symptoms point to urinary tract infection, renal insufficiency, or hypertension. It should always be done in persons with suspected systemic infection or fever of unknown origin. It is desirable for every woman in the first trimester of pregnancy.

Urine secreted in the kidney is sterile unless the kidney is infected. Uncontaminated bladder urine is also normally sterile. The urethra, however, contains a normal flora, so that normal voided urine contains small numbers of bacteria. Because it is necessary to distinguish contaminating from etiologically important organisms, only *quantitative* urine examination can yield meaningful results.

The following steps are essential in proper urine examination:

A. Proper Collection of Specimen: Because of the danger of introducing microorganisms into the bladder, catheterization is to be avoided whenever possible. Satisfactory specimens from males can usually be obtained by cleansing the meatus with soap and water and collecting midstream urine in a sterile container. Satisfactory midstream specimens from females can be obtained after cleansing the vulva and spreading the labia, but catheterization is sometimes unavoidable. Separate specimens from the right and left kidneys and ureters can be obtained by the urologist at cystoscopy using a catheter. When an indwelling catheter and closed collection systems are in place, urine is best obtained by sterile aspiration of the catheter with needle and syringe.

For most examinations, 0.5 mL of ureteral urine or 5 mL of voided urine is sufficient. Urine specimens must be delivered to the laboratory and examined within 1 hour, or refrigerated not longer than overnight. At room or body temperature, many types of microorganisms multiply rapidly in urine. To resolve diagnostic problems, therefore, urine can be aspirated aseptically directly from the full bladder by means of suprapubic puncture of the abdominal wall.

B. Microscopic Examination: A great deal can be learned from the simple microscopic examination of urine. A drop of fresh uncentrifuged urine placed on a slide, covered with a coverglass, and examined with restricted light intensity under the high-dry objective of an ordinary clinical microscope reveals not only leukocytes and epithelial cells but also bacteria if more than 10^4–10^5 organisms per milliliter are present. This procedure informs the physician promptly that significant numbers of organisms are present and also indicates whether cocci (often *S faecalis*) or motile rods (often gram-negative coliform organisms) are causing the infection.

Bacteria are not sedimented by short (3–5 minutes) centrifugation at the usual speeds of the clinical centrifuge. However, brief centrifugation does readily sediment pus cells, which may carry along bacteria and thus may help in rapid microscopic diagnosis of infection in gram-stained smears. The presence of other formed elements in the sediment—or the presence of proteinuria—is of little direct aid in the specific identification of active urinary tract infection. Pus cells may be present without bacteria, and, conversely, bacteriuria may be present without pyuria. The presence of many squamous epithelial cells, lactobacilli, or mixed flora on culture suggests improper urine collection.

C. Urine Cultures: As explained above, culture of the urine, to be meaningful, must be performed quantitatively. Properly collected urine is cultured in measured amounts on solid media, and the number of colonies appearing after incubation is counted to indicate the number of bacteria per milliliter. The usual procedure is to spread 0.1 mL of undiluted urine, 0.1 mL of 1:100 dilution, and 0.1 mL of 1:10,000 dilution on blood agar plates or other solid media for quantitative culture. If desired, a loopful of urine can be cultured anaerobically and inoculated onto a blood agar plate for direct disk sensitivity tests. All media are incubated overnight at 37 °C; colonies are then counted and the number of bacteria per milliliter of urine is estimated. Several simplified methods are available to estimate the number of bacteria in urine (eg, Dip-Slide, spoon with agar, agar-coated pipette, calibrated loop for streaking).

In active pyelonephritis, the number of bacteria in urine collected by ureteral catheter is relatively low. While accumulating in the bladder, bacteria multiply rapidly and soon reach numbers in excess of 10^5/mL, far more than could occur as a result of contamination by urethral or skin flora or from the air. Therefore, it is generally agreed that if more than 100,000 organisms per milliliter are cultivated from a properly collected and properly examined urine specimen, this constitutes strong evidence of active urinary tract infection. The presence of more than 10^5 bacteria of the same type per milliliter in 2 consecutive specimens establishes a diagnosis of active infection of the urinary tract with 95% certainty. If fewer bacteria are cultivated, repeated examination of urine is indicated to establish the presence of infection.

If fewer than 10,000 colonies per milliliter are present (especially if, as is often the case, there are several types), this suggests that the organisms come from normal flora or are contaminants. Intermediate counts (eg, 10,000–100,000 colonies per milliliter) do not permit definitive interpretation from a single specimen and must be repeated with a fresh specimen. Such counts obtained repeatedly suggest persistent, chronic, or suppressed infection. If found only in a single specimen, they suggest contamination. If cultures are negative but clinical signs of urinary tract infection are present, tuberculosis, anaerobic infection, ureteral obstruction, or "urethral syndrome" must be considered.

Bacteria most commonly found in urinary tract infections are coliforms, other gram-negative rods, and enterococci.

Cerebrospinal Fluid

The early, rapid, and precise diagnosis of meningitis ranks high among medical emergencies. It depends upon maintaining a high index of suspicion, securing adequate specimens properly, and examining the specimens promptly. Because the risk of death or irreversible tissue damage is great unless treatment is started immediately, there is rarely a second chance to obtain pretreatment specimens—which are essential for specific etiologic diagnosis and optimal management.

The most urgent diagnostic issue is the differentiation of acute purulent bacterial meningitis from "aseptic" and granulomatous meningitis. The immediate decision is usually based on the results of cell count and glucose content of cerebrospinal fluid (see Table 26–1) and of microscopic search for mi-

Table 26–1. Cerebrospinal fluid findings.

Diagnosis	Some Causative Microorganisms	Cells (per μL)	Protein (mg/dL)	Glucose (mg/dL)	Remarks
Normal	...	0–5 lymphocytes	10–45	50–85	Glucose 20 mg/dL lower than blood level
Acute purulent meningitis (bacterial)	Meningococci, pneumococci, *Haemophilus influenzae*, streptococci, staphylococci, coliform organisms, etc.	200–20,000 or more PMNs	Increased: 50–1000 or more	Low: 0–45 (< 50–70% of normal)	Organisms in smear or culture. Counter-immunoelectrophoresis.
Viral meningoencephalitis ("aseptic")	Viruses of mumps, herpes simplex, lymphocytic chorio-meningitis, poliomyelitis; coxsackievirus, echovirus, arbovirus.	100–1000 or more, mostly lymphocytes	Normal or increased	Normal	Virus isolation or titer rise in paired serum specimens
Granulomatous (tuberculous or fungal) meningitis	*Mycobacterium tuberculosis, Cryptococcus, Coccidioides, Histoplasma*, etc.	10–1000 or more, mostly lympho-cytes	Increased: 45–500 or more	Low: 0–45 (< 50–70% of normal)	Organisms found in smear or culture
Syphilitic or leptospiral meningitis	*Treponema pallidum, Lepto-spira* species.	25–2000 or more, mostly lympho-cytes	Increased: 45–400 or more	15–75	Serologic tests positive
"Neighborhood reaction" (eg, epidural or brain abscess, thrombosis)		Increased	Normal or increased	Normal	Cultures negative

croorganisms. It is subsequently modified by the results of culture, cerebrospinal fluid protein content, serologic tests, and other laboratory procedures. Table 26–1 illustrates some typical findings. In evaluating the results of cerebrospinal fluid glucose determinations, the simultaneous blood glucose level must be considered. In some central nervous system neoplasms, the cerebrospinal fluid glucose is low. In bacterial and fungal meningitis, the cerebrospinal fluid lactic acid is often elevated above 35 mg/dL.

A. Specimens: As soon as infection of the central nervous system is suspected, blood cultures are taken and cerebrospinal fluid is secured. Lumbar puncture is performed with strict aseptic technique, taking care not to risk compression of the medulla by too rapid withdrawal of fluid when the intracranial pressure is markedly elevated. Cerebrospinal fluid is usually collected in 3 or 4 portions (2–5 mL each) in sterile tubes. This permits the most convenient and most reliable examination for the several different values which determine the physician's course of action.

B. Microscopic Examination: Smears are made from fresh uncentrifuged cerebrospinal fluid that appears cloudy or from the sediment of centrifuged cerebrospinal fluid. Smears are stained with Gram's stain and occasionally with Ziehl-Neelsen stain. Ziehl-Neelsen staining is particularly indicated if a pellicle forms on the surface of the fluid, trapping acid-fast organisms. Study of stained smears under the oil immersion objective may reveal intracellular gram-negative diplococci (meningococci), intra- and extra-cellular lancet-shaped gram-positive diplococci (pneumococci), or small gram-negative rods (*H influenzae* or coliform organisms). Cryptococci are organisms best seen in India ink preparations. Common

bacterial causes of meningitis can be rapidly identified by specific immunofluorescence.

C. Counterimmunoelectrophoresis: If stains fail to reveal the presence of a microorganism, specific antisera can be used against important central nervous system pathogens in counterimmunoelectrophoresis against cerebrospinal fluid. An immune precipitate detected in 1 hour suggests the causative organism and can help in the selection of early specific treatment. Cryptococcal antigen in cerebrospinal fluid may be detected by a latex agglutination test.

D. Culture: The culture methods used must be those that will favor the growth of microorganisms most commonly encountered in meningitis. Virus isolation can be attempted in aseptic meningitis or meningoencephalitis. Isolation of the organism in the cerebrospinal fluid is often successful in infections caused by mumps and echo- or coxsackieviruses but not usually successful in the arthropod-borne encephalitides, herpes simplex encephalitis, or lymphocytic choriomeningitis infections.

E. Follow-Up Examination of Cerebrospinal Fluid: The return of cerebrospinal fluid glucose and cerebrospinal fluid cell count toward normal levels is the best evidence of adequate initial therapy.

Respiratory Secretions

Symptoms or signs often point to involvement of a particular part of the respiratory tract, and specimens are chosen accordingly. In interpreting the laboratory results it is necessary to consider the normal microbial flora of the area from which the specimen was collected.

A. Specimens:

1. Throat–Most "sore throats" are due to viral

infection. Only 5–10% of such complaints in adults and 15–20% in children are associated with bacterial infections. The finding of a follicular yellowish exudate or a grayish membrane must arouse the suspicion of hemolytic streptococcal, diphtherial, fusospirochetal (Vincent's), or candidal infection; but such signs may also be present in infectious mononucleosis, adenovirus, and other virus infections.

Throat swabs must be taken from each tonsillar area before a swab is taken from the posterior pharyngeal wall. The normal throat flora includes an abundance of viridans streptococci, neisseriae, diphtheroids, staphylococci, small gram-negative rods, and many other organisms. Microscopic examination of smears from throat swabs is of little value in streptococcal infections because all throats harbor a predominance of streptococci, but it can rapidly identify fusospirochetal disease and may suggest diphtheria. By immunofluorescence, group A streptococci can sometimes be identified rapidly as the predominant organism.

Cultures of throat swabs are most reliable if inoculated promptly after collection, although special swabs are available that permit survival of important pathogens for days. When streaking culture plates (blood agar is used), it is essential to spread a small inoculum thoroughly and avoid overgrowth by normal flora. This can be done readily by touching the throat swab to one small area of the plate and using a second sterile applicator (or sterile bacteriologic loop) to streak the plate from that area. A slash in the agar (to provide reduced oxygen tension) and incubation for 2 days at 37 °C facilitates detection of beta-hemolytic colonies.

Reports on throat cultures should state the types of prevalent organisms. If potential pathogens (eg, beta-hemolytic streptococci) are cultured, their approximate number is important. A few colonies of beta-hemolytic streptococci may well represent only "transients" in the throat without pathogenic meaning. In "strep throat," the group A streptococci prevail. On a blood plate bearing massive growth, the "bacitracin 0.04 unit disk" method most easily establishes the group A nature of the organisms, with greater than 90% accuracy.

2. Nasopharynx–Specimens from the nasopharynx are studied infrequently because they must be obtained by special techniques. (See Viral Diagnosis, below.) Semiquantitative nasopharyngeal culture may indicate the etiologic organism in otitis media of small children.

3. Middle ear–Specimens are rarely obtained because puncture of the drum is necessary. In acute otitis media, 30–50% of aspirated fluids are bacteriologically sterile. The most frequently isolated bacteria are pneumococci, *H influenzae*, and hemolytic streptococci.

4. Lower respiratory tract–Bronchial and pulmonary secretions or exudates are often studied by examining sputum. The most misleading aspect of sputum examination is the almost inevitable contamination with saliva and mouth flora. Thus, finding *Candida* or *S aureus* in the sputum of a patient with pneumonitis has no etiologic significance unless supported by the clinical picture. Meaningful sputum specimens should be expectorated in the physician's presence from the lower respiratory tract and should be grossly distinct from saliva. The presence of many squamous epithelial cells suggests heavy contamination with saliva; a large number of polymorphonuclear leukocytes (PMNs) suggests purulent exudate. Sputum may be induced by inhalation of heated hypertonic saline aerosol for several minutes. Specimens can sometimes be obtained by catheter aspiration, bronchoscopy, or lung biopsy. In pneumonia accompanied by pleural fluid, examination of the latter may yield the etiologic organisms more reliably than sputum. A majority of community-acquired bacterial pneumonias are caused by pneumococci. In suspected tuberculosis or fungal infection, gastric washings (swallowed sputum) may yield organisms when expectorated material fails to do so. Semiquantitative cultures are helpful.

5. Transtracheal aspiration–The flora in such specimens often reflects accurately the events in the lower respiratory tract. Lung puncture or open biopsy of lung tissue may be necessary (eg, in the diagnosis of *Pneumocystis* pneumonia).

B. Microscopic Examination: Smears of purulent flecks or granules from sputum stained by Gram's stain or by acid-fast methods may reveal causative organisms and PMNs. Some organisms (eg, *Actinomyces*) are best seen in unstained wet preparations. A direct "quellung" test for pneumococci with polyvalent serum can be performed on fresh sputum.

C. Cultures: The media used must be suitable for the growth of bacteria (eg, pneumococci, *Klebsiella*), fungi (eg, *Coccidioides immitis*), anaerobes (eg, *Bacteroides*), mycobacteria (eg, *Mycobacterium tuberculosis*), *Mycoplasma*, and others. The relative prevalence of different organisms in the specimen must be estimated. Only a finding of one predominant organism or the simultaneous isolation of an organism from both sputum and blood can clearly establish its role in a pneumonic or suppurative process.

D. Viral Diagnosis: Most upper respiratory tract infections are caused by viruses. Throat swabs, throat washings, and sputum are fertile sources of virus if specialized laboratory facilities for virus isolation are available. Throat swabs immersed in broth, garglings with broth, or sputum must be brought to the virus laboratory promptly or kept frozen until they are inoculated into cell cultures, embryonated eggs, or animals. To support the possible etiologic role of viral agents, a rise in specific antibody titer must be demonstrated. Serum specimens are obtained aseptically as early as possible in the disease and again 2–3 weeks later. The first serum specimen is stored in the refrigerator until the second specimen has been secured. Both serum samples are then submitted to the virus laboratory— with an adequate clinical description—for specific serologic diagnosis.

Gastrointestinal Tract Specimens

Acute symptoms referable to the gastrointestinal tract—particularly nausea, vomiting, and diarrhea—are commonly attributed to infection. In reality most such attacks are caused by intolerance to food or drink, enterotoxins, drugs, or systemic illnesses.

In most forms of acute gastroenteritis, the objectives of management should be to restore water and electrolyte balance, limit the intake of food, and establish an etiologic diagnosis, which must be based on individual and community history as well as appropriate clinical evaluation and laboratory help. In general, antimicrobial drugs should play a secondary role in treatment of acute gastroenteritis.

Many cases of acute infectious diarrheas are due to viruses. On the other hand, many viruses (eg, adenoviruses, enteroviruses) can multiply in the gut without causing gastrointestinal symptoms. Similarly, some enteric bacterial pathogens may establish persistent residence in the gut following an acute infection. Thus, it is often difficult to assign significance to a microbial or viral agent cultured from the stool, especially in subacute or chronic illness.

These considerations should not discourage the physician from attempting laboratory isolation of enteric organisms but should constitute a warning of some common difficulties in interpreting the results.

The lower bowel has an exceedingly high normal bacterial flora. The most prevalent organisms are anaerobes (*Bacteroides*, lactobacilli, clostridia, and streptococci), coliform gram-negative rods, and *S faecalis*. Any attempt to recover pathogenic bacteria from feces involves their separation from the normal flora, usually through the use of differential selective media and enrichment cultures. Important causes of acute gastrointestinal upsets include viruses, toxins (of staphylococci, clostridia, vibrios, toxigenic *E coli*), more or less invasive coliforms, slow lactose fermenters, and shigellae and salmonellae. The relative importance of these groups of organisms differs greatly in various parts of the world.

A. Specimens: Feces and rectal swabs are the most readily available specimens. Bile obtained by duodenal drainage may reveal infection of the biliary tract. The presence of blood, mucus, or helminths must be noted on gross inspection of the specimen. Leukocytes seen in suspensions of stool examined microscopically are a useful differential test for invasive versus noninvasive infectious diarrheas. Special techniques must be used in searching for ova and parasites. Stained smears may reveal a prevalence of leukocytes and certain abnormal organisms, eg, *Candida* or staphylococci, but cannot differentiate enteric bacterial pathogens from normal flora.

B. Culture: Specimens are suspended in broth and cultured on ordinary as well as selective differential media (eg, MacConkey's, EMB agar) to permit separation of non-lactose-fermenting organisms from coliform bacteria. If *Salmonella* infection (typhoid fever or paratyphoid fever) is suspected, the specimen is also placed in an enrichment medium (eg, selenite F broth) for 18 hours before plating on differential media (eg, Hektoen enteric or *Shigella-Salmonella* agar). *Yersinia enterocolitica* is more likely to be isolated after storage of fecal suspensions for 2 weeks at 4 °C. Vibrios and *Campylobacter* grow best on thiosulfate-citrate-bile-sucrose agar. Identification of bacterial colonies proceeds by standard bacteriologic examination, and blood is drawn for serologic diagnosis. The agglutination of bacteria from suspected colonies by pooled specific antiserum is often the fastest way to establish the presence of salmonellae or shigellae in the intestinal tract. Rise in the specific serum antibody titer often supports the diagnosis of *Salmonella* infection.

Gastric washings represent swallowed sputum and may be cultured for tubercle bacilli and other mycobacteria on special media (see Chapter 17). For virus isolation, frozen fecal specimens are submitted to special laboratories, accompanied by paired serum specimens.

Intestinal parasites and their ova are discovered by repeated microscopic study of fresh fecal specimens subjected to specialized handling in the laboratory. (See Chapter 41.)

Puncture Fluids

Exudates that have collected in the pleural, peritoneal, or synovial spaces must be aspirated with the most meticulous aseptic technique to avoid superinfection. If the material is frankly purulent, smears and cultures are made directly. If the fluid is clear, it should be centrifuged at high speed for 10 minutes and the sediment used for stained smears and cultures. The culture method used must be suitable for the growth of organisms suspected on clinical grounds—eg, mycobacteria, anaerobic organisms, neisseriae—as well as the commonly encountered pyogenic bacteria.

Although direct tests for etiologic microorganisms yield the most important answers, indirect supportive evidence of infection is also helpful. This includes tests on oxalated puncture fluids. The following results are suggestive of infection: specific gravity over 1.018; protein content over 3 g/dL, often resulting in clotting; and cell counts over 500–1000/μL. Polymorphonuclear leukocytes predominate in acute untreated pyogenic infections; lymphocytes or monocytes predominate in chronic infections. Transudates resulting from neoplastic growth may grossly resemble infectious exudates in appearing bloody or purulent and in clotting on standing. Cytologic study of smears or of sections of centrifuged cells may prove the neoplastic nature of the process.

Genital Lesions

Prominent among the infections associated with local lesions of the external genitalia, discharge, and regional adenopathy are syphilis, gonorrhea, chancroid, lymphogranuloma venereum, granuloma inguinale, and herpes simplex. Each has a characteristic natural history and evolution of lesions, but one can mimic another. The laboratory diagnosis of most of these infections is covered elsewhere in the text. A few diagnostic tests are listed below.

A. Gonorrhea: Urethral or cervical exudate shows intracellular gram-negative diplococci in stained smear. Exudate, rectal swab, or throat swab must be plated promptly on special media to yield *Neisseria gonorrhoeae*. Serologic tests are not helpful.

B. Syphilis: Darkfield or immunofluorescence examination of tissue fluid expressed from the base of the chancre may reveal typical *Treponema pallidum*. Serologic tests for syphilis become positive 3–6 weeks after infection. A positive flocculation test (eg, VDRL) requires confirmation. A positive immunofluorescence treponemal antibody (FTA-ABS) test (see Chapter 20) proves syphilitic infection.

C. Chancroid: Smears from a suppurating lesion usually show a mixed bacterial flora. Swabs from lesions can be cultured on "chocolate" agar with 1% Isovitalex and vancomycin, 3 μg/mL, to grow *Haemophilus ducreyi*. Serologic tests are rarely done. The Ducrey skin test usually is positive within 3–5 weeks after infection, but it cannot distinguish between an old and a current infection.

D. Chlamydial Genital Infections: The genital tract is the usual source of many types of *Chlamydia trachomatis*, producing either asymptomatic or symptomatic infection. The latter includes urethritis, epididymitis, cervicitis, salpingitis, pelvic inflammatory disease, and lymphogranuloma venereum. These infections are sexually transmitted and may spread readily to the eye to produce inclusion conjunctivitis, which resembles trachoma.

Smears of exudate or scrapings from the eye, urethra, or cervix can be examined by Giemsa's stain or immunofluorescence to reveal typical crescent-shaped inclusions in epithelial cells (see Chapter 22). Culture of exudates or secretions may permit isolation of chlamydiae in specially treated cells.

Serologic tests to show rising antibody titers can be performed—by complement fixation or microimmunofluorescence with group-reactive or immunotype-specific antigens—on sera obtained at intervals of several weeks. Although skin tests (eg, Frei) can indicate past infection, they have been largely abandoned because of inadequate specificity of the antigens.

E. Granuloma Inguinale: The etiologic agent of this hard, granulomatous, proliferating lesion (*Calymmatobacterium* [*Donovania*] *granulomatis*) can be grown in complex bacteriologic media, but this is rarely attempted in practice. Histologic demonstration of intracellular "Donovan bodies" in biopsied material most frequently supports the clinical impression. Serologic tests are not helpful.

F. Herpes Progenitalis: Primary or recurrent herpetic vesicles, evolving to ulcers and crusts and resembling the common "cold sores" on lips or skin, may occur on the genitalia. A positive diagnosis depends upon finding typical multinucleated giant cells or positive immunofluorescence in scrapings from the ulcer base, or isolation and identification of herpes

simplex virus from the aspirated contents of the vesicle. A significant rise in antibody titer occurs during the primary infection.

G. *Trichomonas vaginalis* Vaginitis or Urethritis: Typical organisms can be seen or cultured from genital discharges.

Wounds, Tissue Biopsies, Bone & Joint Infections, Abscesses

Microscopic study of smears and cultures of specimens from wounds or abscesses may often give early and important indications of the nature of the infecting organism and thus help in the choice of antimicrobial drugs. Specimens from diagnostic tissue biopsies should be submitted to bacteriologic as well as histologic examination. They are kept away from fixatives and disinfectants, minced and finely ground, and cultured by a variety of methods.

In closed undrained abscesses, the pus frequently contains only one organism as causative agent—most commonly staphylococci, streptococci, or coliforms. The same is true in acute osteomyelitis, where the organisms can often be cultured from the blood before the local lesion has become chronic. However, in open wounds, a multitude of microorganisms are frequently encountered, which makes it difficult to decide which are significant. When deep suppurating lesions drain onto exterior surfaces through a sinus or fistula, the flora of the surface drainage must not be mistaken for that of the deep lesion.

Only with reservations can organisms obtained from sinus tracts be used to guide therapy. Bacteriologic study of pus from closed or deep lesions must always include anaerobic methods. Anaerobic bacteria (*Bacteroides*, streptococci) sometimes play an essential causative role and are often present as mixtures, whereas aerobes may represent surface contaminants. The typical wound infections due to clostridia are readily suspected in gas gangrene. *Pseudomonas* in wounds gives rise to blue-green pus.

The methods employed must be suitable for the semiquantitative recovery of common bacteria and also for specialized microorganisms such as anaerobes, mycobacteria, and fungi. Eroded skin and mucous membranes are frequently the sites of yeast or fungus infection. *Candida, Aspergillus*, and others can be seen microscopically in smears or scrapings from suspicious areas and can be grown in cultures.

Viral antigens can sometimes be demonstrated directly in specimens from surface lesions by the fluorescent antibody method.

· · ·

ANAEROBIC INFECTIONS

A large majority of the bacteria that make up the normal human flora are anaerobes. When displaced from their normal sites into tissues or body spaces, they may produce disease. Certain characteristics are suggestive of anaerobic infections: (1) They tend to involve mixtures of organisms, frequently several types of anaerobes. (2) They tend to form closed-space infections, either as discrete abscesses (lung, brain, pleura, peritoneum, pelvis) or by burrowing through tissue layers. (3) Pus from anaerobic infections often has a foul odor. (4) Septic thrombophlebitis and metastatic suppuration occur frequently and require surgical drainage in addition to antimicrobial drugs. (5) Most of the pathogenetically important anaerobes except *Bacteroides fragilis* are highly sensitive to penicillin G. (6) Anaerobic infections are favored by reduced blood supply, necrotic tissue, and a low oxidation-reduction potential—all of which also interfere with delivery of antimicrobial drugs. (7) It is essential to use special collection methods, transport media, and sensitive anaerobic techniques and media to isolate the organisms. Otherwise, bacteriologic examination may be negative or yield only incidental aerobes.

The following are sites of important anaerobic infections.

Respiratory Tract

Periodontal infections, sinusitis, and mastoiditis may involve predominantly *Bacteroides melaninogenicus, Fusobacterium*, and peptostreptococci—all susceptible to penicillin. Aspiration of saliva (containing up to 10^8 of these organisms) may result in necrotizing pneumonia, lung abscess, and empyema. Penicillin and postural or surgical drainage are essential for treatment.

Central Nervous System

Anaerobes rarely produce meningitis but are a common cause of brain abscess, subdural empyema, and septic thrombophlebitis. The organisms usually originate in the respiratory tract (via extension or hematogenous spread) and require similar management.

Intra-abdominal & Pelvic Infections

The flora of the colon consists predominantly of anaerobes, 10^{11} per gram of feces. *B fragilis,* clostridia, and peptostreptococci play a main role in abscess formation originating in perforation of the colon or gallbladder and in abscesses of the pelvis originating in the female genital organs. *B fragilis* is often relatively resistant to penicillin; therefore, clindamycin or cefoxitin should be used.

Bacteremia & Endocarditis

About 5–10% of these infections are now caused by anaerobes originating in the gut or the female genital tract. Specific bacteriologic diagnosis is essential for optimal treatment. Otherwise, the rate of treatment failure may be high.

Skin & Soft Tissue Infections

Anaerobes and aerobic bacteria often join to form synergistic infections (gangrene, necrotizing fasciitis, cellulitis). Surgical drainage, excision, and improved circulation are the most important forms of treatment, while antimicrobial drugs act as adjuncts. It is usually difficult to pinpoint one specific organism as being responsible for the progressive lesion, since mixtures of organisms are usually involved.

SEROLOGIC TESTS & THE DEMONSTRATION OF SPECIFIC ANTIBODY

In the course of many infections, serum antibodies are acquired relatively early, as microorganisms multiply, and these antibodies may persist for months or years. Thus, the serologic demonstration of antibody indicates effective exposure (by infection or vaccination) at some time in the past but may have no bearing on the current illness. For the diagnosis of a current infection it is often necessary to demonstrate an increase in antibody concentration, ie, a rise of antibody level in the second of 2 blood specimens obtained at an interval of 10–20 days. The 2 specimens of sera must be examined simultaneously in the same test for meaningful results. Blood specimens must be taken aseptically and the serum separated with sterile precautions.

Diagnostic antibody titers are sometimes obtained in the following infections.

Amebiasis

Latex particles or red blood cells coated with *Entamoeba histolytica* antigens are agglutinated by serum in invasive amebiasis. Gel diffusion or counterimmunoelectrophoresis may reveal antibodies.

Blastomycosis

Complement-fixing and precipitating antibodies appear principally in disseminated and progressive disease, but cross-reactions can occur with histoplasmosis and other mycoses.

Brucellosis

During the acute infection, agglutinating antibodies appear; later, blocking (prozone, see p 243) IgA and IgG antibodies can be observed. Agglutinating IgM antibodies persist for years without manifest activity of the disease. The diagnosis of active brucellosis is suggested by the presence of IgG (over 1:80) agglutinating antibodies. CF tests are rarely employed.

Chlamydial Infections (Psittacosis [Ornithosis], Lymphogranuloma Venereum, Trachoma, Inclusion Conjunctivitis)

Antibodies to the group antigen often become demonstrable by CF tests within 2–4 weeks after symptoms appear. These antibodies cannot differentiate one infection of the group from another. Some group-reactive and species-specific antibodies can be found by immunofluorescence (see Chapter 22).

Coccidioidomycosis

Soon after the initial infection, precipitating and complement-fixing antibodies to *Coccidioides immitis* appear. In the absence of complications, these tend to subside to very low levels within months. Dissemination of the infection is accompanied by a rising titer of complement-fixing antibodies (more than 1:32), which carries a grave prognosis.

Mycoplasmal Pneumonia

In pneumonitis caused by *Mycoplasma pneumoniae*, cold agglutinins develop in the serum during the illness. These are substances that are capable of agglutinating human group O cells at 4 °C but not at 20 or 37 °C. Specific antibodies to *M pneumoniae* can be detected by complement fixation, growth inhibition, or hemagglutination inhibition.

Histoplasmosis

Precipitating and complement-fixing antibodies to antigens of *Histoplasma capsulatum* appear usually within 3–4 weeks of acute infection and, in the absence of complications, revert to low levels. If the infection disseminates and progresses, the complement fixation titer rises in successive serum samples. However, serologic tests are less reliable for diagnosis than isolation of the fungus.

Infectious Mononucleosis

This disease is caused by the Epstein-Barr (EB) herpesvirus. Diagnosis of the clinically suggestive case rests usually on the identification of representative "atypical" lymphocytes in blood smears and on the "heterophil agglutination" test. This is a nonspecific reaction: persons suffering from infectious mononucleosis develop a high titer (usually more than 1:112) of antibodies that agglutinate fresh washed sheep red blood cells or horse red cells. Similar agglutinating antibodies appear in a variety of hypersensitivity reactions but can be differentiated by absorption tests. The mononucleosis agglutinins cannot be absorbed by boiled guinea pig kidney, whereas agglutinins following other reactions are removed by this absorption. Commercial mononucleosis spot tests combine these reactions and yield sensitive and specific results.

In special laboratories, antibodies to EB virus can be demonstrated in sera of mononucleosis patients by immunofluorescence. (See Chapter 38.)

Leptospirosis

Agglutination tests give very high titers (often over 1:1000) following infection.

Parasitic Diseases

In cysticercosis, trichinosis, echinococcosis, and other parasitic infections, CF, precipitin, or HI tests are occasionally employed for diagnosis.

Plague, Tularemia

Agglutination titers of 1:20 or higher, particularly with rising titers, can support the clinical diagnosis of acute infection. Low titers suggest cross-reactions (eg, with *Brucella* or *Shigella* organisms) or long-past infection.

Rheumatoid Factor

In many disorders of possible "autoimmune" origin, antibodies to the host's own antigens are encountered. Antithyroid antibodies are demonstrated in several thyroid disorders; antibodies that fix complement in the presence of nucleoproteins are found in disseminated lupus erythematosus. Anti-DNA antibodies are also demonstrated by immunofluorescence. In rheumatoid arthritis, an IgM ("rheumatoid factor") is present that reacts with human IgG. This can be demonstrated as an agglutination of red cells or other particles coated with IgG by diluted sera from rheumatoid patients. Many individuals with infective endocarditis of more than 6 weeks' duration exhibit a high titer of such "rheumatoid factor." These substances disappear with bacteriologic cure of endocarditis.

Rickettsioses

CF, microagglutination, and immunofluorescence tests permit the demonstration of type-specific antibody rise if specific antigens are available. Various special strains of *Proteus* organisms share antigens with the rickettsiae, and suspensions of these *Proteus* organisms are agglutinated in high titer by the serum of infected persons (Weil-Felix test) (see Chapter 21 for details).

Salmonellosis (Typhoid Fever, Enteric Fever)

A rising agglutination titer to O antigens is suggestive of active infection. Antibodies to H antigens occur commonly with vaccination and may persist for years. In previously vaccinated individuals with residual O or H titers, there may be no further titer rise with active infection.

Staphylococcal Infections

Persons with deep, active, suppurating staphylococcal infections frequently develop antibodies against a variety of staphylococcal antigens and extracellular products. In view of the ubiquity of many staphylococci, most such antibodies have little diagnostic meaning. However, a rise in antibody titer to staphylococcal leukocidin, alpha-hemolysin, or teichoic acid may indicate activity of a deep chronic lesion.

Streptococcal Infections & Poststreptococcal Disease

Persons infected with beta-hemolytic streptococci develop antibodies to a variety of streptococcal antigens and extracellular products. Most conveniently, antibodies to streptolysin O can be detected. If antistreptolysin O (ASO) is repeatedly found to be present in titers exceeding 166 units, this suggests recent infection with beta-hemolytic streptococci or rheumatic disease. Antistreptolysin formation is readily suppressed by early and adequate penicillin therapy. Type-specific bactericidal antibody may also be measured.

Syphilis

Serologic tests for syphilis employ either treponemal or nontreponemal antigens. Nontreponemal tests are based on the accidental relationship between lipid extracts of mammalian tissue and reagin, a substance developing in the serum of persons after treponemal infection. Flocculation tests (VDRL) are standardized and can be automated. All of these tests estimate the presence of reagin and are therefore subject to false-positive results. The latter are particularly frequent in various infectious and febrile disorders, in "collagen diseases," and after vaccinations. Nontreponemal tests can be performed in a quantitative manner if desired. Most biologic false-positive results are of low titer. Nontreponemal positive tests tend to revert to negative in adequately treated syphilis.

Treponemal tests are based on the reaction between treponemal suspensions and specific antitreponemal antibodies. The fluorescent treponemal antibody (FTA-ABS) test, which has high specificity and good sensitivity, is most commonly employed. It becomes positive early in syphilitic infection and tends to remain positive for years after adequate treatment. A treponemal hemagglutination (TPHA) test has similar sensitivity and specificity. The *T pallidum* immobilization (TPI) test requires live (rabbit-grown) treponemes and is thus more complex and less available.

Toxoplasmosis

Toxoplasma gondii, a crescent-shaped protozoon, can be isolated with difficulty by inoculating mice with lymph node material taken from patients with acute infection. Several serologic tests can be applied. The dye test depends upon the ability of antibodies to prevent the uptake of methylene blue by living *Toxoplasma* organisms. The test results become positive (frequently more than 1:1000) in 2–4 weeks after toxoplasmosis is acquired and may remain positive for years. In congenital toxoplasmosis, the dye test is often positive. The CF test becomes positive (up to 1:100) in 4–8 weeks and declines to very low levels in a few months. Immunofluorescent antibody tests in low titer indicate only past infection, but high titers (1:10,000 or more) suggest recent infection. Immunofluorescence tests for IgM antibody reveal congenital infection in newborns. Positive tests in single samples of serum of adults must take into account the high frequency of asymptomatic infection.

Trichinosis

For the diagnosis of acute trichinosis, a bentonite flocculation test is useful. Bentonite particles coated with *Trichinella spiralis* antigen may be agglutinated to high titer by the serum of persons infected for 2 weeks or more.

Viral Infections

The diagnosis of viral infections is discussed in detail in Chapters 28 and 29.

SKIN TESTS

Under the antigenic stimulus of an infectious agent, the host may develop hypersensitivity, manifested by delayed type skin reactivity, to one or more antigens of that agent. The controlled application of known antigens can therefore give evidence of infection and serve as a valuable diagnostic aid. A positive skin reaction indicates only that the individual has, at some time in the past, been infected with the specific agent. It provides information about the relationship of a specific agent to a *current* illness only if conversion from a negative to a positive skin test occurs during or just preceding the current illness. The general skin reactivity declines markedly (anergy) during far-advanced stages of many infections and is a regular feature of sarcoidosis, Hodgkin's disease, and some childhood exanthematous diseases (eg, measles). Similarly, skin reactivity may be suppressed by the administration of corticosteroids or immunosuppressant drugs.

Most skin test reagents are not pure antigens but a complex mixture of potentially reactive substances. For proper interpretation, it is essential to include suitable control materials in the test. Both immediate and delayed skin reactions may occur with some skin test preparations. In general, the delayed reaction is the only meaningful one for the diagnosis of specific infection.

In a properly performed test the entire test volume (usually 0.1 mL) of the standardized preparation must be injected intracutaneously. Unless the injection raises a well circumscribed bleb, it is likely that part of the test volume has escaped into the subcutaneous tissue or onto the surface. This will diminish the reliability of the test. (Patch tests occasionally used in small children are not reliable.) In most instances the test should be read at 48 hours; additional readings at 24 and 72 hours are sometimes helpful.

The size of induration is the only important criterion of positive readings; erythema alone is not meaningful. When several strengths of test preparation are available, the smallest concentration of antigen must be injected initially, followed by increasingly higher concentrations if the previous test result was negative.

Diagnostic skin tests are sometimes applied in the following clinical conditions.

Blastomycosis

Blastomycin is a filtered, concentrated broth in which *Blastomyces dermatitidis* has been grown for long periods. A test dilution of 1:100 gives 5 mm of induration in persons with past infection. Interpretation is analogous to interpretation of the histoplasmin test (see below), but cross-reactions are very frequent.

Brucellosis

A *Brucella* nucleoprotein extract (Brucellergen) or filtrates of old broth cultures of *Brucella* (brucellin) have been used for skin testing. Such preparations cannot be well standardized, and proper controls are not available. Therefore, the usefulness of the skin test is doubtful. Serologic tests are much to be preferred for diagnosis.

Candida

Candida antigens are used in skin tests to ascertain the individual's ability to respond with a delayed type hypersensitivity reaction as an indicator of active cell-mediated reactivity. Virtually all normal adults react positively.

Cat-Scratch Fever

Pus from active cases, diluted 1:5 and heated at 60 °C for 10 hours, can be used as a skin test antigen. It gives a positive reaction in some individuals with a typical clinical picture. The nature of the causative agent and the significance of the test are not known.

Chancroid

A positive Ducrey test, a delayed skin reaction following the injection of a treated suspension of *H ducreyi*, indicates past infection. A positive reaction may persist for years.

Coccidioidomycosis

Coccidioidin is a filtered, concentrated broth in which mycelium of *C immitis* has been grown for long periods. The usual test dilution is 1:100, and a positive reaction (more than 5 mm of induration) occurs in 24–48 hours. In 1:10 dilution the material often gives cross-reactions with other fungal antigens. Positive skin tests commonly denote past subclinical infection and significant specific resistance to reinfection. A skin test with spherulin (derived from culture-grown spherules, rather than mycelium) is more sensitive but less specific.

Echinococcosis

The injection of inactivated hydatid fluid (Casoni reaction) obtained from human or animal cases may give both immediate and delayed reactions in individuals with *Echinococcus* infection. The test is less reliable than antibody demonstrated by immunoelectrophoresis.

Filariasis

Dirofilaria immitis antigens often give positive delayed skin test reactions in infected persons.

Herpes Simplex

Injection of a soluble antigen obtained from growing virus gives a positive result in 18–24 hours in individuals who have had a primary infection with the virus and are latent carriers of virus.

Histoplasmosis

Histoplasmin is a concentrated filtrate prepared from broth in which *H capsulatum* has been grown for long periods. The usual test dilution is 1:100, and a positive reaction (more than 5 mm of induration) occurs in 24–48 hours. Cross-reactions with other fungal products occur relatively frequently. Positive skin tests commonly denote past subclinical infection and significant specific resistance to reinfection. The skin test may raise the antibody titer.

Leishmaniasis

Leishmanin is an inactivated suspension of cultured flagellate *Leishmania*. A positive delayed skin test to this preparation develops within 6–12 weeks after many *Leishmania* infections and remains positive for life. The test is often negative in active kala-azar but becomes positive after effective chemotherapy.

Leprosy

Lepromin, a standardized homogenate of lepromatous skin nodules, has no diagnostic value. Normal persons may react. However, in a person with known leprosy, a positive lepromin test is diagnostic of tuberculoid leprosy and a negative test indicates lepromatous (anergic) leprosy.

Lymphogranuloma Venereum

The Frei test antigen is a chlamydial suspension made from infected chick embryo yolk sacs. An injection of uninfected yolk sac material is used as a control. A positive reaction is induration at least 6 mm larger than the control site; this may occur following infection with any species of *Chlamydia* at any time in the past. The test is probably obsolete.

Mumps

Intradermal injection of inactivated mumps vaccine gives a delayed positive skin test reaction in 18–36 hours provided the individual has had a past infection. A negative mumps skin test is less reliable in identification of susceptible persons than is the absence of neutralizing serum antibodies. A positive mumps skin test does permit demonstration of the ability to respond with a delayed type hypersensitivity reaction.

Paracoccidioidomycosis

Skin tests with paracoccidioidin, a filtrate of an old broth culture of *Paracoccidioides brasiliensis*, are often positive in infected persons, but cross-reactions with blastomycin and histoplasmin are common.

Sarcoidosis

An extract of sarcoid tissue injected into the skin of a person with sarcoidosis results in a papule that persists for months. Excision after 4–8 weeks reveals a histologic pattern of sarcoid (Kveim test). The basis of the reaction is not certain. Reliability depends on standardized materials. (Editorial: *N Engl J Med* 1975;**292:**859.)

Toxoplasmosis

Toxoplasmin is prepared from a suspension of killed *T gondii* and evokes a delayed reaction in some individuals who also give positive serologic tests. Positive reactors are presumed to have been infected at some time in the past. The test has little diagnostic value, but has been employed in epidemiologic surveys.

Trichinosis

Antigens derived from trichinae (*Trichinella* skin test) may give both immediate and delayed reactions in infected individuals, but most commercial antigens are too insensitive and are no longer licensed.

Tuberculosis

The tuberculin skin test is performed with a purified protein derivative (PPD-S) standardized biologically in humans.in terms of tuberculin units (TU) (see Chapter 17).

The initial test dose is usually 5 TU (intermediate strength PPD). Larger doses are injected when smaller doses have given negative results. The test is considered positive if induration 10 mm in diameter or more occurs in 48–72 hours following injection of 5 TU. In hypersensitive persons with erythema nodosum or phlyctenular conjunctivitis, not more than 1 TU should be injected to avoid serious reactions.

Years after a person has exhibited a positive tuberculin test, a repeat test may appear to be negative. However, the repeat test exerts a "booster" effect so that another tuberculin test 1–2 weeks later will give a positive (> 10 mm) induration result.

PPD (-B, -Y) prepared from other mycobacteria are used in epidemiologic surveys. Many of them cross-react.

Tularemia

Antigens extracted from *Francisella (Pasteurella) tularensis* give a delayed skin reaction in persons who have been infected in the past. The test is quite specific and remains positive longer than antibody titers.

•   •   •

Toxin-Neutralization Tests

A. Schick Test: Although it is not designed for the diagnosis of infection, the Schick test is a valuable aid in the determination of probable susceptibility or resistance to diphtheria. The test consists of the intradermal injection of a standard skin test dose of active diphtheria toxin and of an identical amount of heated toxin as control. The test is read in 24 and 48 hours. A positive reaction consists of redness and swelling at the active toxin site that increase for 48 hours and then fade, leaving a brownish pigmented area. The control site shows no reaction. A positive reaction denotes the absence of an adequate amount of neutralizing circulating antitoxin and therefore susceptibility to diphtheria toxin. A negative reaction at both sites suggests the presence of adequate amounts of circulating neutralizing antitoxin (> 0.02 Lf units/mL) and insusceptibility to diphtheria toxin.

The Schick test is at times complicated by individual hypersensitivity to constituents other than toxin contained in the injections.

Individuals who have positive Schick tests should be immunized with diphtheria toxoid.

B. Schultz-Charlton Reaction: If specific antitoxin to the erythrogenic toxin of beta-hemolytic group A streptococci is injected intradermally into a patient with scarlet fever, the rash will blanch and fade at the injection site because the antitoxin has neutralized the toxin. This test is rarely employed.

NONSPECIFIC CLINICAL LABORATORY TESTS

The usual laboratory procedures performed on most patients who undergo detailed medical examination frequently contain clues concerning possible infectious processes. Anemia and leukocytosis are suitable examples. Such abnormalities are compatible with a large variety of diagnoses and are helpful only if integrated with other findings into a meaningful pattern. No attempt is made here to list the many different laboratory findings that can thus aid in the diagnosis of infection. A few specific items will be discussed briefly for the sake of illustration.

Red Cell Count & Packed Cell Volume

Anemia is a feature of many protracted infections, eg, infective endocarditis and malaria. Conversely, in acute diarrheal diseases, there may be dehydration with elevated packed cell volume.

White Cell Count

In most suppurative infections, the white count is elevated and the proportion of young polymorphonuclear cells is increased. A low white count in pneumococcal or staphylococcal pneumonia, especially in elderly patients, is an unfavorable prognostic sign.

In some infections caused by gram-negative bacilli, there is a fall in the total white count and relative lymphocytosis. Similar findings occur in some viral infections (eg, myxoviruses). However, arbovirus infections with encephalitis commonly give rise to high white counts. In whooping cough, the white count is frequently high, with absolute lymphocytosis. Sudden widespread dissemination of any bacterial or fungal pathogen may be accompanied by a very rapid rise in the white count, at times to leukemoid levels. On the other hand, persons with depressed marrow activity do not develop white count elevations with infections.

These examples illustrate the complexity of interpreting white cell counts.

Erythrocyte Sedimentation Rate

In many acute infections, the sedimentation rate is normal; in prolonged infections, it becomes accelerated. However, a rapid sedimentation rate can be associated with so many different processes which produce cell injury or derangements of blood proteins that it is rarely helpful in establishing the diagnosis of infection. It may be of use in evaluating therapeutic response.

C-Reactive Protein

C-reactive protein is a substance in the serum of certain patients that reacts with the somatic C polysaccharide of pneumococci in vitro but is commonly measured by precipitation with a specific antiserum prepared in rabbits. It is a beta-globulin that is found only in minute amounts in normal sera but occurs frequently in markedly increased amounts in sera of patients with inflammatory, neoplastic, or necrotizing processes. The laboratory test for the presence of C-reactive protein thus constitutes a nonspecific test for the presence of inflammation or tissue injury.

Tests for several mucoproteins in serum are likewise entirely nonspecific and so are of little help in specific diagnosis.

Transaminase & Similar Enzyme Tests

Aspartate transaminase (formerly glutamic-oxaloacetic transaminase, GOT), alanine aminotransferase (formerly glutamic-pyruvic transaminase, GPT), lactate dehydrogenase (LDH), and others are intracellular enzymes involved in amino acid or carbohydrate metabolism. In the course of many disease processes involving cellular injury, the enzyme concentration in blood serum increases markedly. Consequently, elevated enzyme levels are found in acute infections, neoplasms, infarctions, and many degenerative processes and are not necessarily due to hepatic insult or myocardial infarction, with which they are commonly associated.

Serum Bilirubin

The serum bilirubin may be elevated, indicating jaundice, particularly in infections of the newborn and those caused by gram-negative enteric organisms.

Biopsy

In many cases of protracted fever of unknown origin, all tests to establish the presence of infection fail to yield a definitive diagnosis. Surgical exploration and histologic examination of tissues may give the final answer.

Nonspecific Organ System Response to Infections

Whenever an infectious process involves primarily one organ system, nonspecific laboratory tests may show abnormal values. For example, in renal infections, proteinuria and abnormal urinary sediment may be present even without bacteriuria. In central nervous system infections, abnormal values of cerebrospinal fluid composition are of great help in diagnosis. In infections of the external eye, the cell picture of the conjunctival exudate assists in etiologic diagnosis. The x-ray appearance of bone or lung may not only support a diagnosis of infection but may even point to the causative agent.

Radioisotope Scanning Methods

Infective processes may alter blood supply to an area, produce necrotic foci, and change tissue cell behavior. Consequently, localized infections in some organs (eg, the liver, spleen, brain) may be found by concentration or by exclusion of isotopes such as gallium, technetium, and others. The technology of scanning methods and the interpretation of results tend to change very rapidly.

LABORATORY AIDS IN THE SELECTION OF ANTIMICROBIAL THERAPY

The first drug used is chosen on the basis of clinical impression after the physician is convinced that a microbial infection exists and has made a tentative etiologic diagnosis on clinical grounds. On the basis of this "best guess," a probable drug of choice can be selected (see Chapter 10). Before the probable drug of choice is administered, specimens are often obtained for laboratory isolation of the causative agent. The results of these examinations may necessitate selection of a different drug. The identification of certain microorganisms that are uniformly drug-susceptible eliminates the necessity for further testing and permits the selection of optimally effective drugs solely on the basis of experience. Under other circumstances, tests for drug susceptibility of isolated microorganisms may be helpful (see Chapter 10).

The commonly performed "disk test" must be used judiciously and interpreted with restraint. In general, only one member of each major class of drugs is represented. For staphylococci, streptococci, and gram-positive rods, penicillin G, nafcillin, cephalothin, erythromycin, gentamicin, and vancomycin are used. For gram-negative rods, ampicillin, carbenicillin, cefoxitin or cefamandole, chloramphenicol, trimethoprim-sulfamethoxazole, and the main aminoglycosides (amikacin, tobramycin, gentamicin) are included. For urinary tract infections with gram-negative rods, nitrofurantoin, nalidixic acid, and trimethoprim may be added.

Isolates of *H influenzae* and of *N gonorrhoeae* should be tested for beta-lactamase production. Isolates of *Bacteroides* might be tested for susceptibility to penicillin G, clindamycin, and cefoxitin. The susceptibility of microbial isolates to different cephalosporins may be sufficiently divergent so that several different drugs may have to be included.

Methenamine salts (eg, methenamine mandelate)

Table 26—2. Bacteriologic diagnosis of specific microorganisms from clinical infections.

Organism	Principal Sources of Clinical Specimens	Preferred Culture Media	Special Conditions and Additional Tests Usually Required
Staphylococcus	Pus or exudate from site of infection; bloodstream, spinal fluid, urine.	Blood agar plates; trypticase-soy broth; brain broth (3 weeks).	Aerobic or micro-aerophilic. Presence of hemolysis; coagulase reaction; mannitol fermentation.
Streptococcus			Aerobic or anaerobic. Type of hemolysis; growth in 6.5% NaCl broth; serologic group.
Pneumococcus	Sputum, bloodstream, spinal fluid, exudates, pus.	Blood agar plates; trypticase-soy broth; blood broth.	Hemolysis—alpha type; solubility in bile; typing with specific serum.
Gonococcus	Exudates from genitalia, eye, joints; blood.	"Chocolate" agar plates incubated in 10% CO_2 (candle jar).	Intracellular diplococci on smear. Oxidase test.
Meningococcus	Bloodstream, spinal fluid, nasopharynx, skin petechiae.		Intracellular diplococci on smear. Oxidase test; maltose fermented.
Corynebacterium diphtheriae	Nasopharynx, wounds, eye.	Löffler's slants; potassium tellurite medium; blood agar plates.	Typical morphology on smear. Virulence test; Schick skin test.
Clostridium	Wounds, exudates, pus, bloodstream.	Blood agar plates; thioglycolate medium; chopped meat broth.	Strictly anaerobic. Type of hemolysis; milk coagulation.
Mycobacterium tuberculosis	Sputum, exudates, pus, spinal fluid, urine.	Petragnani's, Löwenstein's, or Dubos' media (2–4 weeks).	Guinea pig inoculation. Acid-fast stain; concentration.
Actinomyces	Sputum, exudates, pus.	Thioglycolate medium; blood agar plates.	"Sulfur granules" in specimen. Aerobic and anaerobic culture.
E coli-E aerogenes group	Urine, bloodstream, spinal fluid, exudates, pus.	Blood agar plates. MacConkey's or eosin-methylene blue (EMB) agar.	Lactose fermented (paracolon bacilli ferment lactose slowly).
Salmonella	Feces, bloodstream, urine, exudates.	MacConkey's or EMB agar plates; tetrathionate broth; triple sugar iron agar.	Identified by slide agglutination with specific serum; patient's serum for H and O agglutination test.
Shigella	Feces.	EMB, Hektoen agar plates.	Identified by slide agglutination with specific serum.
Klebsiella pneumoniae	Sputum, bloodstream, spinal fluid, exudates, urine.	Blood agar plates; blood broth.	Typing with specific serum.
Proteus-Pseudomonas group	Urine, exudates, bloodstream, spinal fluid.	Blood agar plates; EMB agar.	Characteristic pigment, odor, "swarming"; lactose not fermented.
Yersinia, Francisella (Pasteurella)	Bloodstream, sputum, exudates, pus.	Blood agar plates; cysteine agar.	Patient's serum for agglutination test.
Brucella	Bloodstream, exudates.	Trypticase-soy agar, broth, incubated in 10% CO_2 (candle jar).	Patient's serum for agglutination or precipitin tests.
Haemophilus species	Spinal fluid, bloodstream, sputum, exudates.	"Chocolate" agar plates; blood agar plates with Isovitalex.	Typing with specific serum. Precipitin test in spinal fluid.
Bacteroides	Exudates, bloodstream.	Chopped meat broth; thioglycolate medium; blood agar plates.	Strictly anaerobic. Typical morphology.
Treponema pallidum	Primary or secondary syphilitic lesion, blood serum.	None.	Immunofluorescence microscopy; serologic tests.
Leptospira	Bloodstream, urine.	Serum broth.	Darkfield microscopy.
Borrelia recurrentis	Bloodstream.	Blood broth.	Stained blood film; serologic tests.
Yeasts and fungi	Skin, nails; exudates, pus; sputum, blood, CSF.	Blood agar plates; Sabouraud's medium.	Serologic tests on patient's serum.
Vibrio, Campylobacter	Feces, blood.	Thiosulfate-citrate-bile agar.	Food history important. Contact with salt water.

should never be used in a disk test. If sulfonamides (or their combinations) are to be tested by disk, the media must be free of PABA.

The sizes of zones of growth inhibition vary with the molecular characteristics of different drugs. Thus zone size of one drug cannot be compared to the zone size of another drug acting on the same organism. However, for any one drug the zone size can be compared to a standard, provided media, inoculum size, and other conditions are carefully regulated. This makes it possible to define for each drug a minimum diameter of inhibition zone that denotes "susceptibility" of an isolate by the Kirby-Bauer technique.

The disk test measures the ability of drugs to *inhibit* the growth of microorganisms. Its results correlate reasonably well with therapeutic response in those disease processes where body defenses can frequently eliminate infectious microorganisms.

In a few types of human infections, the results of disk tests are of little assistance (and may be mislead-

Table 26—3. Diagnostic features of some acute exanthems.

Disease	Prodromal Signs and Symptoms	Nature of Eruption	Other Diagnostic Features	Laboratory Tests
Measles (rubeola)	3—4 days of fever, coryza, conjunctivitis, and cough.	Maculopapular, reddish-brown; begins on head and neck, spreads downward. In 5—6 days, rash brownish, desquamating.	Koplik's spots on buccal mucosa. Atypical course in adults or vaccinated persons.	White count low; specialized CF and virus neutralization in tissue culture.
German measles (rubella)	Little or no prodrome.	Maculopapular, pink; begins on head and neck, spreads downward, fades in 3 days. No desquamation.	Lymphadenopathy, post-auricular or occipital.	White count normal or low; virus neutralization in tissue culture or HI tests.
Chickenpox (varicella-zoster)	0—1 day of fever, anorexia, headache.	Rapid evolution of macules to papules, vesicles, crusts; all stages simultaneously present; lesions superficial, distribution centripetal.	Lesions on scalp and mucous membranes. Zoster lesions along sensory nerves.	Specialized CF and virus neutralization in tissue culture. Immunofluoresence in smear of lesion.
Scarlet fever	½—2 days of malaise, sore throat, fever, vomiting.	Generalized, punctate, red; prominent on neck, in axilla, groin, skin folds; circumoral pallor; fine desquamation involves hands and feet.	Strawberry tongue, exudative tonsillitis.	Group A hemolytic streptococci cultures from throat; antistreptolysin O titer rise.
Exanthem subitum (roseola infantum)	3—4 days of high fever.	As fever falls by crisis, pink maculopapules appear on chest and trunk; fade in 1—3 days.		White count low.
Fifth disease (erythema infectiosum)	None.	Red, flushed cheeks; circumoral pallor; maculopapules on extremities.	"Slapped face" appearance.	White count low.
Meningococcemia	Hours of fever, vomiting.	Maculopapules, petechiae, purpura.	Meningeal signs, shock.	Cultures of blood, cerebrospinal fluid.
Rocky Mountain spotted fever	3—4 days of fever, chills, severe headaches.	Maculopapules, petechiae, distribution centrifugal.	History of tick bite.	Agglutination (OX19, OX2), CF.
Typhus fevers	3—4 days of fever, chills, severe headaches.	Maculopapules, petechiae, distribution centripetal.	Endemic area, lice.	Agglutination (OX19), CF.
Infectious mononucleosis	Fever, adenopathy, sore throat.	Maculopapular rash resembling rubella, rarely papulovesicular.	Splenomegaly, adenopathy.	Atypical lymphocytes in blood smears. Mononucleosis spot test.
Enterovirus infections (echo, coxsackie)	1—2 days of fever, malaise.	Maculopapular rash resembling rubella, rarely papulovesicular.	Aseptic meningitis.	Virus isolation from stool or cerebrospinal fluid; CF titer rise.
Drug eruptions	Occasional fever.	Maculopapular rash resembling rubella, rarely papulovesicular.		Eosinophilia.
Eczema herpeticum	None.	Vesiculopustular lesions in area of eczema.		Herpes simplex virus isolated in tissue culture; serology.

ing) because a *bactericidal* drug effect is required for cure. Outstanding examples are infective endocarditis, acute osteomyelitis, and severe infections in a host whose antibacterial defenses are inadequate, eg, persons with neoplastic diseases that have been treated with radiation and antineoplastic chemotherapy, or persons who are being given corticosteroids in high dosage and are immunosuppressed.

The selection of a bactericidal drug or drug combination for each patient can be guided by specialized laboratory tests. Such tests measure either the rate of killing or the proportion of the microbial population that is killed in a fixed time.

Evaluation of the chemotherapeutic regimen in vivo can be performed by **serum assay** (see Chapter 10). This procedure consists of the following steps:

(1) An etiologic microorganism is isolated.

(2) Antimicrobial therapy is started.

(3) Blood is drawn from the patient receiving treatment at the time a peak or a trough (ie, maximum or minimum concentration of drug) is expected.

(4) Dilutions of the separated serum are tested for their ability to kill in vitro the microorganisms isolated from the patient.

This test can sometimes help decide whether the patient is receiving the proper drug in adequate amounts or whether the regimen should be altered.

In urinary tract infections, the antibacterial activity of urine is far more important than that of serum. The disappearance of infecting organisms from the urine during treatment can serve as a partial drug level assay.

Instead of the disk test, a semiquantitative test procedure can be used. It measures more exactly the concentration of an antibiotic necessary to inhibit growth of a standardized inoculum under defined conditions. In the past, this procedure employed individual tubes of broth. At present, a semiautomated microtiter method is used in which defined amounts of drug are dissolved in a measured small volume of broth and inoculated with a standardized number of microorganisms. The end point, or minimum inhibitory concentration (MIC), is considered the last broth cup remaining clear, ie, free from microbial growth. The minimum inhibitory concentration provides a better estimate of the probable amount of drug necessary to inhibit growth in vivo and thus helps in gauging the dosage regimen necessary for the patient.

In addition, bactericidal effects can be estimated by subculturing the clear broth onto antibiotic-free solid media. The result, eg, a reduction of colony-forming units by 99.9% below that of the control, is called the minimal bactericidal concentration (MBC).

In persons with renal impairment who must receive nephrotoxic drugs, concentration of drug in serum can be estimated by an assay of serum against special test microorganisms or by chemical or radioimmunoassay methods.

● ● ●

GRAM & ACID–FAST STAINING METHODS

Gram Stain (Hucker Modification)

(1) Fix smear by heat.
(2) Cover with crystal violet for 1 minute.
(3) Wash with water. Do not blot.
(4) Cover with Gram's iodine for 1 minute.
(5) Wash with water. Do not blot.
(6) Decolorize for 10–30 seconds with gentle agitation in acetone (30 mL) and alcohol (70 mL).
(7) Wash with water. Do not blot.
(8) Cover for 10–30 seconds with safranin (2.5% solution in 95% alcohol).
(9) Wash with water and let dry.

Ziehl-Neelsen Acid-Fast Stain

(1) Fix smear by heat.
(2) Cover with carbolfuchsin, steam gently for 5 minutes over direct flame (or for 20 minutes over a water bath).
(3) Wash with water.
(4) Decolorize in acid-alcohol until only a faint pink color remains.
(5) Wash with water.
(6) Counterstain for 10–30 seconds with Loeffler's methylene blue.
(7) Wash with water and let dry.

Kinyoun Carbolfuchsin Acid-Fast Stain

(1) Formula: Basic fuchsin, 4; phenol crystals, 8; alcohol (95%), 20; distilled water, 100.
(2) Stain fixed smear for 3 minutes (no heat necessary) and continue as with Ziehl-Neelsen stain.

● ● ●

References

Bartlett JG et al: *Cumitech 7: Laboratory Diagnosis of Lower Respiratory Tract Infections*. Washington JA (editor). American Society for Microbiology, 1978.

Bartlett RC et al: *Cumitech 1: Blood Cultures*. Sherris JC (editor). American Society for Microbiology, 1974.

DeLouvois J et al: Bacteriology of abscesses of the central nervous system. *Br Med J* 1977;**2**:98.

Finegold SM et al: *Cumitech 5: Practical Anaerobic Bacteriology*. Shepherd WE (editor). American Society for Microbiology, 1977.

Gorbach SL, Bartlett JG: Anaerobic infections. (3 parts.) *N Engl J Med* 1974;**290**:1177, 1237, 1289.

Jawetz E: The doctor's dilemma: Have I chosen the right drug? An adequate dose regimen? Can laboratory tests help in my decision? In: *Current Clinical Topics in Infectious Diseases*. Remington JS, Swartz MN (editors). McGraw-Hill, 1981.

Jawetz E et al: Laboratory test for antibiotic combinations. *Am J Clin Pathol* 1955;**25**:1016.

Kunin CM: *Detection, Prevention and Management of Urinary Tract Infections*, 3rd ed. Lea & Febiger, 1979.

Lennette EH, Spaulding EH, Truant JP (editors): *Manual of Clinical Microbiology*, 3rd ed. American Society for Microbiology, 1980.

Levison ML, Frank PF: Differentiation of group A from other beta hemolytic streptococci with bacitracin. *J Bacteriol* 1955;**69**:284.

Reller LB, Stratton CW: Serum dilution test for bactericidal action: Standardization and correlation with antimicrobial assays and susceptibility tests. *J Infect Dis* 1977;**136**:196.

Rose NR, Friedman H (editors): *Manual of Clinical Immunology*, 2nd ed. American Society for Microbiology, 1981.

Thornsberry C et al: *Cumitech 6: New Developments in Antimicrobial Susceptibility Testing*. Sherris JC (editor). American Society for Microbiology, 1977.

Vickery DM, Quinnell RK: Fever of unknown origin: An algorithmic approach. *JAMA* 1977;**238**:2183.

27 | General Properties of Viruses

DEFINITIONS

Viruses are the smallest infectious agents (20–300 nm in diameter), containing one kind of nucleic acid (RNA or DNA) as their genome, usually as a single molecule. The nucleic acid is encased in a protein shell, and the entire infectious unit is termed a virion. Viruses replicate only in living cells. The viral nucleic acid contains information necessary for programming the infected host cell to synthesize a number of virus-specific macromolecules required for the production of virus progeny. During the replicative cycle, numerous copies of viral nucleic acid and coat proteins

are produced. The coat proteins assemble together to form the capsid, which encases and stabilizes the viral nucleic acid against the extracellular environment and facilitates the attachment and perhaps penetration of the virus upon contact with new susceptible cells.

The nucleic acid, once isolated from the virion, can be hydrolyzed by either ribo- or deoxyribonuclease, whereas the nucleic acid within the intact virus is not affected by such treatment. In contrast, viral antiserum will neutralize the virion because it reacts with the antigens of the protein coat. However, the same antiserum has no effect on the free infectious nucleic acid isolated from the virion.

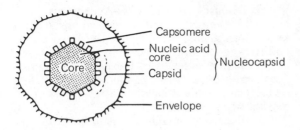

Figure 27–1. Schematic diagram illustrating the components of the complete virus particle, or the virion.

The host range for a given virus may be extremely limited, but viruses are known to infect unicellular organisms such as mycoplasmas, bacteria, and algae and all higher plants and animals.

Much information on virus-host relationships has been obtained from studies on bacteriophages, the viruses that attack bacteria. This subject is discussed in Chapter 9. Properties of individual viruses are discussed in Chapters 30–39.

Some Useful Definitions in Virology (Fig 27–1)

Capsid: The symmetric protein shell that encloses the nucleic acid genome. Often, empty capsids are by-products of the viral replicative cycle.

Nucleocapsid: The capsid together with the enclosed nucleic acid.

Structural units: The basic protein building blocks of the capsid.

Capsomeres: Morphologic units seen in the electron microscope on the surface of virus particles. Capsomeres represent clusters of polypeptides, which when completely assembled form the capsid.

Virion: The complete infective virus particle, which in some instances (adenoviruses, papovaviruses, picornaviruses) may be identical with the nucleocapsid. In more complex virions (herpesviruses, myxoviruses), this includes the nucleocapsid plus a surrounding envelope.

Defective virus: A virus particle that is functionally deficient in some aspect of replication. Defective virus may interfere with the replication of normal virus.

Pseudovirions: During viral replication the capsid sometimes encloses host nucleic acid rather than viral nucleic acid. Such particles look like ordinary virus particles when observed by electron microscopy, but they do not replicate. Pseudovirions contain the "wrong" nucleic acid.

Primary, secondary, and tertiary nucleic acid structure: Primary structure refers to the sequence of bases in the nucleic acid chain. Secondary structure refers to the spatial arrangement of the complete nucleic acid chain, ie, whether it is single- or double-stranded, circular or linear in conformation. Tertiary structure refers to other elements of fine spatial detail in the helix, eg, presence of supercoiling, breakage points, regions of strand separation.

Transcription: The mechanism by which specific information encoded in a nucleic acid chain is transferred to messenger RNA.

Translation: The mechanism by which a particular base sequence in messenger RNA results in production of a specific amino acid sequence in a protein.

EVOLUTIONARY ORIGIN OF VIRUSES

The origin of viruses is not known. Three hypotheses have been proposed:

(1) Viruses became parasites of primitive cells, and the 2 evolved together. Many viruses today cause no host cell damage and remain latent in the host.

(2) Viruses evolved from parasitic bacteria. While this possibility exists for other obligatory intracellular organisms, eg, chlamydiae, there is no evidence that viruses evolved from bacteria.

(3) Viruses may be components of host cells that become autonomous. They resemble genes that escape the regulatory control of the host cell. There is evidence that some tumor viruses exist in host cells as unexpressed genes. The likelihood is great that some small viruses evolved in this fashion. On the other hand, large viruses of the pox or herpes groups show very limited resemblance to host cell DNA.

CLASSIFICATION OF VIRUSES

Basis of Classification

The following properties, listed in the order of preference or importance, have been used as a basis for the classification of viruses. The amount of information available in each category is not uniform for all viruses. For some agents, knowledge is at hand about only a few of the properties listed.

(1) Nucleic acid type: RNA or DNA; single-stranded or double-stranded; strategy of replication.

(2) Size and morphology, including type of symmetry, number of capsomeres, and presence of membranes.

(3) Presence of specific enzymes, particularly RNA and DNA polymerases concerned with genome replication, and neuraminidase necessary for release of certain virus particles (influenza) from the cells in which they were formed.

(4) Susceptibility to physical and chemical agents, especially ether.

(5) Immunologic properties.

(6) Natural methods of transmission.

(7) Host, tissue, and cell tropisms.

(8) Pathology; inclusion body formation.

(9) Symptomatology.

Classification by Symptomatology

The oldest classification of viruses is based on the diseases they produce, and this system offers certain conveniences for the clinician. However, it is not satisfactory for the biologist because the same virus may appear in several groups, since it causes more than one disease depending upon the organ attacked.

A. Generalized Diseases: Diseases in which virus is spread throughout the body via the bloodstream and in which multiple organs are affected. Skin rashes may occur. These include smallpox, vaccinia, measles, rubella, chickenpox, yellow fever, dengue, enteroviruses, and many others.

B. Diseases Primarily Affecting Specific Organs: The virus may spread to the organ through the bloodstream, along the peripheral nerves, or by other routes.

1. Diseases of the nervous system–Poliomyelitis, aseptic meningitis (polio-, coxsackie-, and echoviruses), rabies, arthropod-borne encephalitides, lymphocytic choriomeningitis, herpes simplex, meningoencephalitis of mumps, measles, vaccinia, and "slow" virus infections.

2. Diseases of the respiratory tract–Influenza, parainfluenza, respiratory syncytial virus pneumonia and bronchiolitis, adenovirus pharyngitis, common cold (caused by many viruses).

3. Localized diseases of the skin or mucous membranes–Herpes simplex type 1 (usually oral) and type 2 (usually genital), molluscum contagiosum, warts, herpangina, herpes zoster, and others.

4. Diseases of the eye–Adenovirus conjunctivitis, Newcastle virus conjunctivitis, herpes keratoconjunctivitis, and epidemic hemorrhagic conjunctivitis (enterovirus-70).

5. Diseases of the liver–Hepatitis type A (infectious hepatitis) and type B (serum hepatitis), yellow fever, and, in the neonate, enteroviruses, herpesviruses, and rubella virus.

6. Diseases of the salivary glands–Mumps and cytomegalovirus.

7. Diseases of the gastrointestinal tract–Rotavirus, Norwalk type virus.

8. Sexually transmitted diseases–Until recently, only bacteria (*Neisseria gonorrhoeae, Treponema pallidum,* and *Chlamydia trachomatis*) were included in this category of disease. It is now recognized that herpes simplex virus, hepatitis B virus, papilloma virus, molluscum contagiosum virus, and probably cytomegalovirus are all venereal pathogens.

Classification by Biologic, Chemical, & Physical Properties

Viruses can be clearly separated into families on the basis of the nucleic acid genome and the size, shape, substructure, and mode of replication of the virus particle. Table 27–1 shows one scheme used for classification. However, there is not complete agreement among virologists on the relative importance of the criteria used to classify viruses.

Within each family, genera are usually based on antigenicity. Properties of the major families of animal

Table 27–1. Classification of viruses into families based on chemical and physical properties.

Nucleic Acid Core	Capsid Symmetry	Virion: Enveloped or Naked	Ether Sensitivity	No. of Capsomeres	Virus Particle Size (nm)*	Molecular Weight of Nucleic Acid in Virion ($\times 10^6$)	Physical Type of Nucleic Acid	No. of Genes (Approx.)	Virus Family
DNA	Icosahedral	Naked	Resistant	32	18–26	1.5–2.2	SS	3–4	Parvoviridae
				72	45–55	3–5	DS circular	5–8	Papovaviridae
				252	70–90	20–30	DS	30	Adenoviridae
		Enveloped	Sensitive	162	100†	90–130	DS	160	Herpesviridae
	Complex	Complex coats	Resistant‡		230 × 400	130–240	DS	300	Poxviridae
RNA	Icosahedral	Naked	Resistant	32	20–30	2–2.8	SS	4–6	Picornaviridae
				?§	60–80	12–19	DS segmented	10–12	Reoviridae
		Enveloped	Sensitive	32?	30–90	4	SS	10	Togaviridae
	Unknown or complex	Enveloped	Sensitive		50–300	3–5	SS segmented	10	Arenaviridae
					80–130	7	SS	30	Coronaviridae
					~100	7–10	SS segmented	>4	Retroviridae
	Helical	Enveloped	Sensitive		90–100	6–15	SS segmented	>3	Bunyaviridae
					80–120	5	SS segmented	>8	Orthomyxoviridae
					150–300	5–8	SS	>10	Paramyxoviridae
					70 × 175	3–4	SS	>5	Rhabdoviridae

*Diameter, or diameter × length.

†The naked virus, ie, the nucleocapsid, is 100 nm in diameter; however, the enveloped virion varies up to 200 nm.

‡The genus *Orthopoxvirus*, which includes the better studied poxviruses, eg, vaccinia, variola, cowpox, ectromelia, rabbitpox, monkeypox, is ether-resistant. Some of the poxviruses belonging to other genera are ether-sensitive.

§Reoviruses contain an outer and an inner capsid. The inner capsid appears to contain 32 capsomeres, but the number on the outer capsid has not been definitely established. A total of 92 capsomeres has been suggested.

viruses are summarized in Table 27–1, are discussed briefly below, and are considered in greater detail in the chapters that follow.

DNA-Containing Viruses

A. Parvoviruses: Very small viruses with a particle size of about 20 nm. They contain single-stranded DNA and have cubic symmetry, with 32 capsomeres 2–4 nm in diameter. They have no envelope. Replication and capsid assembly take place in the nucleus of the infected cell. Parvoviruses of rodents and swine replicate autonomously. The adenoassociated satellite viruses are defective, ie, they require the presence of an adenovirus or a herpesvirus as a "helper." Some satellite viruses occur in humans. (See Chapter 37.)

B. Papovaviruses: Small (45–55 nm), ether-resistant viruses containing double-stranded circular DNA and exhibiting cubic symmetry, with 72 capsomeres. Known human papovaviruses are the papilloma (wart) virus (see Chapter 39) and agents isolated from brain tissue of patients with progressive multifocal leukoencephalopathy (JC virus) or from the urine of immunosuppressed renal transplant recipients (BK virus) (see Chapter 33). In animals, there are papilloma, polyoma, and vacuolating viruses. These agents have a slow growth cycle and replicate within the nucleus. Papovaviruses produce latent and chronic infections in their natural hosts, and all can induce tumors in some animal species. (See Chapter 40.)

C. Adenoviruses: Medium-sized (70–90 nm) viruses containing double-stranded DNA and exhibiting cubic symmetry, with 252 capsomeres. They have no envelope. At least 37 types infect humans, especially in mucous membranes, and they can persist in lymphoid tissue. Some adenoviruses cause acute respiratory diseases, pharyngitis, and conjunctivitis. Some human adenoviruses can induce tumors in newborn hamsters. There are many serotypes that infect animals. (See Chapters 37 and 40.)

D. Herpesviruses: Medium-sized viruses containing double-stranded DNA. The nucleocapsid is 100 nm in diameter, with cubic symmetry and 162 capsomeres. It is surrounded by a lipid-containing envelope (150–200 nm in diameter). Latent infections may last for the life span of the host.

Human herpesviruses include herpes simplex types 1 and 2 (oral and genital lesions); varicella-zoster virus (shingles and chickenpox); cytomegalovirus; and EB virus (infectious mononucleosis and association with human neoplasms). Other herpesviruses occur in many animals. (See Chapters 38 and 40.)

E. Poxviruses: Large brick-shaped or ovoid (230 × 400 nm) viruses containing double-stranded DNA, with a lipid-containing envelope. All poxviruses share a common nucleoprotein antigen and contain several enzymes in the virion, including a DNA-dependent RNA polymerase. Poxviruses replicate entirely within cell cytoplasm. All poxviruses tend to produce skin lesions. Some are pathogenic for humans (smallpox, vaccinia, molluscum contagiosum), others for ani-

mals. (Some of the latter can infect humans, eg, cowpox, monkeypox.) (See Chapter 36.)

RNA-Containing Viruses

A. Picornaviruses: Small (20–30 nm), ether-resistant viruses containing single-stranded RNA and exhibiting cubic symmetry. The groups infecting humans are rhinoviruses (more than 100 serotypes causing common colds) and enteroviruses (polio-, coxsackie-, and echoviruses). Rhinoviruses are acid-labile and have a high density; enteroviruses are acid-stable and have a lower density. Picornaviruses infecting animals include foot-and-mouth disease of cattle and encephalomyocarditis of rodents. (See Chapter 31.)

B. Reoviruses: Medium-sized (60–80 nm), ether-resistant viruses containing a segmented double-stranded RNA and having cubic symmetry. Reoviruses of humans include rotaviruses, which cause infantile gastroenteritis and have a distinctive wheel-shaped appearance. Antigenically similar reoviruses infect many animals. Orbiviruses constitute a distinct subgroup that includes Colorado tick fever virus of humans and other agents that infect plants, insects, and animals (blue tongue of cattle and sheep). (See Chapter 39.)

C. Arboviruses: An ecologic grouping of viruses with diverse physical and chemical properties. All of these viruses (more than 350) have a complex cycle involving vertebrate hosts and arthropods as vectors transmitting the viruses by their bite. Arboviruses infect humans, mammals, birds, and snakes, and mosquitoes and ticks as vectors. Human pathogens include dengue, yellow fever, encephalitis viruses, and others. Arboviruses belong to several groups, including toga-, bunya-, rhabdo-, arena-, and reoviruses, described here. (See Chapter 30.)

D. Togaviruses: Most arboviruses of antigenic groups A and B and rubella virus belong here. They have a lipid-containing envelope, are ether-sensitive, and their genome is single-stranded RNA. The enveloped virion measures 40–70 nm. The virus particles mature by budding from the host cell membrane. Some togaviruses, eg, Sindbis virus, possess a 35-nm nucleocapsid and within it a spherical core 12–16 nm in diameter. Sindbis virus may have 32 capsomeres in an icosahedral surface lattice. (See Chapters 30 and 35.)

E. Arenaviruses: RNA-containing, enveloped viruses ranging in size from 50 to 300 nm. They share morphologic, biologic, and antigenic properties of arboviruses of the Tacaribe complex, Lassa fever, and lymphocytic choriomeningitis. Some produce "slow" virus infections. (See Chapters 30 and 33.)

F. Coronaviruses: Enveloped, 80- to 130-nm particles containing an unsegmented genome of single-stranded RNA; the nucleocapsid is probably helical, 7–9 nm in diameter. They resemble orthomyxoviruses, but coronaviruses have petal-shaped surface projections arranged in a fringe like a solar corona. Coronavirus nucleocapsids develop in the cytoplasm and mature by budding into cytoplasmic vesicles. Human coronaviruses have been isolated from acute upper respiratory tract illnesses— "colds." Coronaviruses of animals include avian infectious bronchitis virus among many others. (See Chapter 34.)

G. Retroviruses: Enveloped viruses whose genome contains duplicate copies of high-molecular-weight single-stranded RNA of the same polarity as viral messenger RNA. The virion contains various enzymes including reverse transcriptase (RNA → DNA). Leukemia and sarcoma viruses of animals (see Chapter 40), foamy viruses of primates, and some "slow" viruses (visna, maedi of sheep) are included (see Chapter 33).

H. Bunyaviruses: Spherical, 90- to 100-nm particles that replicate in the cytoplasm and acquire an envelope by budding through the cell membrane. The genome is made up of a triple-segmented, single-stranded RNA. About 70 are antigenically related to Bunyamwera virus; 50 others are not but are morphologically similar. (See Chapter 30.)

I. Orthomyxoviruses: Medium-sized, 80- to 120-nm enveloped viruses containing a segmented single-stranded RNA genome and exhibiting helical symmetry. Particles are either round or filamentous. Most orthomyxoviruses have surface projections as part of their outer wall (hemagglutinin, neuraminidase). The internal nucleoprotein helix measures 6–9 nm, and the RNA is made up of 8 segments. During replication, the nucleocapsid is formed in the nucleus, whereas the hemagglutinin and neuraminidase are formed in the cytoplasm. The virus matures by budding at the cell membrane. Orthomyxoviruses are sensitive to dactinomycin. All orthomyxoviruses are influenza viruses that infect humans or animals. (See Chapter 34.)

J. Paramyxoviruses: Similar to but larger (150–300 nm) than orthomyxoviruses. The internal nucleocapsid measures 18 nm, and the molecular weight of the single-stranded nonsegmented RNA is 4 times greater than that of orthomyxoviruses. Both the nucleocapsid and the hemagglutinin are formed in the cytoplasm. Paramyxoviruses are resistant to dactinomycin. Those infecting humans include mumps, measles, parainfluenza virus, and respiratory syncytial virus. Others infect animals. (See Chapter 35.)

K. Rhabdoviruses: Enveloped virions resembling a bullet, flat at one end and round at the other (Fig 27–35), measuring about 70 × 175 nm. The envelope has 10-nm spikes. The genome is single-stranded RNA. Particles are formed by budding from the cell membrane. Rabies virus is a member of this group along with many other viruses of animals and plants. (See Chapter 33.)

L. Other Viruses: Insufficient information to permit classification. This applies to hepatitis viruses (see Chapter 32), to agents responsible for some immune complex diseases and for some "slow" virus diseases (see Chapter 33), and to some viruses of gastroenteritis (see Chapter 39).

M. Viroids: Small infectious agents causing diseases of plants and possibly animals and humans. They are nucleic acid molecules (MW 70,000–120,000) without a protein coat. Plant viroids are single-stranded, covalently closed circular RNA molecules consisting of about 360 nucleotides and comprising a highly base-paired rodlike structure with unique properties. They are arranged in 26 double-stranded segments separated by 25 regions of unpaired bases embodied in single-stranded internal loops; there is a loop at each end of the rodlike molecule. These features provide the viroid RNA molecule with structural, thermodynamic, and kinetic properties very similar to those of a double-stranded DNA molecule of the same molecular weight and G + C content. Viroids replicate by an entirely novel mechanism in which infecting viroid RNA molecules are copied by the host enzyme normally responsible for synthesis of nuclear precursors to messenger RNA. Thus, DNA-dependent RNA polymerase purified from healthy plant tissue is capable of synthesizing linear (−) viroid RNA copies of full length from (+) viroid RNA templates in vitro.

The infectious agents of degenerative neurologic disorders such as kuru or Creutzfeldt-Jakob disease, or scrapie of sheep, may fit into this category. (The agent of the latter may be a DNA molecule similar in size to plant viroid RNA. See Chapter 33.)

CULTIVATION; QUANTIFICATION; INCLUSION BODIES; CHROMOSOME DAMAGE

Cultivation of Viruses

At present, many viruses can be grown in cell cultures or in fertile eggs under strictly controlled conditions. Growth of virus in animals is still used for the primary isolation of certain viruses and for the study of pathogenesis of viruses and of viral oncogenesis.

A. Chick Embryos: Virus growth in an embryonated chick egg may result in the death of the embryo (eg, encephalitis virus), the production of pocks or plaques on the chorioallantoic membrane (eg, herpes, smallpox, vaccinia), the development of hemagglutinins in the embryonic fluids or tissues (eg, influenza), or the development of infective virus (eg, poliovirus type 2).

B. Tissue Cultures: The availability of cells grown in vitro has facilitated the identification and cultivation of newly isolated and previously known viruses. There are 3 basic types of cell culture. Primary cultures are made by dispersing cells (usually with trypsin) from host tissues. In general, they are unable to grow for more than a few passages in culture, as secondary cultures. Diploid cell strains are secondary cultures which have undergone a change that allows their limited culture (up to 50 passages) but which retain their normal chromosome pattern. Continuous cell lines are cultures capable of more prolonged (perhaps indefinite) culture which have been derived from cell strains or from malignant tissues. They invariably have altered and irregular numbers of chromosomes.

The type of cell culture used for virus cultivation depends on the sensitivity of the cells to that particular virus. In the clinical laboratory, multiplication of the virus can be followed by determining the following:

1. The cytopathic effect, or necrosis of cells in the tissue culture (polio, herpes, measles, adenovirus, cytomegalovirus, etc).

2. The inhibition of cellular metabolism, or failure of virus-infected cells to produce acid (eg, enteroviruses).

3. The appearance of a hemagglutinin (eg, mumps, influenza) or complement-fixing antigen (eg, poliomyelitis, varicella, measles).

4. The adsorption of erythrocytes to infected cells, called hemadsorption (parainfluenza, influenza). This reaction becomes positive before cytopathic changes are visible, and in some cases it is the only means of detecting the presence of the virus.

5. Interference by a noncytopathogenic virus (eg, rubella) with replication and cytopathic effect of a second, indicator virus (eg, echovirus).

6. Morphologic transformation by an oncogenic virus (eg, SV40, Rous sarcoma virus), usually accompanied by the loss of contact inhibition and the piling up of cells into discrete foci. Such alterations are a heritable property of the transformed cells.

Quantification of Virus

A. Physical Methods: Virus particles can be counted directly in the electron microscope by comparison with a standard suspension of latex particles of similar small size. However, a relatively concentrated preparation of virus is necessary for this procedure, and infectious virus particles cannot be distinguished from noninfectious ones.

Hemagglutination. The red blood cells of humans and some animals can be agglutinated by different viruses. Both infective and noninfective particles give this reaction; thus, hemagglutination measures the total quantity of virus present.

The orthomyxoviruses contain a hemagglutinin that is an integral part of the viral envelope. Once these viruses have agglutinated with the cells, spontaneous dissociation of the virus from the cells can occur. The dissociated cells can no longer be agglutinated by the same virus species, but the recovered virus is able to agglutinate fresh cells. (See Chapter 34.) This is due to the destruction of specific mucopolysaccharide receptor sites on the surface of the erythrocyte by the enzyme neuraminidase of the virus particles.

Paramyxoviruses growing in cell culture can be detected by hemadsorption. Erythrocytes adsorb to each infected cell.

Poxviruses have an agglutinin for red cells (a phospholipid-protein complex) that can be separated from the infective virus particle.

Arboviruses and others have hemagglutinins that appear to be identical with the virus particle. The union

between hemagglutinin and red blood cells is irreversible.

B. Biologic Methods: Quantal assays depend on the measurement of animal death, animal infection, or cytopathic effects in tissue culture upon end point dilution of the virus being tested. The titer is expressed as the 50% infectious dose (ID_{50}), which is the reciprocal of the dilution of virus that produces the effect in 50% of the cells or animals inoculated. Precise assays require the use of a large number of test subjects.

The most widely used assay for infectious virus is the plaque assay. Monolayers of host cells are inoculated with suitable dilutions of virus and after adsorption are overlaid with medium containing agar or carboxymethylcellulose to prevent virus spreading. After several days, the cells initially infected have produced virus that spreads only to surrounding cells, producing a small area of infection, or plaque. Under controlled conditions a single plaque can arise from a single infectious virus particle, termed a plaque-forming unit (PFU). The cytopathic effect of infected cells within the plaque can be distinguished from uninfected cells of the monolayer, with or without suitable staining, and plaques can usually be counted macroscopically (see Fig 27–26). The ratio of infectious to physical particles varies widely, from near unity to less than 1 per 1000.

Certain viruses such as herpes or vaccinia form pocks when inoculated onto the chorioallantoic membrane of the embryonated egg. Such viruses can be quantitated by relating the number of pocks counted to the virus dilution.

Inclusion Body Formation

In the course of virus multiplication within cells, virus-specific structures called inclusion bodies may be produced (see Fig 27–29). They become far larger than the individual virus particle and often have an affinity for acid dyes (eg, eosin). They may be situated in the nucleus (herpesvirus), in the cytoplasm (poxvirus), or in both (measles virus). In many viral infections, the inclusion bodies are the site of development of the virions (the virus factories). In some infections (molluscum contagiosum), the inclusion body consists of masses of virus particles that can be seen in the electron microscope to ripen to maturity within the inclusion body. In others (as in the intranuclear inclusion body of herpes), the virus appears to have multiplied within the nucleus early in the infection, and the inclusion body appears to be a remnant of virus multiplication. Variations in the appearance of inclusion material depend largely upon the fixative used.

The presence of inclusion bodies may be of considerable diagnostic aid. The intracytoplasmic inclusion in nerve cells, the Negri body, is pathognomonic for rabies.

Chromosome Damage

One of the consequences of infection of cells by viruses is derangement of the karyotype. Most of the changes observed are random. Frequently, breakage, fragmentation, rearrangement of the chromosomes, abnormal chromosomes, and changes in chromosome number occur. Herpes zoster virus interrupts the mitotic cycle of human cells in culture, resulting in formation of micronuclei and fragmentation of some chromosomes. Chromosome breaks have also been observed in leukocytes from cases of chickenpox or measles. These viruses, as well as rubella virus, cause similar aberrations when inoculated into cultured cells. Cells infected with or transformed to malignancy by SV40, polyoma, or adenovirus type 12 also exhibit random chromosomal abnormalities.

The Chinese hamster cell has a stable karyotype composed of 22 chromosomes. Inoculation of these hamster cells with herpes simplex virus results in chromosome aberrations that are not random in distribution. Most of the breaks occur in region 7 of chromosome No. 1 and in region 3 of the X chromosome. The Y chromosome is unaffected. Replication of the virus is necessary for induction of the chromosome aberrations. To date, no pathognomonic chromosome alterations have been identified in virus-infected cells in humans.

STRUCTURE & SIZE OF VIRUSES

Virus Particles

Advances in x-ray diffraction techniques and electron microscopy have made it possible to resolve fine differences in the basic morphology of viruses. The study of virus symmetry in the electron microscope requires the use of heavy metal stains (eg, potassium phosphotungstate) to emphasize surface structure. The heavy metal permeates the virus particle as a cloud and brings out the surface structure of viruses by virtue of "negative staining."

Virus architecture can be grouped into 3 types based on the arrangement of morphologic subunits: (1) those with helical symmetry, eg, paramyxo- and orthomyxoviruses; (2) those with cubic symmetry, eg, adenoviruses; and (3) those with complex structures, eg, poxviruses. All cubic symmetry observed with animal viruses to date is of the icosahedral pattern. The icosahedron has 20 faces (each an equilateral triangle), 12 vertices, and 5-fold, 3-fold, and 2-fold axes of rotational symmetry. Capsomeres can be arranged to comply with icosahedral symmetry in a limited number of ways, expressed by the formula $N = 10(n-1)^2 + 2$, where N is the total number of capsomeres and n the number of capsomeres on one side of each equilateral triangle. Table 27–2 shows the number of capsomeres where n varies from 2 to 6, in several virus groups.

Icosahedral structures can be built from one simple, asymmetric building unit, arranged as 12 pentamer units and x number of hexamer units. The smallest and most basic capsid is that of the phage ϕX-174, which simply consists of 12 pentamer units.

Viruses exhibiting icosahedral symmetry can also be grouped according to their triangulation number, T,

Table 27–2. Number of capsomeres in several virus groups.

Virus Family	n	T	Capsomeres
Phage (ϕX-174)	2	1	12
Picorna*	2	3	32
Papova†	3	7	72
Reo	4	9	92(?)
Herpes	5	16	162
Adeno	6	25	252

*Picornaviruses are a special case and, for $n = 2$, fit the formula $N = 30(n-1)^2 + 2$.
†Capsomeres in a skew arrangement.

which is the number of small triangles formed on the single face of the icosahedron when all its adjacent morphologic subunits are connected by lines. One class has T values of 1, 4, 9, 16, and 25; a second class, values of 3 and 12; and a third class, values of 7, 13, 19, and 21. The number of morphologic units (capsomeres) is expressed by the formula $M = 10T + 2$. Table 27–2 shows the triangulation number for several virus groups. This formula for triangulation number originated in the idea that those viruses would be formed from small subunits so as to give a surface lattice representing the minimum-energy design for closed shells arranged from identical units.

An example of icosahedral symmetry is seen in Fig 27–2. The adenovirus ($n = 6$) model illustrated shows the 6 capsomeres along one edge (Fig 27–2[a]). Degradation of this virus with sodium lauryl sulfate releases the capsomeres in groups of 9 (Fig 27–2[b], [c]) and possibly groups of 6. The groups of 9 lie on the faces and include one capsomere from each of the 3 edges of the face, and the groups of 6 would be from the vertices. The groups of 9 form the faces of the 20 triangular facets, making the adenovirus icosahedron account for 180 subunits, and the groups of 6 which form the 12 vertices account for 72 capsomeres, thus totaling 252.

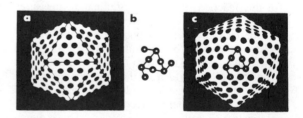

Figure 27–2. *(a)* Representation of the capsomere arrangement of an adenovirus particle, as viewed through the 2-fold axis of symmetry. *(b)* Arrangement of capsomere group of 9, obtained by treatment of an adenovirus with sodium lauryl sulfate. *(c)* Orientation of the capsomere group of 9 on the adenovirus particle. If the model were marked to show the maximum number of small triangles formed on one face of the icosahedron by drawing a line between each adjacent morphologic subunit, it would yield the triangulation number for the adenovirus particle, which in this case turns out to be 25.

Measuring the Sizes of Viruses

Small size and ability to pass through filters that hold back bacteria are classic attributes of viruses. However, because some bacteria may be smaller than the largest viruses, filtrability is no longer regarded as a unique feature of viruses.

The following methods are used for determining the sizes of viruses and their components.

A. Filtration Through Collodion Membranes of Graded Porosity: These membranes are available with pores of different sizes. If the virus preparation is passed through a series of membranes of known pore size, the approximate size of any virus can be measured by determining which membranes allow the infective unit to pass and which hold it back. The size of the limiting APD (average pore diameter) multiplied by 0.64 yields the diameter of the virus particle. The passage of a virus through a filter will also depend on the physical structure of the virus; thus, only a very approximate estimate of size is obtained.

B. Sedimentation in the Ultracentrifuge: If particles are suspended in a liquid, they will settle to the bottom at a rate that is proportionate to their size. In an ultracentrifuge, forces of more than 100,000 times gravity may be used to drive the particles to the bottom of the tube. The relationship between the size and shape of a particle and its rate of sedimentation permits determination of particle size. Once again, the physical structure of the virus will affect the size estimate obtained.

C. Direct Observation in the Electron Microscope: As compared with the light microscope, the electron microscope uses electrons rather than light waves and electromagnetic lenses rather than glass lenses. The electron beam obtained has a much shorter wavelength than that of light, so that objects much smaller than the wavelength of visible or ultraviolet light can be visualized. Viruses can be visualized in preparations from tissue extracts and in ultrathin sections of infected cells. Electron microscopy is the most widely used method for estimating particle size.

D. Ionizing Radiation: When a beam of charged particles such as high-energy electrons, alpha particles, or deuterons passes through a virus, it causes an energy loss in the form of primary ionization. The release of ionization within the virus particle proportionately inactivates certain biologic properties of the virus particle such as infectivity, antigenicity, and hemagglutination. Thus, the size of the biologic unit responsible for a given function in a virus particle can be estimated.

E. Comparative Measurements: (See Table 27-1.) For purposes of reference, it should be recalled that: (1) *Staphylococcus* has a diameter of about 1000 nm. (2) Bacterial viruses (bacteriophages) vary in size (10-100 nm). Some are spherical or hexagonal and have short or long tails. (3) Representative protein molecules range in diameter from serum albumin (5 nm) and globulin (7 nm) to certain hemocyanins (23 nm).

The relative size and morphology of various virus families are shown in Fig 27-3. Particles with a 2-fold difference in diameter have an 8-fold difference in volume. Thus, the mass of a poxvirus is about 1000 times greater than that of the poliovirus particle, and the mass of a small bacterium is 50,000 times greater.

CHEMICAL COMPOSITION OF VIRUSES

Viral Protein

The structural proteins of viruses have several important functions. They serve to protect the viral genome against inactivation by nucleases, participate in the attachment of the virus particle to a susceptible cell, and are responsible for the structural symmetry of the virus particle. Also, the proteins determine the antigenic characteristics of the virus.

Virus structural proteins may be very specialized molecules designed to perform a specific task: (1) vaccinia virus carries many enzymes within its particle to perform certain functions early in the infectious cycle; (2) some viruses have specific proteins for attachment to cells, eg, influenza virus hemagglutinin; and (3) RNA tumor viruses contain an enzyme, reverse transcriptase, that makes a DNA copy of the virus RNA, which is an important step in transformation by these viruses.

Viral Nucleic Acid

Viruses contain a single kind of nucleic acid, either DNA or RNA, that encodes the genetic information necessary for the replication of the virus. The RNA or DNA genome may be single-stranded or double-stranded, and the strandedness, the type of nucleic acid, and the molecular weight are major characteristics used for classifying viruses into families (Table 27-1).

The molecular weight of the viral DNA genome ranges from 1.5×10^6 (parvoviruses) to 160×10^6 (poxviruses). The molecular weight of the viral RNA genome ranges from 1×10^6 (for bromegrass mosaic virus) to 15×10^6 (for reoviruses).

The sequence and composition of nucleotides of each viral nucleic acid are distinctive. One of the properties useful for characterizing a viral nucleic acid is its guanine + cytosine (G + C) content.

Most viral genomes are quite fragile once they are removed from their protective protein capsid, but some nucleic acid molecules have been examined in the electron microscope without disruption, and their lengths have been measured. If linear densities of approximately 2×10^6 per μm for double-stranded nucleic acid and 1×10^6 per μm for single-stranded forms are used, molecular weights of viral genomes can be calculated from direct measurements (Table 27-1).

All major DNA virus groups in Table 27-1 have genomes that are single molecules of DNA and have a linear or a circular configuration. This circle is often supercoiled (Fig 27-4) in the virion.

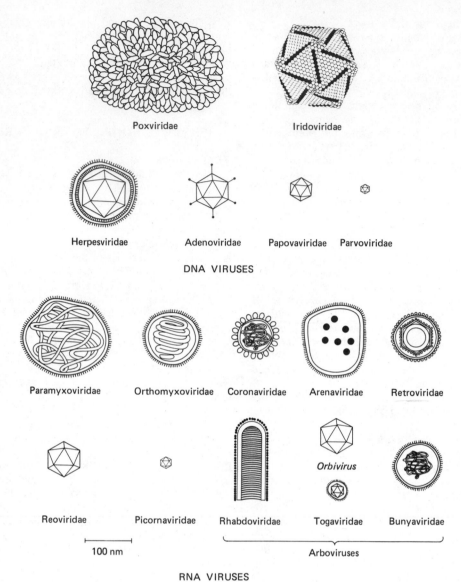

DNA VIRUSES

RNA VIRUSES

Figure 27–3. Diagram illustrating the shapes and relative sizes of animal viruses of the major families. (Reproduced, with permission, from Fenner F, White DO: *Medical Virology,* 2nd ed. Academic Press, 1976.)

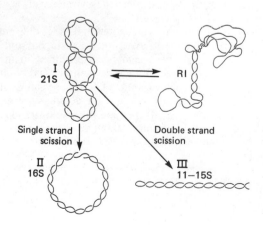

Figure 27–4. Forms of DNA of papovavirus SV40 and sedimentation coefficients in neutral sucrose gradients: supercoiled (I), nicked (II), linear (III), and replicative intermediate (RI). Linear DNA is formed by restriction endonucleases, which cleave both strands of the DNA at a single site. The RI shows 2 forks, 3 branches, and no ends, as seen in electron microscopy. (See Fig 27–24.)

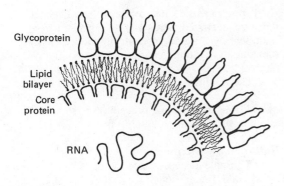

Figure 27–5. Proposed structure of Sindbis virus. (After Harrison et al.)

Glycoprotein

Lipid bilayer

Core protein

RNA

the infected cell. The isolated RNA of other RNA viruses is not infectious. For these virus families, the virions carry an RNA polymerase which in the cell transcribes the genome RNA molecules into several complementary RNA molecules, each of which may serve as a messenger RNA.

Molecular hybridization techniques (DNA to DNA, DNA to RNA, or RNA to RNA) permit the study of transcription of the viral genome within the infected cell as well as the relatedness of different viruses.

The number of genes in a virus can be approximated if one makes certain assumptions about (1) triplet code, (2) the molecular weight of the genome, and (3) the average size of a protein (Table 27–1).

Viral Lipids

A number of different viruses contain lipids as part of their structure (eg, Sindbis virus [Fig 27–5]). Such lipid-containing viruses are sensitive to treatment with ether and other organic solvents (Table 27–1), indicating that disruption or loss of lipid results in loss of infectivity. Non-lipid-containing viruses are generally resistant to ether.

Viral RNAs exist in several forms. The RNA may be a single linear molecule (eg, picornavirus). For other viruses (eg, orthomyxovirus), the genome consists of several segments of RNA that may be loosely linked together within the virion. The isolated RNA of picornaviruses and togaviruses is infectious, and the entire molecule functions as a messenger RNA within

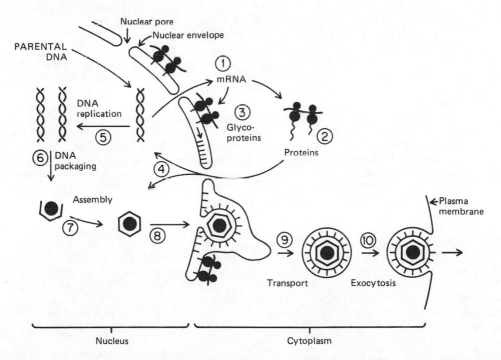

Figure 27–6. Herpesvirus morphogenesis. Diagram begins with parental DNA (upper left) in nucleus of host cell. *(1)* Viral messenger RNAs are synthesized by host cell RNA polymerase on the viral DNA template. Messengers are exported from the nucleus and initiate the synthesis of viral proteins (free polyribosomes) *(2)* and glycoproteins (membrane-bound polyribosomes) *(3)*. Viral proteins enter the nucleus *(4)*, where they promote synthesis of additional classes of viral messenger RNAs. Viral DNA polymerase enters the nucleus and initiates viral DNA replication *(5)*. DNA is cut into unit lengths, packaged into nucleoids *(6)*, and encapsidated *(7)* within an icosahedral shell. The icosahedral shell buds through the nuclear membrane, acquiring a lipoprotein envelope containing viral glycoproteins *(8)*. The mature virus is transported in vesicles to the plasma membrane *(9)*. Fusion of the vesicle with the plasma membrane results in the release of the virus into the extracellular space *(10)*. (Reproduced, with permission, from Silverstein SC: Viral replication. Pages 94–100 in: *International Textbook of Medicine.* Vol 2. *Medical Microbiology and Infectious Diseases.* Braude AI [editor]. Saunders, 1981.)

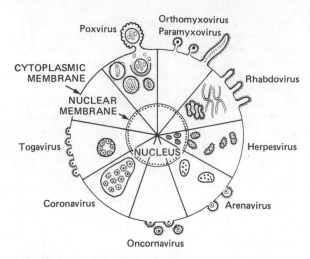

Figure 27–7. Diagrammatic relationship between lipid-containing viruses and host cell membranes. (From Blough & Tiffany.)

The specific phospholipid composition of a virion envelope may be determined by the "budding" of the virus through specific types of cell membranes in the course of maturation. For example, herpesviruses bud through the nuclear membrane of the host cell, and the phospholipid composition of the purified virus reflects the lipids of the nuclear membrane (see Fig 27–6). The different ways in which various animal viruses acquire an envelope are suggested in Fig 27–7. Budding of virions occurs only at sites where virus-specific proteins have been inserted into the host cell membrane.

Glycosphingolipids occur in the surface membrane of animal cells. When cultured cells are transformed by some oncogenic viruses, there are alterations in the various sphingolipids. These may be related to the loss of contact inhibition and to changes in surface antigens that result from viral transformation.

Viral Carbohydrates

Virus envelopes contain glycoproteins. The sugars added to virus glycoproteins often reflect the host cell in which the virus is grown. The glycoproteins are important virus antigens. As a result of their position at the outer surface of the virion, they are frequently involved in the interaction of the virus with neutralizing antibody.

PURIFICATION & IDENTIFICATION OF VIRUSES

Purification of Virus Particles

For purification studies, the starting material is usually large volumes of tissue culture medium, body fluids, or infected cells. The first step involves concentration of the virus particles by precipitation with ammonium sulfate, ethanol, or polyethylene glycol or by ultrafiltration. Hemagglutination and elution can be used to concentrate myxoviruses (see Chapter 34). Once concentrated, virus can be separated from host materials by differential centrifugation, density gradient centrifugation, column chromatography, and electrophoresis.

The minimal criteria for purity are a homogeneous appearance in electron micrographs and the failure of additional purification procedures to remove "contaminants" without reducing infectivity.

Rate-Zonal Centrifugation

A sample of concentrated virus is layered onto a preformed linear density gradient of sucrose or glycerol, and during centrifugation the virus sediments as a band at a rate determined primarily by the size and weight of the virus particle. Samples are collected by piercing a hole in the bottom of the centrifuge tube. The band of purified virus may be detected by optical methods, by radiolabeling the virus, or by assaying for infectivity.

Equilibrium Density Gradient Centrifugation

Viruses can also be purified by high-speed centrifugation in density gradients of cesium chloride (CsCl), potassium tartrate, potassium citrate, or sucrose. The gradient material of choice is the one that is least toxic to the virus. Virus particles migrate to an equilibrium position where the density of the solution is equal to their buoyant density and form a visible band. Virus bands are harvested by puncture through the bottom of the plastic centrifuge tube and assayed for infectivity.

Additional methods for purification are based on the chemical properties of the virus surface.

As shown by column chromatography, virus is bound to a substance such as DEAE or phosphocellulose, then eluted by changes in pH or salt concentration. Zone electrophoresis permits the separation of virus particles from contaminants on the basis of charge.

Identification of a Particle as a Virus

When a characteristic physical particle has been obtained, it should fulfill the following criteria before it is identified as a virus particle.

(1) The particle can be obtained only from infected cells or tissues.

(2) Particles obtained from various sources are identical, regardless of the cellular species in which the virus is grown.

(3) The degree of infective activity of the virus varies directly with the number of particles present.

(4) The degree of destruction of the physical particle by chemical or physical means is associated with a corresponding loss of virus activity.

(5) Certain properties of the particles and infectivity must be shown to be identical, such as their sedimentation behavior in the ultracentrifuge and their pH stability curves.

(6) The absorption spectrum of the purified physical particle in the ultraviolet range should coin-

cide with the ultraviolet inactivation spectrum of the virus.

(7) Antisera prepared against the infective virus should react with the characteristic particle, and vice versa. Direct observation of an unknown virus can be accomplished by electron microscopic examination of aggregate formation in a mixture of antisera and crude virus suspension.

(8) The particles should be able to induce the characteristic disease in vivo (if such experiments are feasible).

(9) Passage of the particles in tissue culture should result in the production of progeny with biologic and serologic properties of the virus.

REACTION TO PHYSICAL & CHEMICAL AGENTS

Heat & Cold

Virus infectivity is generally destroyed by heating at 50–60 °C for 30 minutes, although there are some notable exceptions (eg, hepatitis virus, adenoassociated satellite virus, scrapie virus).

Viruses can be preserved by storage at subfreezing temperatures, and some may withstand lyophilization and can thus be preserved in the dry state at 4 °C or even at room temperature. Viruses that withstand lyophilization are more heat-resistant when heated in the dry state. Enveloped viruses tend to lose infectivity after prolonged storage even at −90 °C and are particularly sensitive to repeated freezing and thawing; however, in the presence of dimethyl sulfoxide (DMSO) at concentrations of more than 5%, these viruses are stabilized.

Stabilization of Viruses by Salts

Many viruses can be stabilized by molar concentrations of salts, ie, they are not inactivated even by heating at 50 °C for 1 hour. The mechanism by which the salts stabilize virus preparations is not known. Viruses are preferentially stabilized by certain salts. Molar $MgCl_2$ stabilizes picorna- and reoviruses, molar $MgSO_4$ stabilizes orthomyxo- and paramyxoviruses, and molar Na_2SO_4 stabilizes herpesviruses.

The stability of viruses is important in the preparation of vaccines. The ordinary nonstabilized poliovaccine must be stored at freezing temperatures to preserve its potency. However, with the addition of salts for stabilization of the virus, potency can be maintained for weeks at ambient temperatures, even in the high temperatures of the tropics.

Heating of some virus preparations in the presence of high salt concentrations can be used to remove adventitious agents. For example, heating poliovirus suspensions in molar $MgCl_2$ will inactivate such simian contaminants as SV40, foamy virus, and herpes B virus but has no deleterious effect on the infectivity and potency of poliovirus.

pH

Viruses are usually stable between pH values of 5.0 and 9.0. In hemagglutination reactions, variations of less than one pH unit may influence the result.

Radiation

Ultraviolet, x-ray, and high-energy particles inactivate viruses. The dose varies for different viruses.

Vital Dyes

Viruses are penetrable to a varying degree by vital dyes such as toluidine blue, neutral red, and proflavine. These dyes bind to the viral nucleic acid, and the virus then becomes susceptible to inactivation by visible light. Impenetrable viruses like poliovirus, when grown in the dark in the presence of vital dyes, incorporate the dye into their nucleic acid and are then susceptible to photodynamic inactivation. The coat antigen is unaffected by the process.

Ether Susceptibility

Ether susceptibility can distinguish viruses that possess a lipid-rich envelope from those that do not. The following viruses are inactivated by ether: herpes-, orthomyxo-, paramyxo-, rhabdo-, corona-, retro-, arena-, toga-, and bunyaviruses. The following viruses are resistant to ether: parvo-, papova-, adeno-, picorna-, and reoviruses. Poxviruses vary in sensitivity to ether.

Antibiotics

Antibacterial antibiotics and sulfonamides have no effect on viruses. However, rifampin can inhibit poxvirus replication.

Antibacterial Agents

Quaternary ammonium compounds are not effective except for a few viruses. Organic iodine compounds are also ineffective. Larger concentrations of chlorine are required to destroy viruses than to kill bacteria, especially in the presence of extraneous proteins. For example, the chlorine treatment of stools adequate for typhoid bacilli is inadequate to destroy poliomyelitis virus present in feces. Formalin destroys resistant poliomyelitis and coxsackieviruses. Alcohols such as isopropanol and ethanol are relatively ineffective against certain viruses, especially picornaviruses.

REPLICATION OF VIRUSES

Viruses multiply only in living cells. The host cell must provide the energy and synthetic machinery and also the low-molecular-weight precursors for the synthesis of viral proteins and nucleic acids. The viral nucleic acid carries the genetic specificity to code for all the virus-specific macromolecules in a highly organized fashion. In some cases, as soon as the viral nucleic acid enters the host cell, the cellular metabolism is redirected exclusively toward the synthesis of new virus particles. In other cases the metabolic pro-

Table 27–3. Pathways of nucleic acid transcription for various virus classes.

Type of Viral Nucleic Acid	Intermediates	Type of mRNA	Example	Comments
± DS DNA	None	+ mRNA	Most DNA viruses (eg, herpesvirus, T4 bacteriophage)	
+ SS DNA	± DS DNA	+ mRNA	φX bacteriophage	See Chapter 9.
± DS RNA	None	+ mRNA	Reovirus	Virion contains RNA polymerase that transcribes each segment to mRNA.
+ SS RNA	± DS RNA	+ mRNA	Picornaviruses, togaviruses	Viral nucleic acid is infectious and serves as mRNA. For togaviruses, smaller + mRNA is also formed for certain proteins.
− SS RNA	None	+ mRNA	Rhabdoviruses, paramyxoviruses, orthomyxoviruses	Viral nucleic acid is not infectious; virion contains RNA polymerase which forms + mRNAs smaller than the genome. For orthomyxoviruses, + mRNAs are transcribed from each segment.
+ SS RNA	− DNA, ± DNA	+ mRNA	Retroviruses	Virion contains reverse transcriptase; viral RNA is not infectious but complementary DNA from transformed cell is.

DS = double-stranded   − indicates negative strand   ± indicates a helix containing a
SS = single-stranded   + indicates positive strand   positive and a negative strand

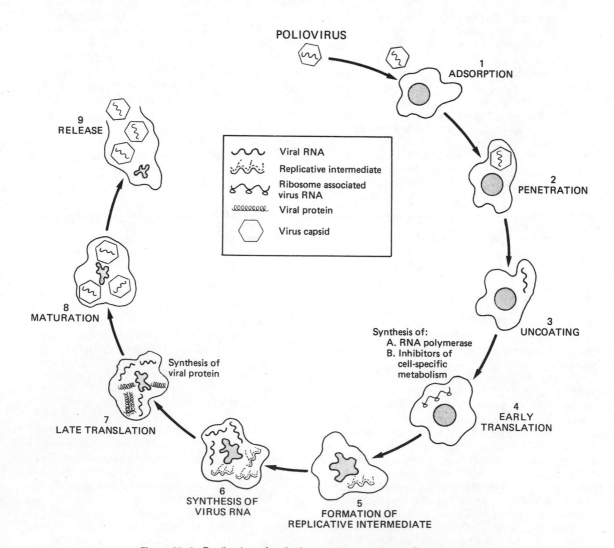

Figure 27–8. Replication of poliovirus, which contains an RNA genome.

cesses of the host cell are not altered significantly, although the cell synthesizes viral proteins and nucleic acids.

During the replicative cycle, viruses transfer genetic information in several ways from one generation to another. The essential theme, however, is that specific mRNAs must be transcribed from the viral nucleic acid for successful expression and duplication of genetic information. Once this is accomplished, viruses use cell components to translate the mRNA. Various classes of viruses use different pathways to synthesize the mRNAs depending upon the structure of the viral nucleic acid. Some viruses (eg, rhabdoviruses, myxoviruses) carry RNA polymerases to synthesize mRNAs. RNA viruses of this type are called negative-strand viruses, since their single-strand RNA genome is complementary to messenger RNA, which is conventionally designated positive-strand. Table 27-3 summarizes the various pathways of transcription (but not necessarily those of replication) of the nucleic acids of different classes of viruses.

Most of the viral mRNAs possess a sequence of polyadenylic acid [Poly (A)] at their 3'-end and an unusual blocked, methylated structure at the 5'-end called a cap. The precise function of these features is yet to be elucidated, but the capped structure appears to enhance initiation of translation. Viral mRNA is not always an exact copy of the genome template, since some mRNAs are processed or spliced to delete certain sequences.

Virus multiplication was first studied successfully in bacteriophages. The mechanism of phage replication is presented in Chapter 9. For animal viruses, some of the steps of the interaction between the infecting virus and susceptible cells have now been elucidated.

The following sections describe the replication of an RNA and a DNA virus.

RNA Virus Replication (Fig 27-8)

Poliovirus contains a single-stranded RNA as its genome. All of the steps are independent of host DNA and occur in the cell cytoplasm. Polioviruses adsorb to cells at specific cell receptor sites (step 1), losing in the process one virus polypeptide (VP4), which may, therefore, be important in adsorption. The sites are specific for virus coat–cell interactions. Whereas intact poliovirus infects only primate cells in culture, the isolated RNA also infects nonprimate cells (rabbit, guinea pig, chick) and completes one cycle of multiplication. Multiple cycles of infection are not observed in nonprimate cells because the resulting progeny possess protein coats and will again infect only primate cells. After attachment, the virus particles are taken into the cell by viropexis (similar to pinocytosis) (step 2), and the viral RNA is uncoated (step 3). The single-stranded RNA then serves as its own messenger RNA. This messenger RNA is translated (step 4), resulting in the formation of an RNA polymerase that catalyzes the production of a replicative intermediate (RI), a partially double-stranded molecule consisting of a com-

plete RNA strand and numerous partially completed strands (step 5). At the same time, inhibitors of cellular RNA and protein synthesis are produced. Synthesis of (+) and (−) strands of RNA probably occurs by similar mechanisms; this is completely elucidated only for (+) strands. Here the RI consists of one complete (−) strand and many small pieces of newly synthesized (+) strand RNA (step 6). The replicative form (RF) consists of 2 complete RNA strands, one (+) and one (−).

The single (+) strand RNA is made in large amounts and may perform any one of 3 functions: (a) serve as messenger RNA for synthesis of structural proteins, (b) serve as template for continued RNA replication, or (c) become encapsidated, resulting in mature progeny virions. The synthesis of viral capsid proteins (step 7) is initiated at about the same time as RNA synthesis.

The entire poliovirus genome acts as its own mRNA, forming a polysome of ~350S, and is translated to form a single large polypeptide that is processed during and after translation to form the various viral polypeptides. Thus, the poliovirus genome serves as a polycistronic messenger molecule. The giant polypeptide is cleaved to form a capsid precursor protein and 2 noncoat proteins one of which undergoes further processing. The capsid precursor protein is cleaved into coat proteins VP0, VP1, and VP3. During encapsidation, VP0 is cleaved into coat proteins VP2 and VP4.

Completion of encapsidation (step 8) produces mature virus particles that are then released when the cell undergoes lysis (step 9).

DNA Virus Replication (Fig 27-9)

In poxvirus replication, synthesis of virus components and assembly of virus particles occur within the cytoplasm of the infected cell. Poxvirus replication is described in Chapter 36.

The replication of other DNA viruses (including the adeno-, herpes-, and papovavirus families) differs in that viral DNA is replicated in the nucleus, whereas viral proteins are synthesized in the cytoplasm, followed by their migration to and assembly within the nucleus. Fig 27-9 shows the steps in the replication of adenovirus, a double-stranded DNA virus. Adsorption (step 1) and penetration (step 2) of the virus into the cell are similar to steps described for poliovirus. In addition to viropexis, enveloped viruses penetrate by fusion of the virus envelope with the plasma membrane, releasing the nucleocapsid into the cytoplasm.

After the virus enters the cell, the protein coat is removed (step 3), presumably by cellular enzymes, and the viral DNA is released into the nucleus. One or both DNA strands are transcribed (step 4) into specific mRNA, which in turn is translated (step 5) to synthesize virus-specific proteins, such as a tumor antigen and enzymes necessary for synthesis of virus DNA. This period encompasses the early virus functions. Host cell DNA synthesis is temporarily elevated and is then suppressed as the cell shifts over to the manufacture of viral DNA (step 6). As the viral DNA continues

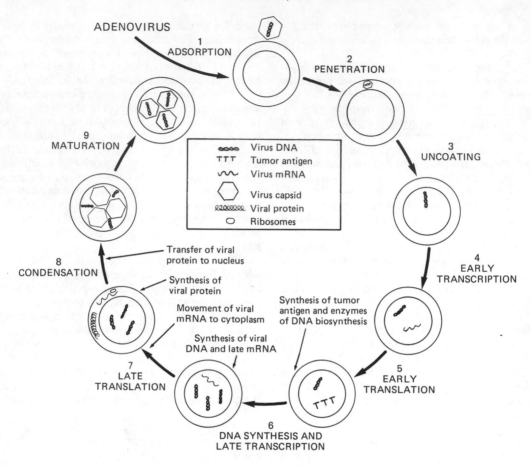

Figure 27–9. Steps in the replication of adenovirus, which contains DNA in its genome. (See text.)

to be transcribed, late virus functions become apparent. Messenger RNA transcribed during the later phase of infection (step 6) migrates to the cytoplasm and is translated (step 7). Proteins for virus capsids are synthesized and are transported to the nucleus to be incorporated into the complete virion (step 8). The migration of some structural proteins of certain viruses from the cytoplasm to the nucleus can be inhibited when arginine is absent from the growth medium. Assembly of the protein subunits around the viral DNA results in the formation of complete virions (step 9), which are released after cell lysis.

Summary of Viral Replication

The molecular events that have been discussed above are summarized in Fig 27–10. Viruses with genomes containing double-stranded (ds) nucleic acid proceed along most of the steps shown in the figure. Viruses with single-stranded (ss) nucleic acid utilize only some of the steps. For the orthomyxoviruses, the RNA template is utilized for the synthesis of a complementary RNA strand that produces the replicative form of the nucleic acid. This in turn serves as the template for the synthesis of the progeny viral RNA. For the retroviruses, the ssRNA acts as a template for

the RNA-dependent DNA polymerase (reverse transcriptase) to synthesize dsDNA. The dsDNA molecules are then used as templates for the transcription and synthesis of ssRNA molecules that serve either as viral mRNA molecules or as viral genomes for encapsidation by the viral structural proteins.

The replication cycle of a typical DNA virus—adenovirus—in human cells is illustrated in Fig 27–11, which shows sequentially the time course of synthesis of viral mRNA, the 75K (75,000 molecular weight) single-stranded DNA binding protein (an early viral gene product), viral DNA, virion proteins, and infectious virus. A dramatic change in macromolecular synthesis occurs at 6-7 hours postinfection, when the cells switch from early to late stages of infection, as signaled by the appearance of the 75K DNA-binding protein in the nucleus and by the onset of viral DNA replication. At the last stages, viral mRNA increases in concentration enormously and represents over 80% of the total mRNA of the cell.

Role of Viruses in the Study of DNA Replication

Several infectious RNAs and DNAs have been synthesized for small viruses. Studies on small DNA phages apply to DNA replication in prokaryotic cells.

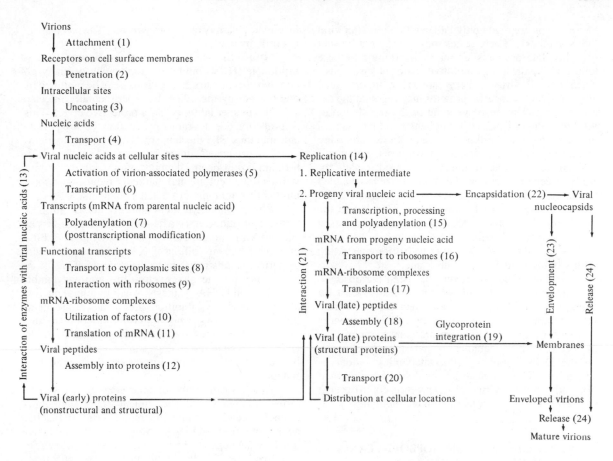

Figure 27–10. Molecular events in the replication of viruses. (From Becker, *Monogr Virol,* Vol 11, 1976.)

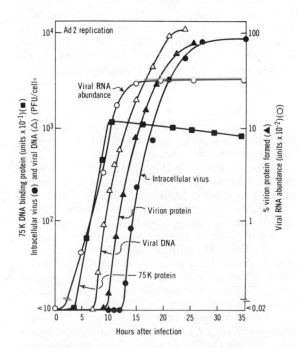

Figure 27–11. Time course of adenovirus replication cycle. (From Green.)

These small phages have limited genetic information and rely on host cell enzymes for DNA replication. The same enzymes appear to be involved in DNA replication of both phage and host-cell DNA.

An example of the kind of problem these systems have helped solve is provided by the research on priming. Since DNA polymerase enzymes can only start synthesis on a double-stranded molecule, cells prime DNA synthesis by first making a short RNA molecule base-paired to the template DNA. Studies with 2 simple phages (ϕX-174 and G4) have shown that this reaction either is catalyzed by a complex series of proteins or is dependent on a very specific DNA template structure, as well as requiring a special RNA polymerase and DNA-binding proteins. These phages are small enough that their entire nucleotide sequence of DNA has been determined. Thus, they serve as simple models for complex biochemical reactions of the host cell.

Control Mechanisms in Virus Replication

In the course of virus replication, all the virus-specified macromolecules are synthesized in a highly organized sequence, although virus components are usually made in excess. In some virus infections, early viral proteins are synthesized soon after infection and late proteins are made only late in infection, after viral DNA synthesis. Early genes may or may not be shut off when late products are made. In addition to these temporal controls, quantitative controls also exist, since not all virus proteins are made in the same amounts. Virus-specific proteins may regulate the extent of transcription of genome or the translation of viral messenger RNA. Although the exact mechanism of these controls is unknown, we do know something about the mechanism of mRNA synthesis. Small animal viruses and bacteriophages are good models for study of gene expression. Their small size has enabled the total nucleotide sequence of a few small DNA phages and SV40 to be elucidated. This led to the discovery that some pieces of DNA are expressed twice by mRNA, being read off either in 2 reading frames or by 2 mRNA molecules with different starting points being read in the same frame.

One surprising discovery has been the observation that animal virus mRNA molecules (at least for adenovirus and SV40) are not direct copies of their DNA genomes. In these viruses, the mRNA sequences coding for a given protein are preceded in the mRNA molecule by short sequences from farther "upstream" on the DNA template, with intervening sequences spliced out. This suggests the possibility that modification and control of virus gene expression could occur at the level of mRNA construction or "splicing."

EXPERIMENTAL CHEMOPROPHYLAXIS OF VIRUS INFECTIONS

Since viruses are obligate intracellular parasites, antiviral agents must be capable of selectively inhibiting viral functions without damaging the host. Only recently have compounds been found that are of value in treatment of virus diseases, and other compounds have been discovered that appear promising. (See Fig 27–12.)

Amantadine (Symmetrel), a synthetic amine, specifically inhibits influenza A viruses by blocking viral penetration into the host cell or by blocking virus uncoating. When administered prophylactically, amantadine has a significant protective effect in experimental animals and humans against influenza A strains but not against influenza B or other viruses.

Methisazone (Marboran), or N-methylisatin-β-thiosemicarbazone (N-methyl IBT), is an inhibitor of many poxviruses. It is highly virus-specific and does not affect normal cell metabolism. The drug inhibits poxvirus replication if given within 24–48 hours after exposure. It blocks the synthesis of certain virus proteins and results in immature, noninfectious virus particle formation.

N-Ethylisatin-β-thiosemicarbazone (N-ethyl IBT) can block the production of infective Rous sarcoma virus by transformed cells. Both N-ethyl and N-methyl IBT—but not the parent IBT molecule itself—interact directly with the virus particle and

inactivate a variety of oncornaviruses. The mechanism is not known.

Guanidine and **2-(α-hydroxybenzyl)-benzimidazole (HBB)** inhibit the replication of many picornaviruses in vitro. Some viruses can be inhibited by one but not by the other. In experimentally infected animals, neither inhibitor has a protective effect. This is probably due to rapid production of drug-resistant mutants. The mechanism of action is uncertain.

Enviroxime (2,amino-1-[isopropyl sulphonyl]-6-benzimidazole phenyl ketone oxime) inhibits rhinoviruses in cell culture and markedly reduced the common cold symptoms in treated volunteers.

Phosphonoacetic acid inhibits herpes simplex virus replication. It is a potent inhibitor of herpes simplex virus–induced DNA polymerase and has little effect on known cellular DNA polymerases. Herpesvirus mutants resistant to the drug arise easily.

Many **purine** and **pyrimidine analogs** inhibit both RNA and DNA synthesis. Analogs inhibit nucleic acid replication by inhibition of enzymes of the metabolic pathways for purines or pyrimidines or by inhibition of polymerases for nucleic acid replication. In addition, some of the analogs can be incorporated into the nucleic acid and block further synthesis or alter its function.

Analogs can inhibit cellular enzymes as well as virus-coded enzymes. The clinical use of such compounds depends on a high therapeutic ratio, so that the benefit of virus inhibition outweighs the inherent toxicity. New analogs are being tested to search for those that may specifically inhibit virus-coded enzymes, with minimal inhibition of analogous cell enzymes.

A number of **halogenated pyrimidines,** which are thymidine analogs, inhibit the replication of members of the major DNA virus families. **Idoxuridine (5-iodo-2'-deoxyuridine [IUDR])** inhibits thymidine kinase and is incorporated into DNA, resulting in the production of a faulty nucleic acid. Drug-resistant mutants of some DNA viruses have been obtained by growth in the presence of IUDR. Topical administration of IUDR is used in humans in the treatment of corneal lesions due to herpes simplex virus. Because of its toxicity and lack of efficacy, it is not used in systemic herpes infections.

5'-Amino-2',5'-dideoxy-5-iodouridine, a thymidine analog, inhibits replication of herpes simplex virus but is much less toxic to normal cells.

(E)-5-(2-bromovinyl)-2'-deoxyuridine appears to offer many advantages over IUDR. It is 60 times less toxic and 20 times more active than IUDR.

Trifluorothymidine (5-trifluoromethyl-2'-deoxyuridine) has also been used successfully in the treatment of corneal lesions due to herpes simplex virus. Trifluorothymidine is also effective against strains of herpesvirus that are resistant to IUDR.

Other halogenated pyrimidines, **5-fluoro-2'-deoxyuridine (FUDR)** and **5-bromo-2'-deoxyuridine (BUDR),** inhibit virus DNA replication and have been useful for the study of virus replication but are not practical as chemotherapeutic agents.

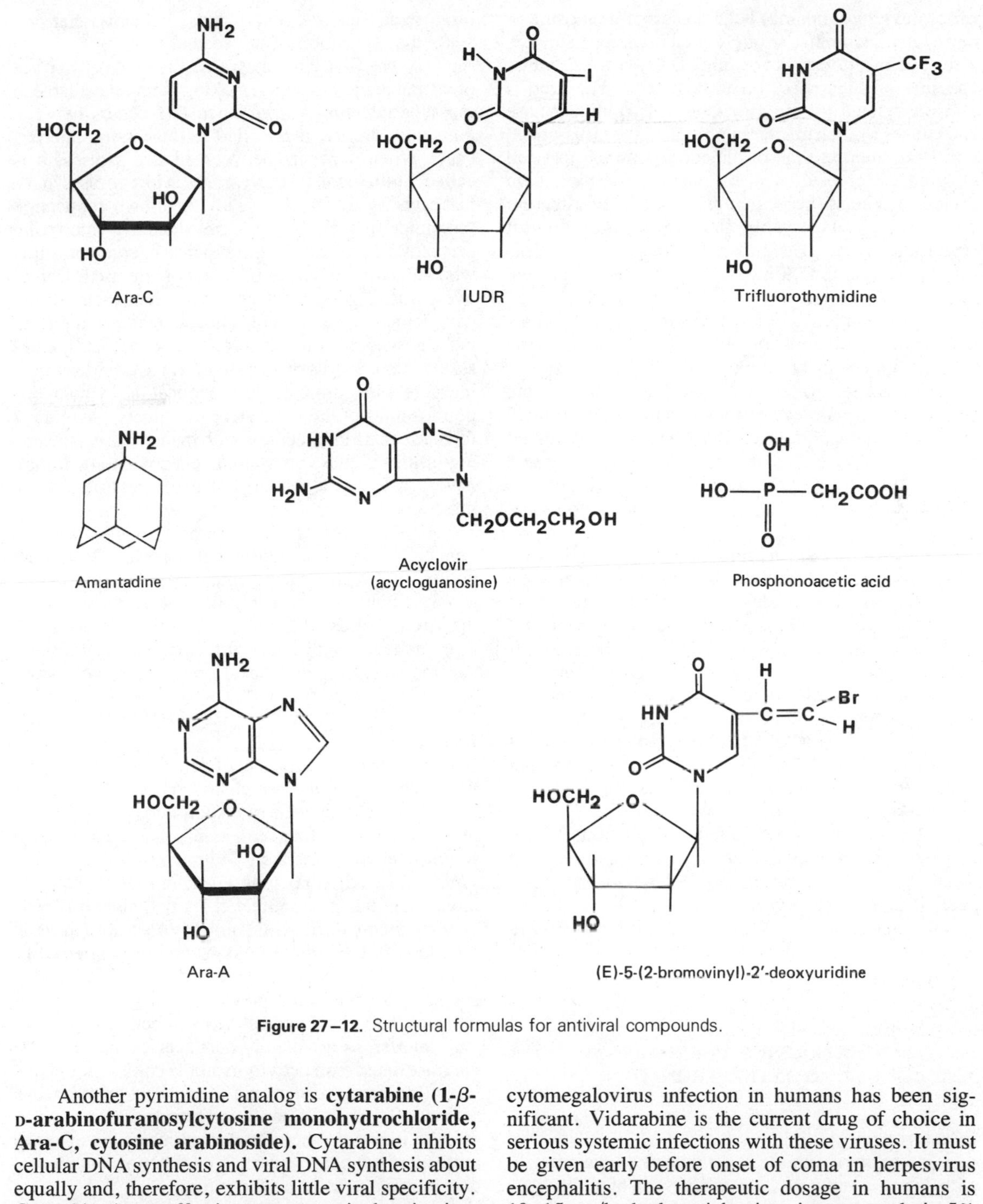

Figure 27–12. Structural formulas for antiviral compounds.

Another pyrimidine analog is **cytarabine (1-β-D-arabinofuranosylcytosine monohydrochloride, Ara-C, cytosine arabinoside).** Cytarabine inhibits cellular DNA synthesis and viral DNA synthesis about equally and, therefore, exhibits little viral specificity. Cytarabine is not effective as a systemic drug in virus infections and is immunosuppressive and cytotoxic.

A purine analog, **9-β-D-arabinofuranosyladenine (ara-A, adenine arabinoside, vidarabine),** is being used in clinical therapeutics. The precise mechanism of action of vidarabine is not clear, but it appears to inhibit DNA polymerase. Vidarabine has been used topically to treat corneal lesions due to herpes simplex virus. The clinical effectiveness of parenteral vidarabine against herpes simplex, varicella-zoster, and cytomegalovirus infection in humans has been significant. Vidarabine is the current drug of choice in serious systemic infections with these viruses. It must be given early before onset of coma in herpesvirus encephalitis. The therapeutic dosage in humans is 10–15 mg/kg body weight given intravenously in 5% dextrose and saline over a 12-hour period. It is relatively nontoxic but may cause nausea and phlebitis. It is not immunosuppressive. It is metabolized slowly in humans by deamination to arahypoxanthine. This metabolite (85% of the excreted product) has some antiviral activity but less than the parent compound. The monophosphate form of the drug is more soluble and may offer therapeutic advantages.

Acyclovir (9-[2-hydroxyethoxymethyl]gua-

nine, acycloguanosine) is an analog of guanosine or deoxyguanosine that strongly inhibits herpes simplex virus but has little effect on other DNA viruses such as vaccinia or adenovirus or on host cells. The drug is phosphorylated by the virus-coded thymidine kinase and causes a much greater inhibition of the virus-coded DNA polymerase than of the corresponding host cell enzymes. Herpesviruses that encode for their own thymidine kinase (herpes simplex, varicella/zoster) are much more susceptible than those that do not (cytomegalovirus, EB virus). Mutants of herpesvirus that lack thymidine kinase fail to phosphorylate the drug and are resistant to it.

Acyclovir has activity in vivo in mice with herpes encephalitis and topically for treatment of herpetic lesions in the eyes of rabbits or skin lesions of guinea pigs. It has been effective in topical application in the control of herpetic eye lesions in humans. In limited trials, parenteral administration of acyclovir prevented the reactivation of latent herpesvirus infections and also was effective in the treatment of active herpetic lesions in patients undergoing immunosuppressive therapy.

Virazole (1-β-D-ribofuranosyl-1,2,4-triazole-3-carboxamide, Ribavirin) is a synthetic nucleoside allegedly effective against many DNA- and RNA-containing viruses both in vitro and in experimental animals. Controlled trial in the USA has been disappointing, but the drug is available in Latin America.

Although not practical as chemotherapeutic agents, protein inhibitors have been useful in the study of viral replication. **Puromycin, cycloheximide,** and **p-fluorophenylalanine** all inhibit synthesis of both viral and cell proteins and can interrupt virus replication at different stages.

Dactinomycin (actinomycin D) inhibits DNA-dependent RNA synthesis and thus the multiplication of DNA viruses but not of most RNA viruses. However, it is toxic to animal cells.

Compounds such as **levamisole** and **isoprinosine** act not as antimetabolites but as stimulants of cellular immunity. They have little effect in humans.

INTERFERENCE PHENOMENON & INTERFERON

Interference

Infection of either cell cultures or whole animals with 2 viruses often leads to an inhibition of multiplication of one virus, an effect called interference. Interference in animals is distinct from specific immunity. Furthermore, interference has not been observed for all virus combinations; 2 viruses may infect and multiply within the same cell (eg, vaccinia and herpesviruses; measles and polioviruses) as efficiently as in single infections.

Two mechanisms have been elucidated as causes of interference:

(1) The first virus may cause the infected cell to produce an inhibitor (interferon, see below) that prevents the replication of the second virus.

(2) The first virus may alter the host cell surface or its metabolic pathways, making them unavailable to the superinfecting virus. When this occurs between unrelated viruses, it is called **heterologous** interference. When it occurs between related viruses, it is called **homologous** interference. Most viruses have the capacity to interfere with their own replication (autointerference). In this case, defective interfering particles are produced at the expense of complete virus when high multiplicities of infection are used. Defective particles generally lack a portion of their normal complement of nucleic acid and are unable to replicate in the absence of complete virus, since for their synthesis they utilize virus precursors. Defective viruses may interfere with complete virus replication by competition for units of the replicative machinery. Autointerference occurs in infections with many viruses, including influenza (the von Magnus phenomenon). It may have a role in the establishment of persistent virus infections.

Interference has been used as a basis for controlling outbreaks of infection with virulent strains of poliovirus by introducing into the population an attenuated poliovirus that interferes with the spread of the virulent virus. Interference between a preexisting virus infection and a superinfecting attenuated virus vaccine has sometimes been a problem in poliovirus vaccination programs.

Interferon

Interferons are a class of proteins which inhibit virus replication and which are produced by intact animals or cultured cells in response to virus infection or other inducers. Interferons appear to be a primary response to virus infection. Within 12–48 hours after virus titers reach a maximum, interferon is produced in large quantities in the infected animal, and virus production rapidly decreases. Antibody does not appear in the blood of the animal until several days after virus production has abated. This temporal relationship suggests that interferon plays a major role in the defense of the animal against virus infections.

Interferons are mainly host species–specific. By contrast, interferon activity is not specific for a given virus. Interferons can inhibit the replication of a wide variety of viruses. When interferon is added to cells prior to infection, there is marked inhibition of virus replication but nearly normal cell function. Interferon does not act directly on the virus.

Interferons are glycoproteins with molecular weights of 20,000–40,000. Virus-induced (type I, IFN-α and IFN-β, pH 2-stable) human interferon differs from the interferon produced by lymphocytes during immune responses (type II, IFN-γ, pH 2-labile). To date, type II interferon has not been produced in sufficient quantity for clinical studies. It may be important as an immune modulator.

Type I interferons can be induced not only by viruses but also by many other inducers, including

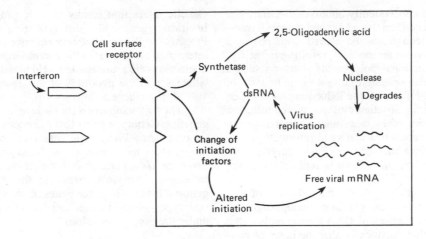

Figure 27–13. Suggested mechanisms of action of interferon.

double-stranded RNA and small molecules such as tilorone. Large-scale production of human leukocyte interferon (from blood leukocytes stimulated with viruses), fibroblast interferon, and lymphoblastoid cell interferon (Namalva cells grown in vat quantities) has permitted clinical studies.

As antiviral agents, interferons act indirectly by binding to specific cell-surface receptors and inducing the production of cellular enzymes that subsequently block viral reproduction by inhibiting the translation of viral mRNA into viral protein (Fig 27–13). At least 3 enzymatic pathways appear to be responsible: (1) a protein kinase that can phosphorylate and inactivate a cellular initiation factor, thus preventing formation of the initiation complex needed for viral protein synthesis; (2) an oligonucleotide synthetase needed for oligoadenylic acid formation (the latter substance activates a cellular endonuclease that degrades viral mRNA); and (3) inhibition of peptide chain elongation by creation of a deficiency in tRNA. At other times, interferons may act not on translation but on viral DNA transcription or on viral assembly.

Preparations of human leukocyte interferon are 1–2% pure and have been injected intravenously into humans in doses of 105–106 units/kg. Interferon was beneficial in early herpes zoster induced by radiation treatment of patients with leukemia; it reduced and delayed cytomegalovirus excretion in renal transplant patients; and, given prophylactically before trigeminal sensory root section, it prevented reactivation of herpes simplex. Topical interferon given repeatedly into the nose before virus challenge was able to reduce "colds" resulting from rhinovirus 4.

However, at this writing the largest quantities of interferon produced are being channeled into adjunctive treatment of patients with carcinoma of the breast, osteosarcoma, and other cancers, where viruses are not known to play a causative role.

Interferons are also being given experimentally to persons with chronic active hepatitis and in the treatment of rabies and severe hemorrhagic fever. Topical

interferon in the eye can suppress herpetic keratitis and accelerate healing.

The interferon preparations available in 1980–1981 are not free from toxicity. They result in gastrointestinal and nervous system side-effects proportionate to the dose given.

It is possible that recombinant DNA techniques will make available larger amounts of interferons at a lower cost in the future.

VIRAL GENETICS & VIRAL INTERACTIONS

Meaningful genetic studies with animal viruses depend on 2 factors. The first is the plaque assay of virus infectivity, a sensitive and accurate quantitative assay method. The second is stable genetic markers, which should ideally result from single mutations. Some markers commonly used include plaque size, specific virus-induced antigens, drug resistance, host range, and inability to grow at high temperatures. Mutants with such markers are obtained either after spontaneous mutation or after treatment with a mutagen.

Conditional-lethal mutants are mutants that are lethal (in that no infectious virus is produced) under one set of conditions—termed nonpermissive conditions—but that yield normal infectious progeny under other conditions—termed permissive conditions. Conditional-lethal mutants include temperature-sensitive (ts) and host range (hr) mutants. Ts mutants have been isolated from nearly all animal viruses; they grow at low (permissive) temperatures but not at high (nonpermissive) temperatures. Host range mutants are able to grow and form plaques in one kind of cell (permissive cell), whereas abortive infection occurs in another type (nonpermissive cell). Hr bacterial virus mutants may possess altered nucleic acid base sequences that are read as nonsense mutations by the nonpermissive host cell, resulting in polypeptide chain termination and consequently abortive infection. The permissive host cell, on the other hand, carries a transfer RNA that recognizes the altered sequence as a codon and inserts an amino acid, resulting in the formation of a functional polypeptide. Perhaps such a mechanism is also operative in host range mutants of animal viruses. Following the induction and isolation of a set of conditional-lethal mutants, mixed infection studies with pairs of mutants under permissive and nonpermissive conditions can yield information concerning gene function, gene sequence (genetic mapping), and mechanisms of virus replication at the molecular level.

Mutagens widely used for the induction of mutants fall into 3 classes: (1) base analogs that can replace the normal bases of DNA during replication; (2) substances that chemically alter the bases of nonreplicating DNA; and (3) those whose action is to remove DNA bases. An example of the first class of mutagens is 5-bromouracil, which replaces thymine quantitatively and which also base-pairs with guanine. This substance can thus induce mutations by causing 2 types of base pair transitions depending upon whether the pairing error occurs during incorporation or during replication following incorporation. Nitrous acid is an example of the second class of mutagens. It can oxidatively deaminate either adenine or cytosine. Representative of the third class of mutagens is ethylene ethanesulfonate, which may remove guanine bases.

When 2 different virus particles infect the same host cell, they may interact in a variety of ways. The types of interactions are summarized in Table 27–4.

Genetic interaction results in some progeny that are **heritably** (genetically) different from either parent. Progeny produced as a consequence of nongenetic interaction are similar to the parent viruses. In genetic interactions the actual **nucleic acid molecules** interact, whereas it is the **products** of the genes that are involved in nongenetic interactions.

The following terms are basic to the discussion of genetics: **Genotype** refers to the genetic constitution of an organism. **Phenotype** refers to the observable properties of an organism, which are produced by the genotype in cooperation with the environment. A **mutation** is a heritable change in the genotype. The **genome** is the sum of the genes of an organism. Several types of interaction can occur simultaneously under the proper conditions.

Genetic Interactions

Recombination results in the production of progeny virus (recombinant) that carries traits not found together in either parent. This type of interaction occurs when both parental viruses are viable (active). It is postulated that the nucleic acid strands break, and part of the genome of one parent is joined to part of the genome of the second parent. The recombinant virus is genetically stable, yielding progeny like itself upon replication. (See Chapter 34.) In the case of viruses with segmented genomes, eg, influenza virus, the formation of recombinants is due to reassortment of individual genome fragments rather than to an actual crossover event.

Marker rescue occurs between the genome of an

Table 27–4. Types and characteristics of interactions between animal viruses.

Type of Interaction	Viability of Parental Viruses	Some Progeny Different From Parental Virus	Progeny Genetically Stable	Example
I. Genetic				
A. Recombination	Active + active	Yes	Yes	Influenza, herpesvirus
B. Marker rescue	Active + inactive	Yes	Yes	Influenza
C. Multiplicity reactivation	Inactive + inactive	Yes	Yes	Vaccinia
II. Nongenetic				
A. Phenotypic mixing	Active + active	Yes	No	Picornaviruses
B. Genotypic mixing	Active + active	Yes	No	Paramyxoviruses
C. Interference	Active + active	No	Yes	Coxsackieviruses
	Defective + active	No	Yes	Satellite + adenovirus
D. Enhancement	Active + active	No	Yes	NDV + parainfluenza
E. Complementation	Active + inactive	No	Yes	Poxviruses
	Active + defective	No*	Yes	(a) Rous-associated virus + Rous sarcoma virus†
				(b) Murine leukemia + sarcoma†
				(c) SV40 + adenovirus
				(d) Adenovirus + satellite
	Defective + defective	No*	Yes	(a) PARA (SV40-adeno) + adenovirus
				(b) MAC-adeno + adenovirus

*In those cases in which the helper virus is supplying the coat (RSV-RAV, MSV-MLV, PARA-adenovirus, MAC-adenovirus), the progeny defective virus will be antigenically different if a heterologous helper virus is present and transcapsidation or pseudotype formation occurs.

†Shares certain similarities with an extreme form of phenotypic mixing.

active virion and the genome of a virus particle that has been inactivated in some way. A portion of the genome of the inactivated virus recombines with that of the active parent, so that certain markers of the inactivated parent are rescued and appear in the viable progeny. None of the progeny produced are identical to the inactivated parent. The progeny carrying the rescued markers of the inactivated parent are genetically stable (see examples in Chapter 34).

Multiplicity reactivation occurs when an inactive virus particle is rendered active by interaction with another inactive virus particle in the same cell. In this case, 2 different parental viruses can be damaged or a single heavily damaged parental virus can be used to infect cells at high multiplicity of infection. Recombination occurs between the damaged nucleic acids of the parents, producing a viable genome that can replicate. The greater the damage to the parental genomes, the larger the number of inactive particles required per cell to ensure the formation of such a viable genome.

Nongenetic Interactions

Phenotypic mixing is the association of a phenotype with a heterologous genotype. This occurs when the genome of one virus becomes randomly incorporated within the capsid of a different virus or a capsid consisting of components of both viruses (Fig 27–14). Progeny are called pseudotypes if the genome is encased in a completely heterologous protein coat (third and fourth progeny from left). Such mixing is not a stable genetic change because, upon replication,

the phenotypically mixed parent will yield progeny encased in capsids homologous to the genotype.

Phenotypic mixing can occur between different genotypes of homologous viruses (eg, entero-, toga-, paramyxo-, orthomyxo-, adeno-, and herpesviruses) as well as between those of certain heterologous viruses (eg, between orthomyxo- and paramyxoviruses or between rhabdoviruses and either paramyxo-, orthomyxo-, retro-, or herpesviruses).

In **genotypic mixing,** a single virus particle can give rise to progeny of 2 distinct parental types. This is not a stable genetic change and probably occurs when 2 complete genomes are accidentally incorporated within a single virus capsid. It has been reported only for the paramyxoviruses.

Interference occurs when the multiplication of a superinfecting virus is inhibited because of the presence of the initially infecting virus. This phenomenon can be mediated either by interferon or by an alteration of cell receptor sites or metabolic pathways necessary for replication of the second virus. Interference may be either reciprocal (markedly reduced yields of both agents) or nonreciprocal (reduced yield of only one agent). (See p 340.)

Enhancement is the increased production of one virus as the result of co-infection with a second virus. All the progeny will be like the parental viruses.

Complementation is the interaction between 2 viruses, one or both of which may be defective, which results in the multiplication of one or both under conditions in which replication would not ordinarily occur. The progeny produced are like the parental viruses.

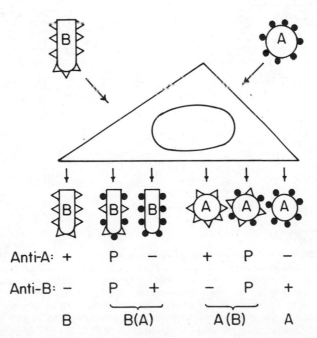

	B	B(A)		A(B)	A
Anti-A:	+	P	–	+	P	–
Anti-B:	–	P	+	–	P	+

Figure 27–14. Schematic diagram of phenotypic mixing and neutralization of pseudotypes. + = Virus lesions present: no neutralization. P = Partial neutralization: resistant fraction present or slower neutralization kinetics. − = No virus lesions: virus completely neutralized. A and B are the pure virus types; A(B) is A genome with B envelope pseudotype; B(A) is B genome with A envelope pseudotype. (Reproduced, with permission, from Boettiger, *Prog Med Virol* 1979; **25**:37.)

Neither the genotype nor the phenotype of either virus is affected. Different types of complementation may occur (Table 27–4), and the mechanisms permitting complementation may vary.

BIOCHEMICAL GENETICS & RECOMBINANT MAPPING

Recent advances in animal virus genetics using restriction enzymes and other biochemical techniques have led to the identification of virus gene products and the mapping of these on the viral genome.

The technique of recombinant mapping has been used with influenza A viruses, which have a genome of 8 segments of RNA, each coding for one virus protein. Under suitable conditions, the RNA fragments and the polypeptides of different influenza A viruses migrate at different rates in polyacrylamide gels, so that strains can be distinguished. By analyzing the recombinants formed between different viruses, the RNA segment coding for each protein has been determined. Similar experiments with temperature-sensitive mutants have shown the biologic function of various polypeptides. Recombinants are being analyzed to determine which virus proteins are responsible for virulence in humans.

For large DNA viruses, restriction endonucleases are used to obtain characteristic fragment patterns for different strains or types. Recombinants between 2 types are then analyzed to see which restricted fragments derive from each parent. By polypeptide analysis of parental and recombinant virus, the virus gene products can be mapped to individual regions of the genome defined by the restriction enzyme fragments.

The use of restriction endonuclease for identification of specific virus strains or isolates is illustrated in Fig 27–15. Viral DNA is isolated and incubated with a specific endonuclease until DNA sequences susceptible to the nuclease are cleaved. The fragments are then resolved on the basis of size by gel electrophoresis. The large fragments are most retarded by the sieving effect of the gel, so that an inverse relationship between size and migration is observed. The position of the DNA fragments can be determined by radioautography on x-ray film if the viral DNA is labeled.

Virus-Mediated Gene Transfer in Mammalian Cells

If external genetic information can be stably introduced into eukaryotic cells, this might permit repair of genetic defects. For instance, congenital galactosemia could be corrected by introducing the galactosidase gene into the patient's cells. No such repair has been accomplished in humans, but there are encouraging results in some experimental systems.

Gene transfer in bacteria can be accomplished by transformation, phage transduction, and conjugation (see Chapter 4). In eukaryotic cells, gene transfer has been accomplished by transformation and DNA recombination (see below). It might be mediated by virus infection. However, there exist the problems of possible immunologic incompatibility of new gene products and of possible transfer of undesirable genes together with desired ones. In addition, regulation of

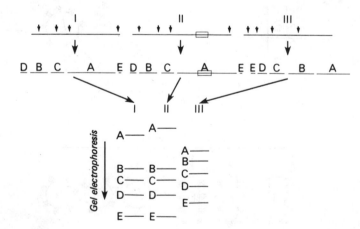

Figure 27–15. Illustration of principles of restriction endonuclease cleavage site analysis. The linear DNA (double-stranded) genomes of 3 hypothetical viruses to be compared are indicated as I, II, III. Suppose a specific nucleotide sequence, eg, GAATTC, the cleavage site for nuclease EcoRI, occurs at 4 sites in each genome as indicated by arrows. Genomes I and II are identical except for a substantial DNA insertion mutation in genome II. Genome III has none of the sequences in question located in positions analogous to genomes I or II. Cleavage of these DNAs at the sites marked by arrows results in 5 fragments (A–E) in each case. If these DNA fragments are separated according to size in adjacent tracks in a gel electrophoresis experiment, the result will be as diagrammed: fragments B, C, D, and E of samples I and II will co-migrate and fragment A from each virus will differ. The fragments from genome III will co-migrate with none of those from genomes I and II. It should be noted that knowledge of the cleavage site maps at the top is not essential to be able to deduce the fact that genomes I and II are related to each other but not to genome III. (Reproduced, with permission, from Summers WC: *Yale J Biol Med* 1980; **53**:55.)

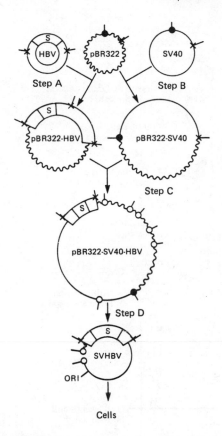

Figure 27–16. Construction of a functional SV40 papovavirus recombinant carrying about 40% of the hepatitis B virus (HBV) genome that includes the sequences coding for the immunizing surface antigen (HBsAg). The HBV DNA fragment is inserted into the late gene region of the papovavirus. **x—** = BamHI site; **●—** = EcoRI site; O—= HaeII site. *Steps A and B:* HBV DNA and SV40 DNA were each cleaved with restriction enzymes, ligated to cleaved plasmid pBR322 DNA, and then cloned and amplified in *E coli. Step C:* The new plasmids containing the viral DNAs were cleaved, ligated, and recloned in *E coli* to yield the double recombinant plasmid. *Step D:* HaeII digestion removed almost all of the plasmid DNA and a small part of SV40. The resultant recombinant DNA retained the SV40 origin of DNA replication (ORI) and the complete SV40 early gene region. For propagation in monkey kidney cells, an SV40 temperature-sensitive early gene mutant had to be used as helper, as it contained the required late genes. The mixed infection at the nonpermissive temperature (39 °C) yielded progeny virions only from cells doubly infected with the SV40-HBV recombinant (functional SV40 early genes) and the helper (functional late genes). The infected monkey kidney cells also synthesized HBsAg but no other HBV antigens. The antigen was excreted into the culture medium as 22-nm particles with the same properties as those found in the blood of patients with type B hepatitis. (Reproduced, with permission, from Moriarty AM et al: *Proc Natl Acad Sci USA* 1981;**78**:2606.)

gene expression may not be active in the recipient cells, and this might be damaging.

Recombinant DNA

The insertion of DNA fragments into plasmids of bacteria has given rise to a new technology that holds great promise for the production of biologic materials, hormones, vaccines, interferon, and other gene products. The principles of recombinant DNA technology were described and illustrated in Chapter 4. Fig 27–16 shows how to derive a recombinant. Fragments of hepatitis B virus DNA have been cloned and the immunizing antigen has been produced in bacteria. This offers the possibility of producing large amounts of such antigen for vaccine. `

PATHOGENESIS OF VIRUS DISEASES

Virus implantation and multiplication occur in different tissues as the infectious agent travels to the target organ from the portal of entry. In the target organ, virus multiplication must reach a critical level before cell necrosis occurs and disease becomes manifest. Viruses call forth a different tissue response than do pathogenic bacteria, not only in the parenchymatous cells but also in cellular infiltration. Whereas polymorphonuclear leukocytes form the principal cellular response to the acute inflammation caused by pyogenic bacteria, infiltration with mononuclear cells and lymphocytes characterizes the inflammatory reaction of uncomplicated viral lesions. In Fig 27–17 are shown examples of mousepox, a disease of the skin, and of human poliomyelitis, a disease of the central nervous system.

In mousepox, the virus enters the body through minute abrasions of the skin and multiplies in the epidermal cells. At the same time, it is carried by the lymphatics to the regional lymph nodes, where multiplication also occurs. The few virus particles entering the blood by way of the efferent lymphatics are taken up by the macrophages of the liver and spleen. In both organs the virus multiplies rapidly. Following release of virus from the liver and spleen, it moves by way of the bloodstream and localizes in the basal epidermal layers of the skin, in the conjunctival cells, and near the lymph follicles in the intestine. The virus may occasionally also localize in the epithelial cells of the kidney, lung, submaxillary gland, and pancreas. A primary lesion occurs at the site of entry of the virus. It appears as a localized swelling that rapidly increases in size, becomes edematous, ulcerates, and goes on to scar formation. A generalized rash follows that is responsible for the release of large quantities of virus into the environment.

In poliomyelitis, virus enters by way of the alimentary tract, multiplies locally at the initial sites of viral implantation (tonsils, Peyer's patches) or the lymph nodes that drain these tissues, and begins to appear in the throat and in the feces. Secondary virus spread occurs by way of the bloodstream to other

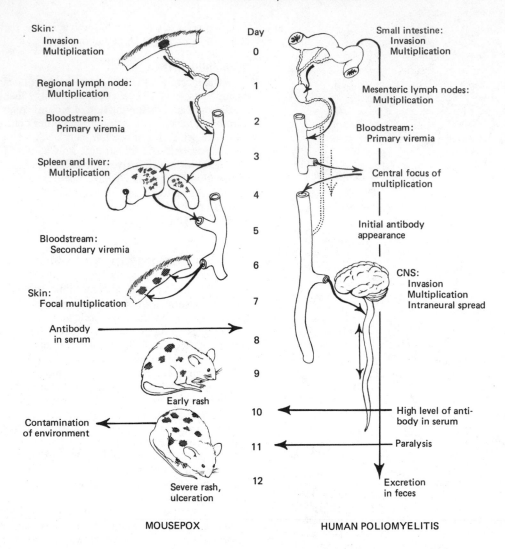

Figure 27–17. Schematic illustrations of the pathogenesis of mousepox and poliomyelitis. (Modified from Fenner.)

susceptible tissues, namely, other lymph nodes, brown fat, and the central nervous system. Within the central nervous system the virus spreads along nerve fibers. If a high level of multiplication occurs as the virus spreads through the central nervous system, motor neurons are destroyed and paralysis occurs. The shedding of virus into the environment does not depend upon secondary virus spread to the central nervous system. Secondary spread to the central nervous system is readily interrupted by the presence of antibodies induced by prior infection or vaccination.

Persistent Viral Infections & Immune Complex Diseases

Certain viruses do not invariably kill the cells they infect. The immunologic response of the host to these viruses may be responsible for the observed pathologic changes and the clinical illness. This phenomenon is exemplified in lymphocytic choriomeningitis virus infection of mice. If adult mice are rendered immunolog-

ically incompetent by x-irradiation, immunosuppressive drugs, or antiserum directed against the lymphoid elements of the mouse, they do not become ill when infected with the virus. The virus replicates in the animal and establishes a chronic infection that persists until the competence of the immunologic response is restored, at which time the animal becomes ill. Infection of newborn mice before they develop immunologic competence results in a lifelong viral infection that is not associated with acute illness; however, after 10 months to 1 year of life, many of the persistently infected mice develop a fatal debilitating disease involving the central nervous system. These animals exhibit chronic glomerulonephritis and hypergammaglobulinemia; the glomerular lesions are thought to be caused by deposition of antigen-antibody complexes (see Chapter 33). Persistent infections occur with a number of animal viruses, and the persistence in certain instances depends upon the age of the host when infected. In human beings, for example, rubella virus and cytomegalovirus infections acquired in utero characteristically result in viral persistence that is of limited duration, probably because of the development of the immunologic capacity to react to the infection as the infant matures.

Persistent ("slow") viral infections may play a far-reaching role in human disease. Persistent viral infections are associated with leukemias and sarcomas of chickens and mice (see Chapter 40) as well as progressive degenerative diseases of the central nervous system of humans and animals (see Chapter 33). The latter may represent a distorted immunopathologic reaction to chronic presence of the virus, leading to "immune complex disease" or chronic central nervous system disease.

Another type of immunopathologic disorder has been observed in humans previously immunized with vaccines containing killed measles or respiratory syncytial virus. Such persons may develop unusual immune responses that give rise to serious consequences when they later are exposed to the naturally occurring infective virus. Dengue hemorrhagic fever with shock syndrome, which develops in dengue infection of persons who already have had at least one prior infection with another dengue serotype, may be a naturally occurring manifestation of the same type of immunopathology (see p 382).

Viruses as Causes of Congenital Defects

Viral infection during pregnancy may be a significant cause of fetal damage and loss. Three principles involved in the production of congenital defects are (1) the ability of the virus to infect the pregnant woman and be transmitted to the fetus; (2) the stage of gestation at which infection occurs; and (3) the ability of the virus to cause damage to the fetus directly, by infection of the fetus, or indirectly, by infection of the mother resulting in an altered fetal environment (eg, fever). The sequence of events that may occur prior to and following viral invasion of the fetus is shown in Fig 27–18.

Rubella and cytomegaloviruses are presently the primary agents responsible for congenital defects in humans (Chapter 35). Congenital infection with herpes simplex, varicella-zoster, and coxsackie B viruses may also be of significance in inducing teratogenic effects in the fetus.

LATENT VIRAL INFECTIONS

Inapparent or subclinical infection covers, at the host-parasite level, the whole field of infections that give no overt sign of their presence.

Latent infections are inapparent infections which are chronic and in which a certain virus-host equilibrium is established. The term occult virus is used in cases where virus particles cannot be detected and in which the actual state of the virus cannot as yet be ascertained. Many terms used for bacteriophage replication have been applied also to animal viruses.

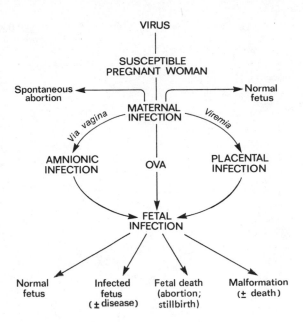

Figure 27–18. Viral infection of the fetus. (After Catalano & Sever.)

Slow virus infections have a prolonged incubation period lasting months or years, during which virus continues to multiply, producing increasing destruction of tissue. The growth of cells in culture for many generations may be accompanied by a concomitant multiplication of virus. The number of cells supporting viral infection in such optimally growing cultures is usually only a small portion of the entire population.

Cells infected with some viruses can divide and grow into infected clones. In such virus carrier cultures, changes that shift the virus-cell complex toward virus release (cell crowding, medium exhaustion, lowering of temperature) also slow cell multiplications.

In Fig 27–19 are presented examples of apparent, inapparent, latent, and occult virus infections.

NATURAL HISTORY (ECOLOGY) & MODES OF TRANSMISSION OF VIRUSES

Viruses may be transmitted in the following ways: (1) direct transmission from person to person by contact, in which droplet or aerosol infection may play the major role (eg, influenza, measles, smallpox); (2) transmission by means of the alimentary tract (intimate association with carrier, food, and drink) (eg, enterovirus infections, infectious hepatitis); (3) transmission by bite (eg, rabies); (4) transmission by means of an arthropod vector (eg, arboviruses).

Some of the viruses may be conveyed in several different ways and may therefore manifest a variable epidemiology.

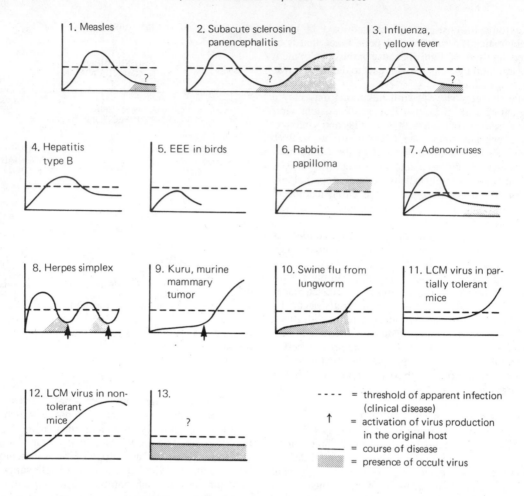

Figure 27–19. Apparent, inapparent, latent, and occult virus infections. *(1)* Measles runs an acute, almost always clinically apparent course resulting in long-lasting immunity. *(2)* Measles may also be associated with persistence of latent infection in sclerosing panencephalitis (see Chapter 35). *(3)* Yellow fever and influenza show a similar pattern except that infection may be more often subclinical than clinical. *(4)* In viral hepatitis type B, recovery from clinical disease may be associated with latent infection in which fully active virus persists in the blood. *(5)* Some infections are, in a particular species, always subclinical, such as equine encephalomyelitis in some species of birds that then act as reservoirs of the virus. *(6)* In rabbit papilloma, the course of infection is chronic, and chronicity is associated with the virus's becoming occult. *(7)* Infection of humans with certain adenoviruses may be clinical or subclinical. There may be a long latent infection during which virus is present in small quantity; virus may also persist after the illness. *(8)* The periodic activation of latent herpes simplex virus, which may recur throughout life in humans, often follows an initial acute episode of stomatitis in childhood. *(9)* In many instances, infection is wholly latent for long periods of time before it is activated. Examples of such "slow" virus infections characterized by long incubation periods are mammary tumor virus in mice, scrapie virus in sheep, and kuru in humans. *(10)* In pigs that have eaten virus-bearing lungworms, swine "flu" is occult until the appropriate stimulus induces virus production and, in turn, clinical disease. *(11)* Lymphocytic choriomeningitis (LCM) virus may be established in mice by in utero infection. A form of modified immunologic tolerance develops in which only low levels of antibody are produced. This antibody and circulating LCM virus form antigen-antibody complexes that ultimately produce immune complex disease in the partially tolerant host. The presence of LCM virus in this latent infection (circulating virus with little or no apparent disease) may be readily revealed by transmission to an indicator host, eg, nontolerant adult mice from a virus-free stock. All nontolerant mice develop classic acute symptoms of LCM and die *(12)*. *(13)* The possibility is shown of latent infection with an occult virus that is not readily activated. Proof of the presence of such a virus remains a difficult task which, however, is attracting the attention of cancer investigators (see Chapter 40).

The following cycles have been recognized among the arthropod-borne viruses:

1. Human-arthropod cycle–***Example:*** Urban yellow fever.

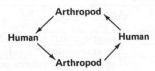

2. Lower vertebrate–arthropod cycle with tangential infection of humans–***Examples:*** Jungle yellow fever, equine encephalitis.

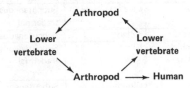

3. Arthropod-arthropod cycle with occasional infection of humans and lower vertebrates–***Example:*** Colorado tick fever.

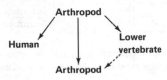

In (3) the virus may be transmitted from the adult arthropod to its offspring by means of the egg (transovarian passage); thus, the cycle may continue with or without intervention of a vertebrate host.

In vertebrates the invasion of most viruses evokes a violent reaction, usually of short duration. The result is decisive. Either the host succumbs or it lives through the production of antibodies that neutralize the virus. Regardless of the outcome, the sojourn of the active virus is usually short (although latent virus infections may occur, as in herpes-, adeno-, and cytomegalovirus infections). In arthropod vectors of the virus, the relationship is usually quite different. The viruses may produce little or no ill effect and remain active in the arthropod throughout the latter's natural life. Thus arthropods, in contrast to vertebrates, act as permanent hosts and reservoirs.

Viral infections have their major impact at different times of life—from rubella, which is most serious during gestation, to St. Louis arboviral encephalitis, which is most serious in the elderly (Table 27–5).

VIRUS VACCINES

The use of vaccines, described in detail in the chapters dealing with specific virus families and diseases, is summarized in Table 27–6. Certain general principles apply to most virus vaccines for use in the prevention of human disease.

Neither vaccination nor recovery from natural infection always results in total protection against a later infection with the same virus. This situation holds for diseases for which successful control measures are available, including polio, smallpox, influenza, rubella, measles, mumps, and adenovirus infections. Control can be achieved by limiting the multiplication of virulent virus upon subsequent exposure and preventing its spread to target organs where the pathologic damage is done (eg, polio and measles viruses kept from the brain and spinal cord; rubella virus from the embryo). Recently, Marek's disease, a widespread lymphoproliferative tumor caused by a herpesvirus of domestic chickens, has been brought under control by an attenuated virus vaccine. The vaccine results in a lifelong active infection of the chicken and does not prevent superinfection of the vaccinated animal with the virulent virus, but it does prevent the appearance of the tumor. This is the first practical cancer vaccine that has been developed. A second cancer vaccine—hepatitis B vaccine to prevent primary hepatocellular carcinoma—is now in field trial.

Table 27–5. Peak ages of incidence of serious viral diseases.*

Before Birth	At Birth	Infants	Children	Adolescents and Young Adults	Older Adults
			Herpes type 1		
	Herpes type 2	Respiratory syncytial disease	Rhinovirus colds	Herpes type 2	
		Parainfluenza	Coronavirus disease	Hepatitis B	
Cytomegalic disease					
Rubella	Hepatitis B	Adenovirus disease	Measles		
			Rubella		
			Mumps		
			Influenza		
			Polio and other enteroviral diseases		
		Rotavirus diarrhea	Hepatitis A	Infectious mononucleosis (EB virus)	St. Louis encephalitis
			Epidemic gastroenteritis (Norwalk virus)		
		Varicella (chickenpox)			Herpes zoster (shingles)

*Adapted from Wilson EB, NIH Publication No. 80–433.

Table 27—6. Principal vaccines used in prevention of virus diseases of humans.

Disease	Source of Vaccine	Condition of Virus	Route of Administration
Recommended Immunization for General Public			
Poliomyelitis	Tissue culture (human diploid cell line, monkey kidney)	Live attenuated	Oral
		Killed	Subcutaneous
Measles*	Tissue culture (chick embryo)	Live attenuated†	Subcutaneous‡
Mumps*	Tissue culture (chick embryo)	Live attenuated	Subcutaneous
Rubella*§	Tissue culture (duck embryo, rabbit, or human diploid)	Live attenuated	Subcutaneous
Immunization Recommended Only Under Certain Conditions (Epidemics, Exposure, Travel, Military)			
Smallpox**	Lymph from calf or sheep (glycerolated, lyophilized) Chorioallantois, tissue cultures (lyophilized)	Live vaccinia	Intradermal: multiple pressure, multiple puncture
Yellow fever	Tissue cultures and eggs (17D strain)	Live attenuated	Subcutaneous or intradermal
Hepatitis type B	Purified HBsAg from "healthy" carriers	Killed	Subcutaneous
Influenza	Highly purified or subunit forms of chick embryo allantoic fluid (formalinized or UV-irradiated)	Killed	Subcutaneous or intradermal
Rabies	Duck embryo or human diploid cells	Killed	Subcutaneous
Adenovirus††	Human diploid cell cultures	Live attenuated	Oral, by enteric-coated capsule
Japanese B encephalitis‡‡	Mouse brain (formalinized), tissue culture	Killed	Subcutaneous
Venezuelan equine encephalomyelitis§§	Guinea pig heart cell culture	Live attenuated	Subcutaneous
Eastern equine encephalomyelitis‡‡	Chick embryo cell culture	Killed	Subcutaneous
Western equine encephalomyelitis‡‡	Chick embryo cell culture	Killed	Subcutaneous
Russian spring-summer encephalitis‡‡	Mouse brain (formalinized)	Killed	Subcutaneous

*Available also as combined vaccines.

†Killed measles vaccine was available for a short period. However, a serious delayed hypersensitivity reaction often occurs when children who have received primary immunization with killed measles vaccine are later exposed to live measles virus. Because of this complication, killed measles vaccine is no longer recommended.

‡With less attenuated strains, gamma globulin is given in another limb at the time of vaccination.

§Neither monovalent rubella vaccine nor combination vaccines incorporating rubella should be administered to a postpubertal susceptible woman unless she is not pregnant and understands that it is imperative not to become pregnant for at least 3 months after vaccination. (The time immediately postpartum has been suggested as a safe period for vaccination.)

**Since smallpox virus seems to have been totally eradicated from the world, vaccination is no longer recommended. However, stocks of vaccine are held in depots if cases should reappear.

††Recently licensed but recommended only for military populations in which epidemic respiratory disease caused by adenovirus is a frequent occurrence.

‡‡Not available in the USA except for the Armed Forces or for investigative purposes.

§§Available for use in domestic animals (from the US Department of Agriculture) and for investigative purposes.

Killed Virus Vaccines

Killed virus vaccines prepared from whole virions generally stimulate the development of circulating antibody against the coat proteins of the virus, conferring some degree of resistance. For some diseases, killed virus vaccines are currently the only ones available. The following disadvantages apply to killed vaccines:

(1) Extreme care is required in their manufacture to make certain that no residual live virulent virus is present in the vaccine.

(2) The immunity conferred is often brief and must be boosted, which not only involves the logistic problem of repeatedly reaching the persons in need of immunization but also has caused concern about the possible effects (hypersensitivity reactions) of repeated administration of foreign proteins.

(3) Parenteral administration of killed virus vaccine, even when it stimulates circulating antibody (IgM, IgG) to satisfactory levels, has sometimes given limited protection because local resistance (IgA) is not induced adequately at the natural portal of entry or primary site of multiplication of the wild virus infection—eg, nasopharynx for respiratory viruses, alimentary tract for poliovirus (see Fig 27–20 and Chapters 31 and 34).

(4) Some killed virus vaccines have induced hypersensitivity to subsequent infection.

Live Attenuated Virus Vaccines

Attenuated vaccines have the advantage of acting like the natural infection with regard to their effect on immunity. They multiply in the host and tend to stimulate longer-lasting antibody production and also to

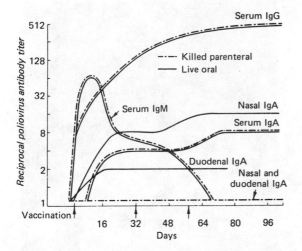

Figure 27–20. Serum and secretory antibody response to orally administered, live attenuated poliovaccine and to intramuscular inoculation of killed poliovaccine. (Reproduced, with permission, from Ogra et al: *Rev Infect Dis* 1980; 2:352.)

induce antibody production and resistance at the portal of entry (see Fig 27–20). The disadvantages of live attenuated vaccines include the following: (1) The risk of reversion to greater virulence during multiplication within the vaccinee. Although reversion has not proved to be a problem in practice, its potential exists. Monitoring should be continued. (2) Unrecognized adventitious agents latently infecting the culture substrate (eggs, primary cell cultures) may enter the vaccine stocks. Viruses found in vaccines have included avian leukosis virus, simian papovavirus SV40, and simian cytomegalovirus. The problem of adventitious contaminants may be circumvented through the use of normal cells serially propagated in culture (eg, human diploid cell lines) as substrates for cultivation of vaccine viruses. Vaccines prepared in such cultures have been in use for years and have been administered to many millions. (3) The storage and limited shelf life of attenuated vaccines present problems, but this can be overcome in some cases by the use of viral stabilizers (eg, $MgCl_2$ for poliovaccine).

The development of virus strains suitable for live virus vaccines previously was done chiefly by selecting naturally attenuated strains or by cultivating the virus serially in various hosts and cultures in the hope of deriving an attenuated strain. The search for such strains is now being approached by laboratory manipulations aimed at specific, planned, genetic alterations in the virus (eg, rabies, influenza, respiratory syncytial virus).

Present Vaccines
    A. Proper Usage: One fact cannot be overemphasized: An effective vaccine does not protect against disease until it is administered in the proper dosage to susceptible individuals. The failure to reach all sectors of the population with complete courses of immunization is reflected in the continued occurrence of paralytic poliomyelitis and measles in unvaccinated persons. Preschool children in poverty areas are the least adequately vaccinated group in the USA.

    B. Simultaneous Administration of Live Vaccines: There was a theoretic possibility that antibody response might be diminished, or that interference might occur if 2 or more live vaccines were given at the same time.

    In practice, however, simultaneous administration of live vaccines can be safe and effective. Trivalent live oral poliovaccine (when given in 3 doses) or a combined live measles, mumps, and rubella vaccine, given by injection, is effective. Antibody response to each component of these combination vaccines is comparable with antibody response to the individual vaccines given separately.

Future Prospects
    A. Local Administration of Vaccine to Stimulate Local Antibody at the Portal of Entry: Intranasally administered aerosol vaccines are being developed, particularly for respiratory disease viruses.

    B. New Vaccines:
    1. Varicella-zoster–Considerable success has been claimed for a varicella vaccine developed in Japan and currently under test in the USA. There is some concern about the possibility of vaccinated subjects contracting zoster in later life.

    2. Cytomegalovirus and Epstein-Barr virus–Vaccines are under development for both of these viruses, but, as with the varicella-zoster vaccine, there is concern about the long-term effects.

    3. Respiratory syncytial virus–A vaccine is currently being tested for this virus.

    C. Purification of Vaccines by New Methods (eg, Zonal Centrifugation): This is being used to eliminate nonviral proteins and thus reduce the possibility of adverse reactions to the vaccine. In some instances, purified material can also be administered in more concentrated form, containing greatly increased amounts of the specifically desired antigen.

    D. Subunit Vaccines: Subviral components are being obtained by breaking apart the virion to include in the vaccine only those viral components that are needed to stimulate protective antibody.

    E. Attenuation of Viruses by Genetic Manipulation: This is being utilized to produce recombinants or temperature-sensitive mutants that can then serve as live virus vaccines.

    F. Human Source of Immunizing Antigen: Hepatitis viruses have not yet been grown in culture; however, a source of vaccine for hepatitis B exists in the large amount of antigen present in healthy carriers. (See Chapter 32.)

    G. Vaccines from Recombinant DNA: The genetic material coding for hepatitis B virus immunizing antigen has been introduced into bacteria. If the bacteria can be made to produce the antigen in quantity,

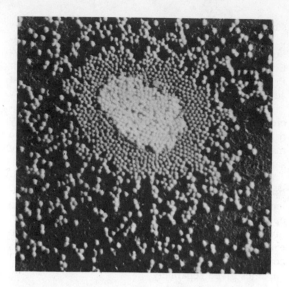

Figure 27–21. Electron micrograph typical of purified preparations of a spherical virus (20,000 ×). Shown are human wart virus particles (papovavirus family) having a diameter of 45 nm. (Melnick & Bunting.)

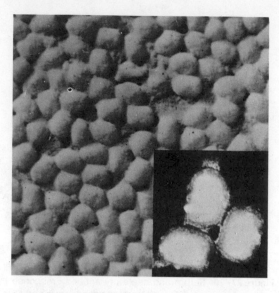

Figure 27–23. Electron micrograph of a purified sample of a brick-shaped poxvirus, molluscum contagiosum (20,000 ×). The virus particles, purified from human skin lesions by differential centrifugation, measure about 330 × 230 nm. (Melnick, Bunting, & Strauss.) *Inset:* Uranyl acetate stain of DNA-containing core of the virus (47,000 ×).

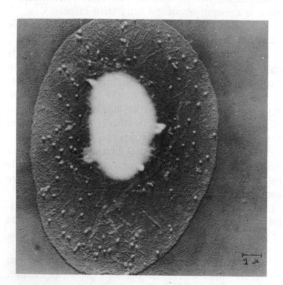

Figure 27–22. Influenza virus particles, PR8 strain, adsorbed on the membranes of a chicken erythrocyte. The particles are about 100 nm in diameter. (Werner & Schlesinger.)

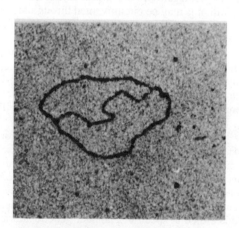

Figure 27–24. Replicating molecule of papovavirus SV40 DNA (see Fig 27–4). The electron micrograph shown above represents about 10% of the population of replicating DNA molecules. Most of the replicating molecules also contain a superhelical branch that is so tightly twisted that in electron micrographic preparations it is usually not possible to distinguish individual DNA duplexes. (Salzman et al.)

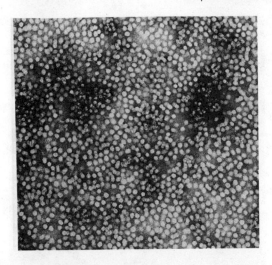

Figure 27–25. Purified hepatitis B surface antigen (HBsAg) (55,000 ×). (McCombs & Brunschwig.)

Figure 27–27. Scanning electron micrograph of a human epithelioid cell infected with herpes simplex virus type 1. Hundreds of virus particles may be seen on the surface of the cell. Bar = 1 μm. (Schlehofer & Hampl.)

Figure 27–26. Plaques produced by poliovirus *(left)* and by an echovirus *(right)*. Both viruses are cultivated in bottle cultures of monkey kidney cells. After the viruses are seeded, the epithelial sheet is covered with an agar overlay containing a vital dye (neutral red). As the cytopathic effect of the virus becomes manifest, the cells lose their vital stain, and clear areas appear in the culture. The progeny of a single virus particle are located in each clear area. The plaque morphology of each of the viruses shown is sufficiently clear so that the 2 virus groups can readily be distinguished from each other by this method. (Hsiung & Melnick.)

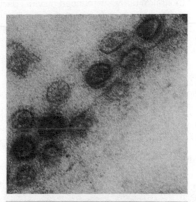

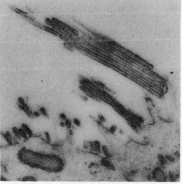

Figure 27–28. *Top:* Spherical forms of influenza virus (116,000 ×). The cell wall passes diagonally across the field, with host cell cytoplasm to the right. Several particles just beneath the cell membrane seem to be undergoing differentiation toward the mature extracellular form. *Bottom:* Influenza virus at the cell surface (31,000 ×). Two bundles of filaments (one cut longitudinally, the other obliquely) extend into the extracellular space. At left, short filaments seem to be budding from the cell (Morgan, Rose, & Moore.)

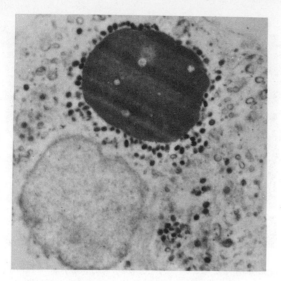

Figure 27–29. Mousepox virus within the infected cell (7400 ×). Nucleus at lower left; above it can be seen a dark cytoplasmic inclusion body surrounded by virus particles. A group of virus particles in the process of development is located to the right of the nucleus. (Gaylord & Melnick.)

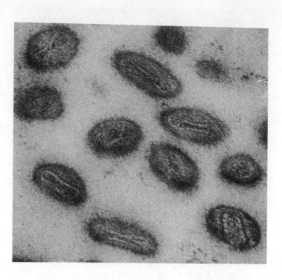

Figure 27–31. Ultrathin section of vaccinia virus-particles within the cytoplasm of an infected cell (74,000 ×). The internal structure of the mature virus is evident. (Morgan, Rose, & Moore.)

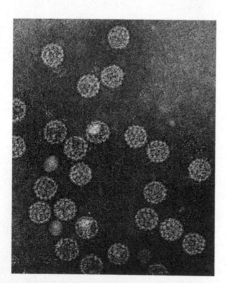

Figure 27–30. Papovavirus SV40. Purified preparation negatively stained with phosphotungstate (150,000 ×). (McGregor & Mayor.)

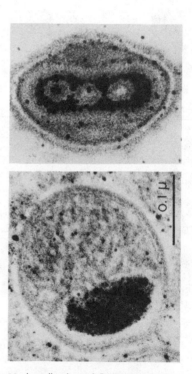

Figure 27–32. Localization of DNA in immature *(bottom)* and mature *(top)* vaccinia particles. After hydrolysis with HCl, a silver methenamine solution has been applied to Epon sections of the virus. Silver granules are specifically deposited at the sites of DNA. Other structures are made visible by counterstaining with uranyl acetate (170,000 ×). (Peters.)

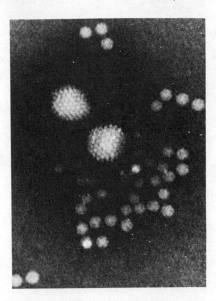

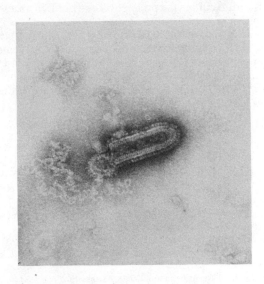

Figure 27–33. A group of adenoassociated satellite viruses surrounding 2 adenovirions that function as helpers for the defective satellites (250,000 ×). (Mayor, Jordan, & Melnick.)

Figure 27–35. Electron micrograph of bullet-shaped particle typical of the rhabdovirus family (100,000 ×). Shown here is vesicular stomatitis virus negatively stained with potassium phosphotungstate. (McCombs, Benyesh-Melnick, & Brunschwig.)

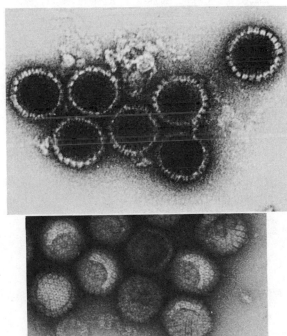

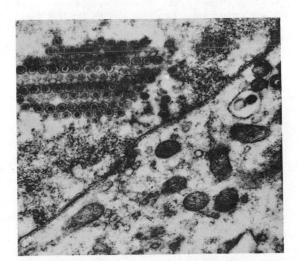

Figure 27–34. Herpesvirus in human amnion cell. The nuclear membrane runs from lower left to upper right. A regular array of virus particles, each possessing a dense central body and a single peripheral membrane, is present within the nucleus (27,000 ×). (Morgan.)

Figure 27–36. *Top:* Herpesvirus particles from human vesicle fluid, stained with uranyl acetate to show DNA core (140,000 ×). *Bottom:* Virions stained to show protein capsomeres of the virus coat (140,000 ×). (Smith & Melnick.)

this will facilitate the production of a purified vaccine containing only the immunizing antigen.

For foot-and-mouth disease virus, another step was necessary. Since the virus has an RNA genome, complementary DNA had to be first prepared for insertion into the bacterial DNA. Immunizing antigen is now being obtained from bacteria containing this recombinant DNA.

H. Synthetic Vaccines: Antigenically active polypeptides have been synthesized for some bacterial viruses. They have produced neutralizing antibodies in animals. The possibility of producing synthetic immunizing antigens for hepatitis B is now being explored.

•   •   •

References

Anderson WF, Diacumakos EG: Genetic engineering in mammalian cells. *Sci Am* 1981;**245**:106.

Arnon R et al: Antiviral response elicited by a completely synthetic antigen with built-in adjuvanticity. *Proc Natl Acad Sci USA* 1980;**77**:6769.

Becker Y, Hadar J: Antivirals 1980: An update. *Prog Med Virol* 1980;**26**:1.

Boettiger D: Animal virus pseudotypes. *Prog Med Virol* 1979; **25**:37.

Choppin PW, Scheid A: The role of viral glycoproteins in adsorption, penetration, and pathogenicity of viruses. *Rev Infect Dis* 1980;**2**:40.

Crumpacker CS: Viral glycoproteins in infectious disease processes. *Rev Infect Dis* 1980;**2**:78.

Dalton AJ, Haguenau F (editors): *Ultrastructure in Biological Systems.* Vol 5: *Ultrastructure of Animal Viruses and Bacteriophages: An Atlas.* Academic Press, 1973.

Diener TO: Viroids. *Sci Am* (Jan) 1981;**244**:66.

Dubois-Dalcq M, Rentier B: Structural studies of the surface of virus-infected cells. *Prog Med Virol* 1980;**26**:158.

Dulbecco R: Contributions of microbiology to eucaryotic cell biology: New directions for microbiology. *Microbiol Rev* 1979;**43**:443.

Edge MD et al: Total synthesis of a human leukocyte interferon gene. *Nature* 1981;**292**:756.

Edman JC et al: Synthesis of hepatitis B surface and core antigens in *E coli. Nature* 1981;**291**:503.

Hsiung GD et al: The use of electron microscopy for diagnosis of virus infections: An overview. *Prog Med Virol* 1979;**25**:133.

Kit S: Viral-associated and induced enzymes. *Pharmacol Ther* 1979;**4**:501.

McIntosh K, Fishaut JM: Immunopathologic mechanisms in lower respiratory tract disease of infants due to respiratory syncytial virus. *Prog Med Virol* 1980;**26**:94.

Matthews REF: Classification and nomenclature of viruses: Third Report of the International Committee on Taxonomy of Viruses. *Intervirology* 1979;**12**:129.

Melnick JL: Taxonomy of viruses, 1980. *Prog Med Virol* 1980; **26**:214.

Murphy FA: Control and eradication of exotic viruses affecting man. *Prog Med Virol* 1979;**25**:69.

Oldstone MBA: Virus neutralization and virus-induced immune complex disease. *Prog Med Virol* 1975;**19**:84.

Oldstone MBA, Fujinami RS, Lampert PW: Membrane and cytoplasmic changes in virus-infected cells induced by interactions of antiviral antibody with surface viral antigen. *Prog Med Virol* 1980;**26**:45.

Robb JA: Virus-cell interactions: A classification for virus-caused human disease. *Prog Med Virol* 1977;**23**:51.

Russell WC, Winters WD: Assembly of viruses. *Prog Med Virol* 1975;**19**:1.

Saral R et al: Acyclovir prophylaxis of herpes-simplex-virus infections: A randomized, double-blind, controlled trial in bone-marrow-transplant recipients. *N Engl J Med* 1981; **305**:63.

Whitley RJ et al: Herpes simplex encephalitis: Vidarabine therapy and diagnostic problems. *N Engl J Med* 1981;**304**:313.

Viruses can be isolated and identified during the course of many diseases, thus establishing the etiologic diagnosis. Often, however, a specific diagnosis cannot be made in the first few days of the infection; the results of many diagnostic tests for viral diseases do not become available until the patient has recovered or died.

The time and cost entailed in isolating and identifying viruses necessitate careful selection of patients and proper collection and handling of specimens. As a general rule, the indications for attempting to isolate a virus from patients include the following: (1) Instances where the established diagnosis will directly affect the management of the patient, eg, laboratory-proved rubella in the first trimester of pregnancy would favor a decision to terminate pregnancy. (2) Instances where the diagnosis is vital to the health of the community, eg, laboratory confirmation of smallpox, poliomyelitis, influenza, or arbovirus encephalitis will provide the information necessary for instituting immunization programs or insect control measures. (3) Instances where the etiologic agent of a disease is being sought. Studies of patients for etiologic association require prior planning and cooperation between the physician, the public health worker, and the virologist and must include the study of samples from control patients.

The laboratory procedures used in the diagnosis of viral diseases in human beings include the following:

(1) Isolation and identification of the agent.

(2) Measurement of antibodies developing during the course of the infection.

(3) Histologic examination of infected tissues. This should be performed on all fatal cases of virus infections and on animals suspected of infection with rabies virus (Negri inclusion bodies).

(4) Detection of viral antigens in lesions by the use of fluorescein-labeled (or peroxidase-labeled) antibody. This method can be used on nasopharyngeal secretions (exfoliated cells), sputum, skin and conjunctival scrapings, brain biopsy (for herpes encephalitis that can be treated), and autopsy tissues.

(5) Electron microscopic examination of vesicular fluids or tissue extracts treated with negative and positive stains to identify and count DNA and RNA virus particles (see Chapter 27). This procedure in the

hands of trained personnel can provide diagnoses within hours in patients with herpesvirus infections. Myxoviruses in respiratory secretions may be identified by this method. An important application in diagnostic virology is the detection of rotavirus in the feces of children suffering from acute gastroenteritis (Fig 28–1). Since the virus does not grow in conventional cell cultures, electron microscopy can serve to directly identify the causative agent.

CONSIDERATIONS IN THE DIAGNOSIS OF VIRAL DISEASES

The choice of methods for laboratory confirmation of a virus infection depends upon the illness. Antibody tests are more readily and cheaply performed than virus isolations, but they require adequately spaced serum samples, and the diagnosis often is not confirmed until convalescence. In addition, antibody tests can be carried out only for those illnesses for which the causative viruses have been grown in the laboratory. Virus isolation is required (1) when new

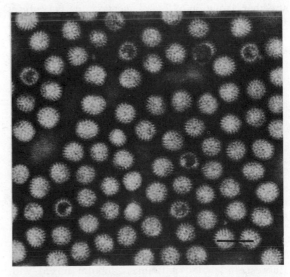

Figure 28–1. Human rotavirus in feces of a child with acute gastroenteritis (125,000 ×). Bar = 100 nm. (Barrera-Oro & Lombardi.)

epidemics occur, as with A2 (Hong Kong) influenza in 1968; (2) when serologic tests overlap and do not allow one to distinguish between 2 viruses, as with smallpox and vaccinia; (3) when it is necessary to confirm a presumptive diagnosis made by direct microscopic observation, eg, detecting a herpesvirus in vesicle fluid; and (4) when the same clinical illness may be caused by many different agents.

In the diagnostic evaluation of a patient with a suspected viral disease, one must bear in mind that the same clinical syndromes may be produced by a variety of agents. For example, aseptic (nonbacterial) meningitis may be caused by many different viruses as well as by spirochetes; similarly, respiratory disease syndromes may be caused by many viruses as well as mycoplasma and other agents.

The isolation of a virus is not necessarily equivalent to establishing the cause of a given disease. A number of other factors have to be taken into consideration. Some viruses persist in human hosts for long periods of time, and therefore the isolation of herpes, poliomyelitis, echoviruses, or coxsackieviruses from a patient with an undiagnosed illness does not prove that the virus is the cause of the disease. A consistent clinical and epidemiologic pattern must be established by repeated studies before one can be sure that a particular agent is responsible for a specific clinical picture.

Dual infections present still another problem. Different viruses may have the same seasonal and geographic occurrence. Enteroviruses and arboviruses sometimes frequent the same area at the same time. Thus in one summer a patient may have inapparent infection with one virus and clinical infection with the other. If the clinical infection should be mild, the syndrome (eg, aseptic meningitis) may have been produced by either virus. Antibody studies must be made for both viruses or the diagnosis may be missed altogether. Isolation of 2 viral agents similarly confuses the etiologic significance of each agent unless their roles in causing illness have been established by prior experience.

DIRECT EXAMINATION OF CLINICAL MATERIAL

The viral diseases for which direct microscopic examination of imprints or smears has been proved useful include rabies, herpes, and varicella-zoster. The staining of viral antigens by immunofluorescence in a smear from a rabid animal is the method of choice for routine diagnosis of rabies. The procedure is carried out as follows:

Two impression smears on a glass slide are made with the suspect brain. The slide is fixed in acetone at −20 °C. One smear (control) is flooded with fluorescein-labeled antirabies globulin mixed with mouse brain containing rabies virus. The other smear (test) is flooded with the same fluorescein-labeled antirabies globulin mixed with normal mouse brain. The

slide is incubated at 37 °C for 30 minutes in a moist chamber, then washed for 10 minutes in buffered saline, air dried, mounted, and examined in the fluorescent microscope by ultraviolet light. The positive test smear gives bright fluorescence, whereas the control smear gives no fluorescence because the specifically labeled antibodies have been bound by the rabies antigen added in mouse brain.

The same principle of identifying viral antigens using immunofluorescence is useful in rapid diagnosis of certain respiratory virus diseases by examining smeared epithelial cells from the nasopharynx, and of herpetic lesions by examining cells scraped from the base of the lesion. Now that herpes encephalitis can be successfully managed if treatment is begun early, immunofluorescence of brain biopsy material may be indicated. Buffy coat leukocytes or leukocytes of the cerebrospinal fluid obtained during the acute illness contain viral antigens (eg, enteroviruses), and this also offers a rapid method for obtaining a diagnosis.

SOLID–PHASE IMMUNOASSAYS

The recognition of hepatitis A virus and rotavirus by direct examination of fecal specimens led to the development of sensitive solid-phase immunoassays for their detection—inasmuch as these important pathogens are not readily grown in cell culture. Both radioimmunoassay (RIA) and enzyme-linked immunosorbent assay (ELISA) are available.

The principles of RIA and ELISA tests have been presented in Chapter 12. RIA applied to viral diagnosis is again discussed in Chapter 29.

ELISA for viral diagnosis consists of the following essential steps: (1) A specific antibody is adsorbed onto the wells in a plastic microtiter plate. (2) The material to be tested is added. If the viral antigen is present, it will combine with the antibody. The excess is washed off. (3) A conjugate is added that consists of antiviral antibody linked to an enzyme. If virus has been fixed to the plate, the antibody portion of the conjugate will attach. Unbound conjugate is washed off. (4) A substrate for the enzyme is added, and the colored product of hydrolyzed substrate is measured in a spectrophotometer. The resulting reading is proportionate to the amount of enzyme bound to the plate, which in turn is related to the quantity of virus antigen in the sample.

A more sensitive technique of antigen detection involves the use of a second specific antibody derived from a different animal species than the one used for preparing the coating antibody. The second antibody is reacted with virus antigen that has been bound to the original coating antibody. A third antibody conjugated with enzyme is added; this antibody is directed against the immunoglobulin of the animal species used to prepare the second specific antibody. Again, the amount of antibody bound, determined by the enzyme activity, is a function of antigen concentration.

VIRUS ISOLATION TECHNIQUE

The isolation of active virus requires the proper collection of appropriate specimens, their preservation both en route to and in the laboratory, and the inoculation of suitable cell cultures, susceptible animals, or embryonated eggs. Prior to the inoculation of the specimen, it may be necessary to eliminate bacteria from the specimen (see below). The presence of a virus is demonstrated by the appearance of characteristic histologic lesions, inclusion bodies, or viral antigens in the inoculated test system. Isolated viruses are specifically identified by using known antibodies that inhibit or neutralize the biologic effects of the virus or react with viral antigens (inhibit hemagglutination, fix complement, or induce specific fluorescence).

SPECIMENS FOR STUDY

Many viruses are most readily isolated in the first few days of the illness (Table 28–1). The specimens to be used in virus isolation attempts are listed in Table 28–2. Tissues obtained at autopsy may also serve this purpose. Each specimen must be handled in such a way that a virus will be kept infectious and will have a chance to grow (see Table 29–8).

Material should, in general, be frozen (preferably at temperatures well below –20 °C) if there is a delay in bringing it to the laboratory. The principal exceptions are (1) whole blood drawn for antibody determination, which must have the serum separated before freezing; and (2) tissue for organ or cell culture (or urine for cytomegalovirus isolation), which should be kept at 4 °C and taken to the laboratory promptly.

In general, virus is present in respiratory illnesses in pharyngeal or nasal secretions. Virus can be demonstrated in the fluid of vesicular rashes. Encephalitides are usually diagnosed more readily by serologic means. Arboviruses and herpesviruses are not usually recovered from spinal fluid, but brain tissue from patients with viral encephalitis may yield the causative virus. In illnesses associated with enteroviruses, such as central nervous system disease, acute pericarditis, and myocarditis, the viruses can be isolated from feces, throat swabs, or cerebrospinal fluid.

Table 28–1. Relation of stage of illness to presence of virus in test materials and to appearance of specific antibody.

Stage or Period of Illness	Virus Detectable in Test Materials	Specific Antibody Demonstrable*
Incubation	Rarely	No
Prodrome	Occasionally	No
Onset	Frequently	Occasionally
Acute phase	Frequently	Frequently
Recovery	Rarely	Usually
Convalescence	Very rarely	Usually

*Antibody may be detected very early in previously vaccinated persons.

PRESERVATION OF VIRUSES

Freezing

A large wide-mouthed thermos jar or insulated carton, half-filled with pieces of solid CO_2 (dry ice), serves for transport and storage of material containing viruses. The temperature in a dry ice storage cabinet is close to –76 °C. Electric deep-freeze cabinets can maintain temperatures of –50 to –105 °C.

Lyophilization

This procedure consists of rapid freezing at low temperature (in a bath containing alcohol and dry ice) and dehydration from the frozen state at high vacuum.

Ten percent to 50% of normal plasma or serum in the fluid menstruum protects the virus to be frozen and dried. The plasma or serum must not contain neutralizing antibodies. Skimmed milk is another "protective" menstruum in which virus-containing material may be suspended.

PREPARATION OF INOCULA

Bacteria-free fluid materials such as cerebrospinal fluid, whole blood, plasma, or serum may be inoculated into cell cultures, animals, or eggs, directly or after dilution with buffered phosphate solution (pH 7.6).

Preparation of Tissues

Tissue is washed in media or sterile water, minced into small pieces with scissors, and ground to make a homogeneous paste. Diluent is added in amounts sufficient to make a concentration of 10–20%. This suspension can be centrifuged at low speed (not more than 2000 rpm) for 10 minutes to sediment insoluble cellular debris. The supernatant fluid may be inoculated; if bacteria are present, they are eliminated as discussed below.

Tissues may also be trypsinized, and the resulting cell suspension may be (1) inoculated on an existing tissue culture cell monolayer, or (2) co-cultivated with another cell suspension of cells known to be virus-free.

Removal of Bacteria

If the material to be tested contains bacteria (throat washings, stools, infected tissue, or insects), they must be inactivated or removed before inoculation.

A. Bactericidal Agents:

1. Antibiotics–Antibiotics are commonly employed in combination with differential centrifugation (see below).

2. Ether–If it is not harmful to the virus in question (eg, enteroviruses, vaccinia), ether may be added in concentrations of 10–15%.

B. Mechanical Methods:

1. Filters–Earthenware, porcelain, and asbestos filters reduce the virus concentration by adsorption and are therefore used infrequently.

Table 28—2. Specimens for isolation of viruses.

Clinical Manifestations and Common Causative Agents	Source of Specimen for Virus Isolation	
	Clinical	Postmortem or Biopsy
Upper respiratory tract infections		
Rhinovirus	Throat swab or nasal secretions	. . .
Parainfluenza		
Respiratory syncytial		
Adenovirus	Throat swab and feces	. . .
Enterovirus		
Reovirus		
Lower respiratory tract infections		
Influenza	Throat swab and sputum	Lung
Adenovirus		
Parainfluenza		
Rhinovirus		
Respiratory syncytial		
Pleurodynia		
Coxsackievirus	Throat swab and feces	. . .
Cutaneous and mucous membrane diseases		
Vesicular		
Smallpox and vaccinia	Vesicle fluid	Liver, spleen, and lung
Herpes simplex		
Varicella-zoster		
Enterovirus	Vesicle fluid, feces, and throat swab	. . .
Exanthematous		
Measles	Throat swab and blood	. . .
Rubella		
Enterovirus	Throat swab and feces	. . .
Diarrhea of infants		
Rotavirus	Feces	Intestinal wall and contents
Central nervous system infections		
Enterovirus	Feces and CSF	Brain tissue and intestinal contents
Herpes simplex	Throat swab and CSF	Brain tissue
Mumps	Throat swab, CSF, urine	Brain tissue
Lymphocytic choriomeningitis	Blood and CSF	Brain tissue
Arboviruses		
Western equine encephalitis	Blood and CSF	Brain tissue
Eastern equine encephalitis		
Venezuelan equine encephalitis		
California encephalitis	Usually not possible to isolate virus from clinical specimens	Brain tissue
St. Louis encephalitis		
Japanese B encephalitis		
Rabies	Saliva	Brain tissue
Chronic central nervous system infections		
Measles (subacute sclerosing panencephalitis)	. . .	Brain tissue
Human papovavirus (progressive multifocal leukoencephalopathy)	. . .	Brain tissue
Parotitis		
Mumps	Throat swab (Stensen's duct) and urine	. . .
Cytomegalovirus		
Severe undifferentiated febrile illnesses		
Colorado tick fever	Blood	. . .
Yellow fever		
Dengue		
Congenital anomalies		
Cytomegalovirus	Urine and throat swab	Kidney, lung, and other tissues
Rubella	Throat swab and CSF	Lymph nodes, lung, spleen, other tissues

2. Differential centrifugation—This is a convenient method of removing many bacteria from heavily contaminated preparations of the small viruses. Bacteria are sedimented at low speeds that do not sediment the virus. High-speed centrifugation then sediments the virus. The virus-containing sediment is then resuspended in a small volume.

CULTIVATION IN CELL CULTURE

Cell culture techniques are the most widely used for isolating viruses from clinical specimens. When viruses multiply in cell culture, they produce biologic effects (cytopathic changes, viral interference, or the production of a hemagglutinin) that permit identification of the agent.

Test tube cultures are prepared by adding cells suspended in 1–2 mL of nutrient fluid that contains balanced salt solutions and various growth factors (usually serum, glucose, amino acids, and vitamins). Cells of fibroblastic or epithelial nature attach and grow on the wall of the test tube, where they may be examined with the aid of a low power microscope.

With many viruses, growth of the agent is paralleled by a degeneration of these cells. (See Fig 28–2.) Some viruses produce characteristic cytopathic effects in cell culture, making a rapid presumptive diagnosis possible when the clinical syndrome is known. As examples, measles, mumps, parainfluenza, and respiratory syncytial viruses characteristically produce multinucleated giant cells, whereas adenoviruses produce grapelike clusters of large round cells, rhinoviruses produce focal areas of rounding and dendritic forms, and herpes simplex virus produces diffuse uniform rounding of cells.

Some viruses (eg, rubella virus) produce no direct cytopathic changes but can be detected by their interference with the cytopathic effect of a second challenge virus (viral interference).

Influenza virus and other orthomyxoviruses may be detected within 24–48 hours if erythrocytes are added to infected cultures. Viruses maturing at the cell membrane produce a hemagglutinin enabling the erythrocytes to adsorb at the cell surface (hemadsorption).

Organ cultures of ferret and human tracheal epithelium may support the growth of many viruses that cause upper respiratory tract disease, including some viruses that do not grow in conventional cell cultures (eg, coronaviruses). Viruses may cause general or focal necrosis of the ciliated epithelial cells or may be detected by a decline in ciliary movement.

The identity of a virus isolate is established with type-specific antiserum, which inhibits virus growth or which reacts with the viral antigens in the tests described in Chapter 29 (eg, complement fixation, hemagglutination inhibition, counterimmunoelectrophoresis, etc).

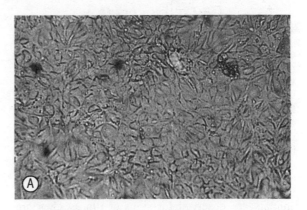

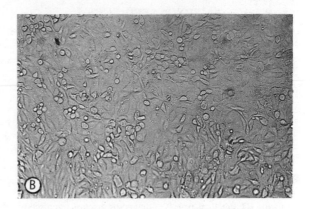

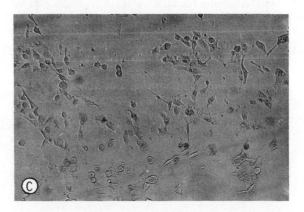

Figure 28–2. *A:* Monolayer of normal unstained monkey kidney cells in culture (120 ×). *B:* Unstained monkey kidney cell culture showing early stage of cytopathic effects typical of enterovirus infection (120 ×). Approximately 25% of the cells in the culture show cytopathic effects indicative of virus multiplication (1+ cytopathic effects). *C:* Unstained monkey kidney cell culture illustrating more advanced enteroviral cytopathic effect (3+ to 4+ cytopathic effects) (120 ×). Almost 100% of the cells are affected, and most of the cell sheet has come loose from the wall of the culture tube.

ANIMAL INOCULATION

In past decades, animal inoculation was often employed for virus isolation. Today, however, only relatively few specialized laboratories perform animal work. The laboratory animals employed include mice, hamsters, cotton rats, guinea pigs, rabbits, and monkeys. In some cases, infant mice (less than 48 hours old) are used. The animals of choice and the route of inoculation are listed in Table 29–8. Intracerebral and intranasal inoculation are employed particularly in mice; these routes require the special experience, skill, and methods available in public health or research laboratories that work with animals. The inoculated animals are observed for signs of illness, then are sacrificed, and their tissues are examined.

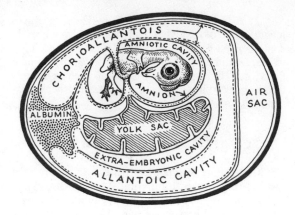

Figure 28–3. Schematic diagram showing developing chick embryo and indicating cavities and other structures used for various routes of inoculation.

EMBRYONATED EGGS

Embryonated eggs in various stages of development (Fig 28–3) can be inoculated by one of several routes. After inoculation, the eggs are reincubated and examined daily for viability. Standardized methods permit inoculation of the chorioallantoic membrane, the amniotic sac, the allantoic sac, the yolk sac, or the embryo. After suitable incubation, fluid or tissue is removed and examined for viral growth or lesions (Table 29–8).

• • •

References

Almeida JD: Practical aspects of diagnostic electron microscopy. *Yale J Biol Med* 1980;**53**:5.

Almeida JD et al: *Manual for Rapid Laboratory Viral Diagnosis.* WHO Publication No. 47. World Health Organization, 1979.

Daisy JA, Lief FS, Friedman HM: Rapid diagnosis of influenza A infection by direct immunofluorescence of nasopharyngeal aspirates in adults. *J Clin Microbiol* 1979;**9**:688.

Fishaut M et al: Cryopreservation of virus-infected cells for use in the fluorescent antibody to membrane antigen test. *J Clin Microbiol* 1980;**11**:687.

Herrmann JE, Hendry RM, Collins MF: Factors involved in enzyme-linked immunoassay of viruses and evaluation of the method for identification of enteroviruses. *J Clin Microbiol* 1979;**10**:210.

Lennette DA, Melnick JL, Jahrling PB: Clinical virology: Introduction to methods. Pages 760–771 in: *Manual of Clinical Microbiology*, 3rd ed. Lennette EH (editor). American Society for Microbiology, 1980.

Lennette EH, Schmidt NJ (editors): Chapters 1 and 3 in: *Diagnostic Procedures for Viral, Rickettsial and Chlamydial Infections,* 5th ed. American Public Health Association, 1979.

McIntosh K et al: Workshop on new and useful techniques in rapid viral diagnosis. *J Infect Dis* 1980;**142**:793.

Schmidt NJ et al: Direct immunofluorescence staining for detection of herpes simplex and varicella-zoster virus antigens in vesicular lesions and certain tissue specimens. *J Clin Microbiol* 1980;**12**:651.

Procedures Available

Typically, a virus infection elicits immune responses directed against one or more viral antigens. Both cellular and humoral immune responses usually develop, and measurement of either may be used to diagnose a virus infection. Cellular immunity may be assessed by dermal hypersensitivity, lymphocyte transformation, and cytotoxicity tests (see p 180). Humoral immune responses are of major diagnostic importance. Antibodies of the IgM class appear initially and are followed by IgG antibodies. The IgM antibodies disappear in several weeks, whereas the IgG antibodies persist for many years. Establishing the diagnosis of a virus infection is accomplished serologically by demonstrating a rise in antibody titer to the virus or by demonstrating antiviral antibodies of the IgM class.

Procedures for quantifying antibodies in virus diseases are based on classic antigen-antibody reactions (see Chapter 12), with some modifications for certain viruses. The commonly used methods include the neutralization (Nt) test, the complement fixation (CF) test, the hemagglutination inhibition (HI) test, and the immunofluorescence test. Less commonly used methods include passive hemagglutination, immunodiffusion, counterimmunoelectrophoresis, and radioimmunoassay. A summary of the tests available for viruses is listed in Table 29–8.

Antibodies measured by different methods do not necessarily give parallel results. This is illustrated in Table 29–1. Antibodies are detected by complement fixation during an enterovirus infection and in the convalescent period, but they do not persist. Antibodies detected by neutralization appear during infection and persist for many years. Assessment of antibodies by several methods in individuals or groups of individuals provides diagnostic information as well as information about epidemiologic features of the disease.

Collection of Blood Specimens

Serial samples of serum are essential for diagnostic purposes if antibodies are to be adequately tested and evaluated. In general, the first sample should be collected as soon as possible after the onset of the illness; the second, 2–3 weeks after onset. A third sample may be required later for special study. Antibodies appear earlier in some viral infections than in others, and so the times of collecting specimens must be varied according to circumstances.

Blood specimens should be drawn with aseptic precautions and without anticoagulants and the serum separated and stored at 4 °C or –20 °C. Before performing serologic tests it may be necessary to heat the serum (56 °C for 30 minutes) to remove nonspecific interfering or inhibiting substances and complement. This is essential for CF tests and also, with certain viruses, for Nt tests.

If paired sera are not available, a presumptive diagnosis can sometimes be made by demonstrating IgM antibodies to the virus. IgM antibodies may be detected by sensitivity to 2-mercaptoethanol or by immunofluorescence. (See Chapter 12.)

NEUTRALIZATION (Nt) TESTS

Virus-neutralizing antibodies are measured by adding serum containing these antibodies to a suspension of virus and then inoculating the mixture into susceptible cell cultures. The presence of neutralizing antibodies is demonstrated if the cell cultures fail to develop cytopathic effects (CPE), while control cell cultures, which have received virus plus a serum free of antibody, develop cytopathic effects. In some instances, the virus-antiserum mixture may be inoculated into susceptible experimental animals (as with type A coxsackieviruses) or embryonated eggs (as with mumps virus). The protection of the host from viral effects demonstrates neutralizing antibody.

Table 29–1. Interpretation of laboratory data in enterovirus infection.

Virus Isolation	Complement-fixing Antibody	Neutralizing Antibody	Antibody of IgM Class	Interpretation of Infection
−	−	−	−	None
+	−	−	−	Early
+	+	+	+	Current
−	+	+	+	Recent
−	−	+	−	Old

The virus in a neutralized mixture is not destroyed. When some virus-antibody mixtures are treated with acid (pH 2.0), the acid denatures the antibody and liberates the virus in its original, fully infectious state.

The level of such antibodies can be determined by using a constant amount of virus and falling concentrations of serum, or undiluted serum and falling concentrations of virus. To establish a diagnosis, one must be able to show a significant rise in antibody titer during the course of the infection.

A positive test in a single sample of serum is not of diagnostic value in acute infections. Neutralizing antibodies can persist for years, and their presence may indicate a past infection in a given individual. Thus, Nt tests are useful in serologic epidemiology, where one is interested in knowing which viral agents have infected a given population in the past.

Although simple in principle, Nt tests are expensive in time and in materials and must be standardized for each viral agent. Among the variables that must be considered are (1) the selection of the cell culture, experimental animal, or embryonated egg; (2) the route of inoculation of the virus-serum mixture; (3) the age of the test animals; (4) the stability of the test virus; (5) the reproducibility of the end point; (6) the relative heat-stability of the specific antibody and of possible interfering substances in serum; (7) the addition of an accessory factor found in fresh normal serum of the homologous species; (8) the use of one concentration of virus and varying dilutions of serum, or vice versa (and the relationship between varying concentrations of each); (9) the temperature of the neutralizing mixture; and (10) the time of incubation of the mixture.

THE NEUTRALIZATION TEST IN CELL CULTURE

The details of this test vary in different laboratories, but the same principle underlies all of them: the viral antibody specifically neutralizes the cytopathogenic effects of the virus.

With each series of Nt tests, control titrations of virus are made. The highest concentration of each serum used is tested for possible nonspecific cell toxicity. A few tubes are left uninoculated to serve as cell controls. The typical results of sera obtained from a patient infected with type 1 poliovirus are shown in Table 29-2. The cultures were incubated at 36 °C for 3 days and then examined microscopically. At the end of that time, the virus titration showed that 100 $TCID_{50}$ doses had been added to each serum.

For viruses such as herpes, polio, or vaccinia, which produce plaques on cell sheets (see Fig 27-26), neutralization may be measured by comparing the number of plaques produced by the virus alone with the number produced in the presence of the serum. Such plaque reduction techniques are available for many viruses grown in cell culture and are commonly used where greater accuracy of quantitation is required.

Suspensions of monkey kidney cells or cells from a continuous cell line may be used directly in Nt tests. The same basic principle that underlies any virus Nt test, ie, antibody specifically neutralizes the infectivity of the virus, also applies to the color (or metabolic inhibition) test. The color test employs known quantities of cell suspensions that are added to test tubes or plastic panel cups 1 hour after the virus-serum mixture. This eliminates the need for cultures in which cells have already grown out on glass. The color test utilizes the fact that with continued cellular growth in control tubes or in the presence of an immune serum-virus mixture, acidic products of metabolism lower the pH of the medium. This effect is readily observed by incorporating the indicator dye phenol red into the medium. This dye is red at pH 7.4-7.8. It becomes salmon pink and finally yellow as the pH drops below 7.0. Conversely, cell necrosis induced by the virus leaves the medium red, for the dying cultures fail to reach the degree of acidity exhibited by the control cultures. The test can thus be read by color change alone rather than by the presence or absence of cellular degeneration as determined microscopically. Neutral-

Table 29-2. Cell culture neutralization test with paired sera of patient infected with type 1 poliovirus.

Virus*	Serum (Day After Onset)	Cellular Degeneration (Cytopathic Effect) Final Serum Dilution					50% Serum Titer	
		1:2	1:10	1:50	1:250	1:1250	Logarithm	Antilog
Type 1	1	000	+++	+++	+++	+++	0.7	5
	20	000	000	000	00+	+++	2.5	320
Type 2	1	000	+++	+++	+++	+++	0.7	5
	20	000	000	0++	+++	+++	1.5	32
Type 3	1	+++	+++	+++	+++	+++	0	0
	20	+++	+++	+++	+++	+++	0	0
None	1	000						
	20	000						

*100 $TCID_{50}$ doses of each virus used in test. Three cultures were inoculated with each virus-serum mixture. + indicates cytopathic change in a culture because of virus growth. 0 indicates no growth of virus. ($TCID_{50}$ = 50% tissue culture infectious dose.)

izing antibodies are measured by determining the serum dilution that in the presence of added virus will allow the cells to metabolize normally and the pH to fall as in the controls.

The test described in the above paragraph is used with the enteroviruses. Because adenoviruses cause a stimulation of cellular metabolism and more rapid lowering of the pH than that in the control cultures, the color reaction is the opposite of that described above.

NEUTRALIZATION TESTS IN EGGS

The embryonated egg may also be used as an indicator system in virus Nt tests. With influenza and mumps viruses, after the inoculation of the virus-serum mixtures, the end point is measured by determining whether viral hemagglutinins have developed in the allantoic fluid (see Fig 29–1).

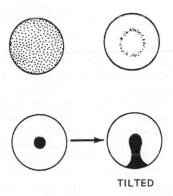

TILTED

Figure 29–1. Patterns of positive (top) and negative (bottom) hemagglutination. When the tube is tilted, only nonagglutinated cells (bottom row) slide down the tube.

NEUTRALIZATION TEST IN MICE

Mice of known uniform susceptibility and standard age are inoculated by a standard route with the virus-serum mixture. They are observed daily for signs of illness, such as weakness or paralysis, to establish specificity of the deaths. Illness and deaths are recorded daily for 21 days. Deaths within 24 hours after inoculation are attributed to traumatic or nonviral causes.

The virus suspension used is titrated by the adopted route of inoculation. The 50% lethal dose (LD_{50}) is calculated by an accepted method (eg, Reed-Muench, Kaerber), and a fixed number of LD_{50} is employed for each virus-serum mixture. Alternatively, the serum is kept constant and the virus dilutions are varied.

INTERPRETATION OF NEUTRALIZATION TESTS

Since neutralizing antibodies for viruses persist for years, it is essential to demonstrate a rise in titer in sequential sera in order to establish current or recent infection by the virus. A positive neutralization test in a single serum specimen is rarely sufficient to establish the clinical diagnosis of acute illness.

COMPLEMENT FIXATION (CF) TESTS

The principles underlying complement fixation (CF) tests have been described in Chapter 12 (p 171). Because antiviral sera fix complement in the presence of the homologous antigens, such CF tests are employed in the diagnosis of many viral infections (see Table 29–3). As in all CF tests, strictly standardized procedures must be employed. The main problem in viral CF tests is the preparation of specific antigens that are stable and not anticomplementary. Most antigens at present are derived from viral cell cultures (fluids or disrupted cells), from embryonated eggs (fluids or tissues), or from extracted tissues of infected animals (eg, mouse brains extracted with acetone for diagnosis of arbovirus infections).

In some instances, viruses may have 2 types of antigens: one associated with the virus particle (V) and the other a separate small, "soluble" entity (S). Antibodies against different antigens may appear at different times during viral infection, as illustrated in mumps (see p 429). The interpretation of complement fixation results depends on the antigen employed in the test and on the antibody titer rise observed.

•　　•　　•

Table 29–3. An example of a complement fixation test response.

Time of Taking Serum	Serum Dilution						Titer
	1:5	1:10	1:20	1:40	1:80	1:160	
Acute phase	0	0	0	0	0	0	0
Recovery phase	4+	3+	0	0	0	0	1:10
Convalescent	4+	4+	4+	3+	2+	0	1:80

4+ indicates complement fixation (no hemolysis); 0 indicates complete hemolysis.

HEMAGGLUTINATION INHIBITION (HI) TEST

Many viruses agglutinate erythrocytes, and this reaction may be specifically inhibited by immune or convalescent sera. As shown in Table 29–8, this reaction forms the basis of many diagnostic tests for viral infections.

Diseases in Which an Antibody Response May Be Demonstrated by the HI Test

Influenza
Rubella
Mumps
Measles
Newcastle disease
Variola
Vaccinia
California virus encephalitis
St. Louis encephalitis
Western equine encephalitis
Japanese B encephalitis
West Nile fever
Dengue
Adenovirus infections
Some enterovirus infections
Reovirus infections

General Principles

The same general principles apply for the HI tests used with different viral agents. However, a distinct species of erythrocytes may be necessary to agglutinate certain viruses, eg, some adenovirus types agglutinate only rat erythrocytes.

To be useful for diagnostic purposes, the erythrocyte suspension must be standardized and the viral antigen standardized and titrated. Positive and negative controls should be included in each test. The results are read (Fig 29–1) as follows:

(1) Positive agglutination is indicated by a red, granular, diffused lining on the bottom of the tube.

(2) Absence of agglutination is indicated by the formation of a compact red button at the bottom of the tube that slides when the tube is tilted.

(3) Partial agglutination is indicated by something in between a diffused lining on the bottom of the tube and a red button. This takes the form of a ring with a hollow center.

Specific antiviral antibody inhibits the agglutination of red cells by virus suspensions. This principle is used to quantify levels of antibody, to demonstrate rises in titer, and to establish the type-specific nature of the antibody rise in viral infections. Two serum specimens are needed from the patient, taken at an interval of 2–3 weeks. The first specimen should be obtained as promptly as possible after the onset of illness. Serial dilutions of the sera are made in diluent, a standard amount (usually 4 hemagglutinating units) of virus suspension is added, and after thorough mixing the red cell suspension is added. Incubation is often at room temperature for 60 minutes. Care must be taken not to

Table 29–4. An example of a hemagglutination inhibition test response.

Time of Taking Serum	Serum Dilution						Titer
	1:8	1:16	1:32	1:64	1:128	1:256	
Acute phase	0	+	+	+	+	+	1:8
Recovery phase	0	0	0	+	+	+	1:32
Convalescent	0	0	0	0	0	+	1:128

+ = Agglutination.
0 = No agglutination.

disturb the mixtures. The test is then read by the criteria outlined above. The highest dilution of serum that inhibits hemagglutination under standard conditions is considered the HI titer (see Table 29–4). A 4-fold or greater titer increase during a 2- to 3-week period is considered proof of active virus infection. For most viruses, HI micromethod tests are now employed.

PASSIVE HEMAGGLUTINATION TEST

The use of a coupling reagent, chromic chloride, to attach proteins to indicator erythrocytes has made possible the hemagglutination of red cells by antigens that otherwise do not demonstrate this property. This indirect, or passive, hemagglutination test has simplified the serologic diagnosis of rhinovirus infections and has made possible the rapid measurement of viral hepatitis B antigen (HBsAg) and antibody. The principle of the method is similar to the hemagglutination test described above, except that agglutination is a function of antibody attaching to antigens (which can be virus particles) permanently fixed onto red cells. The test is analogous to the latex particle agglutination test or bentonite particle agglutination test (see Chapter 12).

IMMUNOFLUORESCENCE TEST

The principles of immunofluorescence tests are described in Chapter 12 (p 168). The direct immunofluorescence (fluorescent antibody, FA) tests use known specific labeled antiviral sera to identify viruses grown in cell culture (as an isolation procedure) or found in exfoliated cells of the respiratory tract (eg, influenza).

The indirect immunofluorescence test may be more sensitive. The unlabeled antiviral serum is used as an unknown reagent, eg, human serum tested against cells grown on coverslips and infected with a virus. Then fluorescein isothiocyanate–labeled antihuman globulin (prepared in an animal) is used as a "stain" for examination in ultraviolet light. Thus, immunofluorescence methods can be used either to identify a virus or to establish the presence of a specific antibody in a series of serum dilutions by employing known virus antigen.

IMMUNODIFFUSION TEST

In immunodiffusion tests, the antigen and antibody are allowed to diffuse toward each other in a semisolid medium such as agar. A line of precipitate is formed at the zone of optimal proportions. The number of precipitin lines formed will depend upon the number of distinct antigen-antibody reactions taking place; each line represents one antigen-antibody system. The technique is well suited for the analysis of soluble antigens associated with viruses (see Chapter 12). The test is more sensitive and rapid if combined with electrophoresis (see below).

COUNTERIMMUNOELECTROPHORESIS TEST

Counterimmunoelectrophoresis methods can be applied to virologic diagnosis. The principles of the method are presented in Chapter 12 (p 169). Counterimmunoelectrophoresis applies when a viral antigen is negatively charged and moves toward the anode when the electric current is applied. Antibody globulin tends to move toward the cathode. When Ag and Ab meet, a precipitin line forms in the gel. An example of hepatitis HBs antigen interacting with human sera is shown in Fig 29–2.

RADIOIMMUNOASSAY

Radioimmunoassay (RIA) techniques measure immunologic rather than biologic activity (Chapter 12, p 169). They are being widely adapted to the detection and measurement of viral antigens and antibodies in picogram concentrations. Two basic assay procedures have been utilized depending on whether the specific compound to be labeled is antigen or antibody. Conventional RIA systems are based on the principle of saturation analysis in which the protein or polypeptide to be measured competes with a labeled antigen for a limited amount of antibody. The final ratio of labeled antigen for the specific antibody depends on the proportion of unlabeled antigen present in the system. To quantify the amount of unlabeled antigen in the system, a means of separating the residual free radioactivity from that complexed with the antibodies is necessary. Such separation techniques include adsorption methods (silicates, coated charcoal), fractional precipitation using staphylococcal protein A that binds the Fc fragment of IgG, and immunologic precipitation of the bound fraction with a second antibody (double antibody) directed against the antigenic determinants of IgG in the first antibody.

Table 29–5 illustrates the general procedure for the double antibody RIA method as applied to the detection of hepatitis B surface antigen (HBsAg) or its antibody (anti-HBs). Antigen detection is based on determining whether a significant reduction occurs in the percentage of counts bound by the test sample when compared with the negative control samples. The amount of reduction is a function of the concentration of unlabeled antigen present. Conversely, antibody detection depends on finding an increased number of counts in the precipitate of the test specimens when compared with the counts observed in the control samples that do not contain antibody.

The second method of immunoassay, which has become a powerful analytic tool for the diagnostic laboratory, is illustrated in Table 29–6. This 2-site, solid-phase immunoradiometric assay involves ad-

CATHODE (−)

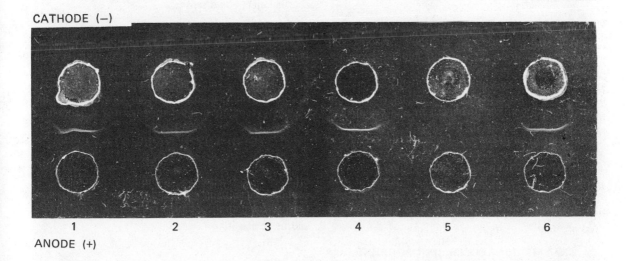

ANODE (+)

Figure 29–2. Counterimmunoelectrophoresis showing formation of precipitin lines between test samples and HBs antibody (anti-HBs). Human serum samples were placed in the top row of wells, and anti-HBs was placed in all wells of the bottom row. In the top row, wells 1–4 contain 4 serum samples from patients with viral hepatitis type B. Well 5 contains a negative normal human serum control; well 6 contains a known positive for HBsAg.

Table 29–5. Double antibody radioimmunoassay.

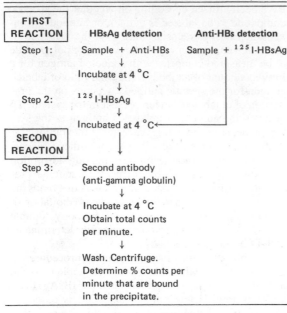

FIRST REACTION	HBsAg detection	Anti-HBs detection
Step 1:	Sample + Anti-HBs	Sample + ^{125}I-HBsAg
	↓	
	Incubate at 4 °C	
	↓	
Step 2:	^{125}I-HBsAg	
	↓	
	Incubated at 4 °C ←	
SECOND REACTION	↓	
Step 3:	Second antibody (anti-gamma globulin)	
	↓	
	Incubate at 4 °C Obtain total counts per minute.	
	↓	
	Wash. Centrifuge. Determine % counts per minute that are bound in the precipitate.	

Table 29–6. Two-site immunoradiometric assay.

Step 1: Specific unlabeled antibody adsorbed to insoluble matrix (polystyrene beads or polyvinyl microtiter wells).

↓

Step 2: Test sample added and antigen extracted immunologically.

↓

Step 3: Labeled antibody added as detector system for antigen bound in step 2.

↓

Wash. Measure radioactivity remaining on insoluble matrix.

sorption of unlabeled antibody to an insoluble matrix, eg, polystyrene beads or polyvinyl microtiter wells. The test sample containing antigen is allowed to complex with the antibody-coated surface. Antigen is literally extracted immunologically from the test specimen by specific binding to its surface; it is measured following a second reaction, now with radioactive labeled antibody. The amount of radioactivity measured is proportionate to the concentration of antigen bound by the initial reaction. The test offers increased sensitivity and specificity and can be completed in a relatively short time.

The RIA technique is 100–200 times more sensitive than the CF test.

ENZYME–LINKED IMMUNOSORBENT ASSAY (ELISA)

The principles of this test are described in Chapter 12 and Chapter 28, where its application to the detection of viral antigen in clinical material is explained.

For serum antibody, the following procedure is used: Viral antigen is first applied to the solid phase. The test serum is added, and any specific antibody is bound to the antigen. Enzyme-linked antiglobulin is added; it attaches to the bound antibody in the test serum. Enzyme substrate is added and the color change measured. It is proportionate to the amount of enzyme bound, and that in turn is related to the amount of antibody in the test serum.

IMMUNE ELECTRON MICROSCOPY

Viruses not detectable by conventional techniques may be observed by immune electron microscopy (IEM). Antigen-antibody complexes or aggregates formed between virus particles in suspension and added homologous antiserum are detected more readily and with greater assurance than individual virus particles. Fig 29–3 shows the IEM examination of human stool filtrates in which hepatitis A virus is demonstrated.

With the IEM technique, the sample is first clarified by centrifugation and then mixed with specific or convalescent serum. Following incubation, the complexes formed are sedimented by centrifugation; the supernatant is discarded and the pellet is resuspended in distilled water, mixed with 3% phosphotungstic acid, and examined by electron microscopy.

The IEM technique may permit the use of convalescent sera from patients with fever of undetermined origin to construct antigen-antibody complexes with serum obtained during the acute phase and to determine if infective agents were associated with the illness. This technique offers a sensitive method of identifying new agents and subsequently determining their role in infectious disease.

DIAGNOSIS OF INFECTIOUS MONONUCLEOSIS

Antibodies against the causative agent of infectious mononucleosis, the EB herpesvirus, can be demonstrated by immunofluorescence and a cell line that carries EB virus (see p 457). Far more commonly, the less specific heterophil agglutination test is used. The principle of the test is briefly described below. In most laboratories, the commercially available mononucleosis spot test is now employed, which is far simpler and more sensitive.

HETEROPHIL AGGLUTINATION TEST

This is a nonspecific phenomenon. In the course of infectious mononucleosis, substances appear in the serum that agglutinate sheep cells. If an early serum is

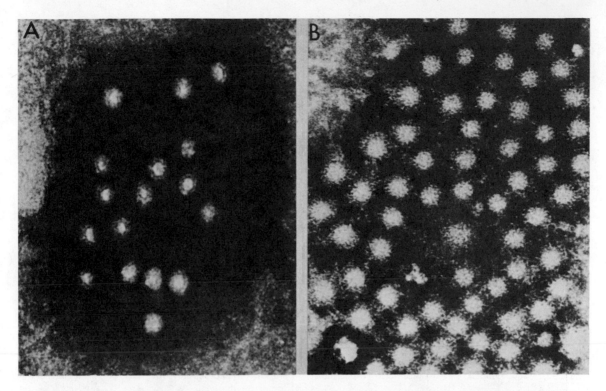

Figure 29–3. Electron micrographs of 27-nm hepatitis A virus (HAV). **A:** HAV particles not treated with antibody, demonstrating the presence of corelike structures (222,000 ×). **B:** HAV particles aggregated with antibody (222,000 ×). Note the presence of an antibody "halo" around each particle. (Bradley, Hornbeck, & Maynard.)

Table 29–7. Absorption reactions of agglutinins in human serum.

Type of Serum	Agglutinins Absorbed By	
	Guinea Pig Kidney	Bovine Erythrocytes
Normal	Yes	No
Infectious mononucleosis	No	Yes
Serum sickness	Yes	Yes

compared to a late one, the rise in titer occurs during mononucleosis. The agglutinins can be removed by absorbing serum with the materials shown in Table 29–7. If the sheep agglutinins are not removed by absorption with guinea pig kidney but are absorbed by beef erythrocytes, the diagnosis of infectious mononucleosis is confirmed. The accidental antigenic relationships that provide for the specificity of this result are not well understood. The heterophil agglutination tube test employing specific absorptions has been replaced largely by the spot test discussed below.

MONONUCLEOSIS SPOT TEST

A reliable, simple, and specific slide test (Mono-Diff, Monospot, Monostico, Monotest) has replaced the traditional sheep cell agglutination test as the most frequently used serologic test in diagnosing infectious mononucleosis.

In this test, the absorbing materials are incorporated in the test circles on the slide. A single drop of serum is placed on each circle, and horse erythrocytes are added. Agglutination of these cells indicates the presence of agglutinins diagnostic for infectious mononucleosis.

TESTS FOR DERMAL HYPERSENSITIVITY
(Skin Tests)

When available, tests for dermal hypersensitivity offer certain advantages in determining, easily and quickly, prior exposure to infectious agents. Tests have been described for mumps, herpes simplex, cat-scratch fever, western equine encephalitis, and vaccinia. The skin test may lead to increase in antibodies, eg, in the CF test.

The skin test antigen (0.1 mL) is injected intradermally into the flexor surface of one arm and the control material into the other arm. The sites of injection are examined after 12–48 hours. The mean diameter of erythematous reaction and induration is measured and compared to the control. A positive reaction is taken to indicate resistance to infection with some viruses.

Table 29—8. Laboratory diagnosis of viral diseases.

(CC, cell culture. Nt, neutralization. CF, complement fixation. HI, hemagglutination inhibition. CAM, chorioallantoic membrane. ID, immunodiffusion. IF, immunofluorescence. CIE, counterimmunoelectrophoresis. RIA, radioimmunoassay. CPE, cytopathic effect.)

Disease	Human Specimens to Be Tested	CC or Animals to Be Inoculated	Primary Isolation of Virus			Diagnostic Serologic Tests	
			Route	Tissue to Be Harvested for Passage	Positive Result in Test System: Signs and Pathology	Type of Test	Source of Virus or Antigen
ARTHROPOD-BORNE							
Encephalitides California St. Louis						Nt in mice or CC	Mouse brain or CC
Japanese B						CF	Mouse brain or CC
Western equine	Brain, blood	Mice	Intracerebral	Brain	Encephalitis	HI	Infant mouse brain
Eastern equine Venezuelan equine Russian spring-summer West Nile fever Bwamba, etc							
Yellow fever	Blood, viscera	Monkeys	Intraperitoneal	Viscera	Hepatic necrosis	Nt	Mouse brain
		Mice	Intracerebral	Brain	Encephalitis		
Rift Valley fever	Blood	Mice	Intraperitoneal	Liver	Hepatitis	Nt, CF	Mouse liver
Dengue	Blood	Mice (difficult)	Intracerebral	Brain	Encephalomyelitis	Nt, CF	Mouse brain
Sandfly fever	Blood	Infant mice	Intracerebral	Brain	Encephalomyelitis	Nt, CF	Mouse brain
Colorado tick fever	Blood	Hamsters	Intraperitoneal	Brain	Encephalitis	Nt	Mouse brain
		Mice	Intracerebral	Brain	Encephalitis	CF	Mouse brain
NEUROTROPIC, NON-ARTHROPOD-BORNE							
Poliomyelitis	Spinal cord, feces, throat swabs	CC		Fluid of infected culture	CPE	Nt, CF	CC
Rabies	Brain	Mice	Intracerebral	Brain	Encephalitis, Negri inclusion bodies in cytoplasm	IF	
Lymphocytic choriomeningitis	Brain, blood, spinal fluid	Mice	Intracerebral	Brain	Encephalitis and choroiditis	Nt	Mouse brain
		Guinea pig	Intraperitoneal	Spleen	Death with pneumonia, focal infiltration in liver	CF	Guinea pig spleen
B virus infection (Herpes B)	Brain, spleen	Rabbit	Intracutaneous	Spinal cord	Necrosis of skin, myelitis, intranuclear inclusion bodies	CF, Nt	Rabbit kidney CC
Herpes simplex		Rabbit kidney CC		CC fluid	CPE	CF, Nt	Rabbit kidney CC
Human papovavirus	Brain	CC			CPE	HI	CC
Measles (SSPE)	Brain	Direct exam (or co-cultivation in cell culture)				IF	
DERMOTROPIC							
Variola (smallpox)	Skin lesions, vesicle fluid, blood	Embryonated egg	CAM	CAM	Pocks on membrane, cytoplasmic inclusion bodies	CF, HI, ID	Vesicle fluid or crusts from patient against standard serum for rapid results

Table 29—8 (cont'd). Laboratory diagnosis of viral diseases.

(CC, cell culture. Nt, neutralization. CF, complement fixation. HI, hemagglutination inhibition. CAM, chorioallantoic membrane. ID, immunodiffusion. IF, immunofluorescence. CIE, counterimmunoelectrophoresis. RIA, radioimmunoassay. CPE, cytopathic effect.)

Disease	Human Specimens to Be Tested	CC or Animals to Be Inoculated	Primary Isolation of Virus			Diagnostic Serologic Tests	
			Route	Tissue to Be Harvested for Passage	Positive Result in Test System: Signs and Pathology	Type of Test	Source of Virus or Antigen
DERMOTROPIC (CONT'D)							
Vaccinia	Skin lesions, vesicle fluid	Embryonated egg	CAM	CAM	Pocks on membrane	CF	CAM, rabbit skin or testicle, mouse brain, CC
		Rabbit	Intracutaneous	Skin	Skin lesion, cytoplasmic inclusion bodies	Nt in eggs, rabbits, mice, CC; HI	
		CC		CC fluid	CPE		
Varicella (chickenpox)	Vesicle fluid	CC		Cells of infected culture	Intranuclear inclusions in skin lesions and in CC	CF, Nt	CC
Zoster	Vesicle fluid	CC		Cells of infected culture	Intranuclear inclusions	CF	CC
Measles	Nasopharyngeal secretions, blood	CC		CC fluid	Multinucleate giant cells and intranuclear inclusions	CF, Nt	CC
Rubella (German measles)	Nasopharyngeal secretions, blood, amniotic fluid	CC		CC fluid	Interference, or CPE	Nt, CF, HI, IF, ID	CC
Congenital rubella syndrome	Throat swabs, urine, feces, spinal fluid, blood, bone marrow, conjunctival swab	CC		CC fluid	Interference, or CPE	Nt, CF, HI, IF	CC
Exanthem subitum	Blood	Monkeys	Intravenous	Blood	Experimental exanthem		
Herpes simplex	Skin lesions, brain	Mouse (newborn)	Intracerebral	Brain	Encephalitis / Intranuclear inclusion bodies	Nt in mice, eggs, or CC	Mouse brain, allantoic fluid
		Embryonated egg	CAM	Allantoic fluid	Pocks /	CF	Allantoic fluid
		CC		Fluid	CPE /	Nt, CF	CC
RESPIRATORY AND PAROTID							
Influenza A Influenza B Influenza C	Throat swabs, nasal washings, lung	Eggs	Amniotic and allantoic sacs	Embryonic fluids	Hemagglutinin produced	HI	Allantoic fluid
		Ferrets, mice	Intranasal	Lung	Pneumonitis	CF	Allantoic fluid
		CC		Fluid phase	CPE, hemadsorption	Nt in eggs, mice, or CC	Allantoic fluid, mouse lung, CC
Parainfluenza		CC			Hemadsorption	Nt, CF	CC
Respiratory syncytial (RS) infection		CC		CC fluid	Multinucleate giant cells with cytoplasmic inclusions	Nt, CF	CC
Common cold (rhinovirus group)	Nasopharyngeal washings, swabs	CC		CC fluid	CPE	Nt	CC
Mumps	Saliva, spinal fluid, urine	Monkeys	Parotid gland	Parotid gland	Parotitis	CF	Amniotic fluid
		Eggs	Amniotic and yolk sac	Amniotic fluid, yolk sac	Hemagglutinin produced	HI	Monkey parotid gland
		CC		Fluid phase	CPE, hemadsorption	Nt in CC	CC

Table 29—8 (cont'd). Laboratory diagnosis of viral diseases.

(CC, cell culture. Nt, neutralization. CF, complement fixation. HI, hemagglutination inhibition. CAM, chorioallantoic membrane. ID, immunodiffusion. IF, immunofluorescence. CIE, counterimmunoelectrophoresis. RIA, radioimmunoassay. CPE, cytopathic effect.)

Disease	Human Specimens to Be Tested	CC or Animals to Be Inoculated	Primary Isolation of Virus			Diagnostic Serologic Tests	
			Route	Tissue to Be Harvested for Passage	Positive Result in Test System: Signs and Pathology	Type of Test	Source of Virus or Antigen
RESPIRATORY AND PAROTID (CONT'D)							
Adenovirus group	Throat swabs, pharyngeal washings, stool	CC		CC cells and fluid	CPE	CF, Nt, HI	CC
HEPATIC							
Infectious hepatitis (type A)	Blood, feces	(No satisfactory experimental system.)				Microtiter RIA	Serum, feces, liver, bile
Serum hepatitis (type B)	Blood, feces, urine					CIE, CF, ID, RIA	Serum, feces, urine
MISCELLANEOUS							
Coxsackie infection	Feces, throat swabs, spinal fluid, vesicle fluid	Infant mice	Subcutaneous	Muscle	Paralysis with myositis and, with certain types, encephalitis, steatitis; pancreatitis	Nt in infant mice or CC	Mouse muscle
		CC		CC fluid	CPE	Nt, CF, HI	CC
Echovirus infection	Feces, throat swabs, spinal fluid	CC		CC fluid	CPE	Nt, CF, HI	CC
Rotavirus infection	Feces	(Electron microscopy to visualize virus.)				CF, IF	(See p 462.)
Reovirus infection	Feces, throat swabs	CC		CC fluid	CPE	Nt, CF, HI	CC
Molluscum contagiosum	Skin lesions	(No satisfactory experimental animal. Characteristic cytoplasmic inclusion bodies. Elementary bodies can be seen in the electron microscope.)					
Verrucae (warts)	Skin lesions	(No satisfactory experimental animal. Electron microscopic examination of warts shows elementary bodies.)					
Encephalomyocarditis (Colombia SK, Mengo)	Blood	Mice	Intracerebral	Brain	Encephalitis	Nt in mice	Mouse brain
Epidemic keratoconjunctivitis	Conjunctivas	CC		CC cells and fluid	CPE	Nt test for adenovirus 8	CC
Foot-and-mouth disease	Skin lesions	Guinea pigs	Intracutaneous, foot pads	Foot pads	Hyperkeratosis with vesicle formation, paralysis with myositis	CF	Guinea pig foot pad
		Newborn mice		Muscle			Mouse muscle
Cytomegalic inclusion disease	Oral swabs, urine, various organs	CC		CC cells and fluid	CPE, inclusion bodies	Nt, CF	CC

• • •

References

Baumgarten A: Viral immunodiagnosis. *Yale J Biol Med* 1980; **53**:71.

Cabau N et al: Freeze-dried erythrocytes for an indirect hemagglutination test for detection of cytomegalovirus antibodies. *J Clin Microbiol* 1981;**13**:1026.

Forghani B, Schmidt NJ: Antigen requirements, sensitivity, and specificity of enzyme immunoassays for measles and rubella virus antibodies. *J Clin Microbiol* 1979;**9**:657.

Friedman MG, Leventon-Kriss S, Sarov I: Sensitive solid-phase radioimmunoassay for detection of human immunoglobulin G antibodies to varicella-zoster virus. *J Clin Microbiol* 1979; **9**:1.

Gallo D et al: Multiple-antigen slide test for detection of immuno-globulin M antibodies in newborn and infant sera by immuno-fluorescence. *J Clin Microbiol* 1981;**13**:631.

Gardner PS: Rapid virus diagnosis. *J Gen Virol* 1977;**36**:1.

Hollinger FB, Dienstag JL: Hepatitis viruses. Pages 899–921 in: *Manual of Clinical Microbiology*, 3rd ed. Lennette EH (editor). American Society for Microbiology, 1980.

Kapikian AZ et al: Visualization by immune electron microscopy of a 27-nm particle associated with acute infectious nonbacterial gastroenteritis. *J Virol* 1972;**10**:1075.

Lennette EH, Schmidt NJ (editors): Chapters 4, 5, 6, and 7 in: *Diagnostic Procedures for Viral, Rickettsial and Chlamydial Infections*, 5th ed. American Public Health Association, 1979.

Minor TE et al: Counterimmunoelectrophoresis test for immuno-globulin M antibodies to group B coxsackievirus. *J Clin Microbiol* 1979;**9**:503.

30 | Arthropod-Borne (Arbo) Viral Diseases

The **arthropod-borne viruses,** or **arboviruses,** are a group of infectious agents that are transmitted by blood-sucking arthropods from one vertebrate host to another. They can multiply in the tissues of the arthropod without evidence of disease or damage. The vector acquires a lifelong infection through the ingestion of blood from a viremic vertebrate. All arboviruses have an RNA genome, and most have a lipid-containing envelope and consequently are inactivated by ether or sodium deoxycholate.

Individual viruses were sometimes named after a disease (dengue, yellow fever) or after the geographic area where the virus was first isolated (St. Louis encephalitis, West Nile fever). Although arboviruses are found in all temperate and tropical zones, they are most prevalent in the tropical rain forest with its abundance of animals and arthropods.

There are more than 350 arboviruses, grouped according to their antigenic relationships. An effort is being made to classify them according to their chemical and physical properties, as described in Chapter 27 and arranged in Table 30–1. Many arboviruses are placed among toga-, bunya-, reo-, arena-, picorna-, and rhabdovirus groups. Definitions of these groups are given in Chapter 27 and are briefly summarized below.

Togaviruses: Spherical particles contain a single-stranded RNA genome (MW 4×10^6) and are surrounded by a lipid-containing envelope. Group A arboviruses are larger (40–80 nm) and are inactivated by proteases, and all multiply in arthropods. Group B arboviruses are smaller (20–50 nm) and are not inactivated by proteases, and not all multiply in arthropods, but all are serologically related. All togaviruses multiply in the cytoplasm and mature by budding. Names of representative group A and group B viruses are given in Table 30–1. Some of the most important ones are discussed below.

Bunyaviruses: Spherical particles contain a single negative strand RNA genome that is segmented. They have a lipid-containing envelope and measure 90–100 nm. The nucleocapsids have helical symmetry and contain a major viral protein. The envelope has 2 glycoproteins in the lipid bilayer and surface projections (10 nm) of glycopeptides clustered to form hollow cylinders. All bunyaviruses multiply in arthropods. Several produce mosquito-borne encephalitides of humans and animals, others hemor-

rhagic fevers. Some are transmitted by sandflies (*Phlebotomus*).

Reoviruses (see Chapter 39): A few arboviruses are placed into this group (subgroup *Orbivirus*), including African horse sickness and Colorado tick fever

Table 30–1. Current taxonomic status of some arboviruses.

Current Taxonomic Classification	Arbovirus Members
Togaviridae Genus *Alphavirus*	*Group A:* Aura, Chikungunya, eastern equine encephalitis, Getah, Mayaro, Middelburg, Mucambo, Ndumu, O'Nyong-nyong, Pixuna, Ross River, Semliki Forest, Sindbis, Una, Venezuelan and western equine encephalitis, and Whataroa viruses
Genus *Flavivirus*	*Group B:* Brazilian encephalitis (Rocio virus), Bussuquara, dengue, Ilheus, Israel turkey meningoencephalitis, Japanese B encephalitis, Kunjin, Kyasanur Forest disease, Langat, louping ill, Modoc, Murray Valley encephalitis, Ntaya, Omsk hemorrhagic fever, Powassan, St. Louis encephalitis, Spondweni, tick-borne encephalitis, Uganda S, US bat salivary gland, Wesselsbron, West Nile fever, yellow fever, and Zika viruses
Bunyaviridae Genus *Bunyavirus*	Bunyamwera (18 members), Bwamba (2), C (11), California (11), Capim (6), Guama (6), Koongol (2), Patois (4), Simbu (16), and Tete (4) serogroups; 7 unassigned viruses
Possible members	Uukuniemi (7 members), *Anopheles* A (3), *Anopheles* B (2), Bakau (2), Crimean-Congo hemorrhagic fever (2), Kaisodi (3), Mapputta (3), Nairobi sheep disease (3), *Phlebotomus* fever (20), and Turlock (3) serogroups; 8 unassigned viruses
Reoviridae Genus *Orbivirus*	African horse sickness, bluetongue, and Colorado tick fever viruses
Rhabdoviridae Genus *Vesiculovirus*	Cocal, Hart Park, Kern Canyon, and vesicular stomatitis viruses
Arenaviridae Genus *Arenavirus*	Junin, Lassa, Machupo, and Pichinde viruses
Nodaviridae	Nodamura virus

(see below). Some infect birds, small mammals, and ticks.

Arenaviruses (see Chapter 27): Pleomorphic particles contain a segmented single negative strand RNA genome (MW $3-5 \times 10^6$), are surrounded by an envelope, and measure 50–300 nm. They contain granules believed to be ribosomes. Several hemorrhagic fever viruses that are antigenically related fall into this group. Most have a rodent host in their natural cycle (see below).

Rhabdoviruses (see p 334): Several bullet-shaped arboviruses fall into this group (Fig 27–35).

Nodavirus: Nodamura virus is an insect pathogen that can infect mammals.

Human Infection

About 75 arboviruses can infect humans, but not all cause overt disease. Those infecting humans are all believed to be zoonotic, with humans the accidental hosts who play no important role in the maintenance or transmission cycle of the virus. Exceptions are urban yellow fever and dengue. Some of the natural cycles are simple and involve a nonhuman vertebrate host (mammal or bird) with a species of mosquito or tick (eg, jungle yellow fever, Colorado tick fever). Others, however, are quite complex. For example, many cases of Central European diphasic meningoencephalitis occur following ingestion of raw milk from goats and cows infected by grazing in tick-infested pastures where a tick-rodent cycle is occurring.

Diseases produced by the arboviruses may be divided into 3 clinical syndromes: (1) fevers of an undifferentiated type with or without a maculopapular rash and usually benign; (2) encephalitis, often with a high case fatality rate; and (3) hemorrhagic fevers, also frequently severe and fatal. These categories are somewhat arbitrary, and some arboviruses may be associated with more than one syndrome, eg, dengue.

The intensity of viral multiplication and its predominant site of localization in tissues determine the clinical syndrome. Thus, individual arboviruses can produce a minor febrile illness in some patients and encephalitis or a hemorrhagic diathesis in others. However, in an epidemic situation, one of the syndromes usually predominates, permitting a tentative diagnosis. A final diagnosis is based on further epidemiologic and serologic data.

After infection with an arbovirus, there is an incubation period during which viral multiplication takes place. This is followed by the abrupt onset of clinical manifestations that are closely related to viral dissemination. Malaise, headache, nausea, vomiting, and myalgia accompany fever, which is an invariable symptom and sometimes the only one. The illness may terminate at this stage, recur with or without a rash, or reveal hemorrhagic manifestations secondary to vascular abnormalities. Frequently, the period of viremia is asymptomatic, with the acute onset of encephalitis following localization of the virus in the central nervous system.

The above clinical categories are utilized in the following sections in discussing some of the most important diseases caused by the arboviruses.

Encephalitis can be produced by many different viruses. Arbovirus encephalitis occurs in distinct geographic distributions and vector patterns (Table 30–2). Each continent tends to have its own arbovirus pattern, and names are usually suggestive, eg, Venezuelan equine encephalitis (VEE), Japanese B encephalitis (JBE), Murray Valley (Australia) encephalitis (MVE). All of the preceding are togavirus infections spread by

Table 30–2. Summary of 6 major human arbovirus infections that occur in the USA.

Diseases	Exposure	Distribution	Vectors	Infection: Case Ratio (Age Incidence)	Sequelae	Mortality Rate (%)
WEE	Rural	Pacific, Mountain, West Central, Southwest	*Culex tarsalis*	50:1 (under 5) 1000:1 (over 15)	+	2–3
EEE	Rural	Atlantic, southern coastal	*Aedes sollicitans* *Aedes vexans*	10:1 (infants) 50:1 (middle aged) 20:1 (elderly)	+	50–70
SLE	Urban-rural	Widespread	*Culex pipiens* *Culex quinquefasciatus* *Culex tarsalis* *Culex nigrapalpus*	>400:1 (young) 64:1 (elderly)	±	5–10
VEE	Rural	South and Central America, southern USA	*Aedes Psorophora Culex*	Unknown ratio	Unknown	0.5
California encephalitis	Rural	North Central, Atlantic, South	(*Aedes* sp?)	Unknown ratio (most cases under 20)	±	Fatalities rare
Colorado tick fever	Rural	Pacific, Mountain	*Dermacentor andersoni*	Unknown ratio (all ages affected)	Rare	Fatalities rare

mosquitoes with a distinct ecologic distribution. California encephalitis is caused by bunyaviruses, as discussed below. However, on a given continent there may be a shifting distribution depending on virus hosts and vectors in a given year.

Encephalitis or meningoencephalitis can also occur with viruses that involve tissues other than the central nervous system—measles, mumps, hepatitis, chickenpox, zoster, herpes simplex, and others. Some of these viruses replicate actively in the central nervous system, producing inflammation. At other times, the viral infection sets off an immunologic reaction that results in "postinfectious" encephalomyelitis, with a prominent demyelinating component.

In some parts of the world, epidemics of arbovirus infection have involved thousands of individuals with symptomatic infection; many more were asymptomatically infected. In 1975 in the USA 4308 cases of encephalitis were reported, with 340 deaths. Cases occurred in almost every state. Of the entire number, 42% were due to St. Louis encephalitis, 7% to other arboviruses, 4% to mumps, 3% to enteroviruses, 2% to herpesviruses, and 40% could not be identified by laboratory means.

TOGAVIRUS ENCEPHALITIS (SLE, WEE, EEE)

Characteristics of Togaviruses

A. Properties: Togaviruses are small viruses (40 nm for group A, 70 nm for group B) that are unstable at room temperature, stable at $-70\ °C$, and rapidly inactivated by ether or by 1:1000 sodium deoxycholate. This property separates them easily from enteroviruses.

The viruses infect many cell lines, embryonated eggs, mice, birds, bats, mules, horses, and other animals. In susceptible vertebrate hosts, primary virus multiplication occurs either in myeloid and lymphoid cells or in vascular endothelium. Multiplication in the central nervous system depends on the ability of the virus to pass the blood-brain barrier and to infect nerve cells. In natural infection of birds and mammals (and in experimental parenteral injection of the virus into animals), an inapparent infection develops in a majority. However, for several days there is viremia, and arthropod vectors acquire the virus by sucking blood during this period—the first step in its dissemination to other hosts. The above characteristics apply to the main togavirus infections in the western hemisphere, particularly St. Louis encephalitis (SLE), western equine encephalitis (WEE), eastern equine encephalitis (EEE), and Venezuelan equine encephalitis (VEE) (see Table 30–2). They also apply to Japanese B encephalitis (JBE), which occurs in the Far East.

B. Replication: All togaviruses replicate in the cytoplasm. The genome RNA, released from virus particles, is infectious and, like picornaviruses, can act as a messenger. However, togaviruses have 2 sizes of mRNA: the virion RNA of 42S and a smaller 26S species containing a subset of the 42S sequences. Each mRNA is translated into a large polypeptide that subsequently undergoes cleavage and processing. The 26S mRNA polypeptide is processed to the capsid protein and 2 envelope proteins, whereas that from the 42S mRNA is processed to nonstructural proteins, 2 of which may be part of the replicase. Except for the smaller-than-genome mRNA, togavirus replication is similar to that of the picornaviruses. Togaviruses, however, have 2 or more structural polypeptides that undergo glycosylation and cleavage and are incorporated into the cytoplasmic membrane of the cell. The virus particle buds through the altered areas of the membrane to acquire its envelope and the glycosylated polypeptides. Only one polypeptide is found in the nucleocapsid of togaviruses, in contrast to the 4 found in picornavirus nucleocapsids.

C. Measurement of Virus Concentration: Viral multiplication can be measured by cytopathic changes, virus-specific immunofluorescence, or the production of viral hemagglutinin as seen directly in the cell culture by the hemadsorption test. Plaque counts can be done with group A and B viruses in most cultures. Arboviruses exhibit homotypic and heterotypic interference, as well as susceptibility to interferon.

D. Antigenic Properties: Complement-fixing antigens and viral hemagglutinins may be prepared from infected brains of newborn mice (because of their low fat content). The hemagglutinins of these viruses are part of the infectious virus particle and can hemagglutinate goose or newly hatched chick red blood cells. The union between hemagglutinin and red cell is irreversible. The erythrocyte-virus complex is still infective, but it can be neutralized by the addition of antibody, which results in large lattice formations.

Some of these viruses have an overlapping antigenicity, most readily demonstrated by cross-reactions in HI tests. The overlapping is due to the presence of one or more cross-reactive antigens in addition to the strain-specific antigen. Thus, immune sera prepared for one strain will contain strain-specific as well as group-specific antibodies.

An immune serum can be made more specific by adsorption with a heterologous virus of the same group. The adsorbed serum tested for hemagglutination-inhibiting (HI) activity reacts only with the homologous and not with the heterologous strain, facilitating the identification of newly isolated strains.

Pathogenesis & Pathology

The pathogenesis of the disease in humans has not been well studied, but the disease in experimental animals may afford a model for the human disease. The equine encephalitides in horses are diphasic. In the first phase (minor illness), the virus multiplies in non-neural tissue and is present in the blood 3 days before the first signs of involvement of the central nervous system. In the second phase (major illness), the virus multiplies in the brain, cells are injured and destroyed, and encephalitis becomes clinically apparent. The 2 phases may overlap. It is not known whether in humans there is a period of primary viral multiplication in the viscera with a secondary liberation of virus into the blood before its entry into the central nervous system. The viruses multiply in nonneural tissues of experimentally infected monkeys.

High concentrations of virus in brain tissue are necessary before the clinical disease becomes manifest. In mice, the level to which the virus multiplies in the brain is partly influenced by a genetic factor that behaves as a mendelian trait.

The primary encephalitides are characterized by lesions in all parts of the central nervous system, including the basal structures of the brain, the cerebral cortex, and the spinal cord. Small hemorrhages with perivascular cuffing and meningeal infiltration—chiefly with mononuclear cells—are common. Nerve cell degeneration associated with neuronophagia occurs. Purkinje's cells of the cerebellum may be destroyed. There are also patches of encephalomalacia; acellular plaques of spongy appearance in which medullary fibers, dendrites, and axons are destroyed; and focal microglial proliferation. Thus, not only the neurons but also the cells of the supporting structure of the central nervous system are attacked.

Widespread neuronal degeneration occurs with all arboviruses producing encephalitis, but some localization occurs.

Clinical Findings

Incubation periods of the encephalitides are between 4 and 21 days. There is a sudden onset with severe headache, chills and fever, nausea and vomiting, generalized pains, and malaise. Within 24–48 hours, marked drowsiness develops and the patient may become stuporous. Nuchal rigidity is common. Mental confusion, dysarthria, tremors, convulsions, and coma develop in severe cases. Fever lasts 4–10 days. The mortality rate in encephalitides varies (see Table 30–2). With JBE, the mortality rate in older age groups may be as high as 80%. Sequelae may include mental deterioration, personality changes, paralysis, aphasia, and cerebellar signs.

Abortive infections simulate aseptic meningitis or nonparalytic poliomyelitis. Inapparent infections are common.

In California, where both WEE and SLE are prevalent, WEE has a predilection for children and infants. In the same area, SLE rarely occurs in infants, even though both viruses are transmitted by the same arthropod vector (*Culex tarsalis*).

Laboratory Diagnosis

A. Recovery of Virus: The virus occurs in the blood only early in the infection, usually before the onset of symptoms. The virus is most often recovered from the brains of fatal cases by intracerebral inoculation of newborn mice, and then it should be identified by serologic tests with known antisera.

B. Serology: Neutralizing and hemagglutination-inhibiting antibodies are detectable within a few days after the onset of illness. Complement-fixing antibodies appear later. The neutralizing and the hemagglutination-inhibiting antibodies endure for many years. The complement-fixing antibody may be lost within 2–5 years.

The HI test with newly hatched chick erythrocytes is the simplest diagnostic test, but it primarily identifies the group rather than the specific causative virus.

It is necessary to establish a rise in specific antibodies during infection in order to make the diagnosis. The first sample of serum should be taken as soon after the onset as possible and the second sample 2–3 weeks later. The paired specimens must be run in the same serologic test.

The cross-reactivity that takes place within group A or B arboviruses must be considered in making the diagnosis. Thus, following a single infection by one member of the group, antibodies to other members may also appear. These group-specific antibodies are usually of lower titer than the type-specific antibody. Serologic diagnosis becomes difficult when an epidemic caused by one member of the serologic group occurs in an area where another group member is endemic, or when an infected individual has been infected previously by a closely related arbovirus. Under these circumstances, a definite etiologic diagnosis may not be possible. Neutralizing, complement-fixing, and hemagglutination-inhibiting antibodies have a decreasing degree of specificity for the causative viral type (in the order listed).

Immunity

Immunity is believed to be permanent after a single infection. In endemic areas, the population may build up immunity as a result of inapparent infections; the proportion of persons with antibodies to the local arthropod-borne virus increases with age.

Effective killed vaccines have been developed to protect horses against EEE and WEE. No effective vaccines for these diseases are at present available for humans.

An excellent attenuated vaccine for VEE is available for curtailing epidemics among horses and has been used experimentally in humans. A vaccine for JBE is being developed.

Because of antigens common to several members within a group, the response to immunization or to infection with one of the viruses of a group may be modified by prior exposure to another member of the same group. In general, the homologous response is greater than a cross-reacting one. This mechanism may be important in conferring protection on a community against an epidemic of another related agent (eg, no Japanese B encephalitis in areas endemic for West Nile fever).

Treatment

There is no specific treatment. In experimental animals, hyperimmune serum is ineffective if given after the onset of disease. However, if given 1–2 days after the invasion of the virus but before the signs of encephalitis are obvious, specific hyperimmune serum can prevent a fatal outcome of the infection.

Epidemiology

In severe epidemics caused by the encephalitis viruses, the case rate is about 1:1000. In the large urban epidemic of St. Louis encephalitis that occurred in 1966 in Dallas (population 1 million), there were 545 reported cases, 145 (27%) laboratory-confirmed cases, and 15 deaths. The overall attack rate was 15 cases per 100,000, with a case fatality rate of 10%. All deaths were in persons age 45 years or older.

SLE is now appearing each year in the USA. In 1976, 372 cases with 17 deaths were reported in the USA.

The epidemiology of the arthropod-borne encephalitides must account for the maintenance and dissemination of the viruses in nature in the absence of humans. Most infections with the arboviruses occur in mammals or birds, with humans serving as an accidental host. The virus is transmitted from animal to animal through the bite of an arthropod vector. Viruses have been isolated from mosquitoes and ticks, which serve as reservoirs of infection. In ticks, the viruses may pass from generation to generation by the transovarian route, and in such instances the tick acts as a true reservoir of the virus as well as its vector. In tropical climates, where mosquito populations are present throughout the year, arboviruses cycle continuously between mosquitoes and reservoir animals.

It is not known whether in temperate climates the virus is reintroduced each year from the outside (eg, by birds migrating from tropical areas) or whether it somehow survives the winter in the local area. The overwintering mechanism is not known. Three possible mechanisms are (1) that hibernating mosquitoes at the time of their emergence could reinfect birds and thus reestablish a simple bird-mosquito-bird cycle; (2) that the virus could remain latent in winter within birds, mammals, or arthropods; and (3) that cold-blooded vertebrates (snakes, turtles, lizards, alligators, frogs) may also act as winter reservoirs—eg, garter snakes experimentally infected with WEE virus can hibernate over the winter and circulate virus in high titers and for long periods the following spring. Normal mosquitoes can be infected by feeding on the emerged snakes and then can transmit the virus. Virus has been found in the blood of wild snakes.

A. Serologic Epidemiology: In highly endemic areas, almost the entire human population may become infected, and most infections are asymptomatic. This is true for Japanese B encephalitis infection in Japan. High infection-to-case ratios exist among specified age groups for many arbovirus infections (Table 30–2).

In the 1964 Houston SLE epidemic (712 reported cases), there was an inapparent infection rate of 8% in a random city survey, but in the epidemic area of the city the inapparent infection rate was 34%. The infection-to-case ratio remained about the same, however. It is obvious that the presence of infected mos-

quitoes is required before human infections can occur, although socioeconomic and cultural factors (air conditioning, screens, mosquito control) affect the degree of exposure of the population to these virus-carrying vectors.

In endemic areas of California, 11% of infants are born with maternal antibody to WEE and 27% have SLE maternal antibody. A direct relationship exists between the length of residence of the mother in the endemic area and the acquisition of antibody.

B. Mosquito-Borne Encephalitis: Infection of humans occurs when a mosquito like *Culex tarsalis, Culex quinquefasciatus, Culex pipiens,* or *Culex tritaeniorhynchus* (Japan) or another arthropod bites first an infected animal and later a human being.

The equine encephalitides, EEE, WEE, and VEE, are transmitted by culicine mosquitoes to horses or humans from a mosquito-bird-mosquito cycle. Equines, like humans, are unessential hosts for the maintenance of the virus. An epizootic of encephalitis in horses should alert physicians to the possibility that an arbovirus epidemic in humans may be developing. EEE and VEE in horses are severe, with up to 90% of the affected animals dying. Epizootic WEE is less frequently fatal for horses. In addition, EEE produces severe epizootics in certain domestic game birds. A mosquito-bird-mosquito cycle also occurs in SLE and JBE. Swine are an important host of JBE. Mosquitoes remain infected for life (several weeks to months). Only the female feeds on blood and can feed and transmit the virus more than once. The cells of the mosquito's mid gut are the site of primary virus multiplication. This is followed by viremia and invasion of organs—chiefly salivary glands and nerve tissue, where secondary virus multiplication occurs. The arthropod remains healthy.

Infection of insectivorous bats with arboviruses produces a viremia lasting 6–12 days without any illness or pathologic changes in the bat. While the virus concentration is high, the infected bat may infect mosquitoes that are then able to transmit the infection to wild birds and domestic fowl as well as to other bats.

In nature, mosquitoes are closely associated with bats, both in summer and during the winter (in hibernation sites). Experimentally, mosquitoes have been shown to transmit virus to bats. Bats thus infected could maintain a latent virus infection, with no detectable viremia, for over 3 months at 10 °C. When bats were returned to room temperature, viremia appeared after 3 days. The mosquito-bat-mosquito cycle may be a possible overwintering mechanism for some arboviruses.

C. Tick-Borne Encephalitis Complex:

1. Russian spring-summer encephalitis–This disease occurs chiefly in the early summer, particularly in humans exposed to the ticks *Ixodes persulcatus* and *Ixodes ricinus* in the uncleared forest. Ticks can become infected at any stage in their metamorphosis, and virus can be transmitted transovarially. The virus persists through the winter in hibernating ticks or in vertebrates such as hedgehogs or bats. Virus is secreted in the milk of infected goats for long periods, and infection may be transmitted to those who drink unpasteurized milk. Characteristics of the disease are involvement of the bulbar area or the cervical cord and the development of ascending paralysis or hemiparesis. The mortality rate is about 30%.

2. Louping ill–This disease of sheep in Scotland and northern England is spread by the tick *Ixodes ricinus*. Humans are occasionally infected.

3. Tick-borne encephalitis (Central European or diphasic meningoencephalitis)–This virus is antigenically related to Russian spring-summer encephalitis virus and louping ill virus. Typical cases have a diphasic course, the first phase being influenzalike and the second a meningoencephalitis with or without paralysis.

4. Kyasanur Forest disease is an Indian hemorrhagic disease caused by a virus of the Russian spring-summer encephalitis complex. In addition to humans, langur *(Presbytis entellus)* and bonnet *(Macaca radiata)* monkeys are naturally infected in southern India.

5. Powassan encephalitis–This tick-borne virus is the first member of the Russian spring-summer complex isolated in North America. Human infection is rare. Since 1959, when the original fatal case was reported from Canada, several additional cases have been confirmed in the northeastern portion of the USA.

Control

Biologic control of the natural vertebrate host is generally impractical, especially when the hosts are wild birds. The most effective method is arthropod control. Since the period of viremia in the vertebrate is of short duration (3–6 days for SLE infections of birds), any suppression of the vector for this period should break the transmission cycle. During the 1966 Dallas SLE epidemic, low-volume, high-concentration malathion mist was sprayed aerially over most of Dallas County. A striking decrease in the number and infectivity rate of the mosquito vectors occurred, demonstrating the effectiveness of the treatment.

Killed vaccines have not met with success. Several live attenuated encephalitis vaccines are being investigated. A live attenuated vaccine was successfully used to halt the severe epidemic of VEE in horses in Texas in 1971.

VENEZUELAN EQUINE ENCEPHALITIS

Venezuelan equine encephalitis (VEE) is a mosquito-borne viral disease that primarily produces an undifferentiated febrile illness in humans and encephalitis in equine animals. It is caused by a group A arbovirus, a typical togavirus. There is a partial cross-immunity between VEE and EEE.

Clinical Findings

Over 50% of equines infected develop central nervous system symptoms after an incubation period of 24–72 hours, while the remainder have an undifferentiated febrile illness. Symptoms include high fever, depression, diarrhea, anorexia, and weight loss. In nonfatal cases, the fever subsides and convalescence is protracted. In fatal cases, fever persists, weakness ensues, and the horse loses balance and dies within 2–4 days.

The disease in humans is influenzalike in about 97% of patients who develop symptoms and consists of high fever, headache, and severe myalgia. Convalescence is often prolonged. Encephalitis occurs in about 3%. A mortality rate of 0.5% has been reported, usually in younger patients who develop neurologic signs. Leukopenia is common in both equines and humans.

Laboratory Diagnosis

The virus may be isolated from whole blood, serum, nasopharyngeal washings, many organs, and occasionally the cerebrospinal fluid during the acute phase of the illness. Isolations are made by intracerebral inoculation of suckling mice or in cell cultures. The antibody response is similar to that found in other arbovirus diseases. Neutralizing and hemagglutination-inhibiting antibodies appear 2–3 weeks after onset but fall within 2–5 years. Serologic tests, listed in order of specificity, include Nt, CF, and HI. Cross-reactions with other members of group A are extensive using the HI test, although homologous titers are higher than the heterologous antibodies.

Epidemiology

The natural cycle for VEE involves mammals and mosquitoes. Birds and bats are susceptible. Humans are tangentially involved.

First reported in Venezuela in 1936, the disease gradually appeared in Panama and Mexico. In 1971, a severe epidemic occurred along the Texas-Mexico border, with the death of several thousand horses and the occurrence of several hundred human cases. Two human cases of VEE were reported in California in 1972. In Florida, VEE is enzootic in rodents. Serologic evidence indicates that much subclinical human infection with this agent occurs in Florida, but clinical central nervous system disease is rare.

Control

Because of the presence of virulent VEE in Mexican border states, immunization of all equines (including revaccination of previously vaccinated equines) with a live attenuated vaccine and local and aerial spraying of mosquitoes were begun on a routine basis in 1972. So far, these measures have proved effective in limiting the spread of the disease. Strict quarantine to prevent movement of equines into areas free of the disease is also necessary. The attenuated VEE vaccine has been used experimentally in humans but is not available for general use.

BUNYAVIRUS ENCEPHALITIS
(California Encephalitis)

The California encephalitis virus complex comprises 11 antigenically related bunyaviruses.

Clinical Findings & Diagnosis

The onset of California encephalitis virus infection is abrupt, typically with a severe bifrontal headache, a fever of 38–40 °C, sometimes vomiting, lethargy, and convulsions. Less frequently, there is only aseptic meningitis.

The white blood cell count is often 10,000–25,000/μL, with polymorphonuclear cells predominating. Cerebrospinal fluid pleocytosis, predominantly lymphocytic, is present. The electroencephalogram reveals generalized cerebral dysfunction with high-amplitude slow activity.

Histopathologic changes include neuronal degeneration and patchy inflammation, with perivascular cuffing and edema in the cerebral cortex and meninges.

The prognosis is excellent, although convalescence may be prolonged. Fatalities and neurologic sequelae are rare.

Serologic confirmation by HI, CF, or Nt tests is done on acute and convalescent specimens.

Epidemiology

These viruses were originally found in California, but they occur mainly in the Mississippi and Ohio river valleys, with scattered cases elsewhere. Cases occur mainly between July and September in the USA, particularly in the young (ages 4–14 years).

These viruses are probably transmitted between various woodland mosquitoes and small mammals such as squirrels and rabbits. Human infection is tangential. The mechanism by which the virus is maintained during the winter months is not known. However, overwintering in diapause eggs of the mosquito vector has been demonstrated. The virus is transmitted transovarially, and adults that develop from infected eggs can transmit the virus by bite.

WEST NILE FEVER

West Nile fever is an acute, mild, febrile disease with lymphadenopathy and rash that occurs in the Middle East, tropical or subtropical Africa, and southwest Asia. It is caused by a group B arbovirus, a typical togavirus.

Clinical Findings

The virus is introduced through the bite of a *Culex* mosquito and produces viremia and a generalized systemic infection characterized by lymphadenopathy, sometimes with an accompanying maculopapular rash. Transitory meningeal involvement may occur during the acute stage. The virus may produce fatal encephalitis in older people, who have a delayed (and low) antibody response.

Laboratory Diagnosis

Virus can be recovered from blood taken in the acute stage of the infection. On paired serum specimens, CF, HI, and Nt titer rises may be diagnostic. Nt antibodies persist longer than CF antibodies. During convalescence, heterologous CF and Nt antibodies develop to JBE and SLE. The heterologous response is shorter and of lower titer than the homologous response.

Immunity

Only one antigenic type exists, and immunity is presumably permanent. Maternal antibodies are transferred from mother to offspring and disappear during the first 6 months of life.

Epidemiology & Control

West Nile fever appears to be limited to the Middle East. Antibodies to the virus have been found in Africa, India, and Korea, perhaps because of an antigenically related virus. In nonimmune populations, subclinical or clinical infections are common. In Cairo, 70% of persons over age 4 years have antibodies.

The disease is more common in summer and more prevalent in rural than urban areas. The virus has been isolated from *Culex* mosquitoes during epidemics, and experimentally infected mosquitoes can transmit the virus. Mosquito abatement appears to be a logical, if unproved, control measure.

YELLOW FEVER

Yellow fever (YF) is an acute, febrile, mosquito-borne illness. Severe cases are characterized by jaundice, proteinuria, and hemorrhage. YF is a group B arbovirus, a typical togavirus. It multiplies in many different types of animals and in mosquitoes. It grows in embryonated chicks and in cell cultures made from chick embryos.

Strains freshly isolated from humans, monkeys, or mosquitoes are pantropic, ie, the virus invades all 3 embryonal layers. Fresh strains usually produce a severe (often fatal) infection with marked damage to the livers of monkeys after parenteral inoculation. After serial passage in the brains of monkeys or mice, such strains lose much of their viscerotropism; they cause encephalitis after intracerebral injection but only asymptomatic infection after subcutaneous injection. Cross-immunity exists between the pantropic and neurotropic strains of the virus.

During the serial passage of a pantropic strain of YF through tissue cultures, the relatively avirulent 17D strain was recovered. This strain lost its capacity to induce a viscerotropic or neurotropic disease in monkeys and in humans and is now used as a vaccine.

Hemagglutinins and complement-fixing antigens

of this group B arbovirus may be prepared from infected tissues. Each antigen has 2 separable components: one is associated with the infectious particle; the other is probably a product of the action of YF virus on tissues it infects.

Pathogenesis & Pathology

Our understanding of the pathogenesis of YF is based on work with the experimental infection in monkeys. The virus enters through the skin and then spreads to the local lymph nodes, where it multiplies. From the lymph nodes, it enters the circulating blood and becomes localized in the liver, spleen, kidney, bone marrow, and lymph glands, where it may persist for days.

The lesions of YF are due to the localization and propagation of the virus in a particular organ. Death may result from the necrotic lesions in the liver and kidney. The most frequent site of hemorrhage is the mucosa at the pyloric end of the stomach.

The distribution of necrosis in the liver may be spotty but is most evident in the midzones of the lobules. The hyaline necrosis may be restricted to the cytoplasm; the hyaline masses are eosinophilic (Councilman bodies). Intranuclear eosinophilic inclusion bodies are also present and are of diagnostic value. During recovery, the parenchymatous cells are replaced, and the liver may be completely restored.

In the kidney, there is fatty degeneration of the tubular epithelium. Degenerative changes also occur in the spleen, lymph nodes, and heart. Intranuclear, acidophilic inclusion bodies may be present in the nerve and glial cells of the brain. Perivascular infiltrations with mononuclear cells also occur in the brain.

Clinical Findings

The incubation period is 3–6 days. At the onset, the patient has fever, chills, headache, and backache, followed by nausea and vomiting. A short period of remission often follows the prodrome. On about the fourth day, the period of intoxication begins with a slow pulse (90–100) relative to a high fever and moderate jaundice. In severe cases, marked proteinuria and hemorrhagic manifestations appear. The vomitus may be black with altered blood. Lymphopenia is present. When the disease progresses to the severe stage (black vomitus and jaundice), the mortality rate is high. On the other hand, the infection may be so mild as to go unrecognized. Regardless of severity, there are no sequelae; patients either die or recover completely.

Laboratory Diagnosis

A. Recovery of Virus: The virus may be recovered from the blood up to the fifth day of the disease by intracerebral inoculation of mice. The isolated virus is identified by neutralization with specific antiserum.

B. Serology: Neutralizing antibodies develop early (by the fifth day) even in severe and fatal cases. In patients who survive the infection, circulating antibodies endure for life.

Complement-fixing antibodies are rarely found after mild infection or vaccination with the attenuated, live 17D strain. In severe infections, they appear later than the neutralizing antibodies and disappear more rapidly.

The serologic response in YF may be of 2 types. In **primary infections** of yellow fever, specific hemagglutination-inhibiting (HI) antibodies appear first, followed rapidly by antibodies to other group B viruses. The titers of homologous HI antibodies are usually higher than those of heterologous antibodies. CF and Nt antibodies rise slowly and are usually specific.

In **secondary infections** where YF occurs in a patient previously infected with another group B arbovirus, HI and CF antibodies appear rapidly and to high titers. There is no suggestion of specificity. The highest HI and CF antibodies are usually heterologous. Accurate diagnosis even by Nt test may be impossible.

Histopathologic examination of the liver in fatal cases is useful in those regions where the disease is endemic.

Immunity

Subtle antigenic differences exist between YF strains isolated in different locations and between pantropic and vaccine (17D) strains.

An infant born of an immune mother has antibodies at birth that are gradually lost during the first 6 months of life. Reacquisition of similar antibodies is dependent upon the individual's exposure to the virus under natural conditions or by vaccination.

Epidemiology

Two major epidemiologic cycles of YF are recognized: (1) classic (or urban) epidemic YF and (2) sylvan (or jungle) YF. Urban YF involves person-to-person transmission by domestic *Aedes* mosquitoes. In the western hemisphere and West Africa, this species is primarily *Aedes aegypti*, which breeds in the accumulations of water that accompany human settlement. Mosquitoes remain close to houses and become infected by biting a viremic individual. Urban YF is perpetuated in areas where there is a constant influx of susceptible persons, cases of YF, and *A aegypti*. With the use of intensive measures for mosquito abatement, urban YF has been practically eliminated in South America.

Jungle YF is primarily a disease of monkeys. In South America and Africa, it is transmitted from monkey to monkey by arboreal mosquitoes (ie, *Haemagogus, Aedes*) that inhabit the moist forest canopy. The infection in animals may be severe or inapparent. Persons such as woodcutters, nut-pickers, or road-builders come in contact with these mosquitoes in the forest and become infected. Jungle YF may also occur when an infected monkey visits a human habitation and is bitten by *A aegypti*, which then transmits the virus to a human being.

The virus multiplies in mosquitoes, which remain infectious for life. After the mosquito ingests a virus-containing blood meal, an interval of 12–14 days is required for it to become infectious. This interval is called the **extrinsic incubation period.**

All age groups are susceptible, but the disease in infants is milder than that in older groups. Large numbers of inapparent infections occur. The disease usually is milder in blacks. Yellow fever has never been reported in India or the Orient, even though the vector, *A aegypti*, is widely distributed there.

New outbreaks continue to occur. In Bolivia, 145 cases of jungle YF, with over 50% mortality, were reported in 1975. The disease occurred in nonimmune persons coming from distant places for the rice harvests. The rice fields, with the jungle adjacent to them, are located near towns. Most cases were in male agricultural workers. The virus had established itself in this area in reservoirs close to the towns. Jungle YF rarely affects the local population, which has developed immunity by having been in contact with the virus through previous minor infections and also by frequent vaccinations. The real number of cases and deaths from jungle YF in such areas is much higher than the reports indicate, as many patients do not go to the hospital but recover or die without any report being made.

Control

Vigorous mosquito abatement programs have virtually eliminated urban YF. The last reported outbreak of YF in the USA occurred in 1905. However, with the speed of modern air travel, wherever *A aegypti* is present, the threat of a YF outbreak exists. Most countries insist upon proper mosquito control on airplanes and vaccination of all persons at least 10 days before arrival in or from an endemic zone. The yellow fever vaccination requirement for travelers entering the USA was eliminated in 1972.

In 1978, a yellow fever outbreak occurred in Trinidad. Eight human cases and a number of infected forest monkeys were detected. The outbreak was quickly stopped by a mass immunization campaign and *A aegypti* control measures.

An excellent attenuated, live vaccine is available in the 17D strain. Vaccine is prepared in eggs and dispensed as a dried powder. It is a live virus and must be kept cold. It is rehydrated just before use and injected subcutaneously by skin scarification or by jet injector. A single dose produces a good antibody response in more than 95% of vaccinated persons that persists for at least 10 years. After vaccination, the virus multiplies and may be isolated from the blood before antibodies develop.

DENGUE
(Breakbone Fever)

Dengue is a mosquito-borne infection characterized by fever, muscle and joint pain, lymphadenopathy, and rash and caused by a group B arbovirus, a togavirus (see above). Dengue and YF are antigeni-

cally related, but this does not result in significant cross-immunity.

Pathogenesis & Pathology

Viremia is present at the onset of fever and may persist for 3 days. The histopathologic lesion is in small blood vessels, with endothelial swelling, perivascular edema, and infiltration with mononuclear cells.

Clinical Findings

The onset of fever may be sudden or there may be prodromal symptoms of malaise, chills, and headache. Pains soon develop, especially in the back, joints, muscles, and eyeballs. The temperature returns to normal after 5–6 days or may subside on about the third day and rise again about 5–8 days after onset (''saddle-back'' form). A rash (maculopapular or scarlatiniform) may appear on the third or fourth day and last for 24–72 hours, fading with desquamation. Lymph nodes are frequently enlarged. Leukopenia with a relative lymphocytosis is a regular occurrence. Convalescence may take weeks, although complications and death are rare. Especially in young children, dengue may occur as a mild febrile illness lasting 1–3 days.

A more severe syndrome—dengue hemorrhagic fever—may occur in individuals with passively acquired (as maternal antibody) or endogenously produced heterologous dengue antibody. Although initial symptoms simulate normal dengue, the patient's condition abruptly worsens and is associated with hypoproteinemia, thrombocytopenia, prolonged bleeding time, and elevated prothrombin time. Dengue shock syndrome, characterized by shock and hemoconcentration, may supervene. These altered manifestations of dengue have been observed, often in epidemic form, in the Philippines, Southeast Asia, and India—regions in which several dengue serotypes are regularly present; the mortality rate is 5–10%. In studies of the dengue diseases in Southeast Asia, dengue hemorrhagic fever, with or without shock, has been found to occur more frequently when dengue type 2 is the secondary infecting virus and the patient is a female age 3 years or older. In 1981, over 40 type 2 dengue deaths occurred in Cuba as a result of hemorrhage and shock. Shock is probably a form of hypersensitivity reaction. It is postulated that virus-antibody complexes are formed within a few days of the second dengue infection which activate the complement system and lead to the disseminated intravascular coagulation seen in the hemorrhagic fever syndrome.

Laboratory Diagnosis

Isolation of the virus is difficult. Injection of early fresh serum into mice rarely produces disease, but the animals may subsequently be immune to challenge. Dengue viruses often grow in cell cultures.

Nt and HI antibodies appear within 7 days of onset of dengue fever and CF antibodies somewhat later. Homotypic antibodies tend to reach higher titers than heterotypic ones.

Immunity

At least 4 antigenic types of the virus exist.

Reinfection with a virus of a different serotype, 2–3 months after the primary attack, may give rise to a short, mild illness without a rash. Mosquitoes feeding on these reinfected patients can transmit the disease.

Epidemiology

The known geographic distribution of the dengue viruses today is India, the Far East, and the Hawaiian and Caribbean Islands. Dengue has occurred in the southern USA (1934) and in Australia. Most subtropical and tropical regions around the world where *Aedes* vectors exist are endemic areas or potential ones. For example, over 500,000 cases of dengue occurred in Colombia in 1972 following reinfestation of the Atlantic coastal areas by *A aegypti*. Over 100,000 cases occurred in 1981 in Cuba.

The infectious cycle is as follows:

Aedes → Human → *Aedes* → Human

Aedes → Monkey → *Aedes* → Monkey

A aegypti is a domestic mosquito; *Aedes albopictus* exists in the bush or jungle and may be responsible for maintaining the infection among monkeys.

In urban communities, dengue epidemics are explosive and involve appreciable portions of the population. They often start during the rainy season, when the vector mosquito, *A aegypti*, is abundant. The mosquito has a short flight range, and urban spread of dengue is frequently house-to-house. The mosquito breeds in tropical or semitropical climates in artificial water-holding receptacles around human habitation or in tree holes or plants close to human dwellings. It apparently prefers the blood of humans to that of other animals. Since *A aegypti* is also the vector of yellow fever, the outbreak of dengue in the Caribbean serves as a warning of even more serious epidemics. Epidemics can be brought under control by aerial spraying with malathion to kill adult mosquitoes and by treatment of breeding sites to kill larvae.

A aegypti is the only known vector mosquito for dengue in the western hemisphere. The female acquires the virus by feeding upon a viremic human. Mosquitoes are infective after a period of 8–14 days (extrinsic incubation time). In humans, clinical disease begins 2–15 days after an infective mosquito bite. Once infective, a mosquito probably remains so for the remainder of her life (1–3 months or more). Dengue virus is not passed from one generation of mosquitoes to the next. In the tropics, mosquito breeding throughout the year maintains the disease.

Epidemics of dengue are usually observed when the virus is newly introduced into an area or if susceptible persons move into an endemic area. The endemic dengue in the Caribbean is a constant threat to the USA, where *A aegypti* mosquitoes are prevalent in the summer months.

In 1977, a dengue type 1 virus was isolated from mosquitoes and from patients in Jamaica, from where it spread to the Bahamas, Trinidad, Cuba, and the USA. This was the first time type 1 virus had been isolated in the western hemisphere.

In 1979, an epidemic of dengue type 4 broke out in Tahiti, the first known appearance of type 4 outside of Southeast Asia. There were 6800 reported cases on the island (population 97,000).

Control

Control depends upon antimosquito measures, eg, elimination of breeding places and the use of insecticides. An experimental attenuated virus vaccine has been produced but not tested.

HEMORRHAGIC FEVER

Hemorrhagic fever has been reported from Africa, Siberia, Central and Southeast Asia, Eastern and Northern Europe, and South America.

Four categories have been suggested for hemorrhagic fevers: (1) tick-borne, which includes some members of the Russian spring-summer encephalitis complex (Omsk hemorrhagic fever and Kyasanur Forest disease), and the Crimean-Congo hemorrhagic fever group; (2) mosquito-borne, which includes the dengue viruses (see above), Chikungunya virus, and yellow fever virus; (3) zoonotic, which includes the viruses of hemorrhagic fever with renal syndrome (Korean hemorrhagic fever), Argentinian hemorrhagic fever (Junin), Bolivian hemorrhagic fever (Machupo), and Lassa fever; and (4) African hemorrhagic fever. The latter is represented by Marburg and Ebola viruses (see p 464).

Common clinical features of the epidemic hemorrhagic fevers include fever; petechiae or purpura; gastrointestinal, nasal, and uterine bleeding; leukopenia; hypotension; shock; proteinuria; thrombocytopenia; and central nervous system signs, often ending in death.

Machupo virus was recovered from a patient in Bolivia who died of hemorrhagic fever in 1963. The virus has been isolated from the mouse *Calomys callosus*. The systematic extermination of this field mouse has been successful in controlling the spread of the disease in Bolivia.

Marburg virus, which was first associated with a 1967 outbreak of hemorrhagic fever in Germany among persons who came in contact with vervet monkeys from Uganda, has an unknown route of transmission.

Outbreaks involving hundreds of cases of African hemorrhagic fever caused by Ebola virus were reported in Sudan and Zaire in 1976–1977. The incubation period was 4–16 days. The mortality rate was as high as 50% in some outbreaks. Transmission required close contact, especially with blood or secretions containing blood. Cases were common among hospital staff members. Barrier nursing and protective clothing permitted containment.

The disease is suspected of being a zoonosis, with rodents or bats as the animal reservoir. It is assumed that "jungle" cases of the virus infection occur in humans from time to time but that the disease dies out spontaneously before reaching epidemic proportions. Exceptionally, as in 1976, nosocomial transmission creates an amplifying cycle of African hemorrhagic fever.

The virus grows in cultures of monkey cells and is infectious for guinea pigs. Virus can be recovered during the incubation period and for several days after onset of illness.

LASSA FEVER

The first recognized cases of this disease occurred in 1969 among Americans stationed in the Nigerian village of Lassa. The causative virus is extremely virulent, with a mortality rate of 36–67% in 4 epidemics in West Africa involving about 100 cases. Transmission can occur by human-to-human contact, presenting a hazard to hospital personnel. Nine of 20 medical workers have died from infections. Lassa fever can involve almost all the organ systems, although symptoms may vary in the individual patient. The disease is characterized by very high fever, mouth ulcers, severe muscle aches, skin rash with hemorrhages, pneumonia, and heart and kidney damage. Benign, febrile cases do occur. The virus can be isolated from the patient's blood in Vero monkey cell cultures.

Lassa virus is an arenavirus (see p 375). Four arenaviruses cause human disease—Lassa, lymphocytic choriomeningitis, Junin, and Machupo. They can be distinguished by immunofluorescent antibody tests.

Lassa virus seems to be transmitted by human contact and also to have a nonhuman cycle. During an epidemic in Sierra Leone in 1972, Lassa virus was isolated from a house rat *(Mastomys natalensis)*. When the virus spreads within a hospital, human contact is the mode of transmission.

The only available therapy for Lassa fever has employed hyperimmune serum from recovered patients. Interferon is being considered now. Rodent control may limit the natural cycle of the virus.

SANDFLY FEVER
(Pappataci Fever, *Phlebotomus* Fever)

Sandfly fever is a mild, insect-borne disease that occurs commonly in countries bordering the Mediterranean Sea and in Russia, Iran, Pakistan, India, Panama, Brazil, and Trinidad. The sandfly *Phlebotomus papatasii* is present in endemic areas between 20 and 45 degrees of latitude. Sandfly fever is caused by a bunyavirus (see p 374).

Clinical Findings

In humans, the bite of the sandfly results in small itching papules on the skin that persist for up to 5 days. The disease begins abruptly after an incubation period of 3–6 days. For 24 hours before and 24 hours after the onset of fever, the virus is found in the blood. The clinical features consist of headache, malaise, nausea, fever, conjunctival injection, photophobia, stiffness of the neck and back, abdominal pain, and leukopenia. All patients recover. There is no specific treatment. The pathology in humans is not known.

Laboratory Diagnosis

The diagnosis is made usually on clinical grounds. It may be confirmed by demonstrating a rise in antibody titer in paired serum specimens by Nt or HI tests.

Immunity

There are at least 20 separate antigenic types, but only 5 appear to cause human illness. Immunity is specific for each type and persists for at least 2 years.

Epidemiology

The disease is transmitted by the female sandfly, a midge only a few millimeters in size. In the tropics, the sandfly is prevalent all year; in cooler climates, only during the warm seasons. Transovarial transmission may occur.

The extrinsic incubation period in the sandfly is about 1 week. The insect feeds at night; during the day, it may be found in dark places (cracks in walls, caves, houses, and tree trunks). Eggs are laid a few days after a blood meal. About 5 weeks are required for the eggs to develop into winged insects. The adult lives only a few weeks in hot weather.

In endemic areas, infection is common in childhood. When nonimmune adults (eg, troops) arrive, large outbreaks can occur among the new arrivals and are occasionally mistaken for malaria.

Control

Sandflies are commonest just above the ground. Because of their small size, they can pass through ordinary screens and mosquito nets. Their flight range is up to 200 yards. Prevention of disease in endemic areas rests on application of insect repellents during the night and the use of residual insecticides in and around living quarters.

COLORADO TICK FEVER
(Mountain Fever, Tick Fever)

Colorado tick fever is a mild febrile disease, without rash, that is transmitted by a tick. It is caused by an orbivirus (Table 30–1). During the acute stage, the virus is present in the blood and can be isolated in cell culture or suckling mice. It appears to be antigenically distinct. The pathologic features of the disease in humans are not known, since the disease is self-limited.

Clinical Findings

The incubation period is 4–6 days. The disease has a sudden onset with chilly sensations and myalgia. Symptoms include headache, deep ocular pain, muscle and joint pains, lumbar backache, and nausea and vomiting. The temperature is usually diphasic. After the first bout of 2 days, the patient may feel well. Symptoms and fever then reappear and last 3–4 more days. The white count falls to 2000–3000/μL.

Laboratory Diagnosis

The virus may be isolated from whole blood by inoculation of suckling mice. Viremia may persist for 2 weeks. Specific Nt and CF antibodies appear in the second week of illness and persist for years.

Immunity

Only one antigenic type is known. A single infection is believed to produce a lasting immunity.

Epidemiology

Colorado tick fever is limited to areas where the wood tick *Dermacentor andersoni* is distributed, primarily Colorado, Oregon, Utah, Idaho, Montana, and Wyoming. Patients have been in a tick-infested area 4–5 days before onset of symptoms, and in many cases ticks are found attached, as their bite is painless. Cases occur chiefly in adult males, the group with greatest exposure to ticks.

D andersoni collected in nature can carry the virus. This tick is a true reservoir, and the virus is transmitted transovarially by the adult female. Natural infection occurs in rodents, which act as hosts for immature stages of the tick.

Control

The disease can be prevented by avoiding tick-infested areas, and by using protective clothing or repellent chemicals. An experimental live vaccine has been made.

RIFT VALLEY FEVER
(Enzootic Hepatitis)

The virus of this disease is primarily pathogenic for sheep and other domestic animals. Humans are secondarily infected during the course of epizootics in domesticated animals in Africa and the Middle East. Infection among laboratory workers is common.

The clinical features are similar to those of dengue: acute onset, fever, prostration, pain in the extremities and joints, and gastrointestinal distress. The temperature curve is like that of dengue and yellow fever (saddle-back type). There is a marked leukopenia. The disease is short-lived, and recovery almost always is complete.

The virus can be isolated from human blood early in the disease. CF, Nt, and HI antibodies develop and persist for years.

The disease is not contagious but is transmitted by a bloodsucking insect active at night, presumably a mosquito. Sheep can be protected if they can be screened at night.

● ● ●

References

Dokisch VA et al: The potential pathogenic role of complement in dengue hemorrhagic shock syndrome. *N Engl J Med* 1973; **289**:996.

Calisher CH et al: Proposed antigenic classification of registered arboviruses. 1. Togaviridae, *Alphavirus. Intervirology* 1980; **14**:229.

Doherty RL: Arthropod-borne viruses in Australia and their relation to infection and disease. *Prog Med Virol* 1974;**17**:136.

Edelman R et al: Evaluation in humans of a new, inactivated vaccine for Venezuelan equine encephalitis virus (C-84). *J Infect Dis* 1979;**140**:708.

Garoff H et al: Nucleotide sequence of cDNA coding for Semliki Forest virus membrane glycoproteins. *Nature* 1980;**288**:236.

Halstead SB: Viral hemorrhagic fevers. *J Infect Dis* 1981; **143**:127.

Henderson BE, Coleman PH: The growing importance of the California arboviruses in the etiology of human disease. *Prog Med Virol* 1971;**13**:404.

Horzinek MC. The structure of togaviruses. *Prog Med Virol* 1973;**16**:109.

Kiley MP, Regnery RL, Johnson KM: Ebola virus: Identification of virion structural proteins. *J Gen Virol* 1980;**49**:333.

Lee HW: Korean hemorrhagic fever. *Prog Med Virol* 1982; **28**:96.

Luby JP: St. Louis encephalitis. *Epidemiol Rev* 1979;**1**:55.

Murphy FA, Harrison AK, Whitfield SG: Bunyaviridae: Morphologic and morphogenetic similarities of Bunyamwera serologic supergroup viruses and several other arthropod-borne viruses. *Intervirology* 1973;**1**:297.

Porterfield JS et al: Bunyaviruses and Bunyaviridae. *Intervirology* 1975/76;**6**:13.

Reeves WC: Overwintering of arboviruses. *Prog Med Virol* 1974;**17**:193.

Theiler M, Downs WG: *The Arthropod-Borne Viruses of Vertebrates: An Account of the Rockefeller Foundation Virus Program, 1951—1970.* Yale Univ Press, 1973.

31 | Picornavirus Family (Enterovirus & Rhinovirus Groups)

Picornaviruses are small (20–30 nm) and nonenveloped and contain a single-stranded RNA genome (MW 2–3×10^6). The nucleocapsid has cubic symmetry. Virus maturation takes place in the cytoplasm. Enteroviruses and rhinoviruses commonly infect humans.

Enterovirus

Enteroviruses exist in many animals, including humans, cattle, pigs, and mice.

Enteroviruses of human origin include the following:

(1) Polioviruses, types 1–3.

(2) Coxsackieviruses of group A, types 1–24.

(3) Coxsackieviruses of group B, types 1–6.

(4) Echoviruses, types 1–34.

(5) Enteroviruses, types 68–71. Since 1969, new enterovirus types have been assigned enterovirus type numbers rather than being subclassified as coxsackieviruses or echoviruses. The vernacular names of the previously identified enteroviruses have been retained.

Enteroviruses are transient inhabitants of the human alimentary tract and may be isolated from the throat or lower intestine. Rhinoviruses, on the other hand, are isolated chiefly from the nose and throat. Among the enteroviruses that are cytopathogenic (polioviruses, echoviruses, and some coxsackieviruses), growth can be readily obtained at 36–37 °C in primary cultures of human and monkey kidney cells and certain cell lines (such as HeLa); in contrast, most rhinovirus strains can only be recovered in cells of human origin (embryonic human kidney or lung, human diploid cell strains) at 33 °C.

The enterovirus capsid is thought to be composed of 32 morphologic subunits, possibly in the form of a rhombic triacontahedron rather than a regular icosahedron. Rhinovirus capsid architecture appears to be similar. Infective nucleic acid has been extracted from several enteroviruses and rhinoviruses.

Enteroviruses are stable at acid pH (3.0–5.0) for 1–3 hours, whereas rhinoviruses are acid-labile. Enteroviruses and some rhinoviruses are stabilized by magnesium chloride against thermal inactivation.

Enteroviruses and rhinoviruses differ in buoyant density. Enteroviruses have a buoyant density in CsCl of about 1.34 g/mL; human rhinoviruses, about 1.40 g/mL.

Rhinovirus

Human rhinoviruses include more than 100 antigenic types. Rhinoviruses of other host species include those of horses and cattle.

Other Genera

Other picornaviruses are foot-and-mouth disease of cattle *(Aphthovirus)* and encephalomyocarditis of rodents *(Cardiovirus)*.

• • •

The host range of the picornaviruses varies greatly from one type to the next and even among strains of the same type. They may readily be induced, by laboratory manipulation, to yield variants that have host ranges and tissue tropisms different from those of certain wild strains; this has led to the development of attenuated poliovirus strains now used as vaccines.

Many picornaviruses cause diseases in humans ranging from severe paralysis to aseptic meningitis, pleurodynia, myocarditis, skin rashes, and common colds. However, subclinical infection is far more common than clinically manifest disease. Different viruses may produce the same syndrome; on the other hand, the same picornavirus may cause more than a single syndrome. For these reasons, clinical disease is not a satisfactory basis of classification.

ENTEROVIRUS GROUP

POLIOMYELITIS

Poliomyelitis is an acute infectious disease that in its serious form affects the central nervous system. The destruction of motor neurons in the spinal cord results in flaccid paralysis. However, most poliovirus infections are subclinical.

Properties of the Virus

A. General Properties: Poliovirus particles are typical enteroviruses, 28 nm in diameter. They are inactivated when heated at 55 °C for 30 minutes, but molar Mg^{2+} prevents this inactivation. Milk or ice cream is also protective, but proper pasteurization inactivates the virus. While purified poliovirus is inactivated by chlorine (0.1 ppm), much higher concentrations of chlorine are required to disinfect sewage containing virus in fecal suspensions and in the presence of other organic matter. In contrast to arboviruses, polioviruses are not affected by ether or sodium deoxycholate.

B. Animal Susceptibility and Growth of Virus: Polioviruses have a very restricted host range. Most strains will infect monkeys by direct inoculation into the brain or spinal cord. Chimpanzees and cynomolgus monkeys can also be infected by the oral route; in chimpanzees, the infection thus produced is usually asymptomatic. The animals become intestinal carriers of the virus; they also develop a viremia that is quenched by the appearance of antibodies in the circulating blood. Unusual strains have been transmitted to mice or chick embryos.

Most strains can be grown in primary or continuous cell line cultures derived from a variety of human tissues or from monkey kidney, testis, or muscle, but not in cells of lower animals.

Poliovirus requires a primate-specific membrane receptor for infection, and the absence of this receptor on the surface of nonprimate cells makes them virus-resistant. This restriction can be overcome by introducing poliovirus into resistant cells by means of synthetic lipid vesicles called liposomes. Once inside the cell, poliovirus replicates normally.

C. Virus Replication: After attaching to virus receptors (which seem to be controlled in humans by genes on chromosome 19), poliovirus undergoes replication as diagrammed in Fig 27–8. Poliovirus RNA serves both as its own messenger RNA and as the source of the genetic information. Viral protein is synthesized on polysomes held together by viral RNA.

Guanidine in concentrations greater than 1 mM and 2-(alpha-hydroxybenzyl)-benzimidazole inhibit poliovirus multiplication in tissue culture. Guanidine acts by inhibiting the release of newly made viral RNA from the replicative complex.

D. Antigenic Properties: There are 3 antigenic types. Complement-fixing antigens for each type may be prepared from tissue culture or infected central nervous system. Inactivation of the virus by formalin, heat, or ultraviolet light liberates a soluble complement-fixing antigen. This antigen is cross-reactive and fixes complement with heterotypic poliomyelitis antibodies. A type-specific precipitin reaction occurs when concentrated virus is used with immune animal or convalescent human sera. Two type-specific antigens are contained in poliovirus preparations and can be detected by precipitin and CF tests. They are the N (native) and H (heated) antigens. The N form can be converted to the H form by heating. The N form represents full particles containing RNA, and the H form empty particles.

Pathogenesis & Pathology

The mouth is the portal of entry of the virus, and primary multiplication takes place in the oropharynx or intestine. The virus is regularly present in the throat and in the stools before the onset of illness. One week after onset there is little virus in the throat, but virus continues to be excreted in the stools for several weeks, even though high antibody levels are present in the blood.

The virus may be found in the blood of patients with abortive and nonparalytic poliomyelitis and in orally infected monkeys and chimpanzees in the preparalytic phase of the disease. Antibodies to the virus appear early in the disease, usually before paralysis occurs.

Viremia is also associated with type 2 oral vaccination. Free virus is usually present in the blood between days 2 and 5 after vaccination, and virus is bound to antibody for an additional few days. Bound virus is detected by acid treatment, which inactivates the antibody and liberates active virus.

These findings have led to the view that the virus first multiplies in the tonsils, the lymph nodes of the neck, Peyer's patches, and the small intestine. The central nervous system may then be invaded by way of the circulating blood. In monkeys infected by the oral route, small amounts of antibody prevent the paralytic disease, whereas large amounts are necessary to prevent passage of the virus along nerve fibers. In humans also, antibody in the form of pooled human gamma globulin may prevent paralysis if given before exposure to the virus.

Poliovirus can spread along axons of peripheral nerves to the central nervous system, and there it continues to progress along the fibers of the lower motor neurons to increasingly involve the spinal cord or the brain. This may occur in children after tonsillectomy. Poliovirus present in the oropharynx may enter nerve fibers exposed during the surgical procedure and spread to the central nervous system.

Poliovirus invades certain types of nerve cells, and in the process of its intracellular multiplication it may damage or completely destroy these cells. The anterior horn cells of the spinal cord are most prominently involved, but in severe cases the intermediate gray ganglia and even the posterior horn and dorsal root ganglia are often involved. In the brain, the reticular formation, vestibular nuclei, and deep cerebellar nuclei are most often affected. The cortex is virtually spared, with the exception of the motor cortex along the precentral gyrus.

Poliovirus does not multiply in muscle in vivo. The changes that occur in peripheral nerves and voluntary muscles are secondary to the destruction of nerve cells. Changes occur rapidly in nerve cells, from mild chromatolysis to neuronophagia and complete destruction. Cells that lose their function may recover completely. Inflammation occurs secondary to the attack on the nerve cells; the focal and perivascular infiltrations are chiefly lymphocytes, with some polymorphonuclear cells, plasma cells, and microglia.

In addition to pathologic changes in the nervous system, there may be myocarditis, lymphatic hyperplasia, ulceration of Peyer's patches, prominence of follicles, and enlargement of lymph nodes.

Clinical Findings

When an individual susceptible to infection is exposed to the virus, one of the following responses may occur: (1) inapparent infection without symptoms, (2) mild illness, (3) aseptic meningitis, (4) paralytic poliomyelitis. As the disease progresses, one response may merge with a more severe form, often resulting in a biphasic course: a minor illness, followed first by a few days free of symptoms and then by the major, severe illness. Only about 1% of infections are recognized clinically.

The incubation period is usually 7–14 days, but it may range from 3 to 35 days.

A. Abortive Poliomyelitis: This is the commonest form of the disease. The patient has only the minor illness, characterized by fever, malaise, drowsiness, headache, nausea, vomiting, constipation, and sore throat in various combinations. The patient recovers in a few days. The diagnosis of abortive poliomyelitis can be made only when the virus is isolated or antibody development is measured.

B. Nonparalytic Poliomyelitis (Aseptic Meningitis): In addition to the above symptoms and signs, the patient with the nonparalytic form presents stiffness and pain in the back and neck. The disease lasts 2–10 days, and recovery is rapid and complete. In a small percentage of cases, the disease advances to paralysis. Poliovirus is only one of many viruses that produce aseptic meningitis.

C. Paralytic Poliomyelitis: The major illness usually follows the minor illness described above, but it may occur without the antecedent first phase. The predominating complaint is flaccid paralysis resulting from lower motor neuron damage. However, incoordination secondary to brain stem invasion and painful spasms of nonparalyzed muscles may also occur. The amount of damage varies greatly. Muscle involvement is usually maximal within a few days after the paralytic phase begins. The maximal recovery usually occurs within 6 months, with residual paralysis lasting much longer.

Laboratory Diagnosis

A. Cerebrospinal Fluid: The cerebrospinal fluid contains an increased number of leukocytes—usually 10–200/μL, seldom more than 500/μL. In the early stage of the disease, the ratio of polymorphonuclear cells to lymphocytes is high, but within a few days the ratio is reversed. The total cell count slowly subsides to normal levels. The protein content of the cerebrospinal fluid is elevated (average, about 40–50 mg/dL), but high levels may occur and persist for weeks. The glucose content is normal.

B. Recovery of Virus: Cultures of human or monkey cells may be used. The virus may be recovered from throat swabs taken soon after onset of illness and from rectal swabs or feces collected for longer periods. The virus has been found in about 80% of patients during the first 2 weeks of illness but in only 25% during the third 2-week period. No permanent carriers are known. Recovery of poliovirus from the cerebrospinal fluid is uncommon, unlike that of the coxsackieviruses or echoviruses.

In fatal cases, the virus should be sought in the cervical and lumbar enlargements of the spinal cord, in the medulla, and in the colon contents. Histologic examination of the spinal cord and parts of the brain should be made. If paralysis has lasted 4–5 days, it is difficult to recover the virus from the cord.

Specimens should be kept frozen during transit to the laboratory. After treatment with antibiotics, cell cultures are inoculated, incubated, and observed. Cytopathogenic effects appear in 3–6 days. An isolated virus is identified and typed by neutralization with specific antiserum.

C. Serology: Paired serum specimens are required to show a rise in antibody titer (see Table 29–2).

During poliomyelitis infection, complement-fixing H antibodies form before N antibodies (see Antigenic Properties, above). The level of H antibodies declines first. Early acute stage sera thus contain H antibodies only; 1–2 weeks later, both N and H antibodies are present; in late convalescent sera, only N antibodies are present. Only first infection with poliovirus produces strictly type-specific complement fixation responses. Subsequent infections with heterotypic polioviruses recall or induce antibodies, mostly against the heat-stable group antigen shared by all 3 types of poliovirus.

Neutralizing antibodies appear early and are usually already detectable at the time of hospitalization. If the first specimen is taken sufficiently early, a rise in titer can be demonstrated during the course of the disease.

Type-specific, short-lived virus-precipitating antibodies develop in convalescence. The microprecipitation test is less useful than the CF and Nt tests.

Immunity

Immunity is permanent to the type causing the infection. There may be a low degree of heterotypic resistance induced by infection, especially between type 1 and type 2 polioviruses.

Passive immunity is transferred from mother to offspring. The maternal antibodies gradually disappear during the first 6 months of life. Passively administered antibody lasts only 3–5 weeks.

Virus neutralizing antibody forms soon after exposure to the virus, often before the onset of illness, and apparently persists for life. Its formation early in the disease implies that viral multiplication occurs in the body before the invasion of the nervous system. As the virus in the brain and spinal cord is not influenced by high titers of antibodies in the blood (which are found in the preparalytic stage of the disease), immunization is of value only if it precedes the onset of symptoms referable to the nervous system.

Operations on the oropharynx and tonsillectomy

enhance the likelihood of central nervous system involvement during prevalence of polioviruses in the community. This may be attributable to the access of cut nerve fibers to virus in the pharynx or to the removal of immunologically active lymphoid tissue.

Treatment

Treatment involves reduction of pain and muscle spasm and maintenance of respiration and hydration. When the fever subsides, early mobilization and active exercise are begun. There is no role for antiserum.

Epidemiology

Poliomyelitis occurs worldwide—year-round in the tropics and during summer and fall in the temperate zones. Winter outbreaks are rare.

The disease occurs in all age groups, but children are usually more susceptible than adults because of the acquired immunity of the adult population. In isolated populations (Arctic Eskimos), poliomyelitis attacks all ages equally. In underdeveloped areas, where conditions favor the wide dissemination of virus, poliomyelitis continues to be a disease of infancy. In developed countries, before the onset of vaccination, the age distribution shifted so that most patients were over age 5 and 25% were over age 15 years. With rising levels of hygiene and sanitation, a similar trend is now occurring in developing countries. Since poliomyelitis in older persons is more likely to be a clinically manifest infection rather than subclinical one, the reported incidence of clinical disease is actually rising in areas where vaccination is not widespread, and outbreaks of poliomyelitis are being recorded in some such areas.

The case fatality rate is variable. It is highest in the oldest patients and may reach 5–10%.

Humans are the only known reservoir of infection. Under conditions of poor hygiene and sanitation in warm areas, where almost all children become immune early in life, polioviruses maintain themselves by continuously infecting a small part of the population. In temperate zones with high levels of hygiene, epidemics have been followed by periods of little spread of virus, until sufficient numbers of susceptible children have grown up to provide a pool for transmission in the area. Warm weather favors the spread of virus by increasing human contacts, the susceptibility of the host, or the dissemination of virus by extrahuman sources. Virus can be recovered from the pharynx and intestine of patients and healthy carriers. The prevalence of infection is highest among household contacts. When the first case is recognized in a family, all susceptibles in the family are already infected, the result of rapid dissemination of virus.

During periods of wide prevalence of poliovirus in an area, flies become contaminated and may distribute virus to food. The role of flies in disease transmission is unsettled. Virus is present in sewage during such periods and can serve as a source of contamination of flies or water used for drinking, bathing, or irrigation.

In temperate climates, infection with enteroviruses, including polio, occurs mainly during the summer. There is a direct correlation between poor hygiene, sanitation, and crowding and the acquisition of infection and antibodies at an early age.

Prevention & Control

Both live and killed virus vaccines are available. Formalinized vaccine (Salk) is prepared from virus grown in monkey kidney cultures. At least 4 inoculations over a period of 1–2 years are recommended in the primary series. A booster immunization is necessary every 2–3 years to maintain immunity. Killed vaccine induces humoral antibodies, but, upon exposure, virus is still able to multiply in the gut (see Fig 27–20).

Oral vaccines contain live attenuated virus now grown in human diploid cell cultures. The vaccine is stabilized by molar $MgCl_2$ so that it can be kept without losing potency for a year at 4 °C and for a month at room temperature. Nonstabilized vaccine must be kept frozen until used.

The live poliovaccine multiplies, infects, and thus immunizes. In the process, infectious progeny of the vaccine virus are disseminated in the community. Although the viruses, particularly type 3 and type 2, mutate in the course of their multiplication in vaccinated children, only extremely rare cases of paralytic poliomyelitis have occurred in recipients of oral poliovaccine or their close contacts. Repeat vaccinations seem to be important to establish permanent immunity. The vaccine produces not only IgM and IgG antibodies in the blood but also secretory IgA antibodies in the intestine, which then becomes resistant to reinfection (see Fig 27–20).

A potential limiting factor for oral vaccine is that of interference. The alimentary tract of the child may be infected with another enterovirus at the time the vaccine is fed. This interferes with the establishment of infection and immunity and is an important problem in areas (particularly in tropical regions) where enterovirus infections are common.

Trivalent oral poliovaccine is used in the USA (see p 173). The American Academy of Pediatrics recommends that primary immunization of infants begin at 2 months of age simultaneously with the first DTP inoculation. The second and third doses should be given at 2-month intervals thereafter, and a fourth dose at 1½ years of age. A trivalent vaccine booster is recommended for all children entering elementary school. No further boosters are presently recommended.

Adults residing in the continental USA have only a small risk of exposure. However, adults who are at increased risk because of contact with a patient or who are anticipating travel to an endemic or epidemic area should be immunized. Pregnancy is neither an indication for nor a contraindication to required immunization.

Before the beginning of vaccination campaigns in the USA, there were about 21,000 cases of paralytic poliomyelitis per year. In 1977, only 18 such cases occurred. Twelve cases of type 1 poliomyelitis occurred in the USA in 1979—all among unvaccinated Amish groups. The disease failed to spread to surrounding vaccinated communities. There is a continuing need for adequate vaccination programs, particularly among underprivileged groups. Whereas in 1964 eighty-seven percent of children age 1–4 years had received a full course of vaccine, in 1971–1975 only about 40% of preschool children from inner cities had been so vaccinated. Obviously, this requires change if clinical poliomyelitis is not to recur on a large scale.

Both killed and live virus vaccines induce antibodies and protect the central nervous system from subsequent invasion by wild virus. Low levels of antibody resulting from killed vaccine have little effect on intestinal carriage of virus. The gut develops a far greater degree of resistance after live virus vaccine, which seems to be dependent on the extent of initial vaccine virus multiplication in the alimentary tract rather than on serum antibody level.

Live vaccine should not be administered to immunodeficient or immunosuppressed individuals. Only killed (Salk) vaccine is to be used.

On very rare occasions, a live vaccine strain can induce neurologic or paralytic disease in persons who are not evidently immunodeficient. Such cases are carefully studied by public health agencies, and it is estimated that there has been one vaccine-associated case for every 10 million persons vaccinated.

Immune human serum globulin (gamma globulin), 0.3 mL/kg, can provide protection for a few weeks against the paralytic disease but does not prevent subclinical infection. Gamma globulin is effective only if given shortly before infection; it is of no value after clinical symptoms develop.

The prevention of poliomyelitis depends on vaccination. Quarantine of patients or intimate contacts is ineffective in controlling the spread of the disease. This is understandable in view of the large number of inapparent infections that occur.

During epidemic periods (defined now as 2 or more local cases caused by the same type in any 4-week period), children with fever should be placed at bed rest. Undue exercise or fatigue, elective nose and throat operations, or dental extractions should be avoided. Food and human excrement should be protected from flies. Once the poliovirus type responsible for the epidemic is determined, oral poliovaccine should be administered to susceptible persons in the population.

Patients with poliomyelitis can be admitted to general hospitals provided appropriate isolation precautions are employed. All pharyngeal and bowel discharges are considered infectious and should be disposed of quickly and safely.

COXSACKIEVIRUSES

The coxsackieviruses comprise a large subgroup of the enteroviruses. They produce a variety of illnesses in human beings, including aseptic meningitis, herpangina, pleurodynia, hand, foot, and mouth disease, myo- and pericarditis, common colds, and possibly diabetes (see Chapter 39). Coxsackieviruses have been divided into 2 groups, A and B, having different pathogenic potentials for mice. Coxsackie B viruses are the most commonly identified causative agents of viral heart disease in humans.

Properties of the Viruses

A. General Properties: Coxsackieviruses are typical enteroviruses, with a diameter of 28 nm.

B. Animal Susceptibility and Growth of Virus: Coxsackieviruses are highly infective for newborn mice. Certain strains (B1–6, A7, 9, 16) also grow in monkey kidney cell culture. Some group A strains grow in human amnion and human embryonic lung fibroblast cells. Chimpanzees and cynomolgus monkeys can be infected subclinically; virus appears in the blood and throat for short periods and is excreted in the feces for 2–5 weeks. Type A14 produces poliomyelitislike lesions in adult mice and in monkeys, but in suckling mice this type produces only myositis. Type A7 strains produce paralysis and severe central nervous system lesions in monkeys.

Group A viruses produce widespread myositis in the skeletal muscles of newborn mice, resulting in flaccid paralysis without other observable lesions. Group B viruses may produce focal myositis, encephalitis, and, most typically, necrotizing steatitis involving mainly fetal fat lobules. The genetic makeup of inbred strains determines their susceptibility to coxsackie B viruses. Some B strains also produce pancreatitis, myocarditis, endocarditis, and hepatitis in both suckling and adult mice. Corticosteroids may enhance the susceptibility of older mice to infection of the pancreas. Normal adult mice tolerate infections with group B coxsackieviruses. However, severely malnourished or immunodeficient mice have greatly enhanced susceptibility.

C. Antigenic Properties: At least 29 different immunologic types of coxsackieviruses are now recognized; 23 are listed as group A and 6 as group B types.

Pathogenesis & Pathology

Virus has been recovered from the blood in the early stages of natural infection in humans and of experimental infection in chimpanzees. Virus is also found in the throat for a few days early in the infection and in the stools for up to 5–6 weeks. The distribution of virus is similar to that found with the other enteroviruses.

Group B coxsackieviruses may cause acute fatal encephalomyocarditis in infants. This appears to be a generalized systemic disease with virus replication and lesions in the central nervous system, heart muscle, and other organs.

Clinical Findings

The incubation period of coxsackievirus infection

ranges from 2 to 9 days. The clinical manifestations of infection with various coxsackieviruses are diverse and may present as distinct disease entities.

A. Herpangina: This disease is caused by certain group A viruses (2, 4, 5, 6, 8, 10). There is an abrupt onset of fever, sore throat, anorexia, dysphagia, vomiting, or abdominal pain. The pharynx is usually hyperemic, and characteristic discrete vesicles occur on the anterior pillars of the fauces, the palate, uvula, tonsils, or tongue. The illness is self-limited and most frequent in small children.

B. Summer Minor Illnesses: Coxsackieviruses are often isolated from patients with acute febrile illnesses of short duration that occur during the summer or fall and are without distinctive features.

C. Pleurodynia (Epidemic Myalgia, Bornholm Disease): This disease is caused by group B viruses. Fever and chest pain are usually abrupt in onset but are sometimes preceded by malaise, headache, and anorexia. The chest pain may be located on either side or substernally, is intensified by movement, and may last from 2 days to 2 weeks. Abdominal pain occurs in approximately half of cases, and in children this may be the chief complaint. The illness is self-limited, and recovery is complete, although relapses are common.

D. Aseptic Meningitis and Mild Paresis: This syndrome is caused by all types of group B coxsackieviruses and by coxsackieviruses A7, A9, and A24. Fever, malaise, headache, nausea, and abdominal pain are common early symptoms. Signs of meningeal irritation, stiff neck or back, and vomiting may appear 1–2 days later. The disease sometimes progresses to mild muscle weakness suggestive of paralytic poliomyelitis. Patients almost always recover completely from nonpoliovirus paresis. Early in aseptic meningitis, the cerebrospinal fluid shows pleocytosis (up to 500 cells/μL) with up to 50% polymorphonuclear neutrophils.

E. Neonatal Disease: Neonatal disease may be caused by group B coxsackieviruses, with lethargy, feeding difficulty, and vomiting, with or without fever. In severe cases, myocarditis or pericarditis can occur within the first 8 days of life; it may be preceded by a brief episode of diarrhea and anorexia. Cardiac and respiratory embarrassment are indicated by tachycardia, dyspnea, cyanosis, and changes in the electrocardiogram. The clinical course may be rapidly fatal, or the patient may recover completely. The disease may sometimes be acquired transplacentally. Myocarditis has also been caused by some group A coxsackieviruses.

F. Colds: A number of the enteroviruses have been associated with common colds; among these are coxsackieviruses A10, A21, A24, and B3.

G. Hand, Foot, and Mouth Disease: This disease has been associated particularly with coxsackievirus A16, but A4, A5, A7, A9, and A10 have also been implicated. Virus may be recovered not only from the stool and pharyngeal secretions but also from vesicular fluid.

The syndrome is characterized by oral and pharyngeal ulcerations and a vesicular rash of the palms and soles that may spread to the arms and legs. Vesicles heal without crusting, which clinically differentiates them from the vesicles of herpes- and poxviruses. The rare deaths are caused by pneumonia.

H. Myocardiopathy: Coxsackievirus B infections are increasingly recognized as a cause of primary myocardial disease in adults as well as children. Coxsackieviruses of group A and echoviruses have been implicated to a lesser degree.

At autopsy, virus has been demonstrated in the myocardium, endocardium, and pericardial fluid by immunofluorescence, peroxidase-labeled antibody, or ferritin-labeled antibody. About 5% of all symptomatic coxsackievirus infections induce heart disease. The virus may affect the endocardium, pericardium, myocardium, or all three. Acute myocardiopathies have been shown to be caused by coxsackieviruses A4, A14, B1–5, and others, and also by echovirus types 9 and 22 and others.

Monkeys infected with coxsackievirus B4 develop pancarditis, with a pathologic picture strikingly similar to that of rheumatic heart disease.

In experimental animals, the severity of acute viral myocardiopathy is greatly increased by vigorous exercise, hydrocortisone, alcohol consumption, pregnancy, and undernutrition and is greater in males than in females. In human illnesses, these factors may similarly increase the severity of the disease.

I. Acute Hemorrhagic Conjunctivitis: Coxsackievirus A24 is one of the agents that can cause this disease (see below).

J. Diabetes Mellitus: Serologic studies suggest an association of diabetes of abrupt onset with past infection by coxsackievirus B4 and perhaps other members of the B group. Experimental studies support the findings in humans. Another picornavirus, encephalomyocarditis virus, induces lesions in mice in the pancreatic islets of Langerhans as well as an accompanying diabetes.

K. Swine Vesicular Disease: The agent of this disease is an enterovirus that antigenically is related to coxsackievirus B5. Furthermore, the swine virus can also infect humans.

Laboratory Diagnosis

A. Recovery of Virus: The virus is isolated readily from throat washings during the first few days of illness and in the stools during the first few weeks. In coxsackievirus A21 infections, the largest amount of virus is found in nasal secretions. In cases of aseptic meningitis, strains have been recovered from the cerebrospinal fluid as well as from the alimentary tract. In hemorrhagic conjunctivitis cases, A24 virus is isolated from eye washings.

Specimens are inoculated into tissue cultures and also into suckling mice. In tissue culture, a cytopathic effect appears within 5–14 days. In suckling mice, signs of illness appear usually within 3–8 days with group A strains and 5–14 days with group B strains.

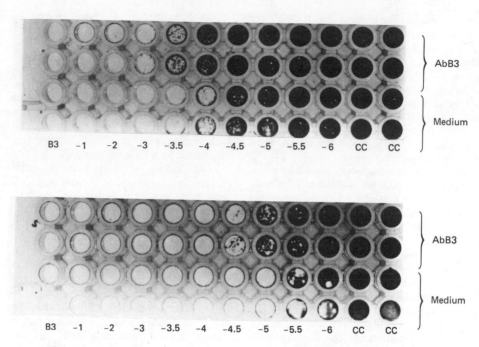

Figure 31–1. Titration of coxsackievirus B3 in the presence of antibody (AbB3) and control medium. From left to right, as the virus dilution increases, complete cytopathic effect, incomplete cytopathic effect, and then individual plaques are seen. The last 2 rows on the right side are cell controls (CC). B3 line shows $0.5 \log_{10}$ dilutions of virus. ***Top:*** Assayed 48 hours postinfection. ***Bottom:*** Assayed 72 hours postinfection; further progression of cytopathic effect is evident. (From Randhawa AS et al: *J Clin Microbiol* 1977;**5**:535.)

The virus is identified by the pathologic lesions it produces and by immunologic means.

B. Serology: Neutralizing antibodies, which are detected as shown in Fig 31–1, appear early during the course of infection. Nt antibodies tend to be specific for the infecting virus and persist for years. CF antibodies exhibit cross-reactions and disappear in 6 months. Serologic tests are difficult to evaluate (because of the multiplicity of types) unless the antigen used in the test has been isolated from a specific patient or during an epidemic outbreak.

Serum antibodies can also be detected and titrated by the immunofluorescence technique, using infected cell cultures on coverslips as antigens. These can be preserved frozen for years.

Immunity

In humans, Nt and CF antibodies are transferred passively from mother to fetus. Adults have antibodies against more types of coxsackieviruses than do children, which indicates that multiple experience with these viruses is common and increases with age.

Epidemiology

Viruses of the coxsackie group have been encountered around the globe. Isolations have been made mainly from human feces, pharyngeal swabbings, sewage, and flies. Antibodies to various coxsackieviruses are found in serum collected from persons all over the world and in pooled gamma globulin.

Coxsackieviruses are recovered much more frequently during the summer and early fall. Also, children develop neutralizing and complement-fixing antibodies during the summer, indicating infection by these agents during this period. Such children have much higher incidence rates for acute, febrile minor illnesses during the summer than children who fail to develop coxsackievirus antibodies.

Familial exposure is important in the acquisition of infections with coxsackieviruses. Once the virus is introduced into a household, all susceptible persons usually become infected, although all do not develop clinically apparent disease.

In herpangina, only about 30% of infected persons within households develop faucial lesions. Others may present a mild febrile illness without throat lesions. Virus has been found in 85% of patients with herpangina, in 65% of their neighbors, in 40% of family contacts, and in 4% of all persons in the community.

The coxsackieviruses share many properties with the echo- and polioviruses. Because of their epidemiologic similarities, enteroviruses may occur together in nature, even in the same human host or the same specimens of sewage or flies.

ECHOVIRUSES

The echoviruses (*e*nteric *c*ytopathogenic *h*uman *o*rphan viruses) are grouped together because they infect the human enteric tract and because they can be recovered from humans only by inoculation of certain tissue cultures. Over 30 serotypes are known, but not all cause human illness. Aseptic meningitis, febrile illnesses with or without rash, common colds, and acute hemorrhagic conjunctivitis are among the diseases caused by echoviruses.

Properties of the Viruses

A. General Properties: Echoviruses are typical enteroviruses measuring 24–30 nm.

B. Growth of Virus: Monkey kidney cell culture is the method of choice for the isolation of these agents. Some also multiply in human amnion cells and cell lines such as HeLa.

Certain echoviruses agglutinate human group O erythrocytes. The hemagglutinins are associated with the infectious virus particle but are not affected by neuraminidase.

Initially, echoviruses were distinguished from coxsackieviruses by their failure to produce pathologic changes in newborn mice, but echovirus-9 can produce paralysis in newborn mice. Conversely, strains of some coxsackievirus types (especially A9) lack mouse pathogenicity and thus resemble echoviruses. This variability in biologic properties is the chief reason why new enteroviruses are no longer being subclassified as echo- or coxsackieviruses.

C. Antigenic Properties: Over 30 different antigenic types have been identified. The different types may be separated on the basis of cross-Nt or cross-CF tests. Variants exist that do not behave exactly like the prototypes. After human infections, Nt antibodies persist longer than CF antibodies.

D. Animal Susceptibility: To be included in the echo group, prototype strains must not produce disease in suckling mice, rabbits, or monkeys. In the chimpanzee, no apparent illness is produced, but infection can be demonstrated by the presence and persistence of virus in the throat and in the feces and by the type-specific antibody responses.

Pathogenesis & Pathology

The pathogenesis of the alimentary infection is similar to that of the other enteroviruses. Virus may be recovered from the throat and stools; in certain types (4, 5, 6, 9, 14, and 18) associated with aseptic meningitis, the virus has been recovered from the cerebrospinal fluid.

Clinical Findings

To establish etiologic association of echovirus with disease, the following criteria are used: (1) There is a much higher rate of recovery of virus from patients with the disease than from healthy individuals of the same age and socioeconomic level living in the same area at the same time. (2) Antibodies against the virus develop during the course of the disease. If the clinical syndrome can be caused by other known agents, then virologic or serologic evidence must be negative for concurrent infection with such agents. (3) The virus is isolated from body fluids or tissues manifesting lesions, eg, from the cerebrospinal fluid in cases of aseptic meningitis.

Echoviruses 4, 6, 9, 11, 14, 16, 18, and others have been associated with aseptic meningitis. Rashes are common in types 9, 16 ("Boston exanthem disease"), 18, and 4. Rashes are commonest in young children. Occasionally, there is conjunctivitis, muscle weakness, and spasm (types 6, 9, and others). Infantile diarrhea may be associated with some types (eg, 18, 20). Echovirus type 28 isolated from upper respiratory illness causes "colds" in volunteers and has been reclassified as rhinovirus type 1. For many echoviruses (and some coxsackieviruses), no disease entities have been defined.

With the virtual elimination of polio in developed countries, the central nervous system syndromes associated with echo- and coxsackieviruses have assumed greater prominence. The latter in children under age 1 may lead to neurologic sequelae and mental impairment. This does not appear to happen in older children.

Laboratory Diagnosis

It is impossible in an individual case to diagnose an echovirus infection on clinical grounds. However, in the following epidemic situations, echoviruses must be considered: (1) summer outbreaks of aseptic meningitis; (2) summer epidemics, especially in young children, of a febrile illness with rash; and (3) outbreaks of diarrheal disease in young infants from whom no pathogenic enterobacteria can be recovered.

The diagnosis is dependent upon laboratory tests. The procedure of choice is isolation of virus from throat swabs, stools, rectal swabs, and, in aseptic meningitis, cerebrospinal fluid. Serologic tests are impractical—because of the many different virus types—unless a virus has been isolated from a patient or during an outbreak of typical clinical illness. Nt and HI antibodies are type-specific and may persist for years. CF antibodies give many heterotypic responses.

If an agent is isolated in tissue culture, it is tested against different pools of antisera against enteroviruses. Determination of the type of virus present depends upon neutralization by a single serum. Infection with 2 or more enteroviruses may occur simultaneously.

Epidemiology

The epidemiology of echoviruses is similar to that of other enteroviruses. They occur in all parts of the globe. Unlike the enterobacteria, which are constantly present in the intestinal tract, the enteroviruses produce only transitory infections. They are more apt to be found in the young than in the old. In the temperate zone, infections occur chiefly in summer and autumn and are about 5 times more prevalent in children of lower income families than in those living in more favorable circumstances.

Studies of families into which enteroviruses were introduced demonstrate the ease with which these agents spread and the high frequency of infection in persons who had formed no antibodies from earlier exposures. This is true for all enteroviruses.

Wide dissemination is the rule. In a period when 149 inhabitants of a city of 740,000 were hospitalized with echo-9 disease, approximately 6% of the population, or 45,000 persons, had a compatible illness.

Control

Avoidance of contact with patients exhibiting acute febrile illness, especially those with a rash, is advisable for very young children. Members of institutional staffs responsible for caring for infants should be tested to determine whether they are carriers of enteroviruses. This is particularly important during outbreaks of diarrheal disease among infants.

OTHER ENTEROVIRUS TYPES

Four enteroviruses (types 68–71) grow in monkey kidney cultures, and 3 of them cause human disease.

Enterovirus 68 was isolated from the respiratory tracts of children with bronchiolitis or pneumonia.

Enterovirus 70 is the chief cause of acute hemorrhagic conjunctivitis. It was isolated from the conjunctiva of patients with this striking eye disease, which occurred in pandemic form in 1969–1971 in Africa and Southeast Asia. It was not diagnosed in the USA until its importation into Florida in 1981. Acute hemorrhagic conjunctivitis has a sudden onset of subconjunctival hemorrhage ranging from small petechiae to large blotches covering the bulbar conjunctiva. There may also be epithelial keratitis and occasionally lumbar radiculomyelopathy. The disease is commonest in adults, with an incubation period of 1 day and a duration of 8–10 days. Complete recovery is the rule. The virus is highly communicable and spreads rapidly under crowded or unhygienic conditions. There is no effective treatment.

Enterovirus 71 was isolated from patients with meningitis, encephalitis, and paralysis resembling poliomyelitis. It continues to be one of the main causes of central nervous system disease, sometimes fatal, around the world. In some areas, particularly in Japan and Sweden, the virus has caused outbreaks of hand, foot, and mouth disease.

RHINOVIRUS GROUP

Rhinoviruses are isolated commonly from the nose and throat but very rarely from feces. These viruses, as well as coronaviruses and some reo-,

adeno-, entero-, parainfluenza, and influenza viruses, cause upper respiratory tract infections, including the "common cold."

Properties of the Virus

A. General Properties: Rhinoviruses are picornaviruses similar to enteroviruses but differing from them in having a CsCl buoyant density of 1.40 g/mL and in being acid-labile.

B. Animal Susceptibility and Growth of Virus: These viruses are infectious only for humans and chimpanzees. They have been grown in cultures of human embryonic lung fibroblasts (WI-38) and in organ cultures of ferret and human tracheal epithelium. They are grown best at 33 °C in rolled cultures.

C. Antigenic Properties: Over 100 serotypes are known. Some cross-react (eg, types 9 and 32).

Pathogenesis & Pathology

The virus enters via the upper respiratory tract. High titers of virus in nasal secretions—which can be found as early as 2–4 days after exposure—are associated with maximal illness. Thereafter, viral titers fall, although illness persists.

Histopathologic changes are limited to the submucosa and surface epithelium. These include engorgement of blood vessels, edema, mild cellular infiltration, and desquamation of surface epithelium, which is complete by the third day. Nasal secretion increases in quantity and in protein concentration.

Experiments under controlled conditions have shown that chilling, including the wearing of wet clothes, does not produce a cold or increase susceptibility to the virus. Chilliness is an early symptom of the common cold.

Clinical Findings

The incubation period is brief, from 2 to 4 days, and the acute illness usually lasts for 7 days although a nonproductive cough may persist for 2–3 weeks. The average adult has 1–2 attacks each year. Usual symptoms in adults include irritation in the upper respiratory tract, nasal discharge, headache, mild cough, malaise, and a chilly sensation. There is little or no fever. The nasal and nasopharyngeal mucosa become red and swollen, and the sense of smell becomes less keen. Mild hoarseness may be present. Prominent cervical adenopathy does not occur. Secondary bacterial infection may produce acute otitis media, sinusitis, bronchitis, or pneumonitis, especially in children. Type-specific antibodies appear or rise with each infection.

Immunity

Natural immunity may exist but may be brief. Only 30–50% of volunteers can be infected with infectious material; yet the "resistant" volunteers may catch colds of the same serotype at other times. Furthermore, people in isolated areas have more severe colds and a higher incidence of infection when a cold is introduced than people in areas regularly exposed to the virus. It has also been observed that older adults experience fewer colds than young adults and children. One 3-year study of acute respiratory tract illness in college and medical students showed that the same serotype was never isolated from separate illnesses in any student who had 2 or more illnesses.

Recent work with human volunteers has shown that resistance to the common cold is independent of measurable serum antibody but perhaps is related to specific antibody in the nasal secretions. These secretory antibodies are primarily 11S IgA immunoglobulins, produced locally in the mucosa and not a transudate from the serum. These 11S IgA antibodies do not persist as long as those in serum, and this could explain the paradox of reinfection in a person with adequate serum antibodies. Results regarding the role of interferon in recovery are inconclusive to date.

Volunteers infected with one rhinovirus serotype resist challenge with both homologous and heterologous virus for 2–16 weeks after the initial infection. Resistance to homologous challenge is complete during this period, while resistance to heterologous challenge is incomplete. This nonspecific resistance may be a factor in the control of naturally occurring colds.

Epidemiology

The disease occurs throughout the world. In the temperate zones, the attack rates are highest in early fall and winter, declining in the late spring. Members of isolated communities form highly susceptible groups.

The virus is believed to be transmitted through close contact, by large droplets. Under some circumstances, transmission of the virus by self-inoculation through hand contamination may be a more important mode of spread than that by airborne particles.

Colds in children spread more easily to others than do colds in adults. Adults in households with a child in school have twice as many colds as adults in households without school children.

In a single community, many rhinovirus serotypes cause outbreaks of disease in a single season, and different serotypes predominate during different respiratory disease seasons.

Treatment & Control

No specific treatment is available. The development of a potent rhinovirus vaccine is unlikely because of the difficulty in growing rhinoviruses to high titer in culture, the fleeting immunity, and the many serotypes causing colds. In addition, many rhinovirus serotypes are present during single respiratory disease outbreaks and may recur only rarely in the same area. Injection of purified vaccines has shown that the high levels of serum antibody are frequently not associated with similar elevation of local secretory antibody, which may be the most significant factor in disease prevention.

FOOT–AND–MOUTH DISEASE
(Aphthovirus of Cattle)

This highly infectious disease of cattle, sheep, pigs, and goats is rare in the USA but endemic in Mexico and Canada. It may be transmitted to humans by contact or ingestion. In humans, the disease is characterized by fever, salivation, and vesiculation of the mucous membranes of the oropharynx and of the skin of the palms, soles, fingers, and toes.

The disease in animals is highly contagious in the early stages of infection when viremia is present and when vesicles in the mouth and on the feet rupture and liberate large amounts of virus. Excreted material remains infectious for long periods. The mortality rate in animals is usually low but may reach 70%. Infected animals become poor producers of milk and meat. Many cattle serve as foci for infection for up to 8 months.

The virus is a typical picornavirus, measuring 24 nm in diameter, and is acid-labile, with a CsCl buoyant density of 1.43 g/mL. There are at least 7 types with over 50 subtypes.

Immunity after infection is adequate but of short duration.

A variety of animals are susceptible to infection. The typical disease can be reproduced by inoculating the virus into the pads of the foot. The reaction in infant mice inoculated with the virus of foot-and-mouth disease is similar to their reaction to inoculation with coxsackieviruses: paralysis results as a consequence of myositis. The virus grows readily in tissue culture of cattle tongue or hamster BHK-21 cells. Formalin-treated vaccines have been prepared from virus grown in such tissue cultures. However, such vaccines do not produce a long-lasting immunity, and frequent booster inoculations are necessary. A vaccine has recently been prepared in bacteria (*E coli*) by recombinant DNA techniques.

The methods of control of the disease are dictated by its high degree of contagiousness and the resistance of the virus to inactivation. When foci of infection occur in the USA, all exposed animals are slaughtered and their carcasses destroyed. Strict quarantine is established, and the area is not presumed to be safe until susceptible animals fail to develop symptoms within 30 days. Another method is to quarantine the herd and vaccinate all unaffected animals. Other countries have successfully employed systematic vaccination schedules. Some nations (eg, the USA and Australia) forbid the importation of potentially infective materials such as fresh meat, and the disease has been eliminated in these areas. Even so, migrating birds may play a role in carrying the virus from one country to another, as from France and Holland to England.

• • •

References

Agol VI: Structure, translation, and replication of picornaviral genomes. *Prog Med Virol* 1980;**26**:119.

Arnow PM et al: Acute hemorrhagic conjunctivitis: A mixed virus outbreak among Vietnamese refugees on Guam. *Am J Epidemiol* 1977;**105**:68.

Brown F et al: Comparison of swine vesicular disease virus and coxsackie B5 virus by serological and RNA hybridization methods. *J Gen Virol* 1976;**31**:231.

Craighead JE: The role of viruses in the pathogenesis of pancreatic disease and diabetes mellitus. *Prog Med Virol* 1975;**19**:161.

El-Hagrassy M, Banatvala JE, Coltart DJ: Coxsackie-B-virus specific IgM responses in patients with cardiac and other diseases. *Lancet* 1980;**2**:1160.

Gwaltney JM Jr, Hendley JO: Rhinovirus transmission: One if by air, two if by hand. *Am J Epidemiol* 1978;**107**:357.

Gyorkey F et al: Coxsackievirus aggregates in muscle cells of a polymyositis patient. *Intervirology* 1978;**10**:69.

Herrmann JE, Hendry RM, Collins MF: Factors involved in enzyme-linked immunoassay of viruses and evaluation of the method for identification of enteroviruses. *J Clin Microbiol* 1979;**10**:210.

Kitamura N et al: Primary structure, gene organization and polypeptide expression of poliovirus RNA. *Nature* 1981;**291**:547.

Melnick JL: Enteroviruses. In: *Viral Infections of Humans: Epidemiology and Control,* 2nd ed. Evans AS (editor). Plenum, 1982.

Melnick JL, Wenner HA, Phillips CA: Enteroviruses. Pages 471–534 in: *Diagnostic Procedures for Viral, Rickettsial, and Chlamydial Infections,* 5th ed. Lennette EH, Schmidt NJ (editors). American Public Health Association, 1979.

Melnick JL et al: Identification of Bulgarian strain 258 of enterovirus 71. *Intervirology* 1979;**12**:297.

Mirkovic RR et al: Enterovirus type 70: The etiologic agent of pandemic acute hemorrhagic conjunctivitis. *Bull WHO* 1973;**49**:341.

Nathanson N, Martin JR: The epidemiology of poliomyelitis: Enigmas surrounding its appearance, epidemicity, and disappearance. *Am J Epidemiol* 1979;**110**:672.

Numazaki Y et al: Serologic diagnosis of enterovirus type 71 infections using selected plaque mutants. *J Infect Dis* 1981;**143**:122.

Sells CJ, Carpenter RL, Ray CG: Sequelae of central-nervous-system enterovirus infections. *N Engl J Med* 1975;**293**:1.

Wilfert CM et al: Persistent and fatal central-nervous-system echovirus infections in patients with agammaglobulinemia. *N Engl J Med* 1977;**296**:1485.

Viral hepatitis is a systemic disease primarily involving the liver. Most cases of acute viral hepatitis in children and adults are caused by one of the following agents: hepatitis A virus (HAV), the etiologic agent of viral hepatitis type A (infectious hepatitis or short incubation hepatitis); hepatitis B virus (HBV), which is associated with viral hepatitis type B (serum hepatitis or long incubation hepatitis); and the more recently recognized hepatitis C, D, etc, viruses. Because these viruses are associated with hepatitis that cannot be ascribed to either HAV or HBV, the disease is designated non-A, non-B hepatitis. They account for most of the transfusion-associated hepatitis cases seen in the United States since 1976 and a sizable portion of sporadic hepatitis. Additional well characterized viruses that can cause sporadic hepatitis, such as yellow fever virus, cytomegalovirus, Epstein-Barr virus (infectious mononucleosis), herpes simplex virus, rubella virus, and the enteroviruses, are discussed in other chapters. Hepatitis viruses produce acute inflammation of the liver, resulting in a clinical illness characterized by fever, gastrointestinal symptoms such as nausea and vomiting, and jaundice. Regardless of the virus type, identical histopathologic lesions are observed in the liver.

HAV, transmitted primarily by the fecal-oral route, may be transmitted rarely by the parenteral route. Correspondingly, HBV produces sporadic infections principally after parenteral inoculation of virus-infected blood or blood products, although transmission by a nonpercutaneous route is also common.

Appreciation of the existence of these lesser known modes of transmission is important when attempting to correlate presently established clinical classifications of viral hepatitis with the presence or absence of hepatitis B surface antigen (HBsAg). This antigen was originally detected in 1963 in the serum of an apparently healthy Australian aborigine by reacting the serum in immunodiffusion tests with serum from a multiply transfused hemophiliac, but the association of the Australia (Au) antigen (HBsAg) with viral hepatitis was not recognized until 1967.

The incidence of this unique antigen in acute hepatitis associated with transfusions was 50–75% prior to the introduction of sensitive screening methods to ban the use of blood donors circulating HBsAg. In chronic active hepatitis, the prevalence rate has varied but is around 30% in most series. A high prevalence of the hepatitis B surface antigen (HBsAg) has been observed in cases of primary liver cancer in most areas of the world. The antigen is not present in sera from well-documented cases of common-source epidemics of viral hepatitis A.

Nomenclature of the hepatitis viruses, antigens, and antibodies is as follows:

HAV	Hepatitis A virus, tentatively classified as an enterovirus.
Anti–HAV	Antibody to HAV
HBV	Hepatitis B virus, a 42-nm double-shelled particle (originally called the Dane particle) that contains a small circular DNA molecule and DNA polymerase.
HBsAg	Hepatitis B surface antigen, which exists as a separate, small 22-nm particle and which is also present on the surface of the larger virus particle.
HBcAg	Hepatitis B core antigen, associated with the 27-nm core of the virus.
HBeAg	Hepatitis B e antigen, which is intimately related to infectivity of a carrier's blood.
Anti-HBs	Antibody to HBsAg
Anti-HBc	Antibody to HBcAg
Anti-HBe	Antibody to HBeAg
Non-A, non-B	Viruses that cause non-A, non-B hepatitis.

General Properties of the Viruses

A. Hepatitis Type A: Recent studies indicate that HAV should be classified with the enteroviruses. It is a 27-nm particle with cubic symmetry, containing a linear single-stranded RNA genome with a molecular weight of about 2.5×10^6. Lipid is not an integral component of HAV, which is stable to treatment with ether, acid, and heat (56 °C for 30 minutes), and its infectivity can be preserved for years at –20 °C. The virus is destroyed by autoclaving (121 °C for 20 minutes), by boiling in water for 1 minute, by dry heat (180 °C for 1 hour), by ultraviolet irradiation (1 minute at 1.1 watts), by treatment with formalin (1:4000 for 3 days at 37 °C), or by treatment with chlorine (10–15 ppm for 30 minutes). The relative resistance of HAV to disinfection procedures emphasizes the need for extra precautions in dealing with hepatitis patients and their products.

Electron microscopic examination of infected liver reveals intracytoplasmic localization of virus particles. Only one serotype is known. There is no crossing with HBV.

HAV initially was identified in stool and liver preparations by employing immune electron microscopy as the detection system (Fig 29–3). The addition of specific hepatitis A antisera from convalescent patients to fecal specimens obtained from patients early in the incubation period of their illness prior to the onset of jaundice permitted concentration and visibility of virus particles by the formation of antigen-antibody aggregates. More sensitive serologic assays such as the microtiter solid-phase immunoradiometric assay and immune adherence have made it possible to detect HAV in stools, liver homogenates, and bile and to measure specific antibody in serum.

Chimpanzees and 2 South American monkeys, the white-moustached (*Saguinus mystax*) and rufiventer marmosets, are susceptible to HAV and have provided laboratories with a source of virus for experimentation and for preparation of diagnostic reagents. HAV from marmoset-adapted material and from extracts of patients' feces has recently been cultivated serially in primary explant cultures of adult *Saguinus labiatus* marmoset livers and in cell culture. A noncytopathic infection occurs, which is identified by immunofluorescence and by radioimmunoassay.

B. Hepatitis Type B: HBsAg is closely associated with hepatitis B infections. Electron microscopy of HBsAg-reactive serum has revealed 3 morphologic forms (Fig 32–1). The most numerous are spherical particles measuring 22 nm in diameter (Fig 27–25). These small particles appear to be made up exclusively of HBsAg—as do tubular or filamentous forms, which have the same diameter but may be over 200 nm long. Larger, 42-nm spherical particles, origi-

nally referred to as Dane particles, are less frequently observed. These particles are more complex. The outer surface, or envelope, contains HBsAg and surrounds a 27-nm inner core that contains HBcAg (Figs 32–2 and 32–3). Overproduction of the surface component apparently results in the 22-nm particles. DNA polymerase activity and endogenous DNA template are associated with the inner core of the Dane particle. The DNA template consists of double-stranded DNA with a molecular weight of approximately 1.6×10^6.

It is the variable length of a single-stranded region of the circular DNA molecules that results in genetically heterogeneous particles with a wide range of buoyant densities.

Two major polypeptides with molecular weights of 22,000 and 25,000 constitute approximately 55% by weight of the HBsAg-containing 22-nm particle. A third major polypeptide has a molecular weight of 68,000, has HBsAg reactivity, and cross-reacts with human serum albumin. The viral envelope may be assembled from the 2 smaller polypeptides, one of which (MW 25,000) is glycosylated.

HBeAg is believed to be an integral, cryptic component of the HBV core particle. A major polypeptide with a molecular weight of approximately 20,000 has been observed in purified preparations.

A new antigen-antibody system, termed the delta (δ) antigen and antibody (anti-δ), is associated with some HBV infections. The antigen is found within certain HBsAg particles. An RNA that co-purifies with the δ antigen may be the genome of a defective δ agent, since experimental studies in chimpanzees indicate that successful transmission requires HBV for expression and replication.

The stability of HBsAg does not always coincide with that of the infectious agent. However, both are stable at $-20\ °C$ for more than 20 years and stable to

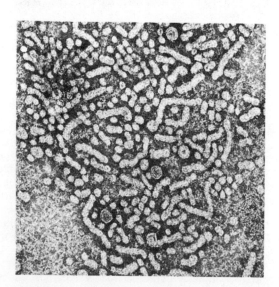

Figure 32–1. Unfractionated HBsAg-positive human plasma diluted 1:10. Filaments, 22-nm spherical particles, and Dane particles are shown (77,000 ×).

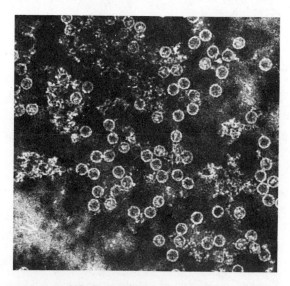

Figure 32–2. HBcAg purified from infected liver nuclei (122,400 ×). The diameter of the core particles is 27 nm. (Fields, Dreesman, and Cabral.)

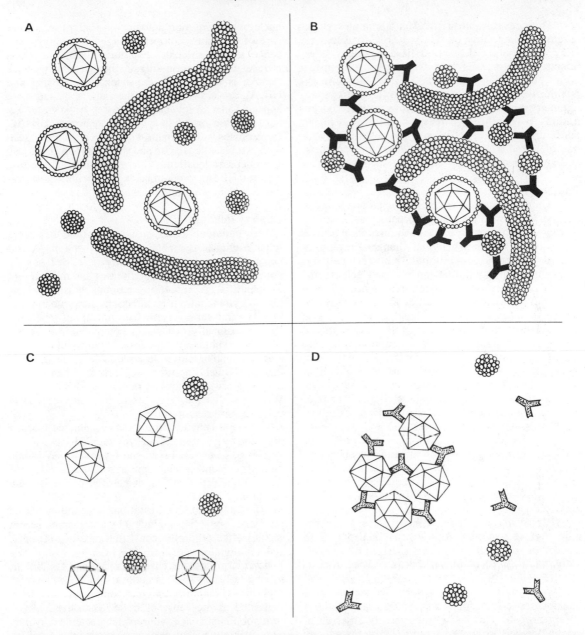

Figure 32–3. Various hepatitis B particles are related and differentiated by their antigenicity. The forms seen in patients' blood are the 22-nm spheres, the filaments 22 nm wide, and the virus itself (Dane particle), which consists of an outer shell and an inner core *(A)*. All 3 forms are characterized by the presence of hepatitis B surface antigen, as indicated by the fact that the antibody (black) to that antigen combines with and agglutinates them all *(B)*. Adding detergent to virus particles strips the surface antigen outer shell off them, yielding free cores *(C)*. These are agglutinated by a different antibody (stippled), the antibody to core antigen, distinguishing them from the surface particles *(D)*. (From: Viral hepatitis, by Melnick JL, Dreesman GR, Hollinger FB. Copyright © 1977 by Scientific American, Inc. All rights reserved.)

repeated freezing and thawing and to plasma fractionation procedures. For example, Cohn ethanol fractionation of HBsAg-positive serum concentrates HBsAg in subfraction III (thrombin), with reduced concentrations found in fraction I (fibrinogen, factor VIII). Low amounts or none are detected in fraction V (albumin) and in fraction II (normal immunoglobulin). Heat inactivation of albumin (60 °C, 10 hours) apparently modifies or inactivates HBV, since infectivity has not been associated with the administration of HBsAg-containing lots. However, immunogenicity is retained. The stability of HBV where noted in the above fractions has resulted in numerous warnings against the indiscriminate use of blood products in therapy. With the advent of donor screening, this problem has virtually been eliminated.

The virus is stable at 37 °C for 60 minutes but not at temperatures above 60 °C. At 100 °C for 1 minute, HBV infectivity is lost but HBs antigenicity is retained. Similarly, HBsAg is stable at pH 2.4 for up to 6 hours, but HBV infectivity is lost. Sodium hypochlorite, 0.5% (eg, 1:10 Clorox), destroys antigenicity within 3 minutes at low protein concentrations, but undiluted serum specimens require higher concentrations (5%). HBsAg is not destroyed by ultraviolet irradiation of plasma or other blood products, and viral infectivity may also resist such treatment.

Pathology

Microscopically, there is spotty parenchymal cell degeneration, with necrosis of hepatocytes, a diffuse lobular inflammatory reaction, and disruption of liver cell cords. These parenchymal changes are accompanied by reticuloendothelial (Kupffer) cell hyperplasia, periportal infiltration by mononuclear cells, and cell degeneration. Localized areas of necrosis with ballooning or acidophilic bodies are frequently observed. Later in the course of the disease, there is an accumulation of macrophages containing lipofuscin near degenerating hepatocytes. Disruption of bile canaliculi or blockage of biliary excretion may occur following liver cell enlargement or necrosis. Preservation of the reticulum framework allows hepatocyte regeneration so that the highly ordered architecture of the liver lobule can be ultimately regained. The damaged hepatic tissue is usually restored in 8–12 weeks.

In 5–15% of patients, the initial lesion consists of bridging hepatic necrosis with impaired regeneration, resulting in collapsed stroma. The occurrence of this lesion in patients over age 40 frequently presages a precarious clinical course leading to fibrosis, cirrhosis, and death.

Persistent (unresolved) viral hepatitis, a mild benign disease that may follow acute hepatitis B in 8–10% of adult patients, is characterized by sporadically abnormal transaminase values and hepatomegaly. Histologically, the lobular architecture is preserved, with portal inflammation, swollen and pale hepatocytes (cobblestone arrangement), and slight to absent fibrosis. This lesion is frequently observed in asymptomatic carriers, does not progress toward cirrhosis, and has a favorable prognosis.

Chronic active (aggressive) hepatitis features a spectrum of histologic changes from inflammation and necrosis to collapse of the normal reticulum framework with bridging between the portal triads or central veins. HBsAg is observed in 10–50% of these patients. The prognosis is guarded, with progression to macronodular cirrhosis frequently occurring.

Occasionally, during acute viral hepatitis, more extensive damage may occur that prevents orderly liver cell regeneration. Such fulminant or massive hepatocellular necrosis is seen in 1–2% of jaundiced patients with hepatitis B but is less common in hepatitis A.

In hepatitis B patients, electron microscopic studies have revealed 27-nm particles in liver cell nuclei which are morphologically similar to the inner core of the virus. Correspondingly, immunofluorescence studies indicate that during HBV infection HBcAg is found primarily in the nucleus, whereas HBsAg is localized in the cytoplasm. HBsAg and HBcAg are rarely found in the same cell, and there appears to be an inverse relationship between the severity of the lesion and the abundance of HBsAg. Hepatocytes with a ground-glass appearance are laden with cytoplasmic HBsAg and are often found in biopsy specimens from patients with persistent viral hepatitis. Nuclear HBcAg predominates in patients whose immune system is compromised.

Clinical Findings (Table 32–1)

In individual cases, it is not possible to make a reliable clinical distinction between hepatitis A and hepatitis B or the more recently described non-A, non-B hepatitis. Other viral diseases that may present as hepatitis are infectious mononucleosis, yellow fever, cytomegalovirus infection, herpes simplex, rubella, and some enterovirus infections. Hepatitis may occasionally occur as a complication of leptospirosis, syphilis, tuberculosis, toxoplasmosis, and amebiasis, all of which are susceptible to specific drug therapy. Other important differential diagnoses include biliary obstruction, primary biliary cirrhosis, Wilson's disease, drug toxicity, and drug hypersensitivity reactions.

In viral hepatitis, the onset of jaundice is often preceded by gastrointestinal symptoms such as nausea, vomiting, severe anorexia, and fever that may mimic influenza. Jaundice may appear within a few days of the prodromal period, but anicteric hepatitis is more common.

Extrahepatic manifestations of viral hepatitis (primarily type B) include (1) a transient serum sickness–like prodrome consisting of urticaria, rash, and nonmigratory polyarthralgia or arthritis occurring 1–6 weeks prior to the onset of hepatitis in 15–20% of patients; (2) polyarteritis nodosa; and (3) glomerulonephritis. Circulating immune complexes have been suggested as the cause of these syndromes. Mixed cryoglobulinemia is a syndrome characterized by purpura, arthralgia, and weakness, often with renal involvement. Vasculitis and immune complex deposition are common. In most cases, the cryoprecipitates contain either HBsAg or anti-HBs.

Complete recovery occurs in most hepatitis A cases and in over 85% of the type B hepatitis cases. Hepatitis A is more severe in adults than in children, in whom it often goes unnoticed. Approximately 3% of patients with acute icteric type B hepatitis ultimately develop chronic active hepatitis. Case fatality rates appear to vary with age and may reflect underlying conditions rather than any increased virulence of the specific causative agent. For the epidemiologic years 1973–1974, the case fatality rate for hepatitis B among persons age 29 years or younger was 0.5–0.6%; for the age group 30 years and over, it was 2%. The rates are highest for transfusion-associated cases (2.7%). Ful-

Table 32—1. Epidemiologic and clinical features of viral hepatitis A, B, and non-A, non-B.

	Viral Hepatitis Type A	Viral Hepatitis Type B	Non-A, Non-B Viral Hepatitis
Incubation period	15—45 days (avg, 25—30)	50—180 days (avg, 60—90)	35—70 days*
Principal age distribution	15—29 years†	15—29 years‡	?
Seasonal incidence	Throughout the year but tends to peak in autumn	Throughout the year	?
Route of infection	Predominantly fecal-oral	Predominantly parenteral	Predominantly parenteral
Occurrence of virus			
Blood	2 weeks before to ≤1 week after jaundice	Months to years	Months to years
Stool	2 weeks before to 2 weeks after jaundice	Absent	?
Urine	?	Absent	?
Saliva, semen	?	Frequently present	?
Clinical and laboratory features			
Onset	Abrupt	Insidious	Insidious
Fever >38 °C (100.4 °F)	Common	Less common	?
Duration of transaminase elevation	1—3 weeks	1—6+ months	1—6+ months
Immunoglobulins (IgM levels)	Elevated	Normal to slightly elevated	?
Complications	Uncommon, no chronicity	Chronicity in 5—10%	Chronicity in 40—60%
Mortality rate	<0.1%	<1%	?
HBsAg	Absent	Present	Absent
Immunity			
Homologous	Yes	Yes	?
Heterologous	No	No	No
Duration	Probably lifetime	Probably lifetime	?
Gamma globulin prophylaxis	Regularly prevents jaundice	Prevents jaundice only if gamma globulin is of sufficient potency against HBV	?

*Shorter (14 days) and much longer (120 days) incubation periods have been observed.
†Nonicteric hepatitis A is common in children.
‡Among the 15—29 year age group, hepatitis B is often associated with drug abuse or promiscuous sexual behavior. Transfusion-associated cases are generally over age 29.

minant hepatitis is lethal in 75–80% of cases and is highly correlated with age. Twenty to 30% of survivors develop chronic active hepatitis.

The potential courses of acute viral hepatitis have been discussed in the section on pathology. Uncomplicated viral hepatitis rarely continues for more than 10 weeks without improvement. Relapses occur in 5–20% of cases and are manifested by abnormalities in liver function with or without the recurrence of clinical symptoms. A posthepatitis syndrome may occur, especially in postmenopausal women. It is characterized by repeated episodes of anorexia, irritability, lethargy, weakness, headaches, and right upper quadrant pain. This syndrome is due to interference with normal estrogen metabolism in the liver and can be successfully treated with estrogens and progesterone in women.

As shown in Fig 32–5, virus persists in the blood and stools of patients with viral hepatitis A for variable times. Transmissibility appears to be minimal 2 weeks after jaundice. HBsAg (and presumably the virus) may persist in the blood of a healthy person for years after infection, and such blood consequently represents a continual potential source of infection. HBV has been detected in nasopharyngeal washings (saliva) and

semen of some patients with hepatitis B.

Non-A, non-B hepatitis is usually clinically mild, with only minimal to moderate elevation of liver enzymes. Hospitalization is unusual, and jaundice occurs in less than 25% of patients. Despite the mild nature of the disease, a relatively large number of cases (40–60%) progress to chronic liver disease. Most patients are asymptomatic, but histologic evaluation often reveals evidence of chronic active hepatitis, especially in those whose disease is acquired following transfusion.

Laboratory Features

Liver biopsy permits a tissue diagnosis of hepatitis. Tests for abnormal liver function, such as serum alanine aminotransferase (ALT; formerly SGPT) and bilirubin, supplement the clinical, pathologic, and epidemiologic findings. Transaminase values in acute hepatitis range between 500 and 2000 units and are almost never below 100 units. ALT values are usually higher than serum aspartate transaminase (AST; formerly SGOT). A sharp rise in ALT with a short duration (3–19 days) is more indicative of viral hepatitis A, whereas a gradual rise with prolongation (35–200 days) appears to characterize viral hepatitis B and non-A, non-B infections.

Leukopenia is typical in the preicteric phase and may be followed by a relative lymphocytosis. Large atypical lymphocytes such as are found in infectious mononucleosis may occasionally be seen but do not exceed 10% of the total lymphocyte population.

Further evidence of liver dysfunction and host response is reflected in a decreased serum albumin and increased serum globulin. Elevation of gamma globulin and serum transaminase is frequently used to gauge chronicity and activity of liver disease. In many patients with hepatitis A, an abnormally high level of IgM is found that appears 3–4 days after the ALT begins to rise. Hepatitis B patients have normal to slightly elevated IgM levels.

The most sensitive and specific method for detecting HBsAg or anti-HBs is the radioimmunoassay (RIA). This test and the red cell agglutination (RCA) technique, which employs HBs antibody-coated cells in a microtiter system, have replaced counterelectrophoresis as the methods of choice for detecting HBsAg. The passive hemagglutination (PHA) technique, which uses HBs antigen–coated cells, is an excellent and rapid method for detecting anti-HBs, rivaling RIA in sensitivity. The enzyme-linked immunosorbent assay (ELISA) (see Chapters 28 and 29) has recently gained acceptance in many countries besides the USA because it circumvents the relatively short half-life of isotopes inherent in RIA systems.

The particles containing HBsAg are antigenically complex. Each contains a group-specific antigen, *a*, in addition to 2 pairs of mutually exclusive subdetermi-nants, *d/y* and *w/r*. Thus, 4 phenotypes of HBsAg have been observed: *adw, ayw, adr,* and *ayr*. In the USA, *adw* is the predominant subtype among asymptomatic carriers, whereas *ayw* has frequently been observed in dialysis-associated outbreaks and among parenteral drug abusers. These virus-specific markers are useful in epidemiologic investigations, since secondary cases have the same subtype as the index case. The evidence indicates that these antigenic determinants are the phenotypic expression of HBV genotypes and are not determined by host factors.

The clinical and serologic events following exposure to HBV are depicted in Fig 32–4 and in Table 32–2. DNA polymerase activity, which is probably representative of the viremic stage of hepatitis B, occurs early in the incubation period, coinciding with the first appearance of HBsAg. The latter is usually detectable 2–6 weeks in advance of clinical and biochemical evidence of hepatitis and persists throughout the clinical course of the disease but typically disappears by the sixth month after exposure. Occasionally, HBsAg persists in patients who develop chronic active hepatitis. In patients destined to become carriers, the initial illness may be mild or inapparent, manifested only by an elevated transaminase determination.

Anti-HBc is frequently detected at the onset of clinical illness approximately 2–4 weeks after HBsAg reactivity appears. Because this antibody is directed against the internal component of the hepatitis B virion, its appearance in the serum is indicative of viral replication. In the typical case of acute type B

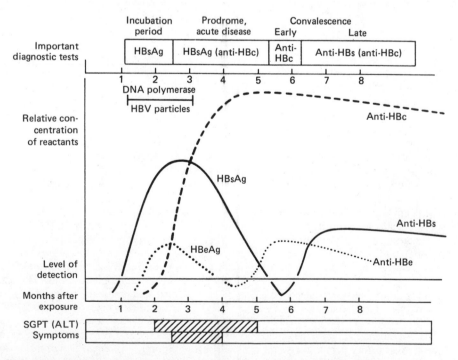

Figure 32–4. Clinical and serologic events occurring in a patient with hepatitis type B. The common diagnostic tests and their interpretation are presented in Table 32–2. (From Hollinger FB, Dienstag JL: *Manual of Clinical Microbiology*, 3rd ed. American Society for Microbiology, 1980.)

Table 32—2. Common serologic tests for HBV and their interpretation.

Positive Tests	Interpretation
HBsAg (surface antigen)	Current active hepatitis infection, acute or chronic.
Anti-HBs (in absence of HBsAg)	Protection against reinfection. Remains for years.
Anti-HBc (in absence of anti-HBs)	Active HBV infection, acute or chronic. Can reveal active infection in some instances when HBsAg is present at concentrations too low to be detected.
HBeAg*	Active hepatitis infection, acute or chronic. Found in presence of HBsAg. Indicates specimens that exhibit potential for enhanced infectivity.
Anti-HBe	When present in HBsAg carrier, blood is potentially less infectious.

*Other HBV serologic markers that may be present at the same time include Dane particles (HBV), observable by electron microscopy. Core antigen and viral DNA polymerase can be measured by disrupting HBV.

hepatitis, the anti-HBc titer falls after recovery. In contrast, high titers of anti-HBc persist in the sera of most chronic HBsAg carriers. Antibody to HBsAg is first detected at a variable period after the disappearance of HBsAg. It is present in low concentrations usually detectable only by the most sensitive methods.

The anti-HBc test is of limited clinical value when the HBsAg test is positive. However, in perhaps 5% of the acute cases of hepatitis B, and more frequently during early convalescence, HBsAg may be undetectable in the serum. Examination of these sera for anti-HBc may help in establishing the correct diagnosis. In the absence of anti-HBc and HBsAg, active hepatitis B disease can be excluded. In contrast, the presence of anti-HBc alone is presumptive evidence for an active HBV infection. However, this relationship is not infallible, and some patients who have recovered from hepatitis B with the development of anti-HBs and anti-HBc eventually lose one or the other antibody.

Another antigen-antibody system of importance involves HBeAg and its antibody. If the specimen contains HBsAg, certain situations may warrant further testing of the serum for HBeAg or anti-HBe. These include assessing the risk of transmission of HBV following exposure to contaminated blood and advising health care professionals who are chronically infected. Specimens positive for HBeAg (or positive for HBsAg at a dilution of 1:10,000) are considered to be very infectious, ie, they contain high concentrations of HBV. Infectivity is reduced, but probably not eliminated, in specimens containing anti-HBe (or low titers of HBsAg).

The clinical, virologic, and serologic events following exposure to HAV are shown in Fig 32–5. Virus particles have been detected by immune electron mi-

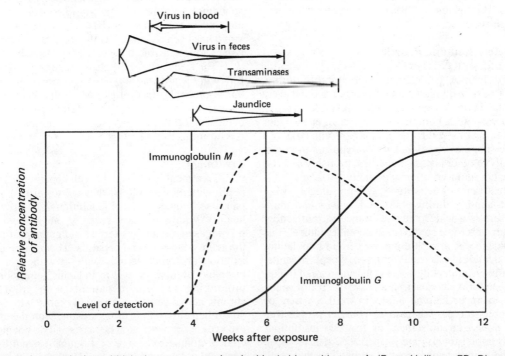

Figure 32–5. Immunologic and biologic events associated with viral hepatitis type A. (From Hollinger FB, Dienstag JL: *Manual of Clinical Microbiology,* 3rd ed. American Society for Microbiology, 1980.)

croscopy in fecal extracts of hepatitis A patients (Fig 29–3). Virus appears early in the disease and disappears within 3 weeks following the onset of jaundice.

By means of RIA, the HAV antigen has been detected in liver, stool, bile, and blood of naturally infected humans and experimentally infected chimpanzees or marmosets. The detection of HAV in the blood of infected chimpanzees supports previous epidemiologic evidence of viremia during the acute stage of the disease. Peak titers of HAV are detected in the stool about 1–2 weeks prior to the first detectable liver enzyme abnormalities.

Anti-HAV appears in the IgM fraction during the acute phase, peaking about 3 weeks after elevation of liver enzymes. During convalescence, anti-HAV is in the IgG fraction, where it persists for decades. The methods of choice for measuring HAV antibodies are RIA, ELISA, and immune adherence hemagglutination (see Chapter 29).

Attempts to isolate HBV in a cell or organ culture system have generally not been successful. In contrast, HAV has recently been propagated in cell culture. Chimpanzees and some species of marmosets have been found to be susceptible to human viral hepatitis type A. HAV infections among imported chimpanzees are well known as an important cause of hepatitis in animal caretakers.

Successful transmission of HBV to chimpanzees has been achieved. The infection results in serologic, biochemical, and histologic evidence of type B hepatitis. Immunofluorescence and electron microscopy reveal HBsAg in the cytoplasm and viruslike particles with HBcAg in the nuclei of hepatocytes. Serial passage has been successful. No evidence for hepatitis B transmission from chimpanzees to humans has been reported.

Virus-Host Immune Reactions

Currently there is evidence for at least 3 hepatitis viruses—type A (short incubation hepatitis virus), type B (long incubation hepatitis virus), and the agent or agents of non-A, non-B hepatitis. A single infection with any confers homologous but not heterologous protection against reinfection. Infection with HBV of a specific subtype, eg, HBsAg/adw, appears to confer immunity to other HBsAg subtypes, probably because of their common group a specificity.

Most cases of hepatitis type A presumably occur without jaundice during childhood, and by late adulthood there is a widespread resistance to reinfection. However, serologic studies in this country indicate that the incidence of infection among certain populations may be declining as a result of improvements in sanitation commensurate with a rise in the standard of living. It has been estimated that as many as 50–75% of young middle to upper income adults in the USA may be susceptible to type A hepatitis. Younger people who live in poorer circumstances or crowded institutions (eg, the armed forces) are at increased risk.

The immunopathogenetic mechanisms that result in viral persistence and hepatocellular injury in type B hepatitis remain to be elucidated. An imbalance between suppressive and cytopathic immune responses of the host has been hypothesized to account for the various pathologic manifestations of this disease. It is postulated that antibody-dependent, complement-mediated cytolysis or cellular effector mechanisms are responsible for the hepatic injury observed, whereas noncytopathic synthesis of viral components, surface expression of viral antigens or liver-specific neoantigens, and shedding of virus are primarily modulated by the humoral immune response.

Various host responses, immunologic and genetic, have been proposed to account for the higher frequency of HBsAg persistence observed in infants or children compared to adults and in certain disease states, eg, Down's syndrome, leukemia (acute and chronic lymphocytic), leprosy, thalassemia, and chronic renal insufficiency. Patients with Down's syndrome are particularly prone to persistent antigenemia (but low antibody frequency) and inapparent infections, and they show a significantly greater prevalence of these disorders than is found in other mentally retarded patients. This does not imply that these patients have an increased susceptibility to HBV. On the contrary, among other equally exposed patients who are residents within the same institution, the total serologic evidence of HBV infection is similar except that the antigen carrier rate is low whereas the antibody prevalence is high. An immunologic difference in the host response to the virus is apparently responsible for this serologic dichotomy.

Persistent antigenemia and mild or subclinical infections are more frequently observed in individuals who have been infected with low doses of virus. Correspondingly, a direct relationship between virus dose and time of appearance of HBsAg or an abnormal ALT value has been reported; ie, the incubation period becomes longer as the dose of virus diminishes.

The frequency of the chronic HBsAg carrier state following acute icteric type B hepatitis is not known but is probably under 10%. More than half of these patients continue to exhibit biochemical and histologic evidence of chronic liver disease, ie, chronic persistent or chronic active hepatitis.

Treatment

Treatment of the patient with hepatitis is directed at allowing hepatocellular damage to resolve and repair itself under optimal conditions. In previously healthy young military recruits, ad libitum ward privileges or strenuous exercise did not appear to alter the acute course of viral hepatitis. Therapeutic administration of corticosteroids with or without azathioprine has been successful in inducing remissions and prolonging survival in patients with progressive chronic active hepatitis, especially those with non-A, non-B hepatitis. These drugs are not recommended for use in cases of acute viral hepatitis and do not alter the clinical course of severe or fulminant hepatitis. Patients should be advised to avoid hepatotoxins such as alcohol during convalescence.

Interferon in large doses has been remarkably successful in reducing the level of HBV and related antigens in the blood of chronic active hepatitis patients and in improving the health of some patients so treated. Vidarabine (ara-A) has also been successful in reducing HBV levels but not as successful as interferon. Combinations of the drug and interferon appear to be synergistic in their effect but are still under investigation.

Epidemiology

The incidence of reported hepatitis in the USA has varied from 26 to 33 cases per 100,000 population, with about 70% categorized as hepatitis A. The actual incidence is undoubtedly much higher because many persons contract so mild a form of hepatitis that they do not seek treatment, and physicians report only 10–20% of the cases they see.

As shown in Table 32–1, there are marked differences in the epidemiologic features of hepatitis A, B, and non-A, non-B infections.

A. Viral Hepatitis Type A (Short Incubation Hepatitis): Outbreaks of type A hepatitis are common in families and institutions, summer camps, and especially among troops. The most likely mode of transmission under these conditions is by the fecal-oral route through close personal contact. Intestinal carriers are either relatively few or epidemiologically unimportant. The clinical disease is most often manifest in children and young adults, with the highest rates in those between 15 and 30 years of age. The ratio of anicteric to icteric cases in adults is about 1:1; in children, it may be as high as 12:1.

Sudden, explosive epidemics of type A hepatitis usually result from fecal contamination of a single source (eg, drinking water, food, milk, or nonhuman primates). The consumption of raw oysters or improperly steamed clams obtained from water polluted with sewage has also resulted in several outbreaks of hepatitis.

Other recently identified sources of potential infection are nonhuman primates. Since 1961, there have been over 35 outbreaks in which primates, usually chimpanzees, have infected humans in close personal contact with them. These animals probably acquire the infection after arrival and transmit the virus to their caretakers. A persistent carrier state is unlikely, since the number of new cases diminishes with residence.

HAV seems to be hardly ever transmitted by the use of contaminated needles and syringes or through the administration of blood. Hemodialysis plays no role in the spread of hepatitis A infections to either patients or staff. The prevalence of anti-HAV is identical in persons with past histories of multiple blood transfusions or accidental inoculations with blood-contaminated instruments and in those from the same socioeconomic background without such exposures. About 30–60% of American adults possess antibodies, with a higher prevalence in those from lower socioeconomic groups.

B. Viral Hepatitis Type B (Long Incubation Hepatitis): The virus of type B hepatitis is also worldwide in distribution. There are about 175 million carriers, of whom 1 million live in the USA.

There is no seasonal trend and no high predilection for any age group, although there are definite high-risk groups such as parenteral drug abusers, institutionalized patients, health care personnel, individuals who have recently received blood transfusions, hemodialysis patients and staff, high promiscuity populations, and newborn infants born to mothers with type B hepatitis. The incidence of hepatitis B among recipients of blood transfusions is about 1%. Since mandatory screening of blood donors for HBsAg was instituted and commercial donors are being replaced with all-volunteer donor sources, the number of icteric cases of transfusion-associated hepatitis has been substantially reduced. At present, non-A, non-B hepatitis accounts for the majority of transfusion-associated hepatitis cases in the USA.

Cases of hepatitis B appear sporadically and are often associated with the parenteral inoculation of infective human blood (or its products), usually obtained from an apparently healthy carrier. Thousands of cases have occurred following parenteral administration of human serum, plasma, whole blood or blood products, or vaccines that contained human serum. Many persons have been infected by improperly sterilized syringes, needles, or scalpels or even by tattooing or ear piercing. The estimated ratio of anicteric to icteric infections is reported to be as high as 10:1.

Other modes of transmission of hepatitis B exist. Volunteers who ingested infectious plasma developed infection. HBsAg can be detected in saliva, nasopharyngeal washings, semen, menstrual fluid, and vaginal secretions as well as in blood. Transmission from carriers to close contacts by the oral route or by sexual or other intimate exposure occurs. There is particularly strong evidence of transmission from persons with subclinical cases and carriers of HBsAg to homosexual and heterosexual long-term partners, although the precise mechanism of transmission is not clear.

Health care personnel (surgeons, pathologists, and other physicians, dentists, nurses, laboratory technicians, and blood bank personnel) have a higher incidence of hepatitis and prevalence of detectable HBsAg or anti-HBs (or both) than those who have no occupational exposure to patients or blood products. The risk that these apparently healthy HBsAg carriers (especially medical and dental surgeons) represent to the patients under their care remains to be determined but is probably small.

Hepatitis B infections are common among patients and staff of hemodialysis units. Family contacts are also at increased risk. As many as 50% of the renal dialysis patients who contract hepatitis B may become chronic carriers of HBsAg compared with 2% of the staff group, emphasizing differences in host response to varying dosage of virus.

The presence of HBeAg, or a high concentration

of HBsAg, in a person's serum may be a useful marker for infectivity; in contrast, lower levels of infectivity appear to correlate best with the presence of anti-HBe.

Persons who have received a transfusion, especially from a paid donor, have a higher incidence of hepatitis and HBs antigenemia than nontransfused persons. This has led to the recommendation that anyone who has received a transfusion should not be allowed to serve as a blood donor. However, as commercial sources of blood donors are eliminated and newer, more sensitive methods for detecting HBsAg (RIA, RCA) are employed, this recommendation is becoming less important.

Engorged mosquitoes and bedbugs, particularly if collected in homes of HBsAg carriers, may be positive for virus. Under suitable circumstances, they may play a role in viral dissemination.

The incubation period of hepatitis B is 50–180 days, with a mean between 60 and 90 days. It appears to vary with the dose of HBV administered and the route of administration, being prolonged in patients infected by a nonpercutaneous route.

Gamma globulin and albumin are blood products that appear free from the risk of hepatitis B. Their method of preparation includes cold ethanol fractionation. In addition, albumin is heated to 60 °C for 10 hours.

C. Non-A, Non-B Hepatitis: Non-A, non-B hepatitis accounts for 90% of the cases of transfusion-associated hepatitis currently seen in the USA. In addition, up to 25% of sporadic hepatitis cases may be caused by the agent or agents responsible for this disease entity. The incubation period ranges from 5 to 10 weeks, although both shorter (2 weeks) and longer (4 months) intervals have been observed. Serologic markers for HAV, HBV, or other viral agents occasionally associated with hepatitis are absent. Thus, the diagnosis is one of exclusion in a patient with biochemical evidence of viral hepatitis. Specific methods for identifying this agent are not yet available. In the absence of such markers, attention has turned to other risk factors associated with this disease. The most meaningful predictor of the disease in a blood donor appears to be a high alanine aminotransferase (ALT, SGPT) value. Transfusion of a donor unit with an elevated ALT level of ≥ 45 IU/L significantly increases the recipient's risk of contracting non-A, non-B hepatitis.

Prevention & Control

A vaccine for hepatitis B is now available. Vaccine is prepared by purifying HBsAg associated with the 22-nm particles from healthy HBsAg-positive carriers. Protection is conferred by antibody to the *a* antigen, an antigen that is common to all subtypes. Preparations containing intact 22-nm particles have been highly effective in reducing HBV infection in hemodialysis patients and staff, among homosexuals, and in neonates born to HBV-infected mothers. Polypeptides derived from the 22-nm particles also have been tested in chimpanzees as a possible vaccine

for hepatitis B. Vaccinated chimpanzees developed antibodies and effectively resisted challenge with live HBV.

Since a source of large amounts of HAV has not been found, the development of a vaccine for hepatitis A depends on the future success of cell culture systems for growing the agent.

Until adequate supplies of vaccines become available, prevention and control of hepatitis must be directed toward interrupting the chain of transmission and using passive immunization.

A. Viral Hepatitis Type A: The appearance of hepatitis in camps or institutions is often an indication of poor sanitation and poor personal hygiene. Control measures are directed toward the prevention of fecal contamination of food, water, or other sources by the individual. Reasonable hygiene—such as hand washing after bowel movements or before meals, the use of disposable plates and eating utensils, and the use of 0.5% sodium hypochlorite (1:10 dilution of Clorox) as a disinfectant—is essential in preventing the spread of HAV during the acute phase of the illness. Extraordinarily conservative measures, such as the use of gowns, masks, and gloves, are usually unnecessary unless there is exposure to feces or fecally contaminated items. Infectivity studies indicate that the risk of transmitting hepatitis A is greatest from 2 weeks before to 1 week after the onset of jaundice. Transmission by the aerosol route appears relatively unimportant. (See General Properties of Viruses.)

Immune human serum globulin (ISG) is prepared from large pools of normal adult plasma and confers passive protection in 80–90% of those exposed when given within 1–2 weeks after exposure to hepatitis A. Its prophylactic value decreases with time, and its administration more than 4 weeks after exposure or after the onset of clinical symptoms is probably not indicated.

ISG does not prevent infection but rather makes the infection mild or subclinical and permits active immunity to develop. For ordinary exposure, the dose is 0.02 mL/kg given once or twice during the incubation period intramuscularly. For persons with continuing exposure (Peace Corps workers, military personnel, chimpanzee handlers, travelers to endemic areas), 0.05–0.1 mL/kg can be given every 4–6 months. Simplified guidelines for ISG prophylaxis against hepatitis A are shown in Table 32–3.

Table 32–3. Guidelines for ISG prophylaxis against hepatitis A.

Person's Weight (kg)	ISG Dose (mL)	
	Routine	High Risk* (Prolonged Exposure)
< 22	0.5	1.0
22–45	1.0	2.5
> 45	2.0	5.0

*Within limits, larger doses of ISG provide longer-lasting but not necessarily more protection. Therefore, more ISG is prescribed in high-risk situations where continuous exposure is anticipated (institutional contacts, travelers to foreign countries).

B. Viral Hepatitis Type B: Persons who have had hepatitis probably should not be used as blood donors. Even persons without a history of hepatitis and with normal liver function tests may be carriers of the virus. In addition, HBV carriers (or those with non-A, non-B hepatitis) may develop acute hepatitis A and the latter disease condition may go unrecognized. Sensitive methods for detecting HBsAg in blood donors are now being employed by all blood banks to avoid administering HBsAg-positive blood. Nevertheless, cases of posttransfusion hepatitis B continue to occur, although at a reduced frequency. Since the incidence of posttransfusion hepatitis (both B and non-B) is higher among recipients of commercial (paid donor) blood or blood from first-time donors, the establishment of an all-volunteer population who donate periodically is an important measure for eliminating transfusion-associated hepatitis. However, registries of minimal-risk donors who are known to be in good health should also provide satisfactory sources of blood, even if such persons are paid.

In transfused patients, the risk of contracting overt hepatitis appears to be reduced in recipients of glycerolized red blood cells. Administration of donor blood containing anti-HBs has not been associated with an increased incidence of hepatitis B following transfusion. Correspondingly, anti-HBs in the sera of recipients prior to transfusion appears to offer some protection against hepatitis B infections.

The resistance of HBV to physical and chemical agents makes it difficult to treat human blood and its products to render them safe for human inoculation. Autoclaving and the use of ethylene oxide gas are both acceptable methods for disinfecting metal objects, instruments, or heat-sensitive equipment. Another useful germicide is 2% activated glutaraldehyde.

Since as little as 0.0001 mL of plasma can transmit the disease, a single carrier of hepatitis B virus might "infect" a large batch of pooled plasma. It has been recommended, therefore, that pooled plasma not be used. If pools must be used, they should be made from no more than 5 donors and each unit tested for HBsAg by one of the more sensitive methods (eg, RIA) prior to pooling. Plasma should be used only in cases of emergency because of the possibility of transmitting hepatitis B to a patient who is already ill.

Studies on passive immunization using specific hepatitis B immune globulin have been encouraging. A special immune globulin from plasma containing anti-HBs with a titer 50,000 times greater than the standard commercial ISG was prepared and administered to 10 susceptible children 4 hours after they had been exposed to infectious serum (MS-2). Six subjects failed to develop HBs antigenemia or biochemical evidence of hepatitis, for a 60% level of protection. In contrast, all 11 control children who received the same dose of virus but without ISG became infected (HBsAg-positive).

Several studies that have compared placebo with ISG containing anti-HBs have indicated a protective effect if the latter is given soon after exposure. However, the concentration of antibody required for protection has not been adequately ascertained. In one study, the protective activity of 3 preparations of immune globulin containing varying levels of antibody to HBsAg was compared. Subjects included hospital personnel accidentally exposed to hepatitis B and newly admitted patients or recently hired employees of renal dialysis units. Since there was no placebo group and the results did not favor one anti-HBs preparation over another, any protective results are difficult to interpret. However, the incubation period of hepatitis B was prolonged significantly in those volunteers receiving the high-titer preparation.

Evidence of passive-active immunity was more frequently observed among newly admitted institutionalized patients who received standard ISG containing a low concentration of anti-HBs than among those treated with an anti-HBs-rich preparation of ISG. It is noteworthy that both preparations successfully prevented the development of a chronic carrier state. Similarly, administration of specific hepatitis B ISG (or conventional ISG with titers of anti-HBs greater than 1:256) to spouses of patients with acute type B hepatitis has been shown to be effective in preventing not only symptomatic type B hepatitis but the infection itself. However, passive-active immunity appeared to occur more frequently in susceptible individuals receiving conventional ISG.

Prevention of transfusion-associated hepatitis by the administration of standard ISG has not been consistently demonstrated in carefully conducted trials. Therefore, although hepatitis B ISG has been officially released for clinical use in exposure to small amounts of HBV, such as might occur with an accidental prick with a contaminated needle or direct mucous membrane contact arising from a splash or pipetting accident, its routine administration to recipients of blood transfusions is not recommended. The early reports on the use of the high-titer ISG to protect infants born to HBV positive mothers are very encouraging.

Proper donor selection and the development of a central registry for identification of carriers can lower the incidence of transfusion-associated hepatitis. In addition, blood or its products should be used only when necessary, since the risk of hepatitis appears to increase with the number of units administered. Hepatitis B virus may be transmitted to personnel in blood transfusion laboratories, but there is no evidence for the transmission of infection from members of the staff to blood or blood products.

Physicians should become aware that despite a low degree of contagiousness, a nonpercutaneous mode of transmission can occur in viral hepatitis type B, especially among sexual consorts and in closed populations (institutions).

The following information on control and prevention of type B hepatitis has been acquired from clinical and epidemiologic studies and is based on recommendations made by the Centers for Disease Control and the Committee on Viral Hepatitis of the National Academy of Sciences.

(1) A confirmed positive test for HBsAg is indicative of acute or chronic viral hepatitis type B or of the healthy carrier state.

(2) The presence of HBsAg in the blood of a patient with acute viral hepatitis type B is usually transient. HBs antigenemia that lasts more than 4 months after the onset of illness should be regarded as persistent antigenemia and specifies those persons likely to become chronic carriers of the antigen.

(3) The chronic carrier of HBsAg may or may not have demonstrable evidence of related liver disease.

(4) Testing for HBsAg by the most sensitive methods is now required for all blood donors. HBsAg carriers should be prohibited from donating blood.

(5) Although the infectiousness of hepatitis patients positive for HBsAg disappears when the antigen is no longer demonstrable in the blood and anti-HBs appears, such people currently are not accepted as blood donors.

(6) With respect to risk of transmission to others, there is no indication at this time that routine HBsAg testing of any specific professional or occupational group should be required. There may be circumstances, such as in dialysis centers or other areas of possible high risk, when it might be prudent to institute regular antigen and antibody testing for various members of the staff but, as a general rule, *routine* testing of professional or occupational groups should not be required on a regular basis.

(7) Immune serum globulin is of no demonstrable value in the treatment of HBsAg carriers.

(8) Persons who sustain percutaneous (eg, needlestick) exposure or contamination of mucosal surfaces with HBV should immediately receive ISG with a high titer of anti-HBs.

(9) All confirmed cases of type B hepatitis should be promptly reported to the local or state health department. This permits more accurate hepatitis surveillance and identifies epidemiologic trends.

(10) Persons identified in the course of diagnostic studies, blood donor testing, or seroepidemiologic investigations as transient or persistent carriers of HBsAg should be so informed and educated regarding the mechanisms of HBV spread so that they might reduce transmission to others. They should be examined for the presence of liver disease.

(11) Patients with acute type B hepatitis generally need not be isolated so long as blood and instrument precautions are stringently observed, both in the general patient care areas and in the laboratories. Staff should wear gloves or other protective clothing when in contact with blood or blood-contaminated objects from these patients.

(12) Because spouses and intimate contacts of persons with acute type B hepatitis are at greater risk of acquiring clinical type B hepatitis than those exposed to healthy carriers, they need to be warned about practices that might increase the risk of infection or transmission.

(13) There is no justification for removing HBsAg-positive carriers from patient contact in the absence of evidence of disease transmission. The use of gloves should reduce the potential for HBV transmission.

(14) There is no evidence that asymptomatic HBsAg-positive food handlers pose a health risk to the general public.

(15) Women who acquire type B hepatitis while pregnant can transmit the disease to their infants. The risk of transmission is increased during the third trimester and the postpartum period. Infants who become HBsAg-positive generally do so within 1–2 months, but testing should continue at monthly intervals for at least 6 months. Most develop persistent antigenemia, especially if the mother is also HBeAg-positive.

(16) The mechanisms that result in HBV dissemination are not well understood but may relate to viral replication reflected by hepatocellular injury, positive tests for DNA polymerase, and the presence of *e* antigen. Until more information is acquired, particularly with regard to the communicability of infection from the healthy carrier, only routine precautions such as those that apply to percutaneous routes of potential transmission should be initiated.

●   ●   ●

References

Blumberg BS: Australia antigen and the biology of hepatitis B. *Science* 1977;**197**:17.

Bradley DW et al: Serodiagnosis of viral hepatitis A by a modified competitive binding radioimmunoassay for immunoglobulin M anti-hepatitis A virus. *J Clin Microbiol* 1979;**9**:120.

Cummings IW et al: Isolation, characterization, and comparison of recombinant DNAs derived from genomes of human hepatitis B virus and woodchuck hepatitis virus. *Proc Natl Acad Sci USA* 1980;**77**:1842.

Daemer RJ et al: Propagation of human hepatitis A virus in African green monkey kidney cell culture: Primary isolation and serial passage. *Infect Immun* 1981;**32**:388.

Deinhardt F: Predictive value of markers of hepatitis virus infection. *J Infect Dis* 1980;**141**:299.

Edman JC et al: Synthesis of hepatitis B surface and core antigens in *E coli. Nature* 1981;**291**:503.

Greenberg HB et al: Effect of human leukocyte interferon on hepatitis B virus infection in patients with chronic active hepatitis. *N Engl J Med* 1976;**295**:517.

Hollinger FB, Dienstag JL: Hepatitis viruses. In: *Manual of Clinical Microbiology*, 3rd ed. Lennette EH (editor). American Society for Microbiology, 1980.

Krugman S, Giles JP: Viral hepatitis, type B (MS-2 strain): Further observations on natural history and prevention. *N Engl J Med* 1973;**288**:755.

Mathiesen LR et al: Enzyme-linked immunosorbent assay for detection of hepatitis A antigen in stool and antibody to hepatitis A antigen in sera: Comparison with solid-phase radioimmunoassay, immune electron microscopy, and immune adherence hemagglutination assay. *J Clin Microbiol* 1978;**7**:184.

Maupas P, Melnick JL (editors): Hepatitis B virus and primary hepatocellular carcinoma. *Prog Med Virol* 1981;No. 27. [Entire issue.]

Maupas P et al: Efficacy of hepatitis B vaccine in prevention of early HBsAg carrier state in children: Controlled trial in an endemic area (Senegal). *Lancet* 1981;**1**:289.

Melnick JL, Dreesman GR, Hollinger FB: Approaching the control of viral hepatitis type B. *J Infect Dis* 1976;**133**:210.

Melnick JL, Dreesman GR, Hollinger FB: Viral hepatitis. *Sci Am* (July) 1977;**237**:44.

Rizzetto M, Purcell RH, Gerin JL: Epidemiology of HBV-associated delta agent: Geographical distribution of anti-delta and prevalence in polytransfused HBsAg carriers. *Lancet* 1980;**1**:1215.

Roggendorf M et al: Immunoglobulin M antibodies to hepatitis B core antigen: Evaluation of enzyme immunoassay for diagnosis of hepatitis B virus infection. *J Clin Microbiol* 1981;**13**:618.

Szmuness W et al: Hepatitis B vaccine: Demonstration of efficacy in a controlled clinical trial in a high-risk population in the United States. *N Engl J Med* 1980;**303**:833.

Szmuness W et al: On the role of sexual behavior in the spread of hepatitis B infection. *Ann Intern Med* 1975;**83**:489.

Tiollais P, Charnay P, Vyas GN: Biology of hepatitis B virus. *Science* 1981;**213**:406.

Tsiquaye KN et al: Ultrastructural changes in the liver in experimental non-A, non-B hepatitis. *Br J Exp Pathol* 1981;**62**:41.

Vyas GN, Cohen SN, Schmid R (editors): *Viral Hepatitis: A Contemporary Assessment of Etiology, Epidemiology, Pathogenesis and Prevention*. Franklin Institute Press, 1978.

Wands JR et al: Immunodiagnosis of hepatitis B with high-affinity IgM monoclonal antibodies. *Proc Natl Acad Sci USA* 1981;**78**:1214.

Rabies & Other Viral Diseases of the Nervous System; Slow Viruses

RABIES

Rabies is an acute infection of the central nervous system that is almost always fatal. The virus is usually transmitted to humans from the bite of a rabid animal.

Properties of the Virus

A. Structure: Rabies virus is a rhabdovirus with morphologic and biochemical properties in common with vesicular stomatitis virus of cattle and several animal, plant, and insect viruses. The rhabdoviruses are rod- or bullet-shaped particles measuring 60–400 nm $\times$ 60–85 nm (Fig 27–35). The particles are surrounded by a membranous envelope with protruding spikes 10 nm long. Inside the envelope is a ribonucleocapsid. The genome is single-stranded RNA (MW 3–5 $\times$ 10^6) that is not infectious and does not serve as a messenger. Virions contain an RNA-dependent RNA polymerase.

B. Reactions to Physical and Chemical Agents: Rabies virus survives storage at 4 °C for weeks but is inactivated by CO_2. On dry ice, therefore, it must be stored in glass-sealed vials. Rabies virus is killed rapidly by exposure to ultraviolet radiation or sunlight, by heat (1 hour at 50 °C), by lipid solvents (ether, 0.1% sodium deoxycholate), and by trypsin.

C. Animal Susceptibility and Growth of Virus: Rabies virus has a wide host range. All warm-blooded animals, including humans, are susceptible. The virus is widely distributed in infected animals, especially in the nervous system, saliva, urine, lymph, milk, and blood. Recovery from infection is rare except in certain bats, where the virus has become peculiarly adapted to the salivary glands. Vampire bats may transmit the virus for months without themselves ever showing any signs of disease.

When freshly isolated in the laboratory, the strains are referred to as street virus. Such strains show long and variable incubation periods (usually 21–60 days in dogs) and regularly produce intracytoplasmic inclusion bodies. Inoculated animals may exhibit long periods of excitement and viciousness. The virus may invade the salivary glands as well as the central nervous system.

Serial brain-to-brain passage in rabbits yields a "fixed" virus that no longer multiplies in extraneural tissues. This fixed virus multiplies rapidly, and the incubation period is shortened to 4–6 days. At this stage, inclusion bodies are found only with difficulty.

The virus may be propagated in chick embryos, baby hamster kidney cells, and human diploid cell cultures. One strain (Flury), after serial passage in chick embryos, has been modified so that it fails to produce disease in animals injected extraneurally. This attenuated virus is used for vaccination of animals.

The replication of rabies virus is similar to that of the most studied rhabdovirus, vesicular stomatitis virus. The single-stranded RNA genome of molecular weight 4.6 $\times$ 10^6 is transcribed by the virion-associated RNA polymerase to 5 mRNA species that are complementary to parts of the genome. These mRNAs code for the 5 virion proteins. The genome is a template for a replicative intermediate responsible for the generation of progeny RNA. After encapsidation, the bullet-shaped particles acquire the envelope by budding through the cytoplasmic membrane.

D. Antigenic Properties: The purified spikes elicit neutralizing antibody in animals. Antiserum prepared against the purified nucleocapsid is used in diagnostic immunofluorescence.

Pathogenesis & Pathology

Rabies virus multiplies in muscle or connective tissue and is propagated through the endoneurium of the Schwann cells or associated tissue spaces of the sensory nerves to the central nervous system. It multiplies there and may then spread through peripheral nerves to the salivary glands and other tissues. Rabies virus has not been isolated from the blood of infected persons.

The incubation period may depend on the amount of inoculum, severity of lacerations, and distance the virus has to travel from its point of entry to the brain. There is a higher attack rate and shorter incubation period in persons bitten on the face or head.

There are hyperemia and nerve cell destruction in the cortex, midbrain, basal ganglia, pons, and especially in the medulla. Demyelinization occurs in the white matter, and degeneration of axons and myelin sheaths is common. In the spinal cord, the posterior horns are most severely involved, with neuronophagia and cellular infiltrates (mononuclear, perivascular, and perineural).

Rabies virus produces a specific cytoplasmic inclusion, the Negri body, in infected nerve cells. The presence of such inclusions is pathognomonic of rabies but may not be observed in all cases. The inclusions are eosinophilic, sharply demarcated, and more or less spherical, with diameters of $2-10$ μm. Several may be found in the cytoplasm of large neurons. They occur throughout the brain and spinal cord but are most frequent in Ammon's horn. Negri bodies contain rabies virus antigens and can be demonstrated by immunofluorescence.

Rabies virus multiplies outside the central nervous system and may produce cellular infiltrates and necrosis in salivary and other glands, in the cornea, and elsewhere.

The post-rabies vaccine reaction is an allergic encephalomyelitis (see Chapter 13).

Clinical Findings

The usual incubation period in dogs ranges from 3 to 8 weeks, but it may be as short as 10 days. Clinically, the disease in dogs is divided into 3 phases: prodromal, excitative, and paralytic. The prodromal phase is characterized by fever and a sudden change in the temperament of the animal; docile animals may become snappy and irritable, whereas aggressive animals may become more affectionate. The excitative phase lasts $3-7$ days, during which the dog shows symptoms of irritability, restlessness, nervousness, and exaggerated response to sudden light and sound stimuli. At this stage the animal is most dangerous because of its tendency to bite. The animal has difficulty in swallowing, suffers from convulsive seizures, and enters into a paralytic stage with paralysis of the whole body, coma, and death. Sometimes the animal goes into the paralytic stage without passing through the excitative stage.

The incubation period in humans varies from 2 to 16 weeks or more, but in many cases it is only $2-3$ weeks. It is usually shorter in children than in adults. The clinical spectrum can be divided into 4 phases: a short prodromal phase, a sensory phase, a period of excitement, and a paralytic or depressive phase. The prodrome, lasting $2-4$ days, may show any of the following: malaise, anorexia, headache, nausea and vomiting, sore throat, and fever. Usually there is an abnormal sensation around the site of infection. The patient may show increasing nervousness and apprehension. General sympathetic overactivity is observed, including lacrimation, pupillary dilatation, and increased salivation and perspiration. The act of swallowing precipitates a spasm of the throat muscles; a patient may allow saliva to drool from the mouth simply to avoid swallowing and the associated painful spasms. (Because of the patient's apparent fear of water, the disease has been known as hydrophobia since ancient days.) This phase is followed by convulsive seizures or coma and death, usually $3-5$ days following onset. Progressive paralytic symptoms may develop before death.

Hysteria may simulate certain features of rabies, particularly in persons who have been near a rabid animal or have been bitten by a nonrabid one.

Laboratory Diagnosis

A. Microscopy: Tissues infected with rabies virus are currently identified most rapidly and accurately by means of direct immunofluorescence using antirabies hamster serum. (See Chapter 28.) Impression preparations of brain or cornea tissue are often used.

A definitive pathologic diagnosis of rabies is based on the finding of Negri bodies in the brain (especially Ammon's horn) or the spinal cord. Negri bodies are found in impression preparations or histologic sections. They are sharply demarcated, more or less spherical, and $2-10$ μm in diameter, and they have a distinctive internal structure with basophilic granules in an eosinophilic matrix. Negri bodies (and rabies antigen) can usually be found in animals or humans suffering from rabies or dead from the infection, but they are rarely found in bats.

B. Virus Isolation: Available tissue (or saliva) is inoculated intracerebrally into mice. Infection in mice results in flaccid paralysis of legs, encephalitis, and death. The central nervous system of the inoculated animal is examined for Negri bodies and rabies antigen. In specialized laboratories, hamster and mouse cell lines can be inoculated for rapid ($2-4$ day) growth of rabies virus; this is much faster than growth in mice. An isolated virus is identified by neutralization tests with specific antiserum.

C. Serology: Antibodies to rabies can be detected by immunofluorescence, complement fixation, or neutralization. Such antibodies may develop in infected persons or animals during progression of the disease.

All animals considered "rabid or suspected rabid" (Table 33–1) should be sacrificed immediately for laboratory examination of tissues. Other animals, if available, should be held for observation for 10 days. If they show any signs of encephalitis, rabies, or unusual behavior, they should be killed humanely and the tissues examined in the laboratory. On the other hand, if they appear normal after 10 days, decisions must be made on an individual basis in consultation with public health officials.

Immunity & Prevention

Only one antigenic type of rabies virus is known. More than 99% of infections in humans and mammals who develop symptoms end fatally. Survival after proved rabies infection is extremely rare. It is therefore essential that individuals at high risk receive preventive immunization, that the nature and risk of any exposure be evaluated (Table 33–1), and that individuals be given postexposure prophylaxis if their exposure is believed to have been dangerous.

A. Pathophysiology of Rabies Prevention by Vaccine: It is likely that rabies virus remains latent in tissues for some time after virus is introduced from a bite. If immunogenic vaccine or antibody can be administered promptly, the virus can be prevented from invading the central nervous system. The action of passively administered antibody is to provide addi-

Table 33—1. Rabies postexposure prophylaxis guide, 1980.*

The following recommendations are only a guide. In applying them, take into account the animal species involved, the circumstances of the bite or other exposure, the vaccination status of the animal, and presence of rabies in the region. *Local or state public health officials should be consulted if questions arise about the need for rabies prophylaxis.*

Animal Species	Condition of Animal at Time of Attack	Treatment of Exposed Person†
Domestic Dog and cat	Healthy and available for 10 days of observation	None, unless animal develops rabies‡
	Rabid or suspected rabid	RIG§ and HDCV**
	Unknown (escaped)	Consult public health officials. If treatment is indicated, give RIG§ and HDCV**
Wild Skunk, bat, fox, coyote, raccoon, bobcat, and other carnivores	Regard as rabid unless proved negative by laboratory tests††	RIG§ and HDCV**
Other Livestock, rodents, and lagomorphs (rabbits and hares)	Consider individually. Local and state public health officials should be consulted on questions about the need for rabies prophylaxis. Bites of squirrels, hamsters, guinea pigs, gerbils, chipmunks, rats, mice, other rodents, rabbits, and hares almost never call for antirabies prophylaxis.	

*Reproduced, with permission, from *MMWR* (June) 1980;29:279.

†*All bites and wounds should immediately be thoroughly cleansed with soap and water.* If antirabies treatment is indicated, both rabies immune globulin (RIG) and human diploid cell rabies vaccine (HDCV) should be given as soon as possible, *regardless* of the interval from exposure.

‡During the usual holding period of 10 days, begin treatment with RIG and vaccine (preferably HDCV) at first sign of rabies in a dog or cat that has bitten someone. The symptomatic animal should be killed immediately and tested.

§If RIG is not available, use antirabies serum, equine (ARS). Do not use more than the recommended dosage.

**If HDCV is not available, use duck embryo vaccine (DEV). Local reactions to vaccines are common and do not contraindicate continuing treatment. Discontinue vaccine if fluorescent antibody (FA) tests of the animal are negative.

††The animal should be killed and tested as soon as possible. Holding for observation is not recommended.

tional time for a vaccine to stimulate active antibody production before the central nervous system is invaded.

B. Types of Vaccines: All vaccines for human use contain only inactivated rabies virus.

1. Nerve tissue vaccine–This is made from infected sheep, goat, or mouse brains and used in many parts of the world including Asia, Africa, and South America. It causes sensitization to nerve tissue and results in postvaccinal encephalitis (an allergic disease) with substantial frequency (0.05%). It has not been used in the USA for several decades. Estimates of its efficacy in persons bitten by rabid animals vary from 5% to 50%.

2. Duck embryo vaccine–This was developed to minimize the problem of postvaccinal encephalitis. The rabies virus is grown in embryonated duck eggs, but the head is removed before the vaccine is prepared so as to remove nervous tissue and avoid allergic encephalitis. It produces local reactions regularly and systemic reactions (fever, malaise, myalgia) in one-third of recipients. Neuroparalytic ($< 0.001\%$) and anaphylactic ($< 1\%$) reactions are infrequent, but the antigenicity of the vaccine is low. Consequently, many (16–25) doses have to be given to obtain a satisfactory postexposure antibody response. This was the vaccine used in the USA in the recent past.

3. Human diploid cell vaccine (HDCV)–To obtain a rabies virus suspension free from nervous system and foreign proteins, rabies virus was adapted to growth in the WI-38 human normal fibroblast cell line. The rabies virus harvest is concentrated by ultrafiltration and inactivated with beta propiolactone or tri-N-butyl phosphate. This material is sufficiently antigenic that only 4–6 doses of virus (Table 33–2) need to be given to obtain a substantial antibody response in most recipients. Local reactions (erythema, itching, swelling at the injection site) occur in 25% of recipients, and mild systemic reactions (headache, nausea, myalgia, dizziness) occur in about one-fifth of recipients. No serious anaphylactic, neuroparalytic, or encephalitic reactions have been reported. This vaccine has been used in the USA since 1979 and is the immunizing agent of choice.

4. Live attenuated viruses adapted to growth in chick embryos (eg, Flury strain) are used for animals but *not* for humans. Occasionally, such vaccines can cause death from rabies in injected cats or dogs. Rabies viruses grown in various animal cell cultures have also been used as vaccines for domestic animals.

C. Types of Available Rabies Antibody:

1. Rabies immune globulin, human (RIG)–This is a gamma globulin prepared by cold ethanol fractionation from the plasma of hyperimmunized humans. The neutralizing antibody content is standardized to contain 150 IU/mL. The dose is 20 IU/kg, half given around the bite wound, half intramuscularly.

Table 33–2. Rabies immunization regimens, 1980.*

Preexposure: Preexposure rabies prophylaxis for persons with special risks of exposure to rabies, such as animal-care and control personnel and selected laboratory workers, consists of immunization with either human diploid cell rabies vaccine (HDCV) or duck embryo vaccine (DEV), according to the following schedule.

Rabies Vaccine	Number of 1-mL Doses	Route of Administration	Intervals Between Doses	If No Antibody Response to Primary Series, Give—†
HDCV	3	Intramuscular	One week between 1st and 2nd; 2–3 weeks between 2nd and 3rd‡	One booster dose‡
DEV	3 or 4	Subcutaneous	One month between 1st and 2nd; 6–7 months between 2nd and 3rd‡ *or* One week between 1st, 2nd, and 3rd; 3 months between 3rd and 4th‡	Two booster doses,‡ 1 week apart

Postexposure: Postexposure rabies prophylaxis for persons exposed to rabies consists of the immediate, thorough cleansing of all wounds with soap and water, administration of rabies immune globulin (RIG) or, if RIG is not available, antirabies serum, equine (ARS), and the initiation of either HDCV or DEV, according to the following schedule.§

HDCV	5**	Intramuscular	Doses to be given on days 0, 3, 7, 14, and 28‡	An additional booster dose‡
DEV	23	Subcutaneous	Twenty-one daily doses followed by a booster on day 31 and another on day 41‡ *or* Two daily doses in the first 7 days, followed by 7 daily doses. Then one booster on day 24 and another on day 34‡	Three doses of HDCV at weekly intervals‡

*Reproduced, with permission, from *MMWR* (June) 1980;**29**:280.

†If no antibody response is documented after the recommended additional booster dose(s), consult the state health department or CDC.

‡Serum for rabies antibody testing should be collected 2–3 weeks after the last dose.

§The postexposure regimen is greatly modified for someone with previously demonstrated rabies antibody.

**The World Health Organization recommends a sixth dose 90 days after the first dose.

2. Antirabies serum, equine (ARS)–This is concentrated serum from horses hyperimmunized with rabies virus. The neutralizing antibody content is standardized to contain 1000 IU per vial (approximately 5 mL). The dose is 40 IU/kg.

D. Choice of Rabies Immunizing Products: This is an application of the risk/benefit ratio, as far as known for each product. HDCV has the greatest efficacy among known vaccines in stimulating antibody production, and few adverse effects are associated with it. There are fewer reactions to RIG (especially rare serum sickness, anaphylaxis) than to ARS, and RIG has a much longer half-life, since it is protein homologous for the human recipient.

E. Preexposure Prophylaxis: This is indicated for persons at high risk of contact with rabid animals. The goal is to attain an antibody level presumed to be protective by means of vaccine administration prior to any exposure. Current suggested schedules are shown in Table 33–2.

F. Postexposure Prophylaxis: Since 1960, 1–5 cases of human rabies have occurred in the USA per year, but every year 20–30 thousand persons receive some treatment for possible bite-wound exposure. *All* bites should be thoroughly cleaned with soap and water immediately, and tetanus prophylaxis should be considered. The decision to administer rabies antibody, rabies vaccine, or both, depends on (1) the nature of

the biting animal (see Table 33–1) and its vaccination status; *all* bites by wild animals and bats require RIG and HDCV; (2) the existence of rabies in the area; (3) the manner of attack (provoked or unprovoked) and the severity of bite and contamination by saliva of the animal; and (4) advice from local public health officials. Schedules for postexposure prophylaxis involving the administration of RIG (or ARS) and HDCV (or DEV) are shown in the 1980 recommendations for the USA (Table 33–2). Different materials and schedules may be proposed in other parts of the world depending on availability of products and local experience.

Epidemiology

About 1000 cases of human rabies are reported each year to the World Health Organization, most of them in developing countries, eg, India, Southeast Asia, the Philippines, North Africa, and South America. In these countries, most human cases develop from the bite of rabid dogs, and perhaps 1 million persons are given postexposure prophylaxis yearly.

In the USA, Canada, and western Europe, cases of human rabies develop from bites of wild animals (especially skunks, foxes, and bats) or are imported by travelers bitten elsewhere in the world. In South America, near Trinidad, rabies is transmitted especially by vampire bats that normally suck the blood of cattle (and may cause outbreaks among them) but may also bite humans. The increase in wildlife rabies in the USA and some other developed countries presents a far greater risk to humans than dogs or cats do. Wild animals trapped and sold as pets can be the source of human exposure.

Bats present a special problem because they may carry rabies virus while they appear to be healthy, excrete it in saliva, and transmit it to other animals, including other bats, and to humans. South American vampire bats may transmit rabies to insectivorous bats living in caves. The latter, in turn, may transmit rabies to fruit-eating bats that visit such caves and migrate elsewhere. Bat caves may contain aerosols of rabies virus and present a risk to spelunkers. Migrating fruit-eating bats exist in all 48 contiguous states of the USA, in Canada, and in Latin America. They are a source of infection for many animals and humans. They may exhibit unusual behavior (because of encephalitis) that attracts the attention of people and leads to bites. *All persons bitten by bats must receive postexposure prophylaxis.*

Human-to-human rabies infection is very rare. It can originate from the saliva of a patient who has rabies and exposes attending personnel. Recently, rabies has been transmitted from corneal transplants—the corneas came from donors who died with undiagnosed central nervous system diseases; the recipients died from rabies 50–80 days later.

Control

Isolated countries, eg, Britain, that have no indigenous rabies in wild animals can establish quarantine procedures. Dogs and other pets to be imported are quarantined for 6–12 months. In countries where dog rabies exists, stray animals should be destroyed and vaccination of pet dogs and cats should be mandatory. In countries where wildlife rabies exists and where contact between domestic animals, pets, and wildlife is inevitable, all domestic animals and pets should be vaccinated and the incidence of rabies in wild animals should be continually ascertained.

Preexposure vaccination is desirable for all persons who are at high risk of contact with rabid animals (Table 33–2). This applies particularly to veterinarians, animal care personnel, certain laboratory workers, and spelunkers. It also applies to persons who expect to live in areas of high rabies prevalence, eg, military personnel, Peace Corps workers, and some travelers.

Animals that appear healthy but have made an unprovoked attack upon and bitten a person should be quarantined for at least 10 days (see Laboratory Diagnosis, above).

ASEPTIC MENINGITIS

This syndrome is characterized by acute onset, fever, headache, and stiff neck. There is pleocytosis of the spinal fluid, consisting largely of mononuclear cells. The fluid is bacteria-free, with a normal glucose content and often a slightly elevated protein content.

Etiology

Aseptic meningitis may be caused by a variety of agents: (1) primarily neurotropic viruses (poliomyelitis, lymphocytic choriomeningitis, and arthropod-borne encephalitis viruses); (2) viruses not primarily neurotropic (enteroviruses, mumps, herpes simplex, herpes zoster, infectious mononucleosis, infectious hepatitis, varicella, and measles); (3) spirochetes (*Treponema pallidum* and leptospirae); (4) bacteria, as in silent brain abscess and inadequately treated bacterial meningitis; and (5) mycoplasmas or chlamydiae.

Diagnosis

The diagnosis of aseptic viral meningitis is made by exclusion of bacterial causes of the symptom complex. Specific etiologic causes of aseptic meningitis can usually be determined only by isolation of the agent or the demonstration of a rise in specific antibodies. However, epidemiologic features have diagnostic value. (See discussions of specific agents.)

Laboratory Findings

The peripheral white count is usually normal, but in lymphocytic choriomeningitis, eosinophilia may appear a few days after onset. There is pleocytosis of the cerebrospinal fluid; polymorphonuclear cells often predominate during the first 24 hours, but a shift to lymphocytes usually occurs thereafter. The range is 100–800 cells or more. In lymphocytic choriomeningitis there may be 500–3000 cells or more. Protein levels of the spinal fluid are often elevated, but the glucose level is within normal limits.

LYMPHOCYTIC CHORIOMENINGITIS

Lymphocytic choriomeningitis (LCM) is an acute disease with aseptic meningitis or a mild systemic influenzalike illness. Occasionally there is a severe encephalomyelitis or a fatal systemic disease. The incubation period is usually 18–21 days but may be as short as 1–3 days. The mild systemic form is rarely recognized clinically. There may be fever, malaise, generalized muscle aches and pains, weakness, sore throat, and cough. The fever lasts for 3–14 days.

LCM is an RNA-containing arenavirus (see Chapter 30) 50–150 nm in diameter.

Diagnosis

Specific diagnosis can be made by the isolation of virus from spinal fluid or blood during the acute phase and by tests demonstrating a rise in antibody titer between acute and convalescent serum specimens. Complement-fixing antibodies rise to diagnostic levels in 3–4 weeks, then fall gradually and reach normal levels after several months. Neutralizing antibodies appear later and reach diagnostic levels 7–8 weeks after onset; they may persist for 4–5 years.

Laboratory Findings

In the prodromal period (or mild systemic form),

leukopenia with relative lymphocytosis is frequently present. In the meningitic form, there is pleocytosis in the spinal fluid (100–3000 cells/μL), with a predominance of lymphocytes. The glucose is normal and the protein content slightly elevated.

Epidemiology & Control

The disease is endemic in mice and other animals (dogs, monkeys, guinea pigs) and is occasionally transmitted to humans. One large epidemic in the USA was caused by infected pet hamsters. There is no evidence of person-to-person spread.

Infected gray house mice, probably the most common source of human infection, excrete the virus in urine and feces. The virus may be harbored by mice throughout their lives, and females transmit it to their offspring, which in turn become healthy carriers. Mice inoculated as adults develop a rapidly fatal generalized infection. In contrast, congenitally or neonatally infected mice do not become acutely ill, but 10–12 months later many develop a fatal debilitating disease involving the central nervous system. The animals exhibit chronic glomerulonephritis and hypergammaglobulinemia; the glomerular lesions are due to deposition of antigen-antibody complexes, and the infection in mice is considered an immune complex disease (see Slow Virus Diseases, below). The mode of transmission from mice to humans is uncertain. Mice and their droppings should be controlled.

ENCEPHALITIS LETHARGICA
(Von Economo's Disease)

Several thousand cases of this acute type of encephalitis occurred during the winter seasons between 1915 and 1926. The disease has not been seen in recent years. A virus is presumed to have been the cause. The pathologic findings were similar to those produced by the neurotropic viruses. Onset was gradual, with malaise, headache, fever, and aching of joints and muscles; this was followed by signs suggesting mesencephalic involvement. Somnolence and stupor were common. The case fatality rate was about 40%. Neurologic sequelae (eg, paralysis agitans) were common in survivors.

EPIDEMIC NEUROMYASTHENIA
(Benign Myalgic Encephalomyelitis)

A number of outbreaks of epidemic neuromyasthenia have been reported in Europe and the USA. No causative agent has been isolated, although viruses are believed to play a role. The main features of the disease are fatigue, headache, intense muscle pain, slight and transient paresis, mental disturbances, and objective evidence of diffuse involvement of the central nervous system. It is sometimes confused with poliomyelitis. Young and middle-aged adults are principally affected. Sporadic cases have also been reported.

ENCEPHALOMYOCARDITIS
VIRUS INFECTION
(Mengo Fever)

The virus has been recovered in several regions of the world, but only rare human infections have been reported. In one well studied case, the patient had fever, headache, nuchal rigidity, vomiting, and short periods of delirium. The virus was isolated from the blood on the first and second days of illness, and antibodies appeared during convalescence. In a few cases, sera from individuals suffering from central nervous system diseases neutralized the virus.

The virus is pathogenic for many animals, including mice, guinea pigs, monkeys, and chick embryos. It has been isolated in nature from the cotton rat, mongoose, rhesus monkey, baboon, chimpanzee, and *Taeniorhynchus* mosquitoes. The virus can cause lesions in the central nervous system and in skeletal and cardiac muscle. An outbreak of fatal myocarditis caused by this virus has been observed in pigs.

The agent belongs to the picornavirus family. It has a diameter of about 25 nm and contains 30% RNA. It is a satisfactory antigen in the CF test and also agglutinates sheep erythrocytes. Antibodies can be measured by Nt, CF, and HI methods.

SLOW VIRUS DISEASES: CHRONIC VIRAL DISEASES OF THE CENTRAL NERVOUS SYSTEM & OTHER PROGRESSIVE DEGENERATIVE DISORDERS

Some chronic degenerative diseases of the central nervous system of humans are caused by "slow" or chronic, persistent virus infections. Among these are kuru, Creutzfeldt-Jakob disease, and subacute sclerosing panencephalitis. For other entities, a viral cause may also be found.

Several animal viruses produce chronic infections of the central nervous system that result in progressive degenerative changes. These animal infections serve as models for similar disorders of humans. These diseases include visna of sheep in Iceland, scrapie of sheep in Britain, and transmissible mink encephalopathy. The progressive neurologic diseases produced by these viruses may have incubation periods of up to 5 years before the clinical manifestations of the infections become evident.

Visna and **progressive pneumonia (maedi) viruses** are closely related agents that cause slow infections in sheep. These viruses share features with RNA tumor viruses, and both are called retroviruses. The similarities include the following: virion assembly and maturation by a budding process, virion size (70–100 nm), the presence of virion-associated RNA-directed DNA polymerase (reverse transcriptase), 4S and 70S RNA, and a similar polypeptide profile (see Chapter 40). Several structural similarities also exist.

Visna virus infects all of the organs of the body of the infected sheep; however, pathologic changes are

Table 33–3. Slow virus infections.

Disease	Virus	Host(s)	Incubation Period	Nature of Disease
Diseases of humans				
Kuru	< 220 nm (probably < 100 nm)	Humans (chimpanzees, monkeys)	Months to years	Spongiform encephalopathy
Creutzfeldt-Jakob (C-J) disease	?	Humans (chimpanzees, monkeys)	Months to years	Spongiform encephalopathy
Subacute sclerosing panencephalitis (SSPE)	Measles variant	Humans	2–20 years	Chronic sclerosing panencephalitis
Progressive multifocal leukoencephalopathy (PML)	Papovavirus	Humans	?	CNS demyelination
Diseases of animals				
Scrapie	< 50 nm, perhaps 14 nm	Sheep (goats, mice)	Months to years	Spongiform encephalopathy
Transmissible mink encephalopathy (TME)	35 nm	Mink (other animals)	Months	Spongiform encephalopathy
Visna	70–100 nm (oncornaviruslike)	Sheep	Months to years	CNS demyelination
Aleutian disease of mink	25 nm	Mink	Months	Immune complex disease
Lymphocytic choriomeningitis (LCM)	50–150 nm	Mice (humans occasionally infected)	Months (in mice)	Immune complex disease (in congenitally or neonatally infected mice)

confined primarily to the brain, lungs, and reticuloendothelial system. There is a long incubation period, and virus can be recovered from the animal as long as 4 years after inoculation. Infected animals develop antibodies to the virus; these can be detected in the cerebrospinal fluid as well as the serum of sick animals.

Spongiform Encephalopathies of Humans & Animals

Four degenerative central nervous system diseases—**kuru** and **Creutzfeldt-Jakob disease** of humans, **scrapie** of sheep, and **transmissible encephalopathy** of mink—have similar pathologic features. There appears to be no antibody or cellular immune response. Although filtration experiments suggest a definite size for the particles, they are not visible by electron microscopy. The agents are extraordinarily resistant to heat, 10% formol saline, and ultraviolet irradiation, but infectivity is destroyed by phenol, ether, and DNase. Perhaps they are small DNA molecules (in the same size range as "viroids"; see Chapter 27) without a protein coat.

Scrapie, which behaves as a recessive genetic trait in sheep, shows marked differences in susceptibility of different breeds. Susceptibility to experimentally transmitted scrapie ranges from zero to over 80% in sheep, whereas goats are almost 100% susceptible. The transmission of scrapie to mice, in which the incubation period is greatly reduced, has facilitated study of the disease. Scrapie has also been transmitted to a laboratory monkey. The scrapie agent has been adapted to mouse passage. The incubation period depends on inoculum size and mouse genotype; it ranges from 100 days to almost the life span of the mouse. The long incubation period is probably due to the slow rate of multiplication of the agent in the brain.

The unusual stability of the scrapie agent (see above) may be attributable to its intimate association with cell membranes. The smallest fragment with infectivity can be removed by filters with a pore diameter of 25 nm.

Transmissible mink encephalopathy (TME) is caused by a virus that induces clinical disease and neurologic lesions in the gray matter of the brain similar to those of scrapie. The virus has properties similar to scrapie. It also has a long incubation period in mink that are naturally infected—presumably by the oral route. Some believe that TME represents a strain of sheep scrapie acquired by mink fed infected sheep meat.

Two human spongiform encephalopathies are caused by "slow viruses," producing lesions similar to those of scrapie and TME. These are Creutzfeldt-Jakob disease and kuru. Brain material from patients who died from either disease can produce similar diseases when injected into chimpanzees. The serial passage of diseased chimpanzee brain into healthy chimpanzees transfers the illness. The viruses have also been transmitted to other primates but not yet to small laboratory animals. Both agents remain infective after brain tissue has been stored in 10% formol saline for 1–2 weeks.

Kuru occurs only in the eastern highlands of New Guinea. The disease consists of relentless progressive cerebellar ataxia, tremors, dysarthria, and emotional lability without significant dementia. It occurs more frequently in women than in men, which coincides with the customs surrounding cannibalism. The remains of dead relatives were handled and eaten primarily by women and children. Since cannibalism has been outlawed, the incidence of the disease has decreased, and it is now felt that this was the primary mode of transmission of the agent.

Creutzfeldt-Jakob disease (C-J disease, subacute presenile dementia) develops gradually, with progressive dementia, myoclonic fasciculations, ataxia, and somnolence, and leads to death in 8–12 months. The histologic lesions resemble those of kuru. C-J disease has been transmitted accidentally from one person to another by a corneal transplant, leading to death of the recipient 18 months later. Brain material from the recipient was kept in 10% formol saline for 7 months, then injected into a chimpanzee who developed signs of C-J disease 17 months later. Both kuru and C-J disease fail to show cerebrospinal fluid pleocytosis or abnormalities in sedimentation rate, blood chemistry, or body temperature. C-J disease is a rare diagnosis.

The histopathology of spongiform encephalopathies (kuru, C-J disease, scrapie, TEM) is fairly similar—intracytoplasmic vacuolation in the axonal and dendritic processes of neurons, with coalescence of vacuoles and destruction of cells. Several other spongiform encephalopathies and progressive dementias (Alpers' disease, Pick's disease, Alzheimer's disease) are also suspected of having a viral cause.

Other Central Nervous System Degenerative Disorders

Subacute sclerosing panencephalitis (SSPE) is a rare disease of teenagers and young adults, with slowly progressive demyelination in the central nervous system ending in death. In involved brain cells, structures are visible in electron microscopic studies that resemble the nucleocapsid of paramyxoviruses. By co-cultivation with HeLa cells, lymph node material or brain material from SSPE patients has yielded isolates of viruses that closely resemble measles virus. Some isolates differ from measles in the electrophoretic behavior of a single protein, the internal membrane or M viral protein, which plays a key role in viral assembly at the cell membrane. SSPE patients have high titers of antimeasles antibody (IgG) in both serum and cerebrospinal fluid. However, antibody to the M protein is lacking. The lack of M protein explains one characteristic of SSPE: persistence of infection but no production of mature infectious virus.

It is possible that SSPE represents a tolerant infection with defective cell-mediated responses in which latent measles virus persists for years. This may be the result of an immunologic dysfunction of the host, of a change in the virus so that some antigens are missing or are not expressed while the viral genetic information persists in host cells, or of both features. Experimentally, persistent infection with measles virus can be established in cell culture where some viral antigens are not expressed on the host cell surface, and such cells are not killed by lymphocytes (see Chapter 35).

A progressive panencephalitis has also been reported in patients with congenital **rubella**. The neurologic illness developed in the second decade and consisted of spasticity, ataxia, seizures, and progressive decline in intellectual ability.

Papovaviruses (see Chapter 40) have been isolated from brain tissue of patients with **progressive multifocal leukoencephalopathy (PML)**, a rare central nervous system complication found in patients suffering from chronic leukemia, Hodgkin's disease, lymphosarcoma, or carcinomatosis or in others receiving immunosuppressants. A causative role for papovaviruses has not been established.

The virus most often isolated, the JC subtype, is distinct antigenically and biologically from known papovaviruses. From the urine of renal transplant patients receiving immunosuppressive therapy, a papovavirus BK subtype has been isolated. JC and BK viruses are antigenically related to each other and to SV40.

The human papovaviruses BK and JC commonly infect humans; antibodies to them are found in 70–80% of human sera. Antibody specific to SV40 occurs in about 3% of human sera.

In hamsters, the JC isolate induces brain tumors that resemble glioblastomas and medulloblastomas but without demyelination. BK lacks this oncogenicity but can transform hamster cells in culture.

A PML-like disease occurs spontaneously in macaques, and papovavirus particles have been isolated from 7 of 8 cases. Additional work is necessary to determine if JC virus is the etiologic agent of PML.

Chronic virus infections may be associated with other progressive degenerative diseases of the central nervous system of humans, eg, **"amyotrophic lateral sclerosis."**

Multiple sclerosis (MS) is a degenerative disorder of the central nervous system, with diffuse involvement beginning in early adult life and a varied course for 10–20 years. The gamma globulin in the cerebrospinal fluid is elevated, but antibodies to no one virus are regularly elevated. While MS has been associated with paramyxovirus and coronavirus isolation occasionally, the etiology is not understood. There may be viral, immunologic, and genetic aspects. Quite possibly, MS represents an autoimmune reaction to central nervous system involvement by viruses, which may remain latent for the life of the host.

In the chronic diseases mentioned above (progressive multifocal leukoencephalopathy, subacute sclerosing panencephalitis, multiple sclerosis), as well as in systemic lupus erythematosus and sarcoidosis, antibodies to different viruses are often present at levels higher than in matched controls. What is not yet known is whether the high levels (1) occur before the chronic disease, indicating a viral cause; (2) occur at the same time the chronic disease becomes manifest, as a result of a common defect in immunity; or (3) occur after the chronic disease is visible, as a result of a decrease in cell-mediated immunity brought on by the disease.

Another cause of persistent infections has been reported. DNA transcripts of an RNA virus (measles) were observed to be integrated into the DNA of chronically infected cell cultures.

Immune Complex Diseases

In a number of the human progressive degenerative disorders of suspected viral cause, the immunologic response of the host to the virus may be responsible for the pathologic changes and for the clinical illness (see Chapter 27). Two diseases of animals that serve as models in exploring this type of pathogenesis are lymphocytic choriomeningitis (LCM) in mice (see above) and Aleutian disease of mink. In both diseases, the virus appears to persist in the chronically infected animal as a virus-antibody complex in which the antibody is unable to neutralize and eliminate the virus. Deposition of these antigen-antibody complexes throughout a relatively long period of infection may produce the basic lesions of the disease.

Aleutian disease of mink is a chronic immune complex disease initiated by a 25-nm virus. Aleutian mink die in 3–6 months after infection, but other genetic types of mink survive longer. Virus circulates from the acute stage of infection onward and can be found in many organs and in serum and urine. Antibody is produced in large quantity, so there is IgG hyperglobulinemia. The virus complexes with the antibody without being neutralized. Virus-antibody complexes circulate and then deposit in glomeruli, leading to renal failure and death. The failure of virus neutralization and elimination by the excess antibody is not entirely understood.

●   ●   ●

References

Anderson LJ et al: Clinical experience with a human diploid cell rabies vaccine. *JAMA* 1980;**244**:781.

Anderson LJ et al: Postexposure trial of a human diploid cell strain rabies vaccine. *J Infect Dis* 1980;**142**:133.

Anderson LJ et al: Rapid antibody response to human diploid rabies vaccine. *Am J Epidemiol* 1981;**113**:270.

Brahic M et al: Gene expression in visna virus infection in sheep. *Nature* 1981;**292**:240.

Buchmeier MJ, Oldstone MBA: Virus-induced immune complex disease: Identification of specific viral antigens and antibodies deposited in complexes during chronic lymphocytic choriomeningitis virus infection. *J Immunol* 1978;**20**:1297.

Chatigny MA, Prusiner SB: Biohazards of investigations on the transmissible spongiform encephalopathies. *Rev Infect Dis* 1980;**2**:713.

Gajdusek DC: Unconventional viruses and the origin and disappearance of kuru. *Science* 1977;**197**:943.

Hall WW, Choppin PW: Measles-virus proteins in the brain tissue of patients with subacute sclerosing panencephalitis: Absence of the M protein. *N Engl J Med* 1981;**304**:1152.

Halsey NA et al: Risk factors in subacute sclerosing panencephalitis: A case-control study. *Am J Epidemiol* 1980;**111**:415.

Kuwert EK et al: Immunization against rabies with Rabies Immune Globulin, Human (RIGH) and a human diploid cell strain (HDCS) rabies vaccine. *J Biol Stand* 1978;**6**:211.

Manuelidis EE et al: Experimental Creutzfeldt-Jakob disease transmitted via the eye with infected cornea. *N Engl J Med* 1977;**296**:1334.

Manuelidis L, Manuelidis EE: Search for specific DNAs in Creutzfeldt-Jakob infectious brain fractions using "nick translation." *Virology* 1981;**109**:435.

Marsh RF et al: Evidence for an essential DNA component in the scrapie agent. *Nature* 1978;**275**:146.

Oldstone MBA: Virus neutralization and virus-induced immune complex disease: Virus-antibody union resulting in immunoprotection or immunologic injury—two sides of the same coin. *Prog Med Virol* 1975;**19**:84.

Plotkin SA: Rabies vaccine prepared in human cell cultures: Progress and perspectives. *Rev Infect Dis* 1980;**2**:433.

Prabhakar BS, Nathanson N: Acute rabies death mediated by antibody. *Nature* 1981;**290**:590.

Rabies prevention. *MMWR* (June) 1980;**29**:265.

Stroop WG, Baringer JR: Persistent, slow and latent viral infections. *Prog Med Virol* 1982;**28**:1.

Wechsler SL, Meissner HC: Measles and SSPE viruses: Similarities and differences. *Prog Med Virol* 1982;**28**:65.

Weiner LP, Johnson RT, Herndon RM: Viral infections and demyelinating diseases. *N Engl J Med* 1973;**288**:1103.

ORTHOMYXOVIRUSES

The name myxovirus was originally applied to influenza viruses. It meant virus with an affinity for mucins. Now there are 2 main groups—the orthomyxoviruses and the paramyxoviruses. Their differences in simple terms are shown in Table 34–1. Paramyxoviruses are discussed in Chapter 35.

All orthomyxoviruses are influenza viruses. Isolated strains are named after the virus *type* (A, B, C), the host and location of initial isolation, the year of isolation, and the antigenic designation of the hemagglutinin and neuraminidase. Eleven hemagglutinin antigenic subtypes and 8 neuraminidase antigenic subtypes are designated. Both of these are glycoproteins under separate genetic control, and they vary independently. Examples of influenza designations follow:

A/swine/New Jersey/8/76 (H1N1), pre-
    viously (Hsw1N1)
A/Brazil/78 (H1N1)
B/Singapore/79
A/Bangkok/79 (H3N2)

The last 3 strains were incorporated in the vaccine for 1981–1982.

Table 34–1. Differences between orthomyxoviruses and paramyxoviruses.

	Orthomyxoviruses	Paramyxoviruses
Viruses and diseases	Influenza A, B, C	Mumps, measles, respiratory syncytial, parainfluenza
Genome	Single-stranded RNA in 8 pieces, MW $2–4 \times 10^6$	Single-stranded RNA in single piece, MW $5–8 \times 10^6$
Inner ribonucleo-protein helix	9-nm diameter	18-nm diameter

INFLUENZA

Influenza is an acute respiratory tract infection that usually occurs in epidemics. Three immunologic types of influenza virus are known: A, B, and C.

Antigenic changes continually take place within the A group of influenza viruses and to a lesser degree in the B group, whereas influenza C appears to be antigenically stable. Influenza A strains are also known for pigs, horses, ducks, and chickens (fowl plague). Some animal isolates are antigenically similar to the strains circulating in the human population.

Influenza virus type C differs from the type A and type B viruses; its receptor-destroying enzyme does not appear to be a neuraminidase, and its virion structure is not fully understood. The following descriptions are based on influenza virus type A.

Properties of the Virus

A. Structure: Influenza virus consists of pleomorphic, approximately spherical particles having an external diameter of about 110 nm and an inner electron-dense core of 70 nm.

The surface of the virus particles is covered with 2 types of projections, or spikes, approximately 10 nm long possessing either the hemagglutinin or the neuraminidase activity of the virus. A model of the influenza virion is shown in Fig 34–1.

The RNA genome consists of 8 distinct pieces with an aggregate molecular weight of $2–4 \times 10^6$.

Because of a divided genome, viruses of this group exhibit several biologic phenomena such as high recombination frequency, multiplicity reactivation, and ability to synthesize hemagglutinin and neuraminidase after chemical inactivation of viral infectivity.

Although viral RNA has not proved to be infectious, viral ribonucleoprotein appears to be so. This structure contains the virion-associated RNA-dependent RNA polymerase as well as the genome. Evidently, all messenger RNA is complementary to the virion RNA.

The results of hybridization studies on RNA have supported the immunologic grouping of the hemagglutinins of the influenza A viruses. Similar studies of the neuraminidase genes have been in agreement with N antigen subtype designations based on the results of serologic tests.

B. Reactions to Physical and Chemical Agents: Influenza viruses are relatively stable and may be stored at 0–4 °C for weeks. The virus is less stable at −20 °C than at +4 °C. Ether and protein denaturants destroy infectivity. The hemagglutinin and CF antigens are more stable than the infective virus. Ultraviolet irradiation destroys infectivity, hemagglutinating activity, neuraminidase activity, and CF antigen, in that order. Infectivity and hemagglutination are more stable at alkaline pH than at acid pH.

C. Animal Susceptibility and Growth of Virus: Human strains of the virus can infect different

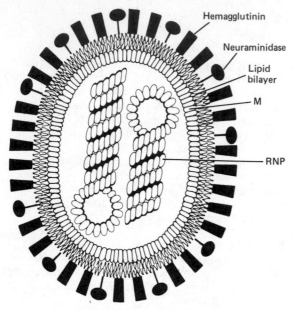

Figure 34–1. A model of the influenza virion. The innermost component is the helical ribonucleoprotein (RNP), which is 9 nm in diameter. It is as yet unknown whether the RNP is one long molecule or is divided into pieces like the virus RNA. The nucleocapsid is further organized by the coiling of the whole RNP strand into a double helix 50–60 nm in diameter. The protein component of this structure has a molecular weight of 60,000 and is associated with the group-specific CF antigen. A protein (M) shell surrounds the nucleoprotein and forms the inner part of the virus envelope. It is composed of a small protein (MW 26,000) and constitutes about 40% of the virus protein. About 20% of the virus particle is composed of lipid, apparently derived from the host cell. The lipid is formed into a bilayer structure. The hemagglutinin spike is responsible for the agglutination of erythrocytes by this virus. It is composed of 2 molecules of a glycoprotein (MW 75,000) that may or may not be cleaved to form 2 disulfide-linked glycopeptides of molecular weight 27,000 and 53,000. The smaller of these is present at the end of the molecule which is attached to the lipid. The neuraminidase spike is responsible for the receptor-destroying activity of the virus; this activity results in elution of the virus from host cells or erythrocytes. The role of its activity in virus replication is unknown. It is composed of 4 polypeptide molecules with a molecular weight of about 60,000. The arrangement of these molecules is still a matter of debate. Both the hemagglutinin and the neuraminidase spikes have been purified, and a study of the purified protein has helped to explain antigenic changes of the virus. (From Compans & Choppin.)

animals; ferrets are most susceptible. Serial passage in mice increases its virulence, producing extensive pulmonary consolidation and death. The developing chick embryo readily supports the growth of virus, but there are no gross lesions.

Wild influenza viruses do not grow well in tissue cultures. In most instances, only an abortive growth cycle occurs, ie, viral subunits are synthesized but little or no new infectious progeny is formed. From most influenza strains mutants can be selected that will grow in cell culture. Because of the poor growth of many strains in cell culture, initial isolation attempts should employ inoculation both of the amniotic cavity of the embryonated egg and of monkey cell cultures.

The process of infection begins by adsorption of the virus onto its receptor sites (neuraminic acid-containing glycoproteins). The hemagglutinin protein is involved in this reaction. The other spike protein, neuraminidase, can destroy the site. The virus particle is taken into the cell, where it is disrupted, causing a decrease in detectable virus shortly after infection.

Intracellular synthesis of the viral RNA and protein then occurs. Viral RNA pieces are synthesized individually in the nucleus within 2–3 hours. All viral proteins are synthesized in the cytoplasm. Structural proteins bind to the cell membrane and are joined by the ribonucleoprotein. At 8 hours, new virus particles bud through the membrane. Neuraminidase may be important in release of the completed virion.

In most influenza virus systems, noninfectious particles capable of hemagglutination are produced (von Magnus phenomenon). These particles, called ''incomplete,'' increase in number upon serial, high-multiplicity passage of the virus. The incomplete particles are smaller and more pleomorphic than standard virus, and they interfere with replication of standard virus. They are known as *d*efective *i*nterfering, or DI, particles. The largest virus RNA piece is missing from such particles.

D. Biologic Properties:

1. Hemagglutination–All strains of influenza virus agglutinate erythrocytes from chickens, guinea pigs, and humans and—unlike paramyxoviruses—agglutinate erythrocytes from many other species as well. Agglutination of red blood cells occurs when the hemagglutinin interacts with a specific receptor on the red blood cell membrane. This receptor is a glycoprotein (MW 3×10^4) that contains sialic acid. This glycoprotein serves both as the receptor site for the hemagglutinin and as the substrate for the viral neuraminidase. Cleavage of the glycoprotein by the enzyme dissociates the virion from the red cell, resulting in spontaneous elution. After elution, the cell receptors are destroyed and hence can no longer be agglutinated with fresh virus; however, the eluted virus can reattach and agglutinate additional cells.

2. Group antigen–All influenza A virus strains share a common antigen, distinct from those of influenza B and C. This soluble (S) antigen is found in the medium from infected cell cultures and is a component of the ribonucleoprotein of the virus. It can be identified by CF. Antibody to this nucleoprotein antigen does not induce resistance to the virus in humans. The other internal proteins and the RNA polymerase also have group-specific antigenic activity.

3. Specific antigens–The infectious virus particles induce in animals the development of virus-neutralizing and other antibodies, and the inoculated animals become resistant to infection. Influenza virus administered in large amounts is toxic. The effect is apparently associated directly with the virus particles and can be prevented by specific antibody.

Virions contain 2 subtype- or strain-specific antigens—the hemagglutinin and the neuraminidase. The hemagglutinin is the principal specific envelope antigen, and differences in this antigen among strains of virus can be shown by HI tests. Antibody to the hemagglutinin neutralizes virus and is a protective mechanism.

Neuraminidase is antigenically distinct from the hemagglutinin and is governed by a separate gene (RNA fragment); hence, it can vary independently of the hemagglutinin. The antigens of the hemagglutinin and the neuraminidase of the virus are the basis for classifying new strains. Antibody against the neuraminidase does not neutralize the virus, but it modifies the infection, probably by its effect on the release of virus from the cells. The antibody against the neuraminidase occurs in sera of humans who experience infection. The presence of antineuraminidase antibody results in marked protection against disease.

4. Filamentous forms–In addition to the spherical particles, elongated forms possessing the same surface projections exist. The filamentous forms also agglutinate red cells and elute from them. In its early passages in chick embryos, the virus is usually in filamentous form, but with serial passage it takes on a spherical appearance.

5. Recombination–The multisegment nature of the influenza virus genome allows recombination to occur with high frequency by reassortment between orthomyxoviruses of the same group. The RNA fragments of different influenza A viruses migrate at different rates in polyacrylamide gels. Similarly, the polypeptides of different influenza A viruses can be differentiated. Thus, using 2 different parental viruses and obtaining recombinants between them, it is possible to tell which parent donated which RNA fragment to the recombinant. These techniques enable rapid and more complete analysis of recombinants that emerge in nature.

Pathogenesis & Pathology

The virus enters the respiratory tract in airborne droplets. Viremia is rare. Virus is present in the nasopharynx from 1–2 days before to 1–2 days after onset of symptoms. The neuraminidase lowers the viscosity of the mucous film in the respiratory tract, laying bare the cellular surface receptors and promoting the spread of virus-containing fluid to lower portions of the tract. Even when neutralizing antibodies are in the blood they may not protect against infection.

Antibodies must be present in sufficient concentration at the superficial cells of the respiratory tract. This can be achieved only if the antibody level in the blood is high or if antibody is secreted locally.

Inflammation of the upper respiratory tract causes necrosis of the ciliated and goblet cells of the tracheal and bronchial mucosa but does not affect the basal layer of epithelium. Interstitial pneumonia may occur with necrosis of bronchiolar epithelium and may be fatal. The pneumonia is often associated with secondary bacterial invaders: staphylococci, pneumococci, streptococci, and *Haemophilus influenzae.*

Clinical Findings

The incubation period is 1 or 2 days. Chills, malaise, fever, muscular aches, prostration, and respiratory symptoms may occur. The fever persists for about 3 days; complications are not common, but pneumonia, myocarditis, pericarditis, and central nervous system complications occur rarely. The latter include encephalomyelitis, polyneuritis, Guillain-Barré syndrome, and Reye's syndrome (see below).

When influenza appears in epidemic form, the clinical findings are consistent enough so that the disease can be diagnosed in most cases. Sporadic cases cannot be diagnosed on clinical grounds. Mild as well as asymptomatic infections occur. The severity of the pandemic of 1918–1919 has been attributed to the fact that bacterial pneumonia often developed.

The lethal impact of an influenza epidemic is reflected in the excess deaths due to pneumonia and cardiovascular and renal diseases. Pregnant women and elderly persons with chronic illnesses have a higher risk of complications and death.

Reye's syndrome occurs mainly in children. It is characterized by encephalopathy and fatty degeneration of the liver, and the mortality rate is high. In 1979–1980, more than 400 cases were reported in the USA, with a mortality rate near 30%. Reye's syndrome is associated with influenza B, rarely with influenza A, and sometimes with other viral diseases such as chickenpox and zoster.

Laboratory Diagnosis

Influenza is readily diagnosed by laboratory procedures. For antibody determinations, the first serum should be taken less than 5 days after onset and the second 10–14 days later.

For rapid detection of influenza virus in clinical specimens, positive smears from nasal swabs may be demonstrated by specific staining with fluorescein-labeled antibody.

A. Recovery of Virus: Throat washings or garglings are obtained within 3 days after onset and should be tested at once or stored frozen. Penicillin and streptomycin are added to limit bacterial contamination, and embryonated eggs are inoculated by the amniotic route. Amniotic and allantoic fluids are harvested 2–4 days later and tested for hemagglutinins. If results are negative, passage is made to fresh embryos. If hemagglutinins are not detected after 2 such passages, the result is negative.

If a strain of virus is isolated—as demonstrated by the presence of hemagglutinins—it is titrated in the presence of type-specific influenza sera to determine its type. The new virus belongs to the same type as the serum that inhibits its hemagglutinating power.

Primate cell cultures (human or monkey) are susceptible to certain human strains of influenza virus. Rapid diagnosis can be made by growing the virus from the clinical specimen in cell culture and then staining the cultured cells with fluorescent influenza antibody 24 hours later, when infected cells are rich in antigen even though they may appear normal.

The phenomenon of hemadsorption is utilized for the early detection of virus growth in cell cultures. Guinea pig red cells or human O cells are added to the cultures 24–48 hours after the clinical specimens have been inoculated and are viewed under the low power lens. Positive hemadsorption shows red blood cells firmly attached to the cell culture sheets as rosettes or chains. The cytopathogenic effects of the influenza viruses are often negligible. Hemadsorption provides a more sensitive testing procedure.

B. Typing of New Isolates: A double immunodiffusion (DID) test is used for typing influenza virus isolates. The allantoic fluid content of a single infected embryonated egg may be used for the DID test. Reference antisera are placed in the outer wells, and the virus harvest, after disruption by detergent, is added to the center well. The plates are incubated overnight in a moist atmosphere, and precipitin lines are read the following morning.

Membrane immunofluorescence has also been recommended as a simple, rapid, and accurate method for typing current influenza A isolates. Surface antigens of infected, unfixed monkey kidney cells are stained in suspension by the indirect immunofluorescence method using anti-H3N2 and anti-H1N1 antisera.

C. Serology: Paired sera are used to detect rises in HI, CF, or Nt antibodies. The HI antibody is used most often. Normal sera often contain nonspecific mucoprotein inhibitors that must first be destroyed by treatment with RDE (receptor-destroying enzyme of *Vibrio cholerae* cultures), trypsin, or periodate. Because normal persons usually have influenza antibodies, a 4-fold or greater increase in titer is necessary to indicate influenza infection. Peak levels of antibodies are present 2–4 weeks after onset, persist for about 4 weeks, and then gradually fall during the course of a year to preinfection levels.

Within one type of influenza virus, strains may differ markedly in antigenicity. It is best to use recently isolated strains.

Complement-fixing antigens are of 2 types. One is soluble (S antigen) and type-specific but not strain-specific. The other is part of the virus particle (V antigen) and is highly strain-specific. It is useful for demonstrating antibody rise when the first serum specimen was not taken early in the disease, because the peak CF titer occurs in the fourth week.

Immunity

Three immunologically unrelated types of influenza virus are known and are referred to as influenza A, B, and C. In addition, the swine, equine, and avian influenza viruses are antigenically related to the human influenza A virus. Influenza C virus exists as a single and stable antigenic type.

At least 18 different antigenic components have been determined in type A strains of influenza virus by quantitative adsorption methods. More undoubtedly exist. Strains share their antigenic components, but in varying proportions. A strain generally shares its antigens with strains prevalent within a few years of its isolation.

Two possible mechanisms for the antigenic variation of influenza virus have been suggested:

(1) All possible configurations may be present in a pool of antigens that exist throughout the globe; from these, highly infectious strains arise and initiate epidemics. High antibody levels to recent strains in the human population will inhibit strains with major antigens that were dominant in recently prevalent strains and will select strains of different antigenic composition.

Serial passage of virus in mice vaccinated with the homologous strain yields a virus with an apparent rearrangement of antigens or the appearance of new antigens. The change in antigenic character evolves slowly on passage (antigenic drift).

(2) Antigenically different strains may be selected by means of genetic recombination induced by selection factors such as passage in a partially immune host. When 2 strains of influenza virus are simultaneously injected into mice or eggs, a new strain sharing the properties of each parent strain may be recovered; this has been attributed to genetic recombination (antigenic shift).

Antibodies are important in immunity against influenza, but they must be present at the site of virus invasion. Resistance to initiation of infection is related to antibody against the hemagglutinin. Decreased extent of viral invasion and decreased ability to transmit virus to contacts are related to antibody directed against the neuraminidase.

Virus-neutralizing antibody occurs earlier in nasal secretions and rises to high titers sooner among those already possessing high concentrations of IgA in their nasal washings prior to the infection. Even though infected with influenza virus, such individuals remain well. In contrast, those with low nasal wash IgA levels prior to infection are highly susceptible not only to infection but also to clinical illness.

Prevention & Treatment by Drugs

Amantadine hydrochloride (see p 143) and its analog rimantadine are antiviral drugs for systemic use in the prevention of influenza A. The drugs block penetration of or uncoat influenza A virus in the host cell and prevent virus replication. The established effect is prophylaxis, and amantadine (200 mg/d) must be given to high-risk persons during epidemics of influenza A if protection is to result. Amantadine is relatively nontoxic but may produce central nervous system stimulation with dizziness and insomnia, particularly in the elderly. It should be considered for persons with chronic obstructive respiratory disease, cardiac insufficiency, or renal disease, particularly if they have not been vaccinated yearly or if a new influenza A strain is epidemic. Amantadine may also modify the severity of influenza A if started within 24–48 hours after onset of illness.

Epidemiology

Influenza occurs in successive waves of infection, with peak incidences during the winter. Influenza A infections may vary from a few isolated cases to extensive outbreaks that within a few weeks involve 10% or more of the population, with rates of 50–75% in children of school age. The period between epidemic waves of influenza A is 2–3 years. All known pandemics were caused by influenza A strains. During the pandemic of 1918–1919 more than 20 million persons died, mainly from complicating bacterial pneumonias. Recent pandemics occurred in 1957–1958 owing to A influenza (H2N2) and in 1968 owing to A influenza (H3N2). In 1976 in New Jersey, a new type of influenza arose that resembled swine influenza (Hsw1N1), but it failed to spread in spite of a lack of immunity in most people under age 50 years. An enormous government-sponsored vaccination campaign was stopped because Guillain-Barré syndrome appeared in some vaccinated individuals. The predominant influenza A in the USA in 1978–1979 was an H1N1 variant of the strains prevalent in the 1950s.

Influenza B tends not to spread through communities as quickly as influenza A. Its interepidemic period is from 3 to 6 years. Small outbreaks of influenza B were frequent in the USA in 1979–1980.

The main reason for the periodic occurrence of epidemic influenza is the accumulation of a sufficient number of susceptibles in a population that harbors the virus in a few subclinical or minor infections throughout the year. Epidemics may be started when the virus mutates to a new antigenic type that has survival advantages and when antibodies in the population are low to this new type. **Antigenic drift** is illustrated in Fig 34–2. A much more drastic change in the segmented RNA genome occurs when **antigenic shift** occurs. This involves the recombination of different segments of the RNA, each of which functions as an individual gene.

In early life, the range of the influenza antibody spectrum is narrow, but it becomes progressively broader in later years. The antibodies (and immunity) acquired from the initial infections of childhood are of limited range and reflect the dominant antigens of the prevailing strains. Later exposures to viruses of related but differing antigenic composition result in an antibody spectrum broadening toward a larger number of the common antigens of influenza viruses. Exposures later in life to antigenically related strains result in a progressive reinforcement of the primary antibody. The highest antibody levels in a particular age group therefore reflect the dominant antigens of the virus responsible for the childhood infections of the group. Thus, a serologic recapitulation of past infection with influenza viruses of different antigenic makeup can be obtained by studying the age distribution of influenza antibodies in normal populations.

Antibodies against swine influenza (perhaps related to the pandemic influenza strain of 1918) have not been found in persons born after 1923. Persons born during 1923–1933 had their first influenza experience with a type A virus closely related to the 1933 WS strain. Those born between 1934 and 1943 do not possess swine or WS antibodies but have antibodies against another type A virus, PR-8 (H0N1).

Another antigenic change occurred among the A viruses in 1946. Strains occurring between 1946 and 1957 have been called A1, or H1N1, strains. The influenza antibodies in persons born between 1946 and 1957 are chiefly against the H1N1 strains. With the widespread appearance of the type A2 Asian strain in 1957, the H1N1 subtypes were replaced by H2N2 viruses.

Type A2 virus seemed to be related to previous influenza viruses, in that sera in 1957 from people who were age 70 years or older often contained antibody against A2 isolates. Furthermore, anti-A2 antibody increases were found in sera from this age group after injections of type A vaccine that did not contain the A2 virus (anamnestic response). This suggests that viruses prevalent during the 1889 pandemic contained H2N2 antigens shared with the 1957 Asian strains.

Influenza B appears to be changing antigenically, since almost all strains isolated in 1965–1966 were closely related to B/Singapore/3/64, which differed significantly from the formerly prevalent variant represented by B/Maryland/1/59. In 1972, a new variant was isolated in Hong Kong (B/HK/5/72) and then became the predominant type B virus around the world. In 1979–1980, for the first time in 6 years, type B viruses caused most of the reported cases in the USA. Most of the type B strains were closely related to B/Singapore/79.

Surveillance for influenza outbreaks is more extensive than for any other disease in order to identify the early appearance of new strains, with the aim of preparing vaccines against them before an epidemic occurs.

Surveillance also extends into animal populations, especially birds, pigs, and horses. Some believe that pandemic strains arise from recombinants of human and animal strains.

Since the virus causing fowl plague was identified as human influenza A type in 1955, many influenza viruses have been isolated from a wide variety of domestic and wild bird species. Some of these include the major H and N antigens related to human strains.

Avian influenza ranges from highly lethal infections in chickens and turkeys to inapparent infections in these and other avian species that harbor the same

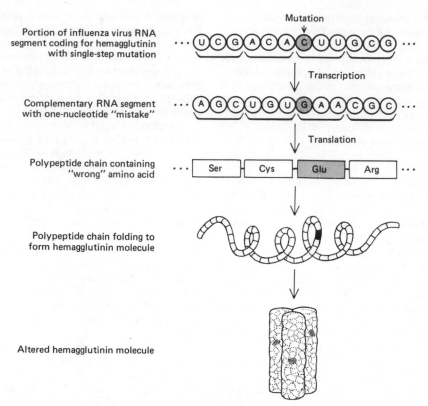

Figure 34–2. Antigenic drift consists of a series of minor genetic alterations within a group of similar strains. One such alteration is depicted here. The short portion of a viral RNA segment shown at the top contains the genetic information that codes for the hemagglutinin molecule; the segment contains a single-step mutation (shaded). The RNA, represented simply as a string of lettered beads, is actually a chain of nucleotides each of which is made up of a ribose sugar, a phosphate group, and one of 4 organic bases: adenine (A), uracil (U), guanine (G), and cytosine (C). The viral RNA is copied by the polymerase in the virion to yield a complementary RNA strand, A generally pairing with U and G with C. In this case, however, a "mistake" has been made: the mutant C pairs with a G. As a result, the 3-letter "triplet" coding for a specific amino acid inserts a "wrong" amino acid in the polypeptide chain of the H protein. The new amino acid may in turn interfere with the folding of the polypeptide chain, distorting the H molecule, or it may appear in the antigenic region of the molecule, producing a minor antigenic variant that cannot be neutralized by antibodies to the parent influenza virus. (Reproduced, with permission, from Kaplan & Webster: The epidemiology of influenza. *Sci Am* [Dec] 1977;**237**:88. Copyright © 1977 by Scientific American, Inc. All rights reserved.)

strains. Domestic ducks and quail often manifest influenza infection by coughing, sneezing, and swelling around the beak, with variable mortality rates. . Wildlife species and most domestic fowl show little or no signs of disease.

The possibility that influenza viruses are transmitted between birds and mammals, including humans, may seem unlikely, particularly if the transfer were to be only by the respiratory route. However, influenza viruses of ducks multiply in the cells lining the intestinal tract and are shed in high concentrations into water. These viruses remain viable for days or weeks in water. It is possible that influenza among birds is a waterborne infection, moving from wild to domestic birds and even to humans.

Control Through Immunization

In the 1940s, it appeared that killed influenza vaccine given by subcutaneous injection might provide protection against epidemic influenza. This hope was dashed when the H1N1 strain appeared in 1947, making existing vaccines useless because of major antigenic changes. Each subsequent major antigenic shift that appeared every 10–15 years made existing vaccines useless.

It is possible that the number of antigens of influenza viruses might be finite but might vary in proportion from one strain to the next. If several strains of broad antigenic composition were combined, such a vaccine might yield an antigenic mass capable of protecting against present and future epidemics. On the other hand, the number of antigenic shifts and the possibility of antigenic drift among influenza viruses might be infinite, rendering the outlook for future control dubious.

A. Who should be vaccinated? At present, it is recommended in the USA that vaccination be limited to those at high risk—the elderly and persons with chronic bronchopulmonary or cardiac disease, or metabolic and renal disorders. They should be vaccinated every year, according to dosage directions provided by the manufacturer. However, if a major antigenic shift becomes apparent, the entire population might be considered for vaccination—as was the case in the 1976 "swine flu" epidemic.

B. When should vaccination be done? At present, yearly vaccinations should be given before the influenza season begins, ie, in early fall.

C. How are antigens for killed influenza vaccines selected and prepared?

1. If only minor antigenic drift is expected for the next influenza season, the most recent strains of A and B viruses representative of the main antigens are included. They are grown in embryonated eggs, harvested, purified, inactivated, concentrated to a standard hemagglutinin content, and stored for administration in the fall.

2. If a strain representing a major antigenic shift has been isolated (usually in Southeast Asia, where influenza occurs 6 months before it becomes epidemic in Europe or the USA), then ways must be found to grow the important new antigen in bulk. This is accomplished by the **recombination** method. Stable hybrids can be made of the low-yield new antigen strain and a high-yield egg-adapted influenza virus. By co-cultivation of the new, different isolate with an established high-egg-yield virus, recombinant progeny are obtained. These hybrids are selected out, grown in bulk, and incorporated into the "vaccine for the next season." Whenever such recombinant vaccines have been tested, their potency was equal to that of wild-strain vaccines.

3. From either of these 2 methods, subviral antigens can be prepared. Such "split viruses" result from chemical treatment of virion suspensions, with subsequent purification and concentration, and they contain the most important antigenic proteins. The split-virus vaccines produce fewer side-effects than whole-virus vaccines. They are preferred for that reason but may require several injections instead of a single one, because of lower antigenicity. They are recommended for children.

D. What are the major risks of and untoward reactions associated with influenza vaccines?

1. All killed vaccines can produce fever, local inflammation at the site of subcutaneous injection, and systemic toxicity with poorly defined nonspecific symptoms of illness for 1–2 days.

2. Since the vaccine strains are grown in eggs, some egg protein antigens are present in the vaccine. Persons allergic to eggs may develop symptoms and signs of hypersensitivity.

3. Whatever immunity results from an inactivated vaccine appears to be of short duration— probably 1–3 years against the homologous virus.

4. Guillain-Barré syndrome, an ascending paralysis, has been statistically associated with mass vaccination programs, eg, the "swine flu" vaccination of 1976. It occurred 5–7 times more frequently in vacci-

nated than in matched, unvaccinated persons. While most persons affected by this syndrome recover completely, 5–10% have residual muscle weakness and 3–5% a fatal outcome. However, no such increased risk of contracting Guillain-Barré syndrome has been associated with subsequent standard influenza vaccines.

E. Current research approaches to better influenza vaccines.

1. A neuraminidase-specific vaccine, which induces antibodies only to the neuraminidase antigen of the prevailing influenza virus. Antibody to neuraminidase reduces the amount of virus replicating in the respiratory tract and the ability to transmit virus to contacts. It reduces clinical symptoms in the infected person but permits subclinical infection that may give rise to more lasting immunity.

2. A live vaccine using temperature-sensitive (ts) mutants. Such ts mutants grow well at the cooler (33 °C) temperature of the upper respiratory tract but fail to grow at the higher (37 °C) temperature of the lung. Mutants selected for this ts property appear to be attenuated or avirulent. Thus, they might be given as a live vaccine into the respiratory tract, stimulating local as well as systemic immunity. By recombination of the *ts* gene with the gene for the current major antigen, potent live vaccines could theoretically be produced and rapidly administered to cope with an influenza epidemic.

Attenuated live influenza virus vaccine has been used in the USSR with reported success. The attenuated virus was selected by serial transfer through embryonated eggs rather than by genetic manipulation.

3. Combined yearly vaccination of persons at high risk, using the best mix of important antigens, and administration of amantadine or other anti-influenza drugs at times of particular stress, eg, surgery, hospitalization.

CORONAVIRUSES

The coronaviruses include human strains from the respiratory tract, avian *i*nfectious *b*ronchitis *v*irus (IBV), *m*ouse *h*epatitis *v*irus (MHV), an enteritis virus of swine, and others. The human coronaviruses cause common colds. Coronaviruses of lower animals establish persistent infections in their natural hosts. Because the murine infection can result in a high incidence of subacute to chronic demyelinating disease, it is being studied as a model for multiple sclerosis in humans.

Properties of the Viruses

Coronaviruses are enveloped, 80- to 130-nm particles that contain an unsegmented genome of single-stranded RNA (MW 7×10^6). The helical nucleocapsid is 7–9 nm in diameter; it matures in the cytoplasm by budding into cytoplasmic vesicles. There are 20-nm-long club-shaped or petal-shaped projections that are widely spaced on the outer surface of the envelope, resembling a solar corona. The 3 chief virus proteins include a 60K phosphorylated nucleocapsid protein, a 90K glycoprotein making up the petal-shaped structures, and a 23K glycoprotein embedded in the envelope lipid bilayer. Viral antigens are found only in the cytoplasm of infected cells.

Growth of Virus

The human coronaviruses are difficult to grow in cell cultures. Some strains require human embryonic tracheal and nasal organ cultures; others will grow in human embryonic intestine or kidney cell cultures. The optimal temperature for growth is 33–35 °C.

Antigenic Properties

The human prototype strain is 229E. Some human isolates are closely related; others are not. Cross-reactions occur between some human and some animal strains, but avian IBV appears to be unrelated to human agents. All or most strains have CF antigens; some have hemagglutinins.

Clinical Features & Laboratory Diagnosis

The human coronaviruses produce "colds," usually afebrile, in adults. If virus is isolated, diagnosis can be confirmed by demonstrating a significant rise in CF or Nt antibody titer in paired serum specimens.

In the absence of virus isolation, serologic diagnosis can be made on the basis of significantly in-creased antibody titers. The CF test is a more sensitive index of human coronavirus infections than is virus isolation with cell and organ culture methods available at present. Serologic diagnosis of infections with strain 229E is now possible by means of passive hemagglutination test. Red cells coated with coronavirus antigen are agglutinated by antibody-containing sera. The test is type-specific, as sensitive as the Nt test, rapid, and convenient.

Epidemiology

As indicated in the foregoing, the coronaviruses are a major cause of respiratory illness in adults during some winter months when the incidence of colds is high but the isolation of rhinoviruses or other respiratory viruses is low. These viruses are a common cause of virus-induced exacerbations in patients with chronic bronchitis.

The apparent infrequency of coronavirus infections in children may be a result of the type of test used: initial infections with strain 229E are accompanied by only a transient CF antibody response, whereas in reinfections in adults, the CF response is enhanced and the Nt antibody response is diminished. Therefore, the Nt test should be the procedure of choice for infants and children and the CF test more sensitive for adults.

Coronaviruses of lower animals can establish long-term infections in their natural hosts (pigs, chickens, mice). They may also set up inapparent persistent infections in humans.

● ● ●

References

Assaad FA et al: A revision of the system of nomenclature for influenza viruses: A WHO memorandum. *Bull WHO* 1980; **58:**585.

Barker WH, Mullooly JP: Influenza vaccination of elderly persons: Reduction in pneumonia and influenza hospitalizations and deaths. *JAMA* 1980;**244:**2547.

Burnet FM: Portraits of viruses: Influenza virus A. *Intervirology* 1979;**11:**201.

Couch RB et al: Efficacy of purified influenza subunit vaccines and relation to the major antigenic determinants on the hemagglutinin molecule. *J Infect Dis* 1979;**140:**553.

Dourmashkin RR, Tyrrell DA: Electron microscopic observations on the entry of influenza virus into susceptible cells. *J Gen Virol* 1974;**24:**129.

Dowdle WR et al: Natural history of influenza type A in the United States, 1957–1972. *Prog Med Virol* 1974;**17:**91.

Hamre D, Beem M: Virologic studies of acute respiratory disease in young adults. 5. Coronavirus 229E infections during six years of surveillance. *Am J Epidemiol* 1972;**96:**94.

Hurwitz ES et al: Guillain-Barré syndrome and the 1978–1979 influenza vaccine. *N Engl J Med* 1981;**304:**1557.

Jackson GG, Stanley ED: Prevention and control of influenza by chemoprophylaxis and chemotherapy. *JAMA* 1976;**235:**2739.

Kaplan MM, Webster RG: The epidemiology of influenza. *Sci Am* (Dec) 1977;**237:**88.

Laver WG, Air GM, Webster RG: Summary of a workshop on influenza B viruses and Reye's syndrome. *J Infect Dis* 1980;**142:**452.

Meiklejohn G et al: Antigenic drift and efficacy of influenza virus vaccines, 1976–1977. *J Infect Dis* 1978;**138:**618.

Murphy BR et al: Hemagglutinin-specific enzyme-linked immunosorbent assay for antibodies to influenza A and B viruses. *J Clin Microbiol* 1981;**13:**554.

Nakajima S et al: Influenza surveillance based on oligonucleotide mapping of RNA of H1N1 viruses prevalent in Japan, 1978–1979. *J Infect Dis* 1980;**142:**492.

Stuart-Harris C: The present status of live influenza virus vaccine. *J Infect Dis* 1980;**142:**784.

Tyrrell DA et al: Coronaviridae: Second report. *Intervirology* 1978;**10:**321.

Tyrrell DAJ: Approaches to the control of respiratory virus diseases. *Bull WHO* 1980;**58:**513.

Young JF, Palese P: Evolution of human influenza A viruses in nature: Recombination contributes to genetic variation of H1N1 strains. *Proc Natl Acad Sci USA* 1979;**76:**6547.

Paramyxoviruses include important human (mumps, measles, parainfluenza, respiratory syncytial) and animal viruses. Some features that distinguish them from orthomyxoviruses are shown in Table 34–1. Rubella virus resembles togaviruses (Chapter 27) in chemical and physical properties but fits with paramyxoviruses on an epidemiologic basis.

Properties of the Paramyxoviruses

A. Structure: The particle has a lipid-containing envelope covered with spikes; a helical ribonucleoprotein nucleocapsid 18 nm in diameter is enclosed. The RNA is a single molecule (MW $5–8 \times 10^6$). Features of the particle are shown in Fig 35–1.

The envelope of paramyxoviruses contains 2 glycoproteins, HN and F, that form spikelike projections from the surface of the viral membrane. These glycoproteins are involved in the early interactions between virus and cell. The larger glycoprotein, HN, has neuraminidase and hemagglutinating activities and is responsible for virus adsorption. The other glycoprotein, F, is involved in virus-induced cell fusion and hemolysis and in virus penetration through fusion of viral and cell membranes. The membrane-fusing activity of the F protein is activated by proteolytic cleavage of a precursor (F_0) by a host enzyme to yield 2 disulfide-linked polypeptides (F_1 and F_2) (Fig 35–2). Only then can viral replication begin.

B. Biologic Properties:

1. Cell fusion–In the course of infection, paramyxoviruses cause cell fusion, long recognized as giant cell formation. This ability to fuse cells is now used for the creation of cell hybrids, an important tool in somatic cell genetics.

2. Persistent infection–Most paramyxoviruses can produce a persistent noncytocidal infection of cultured cells. The clinical importance of this property may explain subacute sclerosing panencephalitis (SSPE) (see p 431).

3. Antigenic properties–Measles, canine distemper, and rinderpest viruses have related antigens. Another antigenically related group includes mumps, parainfluenza, and Newcastle disease viruses.

C. Replication: The RNA genome of viruses of this group is not infectious and does not function as messenger RNA. Instead, the viral genome is transcribed into shorter RNA molecules that serve as messenger and are complementary to the genome. The paramyxoviruses possess an RNA-dependent RNA polymerase that is a structural component of the virion and produces the initial messenger RNA.

MUMPS
(Epidemic Parotitis)

Mumps is an acute contagious disease characterized by a nonsuppurative enlargement of one or both

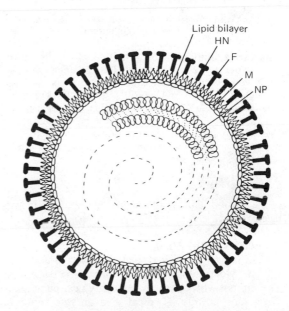

Figure 35–1. The components of paramyxoviruses. HN: Larger virus glycoprotein, responsible both for hemagglutination and receptor-destroying activities of the virus particle. F: Smaller virus glycoprotein, involved in cell fusion by these viruses and probably in the entry of the virus into the cell. F is composed of 2 disulfide bond–linked polypeptides cleaved from a high-molecular-weight precursor. Lipid bilayer: The lipid is cell-derived but probably altered in composition from that of the normal cell. M: Nonglycosylated membrane protein. The HN, F, M, and lipid bilayer can be disrupted, destroying hemolytic activity, and then reassembled without the nucleocapsid, whereupon hemolytic activity is restored. NP: Ribonucleoprotein, the major complement-fixing antigen. There is another small protein of about 47,000 molecular weight whose location and function in the virion are unknown. (From Choppin & Compans.)

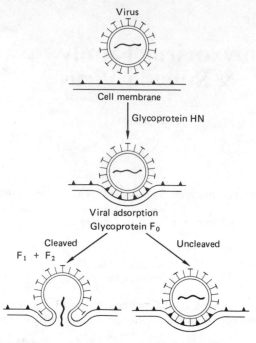

Virus

Cell membrane

Glycoprotein HN

Viral adsorption
Glycoprotein F_0

Cleaved
$F_1 + F_2$

Uncleaved

Fusion with cell membrane
Penetration of viral genome

Attachment but no fusion
No infectivity

Figure 35–2. Initiation of infection. Adsorption of paramyxovirus to receptors on the cell membrane is mediated by the HN glycoprotein. Penetration of the virus into the cell by means of fusion of viral and cell membranes is mediated by the F_0 glycoprotein, which must be cleaved into 2 subunits, F_1 and F_2, to be active. If the F protein is not cleaved, the virus will attach but it will not fuse with the cell membrane and the viral genome cannot penetrate the cell. (After Choppin and Scheid.)

of the parotid glands, although other organs may also be involved.

Properties of the Virus

Mumps virus is a typical paramyxovirus.

A. Morphology and Biochemical Properties: The mumps virus particle has the typical paramyxovirus morphology. Typical also are the biologic properties of hemagglutination, neuraminidase, and hemolysin. Hemagglutination can be inhibited by specific antisera to mumps virus, and this inhibition can be used to measure antibody responses. Similarly, the nucleocapsid of the virus particle forms the major component of the "S" (soluble) complement-fixing antigen.

B. Reactions to Physical and Chemical Agents: The hemagglutinin, the hemolysin, and the infectivity of the virus are destroyed by heating at 56 °C for 20 minutes. The skin test antigen and the complement-fixing antigen are more heat-stable.

C. Animal Susceptibility and Growth of Virus: In monkeys, mumps can produce a disease that is very much like that in human beings. Parotitis is pro-

duced by introducing the virus into Stensen's duct or directly into the gland by injection. By the use of fluorescent antibody, the virus has been located in the cytoplasm of acinar cells.

The virus grows readily in embryonated eggs and in cell culture. Passage in embryonated eggs reduces pathogenicity for humans, and this method was used to obtain a vaccine strain. Mumps virus growing in cell culture produces multinucleated giant cells (syncytia).

D. Skin Test: A skin test antigen for determining hypersensitivity to mumps virus is available. A positive test is considered to be erythema and induration greater than 15 mm 24–48 hours after injection. The skin test is of uncertain value in predicting immune status, since both false positives and false negatives occur frequently.

Pathogenesis & Pathology

Two theories exist regarding the pathogenesis of mumps. (1) The virus travels from the mouth by way of Stensen's duct to the parotid gland, where it undergoes primary multiplication. This is followed by a generalized viremia and localization in testes, ovaries, pancreas, thyroid, or brain. (2) Primary replication occurs in the superficial epithelium of the respiratory tract. This is followed by a generalized viremia and simultaneous localization in the salivary glands and other organs.

Little tissue damage is associated with uncomplicated mumps. The ducts of the parotid glands show desquamation of the epithelium, and polymorphonuclear cells are present in the lumens. There are interstitial edema and lymphocytic infiltration. With severe orchitis, the testis is congested, and punctate hemorrhage as well as degeneration of the epithelium of the seminiferous tubules is observed. Central nervous system pathology may vary from perivascular edema to inflammatory reaction, glial reaction, hemorrhage, or demyelination.

Clinical Features

The incubation period is commonly 18–21 days. A prodromal period of malaise and anorexia is followed by rapid enlargement of parotid glands as well as other salivary glands. Swelling may be confined to one parotid gland, or one gland may enlarge several days before the other. The gland enlargement is associated with pain, especially when tasting acid substances. The salivary adenitis is commonly accompanied by low-grade fever and lasts for approximately a week.

The testes and ovaries may be affected, especially after puberty. Twenty percent of males over 13 years of age who are infected with mumps virus develop orchitis, which is often unilateral and does not usually lead to sterility. Because of the lack of elasticity of the tunica albuginea, which does not allow the inflamed testis to swell, atrophy of the testis may follow secondary to pressure necrosis. Secondary sterility does not occur in women because the ovary, which has no such limiting membrane, can swell when inflamed.

Mumps accounts for 10–15% of aseptic meningitis observed in the USA and is more common among males than females. Meningoencephalitis usually occurs 5–7 days after the inflammation of the salivary glands, but it may occur simultaneously or in the absence of parotitis and is usually self-limiting. The cerebrospinal fluid shows pleocytosis (10–2000/μL, mostly lymphocytes) that may persist after clinical recovery.

Rare complications of mumps include (1) a self-limiting polyarthritis that resolves without residual deformity; (2) pancreatitis associated with transient hyperglycemia, glycosuria, and steatorrhea (it has been suggested that diabetes mellitus may occasionally follow); (3) nephritis; (4) thyroiditis; and (5) unilateral nerve deafness (hearing loss is complete and permanent). Mumps may be a possible causative agent in the production of aqueductal stenosis and hydrocephalus in children. Injection of mumps virus into suckling hamsters has produced similar lesions.

Laboratory Diagnosis

Laboratory studies are not usually required to establish the diagnosis of typical cases. However, mumps can sometimes be confused with enlargement of the parotids due to suppuration, foreign bodies in the salivary ducts, tumors, etc. In cases without parotitis, particularly in aseptic meningitis, the laboratory can be helpful in establishing the diagnosis.

A. Recovery of Virus: Virus can be isolated from saliva, cerebrospinal fluid, or urine collected within 4 days after onset of illness. After treatment with antibiotics, the specimens are inoculated into monkey kidney cell cultures. Virus growth can be detected in 5–6 days by adsorption of suitable erythrocytes by the infected cells. The isolate can be identified with specific antiserum that can inhibit the hemadsorption. Immunofluorescent serum can also identify a virus isolate in cell culture within 2–3 days.

B. Serology: Antibody rise can be detected in paired sera. The CF test is best for specificity and accuracy, although the HI test may be used. A 4-fold or greater rise in antibody titer is evidence of mumps infection.

A CF test on a single serum sample obtained soon after onset of illness may serve for a presumptive diagnosis. S (soluble) antibodies develop within a few days after onset and sometimes reach a high titer before V (viral) antibodies can be detected. In early convalescence, both S and V antibodies are present at high levels. Subsequently, S antibodies disappear more rapidly, leaving V antibodies as a marker of previous infection for several years. The intradermal injection of inactivated virus results in reappearance of V antibodies in high titer. Neutralizing antibodies also appear during convalescence and can be determined in cell culture.

C. Skin Test Antigen: Delayed type hypersensitivity may be noted about 3–4 weeks after onset. The skin test is less reliable than serologic tests to establish evidence of past infection.

Immunity

Immunity is permanent after a single infection. Only one antigenic type exists. Passive immunity is transferred from mother to offspring; thus it is rare to see mumps in infants under age 6 months.

Treatment

Gamma globulin is of no value for decreasing the incidence of orchitis, even when given immediately after parotitis is first noted.

Epidemiology

Mumps occurs throughout the world endemically throughout the year. Outbreaks occur where crowding favors dissemination of the virus. The disease reaches its highest incidence in children age 5–15 years, but epidemics occur in army camps. Although morbidity rates are high, the mortality rate is negligible, even when the nervous system is involved.

Humans are the only known reservoir of virus. The virus is transmitted by direct contact, airborne droplets, or fomites contaminated with saliva and, perhaps, urine. The period of communicability is from about 4 days before to about a week after the onset of symptoms. More intimate contact is necessary for the transmission of mumps than for measles or varicella.

About 30–40% of infections with mumps virus are inapparent. Individuals with subclinical mumps acquire immunity. During the course of inapparent infection, they can serve as sources of infection for others.

Antibodies to mumps virus are transferred across the placenta and are gradually lost during the first year of life. In urban areas, antibodies are then acquired gradually, so that the 15-year-old group has about the same prevalence of persons with antibodies as the adult group. Antibodies are acquired at the same rate by persons living under favorable and unfavorable socioeconomic conditions.

Control

Mumps is usually a mild childhood disease. A live attenuated vaccine made in chick embryo cell culture is available. It produces a subclinical noncommunicable infection.

The vaccine is recommended for children over age 1 year and for adolescents and adults who have not had mumps parotitis. A single dose of the vaccine given subcutaneously produces detectable antibodies in 95% of vaccinees, and antibody persists for at least 8 years.

Combination live virus vaccines (measles-mumps-rubella) produce antibodies to each of the viruses in about 95%.

In 1967, the year mumps vaccine was licensed, there were about 200,000 mumps cases (and 900 patients with encephalitis) in the USA. After 10 years of vaccine use, the number of mumps cases in 1977 was about 22,000, with 70 cases of encephalitis.

PARAINFLUENZA VIRUS INFECTIONS

The parainfluenza viruses are paramyxoviruses with morphologic and biologic properties typical of the genus. They grow well in primary monkey or human epithelial cell culture but poorly or not at all in the embryonated egg. They produce a minimal cytopathic effect in cell culture but are recognized by the hemadsorption method. Laboratory diagnosis may be made by the HI, CF, and Nt tests.

Parainfluenza 1

Included here are **Sendai virus**, also known as the **hemagglutinating virus of Japan (HVJ)**, and **hemadsorption virus type 2 (HA-2)**. Sendai virus may be a causative agent of pneumonia in pigs and newborn infants. Sendai virus is important in somatic cell genetics, where it is used to produce cell fusion. Clinically, the most important member of this group appears to be the widespread HA-2 virus. It is not cytopathogenic for monkey kidney cell cultures but is detected in such cultures by the hemadsorption test. It is one of the main agents producing croup in children, but it can also cause coryza, pharyngitis, bronchitis, bronchiolitis, or pneumonia. In adults it produces respiratory symptoms like those of the common cold, with reinfection occurring in persons with antibodies from earlier infections.

Natural infection stimulates antibody appearance in nasal secretions and concomitant resistance to reinfection. An experimental killed vaccine induces serum antibodies but does not protect against infection.

Parainfluenza 2

This group includes the **croup-associated (CA) virus** of children. The virus grows in human cells (HeLa, lung, amnion) and monkey kidney. Syncytial masses are produced, with loss of cell boundaries. The virus agglutinates chick and human type O erythrocytes. Adsorption and hemagglutination occur at 4 °C, and elution of virus takes place rapidly at 37 °C. However, the cells reagglutinate when returned to 4 °C. Mumps patients develop type 2 antibodies.

Parainfluenza virus 2 occurs spontaneously in 30% of lots of monkey kidney cells grown in culture. The monkey virus SV5 is antigenically related.

Parainfluenza 3

The viruses in this group are also known as **hemadsorption virus type 1 (HA-1)**. They are detected in monkey kidney cultures by the hemadsorption technique. Serial passage in culture may lead to cytopathic changes. Multinucleated giant cell plaques are produced under agar in certain human cell lines.

The virus has been isolated from children with mild respiratory illnesses, croup, bronchiolitis, or pneumonitis. Strains of type 3 virus have been isolated from nasal secretions of cattle ill with a respiratory syndrome known as "shipping fever." At least 70% of market cattle bled at slaughter have parainfluenza 3 antibodies.

Parainfluenza 4 & 5

These viruses are not known to cause any human illness, although antibodies are widespread. Their growth in cell culture can be recognized by the hemadsorption method.

Clinical Features & Control

Children in the first year of life with primary infections caused by parainfluenza virus type 1, 2, or 3 may have serious illness ranging from laryngotracheitis and croup (particularly type 2) to bronchitis, bronchiolitis, and pneumonitis (particularly type 3).

Virtually all infants have maternal antibodies to parainfluenza viruses in serum, yet such antibodies do not prevent infection or disease. Reinfection of older children and adults also occurs in the presence of antibodies arising from an earlier infection. Such reinfections usually present as nonfebrile upper respiratory infections ("colds").

The incubation for type 1 is 5–6 days; that for type 3 is 2–3 days. Most children have acquired antibodies to all 3 types before age 10.

Killed parainfluenza vaccines induce serum antibodies but no immunity. Live vaccines are being investigated.

NEWCASTLE DISEASE CONJUNCTIVITIS

Newcastle disease virus is a typical paramyxovirus that is primarily pathogenic for fowl. It produces pneumoencephalitis in young chickens and "influenza" in older birds. In humans it may produce an inflammation of the conjunctiva. Recovery is complete in 10–14 days. The infection in humans is an occupational disease limited to laboratory workers and to poultry workers handling infected birds.

The virus grows readily in the embryonated egg, in chick embryo cell culture, or in HeLa cells and produces hemagglutination.

Human erythrocytes treated with the virus are agglutinated by specific serum against Newcastle virus.

Newcastle antibodies can be measured by the HI, CF, and Nt tests using chick embryos or tissue cultures. Cross-reacting HI antibodies can develop in mumps, hepatitis, and infectious mononucleosis. Normal human sera possess a heat-labile, nonspecific inhibitor that can be destroyed by heating at 56 °C for 30 minutes.

There are several other avian paramyxoviruses.

MEASLES
(Rubeola)

Measles is an acute, highly infectious disease characterized by a maculopapular rash, fever, and respiratory symptoms.

Properties of the Virus

A. Morphology and Biologic Properties: Measles virus is a typical paramyxovirus, related to canine distemper and bovine rinderpest. All 3 lack neuraminidase activity. Measles agglutinates monkey erythrocytes at 37 °C but does not elute, and it interacts with a distinct cell receptor. Measles virus also causes hemolysis, and this activity can be separated from that of the hemagglutinin.

B. Animal Susceptibility and Growth of Virus: The experimental disease has been produced in monkeys. They develop fever, catarrh, Koplik's spots, and a discrete papular rash. The virus has been grown in chick embryos; in cell cultures of human, monkey, and dog kidney tissue; and in human continuous cell lines. In cell cultures, multinucleate syncytial giant cells form by fusion of mononucleated ones, and other cells become spindle-shaped in the course of their degeneration. Nuclear changes consist of margination of the chromatin and its replacement centrally with an acidophilic inclusion body. Measles virus is relatively unstable after it is released from cells. During the culture of the virus, the intracellular virus titer is 10 or more times the extracellular titer.

Pathogenesis & Pathology

The virus enters the respiratory tract, enters cells, and multiplies there. During the prodrome, the virus is present in the blood, throughout the respiratory tract, and in nasopharyngeal, tracheobronchial, and conjunctival secretions. It persists in the blood and nasopharyngeal secretions for 2 days after the appearance of the rash. Transplacental transmission of the virus can occur.

Koplik's spots are vesicles in the mouth formed by focal exudations of serum and endothelial cells, followed by focal necrosis. In the skin the superficial capillaries of the corium are first involved, and it is here that the rash makes its appearance. Generalized lymphoid tissue hyperplasia occurs. Multinucleate giant cells are found in lymph nodes, tonsils, adenoids, spleen, appendix, and skin. In encephalomyelitis, there are petechial hemorrhages, lymphocytic infiltration, and, later, patchy demyelination in the brain and spinal cord.

Measles nucleoprotein antigens have been identified by immunofluorescence within inclusion bodies in nerve cells of the brain in **subacute sclerosing panencephalitis (SSPE)** (see p 417). The virus has been grown by co-cultivating HeLa cells with brain biopsy material or lymph node material from patients. The presence of latent intracellular measles virus in these specimens suggests a tolerant infection with defective cell-mediated immunity.

If measles antibody is added to cells infected with measles virus, the viral antigens on the cell surface are altered. By expressing fewer viral antigens on the surface, cells may avoid being killed by antibody- or cell-mediated cytotoxic reactions, yet may retain viral genetic information. This may lead to persistent infection as found in SSPE patients.

Clinical Findings

The incubation period is about 10 days to onset of fever and 14 days to appearance of rash. The prodromal period is characterized by fever, sneezing, coughing, running nose, redness of eyes, Koplik's spots (enanthems of the buccal mucosa), and lymphopenia. The fever and cough persist until the rash appears and then subside within 1–2 days. The rash spreads over the entire body within 2–4 days, becoming brownish in 5–10 days. Symptoms of the disease are most marked when the rash is at its peak but subside rapidly thereafter.

In measles, the respiratory tract becomes more susceptible to invasion by bacteria, especially hemolytic streptococci; bronchitis, pneumonia, and otitis may follow in 15% of cases.

Encephalomyelitis occurs in about 1:1000 cases. There appears to be no correlation between the severity of the measles and the appearance of neurologic complications. The cause of measles encephalitis is unknown. It has been suggested that early central nervous system involvement is caused by direct viral invasion of the brain. Later appearance of central nervous system symptoms is associated with demyelination and may be an immunopathologic reaction. Symptoms referable to the brain usually appear a few days after the appearance of the rash, often after it has faded. There is a second bout of fever, with drowsiness or convulsions and pleocytosis of the cerebrospinal fluid. Survivors may show permanent mental disorders (psychosis or personality change) or physical disabilities, particularly seizure disorders. The mortality rate in encephalitis associated with measles is about 10–30%, and many survivors (40%) show sequelae.

Measles virus appears to be responsible for subacute sclerosing panencephalitis (SSPE), a fatal degenerative brain disorder. The disease manifests itself in children and young adults by progressive mental deterioration, myoclonic jerks, and an abnormal electroencephalogram with periodic high-voltage complexes. The disease develops a number of years after the initial measles infection.

Atypical measles. After the introduction of killed measles virus vaccine in 1965, a new clinical syndrome was observed in children who had a history of receiving the vaccine. The syndrome, called atypical measles, was associated with measles virus infection and was characterized by high fever, pneumonia, and an unusual rash (raised papules, wheals, and tiny hemorrhages in the skin) without Koplik's spots. Killed measles virus vaccine is no longer used. Atypical measles is now seen occasionally in young adults.

Laboratory Diagnosis

Measles is usually easily diagnosed on clinical grounds. About 5% of cases lack Koplik's spots and are difficult to differentiate clinically from infection with rubella virus, certain enteroviruses, and adenoviruses.

A. Recovery of Virus: Measles virus can be isolated from the blood and nasopharynx of a patient from

2–3 days before the onset of symptoms to 1 day after the appearance of rash. Human amnion or kidney cell cultures are best suited for isolation of virus.

B. Serology: Specific neutralizing, hemagglutination-inhibiting, and complement-fixing antibodies develop early, with maximal titers near the time of onset of rash. There is only a gradual decline in antibody titer with age.

Measles and canine distemper share an antigen. Measles patients develop antibodies that cross-react with canine distemper virus. Similarly, dogs, after infection with distemper virus, develop antibodies that fix complement with measles antigen. Rinderpest virus is also related to measles.

Immunity

There appears to be only one antigenic type of measles virus, as one attack generally confers lifelong immunity. Most so-called second attacks represent errors in diagnosis of the initial or the second illness.

Epidemiology

Measles is endemic throughout the world. In general, epidemics recur regularly every 2–3 years. The state of immunity of the population is the determining factor. The disease flares up when there is an accumulation of susceptible children. By age 20 years, over 80% have had an attack of the disease. The severity of an epidemic is a function of the number of susceptible individuals. Only about 1% of susceptible persons fail to contract measles on their first close contact with a patient.

When the disease is introduced into isolated communities where it has not been endemic, all age groups develop clinical measles. A classic example of this was the introduction of measles into the Faroe Islands in 1846; only people over age 60 years, who had been alive during the last epidemic, escaped the disease. In places where the disease strikes rarely, its consequences are often disastrous, and the mortality rate may be as high as 25%.

The highest incidence of measles is in the late winter and spring. Infection is contracted by inhalation of droplets expelled in sneezing or coughing. Measles is spread chiefly by children during the catarrhal prodromal period; they are infectious from 1–2 days prior to the onset of symptoms until a few days after the rash has appeared.

Control

Live attenuated measles virus vaccine effectively prevents measles. Prior to the introduction of the vaccine, over 500,000 cases of measles occurred annually in the USA, and over 300 developed encephalitis. Following mass immunization in 1966–1967, the number of cases decreased to 67,000 and 22,000 annually in the next 2 years, with a corresponding decrease in measles encephalitis. Nevertheless, measles continues to occur, and in 1976 and 1977, the reported cases increased to 40,000 and 56,000 respectively — 90% among the nonvaccinated. About 95% of children

properly inoculated with live virus vaccine develop antibodies that persist for at least 14 years.

As of 1979, an effective measles vaccine has been given to 70% of the children in the USA. The result has been the disappearance of the major epidemics of the 1950s that infected and immunized 98% of children by age 10. However, the 30% of children who were not immunized in the 1960s became the susceptible adolescents of the 1970s. In 1977, one-fourth of measles cases in the USA occurred in persons over 15 years of age. To prevent adult measles from becoming a major problem, the vaccination program for children has been intensified, with the result that measles cases in 1981 decreased to about 3000, a record low. From a prevaccination rate of 400 measles deaths per year, the number in 1980 had dropped to only 6.

Less attenuated vaccine virus may produce fever and a modified skin rash in a proportion of vaccinees; this reaction can be prevented by the simultaneous administration of gamma globulin (0.02 mL/kg body weight) *at a separate site from the vaccine*. The more attenuated vaccine viruses do not produce symptoms and do not require the use of gamma globulin. The different vaccine viruses appear to be equally effective in producing immunity.

Measles antibodies cross the placenta and protect the infant during the first 6–10 months of life. Vaccination with the live virus fails to take during this period, and measles immunization should be deferred until 15 months of age. This applies both to monovalent measles vaccine and to combined measles-mumps-rubella vaccine.

When the live vaccine was first introduced, it was often given to infants in the first year of life. This did not produce immunity, and such children must be revaccinated.

Vaccination is not recommended in persons with febrile illnesses or allergies to eggs or other products used in the production of the vaccine, and in persons with immune defects.

Epidemiologic studies have shown that the risk, if any, of SSPE occurring in vaccinated persons is much less than the risk of its occurring in persons who have natural measles.

Killed measles vaccine should not be used, as certain vaccinees become sensitized and develop either local reactions when revaccinated with live attenuated virus or severe atypical measles when infected with wild virus or even with live vaccine virus (see Atypical measles, above).

Measles may be prevented or modified by administering antibody early in the incubation period. Human gamma globulin contains antibody titers of 200–1000 against 100 $TCID_{50}$ of virus. With small doses, the disease can be made mild and immunity ensues. With a large dose of gamma globulin, the disease can be prevented; however, the person remains susceptible to infection at a later date. Antibodies given later than 6 days after exposure are not likely to influence the course of the disease.

RESPIRATORY SYNCYTIAL (RS) VIRUS

This labile paramyxovirus produces a characteristic syncytial effect, the fusion of cells in human cell culture. It is the single most serious cause of bronchiolitis and pneumonitis in infants.

The particle is slightly smaller (80–120 nm) than other paramyxoviruses, and the nucleocapsid measures 11–15 nm. Although RS is one of the most labile of viruses, it can be stabilized by molar $MgSO_4$ (like measles and other paramyxoviruses). RS virus does not hemagglutinate. A soluble complement-fixing antigen can be separated from the virus particle.

RS virus can be grown in cell culture, but it fails to grow in eggs or in laboratory animals. Immunofluorescence can determine the virus antigen in cell culture.

RS virus can be isolated from about 40% of infants under age 6 months suffering from bronchiolitis and from about 25% with pneumonitis, but it is almost never isolated from healthy infants. RS virus infection in older infants and children results in milder respiratory tract infection than in those under 6 months of age. Adult volunteers can be reinfected with RS virus (in spite of the presence of specific antibodies), but the resulting symptoms are those of an upper respiratory infection, a "cold."

Recently, RS viral antigen has been found in osteoclasts in bone sections and in cells cultured from Paget's disease lesions.

RS virus spreads extensively in children every year during the winter season. Reinfection commonly occurs in children, but each subsequent infection is milder than the preceding ones. Nosocomial infections occur in nurseries and on pediatric hospital wards. Transmission occurs primarily via the hands of staff members. Hand washing after every patient contact, wearing gowns and gloves, and isolation of infected patients reduce nosocomial spread.

RS virus grows slowly in cell cultures (4–8 days). For more rapid results, the direct immunofluorescence test with RS antiserum can be applied to nasopharyngeal smears containing exfoliated cells.

Maternal RS antibody is transmitted to the fetus, but it does not protect the infant from disease.

The clinical disease in young infants may actually be the result of an antigen-antibody reaction that results when the infecting virus meets maternally transmitted antibody. Killed RS vaccines may do more harm than good. Efforts to develop an attenuated vaccine that infects subclinically and induces nasal antibody are in progress.

RS virus occurs spontaneously in chimpanzees and has been associated with coryza in these primates.

. . .

RUBELLA (German Measles)

Rubella is an acute febrile illness characterized by a rash and posterior auricular and suboccipital lymphadenopathy that affects children and young adults. Infection in early pregnancy may result in serious abnormalities of the fetus.

Properties of the Virus

The virus is RNA-containing, ether-sensitive, and about 60 nm in diameter. It contains a 30-nm internal nucleocapsid with a double membrane and forms by budding from the endoplasmic reticulum into intracytoplasmic vesicles and at the marginal cell membrane. Projections of the virion, 6 nm long, possess hemagglutinin for some avian erythrocytes. Receptor-destroying enzyme has no effect, and there is no spontaneous elution after hemagglutination.

Rubella virus can be propagated in cell culture. In some cultures, eg, human amnion cells, rabbit kidney cells, and a line of monkey kidney (VERO) cells, the virus produces detectable cytopathologic changes. In other cell cultures, rubella virus replicates without causing a cytopathic effect; however, interference is induced that protects the cells against the cytopathic effect of other viruses. One method of isolating rubella virus consists of inoculating green monkey kidney cells with the specimen and, after 7–10 days of incubation, challenging the cultures with echovirus 11. If echovirus cytopathic effect develops, the specimen is considered negative for rubella virus; conversely, the absence of echovirus cytopathic effect implies the presence of rubella virus in the original specimen.

1. POSTNATAL RUBELLA

Pathogenesis

Infection occurs through the mucosa of the upper respiratory tract. The virus probably replicates primarily in the cervical lymph nodes. After a period of 7 days, viremia develops that lasts until the appearance of antibody on about day 12–14. The development of antibody coincides with the appearance of the rash, suggesting an immunologic basis for the rash. After the rash appears, the virus remains detectable only in the nasopharynx.

Clinical Features

Rubella usually begins with malaise, low-grade fever, and a morbilliform rash appearing on the same day. Less often, systemic symptoms may precede the rash by 1 or 2 days, or the rash and lymphadenopathy may occur without systemic symptoms. The rash starts on the face, extends over the trunk and extremities, and rarely lasts more than 3 days. Posterior auricular and suboccipital lymphadenopathy are present. Transient arthralgia and arthritis are commonly seen in adult females. Rare complications include thrombocytopenia and encephalitis.

Unless an epidemic occurs, the disease is difficult to diagnose clinically, since the rash caused by other viruses such as the enteroviruses is similar. However, rubella has a peak occurrence in the spring, whereas enterovirus infections occur mainly in the summer and fall.

Immunity

Rubella antibodies appear in the serum of patients as the rash fades, and the titer of antibody rises rapidly over the next 1–3 weeks. Much of the initial antibody consists of IgM. IgM rubella antibodies found in a single serum obtained 2 weeks after the rash give evidence of recent rubella infection.

One attack of the disease confers lifelong immunity, as only one antigenic type of the virus exists. A history of rubella is not a reliable index of immunity. The presence of antibody at a 1:8 dilution implies immunity. Immune mothers transfer antibodies to their offspring, who are then protected for 4–6 months.

Treatment

No specific treatment is given unless the patient is pregnant. Rubellalike illness in the first trimester of pregnancy should be substantiated by isolation of the virus from the throat or by demonstrating a 4-fold rise in antibody titer to the virus by means of the HI, CF, or Nt test. Laboratory-proved rubella in the first 10 weeks of pregnancy is almost uniformly associated with fetal infection. Therapeutic abortion is strongly recommended in laboratory-proved cases to avoid the risk of malformed infants.

It should be noted that gamma globulin injected into the mother does not protect the fetus against rubella infection.

2. CONGENITAL RUBELLA SYNDROME

Pathogenesis

Rubella infection during pregnancy may result in infection of the placenta and fetus. A limited number of cells of the fetus become infected. Although the virus does not destroy the cells, the growth rate of the infected cells is reduced, which results in fewer than normal numbers of cells in the organs at birth. The

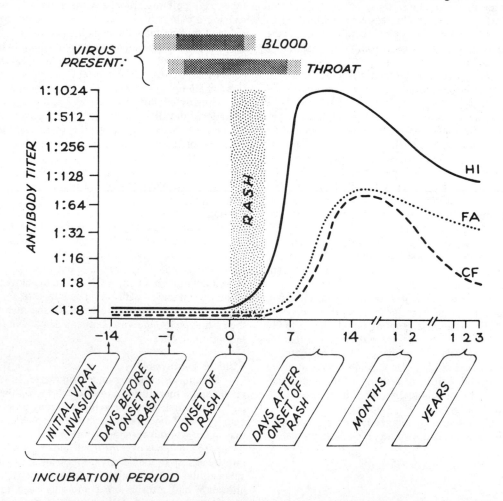

Figure 35–3. Virus and antibody dynamics in rubella. HI = hemagglutination-inhibiting antibody; FA = fluorescent antibody; CF = complement-fixing antibody.

earlier in pregnancy infection occurs, the greater the chance of extensive involvement, with the birth of an infant afflicted with severe anomalies. Infection in the first month of pregnancy results in abnormalities in about 80% of cases, whereas detectable defects are found in about 15% of infants acquiring the disease during the third month of gestation. The intrauterine infection is associated with chronic persistence of the virus in the newborn, which may last for 12–18 months after birth.

Clinical Findings

Infants with congenital rubella syndrome may have one or more abnormalities, which include defects of the heart and great vessels (patent ductus arteriosus, pulmonary artery stenosis, pulmonary valvular stenosis, ventricular septal defect, and atrial septal defect), eye defects (cataracts, glaucoma, and chorioretinitis), and neurosensory deafness. Infants may also display growth retardation, failure to thrive, hepatosplenomegaly, thrombocytopenia with purpura, anemia, osteitis, and an encephalitic syndrome leading to cerebral palsy. The infants often have increased susceptibility to infection and abnormal immunoglobulins, most commonly elevated IgM with low levels of IgG and IgA.

There is a 20% mortality rate among congenitally virus-infected infants symptomatic at birth. Some virus-infected infants appearing normal at birth may manifest abnormalities at a later date. Severely affected infants may require institutionalization.

The spectrum of neurologic and neurosensory involvement in surviving infants is wide. Among 100 patients with congenital rubella infection, neurologic manifestations were found in 81 at some time between birth and 18 months. Sequelae include hearing impairment, visual impairment, growth disturbance, microcephaly, mental retardation, and cerebral dysfunction. Problems with balance and motor skills develop in preschool children. Psychiatric disorders and behavioral manifestations occur in preschool and school age children.

In one study, the neurologic course of congenital rubella syndrome was traced in nonretarded children. During the first 2 years, manifestations involved abnormal tone and reflexes (69%), motor delays (66%), feeding difficulties (48%), and abnormal clinical behavior (45%). Hearing loss was documented in 76%. At 3–7 years, poor balance, motor incoordination (69%), and behavioral disturbances (66%) predominated. Hearing losses increased to 86%. At 9–12 years, the following were noted: residua that included learning deficits (52%), behavioral disturbances (48%), poor balance (61%), muscle weakness (54%), and deficits in tactile perception (41%). Thus, the encephalitic manifestations of congenital rubella syndrome are persistent and diverse.

Immunity

While maternal rubella antibody in the form of IgG is transferred to the infant with congenital rubella, the infant also produces IgM antibodies. Nonaffected infants lose maternal antibody.

Epidemiology

The virus has been recovered from the nasopharynx, throat, blood, cerebrospinal fluid, and urine. The infection is spread by respiratory pathways (droplets).

Infants continue to be infectious, with virus found in the throat for up to 18 months after birth. Virus has been recovered from many tissues tested postmortem.

Congenitally infected infants who appear normal but who shed virus are capable of transmitting rubella to susceptible contacts such as nurses and physicians caring for the infants. This represents a serious hazard to women in the first trimester of pregnancy, who should avoid contact with these babies.

Rubella without rash is of importance because inapparent rubella infection (with viremia) acquired during pregnancy has the same deleterious effect on the fetus as rubella with the typical rash.

3. CONTROL OF RUBELLA

In the 20th century, epidemics of rubella have occurred every 6–9 years. After each epidemic, cases declined for the next 5 years, then increased to epidemic levels 6–9 years after the last major outbreak. In the 1964 epidemic, more than 20,000 infants were born with severe manifestations of congenital rubella.

In the USA, the control of rubella is being attempted by routine vaccination of children age 1–12 years and selected immunization of adolescents and women of childbearing age. Before vaccine became available in 1969, about 50,000 cases were being reported annually. In the next decade, about 100 million doses of vaccine were administered, which resulted in a 70% decrease in rubella incidence. However, the decrease occurred primarily in children. Persons 15 years of age and older experienced only a small decrease in incidence and now account for over 70% of cases. (Before 1969, they accounted for only 20%.) Since vaccine-induced antibodies persist for at least 10 years, the changing pattern may not be due to vaccine failure as much as to failure to adequately vaccinate susceptible adults.

Since the introduction of vaccine, scattered outbreaks have been reported, chiefly among nonvaccinated adolescents in high school and college who had not received vaccine in the routine immunization program. The changing age incidence of rubella since introduction of vaccine is similar to the changing epidemiologic pattern with measles.

In postpubertal females, the vaccine produces self-limited arthralgia and arthritis in about one-third of the vaccinees. Since rubella virus vaccine may infect the placenta, the vaccine should not be given to a postpubertal female unless she is not pregnant, is susceptible (ie, serologically negative), understands that she should not become pregnant for at least 3 months after vaccination, and is adequately warned of the complications of arthralgia. Nevertheless, since rubella vaccination is an effective way of preventing birth defects, it should be vigorously encouraged in women of childbearing age.

In children, the vaccine may also produce mild febrile episodes with arthralgia, often several months after vaccination, but without any permanent residual effects. Vaccinated children are not infectious and do not transmit the virus to contacts at home, even to mothers who are susceptible and pregnant. In contrast, nonimmunized children can bring home wild virus and spread it to susceptible family contacts.

Opinions have been expressed that vaccination of children cannot prevent future infection of pregnant women exposed to wild virus. Therefore, vaccination of prepubertal girls and women in the immediate postpartum period has also been proposed. It would seem wise for all pregnant women to undergo a serum antibody test for rubella and, if found to be susceptible, receive a vaccination immediately after delivery. Conception in the 6–8 weeks after delivery is rare, so the risk of harming a fetus would be minimal.

There is conflicting evidence on the nature and duration of postvaccination immunity with the first (HPV77) rubella vaccine, the risk of superinfection with wild virus, and the subsequent spread of such virus to pregnant women.

In 1979, the second rubella vaccine, RA23/3, grown in human diploid cells, was licensed, and this is the vaccine of choice. It produces much higher antibody titers and a more enduring and more solid immunity than HPV77, and there is evidence that it largely prevents subclinical superinfection with wild virus. This vaccine is available as a single antigen or combined with measles and mumps vaccine. It may effectively produce IgA antibody in the respiratory tract and thus interfere with infection by wild virus.

• • •

References

Albrecht P et al: Persistence of maternal antibody in infants beyond 12 months: Mechanism of measles vaccine failure. *J Pediatr* 1977;**91:**715.

Casali P et al: Purification of measles virus glycoproteins and their integration into artificial lipid membranes. *J Gen Virol* 1981;**54:**161.

Choppin PW, Scheid A: The role of viral glycoproteins in adsorption, penetration, and pathogenicity of viruses. *Rev Infect Dis* 1980;**2:**40.

Desmond MM et al: The longitudinal course of congenital rubella encephalitis in nonretarded children. *J Pediatr* 1978;**93:**584.

Fox JP et al: Rubella vaccine in postpubertal women: Experience in western Washington state. *JAMA* 1976;**236:**837.

Fujinami RS, Oldstone MBA: Antiviral antibody reacting on the plasma membrane alters measles virus expression inside the cell. *Nature* 1979;**279:**529.

Hall WW, Choppin PW: Measles-virus proteins in the brain tissue of patients with subacute sclerosing panencephalitis: Absence of the M protein. *N Engl J Med* 1981;**304:**1152.

Henderson FW et al: Respiratory-syncytial-virus infections, reinfections and immunity. A prospective, longitudinal study in young children. *N Engl J Med* 1979;**300:**530.

Hinman AR, Brandling-Bennett AD, Nieburg PI: The opportunity and obligation to eliminate measles from the United States. *JAMA* 1979;**242:**1157.

Mann JM et al: Assessing risks of rubella infection during pregnancy: A standardized approach. *JAMA* 1981;**245:**1647.

Martin AJ, Gardner PS, McQuillin J: Epidemiology of respiratory viral infections among paediatric inpatients over a six-year period in north-east England. *Lancet* 1978;**2:**1035.

Mills BG et al: Immunohistological demonstration of respiratory syncytial virus antigens in Paget disease of bone. *Proc Natl Acad Sci USA* 1981;**78:**1209.

Morgan EM, Rapp F: Measles virus and its associated diseases. *Bacteriol Rev* 1977;**41:**636.

Preblud SR et al: Current status of rubella in the United States, 1969–1979. *J Infect Dis* 1980;**142:**776.

Rawls WE: Congenital rubella: The significance of virus persistence. *Prog Med Virol* 1968;**10:**238.

Tyeryar FJ, Jr, Richardson LS, Belshe RB: Report of a workshop on respiratory syncytial virus and parainfluenza viruses. *J Infect Dis* 1978;**137:**835.

The **poxviruses** are a large group of agents that are morphologically similar and have a common nucleoprotein (NP) antigen. Some subgroups have a restricted host range and infect only arthropods, or only rodents (fibroma and myxoma), or only birds. Other subgroups infect mainly sheep (orf, sheeppox), goats (goatpox), and cattle (eg, milker's nodule). The so-called orthopoxviruses have a broader host range, affecting several vertebrates. They include ectromelia (mousepox), rabbitpox, cowpox, monkeypox, vaccinia, and variola (smallpox). The last 3, and perhaps others, are infectious for humans.

VACCINIA, VARIOLA, &
RELATED POXVIRUSES
THAT CAN INFECT HUMANS

While smallpox (variola) was declared eradicated from the world in 1979, there is a continuing need to be familiar with vaccinia virus and its possible complications in humans. There is also a need to be aware of other poxvirus diseases that may resemble smallpox and thus must be differentiated from it by laboratory means. Lastly, vaccinia virus has been studied in great detail and provides insight into the properties and replication of this large group of agents.

Vaccinia virus differs in only minor morphologic respects from variola and cowpox. It is described below as the prototype of poxviruses in terms of structure and replication. Monkeypox can infect both monkeys and humans and may resemble smallpox clinically. Yaba virus induces benign tumors in monkeys and can produce similar lesions in humans.

Properties of the Virus
A. Size and Nucleic Acid: Poxviruses are brick-shaped or ellipsoid particles measuring about 230 × 400 nm. There is an outer lipoprotein membrane, or envelope, and a core with a thick membrane, enclosing the genome. The latter is linear double-stranded DNA (MW 130–240 × 10⁶). (See Figs 27–31 and 27–32.) The virion contains several enzymes, including a DNA-dependent RNA polymerase, and about 100 polypeptides. The chemical composition of a poxvirus resembles that of a bacterium.

B. Animal Susceptibility: Both vaccinia and variola viruses grow on the chorioallantoic membrane of the 10- to 12-day-old chick embryo, but the latter produces much smaller pocks. Both grow in several types of chick and primate cell lines. Variola infects only humans and monkeys, whereas vaccinia also infects rabbits.

C. Antigenic Properties: Poxviruses have a complex antigenic pattern, with up to 20 antigen-antibody complexes demonstrable in immunodiffusion tests. Vaccinia and variola differ from each other by only one antigen, but they cross-react little with poxviruses of the myxoma-fibroma group. All poxviruses share a common nucleoprotein (NP) antigen in the inner core.

In addition to structural antigens, poxviruses produce soluble antigens and hemagglutinins. Vaccinia virus contains a heat-labile (L) antigen that is destroyed at 60 °C and a heat-stable (S) antigen that withstands treatment at 100 °C. Both antigens may be present in soluble form in infected tissue. They appear to be different antigenic components of a complex LS antigen, a protein with a molecular weight of about 240,000. Adsorption of immune sera with LS or NP antigens fails to remove neutralizing antibody. Upon the LS antigens depend the serologic tests for smallpox diagnosis. LS antigens from variola and from vaccinia virus are antigenically similar.

The hemagglutinin of vaccinia, variola, or ectromelia (mousepox) is not an integral part of the virion. It is a lipoprotein complex associated with a 65-nm particle. The hemagglutination reaction with chicken red cells can be inhibited by vaccinia immune serum, convalescent smallpox serum, or ectromelia immune serum.

D. Differentiation Among the Poxviruses: The use of restriction enzyme cleavage of viral DNA and the analysis of polypeptides in poxvirus-infected cells can demonstrate distinct characteristics for variola, vaccinia, monkeypox, and cowpox. This is important because smallpoxlike illnesses must be identified to ascertain that variola has indeed been eradicated.

Poxvirus Multiplication
A. Virus Penetration and Uncoating: Virus particles establish contact with the cell surface and are

then engulfed in phagocytic vacuoles of the cell, where first-stage uncoating takes place by means of hydrolytic enzymes in the vacuole. This releases the nucleoprotein core into the cytoplasm. The second uncoating step liberates DNA from the nucleoprotein, and it requires both RNA and protein synthesis in order to occur. Among the several enzymes inside the poxvirus particle, there is a viral RNA polymerase that mediates the synthesis of messenger RNA (mRNA). This mRNA is transcribed within the virus core and then released into the cytoplasm, where it codes for the synthesis of enzyme proteins that release the viral DNA from the nucleoprotein and other enzymes. The synthesis of host cell macromolecules is inhibited at this stage.

Poxviruses inactivated by heat can be reactivated either by viable poxviruses or by poxviruses inactivated by nitrogen mustards (which inactivate the DNA). This process is called nongenetic reactivation and is due to the stimulation of the uncoating protein. Heat-inactivated virus cannot cause second-stage uncoating because of the heat lability of the DNA-dependent RNA polymerase. Any poxvirus can reactivate any other poxvirus, which suggests that all poxviruses carry the RNA polymerase in their cores.

After the release of viral DNA in the second uncoating, additional mRNA is transcribed that codes for additional enzymes and some early structural proteins of the virion, which form part of the core. By 4 hours after cell infection, viral DNA replication occurs in discrete areas of the cytoplasm, which appear as "inclusion bodies" (Fig 27–29) in electron micrographs. After the synthesis of progeny viral DNA has begun, the synthesis of early virus proteins is inhibited, and late viral mRNA is translated into structural proteins and enzymes. DNA replication then ceases.

The assembly of the virus particle from the manufactured components is a complex process. Many of the polypeptides that become part of the virus particle are modified by the addition of sugars (glycosylation) or phosphorus (phosphorylation) or by proteolytic cleavage. Poxviruses are unique in that de novo formation of virus membranes occurs (see Figs 27–31 and 27–32).

Morphogenesis of poxvirus particles can be followed by electron micrographs of thin cell sections. Different structural phases can be correlated with the biochemical steps described above. Mature virions appear as a DNA-containing core encased in double membranes, surrounded by protein, and all enclosed within 2 outer membranes.

Thin sections observed in the electron microscope 24 hours after infection show that the virus is being manufactured throughout the cytoplasm. Ten thousand virus particles per cell are produced.

Release of the virus may be by budding or lysis, and some particles may gain a cell-related envelope.

B. Virus Inhibitors: Cells infected with vaccinia virus and treated with bromodeoxyuridine (BUDR) produce viral antigen in the cytoplasm and yield particles that have incorporated bromodeoxyuridine in their nucleic acid in place of thymidine. Such particles are malformed and noninfectious.

Rifampin can block the formation and assembly of the vaccinia virus envelope, and it also interferes with formation of a core polypeptide in cell culture. Methisazone interferes with the formation of late proteins and assembly of the particle.

Pathogenesis & Pathology of Smallpox

The portal of entry of variola virus is the mucous membranes of the upper respiratory tract. After the entry of the virus, the following are believed to take place: (1) primary multiplication in the lymphoid tissue draining the site of entry; (2) transient viremia and infection of reticuloendothelial cells throughout the body; (3) a secondary phase of multiplication in these cells, leading to (4) a secondary, more intense viremia; and (5) the clinical disease.

The skin lesion follows the localization of virus in the epidermis from the bloodstream. The virus can be isolated from the blood in the first few days of the disease. Clinical improvement follows the development of the skin eruption, perhaps owing to the appearance of antibodies. The pustulation of the skin lesions may give rise to a secondary fever; this may be due to absorption of the products of cell necrosis rather than secondary bacterial infection.

Skin pustules may become contaminated, usually with staphylococci, sometimes leading to bacteremia and sepsis.

In the preeruptive phase, the disease is hardly infective. By the sixth to ninth days, lesions in the mouth tend to ulcerate and discharge virus. Thus, early in the disease, infectious virus originates in lesions in the mouth and upper respiratory tract. Later, pustules break down and discharge virus into the environment of the smallpox patient.

Histopathologic examination of the skin shows that proliferation of the prickle-cell layer occurs early. These proliferated cells contain many cytoplasmic inclusions. There is infiltration with mononuclear cells, particularly around the vessels in the corium. Epithelial cells of the malpighian layer become swollen through distention of cytoplasm and undergo "ballooning degeneration." The vacuoles in the cytoplasm enlarge. The cell membrane breaks down, and coalescence with neighboring, similarly affected cells results in the formation of vesicles. The vesicles enlarge and then become filled with white cells and tissue debris. In variola and vaccinia all the layers are involved, and there is actual necrosis of the corium. Thus, scarring is seen after variola and vaccinia.

The cytoplasmic inclusions (Guarnieri bodies) are round or oval, homogeneous, and acidophilic, but often the inclusion body has a granular appearance with an irregular outline.

Clinical Findings

The incubation period of variola (smallpox) is about 12 days. The onset may be gradual or sudden.

One to 5 days of fever and malaise precede the appearance of the exanthems, which are papular for 1–4 days, vesicular for 1–4 days, and pustular for 2–6 days, forming crusts that fall off 2–4 weeks after the first sign of the lesion and leave pink scars which fade slowly. In each area affected, the lesions are generally found in the same stage of development. The temperature falls within 24 hours after the rash appears.

The nature and extent of the rash are functions of the severity of the disease. Vaccinated contacts may develop a febrile illness without rash that progresses no further. In severe cases, the rash is hemorrhagic. The case mortality rate may vary from 5 to 40%. In mild variola or in vaccinated persons, the mortality rate is under 1%.

Mild variola (variola minor) gives rise to a mild disease in contacts, whereas modified variola major in immunized persons often gives rise to severe smallpox in contacts.

Laboratory Diagnosis

Several tests are available to confirm the diagnosis of smallpox. They are especially important in previously vaccinated persons, in whom the clinical course may be atypical. They depend upon direct microscopic examination of material from skin lesions, recovery of virus from the patient, identification of viral antigen from the lesion, and demonstration of antibody in the blood. The direct examination of clinical material in the electron microscope can also be used for rapid identification of virus particles and can readily differentiate smallpox from chickenpox.

A. Smears: Carefully prepared and properly stained smears from lesions of the papular and vesicular stages may give a positive result within 30 minutes. Smears are made from lesions on slides. The superficial epidermis is removed and the base of the lesion gently scraped with a blade. The dried smears are washed with distilled water and ether, fixed with alcohol, and stained with a mixture of equal parts of 1% gentian violet and 2% sodium bicarbonate for 5 minutes, with steaming. If elementary bodies are seen in large numbers, a presumptive diagnosis of smallpox can be made.

B. Virus Culture: The detection of virus on the chorioallantoic membrane of the 12- to 14-day-old chick embryo is the most reliable laboratory test. It is the easiest way of distinguishing cases of smallpox from generalized vaccinia, for the lesions produced by these viruses on the membrane differ markedly. In 2–3 days, vaccinia pocks are large with necrotic centers whereas variola pocks are much smaller. Cowpox and monkeypox produce hemorrhagic lesions. All of these can also be grown in various cell cultures and identified by hemadsorption or immunofluorescence.

C. Antigen Detection: Antigen can be detected readily by immunodiffusion or by CF test in material collected from the skin lesion.

D. Antibody Determination: After the first week, neutralizing, complement-fixing, and hemagglutination-inhibiting antibodies appear. However, these are of no practical importance in diagnosis and may decline within several months.

Differential Diagnosis

Smallpox may be confused with varicella, pustular acne, meningococcemia, blood dyscrasias, drug rashes, and other illnesses associated with a skin eruption, but none of these illnesses yield materials that give positive laboratory tests for variola virus. The use of restriction enzyme cleavage of the DNA of isolated poxviruses helps in distinguishing related poxviruses from each other.

Immunity

Children of vaccinated, immune mothers receive maternal antibody transplacentally, which persists for several months. After that time artificial immunity can be produced by vaccination (see Control & Eradication of Smallpox, below). Immunity is demonstrable 8 or 9 days following vaccination, reaches its maximum within 2 or 3 weeks, and is maintained at an appreciable level for a few years.

Antibodies alone are not sufficient for recovery from primary poxvirus infection. In the human host, neutralizing antibodies develop within a few days after onset of smallpox but do not prevent progression of lesions, and patients may die in the pustular stage with high antibody levels. Cell-mediated immunity may be as important as circulating antibody. Patients with hypogammaglobulinemia generally react normally to vaccination and develop immunity despite the apparent absence of antibody. Immunity is accompanied by delayed cutaneous hypersensitivity to vaccinia. Patients who have defects in both cellular immune response and antibody response develop a progressive, usually fatal disease upon vaccination.

It is difficult to determine the relative importance of cellular versus humoral immunity to poxviruses. The macrophage migration inhibition test (see Chapter 13) permits correlation between delayed type hypersensitivity, cell-mediated reactions, and immunity to poxvirus infection. Studies with fibroma virus, a poxvirus that produces benign tumors in rabbits, indicate that there is a good correlation between the onset of delayed hypersensitivity to fibroma infection and inhibition of migration (Fig 36–1). Tumor regression does not occur until several days after a positive skin test and a positive migration inhibition test are observed. Increase in tumor size after onset of delayed hypersensitivity is not due to spread of the infection but to a local immune reaction caused by infiltration of inflammatory cells into the lesion. Animals bearing tumors become resistant to reinfection on the fifth day after the primary infection, which correlates with development of delayed hypersensitivity.

Production of interferon (see Chapter 27) is another possible immune mechanism. Irradiated animals without detectable antibody or delayed hypersensitivity recovered from vaccinia infection as rapidly as untreated control animals.

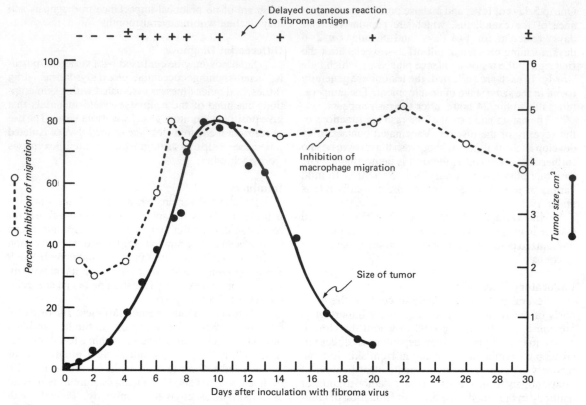

Figure 36–1. Temporal relationship between fibroma virus–induced tumor growth and regression and development of cell-mediated immune response as measured in vivo by skin testing and in vitro by macrophage migration inhibition. (From Tompkins & Rawls.)

Treatment

Vaccinia immune globulin (VIG) is prepared from blood provided by revaccinated military personnel. Indications for use of vaccinia immune globulin are accidental inoculation of vaccine in the eye or eczema vaccinatum.

Methisazone (Marboran) is effective as prophylaxis but is not useful in treatment of established disease (see Chapter 27).

Epidemiology

Transmission of smallpox could usually be traced to contact between cases. Rarely, the dried virus survived on clothes or other materials and resulted in infections.

Patients may be infectious during the incubation period. Virus has been isolated from throat swabs of family contacts of patients with smallpox. Respiratory droplets are infectious earlier than skin lesions.

The following epidemiologic features made smallpox amenable to total eradication: There is no known nonhuman reservoir, and chronic, asymptomatic carriage of the virus does not occur. Since virus in the environment of the patient derives from lesions in the mouth and throat (and later the skin), patients with infection sufficiently severe to transmit the disease are likely to be so ill that they quickly reach the attention of

medical authorities. The close contact requisite for effective spread of the disease generally makes for ready identification of a patient's contacts so that specific control measures can be instituted to interrupt the cycle of transmission.

Control & Eradication of Smallpox

Control of smallpox by deliberate infection with mild forms of the disease was practiced for centuries. This process, called variolation, was dangerous (1% mortality rate) but decreased the effects of major epidemics. Jenner introduced vaccination with live vaccinia virus in 1798.

Vaccinia virus for vaccination is prepared from vesicular lesions ("lymph") produced in the skin of calves or sheep or grown in chick embryos. The latter can be harvested under bacteriologically sterile conditions. The final product contains 40% glycerol and 0.4% phenol to destroy bacteria and keep the vaccine from freezing at its storage temperature of –10 °C. WHO standards require that smallpox vaccines have a potency of not less than 10^8 pock-forming units per milliliter.

Calf-lymph vaccine is kept frozen until issued to physicians. It can then be stored for some weeks in a refrigerator without significant loss of potency, but when removed to room temperature it must be used promptly. Deterioration of vaccine is a problem in tropical countries. There, a stable lyophilized vaccine has been used that is prepared from infected chorioallantoic membranes of embryonated eggs ("avianized vaccine").

In 1967, WHO introduced a worldwide eradication campaign for smallpox. At that time, there were 33 countries with endemic smallpox and 10–15 million cases per year. The last Asiatic case occurred in Bangladesh in 1975, and the last natural victim in Somalia in 1977. There were 3 main reasons for this outstanding success: The vaccine was easily prepared, stable, and safe; it could be given simply by personnel in the field; and mass vaccination of the world population was not necessary. Cases of smallpox were traced, and contacts of the case and those in the immediate area were vaccinated.

The success of smallpox eradication has meant that routine vaccination is no longer recommended. The following summary of vaccination is given because vaccinia virus continues to be administered to millions of persons in military and other populations, and complications from such use continue to occur.

A. Time of Vaccination: Complications of vaccination (see below) occur most commonly under the age of 1 year. Therefore, when necessary, vaccinating between 1 and 2 years of age is preferable to vaccinating in the first year of life. Infants suffering from skin diseases or those with siblings who have skin diseases should not be vaccinated because the vaccinia virus may localize in the lesions of the vaccinated child or of the contact (eczema vaccinatum). Revaccination has been done at 3-year intervals.

B. Technique: The methods used are multiple pressure, multiple puncture, or jet injection. In all techniques, inoculation should be intradermal, never subcutaneous. The skin (arm or thigh) is cleaned with acetone, ether, or soap and water. After the area is dry, a drop of the vaccine is placed on the skin and the side of the needle is then pressed firmly through the drop of vaccine into the superficial layers of the skin. At least 5 pressures should be made. The point of the needle should not draw blood. After the vaccination has been completed, excess vaccine is removed from the skin with dry, sterile gauze. No dressing is applied.

C. Reactions and Interpretations:

1. Primary take–In the fully susceptible person, a papule surrounded by hyperemia appears on the third or fourth day. The papule increases in size until vesiculation appears (on the fifth or sixth day). The vesicle reaches its maximum size by the ninth day and then becomes pustular, usually with some tenderness of the axillary nodes. Desiccation follows and is complete in about 2 weeks, leaving a depressed pink scar that ultimately turns white. The reading of the result is usually made on the seventh day. If this reaction is not observed, vaccination should be repeated with vaccine from another lot until a successful result is obtained.

2. Revaccination–

a. A successful revaccination shows in 1 week (6–8 days) a vesicular or pustular lesion or an area of palpable induration surrounding a central lesion, which may be a scab or an ulcer. Only this reaction indicates with certainty that virus multiplication has taken place.

b. Equivocal reactions may represent immunity but may also represent merely allergic reactions to a vaccine that has become inactivated. When an equivocal reaction occurs, the revaccination should be repeated using a new lot of vaccine known to give "takes" in other persons. A second reading should be made after 6–8 days.

D. Complications of Vaccination:

1. Bacterial infection of the vaccination site–This virtually never occurs.

2. Generalized vaccinia–This is manifested by the occurrence of crops of vaccinial lesions over the surface of the body. Following vaccination, children suffering from eczema may develop vaccinial lesions on the eczematous areas (eczema vaccinatum). Children with a current or past history of eczema should not be vaccinated, since the mortality rate in untreated generalized vaccinia is 30–40%. Neither should children who have siblings with eczema be vaccinated, because of the danger of transmitting the virus and producing generalized vaccinia in the siblings. Generalized vaccinia can occur in the absence of eczema, but this is rare. The use of vaccinia immune globulin has reduced the fatality rate of eczema vaccinatum from 40% to 7%.

3. Postvaccinal encephalitis–The mortality rate of this serious complication may be as high as 40%. The incidence in the USA was about 3 per million among primary vaccinees of all ages. The onset is sudden and occurs about 12 days after vaccination. There is a pleocytosis of the cerebrospinal fluid, the lymphocyte count being 100–200/μL. Focal lesions are widely distributed throughout the gray and white matter of the brain and cord. Perivascular infiltrations of mononuclear cells and areas of demyelination are the chief histologic lesions.

The cause is not clear. Several possibilities exist: (1) Vaccinia virus may invade the central nervous system. (2) Vaccination may activate a latent virus of the nervous system. (3) The reaction may be due to an antigen-antibody reaction that is allergic in character. Similar demyelinating disease may follow infection with variola, measles, and varicella and vaccination against rabies.

4. Vaccinia necrosum or progressive vaccinia–This results from inability to make antibody or to develop cellular resistance and may be fatal. Treatment with vaccinia immune globulin or methisazone (see below) may be of value.

5. Fetal vaccinia–Very rarely, a woman vaccinated late in pregnancy transmitted vaccinia virus to the fetus and stillbirth resulted. Therefore, vaccination should be avoided late in pregnancy.

Smallpox vaccination is associated with a definite measurable risk. In the USA the risk of death from all complications was 1 per million for primary vaccinees and 0.1 per million for revaccinees. For children under

1 year of age, the risk of death was 5 per million primary vaccinations. Among primary vaccinees, the combined incidence of postvaccinal encephalitis and vaccinia necrosum was 3.8 per million in persons of all ages. In revaccinees, these 2 complications occurred at a rate of 0.7 per million.

Even though routine smallpox vaccination of children in the USA was stopped in 1971, more than 4 million doses of smallpox vaccine were administered in 1978. Severe complications of vaccination occurred in conjunction with immunodeficiency, immunosuppression, hematologic or other malignancies, and pregnancy.

E. Drug Prophylaxis: Methisazone (Marboran) can provide transitory protection to an individual who has been exposed to smallpox. The drug is no substitute for vaccination. It is of no value in the treatment of smallpox once the patient has become febrile. It may be beneficial in severe cases of eczema vaccinatum that do not quickly respond to vaccinia immune globulin. Rifampin inhibits the replication of vaccinia virus in cell culture, but it has not been proved to be effective against smallpox in field trials.

F. Variola Virus Stocks: The presence of stocks of virulent smallpox virus in laboratories is of concern because of the danger of laboratory infection and subsequent spread into the community. Variola virus stocks have been destroyed in all laboratories except 5 WHO collaborating centers that pursue diagnostic and research work on variola-related poxviruses.

COWPOX

This disease of cattle is milder than the pox diseases of other animals, the lesions being confined to the teats and udders. Infection of humans occurs by direct contact during milking, and the lesion in milkers is usually confined to the hands. In unvaccinated persons the disease is more severe than in the vaccinated. The local lesion is associated with fever and lymphadenitis. Generalized eruption is rare.

Cowpox virus is similar to vaccinia virus immunologically and in host range. It is also closely related immunologically to variola virus. Jenner observed that those who have had cowpox are immune to smallpox. Cowpox virus can be distinguished from vaccinia virus by the deep red hemorrhagic lesions that cowpox virus produces on the chorioallantoic membrane of the chick embryo. The strains of vaccinia virus used for vaccination of humans are of uncertain origin. If originally derived from cowpox strains, their artificial passage in laboratory animals has resulted in new properties.

MONKEYPOX

This disease is known to occur in monkeys held in captivity. No simian outbreaks in nature have ever been recorded. In 1970, the first known human cases of infection with this virus occurred; these were suspected cases of smallpox occurring in villages in Africa where no smallpox cases had been observed for 2 years. Continued surveillance has led to the diagnosis of 40 human cases from western and central Africa, all in tropical rain forest areas. Most patients experienced what appeared to be reasonably typical smallpox illnesses, but the isolates were found to have properties of typical monkeypox strains and to differ markedly from variola virus. Monkeys are frequently used by the villagers for food and skins. The smallpox surveillance system was able to detect the rare human infections due to monkeypox virus. There does not seem to be a simian reservoir of smallpox, and monkeypox when present does not seem to spread readily among humans. The attack rate in humans has been estimated to be about 4%, in contrast to that of smallpox, which is 30–45%.

YABA MONKEY VIRUS

This simian poxvirus causes benign histiocytomas 5–20 days after subcutaneous or intramuscular administration to monkeys. The tumors regress after about 5 weeks; this is ascribed to the cytopathic effect of the virus itself. Intravenous administration of the virus causes the appearance of multiple histiocytomas in the lungs, heart, and skeletal muscles. The virus is easily isolated from tumor tissue, and characteristic inclusions are found in the tumor cells.

Monkeys of various species and humans are susceptible to the neoplastic effect of the virus, but other laboratory animals are insusceptible. Under natural conditions the virus is possibly transmitted by bloodsucking vectors (as is myxoma, a poxvirus of rabbits).

In morphology, the Yaba virus particles are similar to vaccinia and molluscum contagiosum virions. No immunologic relationship has been found between Yaba virus and other poxviruses. The virus multiplies only in cultures of monkey cells, with cytopathic and proliferative effects. Characteristic eosinophilic inclusions in the cytoplasm of the cell have been found. The virus appears to be transmitted directly from cell to cell in cultures.

The Yaba virus DNA has a guanine plus cytosine (G + C) content of 32.5%, which is significantly different from the 36% G + C content of vaccinia, rabbitpox, cowpox, and ectromelia viruses.

MOLLUSCUM CONTAGIOSUM

The lesions of this disease are small, pink, wartlike tumors on the face, arms, back, and buttocks. The disease occurs throughout the world, in both sporadic and epidemic forms, and is more frequent in children than in adults. It is spread by direct and indirect contact (eg, by barbers, common use of towels).

Histologically, inclusions form in basal layers of the epithelium, gradually enlarge, crowd the nucleus to one side, and eventually fill the cell.

The virus has not been transmitted to animals but has been studied by electron microscopy in the human lesion. The purified virus is oval or brick-shaped and measures 230 × 330 nm.

In ultrathin sections of infected cells, the inclusion bodies are divided into compartments by ex-tremely thin walls, with nests of mature virus particles filling the cavities between the septa. The matrix of the cytoplasm surrounding the cavities appears honeycombed and undergoes segmentation into spherical objects that are larger than the virus itself. The virus appears to form within this larger sphere.

The virus is cytopathic for human and monkey cell cultures but has not yet been serially transferred in culture.

●　　●　　●

References

Arita I: Virological evidence for the success of the smallpox eradication programme. *Nature* 1979;**279**:293.

Baxby D: Identification and interrelationships of the variola / vaccinia subgroup of poxviruses. *Prog Med Virol* 1975;**19**:215.

Baxby D: Poxvirus hosts and reservoirs: Brief review. *Arch Virol* 1977;**55**:169.

Breman JG, Arita I: The confirmation and maintenance of smallpox eradication. *N Engl J Med* 1980;**303**:1263.

Deria A et al: The world's last endemic case of smallpox: Surveillance and containment measures. *Bull WHO* 1980;**58**:279.

Dumbell KR: Laboratory aids to the control of smallpox in countries where the disease is not endemic. *Prog Med Virol* 1968;**10**:388.

Dumbell KR, Archard LC: Comparison of white pock (h) mutants of monkeypox virus with parental monkeypox and with variola-like viruses isolated from animals. *Nature* 1980;**286**:29.

Esposito J, Obijeski JF, Nakano JH: Orthopoxvirus DNA: Strain differentiation by electrophoresis of restriction endonuclease fragmented virion DNA. *Virology* 1978;**89**:53.

Essani K, Dales S: Biogenesis of vaccinia: Evidence for more than 100 polypeptides in the virion. *Virology* 1979;**95**:385.

Fenner F: Portraits of viruses: The poxviruses. *Intervirology* 1979;**11**:137.

Fenner F: The eradication of smallpox. *Prog Med Virol* 1977;**23**:1.

Harper L, Bedson HS, Buchan A: Identification of orthopoxviruses by polyacrylamide gel electrophoresis of intracellular polypeptides. 1. Four major groupings. *Virology* 1979;**93**:435.

37 | Adenovirus Family

Adenoviruses consist of 2 genera, one that infects birds and another that infects mammals. Human adenoviruses are divided into 5 groups (A–E) based on their physical, chemical, and biologic properties. There are at least 37 antigenic types of human adenoviruses that may produce subclinical infection, respiratory tract or eye diseases, and occasionally other disorders. A few types serve as models for cancer induction in animals.

Properties of the Virus

A. Structure: Infective virions, 70–90 nm in diameter, are icosahedrons with capsids composed of 252 capsomeres. Three structural proteins, produced in large excess, constitute "soluble antigens" A, B, and C (Table 37–1). There is no envelope. The DNA is linear and double-stranded (MW $20-30 \times 10^6$). The guanine-cytosine (G + C) content of the DNA is lowest (48–49%) in group A (types 12, 18, and 31), which are the most strongly oncogenic types. The DNA can be isolated in an infectious form capable of transforming cells in culture.

B. Animal Susceptibility and Transformation of Cells: Most laboratory animals are not readily infected with adenoviruses. Newborn hamsters sustain a fatal infection with type 5 and develop malignant tumors when inoculated with any of 8 or more types, including types 12, 18, and 31. Adenovirus cannot be recovered from these tumors, but in the tumor a new antigen can be detected by complement fixation or immunofluorescence. This tumor, or T, antigen also develops in hamster cells that are infected or transformed by oncogenic adenovirus types. Transformed cells produce tumors when inoculated into adult hamsters but do not contain infectious virus. Only a small part (< 10%) of the adenovirus genome is present in many transformed cells. This explains the inability to recover infectious virus from such cells.

Adenovirus messenger RNA (mRNA) can be detected in transformed or tumor cells. Different types of adenovirus result in different mRNA in transformed cells.

In human tumors, adenovirus DNA or mRNA has never been found.

C. Antigenic Properties: All adenoviruses contain a common complement-fixing antigen that persists in suspensions of virus treated with heat or formalin to inactivate infectivity. At least 37 antigenic types have been isolated from humans and many additional ones from various animals. They are typed by cross-neutralization tests or hemagglutination-inhibition.

The major antigens, their size, and their structural position in the virion are shown in Table 37–1. Group-reactive complement-fixing antigens are hexons that form a majority of capsomeres and are 8 nm in diameter. Pentons have a similar size, occur at the 12 vertices of the capsid, and have a fiber protruding from them. The penton base carries a toxinlike activity that results in detachment of cells from the surface on which they are growing. Pentons and fibers are associated with hemagglutinating activity.

Group B adenoviruses (types 3, 7, 11, 14, 16, 21, 34, 35) clump rhesus but not rat erythrocytes; group D (types 8, 9, 10, 13, 15, 17, 19, 22, 23, 24, 26, 27, 29, 30, 32, 33, 36, 37) clump rat but not rhesus erythrocytes; groups C (types 1, 2, 5, 6) and D (type 4) only partly clump rat cells. Types 20, 25, and 28 are atypical in that they have the physical and chemical properties of group D but agglutinate only rhesus cells. Group A (oncogenic types 12, 18, and 31) adenoviruses usually fail to hemagglutinate. Inhibition of hemagglutination by type-specific sera can be used for typing isolates. Some cross-reactions, however, do occur.

D. Virus Growth in Cell Culture: Adenoviruses are cytopathic for human cell cultures, particularly primary kidney and continuous epithelial cells. Growth of virus in tissue culture is associated with a stimulation of acid production (increased glycolysis) in the early stages of infection. The cytopathic effect usually consists of marked rounding and aggregation of affected cells into grapelike clusters. The infected cells do not lyse even though they round up and leave the glass surface on which they have been grown.

In HeLa cells infected with adenovirus types 3, 4, and 7, rounded intranuclear inclusions containing DNA are seen. The virus particles develop in the nucleus and frequently exhibit crystalline arrangement. Many cells infected with type 5 virus also contain crystals, but these crystals are composed of a protein that has not been clearly identified.

During adenovirus replication in cultures of human cells, at least 12 virus-specific polypeptides are synthesized. These peptides are cataloged and their

Table 37–1. Comparative data on adenovirus type 2 morphologic and antigenic subunits and protein components.

Appearance	Name	Number Per Virion	Molecular Weight	Antigen	Specificity	Protein Components
Virion	DNA		23,000,000			
	Protein		150,000,000			
	Hexon	240	210,000 400,000 320,000 360,000	A	Group	II
	Hexons	20	3,600,000			II, VIII, IX
	Penton	12	280,000 1,100,000			III, IV
	Penton base	12	210,000	B	Subgroup	III
	Fiber	12	70,000	C	Type	IV
Core	DNA	1	23,000,000	P		
	Protein		29,000,000			V, VI, VII
	Protein		13,000			VII, IX
	Protein		7,500			X

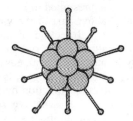

Dodecon: Hemagglutinin made up of 12 pentons with their fibers.

relationship to the virus structure is shown in Table 37–1.

Adenovirus DNA replication occurs in the nucleus and requires host cell DNA polymerase. Adenovirus mRNA is also made in the nucleus in a complex sequence that requires first the synthesis of larger molecules which are broken up and some sections of which are respliced by special enzymes. The spliced mRNA is translated into virus proteins.

Adenovirus-specific proteins are synthesized in the cytoplasm of infected cells and then move rapidly into the nucleus, where viral maturation occurs. In the adenovirus growth cycle in human epithelial cells, new virus particles can be detected about 16–20 hours after inoculation and continue to be formed at a uniform rate for the next 24 hours. About 7000 virus particles are produced per infected cell, and most of them remain intracellular. Particles having a density of 1.34 are infectious (one particle in 5 is infectious), whereas those having densities of less than 1.30 are noninfectious, since they lack the DNA core. Crude infected cell lysates show huge quantities of capsomeres, sometimes partially assembled into viral components.

When infecting cells derived from species other than humans, the human adenoviruses undergo an abortive replication cycle. Adenovirus tumor antigen, mRNA, and DNA are all synthesized, but no capsid proteins or infectious progeny are produced.

For further details on adenovirus replication, see Chapter 27.

E. Adenovirus-SV40 "Hybrids": Certain adenoviruses grown in monkey kidney cell cultures have become "contaminated" with the monkey virus SV40. While some of it was free in the mixture, other SV40 genomes became covalently linked to the adenovirus, so that stable "hybrids" were formed. (See Chapter 40.) Two types of hybrids have been identified. One is a defective adenovirus-SV40 genome encased in an adenovirus capsid. The other consists of nondefective (ie, self-replicating) adenovirus type 2 that carries 5–40% of the SV40 genome. These hybrids have been used in genetic analysis but have no manifest medical relevance.

F. Adenoassociated Virus (AAV): In some adenovirus preparations, small 20-nm particles were found. These proved to be small viruses that could not replicate unless adenovirus (or sometimes herpesvirus) was present as a helper. AAV contains single-stranded DNA (MW 1.6×10^6) and is serologically unrelated to adenovirus. Four antigenic types of AAV are known, 3 of which infect humans but do not seem to produce disease. AAV can infect cells in the absence of an adenovirus helper and induce a latent infection. AAV enters the cell nucleus and is uncoated there, but no mRNA synthesis occurs. Upon addition of an adenovirus, AAV is "rescued" and replication occurs (see Chapter 27).

Pathogenesis

Adenoviruses infect epithelial cells of mucous membranes, the cornea, and other organ systems. They can be isolated from such structures during acute illness and may persist for long periods. Types 1, 2, 5 and 6 can be isolated from surgically removed adenoids or tonsils of most children by growing the epithelium in vitro. Gradual removal of antibody during long culture in vitro permits the viruses to grow, as they cannot be isolated directly from suspensions of such tissues.

Most human adenoviruses grow in intestinal epithelium after ingestion but usually do not produce symptoms or lesions.

Clinical Findings

Adenovirus diseases include syndromes designated as undifferentiated acute respiratory disease, pharyngoconjunctival fever, nonstreptococcal exudative pharyngitis, and primary atypical pneumonia not associated with the development of cold agglutinins.

Pharyngoconjunctival fever may be caused by several adenovirus types. It is characterized by fever, conjunctivitis, pharyngitis, malaise, and cervical lymphadenopathy. The conjunctivitis is readily reproduced when any adenovirus is swabbed onto the eyes of volunteers. However, under natural conditions, only types 3 and 7 regularly cause outbreaks in which conjunctivitis is a predominant symptom. Types 1, 2, 5, 6, 37, and many others have produced sporadic cases of conjunctivitis.

Types 8 and 19 cause epidemic keratoconjunctivitis (shipyard eye). The disease is characterized by an acute conjunctivitis, with enlarged, tender preauricular nodes, followed by keratitis that leaves round, subepithelial opacities in the cornea for up to 2 years. Type 8 infections have been characterized by their lack of associated systemic symptoms except in infants. Intussusception of infancy has been ascribed to adenoviruses 1, 2, 3, and 5.

Types 11 and 21 may be a cause of acute hemorrhagic cystitis in children. Virus commonly occurs in the urine of such patients. Type 37 occurs in cervical lesions and in male urethritis and may be sexually transmitted.

A newly discovered serotype has been associated with infantile gastroenteritis. The virus is abundantly present in stools but has not been grown in cell culture.

Laboratory Diagnosis

A. Recovery of Virus: The viruses are isolated by inoculation of tissue cultures of human cells in which characteristic cytopathic changes are produced.

The viruses have been recovered from throat swabs, conjunctival swabs, rectal swabs, stools of patients with acute pharyngitis and conjunctivitis, and urine of patients with acute hemorrhagic cystitis. Virus isolations from the eye are obtained mainly from patients with conjunctivitis.

A new serotype that has not been isolated in cell cultures can be detected by direct examination of fecal extracts by electron microscopy or by enzyme-linked immunosorbent assay.

B. Serology: In most cases, the neutralizing antibody titer of infected persons shows a 4-fold or greater rise against the type recovered from the patient and a lesser response to other types. Neutralizing antibodies are measured in human cell cultures using the cytopathic end point in tube cultures or the color test in panel cups. The latter test depends upon the phenomenon that adenovirus growing in HeLa cell cultures produces an excess of acid over that of uninfected control cultures. This viral lowering of pH can be prevented by immune serum. The pH is measured by incorporating phenol red into the medium and observing the color changes after 3 days of incubation. Serum and cell control cultures reach a pH of 7.4; virus activity is indicated by a pH of 7.0; and neutralization is presumed to have occurred when the pH is 0.2 unit above that of the virus control.

Infection of humans with any adenovirus type stimulates a rise in complement-fixing antibodies to adenovirus antigens of all types. The CF test, using the common antigen, is an easily applied method for detecting infection by any member of the group.

A sensitive radioimmunoassay can measure serum antibody to type 5 fiber antigen. In response to vaccination with the fiber subunit, volunteers exhibited a 54-fold increase in antifiber antibody.

Immunity

Studies in volunteers revealed that type-specific neutralizing antibodies protect against the disease but not always against reinfection. Infections with the viruses were frequently induced without the production of overt illness.

Neutralizing antibodies against one or more types may be present in over 50% of infants 6–11 months old. Normal healthy adults generally have antibodies to several types. Neutralizing antibodies to types 1 and 2 occur in 55–70% of individuals age 6–15, but antibodies to types 3 and 4 are less prevalent. Neutralizing antibodies probably persist for life.

Infants are usually born without complement-fixing antibodies but develop these by age 6 months. Older individuals with neutralizing antibodies to 4 or more strains frequently give completely negative complement fixation reactions. For military recruits, the incidence of infection (especially due to types 3 and 4) was not influenced by the presence of group complement-fixing antibodies.

Epidemiology

Adenoviruses can readily spread from person to

person. Type 1, 2, 5, and 6 infections occur chiefly during the first years of life and are associated with fever and pharyngitis or asymptomatic infection. These are the types most frequently obtained from the adenoids and tonsils.

In children and young adults, types 3 and 7 commonly cause upper respiratory illness, pharyngitis, and conjunctivitis. While the illness is usually mild, occasionally there is high fever, cervical lymphadenitis, and even pneumonitis. Sometimes enteric infection produces gastroenteritis, but more commonly it is asymptomatic. Types 11 and 21 can produce acute hemorrhagic cystitis in children.

In adolescents and young adults, eg, college populations, only 2–5% of respiratory illness is caused by adenoviruses. In sharp contrast, respiratory disease due to types 3, 4, 7, 14, and 21 is common among military recruits. Adenovirus disease causes great morbidity when large numbers of persons are being inducted into the armed forces; consequently, its greatest impact is during periods of mobilization. During a 1-year study, 10% of recruits in basic training were hospitalized for a respiratory illness caused by an adenovirus. During the winter, adenovirus accounted for 72% of all the respiratory illness. However, adenovirus disease is not a problem in seasoned troops.

The follicular conjunctivitis caused by many adenovirus types resembles chlamydial conjunctivitis (see Chapter 22) and is self-limited.

Epidemic keratoconjunctivitis caused by type 8 spread in 1941 from Australia via the Hawaiian Islands to the Pacific Coast. There it spread rapidly through the shipyards and other industries, thence to the East Coast, and finally to the Midwest. A large outbreak caused by type 8 occurred in 1977 in Georgia among patients subjected to invasive eye procedures by one ophthalmologist. The initial case was a nurse who returned from a vacation in Korea with severe keratoconjunctivitis. In the USA, the incidence of neutralizing antibody to type 8 adenovirus in the general population has been about 1%, whereas in Japan it has been over 30%. In Japan, type 8 spreads via the respiratory route in children. Since 1973, adenovirus type 19 has also caused epidemics of typical epidemic keratoconjunctivitis.

Canine hepatitis virus is an adenovirus. Therefore, humans infected with adenoviruses develop group complement-fixing antibodies that also react with canine hepatitis virus.

In prospective family studies, adenovirus infections have been found to be predominantly enteric; they may be abortive or invasive and followed by persistent intermittent excretion of virus. Such excretion is most characteristic of types 1, 2, 3, and 5, which are usually endemic. Infection rates are highest among infants, but siblings who introduce the infection into a household are more effective in spreading the disease than are infants; similarly, duration of excretion is more important than the mode. In the families studied, neutralizing antibodies provided immunity (85% protective) against homotypic but not heterotypic infection. The contribution of adenoviruses to all infectious illness in the families, based on virus-positive infections only, was 5% in infants and 3% in the 2- to 4-year-old age group.

Prevention & Control

A trivalent vaccine was prepared by growing type 3, 4, and 7 viruses in monkey kidney cultures and then inactivating the viruses with formalin. However, when it was found that the vaccine strains were contaminated genetically with SV40 tumor virus determinants, this vaccine was withdrawn from use. Subsequently, it was found that most adenovirus strains do not replicate in monkey cells unless SV40 is present as a helper virus. Thus, a vaccine had to be made from noncontaminated live virus that could be grown in human diploid cells. The vaccine is given orally in a coated capsule to liberate the virus into the intestine. By this route, the live vaccine produces a subclinical infection that confers a high degree of immunity against wild strains. It does not spread from a vaccinated person to contacts. Such live virus vaccines against type 4 and type 7 are licensed and recommended for immunization of military populations. When both are administered simultaneously, vaccinees respond with neutralizing antibodies against both virus types.

Rigid asepsis during eye examination is essential in the control of epidemic keratoconjunctivitis.

• • •

References

Blanchard JM et al: In vitro RNA-RNA splicing in adenovirus 2 mRNA formation. *Proc Natl Acad Sci USA* 1978;**75**:5344.

D'Angelo LJ et al: Epidemic keratoconjunctivitis caused by adenovirus type 8: Epidemiologic and laboratory aspects of a large outbreak. *Am J Epidemiol* 1981;**113**:44.

De Jong JC et al: Adenovirus 37: Identification and characterization of a medically important new adenovirus type of subgroup D. *J Med Virol* 1981;**7**:105.

Fox JP, Hall CE, Cooney MK: The Seattle virus watch. 7. Observations of adenovirus infections. *Am J Epidemiol* 1977;**105**:362.

Green M et al: Analysis of human tonsil and cancer DNAs and RNAs for DNA sequences of group C (serotypes 1, 2, 5, and 6) human adenoviruses. *Proc Natl Acad Sci USA* 1979;**76**:6606.

Johansson ME et al: Direct identification of enteric adenovirus, a candidate new serotype, associated with infantile gastroenteritis. *J Clin Microbiol* 1980;**12**:95.

Nermut MV, Harpst JA, Russell WC: Electron microscopy of adenovirus cores. *J Gen Virol* 1975;**28**:49.

Rapp F, Melnick JL: Papovavirus SV40, adenovirus and their hybrids: Transformation, complementation, and transcapsidation. *Prog Med Virol* 1966;**8**:349.

Schmidt NJ, Lennette EH, King CJ: Neutralizing, hemagglutination-inhibiting and group complement-fixing antibody responses in human adenovirus infections. *J Immunol* 1966;**97**:64.

Shaw CH, Russell WC, Rekosh DMK: Association of adenovirus early proteins with a nuclear fraction that synthesizes DNA in vitro. *Virology* 1979;**92**:436.

Takafuji ET et al: Simultaneous administration of live, enteric-coated adenovirus types 4, 7, and 21 vaccines: Safety and immunogenicity. *J Infect Dis* 1979;**140**:48.

Taylor JW, Chandler JW, Cooney MK: Conjunctivitis due to adenovirus type 19. *J Clin Microbiol* 1978;**8**:209.

Wadell G et al: Epidemic outbreaks of adenovirus 7 with special reference to the pathogenicity of adenovirus genome type 7b. *Am J Epidemiol* 1980;**112**:619.

All **herpesviruses** have a core of double-stranded DNA surrounded by a protein coat that exhibits icosahedral symmetry and has 162 capsomeres. The nucleocapsid is surrounded by an envelope. The enveloped form measures 150–200 nm; the "naked" virion, 100 nm. The double-stranded DNA (MW $85-150 \times 10^6$) has a wide range of guanine + cytosine content in different herpesviruses. There is little DNA homology among different herpesviruses, except herpes simplex types 1 and 2.

Various classifications for herpesviruses have been proposed, but individual virus names are generally used. Common and important herpesviruses of humans include herpes simplex virus types 1 and 2, varicella-zoster virus, Epstein-Barr (EB) virus, and cytomegalovirus. They have a propensity for subclinical infection, latency following the primary infection, and reactivation thereafter.

Herpesviruses that infect lower animals are B virus of Old World monkeys; herpesviruses saimiri, aotus, and ateles; marmoset herpesvirus of New World monkeys; pseudorabies virus of pigs; virus III of rabbits; infectious bovine rhinotracheitis virus; and many others. Herpesviruses are also known for birds, fish, fungi, and oysters, although the only link between some of these viruses is their appearance in the electron microscope.

Herpesviruses have been linked with malignant diseases in humans and lower animals: herpes simplex virus type 2 with cervical and vulvar carcinoma; EB virus with Burkitt's lymphoma of African children and with nasopharyngeal carcinoma; Lucké virus with renal adenocarcinomas of the frog; Marek's disease virus with a lymphoma of chickens; Hinze virus with a lymphoma of rabbits; and a number of New World primate herpesviruses with reticulum cell sarcomas and lymphomas in these animals.

HERPES SIMPLEX
(Human Herpesvirus 1 & 2)
(Herpes Labialis, Herpes Genitalis,
& Many Other Syndromes)

Infection with herpes simplex virus (herpesvirus hominis) may take several clinical forms. The infection is most often inapparent. The usual clinical manifestation is a vesicular eruption of the skin or mucous membranes. Infection is sometimes seen as severe keratitis, meningoencephalitis, and a disseminated illness of the newborn.

Properties of the Virus

A. The Virion: Morphologically and chemically, herpes simplex virus has been studied in great detail (see Fig 38–1). The envelope is derived from the nuclear membrane of the infected cell (see Fig 27–6). It contains lipids, carbohydrate, and protein and is removed by ether treatment. The double-stranded DNA genome is linear (MW $85-106 \times 10^6$). Types 1 and 2 show 50% sequence homology. Treatment with restriction endonucleases (see Chapter 4 and Chapter 27) yields characteristically different cleavage patterns for type 1 and 2 viruses and even for different strains of each type. This "fingerprinting" of strains allows epidemiologic tracing of a given strain, whereas in the past, the ubiquitousness of herpes simplex virus made such investigations impossible.

B. Animal Susceptibility and Growth of Virus: The virus has a wide host range and can infect rabbits, guinea pigs, mice, hamsters, rats, and the chorioallantois of the embryonated egg.

In rabbits, herpesvirus produces a vesicular eruption in the skin of the inoculated area, sometimes progressing to fatal encephalitis. Corneal inoculation results in dendritic keratitis, which may progress to encephalitis. The virus may remain latent in the brains of survivors, and anaphylactic shock can precipitate an acute relapse of encephalomyelitis. Herpetic keratitis heals, but infective herpesvirus may be recovered from the eye intermittently with or without clinical activity. The virus remains latent in the trigeminal ganglion.

In the chorioallantoic membrane of embryonated eggs the lesions are raised white plaques, each induced by one infectious virus particle. The plaques produced by herpesvirus type 2 are larger than the tiny plaques produced by type 1 virus. The virus grows readily and produces plaques in almost any cell culture. Infected cells develop inclusion bodies and then undergo necrosis (cytopathic effect).

In Chinese hamster cells, which contain 22 chromosomes, the virus causes breaks in region 7 of chromosome No. 1 and in region 3 of the X chromosome. The Y chromosome is unaffected.

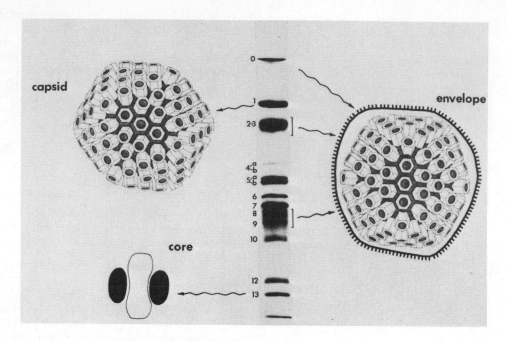

Figure 38–1. Herpesvirus. Several proteins have been identified in the virion. The protein in band number 1 by gel electrophoresis is associated with the viral capsid; the glycoproteins present in bands 0, 2–3, 8, and 9 are associated with the envelope; and a DNA-binding protein (band number 13) is associated with the internal core. (Powell & Purifoy.)

C. Virus Replication: The virus enters the cell either by fusion with the cell membrane or by pinocytosis. It is then uncoated, and the DNA becomes associated with the nucleus. Normal cellular DNA and protein synthesis virtually stop as virus replication begins. The virus induces a number of enzymes, at least 2 of which—thymidine kinase and DNA polymerase—are virus-coded. Thymidine kinases produced by different herpesviruses are serologically different from each other and different from the enzyme in uninfected cells. Phosphonoacetic acid specifically inhibits herpesvirus replication by inhibiting viral DNA polymerase.

Viral proteins are made in a controlled sequence that must proceed stepwise. They are made in the cytoplasm and most are transported to the nucleus, where they take part in virus DNA synthesis and the assembly of nucleocapsids. Maturation occurs by budding of nucleocapsids through the altered inner nuclear membrane. Enveloped virus particles are then released from the cell through tubular structures that are continuous with the outside of the cell or from vacuoles that release their contents at the cell surface (Fig 27–6).

D. Defective Interfering Herpesvirions: Serial passage of undiluted herpes simplex virus results in cyclic production of infectious and defective virions. The DNA in defective virions is made up of reiterated sequences of small fragments of the virus DNA. Defective virions interfere with the replication of standard virus and stimulate overproduction of a large polypeptide, which may have a regulatory function. The biologic role of the defective virions is not known.

E. Antigenic Properties: There are 7–12 precipitating antigens that represent structural and nonstructural viral proteins. Some of these antigens are common to both types 1 and 2 and some are specific for one type. A number of tests, eg, fluorescent antibody, complement fixation, virus neutralization, and radioimmunoassay, have been used to detect herpesvirus antigens.

F. Differentiation of Types 1 and 2: Herpes simplex virus types 1 and 2 cross-react serologically but may be distinguished by a number of tests: (1) The use of type-specific antiserum prepared by adsorption of the viral antiserum with heterotypically infected cells or by inoculation of rabbits with individual type-specific proteins. (2) The greater temperature sensitivity of type 2 infectivity. (3) Preferential growth in different cell species. (4) Restriction enzyme patterns of virus DNA molecules. (5) Differences in the polypeptides produced by type 1 and type 2.

G. Oncogenic Properties: After inactivation of their lytic capabilities by ultraviolet irradiation or other means, herpesvirus types 1 and 2 can cause transformation of cultured hamster cells, which may induce tumors when inoculated into newborn hamsters. Viral genetic information can be demonstrated in the tumor cells. (See Chapter 40.)

Pathogenesis & Pathology

The lesion in the skin involves proliferation, ballooning degeneration, and intranuclear acidophilic inclusions. In fatal cases of herpes encephalitis, there are meningitis, perivascular infiltration, and nerve cell destruction, especially in the cortex. Neonatal generalized herpes infection causes areas of focal necrosis with a mononuclear reaction and formation of intranuclear inclusion bodies in all organs. Survivors may sustain permanent damage.

The fully formed early inclusion (Cowdry type A inclusion body) is rich in DNA and virtually fills the nucleus, compressing the chromatin to the nuclear margin. Later, the inclusion loses its DNA and is separated by a halo from the chromatin at the nuclear margin.

Clinical Findings

Herpesvirus may cause many clinical entities, and the infections may be primary or recurrent. Primary infections occur in persons without antibodies and often result in the virus assuming a latent state in sensory ganglia of the host. Latent infections persist in persons with antibodies, and recurrent lesions are common (eg, recurrent herpes labialis). The primary infection in most individuals is clinically inapparent but is invariably accompanied by antibody production.

The recurrent attacks, in the presence of viral neutralizing antibody, follow nonspecific stimuli such as exposure to excess sunlight, fever, menstruation, or emotional stresses.

A. Herpesvirus Type 1: The clinical entities attributable to herpesvirus type 1 include the following:

1. Acute herpetic gingivostomatitis (aphthous stomatitis, Vincent's stomatitis)–This is the most common clinical entity caused by primary infections with type 1 herpesvirus. It occurs most frequently in small children (1–3 years of age) and includes extensive vesiculoulcerative lesions of the mucous membranes of the mouth, fever, irritability, and local lymphadenopathy. The incubation period is short (about 3–5 days), and the lesions heal in 2–3 weeks.

2. Eczema herpeticum (Kaposi's varicelliform eruption)–This is a primary infection, usually with herpesvirus type 1, in a person with chronic eczema. In this illness, there may be extensive vesiculation of the skin over much of the body and high fever. In rare instances, the illness may be fatal.

3. Keratoconjunctivitis–The initial infection with herpesvirus may be in the eye, producing severe keratoconjunctivitis. Recurrent lesions of the eye appear as dendritic keratitis or corneal ulcers or as vesicles on the eyelids. With recurrent keratitis, there may be progressive involvement of the corneal stroma, with permanent opacification and blindness.

4. Encephalitis–A severe form of encephalitis may be produced by herpesvirus. In adults, the neurologic manifestations suggest a lesion in the temporal lobe. Pleocytosis (chiefly of lymphocytes) is present in the cerebrospinal fluid; however, definite diagnosis during the illness can usually be made only by isolation of the virus (or by demonstrating viral antigens by immunofluorescence) from brain tissue obtained by biopsy or at postmortem. The disease carries a high mortality rate, and those who survive often have residual neurologic defects.

5. Herpes labialis (cold sores, herpes febrilis)–This is the most common recurrent disease produced by type 1. Clusters of localized vesicles occur, usually at the mucocutaneous junction of the lips. The vesicle ruptures, leaving a painful ulcer that heals without scarring. The lesions may recur, repeatedly and at various intervals of time, in the same location. The permanent site of latent herpes simplex virus is the trigeminal ganglion.

B. Herpesvirus Type 2: The clinical entities associated with herpesvirus type 2 include the following:

1. Genital herpes (herpes progenitalis)– Genital herpes is characterized by vesiculoulcerative lesions of the penis of the male or the cervix, vulva, vagina, and perineum of the female. The lesions are more severe during primary infection and may be associated with fever, malaise, and inguinal lymphadenopathy. In women with herpesvirus antibodies, only the cervix or vagina may be involved, and the disease may therefore be asymptomatic. Recurrence of the lesions is common. Type 2 virus remains latent in lumbar and sacral ganglia. Changing patterns of sexual behavior are reflected by an increasing number of type 1 virus isolations from genital lesions and of type 2 from facial lesions, presumably as a result of oral-genital sexual activity.

2. Neonatal herpes–Herpesvirus type 2 may be transmitted to the newborn during birth by contact with herpetic lesions in the birth canal. The spectrum of illness produced in the newborn appears to vary from subclinical or local to severe generalized disease with a fatal outcome. Severely affected infants who survive may have permanent brain damage. To avoid infection, delivery by cesarean section has been used in pregnant women with genital herpes lesions. To be effective, cesarean section must be performed before rupture of the membranes.

Severe generalized disease of the newborn can be acquired postnatally by exposure to either type 1 or 2. Efforts should be made to prevent exposure to active lesions among family and especially among hospital personnel.

Transplacental infection of the fetus with types 1 and 2 herpes simplex virus may cause congenital malformations, but this phenomenon is rare.

C. Miscellaneous: Localized lesions of the skin caused by type 1 or 2 may occur in abrasions that become contaminated with the virus (traumatic herpes). These lesions are seen on the fingers of dentists, hospital personnel (herpetic whitlow), or persons with genital lesions and on the bodies of wrestlers.

Primary and recurrent herpes can occur in the nose (acute herpetic rhinitis).

Mild aseptic meningitis has been attributed to the virus, and recurrent episodes of meningeal irritation have been observed.

Epidemiologic evidence has demonstrated that in most geographic areas, patients with cervical and vulvar cancer have a high frequency of type 2 antibodies. In addition, herpesvirus type 2 nonstructural antigens have been detected by immunofluorescence in biopsies of cervical and vulvar carcinomas. (See Chapter 40.)

Laboratory Diagnosis

A. Recovery of Virus: The virus may be isolated from herpetic lesions (skin, cornea, or brain). It may also be found in the throat, saliva, and stools, both during primary infection and during asymptomatic periods. Therefore, the isolation of herpesvirus is not in itself sufficient evidence to indicate that this virus is the causative agent of a disease under investigation.

Inoculation of tissue cultures is used for virus isolation. The appearance of typical cytopathic effects in cell culture suggests the presence of herpesvirus in 18–36 hours. The agent is then identified by neutralization test or immunofluorescence staining with specific antiserum.

Scrapings or swabs from the base of early herpetic lesions contain multinucleated giant cells.

B. Serology: Antibodies may be measured quantitatively by neutralization tests in cell cultures. In the early stage of the primary immune response, neutralizing antibody appears that is detectable only in the presence of fresh complement. This antibody soon is replaced by neutralizing antibody that can function without complement.

Since the only hope for treatment of herpes simplex virus encephalitis lies in early diagnosis, a rapid means of diagnosis is needed. The fluorescent antibody test using brain biopsy material is the method of choice. Passive hemagglutinating antibodies (see Chapter 29) in the cerebrospinal fluid are a better indicator of the presence of infectious virus than are antibody titers in serum.

A soluble complement-fixing antigen of much smaller size than the virus can be prepared from infected chorioallantoic membranes or from tissue culture. This soluble antigen of herpesvirus can detect dermal hypersensitivity in previously infected persons. There is a good correlation between dermal hypersensitivity and the presence of serum antibodies.

Antibodies appear in 4–7 days; can be measured by neutralization, complement fixation, radioimmunoassay, or immunofluorescence; and reach a peak in 2–4 weeks. They persist with minor fluctuations for the life of the host. The majority of adults have antibodies in their blood at all times.

After a primary type 1 infection, the IgM neutralizing antibody response is type-specific, but after a primary type 2 infection the IgM that develops neutralizes both type 1 and type 2 virus. Subsequently, IgG antibodies react with both type 1 and type 2 antigens, albeit in varying ratios.

There is also some cross-stimulation between herpes simplex and varicella-zoster antigens in patients with preexisting antibody to the other virus.

Immunity

Many newborns have passively transferred maternal antibodies. This antibody is lost during the first 6 months of life, and the period of greatest susceptibility to primary herpes infection occurs between ages 6 months and 2 years. Type 1 antibodies begin to appear in the population in early childhood; by adolescence they are present in most persons. Antibodies to type 2 (genital herpesvirus) rise during the age of adolescence and sexual activity.

After recovery from a primary infection (inapparent, mild, or severe), the virus is usually carried in a latent state, in the presence of antibodies.

Treatment

Topically applied idoxuridine (5-iodo-2'-deoxyuridine, IUDR), trifluorothymidine, vidarabine (adenine arabinoside, ara-A), acyclovir, and other inhibitors of viral DNA synthesis are effective in herpetic keratitis (see Chapter 27). These drugs inhibit herpesvirus replication and may suppress clinical manifestations. However, the virus remains latent in the sensory ganglia, and the rate of relapse is similar in drug-treated and untreated individuals. Some drug-resistant virus strains have emerged. Most strains of type 2 herpesvirus are suppressed less effectively than type 1.

For systemic administration, vidarabine (15 mg/kg/d intravenously) is accepted in herpes encephalitis diagnosed by biopsy. Best results are obtained if treatment is begun early in the disease, before coma sets in. Vidarabine also has some effect in disseminated herpes simplex.

Other drugs, especially acyclovir, are undergoing clinical trial, and many new antiherpes compounds are being developed. Acyclovir has low toxicity and has been administered systemically to suppress the activation of a latent herpes infection in immunosuppressed patients.

Epidemiology

The epidemiology of type 1 and type 2 herpesvirus differs. Herpesvirus type 1 is probably more constantly present in humans than any other virus. Primary infection occurs early in life and is often asymptomatic or produces acute gingivostomatitis. Antibodies develop, but the virus is not eliminated from the body; a carrier state is established that lasts throughout life and is punctuated by transient attacks of herpes. If primary infection is avoided in childhood, it may not occur in later life, perhaps because the thicker adult epithelium is less susceptible or because the opportunity for contact with the virus is diminished (less contact with saliva of infected persons).

The highest incidence of type 1 virus carriage in the oropharynx of healthy persons occurs among children 6 months to 3 years of age. By adulthood, 70–90% of persons have type 1 antibodies.

Type 1 virus is transmitted more readily in families of lower socioeconomic groups; the most obvious explanation is their more crowded living conditions and lower hygienic standards. The virus is spread by direct contact (saliva) or through utensils contaminated with the saliva of a virus shedder. The source of infection for children is usually a parent with an active herpetic lesion.

Type 2 is usually acquired as a sexually transmitted disease, and the age distribution of primary infection is a function of sexual activity. The neonate may acquire type 2 infection from an active lesion in the mother's birth canal.

Control

Neonates and persons with eczema should be protected from evident active herpetic lesions.

Although certain drugs are effective in treatment of herpesvirus infections, once a latent infection is established there has been no known treatment that would prevent recurrences until the recent successful results with acyclovir in immunosuppressed patients.

Little is known about vaccines. Herpes recurs in the presence of circulating antibody, so a vaccine would be of little use in a person who already had a primary infection. A vaccine currently made in Europe has not been adequately tested.

VARICELLA–ZOSTER VIRUS
(Human Herpesvirus 3)

VARICELLA
(Chickenpox)
ZOSTER
(Herpes Zoster, Shingles, Zona)

Varicella (chickenpox) is a mild, highly infectious disease, chiefly of children, characterized clinically by a vesicular eruption of the skin and mucous membranes. However, in immunocompromised children the disease may be severe. The causative agent is indistinguishable from the virus of zoster.

Zoster (shingles) is a sporadic, incapacitating disease of adults (rare in children) that is characterized by an inflammatory reaction of the posterior nerve roots and ganglia, accompanied by crops of vesicles (like those of varicella) over the skin supplied by the affected sensory nerves.

Both diseases are caused by the same virus. Varicella is the acute disease that follows primary contact with the virus, whereas zoster is the response of the partially immune host to a reactivation of varicella virus present in latent form in sensory ganglia.

Properties of the Virus

Varicella-zoster virus is morphologically identical with herpes simplex virus. The virus propagates in cultures of human embryonic tissue and produces typical intranuclear inclusion bodies. Supernatant fluids from such infected cultures contain a complement-fixing antigen but no infective virus. Infectious virus is easily transmitted by infected cells. The virus has not been propagated in laboratory animals. Virus can be isolated from the vesicles of chickenpox or zoster patients or from the cerebrospinal fluid in cases of zoster aseptic meningitis.

Inoculation of vesicle fluid of zoster into children produces vesicles at the site of inoculation in about 10 days. This may be followed by generalized skin lesions of varicella. Generalized varicella may occur in such inoculated children without local vesicle formation. Contacts of such children develop typical varicella after a 2-week incubation period. Children who have recovered from zoster virus–induced infection are resistant to varicella, and those who have had varicella are no longer susceptible to primary zoster virus.

Antibody to varicella-zoster virus can be measured by CF, gel precipitation, neutralization, or indirect immunofluorescence to virus-induced membrane antigens.

The virus has a colchicinelike effect on human cells. Arrest in metaphase, overcontracted chromosomes, chromosome breaks, and formation of micronuclei are often seen.

Pathogenesis & Pathology

A. Varicella: The route of infection is probably the mucosa of the upper respiratory tract. The virus probably circulates in the blood and localizes in the skin. Swelling of epithelial cells, ballooning degeneration, and the accumulation of tissue fluids result in vesicle formation. In nuclei of infected cells, particularly in the early stages, eosinophilic inclusion bodies are found.

B. Zoster: In addition to skin lesions — histopathologically identical with those of varicella — there is an inflammatory reaction of the dorsal nerve roots and sensory ganglia. Often only a single ganglion may be involved. As a rule, the distribution of lesions in the skin corresponds closely to the areas of innervation from an individual dorsal root ganglion. There is cellular infiltration, necrosis of nerve cells, and inflammation of the ganglion sheath.

Varicella virus seems able to enter and remain within dorsal root ganglia for long periods. Years later, various insults (eg, pressure on a nerve) may cause a flare-up of the virus along posterior root fibers, whereupon zoster vesicles appear. Thus, varicella-zoster and herpes simplex viruses are similar in their ability to induce latent infections with clinical recurrence of disease in humans. However, zoster rarely occurs more than once.

Clinical Findings

A. Varicella: The incubation period is usually 14–21 days. Malaise and fever are the earliest symptoms, soon followed by the rash, first on the trunk and then on the face, the limbs, and the buccal and pharyngeal mucosa. Successive fresh vesicles appear in crops during the next 3–4 days, so that all stages of papules, vesicles, and crusts may be seen at one time. The eruption is found together with the fever and is proportionate to its severity. Complications are rare, although encephalitis does at times occur about 5–10 days after the rash. The mortality rate is much less than 1% in uncomplicated cases. In neonatal varicella (contracted from the mother just before or just after birth), the mortality rate may be 20%. In varicella encephalitis, the mortality rate is about 10%, and another 10%

are left with permanent injury to the central nervous system. Primary varicella pneumonia is rare in children but may occur in about 20–30% of adult cases, may produce severe hypoxia, and may be fatal.

Children with immune deficiency disease or those receiving immunosuppressant or cytotoxic drugs are at high risk of development of very severe and sometimes fatal varicella or disseminated zoster.

B. Zoster: The incubation period is unknown. The disease starts with malaise and fever that are soon followed by severe pain in the area of skin or mucosa supplied by one or more groups of sensory nerves and ganglia. Within a few days after onset, a crop of vesicles appears over the skin supplied by the affected nerves. The eruption is usually unilateral; the trunk, head, and neck are most commonly involved. Lymphocytic pleocytosis in the cerebrospinal fluid may be present.

In patients with localized zoster and no underlying disease, vesicle interferon levels peak early during infection (by the sixth day), whereas those in patients with disseminated infection peak later. Peak interferon levels are followed by clinical improvement within 48 hours. Vesicles pustulate and crust, and dissemination is halted.

Zoster tends to disseminate when there is an underlying disease, especially if the patient is taking immunosuppressive drugs or has lymphoma treated by irradiation.

Laboratory Diagnosis

In stained smears of scrapings or swabs of the base of vesicles, multinucleated giant cells are seen. In similar smears, intracellular viral antigens can be demonstrated by immunofluorescence staining.

Virus can be isolated in cultures of human or other fibroblastic cells in 3–5 days. It does not grow in epithelial cells, in contrast to herpes simplex, and does not infect laboratory animals or eggs. An isolate in fibroblasts is identified by immunofluorescence or neutralization tests with specific antisera.

Herpesviruses can be differentiated from poxviruses by (1) the morphologic appearance of particles in vesicular fluids examined by electron microscopy, and by (2) the presence of antigen in vesicle fluid or in an extract of crusts as determined by gel diffusion tests with specific antisera to herpes, varicella, or vaccinia viruses, which give visible precipitation lines in 24–48 hours.

A rise in specific antibody titer can be detected in the patient's serum by CF, Nt (in cell culture), indirect immunofluorescence tests, or enzyme immunoassay. Zoster can occur in the presence of relatively high neutralizing antibody in the blood just prior to onset. The role of cell-mediated immunity is unknown.

Immunity

Varicella and zoster viruses are identical, the 2 diseases being the result of differing host responses. Previous infection with varicella leaves the patient with enduring immunity to varicella. However, zoster may occur in persons who have contracted varicella earlier. This is a reactivation of a varicella virus infection that has been latent for years.

Prophylaxis & Treatment

Gamma globulin of high specific antibody titer prepared from pooled plasma of patients convalescing from herpes zoster (zoster immune globulin) can be used to prevent the development of the illness in immunocompromised children who have been exposed to varicella. Standard immune serum globulin is without value because of the low titer of varicella antibodies.

Zoster immune globulin is available from the American Red Cross Blood Services (through 13 regional blood centers) for prophylaxis of varicella in exposed high-risk immunodeficient or immunosuppressed children. It has no therapeutic value once varicella has started.

Idoxuridine and cytarabine inhibit replication of the viruses in vitro but are not an effective treatment for patients.

Adenine arabinoside (vidarabine, ara-A) has been beneficial in adults with severe varicella pneumonia, immunocompromised children with varicella, and adults with disseminated zoster. (See Chapter 27.) Human leukocyte interferon in large doses appears to be similarly beneficial.

Epidemiology

Zoster occurs sporadically, chiefly in adults and without seasonal prevalence. In contrast, varicella is a common epidemic disease of childhood (peak incidence is in children age 2–6 years, although adult cases do occur). It is much more common in winter and spring than in summer. Almost 200,000 cases are reported annually in the USA.

Varicella readily spreads, presumably by droplets as well as by contact with skin. Contact infection is rare in zoster, perhaps because the virus is absent in the upper respiratory tract.

Zoster, whether in children or adults, can be the source of varicella in children and can initiate large outbreaks.

Control

None is available for the general population.

Varicella may spread rapidly among patients, especially among children with immunologic dysfunctions or leukemia or in those receiving corticosteroids or cytotoxic drugs. Varicella in such children poses the threat of pneumonia, encephalitis, or death. Efforts should be made to prevent their exposure to varicella. Zoster immune globulin may be used to modify the disease in such children who have been exposed to varicella.

A live attenuated varicella vaccine has been developed in Japan and tested in hospitalized immunosuppressed children who were exposed to varicella. It appeared to prevent spread of chickenpox. The vaccine is being used experimentally for similar high-risk children in the USA.

A number of problems are envisioned for the use of such a vaccine for the general population as opposed to high-risk patients. The vaccine would need to confer immunity comparable to that of natural infections. A short-lasting immunity might result in an increased number of susceptible adults, in whom the disease is more severe. Furthermore, any such vaccine would need to be evaluated for later morbidity due to zoster as compared to that following natural childhood infections with varicella virus.

. . .

CYTOMEGALOVIRUS
(Human Herpesvirus 5)
(Cytomegalic Inclusion Disease)

Cytomegalic inclusion disease is a generalized infection of infants caused by intrauterine or early postnatal infection with the cytomegaloviruses. The disease causes severe congenital anomalies in about 10,000 infants in the USA per year. Cytomegalovirus can be found in the cervix of up to 10% of healthy women. Cytomegalic inclusion disease is characterized by large intranuclear inclusions that occur in the salivary glands, lungs, liver, pancreas, kidneys, endocrine glands, and, occasionally, the brain. Most fatalities occur in children under 2 years of age. Inapparent infection is common during childhood and adolescence. Severe cytomegalovirus infections are frequently found in adults receiving immunosuppressive therapy.

Properties of the Virus
A. General Properties: Morphologically, cytomegalovirus is indistinguishable from herpes simplex or varicella-zoster virus.

In infected human fibroblasts, virus particles are assembled in the nucleus. The envelope of the virus is derived from the inner nuclear membrane. The growth cycle of the virus is slower, and infectious virus is more cell-associated than herpes simplex virus.

B. Animal Susceptibility: All attempts to infect animals with human cytomegalovirus have failed. A number of animal cytomegaloviruses exist, all of them species-specific in rats, hamsters, moles, rabbits, and monkeys. The virus isolated from monkeys propagates in cultures of monkey as well as human cells.

Human cytomegalovirus replicates in vitro only in human fibroblasts, although the virus is often isolated from epithelial cells of the host. The virus can transform human and hamster cells in culture, but whether it is oncogenic in vivo is unknown.

Pathogenesis & Pathology
In infants, cytomegalic inclusion disease is congenitally acquired, probably as a result of primary infection of the mother during pregnancy. The virus can be isolated from the urine of the mother at the time of birth of the infected baby, and typical cytomegalic cells, 25–40 μm in size, occur in the chorionic villi of the infected placenta.

Foci of cytomegalic cells are found in fatal cases in the epithelial tissues of the liver, lungs, kidneys, gastrointestinal tract, parotid gland, pancreas, thymus, thyroid, adrenals, and other regions. The cells can be found also in the urine or adenoid tissue of healthy children. The route of infection in older infants, children, and adults is not known.

The isolation of the virus from urine and from tissue cultures of adenoids of healthy children suggests subclinical infections at a young age. The virus may persist in various organs for long periods in a latent state or as a chronic infection. Virus is not recovered from the mouths of adults. Disseminated inclusions in adults occur in association with other severe diseases.

Clinical Findings
Congenital infection may result in death of the fetus in utero or may produce the clinical syndrome of cytomegalic inclusion disease, with signs of prematurity, jaundice with hepatosplenomegaly, thrombocytopenic purpura, pneumonitis, and central nervous system damage (microcephaly, periventricular calcification, chorioretinitis, optic atrophy, and mental or motor retardation).

Infants born with congenital cytomegalic inclusion disease may appear well and live for many years. It has been estimated that one in every 1000 babies born in the USA is seriously retarded as a result of this congenital infection.

Inapparent intrauterine infection seems to occur frequently. Elevated IgM antibody to cytomegalovirus or isolation of the virus from the urine occurs in up to 2% of apparently normal newborns. This high rate occurs in spite of the fact that women may already have cytomegalovirus antibody before becoming pregnant. Such intrauterine infections have been implicated as possible causes of mental retardation and hearing loss.

Many women who have been infected naturally with cytomegalovirus at some time prior to pregnancy begin to excrete the virus from the cervix during the last trimester of pregnancy. At the time of delivery, infants pass through the infected birth canal and become infected, although they possess high titers of maternal antibody acquired transplacentally. These infants begin to excrete the virus in their urine at about 8–12 weeks of age. They continue to excrete the virus for several years but remain healthy.

Acquired infection with cytomegalovirus is common and usually inapparent. In children, acquired infection may result in hepatitis, interstitial pneumonitis, or acquired hemolytic anemia. The virus is shed in the saliva and urine of infected individuals for weeks or months.

Cytomegalovirus can cause an infectious mononucleosis-like disease without heterophil antibodies. "Cytomegalovirus mononucleosis" occurs either spontaneously or after transfusions of fresh blood during surgery ("postperfusion syndrome"). The incubation period is about 30–40 days. There is cytomegaloviruria and a rise of cytomegalovirus antibody. Cytomegalovirus has been isolated from the peripheral blood leukocytes of such patients. Perhaps the postperfusion syndrome is caused by cytomegalovirus harbored in the leukocytes of the blood donors.

Patients with malignancies or immunologic defects or those undergoing immunosuppressive therapy for organ transplantation may develop cytomegalovirus pneumonitis or hepatitis and occasionally generalized disease. In such patients a latent infection may be reactivated when host susceptibility to infection is increased by immunosuppression. In seronegative patients without evidence of previous cytomegalovirus infection, the virus may be transmitted exogenously. Eighty-three percent of seronegative patients who received kidneys from seropositive transplant donors developed infection. Thus, the kidneys seemed to be the source of virus.

Laboratory Diagnosis

A. Recovery of Virus: The virus can be recovered from mouth swabs, urine, liver, adenoids, kidneys, and peripheral blood leukocytes by inoculation of human fibroblastic cell cultures. In cultures, 1–2 weeks are usually needed for cytologic changes consisting of small foci of swollen, rounded, translucent cells with large intranuclear inclusions. Cell degeneration progresses slowly, and the virus concentration is much higher within the cell than in the fluid. Prolonged serial propagation is needed before the virus reaches high titers.

Rapid diagnosis of cytomegalovirus infection in infants is possible by detection of inclusion-bearing "owl cells" in the urine. These are desquamated cells from infected kidney tubules.

B. Serology: Antibodies may be detected by neutralization, complement fixation, or immunofluorescence tests. Such tests may be useful in detecting congenitally infected infants with no clinical manifestations of disease.

Immunity

Complement-fixing and neutralizing antibodies occur in most human sera. In young children possessing CF antibodies, virus may be detected in the mouth and in the urine for many months.

Virus may occur in the urine of children even though serum-neutralizing antibody is present. This suggests that the virus propagates in the urinary tract rather than being filtered from the bloodstream. Virus is not found in young children who lack antibody.

Intrauterine infection may produce a serious disease in the newborn. Infants infected during fetal life may be born with antibody that continues to rise after birth in the presence of persistent virus excretion. (This is similar to the situation in congenital rubella infection.)

Most infants infected with cytomegalovirus in the perinatal period are asymptomatic, and infection continues in the presence of high antibody titers.

Treatment

There is no specific treatment. Neither immune gamma globulin nor DNA virus–inhibitory drugs have any effect.

Epidemiology

The mechanism of virus transmission in the population remains unknown except in congenital infections and those acquired by organ transplantation, blood transfusion, and reactivation of latent virus. Infection with cytomegaloviruses is widespread. Antibody is found in 80% of individuals over 35 years of age. The prolonged shedding of virus in urine and saliva suggests a urine-hand-oral route of infection. Cytomegalovirus can also be transmitted by sexual contact.

Control

Specific control measures are not available. Isolation of newborns with generalized cytomegalic inclusion disease from other neonates is advisable.

Screening of transplant donors and recipients for cytomegalovirus antibody may prevent some transmissions of primary cytomegalovirus. The cytomegalovirus-seronegative transplant recipient population represents a high-risk group for cytomegalovirus infections as well as other lethal superinfections and would be a target population for a vaccine.

A live cytomegalovirus "vaccine" has been developed and has had some preliminary clinical trials. Since cytomegalovirus, like other herpesviruses, causes latent persistent infection, there is doubt that such a "vaccine" would be useful for the population at large. The possible benefits and dangers of a vaccine program for prevention of cytomegalovirus congenital infections require further study.

EB HERPESVIRUS
(Human Herpesvirus 4)
(Infectious Mononucleosis, Burkitt's Lymphoma, Nasopharyngeal Carcinoma)*

EB (Epstein-Barr) virus is the causative agent of infectious mononucleosis and has been associated with Burkitt's lymphoma and nasopharyngeal carcinoma. The virus is an antigenically distinct herpesvirus.

Properties of the Virus

A. Morphology: EB virus is indistinguishable in size and structure from other herpesviruses.

B. Antigenic Properties: EB virus is distinct from all other human herpesviruses. Many different EB virus antigens can be detected by CF, immunodiffusion, or immunofluorescence tests. A lymphocyte-detected membrane antigen (LYDMA) is the earliest-detected virus-determined antigen. EBNA is a complement-fixing nuclear anti-

---

*The oncogenic features of EB herpesvirus are discussed as such in Chapter 40.

gen. Early antigen (EA) is formed in the presence of DNA inhibitors and membrane antigen (MA), the neutralizing antigen, is a cell surface antigen. The virus capsid antigen (VCA) is a late antigen representing virions and structural antigen.

C. Virus Growth: Human blood B lymphocytes infected in vitro with EB virus have resulted in the establishment of continuous cell lines, suggesting that these cells have been transformed by the virus.

This transformation by EB virus enables B lymphocytes to multiply continuously, and all cells contain many EB virus genomes and express EBNA. Some EB virus cell lines express certain antigens but produce no virus particles or VCA; others produce virus particles. EB virus is carried in lymphoid cell lines derived from patients with African Burkitt's lymphoma, nasopharyngeal carcinoma, or infectious mononucleosis. Non-virus-producing B lymphocyte cell lines can be established in vitro from the blood of patients with infectious mononucleosis. Such lines represent a latent state of the virus; the cells contain EB virus genomes but express only the earliest antigen (LYDMA) and possibly EBNA.

Owl monkeys and marmosets inoculated with cell-free EB virus can develop fatal malignant lymphomas. Lymphoblastoid cells from such monkeys cultured as continuous cell lines give positive reactions with EB virus antisera by immunofluorescence.

Immunity

The most widely used and most sensitive serologic procedure for detection of EB virus infection is the indirect immunofluorescence test with acetone-fixed smears of cultured Burkitt's lymphoma cells. The cells containing the EB virus exhibit fluorescence after treatment with fluorescent antibody. Detectable levels of antibody persist for many years.

Early in acute disease, a transient rise in IgM antibodies to VCA occurs, replaced within 2 weeks by IgG antibodies to VCA, which persist for life. Slightly later, antibodies to MA and to EBNA arise and persist throughout life.

Epidemiology

Seroepidemiologic studies using the immunofluorescence technique and CF reaction indicate that infection with EB virus is common in different parts of the world and that it occurs early in life. In some areas, including urban parts of the USA, about 50% of children 1 year old, 80–90% of children over age 4, and 90% of adults have antibody to EB virus.

In groups at a low socioeconomic level, EB virus infection occurs in early childhood without any recognizable disease. These inapparent infections result in permanent seroconversion and total immunity to infectious mononucleosis. In groups living in comfortable social circumstances, infection is often postponed until adolescence and young adulthood. Again, the majority of these adult infections are asymptomatic, but in almost half of cases the infection is manifested by heterophil-positive infectious mononucleosis.

Antibody to EB virus is also present in nonhuman primates.

EB Virus & Human Disease

Most EB virus infections are clinically inapparent. The virus causes infectious mononucleosis and is strongly associated with Burkitt's lymphoma and nasopharyngeal carcinoma.

Infectious mononucleosis (glandular fever) is a disease of children and young adults characterized by fever and enlarged lymph nodes and spleen. The total white blood count may range from $10,000/\mu L$ to $80,000/\mu L$, with a predominance of lymphocytes. Many of these are large "atypical" cells with vacuolated cytoplasm and nucleus. These atypical lymphocytes, probably T cells, are diagnostically important. During mononucleosis, there often are signs of hepatitis.

During the course of infection, the majority of patients develop heterophil antibodies, detected by sheep cell agglutination or the mononucleosis spot test (see Chapter 29).

Although the pathogenesis of infectious mononucleosis is still not understood, infectious EB virus can be recovered from throat washings and saliva of patients ("kissing disease"). Infectious virus is produced by B lymphocytes in the oropharynx and perhaps in special epithelial cells of this region. Virus cannot be recovered from blood, but EB virus genome–containing B lymphocytes are present in up to 0.05% of the circulating mononuclear leukocytes as demonstrated by the establishment of cell lines. These EB virus genome–containing cells express the earliest antigen, LYDMA, which is specifically recognized by killer T cells.

These T cells reach large numbers and can lyse EB virus genome–positive but not EB virus genome–negative target cells. Part of the infectious mononucleosis syndrome may reflect a rejection reaction against virally converted lymphocytes.

Patients with infectious mononucleosis develop antibodies against EB virus, as measured by immunofluorescence with virus-bearing cells. Antibodies appear early in the acute disease, rise to peak levels within a few weeks, and remain high during convalescence. Unlike the short-lived heterophil antibodies, those against EB virus persist for years.

The role that EB virus may play in Burkitt's lymphoma (a tumor of the jaw in African children and young adults) and nasopharyngeal carcinoma (common in males of Chinese origin) is less well established. The association with EB virus is based primarily on the finding that the prevalence of antibody is greater and the antibody titers are higher among patients with Burkitt's lymphoma and nasopharyngeal carcinoma than in healthy matched controls or individuals with other types of malignancies. The significance of these associations is uncertain at present. All cells from Burkitt's lymphoma of African origin and from nasopharyngeal carcinoma carry multiple copies of the EB virus genome and express the antigen EBNA.

B VIRUS
(Herpesvirus of Old World Monkeys)

B virus infection of humans is an acute, usually fatal, ascending myelitis and encephalitis. Cases have followed (1) the bites of apparently normal carrier monkeys or (2) contact with tissue cultures derived from monkeys. Human cases were rare but have increased as the number of persons handling monkeys and preparing vaccines from monkey kidney cultures increased. Herpes B virus is most commonly found in rhesus, cynomolgus, and bonnet macaque monkeys.

Because B virus infection occurs naturally in macaque monkeys, it has been named herpesvirus simiae. It is related as measured by the neutralization test to herpes simplex virus and by one immunoprecipitation line to pseudorabies virus. The virus is transmissible to monkeys, rabbits, guinea pigs, and newborn mice. The virus grows in the chick embryo, producing pocks on the chorioallantoic membrane, and in cultures of rabbit, monkey, or human cells. Experimentally infected animals exhibit intranuclear inclusions and multinucleated giant cells.

The virus enters through the skin and localizes at the site of the monkey bite, producing vesicles and then necrosis of the area. From the site of the skin lesion, the virus enters the central nervous system by way of the peripheral nerves. The picture is predominantly that of a meningoencephalomyelitis. About 3 days after exposure, the patient develops vesicular lesions at the site; regional lymphangitis and adenitis follow. About 7 days later, motor and sensory abnormalities occur; this is followed by acute ascending paralysis, involvement of the respiratory center, and death.

Virus can be recovered from the brain, spinal cord, and spleen of fatal cases. Suspensions of these tissues are inoculated into rabbit kidney cell cultures or intradermally into rabbits; a necrotic lesion of the skin occurs, and the rabbit develops myelitis. The agent is established as B virus by serologic identification. Herpes antiserum hardly neutralizes B virus, whereas B virus antiserum neutralizes both herpes simplex and B viruses equally well.

There is no specific treatment once the clinical disease is manifest. However, gamma globulin containing B virus antibodies is recommended as a preventive measure immediately after a monkey bite.

An experimental killed B virus vaccine has induced antibody responses in human recipients, but its protective value has not yet been proved.

B virus infection occurs in monkeys as a latent infection much as herpes simplex occurs in humans. The virus has been recovered from monkey saliva, brain, and spinal cord and from many lots of monkey kidney culture (once the starting material for preparing poliomyelitis and other vaccines for human use).

In 24 cases of monkey B virus infection, half from the USA, 23 contracted encephalitis and 18 died after a bite wound, a puncture with a contaminated needle, or a cut by glass from monkey tissue cell culture.

MARMOSET HERPESVIRUS
(Herpesvirus of New World Monkeys)

Several herpesviruses have been isolated from New World monkeys, including herpesviruses T, saimiri, ateles, saguinus, and aotus. These viruses seem to have a natural monkey host in which they are present with little apparent effect, but they can produce serious disease when they infect monkeys of another genus. Thus, they resemble herpes simplex virus in humans. Some of these viruses are antigenically related to herpes simplex, and some are distinct.

Two of these viruses—herpesviruses saimiri and ateles—produce malignant disease in other primates. They thus form useful model systems for viral oncologists. Monkeys can be protected from the malignant effect of these viruses by vaccination with live attenuated or killed virus.

•   •   •

References

Barahona H, Melendez LV, Melnick JL: A compendium of herpesviruses isolated from non-human primates. *Intervirology* 1974;**3**:175.

Baringer JR: Herpes simplex virus infection of nervous tissue in animals and man. *Prog Med Virol* 1975;**20**:1.

Chang RS, Rosen L, Kapikian AZ: Epstein-Barr virus infections in a nursery. *Am J Epidemiol* 1981;**113**:22.

Drew WL et al: Prevalence of cytomegalovirus infection in homosexual men. *J Infect Dis* 1981;**143**:188.

Epstein MA, Achong BG: Pathogenesis of infectious mononucleosis. *Lancet* 1977;**2**:1270.

Fleisher G et al: Primary infection with Epstein-Barr virus in infants in the United States: Clinical and serologic observations. *J Infect Dis* 1979;**139**:553.

Galloway DA et al: Detection of herpes simplex RNA in human sensory ganglia. *Virology* 1979;**95**:265.

Hammer SM et al: Temporal cluster of herpes simplex encephalitis: Investigation by restriction endonuclease cleavage of viral DNA. *J Infect Dis* 1980;**141**:436.

Huang E-S et al: Molecular epidemiology of cytomegalovirus infections in women and their infants. *N Engl J Med* 1980;**303**:958.

Kit S et al: Herpesvirus-associated nuclear antigen(s) in cells biochemically transformed by fragments of herpesvirus DNA and in somatic cell hybrids. *Virology* 1980;**105**:103.

Miller G: Epstein-Barr herpesvirus and infectious mononucleosis. *Prog Med Virol* 1975;**20**:84.

Mitchell CD et al: Acyclovir therapy for mucocutaneous herpes simplex infections in immunocompromised patients. *Lancet* 1981;**1**:1389.

Nahmias AJ, Roizman B: Infection with herpes-simplex viruses 1 and 2. *N Engl J Med* 1973;**289**:719.

Openshaw H, Puga A, Notkins AL: Herpes simplex virus infection in sensory ganglia: Immune control, latency, and reactivation. *Fed Proc* 1979;**38**:2660.

Osborn JE: Cytomegalovirus: Pathogenicity, immunology, and vaccine initiatives. *J Infect Dis* 1981;**143**:618.

Roizman B: Genome variation and evolution among herpes viruses. *Ann NY Acad Sci* 1980;**354**:472.

Whitley RJ et al: Herpes simplex encephalitis: Vidarabine therapy and diagnostic problems. *N Engl J Med* 1981;**304**:313.

39 | Reoviruses, Rotaviruses, & Other Human Viral Infections

REOVIRUSES

Reoviruses are 60–80 nm in diameter, contain double-stranded RNA in 10–12 segments, exhibit icosahedral symmetry, and lack an envelope. They mature in the cytoplasm.

Properties of the Viruses

A. Structure: Reovirus virions measure 60–80 nm in diameter and possess 2 distinct capsid shells. The outer shell can be digested by chymotrypsin to reveal the core, which has 12 short spikes at the vertices of the icosahedron. The reovirus genome is unique in that it consists of double-stranded RNA in 10 discrete segments (total MW 15×10^6).

B. Reactions to Physical and Chemical Agents: Reoviruses are unusually stable to heat, acid pH, and many chemicals, but they are inactivated by 70% ethanol. Treatment with proteolytic enzymes increases infectivity.

C. Antigenic Properties: Three distinct but related types of reovirus are demonstrable by Nt and HI tests. All 3 types share a common complement-fixing antigen. Reoviruses contain a hemagglutinin for human O erythrocytes. The human red cell receptors for the reovirus hemagglutinin are not affected by the receptor-destroying enzyme of *Vibrio cholerae* but are destroyed by 1:1000 potassium periodate.

D. Growth of Virus: After adsorption, reovirus reaches the cytoplasm of the host cell. There, the outer shell of the virus is removed and a core-associated RNA transcriptase transcribes mRNA molecules from one strand of the genome RNA still contained in the core. The 10 functional mRNA molecules correspond in size to the 10 genome segments. The reovirus cores contain as structural proteins all enzymes necessary for transcribing, capping, and extruding the mRNAs from the core, leaving the double-stranded RNA genome segments inside.

Once extruded from the core, the 10 mRNA pieces are translated into 10 polypeptides, the primary gene products of reoviruses. Further cleavage of these peptides occurs in the infected cell. Reovirus protein synthesis occurs in the cytoplasm, associated with structures (spindles, centrioles) that are involved in cell mitosis.

A virus-induced RNA-dependent RNA polymerase is responsible for synthesizing minus strands from mRNA-like molecules to form the double-stranded genome segments. Apparently, replication to form progeny RNA thus occurs in partially completed core structures.

Recombinant mapping (see Chapter 27) has been used to identify which RNA segments code for reovirus proteins.

A gene, S1, is responsible for type specificity, hemagglutination, and cell tropism of different reovirus types.

Reoviruses produce a distinctive cytopathic effect in monkey kidney cultures, in which cells separate from the sheet. At this stage, the nuclei are intact but the cytoplasm contains inclusion bodies in which the virus particles are found. The viruses also grow in kidney cultures of other species. Some reoviruses grow in newborn mice or in monkeys, and they may produce central nervous system disease. A strain isolated from a chimpanzee with rhinitis produced the common cold syndrome when passed by nasal instillation into other chimpanzees. The virus also multiplies in chick embryos.

Epidemiology

The reoviruses are found in humans, chimpanzees, monkeys, mice, and cattle. Antibodies are also present in other species.

All 3 types have been recovered from healthy children, from young children during outbreaks of minor febrile illness, from children with diarrhea or enteritis, and from chimpanzees with epidemic rhinitis.

Human volunteer studies have failed to demonstrate a clear cause and effect relationship of reoviruses to human illness. In inoculated volunteers, reovirus is recovered far more readily from feces than from the nose or throat.

ORBIVIRUSES

Orbiviruses are a subgroup of reoviruses that commonly infect insects; many are transmitted by insects to plants or vertebrates. None of these viruses cause serious clinical disease in humans but may cause mild fevers (see Colorado Tick Fever in Chapter 30).

Serious animal pathogens include blue tongue virus of sheep and African horse sickness virus. Antibodies to orbiviruses are found in many vertebrates, including humans.

Some orbiviruses are plant pathogens. Wound tumor virus of plants is an orbivirus that not only multiplies in plant cells but also replicates in the nervous system and other organs of its arthropod vector, the leafhopper.

Orbiviruses have a double protein shell in which a fuzzy, indistinct layer covers the main capsid, which has 32 ring-shaped capsomeres arranged in icosahedral symmetry. This feature gives the group its name (Latin *orbis* "ring").

The genome consists of 10 segments of double-stranded RNA, with a total molecular weight of 12×10^6. The replicative cycle is similar to that of reoviruses. Orbiviruses are sensitive to low pH.

ROTAVIRUSES
(Infantile Gastroenteritis)

The rotaviruses are closely related to reoviruses. They are a major cause of diarrheal illness in human infants and young animals, including calves, mice, piglets, and many others. Among rotaviruses are the agents of human infantile diarrhea, Nebraska calf diarrhea, and epizootic diarrhea of infant mice and SA11 virus of monkeys.

Properties of the Viruses

A. Structure: The name rotavirus (Latin *rota* "wheel") is based on the electron microscopic appearance of the outer capsid margin as the rim of a wheel surrounding radiating spokes from the inner hublike core. The particles have a double-shelled capsid and are about 60–75 nm in diameter. Single-shelled viral particles that lack the outer capsid exhibit rough outer edges and are 50-60 nm in diameter. The inner core of the particles is 33–40 nm in diameter. (See Fig 39–1.)

The virus particle contains 11 segments of double-stranded RNA (total MW 10×10^6). Virions contain an RNA-dependent RNA polymerase that can be activated by chelating agents and a poly A polymerase. The double-shelled particle is the infectious form of the virus. Infectivity of the virions is enhanced by treatment with proteolytic enzymes, eg, trypsin, and this is used in virus isolation in cell culture.

B. Animal Susceptibility and Pathogenesis: Cross-species infections can occur in experimental inoculations, but it is not clear if they occur in nature. In experimental studies, human rotavirus can induce diarrheal illness in newborn colostrum-deprived animals (eg, piglets, calves). Homologous infections may have a wider age range. Swine rotavirus infects both newborn and weanling piglets. Newborns often exhibit subclinical infection due perhaps to the presence of maternal antibody, while overt disease is more common in weanling animals.

Rotaviruses infect cells in the villi of the small intestine. They multiply in the cytoplasm of these enterocytes and damage their transport mechanisms. Damaged cells may slough into the lumen of the intestine and release large quantities of virus, which appear in the stool. The diarrhea caused by rotaviruses may be due to impaired sodium and glucose absorption as the damaged cells on villi are replaced by nonabsorbing immature crypt cells.

C. Virus Replication: Human rotaviruses have not been regularly cultured in vitro, although one human rotavirus strain and several hybrids containing both human and animal rotavirus genes are now cultivable. Rotaviruses from calves, pigs, and monkeys have been grown in cell culture and adapted to laboratory cultivation. This required treatment with proteolytic enzymes (trypsin, pancreatin). Such cultivated viruses now serve as antigens for serologic testing.

In vitro, rotavirus growth is maximal at 18–20 hours. Viral antigens are detected within 4–8 hours in the cytoplasm of infected cells stained by the immunofluorescence technique, where they appear initially as distinct perinuclear granules. Later, antigen is present throughout the cytoplasm. Different types of cell culture manifest great differences in susceptibility to rotavirus infection.

D. Antigenic Properties: The rotaviruses possess common antigens located on the inner shell. These can be detected by immunofluorescence, immune electron microscopy, and many other methods. Type-

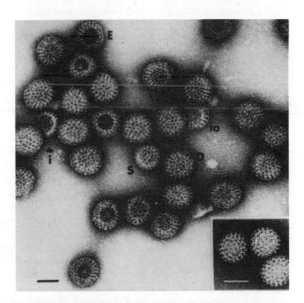

Figure 39–1. Electron micrograph of a negatively stained preparation of human rotavirus. D = double-shelled particles; S = single-shelled particles; E = empty capsids; i = fragment of inner shell; io = fragments of a combination of inner and outer shell. Inset: single-shelled particles obtained by treatment of the virus preparation with $100 \, \mu g/mL$ sodium dodecyl sulfate immediately prior to processing for electron microscopy. Bars = 50 nm. (Esparza & Gil.)

specific antigens are located on the outer capsid layers. These type-specific antigens differentiate among rotaviruses from different species and are demonstrable by immunofluorescence and neutralization tests. At least 4 serotypes have been serologically identified among human rotaviruses, but more may exist.

Molecular epidemiologic studies have analyzed the number of human strains based on differences in the migration of the 11 genome segments following electrophoresis of the RNA in polyacrylamide gels. At least 17 electropherotypes of human virus were observed in one 6-year study, suggesting extensive genome heterogeneity. It remains to be determined whether these differences in electropherotypes reflect changes in serotypes.

Clinical Findings & Laboratory Diagnosis

Rotaviruses cause the major portion of diarrheal illness in infants and children but not in adults. Typical symptoms include diarrhea, fever, abdominal pain, and vomiting, leading to dehydration.

Adult contacts may be infected, as evidenced by seroconversion, but they rarely exhibit symptoms, and virus is infrequently detected in their stool. However, epidemics of clinical disease have occurred in institutionalized adult populations and in adults in nonimmune isolated communities.

In infants and children, severe loss of electrolytes and fluids may be fatal unless treated. Patients with milder cases have symptoms for 3–5 days, then recover completely. Asymptomatic infections, with seroconversion, occur.

Laboratory diagnosis rests on demonstration of virus in stool collected early in the illness and on a rise in antibody titer. Virus in stool is demonstrated by immune electron microscopy, immunodiffusion, and other methods. Many serologic tests can be used to detect an antibody titer rise, particularly CF and ELISA.

Epidemiology & Immunity

Epidemiologic studies on the prevalence of rotavirus infections have shown these ubiquitous agents to be a major cause of gastroenteritis in children. Typically, 50–60% of the cases of acute gastroenteritis of hospitalized children throughout the world are caused by rotaviruses. Rotavirus infections usually predominate during the winter season, with an incubation period of 2–4 days. Symptomatic infections are most common in children between ages 6 months and 12 years, and transmission appears to be by the fecal-oral route. Nosocomial infections are frequent.

Rotaviruses are ubiquitous. By age 6, 60–90% of children have serum antibodies to one or more types. Both humans and animals can become infected even in the presence of antibodies. Local immune factors, such as secretory IgA or interferon, may be important in protection against rotavirus infection. Alternatively, reinfection in the presence of circulating antibody could reflect the presence of multiple serotypes of virus. Asymptomatic infections are common in infants before age 6 months, the time during which protective maternal antibody acquired passively by newborns should be present. Breast-fed babies excrete fewer virus particles per gram of feces than bottle-fed babies, although both groups can become infected. Rotavirus antibody has been detected in colostrum for up to 9 months postpartum.

Treatment

Treatment of gastroenteritis is supportive, to correct the loss of water and electrolytes, which may lead to dehydration, acidosis, shock, and death. Management consists of replacement of fluids and restoration of electrolyte balance either intravenously or orally, as feasible.

The multiplicity of rotavirus serotypes and other factors make the development of vaccines uncertain. In view of the probable fecal-oral route of transmission, waste-water treatment and sanitation are significant control measures.

· · ·

EPIDEMIC GASTROENTERITIS VIRUS

Epidemic nonbacterial gastroenteritis is characterized by (1) the absence of bacterial pathogens; (2) gastroenteritis with rapid onset and recovery and relatively mild systemic signs; and (3) an epidemiologic pattern of a highly communicable disease that spreads rapidly with no particular predilection in terms of age or geography. Although various terms have been used in reports of different outbreaks (eg, epidemic viral gastroenteritis, viral diarrhea, winter vomiting disease, epidemic diarrhea and vomiting) in which a particular clinical feature predominated, studies of outbreaks and of the illness transmitted to volunteers suggest that distinct syndromes may be different manifestations of infection by the same agent.

Virus particles of 27-nm diameter have been demonstrated by immune electron microscopy (see Chapter 29) in stools from adults with acute gastroenteritis in a Norwalk, Ohio, outbreak and other outbreaks. There appear to be at least 3 serotypes.

The "Norwalk" agent has not been grown in tissue culture. However, volunteer experiments have clearly shown that the appearance of the virus coincides with the clinical illness. Antibody develops during the illness and is protective against reinfection with that agent. Experimental infection of chimpanzees results in infection and seroconversion of animals in the absence of clinical illness.

A comparison of the Norwalk agent and rotavirus is shown in Table 39–1.

Viral gastroenteritis has an incubation period of 16–48 hours. Onset is rapid, and the clinical course lasts 24–48 hours; symptoms include diarrhea, nausea, vomiting, low-grade fever, abdominal

Table 39—1. Comparison of proved human gastroenteritis viruses.*

Parameter	Norwalk-like Agents	Rotaviruses
Clinical syndromes	Epidemic diarrhea All age groups	Sporadic seasonal gastroenteritis Infants and young children
Physical properties		
Diameter (nm)	27	60–70
Nucleic acid	?	Double-stranded segmented RNA
Acid-stable	+	+
Heat-stable	+	+
Ether-stable	+	+
Stable to 50 °C in 1 M MgCl$_2$	?	–
Density in CsCl	1.38–1.41	1.36 double-shelled particles 1.38 single-shelled particles
Biologic properties		
Growth in tissue culture	–	±†
Experimental animal infection	± (chimpanzees)	+
Antigens	?	Type-specific and type-common antigens
Serotypes	3	4
Miscellaneous	–	Virion hemagglutinin Virion RNA–dependent RNA polymerase

*From Estes and Graham: *Am J Med* 1979;66:1001.
†Bovine, porcine, and simian isolates adapted to growth in vitro.

cramps, headache, and malaise. No sequelae have been reported.

While immune electron microscopy was required initially for detection of virus and antibody, a radioimmunoassay blocking test and an immune adherence method can now detect antibody to Norwalk type viruses. Whereas rotavirus antibody develops early in childhood (see above), Norwalk virus antibody is acquired later in life; by the fifth decade, 50% of adults have such antibody.

Treatment is symptomatic. Because of the infectious nature of the stools, care should be taken in their disposal.

CROHN'S DISEASE, ULCERATIVE COLITIS, & OTHER CHRONIC DISEASES OF THE GASTROINTESTINAL TRACT

Crohn's disease (regional ileitis) as well as other chronic gastrointestinal diseases have long been suspected of being caused by a transmissible agent. Granulomas can be induced in the footpads of mice inoculated with tissue homogenates from patients with Crohn's disease. Tissue homogenates have also produced the disease in rabbits.

An RNA-containing, ether- and acid-stable virus has been isolated from patients with Crohn's disease, ulcerative colitis, and other chronic gastrointestinal diseases. The virus has been isolated in human diploid fibroblast (WI-38) and rabbit ileum cultures, from surgical resections and biopsy material obtained from many parts of the gastrointestinal tract, and from regional lymph nodes and gallbladder tissue. The etiologic significance of this finding is uncertain but supports the argument that viruses may play a role in these diseases.

WARTS
(Verrucae, Human Papovavirus)

Human wart virus (human papilloma virus) belongs biologically to the papovavirus group (*pa*pilloma, *po*lyoma, *va*cuolating viruses). Papillomaviruses (diameter 55 nm) include viruses of rabbits, cattle, and humans; polyomaviruses (diameter 45 nm) include polyomaviruses of mice, vacuolating viruses of rabbits and monkeys (SV40), and a virus associated with progressive multifocal leukoencephalopathy (PML) of humans. Papovaviruses produce tumors in their natural host or in another species (see Chapter 40).

Common skin warts (verrucae) can be spread by autoinoculation through scratching, or by direct or indirect contact. A filtrable agent recovered from warts has produced warts in volunteers. Virus particles with a diameter of 55 nm can be obtained from those warts that have intranuclear inclusions in their rete cells. Thin sections of such papillomas have revealed crystalline masses within the nucleus. By electron microscopic counting procedures, warts are seen to contain their highest concentration of virus particles when they are about 6 months old; 6–12 months is also the period of peak antibody titers in the patient.

The nuclei of normal skin cells are uniform in size, and the DNA content shows little variation from cell to cell. In contrast, wart-infected skin exhibits large and variable nuclear sizes, and also much higher and more variable DNA values that cannot be explained by increased polyploidy or by increased cell division.

Patients who carry warts possess specific antibodies against this human papovavirus. By immunodiffusion, IgM and IgG antibodies can be measured; by complement fixation, IgG antibodies only.

The outlook for healing and disappearance of warts is best if high-titer IgG antibodies can be measured by complement fixation. Antibodies are detectable also in some persons with no history of warts.

Patients with transplanted kidneys who are receiving immunosuppressive drugs experience an increased incidence of warts and of active infections with herpesviruses (see Chapter 38).

Characteristics of wart viruses have been investigated by restriction enzyme mapping, nucleic acid hybridization, serologic tests, and polypeptide patterns, although no virus has been grown in cell culture. At least 4 antigenic types are known.

Hand warts and plantar warts appear to be antigenically identical. Genital and perianal warts (condylomata acuminata) are caused by a similar but not identical agent. Laryngeal papillomas are caused by a similar and perhaps identical virus, suggesting that infants may be infected by the genital wart virus of their mothers. While laryngeal papillomas are rare, the growths may obstruct the larynx and have to be removed repeatedly by surgical means.

Papovaviruses have also been associated with progressive multifocal leukoencephalopathy (PML). Large numbers of virus particles can be seen under the electron microscope in infected brain cells, and a number of isolates of a human papovavirus resembling SV40 have been made in cell cultures (see Slow Virus Diseases in Chapter 33). The virus can be present in the urine of normal pregnant women and of renal allograft recipients.

EXANTHEM SUBITUM
(Roseola Infantum)

Exanthem subitum is a mild disease occurring mainly in infants between 6 months and 3 years of age. At times it is confused with rubella. The causative agent is found in the serum and throat washings during the febrile period. The febrile disease (but without rash) can be transmitted to monkeys with bacteria-free serum.

The incubation period is about 10–14 days. The onset is abrupt; the temperature may rise to 40–41 °C and last 5 days. There is usually lymphadenopathy. Seizures are frequent. The rubelliform rash characteristically follows the disappearance of fever by a few hours and affects most of the body but not the face. Leukopenia is present with a relative lymphocytosis. All patients recover promptly without any specific therapy.

The disease may occur in small outbreaks, but often only single cases occur in families.

FIFTH DISEASE
(Erythema Infectiosum)

A viral cause has been postulated for this disease. The disease is moderately contagious and occurs mainly in children. There are no prodromal symptoms. Fever, if present, is low-grade. The diagnosis is based on the appearance of a rash, which occurs in 3 stages. It begins with marked erythema of the cheeks, which gives a "slapped cheek" appearance. An erythematous maculopapular rash then spreads over the trunk and extremities. The rash fades with central clearing, giving a lacy appearance. It may be pruritic. Complications are rare. No treatment is necessary.

AFRICAN HEMORRHAGIC FEVER
(Marburg & Ebola Viruses)

These are acute diseases characterized by high fever, with bleeding into skin (petechiae, purpura) and from the nose, gastrointestinal tract, and genitourinary tract; thrombocytopenia; and marked toxicity, often leading to shock and death. Marburg virus disease was recognized in 1967 among laboratory workers exposed to tissues of African green monkeys *(Cercopithecus aethiops)* imported into Germany and Yugoslavia. Transmission from patients to medical personnel occurred, with high mortality rates.

There have been no cases since then in Europe or America, but antibody surveys have indicated that the virus is present in East Africa and causes infection in monkeys and humans.

Marburg virus has been isolated in guinea pigs and various cell culture systems. The virus particle contains RNA and has a cylindric or filamentous shape by electron microscopy. It superficially resembles a rhabdovirus but has no antigenic relationship with any known virus. Experimentally inoculated monkeys developed a uniformly fatal disease resembling hemorrhagic fever in humans.

Treatment is directed at maintaining renal function and electrolyte balance and combating hemorrhage and shock. Transfusion of convalescent plasma may have some benefit. Extreme care is needed to prevent exposure of medical personnel to blood, saliva, and urine of patients.

In 1976 two severe epidemics of hemorrhagic fever occurred in Sudan and Zaire. The virus responsible, provisionally named Ebola virus after a river in Zaire, resembles Marburg virus morphologically but is antigenically distinct. The outbreaks involved over 500 cases and at least 350 deaths. The illness was marked by a sudden onset of severe headache, fever, muscle pains, and prostration, quickly followed by profuse diarrhea and vomiting. In each outbreak, hospital staff became infected through close and prolonged contact with patients, their blood, or their excreta. In one hospital, 41 of 76 infected staff members died.

It is probable that Marburg and Ebola viruses have a reservoir host, perhaps a rodent, and become transmitted to humans only accidentally. Human infection, however, is highly communicable to human contacts. By means of rapid travel, such diseases may spread to distant nonendemic areas and present a risk.

CAT–SCRATCH FEVER
(Benign Lymphoreticulosis)

Cat-scratch fever is characterized by malaise, fever, and regional lymphadenitis. A cat scratch, cat bite, or merely contact with cats often occurs a few days before onset. There may be a local lesion at the site of the scratch, followed by inflammation, and suppuration of the regional lymph nodes. Lymphadenitis may persist for 1–3 weeks or longer.

Heat-inactivated suspensions of pus from a bubo serve as skin-test antigens. They yield a tuberculin type reaction about 24 hours after inoculation into convalescents.

The infectious agent is unknown. The disease is difficult to differentiate from other infections of the lymph nodes. It occurs throughout the world. Cases often occur in children and young adults and have followed insect bites, laceration while cutting meat, and pricks from thorns or splinters. Cats are believed to be merely mechanical transmitters of the infection. They do not become ill.

Tetracycline antibiotics may shorten the course of the disease and prevent suppuration. However, even without treatment, recovery is complete within a few weeks.

GUILLAIN–BARRÉ SYNDROME
(Inflammatory Polyradiculopathy)

This is an inflammatory and demyelinating disorder of the nervous system. It is a rare sequela to acute viral infections, especially measles, rubella, varicella-zoster, or mumps. It can also follow vaccination, especially with vaccinia virus or some types of influenza vaccine. In 1976, swine influenza vaccine inoculation of humans was followed by the Guillain-Barré syndrome 5 times more often than occurred in matched individuals who had not been given this vaccine. Very rarely, this syndrome has followed infections by enteroviruses and cytomegalovirus.

The symptoms may range from minor neuropathy with paresthesias or weakness to rapidly progressive ascending paralysis and occasional death. Treatment is symptomatic.

DIABETES MELLITUS

Since 1899, viruses have been suspected as one of the causes of diabetes mellitus in humans. There have been many reports showing a temporal relationship between onset of various virus infections and the onset of diabetes. Mumps virus has been a popular candidate, but a causal relationship has not been proved. Interest has been rekindled by retrospective serologic studies showing that patients with acute onset diabetes had significantly higher titers or greater prevalence of neutralizing antibodies against coxsackieviruses B1, B4, or B5 than did nondiabetic controls. Furthermore, encephalomyocarditis virus of mice, a member of the same family as the coxsackieviruses, can produce a disease resembling diabetes in mice; development of the disease depends also upon the strain and sex of the mice. In addition, Venezuelan equine encephalitis virus has been found to attack islet cells of monkeys and cause diabetes.

A coxsackie B4 virus has been isolated from a diabetic child. This virus produced diabetes when injected into mice and was recovered from the mice, further substantiating the hypothesis that a viral agent may cause diabetes. Even with this evidence, the role of the virus is probably that of a factor acting in a complex interrelationship with genetic and immunologic features of the host rather than a direct viral cause.

● ● ●

References

Blacklow NR, Cukor G: Viral gastroenteritis. *N Engl J Med* 1981;**304**:397.

Brandt CD et al: Comparison of direct electron microscopy, immune electron microscopy, and rotavirus enzyme-linked immunosorbent assay for detection of gastroenteritis viruses in children. *J Clin Microbiol* 1981;**13**:976.

Craighead JE: The role of viruses in the pathogenesis of pancreatic disease and diabetes mellitus. *Prog Med Virol* 1975;**19**:161.

Esparza J, Gil F: A study on the ultrastructure of human rotavirus. *Virology* 1978;**91**:141.

Esparza J et al: Multiplication of human rotavirus in cultured cells: An electron microscopic study. *J Gen Virol* 1980;**47**:461.

Estes MK, Graham DY: Epidemic viral gastroenteritis. *Am J Med* 1979;**66**:1001.

Gissmann L, Pfister H, zur Hausen H: Human papilloma viruses (HPV): Characterization of four different isolates. *Virology* 1977;**76**:569.

Greenberg HB et al: Role of Norwalk virus in outbreaks of nonbacterial gastroenteritis. *J Infect Dis* 1979;**139**:564.

Halvorsrud J, Örstavik I: An epidemic of rotavirus-associated gastroenteritis in a nursing home for the elderly. *Scand J Infect Dis* 1980;**12**:161.

Hayes EC et al: The interaction of a series of hybridoma IgGs with reovirus particles: Demonstration that the core protein λ2 is exposed on the particle surface. *Virology* 1981;**108**:147.

Jenson AB, Rosenberg HS, Notkins AL: Pancreatic islet-cell damage in children with fatal viral infections. *Lancet* 1980;**2**:354.

Kapikian AZ et al: Approaches to immunization of infants and young children against gastroenteritis due to rotaviruses. *Rev Infect Dis* 1980;**2**:459.

Pfister H, zur Hausen H: Seroepidemiological studies of human papilloma virus 1 (HPV-1) infections. *Int J Cancer* 1978;**21**:161.

Rodger SM et al: Molecular epidemiology of human rotaviruses in Melbourne, Australia, from 1973 to 1979, as determined by electrophoresis of genome ribonucleic acid. *J Clin Microbiol* 1981;**13**:272.

Yoon J-W et al: Virus-induced diabetes mellitus: Isolation of a virus from the pancreas of a child with diabetic ketoacidosis. *N Engl J Med* 1979;**300**:1173.

Oncogenic Viruses | 40

Although a viral origin for cancer has not been demonstrated in humans, it would be illogical to suppose that the human species is unique in the animal world in escaping virus-induced malignant tumors. There are several reasons for believing that proof of viral causation of at least some types of human cancer will be forthcoming: (1) the well-established viral cause of benign warts and of molluscum contagiosum of humans; (2) the many clinical, pathologic, and epidemiologic similarities between other human tumors and those of lower animals that have been shown to be caused by viruses; (3) the proved role of some common viruses (adeno, herpes) in producing experimental cancer in animals; and (4) the biophysical, biochemical, and antigenic similarities between animal tumor viruses and some human viruses. Thus, an understanding of the mechanism of viral oncogenesis by known tumorigenic viruses provides models for the investigation of the possible viral cause of cancer in humans.

Although the first known malignancy of viral origin, avian leukemia, was discovered early in this century, the field of viral oncology has received wide attention for only the last 20 years. Intensified research has resulted in the discovery of the viral etiology of many common tumors in lower animals. Recent advances have been made because of technologic advances in tissue culture methods, in the use of newborn animals of defined genetic constitution for assay, and in the application of modern biophysical, biochemical, and immunologic methods, particularly in genetic engineering.

The tumor-inducing viruses can be classified into 2 main groups with differing physical, chemical, and biologic properties: those which contain RNA as their genetic material and those which contain DNA. This chapter is concerned with in vivo and in vitro carcinogenesis by representative members of the 2 groups of viruses as models in the quest for knowledge of viral carcinogenesis in humans.

VIRUS TRANSFORMATION OF CELLS

Ample evidence indicates that cancer originates as a single cell phenomenon. The altered cell possesses

Abbreviations Used in Chapter 40

ALV	Avian leukemia viruses	MDV	Marek's disease virus
AMV	Avian myeloblastosis virus	M-PMV	Mason-Pfizer monkey virus
ASV	Avian sarcoma viruses	mRNA	Messenger RNA
BPV	Bovine papilloma virus	MSV	Murine sarcoma virus
BUDR	5′-bromodeoxyuridine	MuLV	Murine leukemia virus
CEA	Carcinoembryonic antigen	MuMTV	Murine mammary tumor virus
EBNA	Epstein-Barr virus nuclear antigen	NP	Nonproducer
EBV	Epstein-Barr virus	PARA	Particle aiding the replication of adeno-
FeLV	Feline leukemia viruses		virus
FeSV	Feline sarcoma viruses	PML	Progressive multifocal leukoencepha-
FFU	Focus-forming unit		lopathy
GALV	Gibbon ape leukemia virus	PPV	Pleuropneumonia virus
gs	Group-specific	RaLV	Rat leukemia viruses
HaLV	Hamster leukemia viruses	REV	Reticuloendotheliosis viruses
HaSV	Hamster sarcoma viruses	RSV	Rous sarcoma virus
HPV	Human papilloma virus	SSV	Simian sarcoma virus
HSV	Herpes simplex virus	T Ag	Tumor antigen
HVA	Herpesvirus ateles	tRNA	Transfer RNA
HVS	Herpesvirus saimiri	ts	Temperature-sensitive
IUDR	5-iodo-2′-deoxyuridine	TSTA	Tumor-specific transplantation antigens
LHV	Lucké's herpesvirus	VSV	Vesicular stomatitis virus

new abnormal properties that are genetically transmitted to daughter cells. Viruses have been employed extensively to attempt to delineate the biochemical events responsible for those abnormal properties. The genetic changes in cancer cells may be reflected in morphologic, metabolic, or antigenic alterations. In the animal, the outcome of these phenomena may be one of 2 kinds: either the altered cells invade surrounding tissue and metastasize to distant organs and tissues, resulting in host death; or the host may retain its homeostasis through humoral or cellular immune control mechanisms. Thus, a tumor may be defined as a permanently or temporarily uncontrolled growth of cells. It may be generalized or metastatic, culminating in the death of the animal (malignant tumor), or may remain localized (benign tumor).

The mechanisms by which tumor viruses render cells malignant are not yet fully understood. However, the application of quantitative methods to the study of virus-cell interactions in tissue culture and of sensitive techniques for the detection of virus-induced macromolecules has brought some understanding of molecular changes mediated by tumor viruses. It is apparent that transforming viruses interfere with normal regulatory processes in a eukaryotic cell and that this is accomplished by the induction of a very few virus-specified gene products.

Virus infection of a cell has been described as the penetration of one genetic system into the sphere of action of another. Infection of a cell by a cytocidal virus results in cell death, but infection by a tumor virus leads to a synchronous virus-cell coexistence resulting in profound change in the properties of the infected cells. This phenomenon, called **cell transformation,** has been best studied in vitro, since it is

possible to analyze events at the cellular and subcellular levels. Such studies provide an understanding of what is occurring during tumor induction in an animal.

Transformation may be recognized by an increase in the rate of cellular metabolism and multiplication and by a change in the appearance of the cells or of their arrangement in culture, usually as a result of lack of contact inhibition. When a virus induces transformation, small foci of cells resembling microtumors often appear in the culture. Statistical analyses show that a focus is produced by a single virus particle, so that the number of foci is a measure of the transforming ability of the virus preparation. To establish true oncogenic transformation of an in vitro system, the transformed cells must be able to produce a tumor when injected into the appropriate animal host. This is not always possible, however, and one must rely on heritable changes in cell phenotype as criteria of transformation. The most prominent of these changes are loss of contact inhibition, changes in cell adhesion to substrata, altered morphology to a more rounded cell shape, increase in growth rate, increased cell motility, and acquisition of new antigens. These and other changes in virus-transformed cells—growth in soft agar, decrease in serum requirement for growth and for glycolysis, increased agglutinability of cells by plant lectins, etc—appear to be related to functional changes in cell membranes.

Although the biochemical basis for these functional membrane changes is not well understood, altered synthesis of the carbohydrate-containing lipids and proteins of the cell surface may be involved, including incomplete elongation of the heterosaccharide moiety of glycolipids and loss of a large-molecular-weight glycoprotein from the cell surface. Virus-coded proteins may also be inserted into the cell membrane, but the consequences are unknown. Another manifestation of the cell surface changes that accompany virus transformation is the loss of cytoplasmic microfilaments (Fig 40–1) and the acquisition of numerous fingerlike projections (microvilli) that extend from the cell surface (Fig 40–2).

Even though the DNA and RNA tumor viruses differ profoundly in their mode of replication, the fact that oncornavirus genes, like those of the DNA tumor viruses, become integrated into host cell chromosomal DNA (see below) suggests a possible common mechanism of oncogenesis by the 2 groups of agents. It should be noted that current understanding of virus-induced phenotypic transformation comes exclusively from studies with fibroblasts. Epithelial cells behave differently, and concepts and growth criteria developed with fibroblasts will probably not be directly applicable to cells of epithelial origin.

RNA–CONTAINING TUMOR VIRUSES
(Oncornaviruses)

The oncornaviruses listed in Table 40–1 are similar to each other in structure, chemical composition, reaction to chemical and physical agents, and mode of growth. Based on morphologic, antigenic, and enzymatic differences, they have been divided into A, B, C, and D types of viruses. The oncornaviruses belong to the retroviruses (see Chapter 27), since all its members possess a reverse transcriptase (see below).

Oncornaviruses are widespread in nature and are known to cause natural tumors in the host of origin. With the exception of the murine mammary tumor virus and some more recently recognized viruses, the oncornaviruses fall into species-specific groups of agents inducing either leukemias or sarcomas; hence the term leukemia-sarcoma complex for these agents.

Oncornaviruses have been recognized that are endogenous in the natural hosts, do not produce any known disease, but are capable of replicating in tissue culture. According to their host range in culture, they fall into 3 classes: (1) ecotropic (capable of growth in

Table 40–1. Some properties of RNA-containing tumor viruses (oncornaviruses).

Virus*	Abbreviations Used	Host of Origin	Natural Tumors (Host of Origin)	Experimental Host Range		Size (nm)	Morphology (Particle Type)	Site of Virus Maturation	Persistence of Infectious Virus in Tumor
				In Vivo Tumor	In Vitro Cell Transformation				
Avian complex Leukemia Sarcoma (Rous)	ALV† RSV	Chicken	Yes	Chicken, turkey Avian, rodent, monkey	Chicken‡ Avian, rodent, bovine, monkey, human	70–100	C	Budding at cell membrane	Yes
Murine complex Leukemia	MuLV	Mouse	Yes	Mouse, rat, hamster	Mouse§		C		
Sarcoma	MSV		No	Mouse, rat, hamster	Mouse, rat, hamster				
Murine mammary tumor (Bittner)	MuMTV	Mouse	Yes	Mouse			B		
Feline complex Leukemia	FeLV	Cat	Yes	Cat			C		
Sarcoma	FeSV			Cat, dog, rabbit, monkey	Cat, dog, monkey, human				
Primate Woolly monkey, sarcoma	SSV-1	Monkey	Yes	Monkey	Monkey		C		
Gibbon, leukemia	GALV	Ape	Yes				C		
Monkey, mammary carcinoma (Mason-Pfizer)	M-PMV	Monkey	?		Monkey		D		
Other Viper		Viper	Yes				C		
Hamster, leukemia	HaLV	Hamster	?				C		
Rat, leukemia	RaLV	Rat	?				C		
Bovine, lymphoma		Cow	Yes				C		

*A series of endogenous C type viruses exist that are not oncogenic but replicate in tissue culture; the murine, feline (RD-114), and primate (baboon) viruses are xenotropic (see text).

†The term RAV has been used for ALV strains associated with the defective Bryan strain of RSV (BH-RSV).

‡With avian myeloblastosis virus and avian erythroblastosis virus only.

§With the Abelson strain of MuLV only.

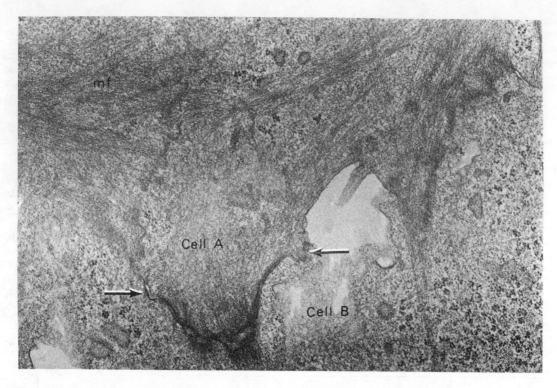

Figure 40–1. Normal rat kidney cells with numerous microfilaments (mf) at intercellular adherens junctions (arrows) between cell A and cell B (32,500 ×). (Altenburg & Steiner.)

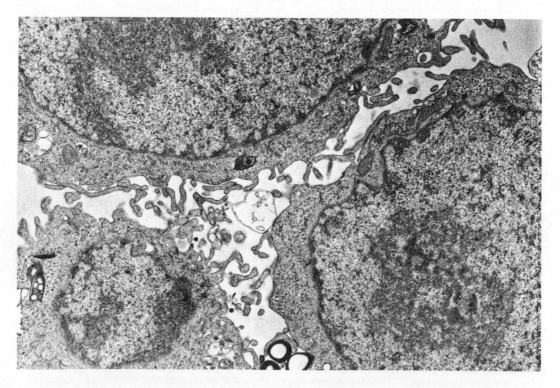

Figure 40–2. Rat kidney cells transformed by murine sarcoma–murine leukemia virus complex (14,100 ×). The cells are held together loosely by intertwining microvilli. Cytoplasmic microfilaments are very sparse. (Altenburg & Steiner.)

cells of the natural host), (2) xenotropic (capable of growth only in cells of a different species), and (3) amphotropic (capable of growth in both autologous and heterologous cells).

Those viruses that have been well studied can be divided into 6 groups on the basis of antigenic makeup, host range, and type of malignancy.

(1) The avian leukemia-sarcoma complex: A group of antigenically related avian agents that are found to cause leukemias (eg, avian leukemia viruses [ALV]) or sarcomas (eg, avian sarcoma viruses [ASV] or Rous sarcoma viruses [RSV]). They have been classified into 7 major groups (A-G) based on envelope antigenicity. This classification, based on antigenic cross-reactions in neutralization and immunofluorescence tests with antisera prepared in chickens, is in agreement with a classification based on virus host range and virus interference in embryonic cells of genetically defined chickens and of other avian species. A dominant cell gene governs the susceptibility of chicken cells to avian oncornaviruses; in susceptible cells, viruses within one antigenic subgroup interfere with the growth of each other but not with viruses of other antigenic subgroups.

Another group of avian C type viruses includes the avian reticuloendotheliosis viruses (REV). REV contain a 60–70S RNA but are antigenically distinct from the avian leukemia-sarcoma group of viruses and lack the p30 antigen (see below). Furthermore, there is no antigenic cross-reactivity between the reverse transcriptase (see below) of REV and the avian leukemia-sarcoma viruses, nor is there homology between their RNAs.

A third group of avian oncornaviruses has been isolated from pheasants and exhibits no immunologic cross-reactivity or nucleic acid homology with the other major groups of avian viruses. Efficient phenotypic mixing with ASV does occur.

(2) The murine leukemia-sarcoma complex: Many different strains of murine leukemia virus (MuLV) have been associated with a variety of leukemias in mice. Four of these have been most prominently used for classification purposes; they bear the name of the investigator first reporting the strain— Gross (G-MuLV), Friend (F-MuLV), Moloney (M-MuLV), and Rauscher (R-MuLV). On the basis of type-specific antigens, found both on the virion surface and on the surface of infected cells, the existing MuLV strains have been divided into 2 major antigenic groups, one carrying the protein coat antigens of the Friend-Moloney-Rauscher (FMR) viruses and the other the antigens of the Gross (G) virus. This classification has been supported by virus neutralization, complement fixation, immunofluorescence, and cytotoxic tests. These agents may also be grouped into N-tropic, B-tropic, and NB-tropic categories, based on host range in genetically defined mouse embryo cells. The first group contains agents capable of replicating best in cells derived from NIH/Swiss (N) mice; the second group of viruses replicates best in cells derived from BALB/c (B) mice; and the third group, composed of laboratory strains only, replicates equally well in both types of cells. Unlike the avian oncornavirus system, this host-range grouping is not in accord with the antigenic classification, since viruses of the G group can be either N- or B-tropic and viruses of both FMR and G groups have been found to be NB-tropic. Furthermore, in contrast to the avian oncornavirus system, a dominant cell gene governs resistance to MuLV rather than susceptibility.

All strains of mice studied to date contain xenotropic C type viruses, which can replicate in cells of other species (human, rat) but not in murine cells. They possess the p30 antigen and reverse transcriptase characteristic (see below) of established MuLV strains but differ from them in envelope antigenicity.

The complex also includes the antigenically related murine sarcoma viruses (MSV) capable of inducing sarcomas. Five different strains of MSV have been recognized to date: H-MSV (Harvey), FJB-MSV (Finkel, Biskis, and Jinkins), M-MSV (Moloney), Ki-MSV (Kirsten), and GZ-MSV (Gazdar). All 5 strains exist as mixtures of MSV and MuLV and bear the antigenicity of the associated MuLV. H-MSV and Ki-MSV, both isolated as a result of passage of a mouse helper virus into rats, have been shown to contain a segment of rat-specific RNA in their genomes.

(3) Murine mammary tumor virus (MuMTV): (Also known as milk factor or Bittner virus.) B type particles, antigenically distinct from the murine oncornaviruses described above, are responsible for mammary carcinomas in certain strains of mice. The known strains of MuMTV, each with a characteristic host cell interaction, have been classified on the basis of biologic behavior. MuMTV-S is the Bittner virus, the virulent virus transmitted by the milk in high tumor incidence strains such as C3H and A. MuMTV-S can be readily transmitted to susceptible strains such as BALB/c. MuMTV-P is the Mühlbock virus, the virulent agent of European strains of mice. The virus is transmitted by the milk route in the RIII strain and by both milk and germ cells in the GR strain.

MuMTV-L, also called nodule-inducing virus (NIV), is retained when MuMTV-S is eradicated from high tumor incidence strains (eg, C3Hf). MuMTV-L is a low-oncogenic virus, is transmitted in the gametes, and has not been removed from any strain carrying it. MuMTV-O has been isolated from old retired BALB/c breeders. It is manifested late in life but once recovered can be passaged in the host of origin. The various strains of MuMTV share protein coat antigens, but antigenic differences can be demonstrated.

The milk-transmitted viruses are also referred to as exogenous agents, while the sequences integrated in the cellular DNA are designated as endogenous proviruses. The latter have been demonstrated in normal mammary gland cells from both high and low mammary tumor–incidence strains. It is currently not clear how dissimilar the exogenous and endogenous viruses may be. Molecular hybridization studies have suggested that they are closely related, although differences do exist between MuMTV-S and MuMTV-L. The biologic significance of the endogenous virus in murine mammary tumorigenesis is unknown.

A virus, similar to the isolates of MuMTV from the laboratory species of mouse *Mus musculus,* has been recovered from an Asian rodent, *Mus cervicolor.* Designated MC-MTV, this agent is the first to be isolated from another species that is immunologically related to MuMTV.

(4) The feline leukemia-sarcoma complex: A group of antigenically related feline leukemia viruses (FeLV), which cause leukemias in the cat, and feline sarcoma viruses (FeSV), which cause sarcomas in the cat as well as in other species such as dogs, rabbits, and monkeys. These agents have been divided into 3 subgroups (A–C) on the basis of protein coat antigenicity and of host range and virus interference patterns in tissue culture.

There are also nontumorigenic endogenous viruses in domestic cats (such as RD-114) that are distinct from the FeLV and FeSV strains and are xenotropic in that they replicate in different mammalian cells but not in feline cells.

(5) The hamster leukemia-sarcoma complex: A group of agents morphologically similar to but antigenically distinct from the murine oncornaviruses. The hamster leukemia viruses (HaLV) appear to be indigenous to the hamster and have best been characterized in tissue culture as nontransforming agents present in stocks of hamster-specific sarcoma viruses (HaSV). These hamster-specific sarcoma viruses have been derived from MSV-induced sarcomas in hamsters and are oncogenic in hamsters but not in mice. They contain the MSV genome in the envelope of the helper HaLV—hence the altered host range and protein coat antigenicity.

(6) Primate oncornaviruses: Three oncornaviruses, antigenically distinct from other simian agents and from oncornaviruses of other species, have been isolated from spontaneous tumors of primates: 2 antigenically related C type agents, from a woolly monkey fibrosarcoma (woolly monkey sarcoma virus or simian sarcoma virus type 1 [SSV-1]) and from gibbon apes with lymphosarcoma or myelogenous leukemia (gibbon ape leukemia virus [GALV]), and an antigenically distinct, apparently D type agent (the Mason-Pfizer monkey virus [M-PMV]) from a rhesus monkey mammary tumor. SSV-1 is tumorigenic for newborn marmosets; both SSV-1 and M-PMV can transform primate cells in vitro, whereas the gibbon virus induces myelogenous leukemia in recipient gibbons but is a nontransforming agent. Like sarcoma viruses of other species, SSV-1 is associated with a nonleukemogenic and nontransforming C type virus termed simian sarcoma-associated virus (SSAV).

D type viruses have also been isolated from langur and squirrel monkeys. Both types appear to represent endogenous viruses in their species of origin. M-PMV appears to be related to the langur monkey isolate, which is horizontally transmitted to rhesus monkeys.

Several oncornaviruses have been isolated from normal baboon cells by co-cultivation with permissive host cell lines. The baboon viruses are infectious for cells from various mammalian species but have not replicated in baboon cell lines, ie, they are xenotropic. These viruses, for which no tumorigenicity has been demonstrated, are distinct from the gibbon and woolly monkey viruses but are closely related to endogenous feline viruses (RD-114). Sequences related to those of the baboon C type viruses have been found to be present in the cellular DNA of other Old World monkeys, higher apes, and humans.

(7) Other: C type oncornavirions have been detected in viper, rat, guinea pig, and bovine malignancies as well as in placentas of normal baboons, rhesus monkeys, and human beings. Of these, the viper and rat agents have been isolated and characterized in culture as nontransforming viruses; akin to the HaLV, the rat virus (termed rat leukemia virus [RaLV]) serves as a helper virus for the replication of defective MSV in rat cells.

There have been reports of C type particles associated with various malignancies of humans and of B type particles associated with human breast cancer. Two C type viruses, ESP-1 and RD-114, initially thought to be of human origin, have been identified as strains of MuLV and an endogenous feline C type virus, respectively. No proven human oncornavirus has yet been recovered.

Properties of Oncornaviruses*

A. Morphology and Size: Electron microscopic studies of infected cells reveal budding virus particles at the cellular membrane and mature particles in intracellular spaces (Fig 40–3). The particles range in size from 100 to 120 nm. The mature particle consists of an RNA- and protein-containing, electron-dense nucleoid (55 nm in diameter) that can be either central (in C type particles) or eccentric (in B type particles). The nucleoid is separated from a glycoprotein- and lipid-containing outer membrane (envelope) by an electron-lucent area (halo). The envelope is derived from the cellular membrane during the process of budding, which is the characteristic mode of release for all oncornaviruses. The nucleoid of intracellular A type particles is electron-transparent. Intracytoplasmic A type particles are precursors of extracellular B type viruses. Intracisternal A type particles appear to be distinct entities that are not a stage in the life cycle of either B type or C type viruses. Biologic activity has been associated only with mature B type and C type particles. The particles associated with biologic activity of the primate virus M-PMV (see Table 40–1) appear to be morphologically distinct and are classified as D type particles.

Purified oncornaviruses stained with phosphotungstic acid (negative staining) reveal superficial similarities with myxoviruses. Like myxoviruses, the envelope of MuMTV (and possibly avian myeloblas-

---

*For general properties of viruses, see Chapter 27.

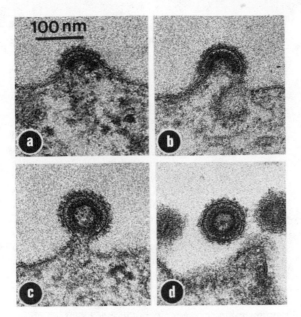

Figure 40–3. Sequential stages of the budding process of replicating oncornaviruses. Pictured is the Friend strain of murine leukemia virus. (Courtesy of H. Frank.)

Table 40–2. Structural components of avian and murine oncornaviruses.

| Virion Polypeptide | | Structural | Virion |
Avian	Murine	Component	Substructure
gp85–S	gp71–S	Knob	Envelope
gp35–S	p15E–S	Spike	
p10	p12E	Envelope associated	
p19	p12	Inner coat	Inner coat
p27	p30	Core shell	Core exterior
p15	p15C	Core associated	
p12	p10	Nucleoprotein	Ribonucleoprotein
p91(β)	p70(a)	Reverse transcriptase	complex
p64(a)			

From Bolognesi et al: *Science* 1978;**199**:184

tosis virus [AMV]) has surface projections about 10 nm long. Treatment of oncornavirus particles with Tween 80-ether results in disruption of the envelope and release of the nucleoids, which have a higher buoyant density (1.22–1.27 g/mL) than that of the intact virion (1.16–1.18 g/mL). Negatively stained nucleoids reveal filamentous nucleoprotein strands (3–4 nm in diameter), often contained within peripheral tightly coiled helical structures (7–9 nm in diameter). The peripheral helical structure (nucleocapsid) has been assumed to form, during virus maturation, a supercoiled hollow sphere that is unstable and in the mature virion uncoils to fill the nucleoid with the nucleoprotein strands (Fig 40–4). The nucleoprotein strands appear to represent the soluble group-specific (gs) antigen characteristic for each group of oncornaviruses (see below), which is also released from the virus particles after Tween 80-ether treatment.

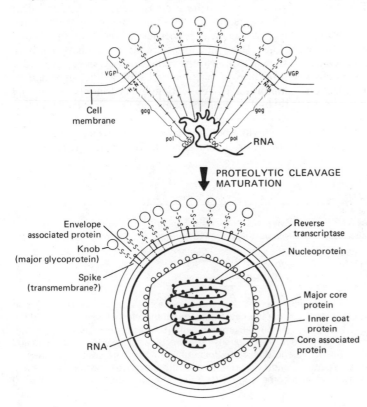

Figure 40–4. Schematic diagram of the postulated mechanism of assembly of a C type oncornavirus. Virus envelope components are inserted in the cell membrane at the site from which virus will bud. Uncleaved "*gag*" precursor molecules, which contain the internal virus polypeptides, migrate to the budding site; one end of the molecule associates with the virus envelope complex and the other end with virus RNA. Proteolytic enzymes cleave the precursor molecules to generate the individual virus polypeptides, the components arrange themselves to form the appropriate substructures, and the mature virion buds from the cell. See Table 40–2 for more detailed designations of the individual murine and avian polypeptides indicated here. (Courtesy of Bolognesi DP et al: *Science* 1978; **199**:183.)

B. Chemical Composition: Oncornavirions consist of approximately 60–70% protein, 30–40% lipids, 1–2.5% RNA, 2% carbohydrates (primarily glycoproteins), and a small amount of double-stranded 7S DNA, presumably of cell origin. The RNA isolated from purified virions is single-stranded and consists of a major 60–70S (MW $1-2 \times 10^7$) viral component and variable amounts of single-stranded small RNA molecules of cell origin. One of these species, tRNA^{trp}, is important because it functions as primer for the synthesis of proviral DNA. The fast-sedimenting 60–70S viral RNA appears to be a dimer structure that can be dissociated by agents capable of breaking hydrogen bonds (heat, dimethyl sulfoxide) into 2 major 30–40S (MW $3-4 \times 10^6$) subunits. Each of the 30–40S subunits resembles eukaryotic cell mRNA in that the 3' end is polyadenylated and the 5' end is capped with an $m^7G^{5'}pppG_m$ group.

Within the avian oncornaviruses, polyacrylamide gel electrophoretic studies have revealed 2 functionally different classes of 30–40S subunit, a larger (class "a") subunit characteristic of transforming sarcoma viruses (ASV), and a smaller (class "b") subunit characteristic of transformation-defective (but not replication-defective) mutants of ASV and of the avian leukemia viruses (ALV). The larger sarcoma RNA subunits appear to contain all the nucleotide sequences present in the smaller leukemia RNA subunits as well as additional sequences, presumably those required for transformation (the src gene). One hypothesis is that the 60–70S RNA of the avian sarcoma viruses constitutes a polyploid genome of 2 genetically identical class "a" subunits and that nontransforming viruses (class "b" subunits) arise through a process of a single deletion of the sequences required for transformation. A similar relationship has not been found between the 30–40S RNA subunits of the mammalian sarcoma-leukemia viruses. The sarcoma virus genome is defective because of the deletion of essential information and therefore is smaller than the leukemia virus genome. The 60–70S viral RNA genome of oncornaviruses appears to be diploid, with each 30–40S subunit representing the entire viral genome, rather than haploid, whereby each 30–40S subunit would contain different genetic information.

A schematic representation of RNA tumor virus genomes and their known gene products is shown in Fig 40–5.

Purified oncornaviruses of all species have been shown to contain a DNA polymerase that can transcribe viral RNA to DNA (RNA-dependent DNA polymerase, also known as reverse transcriptase) and can subsequently synthesize double-stranded DNA molecules after the single-stranded DNA molecules have been liberated from the RNA-DNA hybrid by another enzyme activity (RNase H). These findings lend support to the assumption that oncornavirus RNA replicates in vivo through a DNA intermediate (see below). The reverse transcriptase of oncornaviruses has been purified and shown to be a viral core protein with a molecular weight of 60,000–80,000, separable from the gs antigens of oncornavirions (see below).

Reverse transcriptase activity is not unique to oncornaviruses. Other RNA viruses that are free from demonstrable oncogenicity but induce latent infections in their host of origin also possess the enzyme. This is true for 2 antigenically related viruses inducing "slow" infections of sheep—visna virus and progressive pleuropneumonia virus (PPV)—and for syncytium-forming ("foamy") viruses of primate, bovine, and feline origin. These agents are classified in the same taxonomic order as the oncornaviruses (see above, family **Retroviridae**), since they share other biologic and biophysical properties, in addition to the presence of reverse transcriptase. Visna virus and PPV are able to transform mouse cells in vitro, and their RNA genome is a 60–70S molecule with the same physicochemical properties as those of oncornavirions. The syncytium-forming viruses have not been shown to transform cells but they have revealed a resistance to inactivation by ultraviolet light and an inhibition of replication by dactinomycin and by thymidine analogs similar to that of oncornaviruses. Since these agents do not appear to be oncogenic, it seems that both the presence of reverse transcriptase within virions and genomic RNA replication through a

5' ———	gag	pol	env	onc	c	——— AA . . . A3'
		Polymerase				
	Major Structural	RNase H	Envelope	Transforming	Constant	
	Core Proteins	DNA Endonuclease	Glycoproteins	Protein(s)	Region	
Avian:	p19* p27 p12 p15	p90 p65 p32	gp85 gp37	pp60 ^{src}	?	
Murine:	p15 p12 p30 p10	p84	gp70 p15(E)	p21	?	
Feline:	p15 p12 p30 p10	?	gp70 p15(E)	p85	?	

Figure 40–5. Schematic representation of RNA tumor virus genomes and their known gene products. Starting at the 5' end of the virion RNA, the first gene is gag. Its product is a polyprotein that undergoes posttranslational cleavage to yield the major virus core proteins. The second gene is pol, coding for a pleiotropic enzyme with RNA-dependent DNA polymerase, RNase H, and DNA endonuclease activity. The third gene is env, which codes for a precursor protein that is cleaved and glycosylated to yield virus envelope glycoproteins. The fourth gene, onc, codes for putative primary "transforming proteins" whose presence in the cell leads to malignant transformation. For brevity, intermediate protein processing steps have been excluded. No attempt has been made to illustrate individual genome lengths. (**Note:** * = molecular weight in thousands.) (From Kurth et al: Nature 1979;**279**:197.)

DNA intermediate are phenomena with broader implications as far as pathogenesis is concerned.

Other enzymes (RNA ribonuclease, nucleotide kinase, protein kinase, etc) may also be associated with purified oncornavirus preparations; however, as shown earlier for the enzyme adenosine triphosphatase (ATPase) associated with AMV, they are probably cell enzymes incorporated within the viral envelope during the process of maturation.

C. Reactions to Chemical and Physical Agents: Because of their lipid-containing envelope, the RNA tumor viruses are sensitive to ether. They are readily inactivated by heating (56 °C for 30 minutes), by mild acid treatment (pH 4.5), and by formalin at 1:4000. The RNA tumor viruses can be preserved at −70 °C or lower temperatures.

D. Antigenic Properties: (See Fig 40–4 and 40–5.) Two types of antigens are found in oncornaviruses:

(1) Type-specific or subgroup-specific antigens associated with the viral envelope and characteristic of individual strains, or groups of strains, within oncornaviruses of each species. They are coded for by the *env* gene. They are detectable in neutralization, complement fixation, immunodiffusion, and immunofluorescence tests with sera of animals carrying virus-producing tumors or with antisera prepared against intact virions. The envelope antigens of the avian C type viruses contain at least 2 glycoprotein components with molecular weights of 85,000 and ~35,000. There is no cross-reaction between the envelope antigens of the avian and mammalian oncornaviruses or between oncornaviruses of different mammalian species. Furthermore, there is no cross-reaction between the C type and B type viruses within the murine system and the C type and D type viruses within the primate system.

(2) Group-specific (gs) antigens associated with internal polypeptides of the virion core—cleavage products of the polyprotein coded for by the *gag* gene. They are detectable by complement fixation, immunodiffusion, and immunofluorescence tests and by radioimmunoassay using sera of animals of heterologous species that bear virus-induced (but usually virus-free) tumors, antisera prepared against Tween 80–ether disrupted virions, or monospecific antisera to individual polypeptides. The major gs antigen (p30) is a basic polypeptide with a molecular weight of approximately 30,000; it is shared by all C type viruses within a host species (avian, feline, hamster, murine, primate, rat, viper). No cross-reactions have been observed between the p30 antigens of the avian and mammalian oncornaviruses. Similarly, there is no cross-reaction between the p30 antigens of the C type and B type murine viruses or the C type and D type primate viruses.

Tumor Induction by Oncornaviruses

In contrast to most DNA tumor viruses, oncornaviruses can cause cancer under natural conditions in their hosts of origin (see below). The most common types of malignancies induced are lymphoreticular. A common feature of RNA tumor virus–mediated disease is the synthesis of infectious virus by the neoplastic cells. It should be noted that many morphologically similar viruses, recovered from a variety of animals, have never been shown to cause cancer or any other type of disease; those isolates are designated "leukemia" viruses merely by analogy with the classic members of the group.

A. Avian Leukemia-Sarcoma Complex: Leukemic diseases are common in chickens, and the leukemia-inducing viruses are widespread in normal as well as in diseased chicken populations. The main types of viral leukemias encountered are lymphoid, myeloid, and erythroid. They derive their names from the characteristic primitive cells (lymphoblast, myeloblast, erythroblast) found in large quantities in the blood of the diseased animal, and from this terminology the names of the viruses have evolved: avian lymphomatosis virus, myeloblastosis virus, and erythroblastosis virus.

Infectious virus and physical particles of the virus may be found in high concentration in tumor cells, peripheral blood, and other organs of the affected animals, a phenomenon not encountered with the DNA tumor viruses. Myeloblasts or erythroblasts taken from diseased birds and grown in tissue culture continue to release virus, which in turn can induce the malignancy on inoculation into chickens.

Almost all flocks of chickens are infected with various strains of ALV, especially lymphomatosis virus. The virus is transmitted horizontally through the saliva and feces, producing an infection in the adult animal characterized by transient viremia and enduring antibodies. Relatively few adult birds develop clinical disease. Vertical transmission occurs from the viremic hen but not from the viremic rooster, ie, nongenetic vertical transmission, as distinguished from genetic vertical transmission, in which oncornavirus information is transmitted through the germ line in the form of a DNA provirus (see below). Vertical transmission results in congenitally infected viremic chickens that are tolerant to the virus, free from antibodies, and permanent shedders of the virus. The incidence of leukemia in congenitally infected animals is much higher than in animals infected by contact.

Rous sarcoma virus has undergone countless passages experimentally since it was first isolated in 1911, and it probably now differs from the naturally occurring virus. Several strains of ASV exist that differ in oncogenicity, antigenic structure, and host range.

ASV causes sarcomas in birds of all ages and in chick embryos; unlike lymphomatosis virus, however, it is not naturally transmitted. ASV also induces tumors in ducks, turkeys, pigeons, and other birds. Subgroup D viruses (Schmidt-Ruppin and other strains) can infect mammalian cells and have been shown to induce tumors when inoculated into newborn rats, Syrian and Chinese hamsters, rabbits, mice, guinea pigs, and monkeys. The avian tumors usually contain infectious virus, while the mammalian tumors tend to be virus-free.

B. Murine Leukemia-Sarcoma Complex: Numerous leukemogenic murine viruses have been isolated, with a spectrum of types of leukemia represented. For example, in certain lines of mice, Graffi virus causes myeloid forms of leukemia, whereas in other mouse strains, lymphatic leukemia occurs in a high percentage of cases. Gross virus can cause almost all known types of leukemic disease: lymphatic, stem cell, myeloid, and monocytic leukemia; erythroblastosis; chloroleukemia; lymphosarcoma; and reticulum cell sarcoma. Most murine leukemia viruses are infectious in rats, while Moloney virus is pathogenic in hamsters as well.

Newborn animals are most susceptible to the effects of leukemogenic viruses, but disease can be produced in young and adult animals. Genetic factors play an important role in determining the susceptibility of mice to the virus, the nature of the disease caused, and the transmission of the virus. Large amounts of infectious virus and virus particles are present in the blood and tumor tissue of infected animals. Murine leukemia viruses are widespread in nature. Gross virus is the major cause of naturally occurring disease.

Several different strains of MSV have been isolated; all bear the antigenicity of a helper MuLV that must be present. MSV induces sarcomas in newborn mice, rats, and hamsters. After passage in rats and hamsters, some MSV strains have acquired the protein coat of the endogenous RaLV and HaLV, respectively. Passage of some strains in rat cells has resulted in the acquisition of rat nucleic acid sequences by the RNA of the MSV genome.

C. Murine Mammary Tumor Virus: Tumorigenesis by different strains of MuMTV is a result of a complex interaction between the virus, the genetic constitution of the host, and hormonal factors. The most virulent strain, MuMTV-S, is present in "high mammary cancer" strains of inbred mice (eg, C3H), in which mammary adenocarcinomas develop relatively early in the life of breeding females, with large amounts of infectious virus and B type particles in the tumor, milk, and blood. In such animals, the virus is transmitted from mother to offspring via the milk. The virus induces adenocarcinomas of the mammary gland only, and only in mice of susceptible lines. Animals that do not develop tumors remain subclinically infected and are able to transmit the virus to their progeny.

Studies with a variety of highly inbred strains of mice indicate that the distribution of MuMTV is ubiquitous, with even "low mammary cancer" strains of mice harboring the virus. Virus strains have been described that are transmitted through the ovum and sperm (eg, GR), apparently in the form of an integrated DNA provirus (genetic vertical transmission). In some strains, the virus is rarely expressed in an overt form. Hybridization studies have revealed that tissues of both "low" (eg, BALB/c) and "high" (eg, C3H) mammary cancer strains of mice contain MuMTV DNA

sequences and various amounts of MuMTV RNA. All mice carry endogenous MuMTV sequences in their DNA. The properties and function of the endogenous viruses, as distinct entities from the milk-transmitted exogenous viruses, remain to be established.

D. Feline Leukemia-Sarcoma Complex: Feline leukemia virus (FeLV) and feline sarcoma virus (FeSV) have been derived from cats with leukemia and fibrosarcoma, respectively. FeLV is a common infectious agent in free-roaming cat populations. Most infections are mild and transient, and only a small percentage of cats develop leukemia or lymphoma later in life; of the leukemic cases, about two-thirds express infectious virus. FeLV is efficiently transmitted to close contacts. Newborn kittens are most susceptible to development of persistent viremia and malignancies. FeSV can cause sarcomas in dogs, rabbits, and monkeys as well as in cats.

E. Primate Oncornaviruses: Woolly monkey sarcoma virus (SSV-1) induces sarcomas in newborn marmosets and the gibbon ape leukemia virus (GALV) induces leukemias in gibbons.

Oncornavirus Replication & Cell Transformation

A characteristic property of RNA tumor viruses is that they are not cytocidal for the cells in which they replicate. Similar to other viruses, oncornaviruses pass through an eclipse phase when initiating infection of a new cell. The infected cell then produces new infectious virus, continues to multiply, and may or may not undergo malignant transformation. Infectious virus and virus particles are readily detected in most tumor cells or cells transformed in vitro. As shown by electron microscopic and tissue culture studies, the viruses mature at the cellular membrane; they are continuously released from the cell by budding from the cellular membrane (Fig 40–3).

A. Oncornavirus DNA Copy (Provirus): Early studies with oncornaviruses had shown that inhibitors of DNA synthesis could prevent virus replication and cell transformation if applied during the first 8–12 hours after infection but not thereafter. Low doses of dactinomycin (which blocks DNA-directed RNA synthesis) were inhibitory throughout the replicative cycle. These findings indicated that transient DNA synthesis and continual DNA transcription are required for replication and transformation and led to the assumption that oncornaviruses may replicate through a DNA intermediate. According to the "provirus" theory proposed by Temin, the entering viral RNA is transcribed to DNA early after infection. The RNA-DNA hybrid is then further transcribed to a double-stranded DNA that, during cell division, integrates into the host cell DNA. The newly integrated virus-specific DNA (provirus) serves both as a permanent template for the transcription of progeny viral RNA molecules and as a heritable gene for transformation.

The discovery of the enzyme RNA-dependent DNA polymerase, or reverse transcriptase, present in purified virions and capable of transcribing viral RNA to DNA in an in vitro reaction system, strengthened the assumption that oncornaviruses replicate through a DNA intermediate. The viral DNA polymerase functions during virus replication to make a DNA copy of the RNA genome. Noninfectious variants of ASV and MSV are deficient in the enzyme and certain mutants of ASV with a temperature-sensitive defect for initiation of replication contain a temperature-sensitive enzyme.

Single-stranded DNA copies synthesized in vitro by the reverse transcriptase enzyme are complementary to the viral RNA. The viral DNA products, as well as the 70S viral RNA, have been used as radioactive hybridizing probes to detect virus-specific DNA and RNA species within infected or transformed cells. Studies with both the avian and murine systems indicate the following pattern:

(1) Between 3 and 6 hours after infection, double-stranded viral DNA (provirus) is synthesized and found as a free molecule (MW $\sim 6 \times 10^6$) in the cell cytoplasm, indicating that reverse transcription occurs in the cytoplasm (for RSV this has also been demonstrated to occur in enucleated cells). This process is preceded by the formation of viral RNA-DNA hybrid molecules.

(2) Between 6 and 10 hours after infection, the newly synthesized provirus can be detected in a free form (predominantly as a closed circular duplex with a native molecular weight of 6×10^6) in the cell nucleus.

(3) After 10 hours, the provirus begins to be detected in a covalently integrated form within the cell chromosome, and by 24 hours postinfection most of the provirus is found in an integrated state — presumably as a linear part of the chromosome. Very few copies are integrated per infected cell. There do not appear to be any unique or favored integration sites in the cell genome.

(4) After it is integrated into the cell chromosome, the viral DNA becomes a template for the synthesis of viral genome RNA and of viral messenger (m) RNA — the former being detected first in the nucleus and at a later stage in the cytoplasm. The mRNA molecules are found associated with polysomes and contain nucleotide sequences identical to those of the viral genome RNA (plus strand). The mRNAs are probably complex mixtures of different species, with at least some classes being spliced in different regions to create or remove termination codons. The *gag* and *env* products are translated from different messages. The mechanism of regulation of the splicing events is unknown.

(5) In productive infections, oncornavirus mRNA is translated into viral proteins, and new progeny are produced. In such cells under steady-state conditions, approximately 1% of the cell RNA and protein are viral in origin. It is not known how the virus distinguishes between spliced mRNAs and complete genome RNA copies required for virion maturation. In contrast, cells that have integrated the viral genome (detected as chromosomal proviral DNA by hybridization) but do not produce viral progeny appear to exhibit

varying degrees of transcriptional control; some synthesize appreciable amounts of viral RNA and proteins, whereas others fail to show detectable RNA but can be induced to produce infectious virions after chemical treatment (see below). Infectious DNA has been extracted from mammalian fibroblasts that were transformed by RSV (including a temperature-sensitive mutant) but were virus-free; transfer of the isolated chromosomal DNA into chick embryo fibroblasts resulted in cell transformation and the production of infectious RSV biologically and antigenically identical to the original RSV strain used to transform the cells from which the DNA was derived.

Unlike transformation with DNA tumor viruses, transformation by oncornaviruses occurs with high efficiency, especially in the presence of polyanions such as diethylaminoethyl-dextran. The exact mechanism by which oncornaviruses transform susceptible cells is not clear, but the viral gene (eg, *src*) required for cell transformation has been identified and the *src* product isolated (see below). Studies with nontransforming mutants of RSV showed that the replicating and cell-transforming capacities reside in different subunits of the viral genome. Cells transformed with a particular mutant of RSV at the permissive temperature lost their transformed phenotype within a few hours after a shift to the nonpermissive temperature; conversely, cells that had lost their transformed phenotype at the nonpermissive temperature regained it after a shift to the permissive temperature. These results showed that the continuous presence of a functional viral gene product is necessary for maintenance of the transformed state. Furthermore, since those viral mutants replicated well at the nonpermissive temperature, the gene product necessary for cell transformation is not required for virus replication.

B. Unique Features of the Avian Complex: Most strains of ALV multiply in cultures of chick embryo fibroblasts without causing any cytopathic change or cell transformation. Virus replication in such cells can be detected by means of an immunofluorescence focus assay with type-specific chicken antisera, by the production of virus-specific gs antigen and reverse transcriptase, or by failure of the cells to transform when exposed to RSV, a phenomenon termed **interference** (see Fig 40–6). Cells chronically infected with leukemia viruses can be propagated in serial passage, yielding large quantities of virus capable of inducing neoplasia in vivo or of inducing interference with RSV in vitro.

Morphologic transformation of susceptible mesenchymal target cells into myeloblastlike cells has been achieved only with the avian myeloblastosis virus (AMV). The transformed cells multiply exponentially and produce new virus that in turn is capable of producing neoplasia in vivo or transformation in vitro. This in vitro transforming ability of AMV is used as a means of quantitatively assaying the virus.

Unlike the leukemia viruses, with which they share many physical and antigenic properties, avian sarcoma viruses are unique because of the speed and

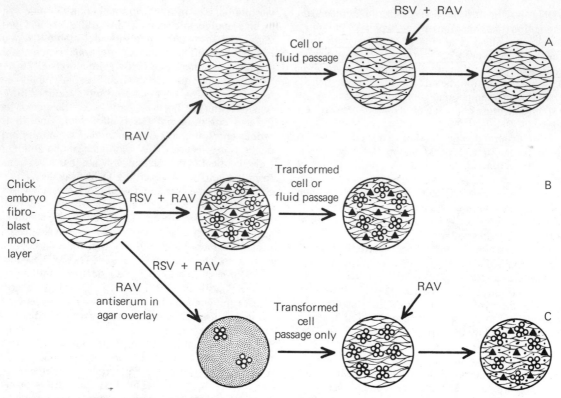

Figure 40–6. *A:* Interference. Chick embryo fibroblasts infected with RAV never transform, continue to produce infectious virus (black dots), and are resistant to superinfection with the (RSV + RAV) "high titer" Bryan strain of RSV. *B:* Transformation. Chick embryo fibroblasts infected with the (RSV + RAV) "high titer" Bryan strain of RSV undergo transformation (foci of rounded cells). The transformed cells release both RSV (black triangles) and RAV (black dots). Transformation of new cultures can be achieved by either passage of intact transformed cells or virus-containing tissue culture fluid. *C:* Selection of nonproducer (NP) cells. Limiting dilution of the (RSV + RAV) "high titer" Bryan strain plated on chick embryo fibroblasts under an agar overlay containing RAV antiserum forms foci of transformed nonproducer (free from infectious virus) cells. Transformation of new cultures can be achieved only by passage of intact nonproducer cells. Nonproducer cells superinfected with a "helper" RAV release both infectious RSV and infectious RAV.

high frequency with which they induce malignant transformation. Infection of chick embryo cells with ASV results in foci of transformed cells, the morphology of which varies for the virus strain used. Virus activity is measured as the number of focus-forming units (FFU) per unit volume. Chick or duck cells transformed in vitro usually continue to release virus; both transformed cells and virus released from them can induce tumors in vivo.

The Schmidt-Ruppin (SR-RSV), Carr-Zilber (CZ-RSV), Prague (PR-RSV), and B77 strains of ASV, which have been shown to induce tumors in mammals (including macaque and marmoset monkeys), can transform mouse, rat, or hamster embryo fibroblast cells in addition to chick embryo cells. Infectious virus cannot be demonstrated in cell-free extracts from the transformed rodent cells by conventional methods. However, those cells usually contain the integrated provirus, the gs antigen (p30), and the *src* gene product (pp60^{src}) characteristic of the avian oncornaviruses. Infectious ASV can be rescued from viable nonpermissive transformed cells either by im-

plantation into chickens or by co-cultivation in vitro with susceptible chick embryo cells, usually in the presence of ultraviolet-inactivated Sendai virus, which facilitates the formation of heterokaryons.

Studies with the avian oncornaviruses have revealed the marked propensity of these agents to exchange and modify their genetic material: Very high frequencies of recombination are exhibited; there are frequent deletions of both nonessential information (ie, *src*) and portions of essential information (eg, *env*); and cellular information may even be incorporated. It is very difficult to maintain pure stocks of oncornaviruses.

Some important features of RSV-cell interactions have emerged from studies with the "defective" Bryan high-titer strain of RSV (BH-RSV): (1) Cell transformation is a function of the RSV genome; and (2) antigenicity, host range, and sensitivity to specific interference by ALV strains are governed by the protein coat in which the RSV genome is encapsidated. Stocks of BH-RSV contain a 10-fold excess of a nontransforming ALV—hence the term Rous-associated virus, or RAV, for the ALV in such preparations. When selective pressures were applied to obtain infection with the RSV component alone, it was found that pure RSV can induce cell transformation but cannot reproduce new, infectious virus (Fig 40–6)—hence the term "defective."

Cells transformed by RSV alone fail to produce infectious virus or protein coat antigen, and such cells are called nonproducer (NP) cells. However, nonproducer cells, capable of multiplying for many generations, contain the p30 antigen of avian oncornaviruses. Superinfection of continuously propagated nonproducer cells with a nontransforming RAV "helper" virus results, through phenotypic mixing, in the production of infectious RSV that possesses the antigenicity of the RAV helper virus but is capable of transforming new cells in vitro and of inducing sarcomas in vivo (Fig 40–6). Different, antigenically distinct RAV strains such as RAV-1, RAV-2, and RAV-0 have been used, and the resulting infectious pseudotypes—RSV (RAV-1), RSV (RAV-2), and RSV (RAV-0)—have been shown to possess the antigenicity, host range, and interference properties of the corresponding helper RAV virus. However, such alteration in the viral envelope does not cause a heritable stable change in the RSV genome.

These alterations occur because BH-RSV contains a deletion in the *env* gene, is unable to code for its own viral envelope, and requires a helper ALV to perform that function. Furthermore, these studies reveal that a sarcoma genome can enter a wide range of otherwise nonpermissive cells provided it is encoded in an envelope to which the cells have receptors for attachment. Indeed, phenotypic mixing can occur between oncornaviruses (both avian and murine) and vesicular stomatitis virus (VSV), an unrelated RNA-containing enveloped rhabdovirus with a very wide host range in tissue culture. An ASV (VSV) pseudotype that can be neutralized only by antiserum to VSV acquires the wide host range of VSV.

C. Unique Features of the Murine Complex:

Laboratory strains of the FMR group can be propagated in vitro in mouse embryo fibroblasts of unrestricted genotype. In contrast, the Gross virus and naturally occurring leukemia viruses can only replicate in cells of certain strains of mice. With the exception of the Abelson strain of MuLV (a defective strain of MuLV that can transform cells in vitro and induce leukemias in mice), replication in susceptible cells is not accompanied by overt morphologic changes, and the infected cells continue to release infectious MuLV for indefinite periods of time. However, the virus released from such chronically infected cells is only about one ten-thousandth as infectious as virus circulating in the blood of the leukemic animal.

Infection of mouse, rat, hamster, or human embryo cells with MSV results in foci of transformed cells, and virus activity can be measured in focus-forming units per unit volume. Some similarity exists between the various strains of MSV and the defective Bryan strain of RSV (BH-RSV). Similar to BH-RSV, MSV preparations contain an excess of nontransforming MuLV, and phenotypic mixing between MSV and MuLV results in the formation of infectious MSV (MuLV) pseudotypes. Pseudotypes can be formed through phenotypic mixing between defective MSV genomes and other nontransforming mammalian C type viruses. Infection of hamsters in vivo or hamster cells in vitro may result in transformed cells that release MSV (HaLV) pseudotype capable of infecting hamster but not mouse cells. Similarly, MSV infection of rat cells that carry the endogenous RaLV results in transformed cells releasing MSV (RaLV) pseudotype; in the case of the Kirsten and Harvey strains of MSV (Ki-MSV; H-MSV), which were originally derived by inoculation of Ki-MuLV and H-MuLV into rats, recombination occurred between the MSV genomes and the endogenous rat C type virus, since the MSV genomes contain both MuLV and RaLV sequences. Feline leukemia virus (FeLV) has been substituted as a helper for the defective MSV, with a resulting MSV (FeLV) pseudotype capable of transforming feline cells and other cells susceptible to FeLV but not mouse cells.

Mechanisms of Cell Transformation by Oncornaviruses

A single avian sarcoma virus gene (*src*) (see Fig 40–5) has been established as being responsible for the induction and maintenance of cell transformation in vitro and tumor induction in vivo. This is the most well characterized RNA tumor virus system. The product of the avian *src* gene was first detected immunologically using antisera from rabbits with tumors induced by ASV. The product is a phosphorylated 60,000-dalton protein, designated pp60^{src}.

At least 10 other transforming genes have been identified among oncornaviruses of avian and mammalian origin. These viral *onc* genes all share homology with sequences found in normal cells (cellular *onc* genes). The cellular sequences were presumably picked up by the different viruses at some time during the past and are now replicated and expressed under viral control.

Elucidation of the function of the viral transforming proteins should eventually reveal the specific biochemical events responsible for malignant transformation of cells by oncornaviruses. The recognized *onc* products possess protein kinase activity, an enzyme that transfers the terminal phosphate group from ATP to an acceptor protein. The virus-induced protein kinases are unique in that they phosphorylate tyrosine residues. (About 90% of the phosphorylated residues in normal cells are serines and about 10% are threonines; phosphorylated tyrosines are very rare.)

The target cell proteins naturally phosphorylated by the viral proteins have not been identified. However, since protein phosphorylation is well documented as being involved in regulation of cellular processes, possession of kinase activity by the viral-coded transforming proteins is intriguing, because transformation includes many changes in cell properties.

Recent observations suggest that the transforming proteins interact with a recently recognized cellular cascade of at least 4 protein kinases located in the plasma membrane. The cascade can be activated by phosphorylation of a tyrosine residue of any of its members, resulting in phosphorylation and inactivation of plasma membrane (Na^+-K^+) ATPase. Members of the cascade serve as substrates for phosphorylation on tyrosine by oncornavirus-transforming proteins. Even more provocative, the avian *src* product appears to be equivalent to one of the cellular components of the kinase cascade.

Normal uninfected vertebrate cells contain very low levels of phosphoproteins antigenically related to the oncornavirus transforming proteins. The normal cellular proteins also have kinase activity. The functions of the proteins during normal cell growth and differentiation are not known. However, it is attractive to speculate that oncornavirus oncogenesis is mediated by aberrantly expressed cellular functions.

The mechanism of transformation by the leukemia viruses is more obscure. There is no evidence that they carry an *onc* gene in their genome. The putative promoter for viral transcription is believed to be contained in a sequence designated the long terminal repeat (LTR). It has been reported that the insertion of the viral promoter adjacent to a critical cellular gene results in the enhanced expression of that gene and, subsequently, neoplasia. Recent data suggest that in many cases of avian lymphomatosis, the c-*myc* gene (the cellular counterpart of the transforming gene of avian MC29 virus) is activated, presumably by the adjacent integration of the leukosis virus promoter. A model of such "promoter-inserting oncogenesis" is shown in Fig 40–7.

In summary, neoplastic transformation by oncornaviruses is the result of a cellular gene normally expressed at low (inactive) levels becoming activated and expressed constitutively. In the case of the acute transforming viruses, such as ASV, a cellular gene has been inserted by recombination into the viral genome and is expressed as a viral gene under the control of the viral promoter. In the case of the leukemia viruses, the viral promoter is inserted adjacent to the cellular gene in the cellular chromosome.

Virus-Induced Cell Surface Antigens

One of the principal characteristics of carcinogenesis by the oncornaviruses is the continuous release of infectious virus from most of the in vivo or in vitro transformed cells. This property has made the assessment of virus-induced surface antigens in these cells more difficult than in cells transformed by DNA-containing viruses, since the latter cells are usually free from infectious virions (see below).

RNA virus-induced tumor cells usually express virus structural antigens on their plasma membranes. This phenomenon has been demonstrated in the avian, murine, and feline systems. The structural antigens may be expressed whether or not the cells are producing infectious virus. Interestingly, the antigens in the

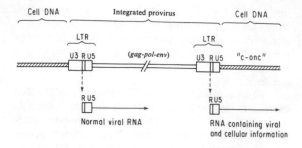

Figure 40–7. Structure and transcriptional products of the integrated ALV provirus. The integrated provirus is flanked by sequences of approximately 350 nucleotides termed long terminal repeats (LTRs). The LTRs, shown greatly enlarged to emphasize structural details, are composed of sequences derived from the 5′ (U5) and 3′ (U3) ends of genomic RNA and a short sequence (R) of approximately 20 nucleotides, present at both ends of genomic RNA. Synthesis of normal viral RNA (genomic RNA and mRNAs) initiates within the left LTR. Initiation within the right LTR would generate a molecule containing viral 5′ sequences (R + U5) plus cellular information encoded in the adjacent cellular DNA. If, as shown, the provirus integrated upstream from a potentially oncogenic cellular gene (designated c-*onc*), initiation within the right LTR could cause elevated expression of the c-*onc* gene. (Courtesy of Hayward et al: *Nature* 1981;**290**:475.)

membrane are usually in the form of high-molecular-weight precursor polyproteins containing all or part of the *env* or *gag* gene products. Host immunity to the structural proteins may abrogate viral infections and afford some protection against tumor formation.

However, there is evidence in all 3 systems that tumor and transformed cells express new cell-surface antigens distinct from the virion structural proteins. Host recognition of these cell-surface antigens appears to be important in resistance to tumor formation. These antigens are induced by the virus, but it has not yet been definitely established whether they are coded for by the virus or the host cell.

Endogenous Oncornavirus Genes

Virus genetic information that is a constant part of the genetic constitution of an organism is designated as "endogenous." An integrated oncornavirus provirus behaves like a cluster of cellular genes, subject to regulatory control by the cell. This cellular control usually results in partial or complete repression of expression of viral genes. In fact, it is not uncommon for normal cells to maintain the endogenous viral information in a quiescent form for extended periods of time.

The same endogenous genome may be actively expressed in one cell and completely repressed in another. A cellular gene (or genes) determines whether an endogenous virus is expressed or not. Many vertebrate animals, including chickens, mice, cats, and baboons, possess endogenous virus sequences. Some species harbor more than one kind of endogenous viral genome; mice are notorious for containing multiple endogenous viruses distinguishable by their host range. The growth of endogenous viruses is usually restricted in cells derived from the original host. Cells from a different, susceptible species must be found in order for propagation to occur.

Endogenous oncornavirus genes are present in the germ cells of animals and are transmitted through an indefinite number of generations with no detriment to the animal. Studies with inbred "virus-free" avian and murine strains showed that tumors induced in such animals by means of irradiation or treatment with carcinogens or tumors occurring spontaneously in old age contained oncornavirus information, such as virus-specific DNA sequences detectable by hybridization and virus-specific gs (*gag*) antigens. The same information was present in virtually all embryonic tissues of "virus-free" chickens or mice.

One method to detect the presence of heritable viral genes in normal avian or murine cells is to "activate" expression in tissue culture. Exposure of normal chick cells derived from leukemia virus–free embryos to ionizing radiation, chemical carcinogens, 5′-bromodeoxyuridine (BUDR), or 5-iodo-2′-deoxyuridine (IUDR) results in the production of an RNA virus with all the tissue culture characteristics of an avian leukemia virus. Similarly, exposure of virus-free mouse embryo cells to IUDR, BUDR, or cycloheximide resulted in the production of an RNA virus with the tissue culture characteristics of a murine leukemia virus. Such experiments prompted the conclusion that normal murine and avian cells have the genetic potential for specifying a complete leukemia C type RNA virus.

Normal cells of many different species have been found to contain DNA sequences homologous to the oncornaviruses of the corresponding species; those sequences are common to all strains within a species. Interactions between exogenous (superinfecting) and endogenous viruses are common, resulting in either genetically stable recombinants or phenotypically mixed particles.

Important features of endogenous viruses can be summarized briefly as follows: (1) DNA copies of the RNA virus genome are covalently linked to cellular DNA and are present in all somatic and germ cells in the host; (2) endogenous viral genomes are transmitted genetically from parent to offspring; (3) the integrated state subjects the endogenous genomes to host genetic control; and (4) the endogenous virus may be induced to replicate either spontaneously or by treatment with extrinsic (chemical) factors.

The discovery of the ubiquitousness of endogenous oncornaviruses led to elegant studies suggesting that their viral genomes have become fixed in the germ line of various animals prior to speciation. For example, the endogenous viruses of Old World primates (baboon, rhesus monkey, green monkey, and others) were found to possess a class of viral DNA sequences (characteristic for the baboon endogenous virus) that is not found in New World monkeys (woolly monkey,

owl monkey, and others), apes (gibbon, gorilla), humans, and other species. Similarly, the endogenous virus of the domestic cat (RD-114) is different from the known feline leukemia virus (FeLV), which is transmitted horizontally. It remains uncertain whether these endogenous viruses have evolved within the germ line or represent a result of exogenous infection that occurred millions of years ago prior to speciation. The finding that the baboon endogenous virus and the RD-114 endogenous virus of the domestic cat (but not the other feline oncornaviruses) share common DNA sequences and antigens suggests that the virus of the Old World primate (baboon) had infected these cats and had become fixed in their germ cell line after they had evolved away from most other feline species. Even though these types of studies open new and exciting avenues for further study of evolutionary fixation of oncornaviral genes, the significance of inherited oncornaviral genes in the process of natural oncogenesis remains unclear. Indeed, most of the rescued endogenous viruses have a very low disease-producing potential; the majority have not yet been demonstrated to transform cells in vitro or to be oncogenic in vivo.

DNA–CONTAINING TUMOR VIRUSES

Of the DNA-containing tumor viruses listed in Table 40–3, the papovaviruses and adenoviruses are the best characterized. Viruses in those 2 groups share basic properties such as cubic symmetry, naked virions, lack of essential lipids, resistance to ether and mild acid (pH 3.0), and multiplication in the cell nucleus (Tables 27–1 and 40–3). They differ, however, in size, virion morphology, antigenic structure, and genetic content.

Papovaviruses

The name papova is derived from the first 2 letters of the names of the oncogenic viruses included in this group: *pa*pilloma viruses of humans, rabbits, cows, and dogs; *po*lyoma virus of mice; and *va*cuolating (SV40) virus of monkeys. Recently, several human papovaviruses have been identified that are serologically related to but not identical with SV40 virus and possess oncogenic potential. Two of these, JC virus and SV40-PML virus, were isolated from brains of patients with progressive multifocal leukoencephalopathy (PML); the JC virus causes transmissible virus-yielding gliomas in newborn hamsters. The third agent, BK virus, isolated from the urine of immunosuppressed renal allograft recipients, causes malignant transformation of hamster cells in vitro and also induces tumors in hamsters. Serologic surveys show that infections with JC and BK viruses are common in humans.

A. Morphology and Nucleic Acid: Papovavirus particles exhibit icosahedral symmetry, have a naked capsid composed of 72 capsomeres, and have diameters of 45–55 nm. They contain double-stranded DNA with a molecular weight of 3×10^6 for polyoma and

Table 40–3. Some properties of DNA-containing tumor viruses.

Virus	Host of Origin	Natural Tumors (Host of Origin)	Experimental Host Range		Size (nm)	Structure	Site of Virus Maturation	Persistence of Infectious Virus in Tumor
			In Vivo Tumors	In Vitro Cell Transformation				
Papovaviruses								
Papilloma								
Human	Human	Yes	Human					
Rabbit	Rabbit	Yes	Rabbit					
Bovine	Cow	Yes	Cow, horse	Bovine, mouse	45–55	Icosahedral symmetry	Nucleus	Yes
Canine	Dog	Yes	Dog					
Polyoma	Mouse	No	Mouse, hamster, other rodents	Mouse, hamster, rat				
SV40	Monkey	No	Hamster	Hamster, mouse, monkey, human				No
BK, JC	Human		Hamster	Hamster				
Adenoviruses								
Human types 3, 7, 11, 12, 14, 16, 18, 21, 31	Human	No						
Simian (some)	Monkey	No	Hamster, rat, mouse	Hamster, rat, human	70–90	Icosahedral symmetry	Nucleus	No
Bovine type 3	Cow	No						
Avian (CELO)	Chicken	No						
Herpesviruses								
Human								
Type 2	Human		Hamster	Hamster				
EB virus	Human		Monkey	Human, monkey				
Monkey (Melendez)	Monkey	No	Monkey		100	Icosahedral symmetry	Nucleus	No
Avian (Marek)	Chicken	Yes	Chicken					
Frog (Lucké)	Frog	Yes	Frog					
Rabbit (Hinze)	Rabbit	No	Rabbit					
Poxviruses								
Molluscum contagiosum	Human	Yes	Human					
Yaba	Monkey	Yes	Monkey		230 × 300	Complex symmetry	Cytoplasm	Yes
Fibroma-myxoma	Rabbit, squirrel, deer	Yes	Rabbit, squirrel, deer					

SV40 viruses and 5×10^6 for the papilloma viruses. Infectious DNA has been isolated from all 3 types of viruses.

Genomic DNA exists as circular molecules. Upon analytical ultracentrifugation, the DNA separates into 2 components with sedimentation constants of 21S and 16S (polyoma, SV40) or 28S and 21S (papilloma). The heavier component has a twisted circular form that converts to the lighter component when single-strand breaks are introduced. Both of these DNA components are known to be infectious, to transform cells in vitro, and to produce tumors in vivo. In addition, a linear component with a sedimentation coefficient of 14S that represents random fragments of host cell DNA is incorporated into some papovavirus capsids (rather than viral DNA), and such particles are termed pseudovirions—a situation akin to the phenomenon of generalized transduction in the bacterial system (see Chapter 4). Hybridization studies also indicate the occurrence of covalent linkage of cell DNA segments into the circular DNA of papovaviruses during replication in cells infected at high multiplicity—similar to the situation with specialized transducing phage (see Chapter 4). Furthermore,

under specialized experimental conditions, a DNA segment containing functional λ phage genes has been incorporated into the circular DNA of SV40. These findings open avenues for study of possible transducing events in eukaryotic cells whereby functionally defined segments of genetic information can be transmitted from cell to cell.

There is some similarity between the DNA of the oncogenic papovaviruses and mammalian cell DNA: (1) The guanine + cytosine (G + C) content of the viral DNA varies between 41% and 49%, which is very similar to mammalian host cell DNA (40–42% G + C). (2) Analysis of nearest neighbor base sequences reveals that the doublet pattern of the viral DNA closely resembles that of the host cell DNA with a rarity of the G + C doublet.

The use of bacterial restriction enzymes, endonucleases that make double-stranded breaks at specific sites in DNA, has permitted the application of physical mapping techniques to analyses of the SV40 genome. These techniques have allowed rapid elucidation of the molecular biology of SV40, since physical mapping of a viral genome can be accomplished much faster than classical genetic analyses, which require

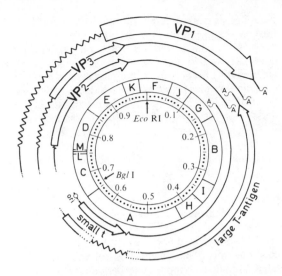

Figure 40–8. Physical map of SV40 DNA indicating localization of the main biological functions. The single cleavage site of the restriction enzyme *Eco*RI is used as a reference point for the physical map (inner circle). The origin of DNA replication (ori) is at or close to 0.663; this site corresponds to a large palindromic sequence, part of which represents the recognition sequence of *Bgl*I. The 5 virus-coded proteins are indicated by blocked arrows; note that the T antigen is coded by 2 noncontiguous segments on the genome (there is some uncertainty in the position of the points as indicated by the dashes). Untranslated parts of the mRNA are shown as solid lines; dots indicate uncertainty as to the exact position of the 5' end. Zigzag lines are used for the segments that are spliced out. A wavy line with an A illustrates the 3' terminal poly(A) tail. (Courtesy of Fiers W et al: *Nature* 1978;**273**:113.)

years for completion. A large battery of restriction endonucleases has been screened for the cleavage patterns generated with SV40 DNA, and it is possible to obtain small, specific, defined regions of the viral genome. A summary of the current status of the SV40 map is shown in Fig 40–8.

The entire nucleotide sequence of SV40 DNA, consisting of 5224 base-pairs, has been determined. The virus is of importance not only as a model DNA tumor virus but as a model of eukaryote gene organization and expression. Several intriguing features of the system are diagrammed in Fig 40–8. At least 15% of the genome is not translated into polypeptides. The coding sequences for the 2 early proteins, small t antigen and large T antigen, originate at the same position; however, large T is coded by 2 noncontiguous regions of the genome, with a splice occurring in the mRNA. Two of the late structural proteins, VP2 and VP3, share tryptic peptides; it is believed that translation of the VP3 gene is initiated within the VP2 gene and is read in the same reading frame. The gene for the major structural protein, VP1, overlaps those for VP2 and VP3 by 122 nucleotides but is read in a different frame. The regulatory sequences for the origin of viral DNA replication (ori) and the initiation of

early and late transcription are all within the same small region of the genome. Therefore, the entire SV40 genome is elegantly organized for the maximum conservation of space.

The polyoma genome is also well characterized. The basic organization closely resembles that of SV40. One major difference is that a third protein is coded for by the early region of the genome; the mRNA for that protein is spliced internally such that a portion of it shifts to a different reading frame.

The ability to recognize and identify specific regions of the viral genome has also permitted the description of a variety of types of variant molecules, most of which are defective for replication. When SV40 is serially passaged in permissive cells at high multiplicity of infection, virus particles with defective genomes accumulate. Some of these SV40 variants contain cellular DNA sequences covalently linked to viral DNA (substituted molecules). Distinctive deletions (loss) of viral DNA may occur at many different sites in the genome; duplicated segments of viral DNA may also be present. Repeated high-multiplicity passage may give rise to viruses with grossly altered genomes that consist predominantly of cellular DNA but retain a small portion of SV40 DNA. It is striking that the initiation site for viral DNA replication is preserved in every variant molecule analyzed. It appears that a genome length 70–100% of the length of parental SV40 DNA is necessary for the molecule to be encapsidated.

Similar studies have been performed with other members of the papovavirus group (polyoma- and papillomavirus) and are now being extended to the adenovirus and herpesvirus molecules. Obviously, the cleavage patterns in the latter 2 systems are more complex, since the genomes are larger. However, the region required for transforming activity by the human adenoviruses has already been localized to the left-hand 7% of the viral DNA molecule on the basis of fragment analysis.

B. Reaction to Chemical and Physical Agents: Papovaviruses are resistant to heating (50 °C for 1 hour), ether, and acid treatment (pH 3.0). SV40 and polyoma viruses can be inactivated at 50 °C in the presence of high concentrations of $MgCl_2$; this has been used to eliminate SV40 virus from stocks of oral poliovaccine, since the infectivity of poliovirus is stabilized under these conditions. Papovaviruses can be stored at −20 °C for long periods with no loss of infectivity. Infectivity of the viruses is decreased by 1:4000 formalin solution, but they are not inactivated as readily as poliovirus and adenovirus. Consequently, live SV40 has been recovered from several lots of killed poliovirus and killed adenovirus vaccines.

C. Antigenic Properties: Each of the papovaviruses is antigenically distinct. The viruses induce the production of specific neutralizing and complement-fixing antibodies. Polyoma, JC, and BK viruses hemagglutinate red blood cells. The nonstructural tumor antigens (see below) induced by JC and BK viruses cross-react antigenically with that induced by

SV40. A plurality of human papillomaviruses has been discovered, although the number and significance of different serotypes remain to be established. Each genus of the papovavirus family contains a group-specific core antigen.

Adenoviruses

Adenoviruses comprise a large group of agents that occur widely in humans, monkeys, cattle, dogs, swine, mice, and chickens. At least 37 antigenic types exist for the human species alone; of these, types 3, 7, 11, 12, 14, 16, 18, 21, 31, and perhaps others cause tumors in newborn animals, particularly hamsters. All of these viruses were isolated from human beings, and serologic surveys show that infection is common with most of these types.

Several simian adenoviruses, bovine adenovirus type 3, and avian adenovirus are tumorigenic when inoculated into newborn hamsters.

The oncogenic adenoviruses are indistinguishable in structure from other adenoviruses and have naked capsids 70–90 nm in diameter, with 252 capsomeres arranged in icosahedral symmetry. They contain double-stranded linear DNA with a molecular weight of 2.3×10^7. The DNA of a highly oncogenic simian adenovirus (SA7) is infectious in tissue culture as well as tumorigenic for newborn hamsters.

The oncogenic human adenoviruses may be classified into 2 subgroups: highly oncogenic (types 12, 18, and 31) and weakly oncogenic (types 3, 7, 11, 14, 16, and 21). Those in the highly oncogenic subgroup are the only adenoviruses with a low G + C content in their DNA (48–49%, a value similar to that of the papovaviruses and cellular DNA). The weakly oncogenic types have an intermediate G + C content of 50–53%. A third subgroup, adenoviruses (types 1, 2, 5, and 6) that are nononcogenic but transform rat embryo cells in vitro, has a high G + C content (55–61%). A further relationship between members within each of the 3 subgroups stems from DNA-DNA or DNA-mRNA homology studies. Maximal DNA-DNA or DNA-mRNA hybridization is attained only between viruses within a subgroup with negligible intersubgroup hybridization. (The highly oncogenic simian adenovirus SA7 has a high G + C content, similar in value to the nononcogenic human adenoviruses.)

Oncogenic Herpesviruses

Herpesviruses of lower animals are the most recent group of DNA-containing viruses shown to possess oncogenic capacity (see Table 40–3). They possess the biophysical and biochemical properties of other members of the herpesvirus group (see Chapter 38).

A. Simian Herpesviruses: Two oncogenic herpesviruses of monkeys have been recognized that are antigenically distinct from each other and from other herpesviruses. Herpesvirus saimiri (HVS) and herpesvirus ateles (HVA) have been isolated from kidney cultures of squirrel and spider monkeys, respectively.

Both agents cause a latent inapparent infection in the host of origin, and a high proportion of the animals possess antiviral antibodies; infection apparently occurs early in life, and the infected animals are virus carriers for life. However, both agents are highly oncogenic for other primates. HVS induces the development of malignant lymphomas in marmosets and owl and spider monkeys, and reticuloproliferative diseases in Cebus and African green monkeys. The virus is especially pathogenic for cottontop marmosets, causing death from lymphoma within 48 days after inoculation. HVA also induces malignant lymphomas in cottontop marmosets and other monkeys. In tissue culture, both agents are capable of replication in a variety of cells, with the production of infectious virus and viral antigens. Both HVS and HVA have been extensively characterized with respect to their biochemical characteristics. Malignant cells derived from inoculated animals or lymphocytes derived from virus carriers within the natural host are free of infectious virus or antigens; however, within 1–3 days after their cultivation in culture, both antigens and infectious virus are produced.

Attenuated and killed vaccines to the viruses have been produced. Monkeys have been protected by the vaccines from the oncogenic effects of the viruses.

Recently, another group of herpesviruses has been discovered. These viruses are similar to the Epstein-Barr virus (EBV) isolated from humans and have been found in Old World nonhuman primates. Like EBV, they are associated with B lymphocytes. They are benign in their natural host but cause lymphoproliferative disease in related species. They include viruses from baboons, orangutans, and chimpanzees.

B. Marek's Disease Virus (MDV): MDV is the causative agent of a highly contagious and apparently malignant lymphoproliferative disease of chickens, with a predilection for nerve tissue (Marek's disease). MDV tumor cells have been found to have T cell markers on their surfaces as do the cells in HVS- and HVA-induced lymphoproliferative disease. Thus, these viruses seem to be T cell–tropic, whereas EBV and the EBV-like primate herpesviruses are B cell–tropic. Strains of MDV with differences in antigenicity, virulence, and tissue tropism have been recognized. The severity of the disease is influenced by both the virus strain and the genetic constitution of the host. In vivo, the virus undergoes an abortive cycle of replication in most tissues of the infected chicken, and the disease can be transmitted by passage of intact lymphoid cells that contain the virus genome but not infectious virus. On the other hand, infectious virus is produced by the epithelial cells of the feather follicle, and such cell-free virus produces the disease when inoculated into susceptible chickens. MDV is stable and remains in infectious form for a long time (over 10 weeks) in contaminated litters and droppings, thus accounting for the high contagiousness and spread of the disease. There have been suggestions that RNA tumor viruses may play a role in Marek's disease.

Although this does not appear to be the usual case, the avian RNA tumor viruses are so widespread that it is difficult to rule out any role for the RNA virus in vivo. The lymphoproliferative disease can be prevented by vaccination with an attenuated strain of MDV or with an antigenically related herpesvirus of turkeys that is nonpathogenic for chickens; the vaccine does not prevent infection with the wild virus, but such infections are not followed by tumor formation. The prevention of cancer by vaccination in this case establishes MDV as the etiologic agent and suggests the possibility of a similar approach to prevention of human tumors if a virus is identified as an etiologic agent.

C. Herpesvirus of Rabbit Lymphoma (Hinze): A herpesvirus (herpesvirus sylvilagus) indigenous to wild cottontail rabbits has been recently recognized as a distinct member of the herpesvirus group. When inoculated into weanling cottontail rabbits (but not domestic rabbits), the virus induces generalized hyperplasia of lymphoid elements and in some instances malignant lymphomas as well. The in vivo virus–lymphoid cell relationship remains to be elucidated; however, leukocytes from infected rabbits have been shown to produce detectable virus after cultivation in culture. In tissue culture, the virus can be propagated equally well in cells of both cottontail and domestic rabbits.

D. Lucké's Herpesvirus (LHV) of Frogs: A renal adenocarcinoma (Lucké tumor) occurs very frequently in a population of wild frogs, *Rana pipiens,* and LHV has been implicated as the etiologic agent. The association of this virus with the frog tumors is most unusual. When tumors are examined from frogs in hibernation or maintained in the laboratory at low temperature, the tumor cells reveal typical inclusion bodies containing numerous herpesvirus particles. The tumors of frogs collected in the spring or summer or maintained at higher temperature, however, do not. The virus cannot yet be grown in cultured cells, but tumor fragments can be cultured in vitro, and these also show this unique temperature dependence for the production of virus particles. Almost all tumors induced by DNA-containing viruses reveal no virus particles in the tumor cells; indeed, many have only fragments of the viral genome present. Virus particles can be partially purified from frog tumor cells; when these cell-free extracts are injected into early stage tadpoles, adenocarcinomas are induced in the developing frogs.

Other viruses, including herpesviruses unrelated to LHV, have been isolated in tissue culture from Lucké tumors; however, they have thus far failed to induce tumors in developing frog embryos. The evidence supports LHV as the causative agent of the tumor. It is significant that the virus induces a carcinoma. In humans, carcinomas are much more prevalent than are sarcomas and lymphoproliferative disease.

Tumor Induction by Papovaviruses & Adenoviruses
A. Papilloma Viruses: Papilloma viruses are the only members of the papovavirus group known to cause natural tumors in their hosts of origin. They cause warts or papillomas in human beings, rabbits, cows, and dogs. The ecology of these viruses is not known, but they are found in large quantities in papillomas. Studies with these agents have been impeded because the agents cannot be cultured in cells in vitro. However, molecular techniques such as nucleic acid hybridization and restriction enzyme analyses have permitted comparisons of various isolates and detection of viral-specific sequences in tumors.

The human papilloma virus (HPV) was the first virus transmitted experimentally from host to host (in 1907). Papilloma viruses have been found associated with several benign epithelial tumors in humans, including skin warts (plantar, common hand, and flat warts), genital condylomas, and laryngeal papillomas. Despite the differences in localization and histologic features, it was long assumed that all wart lesions were caused by the same virus. Recent studies, however, have documented differences among HPV isolates with respect to DNA sequence homologies, restriction enzyme cleavage sites, and antigenic properties. At least 4 serotypes have been distinguished, with HPV-1 mainly associated with plantar warts, HPV-2 preferentially associated with common hand warts, and HPV-3 and HPV-4 present in lesions of epidermodysplasia verruciformis. It is of interest that malignant conversion of the wart lesion was frequently encountered in patients infected with HPV-4.

The rabbit papilloma virus has been studied extensively for its tumor-inducing properties. In the wild cottontail rabbit (the natural host), the virus causes large benign skin papillomas that, on rare occasions, become malignant carcinomas. When inoculated into the domestic rabbit, the virus also produces benign skin papillomas that may either regress or develop into malignant carcinomas. Tumors can be induced in both rabbit species with the DNA isolated from the virus. Infectious virus can be readily recovered from the papillomas of cottontail rabbits but not from their carcinomas; virus cannot be isolated from either papillomas or carcinomas of domestic rabbits. However, infectious DNA has been isolated from such tumors. Transplantation of carcinoma cells results in carcinomas in the new host.

The bovine papilloma virus (BPV) is the most oncogenic of the papilloma viruses. BPV produces fibropapillomas in cattle; experimental inoculation of BPV results in meningiomas in calves and fibromas in hamsters and mice. Both BPV and BPV DNA are able to transform bovine and mouse cells in culture. At least 2 distinct classes of BPV have been isolated, based on nucleic acid analyses. Both types appear to be oncogenic. BPV is implicated as the etiologic agent of naturally occurring equine connective tissue tumors. This observation raises the question of the possibility and extent of transspecies infection and tumor induction, not only by BPV but by all papilloma viruses.

B. Polyoma Virus: Latent infection with polyoma virus is widespread among laboratory and wild mice, with the virus replicating in many different organs. Young mice are infected naturally in the first few weeks by contamination with urine and saliva of adults. Intrauterine infection can occur, often resulting in resorption of fetuses or reduced litter sizes. Not a single natural tumor of mice, the host of origin, has been detected. However, the virus is highly tumorigenic when inoculated into newborn mice or hamsters, which develop tumors within a few weeks of inoculation of large doses of virus. Newborn rats, rabbits, guinea pigs, and ferrets are also susceptible. Infectious DNA isolated from the virus is tumorigenic. The most common tumors are spindle cell sarcomas, but epithelial tumors also occur in mice. The tumors appear in a number of sites—hence the name polyoma. The tumors are usually free from infectious virus or virus particles. As few as 10 tumor cells transplanted into a susceptible adult animal result in new tumors that can be further transplanted. Tumor cells can be serially grown in vitro and retain malignancy.

C. SV40 Virus: SV40 is commonly found in uninoculated cultures of rhesus and cynomolgus monkey kidney cells, in which the virus apparently grows without causing a cytopathic effect. Introduction of fluids from such cultures into renal cell cultures derived from the African green, or grivet, monkey (*Cercopithecus aethiops sabaeus*) is followed by prominent cytoplasmic vacuolization—hence the name vacuolating virus. Isolation of the virus was quickly followed by demonstration of its oncogenic potential when introduced into newborn hamsters. Tumor induction in rhesus monkeys, the natural hosts, has not been demonstrated. Millions of people have been exposed to this virus as a contaminant of viral vaccines, both live and killed. After ingestion of live poliovaccine, many children continued to excrete SV40 for as long as 5 weeks. SV40 virus (as well as its infectious DNA) causes sarcomas at the site of inoculation in newborn hamsters. Virus inoculation by the subcutaneous, intraperitoneal, or intrathoracic route induces tumors with latent periods ranging from 3 months to more than 1 year. Adult animals are resistant to tumor induction when inoculated with SV40 subcutaneously, although intravenous inoculation induces lymphoid tumors in a high percentage of recipients. The tumors are usually free from infectious virus and virus particles. Tumor cells can be serially passed in adult hamsters and cause the same type of tumors as those induced by the virus itself. Both primary and transplanted tumors can be serially propagated in tissue culture and retain malignancy.

D. Adenoviruses: Adenovirus types 12, 18, and 31 cause undifferentiated sarcomas at the site of inoculation—and less commonly at other sites—in newborn hamsters, rats, and mice. Adenovirus type 7 causes tumors in 25% of inoculated newborn hamsters, but the latent period is longer than with other types, and the tumors are usually malignant lymphomas or lymphosarcomas. With adenoviruses 3, 11, 14, 16, and 21, the latent period before the appearance of

sarcomas in newborn hamsters is even longer than that for type 7. Adenovirus tumors contain no infectious virus. Tumors can be maintained in serial passage by means of transplantation of tumor cells into adult animals of the appropriate species; tumor cells may also be grown serially in tissue culture and retain malignancy.

Cell Transformation by Papovaviruses & Adenoviruses

Unlike oncornaviruses, which cause productive infection in permissive cells without killing them, the DNA tumor viruses either cause productive infection and kill the cell in the process of making more virus or transform the cell without subsequent virus production. One or the other may predominate, depending upon the cell; productive infection occurs in permissive cells and transformation in nonpermissive cells. However, the 2 states are not always mutually exclusive, since productive infection can take place in a small percentage of nonpermissive cells; conversely, under conditions preventing virus replication, transformation of permissive cells can be achieved.

The papilloma viruses cannot be readily propagated in culture. The adenoviruses, which induce cytocidal infection in a variety of cells, can transform hamster, rat, and human cells in vitro, but with limited success. The polyoma and SV40 viruses, however, have a marked cell-transforming potential (see Fig 40–9).

Infection of permissive mouse embryo cells with polyoma virus is mainly cytocidal, but infection of nonpermissive hamster embryo cells with the same virus results in transformation of a small fraction of the cell population. Similarly, SV40 almost always undergoes cytocidal multiplication in permissive green monkey kidney cells, but infection of nonpermissive hamster or mouse or semipermissive human fibroblast cells may result in cell transformation. Hamster or mouse cells transformed in tissue culture by either polyoma or SV40 viruses can produce tumors when inoculated into the appropriate host—sometimes when as few as 10–100 cells are used as inoculum.

The time required for transformation of cells by DNA tumor viruses to become evident differs widely for different viruses and different cells. With SV40 and adenovirus, transformation may not be obvious for several weeks, because only a tiny fraction of the infected cell population is transformed. Polyoma virus exhibits a higher frequency of transformation, although a large amount of virus is required to induce transformation. The dose response of cell transformation by polyoma virus is linear—a reflection of a one-hit curve—indicating that a single effective particle is sufficient to cause transformation. It should be noted that with many viruses one infectious unit is equivalent to many virus particles (in some cases up to 10,000). With polyoma virus, 40–100 virus particles are equivalent to one infectious (replicating) unit. For transformation of hamster fibroblasts—the most sensitive system known—one transforming unit is equiva-

A. CELL TRANSFORMATION BY DNA TUMOR VIRUSES

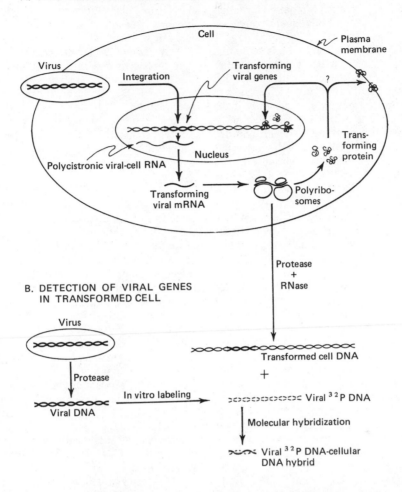

Figure 40–9. *A:* Mechanism of transformation by DNA tumor viruses. Viral genes from virus entering at left are incorporated into host cell chromosomes and direct the production of a polycistronic viral cell RNA transcript. Viral-transforming mRNA processed from this transcript is transported to the cytoplasm and is translated on polyribosomes to form viral-coded proteins. The putative transforming protein is hypothesized to bind either to the plasma membrane or to cellular DNA and alter the cell regulatory mechanism in some manner, resulting in cell transformation. *B:* Detection of viral genes in transformed cells. Viral DNA is extracted from purified virus by treatment with a protease, followed by phenol extraction. Purified viral DNA is labeled in vitro by incorporation of ^{35}P-deoxyribonucleoside triphosphates. The DNA is extracted from transformed cells and is then annealed with a viral ^{32}P-DNA. The positive hybridization, as measured by formation of radioactive hybrid DNA, indicates viral-DNA sequences present in the transformed cell. (From Green, *Perspect Biol Med,* spring 1978.)

lent to 1 million particles. This very low transforming efficiency is probably a reflection of the multiple and complex intracellular events that must occur in order for a viral genome to initiate and maintain the transformed phenotype.

The initial events during productive (cytocidal) and nonproductive (transforming) infection with DNA tumor viruses are common: synthesis of DNA, mRNA, and early antigens (see below); and stimulation of cell DNA synthesis. However, there is then a divergence of pathways leading either to replication of complete virions or to cellular transformation. Fewer viral genes are involved in transformation than in viral

replication. Late events, including replication of viral DNA, synthesis of virion structural proteins, and production of progeny particles, do not occur in transformed cells (see Fig 40–9). Work with temperature-sensitive (ts) mutants of SV40 has identified one viral gene, the A gene, as being involved in transformation. The A gene product is required both for initiation and for maintenance of the transformed state. Cells transformed by tsA mutants lose a variety of properties characteristic of transformed cells when shifted up to the nonpermissive temperature and acquire growth properties typical of normal cells. When the cells are shifted back down to permissive conditions, the transformed phenotype is reacquired. Gene A is an early SV40 gene, the product of which is required for initiation of viral DNA synthesis and subsequent expression of late functions. The gene A protein is the large T antigen (see below). The function of the A protein in the transformed cells remains to be elucidated. Studies with deletion mutants of SV40 have identified a second "early protein," the small t antigen, which appears to be necessary for transformation to occur only if the cells are in a resting state at the time of infection.

The virus-free transformed cells contain a limited number of viral DNA molecules (usually between 1 and 10) detectable by nucleic acid hybridization, as shown in Fig 40–9. Although the entire viral genome appears to be present in most SV40-transformed cells, transformation attempts with restriction enzyme fragments of the viral genome have established that only the early region (50% of the genome) is required for transformation. Only fragments (usually representing about 14%) of the adenovirus genome are retained in transformed cells. In vitro transformation assays with restriction enzyme fragments of viral DNA have localized the transforming activity to the left-hand end 7% of the adenovirus DNA molecule. That amount of genetic information is comparable to that of the early region of SV40 and polyoma virus containing the "transforming" gene or genes.

Fractionation and alkali denaturation studies indicate that the viral DNA present in papovavirus-transformed cells is covalently bound to chromosomal cell DNA (see Fig 40–9), apparently as a provirus, akin to the prophage of lysogenic bacterial cells (see Chapters 4 and 9) and the provirus of oncornaviruses (see above).

Additional evidence for the presence of integrated viral genes stems from transcriptional studies. Cells transformed by adenoviruses as well as by papovaviruses (polyoma and SV40) contain in their cytoplasm a small but highly specific fraction of viral mRNA (see Fig 40–9). This mRNA can be detected by its ability to hybridize with viral DNA. The mRNA is specific for the virus that had originally induced the transformation, since it is not found in normal cells or in cells transformed by a different virus. Further evidence of an integrated viral genome or a portion of it in papovavirus- and adenovirus-transformed cells is the presence in such cells of new virus-specified antigens, one or more of which must be the "transforming protein" (see below and Fig 40–9). Their detection permits recognition of the specificity of viral transformation.

Papovavirus- & Adenovirus-Induced Antigens (T Antigens, TSTA)

Cells transformed by papovaviruses and adenoviruses are free from virion structural antigens but contain several virus-induced antigens that are specific for the transforming virus and are distinct from the antigens induced by a heterologous virus. Their presence in tumor or transformed cells indicates that at least some of the virus-specific mRNA species in such cells are translated into recognizable proteins. An understanding of the functions of these few virus-induced proteins is central to an understanding of the mechanism of mammalian cell transformation by viruses.

A. Tumor or T Antigens: Large tumor (T) antigen appears in the nucleus of tumor cells or cells transformed in vitro, as shown in Fig 40–10. It can be measured by immunofluorescence, immunoprecipitation, or CF tests using antibodies that develop in sera of animals with large primary or transplanted tumors. Distinct T antigens have been demonstrated for polyoma, SV40, and adenoviruses. (Adenovirus T antigen can be detected both in the nucleus and in the cytoplasm.)

The T antigens are unrelated to viral capsid antigens but are specific for the inducing virus and are the same in cells of different species transformed by the same virus. T antigens immunologically identical with those found in transformed cells are also synthesized by papovaviruses and adenoviruses during productive infections in permissive cells. T antigen is formed in the nucleus early during the replicative cycle prior to the synthesis of viral DNA and viral capsid protein.

Large T antigen is a phosphoprotein of molecular weight 90,000–100,000 (see Fig 40–8). It has been purified and shown to bind preferentially to SV40 DNA at the origin of replication. The protein possesses ATPase or protein kinase activities (or both). Large T antigen is the product of the SV40 A gene, is directly required to initiate new rounds of viral DNA replication, is involved in the stimulation of host cell DNA synthesis, and is necessary for the initiation and maintenance of the transformed phenotype. The precise function of T antigen in the transformed cell is not known.

A second protein is also coded for by the early region of the SV40 genome, small t antigen, with a molecular weight of 17,000–20,000 (see Fig 40–8). Small t and large T proteins share common peptides at the amino terminal ends. Small t is not necessary for viral replication; it appears to be involved in stimulation of resting cells to divide, a requisite step during transformation. If growing cells are infected, small t antigen is not obligatory for transformation. SV40 small t antigen is detected by immunoprecipitation using tumor-bearing hamster serum.

Unique to the polyoma system, a middle T antigen of molecular weight 55,000 is synthesized. It is required for maintenance of transformation; large T antigen need not be present in the cells.

B. Tumor-Specific Transplantation Antigens (TSTA): As shown in Fig 40–10, TSTA can be detected by measuring the resistance of virus-immunized animals to challenge with neoplastic cells. Adult animals immunized with active virus are resistant to challenge of large doses (10^5–10^6) of virus-free transformed or tumor cells, whereas nonimmune animals develop tumors when inoculated with as few as 10–100 cells.

This type of immunity is unrelated to circulating viral antibodies but is specifically associated with an

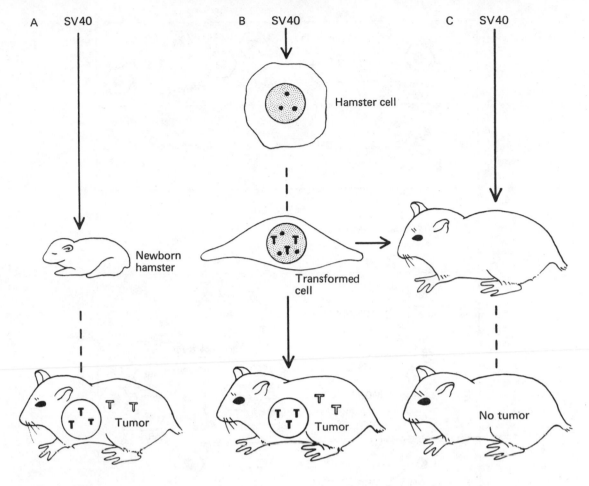

T   Tumor antigen

T   Antibody specific to tumor antigen

Figure 40–10. Tumor (T) antigen. *A:* Newborn hamsters inoculated with SV40 often develop tumors. *B:* Similarly, hamster cells grown in culture and transformed by SV40—meaning that they were given permanent heritable changes—can induce tumors when transplanted to young adult hamsters. The tumor cells as well as the transformed cells contain the T antigen, and the tumor-bearing animal develops antibodies to the T antigen. *C:* Transplantation immunity. A hamster into which transformed cells are transplanted after the adult animal has been inoculated with SV40 virus resists the tumor-causing effect of transformed cells. The virus acts as a vaccine, inducing in certain of the animal's cells a new antigen ("transplantation antigen"); this in turn elicits an immune response, and the animal eliminates the cells bearing the new antigen. The animal also rejects cells that have been transformed in vitro and that evidently carry the same "transplantation antigen." (From: The footprints of tumor viruses, by Fred Rapp & Joseph L. Melnick. Copyright © 1966 by Scientific American, Inc. All rights reserved.)

antigen at the cell surface. It is presumed that this immunity occurs because the active virus induces this new antigen in some cells of the adult animal, and the new antigen in turn elicits a cellular immune response resulting in subsequent rejection of transformed cells carrying the same antigen.

Virus-specific TSTA can also be demonstrated in virus-free transformed cells by their ability to block viral carcinogenesis. Tumors fail to develop in hamsters inoculated at birth with oncogenic virus if they are injected during the latent period with either oncogenic transformed cells (x-ray-treated to prevent

cell replication) or viable nononcogenic transformed cells (derived from a different species, eg, humans). The colony inhibition test has also been used to detect TSTA in virus-induced tumor cells.

The TSTAs of SV40 and polyoma are distinct, although the viruses are both members of the papovavirus group; they have been detected during productive replication in permissive cells. They appear to be early antigens in that their synthesis is not prevented by inhibitors of DNA synthesis. SV40 TSTA seems to be a product of the A gene; it is related to T antigen. Immunization of animals with purified T anti-

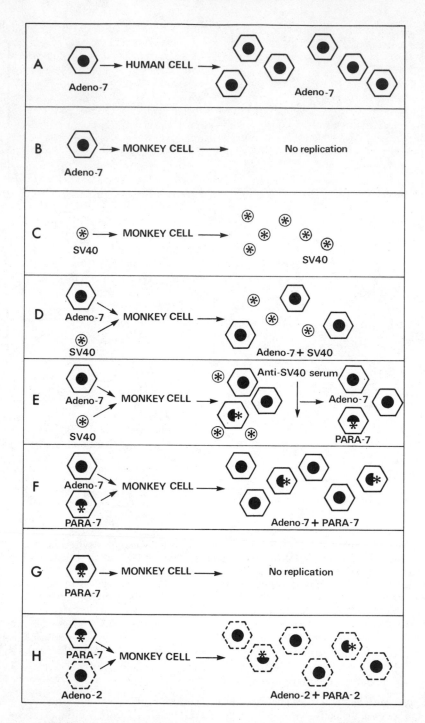

Figure 40–11. Mutual dependence between adeno particles and PARA in "hybrid" populations. The synthesis of SV40 tumor antigen by a "hybrid" requires the multiplication of both adeno particles and PARA. Adenovirus multiplies in human (A) but not in monkey kidney cells (B). SV40 replicates in monkey cells (C), where it also acts as a helper for adenovirus (D). In the product of D, some adenovirus particles exist that contain defective SV40 DNA in their genome. As shown in E, such particles with the hybrid genome induce the formation of SV40 T antigen in the course of infection. Treating the product of the infected cells with anti-SV40 serum binds the SV40 particles, leaving a mixture of pure adenovirus-7 particles and particles containing the combined adeno-SV40 DNA (E). The latter are called PARA because the particles aid in the replication of adenovirus in monkey cells (F). PARA particles are unable to replicate alone in monkey cells (G), but when a cell is infected with both pure adenovirus (type 2) and PARA of another antigenic adenovirus (type 7), transcapsidation occurs and the PARA genome now acquires the coat of the helper adenovirus. This results in an SV40–adenovirus type 2 "hybrid" population containing both pure adeno-2 and PARA-2 particles (H).

gen induces transplantation immunity. Although large T antigen has been detected in the plasma membranes of transformed cells, its identity or relationship to TSTA has not been proved.

Cells transformed by SV40 contain one or more fetal antigens on their surfaces; normal pregnant hamsters contain antibodies (detectable by immunofluorescence) to the surface of SV40-transformed cells. These surface antigens may represent a host protein coded for by a region of the cell genome that has been derepressed by the SV40 genome during the process of transformation. It remains to be seen, however, whether fetal surface antigens are related to the TSTA.

C. Association of Virus-Induced Proteins With Cellular Proteins: A cellular phosphoprotein of molecular weight 53,000 has been detected in SV40-transformed cells. It has been termed nonviral tumor (nvT) antigen, since it is found in immunoprecipitates using tumor-bearing hamster serum. The nvT antigen forms a tight complex with SV40 large T antigen; the biologic function of the complex is unknown. The 53K nvT antigen is induced in nonpermissive cells during SV40 infection and is present in some transformed cells induced by other agents. The elevated levels of 53K nvT antigen may be central to the process of transformation of mammalian cells.

Interaction of Unrelated Tumor Viruses, SV40, & Adenoviruses

In resistant cells derived from monkey kidney, virtually all human adenoviruses are "defective"; they induce the production of T but not of V antigen. If SV40 virus is added to the system, infectious adenovirus is formed abundantly. It appears that the SV40 complementation function affects some post-transcriptional event in the adenovirus replicative cycle.

A virus population was obtained from a preparation of adenovirus type 7 that had been grown in the presence of SV40; it has the ability to replicate in monkey kidney cells and to induce synthesis of both SV40 and adenovirus T antigens; it does not induce SV40 V antigen but induces adeno-7 V antigen. Tumors induced by this population in hamsters bear the T antigen and TSTA of both SV40 and adeno-7.

This population was found to be comprised of 2 types of particles, one being the adenovirus type 7 and the other a stable SV40-adenovirus "hybrid" containing SV40 genetic material encased in an adenovirus type 7 protein coat. The adenovirus particle can readily multiply in human kidney cells but not in monkey kidney cells. The hybrid particle was named PARA (*p*article *a*iding the *r*eplication of *a*denovirus). PARA has properties normally associated with SV40: it induces the synthesis of SV40 tumor and transplantation antigens (the adenovirion does not), and it aids the replication of adenovirus in monkey kidney cell cultures (see Fig 40–11). The genome of PARA consists of defective adenovirus type 7 DNA, representing about 85% of an adenovirus genome, covalently linked to a portion (about 50%) of an SV40 genome.

PARA is defective. By itself, PARA cannot replicate in monkey kidney cells; it requires a helper adenovirus that provides the protein coat. The adenovirus type 7 coat of PARA in the PARA-adenovirus type 7 population can be exchanged for the specific protein coat of unrelated adenovirus types (such as types 1, 2, 3, 5, 6, 12, 16, etc) by a process termed transcapsidation (Fig 40–11). Like the original PARA-adenovirus type 7 population, all PARA-adenovirus serotypes induce the SV40 T antigen and SV40 TSTA. Transfer of the SV40 determinant of PARA into the protein coats of nononcogenic adenoviruses results in the acquisition of oncogenic properties by those viruses. Thus, PARA-adenovirus types 1, 2, 5, and 6 readily induce tumors in newborn hamsters, whereas the parental serotypes do not.

This system illustrates that the tumor-inducing portion of a viral genome (SV40) can masquerade antigenically as an unrelated virus (adenovirus). If it were not for our ability to detect virus-induced, nonstructural antigens (T antigen) as well as nucleic acid sequences, the presence of the defective transforming gene or genes would go unnoticed.

A series of nondefective hybrids exists that consists of a complete adenovirus type 2 genome linked to varying amounts of SV40 DNA and encased in an adenovirus type 2 capsid. These hybrids have been useful in the elucidation of functions expressed by the SV40 genome. Through the use of physical mapping techniques, the precise amount of SV40 information has been determined for each hybrid. Through comparison of the SV40 antigens (T, TSTA) expressed in cells infected by each of the hybrids, a map has been constructed for SV40 genes that code for the different antigens.

VIRUSES & HUMAN CANCER

Experimental systems described above have established the cancer-causing capabilities of many different viruses. Unfortunately, direct extrapolations from those systems to outbred mammals, including humans, are difficult. One reason for that difficulty is that the well-characterized laboratory models employ highly selected, genetically controlled animals and virus strains.

Tumor production in the absence of viral replication is well documented with both DNA and RNA cancer viruses; in fact, the lack of infectious virus is the rule, rather than the exception, with the DNA viruses. Thus, there is no reason to assume that tumors produced in humans should be virus producers. Studies in the model systems have revealed, though, that virus-induced nonstructural proteins are frequently associated with the malignant cells and serve as "footprints" of the transforming agent. However, to detect the nonstructural antigen, the appropriate specific antiserum must be available; such reagents are difficult to prepare.

Many epidemiologic studies have been performed, but none have succeeded in definitely linking a particular agent with human neoplasia, although the strongest evidence suggests an association between certain herpesviruses and human cancer (see below). Some of the difficulties encountered in epidemiologic studies are that long incubation periods may occur between exposure to the agent and appearance of a tumor, the agent involved may not be recoverable using present methodology, specific serologic tests may not be available, the same agent might induce different clinical manifestations, and other factors (such as host age, genetics, or concomitant infections) may play a role in disease development. It is possible that cancer may represent a rare manifestation of a common viral infection.

In spite of these difficulties, several different and promising approaches are being actively pursued in the quest for viral causes of human neoplasia.

Studies Following the Models of Tumorigenesis by Oncornaviruses

Oncornaviruses appear to be ubiquitous in nature and have been associated with leukemias and sarcomas in many animal species. Judged from the known animal systems, lymphoreticular neoplasms would appear most likely to have a viral cause. Following those models, many attempts have been made to determine whether overt infectious oncornaviruslike agents are associated with leukemias or solid tumors of humans. All such studies have yielded negative results.

Particles similar to C type oncornaviruses have been detected by electron microscopy in cells or plasma of patients with leukemia and in solid tumors of humans such as Hodgkin's lymphoma, lymphosarcomas, and sarcomas. Particles similar to C type viruses have also been detected in normal human placental tissue—akin to the findings with placental tissues of subhuman primates. Oncornaviruses have been isolated from leukemic cells grown in culture, but the "isolates" have all been ultimately identified as laboratory contaminants.

Particles resembling the murine mammary tumor oncornaviruses (B type particles) have been detected in human mammary cancer and in the milk of Parsi women (a population in India with a very high incidence of mammary cancer) and of American women with a family history of mammary cancer. Even though the infectious nature of those particles remains questionable, evidence suggests that they contain high-molecular-weight RNA (70S) and reverse transcriptase enzyme activity characteristic of oncornaviruses. There are suggestions of a relationship between the human particles and murine mammary tumor virus. Rabbit antisera to purified MuMTV were reported to precipitate a soluble antigen from sera of women with mammary cancer. An antigen in human breast cancer tissue has been found to react with antibody directed against the major glycoprotein (gp52) of MuMTV. Furthermore, cDNA synthesized in vitro using MuMTV RNA as a template was found to hybridize with polysomal RNA obtained from human mammary adenocarcinomas. No such hybridization was observed with RNA derived from other human malignancies or normal tissues. Other studies have detected evidence of the presence of M-PMV (D type particles)-related material in some human breast tumors. Further studies employing new and more sensitive techniques are needed to define the oncornaviruslike information associated with breast cancer in humans.

Using similar procedures, the presence of RNA related to the RNA of R-MuLV (but not to that of MuMTV) has been observed in human malignancies other than breast cancer. cDNA obtained from R-MuLV by the use of reverse transcription in vitro hybridized with RNA obtained from cells of various leukemias, lymphomas, and sarcomas. A 70S RNA complexed with reverse transcriptase has been detected in cells from human leukemias. The DNA synthesized from that complex hybridized specifically with the RNA of R-MuLV but not with the RNA of MuMTV or of avian myeloblastosis virus. These results appear to be corroborated by a report on the presence of reverse transcriptase activity in cells of patients with acute lymphoblastic leukemia; further work is needed to characterize the enzyme found in leukemic cells, because of the possibility that it may be a cellular enzyme. However, it appears that cells of patients with myelogenous leukemia possess an oncornaviral type reverse transcriptase that is distinguishable from other cell DNA polymerases and serologically related to the reverse transcriptase of primate oncornaviruses and, to a lesser extent, to that of R-MuLV.

The above findings with human malignancies tend to suggest the presence of virus-related information. However, they must be treated with caution inasmuch as other investigators have failed to corroborate the findings. More broadly cross-reactive reagents are needed, since a putative human virus might not be closely related to the known animal agents.

The recent results suggesting promoter-insertion oncogenesis by leukemia viruses (see above) provide a new avenue to be pursued in studies of human disease. Specific cDNA probes able to detect the transcription of recognized cellular *onc* genes can be used to screen for activation of expression in various types of human malignancies.

Studies Following the Models of Tumorigenesis by DNA Tumor Viruses

In view of the fact that solid tumors induced in experimental animals by papovaviruses and adenoviruses are, with few exceptions, free from infectious virus or infectious nucleic acid, it is not surprising that all attempts to isolate viruses from a variety of solid human tumors have met with complete failure.

Following the findings on the presence of virus-specific mRNA in DNA virus–induced (but virus-free) tumors, a search in human tumor tissues for mRNA hybridizable with the DNA of the known oncogenic virus was attempted. Special attention was given to the adenoviruses, since they are oncogenic in experimental animals and are widespread in humans. However, results to date have failed to show that any of the human tumors examined contain adenovirus-specific mRNA.

The presence of papovaviruslike particles has been demonstrated in the brains of patients with progressive multifocal leukoencephalopathy (PML), a rare demyelinating disease of humans usually occurring as a complication of a previous malignancy of the reticuloendothelial system or of immunosuppressive therapy. As indicated earlier (see p 481), 2 human papovaviruses—SV40-PML virus and JC virus—have been isolated from brains of patients with PML, and another human papovavirus, BK, has been isolated from immunosuppressed renal allograft recipients free of PML. The 3 agents are antigenically distinct from each other but share common antigens with the simian papovavirus SV40. All 3 viruses are oncogenic in hamsters and can transform hamster cells in vitro; the same patterns of virus-tumor cell interactions characteristic of SV40 are observed with the human agents—production of T antigen and TSTA, rescue of infectious virus by fusion with susceptible cells, etc. The significance of these viruses to human malignancies remains to be determined. Seroepidemiologic surveys indicate that infections with JC and BK virus are very common in humans (with about 70% of adults having antibodies). The human papovavirus infections do not appear to be related to exposure to the simian SV40 virus, either through contact with rhesus monkeys (the natural host for SV40) or through vaccination with early poliovirus vaccines that may have contained SV40.

Papilloma viral antigen has been identified in cervical biopsies exhibiting dysplasia, suggesting that the virus may play an etiologic role in some cases of cervical neoplasia. The viral antigen has also been found in about 50% of laryngeal papillomas of childhood.

Immunologic Studies

The knowledge of virus-induced T antigens in tumors (or in transformed cells) and of T antibodies in the tumor-bearing animals has led to similar immunologic studies in cancer of humans. Tests of the sera of cancer patients for the presence of complement-fixing or immunofluorescence antibodies to the T antigens of SV40 or adenovirus have yielded negative results.

Carcinomas of the gastrointestinal tract have been found to contain an antigen that is absent from normal adult gut cells but present in embryonal gut cells. This antigen has been named carcinoembryonic antigen (CEA), and it is believed that its appearance in gastrointestinal carcinomas is due to genetic derepression. The antigen can be isolated and purified from the tumor or embryonic tissue and can be detected by means of several different tests with antisera to it prepared in goats or rabbits. Patients with gastrointes-

tinal carcinomas have circulating CEA that is presumably released from the tumor cells. The exact nature of this antigen and the antibody response monitored in the cancer patient remain to be determined.

The identification of the nonstructural transforming proteins of the sarcoma viruses provides a new avenue to be pursued in the search for transforming proteins in human cancer.

Transplantation type antigens have been detected in various human tumors by using the colony inhibition test with the patient's lymphocytes and cells from the autologous tumor. It appears that tumors of certain histologic types in different patients share transplantation type antigens. However, further well-controlled studies are needed before it can be concluded that such tumors possess common antigens. It also appears that cells from patients with leukemia possess antigens to which autologous humoral and cell-mediated immune reactions develop. Evidence is accumulating that—similar to the animal model systems—patients with advanced cancer have circulating serum factors that can block the in vitro reaction of autologous lymphocytes in the colony inhibition test. Further studies in this direction may lead to an understanding of the mechanisms involved in tumor progression or regression in vivo.

Herpesviruses & Human Malignancies

A. Herpes Simplex Virus Type 2: In recent years, a great deal of attention has been focused on herpesviruses of humans as potential oncogenic agents. Herpes simplex virus type 2 is venereally transmitted in humans (see Chapter 38). Seroepidemiologic studies reveal a high degree of association between infection with this virus and invasive carcinoma of the cervix. The prevalence of herpes type 2 antibody in women with the disease was found to be much higher than that in matched controls. In many but not all studies, women with cervical dysplasia and carcinoma in situ (considered by some to be premalignant lesions leading to invasive carcinoma) had an increased prevalence of herpes type 2 antibody. Follow-up of such patients, as well as prospective seroepidemiologic surveys of different populations, may shed further light on whether the association found is covariable or etiologic.

A higher incidence of antibodies to nonstructural antigens induced by herpesvirus has also been observed among patients with cancer of the cervix or vulva (as compared to normal individuals or patients with breast cancer). Nonstructural herpes type 2 antigens have been observed in cancer cells obtained by biopsy from patients with carcinomas of the cervix and the vulva. These findings, together with the capacity of herpesvirus to transform hamster embryo fibroblasts into tumorigenic cells, lend support to the idea of the oncogenic potential of this agent in humans.

Studies with cells transformed by HSV-2 indicate that the entire viral genome is not present but only small fragments of the viral DNA. Recently, a restriction enzyme fragment of HSV-2 has been used to transform cells. To date, hybridization studies (with one unsupported exception) have not revealed the presence of HSV-2 DNA in cervical carcinoma specimens. Future studies using specific probes relevant to the HSV-2 DNA-transforming fragment should be informative.

B. EB Herpesvirus (EBV): The most likely candidate for a virus as an etiologic agent of certain human cancers is the Epstein-Barr virus (EBV), which causes infectious mononucleosis and is widespread in human populations (see Chapter 38). EBV viral DNA and certain antigens are present in 2 human malignancies: Burkitt's lymphoma, a tumor that is most commonly found in children in central Africa and has a predilection for the jaw; and nasopharyngeal carcinoma, found with higher frequency in Chinese male populations in Southeast Asia than in other populations. The virus was detected initially by electron microscopy and subsequently by immunofluorescence in cultured Burkitt's lymphoma cells (but not in the original tumor) that maintain their lymphoid character upon continuous in vitro propagation. The high incidence and high titers of EB antibody (detectable by immunofluorescence, complement fixation, and gel diffusion tests) in patients with Burkitt's lymphoma and nasopharyngeal carcinoma led to the assumption that the association may have a causal role.

Seroepidemiologic surveys showed that infection with EBV in normal populations is widespread not only in Africa and Asia but also all over the world. The virus was subsequently found to be the causative agent of infectious mononucleosis.

EBV has an extreme predilection for cells of lymphoid origin, particularly for human B lymphocytes that have specific EBV receptors. The virus occurs regularly in cell lines derived not only from Burkitt's lymphoma and nasopharyngeal carcinoma but also from peripheral blood leukocytes of patients with infectious mononucleosis and other disease entities, as well as from normal individuals who have EBV antibodies, but not from seronegative persons.

Normal lymphocytes have a limited life span in vitro but can be transformed into continuous cell lines by EBV. Such permanent lines have a diploid (or nearly diploid) karyotype, carry several copies of the viral genome in each cell, and express EBV nuclear antigen, called EBNA. Regardless of whether or not mature virus is produced, all cells that carry EBV genomes express EBNA, the EBV nuclear antigen. Thus, EBNA is diagnostic for viral DNA, usually present in multiple copies in transformed cells and in Burkitt's lymphoma and nasopharyngeal carcinoma. EBNA has been shown to be a DNA-binding protein; ie, it has high affinity for DNA and is associated with the host cell chromosomes. This nonacidic chromosomal protein has recently been purified, but additional work is needed to determine its function, either in virus replication or in the maintenance of the latent virus state.

The question remains whether EBV is causally related to lymphoma and nasopharyngeal carcinoma or whether it represents a passenger virus present in the lymphoid cells of the tumor. Indeed, other viruses — eg, herpes simplex virus and reovirus — have been isolated from Burkitt's lymphomas. The passenger concept assumes that lymphoma cells appearing in EBV-carrying persons — and for EBV-unrelated reasons — pick up the virus. As the cells multiply, the amount of virus is increased and antibody production occurs, similar to the situation with normal lymphocytes. However, the non-Burkitt's lymphomas that are common in the USA and most other areas of the world arise in EBV antibody-positive persons who do not pick up the virus even though their EBV-negative lymphoma cells can be infected and transformed with EBV in vitro. The EBV-sensitive lymphoma cells that appear in seropositive American patients are protected from horizontal spread of the virus in vivo by neutralizing antibodies. This supports the view that EBV-positive Burkitt's lymphomas in African children originate from cells carrying the EBV genome. It has been suggested that EBV may be able to cause oncogenic transformation only in those cells with a special competence, such as a genetic deficiency in some regulatory mechanism. Such cells might be those with the chromosome-14 translocation that has recently been found to be characteristic of malignant Burkitt's lymphoma.

In DNA-DNA hybridization studies, small quantities of EBV DNA have been detected in virus-free biopsy specimens of Burkitt's lymphoma and nasopharyngeal carcinoma; these findings are similar to those obtained with cell lines derived from the same tumors. Each cell carries multiple copies of the viral genome; part is in free circular, covalently closed form and another part is integrated with the cell genome. However, such studies still do not answer the question whether the viral genome detected is the cause of the malignancy or results from a secondary infection of the tumor cells by the virus.

Cells explanted from Burkitt's tumors grow into continuous lines (called lymphoma lines) more easily than cells derived from peripheral blood of persons with infectious mononucleosis or persons who are otherwise antibody-positive. Lymphoma lines, furthermore, differ from lymphoblastoid lines derived in vitro from nonlymphomatous persons. In contrast to the uniform character of the lymphoma lines, lymphoblastoid lines are heterogeneous in morphologic, functional, and growth properties. Perhaps the development of lymphoma involves the appearance in vivo of a particular neoplastic cell type not present in the normal lymphocyte population transformed by EBV. As mentioned, a specific chromosome-14 translocation is present in Burkitt's lymphoma biopsies and established lines but not in EBV lymphoblastoid lines of nonlymphoma origin, and this chromosome translocation might well be the indicator of the EBV-converted cancer cell.

Support for an oncogenic role of EBV comes from studies in the marmoset, a South American monkey. Marmoset lymphocytes (akin to human lymphocytes) can be transformed in tissue culture by cell-free EBV, resulting in continuous virus-positive lines. Cells of such a marmoset lymphoid line (infected with EBV derived from a lymphoid line of a patient with infectious mononucleosis) as well as cell-free virus derived from the cells were found to induce malignant lymphomas in cottontop marmosets. Also, human lymphocytes transformed by EBV (either in vitro or in vivo) can grow as malignant tumors when transplanted into immunologically deficient xenogeneic hosts (nude mice).

In regard to **nasopharyngeal carcinoma,** the EBV genome is regularly present in the tumor regardless of geographic occurrence. However, in these tumors the viral genome and the expressed nuclear antigen are not carried by the T lymphocytes that infiltrate the tumor but by the actual carcinoma cells. Since the tumors occur more frequently in certain ethnic groups, particularly in Chinese, the genetic makeup of the host cell may determine whether an oncogenic transformation may take place. Thus, the situation in principle would be similar to that discussed for Burkitt's lymphoma even though the susceptible cell type, and therefore the resulting tumor, would be different.

Different strains of EBV have been isolated from various sources and have been shown to differ in biologic properties. Notably, certain strains are incapable of causing transformation of normal lymphocytes, which suggests that the various diseases associated with EBV might be a result of different strains. Strains that differ in biologic properties have been found to be similar in the size of their DNA genome, their major structural polypeptides, and various antigens. However, DNA hybridization studies and restriction endonuclease fragment analysis have shown strain differences. A nontransforming strain lacked sequences present in transforming strains. Additional work may establish strain differences in various EBV disease manifestations.

Methods (including vaccines) of intervening in the various clinical manifestations of EBV are under investigation. Such methods may eventually clarify the role of EBV in various human disorders, including the malignancies with which it is associated.

C. Cytomegalovirus: Recently, human cytomegalovirus has been observed to transform human and hamster cells in culture to the malignant state. The less the degree of expression of viral antigens by the transformed cells, the greater the degree of malignancy, as shown by measurements in athymic nude mice. Virus-specific antigens have not been found in human cancer cells. However, when compared with the immunity shown against normal human cells, humoral and cell-mediated immunity against the virus-transformed cells have been reported to increase in patients with prostatic cancer.

Hepatitis B Virus & Primary Liver Cancer

From studies of the natural history of primary hepatocellular carcinoma (PHC), it is clear that persistent or past infection with hepatitis B virus (HBV) is a common feature of the disease. Since few patients with PHC give a history of having had acute hepatitis, the original HBV infection must be subclinical or mild in most patients who subsequently develop PHC.

In the American continent and Europe, whose populations have a rather low prevalence of hepatitis B infection (0.1–1% of blood donors positive for hepatitis B surface antigen [HBsAg]), PHC is an uncommon cancer (1–3 cases per 100,000). One exception is Greece, where the prevalence of HBs antigenemia in the population is 5%; correspondingly, PHC is more frequent (prevalence: 20/100,000), and up to 60% of the PHC cases are HBsAg-positive.

In tropical Africa and the Far East, HBV is clearly associated with cirrhosis and PHC. The prevalence of HBs antigenemia is much higher (10–25%), and PHC is a very common neoplasm, with a prevalence of up to 150/100,000. Moreover, PHC is commonly associated with positive HBs antigenemia (50–80%). Patients with PHC are usually young adults, who seldom have any history of alcoholism.

Epidemiologic and virologic evidence provides telling arguments that HBV is involved in the etiology of PHC:

(1) There is a geographic correlation between areas where hepatitis B infection exhibits high endemicity and those where PHC prevalence is high.

(2) The risk of developing PHC has been shown to be relatively constant in endemic and nonendemic areas among male chronic carriers of HBsAg. The PHC annual death rate varies from 250 to 500 per 100,000 in this population. Given a gross estimate of about 200 million HBsAg chronic carriers in the world, the PHC annual incidence has been calculated to be about 350,000 cases. This indicates that HBV-related PHC is one of the more prevalent cancers in the world population.

(3) HBV infection is found 10–40 times more frequently in PHC patients than in matched controls living in the same area; this occurs in areas of high or low prevalence of the disease.

(4) HBV infection precedes and usually accompanies the development of PHC.

(5) Chronic infection with HBV often leads to cirrhosis. Prospective studies have shown a high frequency of HBsAg-positive patients with cirrhosis who in a few years develop liver cancer, in contrast to HBsAg-negative cirrhosis patients (eg, alcoholic cirrhosis).

(6) In other prospective studies of HBsAg carriers and matched controls over a 4- to 5-year period, the risk of developing PHC was over 200 times higher among the carriers.

(7) The hepatocytes of HBV-infected PHC patients manifest signs of the infection (viral DNA and antigens), but the antigens are not found in the adjacent tumor cells.

(8) Some PHC cell lines that have been grown in culture produce HBsAg. HBV DNA has been shown to

be integrated into the genome of these cells; in addition, RNA molecules containing HBV-specific sequences have been detected in the hepatoma cells.

(9) Viruses similar to HBV in composition and morphology have been detected in lower animals. As with HBV, persistent infection as revealed by antigenemia is common. In the woodchuck, *Marmota monax,* primary liver cancer often occurs. As in human hepatoma, the cancer is usually associated with chronic hepatitis and sometimes with cirrhosis. The virus shares a common core antigen with HBV.

(10) Pekin ducks *(Anas domesticus)* native to China develop liver cancer late in life. A virus, again similar to HBV, has been isolated from Pekin ducks in China and from commercial flocks in the USA that had their origin in ducks transported from China many years ago. The virus is transmitted vertically, and infected ducklings may have persistent viremia.

(11) The final and crucial evidence will come from the application of the new hepatitis B vaccines, which hold the promise of preventing not only infection with the virus but also the cancer that is the result of the infection. Such trials in infants in areas of high prevalence are already under way, and the early results are very encouraging.

•　•　•

References

Bishop JM: The molecular biology of RNA tumor viruses: A physician's guide. *N Engl J Med* 1980;**303**:675.

Butel JS, Tevethia SS, Melnick JL: Oncogenicity and cell transformation by papovavirus SV40: The role of the viral genome. *Adv Cancer Res* 1972;**15**:1.

Camacho A, Spear PG: Transformation of hamster embryo fibroblasts by a specific fragment of the herpes simplex virus genome. *Cell* 1978;**15**:993.

Crawford LV et al: Detection of a common feature in several human tumor cell lines: A 53,000-dalton protein. *Proc Natl Acad Sci USA* 1981;**78**:41.

de The G, Henle W, Rapp F (editors): *Oncogenesis and Herpesviruses III.* International Agency for Research on Cancer, 1978.

Francis DP, Essex M: Leukemia and lymphoma: Infrequent manifestations of common viral infections? A review. *J Infect Dis* 1978;**138**:916.

Hayward WS, Neel BG, Astrin SM: Activation of a cellular *onc* gene by promoter insertion in ALV-induced lymphoid leukosis. *Nature* 1981;**290**:475.

Kaufman RH et al: Herpesvirus-induced antigens in squamous-cell carcinoma in situ of the vulva. *N Engl J Med* 1981;**305**:483.

Kelly TJ Jr, Nathans D: The genome of simian virus 40. *Adv Virus Res* 1977;**21**:85.

Klein G (editor): *Viral Oncology.* Raven Press, 1980.

Maupas P, Melnick JL (editors): Hepatitis B virus and primary hepatocellular carcinoma. *Prog Med Virol* 1981;No. 27. [Entire issue.]

Melnick JL: Hepatitis B virus and liver cancer. In: *Viruses Associated With Human Cancer.* Phillips LA (editor). Marcel Dekker. [In press.]

Melnick JL, Adam E, Rawls WE: The causative role of herpesvirus type 2 in cervical cancer. *Cancer* 1974;**34**:1375.

Moore DH et al: Mammary tumor viruses. *Adv Cancer Res* 1979;**29**:347.

Ohno T et al: Human breast carcinoma antigen is immunologically related to the polypeptide of the group-specific glycoprotein of mouse mammary tumor virus. *Proc Natl Acad Sci USA* 1979;**76**:2460.

Purchio AF et al: Identification of a polypeptide encoded by the avian sarcoma virus *src* gene. *Proc Natl Acad Sci USA* 1978;**75**:1567.

Rentier-Delrue F, Lubiniecki A, Howley PM: Analysis of JC virus DNA purified directly from human progressive multifocal leukoencephalopathy brains. *J Virol* 1981;**38**:761.

Roussel M et al: Three new types of viral oncogene of cellular origin specific for haematopoietic cell transformation. *Nature* 1979;**281**:452.

Takemoto KK: Human papovaviruses. *Int Rev Exp Pathol* 1978;**18**:281.

Tooze J (editor): *The Molecular Biology of Tumor Viruses,* 2nd ed. Cold Spring Harbor Laboratory, 1980.

Although all of the medically significant microorganisms considered in this *Review* are parasitic in their human hosts, the biomedical discipline of **parasitology** has traditionally been concerned only with the parasitic protozoa, helminths, and arthropods. This chapter offers no more than a brief survey of the protozoan and helminthic parasites of medical importance, with particular attention to those forms whose identification depends upon microscopic study. The chapter is designed as a first point of reference; the text is supplemented by tabular materials and by 11 pages of illustrations. The following books and articles are recommended for detailed reference:

Medical Parasitology & Tropical Medicine

Ash LR, Orihel TC: *Atlas of Human Parasitology*. American Society of Clinical Pathologists, 1980.

Bell DR: *Lecture Notes on Tropical Medicine*. Blackwell, 1981.

Catchpool JF: Antiprotozoal drugs. Chap 62, pp 619–646, in: *Review of Medical Pharmacology*, 7th ed. Meyers FH, Jawetz E, Goldfien A (editors). Lange, 1980.

Cohen S, Sadun EH (editors): *Immunology of Parasitic Infections*. Blackwell, 1976.

Desowitz RS: *Ova and Parasites: Medical Parasitology for the Laboratory Technologist*. Harper & Row, 1980.

Drugs for parasitic infections. *Med Lett Drugs Ther* 1982;**24**:5.

Faust EC, Russell PF, Jung RC: *Craig & Faust's Clinical Parasitology*, 8th ed. Lea & Febiger, 1970.

Garcia LS, Ash LR: *Diagnostic Parasitology: Clinical Laboratory Manual*, 2nd ed. Mosby, 1979.

Goldsmith RS: Anthelmintic drugs. Chap 63, pp 647–676, in: *Review of Medical Pharmacology*, 7th ed. Meyers FH, Jawetz E, Goldfien A (editors). Lange, 1980.

Goldsmith RS: Infectious diseases: Helminthic. Chap 26, pp 886–910, in: *Current Medical Diagnosis & Treatment 1982*. Krupp MA, Chatton MJ (editors). Lange, 1982.

Goldsmith RS: Infectious diseases: Protozoal. Chap 25, pp 866–885, in: *Current Medical Diagnosis & Treatment 1982*. Krupp MA, Chatton MJ (editors). Lange, 1982.

Heyneman D: Medical parasitology. Chap 19, pp 335–388, in: *Physician's Handbook*, 20th ed. Krupp MA et al. Lange, 1982.

Hunter GW III, Swartzwelder JC, Clyde DF: *Tropical Medicine*, 5th ed. Saunders, 1976.

Maegraith BG: *Exotic Diseases in Practice: The Clinical and Public Health Significance of the Changing Geographical Patterns of Diseases With Particular Reference to the Importation of Exotic Infections Into Europe and North America*. Heinemann, 1965.

Marcial-Rojas RA (editor): *Pathology of Protozoal and Helminthic Diseases, With Clinical Correlation*. Williams & Wilkins, 1971.

Markell EK, Voge M: *Medical Parasitology*, 5th ed. Saunders, 1981.

Melvin DM, Brooke MM: *Laboratory Procedures for the Diagnosis of Intestinal Parasites*, revised 1974. Centers for Disease Control, Health & Human Services Publication No. (CDC) 79-8282, 1979.

Muller R: *Worms and Disease: A Manual of Medical Helminthology*. Heineman, 1975.

Reeder MM, Palmer PES: *The Radiology of Tropical Disease With Epidemiological, Pathological and Clinical Correlation*. Williams & Wilkins, 1980.

Schmidt GD, Roberts LS: *Foundations of Parasitology*, 2nd ed. Mosby, 1981.

Schultz M (editor): *Current Concepts in Parasitology*. Reprinted from *The New England Journal of Medicine*, 1977–1979. Massachusetts Medical Society, Boston, 1979.

Van den Bossche H: Chemotherapy of parasitic infections. *Nature* 1978;**273**:626.

Warren KS, Mahmoud AAF (editors): *Geographic Medicine for the Practitioner: Algorithms in the Diagnosis and Management of Exotic Diseases*. University of Chicago, 1978.

Wilcocks C, Manson-Bahr PEC: *Manson's Tropical Diseases*, 17th ed. Ballière Tindall, 1972.

Woodruff AW (editor): *Medicine in the Tropics*. Churchill Livingstone, 1974.

Zaman V: *Atlas of Medical Parasitology*. Lea & Febiger, 1979.

Medical Entomology

Harwood RF, James MT: *Entomology in Human and Animal Health*, 7th ed. Macmillan, 1979.

*By Donald Heyneman, PhD, Professor of Parasitology, Department of Epidemiology and International Health, University of California School of Medicine (San Francisco). The illustrations on pp 522–532 are by P.H. Vercammen-Grandjean, DSc.

CLASSIFICATION

The parasites of humans in the kingdom Protozoa are now classified under 3 major categories, or phyla: **Sarcomastigophora** (containing the flagellates and amebas); **Apicomplexa** (containing the sporozoans);

and **Ciliophora** (containing the ciliates). Within these great assemblages are found the important human parasites, listed below within their respective subphyla ([1], [2], and [4]) or class (3):

(1) Mastigophora, the flagellates, with one or more whiplike flagella and, in some cases, an undulating membrane (eg, trypanosomes). These include intestinal and genitourinary flagellates *(Giardia, Trichomonas, Retortamonas, Dientamoeba,* Enteromonas, Chilomastix)* and blood and tissue flagellates *(Trypanosoma, Leishmania).*

(2) Sarcodina, typically ameboid. These parasites are represented in humans by species of *Entamoeba, Endolimax, Iodamoeba, Naegleria,* and *Acanthamoeba.*

(3) Sporozoea undergo a complex life cycle with alternating sexual and asexual reproductive phases, usually involving 2 different hosts (eg, arthropod and vertebrate, as in the blood forms). Coccidia, a subclass of the class Sporozoea, contains both the typical coccidial parasites and the hemosporidial, or malarial, organisms. The former group (suborder Eimeriina) have intestinal and tissue phases, usually alternating between the intestinal (sexual) form in a carnivore and a tissue (asexual or schizogonic) form in a herbivore. *Isospora,* including a species that infects humans, appears to have only the intestinal stage, though the encysted tissue stages may yet prove to be present in other hosts, perhaps as unrecognized, incompletely known species of *Sarcocystis.* The latter are now known to have their sexual phase in gut cells of carnivores, resulting in production of fecally passed infective oocysts, and a nonsexual schizogonic multiplying and eventually encysted phase in tissue cells of prey animals (humans may be in both realms). *Toxoplasma* occurs in its sexual intestinal form *only* in cats or related felines, with production of fecal oocysts very similar to those of *Isospora.* On the other hand, *any* mammal—including the unborn—appears able to serve as an intermediate host for the tissue and central nervous system encysted stage. Humans, for example, become infected with tissue forms of *Toxoplasma* (rapidly dividing tachyzoites in the early acute stages; slowly dividing bradyzoites that become encysted in intracellular muscle, brain, or eye) either from ingestion of undercooked mutton, pork, or other meats that contain tissue cysts or from contamination of food, water, or fingers with infective oocysts from cat feces. Most tragically, the fetus may become infected following transplacental transmission from a mother infected during pregnancy, often with fatal or catastrophic effects on the unborn, while there may be no detectable illness in the mother.

The blood sporozoans (suborder Haemosporina) contain the malarial parasites, *Plasmodium* species. A more distant sporozoan group, the piroplasms, form a distinct subclass, **Piroplasmia,** on a par with the sub-

class **Coccidia.** These unusual parasites have only recently crossed the threshold from animal to human nosology. *Babesia,* a piroplasm of cattle (redwater fever), rodents, and many other animal species, is now a human pathogen as well (babesiosis). Babesiosis has occurred on Nantucket Island and the eastern shoreline of Massachusetts, where conditions for transmission were met in such a way that humans intercepted an endemic tick-rodent-deer cycle of the parasite, and 100 or so human cases have resulted.

(4) Ciliophora, complex protozoa bearing cilia characteristically distributed in highly organized rows or patches, with 2 kinds of nuclei in each individual. *Balantidium coli,* a giant intestinal ciliate of humans and pigs, is the only human parasite representative of this group. Illustrations of parasitic protozoa can be found on pp 522–525.

The parasitic worms, or helminths, of human beings belong to 2 phyla:

(1) Platyhelminthes (flatworms) lack a true body cavity (celom) and are characteristically flat in dorsoventral section. All medically important species belong to the classes **Cestoda** (tapeworms) and **Trematoda** (flukes). The tapeworms, or cestodes, are hermaphroditic, bandlike, segmented intestinal parasites (as adults) with no digestive tract but rather an absorptive surface covered with microtriches. The flukes, or trematodes, are typically leaf-shaped and hermaphroditic and are parasitic in gut, liver, or other viscera, but the schistosomes (*Schistosoma* species) are elongate, have separate sexes, and live in the vascular system. The important tissue and intestinal cestodes of humans belong to the following genera: *Diphyllobothrium, Spirometra, Taenia, Echinococcus, Hymenolepis,* and *Dipylidium.* Medically important trematode genera, in addition to *Schistosoma,* include *Paragonimus, Clonorchis, Opisthorchis, Fasciolopsis, Heterophyes, Metagonimus,* and *Fasciola.*

(2) Nemathelminthes (roundworms) are represented in humans by many parasitic species in the class Nematoda. All are wormlike, unsegmented, round in body section, with a well-developed digestive system and separate sexes. Many families of roundworms have parasitic species that infect humans.

These are listed in Table 41–4 together with the other parasitic helminths. An essential procedure in diagnosis of many helminthic infections is microscopic recognition of ova or larvae in feces, urine, blood, or tissues. Illustrations of diagnostically important stages can be found on pp 526–532; certain important characteristics of the microfilariae, embryonic filariid worms, are also presented in tabular fashion (see Table 41–5). The references listed on p 497 include excellent laboratory diagnostic guides (Desowitz, 1980; Garcia & Ash, 1979; Melvin & Brooke, 1979).

---

*Shown in recent studies to be an ameboflagellate related to the trichomonads and not to the family of true amebae, the Endamoebidae.

GIARDIA LAMBLIA

Giardia lamblia is a flagellated protozoan, the only common protozoan found in the duodenum and jejunum of humans. It is the cause of flagellate diarrhea or giardiasis.

Morphology & Identification

A. Typical Organisms: The trophozoite of *G lamblia* is a heart-shaped, bilaterally symmetric organism 10–18 μm in length. There are 4 pairs of flagella, 2 nuclei with prominent central karyosomes, 2 axostyles, and a single or double parabasal body. A large concave sucking disk in the swollen anterior portion occupies much of the ventral surface. The swaying or dancing motion of *Giardia* trophozoites in fresh preparations is unmistakable. As the parasites are passed into the colon, they dehydrate and typically encyst, the cyst being the normal form found in the stool—often in enormous numbers. These cysts, 8–14 μm in length, are ellipsoid and thick-walled and contain 2–4 nuclei, usually at one end, and various structures of the trophozoite.

B. Culture: This organism has not been cultivated for prolonged periods on artificial media—a testament to its parasitologic specialization.

Pathogenesis & Clinical Findings

G lamblia is usually weakly pathogenic or nonpathogenic for humans. Cysts may be found in large numbers in the stools of entirely asymptomatic persons. In some persons, however, large numbers of parasites attached to the bowel wall may cause irritation and low-grade inflammation of the duodenal or jejunal mucosa, with consequent acute or chronic diarrhea and steatorrhea. The stools may be watery, semisolid, greasy, bulky, and foul-smelling at various times during the course of the infection. Malaise, weakness, weight loss, abdominal cramps, distention, and flatulence may occur. Some of these symptoms may be due to interference with fat absorption as well as to mechanical irritation of the bowel. The bile ducts and gallbladder may also be invaded, causing a mild catarrhal cholangitis and cholecystitis. Children are more liable to clinical giardiasis than adults. Symptoms may continue for long periods and may prove intractable or extremely difficult to eliminate.

Diagnostic Laboratory Tests

Diagnosis depends upon finding the distinctive cysts in formed stools, or cysts and trophozoites in liquid stools. Concentration methods may be necessary to detect asymptomatic infections, but the parasite is usually abundant in the stool when gastrointestinal symptoms are present. Examination of the duodenal contents may be necessary to establish the diagnosis, especially when biliary symptoms predominate. Duodenal aspiration or use of the duodenal capsule technique (Entero-Test) is often superior to fecal examination for diagnosis.

Treatment

Administration of quinacrine hydrochloride (Atabrine) will cure about 90% of *G lamblia* infections. Metronidazole (Flagyl) is an alternative. The course of treatment may be repeated if necessary. Only symptomatic patients require treatment.

Epidemiology

G lamblia is cosmopolitan and common, especially in young children. Humans are infected by ingestion of fecally contaminated water or food containing *Giardia* cysts. Epidemic outbreaks have been reported at ski resorts and other areas in the USA where overloading of sewage facilities or contamination of the water supply has resulted in sudden outbreaks of giardiasis. Numerous reports have been made of giardiasis among American tourists returning from Leningrad, presumably owing to contaminated hotel water supplies. Recent outbreaks among campers in wilderness areas suggest that humans may be infected with various animal *Giardia* species such as *Giardia bovis, Giardia canis, Giardia cati, Giardia equi, Giardia muris,* or other species harbored by beavers or other rodents, deer, cattle, sheep, horses, or household pets. This suggests that human infection can also be a zoonosis and that host specificity among various species is far less than has heretofore been thought. It may also prove that the number of species described may be polytypic forms of a single species, as with *Toxoplasma carinii.*

TRICHOMONAS

The trichomonads are flagellate protozoa with 3–5 anterior flagella, an axostyle, a parabasal body, an anterior pelta, a large vesicular anterior nucleus, an endosome, and an undulating membrane. Of the 3 species infecting humans, only *Trichomonas vaginalis* is pathogenic, causing trichomoniasis.

Morphology & Identification

A. Typical Organisms: *T vaginalis* is pearshaped, with a short undulating membrane extending to mid-body and lined with a posteriorly directed or trailing flagellum, and has 4 anterior flagella. It normally measures 15–20 μm in length but may reach 30 μm. The organism moves with a characteristic wobbling and rotating motion. The nonpathogenic trichomonads, *Trichomonas hominis* and *Trichomonas tenax,* cannot readily be distinguished from *T vaginalis* when alive. When fixed and stained, *T tenax* measures 6–10 μm in length; in other respects it is identical with *T vaginalis*. *T hominis* measures 8–12 μm and bears 5 anterior flagella and a long undulating membrane extending the full length of its body with a free termination of the posterior flagellum, which distinguishes it from the short membrane and trailing flagellum of *T vaginalis*. The parabasal body is small or absent. For all practical purposes, trichomonads found in the mouth are *T tenax;* in the intestine, *T* *hominis;* and in the genitourinary tract (both sexes), *T vaginalis.* Organ specificity is more extreme among these parasites than is host specificity.

B. Culture: *T vaginalis* may be cultivated in a variety of solid and fluid cell-free media, in tissue cultures, and in the chick embryo. *T tenax* and *T hominis* will grow particularly well in sheep serum in saline; media used for culturing the intestinal amebas are also satisfactory. *T vaginalis* requires more complex media for optimal growth. CPLM (cysteine-peptone-liver-maltose) medium is one of the most satisfactory. Simplified trypticase serum is usually used for semen cultures.

C. Growth Requirements: *T vaginalis* grows well under anaerobic conditions, somewhat less well aerobically. The pH optimum is 5.5–6.0; the temperature optimum is 35–37 °C. The following substances appear to be essential for optimal growth: cysteine, a fermentable carbohydrate, 20% animal serum, 0.1% agar, and a heat-labile factor destroyed by autoclaving. The optimal pH for growth in vitro (5.5–6.0) suggests why vaginal trichomoniasis is more severe in women with abnormally low vaginal acidity.

Pathogenesis, Pathology, & Clinical Findings

T hominis and *T tenax* are generally considered to be harmless commensals. *T vaginalis* is capable of causing low-grade inflammation, particularly when the infection is heavy. The organisms have a toxic action on tissue culture cells and will produce extensive lesions in germ-free animals. The intensity of infection, the pH of vaginal and other secretions, the physiologic status of the vaginal and other genitourinary tract surfaces, and the accompanying bacterial flora are among the factors affecting pathogenicity. The organisms cannot survive at normal vaginal acidity of pH 3.8–4.4 or at the nearly neutral vaginal pH found in young girls and elderly women.

In the female, the infection is normally limited to vulva, vagina, and cervix; it does not usually extend to the uterus. The mucosal surfaces may be tender, inflamed, eroded, and covered with a frothy yellow or cream-colored discharge. In the male, the prostate, seminal vesicles, and urethra may be infected. Signs and symptoms in the female, in addition to profuse vaginal discharge, include local tenderness, vulval pruritus, and burning. About 10% of infected males have a thin, white urethral discharge.

Diagnostic Laboratory Tests

A. Specimens and Microscopic Examination: Vaginal or urethral secretions or discharge should be examined microscopically in a drop of saline or *Trichomonas* diluent for characteristic motile trichomonads. Dried smears may be stained with hematoxylin or one of the Romanowsky stains for later study.

B. Culture: Culture of vaginal or urethral discharge, of prostatic secretion, or of a semen specimen may reveal organisms when direct examination is negative.

Immunity

Infection confers no apparent immunity. Little is known about the immune responses to trichomonads.

Treatment

Successful treatment of vaginal infection requires destruction of the trichomonads, for which topical and systemic metronidazole (Flagyl) is the recommended drug; topical treatment for the restoration of normal vaginal epithelium and acidity; and measures to ensure that reinfection will not occur. The patient's sexual partner should be examined and treated simultaneously if necessary. Postmenopausal patients may require treatment with estrogens to improve the condition of the vaginal epithelium. For vaginal infections treated with metronidazole, topical treatment with Floraquin (a mixture containing diiodohydroxyquinoline, dextrose, lactose, and boric acid) or furazolidone-nifuroxime (Tricofuron) is usually effective. Prostatic infection can be cured with certainty only by systemic treatment with metronidazole.

Epidemiology & Control

T vaginalis is a common cosmopolitan parasite of both males and females. Infection rates vary greatly but may be quite high in some populations—often 40% or higher—particularly where the quality of female hygiene is poor. Coitus is the common mode of transmission, but contaminated towels, douche equipment, examination instruments, and other objects may be responsible for some new infections. Infants may be infected during birth. Most infections, in both sexes, are asymptomatic or cause inconsequential symptoms. Control of *T vaginalis* infections always requires detection and treatment of the infected male sexual partner at the same time that the infected female is treated; mechanical protection (condom) should be used during intercourse until the infection is eradicated in both partners.

T hominis is also cosmopolitan and common, particularly in the tropics. Transmission is by the fecal-oral route.

T tenax, apparently transmitted directly from mouth to mouth, is found throughout the world. The prevalence in some populations reaches 10–20%.

OTHER INTESTINAL FLAGELLATES

Retortamonas intestinalis, Chilomastix mesnili, and *Enteromonas hominis* are nonpathogenic intestinal parasites of humans that must be distinguished in the laboratory from the pathogenic amebas and flagellates.

Retortamonas intestinalis

This cosmopolitan but rare parasite lives as a commensal in the human intestine. The trophozoite is small, ovoid, and 4–9 μm long, with a single nucleus, a cytostome, and 2 flagella, one anterior and one emerging from the cytostome. The oval or pear-shaped cyst, 4–7 μm long, has a single nucleus, sometimes dumbbell-shaped, with fibrils along the margins of the cytostome. The organism can be cultivated in media suitable for the trichomonads. Laboratory diagnosis depends upon detection of the cysts or trophozoites in stool specimens. Transmission presumably takes place by ingestion of the cysts.

Enteromonas hominis

Human infections with this very small intestinal flagellate have been reported in many parts of the world. Although it is generally rare, high infection rates have been recorded in some populations. The oval trophozoite is 4–10 μm long, is uninucleate, and bears 4 flagella (3 anterior, one posterior). There is no cytostome. The cyst is oval and 6–8 μm long, with 1–4 nuclei. When the cyst is quadrinucleate, the nuclei are arranged in pairs at the poles. Cultivation is easy on ordinary flagellate media. Laboratory diagnosis and transmission are as for *R intestinalis*.

Chilomastix mesnili

This parasite, which can be confused with *Trichomonas* in the laboratory, is more common than *R intestinalis* and *E hominis*. It is found throughout the world. Some workers consider it to be mildly pathogenic, but there is little evidence to support this. The trophozoite is pear-shaped and 6–24 μm long, with anterior flagella, a large cytostome bearing a fourth flagellum, and a large single anterior nucleus. The spiral motion of the trophozoite is unlike that of *Trichomonas*. The distinctive cyst is lemon-shaped, uninucleate, and 7–10 μm long, with conspicuous fibrils forming the margins of the cytostome. Cultivation, laboratory diagnosis, and transmission are as for the 2 flagellates discussed above.

THE HEMOFLAGELLATES

The hemoflagellates of humans include the genera *Trypanosoma* and *Leishmania*. There are 2 distinct types of human trypanosomes: (1) African, causing sleeping sickness and transmitted by tsetse flies *(Glossina): Trypanosoma rhodesiense** and *Trypanosoma gambiense;** and (2) American, causing Chagas' disease and transmitted by cone-nosed bugs (*Triatoma*, etc): *Trypanosoma (Schizotrypanum) cruzi*. (Another species, *Trypanosoma rangeli* of South America, infects humans without causing disease.) The genus *Leishmania*, usually divided into 3 species infecting humans but more recently divided into 13 or more species, causes cutaneous (Oriental sore), mucocutaneous (espundia), and visceral (kala-azar) leishmaniasis. All forms of these infections are

---

*Sometimes called *Trypanosoma brucei rhodesiense* and *Trypanosoma brucei gambiense* because of the very close relationship and probable origin from *Trypanosoma brucei brucei*, the common antelope form and the cause of frequently fatal nagana in cattle.

transmitted by sandflies (*Phlebotomus* in the Old World, *Lutzomyia* and *Psychodopygus* in the New World).

The genus *Trypanosoma* appears in the blood as trypomastigotes, with elongated bodies supporting a lateral undulating membrane and a flagellum that borders the free edge of the membrane and emerges at the anterior end as a whiplike extension (see p 525). The kinetoplast, present in all forms found in humans, is a darkly staining body containing DNA, lying immediately adjacent to the tiny node (blepharoplast) from which the flagellum arises. Other developmental forms among the hemoflagellates include (1) a leishmanial rounded intracellular stage, the amastigote (see below and p 525); (2) a flagellated extracellular stage, the promastigote (formerly called leptomonad), a lanceolate form without an undulating membrane, with a kinetoplast at the anterior end; and (3) an epimastigote (formerly called crithidia), a more elongated extracellular stage with a short undulating membrane and a kinetoplast placed more posteriorly but still anterior to the nucleus.

In *Leishmania* life cycles, only the amastigote and promastigote are found, the latter being restricted to the insect vector. In *T cruzi*, all 3 may occur in humans, and trypomastigote and epimastigote in the vector. In African trypanosomes, the latter 2 flagellated stages also occur in the tsetse fly vector, but only the trypomastigote has been observed in humans—though recent research suggests that intracellular amastigotes occur in experimental mice and may be present in humans as well.

1. *LEISHMANIA*

The genus *Leishmania*, widely distributed in nature, has a number of species and subspecies that are nearly identical morphologically; in recent years, the number of identified species has increased from 3 to 13 or more. Differentiation is based on DNA buoyant density measurements; lysozyme and other enzyme studies; promastigote growth patterns in vitro in the presence of antisera; developmental characteristics of promastigotes in the specific sandfly vector; vectors, reservoir hosts, and other epidemiologic factors; and the clinical characteristics of the disease produced. Visceral leishmaniasis results from infection with *Leishmania donovani* (India, USSR, North China, East Africa), *Leishmania infantum* (Mediterranean region), and *Leishmania chagasi* (South America). Cutaneous leishmaniasis results from infection with *Leishmania tropica* (urban areas, Near and Middle East, Mediterranean littoral, USSR, Afghanistan, India); *Leishmania major* (ground-squirrel burrows in rural south-central USSR, Iran, Syria, Israel, Jordan, north and west Africa); *Leishmania aethiopica* (highlands of Ethiopia, Kenya, South Yemen); *Leishmania mexicana mexicana* (Mexico, Guatemala); *Leishmania mexicana amazonensis; Leishmania mexicana pifanoi* (diffuse cutaneous leishmaniasis; Venezuela); *Leishmania braziliensis braziliensis*

(Amazon basin, Central America); *Leishmania braziliensis guyanensis* (Guyanas, northern Brazil); *Leishmania braziliensis panamensis* (Panama); and *Leishmania peruviana* (uta; barren western Andes of Peru). The New World forms are all carried by sandflies of the genera *Lutzomyia* and *Psychodopygus;* Old World leishmaniae are transmitted by species of the genus *Phlebotomus*. These 13 forms present a range of clinical and epidemiologic characteristics that for convenience are combined here under 3 familiar clinical groupings: (1) visceral leishmaniasis (kala-azar), (2) cutaneous leishmaniasis (Oriental sore, Baghdad boil, Aleppo sore, wet cutaneous sore, dry cutaneous sore, pian bois, chiclero ulcer, uta, and other names), and (3) mucocutaneous or naso-oral leishmaniasis (espundia).

Morphology & Identification

A. Typical Organism: Only the first stage, the nonflagellated amastigote—formerly called the Leishman-Donovan (LD) body (see p 524)—occurs in the mammalian host. The sandfly transmits the infective promastigotes by bite. The promastigotes rapidly change to amastigotes after phagocytosis by macrophages, then multiply, filling the cytoplasm of the macrophages. The infected cells burst, the released parasites are again phagocytosed, and the process is repeated, producing a cutaneous lesion or visceral infection depending upon the species of parasite. The amastigotes are oval, $2-6 \times 1-3$ μm, with a laterally placed oval vesicular nucleus and a distinct dark-staining (Feulgen-positive) DNA portion of the kinetoplast, which is usually rodlike.

B. Culture and Growth Characteristics: In NNN or Tobie's medium, only the promastigotes are found. *L donovani* usually grows slowly, the promastigotes forming tangled clumps in the fluid. *L tropica* grows more quickly, promastigotes forming small rosettes attached by their flagella in the fluid, producing a fine granular appearance with a distinct surface film, while *L braziliensis* may produce a waxlike surface. In tissue cultures, intracellular amastigotes may be obtained in addition to the extracellular promastigotes.

C. Variations: Strain differences in virulence, tissue tropism or predilection, and biologic, epidemiologic, and pharmacodynamic characteristics have been observed with all species. Consequently, overlap and considerable variability in pathology and clinical pictures occur.

Pathogenesis, Pathology, & Clinical Findings

L donovani, the causative organism of kala-azar, spreads from the site of inoculation to multiply in reticuloendothelial cells, especially macrophages in spleen, liver, lymph nodes, and bone marrow. This is accompanied by vascularity and marked hyperplasia, especially of the spleen. Progressive emaciation is usually accompanied by remarkably little prostration in spite of growing weakness. There is irregular fever, sometimes hectic. Untreated cases showing symptoms of kala-azar usually are fatal. Some forms, especially

in India, develop a postcure florid cutaneous resurgence 1–2 years later (post-kala-azar dermal leishmanoid).

L tropica, L major, L mexicana, and other dermotropic forms induce a dermal lesion at the site of inoculation by the sandfly: cutaneous leishmaniasis, Oriental sore, Delhi boil, etc. Mucous membranes are rarely involved. The dermal layers are first affected, with cellular infiltration and proliferation of amastigotes intracellularly and spreading extracellularly, until the infection penetrates the epidermis and causes ulceration. Satellite lesions may be found (hypersensitivity or recidivans type of cutaneous leishmaniasis), rarely massively proliferated (anergic or diffusa type of cutaneous leishmaniasis). These are tuberculoid, sometimes with few or no parasites, and are regarded as anergic manifestations that may be unresponsive to treatment.

L braziliensis causes mucocutaneous or nasopharyngeal (naso-oral) leishmaniasis in South and Central America. It is known by many local names, the most familiar of which is espundia. The pathologic findings are the same as those of *L tropica* or *L mexicana* infections, but the initial lesions are more superficial and tend to metastasize to mucous surfaces, where they may form polypoid growths and long-lasting, fungating, destructive lesions. This is the characteristic clinical picture of espundia, most commonly found in the Amazon basin. At high altitudes in Peru, the clinical features (uta) tend to resemble those of Oriental sore. In Mexico and Guatemala, the ears are frequently involved (chiclero ulcer), usually with an indolent infection without ulceration and with few parasites.

Diagnostic Laboratory Tests

A. Specimens: Lymph node aspirates, scrapings, and biopsies are important in the cutaneous forms; lymph node aspirates, blood, and spleen or liver puncture are important in kala-azar. Purulent discharges are of no value for diagnosis, although nasal scrapings may be useful.

B. Microscopic Examination: Giemsa-stained smears and sections may show amastigotes, especially in material from kala-azar and under the rolled edges of cutaneous sores.

C. Culture: NNN medium is the medium most generally used. Blood culture is satisfactory only for *L donovani* and then often fails to detect infection; lymph node aspirates are suitable for all forms; and tissue aspirates, biopsy material, scrapings, or small biopsies from the edges of ulcers are useful for the cutaneous forms (and often for kala-azar also). A biphasic blood agar culture, Tobie's medium, is especially suitable. However, only promastigotes can be cultivated in the absence of living cells.

D. Serology: The formol-gel (aldehyde) test of Napier is a nonspecific test that depends on an elevated serum globulin in kala-azar: 1 drop of commercial formalin in 1 mL of serum forms an opalescent gel. The IHA (indirect hemagglutination antibody) test or the IFA (indirect fluorescent antibody) test may be useful but lacks sufficient sensitivity and may cross-react with *T cruzi*. A skin test is epidemiologically important in indicating past exposure to any of the leishmanias (Montenegro test).

Immunity

Recovery from cutaneous leishmaniasis confers a solid and permanent immunity, although it usually is species-specific and may be strain-specific as well. Natural resistance varies greatly among individuals, between different ages and sexes, and among various species of mammals. Vaccination significantly reduces the incidence of Oriental sore, especially if the more florid "wet" type (caused by *L major*) is the vaccine source.

Immunity to kala-azar may develop but varies with the time of treatment and condition of the patient.

Treatment

Single lesions may be cleaned, curetted, treated with antibiotics if secondarily infected, and then covered and left to heal. Pentavalent antimony sodium gluconate (Pentostam, Solustibosan) is the drug of choice for all forms. Pentamidine isethionate (Lomidine) is useful for kala-azar resistant to this drug. Cycloguanil pamoate in oil (Camolar) and amphotericin B (Fungizone) have been recommended for espundia, which is frequently quite unresponsive to treatment.

Epidemiology, Prevention, & Control

Kala-azar is found focally in most tropical and subtropical countries. Its local distribution is related to the prevalence of specific sandfly vectors. In the Mediterranean littoral and in middle Asia and South America, domestic and wild canids are reservoirs, and in the Sudan, various wild carnivores and rodents are reservoirs of endemic kala-azar. Control is aimed at destroying breeding places and dogs and protecting people from sandfly bites. Oriental sore occurs mostly in the Mediterranean region, North Africa, and the Middle and Near East. The "wet" type, caused by *L major,* is rural, and burrowing rodents are the main reservoir; the dry type, caused by *L tropica,* is urban, and humans are presumably the only reservoir. For *L braziliensis*, there are a number of wild but apparently no domestic animal reservoirs. Sandfly vectors are involved in all forms.

2. TRYPANOSOMA

Hemoflagellates of the genus *Trypanosoma* occur in the blood of mammals as mature elongated trypomastigotes. Other stages of the life cycle of *Trypanosoma cruzi* occur in mammalian tissues, but in all species a multiplying epimastigote stage precedes the formation of infective trypomastigotes (metacyclic trypanosomes) in the intermediate host, an insect vector. Trypanosomes cause trypanosomiasis (sleeping

sickness, Chagas' disease, and asymptomatic trypanosomiasis) in humans. The parent form in Africa is *Trypanosoma brucei* (causing nagana in livestock and game animals, with antelopes as a natural reservoir); the 2 human forms, *Trypanosoma rhodesiense* and *Trypanosoma gambiense,* are now regarded by some as subspecies of *T brucei,* as noted above. The 3 forms are indistinguishable morphologically but differ ecologically and epidemiologically.

Morphology & Identification

A. Typical Organisms: African *T gambiense* and *T rhodesiense* both vary in size and shape of the body and length of the flagellum (12–42 μm, usually 15–30 μm) but are essentially indistinguishable. "Slender forms" 25–30 μm long usually predominate over "stumpy forms" with short flagella. The latter form is infective to the insect host and possesses a full battery of enzymes for energy metabolism. The elongated form requires host metabolic assistance and is specialized for rapid multiplication in the vertebrate bloodstream. The same forms are seen in blood as in lymph node aspirates. Somewhat stumpy forms with posterior (as opposed to central) nuclei occur rather more frequently in *T rhodesiense* than in *T gambiense.* The blood forms of American *T cruzi* are present during the early acute stage and at intervals thereafter in smaller numbers. They are typical trypomastigotes, varying about a mean of 20 μm, frequently curved in a C shape when fixed and stained. An unusually large, rounded terminal kinetosome in stained preparations is characteristic and often diagnostic. The tissue forms most common in heart muscle, liver, and brain develop from amastigotes that have multiplied to form an intracellular colony after invasion of the host cell or phagocytosis of the parasite. *Trypanosoma rangeli* of South and Central America infects humans without causing disease and must therefore be carefully distinguished from the pathogenic species (see Table 41–1).

B. Culture: *T cruzi* and *T rangeli* are readily cultivated (3–6 weeks) in the epimastigote form in fluid or diphasic media. Diagnosis of patients in the early, blood-borne (acute) phase of infection can be aided by using the multiplying powers of parasites in

Table 41–1. Differentiation of *T cruzi* and *T rangeli*.

	T cruzi	*T rangeli*
Blood forms		
Size	20 μm	Over 30 μm
Shape	Often C-shaped in fixed preparations	Rarely C-shaped
Posterior kinetoplast	Terminal, large	Distinctly subterminal, small
Developmental stages in tissues	Amastigote to epimastigote	Not found (only trypomastigotes)
Triatomine bugs		
In salivary gland or proboscis (or both)	Always absent	Usually present
In hindgut or feces	Present	Present

laboratory-reared, clean vector insects (cone-nosed, kissing, or triatomine bugs) that have been allowed to feed on patients (xenodiagnosis)—see Diagnostic Laboratory Tests, below. In infected bugs, the 2 species can be distinguished by the fact that *T cruzi* is confined to the hindgut whereas *T rangeli* is usually present in the salivary glands also.

C. Growth Requirements: *T cruzi* requires at least hemin, ascorbic acid, and certain unidentified but dialyzable substances present in serum. The African forms require at least these for development, but neither these nor other known substances suffice to support development to the infective trypanosomal stage. The blood of some apparently uninfected persons inhibits growth of the African species.

D. Variation: The African blood forms are polymorphic, as noted above. The blood trypanosomes of *T cruzi* are monomorphic, but the tissue forms essentially repeat all developmental stages seen in the triatomine vector. Variation in virulence is well recognized: *T rhodesiense* is usually regarded as a virulent zoonotic form and *T gambiense* as a more chronic though still usually fatal form. Both may be morphologically stable or may produce waves of distinct serotypes in the human host, marked by alternation between slender and stumpy trypomastigote populations. These waves of antigenic variants induce a corresponding serologic response by the host. The parasite's antigenic variability is viewed as a means of continuously escaping the host's antibody response by producing a seemingly unlimited series of different antigenic membranes. *T gambiense* is of lower virulence to laboratory animals than *T rhodesiense,* but by passage it can be made to rival the latter in virulence. Strains of *T cruzi* of low virulence to laboratory animals and apparently also to humans are known, mostly from the southern USA and northern Mexico.

Pathogenesis, Pathology, & Clinical Findings

Infective trypanosomes of *T gambiense* and *T rhodesiense* are introduced through the bite of the tsetse fly and multiply at the site of inoculation to cause variable induration and swelling (the primary lesion), which may progress to form a trypanosomal chancre, spreading to lymph nodes, bloodstream, and, in terminal stages, to the central nervous system, where it produces the typical sleeping sickness syndrome: lassitude, inability to eat, tissue wasting, unconsciousness, and death. Infective forms of *T cruzi* pass to humans by inoculation of infected bug feces into the conjunctiva or a break in the skin, *not* by the bite of the bug (which is the mode of entry of the nonpathogenic *T rangeli*). At the site of inoculation, they progress from the amastigote to the promastigote and epimastigote stages and multiply to cause variable induration and swelling; they may form a skin lesion, or chagoma. Chagas' disease is common in infants, who show such dramatic acute responses that it is sometimes described as if it were a purely pediatric disorder. Particularly in children, unilateral swelling of the eyelids (Romaña's sign) is frequent and characteristic at onset. The primary lesion is accompanied by fever, acute regional lymphadenitis, and dissemination to blood and tissues. The parasites can usually be detected within 1–2 weeks as trypomastigotes in the blood. Subsequent developments depend upon the organs and tissues affected and on the nature of multiplication and release of toxins. The African forms multiply extracellularly as trypomastigotes in the blood as well as in the tissues. *T cruzi* multiplies mostly within reticuloendothelial cells, going through a cycle starting with large agglomerations of amastigotes. In both African and American forms, multiplication in the tissues is punctuated by phases of parasitemia with later destruction by the host of the blood forms, accompanied by characteristic bouts of intermittent fever gradually decreasing in intensity. Parasitemia is more common in *T rhodesiense* and is intermittent and scant with *T cruzi*.

The release of toxins explains much of the systemic as well as local or tissue reactions (eg, blood vessels and lymph sinuses in African forms; reaction around infected reticuloendothelial and other cells in the American form). The organs most seriously affected are the central nervous system and heart muscle. Interstitial myocarditis is extreme in Chagas' disease and is the most common serious element in the clinical picture. It is least evident in the chronic Gambian infection. Central nervous system involvement is most characteristic of African trypanosomiasis except that untreated Rhodesian infection often leads to death before brain damage occurs. *T rhodesiense,* a highly virulent organism, appears in the cerebrospinal fluid in about 1 month and *T gambiense* in several months, but both are present in small numbers. *T gambiense* infection is chronic and in about a year leads to progressive diffuse meningoencephalitis. The more rapidly fatal *T rhodesiense* produces the same condition of somnolence and coma only during the final weeks of a terminal infection. Other organs affected are the liver and spleen, especially with chronic *T cruzi* infection, which produces a vigorous reticuloendothelial system response, often simulating kala-azar (splenomegaly, hepatomegaly, bone marrow hyperplasia and engorgement).

Invasion of nerve plexuses in the alimentary tract walls leads to megaesophagus and megacolon, especially in the Brazilian strain of Chagas' disease. All 3 trypanosomes are transmissible through the placenta, and congenital infections are reported in hyperendemic areas.

Diagnostic Laboratory Tests

A. Specimens: Blood (thick and thin films, for culture and for serology), preferably collected when the temperature rises; cerebrospinal fluid, lymph node aspirate, and sometimes marrow primary lesion aspirates or splenic puncture are valuable for diagnostic tests. Uninfected cone-nosed bugs are required if xenodiagnosis of *T cruzi* is intended. The latter test can only be done during the early weeks of infection, the period of parasitemia, although periodic parasitemia may also occur in chronic infections.

B. Microscopic Examination: Fresh blood (or aspirated tissue in saline) is kept warm and examined immediately for the actively motile trypanosomes. Thick films may be stained by Field's rapid method or with Giemsa's stain. Thin films stained with Giemsa's stain are necessary for confirmation. Centrifugation may be necessary. Tissue smears must be stained for identification of the pretrypanosomal stages. Centrifuged cerebrospinal fluid should be similarly examined; there is seldom more than one trypanosome per milliliter. The most reliable tests are blood examinations for *T rhodesiense,* gland puncture for *T gambiense,* and cerebrospinal fluid examination for *T rhodesiense* and advanced *T gambiense.*

C. Culture: Any or all of the specimens required for microscopic examination may be inoculated into media such as Tobie's, Wenyon's semisolid, NNN, or Senekji's medium for attempted culture of *T cruzi* or *T rangeli.* The organisms are grown at 22–24 °C and subcultured every 1–2 weeks, centrifuged material being examined microscopically for trypanosomes. However, trypanosomes are usually very scanty in the blood in Chagas' disease except perhaps in the early acute phase. Culture of the African forms is unsatisfactory.

D. Animal Inoculation: *T cruzi* and *T rangeli* may be detected by inoculating blood intraperitoneally into a number of mice (when available, pups and kittens are animals of first choice). *T rhodesiense* is often detectable (and *T gambiense* with some effort) by this procedure in mice. Trypanosomes appear in the blood in a few days after successful inoculation.

E. Serology: A positive indirect IHA, IFA, or CF (Machado's) test provides confirmatory support in *T cruzi* infection. African forms cause IFA reactions, but these are of limited diagnostic value.

F. Xenodiagnosis: This is the method of choice in suspected Chagas' disease if other examinations are negative, especially during the early phase of disease onset. About 6 clean laboratory-reared triatomine bugs are fed on the patient, and their droppings are examined in 7–10 days for the various developmental forms. Defecation follows shortly after a fresh meal or may be forced by gently probing the bug's anus and then squeezing its abdomen—*taking care that the anus is in contact with a drop of saline or serum to prevent accidental self-infection by a sudden spray from the anus. Laboratory infection with* T cruzi *is a distinct hazard because of the lack of suitable chemotherapy and poor prognosis.* Xenodiagnosis is impracticable for the African forms.

G. Differential Diagnosis: *T rhodesiense* and *T gambiense* are morphologically identical but may be distinguished by their geographic distribution, vector species, and behavior in humans (since they cause different clinical pictures and are distributed differently in tissues and blood). In rats, *T rhodesiense* is usually more virulent. The differentiation of *T cruzi* from *T rangeli (T ariarii, T guatemalense)* is practicable and important, since *T rangeli* is innocuous. The points of differentiation are shown in Table 41–1.

Immunity

Humans apparently show some individual variation in natural resistance to all 3 pathogenic trypanosomes. Strain-specific complement-fixing and protecting antibodies can be detected in the plasma, and these presumably lead to the disappearance of blood forms. Tissue forms are apparently less accessible, and it is significant that each relapse of African trypanosomiasis is apparently due to a strain serologically distinct from the preceding one. Apart from such relapses, Africans free from symptoms may still have trypanosomes in the blood.

Treatment

There is no effective drug treatment for American trypanosomiasis, although Bayer-2502 (nifurtimox) may temporarily relieve some patients with trypomastigotes still present in the blood. African trypanosomiasis is treated principally with suramin sodium (Germanin) or pentamidine isethionate (Lomidine), the former preferably for *T gambiense* and the latter for *T rhodesiense.* Late disease with central nervous system involvement requires melarsoprol (Mel B), as well as suramin or tryparsamide in the presence of parasitemia and active infection of lymph nodes.

Epidemiology, Prevention, & Control

African trypanosomiasis is restricted to recognized tsetse fly belts. Broadly, *T gambiense,* transmitted mostly by the streamside tsetse *Glossina palpalis,* extends from west to central Africa and produces a relatively chronic infection with progressive central nervous system involvement. *T rhodesiense,* transmitted mostly by the woodland-savannah *Glossina morsitans,* is more restricted, being confined to the south and east of Lake Tanganyika, and therefore causes a smaller number of cases; but it is more virulent. Bushbuck and other antelopes may serve as reservoirs of *T rhodesiense,* whereas humans themselves are the principal reservoir of *T gambiense.* Control depends upon searching for and then isolating and treating patients with the disease; controlling movement of people in and out of fly belts; using insecticides in vehicles; and instituting fly control, principally with insecticides and by altering habitats. Contact with reservoir animals is difficult to control.

Chemoprophylaxis, eg, with suramin sodium, is difficult but may be considered.

American trypanosomiasis (Chagas' disease) is especially important in certain parts of Central and South America, although infection of animals with virulent or mild strains extends much more widely, eg, into the southern USA, and a few autochthonous human cases have been recently reported in Texas. Certain triatomine bugs become as domiciliated as bedbugs, and infection may be brought in by rats, opossums, or armadillos—which may themselves become domiciliated and then spread the infection to domestic animals. Since no effective treatment is known, it is particularly important to control the vectors with residual insecticides and habitat destruction and to avoid contact with animal reservoirs. Chagas' disease occurs largely among people in poor economic circumstances. An estimated 8,000,000 persons harbor the parasite, and many of these have an impaired heart and a resulting reduced life expectancy.

ENTAMOEBA HISTOLYTICA

Entamoeba histolytica is a parasite commonly found in the large intestine of humans, certain higher primates, and some domiciliated and commensal animals. Most cases are asymptomatic except in humans or among animals living under stress or unnatural conditions (eg, in zoo-held primates).

Morphology & Identification
A. Typical Organisms: Three stages are encountered: the active ameba, the inactive cyst, and the intermediate precyst. The ameboid trophozoite is the only form present in tissues and is also found in fluid feces during amebic dysentery. Its size is 15–30 μm. The cytoplasm is granular and may contain red cells (pathognomonic) but ordinarily contains no bacteria. Iron-hematoxylin or Gomori's trichrome staining shows the nuclear membrane to be lined by fine, regular granules of chromatin, forming a distinct, even network around the periphery; the karyosome is central, small, and deeply staining. Movement of trophozoites in fresh material is relatively brisk and usually unidirectional. Pseudopodia are fingerlike and broad, reactions that are absent at lower temperatures or with precystic amebas.

Cysts are present only in the lumen of the colon and in mushy or formed feces. Subspherical cysts of actively pathogenic amebas range from 10 to 20 μm, but smaller cysts (of debatable significance but now generally accepted as cysts of a nonpathogenic form, *Entamoeba hartmanni*) range down to 3.5 μm. These small forms (average, below 10 μm) are regarded as a distinct species *(E hartmanni)* or a distinct subspecies *(E histolytica* var *hartmanni).* The cyst wall, 0.5 μm thick, is hyaline. The initial uninucleate cyst may contain a glycogen vacuole and distinctly staining chromatoidal bodies or bars with characteristic rounded ends (in contrast to splinter chromatoidals in developing cysts of *Entamoeba coli*). Nuclear division within the cyst produces the final quadrinucleate cyst, during which time the chromatoid bodies and glycogen vacuoles disappear. Diagnosis in most cases rests on the characteristics of the cyst, since trophozoites usually appear only in diarrheic feces in active cases (see p 522) and survive for only a few hours, though they may be excellently preserved in polyvinyl alcohol (PVA). Stools may contain cysts with 1–4 nuclei depending on their degree of maturation. (See the Keys on pp 509–510.)
B. Culture: Trophozoites are readily studied in cultures; both encystation and excystation can be controlled.
C. Growth Requirements: Growth is most vig-

orous in various rich complex media under partial anaerobiosis at 37 °C and pH 7.0—with a mixed flora or at least a single coexisting species. Growth in tissue culture is also best under partial anaerobiosis.
D. Variation: Variations in cyst size are due to nutritional differences, possible host effects, or the occurrence of the small nonpathogenic form, *E hartmanni*. Possible change in behavior between a generally noninvasive commensal form and an invasive phase of the same population is generally considered unlikely, although use of corticosteroid drugs or other immunosuppressant treatment, concomitant infection, or other immunity-affecting insults could result in sudden upsurge of growth of a virulent strain.

Pathogenesis, Pathology, & Clinical Findings
Multiplication among trophozoites occurs by binary fission. The trophozoite emerges from the ingested cyst (metacyst) after activation of the excystation process in the stomach and duodenum. The metacyst divides rapidly, producing 4 amebulae (one for each cyst nucleus), each of which divides again to produce 8 small trophozoites per infective cyst. These pass to the cecum and produce a population of lumen-dwelling trophozoites. Disease results (in about 10% of infections) when the trophozoites invade the intestinal epithelium. Mucosal invasion by amebas with the aid of proteolytic enzymes occurs through the crypts of Lieberkühn, forming discrete ulcers with a pinhead-sized center and raised edges, from which mucus, necrotic cells, and amebas pass. The mucosal surface between ulcers typically is normal. Amebas multiply rapidly and accumulate above the muscularis mucosae, often spreading laterally. Healing may occur spontaneously with little tissue erosion if regeneration proceeds more rapidly than destruction, or the amebic trophozoites may break through the muscularis into the submucosa. Rapid lateral spread of the multiplying amebas follows, undermining the mucosa and producing the characteristic "flask-shaped" ulcer of primary amebiasis: a small point of entry, leading via a narrow neck through the mucosa into an expanded necrotic area in the submucosa. Bacterial invasion usually does not occur at this time, cellular reaction is limited, and damage is by lytic necrosis. Subsequent spread may coalesce colonies of amebas, undermining large areas of the mucosal surface. Trophozoites may penetrate the muscular coats and occasionally the serosa, leading to perforation into the peritoneal cavity. Subsequent enlargement of the necrotic area produces gross changes in the ulcer, which may develop shaggy overhanging edges, secondary bacterial invasion, and accumulation of neutrophilic leukocytes. Secondary intestinal lesions may develop as progeny spread from the primary lesion (usually in the cecum, appendix, or nearby portion of the ascending colon). The organisms are carried to lower sites in the bowel or may travel anteriorly to the ileocecal valve and terminal ileum, producing a chronic infection. The sigmoid colon and rectum are favored sites for these later lesions. An amebic inflammatory or granulomatous tumor-like

mass (ameboma) may form on the intestinal wall, which rarely will block the lumen. Though the latter condition readily recedes with antiamebic therapy, it usually is not identified until after surgical removal of an assumed carcinoma.

Factors that determine invasion of amebas include the number of amebas ingested, pathogenic capacity of the parasite strain, host condition (such as gut motility, immune competence, environmental, behavioral, and other epidemiologic conditions related to exposure), the presence of suitable enteric bacteria (which apparently produce the low redox potential required at the site of entry and possibly produce metabolic requirements as well), and the history of amebic passage (rapid passage during epidemics appears to enhance virulence). Amebas ingested in large numbers—even if of a relatively noninvasive strain—may have sufficient opportunities for invasion to overcome normal host resistance. Similarly, small numbers of amebas of high pathogenicity or virulence may produce active disease even in a healthy, amebatolerant host. Most infected persons, however, are not diseased but harbor only lumen-dwelling amebas that form cysts passed in the feces. Trophozoites, especially with red cells in the cytoplasm, found in liquid or semiformed stools are pathognomonic. Formed stools usually contain cysts only, while active cases with liquid stools (flecked with blood and mucus strands containing numerous amebas) usually pass trophozoites only. Symptoms vary greatly depending upon the site and intensity of lesions produced. Extreme abdominal tenderness, fulminating dysentery—30 or more movements a day—dehydration, and incapacitation occur in serious cases that involve much of the large intestine. In less acute disease, gradual onset of symptoms is the usual course, with episodes of diarrhea, abdominal cramps, nausea and vomiting, and an urgent desire to defecate. More frequently, there will be weeks of cramps and general discomfort, loss of appetite, and weight loss with general malaise. Symptoms may develop within 4 days of exposure in cases of immediate invasion, or may occur as much as a year later, after a delayed invasion of the intestinal wall. Persons may remain asymptomatic for years, develop tolerance to repeated reinfection, or develop a true immunity—though this is not clearly established. However, a change of host resistance, malnutrition (especially protein deficiency), or other stress conditions, as well as use of immunosuppressants as noted above, predispose the asymptomatic carrier to develop the full syndrome that follows from invasive disease.

Extraintestinal infection is assumed to be metastatic, since it rarely occurs by direct extension from the bowel. By far the most common form is amebic hepatitis or liver abscess (4% or more of clinical infections, with much variation in different populations), which is assumed to be due to microemboli, including trophozoites carried through the portal circulation. Abscess often develops without being clinically evident. It is assumed that hepatic microembolism (with trophozoites) is a common accompaniment of bowel lesions but that these diffuse focal lesions rarely progress. The slight hepatic enlargement and tenderness (and the chronically impaired liver function) encountered in acute, subacute, and chronic intestinal infection may be nonspecific. A true amebic abscess is progressive, nonsuppurative (but occasionally secondarily infected), and destructive without compression and formation of a wall. The contents are necrotic and typically sterile, active amebas being confined to the walls. A characteristic "anchovy paste" is produced in the abscess and is seen on surgical drainage. More than half of patients with amebic liver abscess give no history of intestinal infection, and only one-eighth of them pass cysts in their stools. Amebic abscesses also occur rarely elsewhere (eg, lung, brain, spleen, or draining through the body wall). Any organ or tissue in contact with active trophozoites may become a site of invasion and abscess.

Diagnostic Laboratory Tests

A. Specimens:

1. Fluid feces–

a. Fresh and warm for immediate examination for trophozoites.

b. Preserved in polyvinyl alcohol (PVA) or Merthiolate-iodine-formalin (MIF) fixative for mailing to a diagnostic laboratory (in a waterproofed or double mailing tube, the inner one of metal).

c. After a saline purge (or high enema after saline purge) for cysts and trophozoites.

2. Formed feces for cysts.

3. Scrapings and biopsies obtained through a sigmoidoscope.

4. Liver abscess aspirates collected in a series of samples of about 20 mL for detection of trophozoites. Discard all but the last sample.

5. Blood for serologic tests and cell counts.

B. Microscopic Examination: If possible, always examine fresh warm feces for trophozoites. Otherwise, stain smears with trichrome or iron-hematoxylin stain. The stools in amebic dysentery can usually be distinguished from those in bacillary dysentery by the fact that the former contain much fecal debris; small amounts of blood with strings of nontenacious mucus and red cells often degenerated and clumped; few polymorphonuclear cells or macrophages, though these are not degenerated as in bacillary dysentery; scattered Charcot-Leyden crystals; and trophozoites. Although considerable experience is required to distinguish *E histolytica* from commensal amebas (see below and pp 522–523), it is necessary to do so because misdiagnosis often leads to unnecessary treatment, overtreatment, or a failure to treat.

Differentiation of *E histolytica* (H) and *E coli* (C), the most common other intestinal ameba, can be made in stained smears as follows:

1. Trophozoites–The cytoplasm in H is glassy, with almost no inclusions except perhaps red cells and vacuoles (spherical when present). The cytoplasm in C is granular, with many bacterial and other inclusions and ellipsoid vacuoles. Ectoplasm usually is clearly demarcated in H but not in C. The nucleus of H has a very small central endosome and fine regular chromatin granules lining the periphery (sometimes in a crescentic distribution); that of C has a larger, eccentric endosome, and the peripheral chromatin is more coarsely beaded and less evenly distributed around the nuclear membrane; the nucleus at times appears to rest in a clear vacuole. Moribund trophozoites and precysts of H and C are usually indistinguishable.

2. Cysts–Glycogen vacuoles disappear during successive divisions. Nuclei resemble those of the trophozoites. Rare cysts of H and C may have 8 and 16 nuclei, respectively. Cysts of H in many preparations contain many uninucleate early cysts; these are rarely seen with C. Binucleate developing cysts of C often show the nuclei pushed against the cell wall by the large central glycogen vacuole. Chromatoidal bodies in early cysts of H are blunt-ended bars; those of C are splinterlike; do not have blunt, rounded ends; and often occur in clusters.

C. Culture: Diagnostic cultures are made in a layer of fluid overlying a solid nutrient base, partial anaerobiosis being produced by appropriate incubation or by use of thioglycolate. Dobell's diphasic and Cleveland-Collier media are most often used for diagnosis, and media such as Balamuth's for investigation.

D. Serology: The CF test is not always satisfactory because a good and highly specific antigen is not available. The indirect hemagglutination test is now used routinely and is of value when stool examinations are negative, as in extraintestinal amebiasis. Commercial preparations are available employing the latex agglutination technique (Serameba); Ouchterlony double diffusion (ParaTek); and counterelectrophoresis (Amoebogen). Positive responses to several tests are of value in supporting a tentative diagnosis in doubtful cases of extraintestinal amebiasis.

Treatment

Metronidazole (Flagyl) was considered the drug of choice but has been found to be mutagenic in bacteria and carcinogenic in experimental rats. It is still widely used, however, and is recommended for mild to severe intestinal disease, combined with diloxanide furoate (Furamide) *or* diiodohydroxyquin *or* paromomycin (Humatin) followed by chloroquine. For severe disease, dehydroemetine *or* emetine *or* metronidazole intravenously can be used, along with oral metronidazole *or* a tetracycline. The same drugs in various combinations can also be used for hepatic amebic abscess. For asymptomatic cyst passers, diloxanide furoate or diiodohydroxyquin is recommended. The latter drug may cause optic neuritis at high dosage or after long use, so the recommended dosage should be strictly followed. Owing to varying cure rates when depending upon single-drug therapy and to the danger of undetected liver infections, the following combined drug therapy is currently recommended for symptomatic cases: (1) For mild to moderate intestinal disease: metronidazole plus diloxanide furoate or diiodohydroxyquin; *or* paromomycin followed by chloroquine; *or* diloxanide furoate or diiodohydroxyquin plus a tetracycline followed by chloroquine; (2) For severe intestinal disease (amebic dysentery): dehydroemetine (or emetine), oxytetracycline, and diloxanide furoate, followed by chloroquine; *or* metronidazole followed by diloxanide furoate. (3) For hepatic or other extraintestinal involvement, or for ameboma: metronidazole followed by diloxanide furoate, plus chloroquine; *or* dehydroemetine (or emetine) plus chloroquine and diloxanide furoate. (See Catchpool, 1980, for pharmacology and dosages; see Drugs for parasitic infections, *Med Lett Drugs Ther,* for adverse effects and commercial sources of drugs.)

Epidemiology, Prevention, & Control

Cysts are usually ingested through contaminated water. In the tropics, contaminated vegetables and food are also important cyst sources; flies have been incriminated in areas of fecal pollution. Asymptomatic cyst passers are the main source of contamination and may be responsible for severe epidemic outbreaks where sewage leaks into the water supply or breakdown of sanitary discipline occurs (as in mental, geriatric, or children's institutions). A high-carbohydrate, low-protein diet favors the development of amebic dysentery both in experimental animals and in known human cases. Control measures consist of improving environmental and food sanitation. Treatment of carriers is controversial, although it is agreed that these people should be barred from food handling. The danger of transformation from an asymptomatic lumen infection to an invasive tissue disease as well as possible environmental contamination should be considered in the treatment decision for an asymptomatic cyst passer. No fully satisfactory and safe drug is yet available for chemoprophylaxis, and the mix of drugs required for therapy attests to the problems and still unsatisfactory state of the treatment of amebiasis.

OTHER INTESTINAL AMEBAS

Entamoeba histolytica must be distinguished from 4 other amebalike organisms that are also intestinal parasites of humans: (1) *Entamoeba coli* (see also above), which is very common; (2) *Dientamoeba fragilis,* the only intestinal parasite (actually an ameboflagellate) other than *E histolytica* that has been suspected of causing diarrhea and dyspepsia, but in the manner of *Giardia* and not by invasion; (3) *Iodamoeba bütschlii;* and (4) *Endolimax nana.* These amebas and their cysts are illustrated on pp 522 and 523. To facilitate detection, cysts should be concentrated by the formalin-ether sedimentation technique or the zinc sulfate flotation technique. Unstained, trichrome- or iron-hematoxylin-stained, and iodine-stained preparations should be searched systematically. Mixed infections may occur. Polyvinyl alcohol (PVA) fixation is especially valuable for preservation of trophozoites; Merthiolate-iodine-formalin (MIF) is of particular usefulness for population surveys. The presence of nonpathogenic amebas is strongly indicative of poor sanitation or of accidental fecal contamination—both warnings of possible exposure to pathogenic *E histolytica*.

Key for Identification of Amebic Trophozoites

Examine fresh warm feces or, if this is impracticable, feces that have been promptly preserved while still fresh and warm. Include exudate and flecks of mucus in the specimen.

(1) If all trophozoites have one nucleus, see paragraph (2), below.

If more than half of trophozoites have 2 nuclei, the organism is

Dientamoeba fragilis—a small (mostly 5–15 μm), rounded, amebalike organism with nuclei containing a large chromatin mass in a clear space; no peripheral chromatin and no cysts. *D fragilis* prevalence is sometimes high in institutional populations. Often overlooked.

(2) If nucleus has peripheral granules, see paragraph (3), below.

If the nucleus has no peripheral granules, has a subspherical endosome larger than the radius of the nucleus, and is surrounded by large light granules, the organism is

Iodamoeba bütschlii—an ameba with a characteristic cyst (see below). Its prevalence is usually very low.

(3) If the peripheral granules of the nucleus are regularly arranged and the endosome is small, see paragraph (4), below.

If the peripheral granules are scattered and scarce and the endosome is irregular and much larger than the radius of the nucleus, the organism is

Endolimax nana—a small organism that may be present in 15–20% of some populations.

(4) If the cytoplasm is not coarsely granular, nuclei are always invisible in saline preparations, trophozoites move steadily and in one direction by streaming into blunt pseudopods, and some contain erythrocytes undergoing digestion but not bacteria; or if in a trichrome-stained preparation the nuclear membrane is delicate and lined with a

single layer of fine chromatin granules and the karyosome is minute and central, the organism is either

Entamoeba histolytica—The pathogenic trophozoites are present only in dysenteric or diarrheal fluid feces and are usually large (20–60 μm). (*Do not confuse with macrophages containing erythrocytes;* these may also contain bacteria, and they do not progress in one direction with single blunt pseudopods.) Verify identification by examining a series of stool specimens and searching for identifiable cysts. Pathogenic trophozoites are most often found in flecks of mucoid exudate.

or

Entamoeba hartmanni (*E histolytica* var *hartmanni*, or small race *E histolytica* of some authors)—nonpathogenic and present in fluid or formed feces, always small (8–15 μm). See Cysts, below.

If present in fluid, semiformed, or formed feces; the cytoplasm is coarsely granular; nuclei are sometimes visible in saline preparation; trophozoites do not move progressively but protrude pseudopods in several directions simultaneously; and the cytoplasm contains bacteria but not erythrocytes; or if in trichrome preparations, the nuclear membrane is distinct and lined with large and irregular chromatin granules; or if larger than 15 μm, the organism is

Entamoeba coli—a normal commensal that may be almost impossible to differentiate from *E histolytica* in a fluid stool, except in the cystic state (see below).

Key for Identification of Amebic Cysts

No cysts are known for *Dientamoeba fragilis*.

(1) If mature cysts have 4 nuclei, see paragraph (2), below.

If mature cysts are often irregularly shaped, have 1–2 large nuclei with a large eccentric karyosome and an adjoining cluster of granules and a large iodine-staining vacuole, the organism is

Iodamoeba bütschlii.

If mature cysts have 8 nuclei, the organism is

Entamoeba coli.

(2) If quadrinucleate cysts are oval or ellipsoid and the nuclei have distinct large chromatin masses, the organism is

Endolimax nana.

If the cysts are spherical and the nuclei have regular peripheral chromatin granules and a small karyosome, the organism is

Entamoeba histolytica or *Entamoeba hartmanni* (mean diameters respectively above and below 10 μm).

FREE–LIVING AMEBAS

Primary amebic meningoencephalitis has been reported in about 75 cases in Europe and North America from amebic invasion of the brain. The free-living soil amebas *Naegleria fowleri, Acanthamoeba castellani,* and *Hartmanella* species have been implicated. Most cases have developed in children who were swimming in contaminated outdoor pools. The amebas apparently enter via the nose and the cribiform plate of the ethmoid, passing directly into brain tissue, where they rapidly form nests of amebas that cause extensive hemorrhage and damage, chiefly in the basilar portions of the cerebrum and the cerebellum. In all but a few cases, death ensued in less than a week. Entry of *Acanthamoeba* into the central nervous system from long-lasting sores in the skin has also been reported. Diagnosis is by microscopic examination of the cerebrospinal fluid, which contains the trophozoites and red cells but no bacteria. Amebas can be readily cultured on nonnutrient agar plates seeded with *Escherichia coli.* These soil amebas are distinguished by a large, distinct nucleus, by the presence of contractile vacuoles and mitochondria (absent in *Entamoeba*), and by cysts with a single nucleus and lacking glycogen or chromatoidal bodies. *Acanthamoeba* may encyst in invaded tissues, whereas *Naegleria* does not. Treatment with amphotericin B has been successful in a few cases, chiefly when diagnosis can be made quickly.

THE PLASMODIA

The sporozoan protozoa of the genus *Plasmodium* are pigment-producing ameboid intracellular parasites of vertebrates, with one habitat in red cells and another in cells of other tissues. Transmission to humans is by the bloodsucking bite of females of various species of mosquitoes of the genus *Anopheles.*

Morphology & Identification

A. Typical Organisms: There are at least 5 species of plasmodia that may infect humans: *Plasmodium vivax, Plasmodium ovale, Plasmodium malariae, Plasmodium falciparum,* and *Plasmodium*

knowlesi. Natural transmission of *P knowlesi* to humans has only been demonstrated in Malaysia. In addition, at least 2 species of nonhuman primate plasmodia, *Plasmodium cynomolgi* and *Plasmodium brasilianum,* are transmissible to humans experimentally and probably also in nature. The morphology and certain other characteristics of the 4 principal species that infect humans are summarized in Table 41–2. (See also illustrations on p 525.) *P cynomolgi* is similar to *P vivax* in morphology and in erythrocytic cycle length. *P knowlesi,* morphologically distinct from the other species, is also unique in having a 24-hour erythrocytic cycle.

B. Culture: Human malaria parasites have been successfully cultivated in fluid media containing serum, erythrocytes, inorganic salts, and various growth factors and amino acids. Continuous cultivation of the erythrocytic phase undergoing schizogony (asexual multiple division) has been achieved by Trager and Jensen at Rockefeller University (*Science* 1976;**193:**673). Avian plasmodia also can be grown in tissue cultures as well as in chick or duck embryos. Studies in culture have provided much fundamental biologic information about these protozoa.

C. Growth Characteristics and Requirements: In host red cells, the parasites convert hemoglobin to globin and hematin, which becomes modified into the characteristic malarial pigment. Globin is split by proteolytic enzymes and digested. Oxygen, dextrose, lactose, and erythrocytic protein are also utilized. Growth requirements, in addition to carbohydrates, proteins, and fats, include methionine, riboflavin, ascorbic acid, pantothenic acid, and p-aminobenzoic acid.

D. Variation: Variations of strains exist within each of the 4 typical species that infect humans. Variations have been detected in morphology, pathogenicity, resistance to drug therapy, infectivity for mosquitoes, and other characteristics. Immunity is usually both strain- and stage-specific.

Pathogenesis, Pathology, & Clinical Findings

Human infection results from the bite of an infected female *Anopheles* mosquito, in which occurs the sexual or sporogonic cycle of development (production of infective sporozoites). The first stage of development in humans takes place in parenchymal cells of the liver (the preerythrocytic or exoerythrocytic cycle), after which numerous asexual progeny, the merozoites, leave the ruptured liver cells, enter the bloodstream, and invade erythrocytes. Parasites in the red cells multiply in a species-characteristic fashion, breaking out of their host cells synchronously. This is the erythrocytic cycle, with successive broods of merozoites appearing at 48-hour intervals (*P vivax, P ovale,* and *P falciparum*) or every 72 hours (*P malariae*). The incubation period includes the exoerythrocytic cycles (usually 2) and at least one or 2 erythrocytic cycles. For *P vivax* and *P falciparum,* this period is usually 10–15 days, but it may be much longer (in some cases even months). The incubation

Table 41–2. Some characteristic features of the malaria parasites of humans (Romanowsky-stained preparations).

	P vivax (Benign Tertian Malaria)	*P malariae* (Quartan Malaria)	*P falciparum* (Malignant Tertian Malaria)	*P ovale* (Ovale Malaria)
Parasitized red cells	Enlarged, pale. Fine stippling (Schüffner's dots). Primarily invades reticulocytes, young red cells.	Not enlarged. No stippling (except with special stains). Primarily invades older red cells.	Not enlarged. Coarse stippling (Maurer's clefts). Invades all red cells regardless of age.*	Enlarged, pale. Schüffner's dots conspicuous. Cells often oval, fimbriated, or crenated.
Level of usual maximum parasitemia	Up to 30,000/μL of blood.	Less than 10,000/μL.	May exceed 200,000/μL; commonly 50,000/μL.	Less than 10,000/μL.
Ring stage trophozoites	Large rings (1/3–1/2 red cell diameter). Usually one chromatin granule; accolé forms (adherent to outer surface of red cell) rare; ring delicate.	Large rings (1/3 red cell diameter). Usually one chromatin granule; ring compact.	Small rings (1/5 red cell diameter). Often 2 granules; frequent accolé forms; multiple infections common; ring delicate.	Large rings (1/3 red cell diameter). Usually one chromatin granule; ring dense.
Pigment in developing trophozoites	Fine; light brown; scattered.	Coarse; dark brown; scattered clumps; abundant.	Coarse; black; few clumps.	Coarse; dark yellow-brown; scattered.
Older trophozoites	Very pleomorphic.	Occasional band forms.	Compact and rounded.*	Compact and rounded.
Mature schizonts (segmenters)	More than 12 merozoites (14–24).	Less than 12 large merozoites (6–12). Often in rosette.	Usually more than 12 merozoites (8–32). Very rare in peripheral blood.*	Less than 12 large merozoites (6–12). Often in rosette.
Gametocytes	Round or oval.	Round or oval.	Crescentic.	Round or oval.
Distribution in peripheral blood	All forms.	All forms.	Only rings and crescents (gametocytes).*	All forms.

*Ordinarily, only ring stages or gametocytes are seen in peripheral blood infected with *P falciparum*; postring stages make red cells sticky, and they tend to be retained in deep capillary beds except in overwhelming, usually fatal infections.

period of *P malariae* averages about 28 days. *P falciparum* multiplication is confined to the red cells after the first liver cycle. Without treatment, falciparum infection ordinarily will terminate spontaneously in less than 1 year (usually 6–8 months) unless it ends fatally in a shorter period. The other 3 species continue to multiply in liver cells long after the initial bloodstream invasion, or, it is now thought, there may be a *delayed* multiplication in the liver. These exoerythrocytic cycles coexist with erythrocytic cycles and may persist as "hypnozoites," nongrowing resting forms, after the parasites have apparently disappeared from the peripheral blood. Resurgence of an erythrocytic infection (relapse) occurs when merozoites from the liver are not phagocytosed in the bloodstream and succeed in reestablishing a red cell infection (clinical malaria). *P vivax* and *P ovale* infections may persist without treatment for as long as 5 years. *P malariae*

infections lasting 40 years have been reported, though these are thought to be *recrudescences* of a cryptic erythrocytic infection rather than true relapses from a liver infection.

During the erythrocytic cycles, certain merozoites enter red cells and become differentiated as male or female gametocytes. The sexual cycle therefore begins in the vertebrate host, but then for its continuation into the sporogonic phase, the gametocytes must be taken up and ingested by bloodsucking female *Anopheles* as outlined in Fig 41–1, p 512.

P vivax, *P malariae*, and *P ovale* parasitemias are relatively low-grade, primarily because the parasites favor either young or old red cells but not both; *P falciparum* invades red cells of all ages, and the parasitemia may be very high. *P falciparum* also causes the parasitized red cells to agglutinate and adhere to the endothelial lining of blood vessels, with

Table 41–3. Time factors of the various plasmodia in relation to cycles.

	Length of Sexual Cycle (in mosquito at 27 °C)	Prepatent Period* (in humans) (preerythrocytic cycle)	Length of Asexual Cycle (in humans)
P vivax (tertian or vivax malaria)	8–9 days	8 days	48 hours
P malariae (quartan or malariae malaria)	15–20 days	15–16 days	72 hours
P falciparum (malignant tertian or falciparum malaria)	9–10 days	5–7 days	36–48 hours
P ovale (ovale malaria)	14 days	9 days	48 hours

*Preerythrocytic period only. Full incubation period before clinical malaria usually includes prepatent period (which ends 48 hours after infection of the erythrocytes) plus 2 or 3 erythrocytic schizogonic cycles and may extend over a much longer time.

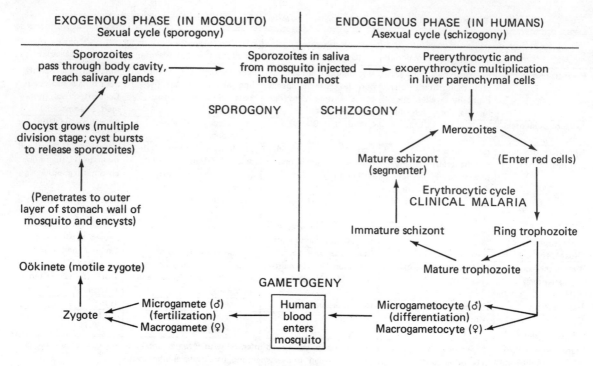

Figure 41–1. Life cycle of the malaria parasites. Continuous cycling or delayed multiplication in the liver may cause periodic relapse over several years (2–3 years in *P ovale*, 6–8 years in *P vivax*), and a low-level blood infection may have a long-delayed resurgence of multiplication (recrudescence) in *P malariae*. However, relapse does not occur with *P falciparum,* though a long prepatent period may occur (perhaps drug-suppressed), resulting in initial symptoms appearing up to 6 months or more after exposure.

resulting obstruction, thrombosis, and local ischemia. *P falciparum* infections are therefore frequently more serious than the others, with a much higher rate of severe or fatal complications (cerebral malaria, malarial hyperpyrexia, gastrointestinal disorders, algid malaria, blackwater fever).

P malariae has also been implicated in a nephrotic syndrome in children—"quartan nephrosis"—with a peak incidence at about age 5. It is characterized by generalized edema, oliguria, massive proteinuria, and hypoproteinemia. Tubular degeneration is visible in renal biopsy specimens. Glomerular lesions include basement membrane thickening and sometimes fibrosis. An antigen-antibody complex to quartan malaria or an autoimmune response to the sensitized kidney may be responsible for the patchy, membranous glomerulonephrosis; progressive sclerosis; and secondary tubular changes. According to Maegraith, it is a degenerative, not an inflammatory, condition and is therefore a nephrosis and not a nephritis. The prognosis is good with early diagnosis, poor in advanced disease. The response to antimalarials given before irreversible renal changes occur is usually good.

Periodic paroxysms of malaria are closely related to events in the bloodstream. An initial chill, lasting from 15 minutes to 1 hour, begins as a generation of parasites rupture their host red cells and escape into the blood. Nausea, vomiting, and headache are common

at this time. The succeeding febrile stage, lasting several hours, is characterized by a spiking fever, sometimes reaching 40 °C or more. During this stage, the parasites presumably invade new red cells. The third, or sweating, stage concludes the episode. The fever subsides, and the patient falls asleep and later awakes feeling relatively well. In the early stages of infection, the cycles are frequently asynchronous and the fever pattern irregular; later, the paroxysms may recur at regular 48- or 72-hour intervals. As the disease progresses, splenomegaly and, to a lesser extent, hepatomegaly appear. A normocytic anemia also develops, particularly in *P falciparum* infections.

Diagnostic Laboratory Tests

A. Specimens and Microscopic Examination: The thick blood film stained with one of the Romanowsky stains (usually Giemsa's) is the mainstay of malaria diagnosis. This preparation concentrates the parasites and permits detection even of light infections. Examination of thin blood films, also stained with Giemsa's stain, is necessary as a second step for parasite species differentiation.

B. Other Laboratory Findings: Normocytic anemia of variable severity, with poikilocytosis and anisocytosis, may be detected. During the paroxysms there may be transient leukocytosis; subsequently, leukopenia develops, with a relative increase in large mononuclear cells. Hepatic function tests may give abnormal results during attacks, but liver function reverts to normal with treatment or spontaneous recovery. The presence of protein and casts in the urine of children with *P malariae* is suggestive of quartan nephrosis. In severe *P falciparum* infections, renal damage may cause oliguria and the appearance of casts, protein, and red cells in the urine.

Immunity

The mechanisms of immunity in malaria have been the cause of considerable study but are still not clearly understood. An acquired strain-specific immunity has been observed that appears to depend upon the presence of parasites in the bloodstream of the host. This so-called **premunition,** or **concomitant immunity,** is soon lost after the parasites disappear from the blood. Exoerythrocytic forms in the liver cannot alone support premunition, and they elicit no host inflammatory response. Hence, superinfection of the liver by homologous strains can continue to occur. Premunition is heavily dependent upon the reticuloendothelial system, which becomes extremely active in patent malaria infections (ie, infection with detectable blood forms). In addition to acquired strain-specific immunity, natural genetically determined partial immunity to malaria occurs in some populations, notably in Africa, where sickle cell disease, glucose-6-phosphate dehydrogenase deficiency, thalassemia, and perhaps other disorders of the hematologic system appear to provide some protection against lethal levels of *P falciparum* infection (though low-level chronic or continually reacquired infection is widespread in these populations). Considerable research efforts to develop a prophylactic vaccine are under way, but so far with limited success.

Treatment & Prevention

Chloroquine (Aralen), the drug of choice for treatment of all forms of malaria during the acute attack, is given as a standard 1.5-g course of chloroquine (base) over a 3-day period. There is no record of *P vivax* resistant to chloroquine, so the standard course should clear the bloodstream of this species. This drug will also terminate susceptible *P falciparum* infections, in which there are no exoerythrocytic forms. Primaquine, which disposes of the exoerythrocytic tissue forms, must be used in conjunction with chloroquine to achieve complete cure of other forms of malaria. There is no satisfactory alternative to primaquine for eradication of tissue forms, but other compounds, eg, amodiaquine (Camoquin), quinine, and proguanil (Paludrine), are available for treatment of acute attacks. Drug-resistant strains of *P falciparum* should be treated with quinine (intravenously in severe cases), with pyrimethamine and either sulfadiazine or dapsone, or with sulfadoxine plus pyrimethamine.

Suppressive prophylaxis can be achieved with chloroquine diphosphate or amodiaquine except in chloroquine-resistant falciparum areas, such as Southeast Asia, parts of South America, and recently Mombasa and other areas of East Africa. In these areas,

various combinations of quinine and sulfonamides, dapsone and sulfadoxine, or pyrimethamine plus sulfadiazine (Fansidar—now available in the USA) must be relied upon, though resistance to these combinations has also been found in many areas of Southeast Asia. The problem is clearly still with us and is probably becoming more acute—one reason for the increased interest in development of an antimalarial vaccine.

In pregnancy, continued prophylaxis with chloroquine (not pyrimethamine or a sulfonamide) is essential, because of the danger of transplacental transmission of malarial agents to the fetus and the highly deleterious effects that can occur.

Epidemiology & Control

Malaria today is generally limited to the tropics and subtropics; in years past, transmission occurred in many temperate regions. Temperate zone malaria is usually unstable and relatively easy to control or eradicate; tropical malaria is often more stable, difficult to control, and far more difficult to eradicate. In the tropics, malaria generally disappears at altitudes above 6000 feet. *P vivax* and *P falciparum*, the most common species, are found throughout the malaria belt. *P malariae* is also broadly distributed but considerably less common. *P ovale* is rare except in West Africa, where it seems to replace *P vivax*. All forms of malaria can be artifically transmitted by blood transfusion or shared needles among addicts when one is infected. Such cases of "needle malaria" do not develop a liver or exoerythrocytic infection; thus, relapse does not occur. Natural infection (other than transplacental transmission) takes place only through the bite of an infected female *Anopheles* mosquito.

Malaria control depends upon elimination of mosquito breeding places, personal protection against mosquitoes (screens, netting, repellents), suppressive drug therapy for exposed persons, and adequate treatment of cases and carriers. Eradication, a highly complex field, requires elimination of contact between *Anopheles* mosquitoes and humans for a sufficient length of time to permit elimination of all cases in an area by treatment and by spontaneous cure. At the end of this period, a state of anophelinism-without-malaria will theoretically have been achieved. The results of massive efforts in highly endemic tropical areas have thus far been disappointing. Many costly eradication projects that have been under way for the past 20 years are being replaced with extended control programs specifically geared to the mosquito vector ecology and the malaria epidemiology of each area.

ISOSPORA

Isospora belli and *Isospora hominis* are sporozoan protozoa of the human intestine, the cause of coccidiosis or isosporosis. Numerous species of intestinal sporozoa or coccidia, some of them important pathogens, occur in other animals and are causes of some of the most pathogenic and economically important diseases of domestic mammals and fowl.

Morphology & Identification

A. Typical Organisms: Although all life cycle stages are known for many species of coccidia, only the elongated ovoid oocysts are known for *I belli* and *I hominis*. The life cycles of these parasites in humans have never been adequately studied, but intestinal biopsies of patients with chronic isosporosis recently demonstrated asexual schizogonic and sexual phases. Important new information is also available from studies with *Sarcocystis* (see *Sarcocystis lindemanni,* below). The oocyst of *I hominis* is about $16 \times 10~\mu m$; that of *I belli* is larger, $25-33 \times 12-16~\mu m$. The oocyst may contain a single sporoblast (developmental stage), 2 sporoblasts, or 2 sporocysts, each with 4 sporozoites (the mature oocyst). *I belli* oocysts are often monosporoblastic; *I hominis* oocysts are more often disporoblastic or even disporocystic. In addition, the *I belli* oocyst wall is often asymmetric, whereas that of *I hominis* is smoothly ovoid or spherical.

B. Culture: These parasites have not been cultivated.

Pathogenesis & Clinical Findings

Isospora species that infect humans inhabit the small intestine, where schizogony takes place below the intestinal epithelial cells. Oocysts are shed into the intestinal lumen and pass out in the stools. Signs and symptoms of coccidiosis apparently are due to the invasion and multiplication of the parasites in the intestinal mucosa. Infections may be silent or symptomatic. About 1 week after ingestion of viable cysts, a low-grade fever, lassitude, and malaise may appear, followed soon by mild diarrhea and vague abdominal pain. The infection has been thought to be self-limited after 1–2 weeks, but a recent review describes cases with diarrhea, weight loss, and fever lasting from 6 weeks to 6 months. Symptomatic coccidiosis is more common in children than in adults. Chronic infections previously recorded were in poorly nourished populations living under unsanitary conditions where continued reinfection was possible.

Diagnostic Laboratory Tests

Diagnosis rests upon detection of the immature oocysts of *I belli* or the mature oocysts and sporocysts of *I hominis* in fresh stool specimens. Stool concentration techniques are usually necessary.

Immunity

Immunity to the coccidia following active infection is well documented in animals, although data from human infection are lacking. The many coccidia species are notably host-specific.

Treatment

Treatment of mild cases consists of bed rest and a bland diet for a few days. No specific treatment has been described for more severe and chronic cases.

Epidemiology

Human coccidiosis is usually sporadic and most common in the tropics and subtropics, although high prevalence rates have been described for Rumania, Holland, and Chile. It is moderately endemic in parts of South Africa, several South American countries, and islands of the southwest Pacific. More than 800 cases have so far been reported in the western hemisphere, including more than 40 from the USA (California and the southeastern states). The infection is easily overlooked on routine stool examination for parasites and is probably more common than the records indicate. New infections result from ingestion of viable cysts.

SARCOCYSTIS LINDEMANNI

Sarcocystis lindemanni of humans, along with other species of *Sarcocystis,* is a protozoan that has recently been shown to be a coccidian. These parasites, some species of which are pathogenic, are found in the muscles of many kinds of vertebrate animals. Human volunteers fed raw beef and pork with *Sarcocystis* cysts later passed *Isospora*-like oocysts in their stools. Similar results have been obtained with dogs and cats. No tissue phase of *Isospora* has yet been found, though recent experimental evidence in laboratory animals suggests that *Sarcocystis* may be the tissue stage of *Isospora* in humans. It now appears likely that *Isospora belli* will prove to be the intestinal, or sexual, phase of a species of *Sarcocystis.* This controversial subject is currently a matter of intensive research interest.

Morphology & Identification

In the muscles, the parasites develop in elongated cysts, known as sarcocysts or "Miescher's tubes," measuring from less than 1 mm to several centimeters in length. The sarcocyst is partitioned by septa into chambers containing many uninucleate crescentic spores, or "Rainey's corpuscles." The mature corpuscle, properly called a **cystozoite,** is a trophozoite comparable to the merozoite of *Plasmodium* that develops into a gametocyte. It is $10-15~\mu m$ in length and pointed at one end and rounded at the other, with an oval vacuole near the pointed end. The cystozoites, when set free by rupture of the cyst, are motile; they have occasionally been found in blood films from mammalian hosts. *S lindemanni* of humans is morphologically indistinguishable from species found in other animals.

Pathogenesis & Clinical Findings

Heavy *Sarcocystis* infections may be fatal in some species of animals (eg, mice, sheep, swine). Extracts of the parasite contain a toxin, sarcocystin, which is probably responsible for the pathogenic effects. This toxin is fatal when injected into rabbits. About 15 cases of human infection have been reported, mostly at autopsy following death due to other causes;

however, inapparent infections are probably common. It is not clear that the parasite is pathogenic for humans. Fleeting subcutaneous swellings, eosinophilia, and heart failure have, however, been attributed to *S lindemanni*. Sarcocysts have been found in humans in the heart, larynx, and tongue as well as in the skeletal muscles of the extremities.

Diagnostic Laboratory Tests

Since the infection ordinarily causes no symptoms or signs in humans, it is usually detected only at autopsy. A reliable CF test has been developed for detection of suspected infections. Other tests should be developed now that *Isospora*-like sporocysts and oocysts have been found in the feces of volunteers fed *Sarcocystis* cysts. The feces of humans, cats, and dogs who have an experimental *Sarcocystis* infection generally demonstrate sporocysts separated from their thin-walled oocysts (rather than the intact oocysts seen in other coccidial infections).

Treatment

There is no known effective treatment.

Epidemiology

Sarcocystis shows little host specificity; cross-infections between various hosts can easily be produced. Since most *Sarcocystis* species are morphologically identical, it is likely that many of the described species (including *S lindemanni*) are not valid. Humans are probably infected by ingestion of raw or poorly cooked infected lamb, beef, or other meats. *Sarcocystis* infections are particularly common in sheep, cattle, and horses. There appears to be a 2-host cycle, with sarcocysts being formed in the muscles of **herbivores** (including humans) and oocysts in the intestines of **predators** such as cats and dogs (and humans). Humans appear to be able to develop both the asexual form of the parasite (sarcocysts in muscles) and the sexual form (oocysts in the intestine). Herbivores are infected by eating grass contaminated with oocysts or sporocysts, and predators are infected when they eat infected herbivore tissues.

TOXOPLASMA GONDII

Toxoplasma gondii is a coccidian protozoan of worldwide distribution that infects a wide range of animals and birds but does not appear to cause disease in them. The normal final hosts are the cat and other members of the family Felidae. The organism in humans produces either neonatal or postnatal toxoplasmosis. The former is usually of great severity and the latter generally much less so. The great majority of human infections are asymptomatic.

Morphology & Identification

A. Typical Organisms: The organisms consist of boat-shaped, thin-walled cells, the rapidly multiplying tachyzoites $4–7 \times 2–4 \ \mu m$ within tissue cells and somewhat larger (up to $10 \times 4 \ \mu m$) outside them. They stain lightly with Giemsa's stain; fixed cells often appear crescentic. Packed intracellular aggregates may be seen (p 524). True cysts are found in the brain or certain other tissues. These cysts contain many thousands of sporelike trophozoites, the slowly dividing bradyzoites, capable of initiating a new infection in the animal ingesting the cyst-bearing tissues.

B. Culture: *T gondii* may be cultured only in the presence of living cells, in tissue culture, or eggs. Typical intracellular and extracellular organisms may be seen.

C. Growth Requirements: Optimal growth is at about 37–39 °C in living cells.

D. Variations: There is considerable strain variation in infectivity and virulence, possibly related to the degree of adaptation to a particular host. Variations in microscopic appearance are negligible, and most workers consider all forms of human and animal toxoplasmosis to be caused by the single species *T gondii*.

Pathogenesis, Pathology, & Clinical Findings

The trophozoite directly destroys cells and has a predilection for parenchymal cells and those of the reticuloendothelial system. Humans are relatively resistant, but a low-grade lymph node infection resembling infectious mononucleosis may occur. Congenital infection leads to stillbirths, chorioretinitis, intracerebral calcifications, psychomotor disturbances, and hydrocephaly or microcephaly. In these cases, the mother was infected during pregnancy. A major cause of blindness and other congenital defects is prenatal toxoplasmosis. Infection during the first trimester generally results in stillbirth or major central nervous system anomalies, though third-trimester infections are far more common. Clinical manifestations of these infections may be delayed until long after birth, even beyond childhood. Neurologic problems or learning difficulties may, in fact, be caused by the long-delayed effects of prenatal toxoplasmosis, effects that may ultimately prove to induce more cumulative, if insidious, damage than the more dramatic, highly visible stillbirths, hydrocephalies, and other gross effects.

Diagnostic Laboratory Tests

A. Specimens: Blood, bone marrow, cerebrospinal fluid, and exudates for direct inspection; lymph node biopsy material; tonsillar and striated muscle biopsies; and ventricular fluid (in neonatal infections) may be required.

B. Microscopic Examination: Smears and sections stained with Giemsa's stain may show the organism. The densely packed cysts, chiefly in the brain or other parts of the central nervous system, suggest chronic infection. Identification must be confirmed by isolation in animals.

C. Animal Inoculation: This is essential for definitive diagnosis. A variety of specimens are inoculated intraperitoneally into groups of mice that have been dye-tested to make certain that they are free from infection. If no deaths occur, the mice are observed for about 6 weeks, and tail or heart blood is then tested for specific antibody. The diagnosis is confirmed by demonstration of cysts in the brains of the inoculated mice.

D. Serology: The Sabin-Feldman dye test is valuable for diagnosis and surveys. It depends upon the appearance in 2–3 weeks of antibodies that will render the membrane of laboratory-cultured living *T gondii* impermeable to alkaline methylene blue, so that organisms are unstained in the presence of positive serum. It is being replaced by the IHA, latex, or IHF test or newer tests like the enzyme-linked immunosorbent assay (ELISA) or fluoroimmunoassay (FIAX), none of which expose technologists to the danger of living organisms, as is required for the dye test, and all of which are easier to run and to read. A CF test may be positive (1:8 titer) as early as 1 month after infection, but it is valueless in many chronic infections. The IFA and IHA tests are routinely used for diagnostic purposes. Frenkel's intracutaneous test is of limited clinical value but is useful for epidemiologic surveys.

Immunity

There are great variations in strains and hosts, and a degree of acquired immunity (or premunition in some cases) may develop. Antibody titers in mothers, as detected in either blood or milk, tend to fall within a few months. Yet, the fact that prenatal infection is limited to babies born of mothers who were first exposed during their pregnancy strongly suggests that the presence of circulating antibodies is at least partially protective.

Treatment

Acute infections can be treated with a combination of pyrimethamine, 25 mg/d for 3–4 weeks, and trisulfapyrimidines, 2–6 g/d for 3–4 weeks.

Epidemiology, Prevention, & Control

Transplacental infection of the fetus has long been recognized as a mode of transmission. Domestic cats have recently been incriminated in the transmission of the parasite to humans. The infective stage is an *Isospora*-like oocyst found in the feces of cats and other felids. Rodents also appear to play a role in transmission, since they harbor in their tissues cysts transmissible to cats. New control recommendations are being devised in the light of many new epidemiologic findings. Measures leading to minimization of human contact with cat feces are clearly important in control, particularly for pregnant women with negative serologic tests. Further work on the similar life histories and relationships of *Toxoplasma, Sarcocystis,* and *Isospora* will lead to greater epidemiologic understanding and improved control.

BABESIA MICROTI

Babesiosis, a red cell–infecting tick-borne piroplasmosis, has in recent years been reported in increasing numbers from Massachusetts, the primary focus being Nantucket Island (Ruebush TK II et al: *Ann Intern Med* 1977;**86:**6). Earlier records involved splenectomized patients, but more recent outbreaks have been in healthy individuals with no record of splenectomy, corticosteroid therapy, or recurrent infection. The illness develops 7–10 days after the tick bite and is characterized by malaise, anorexia, and fatigue followed by fever and frequently sweats, myalgia, arthralgia, nausea, and vomiting. Emotional lability and depression have also been reported. This rodent parasite may be mistaken in humans for *Plasmodium falciparum* in its ring form in red cells. No pigment is produced, however. Human babesiosis appears to be more severe in older individuals; children or young adults may develop self-limited infections. Splenectomy compromises resistance to babesiosis. Earlier reported cases, most ending fatally, were from splenectomized individuals, who developed progressive hemolytic anemia, jaundice, and renal insufficiency. Prolonged parasitemia is common even after clinical recovery. Chloroquine has been used successfully for treatment of these cases, though diminazene aceturate (Berenil, Ganaseg) has been recommended for patients who fail to respond to chloroquine therapy after 3–5 days.

BALANTIDIUM COLI

Balantidium coli, the cause of balantidiasis or balantidial dysentery, is the largest intestinal protozoan of humans. Morphologically similar ciliate parasites are found in swine and lower primates.

Morphology & Identification

A. Typical Organisms: The trophozoite is a ciliated, oval organism, 60×45 μm in average dimensions (occasionally almost twice as large). Its motion is characteristic, a combination of steady, boring progression and rotation around the long axis. The cell wall is lined with spiral rows of cilia that also extend into the deep and conspicuous anterior cytostome. The cytoplasm surrounds 2 contractile vacuoles, food particles and vacuoles, and 2 nuclei—a large, kidney-shaped macronucleus and a much smaller, spherical micronucleus. When the organism encysts, it secretes a spherical or oval double-layered wall. The macronucleus, contractile vacuoles, and portions of the ciliated cell wall may be visible in the cyst, which ranges from 45–65 μm in diameter.

B. Culture: These organisms may be cultivated in a variety of simple media, including those used for cultivation of intestinal amebas.

Pathogenesis, Pathology, & Clinical Findings

When cysts are ingested by the new host, the cyst walls dissolve and the released trophozoites descend to the colon, where they feed on bacteria and fecal debris, multiply, and form cysts that pass out in the feces. It seems apparent that most infections are harmless. However, rarely, the trophozoites invade the mucosa and submucosa of the large bowel and terminal ileum. As they multiply, abscesses and irregular ulcerations with overhanging lips are formed. The number of lesions formed depends upon intensity of infection and degree of individual host susceptibility. Chronic recurrent diarrhea, alternating with constipation, is the commonest clinical manifestation, but attacks of severe dysentery with bloody mucoid stools, tenesmus, and colic may occur intermittently in light as well as heavy infections. Extreme cases may mimic severe intestinal amebiasis. Fatal cases have occasionally been reported.

Diagnostic Laboratory Tests

The diagnosis of balantidial infection, whether symptomatic or not, depends upon laboratory detection of trophozoites in liquid stools or, more rarely, of cysts in formed stools. There are no other constant and distinctive laboratory findings. Sigmoidoscopy may be useful for obtaining material directly from ulcerations for examination. Culturing is rarely necessary.

Immunity

Humans appear to have a high natural resistance to balantidial infection. Factors underlying individual susceptibility are not known.

Treatment

A course of oxytetracycline may be followed by diiodohydroxyquin if necessary.

Epidemiology

B coli is found in humans throughout the world, particularly in the tropics, but it is a rare infection. Only a few hundred cases have been recorded. Infection results from ingestion of viable cysts previously passed in the stools by humans and possibly by swine. Although it has been generally accepted that pigs are important sources of human infections, some epidemiologic evidence suggests that this may not always be so.

PNEUMOCYSTIS CARINII

Pneumocystis carinii, thought by some to be a fungus related to the yeasts and by others a sporozoan, is included here for completeness, though it may have to be placed elsewhere when more life history information becomes available. It appears to be widely distributed among animals in nature—including rats, mice, and dogs—but usually without causing disease. It may cause an interstitial plasma cell pneumonitis in humans, particularly in infants, old people, and patients receiving immunosuppressive therapy.

Morphology & Identification

A. Typical Organisms: The most characteristic stage is a rosette of 8 pear-shaped "sporozoites," each 1–2 μm, in a "cyst" 7–10 μm in diameter. Earlier stages consist of 1–4 nuclei in a mucoid sphere, respectively staining red and blue within a red-violet membrane when heavily stained with Giemsa's stain. Large numbers of organisms are packed in foamy material and among many plasma cells and eosinophils in the pulmonary alveoli and bronchioles of fatal cases. Some may be within histiocytes. Pulmonary infections with pneumonitis have been reported in rats.

B. Culture: Not reported. Attempts to culture the organism in the lungs of cortisone-treated rats or mice should be made.

Pathogenesis, Pathology, & Clinical Findings

Most infections in humans are probably inapparent. Excessive multiplication leading to blocking of the alveolar respiratory surface appears to occur, especially in premature or marasmic infants but also in those whose resistance has been lowered, ie, children and adults receiving corticosteroids, cytotoxic drugs, or antibiotics over extended periods, or those suffering from agammaglobulinemia. An interstitial plasma cell pneumonitis then develops (detectable in x-rays as a "ground glass" appearance), with alveoli filled with organisms and foamy material.

Diagnostic Laboratory Tests

The organism is usually discovered after autopsy, but lung puncture biopsy has been reported to be successful. Staining is difficult. Heavy Giemsa staining should be used simultaneously with Böhmer's hematoxylin (30 minutes, without differentiation) and periodic acid–Schiff stain for mucopolysaccharides.

Treatment

Pentamidine isethionate and pyrimethamine are the drugs with most promise.

Epidemiology, Prevention, & Control

The mode of infection is unknown, but cysts, presumably inhaled, may be derived from domestic rodents or pets or from carrier adults.

HELMINTHS:
OVA IN FECES & MICROFILARIAE IN BLOOD & TISSUES

Table 41–4 shows some diseases that are caused by helminths. Ova (pp 527 and 532) may be detected in feces (or urine, with *Schistosoma haematobium* and sometimes *Schistosoma japonicum*), preferably after concentration by zinc sulfate centrifugal sedimentation or formalin-triton-NE-ether techniques (especially for operculated and schistosome eggs; see Garcia & Ash, Desowitz, and Melvin & Brooke references for further details). Eggs of *Enterobius* may be collected directly from the anal margins with cellulose tape on the end of a spatula.

Microfilariae (see Table 41–5 and p 526) are the embryonic or prelarval stages of filariid worms in humans and are identified in blood smears or concentrate or (especially for *Onchocerca volvulus*) in a skin snip preparation.

Table 41—4. Diseases due to helminths.

C = cestode (tapeworm)		N = nematode (roundworm)		T = trematode (fluke)
Disease and Parasite	**Location in Host**	**Mode of Transmission**	**Geographic Distribution**	**Treatment of Choice**
Angiostrongyliasis; eosinophilic meningoencephalitis *Angiostrongylus cantonensis* (larval) (N), rat lungworm	Larvae in meninges.	Eating raw shrimps, prawns; raw garden slugs; aquatic and land snails; infested lettuce.	Local in Pacific, especially southwest.	Thiabendazole (experimental).
Angiostrongyliasis; intestinal angiostrongyliasis *Angiostrongylus costaricensis* (N), cotton rat arterial worm	Larval stages in bowel wall, especially appendix; also regional lymph nodes in mesenteric arteries.	Ingestion of infected snails, slugs, contaminated salad vegetables.	Central America, Brazil.	Surgical excision.
Ascariasis *Ascaris lumbricoides* (N), common roundworm	Small intestine; larvae through lungs.	Eating viable eggs from feces-contaminated soil or food.	Worldwide, very common.	Pyrantel pamoate, piperazine citrate, mebendazole, levamisole.
Capillariasis *Capillaria philippinensis* (N)	Small intestine.	Undercooked marine fish.	Philippines, Thailand.	Mebendazole.
Clonorchiasis *Clonorchis sinensis* (T), Chinese liver fluke	Liver.	Uncooked freshwater fish.	China, Korea, Indochina, Japan, Taiwan.	Chloroquine, bithionol, hexachloroparaxylol, praziquantel (experimental).
Cysticercosis (bladder worm) *Taenia solium* (larval) (C)	Subcutaneous; eye, meninges, brain, etc.	Ingestion of eggs or regurgitation of gravid proglottid from lower GI tract.	Worldwide.	Surgical excision, mebendazole, praziquantel (experimental).
Dipetalonemiasis *Dipetalonema perstans* (N) *(Acanthocheilonema perstans)* (nonpathogenic?)	Peritoneal and other cavities; microfilariae in blood.	Bite of gnat *Culicoides.*	Equatorial Africa; N coast of S America, Argentina, Panama, Trinidad.	Not treated.
Dracontiasis *Dracunculus medinensis* (N), Guinea worm	Subcutaneous; usually leg, foot.	Drinking water with *Cyclops.*	Africa, Arabia to Pakistan; locally elsewhere in Asia.	Mechanical or surgical extraction; niridazole, metronidazole, thiabendazole.
Echinococcosis, hydatidosis *Echinococcus granulosus* (larval) (C)	Liver, lung, brain, peritoneum, long bones, kidney.	Contact with dogs, foxes, other canids; eggs from feces.	Worldwide but local; sheep-raising areas.	Surgical aspiration and excision, mebendazole, praziquantel (experimental).
Echinococcus multilocularis (larval) (C), hydatid worm		Fox fur trappers.	Northern temperate areas with fox-vole cycle.	
Enterobiasis *Enterobius vermicularis* (N), pinworm	Cecum, colon.	Anal-oral; self-contamination and internal reinfection.	Worldwide.	Pyrantel pamoate, mebendazole, piperazine, pyrvinium pamoate.
Fascioliasis *Fasciola hepatica* (T), sheep liver fluke	Liver.	Watercress, aquatic vegetation.	Worldwide, especially sheep-raising areas.	Bithionol, emetine or dehydroemetine (subcutaneous).
Fasciolopsiasis *Fasciolopsis buski* (T), giant intestinal fluke	Small intestine.	Aquatic vegetation.	E and SE Asia.	Hexylresorcinol (Crystoids), bithionol, stilbazium iodide.
Filariasis *Wuchereria bancrofti,* *Brugia malayi* (N), human filarial worms	Lymph nodes; microfilariae in blood.	Bite of mosquitoes; several species.	Tropical and subtropical, very local but widespread.	Diethylcarbamazine.
Filariasis, occult *Dirofilaria* species (N), heartworm	Lungs (larvae).	Infected mosquitoes?	India, SE Asia.	Diethylcarbamazine or not treated.
Gnathostomiasis *Gnathostoma spinigerum* (N), rat stomach worm	Subcutaneous, migratory.	Uncooked fish.	E and SE Asia.	Surgical excision, diethylcarbamazine.

Table 41—4 (cont'd). Diseases due to helminths.

C = cestode (tapeworm)	N = nematode (roundworm)	T = trematode (fluke)

Disease and Parasite	Location in Host	Mode of Transmission	Geographic Distribution	Treatment of Choice
Heterophyiasis *Heterophyes heterophyes* (T), intestinal fish fluke of humans	Small intestine.	Uncooked fish (mullet).	China, Korea, Japan, Taiwan; Israel; Egypt.	Tetrachloroethylene, hexylresorcinol (Crystoids).
Hookworms *Ancylostoma duodenale,* *Necator americanus* (N)	Small intestine; larvae through lungs.	Through skin, infected soil, from drinking contaminated water *(Ancylostoma).*	Worldwide tropics and North America *(Necator);* temperate zones *(Ancylostoma).*	Mebendazole, pyrantel pamoate, bephenium hydroxynaphthoate, tetrachloroethylene.
Larva migrans: Cutaneous, creeping eruption *Ancylostoma braziliense* and other domestic animal hookworms (N)	Subcutaneous, migrating larvae.	Contact with soil contaminated by dog or cat feces.	Worldwide.	Thiabendazole, levamisole.
Visceral *Toxocara* species (N), cat and dog roundworms	Liver, lung, eye, brain, other viscera; migrating larvae.	Ingesting soil contaminated by dog or cat feces.	Worldwide.	Thiabendazole, levamisole, corticosteroids.
Loiasis *Loa loa* (N)	Subcutaneous, migratory; eye. Microfilariae in blood.	Bite of deer flies, *Chrysops.*	Equatorial Africa.	Surgical removal, diethylcarbamazine, or not treated.
Mansonelliasis *Mansonella ozzardi* (N) (nonpathogenic) Manson's filaria	Body cavities; microfilariae in blood.	Bite of gnat *Culicoides.*	Argentina, N coast of S America; Caribbean islands; Panama, Yucatan.	Not treated.
Metagonimiasis *Metagonimus yokogawai* (T), intestinal fish fluke of humans	Small intestine.	Uncooked fish.	As for *Heterophyes* plus USSR, Balkans, Spain.	Tetrachloroethylene, hexylresorcinol (Crystoids).
Onchocerciasis *Onchocerca volvulus* (N), nodular or blinding worm	Subcutaneous; microfilariae in skin, eyes.	Bite of black fly *Simulium.*	Equatorial Africa; C and S America.	Surgery, diethylcarbamazine
Opisthorchiasis *Opisthorchis felineus,* *Opisthorchis viverrini* (T), Asian liver flukes	Liver.	Uncooked fish.	E Europe, USSR; Thailand.	Chloroquine (treatment unsatisfactory), praziquantel (experimental).
Paragonimiasis *Paragonimus westermani* (T), lung fluke (several species)	Lung.	Raw crabs and other freshwater crustaceans.	E and S Asia; N central Africa; S America; animals in N America.	Bithionol, praziquantel (experimental).
Schistosomiasis *Schistosoma haematobium* (T), schistosomes or *Bilharzia* worms, blood flukes; vesicular blood fluke	Venous vessels of urinary bladder, large intestine; liver.	Cercariae (larvae) penetrate skin in snail-infested water.	Africa, widely; Madagascar; Arabia to Lebanon.	Niridazole, antimony sodium dimercaptosuccinate, stibophen, hycanthone, metrifonate (drug of choice).
Schistosoma japonicum (T), Japanese blood fluke	Venous vessels of small intestine; liver.	Cercariae (larvae) penetrate skin in snail-infested water.	China, Philippines, Japan; potentially Taiwan.	Potassium antimony tartrate (tartar emetic), sodium antimony tartrate; praziquantel (experimental; effective against all 3 species and cestodes).
Schistosoma mansoni (T), Manson's blood fluke	Venous vessels of colon, rectum; liver.	Cercariae (larvae) penetrate skin in snail-infested water.	Africa to Near East; parts of S America; Caribbean tropics and subtropics.	Stibophen, antimony sodium dimercaptosuccinate, hycanthone, niridazole, tartar emetic; oxamniquine (drug of choice).
Sparganosis *Spirometra mansonoides; Spirometra erinacei* (larval) (C), pseudophyllidean larva or sparganum from frogs, snakes, some birds and mammals (adult worms in felids or canids)	Intraorbital wound, other wounds or contusions if used as poultice; subcutaneous tissues if from ingestion of procercoid or sparganum.	Native poultices such as infected raw frog flesh; drinking water with infected copepods; ingestion of raw frogs, tadpoles, snakes.	Orient; occasionally other countries, including N and S America.	Surgical removal.

Table 41—4 (cont'd). Diseases due to helminths.

C = cestode (tapeworm)	N = nematode (roundworm)		T = trematode (fluke)	

Disease and Parasite	Location in Host	Mode of Transmission	Geographic Distribution	Treatment of Choice
Strongyloidiasis *Strongyloides stercoralis* (N), threadworm	Duodenum, jejunum; larvae through skin, lungs.	Through skin and (rarely) by internal autoreinfection.	Worldwide.	Thiabendazole, pyr- vinium pamoate.
Tapeworm disease (see also Cysti- cercosis, Echinococcosis, Spar- ganosis); taeniasis *Diphyllobothrium latum* (C), broad fish tapeworm	Small intestine.	Uncooked freshwater fish.	Alaska, E Canada, Great Lakes area, NW Florida; parts of S America; N Europe; E Mediterranean, Asiatic USSR, Japan; Australia.	Niclosamide, paromo- mycin; praziquantel (experimental).
Dipylidium caninum (C), dog tapeworm	Small intestine.	Ingestion of crushed fleas, lice from pets.	Worldwide.	Niclosamide, paromo- mycin, quinacrine.
Hymenolepis diminuta (C), rat tapeworm	Small intestine.	Indirectly from rats, mice via infected in- sects.	Worldwide.	Niclosamide, paromo- mycin, quinacrine.
Hymenolepis nana (C), dwarf tapeworm	Small intestine.	Anal-oral transfer of eggs or ingestion of infected insects; in- ternal reinfection.	Worldwide.	Niclosamide, paromo- mycin; praziquantel (experimental).
Taenia saginata (C), beef tapeworm	Small intestine.	Uncooked beef.	Worldwide.	Niclosamide, paromo- mycin, quinacrine; praziquantel (experi- mental).
Taenia solium (C), pork tapeworm (see also Cysti- cercosis)	Small intestine.	Uncooked pork.	Worldwide.	Niclosamide, paromo- mycin, quinacrine; praziquantel (experi- mental).
Trichinosis *Trichinella spiralis* (N), trichina worm	Larvae in striated muscle.	Uncooked pork.	Worldwide.	Thiabendazole, corti- costeroids.
Trichostrongyliasis *Trichostrongylus* species (N)	Small intestine.	Ingestion of infective third stage from feces- contaminated food or soil; contact with her- bivore feces.	E Europe, USSR, Iran.	Thiabendazole, pyran- tel pamoate.
Trichuriasis *Trichuris trichiura* (N), whipworm	Cecum; colon.	Ingestion of eggs from feces-contaminated soil.	Worldwide.	Mebendazole, hexyl- resorcinol enema.

Table 41—5. Microfilariae.

Filariid	Disease	Distribution	Vectors	Microfilariae		
				Sheath	Tail Nuclei	Periodicity*
Wuchereria bancrofti	Bancroftian and Malayan filariasis: lymphangitis, hydrocele, elephantiasis	Worldwide 41 N to 28 S	Culicidae (mosquitoes)	+	Not to tip	Nocturnal or non-periodic
Brugia malayi		Oriental region to Japan	Culicidae (mosquitoes)	+	Two distinct	Nocturnal or sub-periodic
Loa loa	Loiasis; Calabar swellings; conjunctival worms	Western and central Africa	*Chrysops*, deer fly, mango fly	+	Extend to tip	Diurnal
Onchocerca volvulus	Onchocerciasis: skin nodules, blindness, dermatitis, hanging groin	Africa, Central and South America	*Simulium*, buffalo gnat, black fly	−	Not to tip	Nonperiodic in skin fluids
Dipetalonema (Acanthocheilonema) perstans	Dipetalonemiasis or acanthocheilonemiasis (minor disturbances)	Africa and South America	*Culicoides*, biting midge	−	Extend to tip	Nocturnal or diurnal or nonperiodic
Dipetalonema streptocerca	Usually nonpathogenic	Western and central Africa	*Culicoides*, biting midge	−	Extend to tip	In skin only
Mansonella ozzardi	Ozzard's mansonelliasis (benign), occasionally hydrocele	Central and South America	*Culicoides*, biting midge	−	Not to tip	Nonperiodic

*Microfilariae are found in peripheral blood (in blood smear) only at night (nocturnal periodicity), largely at night or during crepuscular hours (subperiodicity), largely during daylight hours (diurnal periodicity), or without clear distinction (nonperiodic). Periodicity appears to be correlated with the bloodsucking habits of the chief vector insect in the particular area of transmission of the filaria.

PROTOZOA IN FECES (× 2000)

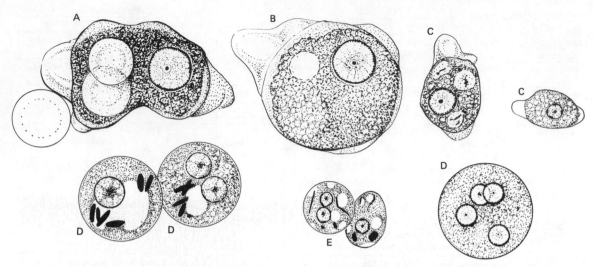

Entamoeba histolytica. A, B: Trophozoite (vegetative form) with ingested red cells in *A; C: Entamoeba hartmanni* trophozoite with food vacuoles, not red cells; *D:* cysts with 1, 2, and 4 nuclei and chromatoid bodies; *E: E hartmanni* binucleate cyst (left), uninucleate precyst (right).

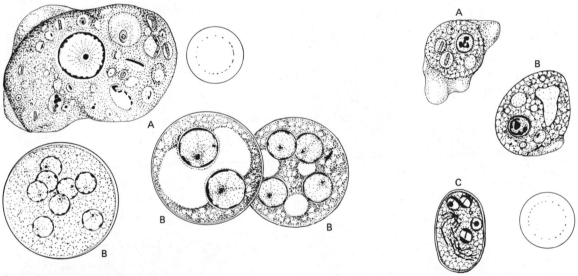

Entamoeba coli. A: Trophozoite with vacuoles and inclusions; *B:* cysts with 2, 4, and 8 nuclei, the latter being mature.

Endolimax nana. A: Trophozoite; *B:* precystic form; *C:* binucleate cyst.

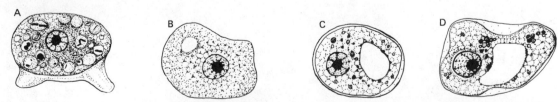

Iodamoeba bütschlii. A: Trophozoite; *B:* precystic form; *C* and *D:* cysts showing large glycogen vacuole (unstained in iron-hematoxylin preparation). Note variable shape of cysts.

[Simple double circles represent the size of red cells.]

PROTOZOA IN FECES (× 2000)*

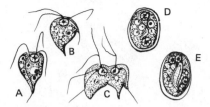

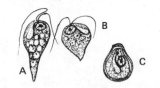

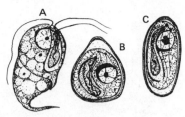

Enteromonas hominis. A, B, C: Trophozoites; *C:* dividing form; *D* and *E:* quadrinucleate cysts.

Retortamonas intestinalis. A and *B:* Trophozoites; *C:* cyst.

Chilomastix mesnili. A: Trophozoite; *B* and *C:* cysts.

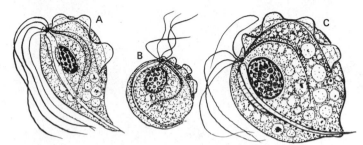

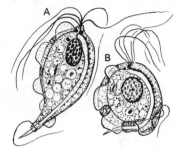

Trichomonas vaginalis. *A:* Normal trophozoite; *B:* round form after division; *C:* common form seen in stained preparation. **Cysts not found.**

Trichomonas hominis. A: Normal and *B:* round forms of trophozoites, probably a staining artifact.

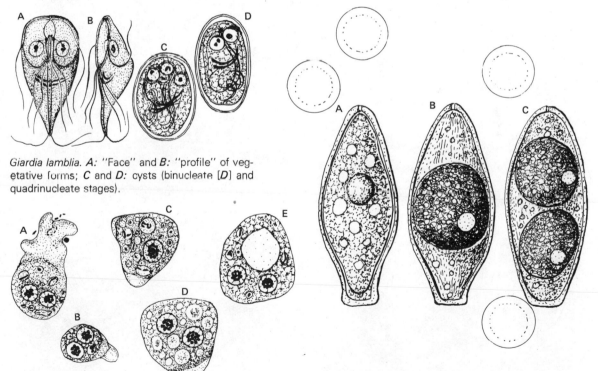

Giardia lamblia. A: "Face" and *B:* "profile" of vegetative forms; *C* and *D:* cysts (binucleate [*D*] and quadrinucleate stages).

Dientamoeba fragilis. Trophozoites (cysts not found). *A:* active; *B:* small; *C:* mononuclear; *D* and *E:* resting.

Isospora hominis. A: Degenerate oocyst; *B:* unsegmented oocyst; *C:* oocyst segmented into 2 sporoblasts after passage into feces. Mature oocyst with sporoblasts developed into sporocysts, each containing 4 sporozoites not shown.

[Simple double circles represent the size of red cells.]

*Trichomonas vaginalis is found in vaginal and prostatic secretions.

PROTOZOA IN FECES (× 2000)

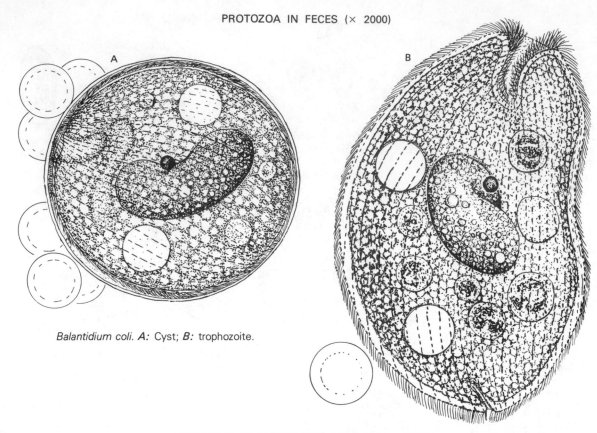

Balantidium coli. A: Cyst; *B:* trophozoite.

PROTOZOA IN BLOOD AND TISSUES (× 2000)

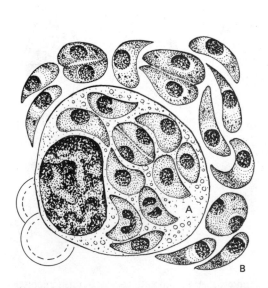

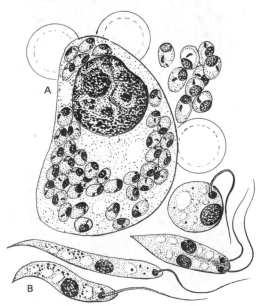

Toxoplasma gondii. A: Trophozoites in large mononuclear cell; *B:* free in blood. Not found within red cells, but parasitize many other cell types, particularly reticuloendothelial. Cyst not shown.

Leishmania donovani. A: Large reticuloendothelial cell of spleen with amastigotes. *B:* Promastigotes as seen in sandfly gut or in culture.

[Simple double circles represent the size of red cells.]

PROTOZOA IN BLOOD (× 1700)

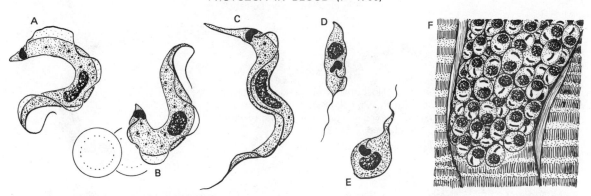

Trypanosoma cruzi. A, B, C: Trypomastigotes in blood; *D, E:* epimastigote (with short anterior undulating membrane); *F:* amastigote colony in heart muscle cell.

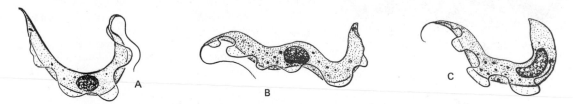

Trypanosoma gambiense (or *Trypanosoma rhodesiense,* indistinguishable in practice).*A, B:* Trypomastigotes in blood; *C:* epimastigote (intermediate type; kinetoplast not yet anterior to nucleus); found in tsetse fly, *Glossina* species.

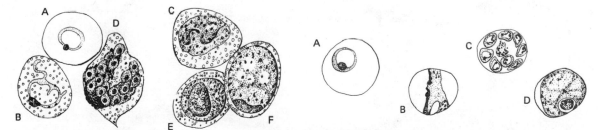

Plasmodium vivax. A: Young signet ring trophozoite; *B:* ameboid trophozoite; *C:* mature trophozoite; *D:* mature schizont, showing a distorted host cell; *E:* microgametocyte; *F:* macrogametocyte with compact nucleus. Note Schüffner's dots and enlarged host cells.

Plasmodium malariae. A: Developing ring form of trophozoite; *B:* band form of trophozoite (note absence of granules); *C:* mature schizont in "rosette" with 8 merozoites; *D:* mature gametocyte.

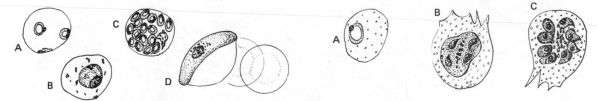

Plasmodium falciparum. A: Ring stage, or young trophozoites (triple infection); *B:* mature trophozoite showing clumped pigment in cytoplasm and Maurer's clefts in erythrocyte; *C:* mature schizont; *D:* mature gametocyte. *B* and *C* stages rarely seen in peripheral blood. Gametocytes in blood are diagnostic.

Plasmodium ovale. A: Young signet ring trophozoite and Schüffner's dots; *B:* ameboid trophozoite developing in fimbriated erythrocyte; *C:* mature schizont showing 8 merozoites.

[Simple double circles represent the size of red cells.]

MICROFILARIAE (× 600)
(in blood or tissue fluids)

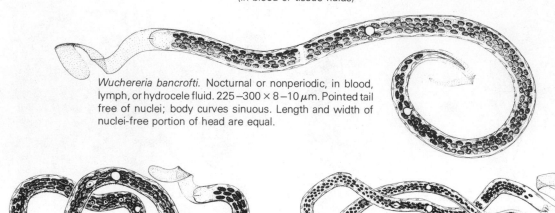

Wuchereria bancrofti. Nocturnal or nonperiodic, in blood, lymph, or hydrocele fluid. 225−300 × 8−10 μm. Pointed tail free of nuclei; body curves sinuous. Length and width of nuclei-free portion of head are equal.

Loa loa. Diurnal periodicity, in blood. 250−300 × 6−9 μm. Nuclei extend to tip of tail.

Brugia malayi. Nocturnal or subperiodic, in blood, lymph, or lymphocele fluid. 160−260 × 5−6 μm. Two nuclei in tip of tail; body curves angular or kinky; nuclei-free portion of head longer than it is wide.

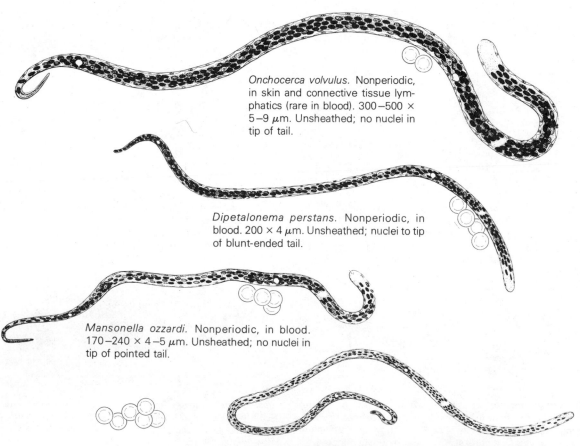

Onchocerca volvulus. Nonperiodic, in skin and connective tissue lymphatics (rare in blood). 300−500 × 5−9 μm. Unsheathed; no nuclei in tip of tail.

Dipetalonema perstans. Nonperiodic, in blood. 200 × 4 μm. Unsheathed; nuclei to tip of blunt-ended tail.

Mansonella ozzardi. Nonperiodic, in blood. 170−240 × 4−5 μm. Unsheathed; no nuclei in tip of pointed tail.

Dipetalonema streptocerca. Nonperiodic. 180 × 2−3 μm. Unsheathed; found in skin only, not in blood. Nuclei to tip of blunt-ended tail.

[Simple double circles represent the size of red cells.]

OVA OF TREMATODES (× 400)
(as seen in feces)

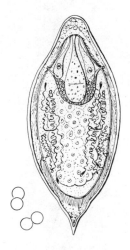

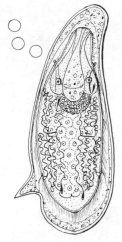

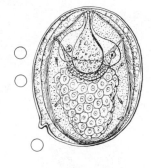

Schistosoma japonicum. Embryonated ovum with small lateral spine, often not visible.

Paragonimus westermani. Unembryonated operculated ovum.

Schistosoma haematobium. Terminally spined embryonated ovum (containing miracidium).

Schistosoma mansoni. Laterally spined embryonated ovum (containing miracidium).

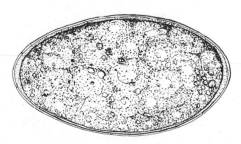

Clonorchis sinensis. Small operculated and embryonated ovum.

A: Heterophyes heterophyes or *B: Metagonimus yokogawai.* Minute embryonated operculated ova.

Fasciola hepatica or *Fasciolopsis buski.* Unembryonated operculated ovum.

OVA OF NEMATODES (× 400)

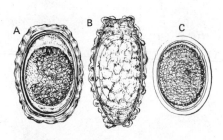

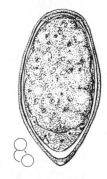

Ancylostoma duodenale or *Necator americanus.* Note shape, thin shell, 4- to 8-cell stage.

Ascaris lumbricoides. A: Fertilized unembryonated ovum; *B:* unfertilized ovum; *C:* fertilized decorticated ovum.

Strongyloides stercoralis. A: Embryonated ovum (rare in feces); *B:* rhabditiform larva (usually seen in feces).

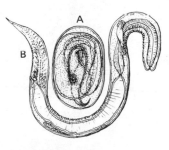

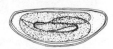

Trichostrongylus orientalis. Unembryonated ovum. (Rare in humans except in specific areas, eg, Iran.)

Trichuris trichiura. Unembryonated double-plug ovum.

Enterobius vermicularis. Embryonated ovum. Note flattening on one side, thin shell. Deposited on perianal skin.

[Simple circles represent the size of red cells.]

ADULT TREMATODES
(in intestine or tissues)

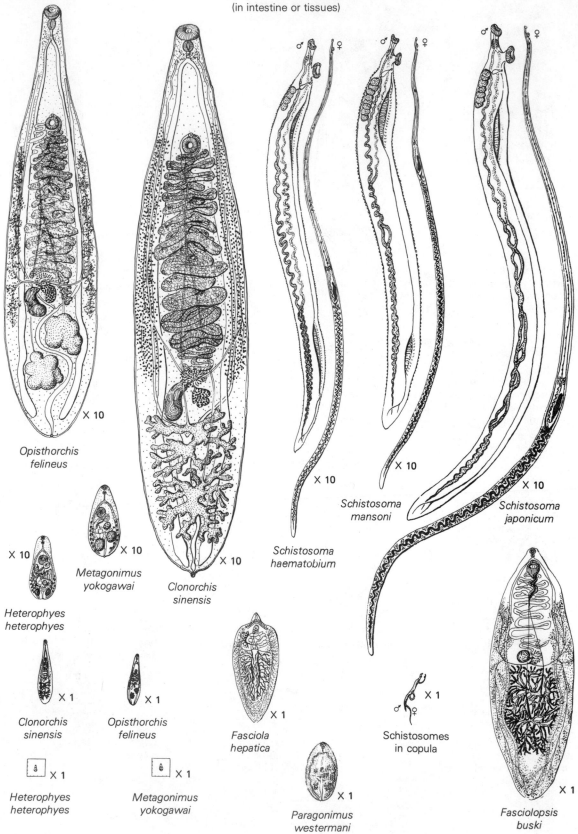

Opisthorchis
felineus

× 10

× 10
Heterophyes
heterophyes

Metagonimus
yokogawai
× 10

Clonorchis
sinensis
× 10

Schistosoma
haematobium
× 10

Schistosoma
mansoni
× 10

Schistosoma
japonicum
× 10

Clonorchis
sinensis
× 1

Opisthorchis
felineus
× 1

Fasciola
hepatica
× 1

Schistosomes
in copula
× 1

Fasciolopsis
buski
× 1

Heterophyes
heterophyes
× 1

Metagonimus
yokogawai
× 1

Paragonimus
westermani
× 1

INTESTINAL AND TISSUE NEMATODES

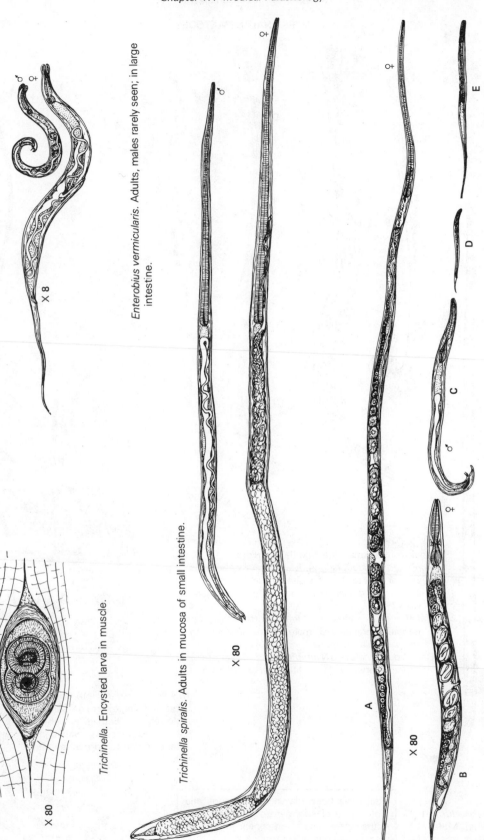

× 80

Trichinella. Encysted larva in muscle.

× 8

Enterobius vermicularis. Adults, males rarely seen; in large intestine.

× 80

Trichinella spiralis. Adults in mucosa of small intestine.

× 80

Strongyloides stercoralis. A: Parasitic female, lateral view, in human intestine; *B:* free-living female in soil; *C:* free-living male in soil; *D:* rhabditiform la va passed in feces or in free-living cycle in soil; *E:* filariform or infective larva in soil, ready to penetrate human skin.

INTESTINAL NEMATODES

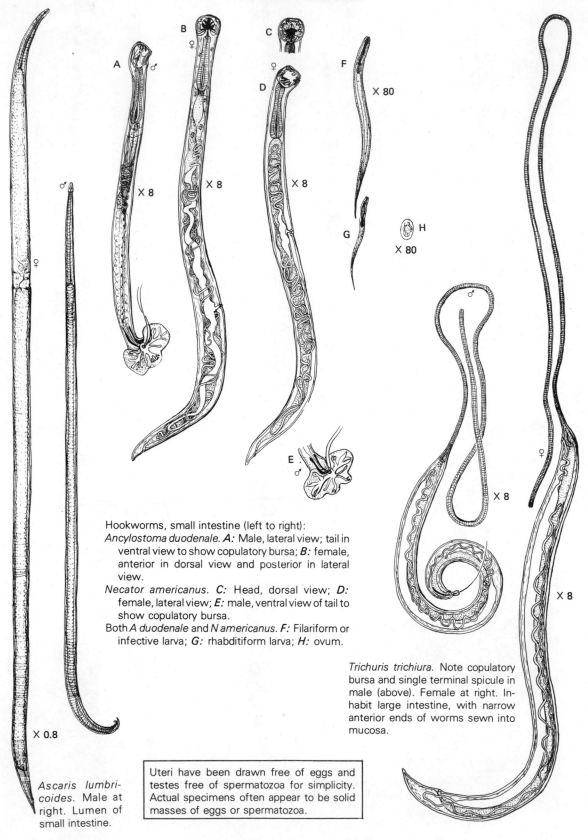

Hookworms, small intestine (left to right):
Ancylostoma duodenale. A: Male, lateral view; tail in
   ventral view to show copulatory bursa; *B:* female,
   anterior in dorsal view and posterior in lateral
   view.
Necator americanus. C: Head, dorsal view; *D:*
   female, lateral view; *E:* male, ventral view of tail to
   show copulatory bursa.
Both *A duodenale* and *N americanus. F:* Filariform or
   infective larva; *G:* rhabditiform larva; *H:* ovum.

Trichuris trichiura. Note copulatory
bursa and single terminal spicule in
male (above). Female at right. Inhabit large intestine, with narrow
anterior ends of worms sewn into
mucosa.

*Ascaris lumbri-
coides.* Male at
right. Lumen of
small intestine.

Uteri have been drawn free of eggs and
testes free of spermatozoa for simplicity.
Actual specimens often appear to be solid
masses of eggs or spermatozoa.

CESTODES (TAPEWORMS)

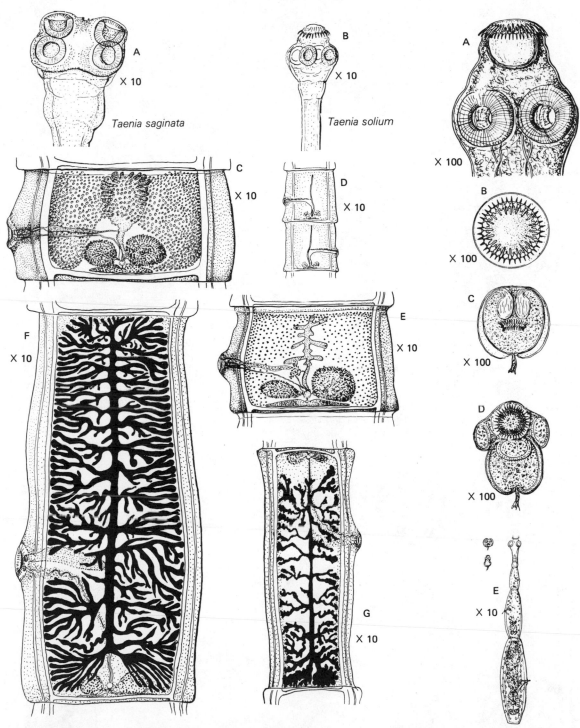

Taenia saginata and *Taenia solium*. *A:* Scolex of *T saginata; B:* scolex of *T solium* with beginning of strobila; *C:* mature proglottid of *T saginata; D:* immature proglottids of *T solium; E:* mature proglottid of *T solium; F:* gravid proglottid of *T saginata* with much more numerous uterine ramifications than in *T solium* (see at right); *G:* gravid proglottid of *T solium.*

Echinococcus granulosus. A: Scolex of adult; *B:* end view of rostellum, showing arrangement of 2 hook rows; *C:* larva from hydatid fluid, invaginated; *D:* same, evaginated; *E:* entire adult worm and larval scoleces (left).

CESTODES

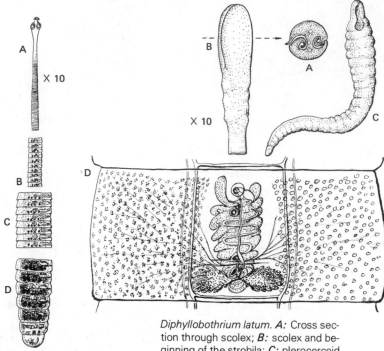

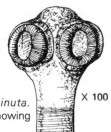

Hymenolepis diminuta. A:
Unarmed scolex and begin-
ning of strobila; *B:* some
genitally mature proglottids;
C: enlarged view; *D:* gravid
proglottids.

Hymenolepis nana. A:
Armed scolex and begin-
ning of strobila; *B:* some
genitally mature proglot-
tids; *C:* enlarged view; *D:*
gravid proglottids.

Diphyllobothrium latum. A: Cross section through scolex; *B:* scolex and beginning of the strobila; *C:* plerocercoid
or sparganum larva (in fish muscles);
D: mature proglottid with egg-filled
uterus.

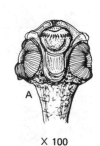

Hymenolepis diminuta.
Scolex and neck, showing
unarmed rostellum.

× 100

× 100   × 100

Hymenolepis nana. A: Scolex
with hooked rostellum re-
tracted; *B:* same with rostellum
everted.

OVA OF CESTODES (× 400)

Hymenolepis
diminuta

Hymenolepis
nana

Taenia saginata, Taenia solium, or *Echinococcus*

Diphyllobothrium
latum

[Simple circles represent the size of red cells.]

Index